W0254276

LEAF PROTEIN CONCENTRATES

Related AVI Books

BASIC FOOD MICROBIOLOGY
Banwart
DIGESTIVE PHYSIOLOGY AND METABOLISM IN RUMINANTS
Ruckebusch and Thivend
DRYING AND STORAGE OF AGRICULTURAL CROPS
Hall
FISH FARMING HANDBOOK
Brown and Gratzek
FOOD PROCESSING WASTE MANAGEMENT
Green and Kramer
FOOD PROTEINS
Whitaker and Tannenbaum
IMPACT OF TOXICOLOGY ON FOOD PROCESSING
Ayres and Kirschman
NUTRITION AND FOOD PROCESSING
Muller and Tobin
NUTRITION AND MEDICAL PRACTICE
Barness, Coble, Jr., Macdonald, and Christakis
NUTRITIONAL EVALUATION OF FOOD PROCESSING
2nd Edition *Harris and Karmas*
NUTRITIONAL QUALITY INDEX OF FOODS
Hansen, Wyse, and Sorenson
POULTRY: FEEDS AND NUTRITION
2nd Edition *Patrick and Schaible*
PROTEIN QUALITY IN HUMANS: Assessment and *In Vitro* Estimation
Bodwell, Adkins, and Hopkins
PROTEIN RESOURCES AND TECHNOLOGY
Milner, Scrimshaw, and Wang
SELENIUM IN BIOLOGY AND MEDICINE
Spallholz, Martin, and Ganther
SOYBEANS: CHEMISTRY AND TECHNOLOGY Vol. 1: Proteins
Revised 2nd Printing *Smith and Circle*
STATISTICAL METHODS FOR FOOD AND AGRICULTURE
Bender, Douglass, and Kramer
THE SAFETY OF FOODS
2nd Edition *Graham*

LEAF PROTEIN CONCENTRATES

Lehel Telek

Research Chemist
Tropical Agriculture Research Station
USDA, SEA, ARS
Mayaguez, Puerto Rico

Horace D. Graham

Professor of Chemistry
University of Puerto Rico
Mayaguez, Puerto Rico

AVI PUBLISHING COMPANY, INC.
Westport, Connecticut

Library of Congress Cataloging in Publication Data

Main entry under title:

Leaf protein concentrates.

Bibliography: p.
Includes index.
1. Plant proteins. 2. Leaves. I. Telek, Lehel.
II. Graham, Horace Delbert, 1925–
TP453.P7L4 1983 664′.64 83-12302
ISBN 0-87055-412-3

Printed in the United States of America

Dedication

Without the pioneering work of Mr. N.W. Pirie and his group, and his tenacity, persistence, and foresight, the field of leaf protein research would not have attained the recognition it has today. Dedication of this volume to this "Moses" of leaf protein research is, therefore, a small but appropriate tribute to his years of unselfish labor.

Contents

Contributors

ADDY, T.O., Director of Applied Research, Johnson & Johnson (Surgikos, Inc.), 250 Arbrook Boulevard, Arlington, TX 76010

BAILEY, R.W., Director, Applied Biochemistry Division, Department of Scientific and Industrial Research (DSIR), Palmerston North, New Zealand ADM 303

BEKERIS, M., Assistant Director of the Augusts Kirhenšteins Institute of Microbiology of the Academy of Sciences of the Latvian SSR, Kleisti, 226067 Riga, Latvian SSR, USSR

BRAY, WALTER J., Arco Solar Industries, Inc., P.O. Box 181, El Centro, CA 92244

BRUHN, H.D., Professor Emeritus, Department of Agricultural Engineering, University of Wisconsin, Madison, WI 53706

BYERS, MARJORIE, Principal Scientific Officer, Biochemistry Department, Rothamsted Experimental Station, Harpenden, Herts. AL5 2JQ, England

CARLSSON, ROLF, Lecturer, Research Leader for Applied Botany Projects, Institute of Plant Physiology, Box 7007, University of Lund, S-220 07, Lund 7, Sweden

CHEEKE, P.R., Professor, Department of Animal Science, Oregon State University, Corvallis, OR 97331

CHEN, C.S., Food Engineer, Florida Department of Citrus, 700 Experiment Station Road, Lake Alfred, FL 33850

DAUGAVIETIS, M., Chief of the Laboratory of Forest Raw Material Processing of the Scientific and Industrial Research Association "Silava," The Latvian Scientific Research Institute for Forestry Problems, 229021 Riga region, 111 Riga Street, Salaspils, Latvian SSR, USSR

DE FREMERY, DONALD, Research Chemist, Western Regional Research Center, Agricultural Research Service, U.S. Department of Agriculture, Berkeley, CA 94710

EDWARDS, RICHARD H., Research Engineer, Western Regional Research Center, Agricultural Research Service, U.S. Department of Agriculture, Berkeley, CA 94710

EL-ALAILY, H.A., Assistant Professor of Animal and Poultry Nutrition, Animal Production Department, Faculty of Agriculture, Ain Shams University, Shoubra El-Kheima, Cairo, Egypt

ENOCHIAN, ROBERT V., Agricultural Economist (Retired), National Economics Division (NED), Economics, Statistics and Cooperatives Service (ESCS), U.S. Department of Agriculture, Berkeley, CA 94710

FESTENSTEIN, GERALD N., Senior Scientific Officer, Rothamsted Experimental Station, Harpenden, Herts. AL5 2JQ, England

FISHMAN, DR. MARSHALL L., Research Chemist, Eastern Regional Research Center, Agricultural Research Service, U.S. Department of Agriculture, 600 East Mermaid Lane, Philadelphia, PA 19118

HANCZAKOWSKI, PIOTR, Research Associate, Research Leader for Leaf Protein Projects, Institute of Animal Production, Department of Animal Nutrition, 32-083 Balice/Kraków, Polska [Poland]

HOLDEN, MARGARET, Principal Scientific Officer (Retired), Rothamsted Experimental Station, Harpenden, Herts. AL5 2JQ, England

HORIGOME, T., Professor, Faculty of Agriculture, Okayama University, Tsushima, Okayama 700, Japan

HOVE, E.L., Director, Applied Biochemistry Division, Department of Scientific and Industrial Research, Palmerston North, New Zealand

IEVIN, I., Professor, Director General of the Scientific and Industrial Research Association "Silava," The Latvian Scientific Research Institute for Forestry Problems, 229021 Riga region, 111 Riga Street, Salaspils, Latvian SSR, USSR

JORGENSEN, N.A., Professor, Department of Dairy Science, University of Wisconsin, Madison, WI 53706

JOSHI, R.N., Professor, Department of Botany, Marathwada University, Aurangabad 431 004, India

KEVINŠ, J., Research Worker of the Scientific and Industrial Research Association "Silava," The Latvian Scientific Research Institute for Forestry Problems, 229021 Riga region, 111 Riga Street, Salaspils, Latvian SSR, USSR

KOCH, LEHEL, Research Associate, Agricultural Chemistry Department, University of Technical Sciences, Budapest, Institute of Agricultural Chemical Technology, Gellért Tér 4, Budapest 1502, Hungary

KOEGEL, R.G., Professor, Department of Mechanical Engineering, University of Wisconsin, Madison, WI 53706

KOHLER, GEORGE O., Technical Advisor, Supervisory Research Chemist (Retired), Western Regional Research Center, Agricultural Research Service, U.S. Department of Agriculture, Berkeley, CA 94710

KUNG, S.D., Department of Biological Science, University of Maryland, Baltimore County, Catonsville, MD 21228

KUZMICKY, DONALD D., Chemist, Western Regional Research Center, Agricultural Research Service, U.S. Department of Agriculture, Berkeley, CA 94710

MARTIN, FRANKLIN W., Research Horticulturist, Tropical Agriculture Research Station, Agricultural Research Service, U.S. Department of Agriculture, P.O. Box 70, Mayaguez, Puerto Rico 00709

NAGY, STEVEN, Research Chemist, Florida Department of Citrus, AREC, P.O. Box 1088, Lake Alfred, FL 33850

NORDBY, HAROLD E., Research Chemist, U.S. Citrus and Subtropical Products Laboratory, Agricultural Research Service, U.S. Department of Agriculture, P.O. Box 1909, Winter Haven, FL 33880

OKE, OLUSEGUN LADIMEJI, Professor, Chemistry Department, University of Ife, Ife-Ife, Nigeria

OSTROWSKI-MEISSNER, HENRY T., Senior Research Scientist, Division of Animal Production, Commonwealth Scientific and Industrial Research Organization, Prospect, P.O. Box 239, Blacktown, N.S.W. 2148, Australia

OSTROWSKI-MEISSNER, TERESA M., Tutor in Sociology/Politics, School of Social Sciences, Deakin University, Waurn Ponds, Victoria 3216, Australia

PIERPOINT, W.S., Principal Scientific Officer, Biochemistry Department, Rothamsted Experimental Station, Harpenden, Herts. AL5 2JQ, England

PIRIE, N.W., Director (Retired), Biochemistry Department, Rothamsted Experimental Station, Harpenden, Herts. AL5 2JQ, England

POLIS, O., Chemistry Engineer, Research Worker of the Scientific and Industrial Research Association "Silava," The Latvian Scientific Research Institute for Forestry Problems, 229021 Riga region, 111 Riga Street, Salaspils, Latvian SSR, USSR

REAM, H.W., Professor Emeritus, Department of Agronomy, University of Wisconsin, Madison, WI 53706

SHAH, F.H., Chief Scientific Officer, Food Technology & Fermentation Division, Pakistan Council of Scientific & Industrial Research (P.C.S.I.R.) Laboratories, Lahore 16, Pakistan

SOLIMAN, H.S., Assistant Professor of Animal and Poultry Nutrition, Animal Production Department, Faculty of Agriculture, Ain Shams University, Shoubra El-Kheima, Cairo, Egypt

TELEK, LEHEL, Research Chemist, Tropical Agriculture Research Station, Agricultural Research Service, U.S. Department of Agriculture, P.O. Box 70, Mayaguez, Puerto Rico 00709

TSO, T.C., Chief, Tobacco Laboratory, Plant Genetics and Germplasm Institute, Beltsville Agricultural Research Center, Agricultural Research Service, U.S. Department of Agriculture, Beltsville, MD 20705

UPĪTIS, A., Chief of the Laboratory of Biotransformation of the Augusts Kirhenšteins Institute of Microbiology of the Academy of Sciences of the Latvian SSR, Kleisti, 226067 Riga, Latvian SSR, USSR

VIEIRA, ENIO C., Fellow from Conselho Nacional de Desenvolvimento Científico e Tecnológico (CNPq), Departamento de Bioquímica, Instituto de Ciências Biológicas, Universidade Federal de Minas Gerais, Caixa Postal 2486, 30000 Belo Horizonte, MG, Brasil

VOSLOH, CARL J., JR., Agricultural Economist, National Economics Division (NED), Economics, Statistics and Cooperatives Service (ESCS), U.S. Department of Agriculture, Washington, DC 20250

WALKER, H.G., JR., Supervisory Research Chemist, Western Regional Research Center, Agricultural Research Service, U.S. Department of Agriculture, 800 Buchanan St., Berkeley, CA 94710

WHITNEY, L.F., Professor, Food Engineering Department, University of Massachusetts, Amherst, MA 01002

WOODHAM, ANTHONY A., Director, Commonwealth Bureau of Nutrition, Bucksburn, Aberdeen AB2 9SB, Scotland

Preface

Several novel sources of protein have been suggested to meet the ever-increasing world demand for this essential and critical nutrient. Of these, leaf protein has been considered to be among the most promising because:

(1) Being a product of photosynthesis, it is a highly renewable resource.
(2) For ages, in most of the world, populations have been eating leaf proteins of one type or another.
(3) Green, lush plants are abundant in the humid tropics where the need for protein is greatest.
(4) Based on the original or modified methods described, preparation of concentrates of leaf proteins is a simple and easy task, capable of being performed on the village level, even in the most remote areas of the world.
(5) The raw material, though more controllable if cultivated plants are used, can be in the form of agricultural by-products or water weeds which are abundant in some lakes, ponds, and streams.

Pioneering work on leaf proteins, particularly at the Rothamsted Experiment Station, under the direction of Mr. N.W. Pirie, was concerned mainly with obtaining a concentrate whose protein, lipid, chlorophyll, and provitamin A (carotenoid) contents varied with the plant species. Since then, emphasis has shifted to the preparation of protein isolates. Investigators in the United States and continental Europe have done much in this respect.

Although the most critical need for food protein exists in the humid tropics where vegetation is more profuse, relatively less work has been done there on leaf proteins, from both the theoretical and applied aspects, as compared with that done in the temperate regions. Significantly, work in the temperate regions has been carried out mainly on crops like alfalfa which can be cultivated on a mass basis. Similar high-protein, multiple-cropping plants, have now been identified in the tropics.

Advocates of the use of leaf proteins differ on where emphasis should be placed. Utilization for animal feed poses less problem than use for human food. In the former case, ruminants have been the principal subject for LPC nutritional studies. Even nonruminants have responded well in some trials. For human feeding, however, leaf protein concentrates have enjoyed less than phenomenal success due to the deep coloration of the product, texture, and acceptability factors. Efforts to use concentrates of proteins from leaves, which themselves are not eaten, probably have deterred progress due to the possible presence of unaccustomed flavors. Not to be overlooked is the possible presence of toxins of various sorts in the crude concentrates. Unless freedom from such compounds is established, the lingering fear of toxicity will continually be a deterrent to the use of leaf protein concentrates in foods. Leaf protein isolates, on the other hand, though not necessarily free of toxic components of the green leaves, would, if properly prepared, probably contain less of the toxic compound, depending on its chemical nature. If the toxic agent is itself a protein, its concentration in an isolate could be the same or even more than in a "crude" concentrate.

A decisive factor in the mode of preparation would be cost. The use of organic solvents in the preparation of isolates could be expensive unless the reagents are recovered economically and reused. In addition, preparation does require special equipment, some technical training, and more time. However, the product is more concentrated, colorless, and bland, and so may be more adaptable to multipurpose food uses and would be more readily acceptable. Disadvantages include the loss of the carotenoids and important lipids, reportedly rich in unsaturated fatty acids.

Chemical analyses attest to the nutritional potential of leaf proteins, their amino acid profile being fairly good. With respect to their content of lysine, tryptophan, and methionine, they are somewhat inferior to the proteins of milk and eggs but better than the proteins of most cereals. Proper admixture into food recipes should, therefore, contribute to the improvement of the nutritional status of protein-deficient populations.

Work on leaf proteins has been in progress in several parts of the world for many years. However, up to now there has been no comprehensive and critical review of the findings, opinions, and projections of these far-flung groups. Therefore, it was considered useful to organize a text containing, insofar as possible, complete coverage of all the work being done on leaf protein. Inasmuch as leading investigators from tropical as well as temperate countries have contributed, the effort may be considered a success. It is hoped that the series of articles contained in this volume will project a true picture of the status of leaf protein research all over the world.

In organizing the material presented in the text, two aims were given consideration.

(1) To seek contributions from investigators whose works have pinpointed the problems in leaf protein research and which can, therefore, offer guidance in future investigations.
(2) To attempt, as far as possible, a global review of leaf protein work which has been done, is being done, or is planned.

This second aim resulted in the acceptance of manuscripts from areas where linguistic difficulties had to be overcome, some of which may be reflected in the articles from some of these areas. The editors take full responsibility for any deviations from standard editorial processes and laud the willingness and efforts of those investigators to contribute to the compilation, and welcome as well the many sound and novel ideas presented. It is hoped that the material presented will further stimulate interest in both the academic as well as the applied aspects of leaf protein research.

Throughout the preparation, each author has been permitted a complete expression of thought. The ideas and opinions offered, therefore, are those of the authors themselves, thus allowing for personal opinions, projections, or evaluations.

Research workers, libraries, administrators, graduate students, and others should benefit from the material presented. It is hoped that information gathered will serve to stimulate further critical and useful fundamental research, as well as applied research, into the utilization of the world's most renewable resource for the alleviation and/or elimination of some of the world's most chronic and severe maladies—hunger, protein deficiency, and starvation.

LEHEL TELEK
HORACE D. GRAHAM

Acknowledgments

Each and every one of the contributors, who dedicated so much time and effort to prepare articles for the text, deserves the deepest and most sincere appreciation of the editors of this book.

The late Dr. Donald K. Tressler, in his capacity as President of the AVI Publishing Company, played a major role in the development of this book. His direction, encouragement, and patience are deeply appreciated. Miss Marjorie Byers, a long-time and dedicated member of the Rothamsted group, did yeoman's work in the organizational phase of its publication. Her suggestions and advice are most gratefully acknowledged. Dr. Rolf Carlsson gave valuable assistance in obtaining the chapters from the authors in Eastern Europe, Brazil, and Egypt, and was always available for advice and discussions. Special thanks are due to all the publishers and scientists who so kindly granted permission to use data, graphs, and other materials from their articles and texts. We are grateful to Barbara Arnold, whose patient retypings and valuable suggestions helped lighten the editorial load in the last phase of the book's preparation. Colleagues who gave enlightened views during discussions, typists whose aching eyes and fingers perfected the task, and, most of all, wives who sacrificed and suffered lonely hours have the thanks and gratitude of the editors.

LEHEL TELEK
HORACE D. GRAHAM

Introduction or the Knowledge Needed for Successful Leaf Protein Production

N.W. Pirie

The use of extracted leaf protein (LP) as a food for people and other nonruminants has been suggested at various times during the past 100 years, and at various times during the past 50 years, samples have been made with which quality and acceptability could be tested. Sustained work started 30 years ago. The reasons for thinking that more effort should be expended on the cultivation of leafy crops and on the fractionation of some of them, if the fractionation can be managed economically, are:

(1) Leaves are potentially the most abundant protein source.
(2) Many leaf crops protect land from erosion.
(3) Leaf Protein (LP), if undamaged in processing, has good nutritive value.
(4) Unpalatable, or even toxic, leaves can be used.
(5) The fiber residue, containing unextracted protein, is a ruminant feed.
(6) This fiber can be more economically conserved than the original crop.

The cogency of these reasons for research on LP or, more generally, on fodder fractionation, has never been seriously questioned. Nevertheless, the idea of making LP was often greeted with ridicule or hostility. The increase in the price of oil has recently jolted critics into rationality. I have outlined some aspects of this farcical history elsewhere (Pirie 1966, 1971, 1975, 1978).

Now that the idea of fodder fractionation is accepted as reasonable, there is some reason to fear that industrialists and controllers of research policy are tending to assume that we have all the knowledge needed for efficient production. Consequently, the methods proposed for fractionation, and the situations envisaged for it, do not always seem to be reasonable. Four questions may be asked. (1) What leafy material should be fractionated? (2) What equipment should be used to make the leaf extract? (3) In what form would LP be used? (4) To whom will it be most useful? It will be difficult to get adequate funding for research until there are convincing answers to these questions, but getting answers to at least two of the questions involves research. This logical conflict is one reason for the slow development of the subject. Another reason is premature attempts at economic forecasting. Forecasts are meaningless until the first two questions have been answered. It is worth bearing in mind that various forms of dried and powdered fish have been used for at least 2500 years and produced commercially for 50 years. Nevertheless, a recent comment (Crisan 1978) ran: "It is difficult, if not impossible, to predict accurately what a marketable FPC will cost at this point in its development since commercial production is yet to be realized." Much the same can be said for yeast grown on oil in spite of the vast amount of effort put into that form of production.

With all these uncertainties, it is pleasant to note the absence of one potential restraint on development. Every point of any significance for LP production either has been published in the open literature or is covered by a patent that has by now expired.

It is obviously convenient to use readily available crops when work on LP is being initiated in an institute. There are so many urgent and novel problems that agronomic problems can be left till later on. Nevertheless, it is a pity that so many institutes, having sensibly started work on a crop such as lucerne, get "hooked" on it. Availability is its main merit. A subsidiary benefit coming from the human feeding experiments with lucerne LP is that they show that even a strongly flavored LP is acceptable. Many other species of leaf give LP with much less flavor, some give a greater annual yield, and very few give juice with such an inconvenient tendency to froth. The amount of agronomic work that has been done on LP sources in temperate climates is still small—in spite of the potentialities of LP, more work is probably being done on such topics as the cultivation of mushrooms. Work on agronomy is more adequate in the tropics, especially at Aurangabad (India). I have summarized this agronomic work elsewhere (Pirie 1978, 1979). Measurements are still needed on many more commercial varieties of conventional crops, and on varieties rejected by plant breeders. A variety giving abundant leaf may have been rejected because it yielded little seed. That would probably be advantageous for LP production because flowering and the development of seed usually accompany a diminution in protein extractability. With cooperation from plant breeders, it should be possible to select better varieties than any hitherto tested.

Crops grown primarily for fractionation will be the main source of LP. Other sources of leaf should not, however, be overlooked. It should be borne in mind that undesirable texture or extractable toxic substance, which makes some leaves unattractive as fodder, will probably not affect their use as sources of LP. So much juice is expressed during fractionation that toxic substances will largely be removed from the fiber residue.

LP can be extracted from by-products such as beet tops, pea vines, potato haulm, and discards from vegetables. In Britain, as much protein could be extracted from them as is present in home-grown beef. Water weeds are a menace in many parts of the world, and vastly expensive attempts are made to control them. It would be more sensible to devise fractionation equipment that could be mounted on a barge, and combine weed control with the production of useful commodities. Protein is not readily extractable, by present methods, from the abundant floating weeds. This is a pity, but it does not demolish the case for fuller investigation of water weeds; money will be spent on controlling them in any event, so we should try to get something back in return.

The position with tree leaves is somewhat similar. With curious consistency, extraction of LP from the leaves of most species is difficult. Furthermore, it would be difficult to collect leaves from a mature tree. There is now great interest in coppiced trees as a source of fuel and paper pulp. The regular form of a coppice would make the collection of leaves easier. It would therefore be worthwhile searching for species or varieties from which extraction is easy, or for new methods of extraction that will work on leaves that have hitherto been intractable.

The extraction of LP from the leaves of crops, trees, or water weeds that are already being eaten in the normal way as green vegetables would seldom be sensible. Few communities eat green vegetables to the extent that is possible and desirable. Therefore, it would be more practical to popularize their use as it is unlikely that a community unaccustomed to eating green vegetables will take readily to LP. Young children are an exception to this generalization because their small stomachs cannot cope with much leaf. If it is felt that LP would be more acceptable if it were made from a familiar vegetable, it would be reasonable to extract it for children. In regions where children who are being weaned are the important malnourished group, it would probably be better to give the LP to the mother rather than the infant.

It is essential to rub the mass of leaf thoroughly before trying to press out juice from it; therefore, it would be convenient to do both jobs in one machine. In small-scale agronomic work, convenience has to be disregarded for the sake of establishing extraction conditions that are the same in all experiments. Early units for bulk extraction simply used scaled-up versions of the analytical procedure. Leaf was pulped into one machine and the pulp was transferred to a batch or continuous press. In all the human trials of nutritive value, the LP was made in this way.

Many attempts have been made to use 3-roll mills and screw expellers as extraction units. No one now advocates the use of the former; attempts are still being made to use standard expellers. In a conventional expeller, feeding and the application of pressure are so inefficient that there is a considerable amount of inadvertent rubbing of leaf against leaf, and leaf against parts of the machine; there is therefore some liberation of juice. But most of those who use screw expellers have reverted to the two-unit system and pass the crop through a pulper before feeding it to the screw expeller. Conventional screw expellers are designed to exert much more pressure than is needed to express juice if the juice has been adequately released from the cell structure of the leaf. With unlubricated material, such as leaf pulp, this increases the waste of energy in friction, as well as increasing the weight and cost of the machine. When the fluid that is being expressed has the commercial value of oil, such an expense is tolerable. Leaf juice, however, is less valuable, containing only 2 to 5% protein. If such a fluid is to be expressed economically, it is essential that the machinery not be unnecessarily expensive. Furthermore, juice pressed out from tightly compacted leaf, even if it has been adequately pulped, contains less protein than juice pressed out more gently.

Some progress has been made (Pirie 1977; Butler and Pirie 1977) toward reconciling these requirements. The first section of a modified screw expeller is a set of angled paddles that disintegrate the mass of leaf thoroughly before pushing it into the section of the unit in which pressure is applied. Juice comes through the casing in both sections. Because pressure is gentle, some juice can still be pressed out from the fiber. This is immaterial if the fiber is to be ensiled or used fresh; however, if the fiber is to be dried, the residual juice would be pressed out in a machine in which there is no relative motion between metal and compressed fiber.

The optimum size of an extraction unit will depend on the circumstances in which fodder fractionation is undertaken. If the primary objective is the production of partly dewatered fiber that can be incorporated into industrially produced ruminant feed, in the hope thus "to delay the demise of the dehydration industry now operating on gas or liquid fuel (Bruhn *et al.* 1977)," installations handling several hundred tons of leaf per day would be reasonable. Even in such an installation, it will probably be better to have several units in parallel, each handling a few tons per hr, rather than one Brobdingnagian unit. Units of that size would also be convenient on the average farm. The most urgent need, however, is for units handling a few hundred kg per hr (wet weight of crop) with which 20 to 30 kg per day of LP (dry matter) could be made.

The question of scale is inextricably bound up with the question of the proposed recipient of the LP. Because banana, cassava, and yams are important dietary components in many parts of the wet tropics, these areas tend to be regions of protein deficiency; they also are regions peculiarly well adapted to the growth of leaf crops. They seem therefore to be regions where LP could be a useful human food. According to many surveys (Valverde and Rawson 1976; Scoville and Due 1977; van Ginneken 1976), nutritional conditions are worse in rural areas, with poor communications and little contact with industrialized production, than in urban areas. It is for regions such as these that extraction units should be designed: they should be cheap, and robust; ideally it should be possible to use an animal rather than a motor as the drive.

The process of juice extraction from leaves has no close analogues in traditional food handling and cooking. That is probably why the potentialities of LP have been overlooked for so long. Many standard processes, e.g., cheese making, are analogous to the separation of LP from the extract. Some suggested methods, however, should be viewed skeptically. For example: any process that involves prolonged contact between coagulated LP and the soluble components of the juice is likely to diminish the nutritive value of the LP because associations form between protein and phenolics; any process that encourages enzyme actions in the juice will diminish LP yield because of autolysis and increase the risk that the photosensitizing agent, pheophorbide, will be formed as a result of the action of chlorophyllase and acid. Fortunately, the reliable methods of separation are simpler than the suggested alternatives.

After LP has been extracted from the leaf, coagulated, and filtered from the extract, and, if necessary, washed by resuspending in water and filtering again, every subsequent form of treatment is likely to be deleterious. If LP is being made for local use, there is no need for preservation; it keeps as well as cheese and better than most other fresh foods. If some preservation is essential, it can be managed by adding salt or sugar to moist coagulum that has been thoroughly pressed. Drying is usually unnecessary. If, for prolonged storage or to economize on the transport of moist material, drying is thought to be essential, careful attention should be given to the precautions that must be taken to minimize Maillard reactions and conjugation between the protein and unsaturated fatty acids. The differences in nutritive value that have been observed among preparations of LP are more likely to be the result of differing amounts of damage during processing than of genuine differences among species. To minimize loss of β-carotene, dry LP should be stored in nitrogen; LP that is preserved in the moist state in a jar will automatically be protected from oxygen.

Removal of chlorophyll and its breakdown products from LP by solvent extraction, and the separation of part of the LP in a water soluble form, are familiar processes in the laboratory. There is no obvious obstacle to managing them on an industrial scale, but it is difficult to envisage circumstances in which these processes would be useful. LP is not likely to be made in a region where people are not already eating, or have not been persuaded to eat, leafy vegetables on a considerable scale. Many communities already use powdered dried leaves as a relish. There is therefore no reason to think that green material is necessarily unattractive. Anyone who wants to prepare a soluble white protein would be better advised to start with cottonseed, ground nut, or soy, rather than leaves. Furthermore, solvent extraction removes β-carotene and other lipids as well as the green pigments. Vitamin A deficiency is so widespread in tropical countries that the β-carotene is nearly as important a component as the protein; the lipid component of LP contributes nearly as much energy as the protein.

Unfractionated LP, made on an industrial scale, will probably have an important role in pig and chicken feeding in wealthy countries. When carefully prepared from a local crop for local consumption, it could meet part of the protein requirement in regions where protein is now scarce. It is not easy to see what use would be made of a sophisticated and fractionated product. The wealthy do not need it; the poor could not afford it.

The potential abundance of LP is the primary reason for confidence that it will be used in some form and for advocating more diversified and extensive research on its production. Though the fundamental principles of production will remain the same, differing forms of production suit an isolated village and a commercial farm, or the humid tropics and a region with prolonged winters. Machinery suited to many different crops and conditions will have to be designed and tested. Production is already starting in several countries: some of these projects will probably fail. Failure will often depend on social or political factors, but will sometimes be caused by the use of inappropriate crops or methods of processing. At this stage of research, therefore, it is important to keep as many options open as possible. It would be unfortunate if the priniciple of fodder fractionation were to be judged impractical because faults in technique were mistaken for faults in objective

REFERENCES

BRUHN, H.D., STRAUB, R.J. and KOEGEL, R.G. 1977. On farm forage protein—the potential and the means. Agric. Eng. *32* (3) 66.

BUTLER, J.B. and PIRIE, N.W. 1977. A simple unit for extracting protein in bulk from leaves. Proc. Nutr. Soc. *36*, 133A.

PETERSON, M.S., JOHNSON, A.H. and CRISAN, E.V. 1978. Fish protein concentrate (FPC). *In* Encyclopedia of Food Science. M.S. Peterson and A.H. Johnson (Editors). AVI Publishing Co., Westport, CT.

PIRIE, N.W. 1966. Leaf protein as a human food. Science *152*, 1701.

PIRIE, N.W. 1971. Leaf Protein: Its Agronomy, Preparation, Quality and Use. IBP Handb. *20*. Blackwell's Scientific Publishers, Oxford.

PIRIE, N.W. 1975. Leaf protein: A beneficiary of tribulation. Nature *253*, 239.

PIRIE, N.W. 1977. A simple unit for extracting leaf protein in bulk. Exp. Agric. *13*, 113.

PIRIE, N.W. 1978. Leaf Protein and Other Aspects of Fodder Fractionation. Cambridge University Press, London.

PIRIE, N.W. 1979. Leaf protein as a source of food. Appl. Biol. *4*, 2.

SCOVILLE, M. and DUE, J.M. 1977. The rural-urban income profile of Uganda. Ill. Agric. Econ. *17*, 28.

VALVERDE, V. and RAWSON, I.G. 1976. Dietetic and anthropometric differences between children from the center and surrounding villages of a rural region of Costa Rica. Ecol. Food Nutr. *5*, 197.

VAN GINNEKEN, W. 1976. Rural and urban income inequalities in Indonesia, Mexico, Pakistan, Tanzania and Tunisia. International Labour Office, Geneva.

Part I

Plant Sources of LPC

1

Protein Extraction from Grasslands

Henry T. Ostrowski-Meissner[1]

WORLD'S PROTEIN DEMANDS AND AVAILABLE RESOURCES

The problem of feeding the world's exploding population has today become a sociopolitical dilemma. Since the population growth rates, particularly in Asia, Africa, and Latin America, are increasing rapidly (Fig. 1.1), the availability of food resources for millions has become a critical and challenging problem. If the world population will really double in the next 22 years, can agricultural productivity keep up with such a pace?

The 3.5 billion people in the world today live off an agricultural output of 1.4 billion hectares (ha) of arable land, the animal output from grasslands, plus small amounts of food from forests and from the sea. Present total world annual protein production has been estimated by Arnott (1974) as approximately 35 million metric tons (MT). If every person in the world consumed protein at the rate that people do in developed countries, the world demand would be approximately 80 million MT. Calculating world protein resources, it can be assumed that, theoretically, protein demands can be met by an immediate substantial increase in overall efficiency of farming within the existing agricultural ecosystems with much more conventional protein being recoverable as compared to present production and/or by producing a large proportion of unconventional consumable protein.

Changes in the improvement of the efficiency of conversion of the earth resources into food cannot be done without changing the traditional concept of agriculture in relation to the two interrelated areas—plant and animal production—and without breaking the conservative approach to foods, nutrition, and dietetics. In fact, nobody at the moment can definitely describe the agricultural system which would cover future protein demands. Al-

[1] Balai Penelitian Ternak, Project for Animal Research and Development, Bogor, Indonesia (Commonwealth Scientific and Industrial Research Organization—Australia).

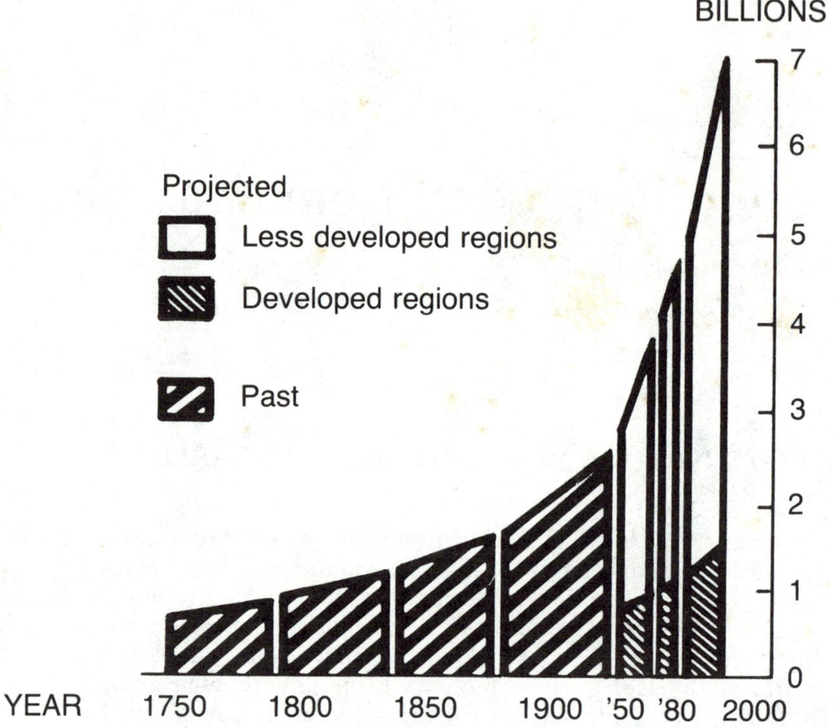

Fig. 1.1. Past and projected world human population in developed and less developed regions.
From data by FAO-WHO (1965).

though research has turned to several relevant areas having a possibility of additional protein production, progress in agricultural practice has been much slower, particularly in relation to unconventional food production.

Unconventional proteins fall conveniently into two major classes. Within the first group are those products not yet used for food but now available in major quantities. This includes protein isolates from fish not used for consumption, and protein concentrates from oil seeds and nuts such as cottonseed, peanuts, sunflower, sesame, and coconut, as well as those proteins which are, or which can be, recovered from the *fresh green parts of plants (leaves).* The second major group of unconventional proteins would include those produced by microorganisms, comprising yeasts, algae, and bacteria, growing on simple substrates. This group of proteins is fashionably termed single cell proteins.

The major objective of this presentation is a discussion of those unconventional proteins derived from the fresh parts of herbage such as leaf protein concentrate (LPC). The principles of the process and its application in practice will be discussed. This is in order to increase the recovery of yields of edible protein from existing resources within the agricultural ecosystems. It is assumed that the results discussed in this presentation and which were obtained in Australia are analogous to those which can generally be obtained under most temperate and subtropical climatic conditions. Hence, it should be possible to use them in areas where there is a high protein deficit and where leaf protein extracts might be produced locally for use as a feedstuff for monogastric animals or be fed directly to young children and adults who do not have a wide choice of foods.

POTENTIAL PROTEIN PRODUCTION IN AGRICULTURAL ECOSYSTEMS

Agricultural Production and the Earth's Solar Radiation

Analyzing world feed and food supplies from agricultural ecosystems and relating those supplies to unconventional proteins in terms of potential production, it appears that protein as obtained from green vegetation is the most potential pool of protein within any agricultural ecosystem, irrespective of geographical position. The quantities of the recovered food- and/or feed-grade proteins from the ecosystem are a function of yields of vegetation being achieved through photosynthesis. These yields from the land area are, however, heavily dependent on the available energy (solar radiation, fuel, fertilizers, etc). According to Blaxter (1974), energy is obviously the control which will help us to hold what we have gained and to increase productivity to levels beyond our present vision.

Production of protein in the world agricultural ecosystem is dependent on available energy resources limiting this production (Phillipson 1973). The distribution of the earth's solar radiation, as thus far recorded, is schematically presented in Fig. 1.2. Approximately 20% of the total earth's solar radiation is reaching the nonwoodland ecosystem, i.e., agricultural and other productive land, in an average ratio of 2.4×10^{13} J ha^{-1}. This energy, in turn, can be converted into plant material with an average efficiency of 2.6% as calculated by Bonner (1962).

According to Phillipson (1973), the potential maximum above-ground net primary production of plant material, dry weight, within the nonwoodland ecosystem approximates 3.72×10^4 kg ha^{-1} per annum. In most cases, however, due to numerous agronomic and other limitations, practically achieved yields of organic matter derived as a result of energy fixation through photosynthesis in the manmade agricultural ecosystems reach only 10 to 20% of the potential maximum value.

Nitrogen Cycle in the Biosphere and Protein Production

The biological efficiency of production of plant proteins in the form of net primary production above the ground depends on the region of the world and the type of agricultural system. It has been calculated that only 1.7% of the total protein synthesized by plants as a result of biological and chemical

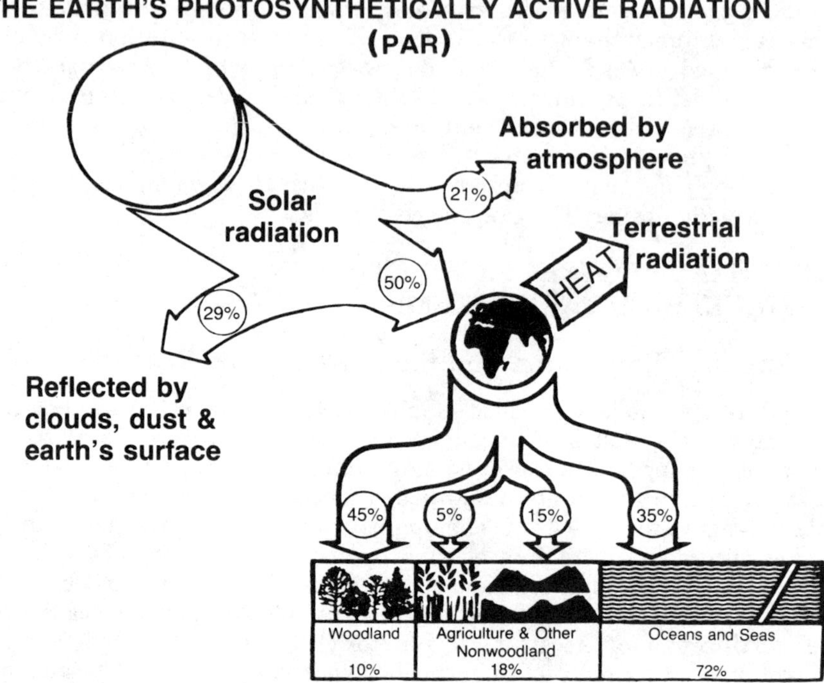

Fig. 1.2. The earth's photosynthetically-active radiation (PAR) and its conversion into the energy of the major ecosystems.

fixation in the nitrogen cycle after being consumed by animals is converted to high biological value protein representing feed and foodstuffs of animal origin. Figure 1.3 shows schematically the major pathways of nitrogen cycle in the biosphere and the nitrogen pool of plant origin (12 billion MT) from which only 0.2 billion MT of nitrogen of animal origin is recovered at present from agricultural ecosystems in conventional farming operations. Taking potential aboveground net primary production as calculated by Phillipson (1973) from the total earth's solar radiation reaching 1 ha of land in the nonwoodland ecosystem, approximately 9×10^3 kg crude protein ($N \times 6.25$) can be derived per annum as primary production of protein of plant origin.

Comparing various crops and sources of protein derived directly from agricultural ecosystems (Table 1.1), permanent grasslands have been shown to be outstanding, high dry-matter and protein-yielding performers. Also, the comparative cost of the unit of protein in various feedstuffs related to the yield of protein achieved from the land area shows pasture herbage as the cheapest source of feed-grade protein. On the other hand, milk protein

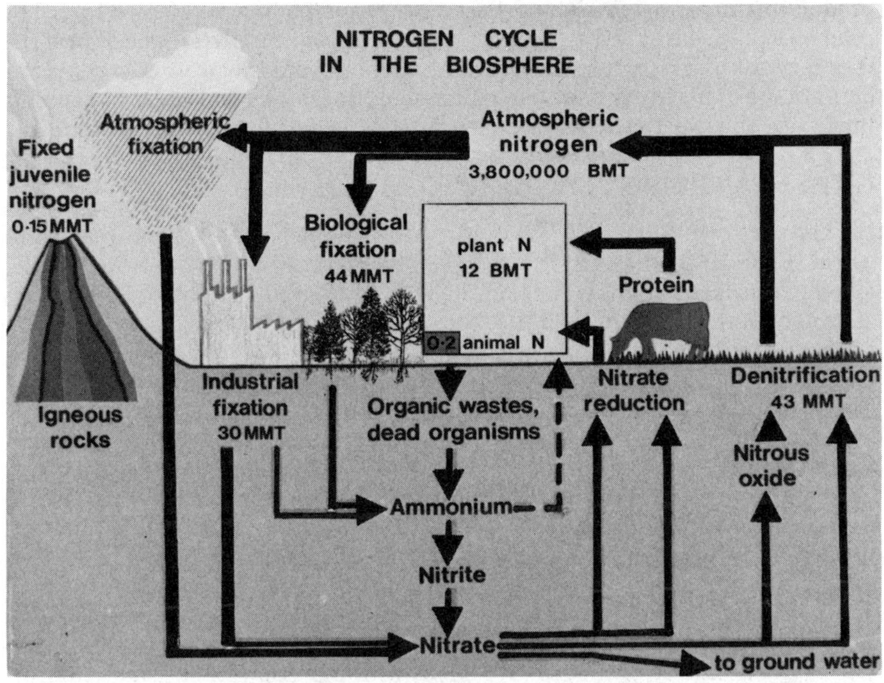

Fig. 1.3. Nitrogen cycle in the biosphere, and conversion of nitrogen into two main nitrogen pools: of plant and of animal origin.

TABLE 1.1. POTENTIAL YIELDS OF SOME FOODS AND FEEDS DERIVED FROM 1 HA OF AGRICULTURAL LAND PER ANNUM AND COST OF PROTEIN ($/KG)

Food- or Feedstuff	Production (kg × 10³)			Comparative Costs of Protein ($/kg)[1]
	Protein	Essential Amino Acids	Dry Matter	
Maize	0.70	0.25	6.22	0.66
Soybean	1.35	0.49	2.47	0.27
Pasture herbage	2.70	1.15	13.5–17.0	0.06
Beef				
based on crops[2]	0.29	0.11		2.4
based on pasture[3]	0.18	0.07		0.6
Milk				
based on crops[2]	0.42	0.20	1.40	1.1
based on pasture[3]	0.58	0.28	1.94	0.2
Fish (farmed)	0.65			
Hydrocarbon-based yeast	44		73	0.2

Source: Adapted from Hutton (1970, 1972) and Whittlestone (1972).
[1]Based on farmer prices.
[2]Under crop system of feeding (United States).
[3]Under grassland-based system of feeding (New Zealand).

production under the grassland-based system of feeding in relation to cost of production appeared to be the most potential and favorite means of protein recovery from agricultural ecosystems. Hence, from the protein production point of view, highly productive cultivated grasslands and natural grazing lands are the most efficient for either feed- and/or food-grade proteins.

GRASSLANDS AS A SOURCE OF PROTEIN

There are over 3.01×10^9 ha of meadows and permanent pastures in the world (FAO 1971) that are still far from being properly utilized as a source of fodder for farm animals in terms of both gross productivity and efficiency of conversion into high protein foods. The most advantageous, from the herbage productivity and conversion efficiency point of view, are grasslands in the regions where climate and agricultural conditions allow dairy farming to be based exclusively on grazing pastures. The typical examples of such farming systems were demonstrated by Hutton (1970) and King and Stockdale (1978). Some of the practical results of the former are given in Table 1.1 in relation to milk protein production as derived from pasture. The potential primary protein production from grasslands can be characterized by protein yields practically achieved from permanent, irrigated, and topdressed pastures involved in intensive dairying being as high as 6×10^3 kg ha^{-1} year^{-1} (Ostrowski-Meissner 1976A). This yield is only some 30% lower than that calculated by Phillipson (1973) as a possible maximum yield which can be achieved in a nonwoodland ecosystem. The gross efficiency of conversion of available pasture protein on high-yielding grasslands into milk protein in intensive dairy farming systems based entirely on pasture grazing averages 13% (Hutton 1970; Ostrowski-Meissner 1976A, 1978A).

The question which arises is: By what means can one improve this conversion efficiency and how can one recover some more of the remaining 87% pasture protein which at present is being wasted by dairy cows and other ruminant farm animals within the conventional process of milk and/or meat production?

Depending on the botanical composition and herbage regrowth stage, average concentrations of 20 to 30% crude protein (CP) on a dry matter (DM) basis were recorded (Ostrowski-Meissner 1978C; Ostrowski-Meissner *et al.* 1975). On the other hand, according to the nutrient requirements of beef cattle (Natl. Res. Counc. 1970), growing steers and heifers require in their fodder only some 9 to 13% CP on DM basis, depending on the stage of their growth; dry pregnant mature cows need only some 6% CP, while dairy cattle during lactation require some 15% CP in the fodder's DM (Natl. Res. Counc. 1971).

Since protein requirements of beef and dairy cattle are appreciably lower than normally present in pasture herbages throughout the year, the surplus of protein in consumed fodder which is additional to animals' needs is de-aminated in the rumen to ammonia, which, after absorption followed by the conversion to urea in the liver, is finally eliminated in the urine. This causes a low degree of protein conversion from pasture herbage to high protein products such as milk and/or meat. Hence, it is reasonable to suppose that by "skimming off" the surplus protein from herbage and feeding the remaining partly deproteinized herbage residue to cattle, there should be a notable increase in the efficiency of grassland use as a protein source.

PROTEIN EXTRACTION FROM GREEN VEGETATION: THE CONCEPT AND DEVELOPMENT

The year 1973 marked the bicentenary of the discovery by G.F. and H.M. Rouelle that the coagulum which was separated from a heated leaf extract was nutritionally similar to the curd obtained from milk (Rouelle 1773). In 1926 Ereky developed a mill which macerated herbage, and the expressed juice, after further treatment, was used for feeding pigs and other nonruminant farm animals. A few years later Slade (1937) and then Pirie (1942) described the procedure suggested for extracting proteins from herbage for human consumption. Subsequently several workers designed, tested, and described alternative equipment which could be used for protein extraction from green vegetation. The most notable of these is Pirie, whose international contribution to the protein extraction problem has been underlined by a book on leaf protein published under the auspices of the International Biological Programme (Pirie 1971). Most of the world research on protein extraction summarized in Pirie's book was, however, related to extraction of protein from forage crops, and was directed toward the production of isolates for human and animal feeding. Hence, the emphasis was placed on the maximum extraction of protein from forage with the residual pulp being considered as a by-product.

A recent review of the protein extraction problem in the United Kingdom is a symposium on Green Crop Fractionation in Harrogate in 1976 (Jones 1977). The objective of this symposium was to review the results of the current research programs in the U.K., Europe, and the United States and to define the systems and economic conditions under which the process of green crop fractionation is likely to be a viable proposition under U.K. agricultural conditions. As a result, the entire crop fractionation program, as carried out in the U.K. and the United States, was analyzed with areas considered important being outlined for further research and development.

The interest in leaf protein research had its origin in economic circumstances related to the costs of production of dried forage crops such as grass and lucerne. Economically, the most promising area in grass- or lucerne-drying lay in reducing direct fuel consumption for drying. Pressing some of the juice out before drying has offered the greatest advantages since this operation requires considerably less fuel than does the drying of the extracted moisture (juice) originally present in the conventionally dried forage crops, that is, without mechanical dejuicing prior to drying.

From the massive number of papers dealing with various aspects of protein extraction from different crops it could be concluded that:

(1) There is sufficient evidence available to indicate that the nutritional value of protein concentrates extracted from green vegetation is comparable to that of protein isolates of animal origin and superior or similar to protein isolates of seeds (Morris 1977).
(2) Processed herbage pulp with a reduced level of protein still appeared to be good (full, productive) fodder for beef cattle and sheep (Connell and Houseman 1977; Stahmann 1975).
(3) Crop fractionation and protein concentrate production in large commercial-scale operations, despite the high costs of fuel, still have economic advantages to be gained within agricultural ecosystems based on seasonal production (Wilkins *et al.* 1977; Vosloh *et al.* 1976).
(4) With protein extraction applied to conventional farming operations in the U.K., with both pigs and cattle being involved in utilization of the extracted juice and the pressed forage, respectively, the efficiency of agricultural land utilization has substantially increased (Jones and Houseman 1975).

Even though this increase was observed in relation to summer production only, it can be assumed that, had the fractionation been an all-year-round process, with fresh crops being available as a source for fractionation throughout the whole year, the results would be much more favorable.

Taking into account the preceding conclusions and the data presented in Table 1.1 showing the superiority of farming in agricultural ecosystems based on grasslands and acknowledging all pioneering efforts upon which most modern developments and the world's up-to-date appraisal in leaf protein are based, there has grown a new concept of dairying founded on protein extraction from pasture herbage.

PROTEIN EXTRACTION FROM GRASSLANDS INVOLVED IN DAIRY FARMING IN AUSTRALIA

The Principles of the System

Pasture as a potential source of extracted protein in the future of dairy farming has been described by Hutton (1970), the practical results presented later (Ostrowski-Meissner 1976A,B; 1978A,B) showed a high feasibility of applying the protein extraction operation to dairy farming based on grasslands in temperate and subtropical regions. The yields of protein recovered from pasture involved in simultaneous protein extraction and dairying showed a four- to five-fold increase as compared to conventional farming based on pasture grazed by herds of dairy cows without involvement in protein extraction activities (Ostrowski-Meissner 1976B).

Present agricultural conditions in Australia, particularly in Victoria, New South Wales, and Queensland, appear to be most favorable for the development of a project for commercial plant fractionation and direct protein recovery from crops and/or pasture herbage. This is due mainly to climatic conditions which allow the cultivation of a variety of year-round harvested tropical, subtropical, and temperate high-yielding crops and grasslands. Under such conditions (Fig. 1.4), an extraction project on grasslands could be advantageous and economic and certainly has a head start over similar projects already established in the U.K. and Europe, where climate allows for only a 6 to 8 month production season annually.

There are about 5 million dairy cattle in Australia, Victoria being the leading state with approximately 1.5 million, Queensland 1.4 million, New South Wales 1.2 million, and other states sharing the remaining 0.9 million (Anon. 1955). Victoria leads in intensive dairy production in Australia, since rainfall and soil fertility are favorable and irrigation is available, ensuring high productivity of grasslands involved in dairying. Hence, this agricultural region has been chosen to develop a system of protein extraction from those grasslands which are involved in intensive dairy farming so as to increase the recovery of edible protein from the agricultural ecosystem.

The protein extraction from pasture herbage in Australia has been based on Rouelle's (1773) and Pirie's (1971) concept of protein recovery from green vegetation. In this system, demonstrated schematically in Fig. 1.5., herbage, after harvesting from pasture followed by the mechanical process of maceration and dejuicing, during which part of the crude protein is removed, could either be fed as fresh-pressed herbage cakes to livestock on the same paddock from where it was cut and processed or be conserved as either dried or ensilate (Ostrowski-Meissner 1976A,B).

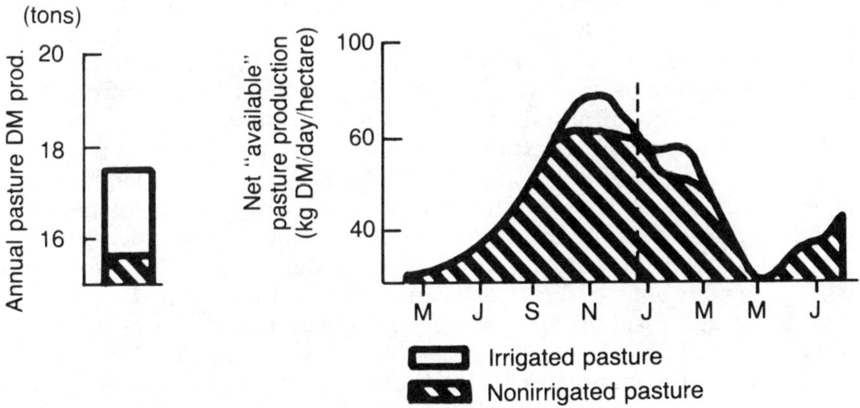

Fig. 1.4. Annual productive characteristics of permanent topdressed pasture in Australia (Victoria) with and without irrigation applied during the summer and autumn seasons.

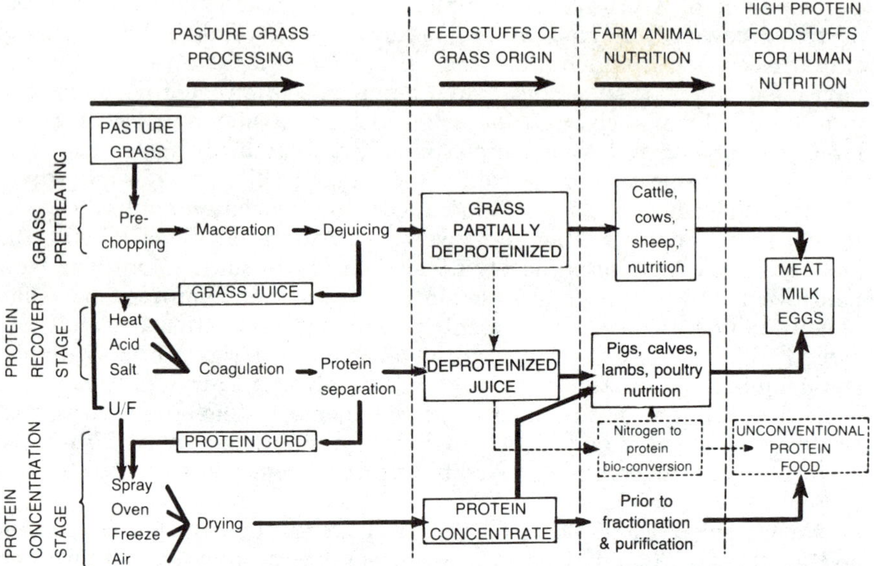

Fig. 1.5. Diagram of protein extraction from green plants using pasture herbage as an example; processing stages and conversion of pasture through feedstuffs into both conventional and/or unconventional edible protein products of food grade, with farm animals and, alternatively, single cell organisms being pasture nitrogen converters.
From Ostrowski-Meissner (1976A).

Proteins extracted from herbage juice, after concentration by the use of different technologies to about 50% dry matter content as protein concentrate (LPC), could be used as either a high protein concentrate for monogastric farm animals (poultry, pigs) or, after fractionation and purification, as an unconventional protein source for human nutrition.

Unextracted protein, together with most of the other nutrients in processed pasture herbage, provides a suitable (still full-productive) fodder for the ruminant livestock which could be associated with this development. A research project initiated in New Zealand (Ostrowski-Meissner 1976A,B) and then carried out in Australia (Ostrowski-Meissner 1978A,B) examined ways of combining the direct extraction of protein from pasture herbage with using the residues for feeding grazing ruminants. Locating protein extraction and livestock enterprises based on pasture together confers advantages in the costs of producing the raw plant materials, in the productive use of plant residues, in the maintenance of soil and sward productivity and in the collection, transport, and processing of protein extracts. It appears that dairy farming is most adaptable to these procedures since the extracted juice collected and stored on the farm would be transported by bulk tanker to the milk factory using the same transport as presently used for milk collection.

There are two versions of the system which could be applied to dairy farming. *Version I* envisages juice transport from farm to a centrally located milk factory. Using the transport vehicles which at present collect milk from dairy farms on a daily basis, the herbage juice, collected from the protein extraction operation, would also be sent, in a separate tank, for further processing and final LPC drying (Fig. 1.6A). In this version, juice volume to be transported annually from the farm would be more than twice the amount of milk. In *version II* (Fig. 1.6B), juice is processed on the farm and concentrated protein is sent to the milk factory instead of juice. In this alternative method, the transported volume would be reduced by more than half. In both versions, the system is composed of a harvester and herbage processing unit. In *version II*, together with an herbage processing unit, additional, mobile, or stationary juice processing devices will be located on the dairy farm.

As opposed to the "on-the-farm" scale operation just outlined, all protein extraction processes under consideration in the U.K. (Jones 1977), in the United States (Kohler and de Fremery 1977; Koegel and Bruhn 1977), and in Hungary (Hollo 1969) have been designed as stationary large-scale commercial operations. They lead to production of the pressed forage, in most cases used further for drying or as a silage for cattle and/or sheep (Connell and Houseman 1977). It has been suggested that the juice expressed from grass or from lucerne in U.K. agricultural conditions be used, after preservation without any processing, as a protein supplement in pig nutrition (Braude *et al.* 1977). Processes developed in the United States (Kohler and de Fremery 1977) and in Europe (Hollo 1969) envisaged further juice processing for recovery of food- and/or feed-grade protein concentrates which can be distributed on the market in dried form.

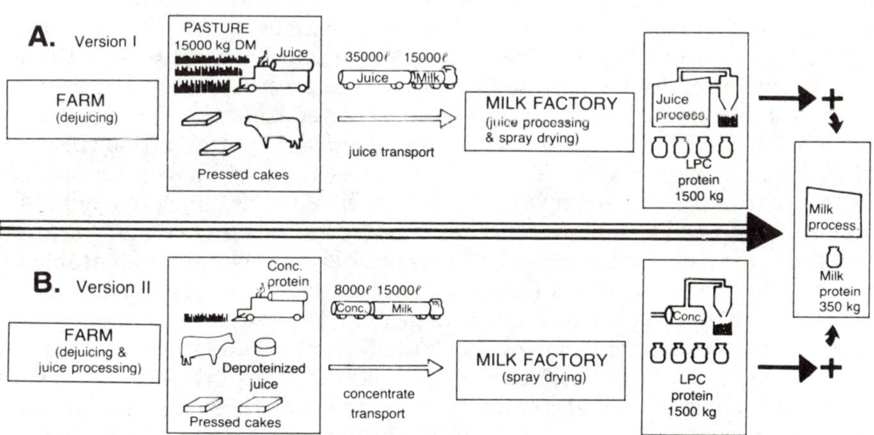

Fig. 1.6. Suggested versions of the practical application of the protein extraction from pasture herbage in dairy farming operations. A—Version I—Herbage juice transport. B—Version II—Concentrated herbage protein transport.

Protein Extraction Equipment and Herbage Processing

In Australia, a plant capable of processing up to 300 kg of fresh herbage per hr has recently been assembled for operation in an "on-the-farm" system (McKenzie 1978). The plant consists of a Pirie (1971) pulper, a roller press, a juice line permitting the mixing of steam from a boiler, and a filtering rack for separation of the coagulum. The pulper operates in an automatic feeding mode by means of the specially designed endless belt. The herbage harvested from pasture after maceration is discharged from the pulper on a polyvinylchloride belt. The belt carries pulp through the nip between two vulcanized rollers of different diameter in the press built up on a simple and inexpensive grain crusher. The aforementioned herbage processing unit designed for "one man, on-the-farm operation" gave consistent yields amounting to approximately 20% of the original dry weight of herbage. The typical distribution of pasture DM during its processing and pasture herbage fractionation is shown in Fig. 1.7.

Multidisciplinary research on protein extraction from grasslands was initiated in 1973 in the Nutrition Centre, Ruakura Research Station, Hamilton, N.Z. (Ostrowski-Meissner 1975A, 1976A,B,C,D, 1979D) and later on (Swan *et al.* 1980) led to the construction of the on-the-farm mobile protein extraction unit (Donelly *et al.* 1980). An advantage of using a mobile protein extraction unit in agricultural practice is that it may be used for processing a variety of green vegetation grown under various productive circumstances and in various geographical locations.

HERBAGE JUICE PROCESSING

Whole juice, mechanically expressed from herbage that had been preserved, is considered in some countries, e.g., in Great Britain, as a most economical form for extracted herbage proteins to be used for farm animal nutrition—mainly for pigs (Jones and Houseman 1975; Braude *et al.* 1977).

In order to reduce the input of energy in the process of protein recovery of the juice (approximately 10% solids) extracted from the herbage, there have been attempts to apply whole juice in practical pig nutrition (Braude *et al.* 1977). The initial results were inconsistent. When whole juice was fed to pigs throughout the growing period (from 20 to 90 kg liveweight) in amounts required to replace half the protein usually supplied by 7% whitefish meal, then performance and carcass quality were closely comparable to those of control pigs fed on fish meal only (Barber *et al.* 1979). However, when juice replaced 7% whitefish meal protein, the results were poorer than those of the all-fishmeal control pigs. Satisfactory results were also obtained when juice was fed in conjunction with liquid cheese whey (Barber *et al.* 1979). Barber *et al.* (1980), however, reported that those pigs given juice grew at the same rate but had a significantly poorer gain ratio and greater daily feed intake. They also had a thicker backfat layer and somewhat poorer commercial grading.

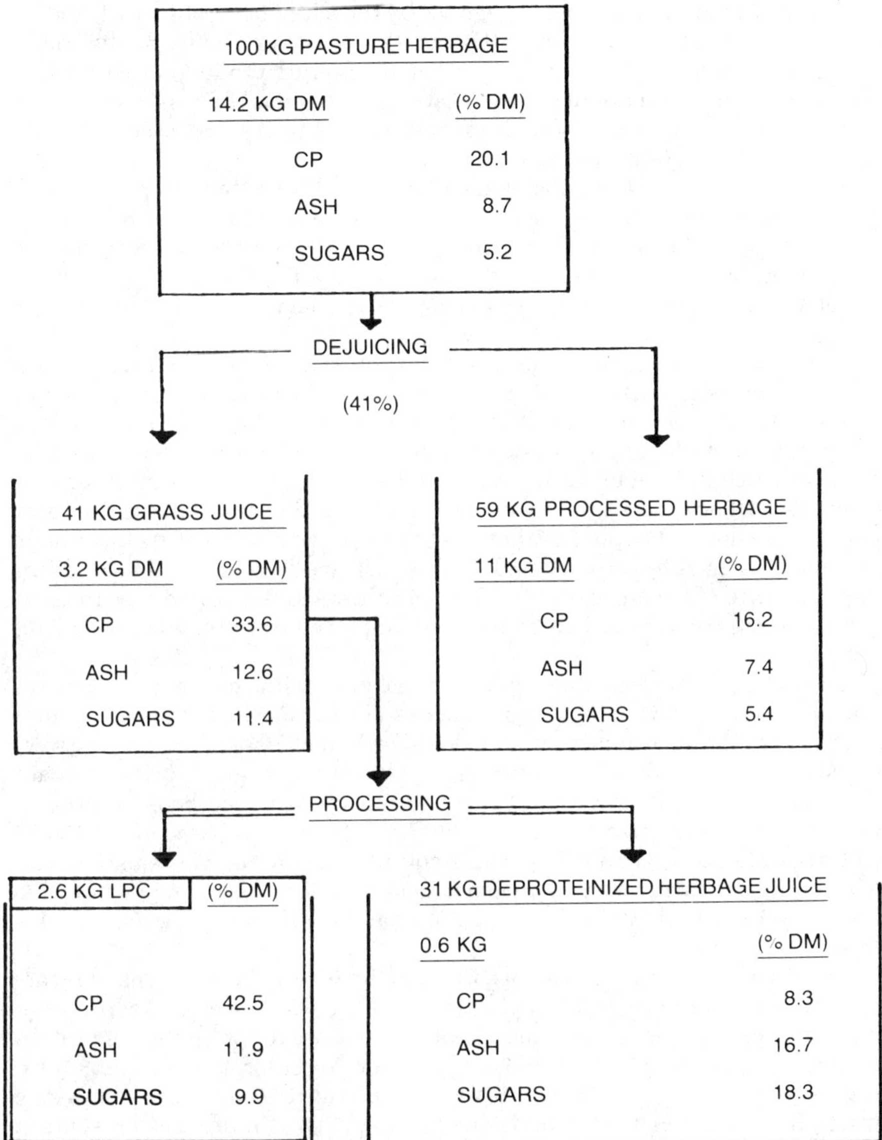

Fig. 1.7. Efficiency of pasture herbage processing as achieved in a typical protein extraction operation with heat coagulation at 85°C.

The reason given by Braude *et al.* (1977) for the inconsistency of the results in the initial trials on pigs was that it is difficult to standardize the chemical characteristics of herbage juice. The most common practice is to recover proteins from the extracted juice by the use of heat, chemical, and/or membrane filtration techniques (Ostrowski-Meissner 1979A,B, 1980B,C). The dried product LPC, irrespective of its higher production costs, has certain chemical and nutritional characteristics and is the most convenient form in which extracted protein from herbage can be incorporated in practical rations for farm animals.

Most commercial technologies developed in the United States, Europe, New Zealand, and Australia envisage juice processing in order to produce the protein concentrate, LPC. When extended LPC storage and/or transport is unavoidable, drying, particularly spray-drying, maintains the high quality of the protein recovered from pasture herbage (Ostrowski-Meissner 1976A).

In this system adapted for "on-the-farm" protein extraction from pasture herbage in Australia, the juice expressed from herbage is filtered by passing through the set of 1.5 mm sieves followed by coagulation of protein at a temperature of 85° to 90°C, using steam injection. Precipitated protein is then collected in a set of calico sacks and the coagulum is accumulated and drained until processing for the day is completed. Wet coagulum is used as a protein supplement in poultry diets by mixing it with crushed grain without preservation or after previous addition of 3% acetic acid and 0.3% sodium metabisulfite (McKenzie 1978). The coagulum can be stored wet in commercial deep freezers or can be dried, using any large commercial drying system.

Because protein separation from herbage juice using conventional steam and/or acid coagulation technique causes some damage to the protein (Lund 1973), ultrafiltration has been considered by Knuckles *et al.* (1975), Ostrowski-Meissner (1975B), and Singh *et al.* (1974) as an alternative to coagulation. Ultrafiltration is one of the most inexpensive methods for protein isolation and concentration (Payne *et al.* 1973). Spray-dried, ultrafiltered LPCs from herbage are not only water-soluble (Ostrowski-Meissner 1976D), a form which is favored in modern food and feed technology, but also are of higher nutritive value than the heat-coagulated LPCs (Ostrowski-Meissner 1976A).

Protein extracted with the juice from pasture herbage can be easily fractionated into dark green chloroplastic—feed-grade—and cream-white cytoplasmic—food-grade—fractions. The most advantageous method of protein separation appeared to be steam coagulation for chloroplastic fraction recovery followed by membrane filtration (ultrafiltration) for cytoplasmic fraction separation (Ostrowski-Meissner 1976D). Figure 1.8 presents a schematic diagram of the separation of protein fractions from herbage juice as achieved in this laboratory showing approximate recoveries of protein fractions of feed- and food-grade. The diagram also indicates possible ways of utilizing the deproteinized liquor in farm animal nutrition or its use as a substrate for microbial growth, allowing for the production of approximately 14 to 20 g of microbial protein from 1 liter of deproteinized herbage juice. When not being used, the liquor containing minerals and nitrogen compounds is returned to pasture as a topdressing.

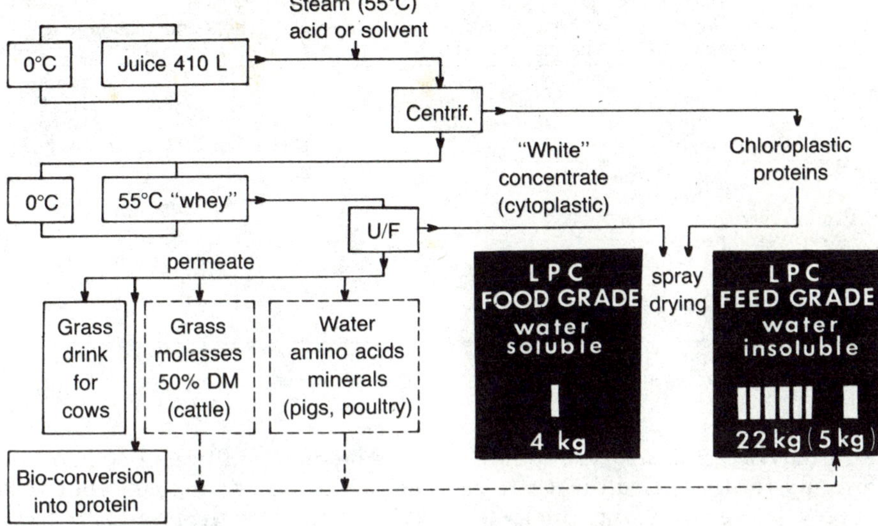

Fig. 1.8. Processing of juice extracted from pasture herbage and average balance of dry matter and protein as achieved during fractionation of herbage proteins into chloroplastic (feed-grade) and cytoplasmic (food-grade) protein fractions. Based on processing of juice extracted from 1 MT of fresh weight herbage as in Table 1.2.

LEAF PROTEIN CONCENTRATES FROM PASTURE

Efficiency of Production

Yields of unfractionated LPC feed-grade achieved from the unit of fresh or dry weight herbage were higher with ultrafiltration as compared to heat coagulation at 85°C (Table 1.2). This was achieved despite the botanical composition and pasture regrowth stage (Ostrowski-Meissner 1978C).

With protein extraction applied to topdressed and irrigated permanent pasture in northern Victoria, yields of 2.6 to 3.3 kg LPC DM per 100 kg of fresh herbage were achieved. Depending on the technique of protein recovery, steam coagulation or membrane filtration, the recoveries of protein were maintained at approximate levels of 39 and 44%, respectively.

To achieve high yields of LPC from grasslands, pasture herbage should be processed when green, rapidly growing, and vegetative, not when mature and fibrous (McKenzie 1977; Ostrowski-Meissner 1978C). Therefore, LPC is most readily produced in northern Victoria from herbage grown under irrigation. White clover and lucerne showed greatest potential for LPC production in spring, summer, and autumn, and grass had the greatest potential in winter (McKenzie 1977).

The obvious question under consideration in the 1980s will be whether protein extraction from grasslands and other green vegetation is a feasible

TABLE 1.2. PRODUCTION EFFICIENCY CHARACTERISTICS OF LPC
LPC obtained from pasture herbage processed alternatively by heat coagulation at 85°C or by membrane filtration using DIAFLO 2 × 10^4 MW cutoff membrane.

Measurement[1]	Heat Coagulation (85°C)	Membrane Filtration	Average S.E. of Mean Difference
Yield of LPC (kg DM from 100 kg fresh herbage)	2.6	3.3	0.19
Protein nitrogen recovery (recovered protein as % of the total N × 6.25 in herbage)	38.7	44.1	2.1
Protein yield (g per kg herbage DM)	77.8	88.7	5.8

Source: Ostrowski-Meissner (1978B,C).
[1]Each value represents the mean of four extraction procedures.
DM—Dry matter.

alternative technical operation which could be successfully applied in present and future agricultural circumstances. Taking into account that the supply of support energy (fuel, electricity) required for the protein extraction purpose is limited in many countries and that the cost of conventional energy sources is increasing rapidly, there are certain reservations as to the feasibility of the process being incorporated into agricultural practice irrespective of its potential in productive terms. It is reasonable to suppose, however, that with the protein extraction process being less dependent on conventional energy support and being more involved with the solar or geothermal energy available within the ecosystem as a source for extraction purposes, the whole operation will become less expensive. Therefore, the future application of the protein extraction system in agricultural practice should eventually be proved as an acceptable and reliable proposition.

Chemical Characteristics

The LPC recovered at rates of approximately 78 to 89 g of protein per kg of herbage DM (summer-grown herbage at fifth week of regrowth) is characterized by the typical chemical composition as given in Table 1.3. There were, however, slight differences in chemical composition of LPC recovered from pasture herbage grown in various seasons of the year (Table 1.4). Apart from the total nitrogen concentration being highest in the LPC produced in autumn, and the soluble sugars content being lowest in summer and highest in the spring season, there were no significant differences in organic matter, lysine, methionine, tryptophan, and *in vitro* protein digestion due to season of the year when LPC was produced (Ostrowski-Meissner 1978C). Protein recovery from spring-grown herbage is generally higher as compared to other seasons. It has been shown that, despite the

TABLE 1.3. CHEMICAL CHARACTERISTICS OF LPC
LPC obtained from pasture herbage processed alternatively by heat coagulation at 85°C or by membrane filtration using the DIAFLO 2×10^4 MW cutoff membrane.

Measurement[1]	Heat Coagulation (85°C)	Membrane Filtration	Average S.E. of Mean Difference
Composition of LPC (% DM)			
crude protein (N × 6.25)	42.5	46.8	1.1
ash	11.9	9.6	0.83
soluble carbohydrates	9.9	6.7	0.96
total essential amino acids (EAA)[2] (g per 100 g recovered)	44.8	48.7	2.2

Source: Ostrowski-Meissner (1978B,C).
[1]Each value represents the mean of four extraction procedures.
[2]Cystine excluded.

irrigation and topdressing, recovery of protein from mixed pasture in Victoria decreased substantially as the season progressed toward the summer (McKenzie 1977).

Biochemical and Nutritional Implementations

The biological evaluation of grass protein concentrates produced from summer-grown herbages, using two different extraction methods (Table 1.5), indicates that the membrane filtration (ultrafiltration) technique used for LPC production is superior to that of steam coagulation (Ostrowski-Meissner 1978C). This is in terms of total essential amino acids content; lysine, methionine, and tryptophan availability; protein digestibility *in vivo*; and its biological value as measured by PER (protein efficiency ratio). Ultrafiltration also enabled the production of a water-soluble (dispersible) powder. PER of ultrafiltered concentrate, after methionine and lysine supplementation, and of heat-coagulated LPC, after simultaneous lysine, methionine, and tryptophan supplementation, were similar to that of casein which was used as a standard control protein. According to the essential amino acid concentration, as shown in Table 1.6, the LPC contained significantly less lysine, threonine, tryptophan, and tyrosine, while the concentration of other amino acids did not differ statistically.

In general, concentrations of the essential amino acids, detected in LPCs, despite the technique used for their production, were in the range of concentrations as reported by Byers (1971B) except for the lower lysine and threonine values in the heat-coagulated LPC. A number of authors indicated that, on the average, the amino acid compositions of protein concentrates extracted from various plants do not show large variations (Byers 1971B; Gerloff *et al.* 1965; Holló 1969; Hove 1972; Parrish *et al.* 1974). The differences in amino acid concentrations, due to the technique used for

TABLE 1.4. CHEMICAL COMPOSITION OF THE FREEZE-DRIED PROTEIN CONCENTRATES (LPC)
LPC obtained by heat coagulation at 85°C from juice extracted from pasture herbage cut in three seasons of the year.

Season of the Year[1]	Total Nitrogen (% DM)	Organic Matter (% DM)	Soluble Sugars (% DM)	Amino Acids (g per 100 g Recovered Amino Acids)			*In Vitro* Digestion (%)
				Methionine	Lysine	Tryptophan	
Spring	6.6[ab]	87.9[a]	15.7[ab]	1.7[a]	4.6[a]	1.5[a]	85.2[a]
Summer	6.2[b]	85.2[a]	5.2[c]	1.9[a]	4.8[a]	1.3[a]	84.3[a]
Autumn	6.9[a]	88.3[a]	10.4[bc]	1.8[a]	5.0[a]	1.3[a]	84.9[a]
Average S.E. of mean differences	0.21	2.9	2.7	0.25	0.32	0.14	1.9

Source: Ostrowski-Meissner (1978C).
[1]Each value represents the mean of two LPC samples (each analyzed in duplicate), each of which was obtained as a result of protein extractions from bulked pasture samples in their fifth week of regrowth. Values in the same column with unlike superscripts showed significant differences at $P = 0.05$ as determined using Duncan's multiple range test.
DM—Dry Matter.

TABLE 1.5. NUTRITIONAL CHARACTERISTICS OF LPC
LPC obtained from pasture herbage processed alternatively by heat coagulation at 85°C or by membrane filtration using the DIAFLO 2 × 10^4 MW cutoff membrane.

Measurement[1]	Heat Coagulation (85°C)	Membrane Filtration	Average S.E. of Mean Difference
Protein digestibility (%)			
in vivo	73	78	3.6
in vitro	85	80	2.1
Availability (%)			
lysine	77	81	3.3
methionine	82	85	2.4
tryptophan	78	72	2.7
PER[2]			
LPC supplemented with DL-methionine (0.2%)	1.4	2.2	0.18
LPC supplemented with DL-methionine (0.2%) and L-lysine (0.5%)	2.2	2.7	0.14
LPC supplemented with DL-methionine (0.2%), L-lysine (0.5%), and L-tryptophan (0.3%)	2.7	2.6	0.17

Source: Ostrowski-Meissner (1978B,C).
[1]Each value represents the mean of four extraction procedures.
[2]Casein control group PER: 2.8; all groups of rats fed LPC without amino acid supplementation gave negative weight gains.

protein separation from juice, were also demonstrated by Girault (1973). He observed distinctive differences in the amino acid composition of protein extracts obtained as a result of different protein recovery procedures. Byers (1971A) also reported that the method of protein separation from juice may influence the amount of lysine in the final product. This is confirmed by the results presented in Table 1.6 in reference to lysine and also to threonine, tryptophan, and tyrosine.

In vivo and *in vitro* digestibilities of both LPCs, as obtained by two different production procedures, were in the range of values reported by Byers (1971B), Subba Rau *et al.* (1969, 1972), and Hartman *et al.* (1967); satisfactory for such a type of product, but lower than those reported by Akeson and Stahmann (1965) and Saunders *et al.* (1973).

The total essential amino acids and chemically-determined lysine availability correspond with the nutritional value of LPCs measured in biological tests with rats. A similar relationship between PER values and amino acid composition of LPCs was shown by Hansen and Eggum (1973) and Sikka *et al.* (1975), and a relationship between PER and chemically-determined lysine availability was also reported (Ostrowski-Meissner *et al.* 1972).

LPC produced by the ultrafiltration procedure was superior to heat-coagulated LPC in terms of its nutritional value. The ultrafiltered LPC supplemented with synthetic methionine and lysine showed a PER value

TABLE 1.6. THE AMINO ACID COMPOSITION OF THE TWO FREEZE-DRIED LPC'S AND COMPARISON WITH REFERENCE DATA

	Protein Concentrate from Pasture Herbage			Reference		
Amino Acid	Heat Coagulation (85°C)	Membrane Filtration	Average S.E. of Mean Difference[1]	Byers (1971B) (Range: from	–to)	FAO (1965)
Histidine	2.2	2.0	0.13	1.8	2.8	—
Isoleucine	4.6	4.6	0.37	4.5	5.5	4.2
Leucine	9.5	9.9	0.42	8.8	10.2	4.8
Lysine	4.8	6.2	0.33[1]	5.6	7.3	4.2
Methionine	1.9	2.1	0.20	1.6	2.6	2.2
Phenylalanine	6.1	5.9	0.28	5.5	6.8	2.8
Threonine	4.3	5.0	0.22[1]	4.7	5.8	2.8
Tryptophan	1.3	2.0	0.17[2]	1.2	2.3	1.4
Tyrosine	3.9	4.3	0.14[1]	3.7	4.9	2.8
Valine	6.2	6.7	0.35	5.9	6.9	4.2

Source: Ostrowski-Meissner (1978B,C).
[1]Significance of difference at $P = 0.05$ level.
[2]Significance at $P = 0.01$ level.

similar to casein. These results agree with those reported by Hanczakowski (1974), Saunders *et al.* (1973), and Subba Rau *et al.* (1972), who showed that protein concentrates from green plants, supplemented with methionine only or methionine with lysine, were nutritionally equivalent to casein. However, to the heat-precipitated LPC, synthetic tryptophan as well as lysine and methionine had to be added so as to increase the PER value of the LPC to the casein value level. The ultrafiltered LPC slightly decreased in PER value when tryptophan as well as lysine and methionine was added.

According to the amino acid composition (Table 1.6) in both LPCs, irrespective of technique used, methionine was the only limiting amino acid. This has not been proved by the response of rats to synthetic DL-methionine supplementation. Depending on the process used for the LPC production, addition of synthetic lysine or lysine and tryptophan were necessary to improve the PER of the LPC to the value achieved with casein, which is used as a reference protein. The PER values in the steam-coagulated LPC, as obtained after the methionine supplementation, were low as compared to the PER values of the ultrafiltered LPC. This could be due to insufficient methionine supplementation. The low analytical value for methionine in heat-coagulated LPC would indicate that this is the case. However, despite the total lysine and tryptophan "sufficiency" in both LPCs, the response of rats to added lysine may indicate loss of lysine availability which was slightly greater in the heat processed LPC as opposed to the ultrafiltered LPC. This can be explained by heat processing (Lund 1973), since in the presence of reducing sugars, proteins are degraded via the Maillard reaction, the basic amino acids being especially reactive. Even though the heat-coagulated LPC was supplemented with methionine and lysine, it had a lower PER value which may indicate that, due to processing (protein separation procedure followed by drying), amino acids other than methionine or lysine became limiting, too. This may be due to the decrease in content and/or the lowering in availability (Ostrowski-Meissner 1978D). Of all the essential amino acids, lysine and threonine were pointed out by Lund (1973) as the most heat-labile, but it was shown by Meredith *et al.* (1974) that during processing, histidine, threonine, and valine also are subject to an even higher degree of degradation than are methionine and lysine. Wallace (1973), however, indicated that processed protein products tend to be limited by the sulfur amino acids rather than by lysine and so damage to sulfur amino acids and supplementation with these is generally more significant than damage to lysine and supplementation with lysine. Fetuga *et al.* (1973), on the other hand, showed that apart from methionine both lysine and tryptophan are the amino acids in shortest supply in most proteins of plant origin. The results shown in Tables 1.5 and 1.6 with heat-coagulated LPC would indicate that this is so. However, in the analyzed LPCs, both these amino acids were found in amounts exceeding the FAO (1965) amino acid standard.

Herbage as a Source of Food-grade LPC

Protein concentrates recoverable from green herbage represent a mixture of different types of proteins (Ostrowski-Meissner 1979B), but due to the distinctive dark color, bitter taste, and strong grassy smell, unfractionated product is not readily acceptable for direct human consumption (Pirie 1971). To recover purified LPC suitable for human nutrition, first chloroplast-containing (feed-grade) proteins are separated from the crude plant extracts by the use of various chemical and/or physical techniques. Second, the remaining chloroplast-free (cytoplasmic, food-grade) protein fraction may be isolated by heat precipitation, by chemical coagulation, or by membrane filtration. After concentration, the cytoplasmic fraction is cream-white with a greenish tint in color and tasteless. Various isolation techniques for the recovery of food-grade LPC have been demonstrated as commercially feasible (Ostrowski-Meissner 1980C; Ostrowski-Meissner *et al.* 1980).

Yields, composition, and nutritive quality of recovered LPC from herbage depend on the protein recovery technique from the herbage juice (Ostrowski-Meissner 1975A, 1979B, 1980C). Membrane filtration has been shown as a superior technique in recovering chloroplast-free proteins with the final product, after drying, being water dispersible and showing lower hemolytic activity as opposed to the heat-coagulated, water-insoluble product.

Typical chemical and biological characteristics of food- and feed-grade LPC from herbage are given in Table 1.7. Mixed herbage, however, as well as pure species of perennial grasses (paspalum and perennial ryegrass) are yielding much less protein compared with legumes (white clover and lucerne) (Table 1.8). From the various plant species used for food-grade LPC production, the most superior in terms of yields of recoverable cytoplasmic protein fraction and *in vitro* digestibility was *Chenopodium quinoa* (Ostrowski-Meissner *et al.* 1980). Mixed herbage grown in the humid tropics have much less yields of recoverable protein compared with mixed herbage grown in temperate climate conditions on cultivated grasslands. This low recovery may be explained by the initial low protein contents in herbage (14%). According to Byers (1961) and Telek (1979), low protein content in processed green material may restrict recovery of protein from herbage species grown in tropical countries.

LPC from Pasture in Poultry Nutrition

Chickens. Protein concentrates recovered from pasture herbage have been used to replace soybean meal as a source of protein in diets for growing chickens (McKenzie 1978). Amino acid composition (Table 1.9) was notably affected by the method of LPC drying. In the trials with growing chickens it was shown that oven-dried LPCs produced from White Clover had a biological value 15 to 20% lower than that of soybean meal (Table 1.10). Methionine

TABLE 1.7. PRODUCTION EFFICIENCY AND CHEMICAL AND NUTRITIONAL CHARACTERISTICS OF LPC
LPC obtained from pasture herbage processed alternatively without or with fractionation into concentrates of feed- and food-grade products using different processing and fractionation techniques.

	Protein Concentrate from Herbage				
	Heat Precipitation			Membrane Filtration	
		Fraction			
Measurement[1]	Without Fractionation	Chloroplastic (55°C)	Cytoplasmic (55°/85°C)	Fractionation	Cytoplasmic Fraction
Protein Concentrate (Grade)	Feed	Feed	Food	Food	Food
LPCs Production Efficiency					
yields of LPC (kg DM from 100 kg of fresh herbage)	2.6	2.2	0.4	3.3	0.4
protein nitrogen recovery (recovered protein as percentage of the total N × 6.25 in herbage)	38.7	32.1	6.2	44.1	6.6
protein yield (g per kg herbage DM)	77.8	64.6	12.5	89.7	13.2
Chemical characteristic of LPC (% DM)					
crude protein (N × 6.25)	42.5	41.2	57.4	46.8	52.0
ash	11.9	13.1	5.5	9.6	3.6
soluble carbohydrates	9.9	11.7	9.1	6.7	6.4
total essential amino acids (EAA)[2] (g per 100 g recovered)	44.8	44.3	47.4	48.7	49.0
Protein digestibility (%)					
in vivo	73	71	80	78	82
in vitro	85	78	84	80	93
Availability (%)					
lysine	77	73	82	81	86
methionine	82	80	81	85	91
tryptophan	78	75	80	72	94
Protein Efficiency Ratio (PER)[3]					
LPC supplemented with DL-methionine (0.2%)	1.4	1.1	2.0	2.2	2.6
LPC supplemented with DL-methionine (0.2%) and L-lysine (0.5%)	2.2	1.9	2.4	2.7	2.6
LPC supplemented with DL-methionine (0.2%), L-lysine (0.5%), and L-tryptophan (0.3%)	2.7	2.6	2.8	2.6	2.8

Source: Ostrowski-Meissner (1979B).
[1]Each value represents the mean from eight processed herbages.
[2]Cystine excluded.
[3]Casein control group PER: 2.8; all groups of rats fed LPC without amino acid supplementation gave negative weight gains.

TABLE 1.8. EFFICIENCY OF CYTOPLASMIC PROTEIN RECOVERY FROM VARIOUS HERBAGES, LEGUMES, AND OTHER SPECIES GROWN AT VARIOUS GEOGRAPHICAL LOCATIONS (FRACTIONATED HEAT PRECIPITATION AT 85°C)

		Cytoplasmic Protein Fraction			
Herbage Species	Location[1]	Yield (g/kg Herbage) Dry Matter)	Protein Nitrogen (% DM)	Cytoplasmic LPC as a Percentage of the Total Recoverable Proteins	*In Vitro* Digestion (%)
Mixed herbage	NZ[2]	36	12.14	35	90
	A[3]	30	12.41	33	91
	I[4]	7	12.03	24	93
Perennial ryegrass	A[3]	18	11.90	32	92
(Lolium perenne)	NZ[4]	19	11.72	34	91
Paspalum	A[3]	12	12.47	34	87
(Paspalum dilitatum)	NZ[4]	14	12.02	32	91
White Clover	A[3]	58	12.16	37	91
(Trifolium repens)	NZ[4]	61	11.97	35	94
Lucerne					
(Medicago sativa)	A[3]	61	12.33	46	89
Atriplex hortensis	A[3]	92	14.04	56	89
	S[3]	90	14.51	58	87
Chenopodium quinoa	A[3]	75	13.73	45	94
	S[3]	73	13.50	47	94

[1] A—Grown in Australia. S—Grown in Sweden. NZ—Grown in New Zealand. I—Grown in Indonesia.
[2] Source: Ostrowski-Meissner (1976E).
[3] Source: Ostrowski-Meissner *et al.* (1980).
[4] Source: Ostrowski-Meissner, unpublished data.

TABLE 1.9. AMINO ACID COMPOSITION OF LPC EXTRACTED FROM WHITE CLOVER AS A RESULT OF DIFFERENT METHODS OF DRYING (PERCENTAGE OF TOTAL AMINO ACIDS)

Amino Acid	Freeze-Dried	Oven-Dried (121°C)	Tumble-Dried
Lysine (availability %)	6.4 (89%)	5.6 (68%)	6.4
Cysteine and cystine	1.6	1.7	1.7
Methionine (availability %)	2.1 (75%)	2.0 (40%)	2.3
Histidine	2.5	2.4	2.4
Arginine	6.3	6.4	6.5
Tryptophan	ND	ND	ND
Aspartic acid	9.7	10.0	9.9
Threonine	5.0	5.3	5.2
Serine	4.4	4.7	4.6
Glutamic acid	11.1	11.6	11.3
Proline	5.2	5.1	5.1
Glycine	5.2	5.7	5.5
Alanine	6.2	6.3	6.2
Valine	6.5	6.1	6.0
Isoleucine	5.3	4.7	4.7
Leucine	9.4	9.5	9.3
Tyrosine	4.8	5.0	5.0
Phenylalanine	6.2	6.1	6.1
Crude protein (N × 6.25) (% DM)	60.1	59.8	

Source: McKenzie (1978).
ND—Not determined.

TABLE 1.10. GROWTH OF CHICKENS (12 TO 18 DAYS) AND PROTEIN EFFICIENCY RATIO (PER) ACHIEVED WITH LPC
LPC extracted from white clover and soybean meal at two dietary levels without and with synthetic amino acids supplementation.

	Crude Protein in the Ration (N × 6.25)			
	18.7% DM		20.0 to 21.8% DM	
Diet	Weight Gain (g)	PER	Weight Gain (g)	PER
LPC				
preserved (wet)	50.0	3.05	—	—
freeze-dried	50.4	2.84	32.9	1.83
oven dried	44.1	2.39	21.7	1.30
Soybean meal	56.1	2.84	—	—
LPC freeze-dried + L-lysine	52.8	3.00	—	—
LPC oven dried + L-lysine	49.9	2.49	—	—
Soybean meal + L-lysine	66.1	3.38	52.1	2.67
LPC freeze-dried + DL-methionine	—	—	34.2	2.00
LPC freeze-dried + DL-methionine + L-lysine	—	—	49.9	2.64
LPC oven dried + DL-methionine	—	—	22.7	1.40
LPC oven dried + DL-methionine + L-lysine	—	—	48.0	2.73

Source: McKenzie (1978).

and lysine appeared to be the amino acids limiting the biological value of a wheat-based diet for chickens. In order to reduce the losses of limiting amino acids with simultaneous reduction of the costs of LPC production, it is recommended to mix preserved LPC with crushed grain rather than drying it before mixing into the diets. Under practical farm conditions, the use of wet LPC as a dietary ingredient seems to be most practical and convenient since drying at high temperatures (oven drying) resulted in a substantial reduction of the contents and/or availability of the most limiting amino acids in LPCs.

Laying Hens. Preserved LPC used in the diet for laying hens at the levels of 0, 1, 3, and 9% as a substitute of meat meal increased egg production slightly, with a simultaneous increase in density of yolk color (Table 1.11). The quantity of xanthophyll determined in freeze-dried LPCs was in the range of 480 to 580 mg/kg LPC (McKenzie 1978).

TABLE 1.11. YOLK COLOR AND EGG PRODUCTION AS A RESULT OF MEAT MEAL SUBSTITUTION BY LPC IN DIET FOR LAYING HENS (15% CP)

Protein Supplement In Ration (% DM)			
LPC	Meatmeal	Roche Color Score	Egg Production (g/day)
0	10	5.1	143
1	9	6.6	153
3	7	7.3	165
9	0	8.0	Not recorded

Source: McKenzie (1978).

The dried unfractionated leaf protein concentrates produced from mixed herbage when supplemented with methionine gave chick growth efficiency results similar to those results obtained from a soybean meal supplemented with methionine (Johns 1980; McKenzie 1978). The relatively high fat level in the LPC contributed significantly to its energy content and thus it had a higher productive energy value than that found with the soybean meal. In general, unfractionated LPC, recovered from mixed herbage, compared favorably with soybean meal as protein concentrate for poultry rations (Johns 1980; McKenzie 1977; Ostrowski-Meissner 1979E).

LPC also contains the pigment xanthophyll (1.1 to 1.5 g/kg) which is responsible for imparting the orange color to egg yolks and broiler skins. In many countries, such as Japan, the United States, France, and Spain, poultry rations have traditionally been supplemented with dried lucerne and other concentrates to supply this pigment and hence satisfy consumer preferences for eggs with well-colored yolks and broiler carcasses with like skins. Research in Japan (Yoshida and Hoshii 1980) with unfractionated protein concentrates, from mixed pastures produced in New Zealand, has shown that the xanthophyll in LPC used for pigmentation has a similar efficiency to that in dried lucerne. However, compared with dried lucerne, LPC contains about five times as much xanthophyll. It also has higher productive energy, digestible protein contents, and lower fiber contents. Thus, LPC is a more suitable product for inclusion in poultry rations than is dried lucerne. It is already used for this purpose in France where commercial LPC production is well advanced.

LPC and Fiber Residues in Feeding Wool-producing Sheep

In Australia, using wool-producing sheep, the feeding value of protein expressed from lucerne and the fibrous residue fractions were investigated by Weston *et al.* (1978). Herbage containing on the average 17.2% organic matter (OM) and 3.9% crude protein (CP) was processed using the pulper and press technique. The feeding value of the protein concentrate obtained (steam coagulation at 94°C), deproteinized juice, and pressed fibrous residues for Border Leicester × Merino sheep was determined.

Juice expressed from lucerne contained on the average 9.1% OM and 4.1% CP and had a net energy value of 7.9 (± 0.5) MJ × kg^{-1} OM. When the juice was incorporated into the roughage and maize diet instead of soybean for weaner lambs, daily live weight gains of 283 g (± 14) were obtained as compared with 316 g (± 9) on a soybean diet. Herbage juice providing 160 g CP daily increased greasy wool growth in roughage-fed sheep by 5.3 (± 0.4) g/100 g CP.

The digestibility of protein in concentrate from lucerne as determined with sheep was 84% ± 1. When the concentrate was given to provide 87 g CP daily, greasy wool regrowth increased by 10.1 g ± 0.9/100 g CP, as compared with 9.3 g ± 0.4/100 g CP obtained with casein.

The digestibility of OM and cell wall constituents in fibrous residues were 65% ± 1 and 62% ± 2, respectively.

The data presented by Weston *et al.* (1978) indicate a high energy value for the lucerne juice and a high biological value for wool growth for the protein concentrate. The fiber residues have the nutritive value of a medium quality roughage.

PARTIALLY DEPROTEINIZED PASTURE HERBAGE AS FODDER FOR DAIRY COWS

The chemical composition of the freshly-cut, unprocessed pasture herbage and the partially deproteinized herbage fed to cows either fresh or as silage is given in Table 1.12 (Ostrowski-Meissner 1978B).

Protein extractability figures achieved in a farm-scale operation ranged from 22 to 52% of the total CP determined in the freshly harvested herbage used for protein extraction. The chemical analyses revealed that the partially deproteinized pasture herbage still contained more than 15% CP on a DM basis, which is considered sufficient to meet the requirements of dairy cows, beef cattle, and bulls (Natl. Res. Counc. 1970, 1971). This has been confirmed by the practical results on dairy cows fed partially deproteinized herbage (Table 1.13). It has also been shown by Jones and Houseman (1975), Maguire and Brookes (1973), Vartha and Allison (1973A,B), and Weston *et al.* (1978) that deproteinized herbage can be a fully productive fodder for cattle and sheep. Silage made from partially deproteinized pasture herbage as shown in Table 1.14 is comparable to good quality silages from unprocessed herbage (Ostrowski-Meissner 1976A).

The protein extraction system from grasslands has been considered in an independent economy and marketing analyses (Hutton 1975) as a feasible and profitable alternative to be applied under the agricultural circumstances characteristic of dairying in the Waikato (New Zealand), considered the world's most intensive dairy farming area. However, in a series of experiments conducted on highly productive lactating cows involved in the protein extraction operation in this area, a 10% reduction in the intake of partially deproteinized (processed) pasture has been observed. This resulted in a 15% decrease in milk production and a lowering in both fat and protein contents as compared with results with nonprocessed ryegrass-white clover pasture (Donelly *et al.* 1980). In dry cows and beef cattle, however, even though the consumption of partially-deproteinized herbage was not reduced but remained the same, 14% higher live weight gains were recorded in animals fed partially-deproteinized herbage as compared with the animals fed unprocessed herbage.

EFFICIENCY OF PASTURE ENERGY AND PROTEIN CONVERSION IN PROTEIN EXTRACTION SYSTEM

The efficiency of pasture energy and nitrogen conversion into dairy products depends on the stocking rate, which affects milk production from the unit of pasture area. The relationship between stocking rate and milk protein production was calculated as $Y = 14.3\ SR \pm 1.1 + 172$ with S.E. =

TABLE 1.12. AVERAGE CHEMICAL CHARACTERISTICS OF UNPROCESSED AND MECHANICALLY PROCESSED PASTURE HERBAGE

LPC obtained during protein extraction in large-scale operation.

Product[1]	DM (%)	CP (% DM)	Ash (% DM)	Soluble Sugars (% DM)	Fiber (% DM)	Energy (Joules $\times 10^3$)	*In Vitro* Digestion (%)
Pasture herbage	14.2	20.1	8.7	5.2	22.6	17.4	69.6
Processed herbage (partially deproteinized)	18.6	16.2	7.4	3.4	28.3	18.1	70.8
Silage from partially deproteinized herbage (pH 4.1)	20.1	16.9	7.0	9.6	26.5	18.4	72.0

Source: Ostrowski-Meissner (1978B).

[1]Pasture of botanical composition: 55% white clover, 44% perennial grasses, and 1% weeds (fourth week of herbage regrowth).

TABLE 1.13. PERFORMANCE OF DAIRY COWS GIVEN UNPROCESSED FRESH PASTURE HERBAGE OR MECHANICALLY PROCESSED, PARTIALLY DEPROTEINIZED HERBAGE

	Pasture Herbage	
Criterion[1]	Unprocessed	Processed (Partially Deproteinized)
Average live weight (kg)	397	391
Fresh matter intake (kg/day)	111	83
Dry matter intake (kg/day)	15.8	15.4
Milk production (kg/day)	17.7	17.5
Milk composition		
protein (%)	3.0	2.9
fat (%)	4.2	3.9
Efficiency of herbage protein (CP) conversion into milk protein (%)	23.3	27.3

Source: Ostrowski-Meissner (1978B).
[1]Six cows in each group selected from the same herd. Feeding trials during late spring and summer (between November and mid-February).

± 5.4 (King 1978), where Y is the annual milk protein production per year and SR is the stocking rate. Based on both dairy production and protein extraction figures, as presented in Table 1.15, the efficiency of pasture production has been compiled as an effect of stocking rate.

Energy Conversion

The question arises as to what the potential productivity limit in agricultural systems is in northern Victoria, taking into account the conversion of the photosynthetically-active radiation (PAR) into net above-the-ground "available" pasture DM production.

Using the mean daily totals of the incoming solar radiation at latitudes characteristic to northern Victoria (37°) and using the data given by Baumgartner (1973) on the partition of extraterrestrial radiation, approximately 50% of which is within the visible range (400 to 760 nm), PAR has been calculated as a fraction of total radiation on an annual basis (Fig. 1.9). The net primary pasture production calculated from PAR (2.5 kJ $\times 10^{13}$ ha^{-1} $year^{-1}$) was estimated as an average of 1.9 kg DM $\times 10^4$ ha^{-1} $year^{-1}$ with an average conversion efficiency of 1.5%. This net photosynthetic efficiency of primary pasture productivity was far below the average 2.6% possible maximum achievable under optimum agricultural conditions (Bonner 1962; Phillipson 1973).

The secondary PAR conversion—from energy of pasture to energy of dairy products—in northern Victoria has been calculated as 0.11%. With an involvement of such a pasture in a protein extraction system, an average

TABLE 1.14. CHEMICAL COMPOSITION (%) OF SILAGES OBTAINED FROM PARTIALLY DEPROTEINIZED GRASS GROWN ON CONVENTIONALLY GRAZED OR ON "0 GRAZED" PASTURES

Silage[1]	DM	Ash	N	NH_3[2]	pH	Acids: Lactic	Acetic	Propionic	Butyric
Processed grass (cakes) from pasture:									
(a) Conventionally grazed	21.0	10.1	3.05	6.9	4.05				
(b) Used during 3 years exclusively for protein extraction in "0 grazing" system	22.0	10.7	2.94	6.7	4.08	NA[3]	1.61	0.14	0.16
Unprocessed pasture grass	18.7	19.6	2.93	10.7	4.33	5.95	1.72	0.14	3.6

Source: Ostrowski-Meissner (1976A).
[1] Silages prepared in miniscale (5 kg in plastic buckets) during 5 weeks at 22°C.
[2] NH_3—Ammonia N as a percentage of the total N.
[3] Not analyzed.

TABLE 1.15. ANNUAL PASTURE, MILK, AND LPC PRODUCTION (KG × 10^3 HA^{-1}) AND PROTEIN (N × 6.25) CONVERSION EFFICIENCY (%) IN DAIRY FARMING IN EITHER CONVENTIONAL OR PROTEIN EXTRACTION SYSTEMS AT THREE DIFFERENT STOCKING RATES

Measurement	Stocking Rate (Cows per ha): 4.4		6.6		8.6	
	CD[1]	PE[2]	CD	PE	CD	PE
Pasture (with an extra hay supplement)—DM	17.8	13.8	20.4	15.8	22.2	17.2
—CP	3.6	2.3	4.1	2.6	4.5	2.8
Protein recovery in the form of: —milk	0.5	0.4	0.5	0.4	0.4	0.3
—unfractionated LPC	—	1.4	—	1.6	—	1.7
(food-grade fraction)		(0.2)		(0.3)		(0.3)
Efficiency of protein converson (%) from pasture into:						
milk	13	17	12	15	10	11
milk and unfractionated LPC	—	78	—	77	—	71
milk, meat,[3] and LPC—food-grade	—	42	—	41	—	38

Source: Ostrowski-Meissner (1978B).
[1] Conventional dairying based on pasture grazing.
[2] Dairying in protein extraction system which resulted in part of the pasture DM and protein being extracted during herbage processing.
[3] Chicken meat obtained as a result of a feeding diet containing 9% LPC.

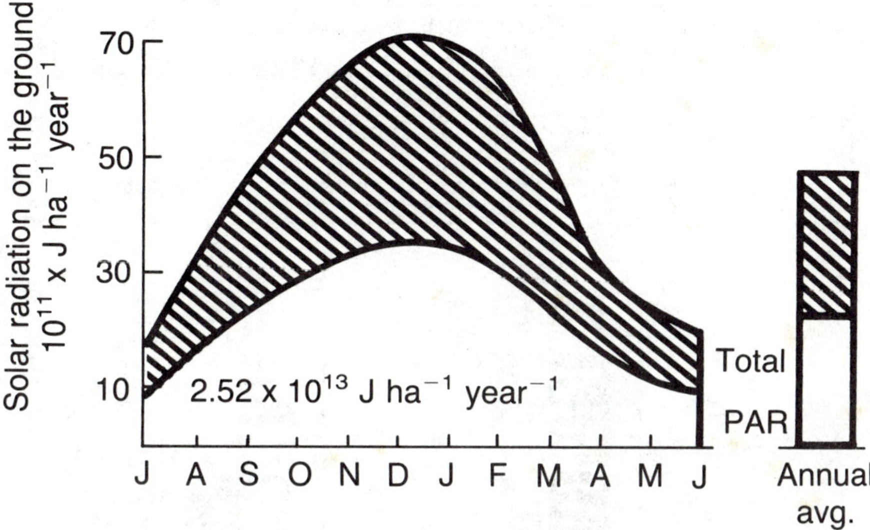

Fig. 1.9. Mean monthly totals of incoming solar radiation available in agricultural ecosystem in Northern Victoria, Australia, at 37° latitude.

annual PAR conversion into protein products as recovered in milk, meat, and LPC form reached the 0.58% level. The primary and secondary PAR conversion and the distribution of the pasture energy and energy of the proteinaceous products derived from pasture in both conventional dairying and within a protein extraction system on a dairy farm are schematically presented in Fig. 1.10.

Pasture Nitrogen Conversion

Primary Nitrogen Production from Pasture. Nitrogen production on irrigated and topdressed pastures in northern Victoria has been calculated as approximately 725 kg ha^{-1}, this being annual "available" herbage nitrogen production. With protein extraction applied to such a pasture, a large proportion of the herbage nitrogen is separated, in LPC form, with the further subdivision into feed- and food-grade edible protein products (Fig. 1.11).

Secondary Nitrogen Production from Pasture. Using pasture herbage for pasture protein conversion into dairy products, an efficiency of 13% has been determined. Applying protein extraction to pasture herbage prior to feeding dairy cows, the quantity of recoverable proteins in milk, meat, and LPC form—both food- and feed-grade—is notably increased from 13 to 78% (Fig. 1.12). When LPC feed-grade was used as a protein source in the diet of growing chickens, then the conversion of nitrogen from pasture to nitrogen recovered in the form of highly proteinaceous products (such as milk, beef,

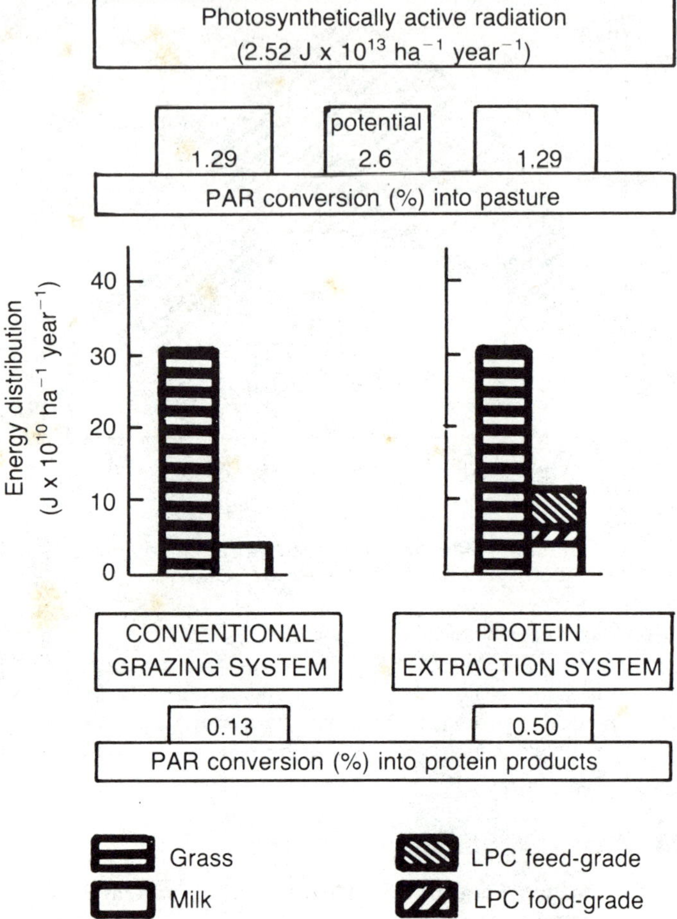

Fig. 1.10. Conversion of photosynthetically-active radiation into energy of food and feed products in conventional and protein extraction systems.

chicken meat, and unconventional food-grade protein LPC) reached the level of 42%.

Similar performances with dairy cows, fed either with unprocessed fresh pasture or mechanically processed, partially deproteinized pasture herbage (see Table 1.14), showed higher protein conversion efficiency by cows fed with partially deproteinized pasture (27.3%) compared with unprocessed herbage (23.3%). In addition to the higher protein conversion efficiency with the application of protein extraction from pasture before its utilization by dairy cows, approximately 1 kg of protein per animal daily has been recovered from herbage in LPC form as a result of pasture processing prior to its feeding to dairy cows.

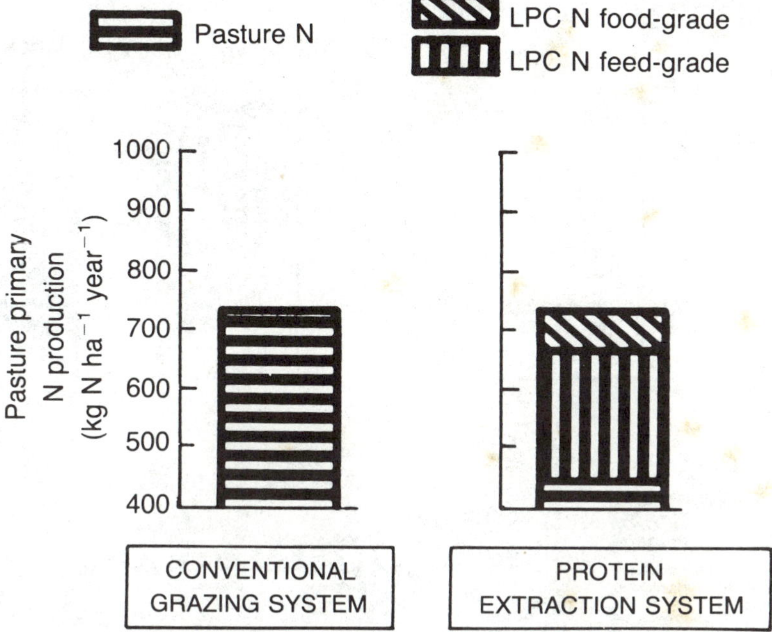

Fig. 1.11. Annual primary "available" nitrogen production from pasture in conventional and protein extraction systems.

ADVANTAGES AND POTENTIAL OF PROTEIN EXTRACTION FROM GRASSLANDS IN AUSTRALIA

The introduction of the protein extraction system to conventional dairy farming in northern Victoria resulted in yields of approximately 1.4 to 1.7×10^3 kg protein ha^{-1} $year^{-1}$ in LPC form from irrigated and top-dressed pastures characterized by a production of 1.4 to 1.7×10^4 kg DM ha^{-1}. In addition to the LPC protein, approximate yields of milk protein amounting 0.3 to 0.4×10^3 kg ha^{-1} $year^{-1}$ were maintained, depending on the stocking rate of dairy cows. In a tropical climate, where comparative yields of pasture herbage DM can exceed 50 MT per ha annually (Vincente-Chandler 1973), involvement of such grasslands in a protein extraction system could bring hypothetical yields of 4.5×10^3 kg CP per ha annually in LPC form and a further 1.78×10^3 kg of milk protein from intensive dairying. It has been calculated that the new technology—protein extraction from grasslands—applied to dairy farming in Australia in Victoria, New South Wales, and Queensland, which are the leading states in intensive dairy production, could increase present protein production from the estimated 6.5×10^8 kg being achieved in these three states through conventional farming to approximately 1.9×10^{10} kg. Of this amount approximately 1.4 to 1.6×10^{10} kg would be leaf protein concentrate feed-grade

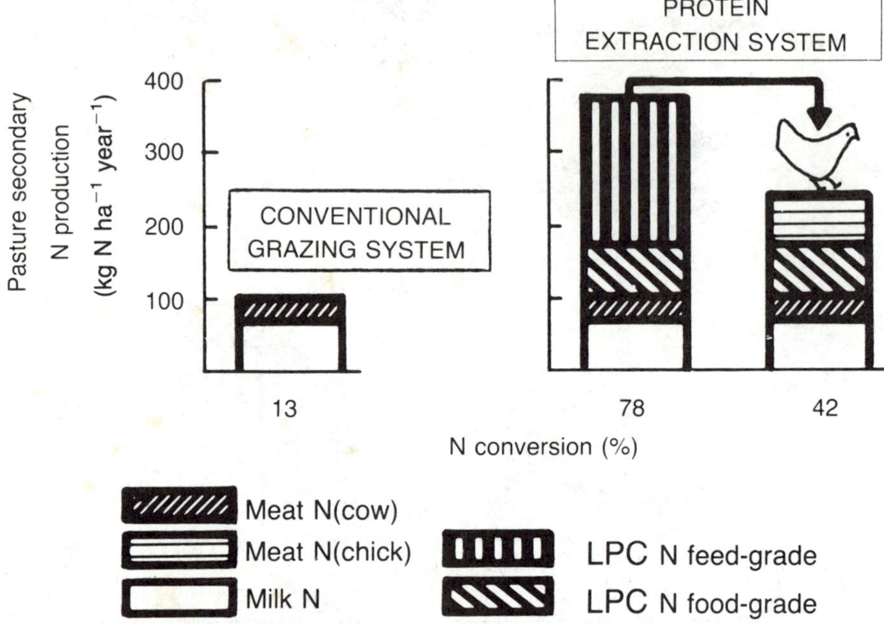

Fig. 1.12. Annual secondary protein production from mixed pasture and its conversion into high protein dairy products in conventional pasture management system and with the application of the protein extraction procedure. Growing chickens used as converters of LPC N feed-grade into meat protein.
From Ostrowski-Meissner (1978B).

and nutritionally equivalent to soybean meal. Selling dried LPC at the international market price similar to soybean meal, it is possible to obtain additional agricultural production from Australian dairy farming worth approximately $2 billion annually, with meat and dairy production still remaining at the present level.

With fractionation of the total recoverable protein, approximately 3×10^9 kg food-grade protein could be recovered as unconventional protein suitable for direct human consumption.

The remaining feed-grade LPC, after being used as a protein source in poultry nutrition, can hypothetically be converted into broiler meat giving a yield of approximately 4×10^9 kg high quality animal protein.

The hypothetical figures just given indicate an enormous potential in protein of both feed- and food-grade quality in the grasslands of the temperate and subtropical regions. Whether hypothetical figures can be achieved in real practice, in routine farm operations, is a matter for agricultural engineering involvement in the whole protein extraction process and optimization of the efficiency of the entire extraction system which, as has been shown, depends on many factors limiting the final protein recovery from pasture (Ostrowski-Meissner 1975A, 1976C, 1977). Further research is needed in order to develop a whole system of protein extraction feasible to be introduced to dairy farming practice under various agricultural conditions specific to particular state and/or climatic regions in Australia. This is where net primary protein production derived from the grassland ecosystem indicates tremendous potential for further development.

Various aspects of protein extraction from grasslands have been investigated mainly in relation to New Zealand and Australian (Victoria) agricultural circumstances (Donelly *et al.* 1980; Johns 1980; Ostrowski-Meissner 1979A,B,C,D,E, 1980A,B,C; Stockdale *et al.* 1981). Some comparative studies have also been conducted on the same species grown in Victoria (Australia) and in Sweden (Ostrowski-Meissner *et al.* 1980). From the results of this research, one important conclusion is that protein extraction from herbage is a feasible practical alternative to the conventional use of agricultural land and it is only matters of economy, management, and the availability of suitable equipment that will enable grasslands to become a high yielding source of unconventional protein for direct animal and human consumption (Ostrowski-Meissner 1979D,E, 1980A, 1981).

Australian and New Zealand involvement in protein extraction from grasslands, apart from the substantial improvement to the national protein economy, may result in the development of a complete technological process which could be used as an emergency tool to supply protein and equipment for recovery of protein from local resources to communities suffering from natural disasters, war, and/or crop failure. Once the extraction process is developed as a complete "on-the-farm" technology, it could be distributed as international agricultural aid to countries and/or areas suffering from protein deficiency so as to give the local communities a tool for feed and/or food production directly from locally-grown herbage and other vegetation and, moreover, using local available energy resources and indigenous labor. An example of the latter has been demonstrated by Pirie (1971) in reference to a nutritional project carried out within the International Biological Programme and, recently, by Kamalanathan and Devadas (1975) and Bray (1977) in relation to children fed with LPC in India and by Olatunbosun *et al.* (1972) in Nigeria.

It is reasonable to suppose that protein extraction from green vegetation as a complete technology offered to village and/or farming communities in developing countries suffering from malnutrition would be a favorable strategy for development and technical assistance. The technology in combination with other relevant aids (education) would encourage the recipient regions to contribute toward building their own, not only political, but economic, independence. It would also help to develop a sense of planned action and reliance on their own natural resources in terms of self-sufficiency in food/feed supplies. Such an active approach to self-sufficiency by the recipient region of the new technological development in a food production process is much more effective in long terms than awaiting foreign aid relief gifts from more developed countries, which are at present experiencing their own economic problems. The outline and institutional aspects of such a strategy were most recently demonstrated by Gurnett-Smith (1978) in relation to Australian assistance and contribution to animal production in developing countries.

ECONOMIC CONSIDERATIONS

LPC will command its highest market value when it is costed into poultry rations as a source of all xanthophyll, protein, and energy. Under these conditions, its likely inclusion rate is quite low (1–2%) but will probably command a price in the range of $550–$700/MT. Where it is costed into rations as a source of protein and energy only, although its inclusion rates could be much higher (approximately 10–15%), the selling price will be somewhat lower ($100–$300/MT) (Donelly *et al.* 1980). Large markets do exist for LPC at a high price in countries where large quantities of dried lucerne and xanthophyll concentrates are included in poultry rations to achieve pigmentation.

Due to the problems of low intake and high wastage of pressed herbage by high milk-yielding cows under New Zealand agricultural conditions, the economic returns to a combined protein extraction-dairying system are not envisaged at present. However, because of the excellent growth of the steers fed pressed herbage and lucerne in particular, an economic analysis has been carried out for a hypothetical protein extraction-beef growing/finishing system with lucerne as the forage. It has been calculated that where 50% of the farm is involved in lucerne and committed to protein extraction, the per ha gross margin for the whole farm is more than two-fold higher than that for the prime beef system alone (Donelly *et al.* 1980). This is assuming the stocking rate of 3.6 to 3.8 steers per ha. These economic returns are based on hypothetical, and as yet untested, farm livestock systems and should accordingly be interpreted with caution. However, they are sufficiently high to justify an investment in such a research program in countries with large grazing areas.

According to estimates made for the protein extraction operation, in New Zealand, an optimum-sized, centrally-located factory would draw on 6000 ha of grassland (Donelly *et al.* 1980). With the involvement of a mobile protein extraction unit in a whole on-the-farm operation, the optimum size of the area under the extraction system would be much smaller. This is on the basis of both the number and size of individual farms involved in the whole cooperative type of operation.

Changes in the improvement of the efficiency of conversion of the earth's resources into food cannot be done without, first, changing our traditional concept of agricultural practices in relation to two interrelated areas: plant production and animal production; and second, without breaking our conservative approach to foods, nutrition, and dietetics. If fact, nobody at the present time can definitely describe the agricultural system which would embrace future protein demands without changing the present conservative model of food production and consumption. Fortunately enough, there is plenty of sunlight, water, carbon dioxide, inorganic nitrogen, and phosphorus in the world, i.e., the essential ingredients for food production by means of photosynthesis. According to Schmitt (1965), 30 billion people may ultimately lead fairly free and enriched lives on this planet, and the resources of the earth for the production of food are many times greater than man's needs as far ahead as one can see. To make this optimistic forecast technically possible, the ecosystems all around the world have to be utilized much more efficiently than at present. The example of an efficient utilization of grasslands as given in this chapter is one of many possible ways by which mankind now or in the future can be sufficiently fed by food supplied by advanced agriculture, effectively recovering nutrients from world ecosystems without destroying the balance of the natural environment and preserving for generations to come the most wonderful creation—nature, with man being an integral part of it.

ACKNOWLEDGMENTS

The review presented here relates to studies conducted in Australia and New Zealand prior to appointment to the Centre for Animal Research and Development in Bogor, Indonesia.

The author gratefully acknowledges the receipt of a Research Fellowship from the New Zealand National Research Advisory Council which enabled him to undertake the research on protein extraction from herbage.

The research reported here was made possible by the interest and cooperation of Dr. J.B. Hutton, then the Head of the Nutrition Centre, Ruakura Animal Research Station, Hamilton, New Zealand, who provided laboratory, facilities, and assistance within the Nutrition Centre and other Ruakura Departments and also arranged assistance from the N.Z. Co-operative Dairy Company at Matangi and the Applied Biochemistry Division, Department of Scientific and Industrial Research. Thanks are also due to Mr. R.I. Hall, J. Hughes, and R. Newth for their excellent technical assistance during the development and initiation of the protein extraction project.

The author is also grateful to D.R. McKenzie, Head of the Biochemistry Department, Bendigo College of Advanced Education (BCAE), for allowing the use of protein extraction facilities in his department and also for his permission to quote some of the data on mixed pasture in Northern Victoria. The receipt of a Research Grant from the BCAE, which enabled the continuation of the project in Victoria, Australia, is gratefully acknowledged.

REFERENCES

AKESON, W.R. and STAHMANN, M.A. 1965. Nutritive value of leaf protein concentrate, an *in vitro* digestion study. Agric. Food Chem. *13*, 145–148.

ANON. 1955. Distribution of stock. *In* Atlas of Australian Resources. Dep. Nat. Developm., Canberra.

ARNOTT, K.J. 1974. Review of the world protein situation. Presented at the Farmers Club Meeting: Protein Sources in the Future. Feb. 1974, London.

BARBER, R.S., BRAUDE, R., MITCHELL, K.G., PARTRIDGE, I.G. and PITT-

MAN, R.J. 1979. Value of lucerne juice and grass juice as sources of protein for the growing pig. Anim. Feed Sci. Technol. *4*, 233–262.

BARBER, R.S, BRAUDE, R., MITCHELL, K.G., PARTRIDGE, I.G. and PITTMAN, R.J. 1980. Value of freshly produced lucerne juice as a source of supplemented protein for the growing pig. Anim. Feed Sci. Technol. *5*, 215–220.

BAUMGARTNER, A. 1973. Plant response to climatic factors. Proc. Uppsala Symp. Ecology and Conservation. 1970, Uppsala, Sweden, UNESCO.

BLAXTER, K.L. 1974. Alternative sources of protein for animal feeding stuffs. Presented at the Farmers Club Meeting: Protein Sources in the Future. Feb. 1974, London.

BONNER, J. 1962. The upper limits of crop yield. Science *137*, 11–15.

BRAUDE, R., JONES, A.S. and HOUSEMAN, R.A. 1977. The utilisation of the juice extracted from green crops. *In* Green Crop Fractionation. R.J. Wilkins (Editor). Br. Grassl. Soc. Ocass. Symp. *9*.

BRAY, W. 1977. The processing of leaf-protein to obtain food-grade products. *In* Green Crop Fractionation. R.J. Wilkins (Editor). Br. Grassl. Soc. Occas. Symp. *9*.

BYERS, M. 1961. Extraction of protein from the leaves of some plants growing in Ghana. J. Sci. Food Agric. *12*, 20–30.

BYERS, M. 1971A. The amino acid composition and *in vitro* digestibility of some protein fractions from three species of leaves of various ages. J. Sci. Food Agric. *22*, 242–247.

BYERS, M. 1971B. The amino acid composition of some leaf protein preparations. *In* Leaf Protein. International Biological Program Handbook *20*. N.W. Pirie (Editor). Blackwell's Scientific Publications, Oxford.

CONNELL, J. and HOUSEMAN, R.A. 1977. The utilisation by ruminants of the pressed green crops from fractionation machinery. *In* Green Crop Fractionation. R.J. Wilkins (Editor). Br. Grassl. Soc. Occas. Symp. *9*.

DONELLY, P.E., McDONALD, R.M. MILLS, R.A., RITCHIE, J.M., SWAN, J.E., TRIGG, T.E. and BRYANT, A.M. 1980. Protein from pasture. 1980 Ruakura Farm Conf. Proc. *43*, Hamilton, New Zealand.

EREKY, K. 1926. Vegetable foods and medicines for men and animals. Br. Pat. 270629. May 7.

FAO. 1965. Protein requirements. Rep. Joint FAO/WHO Expert Group. FAO Nutr. Meet. Rep. Ser. *37*. Food Agric. Organ. U.N., Rome.

FAO. 1971. Production Yearbook, Vol. 25. Food Agric. Organ. U.N., Rome.

FAO-WHO. 1965. Joint Expert Group on Protein Requirements. FAO Nutr. Meet. Rep. Ser. *37*. Food Agric. Organ. U.N., Rome.

FETUGA, B.L., BABATUNDE, G.M. and OYENUGA, V.A. 1973. Protein quality of some Nigerian feedstuffs. II. Biological evaluation of protein quality. J. Sci. Food Agric. *24*, 1505–1514.

GARLAND, K.R. 1975. Protein production in Victoria and areas for the development of leaf protein extraction. Presented at the Seminar LPC Production in Victoria. Bendigo College of Advanced Education, July 1975, Bendigo, Victoria.

GERLOFF, E.D. LIMA, I.H. and STAHMANN, M.A. 1965. Amino acid composition of leaf protein concentrates. J. Agric. Food Chem. *13*, 139–143.
GIRAULT, A. 1973. The study of some properties of rapeseed protein with a view to protein concentrate production. J. Sci. Food Agric. *24*, 509.
GURNETT-SMITH, A.F. 1978. Australia's contribution to overseas animal production in developing countries. Proc. Aust. Soc. Anim. Prod. *12*, 13–22.
HANCZAKOWSKI, P. 1974. The influence of the addition of synthetic methionine and lysine on the nutritive value of leaf protein concentrates. Rocz. Nauk Zootechn. *1*, 139–145. (Polish)
HANSEN, N.G. and EGGUM, B.O. 1973. The biological value of proteins estimated from amino acid analysis. Acta Agric. Scand. *23*, 247–251.
HARTMAN, G.H., JR., AKESON, W.R. and STAHMANN, M.A. 1967. Leaf protein concentrate prepared by spray drying. J. Agric. Food Chem. *15*, 74–79.
HOLLO, J. 1969. Green plant concentrates of high biological activity as potential protein and other nutrient resources. Aust. Chem. Eng. *10* (Feb.) 9–15.
HOVE, E.L. 1972. Developments and future trends in non-animal sources of protein. Proc. N.Z. Soc. Anim. Prod. *32*, 147–159.
HUTTON, J.B. 1970. Crops or grasses for efficient low-cost livestock production. Proc. 11th Int. Grassl. Congr., 1970. Univ. of Queensland Press *A78*, St. Lucia, Queensland, Australia.
HUTTON, J.B. 1972. Milk protein production: An analysis of New Zealand's present and potential capabilities. Proc. N.Z. Soc. Anim. Prod. *32*, 160–169.
HUTTON, J.B. 1975. Review of the workshop on leaf protein production. *In* Leaf Protein Concentrate (New Zealand Scene). G.M. Wallace (Editor). Ruakura Agric. Res. Centre Publication, Palmerston North, Hamilton, New Zealand.
JOHNS, D.C. 1980. Amino acid supplementation of leaf protein concentrate. Proc. South Pac. Poultry Sci. Conv., WPSA, N.Z. Branch, 1980, Auckland.
JONES, A.S. 1977. The principles of green crop fractionation. *In* Green Crop Fractionation. R.J. Wilkins (Editor). Br. Grassl. Soc. Occas. Symp. *9*.
JONES, A.S. and HOUSEMAN, R.A. 1975. Forage crop fractionation. Rep. Rowett Inst. *31*, 136–149.
KAMALANATHAN, G. and DEVADAS, R.P. 1975. Leaf protein as a supplement in preschool feeding programs. Presented at 10th Int. Congr. Nutr., Kyoto, Aug. 1975, Int. Union Nutr. Sci.
KING, K. 1978. Personal communication. Irrigation Research Station, Kyabram, Victoria, Australia.
KING, K. and STOCKDALE, R. 1978. The effects of stocking rate and nitrogen fertiliser on the productivity of grazing dairy cows and irrigated perennial pasture. Proc. 20th Int. Dairy Congr., Paris, June 1978.
KNUCKLES, B.E., DE FREMERY, D., BICKOFF, E.M. and KOHLER, G.O. 1975. Soluble protein from alfalfa juice by membrane filtrations. J. Agric. Food Chem. *23*, 209–212.
KOEGEL, R.G. and BRUHN, H.D. 1977. Requirements for expression of plant juice. *In* Green Crop Fractionation. R.J. Wilkins (Editor). Br. Grassl. Soc. Occas. Symp. *9*.

KOHLER, G.O. and DE FREMERY, D. 1977. Production and processing of alfalfa protein for foods and feeds. Int. Workshop Utilisation of Agric. Wastes for Feed and Food, Belo Horizonte, Brazil, Dec. 1977, Cent. Tecnol. de Minas Gerais.

LUND, D.B. 1973. Effects of food processing. Food Technol. *27* (Jan.) 16–18.

MAGUIRE, M.F. and BROOKES, I.M. 1973. The effect of juice extraction on the composition and yield of grass crops for dehydration. Proc. 1st Int. Crop Drying Congr., Oxford, 1973. C.L. Skidmore (Editor). E. & E. Plumridge, Linton, Cambridge.

McKENZIE, D.R. 1976. Leaf protein concentrate as a poultry protein supplement. Proc. 1st Australasian Poultry and Stock Feed Conv., Melbourne, Oct. 1976, ACMF, ASFMA, and WPSA—Australian Branch.

McKENZIE, D.R. 1977. Yields of protein extracted from a range of Northern Victorian herbage. Aust. J. Exp. Agric. Anim. Husb. *17*, 268–276.

McKENZIE, D.R. 1978. Farm scale production of leaf protein concentrate and its utilisation as a protein supplement in intensive livestock production. Proc. 2nd Australasian Poultry and Stock Feed Conv., Sydney, March 1978, ACMF, ASFMA, and WPSA—Australian Branch.

MEREDITH, F.I., GASKINS, M.A. and DULL, G.G. 1974. Amino acid losses in turnip greens during handling and processing. J. Food Sci. *39*, 689–691.

MORRIS, T.R. 1977. Leaf protein concentrates for non-ruminant farm animals. *In* Green Crop Fractionation. R.J. Wilkins (Editor). Br. Grassl. Soc. Occas. Symp. *9*.

NATL. RES. COUNC. 1970. Nutrient Requirements of Beef Cattle, 4th Revised Edition. National Academy of Science, Washington, D.C.

NATL. RES. COUNC. 1971. Nutrient Requirements of Dairy Cattle, 4th Revised Edition. National Academy of Science, Washington, D.C.

OLATUNBOSUN, D.A., ADADEVOK, B.K. and OKE, O.L. 1972. Leaf protein: A new protein source for the management of protein calorie malnutrition in Nigeria. Niger. Med. J. *2*, 195–199.

OSTROWSKI-MEISSNER, H.T. 1975A. Factors limiting protein extraction from pasture—summary. *In* Leaf Protein Concentrate (New Zealand Scene). G.M. Wallace (Editor). Ruakura Agric. Res. Centre Publication, Palmerston North, Hamilton, New Zealand.

OSTROWSKI-MEISSNER, H.T. 1975B. Concentration of grass proteins by ultrafiltration and reverse osmosis. *In* Leaf Protein Concentrate (New Zealand Scene). G.M. Wallace (Editor). Ruakura Agric. Res. Centre Publication, Palmerston North, Hamilton, New Zealand.

OSTROWSKI-MEISSNER, H.T. 1976A. Pasture production in protein extraction system. Proc. N.Z. Soc. Anim. Prod. *36*, 31–41.

OSTROWSKI-MEISSNER, H.T. 1976B. Protein extraction from pastures in temperate regions—present and potential capabilities. Proc. 1st Int. Congr. Eng. Food, Boston, Aug. 1976.

OSTROWSKI-MEISSNER, H.T. 1976C. Limitations in protein extraction efficiency from grasses due to technology applied in processing. Proc. 1st Int. Congr. Eng. Food, Boston, Aug. 1976.

OSTROWSKI-MEISSNER, H.T. 1976D. Ultrafiltration as a method for recovery of proteins from grass—their fractionation and purification. Proc. 1st Int. Congr. Eng. Food, Boston, Aug. 1976.

OSTROWSKI-MEISSNER, H.T. 1976E. Protein Extraction from Pastures, 1973 to 1976. (Relevant papers.) Final Rep. N.Z. Res. Advisory Counc. Res. Fellowship, Ruakura Research Centre, Hamilton, New Zealand.

OSTROWSKI-MEISSNER, H.T. 1977. Development of a new protein source: Leaf protein concentrate. Pap. presented Meet. Victorian Branches Aust. Soc. Anim. Prod. Agric. Eng. Soc. Engineering in Intensive Livestock Production, Bendigo, Victoria, Aust., Oct. 1977.

OSTROWSKI-MEISSNER, H.T. 1978A. Protein extraction from herbage: New development and its potential. Proc. 3rd Conf. Sci. Technol. Aust. N.Z. Assoc. Adv. Sci. (ANZAAS), Canberra, May 1978.

OSTROWSKI-MEISSNER, H.T. 1978B. Protein extraction from pasture: A new concept in efficient dairy farming in temperate and subtropical regions. Proc. 4th World Conf. Anim. Prod., Buenos Aires, Aug. 1978.

OSTROWSKI-MEISSNER, H.T. 1978C. Fractionation of chloroplast-free proteins from herbage for human consumption. Proc. 3rd Conf. Sci. Technol. Aust. N.Z. Assoc. Adv. Sci. (ANZAAS), Canberra, May 1978.

OSTROWSKI-MEISSNER, H.T. 1978D. Analysis for availability of amino acid supplements in foods and feeds: Biochemical and nutritional implications. *In* Protein Nutritive Quality Improvement: Genetic Selection—Fortification—Supplementation. M. Friedman (Editor). Plenum Publishing, New York and London.

OSTROWSKI-MEISSNER, H.T. 1979A. Membrane filtration for isolation, fractionation and purification of food- and feed-grade proteins from pasture herbage. J. Food Processing Preserv. *3*, 59–84.

OSTROWSKI-MEISSNER, H.T. 1979B. The isolation of protein concentrates from pasture herbage and their fractionation into feed- and food-grade products. J. Food Processing Preserv. *3*, 105–124.

OSTROWSKI-MEISSNER, H.T. 1979C. Seasonal variations in protein fractions, yields and quality of leaf protein concentrates extracted from pasture herbage. J. Food Processing Preserv. *3*, 225–239.

OSTROWSKI-MEISSNER, H.T. 1979D. Grasslands as a source of unconventional protein for direct animal and human consumption. Proc. 10th N.Z. Geogr. Conf. & 49th ANZASS Congr., Auckland, Jan. 1979. N.Z. Geogr. Soc. Conf. Ser. *10*. W. Morgan *et al.* (Editors). N.Z. Geogr. Soc., Auckland.

OSTROWSKI-MEISSNER, H.T. 1979E. Protein extraction from grasslands. Sci. Technol. *16*, 4–11.

OSTROWSKI-MEISSNER, H.T. 1980A. The effects of storage and heating on lysine availability of food-grade proteins from pasture herbage as measured by chemical, biological and microbiological assays. J. Food Qual. *3*, 275–282.

OSTROWSKI-MEISSNER, H.T. 1980B. Protein degradation in herbage extract during membrane filtration process: The effect of reducing agents addition. J. Food Processing Preserv. *4*, 261–279.

OSTROWSKI-MEISSNER, H.T. 1980C. Quantities and quality of protein extracted from pasture herbage using heat precipitation or ultrafiltration procedures. J. Sci. Food Agric. *31*, 177–187.

OSTROWSKI-MEISSNER, H.T. 1981. Optimization of protein extraction from pasture herbage and qualitative considerations. J. Food Processing Preserv. *5*, 7–22.

OSTROWSKI-MEISSNER, H.T., CARLSON, R. and TRAGARDH, C. 1980. Isolation and purification of proteins from green vegetation for direct human consumption. *In* Food Process Engineering. P. Linko, Y. Maiki, and J. Olkku (Editors). Applied Science Publisher, London.

OSTROWSKI-MEISSNER, H.T., HALL, R.I., HUGHES, J.W. and NEWTH, R.P. 1975. Field studies on protein recovery limitations during protein extraction from pasture grass. *In* Leaf Protein Concentrate (New Zealand Scene). G.M. Wallace (Editor). Ruakura Agric. Res. Centre Publication, Palmerston North, Hamilton, New Zealand.

OSTROWSKI-MEISSNER, H.T., MORSTIN, E. and KOSCINSKA, A. 1972. A comparison of nutritional value of feed mixtures for pigs in experiments on rats and pigs. Zesz. Probl. Postepow Nauk Roln. *126*, 143–149. (Polish)

PARRISH, G.K., KROGER, M. and WEAVER, J.C. 1974. The prospects of leaf protein as a human food and a close look at alfalfa. Crit. Rev. Food Technol. *5*, 1–13.

PAYNE, R.E., HILL, CH.G. and AMUNDSEN, C.H. 1973. Concentrations of egg white by ultrafiltration. J. Milk Food Technol. *36*, (7) 359–363.

PHILLIPSON, J. 1973. The biological efficiency of protein production by grazing and other land-based systems. *In* The Biological Efficiency of Protein Production. J.G.W. Jones (Editor). University Press, Cambridge.

PIRIE, N.W. 1942. Green leaves as a source of proteins and other nutrients. Nature (London) *149*, 251.

PIRIE, N.W. 1971. Leaf Protein: Its Agronomy, Preparation, Quality and Use. IBP Handb. *20*. Blackwell's Scientific Publishers, Oxford.

ROUELLE, H.M. 1773. Observations on the sediments on green parts of plants and on glutinous or vegeto-animal matter. J. Med. Chir. Pharm. *40*, 59. (French)

SAUNDERS, R.M., CONNOR, M.A., BOOTH, A.N., BICKOFF, E.M. and KOHLER, G.O. 1973. Measurement of digestibility of alfalfa protein concentrates by in vivo and in vitro methods. J. Nutr. *103*, 530–535.

SCHMITT, W.R. 1965. The planetary food potential. Ann. N.Y. Acad. Sci. *118*, 645.

SIKKA, K.C., JOHARI, R.P., DUGGAL, S.K., AHUJA, V.P. and AUSTIN, A. 1975. Comparative nutritive value and amino acid content of different extractions of wheat. J. Agric. Food Chem. *23*, 24–26.

SINGH, R., WHITNEY, L.F. and CHEN, C.S. 1974. Recovery of alfalfa protein by membrane ultrafiltration. Proc. Annu. Meet. Am. Soc. Agric. Eng., Oklahoma, June 1974, Pap. *74-6003*.

SLADE, R.E. 1937. Grass and the national food supply. Rep. Br. Assoc. Advmt. Sci. *457*.

STAHMANN, M.A. 1975. The Wisconsin work. 12th Tech. Alfalfa Conf. Proc., 1975, Berkeley, Agric. Res. Serv., U.S. Dep. Agric.

STOCKDALE, C.R., KING, K.R., McKENZIE, D.R. 1981. Nutritive value for lactating dairy cows of the pressed herbage remaining after the partial extraction of leaf juice. Aust. J. Exp. Agric. Anim. Husb. *21*, 376–381.

SUBBA RAU, B.H., MAHADEVIAH, S. and SINGH, N. 1969. Nutritional studies on whole-extract coagulated leaf protein and fractionated chloroplastic and cytoplasmic proteins from lucerne. J. Sci. Food Agric. *20*, 355–358.

SUBBA RAU, B.H., RAMANA, V.R. and SINGH, N. 1972. Studies on nutritive value of leaf proteins and some factors affecting their quality. J. Sci. Food Agric. *23*, 233–245.

SWAN, J.E., DONELLY, P.E., McDONALD, R.M., MILLS, R.A., RITCHIE, J.R. and TRIGG, T.E. 1980. Leaf protein concentrate from pasture for poultry rations. Proc. South Pac. Poultry Sci. Conv., Auckland, World's Poultry Sci. Assoc. (WPSA)—N.Z. Branch.

TELEK, L. 1979. Preparation of leaf protein concentrates in lowland humid tropics. *In* Tropical Foods: Chemistry and Nutrition, Vol. 2. G.E. Inglett and G. Charalambous (Editors). Academic Press, New York.

VARTHA, E.W. and ALLISON, R.M. 1973A. Extractable protein from "Grasslands Tama" Westworlds rye grass. N.Z. J. Exp. Agric. *1*, 239–244.

VARTHA, E.W. and ALLISON, R.M. 1973B. Protein extracted herbage for sheep feeding. N.Z. J. Exp. Agric. *1*, 171–177.

VICENTE-CHANDLER, J. 1973. Fertiliser unlocks the potential to tropical grasslands. World Farming *15* (Jan.) 20–24.

VOSLOH, C.J., JR., EDWARDS, R.H., ENOCHIAN, R.V., KUZMICKY, D.D. and KOHLER, G.O. 1976. Leaf protein concentrate (Pro-Xan) from alfalfa: An economic evaluation. Agric. Econ. Rep. *346*. U.S. Dep. Agric. Econ. Res. Serv., Berkeley, Calif.

WALLACE, G.M. 1973. Nutrient loss during food processing. Food Technol. N.Z. *8* (March) 11–12.

WESTON, R.H., HOGAN, J.P. and GRAHAM, N.McC. 1978. The feeding value of various fractions prepared from lucerne. Proc. Aust. Soc. Anim. Prod. *12*, 129.

WHITTLESTONE, W.G. 1972. Sources of world food protein and the New Zealand contribution. Proc. N.Z. Soc. Anim. Prod. *32*, 139–146.

WILKINS, R.J., HEATH, S.B., ROBERTS, W.P. and FOXELL, P.R. 1977. A theoretical economic analysis of systems of green crop fractionation. *In* Green Crop Fractionation. R.J. Wilkins (Editor). Br. Grassl. Soc. Occas. Symp. *9*, Hurley, England.

YOSHIDA, M. and HOSHII, H. 1980. Nutritive and economical evaluation of leaf protein concentrates produced in New Zealand. Proc. South Pac. Poultry Sci. Conv., Auckland, World's Poultry Sci. Assoc. (WPSA)—N.Z. Branch.

2

Leaf Protein Concentrate from Plant Sources in Temperate Climates

Rolf Carlsson

Several plants growing in or originating from temperate areas have been studied for production of leaf protein concentrate (LPC) or leaf nutrient concentrate. Most of the work has been performed on *Medicago sativa* (alfalfa) and has been extensively reviewed (Kohler and Edwards 1980; Fiorentini and Galoppini 1981; Vinconneau 1979). Since most green plant protein originates from the leaves, the term LPC will be used instead of plant protein concentrates, perhaps the more logical term, since, in most cases, the whole plant is harvested and processed.

PLANT MATERIAL

Plants for production of LPC are logically chosen from quickly growing, lush vegetation. Forage crops and other agricultural plants as well as leafy vegetables have often been examined. Many agricultural crops also give an abundance of by-product leaves. (A list of plant species suitable for LPC production is given in Table 2.1 with identification according to normal use: agricultural crop, leafy vegetable, or by-product leaves. Research done on general and specific cultivars is cited.) The possible introduction of short-rotation forests for energy production may add another by-product leaf source.

Leguminous Species

These species do not need nitrogen fertilization. However, to maximize the production of protein in the plant and the yield of extractable protein, potassium has to be used in intensive cropping systems.

The perennial legume *Medicago sativa* has been and is the basic plant material for all green crop driers with wet fractionation systems (Vepex and Pro-Xan). However, other perennial legumes, *Trifolium* spp., for instance,

TABLE 2.1. PLANT SPECIES SUITABLE FOR LEAF PROTEIN CONCENTRATE PRODUCTION

Latin Name	Author
Papilionaceae (Leguminosae)	
Glycine max[1]	Carlsson (1971); Betschart and Kinsella (1973); Kawabata and Taguchi (1975);
Lupinus sp.[1]	Ostrowski (1978)
L. albus[1]	Byers (1967, 1971A)
L. angustifolius[1]	Hove (1976); McKenzie (1977)
L. luteus[1]	Carlsson (1975A: I)
Melilotus alba[1]	Byers (1967); Festenstein (1972)
M. officinalis	Carlsson (1975A: I)
Phaseolus lunatus[1,3]	Stahmann (1970)
P. vulgaris[1]	Subba Rau *et al.* (1972)
Pisum sativum[1,2,3]	Byers (1967); Varga and Nosticzius (1968); Huang *et al.* (1971); Holló (1973); Lexander and Lundborg (1973); Pirie (1976)
Trifolium alexandrinum[1]	Malik and Ulla (1969); Aziz *et al.* (1971); Kawatra *et al.* (1974); Munshi *et al.* (1974, 1975); Mungikar *et al.* (1976)
T. fragiferum[1]	Byers (1967)
T. hybridum[1]	Byers (1967)
T. pratense[1]	Lexander *et al.* (1970); Festenstein (1972, 1976); Carlsson (1975A: I); Igarashi *et al.* (1976); Hove (1976); McKenzie (1976, 1977, 1978); Ostrowski (1976, 1978); Vartha and Brusse (1977)
T. repens[1]	Horigome and Kandatsu (1968); Huang *et al.* (1971); Carlsson (1975A: I); Kawabata and Taguchi (1975); Festenstein (1976); Hove (1976); McKenzie (1976, 1977, 1978); Ostrowski (1976); Vartha and Brusse (1977)
T. repens latum[1]	Horigome (1977)
T. resupinatum[1]	Nazir and Shah (1966)
T. subterraneum[1]	McKenzie (1977)
Vicia faba[1,3]	Lexander *et al.* (1970); Festenstein (1972)
V. dasycarpa[1]	McKenzie (1978)
V. sativa[1]	Byers (1967); Hanczakowski (1970); Lexander *et al.* (1970); Festenstein (1972); Holló (1973); Thomke (1976)
V. villosa[1]	Gonzalez *et al.* (1974)
Gramineae	
Avena sativa[1]	Horigome and Kandatsu (1964); Nanda *et al.* (1975); McKenzie (1977); Horigome (1977)
Bromus arvensis[1]	Lexander *et al.* (1970)
Cynodon dactylon[1]	Fishman and Burdick (1977)
Dactylis glomerata[1]	Horigome and Kandatsu (1964); Lexander *et al.* (1970); Festenstein (1972, 1976); Arkcoll and Davys (1973); Woodham *et al.* (1974); Carlsson (1975A: I); Heath and King (1977); Ostrowski (1978)
Festuca arundinacea[1]	Heath and King (1977); Ostrowski (1978)
F. pratensis[1]	Lexander *et al.* (1970); Carlsson (1975A: I)
Holcus lanatus[1]	Carlsson (1975A: I)
Hordeum vulgare[1]	Varga and Nosticzius (1968); Byers (1967, 1971A); Festenstein (1976); Ströbäck and Gibbons (1976); McKenzie (1977)
Lolium multiflorum[1]	Lexander *et al.* (1970: Westerwolds ryegrass); Vartha and Allison (1973); Vartha *et al.* (1973); McKenzie (1977); Thomke (1976); Bugge (1977)

(continued)

TABLE 2.1. *(Continued)*

Latin Name	Author
L. perenne[1]	Lexander *et al.* (1970); Festenstein (1972, 1976); Hove (1976), Ostrowski (1976, 1978); Heath and King (1977); Vartha and Brusse (1977); Wieringa (1977)
Paspalum dilitatum[1]	McKenzie (1977); Ostrowski (1978)
Phalaris arundinacea[1]	McKenzie (1976); Ostrowski (1978)
Secale cereale[1]	Carlsson (1971, 1975A: I); Hanczakowski (1975); Festenstein (1976); Braude *et al.* (1977)
Triticum aestivum[1]	Byers (1967); Varga and Nosticzius (1968); Festenstein (1972, 1976); Woodham *et al.* (1974); Carlsson (1975A: I); Hanczakowski (1975)
Zea mays[1]	Festenstein (1972, 1976); Holló (1973); Bahr *et al.* (1977)
Cruciferae	
Armoracia rusticana[1,3]	Carlsson (1975A: I)
Brassica spp.[1,2,3]	Carlsson (1978C: I, II)
B. carinata[1,2]	Brown *et al.* (1975)
B. chinensis[2]	Byers (1971A)
B. hirta[1,2] *(Sinapis alba)*	Byers (1967); Festenstein (1972, 1976); Holló (1973)
B. napus[1]	Byers (1967); Holló *et al.* (1969); Lexander *et al.* (1970); Carlsson (1975A: I); Hanczakowski (1975); Hove (1976); Lundborg (1979)
B. oleracea[1,2]	Byers (1967: cv acephala); Lexander *et al.* (1970: cv acephala); Subba Rau *et al.* (1972: cv botrytis, cv capitata, cv caulorapa); Holló (1973: cv acephala); Carlsson (1975A: I: cv acephala, cv gemmifera); Hanczakowski (1975, 1977); Munshi *et al.* (1975); Nanda *et al.* (1975: cv botrytis); Kawabata and Taguchi (1975); Pirie (1976); Tekale and Joshi (1976); Thomke (1976: cv acephala); Goel *et al.* (1977: cv botrytis); Heath and King (1977: cv acephala); Lundborg (1979; several cv's)
Campestris var. *rapa*[1,3]	Subba Rau *et al.* (1972)
Raphanus sativus[1]	Arkcoll (1971); Festenstein (1972, 1976); Subba Rau *et al.* (1972); Kawabata and Taguchi (1975); Heath and King (1977)
Amaranthaceae	
Amaranthus spp.[1,2]	Koch *et al.* (1967); Holló (1968); Koch (1973); Carlsson (1972–1973, 1975A: I, II, III, IV; 1977, 1978C)
A. caudatus[1,2]	Lexander *et al.* (1970); Carlsson (1975A: II, III, IV)
A. hybridus[1,2]	Koch *et al.* (1965)
Chenopodiaceae	
Atriplex spp.[1,2]	Carlsson (1972–1973, 1975A: I, II, III, IV); Silva and Pereira (1976)
A. hortensis[2]	Holló (1968); von Krampitz *et al.* (1970); Lexander *et al.* (1970); Carlsson (1972–1973: several provenances, 1975A: II, III, IV; 1978C: I, II, III; 1980, 1982)
Beta vulgaris[1,2,3]	Garcha *et al.* (1971); Subba Rau *et al.* (1972); Boldizsár *et al.* (1975); Carlsson (1975A: I, II: several cv's); Pirie (1976); Tekale and Joshi (1976); Nörgaard-Pedersen (1977B)
Chenopodium spp.[1,2]	Carlsson (1975A: I, II, III, IV; 1978C: I, II, III)
C. album[1,2]	Festenstein (1972, 1976); Carlsson (1975A: I, II:

TABLE 2.1. *(Continued)*

Latin Name	Author
	several provenances/varieties); Heath and King (1977); Ferrer *et al.* (1977)
C. nuttalie[1]	Byers (1964)
C. quinoa[1,2]	Byers *et al.* (1965); Lexander *et al.* (1970); Carlsson (1979: several provenances, 1975A: I, II, III, IV; 1978C: I, II, III); Carlsson *et al.* (1975); Anon. (1976); El-Alaily and Woodham (1976); Smith and Pena (1977); Ostrowski (1978)
Kochia scoparia[1]	Byers *et al.* (1965); Stovall (1970); Carlsson (1975A: II)
Spinacea oleracea[2]	Carlsson (1975A: I, II); Hove (1976); Bahr *et al.* (1977)
Tetragonia spp.[2]	Koch *et al.* (1965); Carlsson (1975A: II)
Other nonwoody species	
Cucurbitaceae spp.[1,3]	Crook and Holden (1948); Byers (1967); Carlsson (1968–1970, 1978C: I, II)
Daucus carota[3]	Stahmann (1970); Subba Rau *et al.* (1972); Omole *et al.* (1976: leaves)
Erigeron annuus[1]	Kawabata and Taguchi (1975)
Helianthus annuus[1]	Varga and Nosticzius (1968); Lexander *et al.* (1970); Holló (1973); Carlsson (1978C: I, II, III); Lundborg (1979)
H. annuus × tuberosus[1]	Lexander (1969–1972)
H. tuberosus[1]	Carlsson (1971, 1975A: I)
Nicotiana spp.[1]	Chan *et al.* (1972); Sakano *et al.* (1974)
N. tabacum[1]	Chan *et al.* (1972); Sakano *et al.* (1974); Anon. (1977); Bahr *et al.* (1977)
Pastinaca sativa[1,3]	Lexander *et al.* (1970); Carlsson (1975A: I)
Solanum melongena[1]	Wildman (1973); Sakano *et al.* (1974)
S. tuberosum[1,3]	Carlsson (1971: several cv's, 1975A: I); Hanczakowski (1970, 1975); Hanczakowski and Makuch (1980: several cv's); Stahmann (1970); Subba Rau *et al.* (1972); Carruthers and Pirie (1975); Pirie (1976)
Typha latifolia[2]	Boyd (1971); Carlsson (1975A: I, 1981)
Urtica dioica[1]	Lexander *et al.* (1970); Carlsson (1971, 1975A: I); Hughes *et al.* (1980); Carlsson *et al.* (1982)
Woody species	
Alnus incana[3]	Bruvere *et al.* (1978)
Betula pubescens[3]	Bruvere *et al.* (1978)
Gossypium hirsutum[3]	Pirie (1976); Bahr *et al.* (1977)
Picea sp.[3]	Ladinskaja *et al.* (1974)
Pinus sp.[3]	Ladinskaja *et al.* (1974)
Populus spp.[3]	Sirén *et al.* (1970: leaves); Sirén (1973: leaves); Carlsson (1975B, 1978B); Chedd (1975); Bruvere *et al.* (1978)
Salix spp.[3]	Sirén (1973: leaves); Carlsson (1975B, 1978B)
Sambusa niger[3]	Butler and Pirie (1977)

[1] Agricultural crop.
[2] Vegetables (leafy).
[3] By-product leaves.

may play the same role in areas where *M. sativa* does not grow well. Much effort has also been directed toward the study of *T. repens* (white clover) for LPC production. The yield of expressed protein per season from white clover can be 2 MT/ha (McKenzie 1978). In more northern areas with a cool, temperate climate, only *T. pratense* (red clover) or *Trifolium hybridum* (alsike clover) can be grown. *T. pratense* has been used for wet fractionation in Aberdeen, Scotland (Connell and Houseman 1977) and can yield 1.2 MT/ha (Arkcoll 1971). Yield is probably correlated with water availability.

Cost of fertilizer may also favor the selection of legumes for LPC use. In Egypt, with a hot, temperate climate, the relatively high cost of nitrogen fertilizers may allow only leguminous plants of such types as *Trifolium alexandrinum* (berseem) to be grown for LPC production.

White and red clover are commonly grown perennials. Crops like these reduce management costs and often have a longer growing/harvesting season than annual crops. Thus, perennial crops are generally preferred for wet fractionation (Wilkins 1977).

In mixed swards, both perennial and annual legumes are combined with grasses or with green cereals. Perennial legumes *T. repens* and *T. pratense* (white and red clover), annual legumes *Pisum sativum* (field pea) and *Vicia sativa* (vetch), grasses *Lolium perenne* (perennial ryegrass) or *Festuca* species, and green cereals *Avena sativa* (oats) and *Secale cereale* (winter rye) are used for such swards.

The mixture of plants enhances the value of the swards as cattle feed and green fertilizer since the legumes fix nitrogen and have high nitrogen contents. Furthermore, the presence of fibrous grass constituents can enhance the efficiency of disintegrating and pressing plant material when it is wet fractionated in a screw-expeller. Without the fibrous grass, juicy legumes have a tendency to slide backward against the feed entrance of the screw press. Ostrowski (1976) reported a yield of 1.9 MT/ha of extractable protein from a mixed *T. repens* and *L. perenne* pasture. Connell and Houseman (1977) reported using tetraploid *T. pratense* mixed with *L. perenne* for wet fractionation.

Among the annual legumes, *Lupinus* spp. (lupine), *P. sativum*, *T. alexandrinum*, *Vicia sativa*, and *Vicia faba* (broad or horse bean) are generally recommended for protein extraction. In spite of favorable extraction ratios of protein nitrogen, very little is recorded about their yields of extracted protein per ha. *T. alexandrinum* has yielded 700 kg/ha extractable protein (Mungikar *et al.* 1976). The by-product leaves and stems of *P. sativum* have been extracted after harvesting the green peas, and 22 to 47% of the total nitrogen has been obtained as protein nitrogen in LPC (Pirie 1976). Up to 600 kg/ha of protein can be extracted from a fresh crop processed without delay. Residual pea haulm yielded a few hundred kilograms of extracted leaf protein in southern Sweden (Ahmad 1967).

Vicia faba, reintroduced as animal feed in Scandinavia, can yield 800 kg/ha bean protein. The yield of leaf protein should be much higher from that crop, as protein transformation losses from leaf protein into seed protein would not occur. Lexander *et al.* (1970) found that the green protein fraction of this crop had a high pepsin digestibility in spite of a rapidly darkening extracted juice. The high-producing seed crop *Glycine max* (soybean) and other *Glycine* spp. such as the perennial *Glycine wightii* are potential but neglected leaf protein sources. *Lupinus* spp. are interesting annual legumes, as a high proportion of the easily extractable protein can be fractionated off as a white protein fraction at low temperatures +43°C (Byers 1971A). Since *Lupinus albus* grows luxuriantly in southern South America, it may be a worthwhile crop there for wet fractionation.

Grass Species

The most widely used perennial grass for wet fractionation is *Lolium perenne*. Its use is due to its abundance on present-day farms and is not connected with any specific good performance for LPC production. Other commonly found perennial grasses that have been tested for LPC include: *Festuca arundinacea* (tall fescue), *Dactylis glomerata* (orchard grass, cocksfoot), and *Phalaris arundinacea* (reed canary grass). Annual grasses such as *Lolium multiflorum* (Italian ryegrass) and the tetraploid cultivar Westerwolds ryegrass have also been tested because they are easily available. The yield of extractable protein from *D. glomerata* can be 2.0 MT/ha (Arkcoll and Davys 1973). The yield of extracted crude protein [TN × 6.25] from *L. perenne* was found to reach 1.3 MT/ha (Wieringa 1977), although only one-third of the produced protein was extracted. Vartha and Allison (1973) obtained a slightly lower yield from the annual *L. multiflorum* cv Westerwoldicum. In Sweden, Westerwolds ryegrass has given favorable results as an LPC crop.

There is a relatively high yield of protein from green cereals. Cut twice during half a growing season, their extraction yield is 0.6 to 0.7 MT/ha (Arkcoll 1971). This high yield is due to a high extraction ratio of protein.

Other Nonwoody Species

A few hundred plant species and seed stock have been checked to find "a high yield of good quality LPC" at Rothamsted Experimental Station, England (Crook and Holden 1948; Byers 1958–1965, Personal communication—Rothamsted, U.K.), and at the Department of Plant Physiology, University of Lund, Sweden (Lexander *et al.* 1970; Carlsson 1975A: I; Lundborg 1979). Both groups came to a similar conclusion after examining both agricultural and wild species. Although LPC can be obtained from many conventional plants, wild plants may constitute the largest plant source for production of LPC. A few wild species, e.g., *Chenopodium album* (fat hen, goosefoot, lamb's quarters) and *Urtica dioica* (stinging nettle), are represented in Table 2.1. *Heracleum sosnowski* (cow parsnip, hogweed), another wild plant, belongs to a group of species with high dry matter and protein production which has been tested for LPC production (Hanczakowski and Lutynska 1976). Among the domestic plants, species suitable for LPC production often belonged to the plant families Amaranthaceae (pseudocereals, vegetable species), Chenopodiaceae (goosefoot family), Cruciferae (cabbage/kale family), Cucurbitaceae (cucumber family), Papilionaceae (legumes) and Solanaceae (potato-tomato family). This does not, of course, mean that all species of these groups are suitable. On the other hand, it was often found that species of the plant families Compositae (aster family; sunflower family), Polygonaceae (knotgrass family), and Umbelliferae (carrot family) contained plants with low protein extraction ratios (Carlsson 1975A: I). Low protein extractibility for plants of these families is not always the case. *Helianthus annuus* (sunflower) has often shown low extraction ratios; however, by examining more than 10 cultivars, Lundborg (1979) found extraction ratios of 50%, using the laboratory-scale pulper of Davys and Pirie (1969).

Amaranthaceae and Chenopodiaceae Species. These families contain leafy vegetables and pseudocereals (Sauer 1950, 1967; Singh 1961; Simmonds 1965; Brücher 1968). Plants from these families have received renewed interest as cattle feed (Ariotti *et al.* 1974), as pseudocereals (Ruskin 1975), and as LPC species (Carlsson 1975A, 1980). The main features for plants of these families that make them suitable for LPC production are their high protein production when given nitrogen fertilizer, their high protein extraction ratio, especially for the Chenopodiaceae species *Atriplex* and *Chenopodium*, and the high proportion of white protein that can be obtained from them by heat fractionation of extracted proteins (Carlsson 1975A: II, III, IV, 1978A; Ostrowski 1978; Ostrowski-Meissner *et al.* 1980).

Amaranthus cruentus and *Amaranthus hypochondriacus* are two pseudocereals that give high protein production in their leaves, about 1.4 MT/ha crude protein (200 kg N/ha, 11 weeks) in hot temperate climates (Carlsson 1978C), while *Amaranthus hybridus*, *A. paniculatus*, and *A. retroflexus* (not the weedy type) seem to be better adapted to cooler regions (Carlsson 1979). The possible advantage of a C_4 trait of amaranth species—an especially efficient photosynthesis system in hot, dry climates—may be of value in those regions, but does not seem to be so in cool regions (Laetsch 1971).

In the family Chenopodiaceae, the mountain spinach plant *Atriplex hortensis* (garden *Atriplex*) and the pseudocereal *Chenopodium quinoa* (rice goosefoot, quinoa) are the most examined genera (Lexander *et al.* 1970; Carlsson 1975A, 1980, 1982; Ostrowski 1978) (Fig. 2.1–2.3). The true protein production in Sweden for both plants was about 1.2 MT/ha (200–400 kg N/ha at 14 weeks). Two consecutive harvests from two sowings of *C. quinoa* gave a true protein production of 2.0 MT/ha (2 × 300–400 kg N/ha; 20–21 weeks in total) (Carlsson 1968–1970; Carlsson *et al.* 1982). The protein extraction ratios for *Amaranthus*, *Atriplex*, and *Chenopodium* species field grown in Sweden were from 50 to 60% (Carlsson 1975A: III) using the laboratory-scale pulper of Davys and Pirie.

Chenopodium album is looked upon by most people as a wild species. It has, however, accompanied mankind since long ago (Brouks 1975). During wartimes in Sweden, it has been a popular spinach plant and is still used by vegetable lovers. In northern India, it is used as a grain crop (Singh 1961). Its drought resistance, which it shares with other Chenopodiaceae species, makes it often the only survivor in drying meadows harvested for "hay." Its

Fig. 2.1. Harvest of *Atriplex hortensis* L. for production of LPC.

Fig. 2.2. Cultivation of *Chenopodium quinoa* Willd. for LPC production on a farm in southern Sweden.

digestibility as cattle feed can be comparable to *Medicago sativa* (Jones *et al.* 1971). The dry matter of pressed, dewatered crop residues of *C. quinoa* is more digestible than the whole crop according to *in vitro* experiments with cellulase (Carlsson 1978C). *Kochia scoparia* (fireweed, summer cypress) is

Fig. 2.3. Surface view of *Chenopodium quinoa* Willd. at the age of 6 weeks. The area within the square is 1 m^2. Plant and row distances are 15 cm.

another drought-resistant plant that has good forage value (Hughes *et al.* 1951), from which 40 to 60% of the crude protein in the plant can be extracted (Stovall 1970). Another well known Chenopodiaceae plant is *Beta vulgaris* (sugar beet). The leaves are often left unused on the fields after the root harvest or are used as cattle feed to a limited extent. The protein yield can be up to 0.8 MT/ha from by-product leaves (Pirie 1976). In Denmark, the loss of protein from ensilaged, whole beet tops can be 50% (Nörgaard-Pedersen 1977A). The tops have been wet fractionated instead to get a protein-rich juice for pig feeding and a better fiber product for silage.

Cruciferae Species. Investigated *Brassica* species have the same advantages as Amaranthaceae and Chenopodiaceae species suitable for LPC production and have been extensively studied. The fast-growing *Brassica* species are excellent for extending the harvest season both as early spring and late autumn crops. Annual green cereals with one regrowth followed by *Brassica hirta* (mustard), *Brassica oleracea* (kale), or *Raphanus sativa* (fodder radish) give a total yield of about 2 MT/ha extracted true protein (Arkcoll 1971). Lundborg (1979) examined 18 species and cultivars of *Brassica* supposedly yielding high biomass to determine their potential use for LPC production and to study the separation of green and white protein fractions in the plants. It seemed especially easy to separate the green protein fraction (particle fragments of chloroplasts, etc.) with a low-speed centrifuge after heating the extracted juice to a relatively low temperature.

The by-product leaves of *Brassica* species such as *B. oleracea* cv Botrytis (cauliflower) have been extracted several times, and the LPC obtained has often had a good quality. The good feeding value of the residual pressed crop from cauliflower leaves has been shown by Livingston *et al.* (1972).

Cucurbitaceae and Solanaceae Species. These are less exploited species for LPC extraction, although the by-product vines of *Cucurbita* spp. have high protein extraction ratios and the extraction ratio generally is high for *Solanum tuberosum* (potato) haulm as well as other Solanaceae species. A study of 11 cultivars in Sweden showed a range of extraction ratios from 20 to 65% of the crude protein in the tops when plants were minced (Carlsson 1971). Extracting about half of the protein from potato haulm at the normal time for tuber harvest, Carruthers and Pirie (1975) obtained 200 to 300 kg/ha protein as LPC. For potato-growing countries, this represents a large native protein source (Shmanenkov *et al.* 1970; Hanczakowski 1975; Pirie 1976).

Among Solanaceae species, *Nicotiana* spp. and *Solanum melongena* have a special property. It is possible to obtain a crystalline, white Fraction I protein (ribulose-1,5-diphosphate carboxylase, F I protein, RuDPase) from extracted, soluble leaf proteins (Sakano *et al.* 1974; Bahr *et al.* 1977). A very pure protein can thus be produced from the toxic tobacco plant, and the protein extraction as such is a detoxification process. Due to intensive tobacco cultivation in many areas of the world, large quantities of leaf protein can be produced per ha (Tso and Kung, Chapter 4). This white Fraction I protein is the most abundant single protein on earth. There has been little success with obtaining crystalline protein from other Solanaceae species or members of other plant families, e.g., *Beta vulgaris* and *Brassica sinensis* (Chinese cabbage) (Sakano *et al.* 1974; Bahr *et al.* 1977) and Cruciferae species (Carlsson 1978C).

Miscellaneous Species

Only a few of the wild species examined (Crook and Holden 1948; Byers 1958–1965; Boyd 1971; Carlsson 1975A: I) will be mentioned. *Urtica dioica* (nettle-cloth plant, stinging nettle) has luxuriant growth capacity and good regrowth ability according to harvests from the same plots 8 years in succession in southern Sweden. The perennial plants were cut 3 to 4 times per season and produced 3 MT/ha true protein (Carlsson *et al.* 1982). The stands were based on a commercial plant type for nettle-cloth production. The indigenous Swedish plants were somewhat less productive in a greenhouse test under controlled conditions (Lexander *et al.* 1970). Depending on processing conditions, 25 to 60% of total plant nitrogen was extractable. In spite of a quickly darkening extract (due to phenolics), a good nutritive value can be given by the LPC if properly processed (Carlsson *et al.* 1982). A tropical relative, *Boehmeria nivea* (ramie) that is also a fiber crop has been advocated for LPC by Pirie (1976).

The LPC potential of aquatic plants was reviewed earlier by Boyd (1971), who found *Typha latifolia* (cattail) unsuitable for protein extraction. This contrasted with the results from plants growing in southern Sweden (Carlsson 1975A: I). About half of the crude protein was extracted as true protein by Carlsson (1975A: I). Perhaps different ecotypes of *Typha latifolia* behave differently during processing.

Helianthus annuus, Helianthus tuberosus (Jerusalem artichoke), and hybrids between the two species have high dry matter content and are good sources of protein production (Schuster and Boye 1971; Rai and Shukla 1977). As mentioned earlier, these species may contain varieties with a fairly high extraction ratio for protein. The hybrid crop that is perennial due to its tubers could be interesting for production of LPC and inulin (fructofuranose) preparation from the same expressed juice.

Woody Species

The possibility of production of LPC (also called protein-vitamin concentrate/paste) from forest tree leaves has lately been reviewed by Carlsson (1975B, 1978B) and Chedd (1975). Most common trees in the temperate zones have been investigated regarding the qualitative and quantitative composition of their leaves, including needles (Carlsson 1978B). Many types of products from forest leaves have been produced using green leaf meal, chlorophyll-vitamin paste, and LPC. The amino acid composition of whole leaves indicates that the protein in the leaves is comparable to good quality forage protein (Sirén *et al.* 1970; Kudasheva and Chestak 1973). Its digestibility by cattle is good (Nedorizescu 1972).

Among woody plants, the most promising ones for LPC production are those from fast-growing, short-rotation forests (energy forests) and from plantations of woody shrubs. In the former case, *Eucalyptus*, *Populus* (aspen, poplar, cottonwood), and *Salix* (sallow, willow) species are the most promising. In the latter case, by-product leaves from hedges or *Gossypium hirsutum* (cotton) could be investigated.

LPC has been produced from *Populus* and *Salix* species in Sweden (Carlsson 1968–1970). There exist problems with the extraction procedure and the relatively low *in vitro* digestibility of the protein in these LPCs (about 50%), due partly perhaps to the high fiber and polyphenolic contents of the plant material, leaves, and small twigs. However, such problems could be solved by a quick processing under reducing extraction conditions. A vitamin A-protein concentrate from coniferous needles has been produced by Ladinskaja *et al.* (1974) in the USSR at the Kirov Forest Academy in Leningrad. The concentrate was fed to pigs and calves, who readily consumed it.

GENETIC VARIABILITY FOR SELECTION OF LEAF PROTEIN CONCENTRATE PLANTS

Some preliminary studies to select especially suitable cultivars, seed sources, breeding lines (strains), and even individual plants from established LPC crops have been performed since the beginning of the 1970s. Cultivars of *Brassica* spp. (Hanczakowski 1977; Lundborg 1979), *Helianthus annuus* (Lundborg 1979), *Medicago sativa* (Jelinowska 1979), and *Solanum tuberosum* (Carlsson 1971; Hanczakowski and Makuch 1980) have shown quantitative and qualitative traits.

In 1972 and 1973, more than 150 seed sources of selected *Amaranthus* species *(A. caudatus, A. hybridus/hypochondriacus, A. gangeticus, A. paniculatus), Atriplex* species *(A. hastata, A. hortensis, A. nitens)*, and *Chenopodium* species *(C. giganteum, C. quinoa, C. urbicum)* were studied by Carlsson. The following factors were investigated: protein production per plant, protein extraction ratio, nitrogen content of the LPC, pepsin/pancreatin *in vitro* protein digestibility of the LPC, foaming ability during processing (indicationg saponins), hemolytic values of freeze-dried plant material and LPC (also indicators of saponins). Differences were found mostly between species but also between seed sources. Jelinowska (1979) showed yield data variations for different strains of *Medicago sativa.*

In combination with plant breeding of *M. sativa* and *Trifolium pratense* for better quality as cattle feed (Julén and Mårtensson 1974), the LPC group at the Department of Plant Physiology, University of Lund (Carlsson 1979) investigated for individual, field-grown plants of *M. sativa* and *T. pratense* the protein extraction ratio, the yield of LPC from the plant, the nitrogen content of the LPC, the methionine content of the extracted leaf protein, and the pepsin/pancreatin *in vitro* protein digestibility of LPC. The variations noted could be used for selection work. The content of nitrogen in the LPC varied from 5.8 to 9.8% of the dry matter for *M. sativa* and from 6.5 to 8.3% for *T. pratense.* The nitrogen levels were the same or lower than for the previously mentioned *Amaranthus* sources [7.1 to 8.4% N in the LPC DM (dry matter)], and those of *Atriplex/Chenopodium* (9.0 to 10.0%). The L-methionine contents for *M. sativa* LPC varied from 1.0 to 2.0 g per 16 g nitrogen, and for *T. pratense* from 1.2 to 1.8 g per 16 g nitrogen. A slightly positive correlation between L-methionine contents and the pepsin/pancreatin digestibility values seemed to be present. *Lolium multiflorum*, especially its F_1 generation, has lately been intensively investigated by Bugge (1977). The protein extraction ratio, the yield of LPC, the nitrogen content in LPC, and the methionine content in the plant material and LPC were investigated. The nitrogen content in the LPC varied from 6.6 to 8.9% for the F_1 plants, with a mean value of 7.8%, and with a parental control of 8.6%. In similar ways, the other factors varied. In general, however, the methionine values seemed lower than the ones for *M. sativa* and *T. pratense.*

Selection work for plant breeding has also been done for purposes other than the production of LPC. However, as the selection deals with soluble proteins and Fraction I protein (Rommann *et al.* 1971) and ribulose-1,5-diphosphate carboxylase (F I) acitvity (Frey and Moss 1976), it can be useful for the production of white LPC for human consumption. Also, soluble proteins from *Lotus corniculatus* (bird's-foot trefoil), *M. sativa*, *Trifolium pratense*, and *T. repens* are claimed to be a partial cause of bloat in cattle (McArthur and Miltimore 1969; Rommann *et al.* 1971; Jones and Lyttleton 1972). Part of the selection work for these legumes is aimed at reducing the amount of soluble protein (Gutek *et al.* 1976). The heritability value (amount of genetically determined variability) for soluble protein suggested that selection can be done either to decrease or increase the yield of extractable white protein that is soluble. In relation to an increase in the amount of white LPC for human consumption, an effort to accomplish the latter would be most rewarding. The genetic variation of RuDP carboxylase in one grass, *Hordeum vulgare* (barley) has also been chosen for studies (Frey and Moss 1976; Ströbäck and Gibbons 1976).

Should perennial or annual crops be used for LPC production? The advantage of perennial crops was noted earlier (leguminous species). However, most farmers also use annual, winter annual, or short-duration crops for crop rotation systems. Such arrangements help to avoid the establishment of harmful insect populations and fungal diseases. Thus, there is always the option to utilize suitable annual species for an extension of the season for LPC production. Annual crops for wet fractionation during a whole season have been tried by Arkcoll (1971).

Medicago sativa is the basic crop for the green crop drying industry, but its availability varies with the time of the year. In cool, temperate climates, the production of the crop is very low in the late summer and at the end of the year. The green crop driers have, therefore, a need for other, supplementary crops during part of the season to economize the cost of their processing equipment. Plants like *Brassica* species are suitable for covering the additional needs at the beginning and end of a growth season. The farmer supplying these crops can still grow spring or autumn/winter-sown cereals. The France Luzerne Society in France is already using *Brassica* green fodder crops for LPC production.

The gap at the late summer period could be closed by use of annuals as well. *Chenopodium album* and *C. quinoa* (Ariotti *et al.* 1974) and *Helianthus annuus* (Schuster and Boye 1971) are crops that have already been examined for green fodder crop production. Other, less common, forage crops are the drought-hardy "shrubs" *Atriplex nummularia* and *Atriplex repanda* (Silva and Pereira 1976). Such plants could be used to supply extra plant material in the late summer. Their merits as LPC plants have already been investigated. *C. quinoa* has been used by green crop driers to close the late summer gap between seasons in southern Sweden and Denmark (Anon. 1976). The composition of the dried product from *C. quinoa* was similar to that of *M. sativa* and good quality grasses. In several countries, *C. quinoa* has been studied with success for wet fractionation, in both cool and hot climates.

PROCESSING OF PLANT MATERIAL

Different plant materials behave differently during the processing in different types of machinery. Using the screw presses seems to create problems for different crops, which is a pity as they are commonly used for juice expression. Normally, the presses work well with fibrous crops such as grasses. However, lush, green plants like *Beta vulgaris*, *Brassica* species, and *Chenopodium quinoa* are sometimes too soft and turn into a slurry-like pulsating pulp in the press. To alleviate the problems in grinding lush materials, grass, hay, or straw can be mixed with the soft plant materials. A minor loss of true protein may appear, which is compensated for by the greater grinding efficiency. Vines and unchopped, fibrous materials may wind themselves around the screw in the press during processing. Chopping alleviates this problem. The rotary pulpers and extruders seem to work satisfactorily with most crops.

To remove juice from disintegrated crops, both screw presses and belt presses seem to handle most materials. Again, for wet/lush crops, especially short-chopped grass (10 mm), the screw press can produce the aforementioned slurry. A wet crop can also slip on the belt in a belt press. When chopped crops were pressed in either of the two press types, the belt press produced more dry matter and true protein (Shepperson *et al.* 1977).

Some plants have a large quantity of organic acids or phenolic acids in their vacuoles. When the vacuole breaks during cell maceration, these compounds can cause an immediate precipitation of protein in the plant material before it can be extracted or expressed (Arkcoll 1971). The organic acids from the plant cell vacuole cause autoprecipitation before the juice is expressed and in the expressed juice as such. Plants of the family Polygonaceae have a characteristic extract pH between 4 and 5 (Carlsson 1975A: I), and mucilaginous pulps form during the disintegration (Byers 1961). Tannins can also have negative effects on protein extraction (Anderson 1968; Butler and Pirie 1977). *Helianthus annuus, Populus* spp., *Salix* spp., and *Urtica dioica* are plants with darkening extract and high phenolic contents (Carlsson 1975A: I).

Chenopodiaceae, Cruciferae, and Cucurbitaceae species often have a relatively high pH in the expressed juice and seem to lack high amounts of phenolics or easily oxidizable phenolics (Carlsson 1975A: I, II, III; 1978C). Subsequently, high protein extraction ratios are often found for these species (Carlsson 1975A: I, II, III).

Separation of Extracted Leaf Protein from the Juice

The juice contains several substances that can affect the separation of protein such as saponins (protein foam stabilizers), organic acids (pH effects on protein solubility and denaturation), and phenolics (denaturation of proteins). Among the plant species that give a foam-rich, expressed juice are *M. sativa* and *Amaranthus* spp. This foaming causes problems in further processing unless the foam volume is reduced. Saponins are a probable cause of the stable foam. For *M. sativa*, a silicone antifoam can be used (Edwards 1977). The froth of *Amaranthus* has to be treated by a silicone antifoam and NaOH added to increase the pH to 8.5 (Carlsson 1977). Another antifoam, *n*-octanol, can also be used.

Foam-free juice can be treated in different ways to precipitate the protein. The protein can be precipitated by heating the juice, by acidifying it to the isoelectric point of the proteins, or by organic solvent precipitation.

The size of the protein coagulum can vary, depending on the pH of the juice and the protein concentration in the juice. These two variable factors are different for different species. Under standard conditions, e.g., at pH 8.5, the coagulum is easy to separate from the deproteinized juice. On the other hand, *C. quinoa* can give a thick coagulum filling the whole juice volume. The juice then has to be diluted before the separation of the coagulum. Other plants, *Amaranthus* spp. for example, can produce a curd too fine for a commercial separator (de Laval milk separator) to completely remove the coagulum. The juice is then only partly deproteinized. One way to solve this is to add $CaCl_2$ before the separation (Carlsson 1977).

Acid precipitation of protein often yields curds that are finer than the ones obtained by heat precipitation. Depending on the species, organic solvent precipitation can give a relatively fine coagulum or a more voluminous one. In the latter case, it is probably due to a co-precipitation of other organic compounds.

Fractionation Products

Species with a relatively high yield of white coagulum often belong to the genera *Atriplex*, *Brassica*, *Chenopodium*, and selected legumes, while grasses often give low yields (Lexander *et al.* 1970; Carlsson 1975A: I, II, IV, 1980, 1982; Ostrowski 1978; Lundborg 1979). All species with a high proportion of white protein in the extract also have a high protein production in the plant or per ha. The yield of white leaf protein per ha is about 200 kg during a three-month period for *Atriplex hortensis* and *Chenopodium quinoa* (Carlsson 1975A: IV, 1980, 1982; Fig. 2.1–2.3).

A small amount of green color in the white protein did not impair the nutritive value of *C. quinoa* LPC (pepsin/pancreatin *in vitro* protein digestibility), heat-precipitated after separation of a low-temperature green protein fraction. The total nitrogen content in the second white fraction ranged from 7.8 to 12.5% of the LPC dry matter, but the digestibility was independent of the protein content of the LPC and was high (85 to 96% of the protein was digestible) (Carlsson 1975A: II). With that background, it is of interest that a large proportion of that same second heat-precipitated fraction can be obtained from *Urtica dioica* (Carlsson 1975A: I), which can produce in

Sweden 3000 kg/ha true protein during one season with 3 to 4 cuttings of regrowth. Also, *Helianthus annuus* can give a large amount of the second heat-precipitated fraction (Lundborg 1979).

***In Vivo* Test with Rats and Chickens.** The quality of the protein in the LPC is a function of the reactions between the protein and other substances during LPC production and of the composition of the LPC. Both factors are related to plant material and developmental stage of the plant at harvest. A positive effect of increased plant age on the net protein utilization (NPU) value of the protein in the LPC from *Triticum aestivum* (wheat) until the stage with ears, and from *Vicia sativa* (tares) until the pod stage, has been shown by Henry and Ford (1965). An opposite result was indicated in an early work on LPC from pasture plants *Dactylis glomerata* and leguminous species by Davies *et al.* (1952).

No consistent effects of different nitrogen fertilizer levels have been found on the nutritive value of LPCs (Hanczakowski and Lutynska 1976: *Heracleum sosnowski*, 240 kg/ha N and 480 kg/ha N; Hanczakowski 1977: four *Brassica oleracea* cultivars, 200 kg/ha N and 400 kg/ha N). For whole freeze-dried plant shoots, however, Eppendorfer (1977) found a negative correlation between NPU and increased fertilizer levels. The possible effects of plant physiological stages and other cultivation conditions indicate that one should be cautious when comparing the quality of different plant species and cultivars.

In many cases, plants in very leafy stages have been harvested for LPC production. This may make a comparison justified. Leafy plants have been studied for species of Cruciferae *(Brassica, Sinapis)*, Gramineae (green cereals), and Leguminosae *(Medicago, Lupinus, Trifolium, Vicia)* (Henry and Ford 1965; Subba Rau *et al.* 1972; Hanczakowski 1975, 1977; Munshi *et al.* 1975; McKenzie 1976; Lundborg 1979). In some cases, the LPCs have been produced at a stage when the leaves/residual plant parts can be harvested as a by-product (Subba Rau *et al.* 1972) at the normal harvest time for the main product. From a practical point of view, plants can be compared, although "true" species differences cannot be counted on.

Effects of Nonprotein Constituents on *In Vivo* Value of LPC

Trifolium pratense phenolics and *o*-diphenolases have been shown to reduce both the availability of lysine in casein and the biological value of it (Horigome and Kandatsu 1968). Allison found a correlation between available lysine contents and BV's of various LPCs. *M. sativa* LPC that was produced under reducing conditions, under normal oxidative conditions, and, finally, under oxidative conditions with the addition of chlorogenic acid showed a decrease of lysine availability in this sequence (Allison 1971). Igarashi *et al.* (1976) showed a correlation between available lysine content and *in vitro* trypsin digestibility of *T. pratense* LPC.

CONCLUSION

A good yield of LPC with good quality can be obtained from selected plant species, while, in other cases, an adjustment of the processing method to the plant species has to be made.

REFERENCES

AHMAD, J. 1967. Biochem. Dep. Sect. Rothamsted Exp. Stn. Rep. *1967*, 117.

ALLISON, R.M. 1971. Factors influencing the availability of lysine in leaf protein. *In* Leaf Protein: Its Agronomy, Preparation, Quality, and Use. IBP Handb. *20*. N.W. Pirie (Editor). Blackwell, Oxford.

ANDERSON, J.W. 1968. Extraction of enzymes and subcellular organelles from plant tissues. Phytochemistry (Oxford) *7*, 1973–1978.

ANON. 1976. Are we going to grow chenopods? KI-SAM Nyt *10* (Aug.) 42. (Danish)

ANON. 1977. Protein from tobacco. J. Am. Diet. Assoc. *70*, 58.

ARIOTTI, M.P., BOCCIGNONE, M., CAMPOS MERINO, J., MALETTO, S., MUSSA, P.P., SALAZAR, F. and SARRA, C. 1974. Evaluation of the forage value of *Chenopodium quinoa*. Ann. Fac. Med. Vet. Torino *21*, 133–140. (Italian)

ARKCOLL, D.B. 1971. Agronomic aspects of leaf protein production in Great Britain. *In* Leaf Protein: Its Agronomy, Preparation, Quality and Use. IBP Handb. *20*. N.W. Pirie (Editor). Blackwell, Oxford.

ARKCOLL, D.B. and DAVYS, M.N.G. 1973. Mechanical fractionation as an aid to crop drying. Proc. 1st Int. Green Crop Drying Congr., Oxford, April 1973.

AZIZ, T.A., EL-SHAZLY, K., EL-ZAYAT, S., ABOU AKKADA, A.R. and NAGA, M.A. 1971. The use of leaf proteins in poultry nutrition. Alexandria J. Agric. Res. *19*, 193–198.

BAHR, JT., BOURQUE, D.P. and SMITH, H.J. 1977. Solubility properties of fraction I proteins of maize, cotton, spinach and tobacco. J. Agric. Food Chem. *25*, 783–789.

BETSCHART, A.A. and KINSELLA, J.E. 1973. Extractibility and solubility of leaf protein. J. Agric. Food Chem. *21*, 60–65.

BICKOFF, E.M., BOOTH, A.N., DE FREMERY, D., EDWARDS, R.H., KNUCKLES, B.E., MILLER, R.E., SAUNDERS, R.M. and KOHLER, G.O. 1975. Nutritional evaluation of alfalfa leaf protein concentrate. *In* Protein Nutritional Quality of Foods and Feeds, Vol. 1. M. Friedman (Editor). Marcel Dekker, New York.

BIRK, Y. 1969. Saponins. *In* Toxic Constituents of Plant Foodstuffs. I.E. Liener (Editor). Academic Press, New York.

BOLDIZSÁR, H., RIBICZEY-SZABÓ, P. and KOZMA, M. 1975. Degradation of leaf protein concentrates by pepsin and trypsin. Acta Aliment. Acad. Sci. Hung. *4*, 217–227.

BOYD, C.E. 1971. Leaf protein from aquatic plants. *In* Leaf Protein: Its Agronomy, Preparation, Quality and Use. IBP Handb. *20*. N.W. Pirie (Editor). Blackwell, Oxford.

BRAUDE, R., JONES, A.S. and HOUSEMAN, R.A. 1977. The utilization of the juice extracted from green crops. *In* Green Crop Fractionation. R.J. Wilkins (Editor). Br. Grassl. Soc. Occas. Symp. *9* and Br. Soc. Anim. Prod., Grassland Research Inst., Hurley, U.K.

BRAY, W.J., HUMPHRIES, C. and INERITEI, M.S. 1978. The use of solvents to decolorise leaf protein concentrate. J. Sci. Food Agric. *29*, 165–171.

BROUKS, B. 1975. Plants Consumed by Man. Academic Press, New York.

BROWN, H.E., STEIN, E.R. and SALDANA, G. 1975. Evaluation of *Brassica carinata* as a source of plant protein. J. Agric. Food Chem. *23*, 545–547.

BRUVERE, V.A., ALKENE, A.J. GALBANS, U.I. and POLJE, O.R. 1978. Extraction and studies of protein from tree leaves. "Wood Chemistry" *4*, 106–108. (Russian)

BRÜCHER, H. 1968. The genetic reserves of South America for crop breeding. Theor. Appl. Genet. *38*, 9–22. (German)

BUCHANAN, R.A. 1969. Effect of storage and lipid extraction on the properties of leaf protein. J. Sci. Food Agric. *20*, 359–364.

BUGGE, G. 1977. Quantity and quality of nitrogen substances in green crop and leaf protein concentrate from *Lolium multiflorum*. Unpublished Rep. 3rd EEC Veg. Prot. Work. Group Meet., Feb. 8–10, 1977, Wageningen, Netherlands.

BUTLER, J. and PIRIE, N.W. 1977. Leaf protein extraction. Rothamsted Exp. Stn. Rep. *1977*, 291.

BYERS, M. 1958–1965. Biochemistry Sections. Rothamsted Exp. Stn. Rep. *1958–1965*.

BYERS, M. 1961. Extraction of protein from the leaves of some plants growing in Ghana. J. Sci. Food Agric. *12*, 20–30.

BYERS, M. 1964. On Chenopodium nuttalie and C. quinoa. *In* Biochem. Sect. Rothamsted Exp. Stn. Rep. *1964*, 122.

BYERS, M. 1967. The *in vitro* hydrolysis of leaf proteins. II. The action of papain of protein concentrates extracted from leaves of different species. J. Sci. Food Agric. *18*, 33–38.

BYERS, M. 1971A. Amino acid composition and *in vitro* digestibility of some protein fractions from three species of leaves at various ages. J. Sci. Food Agric. *22*, 242–251.

BYERS, M. 1971B. The amino acid composition of some leaf protein preparations. *In* Leaf Protein: Its Agronomy, Preparation, Quality and Use. IBP Handb. *20*. N.W. Pirie (Editor). Blackwell, Oxford.

BYERS, M., DAVYS, M.N.G., PIRIE, N.W. and STURROCK, J.W. 1965. Production of leaf protein as human food. Rothamsted Exp. Stn. Rep. *1965*, 106–107.

CARLSSON, R. 1968–1970. Unpublished material. Dep. Plant Physiol., Univ. Lund, Lund, Sweden.

CARLSSON, R. 1971. Investigation of leaf protein production of wild and conventional species and leaf protein extraction ratios. Unpublished Rep. to Bank of Sweden Tercentenary Fund, Feb. 1971, Stockholm. (65 pp, 28 tables) (Swedish)

CARLSSON, R. 1972–1973. Unpublished material. Selection among *Amaranthus, Atriplex* and *Chenopodium* species provenances for production of leaf protein concentrates. Dep. Plant Physiol., Univ. Lund, Lund, Sweden.

CARLSSON, R. 1975A. Selection of Centrospermae and other species for production of leaf protein concentrates. Ph.D. Thesis, May 1975. Univ. Lund, Lund, Sweden. */LUNBDS/(NBFB-1004)/1–8/* [With additional separate papers (many thesis copies are circulated)]:

I: Extraction and fractionation of leaf proteins from wild and cultivated species grown in southern Sweden. (28 pp)

II: Centrospermae species as raw material for production of leaf protein. (68 pp)

III: Leaf protein production of *Atriplex hortensis* L., *Chenopodium quinoa* Willd. and *Amaranthus caudatus* L., field-grown in southern Sweden. (23 pp)

IV: Qualities of leaf protein concentrates from *Atriplex hortensis* L., *Chenopodium quinoa* Willd. and *Amaranthus caudatus* L., field-grown in southern Sweden. (29 pp)

CARLSSON, R. 1975B. Increased utilization of whole trees.—Production of protein-vitamin concentrate from leaves. Skog i Skåne *4*, 20–21. (Swedish).

CARLSSON, R. 1977. Personal communication. Western Regional Research Center, U.S. Dep. Agric., Berkeley, CA.

CARLSSON, R. 1978A. Leaf protein from non-agricultural plants. Proc. Int. Workshop Utilization Agric. Waste for Feed and Food, CETEC, Belo Horizonte, Minas Gerais, Brazil, Dec. 1977.

CARLSSON, R. 1978B. Production of animal feed and protein-vitamin concentrates from leaves of forest trees: A review. Proc. Int. Workshop Utilization Agric. Waste for Feed and Food, CETEC, Belo Horizonte, Minas Gerais, Brazil, Dec. 1977.

CARLSSON, R. 1978C. Unpublished Reports to Western Regional Research Center, U.S. Dep. Agric., Berkeley, CA., March 1978, with collaborators, as follow:

I: Production of leaf protein concentrates from *Amaranthus* species and other species, grown in a hot, temperate climate. CARLSSON, R., DE FREMERY, D. and KOHLER, G.O.

II: Quality of leaf protein concentrates and fibre residues from various species grown in a hot, temperate climate. CARLSSON, R., GUMBMAN, M.R. and KOHLER, G.O.

III: Composition of leaf protein concentrates: Contributions from different parts of plant shoots. CARLSSON, R. and KOHLER, G.O.

CARLSSON, R. 1979. Plant selection among temperate species for production of leaf protein concentrate. Proc. Eucarpia Fodder Crops Sect. Meet., Sept. 4–9, 1978, Radzikow, Poland. *In* Biuletyn *135*/1979. Instytutu Hodowli i Aklimatyzacji Roslin, Suppl. 1, 239–248.

CARLSSON, R. 1980. Quantity and quality of leaf protein concentrates from *Atriplex hortensis* L., *Chenopodium quinoa* Willd. and *Amaranthus caudatus* L. grown in southern Sweden. Acta Agric. Scand. *30*, 418–426.

CARLSSON, R. 1981. Leaf protein in aqua-culture. Unpublished Rep. for Institutet för Vatten och Luftvård—IVL, Aneboda, Sweden.

CARLSSON, R. and CLARKE, E.M.W. 1983. *Atriplex hortensis* L. as a leafy vegetable, and as a leaf protein concentrate plant. *In* Plant Food for Human Nutrition. C.E. Bodwell, L. Petit and J. Gueguen (Editors). Martinus Nijhoff/ Dr. W. Junk Publishers, The Hague, Netherlands.

CARLSSON, R., CLARKE, E.M.W. and WOODHAM, A.A. 1975. The effects of plant physiological stages on the nutritive value of leaf protein concentrates. Unpublished Rep. for Rowett Res. Inst., Aberdeen, Scotland.

CARLSSON, R., HANCZAKOWSKI, P. and ISRAELSEN, M. 1982. New forage crops for wet-fractionation to produce leaf protein concentrate. Rocz. Nauk. Zootechn. [J. Anim. Sci. Technol., Poland] *9*, 263–270.

CARLSSON, R. and KNUCKLES, B.E. 1978. Quantity and quality of non-green leaf protein fraction of *Brassica* and *Eruca* cultivars. Personal communication. Western Regional Research Center, U.S. Dep. Agric., Berkeley, CA.

CARLSSON, R. and LEXANDER, K. 1972. Possible, genetic variation in factors for production of good quality leaf protein concentrates among individual plants of *Medicago sativa* L. and *Trifolium pratense* L. Unpublished material. Dep. Plant Physiol., Univ. Lund, Lund, Sweden.

CARR, J.R. and PEARSON, G. 1976. Photosensitisation, growth, performance and carcass measurements of pigs fed diets containing commercially prepared lucerne leaf protein concentrate. N.Z. J. Exp. Agric. *4*, 45–50.

CARRUTHERS, I.B. and PIRIE, N.W. 1975. The yields of extracted protein and of residual fibre from potato haulm taken as a by-product. Biotechnol. Bioeng. *17*, 1775–1782.

CHAN. P.H., SAKANO, K., SINGH, S. and WILDMAN, S.G. 1972. Crystalline fraction I protein: Preparation in large yield. Science *176*, 1145–1146.

CHEDD, G. 1975. Cellulose from sunlight. New Sci. *65*, 572–575.

CHEEKE, P.R. 1976. Nutritional and physiological properties of saponins. Nutr. Rep. Int. *13*, 315–324.

CLIFFORD, A.J., VASCONCELLOS, J.A., FORMAN, L.P., LUMIJARVI, D. and WIER, W.C. 1977. Nucleic acid content and nutritive value of green and white leaf proteins of alfalfa. Nutr. Rep. Int. *15*, 511–518.

CONNELL, J. and HOUSEMAN, R.A. 1977. The utilization by ruminants of the pressed crop from fractionation machinery. *In* Green Crop Fractionation. R.J. Wilkins (Editor). Br. Grassl. Soc. Occas. Symp. *9* and Br. Soc. Anim. Prod., Grassland Research Inst., Hurley, U.K.

CROOK, E.M. and HOLDEN, M. 1948. Some factors affecting the extraction of nitrogenous materials from leaves of various species. Biochem. J. *43*, 181–185.

DAVIS, M., EVANS, W.C. and PARR, W.H. 1952. Biological values and digestibilities of some grasses and protein preparations from young and mature species by the Thomas-Mitchell method, using rats. Biochem. J. *52*, xxiii.

DAVYS, M.N.G. and PIRIE, N.W. 1960. Protein from leaves by bulk extraction. Engineering (London) *190*, 274–275.

DAVYS, M.N.G. and PIRIE, N.W. 1965. A belt press for separating juices from fibrous pulps. J. Agric. Eng. Res. *10*, 142–145.

DAVYS, M.N.G. and PIRIE, N.W. 1969. A laboratory-scale pulper for leafy plant material. Biotechnol. Bioeng. *11*, 517–528.

DE FREMERY, D., MILLER, R.E., EDWARDS, R.H., KNUCKLES, B.E., BICKOFF, E.M. and KOHLER, G.O. 1973. Centrifugal separation of white and green protein fractions from alfalfa juice following controlled heating. J. Agric. Food Chem. *21*, 886–889.

EDWARDS, R.H. 1977. Personal communication. Western Regional Research Center, U.S. Dep. Agric., Berkeley, CA.

EDWARDS, R.H., MILLER, R.E., DE FREMERY, D., KNUCKLES, B.E., BICKOFF, E.M. and KOHLER, G.O. 1975. Pilot plant production of an edible white fraction leaf protein concentrate from alfalfa. J. Agric. Food Chem. *23*, 620–626.

EIPESON, W.E., SINGH, N. and MANJREKAR, S.P. 1974. Kinetics of thermal precipitation of leaf proteins from lucerne *(Medicago sativa)*. J. Food Sci. Technol. (India) *11*, 66–70.

EL-ALAILY, H.A. and WOODHAM, A.A. Unpublished material. Rowett Res. Inst., Aberdeen, Scotland.

EPPENDORFER, W.H. 1977. Amino acid composition and nutritive value of Italian rye-grass, red clover and lucerne as influenced by application and content of nitrogen. J. Sci. Food Agric. *28*, 607–614.

FAO/WHO. 1965. Protein requirements. FAO Nutr. Meet. Rep. Ser. *37*. Food Agric. Organ. U.N., Rome.

FAO/WHO. 1973. Protein requirements. FAO Nutr. Meet. Rep. Ser. *52*. Food Agric. Organ. U.N., Rome.

FEENY, P.P. 1969. Inhibitory effect of oak leaf tannins on the hydrolysis of protein by trypsin. Phytochemistry (Oxford) *8*, 2119–2126.

FERRER, I., SILVA, E. and BARRIGA, R. 1977. Extraction of proteins from leaves of *Chenopodium album*. Aliment. Soc. Chilena Tecnol. Aliment. *2*, 19–26. (Spanish)

FESTENSTEIN, G.N. 1972. Water-soluble carbohydrates in extracts from large-scale preparation of leaf protein. J. Sci. Food Agric. *23*, 1409–1415.

FESTENSTEIN, G.N. 1976. Carbohydrates associated with leaf protein. J. Sci. Food Agric. *27*, 849–854.

FIORENTINI, R. and GALOPPINI, C. 1981. Pilot plant production of an edible alfalfa protein concentrate. Food Sci. *46*, 1514–1517, 1520.

FISHMAN, M.L. and BURDICK, D. 1977. Extractability, solubility and molecular size distribution of nitrogenous constituents in Coastal Bermuda grass. J. Agric. Food Chem. *25*, 1122–1127.

FREY, N.M. and MOSS, D.N. 1976. Variation in RuDPCase activity in barley. Crop Sci. *16*, 209–213.

GARCHA, J.S., KAWATRA, B.L. and WAGLE, D.S. 1971. Nutritional evaluation of leaf proteins and the effect of their supplementation to wheat flour by rat feeding. J. Food Sci. Technol. (India) *8*, 23–25.

GERLOFF, E.D., LIMA, I.H. and STAHMANN, M.A. 1965. Amino acid composition of leaf protein concentrates. J. Agric. Food Sci. *13*, 139–143.

GLENCROSS, R.G. FESTENSTEIN, G.N. and KING, H.G.C. 1972. Separation and determination of isoflavones in the protein concentrate from red clover leaves. J. Sci. Food Agric. *23*, 371–376.

GOEL, U., KAWATRA, B.L. and BAJBAJ, S. 1977. Nutritional evaluation of a cauliflower leaf protein concentrate by rat feeding. J. Sci. Food Agric. *28*, 786–790.

GONZALEZ, G., OCIO, E., TREVINO, J., TORUERO, F. and GONZALEZ, V. 1974. Preliminary trials with Aragon and Du Puits alfalfas (*Medicago sativa* L.) and hairy vetch (*Vicia villosa* Roth) as a sources of LPE. Växtodling-Plant Husb. *29*, 89–94.

GRUMME, R.H., HOLL, N. and JORGENSEN, N. 1977. Personal communication. Univ. Wisconsin, Madison.

GUTEK, L.H., GOPLEN, B.P. and HOWARTH, R.E. 1976. Heritability of soluble proteins in alfalfa. Crop Sci. *16*, 199–201.

HANCZAKOWSKI, P. 1970. Production and properties of protein concentrates from green plants. Przem. Ferment. Rolny *10*, 25–27. (Polish)

HANCZAKOWSKI, P. 1975. Composition and nutritive value of leaf protein concentrates. Rocz. Nauk Roln. Ser. B: Zootechn. *97*, 85–95. (Polish)

HANCZAKOWSKI, P. 1977. Composition and feeding value of leaf protein concentrates from four varieties of cabbage grown at various nitrogen fertilizer levels. Rocz. Nauk Roln. Ser. B: Zootechn. *4*, 227–235. (Polish)

HANCZAKOWSKI, P. and LUTYNSKA, R. 1976. Leaf protein extraction from *Heracleum sosnowski*, grown at various nitrogen fertilizer levels. Rocz. Nauk Roln. Ser. B: Zootechn. *3*, 143–150. (Polish)

HANCZAKOWSKI, P. and MAKUCH, M. 1980. The composition and nutritive value of protein concentrates from potato haulms. Potato Res. *23*, 1–8.

HEATH, S.B. and KING, M.W. 1977. The production of crops for green crop fractionation. *In* Green Crop Fractionation. R.J. Wilkins (Editor). Br. Grassl. Soc. Occas. Symp. *9* and Br. Soc. Anim. Prod., Grassland Res. Inst., Hurley, U.K.

HENRY, K.M. and FORD, J.E. 1965. The nutritive value of leaf protein concentrates determined in biological tests with rats and by microbiological methods. J. Sci. Food Agric. *16*, 425–432.

HOLDEN, M. 1974. Chlorophyll degradation products in leaf protein preparations. J. Sci. Food Agric. *25*, 1427–1432.

HOLLÓ, J. 1968. Production of a cellulose-free protein extract from plants useful as forages. C.R. Seances Acad. Agric. Fr. *54*, 659–664. (French)

HOLLÓ, J. 1973. Production of a cellulose-free protein extract from forage plants.—The yield of leaf protein from various forage plants. C.R. Seances Acad. Agric. Fr. *59*, 89–96. (French)

HOLLÓ, J., KOCH, L. and KOCH, B. 1969. Some aspects on the utilization of leaf protein to improve the production of nutritive substances. Voeding (The Hague) *30*, 489–498. (French)

HORIGOME, T. 1977. Nutritional studies of fractionated cytoplasmic and chloroplastic protein from leaves of oats and Ladino clover. Jpn. J. Zootech. Sci. *48*, 267–272.

HORIGOME, T. and KANDATSU, M. 1960. The nutritive value of grass proteins. X. Digestibilities of various proteins isolated from white clover leaf. Nippon Chikusan Gakkai-Ho *30*, 381–385. (Japanese)

HORIGOME, T. and KANDATSU, M. 1964. Studies on the nutritive value of grass proteins. XII. Digestibility of isolated grass proteins. Nippon Nogei Kagaku Kaishi *38*, 121–127. (Japanese)

HORIGOME, T. and KANDATSU, M. 1966A. Nutritive value of grass proteins. XIII. Phenolic substances of red clover leaves and effects of p-coumaric, caffeic and chlorogenic acids on the digestibility of the leaf proteins. Nippon Nogei Kagaku Kaishi *40*, 246–251. (Japanese)

HORIGOME, T. and KANDATSU, M. 1966B. Studies on the nutritive value of grass proteins. XIV. Lowering effects of phenolic compounds and o-diphenolase on the digestibility of protein in pasture plants. Nippon Nogei Kagaku Kaishi *40*, 449–455. (Japanese)

HORIGOME, T. and KANDATSU, M. 1968. Biological value of proteins allowed to react with phenolic compounds in the presence of o-diphenol oxidase. Agric. Biol. Chem. *32*, 1039–1102.

HOVE, E.L. 1976. High-protein food prepared from fresh leafy material by alcohol drying and mechanical defibering. N.Z. J. Agric. Res. *20*, 309–313.

HUANG, K.H., TAO, M.C., BOULET, M., RIEL, R.R., JULIEN, J.P. and BRISSON, G.J. 1971. A process for the preparation of leaf protein concentrates based on the treatment of leaf juices with polar solvents. J. Inst. Can. Technol. Aliment. *4*, 85–90.

HUGHES, H.D., HEATH, M.E. and METCALFE, D.S. 1951. Forages: The Science of Grassland Agriculture. Iowa State College Press, Ames.

HUGHES, R.E., ELLERY, P., HARRY, T., JENKINS, V. and JONES, E. 1980. The dietary potential of the common nettle. J. Sci. Food Agric. *31*, 1279–1286.

IGARASHI, K., SAKAMOTO, Y. and YASUI, T. 1976. Changes in the constituents of the leaves of red clover due to the length of drying time in the sun, and the digestibility of isolated protein preparations and impurities. Nippon Nogei Kagaku Kaishi *50*, 67–75. (Japanese)

ISHAYA, I., BIRK, Y., BONDI, A. and TENCER, Y. 1969. Soybean saponins. IX. Studies on their effect on birds, mammals and cold-blooded organisms. J. Sci. Food Agric. *20*, 433–436.

JELINOWSKA, A. 1979. Suitability of some lucerne cultivars to obtain leaf protein. Proc. Eucarpia Fodder Crops Sect. Meet. Sept. 4–9, 1978. *In* Biuletyn *135*/1979. Instytutu Hodowli i Aklimatyzacji Roslin, Suppl. 1, 214–220.

JENNINGS, A.C., PUSZTAI, A., SYNGE, R.L.M. and WATT, W.B. 1968. Fractionation of plant material. III. Two schemes for chemical fractionation of fresh leaves, having special applicability for isolating bulk protein. J. Sci. Food Agric. *19*, 203–213.

JONES, D.B., CHRISTIAN, K.R. and SNAYDON, R.W. 1971. Chemical composition and *in vitro* digestibility of some weed species during summer. Aust. J. Exp. Agric. Anim. Husb. *11*, 403–406.

JONES, W.T. and LYTTLETON, J.W. 1972. Bloat in cattle. XXXVI. Further studies on foaming properties of soluble leaf proteins. N.Z. J. Agric. Res. *15*, 267–278.

JONES, W.T. and MANGAN, J.L. 1977. Complexes of the condensed tannins of sanfoin (*Onobrychis viciifolia* Scop.) with fraction I leaf protein and with submaxillary mucoprotein, and their reversal by polyethylene glycol and pH. J. Sci. Food Agric. *28*, 126–136.

JULÉN, G. and MÅRTENSSON, P. 1974. Breeding for better quality in fodder plants. Sver. Utsaedesfoeren. Tidskr. *84*, 143–154. (Swedish)

JURZYSTA, M. 1979. Biochemical characteristic and feeding value of alfalfa selected for saponin content. Proc. Eucarpia Fodder Crops Sect. Meet., Sept. 4–9, 1978. *In* Biuletyn *135*/1979. Instytutu Hodowli i Aklimatyzacji Roslin, Suppl. 1., 316–327.

KAWABATA, M. and TAGUCHI, K. 1975. Leaf protein as human food. I: Separation of cytoplasm protein by aceton powder method. Kyoto Furitsu Daigaku Gakujutsu Hokoku: Rigaku, Seikatsu Kagaku *26*, 25–29. (Japanese)

KAWATRA, B.L., GARCHA, J.S. and WAGLE, D.S. 1974. Effects of supplementation of leaf protein extracted from berseem *(Trifolium alexandrinum)* to wheat flour diet. J. Food Sci. Technol. (India) *11*, 241–242.

KNUCKLES, B.E., DE FREMERY, D., BICKOFF, E.M. and KOHLER, G.O. 1975. Soluble protein from alfalfa juice by membrane filtration. J. Agric. Food Chem. *23*, 209–212.

KNUCKLES, B.E., DE FREMERY, D. and KOHLER, G.O. 1976. Coumesterol content of fractions obtained during wet processing of alfalfa. J. Agric. Food Chem. *24*, 1177–1180.

KOCH, B., KOTA, M. and HORWATH, I.M. 1965. Fodder crops as leaf protein sources. Agrobotanika *7*, 19–28. (Hungarian)

KOCH, B., KOTA, M. and HORWATH, I.M. 1967. Essential amino acid production of some fodder crops. Agrobotanika *9*, 115–130. (Hungarian)

KOCH, L. 1973. Producing protein concentrates from green plants. Växtodling-Plant Husb. *28*, 129–134.

KOEGEL, R.G. and BRUHN, H.D. 1977. Requirements for expression of plant juice. *In* Green Crop Fractionation. R.J. Wilkins (Editor). Br. Grassl. Soc. Occas. Symp. *9*, and Br. Soc. Anim. Prod., Grassland Research Inst., Hurley, U.K.

KOHLER, G.O. 1976. Personal communication. Western Regional Research Center, U.S. Dep. Agric., Berkeley, CA.

KOHLER, G.O. and EDWARDS, R.E. 1980. Researchers find multiple Pro-Xan potentials while plant works on process improvements. Feedstuffs *52*, 30–33.

KOHLER, G.O. and KNUCKLES, B.E. 1977. Edible protein from leaves. Food Technol. *31*, 191–195.

KUDASHEV, A.V. and SHESTAK, S.S. 1973. Amino acid composition of spring forage. Zhivotnovodstvo *9*, 44–45. (Russian)

LADINSKAYA, S.I., HUDASHEVA, G.S., GRATSIANOVA, O.V. and MEDNIKOV, F.A. 1974. Proteins in needles of pine and spruce, and the possibility to extract them. "Forest J." *4*, 99–103. (Russian)

LAETSCH, W.M. 1971. Chloroplast structural relationships in leaves of C4 plants. *In* Photosynthesis and Photorespiration. M.D. Hatch, C.B. Osmond and R.O. Slatyer (Editors). Wiley-Interscience, New York.

LEXANDER, K. 1969–1972. Personal communication. Dep. Plant Physiol., Univ. Lund, Lund, Sweden.

LEXANDER, K., CARLSSON, R., SCHALÉN, V., SIMONSSON, Å. and LUNDBORG. T. 1970. Quantity and quality of leaf protein concentrates from wild species and crop species grown under controlled conditions. Ann. Appl. Biol. *66*, 193–216.

LEXANDER, K. and LUNDBORG, T. 1973. Unpublished material. Dep. Plant Physiol., Univ. Lund, Lund, Sweden.

LIVINGSTON, A.L., KNOWLES, R.E., PAGE, J., KUZMICKY, D.D. and KOHLER, G.O. 1972. Processing of cauliflower waste for poultry and animal feed. J. Agric. Food Chem. *20*, 277–281.

LOHREY, E., TAPPER, B. and HOVE, E.L. 1974. Photosensitization of albino rats fed lucerne-protein concentrates. Br. J. Nutr. *31*, 159–166.

LU, P.S. and KINSELLA, J.E. 1972. Extractability and properties of protein from alfalfa leaf meal. J. Food Sci. *37*, 94–99.

LUNDBORG, T. 1979. Protein fractionation and solvent extraction as methods for production of leaf protein concentrates for human consumption. Ph.D. Thesis, Jan. 1979, Univ. Lund, Lund, Sweden. *LUNDBS/(NBFB-1003)/1–12/*.

LUNDBORG, T. and TRÄGÅRDH, C. 1972. Leaf protein concentrate for human consumption. Unpublished Rep. for Swedish Board for Technical Development (STU), *70-1426/U1072*. (39 pp plus tables and figures) (Swedish)

MAGUIRE, M.F. 1977. Green crop fractionation on the farm. *In* Green Crop Fractionation. R.J. Wilkins (Editor). Br. Grassl. Soc. Occas. Symp. *9*, and Br. Soc. Anim. Prod., Grassland Research Inst., Hurley, U.K.

MALIK, Z.R. and ULLA, H.H. 1969. Comparative value of sesamum cakes, soybean meal, sunflower oilcake and leaf protein concentrate in the ration of broiler chicks. West Pak. J. Agric. Res. *7*, 94–101.

MATRAI, T. and TRÄGÅRDH, C. 1977. Processing methods in leaf protein production and their influence on biological value and chemical composition of the product.—Hungarian-Swedish cooperation research 1972–1976. *In* Leaf Protein Concentrate for Human Consumption. Unpublished Rep. for Swedish Board for Technical Development (STU), *75-4439*. (Swedish)

MAURON, J. 1970. Nutritional evaluation of proteins by enzymic methods. *In* Evaluation of Novel Protein Products. A.E. Bender, R. Kihlberg, B. Löfqvist and L. Munck (Editors). Pergamon Press, Oxford and New York.

McARTHUR, J.M. and MILTIMORE, J.E. 1969. Bloat investigations. Studies on soluble proteins and nucleic acids in bloating and non-bloating forages. Can. J. Anim. Sci. *49*, 69–75.

McKENZIE, D.R. 1976. Leaf protein concentrate as a poultry protein supplement. Proc. 1st Australas. Poult. and Stock Feed Conv., Oct. 1976, Melbourne.

McKENZIE, D.R. 1977. Yields of protein extracted from a range of northern Victorian herbage. Aust. J. Exp. Agric. Anim. Husb. *17*, 268–276.

McKENZIE, D.R. 1978. Farm scale production of leaf protein concentrate and its utilization as a poultry supplement in intensive livestock production. Proc. 2nd Australas. Poult. and Stock Feed Conv., March 1978, Sydney.

MUNGIKAR, A.M., TEKALE, N.S. and JOSHI, R.N. 1976. The yields of leaf protein and fibre that can be obtained from fractionated berseem (*Trifolium alexandrinum* L.). Indian J. Nutr. Diet. *13*, 114–118.

MUNSHI, S.K., WAGLE, D.S. and THAPAR, V.K. 1974. The nutritive value of leaf protein and the xanthine oxidase activity in the rat liver. J. Res. Punjab Agric. Univ. *11*, 412–417.

MUNSHI, S.K. WAGLE, D.S. and THAPAR, V.K. 1975. The nutritive value of leaf proteins isolated from the leaves of different crop plants. J. Food Sci. Technol. (India) *12*, 23–26.

NANDA, C.L., KONDOS, A.S. and TERNOUTH, J.H. 1975. An improved technique for plant protein extraction. J. Sci. Food Agric. *26*, 1917–1924.

NAZIR, M. and SHAH, F.H. 1966. Extraction of proteins from various leaves. Pak. J. Sci. Ind. Res. *9*, 235–238.

NEDORIZESCU, M. 1972. Production of some fodder meals from different forest products. Rev. Zooteh. Med. Vet. *22*, 31–40. (Roumanian)

NÖRGAARD-PEDERSEN, E.J. 1977A. Beet top juice as a protein source. Unpubl. Rep. 3rd EEC Veg. Prot. Work. Group Meet., Feb. 8–10, 1977, Wageningen, Netherlands.

NÖRGAARD-PEDERSEN, E.J. 1977B. Personal communication. 3rd EEC Veg. Prot. Work. Group Meet., Feb. 8–10, 1977, Wageningen, Netherlands.

OHSHIMA, M. and OOCHI, K. 1976. The order of limitation of amino acids in ladino clover leaf protein concentrates for growing rats. Nutr. Rep. Int. *14*, 611–620.

OMOLE, T.A., OKE, O.L. and MFON, B.P. 1976. Carrot leaf protein: Preliminary trials with whole leaf using rabbits. Nutr. Rep. Int. *14*, 173–178.

OSTROWSKI, H.T. 1976. Pasture production in a protein extraction system. Proc. N.Z. Soc. Anim. Prod. *36*, 30–41.

OSTROWSKI, H.T. 1978. Protein recovery from agricultural ecosystem in Victoria. II. Fractionation of chloroplast-free proteins from herbage for human consumption. Proc. 3rd Aust. Conf. Sci. Technol., ANZAAS (Aust. N.Z. Assoc. Adv. Sci.), May 1978, Canberra.

OSTROWSKI-MEISSNER, H.T., CARLSSON, R. and TRÄGÅRDH, C. 1980. Isolation and purification of proteins from green vegetation for direct human consumption. *In* Food Process Engineering, Vol. 1. Food Processing Systems. P. Linko, Y. Mälkki, J. Olkku and J. Larinki (Editors). Applied Science Publishers, London.

PEDERSEN, M.W., BERRANG, B., WALL, M.E. and DAVIES, K.H., JR. 1973. Modification of saponin characteristics of alfalfa by selection. Crop Sci. *13*, 731–735.

PIENAZEK, D., RAKOWSKA, M. and KUNACHOWICZ, H. 1975. The participation of methionine and cysteine in the formation of bonds resistant to the action of proteolytic enzymes in heated casein. Br. J. Nutr. *34*, 163–173.

PIERPOINT, W.S. 1970. Formation and behaviour of o-quinones in some processes of agricultural importance. Rothamsted Exp. Stn. Rep. *1970* (Part 2) 199–218.

PIRIE, N.W. 1976. Food from waste: Leaf protein. *In* Food from Waste. G.G. Birch, K. Parker and J.T. Worgan (Editors). Applied Science Publishers, London.

PIRIE, N.W. 1977A. A simple unit for extracting leaf protein in bulk. Exp. Agric. (U.K.) *13*, 113.

PIRIE, N.W. 1977B. The role of leaf protein in animal feeding. World Anim. Rev. *22*, 11–14.

POMERANZ, Y. 1975. Proteins and amino acids in barley, oats, and buckwheat. *In* Protein Nutrition Quality of Foods and Feeds, Part 2. M. Friedman (Editor). Marcel Dekker, New York.

POPPE, J., TOBBACK, P.P. and MAES, E. 1970. Factors influencing protein extraction from lucerne *(Medicago sativa)*. Lebensm. Wiss. Technol. *3*, 67–70.

RAI, S.N. and SHUKLA, P.C. 1977. Utilization of sunflower (*Helianthus annuus* L.) as green fodder for bullocks. Gujarat Agric. Univ. Res. J. (India) *2*, 101–104.

RAMA RAO, P.B., NORTON, H.W. and JOHNSON, B.C. 1964. The amino acid composition and nutritive value of proteins. V. Amino acid requirements as patterns for protein evaluation. J. Nutr. *82*, 88–92.

RESHEF, G., GESTETNER, B., BIRK, Y. and BONDI, A. 1976. Effect of alfalfa saponins on the growth and some aspects of lipid metabolism of mice and quails. J. Sci. Food Agric. *27*, 63–72.

ROMMANN, L.M., GERLOFF., E.D. and MOORE, R.A. 1971. Soluble proteins of alfalfa, white clover and birdsfoot trefoil. Crop Sci. *11*, 792–795.

RUSKIN, F.R. 1975. Underexploited tropical plants with promising economic value. Nat. Acad. Sci. Contract *csd. 2584*, Washington, DC.

SAKANO, K., KUNG, S.D. and WILDMAN, S.G. 1974. Change in solubility of crystalline fraction I proteins correlated with change in composition of the small sub-unit. Plant Cell Physiol. *15*, 611–617.

SAUER, J.D. 1950. The grain amaranths: A survey of their history and classification. Ann. Mo. Bot. Gard. *37*, 561–632.

SAUER, J.D. 1967. The grain amaranths and their relatives: A revised taxonomy and geographical survey. Ann. Mo. Bot. Gard. *54*, 103–137.

SCHUSTER, W. and BOYE, R. 1971. The production capacity of physiologically and strongly differentiated sunflower varieties. Z. Acker Pflanzenbau *133*, 182–199. (German)

SHAH, F.H., UD-DIN, R. and SALAM, A. 1967. Effect of heat on the digestibility of leaf proteins. I. Toxicity of the lipids and their oxidation products. Pak. J. Sci. Ind. Res. *10*, 39–41.

SHEPPERSON, G., CONNELL, J., HOUSEMAN, R.A. and HEATH, S.B. 1977. The performance of the machinery at present available for the expression of juice from forage crops. *In* Green Crop Fractionation. R.J. Wilkins (Editor). Br. Grassl. Soc. Occas. Symp. *9* and Br. Soc. Anim. Prod., Grassland Research Inst., Hurley, U.K.

SHMANENKOV, N.A., SADOKOVA, A.P., POTAPENKO, V.A., KOSHAROVA, L.M. and USPENSKAJA, E.V. 1970. Potato tops as a source of isolated feed protein for farm animals. Tr. Vses. Nauchno-Issled. Inst. Fiziol. Biokhim. Skh. Zhivotn. *9*, 227–237. (Russian)

SILVA, E. and PEREIRA, C. 1976. Isolation and composition of leaf proteins from *Atriplex nummularia* and *Atriplex repanda*. Cienc. Invest. Agrar. (Chile) *3*, 169–174. (Spanish)

SIMMONDS, N.W. 1965. The grain chenopods of the tropical American highlands. Econ. Bot. *19*, 223–235.

SINGH, H. 1961. Grain amaranths, buckwheat and chenopods. Indian Counc. Agric. Res. Cereal Crop Ser. *1* (New Delhi).

SIRÉN, G. 1973. Protein from forest trees. Sven. Naturvetensk. *26*, 41–46. (Swedish)

SIRÉN, G., BLOMBÄCK, B. and ALDEŃ, T. 1970. Protein in forest tree leaves. R. Coll. For., Stockholm, Res. Notes *28*.

SMITH, A.M. and AGIZA, A.H. 1951. The amino acids in several grassland species, cereals and bracken. J. Sci. Food Agric. *2*, 503–520.

SMITH, E.B. and PENA, P.M. 1977. Use of *Tetrahymena pyriformis* W. to evaluate protein quality of leaf protein concentrates. J. Food Sci. *42*, 674–676.

STAHMANN, M.A. 1970. Alfalfa protein concentrate for human and animal consumption. Agric. Eng. *51*, 412–413.

STARON, T. 1975. A method to obtain proteins by fractionation of green plants. C.R. Seances Acad. Agric. Fr. *61*, 446–458.

STOVALL, R.A. 1970. Protein concentrate from Kochia. M.Sc. Thesis, May 1970. Texas Tech. Univ., Lubbock, TX.

STRÖBÄCK, S. and GIBBONS, G.C. 1976. Ribulose-1,5-diphosphate carboxylase from barley *(Hordeum vulgare)*. Isolation, characterization, and peptide mapping studies of the sub-units. Carlsbergs Res. Commun. *41*, 57–72.

SUBBA RAU, B.H., RAMANA, K.V.R. and SINGH, N. 1972. Studies on the nutritive value of leaf proteins and some factors affecting their quality. J. Sci. Food Agric. *23*, 233–245.

TAO, M., BOULET, M., BRISSON, G.J., HUANG, K.H., RIEL, R.R. and JULIEN, J.P. 1972. A study of the chemical composition and nutritive value of leaf protein concentrates. Can. Inst. Food Sci. Technol. J. *5*, 50–54.

TAPPER, B.A., LOHREY, E., HOVE, E.L. and ALLISON, R.M. 1975. Photosensitivity from chlorophyll-derived pigments. J. Sci. Food Agric. *26*, 277–284.

TEKALE, N.S. and JOSHI, R.M. 1976. Extractable protein from the by-product vegetation of some cole and root crops. Ann. Appl. Biol. *82*, 155–157.

THOMKE, S. 1976. Results from some experiments with new protein sources to monogastric animals. French-Swedish Symp. Monogastric Anim. Feed., Mar. 22–28, 1976, Uppsala, Sweden.

TRÄGÅRDH, C. 1978. Leaf protein for human consumption.—Investigations of some unit operations included in a solvent extraction process. Ph.D. Thesis. Univ. Lund (Lund Inst. Technol.), Alnarp, Sweden.

VARGA, J. and NOSTICZIUS, A. 1968. Experiments to produce plant protein concentrates. Mosonmagyarovari Agrartud. Foiskola Kozl. *11*, 61–71. (Hungarian)

VARTHA, E.W. and ALLISON, R.M. 1973. Extractable protein from "Grassland Tama" Westerwolds rye-grass. N.Z. J. Exp. Agric. *1*, 239–242.

VARTHA, E.W. and BRUSSE, M.J. 1977. Yields of nitrogen and extractable leaf protein from an irrigated rye-grass-white clover pasture. N.Z. J. Exp. Agric. *5*, 151–155.

VARTHA, E.W., FLETCHER, L.R. and ALLISON, R.M. 1973. Protein-extracted herbage for sheep feeding. N.Z. J. Exp. Agric. *1*, 171–174.

VIEIRA, E.C. 1978. Leaf protein from cassava and pereskia. Proc. Int. Workshop Utilization Agric. Waste for Feed and Food, CETEC, Belo Horizonte, Minas Gerais, Brazil, Dec. 1977.

VINCONNEAU, H.F. 1979. Processing of leaf proteins into food ingredients. J. Am. Oil Chem. Soc. *56*, 469–470.

von BAER, E. 1972. Personal communication. Gorbea, Chile.

von KRAMPITZ, G., HAAS, W. and HARDEBECK, H. 1970. Lysine-rich proteins in leaves and seeds of garden Atriplex (*Atriplex hortensis* L.). Z. Tierphysiol. Tierernaehr. Futtermittelk. *27*, 1–9. (German)

WIERINGA, I.R. 1977. Influence of nitrogen fertilization and cutting frequency on perennial rye-grass yield and crude protein extractability. Unpublished Rep. 3rd EEC Veg. Prot. Work. Group Meet., Feb. 8–10, 1977, Wageningen, Netherlands.

WILDMAN, S.G. 1973. Tobacco plants as a potential source for large scale production of pure protein for human consumption. Unpublished Rep. Dep. Biol., Molecular Biology Inst., Univ. California at Los Angeles (UCLA).

WILKINS, R.J. 1977. Green Crop Fractionation. Br. Grassl. Soc. Occas. Symp. *9* and Br. Soc. Anim. Prod., Grassland Research Inst., Hurley, U.K.

WILSON, R.F. and TILLEY, J.M.A. 1965. Amino acid composition of lucerne and of lucerne and grass protein preparations. J. Sci. Food Agric. *16*, 173–178.

WOODHAM, A.A. 1965. The nutritive value of leaf protein concentrates. Proc. Nutr. Soc. *24*, xxiv.

WOODHAM, A.A., ARKCOLL, D.B., KARMALI, R.A. and CLARKE, E.M.W. 1974. The effect of processing conditions on the nutritive value of protein concentrates prepared from green leaves. Proc. 4th Int. Congr. Food Sci. Technol., Madrid, Sept. 1974.

YASUI, T. and IWAMATSU, K. 1972. Studies on the nutritive value of grass proteins. XIX. A new method for the preparation of proteins from several leaves and amino acid composition of these proteins. Nippon Nogei Kagaku Kaishi *46*, 597–602. (Japanese)

3

Tropical Plants for Leaf Protein Concentrates

Lehel Telek and Franklin W. Martin

At the present growth rate, world population will double in the next 30 to 40 years. This population increase will not be equally distributed; it will mostly burden the developing countries spread along the humid lowland tropics. The developed nations with declining birth rates are approaching zero-population growth and show a steady increase in food production. However, in the developing countries, with current yearly population growth of 2.3%, the increase in yearly food production has declined from 0.7 to 0.3%. This ever-widening food shortage cannot be alleviated by conventional agriculture alone. New sources of food and feed must be found. As a source, leaves offer the highest yield of protein of all crops. With suitable plant material the yield of leaf protein in ha/year is at least four times that of the soybean.

Leaf protein concentrates for animal production are manufactured mainly from alfalfa in Hungary, France, and Denmark; new plants are under construction in the United States and Great Britain. In spite of efforts to adapt alfalfa to the tropics, it has been only marginally successful in a few areas, and an extensive search for tropical plant sources of LPC is being conducted. The tropics is the geographical zone between latitudes 23°27′ north and south of the equator. There are only a few generalizations concerning tropical climates: there is no wide seasonal variation, and daylight length changes but slightly. The changes in annual rainfall cycles are marked. Some areas of the tropics have definite rainy and dry seasons; a few get no rain at all or are always humid and rainy.

It has been estimated that the tropics contain 3 million plant species, as compared to 1.5 million species in the temperate zones. Travel through the tropics impresses one with the variety of plants, the density of the forests, and the appearance of richness. Working with any particular group of plants, one becomes aware of an amazing number of legumes, of forage grasses, or of green-leaved vegetables. Where typical tropical rainy seasons occur, the overwhelming appearance of green foliage suggests that plentiful food is available.

Working within a specific area, however, one quickly finds that most of the protein of the tropics is not available for human consumption. The bulk of the protein on any piece of land is in leaves and stems, which cannot be utilized by humans. In spite of the wide use of leaves, tubers, flowers, pods, and seeds as vegetables in the tropics, the lush tropics are often not a copious source of food.

The search for appropriate tropical sources of leaf protein concentrate is a search involving hundreds of plant species. Fortunately, many tropical species are already known for other uses, and the literature is rich in data on protein content. Thus, there is a considerable body of literature to begin with and several studies of leaf protein extraction from tropical plants to provide guidelines.

In Ghana, Byers (1961) tested the protein content of 60 tropical plant species by mincing in a home grinder and extracting the protein by adding water and filtering. The protein was precipitated by trichloroacetic acid and estimated from total nitrogen determinations. Very good results were obtained, especially with legumes.

A wide variety of plants were tested as a source of LPC in Jamaica by Mendes (1965). These included many species of the tropics that are present everywhere—grains and grasses, cover crops and fodders, miscellaneous plants, and plants whose leaves are normally discarded. A small extraction plant was used for this purpose. Percentage protein extracted varied from 3 to 67%. In only 4 of 58 species were 10 g or more protein recovered from 100 g leaves (dry weight basis). Protein was coagulated and precipitated by steam at 80–85°C. The protein precipitate was stored until used, and then incorporated into typical foods of Jamaica using many different recipes. Finally, the economic aspects of LPC were studied.

Protein extractability of tropical as well as temperate zone crops was studied in India by Singh (1964), Devi *et al.* (1965), and Joshi (1971).

Protein content of randomly collected wild or cultivated tropical plants was studied by Martin *et al.* (1977) in Puerto Rico.

The potential usefulness of tropical and subtropical leaves as a source of leaf protein concentrate has been reviewed by Nagy *et al.* (1978), listing 60 tropical plants with crude protein content higher than 20%. The table of plants was compiled from previous reports, based mostly on data of randomly collected plants.

In 1978, a broad research program on tropical leaf protein was organized at the Tropical Agriculture Research Station (TARS), U.S. Dept. of Agric., S.E.A., A.R.S., in Mayaguez, Puerto Rico, for systematic evaluation of tropical plants suitable for leaf protein fractionation. We considered the ideal plant for LPC to be one that was high in protein, dry matter, protein extractability, and regrowth potential; also, one that would be able to fix nitrogen, be machine harvestable, nontoxic, and low in antinutritional factors.

Table 3.1 lists the evaluated species. The seeds were received from the Southern Region Plant Introduction Station of U.S. Dept. of Agric., Experiment, Georgia. Toward the close of the rainy season, 10 to 15 plants of each species were planted in jiffy pots in the greenhouse. The seedlings were planted out in the field in rows for general observations of growth and insect and disease problems. In the prebloom stage, leaves were collected for dry matter and protein determinations, and the extraction and heat fractionation behavior were observed. Ripe seeds were collected from plants for future plantings. The following year, a worldwide seed collection of promising species was received and planted in the field to select the best varieties for humid lowland tropics. Table 3.3 shows the plants selected for leaf protein concentrate production and their essential amino acid contents.

PREPARATION OF LEAF PROTEIN CONCENTRATES (LABORATORY METHOD)

Leaves and stems of freshly harvested plants are washed with tap water to remove adherent soil and chopped with a sharp knife to 2–3 cm pieces (Fig. 3.1). Two hundred grams of chopped plant are extracted in a blender with 600 ml ice water. This mixture is blended at high speed for 5–10 min (Fig. 3.2). The slurry is transferred into a filter bag made of closely woven fabric and is pressed (Fig. 3.3). The fibrous residue is partially dehydrated by pressing the filter bag between two wooden panels in a hydraulic press and is then dried to a constant weight in a microwave oven. The fibers are ground in a Wiley mill with a 20-mesh screen to obtain a homogeneous sample for protein analysis by the Kjeldahl method. The green juice is heated carefully in a 2-liter Erlenmeyer flask immersed in boiling water and agitated with a slow motion stirrer (Fig. 3.4). At 55°C, a green coagulum forms and is separated by centrifugation in large centrifuge bottles (Fig. 3.5). The liquid phase is collected in a 1-liter Erlenmeyer flask. The

TABLE 3.1. CRUDE PROTEIN CONTENT OF TROPICAL PLANTS

Plant	Origin	Percentage		Type[1]
		Dry Matter	Crude Protein	
Amaranthaceae				
Amaranthus anclancalius	Hungary	12.3	26.6	IV
A. caudatus	Sweden	13.0	27.7	IV
A. cruentus	Taiwan	14.6	28.3	IV
A. gangeticus	Hungary	14.5	24.4	IV
A. hypochondriacus	Sweden	11.5	27.9	IV
A. mantegazzianus	Sweden	16.2	30.0	IV
Compositae				
Helianthus uniflorus	Hungary	26.6	29.9	II
H. annuus	Sweden	24.6	25.4	II
Cruciferae				
Brassica alba	Hungary	22.5	39.8	III
B. campestris	Pakistan	14.2	19.1	III
	Guatemala	10.8	21.0	III
B. hirta	Yugoslavia	10.4	30.0	III
	Poland	12.6	30.8	III

(continued)

TABLE 3.1. *(Continued)*

Plant	Origin	Percentage		Type[1]
		Dry Matter	Crude Protein	
B. napus	Hungary	11.8	21.1	III
	France	11.6	26.4	III
	China	14.4	24.4	III
B. juncea	India	13.8	27.1	III
	Cuba	12.2	22.3	III
	Nepal	14.2	24.8	III
B. nigra	India	10.2	26.4	III
	Turkey	10.8	24.0	III
	Greece	14.1	20.6	III
B. oleracea	United States	14.0	19.4	III
B. oleracea var. *gongyloides*	United States	12.6	19.4	III
Lepidium sativum	Puerto Rico	12.3	17.6	III
Nasturtium officinale	Puerto Rico	18.2	22.6	IV
Cucurbitaceae				
Benincasa hispida	India	18.0	18.0	II
Lagenaria siceraria	South Africa	11.4	26.3	II
Luffa cylindrica	India	19.3	26.3	II
Euphorbiaceae				
Cnidoscolus chayamansa	Mexico	18.8	26.3	II
Manihot esculenta	Colombia	20.8	25.5	I
Leguminosae				
Aeschynomene falcata	Brazil	20.2	13.5	III
A. scabra	Mexico	20.8	15.5	III
A. indica	India	20.8	16.9	III
Alysicarpus vaginalis	India	20.1	20.0	III
	Ceylon	18.6	20.3	III
Cajanus cajan	India	24.0	22.5	III
	Mexico	28.0	20.6	III
Calopogonium muconoides	Indonesia	20.0	19.7	III
Canavalia ensiformis	India	21.5	18.4	III
	Brazil	19.8	22.1	III
C. gladiata	Philippines	20.9	21.9	III
Centrosema pubescens	India	23.5	18.9	III
	Philippines	25.0	23.2	III
	Ivory Coast	20.0	19.4	III
Clitoria ternatea	Brazil	16.1	23.6	III
	Cuba	20.6	23.0	III
	Australia	19.2	24.3	III
Crotalaria alata	India	18.6	19.9	II
C. argyrolobioloides	Kenya	20.4	23.9	II
C. brachystachya	Brazil	19.2	27.4	II
C. incana	Argentina	19.3	22.9	II
C. juncea	India	21.4	25.8	II
	USSR	24.0	26.3	II
Cyamopsis tetragonoloba	India	14.2	19.2	III
Desmodium canum	Brazil	20.8	18.9	I
D. distortum	Hawaii	16.8	17.8	III
D. intortum	Spain	25.0	18.7	III
	Brazil	25.0	23.5	III
D. perplexum	Brazil	20.0	16.2	II
D. sandwicense	Australia	21.7	23.0	I
Glycine wightii	South Africa	19.2	19.6	III
Indigofera arrecta	Ghana	31.2	15.1	II
I. brevipes	Costa Rica	18.3	26.8	II
I. cireinella	Korea	17.6	26.2	I
	South Africa	16.4	28.1	I
I. colutea	Australia	20.2	28.7	III
I. confusa	Indonesia	19.8	14.6	II
I. cryptantha	South Africa	19.8	24.0	III
I. echinata	Tanzania	21.0	21.4	II

TABLE 3.1. *(Continued)*

Plant	Origin	Percentage Dry Matter	Percentage Crude Protein	Type[1]
I. hirsuta	Nigeria	22.1	24.2	II
	Brazil	21.0	27.9	II
	Rhodesia	23.4	30.6	II
I. hochstetteri	Rhodesia	18.3	21.2	II
I. microcarpa	Argentina	34.9	22.3	II
I. mucronata	Peru	20.8	22.4	II
	Brazil	23.7	24.4	II
I. retroflexa	Kenya	21.8	21.2	II
I. schimperi	Africa	14.6	23.3	II
I. semitijuga	India	31.8	17.2	II
I. spicata	Tanzania	16.5	35.7	II
I. subulata	Kenya	27.2	12.3	II
	Cuba	26.4	10.8	II
I. suffruticosa	Brazil	21.4	25.3	II
	Mexico	20.7	32.4	II
I. sumatrana	Australia	21.8	28.2	II
I. tetlensis	Africa	20.2	20.5	III
I. teysmannii	Malaya	21.6	31.0	II
I. tinctoria	Dominican Republic	20.6	15.2	II
Lablab purpureus	Malaysia	21.5	27.7	III
Lupinus albus	Turkey	18.8	19.5	III
L. angustifolius	Hungary	20.4	18.8	III
	South Africa	22.6	16.6	III
L. luteus	Hungary	22.2	16.1	III
	Spain	20.4	19.2	III
L. hispanicus	Portugal	20.6	19.8	III
	Spain	20.2	19.2	III
Macroptilium lathyroides	Australia	18.8	19.5	III
Macrotyloma uniflorum	Puerto Rico	18.6	26.4	III
	South Africa	21.0	21.3	III
Mucuna deeringiana	Mozambique	17.2	32.6	II
Phaseolus acontifolius	India	18.8	18.3	III
	Afghanistan	22.2	15.8	III
P. calcaratus	Ivory Coast	19.7	20.8	III
	Honduras	20.1	23.7	III
Psophocarpus tetragonolobus	Puerto Rico	20.6	22.0	III
Sesbania arabica	Turkey	21.8	29.9	III
	Afghanistan	22.2	30.0	III
S. cannabina	India	19.8	21.4	III
S. exasperata	Brazil	20.4	20.9	III
	Argentina	20.6	20.6	III
S. macrocarpa	Australia	22.0	19.2	III
	Mexico	19.8	19.9	III
S. sesban	India	20.6	27.6	III
	China	19.4	29.4	III
Stizolobium aterrimum	Mexico	20.6	27.4	III
Stylosanthes gracilis	Paraguay	21.2	22.3	IV
S. humilis	Australia	22.0	20.9	IV
	Brazil	21.8	18.9	IV
Tephrosia adunea	Venezuela	22.2	18.0	II
T. cinerea	Uruguay	24.2	14.0	II
T. incana	Kenya	23.8	19.3	II
	Indonesia	24.4	21.4	II
T. noctiflora	Brazil	23.6	13.2	II
T. vogelii	Puerto Rico	20.4	12.3	II
Vigna mungo	Pakistan	19.3	23.6	III
	China	21.0	24.0	III
	Iran	19.3	16.9	III

(continued)

TABLE 3.1. *(Continued)*

Plant	Origin	Percentage		Type[1]
		Dry Matter	Crude Protein	
V. radiata	Turkey	18.9	22.9	III
	India	21.1	22.2	III
V. unguiculata	Guatemala	18.8	19.5	III
	Mexico	19.0	19.4	III
Zornia brasiliensis	Brazil	20.2	15.8	III
Z. diphylla	Brazil	19.8	16.8	III
Z. latifolia	Brazil	20.0	15.8	III
Malvaceae				
Abelmoschus manihot	Japan	14.6	14.0	III
Solanaceae				
Capsicum annuum	Yugoslavia	20.0	22.4	III
	Ecuador	12.5	19.9	III
	Israel	20.0	21.8	III
C. chinense	Georgia-USA	15.3	20.0	III
	Guatemala	15.3	23.4	III
	Colombia	16.7	19.9	III
C. pendulum	Mexico	18.0	19.8	III
	Chile	22.2	21.0	III
	California-USA	16.0	20.2	III
Solanum melongena	India	21.0	21.2	III
	China	21.4	21.4	III

[1] Yield of different fractions after extraction: I—Only one green fraction coagulated at room temperature. II—One green fraction on heating to 55°C and one minute amount of light tan fraction at 82°C. III—One green fraction at 55°C, one white fraction at 64°C, and another light tan fraction at 82°C. IV—No distinct separable coagulum by heat fractionation.

green coagulum is washed twice with a small amount of distilled water, then resuspended with vigorous shaking. After repeated washing and centrifugation, the green coagulum is spread in thin layers on glass plates and dried overnight in a cold room or in a microwave oven for 5 min at a low energy setting (Fig. 3.6 and 3.7A).

When the supernatant from centrifugation is heated carefully to 64°C, a white curd coagulates and is separated by centrifugation (Fig. 3.4 and 3.5). The greenish-white precipitate is washed with 0.01 *N* hydrochloric acid, then distilled water and acetone, and dried in a rotary evaporator to a free-flowing off-white powder (Fig. 3.7B). The liquid phase after centrifugation is collected in a 1 liter Erlenmeyer flask and heated again, this time to 82°C. When it is cooled in a refrigerator, a light tan precipitate separates and is collected in centrifuge bottles. It is washed with 0.01 *N* hydrochloric acid and acetone, then dried in a rotary evaporator heated in a boiling water bath (Fig. 3.7C). The samples are analyzed for dry matter, and crude protein is determined by the Kjeldahl method. If determination of extractability is needed, the pressed fibrous residue is blended a second time with 300 ml distilled water and is then pressed again and dried (Fig. 3.7D). Nitrogen is determined in the extracted pressed residue.

EXTRACTION CHARACTERISTICS OF TROPICAL PLANTS

During our survey of hundreds of tropical plants, it was observed that the pressed juice of certain plants coagulated spontaneously. This reaction occurred during extraction, or in the screw press, or after standing at room temperature for a few minutes or hours. This phenomenon was observed first during extraction of cassava leaf varieties. Later, similar behavior was noticed with *Leucaena leucocephala* and some wild growing *Desmodium* and *Mimosa* species. It was also true for many of the tree legumes of Mimosa, Cassia, and pea subfamilies. In extracts of this type of plant, no additional protein separated on heating to 55° or 64°C or only a trace amount of protein fraction separated after heating to 82°C. In Table 3.1 these plants are classified as Type I.

Another group of plants yielded a green protein coagulum only after the extracted green plant juice was heated to 55°C. After separation of the green protein, the brown juice was reheated slowly. Only a very small quantity of light tan precipitate occurred at 82°C. A white proteinaceous precipitate could be formed by adding two volumes of acetone or ethyl alcohol. The solvent-precipitated fraction contained very large amounts of inorganic salts. This kind of behavior was initially observed with the leaf protein extract of *Cnidoscolus chayamansa*, sorghum-Sudan grass hybrids, with several grasses, and some indigoferas. Plants of this group are classified as Type II.

A third and most important group of plants is listed as Type III. Careful heat fractionation of protein extracts of these plants yields three distinct protein fractions: a green coagulum at 55°C, a copious white protein precipitate at 64°C, and a lesser amount of light tan precipitate at 82°C.

A final group, Type IV plants, includes those whose proteins do not precipitate either spontaneously or by heat treatment. This negative reaction may be caused by extracts of pectinaceous material acting as a protective colloid as in the case of *Stylosanthes gracilis* and *S. humilis*, *Nasturtium officinale*, and *Amaranthus* species. Conclusive proof was found that high concentrations of tannin and polyphenols are responsible for the spontaneous precipitation of the extracted plant proteins at room temperature. Lower tannin and polyphenol content will limit the heat fractionation to green protein coagulation only. Plants yielding three protein fractions by differential heat treatment were found to have very low condensed tannin and polyphenol content. This correlation could be utilized in rapid screening of plants for potential leaf protein sources. If using the preceding preparation method and three distinct protein fractions are separated, the plant is a preferable source, since its protein fractions are affected only slightly by phenol-protein interactions.

NUTRITIONAL EVALUATION OF LEAF PROTEIN CONCENTRATES PREPARED FROM SELECTED TROPICAL PLANTS

Leaf protein concentrates from tropical legumes (*Leucaena leucocephala*, *Vigna unguiculata*, *Clitoria ternatea*, *Desmodium distortum*, *Psophocarpus tetragonolobus*, *Macroptilium lathyroides*, *Phaseolus calcaratus)* and *Brassica napus*, and *Manihot esculenta* were prepared and evaluated nutritionally with rats (Cheeke *et al.* 1980).

The plants used as sources of LPC were selected and grown in plots at the

Fig. 3.1. Cutting the plants.

Fig. 3.2. Mincing the plants.

Tropical Agriculture Research Station in the years 1977–1978 (Telek 1979). The individual plot areas were 13.5 m^2, except for *M. esculenta* for which 45 m^2 plots were used. Nonlegumes were fertilized with 105 kg N, 105 kg K, and 90 kg P/ha. The plots were irrigated as needed. The plants were harvested in the vegetative stage of growth, with sequential cuttings taken every four weeks. The harvested material was pooled in polyethylene bags and stored in a freezer until processed in the pilot plant of the Food Technology Department, University of Puerto Rico, Rio Piedras. Processing consisted of chopping the leaves into 2 cm pieces, followed by soaking them in 2% Na_2SO_3 at pH 9. The soaked material was disintegrated in a hammer mill and pressed in a single-screw press. The expressed juice was heated at 82°C with steam until protein coagulum appeared. The hot coagulum was collected in a basket centrifuge, and then pressed in a canvas bag in a hydraulic press. Finally, the green protein was spread in a thin layer on glass plates, and dried in an air-conditioned, dehumidified room.

The *Leucaena leucocephala* and cassava were handled differently. Following extraction, the juice was left for 20 hr for self-precipitation of proteins at ambient temperatures (29°–31°C). The settled precipitates were drained and pressed as before. One sample of *L. leucocephala* was acid-washed twice with 0.05 *N* hydrochloric acid, while another was washed with acetone (1 part precipitate to 4 parts acetone). The acid-washed LPC was rinsed with distilled water, while the acetone-extracted LPC was washed with ethanol. One sample of *Desmodium distortum* LPC was washed with acetone and with 5% dimethylformamide to break phenol-protein complexes. This was followed by three ethanol rinses. One sample of the cassava LPC was dried in a household microwave oven at the lowest setting.

Fig. 3.3. Filtering through dacron cloth.

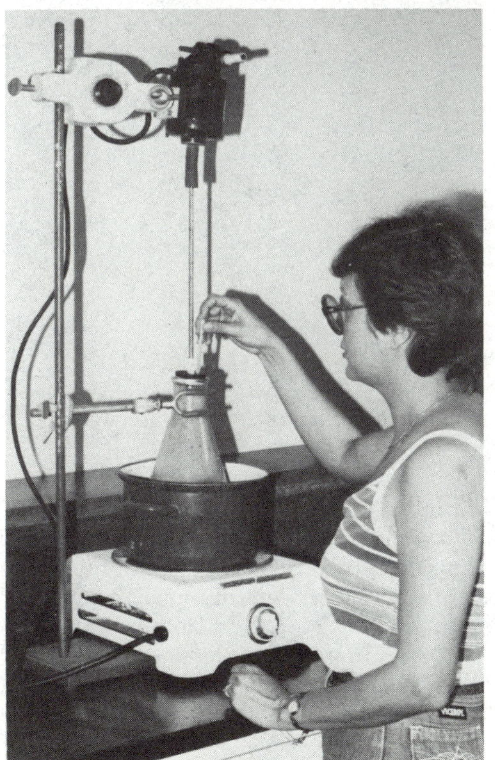

Fig. 3.4. Heat fractionation.

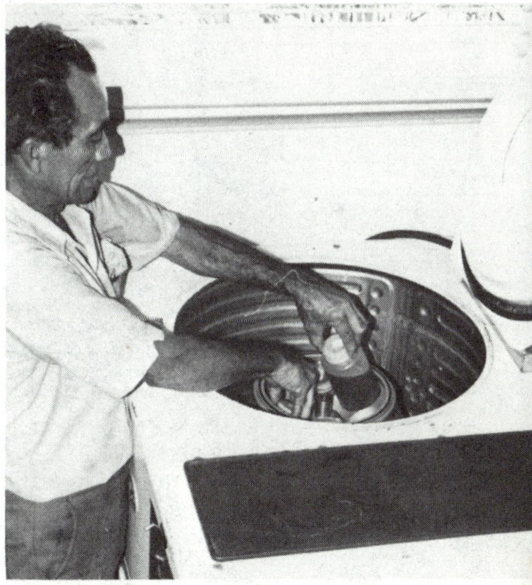

Fig. 3.5. Separation of protein by centrifugation.

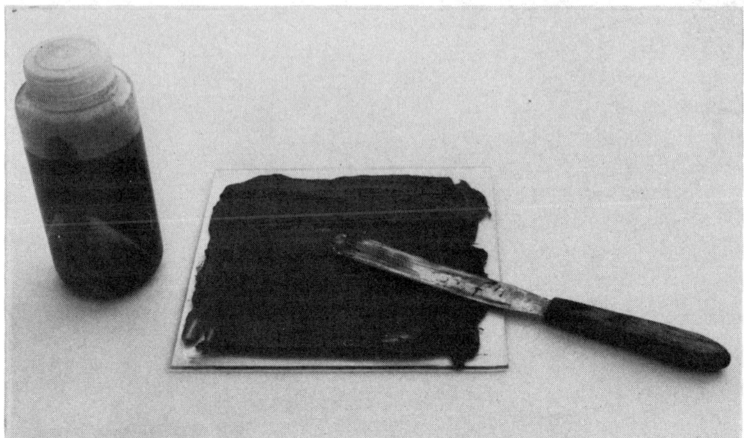

Fig. 3.6. Drying the protein fraction on glass plate.

Fig. 3.7. Protein fractions. From left to right: A—Green protein coagulated at 55°C. B—White protein coagulated at 64°C. C—White protein coagulated at 82°C. D—Fibrous residue.

The protein quality of the LPC samples was estimated by using the LPC as a supplement to corn grain. This procedure was used because it is representative of the way protein supplements are used in animal feeding. The rat diets were formulated to contain 16% crude protein, with corn and soybean meal providing 10% protein and LPC 6%. Additional dietary ingredients were 4% mineral mix, 1% vitamin mix (Cheeke *et al.* 1977), and 4% corn oil. The amounts of LPC, ground yellow corn, and soybean meal were variable and are listed in Table 3.2.

TABLE 3.2. PROTEIN CONTENT OF TROPICAL PLANT LPC, DIET COMPOSITION, AND RAT GROWTH PERFORMANCE

			Diet Composition			Rat Performance			
Source of LPC	Common Name	Crude Protein[5] (%) of LPC	% LPC	% Corn	% Soy-bean Meal	Avg Daily Gain (g)	Avg Daily Gain as % of Control	Avg Daily Feed Intake (g)	Protien Effi-ciency Ratio
Corn-soy control	—	—	—	69	22	7.2±	100	16.4±	2.7
Leucaena leucocephala	ipil-ipil	31.3	31.9	57	2.1	0.9±	12.5	11.0±	0.4
L. leucocephala—acetone-washed		38.2	26.1	64.5	0.4	0.7±	9.7	11.6±	0.4
L. leucocephala—acid-washed		28.2	35.5	52.7	2.8	1.0±	13.9	9.7±	0.5
Manihot esculenta[1]	cassava	36.2	27.6	62.6	0.8	1.8±	25.0	11.7±	0.9
M. esculenta[2]		32.1	31.2	58.1	1.7	2.0±	27.8	11.1±	0.8
M. esculenta[3]		33.3	30.0	59.6	1.4	1.2±	16.7	11.7±	0.6
M. esculenta[4]		41.4	24.2	66.8	—	2.0±	27.8	14.8±	0.8
Vigna unguiculata	cowpea	51.9	19.3	71.7	—	5.8±	80.6	18.2±	2.0
Clitoria ternatea	butterfly pea	59.3	16.9	74.1	—	6.7±	93.1	17.7±	2.4
Desmodium distortum	Spanish clover	36.5	27.4	62.8	0.8	5.4±	75.0	13.0±	2.0
D. distortum[4]		47.0	21.3	69.7	—	6.6±	91.7	16.6±	2.3
Psophocarpus tetragonolobus	winged bean	51.9	19.3	71.7	—	6.0±	83.3	17.2±	2.2
Macroptilium lathyroides		44.6	22.4	68.6	—	3.0±	41.7	14.9±	1.3
Phaseolus calcaratus	rice bean	38.0	26.3	64.2	0.5	6.0±	83.3	13.5±	2.1
Brassica napus **cv Early Giant**	forage rape	40.4	24.8	66.1	0.1	6.1±	84.7	17.4±	2.1

[1] 1st extraction; dried in microwave.
[2] 1st extraction; dried with air conditioner.
[3] 2nd extraction; dried in microwave.
[4] Acetone-washed.
[5] N × 6.00.

Five male Long-Evans rats of about 75 g initial weight were assigned to each dietary treatment, and fed *ad libitum* for 21 days. Growth rate was measured and expressed as a percentage of the gains of the control animals. A modified PER value was calculated, being g of gain per g of protein consumed. The modifications from standard PER determination were that the diets contained 16% crude protein, and the test proteins were not the sole source of dietary protein.

The following tropical legumes, *Vigna unguiculata* (Fig. 3.8), *Desmodium distortum*, *Phaseolus calcaratus*, and *Psophocarpus tetragonolobus*, gave excellent results, comparable to what would be obtained with alfalfa LPC. These plants have low contents of polyphenols. Another legume low in phenolics, *Macroptilium lathyroides* (Fig. 3.9), gave relatively poor results (Table 3.2). This is unfortunate, as it is an erect, free-standing plant well-suited for machine harvest. It tolerates repeated cutting. Identification of the factor(s) responsible for the poor results with this plant should be pursued.

The amino acid profile (Table 3.3) is similar for the various LPC samples, and similar to reported values for alfalfa LPC and for soybean meal. The differences in rat growth performance are due likely to different amino acid availabilities, as influenced by phenolics and other compounds that may react with protein or other antinutrients. Extraction of *Desmodium* LPC with acetone-dimethyl-formamide did improve rat growth (Table 3.2), sug-

Fig. 3.8. *Vigna unguiculata.*

Fig. 3.9. *Macroptilium lathyroides* (L.) Urb.

gesting that phenolics had an adverse effect on growth in the nonwashed material.

In summary, this study has shown that several tropical legumes can be used to produce LPC which will give acceptable animal performance. *Clitoria*

TABLE 3.3. ESSENTIAL AMINO ACID COMPOSITION OF LPC FROM SELECTED TROPICAL SPECIES

	Amino Acids[5]									
Source of LPC	Arg	His	Ile	Leu	Lys	Met	Phe	Thr	Val	1/2Cys
L. leucocephala	6.4	2.2	5.0	9.1	6.3	2.4	5.9	4.8	6.0	0.7
M. esculenta[1]	6.3	2.4	5.4	9.3	6.5	2.5	7.0	4.9	6.0	0.8
M. esculenta[2]	6.0	2.4	5.2	9.1	6.4	2.4	6.8	5.2	5.7	0.8
V. unguiculata	6.7	2.4	5.4	9.4	5.8	2.7	7.5	5.3	6.4	0.7
C. ternatea	6.0	2.2	5.8	9.1	6.1	2.4	7.2	5.2	6.2	2.1
D. distortum	6.1	2.6	5.5	9.4	6.5	2.6	7.3	5.0	6.0	0.7
P. tetragonolobus	6.2	2.6	5.4	9.3	6.4	2.5	7.1	5.2	6.4	0.7
M. lathyroides	6.6	2.5	5.6	9.7	5.4	2.7	7.5	5.0	6.4	0.7
P. calcaratus	6.0	2.5	5.4	9.2	6.4	3.0	7.1	5.1	6.2	0.9
B. napus	6.2	2.6	5.3	9.3	5.8	2.6	7.5	5.3	6.4	0.8
M. sativa (alfalfa)[3]	6.5	2.3	5.6	9.3	5.9	2.3	5.9	5.1	6.3	0.6
Soybean meal[4]	7.3	2.7	5.3	8.2	6.5	1.3	5.3	1.3	5.3	1.5

Source: Cheeke *et al.* (1980).
[1] Dried in air-conditioned room.
[2] Dried in microwave oven.
[3] Kuzmicky and Kohler (1977).
[4] Natl. Res. Counc. (1971).
[5] g amino acid/100 g recovered amino acids.

ternatea, *Desmodium distortum*, *Phaseolus calcaratus*, and *Psophocarpus tetragonolobus* appear especially promising. The protein concentrate of *Brassica napus* also showed good results.

Cassava and *Leucaena* were included in this nutritional evaluation alongside the selected plant sources to support our classification of plants based on number of protein fractions. Since they were Type I plants, it was suspected that the spontaneously precipitated protein concentrate would have diminished nutritional value. The LPC from cassava and *Leucaena* gave extremely poor growth rates (Table 3.2). Acid or acetone washing did not improve gains. Both of these plants are known to contain toxic ingredients; cassava leaves contain cyanogenic glycosides while *Leucaena* contains the toxic amino acid mimosine. However, the evaluated protein concentrates were free of cyanides or mimosine, respectively. The obtained data show that, from these two potential leaf protein sources, protein concentrates cannot be produced by the accepted LPC processes.

PLANTS SELECTED FOR LPC EXTRACTION

Leguminosae

***Clitoria ternatea* (L.).**

Common names: Butterfly pea, kordofan pea

Description: Bogdan (1977); Skerman (1977)

It is native in tropical America; it occurs naturally in tropical Africa, India, China, Malaysia, and Indonesia. After introduction, encouraging results were obtained in Australia, the Philippines, Senegal, and Zambia.

It is adapted to a wide range of soils from sandy to heavy black clays (Lee 1954). In Puerto Rico, it nodulated without *Rhizobium* inoculation.

It grows rapidly in warm, humid weather, producing a dense cover, and flowers in two months after seeding. The flowers are deep blue. It is an erect plant and machine harvestable. After cutting, new lateral branching occurs, and the plant is bushy, forming a dense foliage. It has good regrowth potential. *Clitoria* is drought tolerant; however, it responds to irrigation. It is sensitive to flooding (Farinas 1966). A yield of 13.4 MT dry matter/ha was obtained in Australia (Parbery 1967A). In Cuba, the Mexican cultivar "Conchita clara" produced 81.8 MT fresh herbage/ha under dry land conditions and 84.0 MT with irrigation. Seed production is adequate. Disintegration for leaf protein extraction was performed smoothly, and pressing in a single-screw press produced relatively dry residue.

***Desmodium distortum* (Aubl.) Macbride.**

Description: Smartt (1976); Bogdan (1977)

Desmodium distortum (Fig. 3.10) is an upright perennial plant growing to 2 m woody bush. In Zambia, it yielded 7355 kg dry matter/ha (Bogdan 1977). In the rainy season, it produced a large amount of leaves separated from woody stems. The leaves were processed (11 MT/ha) directly by the disintegrator. The plant would merit further exploration by using germ plasm of a wider geographic distribution.

Fig. 3.10. *Desmodium distortum* (Aubl.) Macbride.

***Lablab purpureus* (L.) Sweet; *Lablab niger* Medik, syn. *Dolichos lablab*.**
Common name: Hyacinth bean
Description: Purseglove (1968); Smartt (1976); Bogdan (1977)

Hyacinth beans are widely grown in Southeast Asia, Egypt, and Sudan and have been introduced into Brazil, the Philippines, and Australia (Barnard 1972). The plant can grow on a variety of soils. It resists drought but cannot tolerate waterlogging. It remains green and vigorous during the dry season. In Puerto Rico, it grows without inoculation. For seed inoculation, the cowpea group strain of *Rhizobium* is recommended. *Lablab purpureus* (Fig. 3.11) is a fast-growing annual legume; cutting can begin 7–10 weeks after sowing. The Rongal variety of Australia survived three close grazings (Philpotts 1967).

It is a short-day plant and flowers with less than 11 hr of daylight. During our studies of tropical plants for leaf protein extraction, we found two cultivars which did not flower in the dry season and produced large amounts of green biomass without support. These had to be harvested by cutting with machete.

In 287 days in Australia, Parbery (1967B) obtained DM yields of 44.8 MT/ha, which contained 6.27 MT crude protein.

Lablab grows well in a warm climate. It needs rainfall or irrigation during the first two or three months after planting; afterward, it is tolerant to drought and very sensitive to flooding.

Experiments were performed in Brazil to evaluate the potential uses of

Fig. 3.11. *Lablab purpureus* (L.) Sweet.

the hyacinth bean. The practical effects as a green manure on corn and beans were measured. It was also used as cattle feed. Good results were obtained in trial feedings. Cattle consumed it readily even at first grazing. Thirty-three to 40 MT green mass were harvested/ha with a crude protein content of 28%. It is a palatable fodder, a good source of LPC extraction, and makes good silage (Schaaffhausen 1963).

Because of the large percentage of vines and leaf stems, the green biomass must be chopped prior to disintegration. The produced leaf protein has an aromatic fragrance. Hamilton *et al.* (1969) reported that milk from the cows fed on hyacinth bean was tainted.

***Macroptilium lathyroides* (L.) Urb.**

Common names: Phasey bean, wild pea bean

Description: Bogdan (1977); Skerman (1977)

Our first plant was collected in TARS's parking area, where the grass is cut regularly. Three protein fractions were first observed during heat fractionation of this plant. Its high protein content, good extraction characteristics, rich nodulation, and rapid regrowth directed our interest toward forage legumes.

This annual or short-lived perennial herb, with support, is twining. If cut regularly, the stem will branch and will form a dense stand, similar to well managed alfalfa. It can be machine harvested. In Puerto Rico, it nodulates profusely without inoculation.

It originates in tropical America. In Puerto Rico, it is widespread on roadsides and empty lots. It was introduced into India, Australia, Africa, and the southeastern United States. It is also grown in Rhodesia, Sudan, and Mali for grazing or green manure (Tontain 1973). It is day-neutral and adapted to a wide range of climates. It survives drought and is fairly tolerant to waterlogging. It is adapted to a wide range of soils, and is tolerant to acid and alkaline soils and slightly saline environment (Fretes *et al.* 1970). Aluminum toxicity could be eliminated by liming (Russell 1966).

Flowers are purple. It has characteristic long and narrow pods which contain 20–24 seeds. Seed production is high; however, they are difficult to collect since pods are sensitive to shattering. Seeds should be harvested carefully by hand. There are 120,000 seeds/kg. The plant is sensitive to virus infections (Alconero and Santiago 1973).

Leaf protein extraction was trouble-free.

***Psophocarpus tetragonolobus* (L.) DC.**

Common names: Winged bean, asparagus bean, Goa bean

Description: Smartt (1976); Purseglove (1968); Allen and Allen (1981)

The geographic origin of the winged bean is still uncertain; the center of genetic diversity is probably Papua, New Guinea (Khan 1976). The origin and ethnobotany of the winged bean are widely discussed by Strathern (1978). It is well distributed in Southeast Asia. It is not cultivated in tropical America.

The winged bean is cultivated for its young, tender pods, which can be harvested 10 weeks after sowing. The young leaves and shoots can be eaten as a leafy vegetable. It was reviewed by Martin and Delpin (1978) as a vegetable for the hot humid tropics. The winged bean thrives in tropical monsoon climates, where rains quickly destroy other beans. When planted during the season of long days, most winged bean varieties will develop considerable biomass before flowering begins. The leaves are palatable for livestock (Pospišil *et al.* 1971).

The soils for the winged bean can be extremely varied. Excellent nodulation occurred without inoculation in our experimental plots in Puerto Rico. It grows well in extremely poor soils, although loamy soils are regarded as the most suitable. It is sensitive to prolonged drought conditions and cannot tolerate waterlogging.

The plants develop vines, which need support. Usually fine bamboo poles are used as stakes. For leaf production, strong wire was stretched horizontally over the planting, to which light strings were fastened for every plant and staked into the ground. The vines climbed the strings. The plants were harvested with a sharp machete by cutting the strings with the attached green biomass. For leaf protein extraction, the vines and leaves were chopped before transferring them to the disintegrator.

Brassicas

On larger plots, we have investigated black mustard, *Brassica nigra* (L.) Koch; white mustard, *Brassica alba* (L.) Rabech; and collard, *Brassica oleracea* var. acephala. These are erect, branched plants which do not form heads like cabbage. Thousand-headed kale, which produces rich foliage, and narrow-stemmed kale, with thick, juicy stems, are grown for feeding livestock. Collards are usually grown to be eaten as a boiled green vegetable. They produce a rich, lush plant material with slow regrowth potential.

Rape, *Brassica napus*, is grown in Europe as a green fodder for livestock and its seeds are used for oil production. It is not grown extensively in the tropics; however, in Mayaguez it produced erect, machine harvestable, juicy green plants. The brassicas, in general, produced large amounts of lush plant material on slightly fertilized soil, but in our experiments, the regrowth was slow and poor. Therefore, it is suggested that they be used as a single crop, and replanted on lands where legumes were grown in the previous year. The workup in disintegrator and press was trouble-free. Their proteins had a cooked cabbage smell. In *in vitro* digestibility experiments in our laboratory, the pressed residue of kale showed poor results, which was surprising, since the brassicas, in general, are plants of low phenolic content. This apparent limitation merits further investigation. The green proteins had good nutritional values (PER), and the proteins separated at 64° and 82°C had the lightest color of the fractions we obtained in our investigations.

PLANTS WHICH SHOW NO POTENTIAL FOR LPC PRODUCTION

In this section, those plants will be discussed which showed much promise to many well-known researchers of leaf protein. Certain species are still considered desirable by some of them. Tropical forage plant breeders recommended some species, and our laboratories considered all of them as sources with good potential until the plants were scrutinized for their physical features, their crude protein content, and dry matter yield/ha. However, every plant in this group failed the final tests: the extraction process or the nutritional evaluation of the protein concentrate. These plants, however, have other important merits and good utilization records as forages for ruminants and as small animal feed. *Leucaena leucocephala* serves as a good browse forage for cattle. Cassava leaves were well accepted as rabbit feed (Harris *et al.* 1980). *Stylosanthes* is a very valuable forage legume, especially in mixed pastures. Under intensive management, sorghum and Sudan grass hybrids offer the highest dry matter and protein yield/ha/annum in the humid tropics and are especially suitable for silage for the dry season.

***Manihot esculenta* Crantz.** Cassava, *Manihot esculenta* Crantz, is an important dietary staple for 300 million people in the humid tropics. Because the tubers are very low in protein, the geographic cassava belt is associated with widespread protein malnutrition. However, the leaves of cassava are rich in crude protein. Therefore, it was logical to consider their leaves as a potential source of protein to supplement the nutritionally unbalanced foods prepared from the tubers. Byers (1961), who studied tropical leaves in Ghana, reported that protein was poorly extracted from the cassava leaf. Singh (1964) in India also reported poor extractions from cassava leaves. In contrast, Oke (1973) obtained extractability of 70% in Nigeria. After precipitation of protein by heat, the coagulum contained only a low level of cyanide (Oke 1973). Renewed interest in cassava is especially evidenced in Brazil. In 1977, an international workshop on the use of agricultural waste for feed and food was organized in Belo Horizonte, where problems with the extraction and fractionation of leaf proteins were reviewed. Cassava leaf protein concentrates were discussed in general without reporting any new results or suggesting new directions in research (Kinsella 1978; Stahmann 1977).

In the Institute of Tropical Agriculture in Mayaguez, Puerto Rico, 11 cultivars of cassava were planted and leaves were periodically harvested for leaf protein extraction. It was found that a green protein fraction spontaneously coagulated at room temperature from the extracted plant juice from every cultivar and yielded as much green protein concentrate as conventional precipitation with heat. The coagulum formed by spontaneous precipitation was settled in large glass tubes (10 cm diameter) which had a conical bottom and outlet. The outflow was controlled by a rubber hose and pinch closure. The settled green protein concentrate could be further separated by centrifuging or filtering in cone-shaped filter bags made from closely woven dacron fabric, and, after draining, pressing the bags carefully between wooden plates in a hydraulic press. The protein was dried and spread in a thin layer on a glass plate in an air-conditioned room. The liquid phase of the coagulation still contained sufficient active principle to coagulate green protein extracts of *Brassica oleracea*, *Clitoria ternatea*, and *Macroptilium lathyroides*.

The spontaneous coagulation can be explained by the complicated reactions that occurred between polyphenols and proteins after they were separated by the disintegration process of their natural tissues. The polyphenol complexes in leaf protein concentrate interfere with the extractability of proteins and with enzyme digestibility *in vitro* and *in vivo*, and decrease the nutritional value of the proteins.

The contents of tannin and polyphenol in leaves of every cultivar were much higher for cassava than for legumes that yielded three protein fractions during different heat treatments.

Quinoids formed by polyphenol oxidase during extraction could also react with proteins to adversely affect nutritional value. In a thin layer chromatographic study of cassava leaves, Thakur *et al.* (1974) found 55 phenolic constituents. Of these, 20 compounds were identified as quercetin and luteolin glycosides and chlorogenic, coumaric, ferulic, and sinapic acid esters. Many such compounds can form quinoids and react with the amino group of lysine. Possible unavailability of lysine could explain the poor response of animals to cassava proteins.

Nutritional evaluation of cassava leaf protein concentrates showed poor animal performance (Cheeke *et al.* 1980) (Table 3.3).

Leucaena. Few sources of vegetable protein can compete economically in the lowland tropics with *Leucaena leucocephala* of the legume subfamily Mimosaceae, which is widespread in the tropics of Central America, Africa, India, the Philippines, and Australia. This deep-rooted, woody legume is drought resistant, yields copious amounts of seed, and has a rapid regrowth rate. When managed as a forage crop, after multiple cutting it yields more protein than alfalfa (Takahashi and Ripperton 1949).

Leucaena grows abundantly in the humid tropics without fertilization. The description, culture, and utilization of *L. leucocephala* were reviewed by Oakes (1968), Gray (1968), and Brewbaker (1976). Yield trials in Hawaii were reported by Brewbaker *et al.* (1972), in the U.S. Virgin Islands by Oakes and Skov (1967), and in the northern territory of Australia by Falvey (1976). The economic importance of this tropical legume has generated considerable interest, and an international symposium in the Philippines was cosponsored by the U.S. National Academy of Sciences (Natl. Acad. Sci. 1977).

In Mayaguez, Puerto Rico, we planted a collection of 82 varieties of germ plasm originating from all around the world. The seedlings grew well. Addition of *Rhizobium* did not improve the growth.

The standard extraction procedure yielded a thick jelly-like extract, which could not be separated by filtration from the pressed fibrous residue. With a double amount of added water and quick processing, the extraction was improved. However, it was observed that, on standing, every extract coagulated at room temperature, and the green coagulum settled on the bottom of the flasks. The sediment was centrifuged. The precipitation was found to be complete. No further fraction could be isolated by heating the separated aqueous phase. The coagulum was washed twice in a blender with 0.1 *N* hydrochloric acid and centrifuged again, then washed with distilled water until free of chloride. Similarly, the pressed residue was washed with 0.1 *N* HCl. Both products were found to be free of mimosine (see Chapter 12, page 347). The washed green protein was spread in a thin layer on glass plates and dried in an air-conditioned room or in a microwave oven. The dry powder from the free-flowing green protein concentrate contained 40–46% protein. Some of the fibrous particles were seen in the concentrate. This could be eliminated by a vibrating screen filtration of the green juice. The distribution of mimosine in the extraction process was followed by using a commercial amino acid analyzer which gave a specific method of determination of mimosine in *Leucaena leucocephala* or in the leaf protein fractions (Telek and Evans 1978).

Nutritional evaluation of the mimosine-free product disclosed a poor quality protein for monogastric animals (Cheeke *et al.* 1980) (Table 3.3).

LEAF PROTEINS OF TROPICAL LEGUME TREES

About two decades ago, the potential use of tree leaves as a source of leaf protein concentrate was suggested (Pirie 1968). In a review, Keays and Barton (1975) estimated that yearly 15 million MT of commercial foliage could be utilized as animal feed, and 10 million MT of grain could be diverted to human nutrition. Carlsson (1975, 1978) reviewed the production of animal feed and protein-vitamin concentrates from leaves of forest trees, listing Russian references for utilization of spruce and pine needles as protein-vitamin concentrate for swine and calves, and Swedish studies of such fast-growing trees as aspen, poplar, sallow, sycamore, and willow. These short-rotation forests could produce large quantities of green leaves and wood for charcoal production simultaneously.

The utilization of tree leaves as a source for animal feed could be important if lumbering is done on a large scale. The fast growing trees are harvested young for fuel energy, and the needles and leaves are by-products. In this case mobile manufacturing equipment would have to be designed to avoid long-distance transportation of the leafy material.

The phenol-tannin content should be investigated year-round. Nutritional value of the products should be determined by rat feeding experiments. From the available literature of experiments in temperate zone regions, some difficulties can be noted. Law *et al.* (1978) experienced spontaneous precipitation working with white spruce needles. Carlsson (personal communication) found that proteins prepared from short rotation forest species had low *in vitro* digestibility. He also recognized that the presence of phenolic substances negatively affects the nutritional value of the proteins prepared from tree leaves. However, he did not report any analytical data.

After our studies of *Leucaena leucocephala*, a rapidly growing tree of the Mimosaceae subfamily of Leguminosae, we extended our investigations to the other tree legumes we could locate in the arboretum of the Tropical Agriculture Research Station and in natural locations in western Puerto Rico.

The huge family of the Leguminosae with 13,000 plant species is second only to the Gramineae in size. Extremely diverse in form, they range from forest trees to shrubs and herbaceous annuals and are grouped into three main subfamilies. Members of the Papilionoideae (pea) subfamily are mostly herbaceous plants of agronomic importance. The other two subfamilies (Caesalpinioideae and Mimosoideae) (*Cassia* and *Mimosa*) contain tropical and subtropical trees and herbaceous plants. In identification of species, the monumental books *Common Trees of Puerto Rico and the Virgin Islands, Vol. 1* (Little and Wadsworth 1964) and *Vol. 2* (Little *et al.* 1974) were a valuable aid.

Leaves were collected randomly for protein and dry matter and leaf protein extraction and fractionation. The results are summarized in Table 3.4, indicating that, with currently known methods, good quality leaf pro-

TABLE 3.4. TANNIN, PHENOL, AND PROTEIN CONTENT OF LEGUME TREE LEAVES

	DM%			
Legume Tree	Total Phenols	Nontannin Phenols	Condensed Tannins	Protein
Cassia subfamily (Caesalpinioideae)				
Bauhinia alba	4.92	1.80	3.12	24.68
Bauhinia candida	5.93	1.53	3.70	13.15
Bauhinia galpini	9.97	1.58	8.39	14.36
Bauhinia purpurea	7.12	2.37	4.75	9.95
Bauhinia reticulata	6.10	1.37	4.73	8.44
Bauhinia violacea	5.35	2.64	2.71	9.42
Brownea grandiceps	11.12	1.45	9.67	5.69
Brownea macrophylla	6.27	1.13	5.14	7.72
Cassia moschata	5.00	3.61	1.39	17.39
Cassia nodosa	7.74	1.22	6.52	18.86
Cassia spectabilis	1.48	1.24	0.24	30.72
Delonix regia	10.23	1.96	8.27	8.58
Tamarindus indica	4.06	1.23	2.83	8.17
Mimosa subfamily (Mimosoideae)				
Albizia adinocephala	2.09	1.33	0.76	26.97
Calliandra inaequilatera	10.38	4.25	6.13	21.01
Calliandra surnamensis	7.25	1.85	5.44	18.30
Enterolobium cyclocarpum	3.53	0.99	2.54	30.14
Inga laurina	7.73	3.41	4.32	14.58
Inga vera	5.95	1.33	4.62	19.27
Leucaena leucocephala	6.38	1.82	4.56	21.32
Parkia biglandulosa	8.95	1.70	7.25	6.88
Pithecelobium dulce	3.01	1.50	1.51	18.60
Samanea saman	3.09	1.50	1.59	19.46
Pea subfamily (Faboideae)				
Dalbergia sissoo	4.54	2.72	1.82	10.75
Erythrina poeppigiana	1.68	1.23	0.45	23.61
Erythrina variegata orientalis	2.40	1.80	0.60	21.74
Myrospermum frutescens	1.77	1.21	0.56	20.68

tein concentrates for nonruminants cannot be prepared from tree leaves, especially from plants of Type I.

Our survey of tropical legume trees was only a small sampling of available tropical tree leaves. Evaluation should be continued in the vast tropical regions of South America and Africa, where only 10% of the land is cultivated by man and the remainder is covered by forests or pastures. Only 7% of 1,000,000 km^2 in northeastern Brazil is cultivated. In this vast area, 250 legumes were collected by Duke (1959), including 115 from the subfamily of papilionoideae and 50 species of the Mimosoideae. Several important fodder trees are of the latter subfamily, such as bauhinias and mimosas. In the 20 million km^2 Cerrado regions of Brazil, which are watered by heavy rain for six months, the soil is leached, deficient in minerals, and of extensive aluminum toxicity. Here, legumes are predominant plants. These areas should be the grounds of systematic research of leguminous varieties for pastures and tree species for maintaining nitrogen balance in the soil.

The Amazon rain forest could offer an array of high trees for study as possible sources for animal feed. Döbereiner and Campelo (1977) extensively reviewed the importance of legumes and their contribution to tropical areas of Brazil. Some of the leaves of the Leguminosae definitely could be used as feed for ruminants. However, for leaf protein concentrate fractionation, a new process has to be found in which the phenol-protein interactions could be inhibited or the protein-phenol complex could be cleaved by economical methods. Until this is achieved, food from the forest remains a dream.

Indigofera. We were initially attracted to indigo for its rapid regrowth potential. We noticed its vigorous growth along the roadsides where it had been drastically cut back recently by road cleaning crews using machetes. In the processing of the trailing indigo *(Indigofera spicata)*, it behaved as a Type III plant, yielding three distinct protein fractions on differential heat treatment. This observation prompted us to investigate a large number of *Indigofera* species which had been widely cultivated for preparation of the blue indigo dyes in India, Thailand, and Indonesia. Twenty to 22 MT of green material have been harvested as first cut in plantings of indigo in India. Some of the plants attain a height of 1.83 m (6 ft). Since the year 1880, synthetic indigo dye has made the cultivation of indigo unprofitable. Plants readily escaped from the discontinued cultivation, covering large areas as weeds, and have become distributed in nearly all tropical countries. Only four species contain the toxic amino acid indospicine (Charlwood and Bell 1977).

We planted several species of indigoferas at the Institute (Table 3.1). The growth of some cultivars was impressive, especially when compared to alfalfa, which was planted simultaneously alongside the indigos. However, during the extraction and fractionation, the indigos yielded purple- or blue-colored proteins, some of which precipitated spontaneoulsy, indicating a possible high tannin or polyphenol content.

***Stylosanthes humilis* H.B. and K.**
Common name: Townsville stylo
Description: Bogdan (1977); Skerman (1977)

It is indigenous to central Mexico, south through Central America, to Northeast Brazil. It is now widespread in the tropics, where it is considered an outstanding pasture legume because of its adaptability to a variety of soil conditions, high protein content, regrowth potential, and ease of establishment. Herbage production in the first year is 0.6–4.8 MT/ha dry matter and, in subsequent years, between 1.8 and 2.4 MT. Kretschmer (1968) studied *Stylosanthes humilis* in Florida in pangola grass pastures. Inclusion of *S. humilis* with pangola resulted in higher dry matter and crude protein yields/ha. In all stages of growth, it is readily eaten by cattle and will regenerate from year to year under heavy grazing. It can be green chopped or can be used as an early winter hay crop.

***Stylosanthes guianensis* (Aubl.) SW. (formerly *S. gracilis*).**
Common name: Stylo
Description: Bogdan (1977); Skerman (1977)

Stylosanthes guianensis is one of the new and most promising legumes for the tropics.

Naturally occurring throughout Central and South America, mainly in the northern states of Brazil, it is adapted to a rainfall range of 900–4000 mm/year. It can tolerate highly acid soils and it is a short-day plant. The vigorous adult plant can be harvested continuously from 6 months after planting to about 6 years. It is capable of fixing substantial amounts of nitrogen without inoculation (Tuley 1968). It makes a good hay containing 14–16% protein. Gilchrist (1967) reported a yield of 11 MT/ha/year in Queensland; however, the average yield is between 2.5 and 10 MT (DM)/ha annum. The crude protein content ranges from 12 to 18%. In Puerto Rico, stylo is utilized in mixed swards, where its presence increases the live-weight gains of grazing cattle. The average DM yield in Puerto Rico was reported to be between 21 and 24 MT/ha/164 days, with a crude protein yield of 3.6–4.0 MT/ha/164 days (Velez-Santiago *et al.* 1981).

The characteristics of both *Stylosanthes* offered promise of excellent plant material for leaf protein extraction in the tropics to compete in yield with alfalfa in temperate climates. However, hopes vanished at the first step of the processing. During maceration in the Waring Blendor or in pilot plant-scale disintegration, a thick emulsion formed which could not be separated from the fibrous material either by centrifuging or by pressing. On heating, the emulsion thickened and the separation became even more difficult. After unsuccessful processing experiments with 10 different cultivars, further research was abandoned. Breeding *Stylosanthes* for low pectin content probably would make this otherwise ideal plant an excellent source for leaf protein extraction in the tropics.

TROPICAL GRASSES

The lush vegetation of the humid tropics is often considered as having a high potential for animal production. Grasses and forage legumes are the two most important groups of plants for grazing animals. The forage legumes have been discussed in detail on previous pages. The grasses are an extremely large family of more than 10,000 species. Tropical grasses have a capacity for a high rate of photosynthesis (Ludlow and Wilson 1968); they grow year-round and show excellent regrowth after repetitive cuttings (Sotomayor-Rios *et al.* 1976); but the natural N content of the grasses is relatively low. High dry matter production in the range of 12 MT/ha in response to nitrogen fertilization is common (Vicente-Chandler *et al.* 1961).

Quality and Digestibility

Improved tropical grasses are often good quality when fed at immature stages of growth, but the maximum attainable intake and digestibility are lower than in immature temperate grasses. This may be related to the high proportion of indigestible cell wall constituents and the extent of lignification. Histochemical examination has revealed that tropical species have lignified sheath cells and vascular bundles; these structures are not degraded in the rumen (Moore and Mott 1973).

The low quality of tropical grasses at the beginning of and during the dry season is a major problem (Pfander 1971).

Minson and McLeod (1962) found that mean digestibility of tropical forages was 12.8% lower than that for the temperate varieties. The lower milk production per cow on tropical pasture is primarily due to low digestibility (Hamilton *et al.* 1970), although low protein is also an important cofactor (Hardison 1966). The level of crude protein below which nitrogen is the first limiting factor in tropical grasses is 7% (Milford and Haydock 1965). Vicente-Chandler *et al.* (1964) concluded, however, that several improved tropical grasses are palatable and nutritious if properly managed. Young growth of tropical grasses usually provides sufficient protein for the animal, but Milford and Haydock (1965) showed that content and digestibility of crude protein declined rapidly with age in tropical grasses; the decline was found to be greatest in buffel and pangola.

Forage Yields

Forage yields in the humid tropics during the dry season are only about half of those during the remaining part of the year (Vicente-Chandler *et al.* 1974). Lower rainfall, shorter days, cooler weather during the winter months, and flowering of the plants reduce growth. The storage of the excess herbage harvested during the high growing season is essential for the winter months.

Good haymaking conditions in the tropics often do not occur until the grasses are mature; thus, low quality of the dried forage is unavoidable (Miller 1969). Haymaking from young regrowth forages in the field, using sun drying, is difficult in the humid tropics because of heavy rainfall and high relative humidity during the lush growth period. A small increase in relative humidity, not even detectable by human senses, would extend the necessary field drying time for 2–3 days. Thus, in the rainy season, during the best growing period of tropical grasses, the daily heavy rains make field drying impossible, and with the ever-increasing cost of fossil fuels, mechanical drying would be a costly process.

Leaf Protein Extraction as a Solution

Leaf protein extraction of tropical grasses would be a rational approach to prepare stored feed for the dry season. The pressing of disintegrated plant material having a moisture content of 83% physically removes water, and the moisture content is lowered to 74% (Connell and Houseman 1977). The bulk is also reduced considerably. The more effective double-screw press reduces the water content of disintegrated alfalfa by 20% with a single pressing. The pressed residues can be dried artificially more economically than the unpressed crop because their disintegrated structure allows more ready diffusion of water vapor. The dried residue could be fed as hay or as pelleted feed, which is usually digested with better efficiency. The fibrous residues could be ensiled with the addition of molasses or mixed with another fresh forage crop in order to increase palatability, and the extracted green protein processed for poultry and swine feed.

Dry Matter and Protein Yields

Figure 3.12 shows that, in a 2-year study of tropical grasses in Brazil, the dry matter content of the grasses increased linearly with advance in age of the forages (Gomide *et al.* 1969). At 4 weeks of age, the average dry matter percentages of the grasses varied from as low as 12.2% for Napier grass to as high as 31.4% for Bermuda grass. The crude protein percentage decreased with advance of plant age (Fig. 3.13). It is observed that most of the change

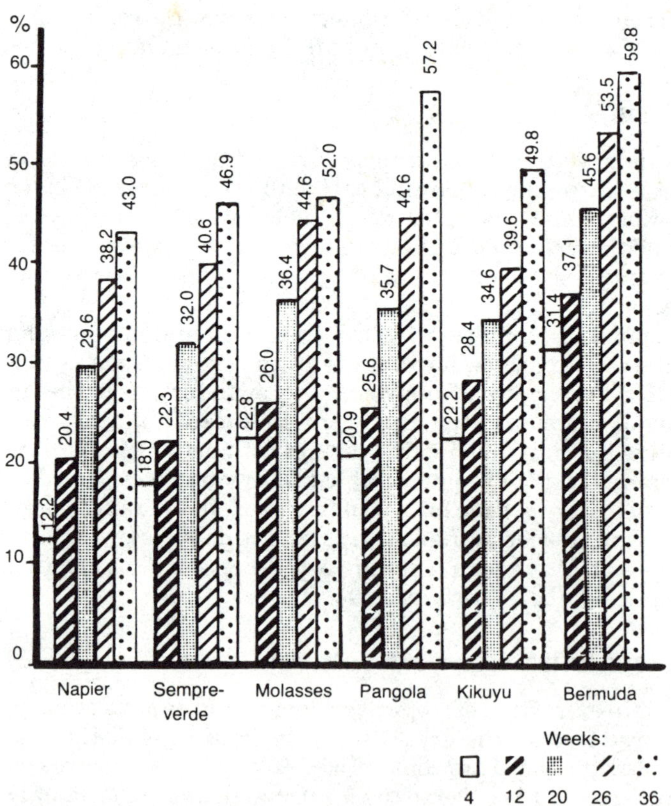

Fig. 3.12. Dry matter (%) vs. plant age of tropical grasses in Brazil.

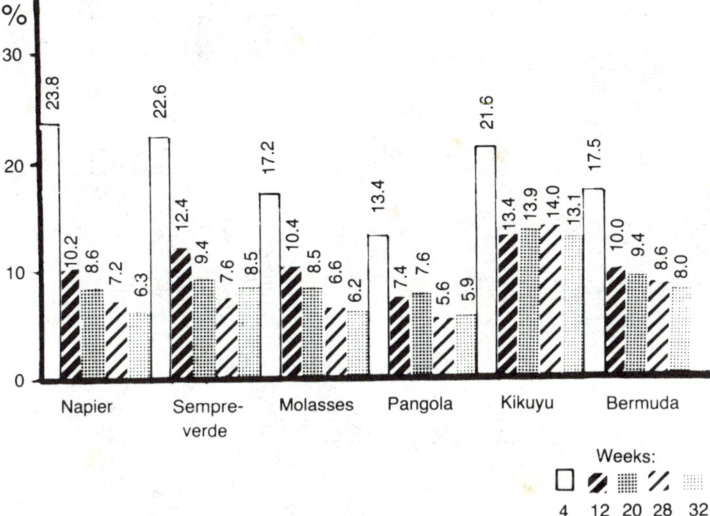

Fig. 3.13. Crude protein (%) vs. plant age of tropical grasses in Brazil.

occurred between 4 and 12 weeks of plant age except in Kikuyu grass, which maintained a relatively high crude protein content throughout the growing period.

The developers of the Vepex process were impressed by the high protein yield of the managed tropical grasses. They postulated that the periodically cut grasses would produce sufficient yields year-round for the extraction plant and that it would be possible to use raw material of one plant culture (Holló and Koch 1970).

During our early investigations, we were also impressed by the reported high yields. A visit to the experiment stations in Puerto Rico left the impression of easy machine harvesting and transportation of green crops, similar to the practice with alfalfa. The regrowth rate of the experimental plot was impressively uniform. Our creed (Nagy *et al.* 1978) was summarized as follows:

"The tropical forage grasses are unexploited leaf sources that could supply large quantities of protein. Tropical forage grasses photosynthesize more efficiently, grow during most of the year, show excellent regeneration after repetitive cuttings, and with increased nitrogen fertilization respond with increased green forage and protein yields. Extensive investigations of tropical grasses by Caro-Costas *et al.* (1960, 1961, 1972); Vicente-Chandler *et al.* (1959, 1961, 1964); and Sotomayor-Rios *et al.* (1973, 1974, 1976) have considerably broadened our understanding of the effects of fertilization and repetitive cutting on green forage, dry matter, and protein yields.

"As a rule, under constant fertilization conditions, yields of green forage and dry forage increase with length of cutting interval (usually 30 to 90

TABLE 3.5. CRUDE PROTEIN CONTENT OF TROPICAL FORAGE GRASSES HARVESTED AT THREE INTERVALS OVER A 2-YEAR PERIOD[1]

Species	PRPI[2]	30 Days		45 Days		60 Days	
		Crude Protein as % of Dry Matter	Crude Protein Yields (kg ha^{-1} Year^{-1})	Crude Protein as % of Dry Matter	Crude Protein Yields (kg ha^{-1} Year^{-1})	Crude Protein as % of Dry Matter	Crude Protein Yields (kg ha^{-1} Year^{-1})
Digitaria setivalva	6402	13.3	1946	11.1	2066	9.3	1790
Brachiaria sp.	9626	11.1	1870	9.0	1824	8.3	1617
Brachiaria mutica	6451	13.8	2051	10.3	1902	9.3	1790
Digitaria decumbens	6439	13.8	2179	10.3	1834	9.5	1859
Brachiaria decumbens	5365	11.6	1866	9.5	1961	7.9	1887
Brachiaria brizantha	5909	12.0	1958	9.3	1907	7.8	1696
Digitaria pentzii × *D. sumtsii*	9621	14.3	1929	11.5	1836	9.7	1764
Digitaria milanjiana	6416	13.8	1938	10.8	2009	9.5	1925
Brachiaria brizantha	5569	14.0	2062	11.4	2018	9.7	1711
Brachiaria decumbens	9625	13.3	1910	10.1	1800	8.5	1718
Digitaria smutsii	6434	13.8	1830	11.2	1864	9.7	1721
Brachiaria ruziziensis	5366	11.2	1437	9.7	1460	8.9	1483
Digitaria decumbens	5124	13.8	1757	11.6	1811	10.1	1567
Digitaria decumbens	0560	13.3	1711	10.5	1622	9.6	1546
Brachiaria brizantha	5567	12.8	1758	10.4	1754	7.7	1827
Brachiaria brizantha	1525	12.0	1618	9.8	1504	8.8	1401
Cynodon nlemfuensis var. *nlemfuensis*	2341	14.0	1883	10.3	2141	9.2	2030
Digitaria pentzii × *D. pentzii*	9620	13.8	1525	11.3	1482	11.1	1158
Digitaria pentzii × *D. milanjiana*	9619	14.0	1440	12.0	1642	10.3	1437
Average		13.1	1824	10.5	1814	9.2	1692

[1]Published with permission of Sotomayor-Rios *et al.* (1976).
[2]Puerto Rico plant introduction number (1976).

days; Vicente-Chandler *et al.* 1964; Sotomayor-Rios *et al.* 1976): As shown in Table [3.5], crude protein contents show a reverse trend; i.e., as harvest intervals increase, crude protein decreases. At the 30-, 45-, and 60-day cutting intervals, the average crude protein yields (Table [3.5]) of 19 grasses were 1824, 1814, and 1692 kg/ha/year, respectively. As the length of cutting increases, the proportion of leaf blades decreases and of stems increases. Since leaves possess a higher proportion of protein than stems, the end result is lower protein yields. In addition, protein contents of both leaf blades and stems drop sharply with age (Vicente-Chandler *et al.* 1964). Therefore, if forage grasses are to be seriously considered as an LPC source, a compromise would be required between long harvesting intervals, which produce high forage yields, and short harvest intervals which produce high-protein contents."

Results of Extraction

Our experiments with *Sorghum bicolor* (Millo blanco) and sorghum hybrids gave encouraging yields (Sotomayor-Rios and Telek 1977). However, the extractions were disappointing. The fibrous grasses produced less green juice than legumes, and their initial protein content was lower. Therefore, more plant material had to pass through the disintegrator, and the extractable protein was found on average to be 28.6% compared with the extractability of 52.4% for legumes. The extraction was worked up by the method of Bickoff and Kohler (1974). It was found from the sorghum-Sudan extracts that, in general, the white protein fraction could not be isolated by differential heat fractionation. In some cases, traces of protein coagulates could be observed when the mother liquor of green protein precipitate was heated to 82°C. Several other grasses were worked up with similar discouraging results (Table 3.6), and further investigations of tropical grasses as sources for leaf protein extraction were suspended. It was concluded that the ever-increasing cost of nitrogen fertilizer, the higher processing cost due to lower crude protein content and tough fibrous plant material, the higher energy requirement of the disintegrator, and the lower quality of protein would make the process uneconomical.

TABLE 3.6. EXTRACTABILITY OF PROTEINS FROM TROPICAL GRASSES

Tropical Grass	% Protein	% Extractability of Crude Protein
Guinea grass, *Panicum maximum* Jacq.	13.1	19.2
Napier grass, *Pennisetum purpureum,* Sebum	10.7	19.6
Forage hybrid sorghum (Millo blanco)	12.8	28.2
Pangola grass, *Digitaria decumbens,* Stant	11.2	29.0
Sorghum-Sudan hybrid	12.4	24.6
Star grass, *Cynodon nlemfuensis*	11.6	18.8

CONCLUSION

Our relatively short systematic investigation in search of tropical plant sources for leaf protein extraction and fractionation produced valuable results.

(1) Plants were selected which are equivalent in yield, extractability, and nutritional quality to alfalfa, the preferred plant material for commercial manufacturing of leaf protein concentrates in the temperate zone.

(2) It was recognized that, in the tropics, year-round production cannot be obtained by a single culture, and a pattern of different species plantings has to be formulated.

The assessment concerning the possibilities as stated by Holló and Koch (1970) now seems wrong: "When it is possible to use the raw material of one or only a few plant cultures—e.g. in tropical regions, the technological problems are not great. However, in the temperate zone, the raw materials involved extend over a very large number of plant species and the technical problems are increased."

(3) It is suggested that, being considered for commercial exploitation, at every new location, the use of plant species should be reinvestigated, and a growing schedule for year-round use should be devised which is strongly influenced by climatic variation. A small extraction plant for direct utilization on-farm should evaluate the selected plants before a larger-scale operation is selected.

(4) It was found that the protein pattern of heat fractionation, i.e., the number of obtained protein fractions, is a rapid preliminary selection method in screening plants for leaf protein extraction.

(5) Our studies shattered the popular belief that cassava leaves, tree leaves of such species as *Leucaena leucocephala*, and tropical grasses are rich sources of available proteins for human or nonruminant nutrition.

As mentioned earlier, the most crucial problem is the phenol-protein interaction. Every plant contains *o*-diphenols and polyphenol oxidases which catalyze the oxidation to an *o*-quinone which will bind with protein. Even more important are the condensed tannins in the leaves, which are present in every plant source at lower or higher levels, and which we found readily bound proteins and formed insoluble complex molecules with them. A high tannin level can precipitate the entire protein content (cassava, *Leucaena*). A detailed study should be made of tannin formation in the plant selected and how it is affected by age, climate, stress, sampling, and harvesting method, and cutting times, followed by parallel nutritional evaluation. The characterization of tannins and phenolics in the plant sources is of great importance to the problem of the insolubility of tannin-protein complexes, and makes the development of a direct chemical analytical method extremely difficult.

Agronomic research should be continued, with interested collaborators at different locations evaluating a diverse germ plasm collection.

Protein fractionation cannot be profitable without the proper utilization of the pressed residue. The nutritional evaluation of this fraction in the form of direct feeding or as dried, pelleted feed is of primary importance. The technology of silage and haylage making from pressed residue of tropical plant sources should also be investigated in depth.

On-farm utilization with a small pilot plant is suggested as a next step of *evaluation* in large animal feeding. The pressed residue should be fed directly to ruminants and should be ensiled for the dry season. After these agronomical, industrial, and feeding experiments, economic feasibility studies should be done with careful investigation of available manpower, land, energy supply, and marketing potential. The first industrial leaf protein production in Europe became a successful enterprise because the manufacturing concern was well organized in its alfalfa dehydrating process and had made certain that the best possible resources and market would be available to it.

REFERENCES

ALCONERO, R. and SANTIAGO, A. 1973. *Phaseolus lathyroides* as a reservoir of cowpea mosaic virus in Puerto Rico. Phytopathology *63*, 120–123.

ALLEN, O.N. and ALLEN, E.K. 1981. The Leguminosae. A Source Book of Characteristics, Uses and Nodulation. University of Wisconsin Press, Madison.

BARNARD, C. 1972. Register of Australian Herbage Plant Cultivars. CSIRO, Canberra.

BICKOFF, E.M. and KOHLER, G.O. 1974. Preparation of edible protein of leafy green crops such as alfalfa. U.S. Pat. 3,823,128. July 9.

BOGDAN, A.V. 1977. Tropical pasture and fodder plants. *In* Tropical Agriculture Series. D. Rhind (Editor). Longman, New York.

BREWBAKER, J.L. 1976. Establishment and management of *Leucaena* for livestock production. Manuscript presented March 10, 1976 at International Seminar on Livestock Production in the Tropics, Acapulco.

BREWBAKER, J.L., PLUCKNETT, D.L. and GONZALEZ, V. 1972. Varietal variation and yield trials of *Leucaena leucocephala* (Koa haole) in Hawaii. Hawaii Agric. Exp. Stn. Res. Bull. *166*.

BROWN, H.E., STEIN, E.R. and SALDAÑA, G. 1975. Evaluation of *Brassica carinata* as a source of plant protein. J. Agric. Food Chem. *3*, 545.

BYERS, M. 1961. The extraction of protein from the leaves of some plants growing in Ghana. J. Sci. Food Agric. *12*, 201.

CARLSSON, R. 1975. Increased utilization of whole trees.—Production of protein-vitamin concentrate from leaves. Skog i Skåne *4*, 20–21 (Swedish).

CARLSSON, R. 1978. Production of animal feed and protein-vitamin concentrates from leaves of forest trees: A review. Proc. Int. Workshop Utilization

Agric. Waste for Feed and Food, CETEC, Belo Horizonte, Minas Gerais, Brazil, Dec. 1977.

CARO-COSTAS, R., ABRUÑA, F. and FIGARELLA, J. 1972. Effect of nitrogen rates, harvest interval and cutting heights on yield and composition of Star grass in Puerto Rico. J. Agric. Univ. P.R. *56*, 267–279.

CARO-COSTAS, R. and VICENTE-CHANDLER, J. 1961. Effect of fertilization on carrying capacity and beef production by Napier grass pasture. Agron. J. *53* (3) 204–205.

CARO-COSTAS, R., VICENTE-CHANDLER, J. and FIGARELLA, J. 1960. The yields and composition of five grasses growing in the humid mountains in Puerto Rico as affected by nitrogen fertilization, season, and harvest procedures, J. Agric. Univ. P.R. *44*, 107–120.

CHARLWOOD, B.V. and BELL, E.A. 1977. Qualitative and quantitative analysis of common and uncommon amino acids in plant extracts. J. Chromatogr. *135*, 377–384.

CHEEKE, P.R., KINZELL, J.H., DE FREMERY, D. and KOHLER, G.O. 1977. Freeze dried and commercially prepared alfalfa protein concentrate evaluation with rats and swine. J. Anim. Sci. *44*, 772–777.

CHEEKE, P.R., TELEK, L. and CARLSSON, R. 1980. Nutritional evaluation of leaf protein concentrates prepared from selected tropical plants. Nutr. Rep. Int. *22*, 717–721.

CONNELL, J. and HOUSEMAN, R.A. 1977. The utilization by ruminants of the pressed green crops from fractionation machinery. *In* Green Crop Fractionation. R.J. Wilkins (Editor). Br. Grassl. Soc. Occas. Symp. *9*.

DEVI, A.V., RAO, V.A.N. and VIJAYARAGHAYAN, P.K. 1965. Isolation and composition of leaf protein from certain species of Indian flora. J. Sci. Food Agric. *16*, 116.

DÖBEREINER, J. and CAMPELO, A.B. 1977. Importance of legumes and their contribution to tropical agriculture. *In* A Treatise on Dinitrogen Fixation. Section IV. Agronomy and Ecology. R.W.F. Hardy and A.H. Gibson (Editors). John Wiley & Sons, New York.

DUKE, A. 1959. Papilionoidae. Ann. Acad. Bras. Cienc. *31*, 211.

FALVEY, L. 1976. Productivity of *Leucaena leucocephala* in the Daly Basin, Northern Territory. Trop. Grassl. *10*, 117–122.

FARINAS, E.C. 1966. Production and distribution of forage seed and vegetative propagation materials in the Philippines. Proc. 9th Int. Grassl. Congr. São Paulo, Brazil, 1965.

FRETES, R., SAMUDO, R. and GAY, C. 1970. Natural pasture grounds of Paraguay. I. Classification and description. Min. Agric. Gan. Publ. Misc. *5* (Spanish).

GILCHRIST, E.L. 1967. A place for stylo in North Queensland pastures. Queensl. Agric. J. *93*, 344–349.

GOMIDE, J.A., NOLLER, C.H., MOTT, G.O., CONRAD, J.H. and HILL, D.L. 1969. Effect of plant age and nitrogen fertilization on the chemical composition and in vitro cellulose digestibility of tropical grasses. Agron. J. *61*, 116–120.

GRAY, S.G. 1968. A review of research on *Leucaena leucocephala*. Trop. Grassl. *2*, 19–30.

HAMILTON, R.I., FRASER, J. and ARMITT, J.D. 1969. Preliminary assessment of tropical pasture species for taint in milk. Aust. J. Dairy Tech. *24*, 62–65.

HAMILTON, R.I., LAMBOURNE, L.J., ROE, R. and MINSON, D.J. 1970. Quality of tropical grasses for milk production. Proc. 11th Int. Grassl. Congr., Surfers Paradise, Australia. 1970.

HARDISON, W.A. 1966. Chemical composition, nutrient content and potential milk production capacity of fresh tropical herbage. Dairy Training Res. Inst., Univ. Philippines, Coll. Agric. (Laguna) Tech. Bull. *1*.

HARRIS, D.J., CHEEKE, P.R. and TELEK, L. 1980. Utilization of alfalfa meal and tropical forages by weanling rabbits. Proc. West. Sect. Am. Soc. Anim. Sci. *31*, 113–115.

HOLLÓ, J. and KOCH, L. 1970. Protein from green matter. Process Biochem. *5*, 37–39.

HOLLÓ, J., ZAGYVAI, I. and KOCH, L. 1971. Vepex process: Process for the production of fiberless green plant concentrate of full biological value. U.S. Pat. 3,637,396. Jan. 25.

JOSHI, R.N. 1971. The yields of leaf protein that can be extracted from crops in Aurangabad. *In* Leaf Protein: Its Agronomy, Preparation, Quality and Use. IBP Handb. *20*. N.W. Pirie (Editor). Blackwell, Oxford.

KEAYS, J.L. and BARTON, G.M. 1975. Recent advantages in foliage utilization. Can. For. Serv. Inf. Rep. *VP x-137*.

KHAN, T.N. 1976. Papua New Guinea: A centre of genetic diversity in winged bean [*Psophocarpus tetragonolobus* (L.) DC.]. Euphytica *25*, 693–706.

KINSELLA, J.E. 1978. Cassava leaf protein: Summary. Proc. Int. Workshop on Utilization of Agric. Wastes for Feed and Food, Belo Horizonte, M.G., Brazil, 1977.

KRETSCHMER, A.E., JR. 1968. *Stylosanthes humilis*, a summer growing self generating annual legume for use in Florida pastures. Fla. Agric. Exp. Stn. Circ. *S-184*.

KUZMICKY, D.D. and KOHLER, G.O. 1977. Nutritional value of alfalfa leaf protein concentrate (Pro-Xan) for broilers. Poult. Sci. *56*, 1510–1516.

LAW, K.N., LO, S.N. and KORAN, Z. 1978. Utilization of spruce foliage. Extraction of protein and chlorophyll-carotene. Wood Sci. *11*, 91.

LEE, L.C. 1954. *Clitoria ternatea*. Proc. Pan Indian Ocean Sci. Congr., Pt. 11, Perth, W. Australia, 1953.

LITTLE, E.L. and WADSWORTH, F.H. 1964. Common Trees of Puerto Rico and the Virgin Islands, Vol. 1. Agric. Handb. *249*, U.S. Dep. Agric. Forest Service, Washington, DC.

LITTLE, E.L., WOODBURY, R.O. and WADSWORTH, F.H. 1974. Common Trees of Puerto Rico and the Virgin Islands, Vol. 2. Agric. Handb. *449*, U.S. Dep. Agric. Forest Service, Washington, DC.

LUDLOW, M.M. and WILSON, G.L. 1968. Studies on the productivity of tropical pasture plants. Aust. J. Agric. Res. *19*, 35–45.

MARTIN, F.W. and DELPHIN, H. 1978. Vegetables for the hot humid tropics. Part 1. The winged bean, *Psophocarpus tetragonolobus*. U.S. Dep. Agric., Agric. Res. Serv., New Orleans.

MARTIN, F.W., TELEK, L. and RUBERTE, R. 1977. Some tropical leaves as feasible sources of dietary protein. J. Agric. Univ. P.R. *61*, 32–40.

MENDES, C.B. 1965. Investigations into the production of high protein concentrate from leaves for inclusion in the diet of infants and children. SRC Tech. Rep. *1/65*. Scientific Res. Council, Hope, Kingston, Jamaica.

MILFORD, R. and HAYDOCK, K.P. 1965. The nutritive value of protein in subtropical pasture species grown in southeast Queensland. Aust. J. Exp. Agric. Anim. Husb. *5*, 13–17.

MILLER, T.B. 1969. Forage conservation in the tropics. J. Br. Grassl. Soc. *24*, 158–162.

MINSON, D.J. and McLEOD, M.N. 1962. The in vitro technique: Its modification for estimating digestibility of large numbers of tropical pasture samples. Aust. CSIRO Div. Trop. Pastures Tech. Pap. *8*.

MOORE, J.E. and MOTT, G.O. 1973. Structural inhibitors of quality in tropical grams. *In* Antiquality Components of Forages. A.G. Matches (Editor). Crop Science Society of America, Madison, WI.

NAGY, S., TELEK, L., HALL, N.T. and BERRY, R.E. 1978. Potential food uses for protein from tropical and subtropical plant leaves. J. Agric. Food Chem. *26*, 1016–1028.

NATL. ACAD. SCI. 1977. Leucaena. Promising Forage and Tree Crop for the Tropics. National Academy of Sciences, Washington, DC.

NATL. RES. COUNC. 1971. Atlas of Nutritional Data on United States and Canadian Feeds. National Research Council, National Academy of Sciences, Washington, DC.

OAKES, A.J. 1968. *Leucaena leucocephala*. Description, culture, utilization. Adv. Front. Plant. Sci. *20*, 1–114.

OAKES, A.J. and SKOV, O. 1967. Yield trials of *Leucaena* in the U.S. Virgin Islands. J. Agric. Univ. P.R. *51*, 176–181.

OKE, O.L. 1973. Leaf protein research in Nigeria. A review. Trop. Sci. *15*, 139.

PARBERY, D.P. 1967A. Pasture and fodder crop plant introduction at Kimberley Research Station, W.A., 1963–64. Part 1. Perennial legumes. Aust. CSIRO Div. Land Res. Tech. Pap. *6716*.

PARBERY, D.P. 1967B. Pasture and fodder crop plant introduction at Kimberley Research Station, W.A., 1963–64. Part II. Annual Legumes. Aust. CSIRO Div. Land Res. Tech. Pap. *67/10*.

PFANDER, W.H. 1971. Animal nutrition in the tropics—Problems and solutions. J. Anim. Sci. *33*, 843–849.

PHILPOTTS, H. 1967. The effect of soil temperature on nodulation of cowpea (*Vigna sinensis*). Aust. J. Exp. Agric. Anim. Husb. *7*, 372–376.

PIRIE, N.W. 1968. Food from the forests. New Sci. *40*. 420–422.

POSPIŠIL, F., KARIKARI, S.K. and BOAMAN-MENSH, E. 1971. Investigations of winged bean in Ghana. World Crops *23*, 260–264.

PURSEGLOVE, J.W. 1968. Tropical crops. Dicotyledons I. Longmans Green & Co., London.

RUSSELL, J.S. 1966. Plant growth on a low calcium status solodic soil in a subtropical environment. I. Legume species, calcium carbonate, zinc, and other minor element interactions. Aust. J. Agric. Res. *17*, 673-686.

SCHAAFFHAUSEN, R.V. 1963. *Dolichos lablab* or hyacinth bean: Its uses for feed, food and soil improvement. Econ. Bot. *17*, 146–153.

SINGH, N. 1964. Leaf protein extraction from some plants of Northern India. J. Food Sci. Technol. *1*, 37.

SKERMAN, P.J. 1977. Tropical forage legumes. FAO Plant Production and Protection Series *2*. Food Agric. Organ., Rome.

SMARTT, J. 1976. Tropical pulses. *In* Tropical Agriculture Series, Longman Group, London.

SOTOMAYOR-RIOS, A., JULIA, F.J. and ARROYO-AGUILU, J.A. 1974. Effects of harvest intervals on the yield and composition of ten forage grasses. J. Agric. Univ. P.R. *67*, 448–455.

SOTOMAYOR-RIOS, A., MATIENZO, A.A. and VELEZ-FORTUÑO, F. 1973. Evaluation of seven forage grasses at two cutting stages. J. Agric. Univ. P.R. *57* (3) 173–185.

SOTOMAYOR-RIOS, A. and TELEK, L. 1977. Forage yield and protein content of millo blanco (*Sorghum bicolor*) and two F_1 hybrids. J. Agric. Univ. P.R. *61*, 300–304.

SOTOMAYOR-RIOS, A., TORRES-RIVERA, S. and SILVA, S. 1976. Effect of three harvest intervals on yield and composition of nineteen forage grasses in the humid mountain region of Puerto Rico. J. Agric. Univ. P.R. *60*, 294–309.

STAHMANN, M.A. 1978. Coagulation and preservation of plant juice protein by anaerobic fermentation. Proc. Int. Workshop on Utilization of Agric. Wastes for Feed and Food, Belo Horizonte, M.G., Brazil, 1977.

STRATHERN, A. 1978. Ethnobotany and plant geography of the winged bean. *In* The Winged Bean. Pap. presented 1st Int. Symp. on Dev. Potential of Winged Bean. Philippine Counc. Agric. Resour. Res. (Editors). Los Baños, Philippines.

TAKAHASHI, M. and RIPPERTON, J.C. 1949. Kao Haole (*Leucaena glauca*). Univ. Hawaii Agric. Exp. Stn. Bull. *100*.

TELEK, L. 1979. Preparation of leaf protein concentrates in lowland humid tropics. *In* Tropical Foods: Chemistry and Nutrition, Vol. 2. G.E. Inglett and G. Charalambous (Editors). Academic Press, New York.

TELEK, L. and EVANS, J. 1978. Preparation of detoxified leaf protein concentrate from *Leucaena leucocephala*. Presented Annu. Meet. Am. Chem. Soc., Miami, Sept. 10–15, 1978.

THAKUR, M.L., SOMAROO, S.H. and GRANT, W.F. 1974. The phenolic constituents from leaves of *Manihot esculenta*. Can. J. Bot. *52*, 2381.

TONTAIN, B. 1973. Principal cultivated tropical forage plants. Inst. Elevage Med. Vet. Pays Trop. Note Synthese *3*.

TULEY, P. 1968. *Stylosanthes gracilis*. Herb. Abstr. *38*, 87–94.

VELEZ-SANTIAGO, J., SOTOMAYOR-RIOS, A. and LUGO-LOPEZ, M.A. 1981. Potential of *Stylosanthes guianensis* as a forage crop in the humid mountain region of Puerto Rico. J. Agric. Univ. P.R. *65*, 232.

VICENTE-CHANDLER, J., ABRUÑA, F., CARO-COSTAS, R., FIGARELLA, J., SILVA, S. and PEARSON, W.R. 1974. Intensive grassland management in the humid tropics of Puerto Rico. Univ. P.R., Mayaguez, Coll. Agric. Sci., Agric. Exp. Stn., Rio Piedras, P.R. Bull. *233*.

VICENTE-CHANDLER, J., CARO-COSTAS, R., PEARSON, R.W., ABRUÑA, F., FIGARELLA, J. and SILVA, S. 1964. The intensive management of tropical forages in Puerto Rico. Univ. P.R. Agric. Exp. Stn. Bull. *187*.

VICENTE-CHANDLER, J., FIGARELLA, J. and SILVA, S. 1961. Effects of nitrogen fertilization and frequency of cutting on the yield and composition of pangola grass in Puerto Rico. J. Agric. Univ. P.R. *45*, 37–45.

VICENTE-CHANDLER, J., SILVA, S. and FIGARELLA, J. 1959. The effect of nitrogen fertilization and frequency of cutting on the yield and composition of three tropical grasses. Agron. J. *51*, 202–206.

4

Soluble Proteins in Tobacco and Their Potential Use

T.C. Tso and S.D. Kung

Leaf protein is the most important protein in nature because all forms of life ultimately depend on it. Its abundance has prompted numerous studies to determine the feasibility of using it as food or feed. The tobacco leaf protein has recently been reviewed by DeJong and Lam (1977) and recent studies have pointed out the potential usefulness of soluble proteins extracted from tobacco leaves (Wildman and Bonner 1947; Ershoff *et al.* 1978; Tso 1977; Kung and Tso 1978). Until recently however, tobacco had not been considered a likely commercial source of protein. Tobacco is a crop that demands more energy to produce than any other crop. In the United States, for example, 20.8 barrels of oil equivalent is needed to produce 0.4 ha (1 acre) of tobacco per year in comparison with 18.4 for tomato, 15.0 for lettuce, 9.6 for potato, 8.2 for rice, 4.1 for corn silage, 2.0 for soybean, and 0.6 for wheat. Generally, 1 kcal of energy enters the plant through its photosynthetic system, and represents about 2.6 g of mass as glucose, but only 0.12 g of mass as amino acids (Tso 1977). Thus, from an economic point of view, tobacco cannot be commercially grown solely for its protein. Moreover, extraction of leaf proteins involves maceration of the leaves; hence, the by-product—a fibrous macerate—cannot be processed by the conventional curing method for use in smoking products because only intact leaves can be so cured.

Recent advances in technology and a better understanding of biochemical changes during tobacco curing make it possible to extract soluble protein and at the same time to make use of leaf material for smoking. This is due to the development of a new curing process and the use of reconstitution method.

The HLC Procress

In 1975, the homogenized-leaf curing (HLC) process was developed (Tso *et al.* 1975), and this has made the removal of undesirable components (Tso and Gori 1975) and the utilization of tobacco proteins possible. By this process, harvested leaf material is homogenized, and part of the protein in the aqueous phase is removed. The remaining mother liquor is recombined with the fibrous residue, and the mixture is incubated under conditions that cause biochemical changes similar to those caused by conventional curing. The mixture is then dehydrated, reconstituted, and converted to smoking products.

Advantages of the HLC Process

The advantages of the HLC process include substantial savings in labor and time, and protein—which serves as precursors of some undesirable smoking products—is recovered as a useful by-product.

Leaf proteins contribute little to smoking quality, but are precursors of harmful smoke components, including quinoline, HCN, and several other nitrogenous compounds (Tso 1977; Dong *et al.* 1978). Using a purified sample of soluble tobacco protein Dong *et al.* recently demonstrated that quinoline is the main combustion product of Fraction I protein (F I protein) (Dong *et al.* 1978). More recently, several amino acids, especially tryptophan, glutamic acid, and lysine, have been reported to form mutagens when subjected to high temperature (Sugimura 1978). Therefore, removal of proteins from tobacco leaf before the curing process may result in a safer smoking product.

THE NATURE OF FRACTION I PROTEIN

The most well-characterized leaf protein, known as F I protein, was first isolated 30 years ago from spinach by Wildman and Bonner (1947). This soluble protein is found in all organisms containing chlorophyll *a*, including the procaryotic blue-green algae (Kawashima and Wildman 1970), and is identical to ribulose-1,5-biphosphate (RuBP) carboxylase-oxygenase in higher plants. This enzyme has a dual function in that it catalyzes both the carboxylation and the oxygenation of RuBP (Marsho and Kung 1976). Therefore, it catalyzes the crucial reactions of both photosynthesis and photorespiration, the ratio of these two processes determining the plant's productivity (Zelitch 1973).

F I protein has a molecular weight of 550,000 and consists of eight large and eight small subunits arranged into a two-layered structure, each layer consisting of four large and four small subunits (Baker *et al.* 1975). Hirai (1977) has shown that when two or more types of small subunits are present, they are distributed randomly, producing a hybrid molecule. The large subunit, molecular weight 55,000 contains the catalytic site of the enzyme, whereas the small subunit, molecular weight 12,500, may have a regulatory function (Nishimura and Akazawa 1974).

Studies with the *Nicotiana* and cell-free systems have shown that chloroplast genes contain the genetic information for the large subunit, whereas nuclear genes code for the small subunits (Kawashima and Wildman 1972; Kung 1977; Chan and Wildman 1972; Sakano *et al.* 1974B; Ellis 1975). Also, immunological evidence has demonstrated that cytoplasmic ribosomes (80S) control the synthesis of the small subunit of F I protein, while the large subunit is synthesized by chloroplastic ribosomes (70S) (Gooding *et al.* 1973; Gray and Kekwick 1974). Ellis (1975) suggested that the small subunit acts as an initiation factor in the translation of the mRNA for the large subunit. This suggestion implies that the nuclear genome controls the overall rate at which F I protein is synthesized; however, the mechanism of the control is not yet known. Recent evidence indicates that the small subunit is synthesized in the cytoplasm as a precursor of a higher molecular weight intermediate (Chua *et al.* 1978), which is transported across the chloroplast membrane to link up with the large subunit. The intermediate may be involved in regulating the synthesis of the large subunit and assembling the functional molecule. Its need in the assembly of the molecule would explain why attempts to reconstitute the enzyme from isolated subunits have not been successful (Nishimura and Akazawa 1974). New combinations of large and small subunits of the enzyme could only be assembled *in vivo* (Kung and Rhodes 1978).

Recently, isoelectric focusing of *S*-carboxymethylated F I protein from *N. tabacum* in polyacrylamide gel resolved the subunits into their component polypeptides (Kung *et al.* 1974). Each large subunit was resolved into three polypeptides; and each small subunit was resolved into two polypeptides. The subsequent study of F I protein from over 10 plant species revealed that the large subunits consist of three polypeptides whereas the small subunits comprise from one to four polypeptides (Fig. 4.1) (Kung 1976). The study further showed that the three polypeptides of the large subunit are inherited via the maternal line whereas the polypeptides of the small subunit are inherited via both maternal and paternal genes (Fig. 4.1). This pattern of inheritance manifested in F I protein provides us with a unique genetic marker for both chloroplast and nuclear genomes. Consequently, it has been successfully used as a genetic probe in the examination of several plant developmental processes (Kung 1976).

Since the multiple polypeptide composition of the large and small subunits of *N. tabacum* F I protein was first demonstrated by Kung *et al.* (1974) some attempts have been made to determine differences among the three polypeptides composing the large subunits. These polypeptides might originate (1) from three distinct mRNAs coded by separate chloroplast genes, or (2) as a result of post-translational modification, such as deamidation of glutaminyl or asparaginyl residues (Robinson and Rudd 1974) of a single gene product to produce three polypeptides of different charge. Since these polypeptides cannot be differentiated by amino acid analysis or by fingerprinting of trypsin or chymotrypsin digests (Gray *et al.* 1978), the second alternative is currently favored. This alternative is in agreement with the recent finding that a single segment of maize chloroplast DNA (Link *et al.*

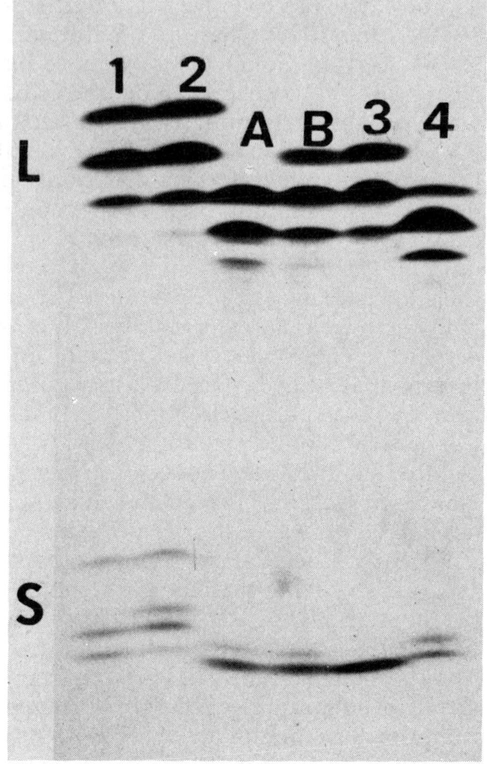

Fig. 4.1. Genetic analysis of *Nicotiana* F I protein by isoelectric focusing. The polypeptide composition of large (L) and small (S) subunits of F I protein from *N. gossei* (1), *N. excelsior* (2), *N. tabacum* × *N. glauca* (A), *N. glauca* × *N. tabacum* (B), *N. glauca* (3), and *N. tabacum* (4).

1978) contains the information for the large subunit. This segment, with 2000 to 2200 base pairs, is not large enough to hold the codes for three distinct polypeptides of 450 amino acid residues each. Moreover, if the first alternative were true, one would expect to find some isoelectric focusing patterns showing unequally spaced polypeptides arising from independent mutation of the separate genes during the course of plant evolution, but such patterns have not been found. Instead, the relative intensities of these polypeptide bands, which are evenly spaced, vary from experiment to experiment. Also, in virtually all isoelectric focusing runs, whether the proteins have been *S*-carboxymethylated with iodoacetic acid or modified with iodoacetamide (Fig. 4.1) the center band is the most intense. Differences in band intensities among experiments probably reflect different degrees of modification rather than gene regulation. On the other hand, most plant

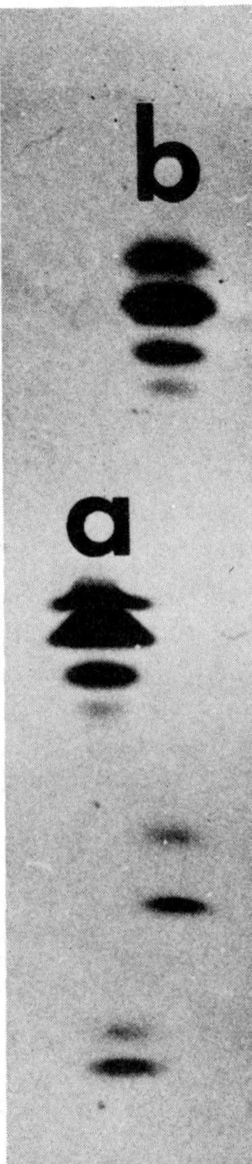

Fig. 4.2. Isoelectric focusing of subunit polypeptides from *N. tabacum* F I protein. The isoelectric points were altered (a) through chemical modification of thiol groups with iodoacetic acid and (b) with iodoacetamide. The pH gradients are from 5 to 7 (bottom to top).

species contain a single polypeptide for the small subunit, and it is coded by the nuclear genome. Multiple polypeptides have been shown to constitute the small subunits isolated from tobacco, tomato, and spinach (Chen *et al.* 1976). These polypeptides, unlike those in the large subunit, have been proven to be separate gene products by sequence analysis (Stroback *et al.* 1976).

The relative frequencies at which both chloroplast and nuclear genes mutate can be estimated from comparisons between progeny and progenitor species with respect to the polypeptide compositions of their large and small subunits. The findings could provide an insight for understanding how F I protein evolves and the sequence in which the genus of *Nicotiana* speciates (Gray *et al.* 1974). Evidence currently available indicates a close correlation between the number of polypeptides in the small subunit and the ploidy level of *Nicotiana* species (Kung *et al.* 1975; Chen *et al.* 1975).

Tobacco plants provide several unique advantages in studies concerning the polypeptide composition of F I protein. First, this protein can be purified by a simple direct crystallization from most tobacco species. Second, there is a wide variety of large and small subunits. Third, many interspecific reciprocal hybrids can be made.

EXTRACTION OF SOLUBLE TOBACCO LEAF PROTEINS

Of the total leaf proteins in tobacco, approximately half are soluble and half insoluble (Fig. 4.3). F I protein can be as much as 50% of the total soluble leaf proteins. Soluble proteins other than F I protein, both chloroplastic and cytoplasmic, are called F II protein, which is unfractionated. The nature of F II protein has not been well defined, although the general composition has been examined (Kung and Tso 1978).

The extraction of soluble leaf proteins from most forage or nonforage crops has been unsuccessful. Most leaf protein preparations contain appreciable amounts of pigments and other contaminants which impart an undesirable color, odor, taste, and texture. In addition, the cost of production by available techniques has been prohibitive.

In this section, we report the techniques we used to maximize the laboratory-scale production of tobacco F I and F II proteins. The crystallization procedure for the F I protein is essentially that developed by Lowe (1977), with further modifications (Kung *et al.* 1978).

Crystallization Procedure for F I Protein

Whole young tobacco plants, including stalks, or regular near-mature leaves, including midribs, were harvested in 2 kg batches and homogenized in 400 ml of 2.0 *M* NaCl plus 2-mercaptoethanol in a Waring Blendor. The resulting slurry was squeezed through four layers of cheesecloth and one layer of Miracloth. The green filtrate was immediately heated in a water bath with occasional stirring until the filtrate reached 45° to 48°C. It was held at those temperatures for a short time and then rapidly cooled to 15° to 20°C in an ice bath. For every 100 ml of filtrate, 2 ml of 10% Na_2EDTA was added, and the pH adjusted to 7.5 with 1.0 *M* Tris (about 4 to 5 ml per 100 ml of filtrate). The green suspension was centrifuged for 15 to 20 min at 16,000 *g*, and the supernatant was passed through a Sephadex G-50 column equilibrated with Tris-EDTA buffer (25 m*M* Tris-HCl buffer containing 0.2 m*M* EDTA, pH 8.0). Crystals usually formed as the eluate emerged from the column; otherwise, they formed overnight at 4°C.

For recrystallization, the mother liquor was suctioned off and the protein was washed twice with Tris-EDTA. The crude crystals were resuspended in a small volume of Tris-EDTA and solubilized by the addition of saturated

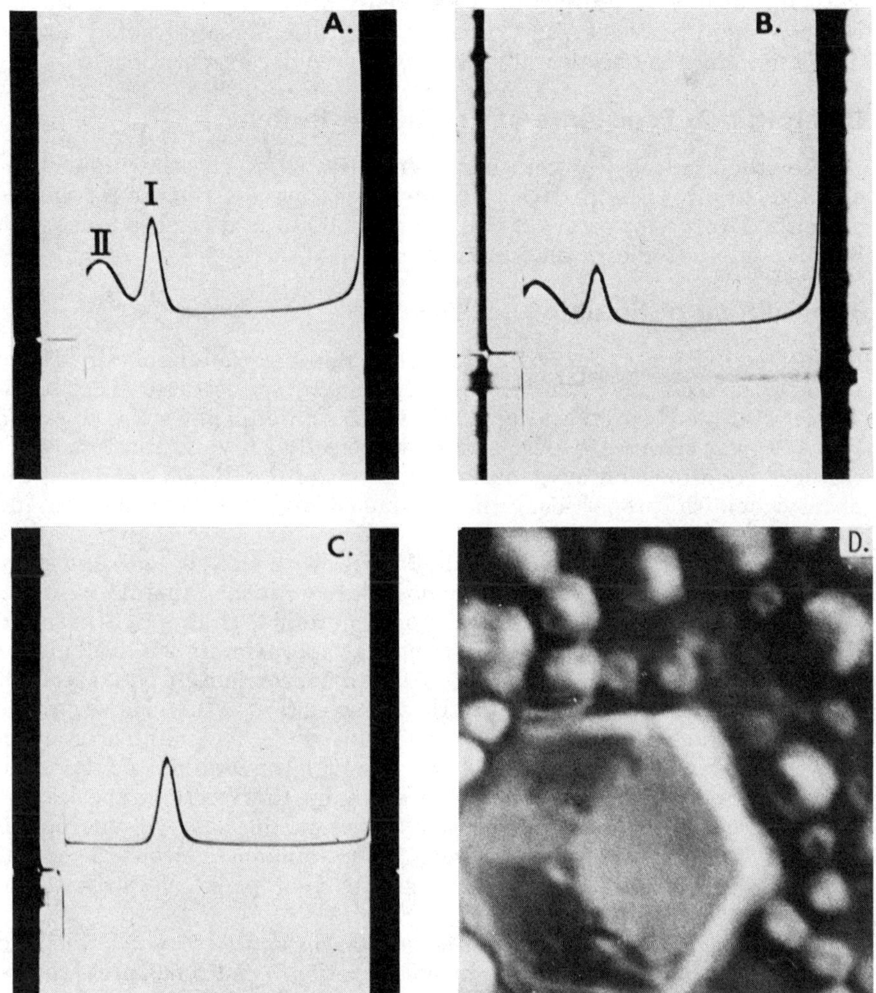

Fig. 4.3. Analytical ultracentrifuge schlieren patterns of tobacco leaf proteins (A–C). A—Aqueous extract of leaf homogenate consisting of F I (I) and F II (II) proteins. B—Aqueous extract of leaf homogenate after it had been heated at 45°–48°C for 10 min; only about half of the leaf protein remained soluble (compare A with B). C—F I protein after one recrystallization. D—F I protein crystals. The largest crystal is more than 0.3 mm in diameter.

NaCl. Centrifugation at 10,000 *g* for 10 min was sufficient to precipitate any residues. The solution was passed through a Sephadex G-50 column, and the column eluate containing the protein was collected and stored at

4°C. One such recrystallization was usually performed before the protein was used in nutritional tests. The recrystallization procedure may also be used to remove bacterial contamination from older preparations.

Precipitation Procedure of Fraction II Protein

After the crude F I protein had been collected, the mother liquor was acidified to pH 4.5 with HCl (6 *N*) to precipitate the remaining soluble proteins. This precipitate was pelleted at 12,000 *g* and washed twice with 80% acetone to remove contaminating pigments.

The Content of Soluble Leaf Proteins

The distribution of the two fractions of soluble leaf proteins obtained from young tobacco plants, F I protein and F II protein, is illustrated in Fig. 4.3A. The crystalline F I protein (Fig. 4.3D) whose schlieren pattern is shown in Fig. 4.3C was chemically pure and enzymatically active. It catalyzed both the carboxylation and oxygenation reactions of RuBP and exhibited the physicochemical properties of the enzyme (Kung *et al.* 1978; Jensen and Bahr 1977).

The ratio of F I protein to chlorophyll varies with plant species and stage of development. In the young greenhouse-grown tobacco plants (6 weeks after transplanting) we used, the ratio of F I protein to chlorophyll, based on the analysis of four species of *Nicotiana*, was approximately 8 to 10 mg F I protein per mg of chlorophyll (Table 4.1). An approximately equal amount of F II protein was also present in these leaves (Fig. 4.3A). However, the ratio of F I and F II protein contents may also vary, depending on stage of growth and development. In this study, although the contents of F I protein determined on a fresh weight basis varied among the *Nicotiana* species, the yields were rather uniform when expressed on the basis of chlorophyll content. The close correlation between F I protein and chlorophyll content in spinach was originally used to deduce its chloroplast origin (Lyttleton and Ts'o 1958).

The yield of leaf protein depends largely on the degree to which cells and chloroplasts are ruptured during homogenization. The French press can be

TABLE 4.1. THE CONTENTS[1] OF CHLOROPHYLL (CHL.) AND F I PROTEIN IN LEAVES FROM FOUR SPECIES OF *NICOTIANA*

Species	mg Chl./g Fresh Weight	mg F I Protein/g Fresh Weight	mg F I Protein/mg Chl.
N. tabacum	0.74	6.4	8.6
N. gossie	0.94	7.8	8.3
N. excelsior	0.55	5.5	10.3
N. suaveolens	0.94	9.9	10.5

[1] Average of 4–6 experiments.

used efficiently, but not routinely, to extract leaf proteins. We used it to determine the total soluble protein content of tobacco leaves, assuming 100% recovery in the extract. We obtained lesser amounts of soluble leaf protein using the blender. Extractability of the soluble leaf proteins during homogenization could be maximized by use of enough solvent. However, an appreciable amount of protein was usually lost during the subsequent heating and crystallization steps (Fig. 4.3B) (Table 4.2). Since only 30–40% of the total amount of F I protein could be obtained as recrystallized product (Fig. 4.3D), the procedure we used is not totally satisfactory with respect to recovery efficiency. We are hopeful, however, that future technology will permit high recoveries of this protein. The F II protein we isolated contained some 20–30% of previously unprecipitated F I protein. Unlike the recrystallized F I protein, the twice-washed F II protein contained pigments and was slightly brownish (Fig. 4.4). Table 4.2 lists the percentage recoveries of both fractions after different steps of the extraction process. In our more recent laboratory tests with small amounts (100–200 g) of samples at different growth stages, recovery efficiencies were much higher.

TABLE 4.2. PERCENTAGE RECOVERY OF TOTAL SOLUBLE LEAF PROTEINS[1] DURING VARIOUS STEPS OF EXTRACTION[2]

Steps of Extraction	F I Protein	F II Protein
Homogenization	80	80
Heating	50–60	50–60
Crystallization	30–40	—

[1]The release of soluble leaf proteins by French press is assumed as 100%.
[2]Average of 4–6 experiments.

AMINO ACID COMPOSITIONS OF F I AND F II PROTEINS

Both the recrystallized F I protein and the aqueous-acetone-washed F II protein from each of the four *Nicotiana* species were washed twice with distilled water and lyophilized to salt-free powders. Portions were then hydrolyzed in 1 ml of constant-boiling HCl (5.7 *N*) at 100°C for 20 hr under vacuum. Amino acid analyses were performed on a Technicon TSM Amino Acid Analyzer as previously described (Kung *et al.* 1977).

The amino acid compositions of the F I proteins shown in Table 4.3 agree well with those previously reported (Kung *et al.* 1977; Kawashima *et al.* 1971). Table 4.3 shows that the amino acid compositions of the F II proteins were nearly identical and were remarkably similar to those of the F I proteins. These relative amino acid compositions suggest that both the F I

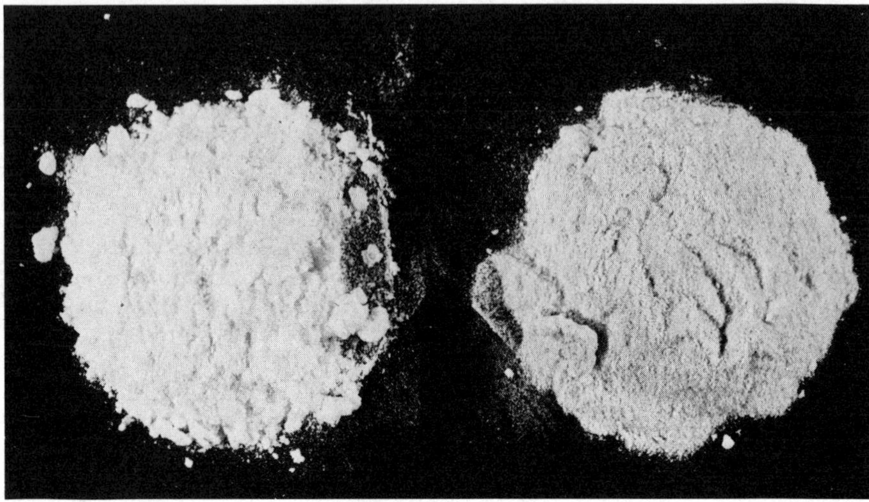

Fig. 4.4. Lyophilized F I (left) and F II (right) tobacco proteins. F I protein was recrystallized once and is a white powder. F II protein was washed twice with 80% acetone and appears brownish.

and F II proteins have a high nutritional value. Comparison with the FAO (Food Agric. Organ. U.N. 1957) reference protein (Table 4.4) showed that the F I and F II proteins contained all the essential amino acids and, in fact, generally more of each. The percentage of almost all essential amino acid in the F II protein of tobacco fell within the range of percentages reported for that amino acid in 56 F II proteins of 21 species (Byers 1971). The levels of methionine reported for these soluble tobacco leaf proteins are probably low estimates because the oxidized forms of methionine were not determined.

PURITY OF THE SOLUBLE, TOBACCO LEAF PROTEINS

Recrystallized F I protein from tobacco is essentially pure. It contains no minerals except sulfur from sulfur-containing amino acids (Chollet *et al.* 1975). By comparison, F I proteins isolated from other plant species may contain considerable amounts of carbohydrate. Unlike spinach F I protein, for example, tobacco F I protein is soluble only in the presence of its substrate RuBP or in high salt (NaCl) concentrations (Kwok *et al.* 1971). Under defined conditions, removal of salt from the solution will cause the F I protein to crystallize (Sakano *et al.* 1974A). Recent attempts to crystallize F I protein from other plant materials including spinach and maize and cotton have been unsuccessful (Bahr *et al.* 1977). Currently, efforts to crystallize F I protein from another relative of tobacco, tomato, have resulted in some success.

TABLE 4.3. THE AMINO ACID COMPOSITIONS (TRYPTOPHAN EXCLUDED) OF CRYSTALLINE F I PROTEIN AND WASHED F II PROTEIN (EXPRESSED AS G AMINO ACID PER 100 G RECOVERED AMINO ACIDS)
Determinations were made on four different preparations.

	F I Protein (Crystals) Preparations					Unfractionated Leaf Proteins (Acid Precipitate) Preparations				
Amino Acid	1	2	3	4	Average	1	2	3	4	Average
Aspartic acid	8.7	9.3	9.3	8.9	9.05	9.5	9.6	9.5	8.4	9.25
Threonine	5.4	5.6	5.1	4.8	5.23	4.8	5.2	5.1	4.5	4.90
Serine	3.2	3.2	3.7	2.2	3.08	3.8	4.1	5.2	3.6	4.18
Glutamic acid	11.3	11.8	11.3	11.5	11.48	11.0	11.0	10.8	10.8	10.90
Proline	4.8	5.3	4.8	5.5	5.10	4.7	4.5	4.7	4.9	4.70
Glycine	9.9	10.2	10.9	10.1	10.28	11.1	10.9	10.6	11.2	10.95
Alanine	9.2	9.4	9.6	9.3	9.38	9.5	9.4	9.6	9.7	9.55
Valine	7.8	8.0	8.2	8.0	8.00	8.1	8.0	8.2	8.4	8.18
Methionine[1]	1.5	0.8	1.0	1.4	1.18	1.2	—	1.2	1.6	1.33
Isoleucine	4.5	4.3	4.6	4.6	4.50	5.0	5.2	4.9	5.3	5.10
Leucine	8.9	8.8	8.7	9.2	8.90	9.0	9.5	8.6	9.1	9.05
Tyrosine	5.1	4.2	3.4	5.0	4.43	3.6	3.8	2.7	3.5	3.40
Phenylalanine	4.5	3.7	3.9	4.2	4.08	4.0	4.5	3.7	3.9	4.03
Lysine	5.8	6.0	6.3	6.0	6.03	6.3	6.3	7.0	6.8	6.60
Histidine	2.7	2.9	2.6	3.0	2.80	2.5	2.6	2.3	2.3	2.43
Arginine	6.9	6.4	6.4	6.4	6.53	6.0	5.9	5.9	6.1	5.98

[1]Methionine determined directly on normal hydrolysate.

F II protein from tobacco leaf cannot be crystallized, as it is a mixture of several different proteins. However, it can be purified free from other contaminants, such as pigments and phenolics, by acetone extraction and water washing. A very low amount of carbohydrate may still be present as a minor contaminant.

TABLE 4.4. COMPARISON OF THE ESSENTIAL AMINO CONTENTS[1] OF F I PROTEIN AND UNFRACTIONATED LEAF PROTEINS FROM TOBACCO WITH UNFRACTIONATED LEAF PROTEINS FROM OTHER PLANTS AND FAO REFERENCE PROTEIN (EXPRESSED AS G AMINO ACID PER 100 G RECOVERED AMINO ACIDS)

Amino Acid	Tobacco Leaf (F I Protein)	F II Leaf Protein (Tobacco)	F II Leaf Protein (21 Plant Species)	FAO[2]
Isoleucine	4.5	5.1	4.5–5.5	4.2
Leucine	8.9	9.1	8.8–10.2	4.8
Lysine	6.0	6.6	5.6–7.3	4.2
Methionine	1.2	1.3	1.6–2.6	2.2
Phenylalanine	4.1	4.0	5.5–6.8	2.8
Threonine	5.2	4.9	4.7–5.8	2.8
Tryptophan	1.5	1.5	1.2–2.3	1.4
Tyrosine	4.4	3.4	3.7–4.9	2.8
Valine	8.0	8.2	5.9–6.9	4.2

[1]The range of amino acid analyses on 56 unfractionated leaf proteins made from 21 species (Byers 1971).
[2]1965 provisional recommendation.

POTENTIAL USE OF TOBACCO LEAF PROTEINS

Ershoff *et al.* (1978) fed weanling male rats diets containing 10% protein in the form of either casein or recrystallized F I protein from tobacco. Findings indicated that the average weight increment as PER (protein efficiency ratio) of rats fed the diet containing F I protein from tobacco was significantly higher throughout a 28-day experimental period than that of rats fed the diet containing casein. No significant differences in hematological findings were noted between rats in the two dietary groups.

In a similar study conducted in the protein laboratory at the U.S. Dept. of Agriculture, Beltsville Agricultural Research Center, results indicate almost equal PER values for test animals fed three different diets—one with tobacco F I protein, another with tobacco F II protein, and a third with casein (Kung *et al.* 1980).

The essential amino acid compositions of tobacco F I protein, egg protein, and milk proteins are similar (Table 4.5). Because of its high purity and high nutritional value, Ershoff *et al.* (1978) suggested that F I protein from tobacco has a great potential to be formulated into important therapeutic products.

Other potential uses of F I protein are almost unlimited. Because it is colorless, tasteless, and odorless, and also because of its long shelf-life, F I protein might be used as a diet staple—in liquid, semisolid, and solid foods. Thus, soft drinks and food gels might be made more nutritive; and meats could be extended with this protein.

Tobacco F II protein is very similar to the F I protein in amino acid composition. In contrast to seed proteins, the tobacco leaf proteins are rich in lysine, threonine, and valine (Table 4.5), and the average content is more than 150% that of the FAO reference protein (Table 4.4). F II protein in its present state can safely be used as feed for animals. With additional purification it may also provide food for humans.

TABLE 4.5. ESSENTIAL AMINO ACIDS IN F I PROTEIN FROM TOBACCO, SOME MAJOR CROP PROTEINS, AND MILK AND EGG PROTEINS (EXPRESSED AS G AMINO ACID PER 100 G RECOVERED AMINO ACID)

Amino Acid	F I Protein	Soybean[1]	Rice[2]	Wheat[2]	Corn[2]	Egg[2]	Milk Human[3]	Milk Cow
Isoleucine	4.5	5.8	5.2	4.0	6.4	6.8	6.4	6.4
Leucine	8.9	7.6	8.2	7.0	15.0	9.0	8.9	9.9
Lysine	6.0	6.6	3.2	2.7	2.3	6.3	6.3	7.8
Methionine	1.2	1.1	3.0	2.5	3.1	3.1	2.2	2.[illegible]
Phenylalanine	4.1	4.8	5.0	5.1	5.0	6.0	4.6	4.[illegible]
Threonine	5.2	3.9	3.8	3.3	3.7	5.0	4.6	4.[illegible]
Tryptophan	1.5	1.2	1.3	1.2	0.6	1.7	1.6	1.[illegible]
Tyrosine	4.4	3.2	5.7	4.0	6.0	4.4	5.5	5.[illegible]
Valine	8.0	5.2	6.2	4.3	5.3	7.4	6.6	6.[illegible]

[1] Source: Block and Weiss (1956).
[2] Source: Block and Bolling (1951).
[3] Source: Food Agric. Organ. U.N. (1957).

The total content of soluble leaf protein decreases with senescence. It is estimated that mature tobacco leaves contain about 3 to 4 mg of F I protein per g of fresh weight. An equal or greater amount of F II protein should also be present. Even if only 60% of all soluble proteins could be recovered during HLC processing of one year's production of tobacco, enough protein would be obtained to feed many millions for one year, based on the FAO recommended protein need. Table 4.6 shows the projected yields of F I and F II protein as by-products of tobacco production in the years 1985 and 2000. The figures are based not on any expected increase in world tobacco hectarage, but on the expected increase in the efficiency of tobacco production. From tobacco alone, enough proteins could be obtained as by-products to meet the protein need of more than 32 million people by the year 2000 (Tso 1977).

TABLE 4.6. PROJECTED YIELDS OF F I AND F II PROTEINS AS BY-PRODUCTS FROM TOBACCO

	Year 1985	Year 2000
Tobacco yields (lb)	12.5×10^9	20.0×10^9
Extractable protein yields (lb)		
Fraction I protein	3×10^8	4.8×10^8
unfractionated proteins	3×10^8	4.8×10^8
total	6×10^8	9.6×10^8
Protein food value for human need[1]		
(no. of people)	20.4×10^6	32.6×10^6

[1] 36.6 g/person/day (FAO).

The idea of using crystalline F I protein and other soluble proteins as by-products of the HLC process thus has great potential (Tso 1977), and the potential can be further strengthened by the availability of a simple large-scale crystallization procedure for producing pure tobacco F I protein.

SUMMARY

Soluble proteins in tobacco have high nutritive value and are easy to purify for human food, animal feed, and other beneficial use. Even without further increase in tobacco growing area, the soluble proteins recovered as a by-product from a year's crop of tobacco should provide a year's supply of protein for 32 million people by the year 2000. The added advantage of extracting tobacco proteins is that a much safer smoking product would result, because proteins may serve as precursors of many undesirable smoke components.

REFERENCES

BAHR, J.T., BOURQUE, D.P. and SMITH, H.J. 1977. Solubility properties of fraction 1 protein of maize, cotton, spinach and tobacco. J. Agric. Food Chem. *25*, 783.

BAKER, T.S., EISENBERG, D., EISERLING, I.A. and WEISSMAN, L. 1975. The structure of form 1 crystals of RuDP carboxylase. J. Mol. Biol. *91*, 391–399.

BLOCK, R.J. and BOLLING, D. 1951. Amino Acid Composition of Proteins and Foods, 2nd Edition. Charles C. Thomas, Springfield, IL.

BLOCK, R.J. and WEISS, K.W. 1956. Amino Acid Handbook. Charles C. Thomas, Springfield, IL.

BYERS, M. 1971. The amino acid composition of some soluble protein preparations. *In* Leaf Protein: Its Agronomy, Preparation, Quality and Use. N.W. Pirie (Editor). IBP Handb. *20*. Blackwell, Oxford.

CHAN, P.H. and WILDMAN, S.G. 1972. Chloroplast DNA codes for the primary structure of the large subunit of fraction 1 protein. Biochim. Biophys. Acta *277*, 677–680.

CHEN, K., KUNG, S.D., GRAY, J.C. and WILDMAN, S.G. 1975. Polypeptide composition of fraction 1 protein from *Nicotiana glauca* and from cultivars of *Nicotiana tabacum*, including a male sterile line. Biochem. Genet. *13*, 11–12.

CHEN, K., KUNG, S.D., GRAY, J.G. and WILDMAN, S.G. 1976. Subunit polypeptide composition of fraction 1 protein from various plant species. Plant Sci. Lett. 7, 429–434.

CHOLLET, R., ANDERSON, L.L. and HOVSEPIAN, L.C. 1975. The absence of tightly bonded copper, iron and flavin nucleotide in crystalline ribulose-1, 5-biphosphate carboxylase oxygenase from tobacco. Biochem. Biophys. Res. Commun. *64*, 97.

CHUA, N.H., SCHMIDT, G.W., and MALTIN, K.S. 1978. *In Vitro* Synthesis of Transport and Assembly of RuBPCase Subunits in Photosynthetic Carbon Assimilation. H.W. Siegelman and G. Hind (Editors). Plenum Publishing Corp., New York.

DeJONG, D.W. and LAM, J.J., JR. 1977. Protein content of tobacco. *In* Proc. Am. Chem. Soc. Symp. Recent Advances in the Chemical Composition of Tobacco and Tobacco Smoke. J.L. McKenzie (Editor). 173rd Am. Chem. Soc. Meet., Agric. Food Chem. Div., 1977, New Orleans.

DONG, M., SCHMELTZ, I., JACOBS, E. and HOFFMANN, D. 1978. Aza-arenes in tobacco smoke. J. Anal. Toxicol. *2*, 21–25.

ELLIS, R.J. 1975. Inhibition of chloroplast protein synthesis by lincomycin and MDMP. Phytochemistry *14*, 89–93.

ERSHOFF, B.H., WILDMAN, S.G. and KWANYUEN, P. 1978. Biological evaluation of crystalline fraction-1-protein from tobacco. Proc. Soc. Exp. Biol. Med. *157*, 626–630.

FOOD AGRIC. ORGAN. U.N. 1957. Protein Requirements. FAO Nutr. Stud. *16*. Food Agric. Organ. U.N., Rome.

GOODING, L.R., ROY, H. and JAGENDORF, A.T. 1973. Immunological identification of nascent subunits of wheat RuDP carboxylase on ribosomes of both chloroplast and cytoplasmic origin. Arch. Biochem. Biophys. *159*, 324–355.

GRAY, J.C. and KEKWICK, R.G.O. 1974. The synthesis of the small subunit of RuDP carboxylase in the French bean *Phaseolus vulgaris*. Eur. J. Biochem. *44*, 491–500.

GRAY, J.C., KUNG, S.D. and WILDMAN, S.G. 1978. Polypeptide chains of the large and small subunits of fraction 1 protein from tobacco. Arch. Biochem. Biophys. *185*, 272–281.

GRAY, J.C., KUNG, S.D., WILDMAN, S.G. and SHEEN, S.J. 1974. Origin of *Nicotiana tabacum* L. detected by polypeptide composition of fraction I protein. Nature *252*, 226–227.

HIRAI, A. 1977. Random assembly of different kinds of small subunit polypeptides during formation of fraction 1 protein macromolecules. Proc. Natl. Acad. Sci. U.S.A. *74*, 3443–3445.

JENSEN, R.G. and BAHR, J.T. 1977. Ribulose 1,5-biphosphate carboxylase-oxygenase. Annu. Rev. Plant Physiol. *28*, 379–400.

KAWASHIMA, N., KWOK, S.Y. and WILDMAN, S.G. 1971. Studies on fraction 1 protein. III. Comparison of the primary structure of the large and small subunits obtained from five species of *Nicotiana*. Biochim. Biophys. Acta *236*, 578.

KAWASHIMA, N. and WILDMAN, S.G. 1970. Fraction 1 protein. Annu. Rev. Plant Physiol. *21*, 325–358.

KAWASHIMA, N. and WILDMAN, S.G. 1972. Studies on fraction 1 protein. IV. Model of inheritance of primary structure in relation to whether chloroplast or nuclear DNA contains the code for a chloroplast protein. Biochim. Biophys. Acta *262*, 42–49.

KUNG, S.D. 1976. Tobacco fraction 1 protein—A unique genetic marker. Science *191*, 429–434.

KUNG, S.D. 1977. Expression of chloroplast genomes in higher plants. Annu. Rev. Plant Physiol. *28*, 401–437.

KUNG, S.D., CHOLETT, R. and MARSHO, T.V. 1978. Crystallization and assay procedures of ribulose-1,5-biphosphate carboxylase-oxygenase. Methods Enzymol. *69*, 326–336.

KUNG, S.D., LEE, C.I., WOOD, D.D. and MOSCARELLO, M.A. 1977. Evolutionary conservation of chloroplast genes coding for the large subunits of fraction 1 protein. Plant Physiol. *60*, 89.

KUNG, S.D. and RHODES, P. 1978. Interaction of Chloroplast and Nuclear Genomes in Regulating RuBPCase Activity in Photosynthetic Carbon Assimilation. H.W. Siegelman and G. Hind (Editors). Plenum Publishing Corp., New York.

KUNG, S.D., SAKANO, K., GRAY, J.C. and WILDMAN, S.G. 1975. The evolution of fraction 1 protein during the origin of the new species of *Nicotiana*. J. Mol. Evol. 7, 59–64.

KUNG, S.D., SAKANO, K. and WILDMAN, S.G. 1974. Detection of multiple peptide composition of the large and small subunit structure of *Nicotiana tabacum* fraction 1 protein by finger-printing and electrofocusing. Biochim. Biophys. Acta *366*, 138–143.

KUNG, S.D., SAUNDERS, J.A., TSO, T.C., VAUGHN, D.A., WOMACK, M., STAPLES, R.C. and BEECHER, G.R. 1980. Tobacco as a potential food source and smoke material: Nutritional evaluation of tobacco leaf protein. J. Food Sci. *45*, 320–322.

KUNG, S.D. and TSO, T.C. 1978. Tobacco as a potential food source and smoke material. II. Soluble protein content, extraction, and amino acid composition. J. Food Sci. *43*, 1844–1848.

KWOK, W.Y., KAWASHIMA, N. and WILDMAN, S.G. 1971. Specific effect of ribulose-1,5-biphosphate on the solubility of tobacco fraction 1 protein. Biochim. Biophys. Acta *234*, 293.

LINK, G.L., BOGSRAD, L., BEDBROOK, J.R., COLN, D.M. and RICH, A. 1978. The Expression of the Gene for the Large Subunit of RuBPCase in Maize in Photosynthetic Carbon Assimilation. H.W. Siegelman and G. Hind (Editors). Plenum Publishing Corp., New York.

LOWE, R.H. 1977. Crystallization of fraction I protein from tobacco by a simplified procedure. FEBS Lett. *78*, 98–100.

LYTTLETON, J.W. and TS'O, P.O.P. 1958. The localization of fraction 1 protein of green leaves in the chloroplasts. Arch. Biochem. Biophys. *73*, 120.

MARSHO, T.V. and KUNG, S.D. 1976. Oxygenase activity in crystallized fraction 1 protein from tobacco. Arch. Biochem. Biophys. *173*, 341–346.

NISHIMURA, M. and AKAZAWA, T. 1974. Studies on spinach leaf RuDP carboxylase. Biochemistry *13*, 2277–2281.

ROBINSON, A.B. and RUDD, C.J. 1974. Deamidation of glutaminyl and asparaginyl residues in peptides and proteins. Curr. Top. Cell. Regul. *8*, 247–295.

SAKANO, K., KUNG, S.D. and WILDMAN, S.G. 1974A. Change in solubility of crystalline fraction 1 protein correlated with change in the composition of the small subunit. Plant Cell Physiol. *15*, 611.

SAKANO, K., KUNG, S.D. and WILDMAN, S.G. 1974B. Identification of several chloroplast DNA genes which code for the large subunit of *Nicotiana* fraction 1 protein, Mol. Gen. Genet. *130*, 91–99.

STROBACK, S., GIBBONS, G.C., HASLETT, B. and WILDMAN, S.G. 1976. On the nature of the polymorphism of the small subunit of RuBPcase in the amphidiploid *Nicotiana tabacum*. Carlsberg Res. Comm. *41*, 335–339.

SUGIMURA, T. 1978. an interview with Sugimura by S. Fox. Chem. Eng. News *56* (1) 24.

TSO, T.C. 1977. Tobacco as a potential food source and smoke material. Beitr. Tabakforsch. *9*, 63–66.

TSO, T.C. and GORI, G.B. 1975. Leaf quality and usability: Theoretical model I. *In* Proc. Symp. Chemical Requirements of the Tobacco Industry. Div. Chem. Market. Econ., Am. Chem. Soc. Meet., 1975, Philadelphia.

TSO, T.C., LOWE, R.H. and DeJONG, D.W. 1975. Homogenized leaf curing. I. Theoretical basis and preliminary results. Beitr. Tabakforsch. *8*, 44–51.

WILDMAN, S.G. and BONNER, J. 1947. The proteins of green leaves. I. Isolation, enzymatic properties and auxin content of spinach cytoplasmic proteins. Arch. Biochem. *14*, 381–413.

ZELITCH, I. 1973. Plant productivity and control of photorespiration. Proc. Natl. Acad. Sci. *70*, 579–584.

Part II

Chemistry and Nutrition of LPC

5

Extracted Leaf Proteins: Their Amino Acid Composition and Nutritional Quality

Marjorie Byers

Great confusion has been created in the literature by the indiscriminate use of the term "leaf protein" to describe both the "protein" in the whole leaf calculated from its total N content, e.g., Rogers (1959), and the lipoprotein complex which can be extracted from it. Most agriculturists and many agricultural chemists still define the protein content of a leaf by multiplying its total N content by a factor, usually 6.25.[1] This so-called "crude protein content" is very crude indeed, including as it does all inorganic N and that proportion of the organic N not present as protein, i.e., the amides and amino acids comprising the free amino acid pool, amines, alkaloids, etc. (see Fig. 5.1). The situation is further exacerbated by some authors who incorrectly refer to the amino acid composition of leaf protein when what they are really discussing is the amino acid profile (or more usually the partial profile) of the whole leaf, which is not the same thing at all (Rogers and Milner 1963; Beaton 1966). This difference in definition accounts for what appears to be conflicting reports about induced changes in the amino acid composition of "leaf protein."

[1] The traditional factor of 6.25 for converting N to protein was based on the early assumption that all purified proteins contained 16% N, but Pirie (1955), using data of Chibnall, argued that a factor of 6.0 was probably more accurate for plant material. Factors for converting the N content of cereal grains to protein (all at < 6.0) have subsequently been established, but the correct factor(s) to apply to extracted leaf protein complexes have not been calculated. For practical purposes, when dealing with raw material, or crude products containing little protein, it makes little difference which factor is used, but once a relatively pure preparation is obtained, errors could arise from the use of an incorrect value.

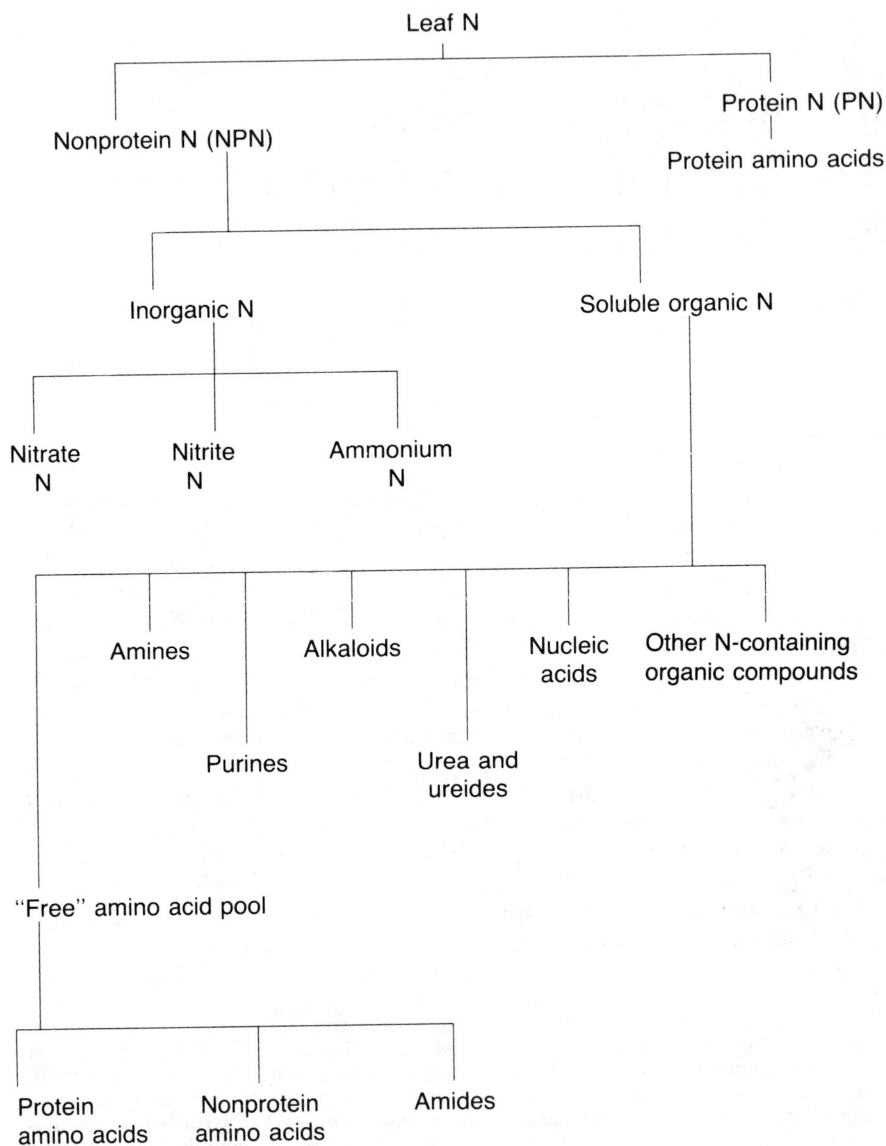

Fig. 5.1. Distribution of N in the leaf.

AMINO ACIDS AND PROTEINS IN LEAVES

Distribution of Amino Acids

Both protein and nonprotein amino acids are present in leaves. Protein amino acids occur not only in the bound state in leaf proteins but are also found, free, in the soluble nonprotein N (NPN) fraction. Collectively the "free" amino acids, both protein and nonprotein, and the amides comprise the free amino acid pool which, in turn, forms part of the soluble organic N fraction (Fig. 5.1).

Of the nonprotein amino acids and simple peptides, of which more than 200 have now been isolated from plants (Fowden *et al.* 1979), some are specific to a particular species or genus, e.g., homoserine in young pea plants; the occurrence of others is universal, e.g., 4-aminobutyric acid, which can sometimes account for as much as half the total free amino acid content in a leaf extract. A few others are produced in measurable amounts only when the plant is under stress.

To obtain a complete amino acid spectrum of a leaf, the nonprotein acids and amides must be included in any analysis. Published results which omit these have only a limited value and can sometimes mislead the unwary. For example, if the amount of an amino acid is expressed as a percentage of only those determined, a thoroughly inaccurate impression about leaf amino acid composition and content is obtained.

Distribution of N

The total N (TN) content of a leaf, and the distribution of N within it, varies according to the physiological state of the plant, which itself is governed by age, nutritional status, and other stresses induced by environmental conditions or disease. For example, as the leaf matures, the TN content decreases as N is transported away from the leaf, and the proportion of N present as protein N (PN) decreases because soluble amino acids, consisting mainly of amides, are being catabolically derived from protein in the senescing leaves.

Application of nitrogen fertilizer can also produce an increase in the proportion of NPN due to the accumulation of nitrate. In one reported experiment with sugar beet, nitrate-N accounted for 88 and 38% of the total N content of the petioles and blades, respectively (Lorenz 1978). Other plants showed a similar, although less spectacular, response.

Plants suffering nutritional stress also have more NPN than is usual because N in excess of that used for protein synthesis is stored usually as asparagine and/or glutamine, although amines are also produced (Smith 1975). There are also several specific responses to other forms of stress which take the form of the appearance of, or a large increase in, one individual amino acid in the free state, e.g., β-alanine, which is symptomatic of K-deficiency (Nowakowski and Byers 1972) or the accumulation of proline in water-stressed plants (Singh *et al.* 1973). Methylated quaternary ammonium compounds such as glycine betaine appear in many species when grown under saline conditions (Stewart and Lahrer 1979).

The Proteins in Leaves

The protein in leaves, unlike that of the seed storage proteins, consists largely of enzymes, the main exception to this being the structural protein of the cell. The two main groups of soluble proteins, known as Fractions I and II (F I and F II), are usually classified on the basis of their MW (molecular weight) range, isoelectric points, or by their sedimentation constants.

Fraction I protein, the main component of which is ribulose-1,5-bisphosphate carboxylase (RuBP carboxylase) (EC 4.1.1.39), the carboxylation enzyme of photosynthesis, is the major soluble protein of the chloroplast, and can account for up to 50% of the protein found in a leaf extract. All RuBP carboxylase preparations, irrespective of the species of leaf from which they were made, have a MW of between 500,000 and 600,000 daltons, a sedimentation constant of around 18S, and a similar amino acid composition. RuBP carboxylase consists of one large and one small subunit, which are thought to be synthesized in the chloroplast and cytoplasm, respectively (Cashmore 1976). Their MW's are around 55,000 and 12,000 daltons, respectively, and they have different amino acid compositions (Seigel *et al.* 1972; Jones and Mangan 1976; Jensen and Bahr 1977; Bahr *et al.* 1977). As with RuBP carboxylase itself, the large subunit from different species is homologous, but there is considerable variation in the amino acid composition between the small subunits from different species (Seigel *et al.* 1972; Jensen and Bahr 1977). While RuBP carboxylase is the major component in all Fraction I proteins, additional polypeptides have been found in preparations made from C_4 plants, which fix CO_2 via the dicarboxylic acid pathway. These latter polypeptides, which are thermolabile, have been tentatively identified as coming from phosphoenolpyruvate carboxylase (EC 4.1.1.31), which occurs primarily in C_4 plants (Bahr *et al.* 1977).

Fraction II protein, which consists of a mixture of proteins originating from the chloroplasts and the cytoplasm, ranges in MW from 10,000 to 300,000 daltons and has a sedimentation constant of from 4S to 10S (Jones and Mangan 1976). A preparation from tobacco leaves was found to have a much higher lysine content than the corresponding Fraction I protein (Knuckles *et al.* 1979). Fraction II protein can be subdivided into a high MW fraction, consisting of two major components, and a low MW fraction consisting of many proteins. The sedimentation constant of these two fractions from alfalfa averaged 6.8 and 3.8, respectively (Sarkar *et al.* 1975).

Amino Acid Composition and Taxonomic Classification

Because the ratio of PN:NPN in the leaf and the distribution of N within the NPN fraction vary, neither leaf amino acid composition nor content is constant. It is, therefore, illogical to try to correlate the total amino acid profile of a leaf with its taxonomic classification in the fashion attempted by Watson and Creaser (1975). A chemotaxonomic classification based on the occurrence of specific nonprotein amino acids is possible with many seeds and some vegetative tissue (Fowden *et al.* 1979), but some amino acids previously thought to be restricted to one genus or species are now known to be more widespread, e.g., azetidine-2-carboxylic acid is not found solely in the Liliaceae.

In theory, there is a valid argument for trying to correlate taxonomic characteristics with the amino acid composition of the protein fraction because this does not appear to be influenced by age or environmental conditions (Gerloff *et al.* 1965; Kawashima and Tamaki 1967; Byers 1971A, B; Bolton *et al.* 1976). However, because of the preponderance of RuBP carboxylase in extracted leaf proteins, no great variation in amino acid composition would be expected. Nevertheless, small differences between proteins extracted from different species, and between fractions from the same species, have been found, but only after an elaborate statistical analysis (Byers 1971A; Pirie 1978).

The distribution of amino acids within a leaf is relevant to the work on extracted leaf protein because it is often stated that the leaf protein composition changes with age, or with the nutritional status of the plant (Coïc *et al.* 1962; Beaton 1966; Garcha *et al.* 1970A; Stabursvik and Heide 1974). However, if such papers are read thoroughly, it becomes apparent that most authors are referring to changes in the amino acid composition of the whole leaf and not of the protein fraction. This is not always apparent from the summaries or table headings, and abstracts based on these only perpetuate this erroneous impression. Therefore, it is always advisable to check definitions of "leaf protein" before quoting results, and to compare like with like. Also, make sure your own definition is correct.

WHY EXTRACT THE PROTEIN FROM LEAVES?

Some Nutritional Considerations with Regard to Leaves, Leaf Extracts, and Extracted Leaf Protein

Views are divided as to the merits of extracting leaf protein. At one extreme are those who advocate just eating more leaves; opposing them are those who regard extracted leaf protein as a major potential contributor to protein-deficient diets, especially in tropical areas with a high rainfall, where vegetation is dense. Personal preferences apart, there are technical aspects to consider.

Nutritionally, only herbivores are able to extract the maximum benefit from leaves because nonruminants lack the mechanism necessary for rupturing plant cell walls and thus releasing the protein. Nevertheless, leaves are valuable in the human diet as a source of those protein amino acids present in the free state, mineral salts, and some vitamins (or their precursors), as well as providing necessary roughage. Their consumption, therefore, should be encouraged (Pirie 1975). The eating of leaves is, however, governed by social and economic factors, and in many of the developing countries, consumption drops as the inhabitants turn toward a more sophisticated (usually western-style) diet. Their consumption can rise in times of shortage, but some species are considered edible only in times of famine. In addition, many species of leaves, of which there are some 250,000–300,000 (Princen 1977), cannot be eaten at all, or at best, sparingly, because they contain undesirable components, e.g., alkaloids, certain phenolics (Singleton and Kratzer 1969), or nonprotein amino acids (Hylin 1969; Fowden *et al.* 1979), saponins (Livingston *et al.* 1979), estrogens (Glencross *et al.* 1972), cyanogenetic glycosides (Conn 1969), or growth depressants (Peterson 1950). Clinically, consumption is limited by the amount of roughage the human gut can cope with.

Fibrous matter, i.e., potential roughage, can usually be separated from the other components by macerating the leaf and squeezing the resultant pulp. Only a few species, usually those containing a large amount of mucilage, or having an extremely high fiber content, cannot be handled this way. The direct use of these protein-rich extracts in nonruminant diets was advocated by Hartman *et al.* (1967), but Pirie (1969) objected to this because undesirable components might still be present in the NPN fraction. Whole leaf extracts have subsequently been fed to pigs, with some success (Houseman and Connell 1976; Braude *et al.* 1977; Mansfield and Connell 1977), although there were some anomalous results. Precipitating the extracted protein offers the dual advantage of concentrating it and, providing it is well washed, freeing it from soluble contaminants.

EXTRACTED LEAF PROTEIN

Some Compositional Considerations

Before discussing the amino acid profile of extracted leaf proteins, some comment about the overall composition of these precipitated complexes is necessary. The detailed composition of some components other than protein is discussed elsewhere in this book, but because as groups they can influence the availability of the nutritionally essential amino acids, and hence the nutritive value of preparations, they should also be considered in relation to protein and amino acid content and composition. For a comprehensive discussion of leaf protein composition, see Pirie (1978).

The relative proportions of the major components of preparations made from unfractionated leaf extracts, i.e., protein, lipid, and carbohydrate, depend upon the method of precipitation. Heat (preferably by injection of steam rather than a slow raising of the temperature), addition of acids or solvents, and flocculation with salts have all been used. More sophisticated methods of separating the protein from extracts, such as ultrafiltration, ion exchange, or gel chromatography, have been used in the laboratory, but are unsuited to large-scale preparative work. All these techniques can also be used with fractionated leaf extracts, but it follows that the composition of the final product is influenced by the initial fractionation procedure as well as by the method used to coagulate the protein.

Composition of Unfractionated Leaf Proteins

Definition. Unfractionated leaf protein is defined here as the complex precipitated from a leaf extract which has not been subject to any fractionation procedure other than filtration through a coarse sieve to remove any stray fiber and cell debris.

Heat-, Acid-, and Salt-precipitated Preparations. A typical complex precipitated from a leaf extract by any of these methods is dark green and contains (on a dry matter basis) from 50 to 65% protein (calculated as N × 6.0), from 15 to 30% lipids and other substances soluble in organic solvents, e.g., chlorophylls and carotenoids, and around 5% ash. The difference between the sum of these three components and 100% is usually classified as % carbohydrate, but it is probably more accurate to call this portion "unaccounted for, but including carbohydrate" (Byers 1971A).

There can be exceptions to the 5–10% "carbohydrate" usually found. The extract obtained from pea vines, processed after removal of the seeds, contains large amounts of starch which quickly deposits itself as a white sediment (Pirie 1978). If this is not removed (most conveniently by low-speed centrifugation), the "carbohydrate" content of the protein subsequently precipitated will be much higher than usual. The starch in this instance came from the mature (empty) pods and not the leaves, and illustrates one of the problems which can arise from using by-product materials.

Acid-precipitated preparations usually have a greater N content than the corresponding heat-coagulated proteins made from the same extract (Table 5.1) because nucleic acids are co-precipitated with the protein when a leaf extract is acidified (Singh 1960).

TABLE 5.1. THE EFFECT OF METHOD OF PRECIPITATION ON THE GROSS COMPOSITION OF UNFRACTIONATED LEAF PROTEIN (LPC)

Leaf	Method of Precipitation	Composition of LPC (as % of DM) Protein[1]	Lipid[2]	Ash	Reference
Barley	Heat (80°C)	58.7	23.0	5.7	Byers (1971A)
	Acid (TCA)	63.3	23.0	3.6	
Alfalfa	Heat (75°C)	72.1	14.5	6.1	Huang *et al.* (1971)
	Acetone	59.0	1.8	16.6	
	Ethanol	65.0	1.0	17.5	

[1]Protein calculated as either N × 6.25 or N × 6.0.
[2]Lipid extracted with 2:1 (v/v) chloroform:methanol.

Fractionation of proteins by ammonium sulfate flocculation is one of the oldest separation techniques in biochemistry, but for practical reasons has not been used for large-scale preparative work. Experiments at Rothamsted (unpublished) using various salts, including ammonium sulfate and calcium chloride, to precipitate protein from whole leaf extracts showed that, in comparison with the heat-coagulated product, the flocculated proteins contained much less N and yields were smaller. Recently, Bray and Humphries (1979) reported the yields (though not the protein content) of precipitated material obtained by adding various flocculating agents to leaf extracts. The polyanionic flocculant Superfloc A150, which gave the largest yields, was subsequently used to develop a fractionation procedure.

The amounts of lipid extractable from complexes precipitated by these methods varies. It depends not only on the species of leaf from which the protein was extracted (Byers 1961), but also on the subsequent treatment of the extracted protein and on the solvent-mixtures used for lipid extraction (Lima *et al.* 1965; Byers 1967; Buchanan 1969A,B). There have been some exceedingly low "crude fat" contents published which, if used in the formula given earlier to calculate "carbohydrate" content, give erroneous results. It is too often assumed that all fat is extracted by diethyl ether (AOAC 1970), whereas a judicious mixture of polar solvents is required. Further, if the extracted protein is dried at temperatures exceeding 60°C, there is a decrease in the amount of lipid extractable (Buchanan 1969A,B). Therefore, only freshly made moist preparations, or samples which have been air-dried (below 60°C) or lyophilized, should be used for analytical purposes.

Solvent-precipitated Preparations. Although organic solvents have been used to remove lipids and associated pigments from extracted leaf protein, their use as precipitating agents, except in laboratory-scale experiments, has been limited because of their cost. They have been used mainly to precipitate protein fractions; nevertheless, acetone (Huang *et al.* 1971; Brown *et al.* 1975) and ethanol (Huang *et al.* 1971) have been used to precipitate the protein from whole leaf extracts.

The composition of some of these solvent-precipitated proteins can be compared with that of the corresponding heat-coagulated preparations in Table 5.1. The texture of these solvent-precipitated proteins was superior to that of the heat-coagulated products, and they had a greater dispersibility in water (Tao *et al.* 1972). Accounts of experiments in New Zealand using organic solvents were reported at a workshop held there (Hove and Bailey 1975; Wallace 1975): the best-textured product was made by pretreating the leaf extract with butan-1-ol and then adding an excess of propan-2-ol.

These solvent-precipitated unfractionated proteins are never entirely colorless, and the buff or light-brown products are similar in appearance to those obtained by solvent extraction of heat- or acid-precipitated preparations.

Solvent Extraction of the Unfractionated Protein. To some the green color of the unfractionated heat- or acid-coagulated protein is an obstacle to its acceptance in the human diet and several methods have been proposed to arrive at a white or neutral-colored product. In theory, solvent extraction of the unfractionated product, simultaneously removing lipids and pigments, seemed an attractive proposition since protein content would also be enhanced. Early experiments at Rothamsted, and elsewhere, were discouraging. The end products were seldom free from color (ranging from light green to brown depending on the solvent system used) and often had a gritty texture. Wallace (1975) found that most chlorophyll was removed by 2:1 (v/v) chloroform:methanol but that a paler-colored product was obtained by sequentially extracting with butan-1-ol and then propan-2-ol (cf. solvent-precipitated proteins). In a recent series of experiments designed to test the color and texture of solvent-extracted proteins, Bray *et al.* (1978) found that the best results were obtained by propan-1-ol or butan-1-ol.

To summarize: Although products of good texture and color can now be made, it would be premature to advocate solvent extraction as a routine procedure. Organic solvents are expensive and not always recoverable, and not enough is known about the *in vivo* nutritional behaviors of such preparations.

Ash Content of Unfractionated Proteins. An International Biological Programme (IBP) Technical Group suggested maximum ash content of 3% (on a dry matter basis) if the product was for human consumption (Pirie 1971), but experience has shown that very few large-scale preparations of unfractionated protein meet this requirement. Preparations made from very young leaves, especially those from cereal crops, usually fall within the proposed limit, but those from most other crops exceed it.

The main source of ash is in the dust or mud adhering to the harvested crop, much of which can be removed if the crop is thoroughly washed before pulping. A less obvious source of ash is the high silica content of some species. Pirie (1978) is of the opinion that silica is probably a harmless constituent of leaf protein, but there is some evidence to the contrary. Subba Rau *et al.* (1972) reported that carrot leaf protein made from unwashed foliage was much less digestible than that made from (the same batch) of washed leaves: the ash contents of these two preparations were 20.0 and 11.6%, respectively. Omole *et al.* (1976) in discussing these results thought the failure of the protein made from the unwashed leaves to support growth (the rats went into negative nitrogen balance) might be due to a toxic component in the leaves. This was subsequently disproved by their own experiments when rats fed whole carrot leaves grew well. While it has not been positively proved that a high ash content *per se* is responsible for poor digestibility in rats it must, nevertheless, remain suspect. The most sensible course on obtaining an otherwise acceptable preparation (but with a high ash content) is to follow Pirie's advice (1978) and find out whether it is due to bad preparative technique or the species used.

Composition of Fractionated Leaf Proteins

Because of the early discouraging results in trying to produce a colorless product by solvent extraction, attention was turned to methods of separating the pigmented material from leaf extracts, leaving the protein not associated with the chloroplasts in solution. The fractionation of leaf extracts is not a new concept. Rouelle in 1773 used controlled heating to make two fractions [for a review of this and associated papers, see Osborne (1921), and for a translation of the 1773 paper, see Pirie (1971, 1978)].

Until recently, there have been different approaches to the separation of proteins from leaf extracts. Those interested in isolating and characterizing individual proteins and polypeptides employed different criteria and techniques from those whose aim was the large-scale production of a protein-rich concentrate of high nutritive value. In the leaf protein field, the term "chloroplastic" was originally used to describe that fraction containing the pigmented material; others at a later date have used the term "green" protein. The protein precipitable from the pigment-free (but not necessarily thylakoid-free) extracts has been variously called "cytoplasmic" or "white" protein.

The terms "chloroplastic" and "cytoplasmic" were in general use long before modern methods of protein separation and identification were introduced. It has been suggested that these names should no longer be used (Bickoff *et al.* 1975), but Nagy *et al.* (1978) have proposed their retention on practical grounds. However, whatever terminology is adopted in the future, it must be remembered that the names are descriptive of crude fractions, and do not imply proteins of definitive composition.

Chloroplastic Proteins. These have been separated by:

(1) Controlled heating of a leaf extract to between 45° and 60°C; the exact temperature of precipitation varies with species (Byers 1965, 1971A; Subba Rau *et al.* 1969, Lexander *et al.* 1970; de Fremery *et al.* 1973; Edwards *et al.* 1975; Nagy *et al.* 1978)
(2) Centrifuging the untreated extract (Wilson and Tilley 1965; Smith 1966; Byers 1971A; Bickoff *et al.* 1975) and then solvent-extracting the precipitate (Horigome 1977)
(3) Adding organic solvents (Slade *et al.* 1945; Hove and Bailey 1975; Wallace 1975; Bray and Humphries 1978)
(4) Flocculating with salts or other flocculating agents (Bray and Humphries 1979)

Cytoplasmic Proteins. These have been precipitated from pigment-free extracts by:

(1) Heating to around 80°C (Byers 1965, 1971A; Subba Rau *et al.* 1969; Lexander *et al.* 1970; Edwards *et al.* 1975; Hove and Bailey 1975)
(2) Acidification (Yemm and Folkes 1953; Byers 1971A; Hove and Bailey

1975; Miller *et al.* 1975; Bray and Humphries 1978, 1979) and then solvent-extracting the precipitate (Horigome 1977)

(3) Adding organic solvents (Wilson and Tilley 1965; Nagy *et al.* 1978)

(4) Concentrating the extract by ultrafiltration, then heating or acidifying it (Knuckles *et al.* 1975)

Nagy *et al.* (1978) gave flow diagrams for some of the various permutations that have been used to produce these fractions. The proportion of chloroplastic:cytoplasmic protein produced is an important consideration if a process is to be developed commercially, but this aspect is outside the scope of this chapter.

Overall Composition of Fractionated Proteins. Some figures relating to the composition of proteins made by different methods, and from different species, are shown in Table 5.2. Least protein is found in the chloroplastic fractions, which contain much more lipid and ash than the other preparations. Conversely, the cytoplasmic fractions have the highest protein content and only about 5% each of lipid and hydrolyzable carbohydrate, and < 1% ash. More analytical data on fractionated proteins can be found in papers by Subba Rau *et al.* (1969), Byers (1971A), Bickoff *et al.* (1975), Edwards *et al.* (1975), Knuckles *et al.* (1975), Miller *et al.* (1975), and Pirie (1978).

AMINO ACID COMPOSITION OF EXTRACTED LEAF PROTEINS

Analytical Problems

The problems of comparing results obtained by different methods of analysis, using hydrolysates which themselves have been prepared by different techniques, have been discussed in an earlier review (Byers 1971B). The comments made then are still valid. It is also inevitable, given the wide choice available, that results are still being expressed in many different ways, hence the need for care when interpreting, or making a comparison with, other published values. The difference this can make, especially to basic amino acid content, is illustrated in Table 5.3, where the analysis on one sample is presented in five ways.

The results obtained in recent years using modern methods of amino acid analysis confirmed earlier observations that there was a similarity in composition between various protein fractions extracted from a leaf and between preparations made from different species. This can be seen in Table 5.4, which gives the total amino acid composition (tryptophan excepted) of some proteins made from whole and fractionated extracts of barley and lupine leaves. However, although similar, the composition of the various preparations is not identical, and the question arises as to how to distinguish between those differences which, however small, are real and those differences which stem from imperfect analytical techniques.

TABLE 5.2. THE GROSS COMPOSITION OF SOME FRACTIONATED LEAF PROTEINS PREPARED BY DIFFERENT METHODS

Leaf	Fraction	Composition as % of Dry Matter				Reference
		Protein[1]	Lipid[2]	Ash	Other	
Alfalfa	Pro-Xan II (green LPC)	47.2	13.7	16.0	4.1[3]	Bickoff *et al.* (1975)
	Welpro (white LPC)	88.7	<0.5	<0.5	<0.5[3]	Edwards *et al.* (1975)
Alfalfa	Chloroplast-free extract precipitated at					
	pH 3.5	73.8	ND	<1.0		Miller et al. (1975)
	4.0	79.4	ND	<1.0		
	4.5	85.0	ND	<1.0		
Barley	1600 *g* sediment	44.9	34.6	8.3	12.2[4]	Byers (1971A)
	1600 *g* supernatant } TCA-pptd	79.1	9.4	0.8	10.7[4]	
	50,000 *g* supernatant } TCA-pptd	86.9	5.5	<0.1	1.8[5]	
Lupine	70 *g* sediment	40.3	35.2	2.8	21.7[4]	Byers (1971A)
	43°C precipitate	40.9	30.6	3.0	25.6[4]	
	50,000 *g* supernatant } TCA-pptd	87.8	ND	<0.1	1.8[5]	
	43°C supernatant } TCA-pptd	86.9	7.6	<0.1	1.3[5]	

[1] Protein calculated as either N × 6.0 or N × 6.25.
[2] Lipid extracted by ether (alfalfa) or 2:1 (v/v) chloroform:methanol (barley and lupine).
[3] Fiber content.
[4] Carbohydrate and unaccounted for.
[5] Acid-hydrolyzable carbohydrate.
ND—Not determined.

TABLE 5.3. THE AMINO ACID COMPOSITION (EXCLUDING TRYPTOPHAN BUT INCLUDING AMMONIA) OF AN UNFRACTIONATED WHEAT LEAF PROTEIN CONCENTRATE (LPC) EXPRESSED IN FIVE DIFFERENT WAYS

N as % of DM on sample = 9.60; protein content (N × 6.0) = 57.6.

Amino Acid	g Amino Acid Residue per 100 g LPC	g Amino Acid per 100 g LPC	g Amino Acid per 100 g Recovered Amino Acids	g Amino Acid per 16 g N	g Amino Acid N as % of Total Recovered N
Aspartic acid	5.41	6.25	9.70	10.48	6.89
Threonine	2.78	3.27	5.06	5.48	4.03
Serine	2.53	3.05	4.72	5.11	4.26
Glutamic acid	6.37	7.26	11.25	12.17	7.24
Proline	2.69	3.19	4.93	5.34	4.06
Glycine	2.77	3.64	5.64	6.11	7.11
Alanine	3.56	4.46	6.91	7.47	7.34
Valine	3.47	4.10	6.34	6.86	5.13
Cystine	0.84	0.98	1.52	1.52	1.65
Methionine	1.30	1.48	2.29	2.47	1.45
Isoleucine	2.74	3.17	4.91	5.31	3.54
Leucine	5.08	5.89	9.13	9.87	6.59
Tyrosine	2.55	2.83	4.38	4.74	2.29
Phenylalanine	3.50	3.92	6.08	6.57	3.48
Ammonia	0.91	0.91	1.41	1.52	7.83
Lysine	3.77	4.29	6.65	7.20	8.61
Histidine	1.33	1.51	2.34	2.53	4.28
Arginine	3.91	4.36	6.75	7.30	14.67
Total	55.51	64.56	100.01	108.18	100.00

TABLE 5.4. THE AMINO ACID COMPOSITION (EXCLUDING TRYPTOPHAN) OF SOME UNFRACTIONATED, CHLOROPLASTIC, AND CYTOPLASMIC PROTEINS FROM THE LEAVES OF BARLEY AND LUPINE

Results expressed as g amino acid per 100 g recovered amino acids.

	Chloroplastic			Unfractionated				Cytoplasmic	
	Sedimented		43°C Precipitate	TCA-precipitate	80°C Precipitate		TCA-precipitate	TCA-precipitate	
Amino Acid	Barley	Lupine	Lupine	Barley	Barley	Lupine	Lupine	Barley	Lupine[1]
Aspartic acid	9.75	9.94	10.26	9.63	9.52	10.29	10.20	9.62	10.06
Threonine	4.82	4.99	4.95	5.19	4.95	5.07	4.98	5.41	4.98
Serine	4.85	5.21	5.08	4.43	4.37	4.59	4.77	4.10	4.17
Glutamic acid	11.00	11.32	11.38	11.61	11.20	11.97	11.85	11.94	12.16
Proline	4.88	5.07	5.05	4.70	4.65	5.11	4.68	4.62	4.54
Glycine	6.12	5.93	6.01	5.68	5.60	5.58	5.73	5.38	5.26
Alanine	7.05	6.37	6.42	6.78	6.63	6.19	6.21	6.52	5.90
Valine	6.16	5.96	6.24	6.38	6.36	6.23	6.28	6.50	6.34
Cystine	1.00	0.71	0.66	1.86	1.95	1.33	1.03	1.72	1.78
Methionine	2.28	1.92	1.88	2.14	2.35	1.73	1.69	2.39	1.72
Isoleucine	5.25	5.63	5.89	4.88	5.02	4.95	4.92	4.74	4.48
Leucine	10.43	10.61	10.75	9.14	9.52	9.84	9.72	8.42	9.18
Tyrosine	4.49	4.40	4.00	4.50	4.50	4.91	4.51	4.92	5.48
Phenylalanine	6.97	7.35	6.96	6.03	6.41	6.38	6.20	5.84	5.87
Lysine	5.60	4.77	4.79	6.85	6.36	5.83	6.98	7.06	7.44
Histidine	1.82	1.91	1.91	2.34	2.33	2.27	2.39	2.66	2.82
Arginine	6.29	6.29	5.96	6.77	7.01	6.51	6.30	7.01	6.64

Results, except for the single result on lupine 80°C precipitate, are the mean percentages of analyses of three preparations in each group calculated from data in Byers (1971A); ammonia is not included in this table.

[1]Identical results obtained with TCA-precipitates from both sedimented and 43°C precipitate supernatants.

Proline and Lysine. Even using comparable preparations and standard hydrolysis conditions, variation in content is greater for some amino acids than others, the largest differences being found with the S-amino acids, proline, and lysine. For example, proline values (as g amino acid per 100 g recovered amino acids) ranged from 3.5 to 5.4 in 27 unfractionated leaf proteins made from 9 species (Gerloff *et al.* 1965) and from 4.2 to 5.1 in 13 unfractionated preparations made from 3 species (Byers 1971A) in a completely random fashion. This is probably due to the less accurate results obtained when ninhydrin reacts with an imino group (as in proline) rather than with an α-amino group as in other protein amino acids.

The comparable ranges for lysine from the same series of analyses were from 4.5 to 7.3 and 5.8 to 7.3, respectively, but in this instance it is unclear whether the differences are real or induced. Some proteins precipitated by trichloroacetic acid (TCA) from whole leaf extracts contain from 10 to 15% more lysine than complexes precipitated by heating the same extract (Byers 1971A; Chou *et al.* 1975), although not all (Betschart and Kinsella 1974). Most solvent-precipitated proteins also have a greater lysine content than the corresponding heat-coagulated product (Chibnall *et al.* 1963; Wilson and Tilley 1965; Tao *et al.* 1972; Brown *et al.* 1975). Heat damage to protein-containing foodstuffs is known to adversely affect the amount of nutritionally available lysine but it is still widely assumed that total lysine content of such samples is not affected. However, under certain processing conditions, condensation products can be formed between the ε-amino group of lysine and aldehyde groups which are resistant to acid hydrolysis (Mauron 1970).

S-Amino Acids. Cyst(e)ine and methionine together account for only 3–4% of the total amino acid content in extracted leaf proteins, which makes it difficult to determine whether a change in their content is real or is due to analytical error. This is a major problem, especially with cyst(e)ine, as duplicate analyses of the same sample seldom give identical results. The difficulties in determining S-amino acids relate to their instability in oxygen (air) during protein hydrolysis rather than to their actual analysis: cyst(e)ine is totally destroyed under such conditions. Using a sealed evacuated tube technique, or replacing the air with oxygen-free nitrogen, offers only partial protection to cyst(e)ine (and then only if the dissolved air in the hydrolyzing acid is first removed), but methionine can be satisfactorily determined using samples prepared in this way (Byers 1971A; Byers and Bolton 1979). Cyst(e)ine is usually determined as cysteic acid after a controlled oxidation of the sample, usually with performic acid (Bidmead and Ley 1958). Although theoretically this should lead to a quantitative conversion, this is by no means certain (Lipton *et al.* 1977). Certainly the reported cyst(e)ine contents of leaf proteins obtained via cysteic acid determination are just as variable as those obtained by direct measurement of a protected hydrolysate. This variability was confirmed in a recent collaborative trial (Williams *et al.* 1979) to determine the cyst(e)ine content of feedstuffs (including a leaf protein preparation) by oxidizing them with either performic acid (PA) or dimethylsulfoxide (DMSO). The cystine content of the leaf protein (as g per 100 g sample weight) ranged from 0.68 to 1.06 (PA) and from 0.54 to 1.00 (DMSO). This range of values—which was produced by experienced analysts—when averaged and converted came to 1.25 and 1.18 g cystine per 16 g N for PA and DMSO, respectively, which come within the accepted range of between 1 and 2%.

Methionine can be determined either directly or as methionine sulfone ($MetO_2$), following a deliberate oxidation of the protein by, for example, performic acid [cf. cyst(e)ine]. The advantage of the former method is that any methionine sulfoxides (MetO)—there are two stereoisomeric forms—present in the hydrolysate can be measured separately, whereas in a deliberately oxidized sample they are converted to $MetO_2$. The occurrence of MetO is usually considered to arise from the casual oxidation of methionine *in situ* during hydrolysis, but its occurrence in proteins cannot be excluded. With leaf protein there is the possibility that the sulfoxides might be produced during the extraction process: there is some evidence for this (Byers 1970, 1971A,B; Bickoff *et al.* 1975; Pirie 1978). In two heat-coagulated preparations made from the same extract, 18% of the methionine appeared as MetO in the protein made with minimum delay at all stages of processing, whereas 30% was found as MetO in a sample made from a 2-hr-old extract and processed over 14 hr. Amounts of MetO of this order were not found in hydrolysates of laboratory-prepared TCA-precipitated proteins. There was also about 10% less lysine in the protein from the slow processing (Byers 1971A,B).

For more details of techniques and problems in S-amino acid analysis, see articles by Eaker (1970), Friedman and Noma (1975), and Walker *et al.* (1975).

Tryptophan. This amino acid is not always included in published analyses of leaf proteins mainly because it has to be determined separately due to its complete decomposition during a conventional acid hydrolysis. Tryptophan determinations, especially on plant material, are not always satisfactory, and different results are often obtained from the same sample using different techniques (Miller 1967). For a review of methods, and an evaluation of their applications to proteins, see Friedman and Finley (1975).

The range of values reported for leaf proteins, from 0.5 to 2.5 (g amino acid per 100 g protein), reflects this uncertainty. In the absence of comparative results, and of any systematic study of a series of preparations of known provenance, it must be assumed that the tryptophan content of leaf proteins is around 1.5–2.0%. It is impossible, looking at the published values, to make any distinction between the tryptophan contents of unfractionated and fractionated preparations. For a list of publications which include tryptophan in the analysis, see Table 5.5.

Differences in Amino Acid Composition

Despite the analytical problems, apparent differences gradually emerged between the amino acid composition of proteins precipitated from whole

TABLE 5.5. SOME REFERENCES TO PUBLISHED ANALYSES ON THE AMINO ACID COMPOSITION OF EXTRACTED PROTEINS FROM DIFFERENT SPECIES OF LEAVES

All analyses are by ion exchange chromatographic methods unless otherwise stated. Presentation of amino acid results:
A—g amino acid per 100 g recovered amino acids (or 100 g protein).
B—g amino acid per 16 g N.
C—Amino acid N as % of total protein N.
D—Amino acid N as % of amino acid N recovered.
E—Amino acid mole %.

Species of Leaf			Amino Acid Analysis			
Latin Name	Common Name	Preparation	Presentation of Results	Trp	Other Comment	Reference
Amaranthus caudatus	Tete (in Nigeria)	Unfractionated	A	ND		Oke (1973)
Avena sativa	Oat	Chloroplastic Cytoplasmic	A	ND	Cys ND	Horigome (1977)
Beta vulgaris	Beetroot	Unfractionated	B	Inc.		Oelshlegel *et al.* (1969)
			B	ND		Subba Rau *et al.* (1972)
Brassica carinata		Unfractionated	A	ND		Brown *et al.* (1975)[3]
Brassica chinensis	Chinese cabbage	Unfractionated Chloroplastic Cytoplasmic	A	ND		Byers (1971A,B)[3]
Brassica napus	Turnip	Unfractionated	A	Inc.		Gerloff *et al.* (1965)
Brassica oleracea	Cabbage	Unfractionated	C	Inc.		Chibnall *et al.* (1963)
Brassica oleracea cv Botrytis	Cauliflower	Unfractionated	B	ND		Subba Rau *et al.* (1972)
Celosia argentea	Soko (in Nigeria)	Unfractionated	A	ND		Oke (1973)
Chenopodium amaranticolor	Chenopodium	Unfractionated	A	Inc.		Gerloff *et al.* (1965)[3]
Cnidoscolus chayamansa	Chaya	Chloroplastic Cytoplasmic	A	Inc.		Nagy *et al.* (1978)
Cucurbita ovifera	Marrow	Chloroplastic Cytoplasmic	A	Inc.		Gerloff *et al.* (1965)
Cynodon dactylon L. Pers	Coastal Bermuda grass	Chloroplastic Cytoplasmic	B	Inc.		Fishman and Evans (1978)
Daucus carota	Carrot	Unfractionated	B	Inc.		Oelshlegel *et al.* (1969)
			B	ND		Subba Rau *et al.* (1972)

(continued)

TABLE 5.5. *(Continued)*

Species of Leaf			Amino Acid Analysis			
Latin Name	Common Name	Preparation	Presentation of Results	Trp	Other Comment	Reference
Dolichos lablab	Bonavist bean	Chloroplastic	A	Inc.		Nagy *et al.* (1978)
Eupatorium odoratum	Queen's weed	Unfractionated	B	Inc.	Pro ND	Eggum (1970A)
Hordeum murinum	Barley grass	Unfractionated	C	Inc.		Chibnall *et al.* (1963)
Hordeum vulgare	Barley	Unfractionated	C	Inc.	M.B.A.	Yemm and Folkes (1953)
		Chloroplastic Cytoplasmic	A	ND		Byers (1971A,B)[3]
Lemna minor	Pondweed	Unfractionated	A	Inc.		Maciejewska-Potapczyk *et al.* (1975)
Lolium perenne	Perennial ryegrass	Unfractionated	A	Inc.		Gerloff *et al.* (1965)
		Cytoplasmic	C	Inc.		Chibnall *et al.* (1963)
	Mixed grasses	Unfractionated	C	Inc.		Wilson and Tilley (1965)
Lupinus albus	Lupine	Unfractionated Chloroplastic Cytoplasmic	A	ND		Byers (1971A,B)
Manihot utilissima	Cassava	Unfractionated	B	Inc.	Pro ND	Eggum (1970A)
Medicago denticulata	Burr medic	Unfractionated	C	Inc.		Chibnall *et al.* (1963)
Medicago sativa	Alfalfa	Unfractionated	A	Inc.		Gerloff *et al.* (1965)[1,2]
	Lucerne		A	ND		Byers (1971B)[2]
			B	ND		Subba Rau *et al.* (1972)
			B	ND		Tao *et al.* (1972)
			A	ND		Fafunso and Byers (1977)
		Unfractionated Cytoplasmic	C	Inc.		Chibnall *et al.* (1963)[1,2]
			C and D	Inc.		Wilson and Tilley (1965)[1,2]
		Unfractionated Chloroplastic Cytoplasmic	B	Inc.		Smith (1966)[1,2]
			B	Inc.		Bickoff *et al.* (1975)[3]
Miscanthus floridulus	(Taiwan—indigenous grass)	Unfractionated	A	ND	Cys ND	Chou *et al.* (1975)[3]

Myriophylum sp.	"Lakeweed" (water pepper)	Unfractionated	B	Inc.		Oelshlegel *et al.* (1969)
Nicotiana tabacum L.	Tobacco	Chloroplastic, Cytoplasmic	E	ND	Cys ND	Kawashima and Tamaki (1967)
		Chloroplastic Fraction I, Fraction II	B	ND		Knuckles *et al.* (1979)
Onobrychis sativa	Sanfoin	Unfractionated	A	Inc.		Gerloff *et al.* (1965)
Panicum maximum	Guinea grass	Unfractionated	B	Inc.	Pro ND	Eggum (1970A)
Phalaris tuberosa	Towoomba canary grass	Unfractionated	C	Inc.		Chibnall *et al.* (1963)
Phaseolus limensis	Lima bean	Unfractionated	B	Inc.		Oelshlegel *et al.* (1969)
Pisum sativum	Pea	Unfractionated	B	Inc.		Oelshlegel *et al.* (1969)
Solanum incanum	Ogba (in Nigeria)	Unfractionated	A	ND		Oke (1973)
Solanum nodiflorum	Ogunmo (in Nigeria)	Unfractionated	A	ND		Oke (1973)
Solanum tuberosum	Potato	Unfractionated	B	Inc.		Oelshlegel *et al.* (1969)
Sorghum sudanensis	Sorghum	Chloroplastic	A	Inc.		Nagy *et al.* (1978)
Spinacea oleracea	Spinach	Unfractionated, Cytoplasmic	C	Inc.		Chibnall *et al.* (1963)
Trifolium pratense	Red clover	Unfractionated	A	Inc.		Gerloff *et al.* (1965)
Trifolium repens	White clover	Unfractionated	B	ND		Tao *et al.* (1972)
Trifolium repens latum	Ladino clover	Chloroplastic, Cytoplasmic	A	ND	Cys ND	Horigome (1977)
Triticum aestivum	Wheat	Unfractionated	A	Inc.		Gerloff *et al.* (1965)
			A[4]	ND		Buchanan (1969B)
Tropaeolum lobianum	Nasturtium	Unfractionated	A	Inc.		Gerloff *et al.* (1965)
Zea mays	Corn Maize	Unfractionated	A	Inc.		Gerloff *et al.* (1965)

Data also quoted in: [1]Byers (1971B).
[2]Wang and Kinsella (1975).
[3]Nagy *et al.* (1978).
[4]Results wrongly given in paper as g per 16 g N.

Trp—Tryptophan. Cys—Cystine. Pro—Proline. M.B.A.—Microbiological assay. ND—Not determined. Inc.—Included.

and from fractionated leaf extracts. Greater amounts of lysine (Yemm and Folkes 1953), lysine and histidine (Wilson and Tilley 1965; Kawashima and Tamaki 1967), histidine (Smith 1966), and less leucine (Smith 1966; Kawashima and Tamaki 1967) were found in cytoplasmic preparations than in the unfractionated or chloroplastic proteins made from the same extract. These random observations were confirmed when the amino acid composition of 39 preparations made from three species of leaves was statistically analyzed by a principal coordinates method using a specially designed computer program: a detailed description of this is given in Byers (1971A).

Briefly, the amino acid contents of each sample were compared, in turn, with the amino acid contents of the other 38 preparations to give ½ (38 × 39) similarity coefficients covering every possible combination of the 39 preparations. Using matrix algebra, the 38 dimensions normally needed to represent this number of similarity coefficients were condensed and surveyed, on the computer, until a position was located where most variation between samples was found in as few dimensions as possible. In this study only 2 of the 38 coordinates showed much variation, and these are shown plotted one against the other in Fig. 5.2. Coordinate 1 (which brings out the greatest variations) divided the 39 preparations into three groups which corresponded to the cytoplasmic, unfractionated, and chloroplastic proteins (negative, neutral, and positive, respectively) and coordinate 2 divided each of these into three subgroups which corresponded to the species of leaf.

Only 16 amino acids were used in this analysis: tryptophan had not been determined on these samples, and the cyst(e)ine values were omitted as being not entirely reliable. Correlation coefficients calculated for all 39 preparations between the percentages of the 16 amino acids and the values of each of the two coordinates showed that 11 of the amino acids correlated with coordinate 1, the most highly correlated being lysine and histidine (negatively) and leucine, serine, phenylalanine, and isoleucine (positively) (Table 5.6). These compositional differences between fractions have been confirmed by more recent analyses (Bickoff *et al.* 1975; Horigome 1977; Nagy *et al.* 1978). Coordinate 2 was most highly correlated with methionine content (Table 5.6), indicating that this amino acid was species dependent, which agreed with the observation that the methionine content of all lupine leaf proteins seemed to be slightly, but consistently, lower than in preparations made from barley or Chinese cabbage. Because of the problems associated with the analysis of methionine this result should not be regarded as definitive, but it is interesting to note that Horigome (1977) also found less methionine in protein extracted from ladino clover, another legume, than in that from oats.

Factors Affecting Amino Acid Composition

Having found small, but real, differences in the amino acid composition between fractions (and possibly between proteins from different species), the influence of other factors on composition had to be considered. On the

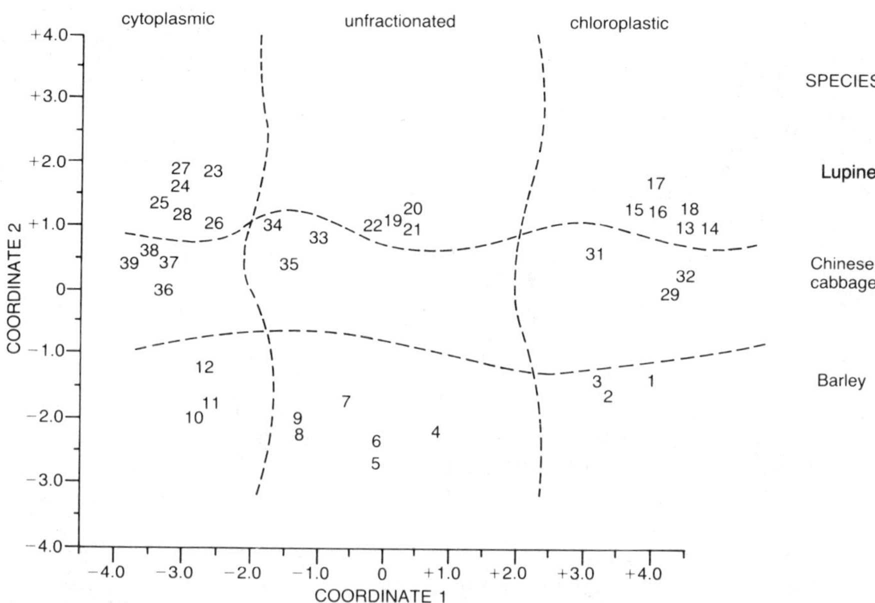

Fig. 5.2. Principal coordinate analysis of 39 leaf protein preparations compared by their amino acid composition [cyst(e)ine and tryptophan excluded]. The numbers identify preparations: No. 1–12, 13–28, and 29–39 correspond to barley, lupine, and Chinese cabbage preparations, respectively.

agronomic side this was found to be unaffected by either the physiological age or state of the leaf (Gerloff *et al.* 1965; Kawashima and Tamaki 1967; Byers 1971A,B) or by the nutrient status of the plant (Gerloff *et al.* 1965; Kawashima and Tamaki 1967; Bolton *et al.* 1976), although both leaf age and fertilizers have a considerable effect on the crude protein content of a leaf and its amino acid profile.

The formation of condensation products resistant to acid hydrolysis can account for the underestimation of lysine content. One such reaction (that between the ϵ-amino and aldehyde groups) has already been discussed. However, with leaf proteins, condensation reactions are much more likely to occur during the extraction process because several amino acids, especially lysine and cysteine, can couple with quinones (enzymatically produced when the leaf is disintegrated), and with polyphenols (Anderson 1968; Pierpoint 1969, 1971; and Chapter 10 in this book). Allison *et al.* (1973) cite several references for the incomplete release of amino acids from such products when hydrolyzed in strong mineral acid. Such condensation products are, however, of two sorts, and a careful distinction must be made between them. Those just discussed interfere with amino acid deter-

TABLE 5.6. CORRELATION COEFFICIENTS BETWEEN VALUES OBTAINED IN COORDINATES 1 AND 2[1] AND AMINO ACID CONTENT OF THE 39 PROTEINS

Coordinate 1		Coordinate 2	
Amino Acid	Correlation Coefficient	Amino Acid	Correlation Coefficient
Leucine	+0.94	Aspartic acid	+0.78
Phenylalanine	+0.94	Alanine	−0.70
Scrine	+0.91	Methionine	−0.85
Isoleucine	+0.88		
Glycine	+0.83		
Threonine	−0.70		
Arginine	−0.71		
Tyrosine	−0.81		
Glutamic acid	−0.84		
Histidine	−0.94		
Lysine	−0.95		

[1]See Fig. 5.2.

minations, whereas the other sort, which are more common, render an amino acid nutritionally unavailable. The failure of digestive enzymes to release an amino acid must not be equated with incomplete release on acid hydrolysis.

The use of reducing agents or polymers has been advocated to prevent coupling with phenolics during the processing of plant tissues (Anderson 1968; Stokes *et al.* 1968). Jones and Lyttleton (1972) and Sarkar *et al.* (1975) have successfully used sodium diethyldithiocarbamate and metabisulfite, respectively, to inhibit polyphenol oxidase activity, and hence quinone formation, during the extraction of Fraction I protein from legumes. Adding polyvinylpyrrolidone (PVP) at the start of the extraction process seemed successful in that both heat- and acid-precipitated proteins made from an alfalfa extract prepared with PVP had the same lysine contents (Fafunso and Byers 1977), while less lysine was found in the heat-precipitated protein made from the (untreated) control extract.

Except for these differences in lysine content the method used to coagulate the protein does not seem to greatly affect the content of other amino acids. Likewise, solvent extraction of the protein concentrate makes no difference to amino acid composition (Buchanan 1969B), and indeed some routinely defat their samples before hydrolysis (Garcha *et al.* 1970A). Storage also has little effect on protein composition and only small variations in the contents of glutamic acid, methionine, and tyrosine were found in a lyophilized sample stored in air at 27°C over a 24 week period (Betschart and Kinsella 1974), and of these variations only that of tyrosine exhibited a linear trend.

The most interesting alteration to leaf protein composition so far reported is that of Bickoff *et al.* (1975) who found greatly enhanced levels of S-amino acids in a cytoplasmic (white) fraction made from alfalfa which had been sprayed with sodium bisulfite before pulping. The methionine content (as g per 16 g N) of this cytoplasmic protein was 2.65 compared with 2.27 in the corresponding preparation made from untreated alfalfa. The comparative values for cystine were 1.68 and 1.44, respectively. De Groot and Slump (1969) found that if protein-containing foodstuffs were treated with alkali this could result in the formation of lysinoalanine (LAL) in amounts depending on reaction conditions. They also found that the occurrence of LAL in hydrolysates of soybean protein was accompanied by a concomitant decrease in the contents of both lysine and cystine. Recently, Finley and Kohler (1979), also using soybean protein, reported that LAL formation could be inhibited by adding reducing anions (e.g., bisulfite) during the alkali processing. No measurements of cystine or lysine were reported, but on the evidence of de Groot and Slump (1969), the contents of these amino acids should remain unchanged if no LAL is formed. The relevance of these results to both the composition and nutritional properties of the white protein prepared from bisulfite-treated alfalfa is discussed later under "Availability of Nutritionally Essential Amino Acids."

Published Amino Acid Analyses of Extracted Leaf Proteins

There are now plenty of reliable total amino acid analyses of extracted leaf proteins, and there is little point in routinely analyzing proteins extracted and precipitated by standard methods. Analyses can, without detriment to a project, be restricted to preparations which, because of modified techniques, might have altered composition. There are fewer analyses of preparations made from tropical species of leaves but, in general, the values found do not differ significantly from those of other leaf proteins. However, Nagy *et al.* (1978) reported that two chloroplastic fractions made from tropical plants had an increased valine content. Table 5.5 lists species from which protein has been extracted and analyzed for total amino acid content in recent years, mainly by ion exchange chromatographic (IEC) methods. With a few exceptions, analyses done in the pre-IEC era are not very reliable because of imperfect techniques (for a survey of these, see Byers 1971B) and they should not now be used for comparative purposes. Table 5.5, which is arranged alphabetically by Latin name, although long, is not comprehensive, and exclusion of a particular reference from it does not necessarily imply that the work is untrustworthy. Consultation of this list before contemplating an amino acid analysis may prevent much unnecessary duplication.

Several other papers give the contents of some of those amino acids nutritionally essential for man (EAA's). Many of these analyses have been done by methods other than IEC, microbiological assay (MBA) or colorimetric reactions specific to a particular amino acid being the most common. Results are usually given as g amino acid per 16 g N. Henry and Ford (1965), using a large number of preparations made at Rothamsted from different species and by different techniques, gave values for all EAA's except tyrosine and threonine, but included histidine which is essential for rats. Values for methionine and/or lysine in preparations made from a total of 37 species of leaves grown in India have been reported by Valli Devi *et al.* (1965) and Garcha *et al.* (1970A,B) and from 20 species grown in Sweden by Lexander *et al.* (1970). Garcha *et al.* (1970A) also gave the amounts of tryptophan and the nonessential arginine found in 20 of the Indian preparations. Values for some of the EAA's in soybean leaf protein (cystine, tryptophan, and tyrosine were missing) have also been determined (Betschart and Kinsella 1974); these can be seen in Table 5.7. All the results given in these papers fall within the range of values obtained by IEC methods except those for lysine reported by Valli Devi *et al.* (1965), which were only about that usually found, and those for arginine (Garcha *et al.* 1970A), which were nearly double.

NUTRITIONALLY ESSENTIAL AMINO ACIDS (EAA'S)

The Food and Agriculture Organization's (FAO) recommended requirements of EAA's for human nutrition, first introduced in 1957 and reconfirmed in 1965, were drastically altered in 1973. The requirements for threonine, valine, leucine, and lysine were all considerably increased,

TABLE 5.7. THE AMINO ACID COMPOSITION (AS G AMINO ACID PER 100 G PROTEIN) OF LEAF AND SEED PROTEINS FROM A CEREAL (WHEAT) AND LEGUMES (ALFALFA AND SOYBEAN) AND THEIR COMPARISON WITH THE FAO/WHO RECOMMENDED REQUIREMENTS OF NUTRITIONALLY ESSENTIAL AMINO ACIDS FOR HUMANS

Amino Acid	Whole Seed	Unfractionated Leaf Protein			Whole Seed	FAO/WHO Recommendation	
	Wheat[1]	Wheat[2]	Alfalfa[3]	Soybean[4]	Soybean[5]	1965	1973
Asp	5.4[a]	10.5	10.2		11.0[a]		
Thr	3.3	5.5	5.2	5.3	3.9	2.8	4.0
Ser	4.8	5.1	4.3		5.1		
Glu	26.7[b]	12.2	11.1		19.2[b]		
Pro	9.2	5.3	4.8		5.7		
Gly	4.4	6.1	5.3		4.1		
Ala	3.9	7.5	6.0		4.1		
Val	4.6	6.9	6.8	6.7	4.9	4.2	5.0
Cys	3.1	1.7	1.3	ND	1.4	2.0	3.5 (Cys + Met)
Met	1.7	2.5	2.3	1.1	1.4	2.2	
Ile	3.6	5.3	5.3	5.0	4.7	4.2	4.0
Leu	6.8	9.9	8.9	10.0	7.0	4.8	7.0
Tyr	3.4	4.7	4.4	ND	3.6	2.8	6.0 (Tyr + Phe)
Phe	4.7	6.6	5.7	5.8	4.6	2.8	
Lys	3.0	7.2	6.7	7.2	6.3	4.2	5.5
His	2.6	2.5	2.5		2.3		
Arg	6.1	7.3	6.5		7.7		
Trp	(1.5)[6]	(1.7)[7]	1.5	ND	1.2	1.4	1.0

[a] Aspartic acid + asparagine.
[b] Glutamic acid + glutamine.
ND—Not determined.
Ammonia is not included in this table.
[1] Byers and Bolton (1979).
[2] Buchanan (1969B) (whose results were wrongly given as g amino acid/16 g N).
[3] Bickoff *et al.* (1975) (results converted from g amino acid/16 g N).
[4] Betschart and Kinsella (1974) (some essential amino acids only).
[5] Rackis *et al.* (1961) (results converted from g amino acid/16 g N).
[6] Lyman *et al.* (1956) (average values for 5 samples).
[7] Gerloff *et al.* (1965) (average values for 5 samples).

whereas the recommended amounts of cystine plus methionine, and tryptophan, were decreased. These FAO "provisional patterns" are based on existing knowledge at the time of publication and are, therefore, liable to periodic modification. Hence, conclusions drawn from comparisons with the 1965 standards are now incorrect, and should be reassessed.

The composition of three unfractionated proteins extracted from wheat, alfalfa, and soybean leaves, respectively, and of both the 1965 and 1973 reference proteins are given in Table 5.7. When compared with the 1965 standard, the first (joint) limiting amino acids in all extracted leaf proteins were taken to be cyst(e)ine plus methionine, followed by tryptophan, which was occasionally below the recommended level. Although the combined S-amino acid content is no longer below that of the current (1973) standard, cyst(e)ine and methionine are still limiting because all other EAA's, including tryptophan, are well above the new minimum recommended levels. The large increase in the requirement for lysine in 1973 (from 4.2 to 5.5 g per 100 g protein) can still be met by all preparations except possibly a few chloroplastic fractions in which the lysine content might be marginal (see Table 5.4).

The amino acid composition of extracted leaf protein is very different from that of the protein in either cereal or legume grain: the composition of leaf and seed protein from both wheat and soybean can be compared in Table 5.7. The most important differences are in the complements of certain EAA's. In contrast to cereal seeds, all of which are deficient in lysine, there is an adequate amount of this amino acid in most leaf protein preparations. The latter also contain adequate amounts of tryptophan, which, along with lysine, is limiting in maize. Legume grains on the other hand contain sufficient lysine, but are deficient in S-amino acids, the values found being well below those of the 1973 FAO reference protein, or those of leaf proteins.

AVAILABILITY OF NUTRITIONALLY ESSENTIAL AMINO ACIDS (EAA'S)

A total amino acid analysis is necessary to establish overall composition and to determine the limiting EAA's. However, it is the nutritional availability of the EAA's rather than their absolute amount which determines protein quality. Factors influencing this, and methods by which quality can be evaluated, are extensively covered in Bender *et al.* (1970) and Friedman (1975): for a résumé of methods that can be used for measuring the availability of amino acids, see Meade (1972). With leaf proteins, lysine, because of the many factors which can render it both chemically and nutritionally unavailable, and the S-amino acids, which are themselves limiting, are the most important in relation to quality.

S-Amino Acids

Initially, and on the basis of total content, methionine alone was regarded as the limiting EAA in leaf protein, but it is now generally agreed, especially since the publication of the 1973 FAO reference standard, that the total

S-amino acid content is more relevant. This arises from the fact that both cystine and cysteine, although not EAA's, can spare (i.e., partially replace) dietary methionine (Rose *et al.* 1948). Subsequent *in vivo* experiments using rats universally supported this view; if methionine was added to diets containing unfractionated leaf protein, their nutritive value improved (Henry and Ford 1965; Mokady and Zimmerman 1967; Shurpalekar *et al.* 1969; Eggum 1970A; Gordon 1970; Garcha *et al.* 1971; Trigg 1971; Woodham 1971; Lu and Kinsella 1972; Trigg and Topps 1972; Hove *et al.* 1974; Bickoff *et al.* 1975). Both Trigg (1971) and Hove *et al.* (1974) reported a growth response in rats when diets were supplemented with cystine instead of methionine, but Trigg found no additional response when both methionine and cystine were given. However, rats have a greater requirement for methionine than most other species (Eggum 1970B), and in the one reported experiment with pigs, there was no additional response if methionine was added to diets containing unfractionated leaf protein (Carr and Pearson 1976).

The poorer *in vivo* results obtained using rats fed either unfractionated or chloroplastic protein could not be attributed to a deficiency of either methionine or total S-amino acids because cytoplasmic fractions, having a similar S-amino acid content, had nutritive values approaching that of casein (Henry and Ford 1965; Subba Rau *et al.* 1969; Bickoff *et al.* 1975). Cytoplasmic protein extracted from bisulfite-treated alfalfa was found to be nutritionally superior to casein, having a greater protein efficiency ratio (PER), which was in line with its greater S-amino acid content (Bickoff *et al.* 1975). Adding methionine to this fraction, or to the corresponding fraction made from untreated leaves, increased the PER of the diet still more, to approximately equal values for both preparations, indicating that methionine was also the limiting amino acid in cytoplasmic proteins.

The unavailability of S-amino acids could be associated with the presence of chloroplastic material. Some analyses on barley proteins supported this view; the availability of methionine was found to be 100, 90, and 40 (as % of total content) in cytoplasmic, unfractionated, and chloroplastic proteins, respectively (Ford 1964; Buchanan 1969B; Byers 1970, 1971A,B). The paucity of available methionine values for leaf (or any other) proteins is due to the fact that determinations have to be done by *in vivo* or MBA methods. Only recently have chemical approaches to this problem been considered (Dévényi *et al.* 1974; Lipton and Bodwell 1975, 1977), but none are yet fully developed.

Several other factors can affect the availability of S-amino acids in leaf protein (Byers 1971A, B; Bickoff *et al.* 1975; Pirie 1978). Both methionine and cyst(e)ine are easily oxidized and most of their oxidation products cannot spare methionine (Miller and Samuel 1968). Neither cysteic acid nor $MetO_2$ (the fully oxidized products) has any nutritional value, but there is conflicting evidence about the sparing action of MetO (Miller and Samuel 1968; Bickoff *et al.* 1975; Sjöberg and Boström 1977). It is often convenient to determine cyst(e)ine and methionine by converting them to cysteic acid and $MetO_2$, respectively, which are easily measured, but this does not allow measurement of the intermediate oxidation products, of which, in this instance, MetO is the most important. Methionine and MetO can be measured separately using a suitably prepared hydrolysate, but one still cannot distinguish between MetO produced during the extraction process and that resulting from oxidation during hydrolysis. Several methods have been suggested for the direct measurement of MetO in intact proteins; for a review of these, and a description of a novel approach using electron spectroscopy, see Walker *et al.* (1975). Another possible method has recently been investigated by Lipton and Bodwell (1977), but none of these methods is yet suitable for routine use.

The S-amino acids can also react with phenolics (Pirie 1978). In particular, the *o*-quinones produced by enzymatic oxidation of chlorogenic and caffeic acids in plant extracts can couple with both free and peptide-bound cysteine (Pierpoint 1969, 1971). A conjugation of this sort could be responsible for the lack of free sulfhydryl groups noted in unfractionated and chloroplastic proteins (Byers 1967, 1971A,B).

Bickoff *et al.* (1975) are of the opinion that cyst(e)ine and methionine are being lost during the extraction process and that they are consequently being underestimated. Their analyses on protein extracted from bisulfite-treated alfalfa support this view, as do the results of Byers (1975A,B) whose cystine values, calculated from the difference between total S and S due to methionine, were greater than those obtained by direct measurement. The role of bisulfite in protecting S-amino acids is not understood, but its use in preventing the formation of LAL in alkali-treated proteins, which is accompanied by a decrease in measurable cyst(e)ine and lysine (whose availability is discussed next), has been noted by Finley and Kohler (1979). Betschart (1974) failed to detect any LAL when solubilizing leaf proteins in dilute alkali (up to pH 9.0), and there have been no reports of its occurrence in hydrolysates of extracted leaf proteins. However, this does not mean it is absent. The now almost universal use of short runs (between 1 and 2 hr) for amino acid analyses does not easily allow for the detection of small peaks of unknown origin, especially in the basic region where LAL elutes. There are conflicting reports about the toxicity of LAL (Finley and Kohler 1979), but as long as there is uncertainty about its physiological effects, processes likely to produce it (e.g., alkaline extraction of leaf protein) are best avoided. While adding bisulfite might counteract the adverse effects due to an alkaline pH, it could also possibly induce the destruction of β-carotene (Peiser and Yang 1979); its use, therefore, would need careful investigation.

Lysine

The lack of extra response when lysine is added to diets containing unfractionated or cytoplasmic leaf protein (Shurpalekar *et al.* 1969; Reddy, in Woodham 1971; Bickoff *et al.* 1975) indicates that sufficient lysine is available in such preparations. Nevertheless, values for the several criteria used to measure nutritive value vary considerably (Duckworth and Woodham 1961; Henry and Ford 1965; Woodham 1965, 1971; Buchanan 1969B; Subba Rau *et al.* 1972), and factors which influence lysine availability, e.g., heat damage, conjugation with polyphenols, etc., must be suspect.

The results of Duckworth and Woodham (1961), Henry and Ford (1965), Buchanan (1969B), Subba Rau and Singh (1970), and Woodham (1971) showed that improper drying of the protein probably accounted for many of the poor results in early feeding trials, but delay during processing, either before or after protein precipitation, is also likely to adversely affect lysine availability (Pirie 1975, 1978). Lysine which has reacted to form acid-unhydrolyzable condensation products is at the same time rendered nutritionally unavailable.

There are many procedures, both chemical and biological, for determining available lysine. Most of the chemical methods are modifications of Carpenter's (1960) FDNB method, which directly determines those ε-groups left unbound, but this has never given satisfactory results with proteins of vegetable origin (Booth 1971). Inversion of this procedure to measure unmodified lysine (i.e., that not derivatized) has been more successful (Roach *et al.* 1967; Allison *et al.* 1973; Couch and Thomas 1976).

Chemically determined available lysine values (as % of total lysine content) in 20 unfractionated preparations of Indian origin were all > 75% (Garcha *et al.* 1970A) and in 9 Rothamsted preparations ranged from 74 to 88% (Allison 1971; Allison *et al.* 1973). The latter results, and those found using chloroplastic (62–70%) and cytoplasmic (85–86%) fractions, all correlated with previously reported values for the biological value and true digestibility of these preparations (Henry and Ford 1965). The percentage of available lysine in these, and in other samples, obtained by biological methods fell within the ranges just given (Henry and Ford 1965; Buchanan 1969B; Lexander *et al.* 1970; Trigg 1971; Cheeke and Myer 1975).

There are now sufficient available lysine determinations on extracted leaf proteins to indicate the range of values found in bulk preparations. What is lacking, however, is any systematic study of both the total and available lysine values (preferably by reliable chemical methods) in preparations made under different processing conditions. In the absence of such information one can only speculate on the effects of, for example, extracting with alkali, temperature, elapsed time during processing, etc. The effect of species, or variety, on availability (some plants contain large amounts of tannin) should only be studied using standardized conditions, otherwise differences due to cause and effect cannot be distinguished. Any work along these lines would be invaluable, as the lack of knowledge in this area constitutes one of the largest gaps in our understanding of the nutritional quality of extracted leaf proteins.

Is Lysine the Second Limiting EAA?

A greater response than to methionine alone was found when both methionine and lysine were added to diets containing unfractionated alfalfa (Larson and Halverson 1962; Reddy, in Woodham 1971; Bickoff *et al.* 1975) or ladino clover (Ohshima and Oouchi 1976) protein. Bickoff *et al.* (1975) also obtained a similar result using an alfalfa cytoplasmic protein, and found that the response to added lysine increased as more methionine was given. On the other hand, neither Henry and Ford (1965) nor Shurpalekar *et al.* (1969; also cited by Woodham 1971) got any additional response when both amino acids were added to diets containing unfractionated tare (vetch) *(Vicia sativa)* or alfalfa protein, respectively.

The problem in assessing this conflicting evidence is that there are available lysine values for only a few of these proteins (Henry and Ford 1965), but indirect information can be obtained by looking at the techniques used in their preparation. Two of the preparations whose nutritive values were improved when fed with lysine and methionine were processed slowly, the precipitated protein being allowed to stand for several hours before filtration (Halverson 1962; Ohshima and Oouchi 1976); the latter also precipitated the protein by slowly raising the temperature. Bickoff *et al.* (1975) refer to their published methods for preparative details, but these can vary. Pro-Xan (whole or unfractionated protein), while precipitated instantly by steam injection, can be separated slowly by flotation or sedimentation (Kohler and Bickoff 1971; Spencer *et al.* 1971) or more quickly by mechanical separation (Lazar *et al.* 1971). Several methods, including heating, can also be used to separate Pro-Xan II (the chloroplastic fraction) before precipitation of the white (cytoplasmic) protein. There is no information about the origin of the preparations used by Reddy.

The feature common to all the preceding preparations is that, with the possible exception of the white protein, the precipitated material is allowed to stand in contact with the carbohydrate-rich nonprotein fraction for varying lengths of time, thus increasing the possibility that conjugation products may be formed. In contrast, the preparations used by Henry and Ford (1965) and by Shurpalekar *et al.* (1969), which showed no extra response when fed with lysine and methionine, were immediately coagulated by steam injection and separated, by filtration, as soon as possible to minimize contact between precipitated protein and the nonprotein fraction.

There is no dispute that adding lysine as well as methionine can enhance the nutritive value of certain preparations, but just the same not all preparations have shown this response. Further experiments, using preparations made by different techniques, and of known available lysine content, seem indicated in order to examine the claim that lysine is the second limiting EAA in leaf protein (Bickoff *et al.* 1975).

Other Essential Amino Acids

Values for the availability of some of the other essential amino acids in proteins made from a wide range of species have been determined by biological methods by Ford (1964), Henry and Ford (1965), Buchanan (1969B), and Byers (1970), all using MBA, and Henry and Ford (1965) and Trigg (1971), using rats. No comparison of these results has been attempted because of the assortment of preparations used and the variation in methodology.

Threonine. The sole values reported seem to be those of Trigg, who found from 80 to 86% availability, which would make this amino acid rather marginal in relation to the 1973 (increased) recommended amount.

Valine. In comparison with the (increased) recommended amount by FAO in 1973 there is an adequate amount of valine in unfractionated preparations, which is from 90 to 100% available (Ford; Henry and Ford; Byers). However, Trigg found only 68–78% availability and he thought that valine might be the second limiting amino acid, after methionine. The percentage availability in a chloroplastic and cytoplasmic fraction made from barley leaves was 40 and 93%, respectively (Byers).

Isoleucine. Results are scattered, and values ranging from 72 to 100% have been reported with unfractionated protein (Ford; Henry and Ford; Buchanan; Byers; Trigg). If completely available the isoleucine content would exceed the 1973 FAO requirement, but if availability fell to 80% or less it would become marginal. Heat damage to the protein results in a marginal value (Buchanan). Trigg, on the basis of percentage availability, thought that isoleucine might be the third limiting EAA in leaf protein, but Henry and Ford got no additional response over that for methionine when they gave isoleucine and methionine together in diets fed to rats. Values of 31 and 86% available isoleucine were reported in barley chloroplastic and cytoplasmic fractions, respectively (Byers).

Leucine. Despite the large increase (from 4.8 to 7.0 g per 100 g protein) in the FAO recommended amount in 1973, the leucine content of leaf protein is well above this level. However, the amount available in unfractionated protein ranges from 63 to 75% (Byers) and from 80 to 90% (Ford; Henry and Ford; Buchanan; Trigg); a leucine availability of 80% would still exceed the FAO value. Availability is decreased if the protein is heat damaged (Buchanan). Adding extra leucine, or leucine plus lysine, to unfractionated protein fed to rats did not improve the nutritive value of either diet, but leucine and lysine plus methionine gave a greater response than when lysine and methionine, or leucine and methionine, were given together (Reddy, cited in Woodham 1971). In sedimented and heat-coagulated cholorplastic fractions, only 28 and 75% leucine was available, respectively, rising to 90% with a cytoplasmic fraction (Byers).

Tyrosine and Phenylalanine. Trigg reported values ranging from 77 to 93% for tyrosine and from 67 to 80% for phenylalanine. Both total and available content of both these amino acids is well in excess of the 1973 FAO recommendations.

Tryptophan. The tryptophan content of all leaf proteins is well above the recommended value in the FAO reference protein, which itself was decreased from 1.4 to 1.0 g per 100 g protein in 1973, and it appears to be 100% available (Ford; Henry and Ford; Buchanan), unless overheated during drying (Buchanan). Tryptophan does not appear to have been added to diets for feeding trials, and there have been no determinations of availability in fractionated proteins.

CURRENT DEVELOPMENTS AND POSSIBILITIES IN LEAF PROTEIN TECHNOLOGY

Fraction I protein became of more than academic interest when it was thought to be implicated in causing bloat in ruminants feeding on legume pastures. Jones and Mangan (1976) were the first to elegantly fractionate large amounts of leaf extract using heat, ammonium sulfate precipitation, and gel filtration on Sephadex, in that order, with the object of making a sufficiently large sample of Fraction I protein of high purity for animal experiments. Coincidentally, they confirmed the observations of de Fremery *et al.* (1973) that unless the pH of the extract was adjusted to about 6.8 before heat denaturation, a low yield of white (or cytoplasmic) protein was obtained. Further they confirmed that this fraction did not have its origin in the cytoplasm, and was, in fact, Fraction I protein.

Another theoretical approach with a possible practical application to leaf protein technology was that of Bahr *et al.* (1977) and Fishman and Burdick (1977). Both pointed out the superior photosynthetic capacity (and hence yield) of C_4 plants over those of the C_3 species which fix CO_2 via the phosphoglyceric acid pathway. Using the C_4 Coastal Bermuda grass, Fishman and Burdick (1977) studied the extractability, solubility, and MW distribution, and subsequently (Fishman and Evans 1978) the amino acid composition of these fractions, but no comparisons were made with a C_3 species. However, Bahr *et al.* (1977), using three C_3 plants (tobacco, spinach, and cotton) and one C_4 species (maize), found that proteins extracted from all four species had identical solubilities in ammonium sulfate and identical isoelectric points, at pH 4.5. Although there was a difference in the temperature at which protein was precipitable from the extracts (about 45°C for maize and >60°C for the other extracts), this cannot be used as a criterion to distinguish between C_3 and C_4 plants as claimed because extracts from lupine and Chinese cabbage (both C_3 plants) also precipitate at the lower temperatures (Byers 1971A). However, the heat-precipitated maize protein contained at least two (thermolabile) polypeptides more than the corresponding preparations from spinach.

Finally, Knuckles *et al.* (1979) described a large-scale method for extracting the protein from tobacco leaves, and the subsequent isolation and crystallization of the Fraction I protein. Fraction II protein, not yet crystallized, was found to have a much larger lysine content than either Fraction I protein or the green (chloroplastic) protein precipitated at 50°C, which confirmed the results of Fishman and Evans (1978). Comparison of the amino acid analyses of these proteins with a chloroplastic and a cytoplasmic fraction (also from tobacco leaf) made by a less sophisticated method (Table 5.8) shows that Fraction II protein and the cytoplasmic fraction have similar, enhanced, lysine contents (cf. Table 5.4).

In conclusion, these experiments show how different approaches to the same problem have eventually proved to be mutually beneficial. Enough is now known about the identity of the soluble proteins of the leaf, and about some of the reactions they can undergo during their extraction and pro-

TABLE 5.8. A COMPARISON OF THE AMINO ACID COMPOSITION (EXCLUDING TRYPTOPHAN, BUT INCLUDING AMMONIA) OF SOME PROTEIN FRACTIONS EXTRACTED FROM TOBACCO *(NICOTIANA TABACUM)* LEAVES
Results expressed as g amino acid per 16 g N.

Amino Acid	Kawashima and Tamaki[1]	Knuckles *et al.*[2]			Kawashima and Tamaki[1]
	Green	Green	Fraction I	Fraction II	Supernatant
Asp	8.29	8.72	9.21	10.50	10.89
Thr	4.27	4.28	5.37	5.12	5.10
Ser	4.54	4.62	3.18	4.37	3.51
Glu	10.14	10.23	12.24	12.66	14.15
Pro	5.34	4.36	4.74	4.87	5.27
Gly	5.49	5.13	5.58	5.58	5.83
Ala	6.31	5.62	6.13	6.44	7.38
Val	5.64	5.90	7.48	7.62	7.99
Cys	ND	0.99	2.00	1.78	ND
Met	1.88	2.27	2.13	2.50	1.89
Ile	4.90	4.95	4.76	5.32	5.79
Leu	9.65	8.78	9.16	9.64	9.56
Tyr	3.56	3.62	6.58	6.03	5.27
Phe	6.06	5.72	5.68	5.81	5.49
Amm	ND	1.04	1.06	0.70	ND
Lys	5.89	5.69	6.25	7.16	7.97
His	1.96	1.89	3.09	2.88	2.74
Arg	4.98	5.12	8.06	7.00	7.15

[1]Kawashima and Tamaki (1967): Results converted from μmole % to g per 16 g N and adjusted to % recovery of N quoted by Knuckles *et al.* (1979).
[2]Knuckles *et al.* (1979).
ND—Not determined.

cessing, to enable the production of a leaf protein concentrate (as a food or feed) to be put on a less empirical basis. On the other hand, those wanting to process large quantities of leaves in order to extract a measurable quantity of a specific protein have highly-developed pilot plant facilities at their disposal.

REFERENCES

ALLISON, R.M. 1971. Factors influencing the availability of lysine in leaf protein. *In* Leaf Protein: Its Agronomy, Preparation, Quality and Use. N.W. Pirie (Editor). Blackwell Scientific Publications, Oxford.

ALLISON, R.M., LAIRD, W.M. and SYNGE, R.L.M. 1973. Notes on a deamination method proposed for determining "chemically available lysine" of proteins. Br. J. Nutr. *29*, 51–55.

ANDERSON, J.W. 1968. Extraction of enzymes and subcellular organelles from plant tissues. Phytochemistry *7*, 1973–1988.

AOAC. 1970. Official Methods of Analysis, 11th Edition. Assoc. of Official Analytical Chemists, Washington, D.C.

BAHR, J.T., BOURQUE, D.P. and SMITH, H.J. 1977. Solubility properties of Fraction I proteins of maize, cotton, spinach and tobacco. J. Agric. Food Chem. *25*, 783–789.

BEATON, J.D. 1966. Sulfur requirements of cereals, fruit trees, vegetables and other crops. Soil Sci. *101*, 267–282.

BENDER, A.E., KIHLBERG, R., LÖFQVIST, B. and MUNCK, L. 1970. Evaluation of Novel Protein Products. Pergamon Press, Oxford.

BETSCHART, A.A. 1974. Nitrogen solubility of alfalfa protein concentrate as influenced by various factors. J. Food Sci. *39*, 1110–1115.

BETSCHART, A.A. and KINSELLA, J.E. 1974. Influence of storage on composition, amino acid content, and solubility of soybean leaf protein concentrate. J. Agric. Food Chem. *22*, 116–123.

BICKOFF, E.M., BOOTH, A.N., DE FREMERY, D., EDWARDS, R.H., KNUCKLES, B.E., MILLER, R.E., SAUNDERS, R.M. and KOHLER, G.O. 1975. Nutritional evaluation of alfalfa leaf protein concentrate. *In* Protein Nutritional Quality of Foods and Feeds, Part 2. M. Friedman (Editor). Marcel Dekker, New York.

BIDMEAD, D.S. and LEY, F.J. 1958. Quantitative amino acid analysis of food proteins by means of a single ion-exchange column. Biochim. Biophys. Acta *29*, 562–567.

BOLTON, J., NOWAKOWSKI, T.Z. and LAZARUS, W. 1976. Sulphur-nitrogen interaction effects on the yield and composition of the protein-N, non-protein-N and soluble carbohydrates in perennial ryegrass. J. Sci. Food. Agric. *27*, 553–560.

BOOTH, V.H. 1971. Problems in the determination of FDNB-available lysine. J. Sci. Food Agric. *22*, 658–666.

BRAUDE, R., JONES, A.S. and HOUSEMAN, R.A. 1977. The utilization of the juice extracted from green crops. *In* Green Crop Fractionation. R.J. Wilkins (Editor). British Grassland Society, Maidenhead, England.

BRAY, W.J. and HUMPHRIES, C. 1978. Solvent fractionation of leaf juice to prepare green and white protein products. J. Sci. Food Agric. *29*, 839–846.

BRAY, W.J., and HUMPHRIES, C. 1979. Preparation of a white leaf protein concentrate using a polyanionic flocculant. J. Sci. Food Agric. *30*, 171–176.

BRAY, W.J., HUMPHRIES, C. and INERITEI, M.S. 1978. The use of solvents to decolorise leaf protein concentrates. J. Sci. Food Agric. *29*, 165–171.

BROWN, H.E., STEIN, E.R. and SALDANA, G. 1975. Evaluation of *Brassica carinata* as a source of plant protein. J. Agric. Food Chem. *23*, 545–547.

BUCHANAN, R.A. 1969A. Effect of storage and lipid extraction on the properties of leaf protein. J. Sci. Food Agric. *20*, 359–364.

BUCHANAN, R.A. 1969B. *In vivo* and *in vitro* methods of measuring nutritive value of leaf protein preparations. Br. J. Nutr. *23*, 533–545.

BYERS, M. 1961. Biochem. Sect. Annu. Rep. Rothamsted Exp. Stn. *1960*, 109.

BYERS, M. 1965. Biochem. Sect. Annu. Rep. Rothamsted Expt. Stn. *1964*, 121–122.

BYERS, M. 1967. *In vitro* hydrolysis of leaf proteins. I. The action of papain on protein concentrates extracted from the leaves of *Zea mays*. J. Sci. Food Agric. *18*, 28–33.

BYERS, M. 1970. Biochem. Sect. Annu. Rep. Rothamsted Exp. Stn. *1969*, 133–134.

BYERS, M. 1971A. Amino acid composition and *in vitro* digestibility of some protein fractions from three species of leaves of various ages. J. Sci. Food Agric. *22*, 242–251.

BYERS, M. 1971B. The amino acid composition of some leaf protein preparations. *In* Leaf Protein: Its Agronomy, Preparation, Quality and Use. N.W. Pirie (Editor). Blackwell Scientific Publications, Oxford.

BYERS, M. 1975A. Determination of S in extracted leaf protein. J. Sci. Food Agric. *27*, 131–134.

BYERS, M. 1975B. Relationship between total N, total S, and the S-containing amino acids in extracted leaf protein. J. Sci. Food Agric. *27*, 135–139.

BYERS, M. and BOLTON, J. 1979. Effects of nitrogen and sulphur fertilisers on the yield, N and S contents, and amino acid composition of the grain of spring wheat. J. Sci. Food Agric. *30*, 251–263.

CARPENTER, K.J. 1960. The estimation of available lysine in animal-protein foods. Biochem. J. *77*, 604–610.

CARR, J.R. and PEARSON, G. 1976. Photosensitisation, growth performance and carcass measurements of pigs fed diets containing commercially prepared lucerne leaf-protein concentrates. N.Z. J. Exp. Agric. *4*, 45–50.

CASHMORE, A.R. 1976. Protein synthesis in plant leaf tissue. The sites of synthesis of the major proteins. J. Biol. Chem. *251*, 2848–2853.

CHEEKE, P.R. and MYER, R.O. 1975. Protein digestibility and lysine availability in alfalfa meal and alfalfa protein concentrate. Nutr. Rep. Int. *12*, 337–344.

CHIBNALL, A.C., REES, M.W. and LUGG, J.W.H. 1963. The amino acid composition of leaf proteins. J. Sci. Food Agric. *14*, 234–239.

CHOU, C.H., YOUNG, C.C. and HUANG, C. 1975. Quality of leaf protein concentrates in *Miscanthus floridulus*. Bot. Bull. Acad. Sin. *16*, 191–199.

COÏC, Y., FAUCONNEAU, G., PION, R., LESAINT, G. GODEFROY, S. 1962. Influence of sulphur deficiency on the absorption of minerals and on the metabolism of nitrogen and organic acids in barley. Ann. Physiol. Veg. *4*, 295–306. (French)

CONN, E.E. 1969. Cyanogenic glycosides. J. Agric. Food Chem. *17* 519–526.

COUCH, J.R. and THOMAS, M.C. 1976. A comparison of chemical methods for the determination of available lysine in various proteins. J. Agric. Food Chem. *24*, 943–946.

DE FREMERY, D., MILLER, R.E., EDWARDS, R.H., KNUCKLES, B.E., BICKOFF, E.M. and KOHLER, G.O. 1973. Centrifugal separation of white and green protein fractions from alfalfa juice following controlled heating. J. Agric. Food Chem. *21*, 886–889.

DE GROOT, A.P. and SLUMP, P. 1969. Effects of severe alkali treatment of proteins on amino acid composition and nutritive value. J. Nutr. *98*, 45–56.

DÉVÉNYI, T., BÁTI, J., HALLSTRÖM, B., TRAGARDH, CH., KRALOVÁNSZKY, P.U. and MÁTRAI, T. 1974. Determination of available methionine in plant materials. Acta Biochim. Biophys. Acad. Sci. Hung. *9*, 395–398.

DUCKWORTH, J. and WOODHAM, A.A. 1961. Leaf protein concentrates. I. Effect of source of raw material and method of drying on protein value for chicks and rats. J. Sci. Food Agric. *12*, 5–15.

EAKER, D. 1970. Determination of free and protein-bound amino acids *In* Evaluation of Novel Protein Products. A.E. Bender *et al.* (Editors). Pergamon Press, Oxford.

EDWARDS, R.H., MILLER, R.E., DE FREMERY, D., KNUCKLES, B.E., BICKOFF, E.M. and KOHLER, G.O. 1975. Pilot plant production of an edible white leaf protein concentrate from alfalfa. J. Agric. Food Chem. *23*, 620–626.

EGGUM, B.O. 1970A. The protein quality of cassava leaves. Br. J. Nutr. *24*, 761–768.

EGGUM, B.O. 1970B. Nutritional evaluation of proteins by laboratory animals. *In* Evaluation of Novel Protein Products. A.E. Bender *et al.* (Editors). Pergamon Press, Oxford.

FAFUNSO, M. and BYERS, M. 1977. Effect of pre-press treatments of vegetation on the quality of the extracted leaf protein. J. Sci. Food Agric. *28*, 375–380.

FAO/WHO. 1965. Protein requirements. FAO Nutr. Meet. Rep. Ser. *37*. Food and Agriculture Organization, Rome.

FAO/WHO. 1973. Energy and protein requirements. FAO Nutr. Meet. Rep. Ser. *52*. Food and Agriculture Organization, Rome.

FINLEY, J.W. and KOHLER, G.O. 1979. Processing conditions to inhibit lysinoalanine formation in alkali-treated proteins. Cereal Chem. *56*, 130–132.

FISHMAN, M.L. and BURDICK, D. 1977. Extractability, solubility and molecular size distribution of nitrogenous constituents in Coastal Bermuda grass. J. Agric. Food Chem. *25*, 1122–1127.

FISHMAN, M.L. and EVANS, J.J. 1978. Amino acid composition of Coastal Bermuda grass fractions. J. Agric. Food Chem. *26*, 1447–1451.

FORD, J.E. 1964. A microbiological method of assessing the nutritional value of proteins. 3. Further studies on the measurement of available amino acids. Br. J. Nutr. *16*, 449–460.

FOWDEN, L., LEA, P.J. and BELL, E.A. 1979. The nonprotein amino acids of plants. *In* Advances in Enzymology, Vol. 50. A. Meister (Editor). John Wiley & Sons, New York.

FRIEDMAN, M. 1975. Protein Nutritional Quality of Foods and Feeds, Part 1 and Part 2. Marcel Dekker, New York.

FRIEDMAN, M. and FINLEY, J.W. 1975. Evaluation of methods for tryptophan analysis in proteins. *In* Protein Nutritional Quality of Foods and Feeds, Part 1. M. Friedman (Editor). Marcel Dekker, New York.

FRIEDMAN, M. and NOMA, A.T. 1975. Methods and problems in chromatographic analysis of sulfur amino acids. *In* Protein Nutritional Qualtiy of Foods and Feeds, Part 1. M. Friedman (Editor). Marcel Dekker, New York.

GARCHA, J.S., KAWATRA, B.L. and WAGLE, D.S. 1970A. Evaluation of different leaf protein concentrates for some essential amino acids. Curr. Sci. *39*, 269–270.

GARCHA, J.S., KAWATRA, B.L. and WAGLE, D.S. 1971. Nutritional evaluation of leaf proteins and the effect of their supplementation to wheat flour by rat feeding. J. Food Sci. Technol. *8*, 23–25.

GARCHA, J.S., KAWATRA, B.L., WAGLE, D.S., and BHATIA, I.S. 1970B. Studies on extraction and isolation of leaf proteins of various crops grown in the Punjab. J. Res. Punjab Agric. Univ. *7*, 211–215.

GERLOFF, E.D., LIMA, I.H. and STAHMANN, M.A. 1965. Amino acid composition of leaf protein concentrates. J. Agric. Food Chem. *13*. 139–143.

GLENCROSS, R.G., FESTENSTEIN, G.N. and KING, H.G.C. 1972. Separation and determination of isoflavones in the protein concentrate from red clover leaves. J. Sci. Food Agric. *23*, 371–376.

GORDON, T. 1970. Quality of leaf protein concentrates as measured with rats and the usefulness of the TOH dilution technique to measure their body composition. M.Sc. Thesis. University of Aberdeen, Aberdeen, Scotland.

HALVERSON, A.W. 1962. Effects of various procedures in laboratory processing of fresh alfalfa on separation of nitrogen and solids from fiber. J. Agric. Food Chem. *10*, 419–422.

HARTMAN, G.H., JR., AKESON, W.R. and STAHMANN, M.A. 1967. Leaf protein concentrate prepared by spray-drying. J. Agric. Food Chem. *15*, 74–79.

HENRY, K.M. and FORD, J.E. 1965. The nutritive value of leaf protein concentrates determined in biological tests with rats and by microbiological methods. J. Sci. Food Agric. *16*, 425–432.

HORIGOME, T. 1977. Nutritional studies on fractionated cytoplasmic and chloroplastic proteins from leaves of oats and ladino clover. Jpn. J. Zootech. Sci. *48*, 267–272.

HOUSEMAN, R.A. and CONNELL, J. 1976. The utilization of the products of green-crop fractionation by pigs and ruminants. Proc. Nutr. Soc. *35*, 213–220.

HOVE, E.L. and BAILEY, R.W. 1975. Towards a leaf protein concentrate industry in New Zealand. N.Z. J. Exp. Agric. *3*, 193–198.

HOVE, E.L., LOHREY, E., URS, M.K. and ALLISON, R.M. 1974. The effect of lucerne-protein concentrate in the diet on growth, reproduction and body composition of rats. Br. J. Nutr. *31*, 147–157.

HUANG, K.H., TAO, M.C., BOULET, M., RIEL, R.R., JULIEN, J.P. and BRISSON, G.J. 1971. A process for the preparation of leaf protein concentrates based on the precipitation of leaf juices with polar solvents. Can. Inst. Food Sci. Technol. J. *4*, 85–90.

HYLIN, J.W. 1969. Toxic peptides and amino acids in foods and feeds. J. Agric. Food Chem. *17*, 492–496.

JENSEN, R.G. and BAHR, J.T. 1977. Ribulose-1,5 diphosphate carboxylase-oxygenase. Annu. Rev. Plant Physiol. *28*, 379–400.

JONES, W.T. and LYTTLETON, J.W. 1972. The importance of inhibiting polyphenol oxidase in the extraction of Fraction 1 leaf protein. Phytochemistry *11*, 1595–1596.

JONES, W.T. and MANGAN, J.L. 1976. Large-scale isolation of Fraction 1 leaf protein (18S) from lucerne *(Medicago sativa)*. J. Agric. Sci. (Cambridge) *86*, 495–501.

KAWASHIMA, N. and TAMAKI, E. 1967. Studies on protein metabolism in higher plant leaves. I. Amino acid composition of tobacco leaf proteins at various stages. Phytochemistry *6*, 329–338.

KNUCKLES, B.E., DE FREMERY, D., BICKOFF, E.M. and KOHLER, G.O. 1975. Soluble protein from alfalfa by membrane filtration. J. Agric. Food Chem. *23*, 209–212.

KNUCKLES, B.E., KOHLER, G.O. and DE FREMERY, D. 1979. Processing of fresh tobacco leaves for protein fractions. J. Agric. Food Chem. *27*, 414–418.

KOHLER, G.O. and BICKOFF, E.M. 1971. Commercial production from alfalfa in U.S.A. *In* Leaf Protein: Its Agronomy, Preparation, Quality and Use. N.W. Pirie (Editor). Blackwell Scientific Publications, Oxford.

LARSON, R.L. and HALVERSON, A.W. 1962. Protein quality of an alfalfa concentrate. J. Agric. Food Chem. *10*, 422–425.

LAZAR, M.E., SPENCER, R.R., KNUCKLES, B.E. and BICKOFF, E.M. 1971. Pro-Xan process: Pilot plant for separation of heatprecipitated leaf protein from residual alfalfa juice. J. Agric. Food Chem. *19*, 944–946.

LEXANDER, K., CARLSSON, R., SCHALÉN, V., SIMONSSON, Å. and LUNDBORG, T. 1970. Quantities and qualities of leaf protein concentrates from wild species and crop species grown under controlled conditions. Ann. Appl. Biol. *66*, 193–215.

LIMA, I.H., RICHARDSON, T. and STAHMANN, M.A. 1965. Fatty acids in some leaf protein concentrates. J. Agric. Food Chem. *13*, 143–145.

LIPTON, S.H. and BODWELL, C.E. 1975. Chemical approaches for estimating nutritionally available methionine. *In* Protein Nutritional Quality of Foods and Feeds, Part 1. M. Friedman (Editor). Marcel Dekker, New York.

LIPTON, S.H. and BODWELL, C.E. 1977. A rapid method for detecting chemical alteration of methionine. J. Agric. Food Chem. *25*, 1214–1216.

LIPTON, S.H., BODWELL, C.E. and COLEMAN, A.H., JR. 1977. Amino acid analyser studies of the products of peroxide oxidation of cystine, lanthionine, and homocystine. J. Agric. Food Chem. *25*, 624–628.

LIVINGSTON, A.L., KNUCKLES, B.E., EDWARDS, R.H., DE FREMERY, D., MILLER, R.E. and KOHLER, G.O. 1979. Distribution of saponin in alfalfa protein recovery systems. J. Agric. Food Chem. *27*, 362–365.

LORENZ, O.A. 1978. Potential nitrate levels in edible plant parts. *In* Nitrogen in the Environment, Vol. 2. D.R. Nielsen and J.G. MacDonald (Editors). Academic Press, New York.

LU, P.S. and KINSELLA, J.E. 1972. Extractability and properties of protein from alfalfa leaf meal. J. Food Sci. *37*, 94–99.

LYMAN, C.M., KUIKEN, K.A. and HALE, F. 1956. Essential amino acid content of farm feeds. J. Agric. Food Chem. *4*, 1008–1013.

MACIEJEWSKA-POTAPCZYK, W., KONOPSKA, L. and OLECHNOWICZ, K. 1975. Protein in *Lemna minor*. Biochem. Physiol. Pflanz. *167*, 105–108.

MANSFIELD, G.A. and CONNELL, J. 1977. A report of the Agricultural Development Advisory Service/National Institute for Research in Dairying forage fractionation programme. *In* Green Crop Fractionation. R.J. Wilkins (Edor). British Grassland Society, Maidenhead, England.

MAURON, J. 1970. *Cited by* ALLISON, R.M., LAIRD, W.M. and SYNGE, R.L.M. Notes on a deamination method proposed for determining "Chemically available lysine" of proteins. Br. J. Nutr. *29*, 51–55.

MEADE, R.J. 1972. Biological availability of amino acids. J. Anim. Sci. *35*, 713–723.

MILLER, D.S. and SAMUEL, P. 1968. Methionine sparing compounds. Proc. Nutr. Soc. *27*, 21A.

MILLER, E.L. 1967. Determination of the tryptophan contents of feedingstuffs with particular references to cereals. J. Sci. Food Agric. *18*, 381–386.

MILLER, R.E., DE FREMERY, D., BICKOFF, E.M. and KOHLER, G.O. 1975. Soluble protein concentrate from alfalfa by low-temperature acid precipitation. J. Agric. Food Chem. *23*, 1177–1179.

MOKADY, S. and ZIMMERMAN, G. 1967. The effect of different lipid extractants used with impulse-rendered lucerne paste on the nutritional and calorigenic properties of its proteins. Proc. 7th Int. Congr. Nutr., 1966, Hamburg, Vol. 5. Pergamon Press, Oxford.

NAGY, S., TELEK, L., HALL, N.T. and BERRY, R.E. 1978. Potential food uses for protein from tropical and sub-tropical plant species. J. Agric. Food Chem. *26*, 1016–1028.

NOWAKOWSKI, T.Z. and BYERS, M. 1972. Effects of nitrogen and potassium fertilisers on contents of carbohydrates and free amino acids in Italian ryegrass. II. Changes in the composition of the non-protein nitrogen fraction and the distribution of individual amino acids. J. Sci. Food Agric. *23*, 1313–1333.

OELSHLEGEL, F.J., JR., SCHROEDER, J.R. and STAHMANN, M.A. 1969. Potential for protein concentrates from alfalfa and waste green plant material. J. Agric. Food Chem. *17*, 791-795.

OHSHIMA, M. and OOUCHI, K. 1976. The order of limitation of amino acids in ladino clover leaf protein concentrate for growing rats. Nutr. Rep. Int. *14*, 611–620.

OKE, O.L. 1973. Leaf protein research in Nigeria: A review. Trop. Sci. *15*, 139–155.

OMOLE, T.A., OKE, O.L. and MFON, B.P. 1976. Carrot leaf protein, preliminary trials with whole leaf using rabbits. Nutr. Rep. Int. *14*, 173–178.

OSBORNE, T.B. 1921. The proteins of the alfalfa plant. J. Biol. Chem. *49*, 63–91.

PEISER, G.D. and YANG, S.F. 1979. Sulfite-mediated destruction of β-carotene. J. Agric. Food Chem. *27*, 446–449.

PETERSON, D.W. 1950. Some properties of a factor in alfalfa meal causing depression of growth in chicks. J. Biol. Chem. *183*, 647–653.

PIERPOINT, W.S. 1969. *o*-Quinones formed in plant extracts. Their reactions with amino acids and peptides. Biochem. J. *112*, 609–616.

PIERPOINT, W.S. 1971. Formation and behaviour of *o*-quinones in some processes of agricultural importance. Rep. Rothamsted Exp. Stn. *1970*, 199–218.

PIRIE, N.W. 1955. Leaf proteins. *In* Modern Methods of Plant Analysis, Vol. 4. K. Paech and M.V. Tracey (Editors). Springer-Verlag, Berlin.

PIRIE, N.W. 1969. The present position of research on the use of leaf protein as a human food. Plant Foods Hum. Nutr. *1*, 237–246.

PIRIE, N.W. 1971. Conclusion. *In* Leaf Protein: Its Agronomy, Preparation, Quality and Use. N.W. Pirie (Editor). Blackwell Scientific Publications, Oxford.

PIRIE, N.W. 1975. The potentialities of leafy vegetables and forages as food protein sources. Baroda J. Nutr. *2*, 43–58.

PIRIE, N.W. 1978. Leaf Protein and Other Aspects of Fodder Fractionation. Cambridge University Press, Cambridge.

PRINCEN, L.H. 1977. Potential wealth in new crops: Research and developement. *In* Crop Resources. D.S. Seigler (Editor). Academic Press, New York.

RACKIS, J.J., ANDERSON, R.L., SASAME, H.A., SMITH, A.K. and VANETTEN, C.H. 1961. Amino acid in soybean hulls and oilmeal fractions. J. Agric. Food Chem. *9*, 409–412.

ROACH, A.G., SANDERSON, P. and WILLIAMS, D.R. 1967. Comparison of methods for the determination of available lysine value in animal and vegetable protein sources. J. Sci. Food Agric. *18*, 274–278.

ROGERS, D.J. 1959. Cassava leaf protein. Econ. Bot. *13*, 261–263.

ROGERS, D.J. and MILNER, M. 1963. Amino acid profile of manioc leaf protein in relation to nutritive value. Econ. Bot. *17*, 211–263.

ROSE, W.C., OESTERLING, M.J. and WOMACK, M. 1948. Comparative growth on diets containing 10 and 19 amino acids, with further observations upon the role of glutamic and aspartic acids. J. Biol. Chem. *176*, 753–762.

SARKAR, S.K., HOWARTH, R.E., HIKICHI, M. and McARTHUR, J.M. 1975. Soluble protein of alfalfa *(Medicago sativa)* herbage. Fractionation by ammonium sulfate and gel chromatography. J. Agric. Food Chem. *23*, 626–630.

SHURPALEKAR, K.S., SINGH, N. and SUNDARAVALLI, O.E. 1969. Nutritive value of leaf protein from lucerne *(Medicago sativa)*: Growth responses in rats at different protein levels and to supplementation with lysine and/or methionine. Indian J. Exp. Biol. *7*, 279–280.

SIEGEL, M.I., WISHNICK, M. and LANE, M.D. 1972. Ribulose-1,5 diphosphate carboxylase. *In* The Enzymes, Vol. 6, 3rd Edition. P.D. Boyer (Editor). Academic Press, New York.

SINGH, N. 1960. Differences in the nature of N precipitated by various methods from wheat leaf extracts. Biochim. Biophys. Acta *45*, 422–428.

SINGH, T.N., PALEG, L.G. and ASPINALL, D. 1973. Stress metabolism. I. Nitrogen metabolism and growth in the barley plant during water stress. Aust. J. Biol. Sci. *26*, 45–56.

SINGLETON, V.L. and KRATZER, F.H. 1969. Toxicity and related physiological activity of phenolic substances of plant origin. J. Agric. Food Chem. *17*, 497–512.

SJÖBERG, L.B. and BOSTRÖM, S.L. 1977. Studies in rats on the nutritional value of hydrogen peroxide-treated fish protein and the utilization of oxidized sulphur-amino acids. Br. J. Nutr. *38*, 189–205.

SLADE, B.R.E., BRANSCOMBE, D.J. and McGOWAN, J.C. 1945. Protein extraction. Chem. Ind. (Soc. Chem. Ind.) *25*, 194–197.

SMITH, R.H. 1966. Lipid-protein isolates. *In* Adv. Chem. Ser. *57*. American Chemical Society, Washington, D.C.

SMITH, T.A. 1975. Recent advances in the biochemistry of plant amines. Phytochemistry *14*, 865–890.

SPENCER, R.R., MOTTOLA, A.C., BICKOFF, E.M., CLARK, J.P. and KOHLER, G.O. 1971. The Pro-Xan process: The design and evaluation of a pilot plant system for the coagulation and separation of the leaf protein from alfalfa juice. J. Agric. Food Chem. *19*, 504–507.

STABURSVICK, A. and HEIDE, O.M. 1974. Protein content and amino acid spectrum of finger millet *(Eleusine coracana)* as influenced by nitrogen and sulphur fertilizers. Plant Soil *41*, 549–571.

STEWART, G.R. and LAHRER, F. 1979. The accumulation of amino acids and related compounds in relation to environmental stress. *In* The Biochemistry of Plants, Vol. 5. B.J. Miflin (Editor). Academic Press, New York.

STOKES, D.M., ANDERSON, J.W. and ROWAN, K.S. 1968. The isolation of mitochondria from potato-tuber tissue using sodium metabisulphite for preventing damages by phenolic compounds during extraction. Phytochemistry *7*, 1509–1512.

SUBBA RAU, B.H., MAHADEVIAH, S. and SINGH, N. 1969. Nutritional studies on whole-extract coagulated leaf protein and fractionated chloroplastic and cytoplasmic proteins from lucerne *(Medicago sativa)*. J. Sci. Food Agric. *20*, 355–358.

SUBBA RAU, B.H., RAMANA, K.V.R. and SINGH, N. 1972. Studies on nutritive value of leaf proteins and some factors affecting their quality. J. Sci. Food Agric. *23*, 233–245.

SUBBA RAU, B.H. and SINGH, N. 1970. Studies on nutritive value of leaf protein from lucerne *(Medicago sativa)*. Part II. Effect of processing conditions. Indian J. Exp. Biol. *8*, 34–36.

TAO, M., BOULET, M., BRISSON, G.J., HUANG, K.H., RIEL, R.R. and JULIEN, J.P. 1972. A study of the chemical composition and nutritive value of leaf protein concentrates. Can. Inst. Food Sci. Technol. J. *5*, 50–54.

TRIGG, T.E. 1971. The effect of various additional amino acids on the quality of several leaf protein concentrates given to rats. M.Sc. Thesis. University of Aberdeen, Aberdeen, Scotland.

TRIGG, T.E. and TOPPS, J.H. 1972. The effects of additional methionine on the quality of leaf protein concentrates differing in nutritive value. Proc. Nutr. Soc. *31*, 45A-46A.

VALLI DEVI, A., RAO, N.A.N. and VIJAYARAGHAVAN, P.K. 1965. Isolation and composition of leaf protein from certain species of Indian flora. J. Sci. Food Agric. *16*, 116–120.

WALKER, H.G., KOHLER, G.O., KUZMICKY, D.D. and WITT, S.C. 1975. Problems in analysis for sulfur amino acids in feeds and foods. *In* Protein Nutritional Quality of Foods and Feeds, Part 1. M. Friedman (Editor). Marcel Dekker, New York.

WALLACE, G.M. 1975. The recovery of a leaf-protein concentrate: A review. *In* Leaf Protein Concentrates (New Zealand Scene). G.M. Wallace (Editor). Ruakura Agricultural Research Centre, Hamilton, New Zealand.

WANG, J.C. and KINSELLA, J.E. 1975. Composition of alfalfa leaf protein isolates. Food Sci. *40*, 1156–1161.

WATSON, L. and CREASER, E.H. 1975. Non-random variation of protein amino acid profiles in grass seeds and dicot leaves. Phytochemistry *14*, 1211–1217.

WILLIAMS, A.P., HEWITT, D. and COCKBURN, J.E. 1979. A collaborative study on the determination of cyst(e)ine in feeding stuffs. J. Sci. Food Agric. *30*, 469–474.

WILSON, R.F. and TILLEY, J.M.A. 1965. Amino acid composition of lucerne and grass protein preparations. J. Sci. Food Agric. *16*, 173–178.

WOODHAM, A.A. 1965. The nutritive value of leaf protein concentrates. Proc. Nutr. Soc. *24*, xxiv–xxv.

WOODHAM, A.A. 1971. The use of animal tests for the evaluation of leaf protein concentrates. *In* Leaf Protein: Its Agronomy, Preparation, Quality, and Use. N.W. Pirie (Editor). Blackwell Scientific Publications, Oxford.

YEMM, E.W. and FOLKES, B.F. 1953. The amino acids of cytoplasmic and chloroplastic proteins of barley. Biochem. J. *53*, 700–707.

6

Gas-Liquid Chromatographic Analysis of Amino Acids

Steven Nagy

Gas-liquid chromatography (GLC) has become an important method for the analysis of amino acids because: (1) it is quantitatively as accurate and as reliable as classical ion exchange chromatography (Gehrke *et al.* 1968A), (2) the speed of analysis of an amino acid mixture (about 35 min; Nagy and Hall 1979) is unequalled by any other analytical procedure, and (3) the cost of gas chromatographic equipment is markedly less than ion exchange instruments.

The ease with which amino acids may be chemically modified has resulted in a plethora of studies on volatile derivatives. Some derivatives investigated have included the N-trimethysilyl trimethylsilyl esters (Ruhlmann and Giesecke 1961; Gehrke *et al.* 1969), N-acetyl *n*-amyl esters (Johnson *et al.* 1961), N-trifluoroacetyl (TFA) *n*-amyl esters (Darbre and Blau 1963), phenylthiohydantoin and methyl 2,4-dinitrophenyl esters (Pisano *et al.* 1962), N-acetyl *n*-propyl esters (Adams 1974), N-heptafluorobutyryl (HFB) *n*-propyl esters (Moss *et al.* 1971), N-HFB *n*-isobutyl esters (MacKenzie and Tenaschuk 1974), and N-TFA *n*-butyl esters (Lamkin and Gehrke 1965).

The most extensively studied volatile derivative has been the N-TFA *n*-butyl amino acid ester. In a series of publications, Gehrke and co-workers described the experimental conditions for protein hydrolysis (Roach and Gehrke 1970), quantitative conversion of amino acids to volatile N-TFA *n*-butyl esters (Stalling *et al.* 1967; Roach and Gehrke 1969A), and gas-liquid chromatographic methods for separation and quantitation of the amino acids (Gehrke and Stalling 1967; Gehrke *et al.* 1968B; Roach and Gehrke 1969B; Gehrke and Takeda 1973; Kaiser *et al.* 1974). Polyester stationary phases, such as ethylene glycol adipate, diethylene glycol succinate, neopentyl glycol succinate, and Carbowax 20M possess excellent resolving capabilities for the N-TFA *n*-butyl esters (Gehrke and Shakrokhi 1966; Gehrke *et al.* 1968B; Appelqvist and Nair 1976), but their disadvantages are high stationary phase bleed above 200°C and the requirement for extensive column conditioning. In addition, peaks for trifluoroacetic acid (reagent) and trifluoroacetamide (ammonia derivative) interfere with the accurate quantitation of some amino acid derivatives on these phases (Gehrke *et al.* 1968A). Nagy and Hall (1979) found that Silar® (phenyl and cyanoalkyl polysiloxane) stationary phases separate N-TFA *n*-butyl esters as effectively as the polyester phases and without their disadvantages.

APPARATUS

(1) A gas chromatograph equipped with a flame ionization detector, glass-lined injection port, glass columns, and capable of temperature programming. There should be minimal exposure of the volatile amino acid derivative to any metal surface between the injection port and detector.
(2) A 1 mV recorder connected to a data reducer (e.g., Autolab System IV-B Chromatography Data Analyzer-Spectra Physics; Hewlett-Packard Model 5880 A Level Four)
(3) Carrier (helium or nitrogen), air, and hydrogen gas lines to the gas chromatograph should be equipped with filters which contain a molecular sieve and drierite (gas purifier—Alltech Associates) and, in addition, an oxygen-absorbing trap (Oxisorb—Alltech Associates) for the carrier gas line
(4) An oil bath equipped with a thermostat to control temperatures of ± 2°C, and positioned over a magnetic stirring plate
(5) Magnetic stirring bars, PTFE-coated
(6) An all-glass rotary evaporator fitted with a temperature-controlled water bath
(7) Vacuum pump
(8) Pyrex glass, screw-top culture tubes with Teflon®-lined caps:
    (a) 25 × 150 mm for hydrolysis of small protein samples (about 10 mg) or 25 × 200 mm for larger samples (about 20 mg) and
    (b) 13 × 100 mm tubes for acylation of amino acids
(9) Ion exchange columns (30 cm × 0.9 cm id)
(10) HI-EFF Fluidizer (Applied Science Labs)
(11) Round-bottom flasks (100 to 500 ml)
(12) Disposable transfer pipets
(13) Pipets (1 to 25 ml)
(14) Syringes (5 to 25 μl) (Hamilton)
(15) Ultrasonic bath (Cole Parmer)
(16) Fritted-glass funnels
(17) Microvials with open top caps equipped with Teflon® septa

REAGENTS

(1) Chromatographically pure amino acid standards (Mann Research Labs)
(2) Cation exchange resin, H^+ form, 100–200 mesh

(3) 0.1 *N* Hydrochloric acid
(4) Chloroform, reagent grade, distilled in glass
(5) Methylene chloride, reagent grade, distilled in glass
(6) *n*-Butanol, reagent grade, distilled in glass
(7) Hydrogen chloride gas, anhydrous, 99.7% min. purity
(8) Trifluoroacetic anhydridc in methylene chloride (25% V/V) (Regis)
(9) *Trans*-4-(aminomethyl) cyclohexane carboxylic acid (tranexamic acid)—internal standard
(10) Gas-Chrom Q (solid support) (Applied Science Labs)
(11) Silar 10C (stationary phase) (Applied Science Labs)
(12) OV-7, OV-17, OV-210 (stationary phases)

PROCEDURES

(A) Protein Hydrolysis and Amino Acid Preparation

(1) A sample containing 20 mg of leaf protein concentrate (LPC) is weighed into a 25 × 200 mm tube, and about 65 ml of 6 *N* HCl is added. The ratio of HCl to protein (W/W) should be about 1000–3000 to 1.
(2) The tube is placed in a sonicator bath and evacuated with a vacuum pump to remove dissolved air. The tube is repeatedly flushed with nitrogen during evacuation and, finally, the tube is sealed under nitrogen.
(3) The sample is hydrolyzed in an oven at 145°C for 4 hr.
(4) After hydrolysis, the sample is filtered through a glass funnel equipped with a coarse-fritted disc to remove insoluble materials.
(5) The filtrate is poured into a 200 ml round-bottom flask and 0.5 mg of tranexamic acid (internal gas chromatograph standard) is added. The solution is concentrated to dryness on a rotary evaporator at about 50° to 60°C. Methylene chloride is added to the flask to azeotropically remove the last traces of water.
(6) Interfering materials must be removed from the hydrolyzed protein prior to derivatization, and this is done by passage through a cation exchange column.
  (a) The concentrated mixture (amino acids derived from the hydrolyzed protein, internal standard, other materials) from step (5) is dissolved in 0.1 *N* HCl. An aliquot containing about 5 mg of amino acids is percolated into a cation resin bed (about 5 to 7 ml of a resin bed packed in a 30 cm × 0.9 cm id ion exchange column).
  (b) Nonionic materials and anions are eluted from the resin bed with about 20 ml of deionized water at 3 ml/min and 30 ml of deionized water at full flow. Discard this eluent.
  (c) Free amino acids are eluted from the column with 20 ml of 7 *N* NH_4OH at about 3 ml/min and, finally, the column is rinsed with about 5 ml of deionized water at about 3 ml/min.
(7) The combined eluent is collected in a 250 ml round-bottom flask and concentrated to dryness on a rotary evaporator at about 55°C.

(B) Sample Derivatization

(1) To the dried eluent from the ion exchange column [step (7) of "Protein Hydrolysis and Amino Acid Preparation"] is added 10 ml of the butylation reagent (3 *N* HCl-*n*-butanol). The flask is placed in an ultrasonic bath for 5 min.

(2) A magnetic stirring bar is added and the flask is placed in an oil bath positioned over a magnetic stirring plate. A condenser is attached and esterification is conducted at 115°C for 15 min.

(3) Following esterification, evaporate the mixture to dryness under vacuum at 55°C.

(4) To the dried mixture is added 4 ml of acylating reagent (trifluoroacetic anhydride in methylene chloride). The flask is placed in an ultrasonic bath for about 1 min, and then the mixture is transferred with a disposable pipet to a 13 × 100 mm acylation tube. The tube is capped with a Teflon®-lined screw cap.

(5) The acylation tube is placed in an oil bath at 150°C for 5 min. Time and temperature (±2°C) of acylation must be rigidly controlled.

(6) Following acylation, samples are transferred to microvials with open top caps equipped with Teflon® septa and stored at 4°C until chromatography is performed.

(C) Reagent Preparation

(1) Butylation Reagent.

(a) Anhydrous HCl gas is bubbled through cooled *n*-butanol in a nitrogen-purged flask. The process is continued until the alcohol is 3 *M* in HCl on a W/W basis.

(b) The reagent is stable for several months if stored at 4°C in a polypropylene bottle.

(2) Acylation Reagent.

(a) Reagent can be made by mixing methylene chloride and trifluoroacetic anhydride (TFAA) in a ratio of 2:1 (V/V) or purchased from Regis (25% TFAA in methylene chloride).

(D) Column Preparation

(1) Packing A. 0.75% (W/W) Silar 10C on 100–120 mesh Gas-Chrom Q

(a) Weigh out separately 19.85 g Gas-Chrom Q and 0.15 g Silar 10C.

(b) Evenly spread the Gas-Chrom Q (19.85 g) in a porcelain plate (1500 ml cap).

(c) Dissolve the Silar 10C (0.15 g) in acetone, and evenly pour the solution over the Gas-Chrom Q, wetting it completely. If necessary, more acetone is used for quantitative transfer of the Silar 10C and for making a slurry of the mixture. The surface of the Gas-Chrom Q should barely be covered with acetone.

(d) The plate containing the slurry is placed on a hot water bath (80°–90°C) and stirred with a gentle folding action (spoon) until it becomes free-flowing from loss of solvent.

(e) The semidry packing is transferred to the HI-EFF fluidizer and any residual solvent is removed by passing N_2 through the fluidized bed at 60°C (Kruppa *et al.* 1967).

(f) Under positive N_2 pressure, the dried, coated support is packed into a 183 cm × 0.4 cm id glass column. Both column ends are plugged with silanized glass wool.

(g) For conditioning, N_2 or He gas (30 ml/min) is used. The column temperature is raised at 2°C/min until it reaches an upper limit of about 250°C and then is maintained at that limit for about 15 to 30 min. Additional conditioning may be necessary if the baseline is not stable. [In general, Silar phases show excellent resolving capabilities and minimal bleed after only a short conditioning period (Nagy and Hall 1979).]

(2) Packing B. 0.5% (W/W) OV-210 + 0.5% (W/W) OV-17 + 0.4% (W/W) OV-7 on 100–120 mesh Gas-Chrom Q. Prepare in a manner similar to Packing A using 19.72 g Gas-Chrom Q, 0.10 g OV-210, 0.10 g OV-17, and 0.08 g OV-7; use acetone as the solvent.

(a) After fluidized bed drying, pack the coated support into an all-glass 183 cm × 0.4 cm id column.

(b) The column is conditioned with N_2 or He (30 ml/min) by raising the temperature to about 250°C at 1°–2.5°C/min; it is maintained at that limit for about 15 min. For good column performance, this type of slow heat conditioning should be repeated several times.

(E) Gas Chromatographic Conditions

(1) Silar 10C.

(a) Gas flow rates: Carrier 60 ml/min; hydrogen 30 ml/min; air 350–400 ml/min

(b) Injector temp. –200°C

(c) Detector temp. –245°C

(d) The N-TFA *n*-butyl derivatives are injected on-column at 110°C, held at 110°C for 5 min, and then programmed at 8°C/min to 230°C (see Fig. 6.1 for the separation of 17 α-amino acids on 0.75% Silar 10C). N-TFA *n*-butyl derivatives of arginine, histidine, and cystine are not determined on this column because they cannot be quantitatively eluted (Nagy and Hall 1979).

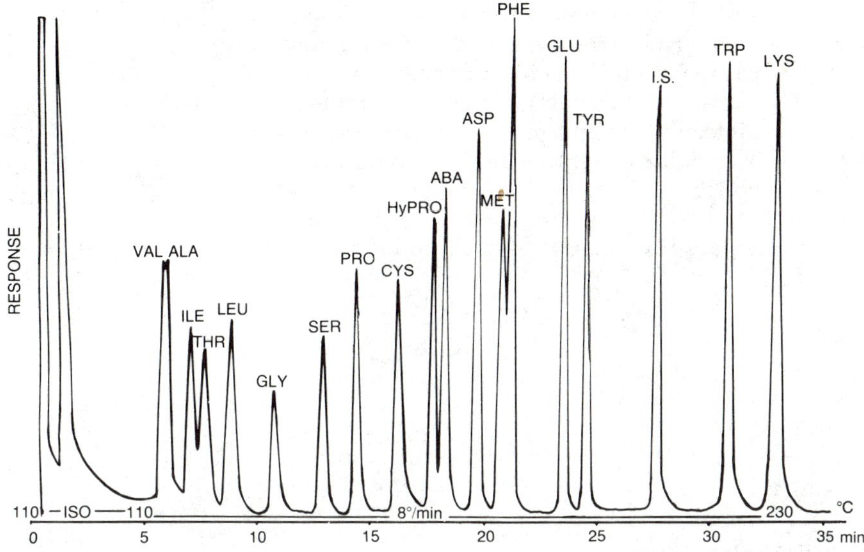

Fig. 6.1. Separation of γ-aminobutyric acid and 17 α-amino acids on 0.75% Silar 10C.

(2) OV-210-OV17-OV7. This column is used for the quantitative determination of arginine, histidine, and cystine.

(a) Gas flow rates: Carrier 60 ml/min; hydrogen 30 ml/min; air 350–400 ml/min

(b) Injector temp. −245°C

(c) Detector temp. −250°C

(d) *Histidine*—The derivatized amino acid mixture in an excess of TFAA is injected on-column at 140°C, held isothermally for 6 min, and programmed at 210°C at 8°C/min (Hall and Nagy 1979). *Arginine and cystine*—The derivatized sample is injected on-column at 90°C, held isothermally for 2 min, and programmed to 210°C at 8°C/min.

CALCULATIONS

(1) Determine relative molar responses (RMR) of each standard amino acid (aa) to the internal standard (is).

$$RMR_{aa/is} = \frac{A_{aa}/G_{aa}/MW_{aa}}{A_{is}/G_{is}/MW_{is}} = \frac{A_{aa}}{moles_{aa}} \Big/ \frac{A_{is}}{moles_{is}}$$

A_{aa} = Area or electronic count of amino acid peak
A_{is} = Area or electronic count of internal standard peak
G_{aa} = Grams of amino acid in sample
G_{is} = Grams of internal standard in sample
MW_{aa} = Molecular weight of amino acid
MW_{is} = Molecular weight of internal standard
moles = g/MW

(2) Calculate the amount of each amino acid present in the sample.

$$G_{aa} = \frac{A_{aa}}{A_{is}} \left[\frac{MW_{aa}}{RMR_{aa/is}} \times \frac{G_{is}}{MW_{is}} \right]$$

$$W/W\%_{aa} = \frac{G_{aa}}{G_{\text{total recovered amino acid}}} \times 100$$

REFERENCES

ADAMS, R.F. 1974. Determination of amino acid profiles in biological samples by gas chromatography. J. Chromatogr. *95*, 189–212.

APPLEQVIST, L.A. and NAIR, B.M. 1976. An improved technique for the gas-liquid chromatographic separation of the N-trifluoroacetyl n-butyl derivatives of amino acids. J. Chromatogr. *124*, 239–245.

DARBRE, A. and BLAU, K. 1963. Quantitative estimation of some amino acids by gas chromatography. Biochem. J. *88*, 8P–9P.

GEHRKE, C.W., NAKAMOTO, H. and ZUMWALT, R.W. 1969. Gas-liquid chromatography of protein amino acid trimethylsilyl derivatives. J. Chromatogr. *45*, 24–51.

GEHRKE, C.W., ROACH, D., ZUMWALT, R.W., STALLING, D.L. and WALL, L.L. 1968A. Quantitative Gas-Liquid Chromatography of Amino Acids in Proteins and Biological Substances. Analytical Biochemical Laboratories, Columbia, MO.

GEHRKE, C.W. and SHAHROKHI, F. 1966. Chromatographic separation of n-butyl N-trifluoroacetyl esters of amino acids. Anal. Biochem. *15*, 97–108.

GEHRKE, C.W. and STALLING, D.L. 1967. Quantitative analysis of the twenty natural protein amino acids by gas-liquid chromatography. Sep. Sci. *2*, 101–138.

GEHRKE, C.W. and TAKEDA, H. 1973. Gas-liquid chromatographic studies on the twenty protein amino acids: A single-column separation. J. Chromatogr. *76*, 63–75.

GEHRKE, C.W., ZUMWALT, R.W. and WALL, L.L. 1968B. Gas-liquid chromatography of protein amino acids: Separation factors. J. Chromatogr. *37*, 398–413.

HALL, N.T. and NAGY, S. 1979. Response amplification of histidine in gas-liquid chromatographic analysis of amino acid mixtures. J.Chromatogr. *171*, 392–397.

JOHNSON, D.E., SCOTT, S.J. and MEISTER, A. 1961. Gas-liquid chromatography of amino acid derivatives. Anal. Chem. *33*, 669–673.

KAISER, F.E., GEHRKE, C.W., ZUMWALT, R.W. and KUO, K. 1974. Amino Acid Analysis: Hydrolysis, Ion-Exchange Clean-up, Derivatization, and Quantitation by Gas-Liquid Chromatography. Analytical Biochemistry Laboratories, Columbia, MO.

KRUPPA, R.F., HENLY, R.S. and SMEAD, D.L. 1967. Improved gas chromatography packings with fluidized drying. Anal. Chem. *39*, 851–853.

LAMKIN, W.M. and GEHRKE, C.W. 1965. Quantitative gas chromatography of amino acids: Preparation of n-butyl N-trifluoroacetyl esters. Anal. Chem *37*, 383–389.

MacKENZIE, S.L. and TENASCHUK, D. 1974. Gas-liquid chromatography of N-hepta-fluorobutyryl isobutyl esters of amino acids. J. Chromatogr. *97*, 19–24.

MOSS, C.W., LAMBERT, M.A. and DIAZ, F.J. 1971. Gas-liquid chromatography of twenty protein amino acids on a single column. J. Chromatogr. *60*, 134–136.

NAGY, S. and HALL, N.T. 1979. Gas-liquid chromatographic separation on Silar™ stationary phases. J. Chromatogr. *177*, 141–144.

PISANO, J.J., VANDEN HEUVEL, W.J.A. and HORNING, E.C. 1962. Gas chromatography of phenylthiohydantoin and dinitrophenyl derivatives of amino acids. Biochem. Biophys. Res. Commun. 7, 82–86.

ROACH, D. and GEHRKE, C.W. 1969A. Direct esterification of the protein amino acids: Gas-liquid chromatography of N-TFA n-butyl esters. J. Chromatogr. *44*, 269–278.

ROACH, D. and GEHRKE, C.W. 1969B. The gas-liquid chromatography of amino acids. J. Chromatogr. *43*, 303–310.

ROACH, D. and GEHRKE, C.W. 1970. The hydrolysis of proteins. J. Chromatogr. *52*, 393–404.

RUHLMANN, K. and GIESECKE, W. 1961. Gas chromatography of silylated amino acids. Angew. Chem. *73*, 113.

STALLING, D.L., GILLE, G. and GEHRKE, C.W. 1967. Quantitative gas chromatography of amino acids. Anal. Biochem. *18*, 118–125.

7

Characterization of Leaf Protein Concentrate by Gel Chromatography

Dr. Marshall L. Fishman

Although proteins were first extracted from green plants by H.M. Rouelle in 1773 (Pirie 1971), the characterization of these proteins is far from complete because of the structural complexity of proteins, the large variety found in one plant, and the probability of alterations during extraction. There is no one chemical or physical measurement which will uniquely characterize all the proteins in plants individually or as a group. Nevertheless, once total nitrogen has been established by Kjeldahl analysis and amino acid content by ion exchange chromatography, gel chromatography is the single most powerful and versatile tool for the characterization of the complex mixture of proteins from plants called leaf protein concentrate (LPC).

The versatility of gel chromatography has permitted its use as a preparative and as an analytical technique for the characterization of LPC. Used as a preparative technique, the goal of gel chromatography is to concentrate the leaf proteins in the extract and to collect sufficient quantities of LPC for further use. As an analytical tool, gel chromatography is used to quantitate the molecular size and amount of LPC in a mixture. Recovery of the sample components in purer form is not necessary.

GEL CHROMATOGRAPHY OF LEAF PROTEIN CONCENTRATE

Historical

Initially, gel chromatography developed along parallel and distinct lines. Porath and Flodin (1959) are generally credited with developing and popularizing the separation and characterization of macromolecules soluble in aqueous media, i.e., hydrophilic ones such as proteins, by their introduction of crosslinked dextran beads as the stationary phase. Porath and Flodin called this form of gel chromatography gel filtration. J.C. Moore (1964) developed and popularized the fractionation and characterization of macromolecules soluble in organic media, i.e., hydrophobic ones such as synthetic polymers, by his introduction of crosslinked polystyrene beads as the stationary phase. This form of gel chromatography he called gel permeation.

After the introduction of porous glass beads, a gel chromatographic stationary phase which can separate hydrophilic and hydrophobic macromolecules alike (Haller 1965), it became increasingly apparent that the similarities in the mechanism of separation by gel permeation and gel filtration far outnumbered the differences. Moreover, following the suggestion of Determann (1968), the term gel chromatography will be used to refer to gel filtration chromatography, steric exclusion chromatography, size exclusion chromatography, sieve chromatography, gel permeation chromatography, and hydrodynamic volume exclusion chromatography.

Theory of Separation

In gel chromatography, separation is according to the hydrodynamic volume (HV) of the dissolved solute molecules (i.e., the molecular volume in the solvated state). Uniquely, among chromatographic techniques, the molecule with the largest HV elutes first, the smallest last. The mobile phase is generally, but not necessarily, a liquid (Giddings *et al.* 1977). The stationary phase is a crosslinked macromolecule or a porous silica, usually in the form of a spherical particle. In column gel chromatography, the solute molecule is dissolved in the mobile phase and allowed to elute (percolate) through a tubular column packed with stationary phase, and presaturated with mobile phase. Wheaton and Bauman (1953) showed that the elution volume, V_e, of a solute at its maximum concentration (i.e., the peak mean) was related to the volume of the mobile phase, V_o, the volume of the stationary phase, V_S, and partition coefficient, K, by the equation:

$$V_e = V_o + KV_S \tag{7.1}$$

Equation (7.1) is the basic equation of gel chromatography and partition chromatography, in general.

If K = 0 for the solute molecules, then

$$V_e = V_o \tag{7.2}$$

meaning the HV of the solute molecules is only sufficiently large to permit them access to the volume occupied by the mobile phase. In gel chromatography V_o is also called the void volume and is the volume between beads. If K = 1 for the solute molecules, then

$$V_e = V_o + V_S \tag{7.3}$$

meaning the solute molecules have a hydrodynamic volume sufficiently small to have access to all the volume occupied by the mobile phase and the stationary phase. The volume of the stationary phase is the volume of the micropores within the gel particles. However, all of V_S is probably not accessible to the smallest of solute molecules and, therefore, not readily measured (Determann and Brewer 1975). Laurent and Killander (1964), redefined the stationary phase as the volume of micropores within the gel particles available to eluent from the mobile phase. The redefined stationary phase, V_{AV}, is related to V_o by the equation

$$V_{AV} = V_T - V_o \tag{7.4}$$

where V_T is the elution volume at maximum concentration of a molecule which occupies the same volume of micropores within the gel as eluent from the mobile phase. A new partition coefficient, K_{AV}, is now defined in terms of measurable parameters by replacing V_S with $V_T - V_o$, and K with K_{AV} in equation (7.1) and rearranging the relation

$$K_{AV} = \frac{V_e - V_o}{V_T - V_o} \tag{7.5}$$

Determann (1968) discusses the advantages and disadvantages of K_{AV} as a parameter for characterizing the behavior of a solute in gel chromatography; in addition, he discusses other commonly used parameters. Physically, K_{AV} for a solute molecule is the volume fraction of eluent-available pores within the gel bead which are accessible to the solute. Since equations (7.1) and (7.5) are essentially mass balance equations, they hold for equilibrium and nonequilibrium conditions. Near or at equilibrium, K_{AV} and column resolution are maximum for a specific solvent and packing. The chromatographic process is at or near equilibrium if a narrow band of dilute solute is applied to the column and the flow rate of the mobile phase is sufficiently low that the number of transfers from mobile to stationary phase or vice versa per unit length of column is independent of flow rate (Cassassa 1971). At higher flow rates (i.e., under nonequilibrium conditions), the number of transfers, column resolution, and K_{AV} decrease with increasing flow rate.

Experimentally, V_o is determined by injecting a substance onto the column which is totally excluded from the micropores of the stationary phase (e.g., blue dextran) and measuring its elution volume at peak mean. Experimentally, V_T is determined by injecting a substance onto the column which totally penetrates the micropores of the stationary phase (e.g., sodium azide) and measuring its elution volume at peak mean. Blue dextran and sodium azide can be detected by their ultraviolet absorption spectra.

"Goodness" of Separation by Gel Columns

With the inception of column chromatography, chromatographers have found the need to quantitatively describe the ability of a column to separate two or more substances. Two of the most widely used terms are resolution, R_S, and height equivalent to a theoretical plate, H, as defined by equations (7.6) and (7.7) in terms of measurable quantities. A more complete discussion of the meaning of R_S, H, and measures of "goodness" of separation as they apply to liquid chromatographs are given by Snyder and Kirkland (1974).

$$R_S = \Delta z / 4\sigma_{AV} \tag{7.6}$$

$$H = \sigma^2 / L \tag{7.7}$$

where σ is the quarter width of an elution peak, σ_{AV} is the arithmetic mean for σ's of two peaks, Δz is the distance between the means of two elution peaks, L is column length. The separating power of a column is measured by R_S, whereas peak broadening is measured by H. The ability of a column to separate is directly proportional to R_S and inversely proportional to H. In gel chromatography, H is best determined by measuring the σ of a substance of monodispersed molecular weight which penetrates 50% of the micropores in the stationary phase.

Gels

The mutual compatibility of solvent, solute, and gel matrix is the most important criterion for determining the appropriate gel to use. Ideally, the solvent should dissolve infinite solute, and freely penetrate all of the micropores within the gel bead, whereas the solute should not adsorb onto the gel matrix. Since LPC only dissolves in aqueous solvents, only gels which absorb aqueous solvents can be used. Hence, nonpolar crosslinked gels such as polystyrene, polyvinylacetate, and silica gel cannot be used to separate or characterize LPC.

Two types of gels will absorb aqueous solvents. The soft gels, xerogels, are made from polymers which are water soluble prior to crosslinking, and rigid gels, aerogels, are made of porous glasses. Among the soft crosslinked gels are dextrans, polyacrylamide, agarose-acrylamide composites, and dextran-acrylamide composites. Nevertheless, it appears that the dextran-acrylamide composites are useful only over the pH range 5.5–8 for size separations as adsorption occurs below pH 5.5 and cation exchange above pH 8 (Belew *et al.* 1978). The latter two gels are attempts to increase the mechanical strength of the soft gels.

Since the composite gels have been introduced only recently, there has not been time for a critical evaluation of them. The porous glasses adsorb proteins so strongly that they have not been used extensively to characterize them. However, the use of glass beads for protein separation may increase markedly if efforts are successful to eliminate or substantially diminish adsorption for a wide variety of proteins by covalently bonding inert organic surfaces onto the glass. Then it is expected that better separation will be obtained with rigid gels than with soft as the greater mechanical strength of the rigid gels over the soft ones will permit smaller particle sizes to be used (e.g., 5–10 μ for glasses compared to 20–120 μ for cross-linked dextrans).

Recently, Chang *et al.* (1976) reported that by bonding a glycerylpropylsilyl (named glycophase) layer onto glass, they obtained separations of proteins up to 68,000 daltons which were at higher resolutions than had been obtained for the same proteins on soft gels. Engelhardt and Mathes (1977) reported that glycerylpropylsilyl-coated glass will retard some protein and that glass coated with an amidepropylsilyl layer is superior in its inertness toward proteins while giving resolution comparable to the glycerylpropylsilyl-coated glass. Most recently, the Toyo Soda Manufacturing Co., Ltd., has reported developing a series of proprietary, rigid, hydrophilic gels (10–13 μ particle size with a molecular weight operating range between 6×10^5 and 2×10^4) (Rokushika *et al.* 1978; Anon. 1978). These gels, when packed in columns, have an H value of 0.06 mm compared to 0.5–1.5 mm for soft gels. Therefore separations which would take 3.5 hr by soft gel take less than 0.75 hr with these gels. At present, the gels are being marketed by the name TSK-SW columns.

Although there is promise that high performance rigid gels will be available eventually for leaf protein analysis, at present only the soft gels have been used successfully. Therefore, the remainder of the chapter will concern itself with methodology and application involving soft gels. A comprehensive review of high performance liquid chromatography (HPLC) including applications involving rigid microporous gels has been recently written by Snyder and Kirkland (1974).

Analytical Gel Chromatography

A gel chromatograph is an instrument which stores and drives the mobile phase, permits sample introduction, and separates samples by hydrodynamic volume by forcing the sample through a tubular column packed with gel and detecting the components after separation. Figure 7.1 is a typical schematic of the gel chromatograph. The gel and whether preparative or analytical gel chromatography is to be performed are the most important factors in determining equipment requirements.

Solvent Delivery

Components for an analytical gel chromatograph are chosen to obtain constant and reproducible flow rates and to minimize sample dilution which

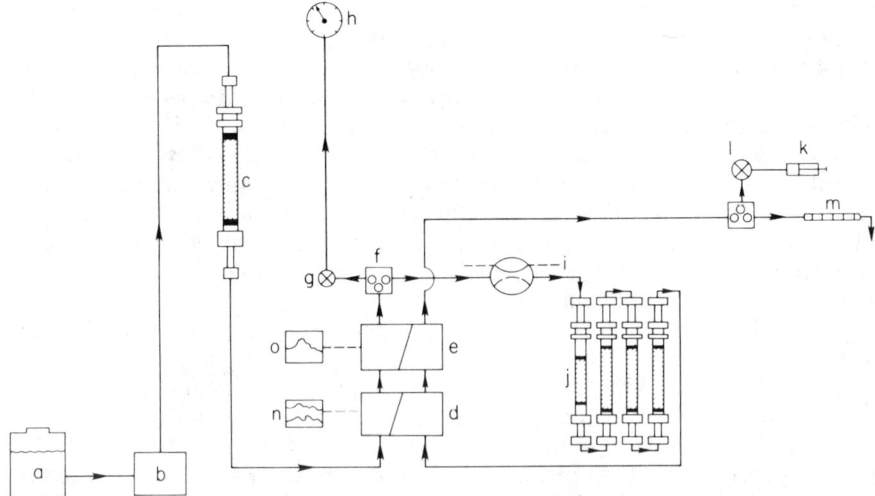

Fig. 7.1. Schematic of gel chromatograph. Components: A—Reservoir. B—Peristaltic pump. C—Safety column. D—Ultraviolet absorptometer. E—Differential refractometer. F—T-connector. G and L—One-way slider valve. H—Pressure gauge. I—Six port injection valve. J—Columns. K—Syringe. M—Pipet. N—Dual channel potentiometric recorder. O—Single channel potentiometric recorder.
From Fishman (1976).

is not associated with the process of size separation. The most inexpensive method for forcing mobile phase through a gel column is gravity flow while maintaining a constant head pressure with a simple device such as a Marriotte flask (Anon. 1973). If the resistance to flow during the life of a packed column is relatively constant and low, gravity flow of the mobile phase is the method of choice because of low cost and simplicity. We have found for the gel chromatography of LPC that column resistance rises slowly with the number of samples injected onto the column. Increased column resistance occurs even when pure protein standards are used to calibrate the column, but the rise occurs to a far lesser extent than with LPC. Even passing the sample through a 0.45 μm membrane filter does not prevent column resistance from rising with number of samples injected, although it slows down the rise in resistance. Therefore in analytical gel chromatography of LPC, it is almost mandatory to use a pump to drive the mobile phase. Moreover, inadvertently injecting small quantities of air into the system will affect the flow rate in a pump driven system to a lesser extent than in a gravity flow system.

If column inlet pressures are below 345 kPa (50 psi), a peristaltic pump can be used. In the 345–621 (50–90 psi) range, peristaltic pumps can be used only with heavy walled tubing, and the tubing in contact with rollers in the pump head must be changed frequently, approximately every 96 hr of use. Peristaltic pumps are advantageous in that they are inexpensive in comparison to piston pumps, relatively pulseless, and do not permit metal parts to come in contact with the mobile phase. Disadvantages of peristaltic pumps are that columns can run dry if tubing breaks, flow rates change slowly because plastic-walled tubing flows under stress, flow rates below 0.5 ml/hr are difficult to reproduce, and they cannot pump liquids against head pressures in excess of 621 kPa (90 psi). Important features to look for in a peristaltic pump are sufficient roller head area in contact with tubing to prevent pulsing and a motor which maintains its speed in spite of line voltage fluctuations or heating.

The dual piston pump is widely used in gel chromatography to drive the mobile phase. These pumps maintain constant flow, flow rates can be reproduced to 0.1 ml/hr, and they pump long periods without stopping for maintenance. Also, they pump against head pressures of 3450 kPa (500 psi) if internal parts are nonmetallic, or up to 48,300 kPa (7000 psi) if 316 stainless steel is used. At present, with soft gels, pumps which are rated to pump against 3450 kPa (500 psi) are adequate. The main disadvantages of dual piston pumps are that they are 3 to 10 times more expensive than peristaltic pumps and if internal parts are 316 stainless steel, they are corroded by aqueous solutions containing halide ions. Leaking is a problem with piston pumps employing Teflon slider valves. Pulsing is a problem with the less expensive single piston pumps, unless damping devices are incorporated into the system. Pulsing is not desirable as it causes a noisy output signal from the detector, particularly at high sensitivities [i.e., full scale 0.2 AU (Absorbance Units)].

Sample Application

Sample application falls into two broad categories, manual or automatic. The least expensive manual method is to stop flow, layer the sample onto the gel bed, allow the sample to penetrate into the gel, wash sample into bed with two sample volumes of eluents, and reconnect column to the pump. A four port switching valve above the top of the column can be used to apply a measured volume of sample by gravity flow from a syringe while the eluent from the reservoir is diverted to drain. The four port valve eliminates the need to stop flow from the reservoir or disconnect tubing between the pump and the top of the column. The most convenient manual injector is the six port rotary loop valve (Fig. 7.2A). In one position, the valve connects the pump directly to the column. In this same position a loop of known volume can be filled with sample. By turning the valve to a second position (Fig. 7.2B), the loop is placed in series with the pump and the column. Hence, a sample equal in volume to that of the loop is pumped onto the column. The loop valve permits injection of a measured volume of sample without disconnecting the column and with only slight change in flow rate.

Even more convenient than the manual loop valve is the loop valve

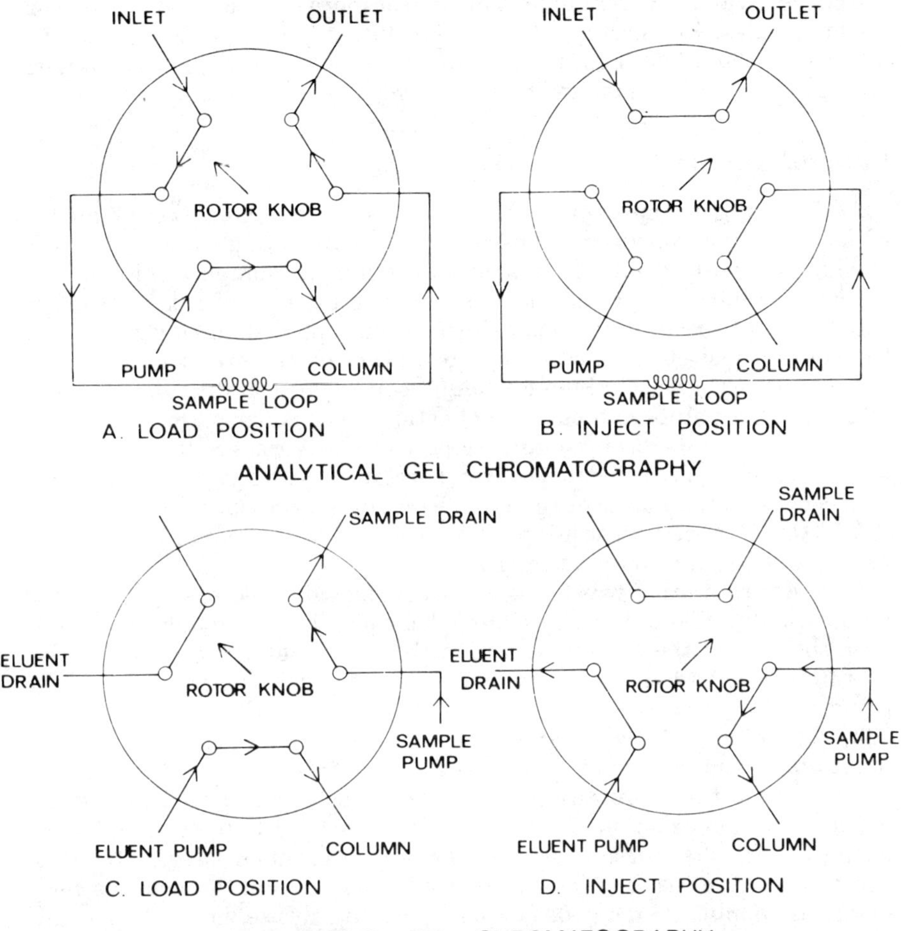

Fig. 7.2. Flow patterns of a six port sample application valve.

powered by an electric motor. In one relatively inexpensive version, six loops are placed in parallel with each other and one of the six is in series with the pump and column; the rest are closed at each end. By causing rotary valves at each end of the loop to rotate through an arc subtending an angle of 60°, that loop is blocked off and the loop next to it is placed into series with the pump and the column. By connecting the motor-driven valves to an electric timer and counter, it is possible to obtain up to six sample applications automatically at timed intervals. Other variations of the six port valve are available to give 40 or more injections with one loading of samples. An injector valve rated to withstand pressures of 3450 kPa (500 psi) without leaking should prove adequate for most applications with agarose, polyacrylamide, and dextran gels.

Column Tubing

At operating pressures of 3450 kPa (500 psi) or less, glass is the material of choice for column tubing. The main advantages of glass are that it is chemically inert to all buffer solutions commonly employed in the gel chromatography of proteins and it is transparent. The transparency of the tubing is an important aid in packing columns and in detecting changes in the column bed such as occur by adsorption or compression. The chief disadvantages of glass tubing for columns are their fragility and tendency to break at the inlet and outlet connections. The inner diameter, id, of a glass column limits its maximum pressure of use. A glass column with an id of 9 mm or less is not rated to withstand pressures in excess of 3450 kPa (500 psi). A column with an id of 13 mm has maximum pressure rating of about 2070 kPa (300 psi), whereas 690 kPa (100 psi) is the maximum pressure rating for a column with an id of 25 mm.

Initially, resolution was thought to increase with decreasing column id because of diminished band spreading. However, interactions of the sample with the wall of the column also cause band spreading (i.e., the so-called "wall effect"), and these become more serious with decreasing id of the column. More recent work indicates that the resolution is not related simply to column id (De Stefano 1974). Other factors such as configuration of the applied sample, particle size, and shape of the packing are important in determining the column id to maximize resolution. Since soft gels are deformable, the exact shape can vary from packing to packing and even change during the course of an experiment. At present for soft gels, trial and error are still necessary for choosing the best column dimensions for a particular application. A good rule of thumb is to choose the smallest id and shortest length of column consistent with the resolution requirements of the separation and pressure requirements of the system. Accordingly, the separation will be optimized for speed and minimized for sample size. For the analysis of LPC, we have found that glass columns, 6 × 330 mm, with adjustable end pieces are useful. The end pieces should be covered by a bed support followed by a 5 μm filter sandwiched between two 30 μm filters to permit flow but prevent loss of gel. The adjustable end pieces permit the column length to be varied continuously between 300 and 30 mm. It may be necessary to place several columns in series, each with a different gel or combination of gels, to cover the broad molecular distribution of proteins found in leaves.

Detectors

The perfect detector for the gel chromatography of leaf proteins should respond specifically to proteins, polypeptides, and amino acids with high sensitivity and low baseline noise and drift; and linearly over a wide range of concentrations. It should not respond to changes in effluent temperature and flow rate. Moreover, the perfect detector should have a flow cell whose volume is small in comparison to the volume of the peak of interest (i.e., 1/10) to prevent extra column band spreading. The flow cells should be completely swept by the column effluent to prevent stationary phase formation and diminish bubble hangup. Bubble hangup in the detector is one of the major causes of baseline noise and it can be reduced if not eliminated by completely degassing all solvent prior to filling the resevoir.

There is no detector for proteins which follows all the criteria just listed. The flow-through ultraviolet absorption photometer comes closest to perfection as judged by its overwhelming use compared to other detectors. The popularity of the UV photometer in protein analysis can be accounted for by its high baseline stability (very important in soft gel chromatography as run times are minimum of 3 hr), low noise to signal ratio, and convenience of use. Three commonly used wavelengths in protein analysis are 280 nm, 254 nm, and 206 nm.

The broad molecular weight distribution of leaf protein concentrate causes dilution within the column in the range of 50–100:1. Fishman and Burdick (1977) found that LPC prepared from Coastal Bermuda grass could be monitored at 254 nm and at 206 nm. The sensitivity at 206 nm was 8.5 times greater than at 254 nm. In addition to high sensitivity for proteins, measurements at 206 nm show less variability with amino acid composition than measurements at 254 or 280 nm (Scopes 1974). The amide bond is the major contributor to protein absorbance at 206 nm, which accounts for the comparatively high sensitivity of 206 nm for proteins. Unfortunately, practically all the salts employed in buffer solutions, except sodium and potassium halides, absorb at 206 nm. Fishman (1976) found that the background absorbance due to 0.02% sodium azide, a commonly used bacteriostat, reduced the absorbance at 206 nm from 8.5 to 1.9 times that found at 254 nm. In this same study, although unreported, it was found that absorption at 280 nm was not sufficient to measure protein if a partial separation of the high molecular weight proteins was made.

The second most useful technique for monitoring LPC is differential refractometry. Refractometry comes closest to a universal detector for liquid chromatography. Any solute whose refractive index is different from the solvent can be detected. Sensitivity is proportional to the difference in refractive index between solute and solvent. Virtually all substances extractable from leaves and soluble in aqueous buffer can be detected by differential refractometry. The major drawbacks to refractometry are the need for temperature control and the lack of sensitivity compared to detection at 206 nm. Fishman (1976) found that even in the presence of 0.02%

NaN_3, measurement at 206 nm was 3.4 times as sensitive as the refractive index. Surprisingly, refractive index was almost as sensitive a measure of protein concentration as measurement at 254 nm for proteins whose molecular weights were in excess of 25,000. In this particular study a Fresnel type of refractometer was used. Protein was found to absorb on the surface of the glass prism, thereby decreasing sensitivity. At the same time that absorption decreased, so did background noise, so that the signal could be more highly amplified by the recorder. The net result was that absorption caused no net decrease in the lowest detectable quantity of solute.

A second type of refractometer available is the deflection differential refractometer. Its main advantage over the Fresnel refractometer is that it requires only one cell over the entire refractive index range whereas the Fresnel cell requires two. Nevertheless, one Fresnel cell is sufficient for virtually all applications involving aqueous solvents.

In principle, several other detectors are available for the detection of LPC (e.g., visible photometers, conductometers, fluorimetry, infrared photometry); nevertheless, none of these have been used to date. For example, it would be possible to detect the reaction product of ninhydrin and proteins with a visible photometer, or fluorescamine and proteins with a fluorimeter. These detectors would have higher sensitivity and specificity than UV photometers. On the other hand, they would require more elaborate equipment (i.e., a reactor and extra pump) and would be less convenient than the UV photometer.

Fittings and Connectors

Fittings and connectors should be chosen which minimize dead volume, are completely swept by the mobile phase, and whose wetted parts are chemically inert to the mobile phase. Teflon tubing connected with "Cheminert" types of fittings meets the suggested requirements for tubing and connectors. Tubing id between injection point and detector should be sufficiently small to minimize extra column band spreading and yet not be subject to plugging. Experience has indicated that 0.0305 cm (0.012 in.) id is a good compromise. Teflon tubing with an id of 0.0305 cm (0.012 in.), an od of 0.1588 cm (0.0625 in.), and connected with Cheminert® type fittings [see connector (E) in Fig. 7.3] is rated to withstand pressures of 3450 kPa (500 psi).

Data Acquisition

A potentiometric recorder is required to monitor the analogue signal from the detector. Features of the recorder important to the soft gel chromatography of LPC are multiple chart speeds (2.5, 5, 12.7, 25.4, and 50.8 cm/hr and min or 1, 2, 5, 10, and 20 in./hr and min), multiple input spans (1, 10, 100 mv; 1, 10 v), two or more input channels, freedom from drift ($<0.25\%$ full scale/24 hr), good AC noise rejection, high input impedance, reliable

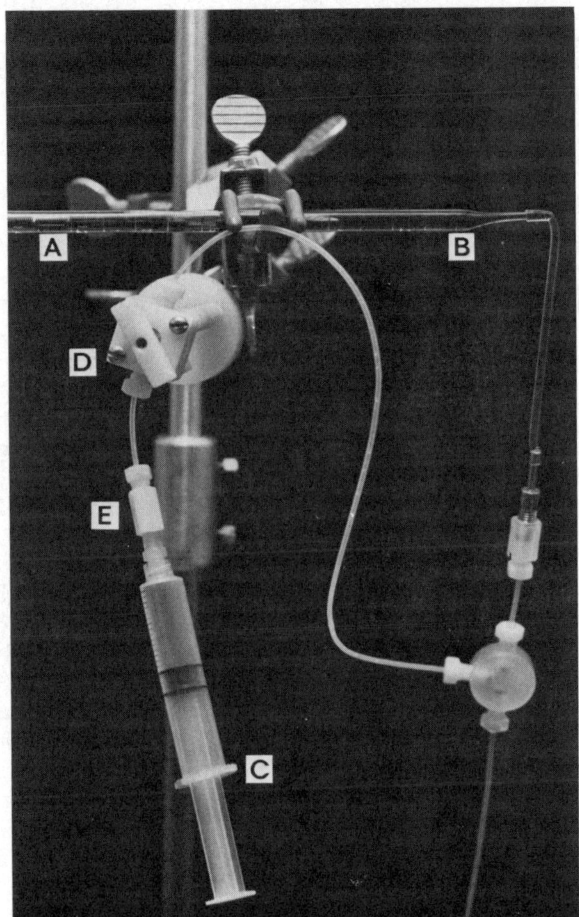

Fig. 7.3. Simple device for measuring flow rate. Components: A—Bubble. B—2 ml graduated pipet drawn out at one end. C—Plastic syringe. D—One-way slider valve. E—Cheminert® fitting [tube end fittings (2) and connector (1) for rapid connection of Teflon tubing].

inking system (e.g., disposable fiber tip pen), and a pen response of 1 sec full scale or less.

Periodic sampling and storage of the detector signal by a data acquisition system can speed up data handling and reduce or eliminate the manual labor of calculating data. A simple data acquisition system would consist of an analogue to digital (A/D) converter (e.g., a digital millivolt meter), a device to control sampling and to measure the time of day (e.g., digital clock), and a device to produce output in a format that can be stored (e.g., printer or tape punch). In LPC analysis, simultaneous detection of the column effluent with two or more detectors has proved useful (Fishman

1976). Incorporation of a multiplexer, also called a scanner, in the data acquisition system would permit acquisition of data from several detectors. Such a system is called a data logger and is the most inexpensive method of acquiring data from multiple detectors. A data logger with the capability of calculating such chromatographic parameters as peak areas, peak maxima, and various statistical averages of the chromatographic curves (e.g., by incorporating a preprogrammed computer) is called a digital integrator.

We have found that the most economical and flexible arrangement is to collect data via a data logger with a punched tape output. The data are fed into an off- line programmable electronic calculator via a tape editor. The calculator can be programmed to calculate and print out the desired quantities. Off-line processing of data requires about 15 min/run or less depending on the complexity of the sample and the speed of the printer. Therefore, the calculator could be used for many other purposes, such as processing data from an amino acid analyzer or doing routine statistical calculations. The main disadvantage of a programmable electronic calculator is the necessity of programming. For multi-channel uses, integrators are more expensive per channel and are somewhat inflexible. Nevertheless, they are preprogrammed.

It would also be possible to interface the detectors directly to a minicomputer and have the computer perform the calculations and print out a finished report. Recently, minicomputers have been used to control the operation of automated High Performance Liquid Chromatographs in addition to performing calculations. Potential application of minicomputers to control gel chromatography is somewhat more limited than in HPLC since solvent gradients are not normally used in separation. Full-sized computers can be used to process the data directly by interfacing and time sharing. A full discussion of the application of computers to the control and processing of data from scientific instruments is beyond the scope of this chapter, but has been treated fully elsewhere (Perone and Jones 1973).

Measurement of Elution Volume

Molecular weight determinations by gel chromatography require quantitative measurement of the volume of mobile phase and the time necessary to move solute molecules from point of injection to point of detection in the chromatograph. These same volume and time measurements in addition to the concentration at the point of detection permit quantitation of the amount of solute injected into the chromatograph. Transport of mobile phase can be measured by flow meter, gravimetrically, and volumetrically. The flow meter is semiquantitative whereas the gravimetric method is very accurate but time consuming (Snyder and Kirkland 1974).

Variations of the volumetric method offer the best compromise between convenience and reproducibility. The basic volumetric method measures the time required for water to fill a calibrated volume in a vessel (e.g., a volumetric flask or a buret). At constant flow rate and eluent composition, flow rates can be measured conveniently with a standard error of ± 1% by injecting an air bubble into a tube with a calibrated volume. A simple device made from Cheminert fittings, a plastic syringe, and a 2 ml pipette drawn out at one end is shown in Fig. 7.3. The flow rate was obtained by measuring the time for the trailing meniscus of an air bubble (A) to tranverse a preselected volume in the graduated pipet (B). The bubble was created when the air between the plunger of the syringe (C) and the one-way slider valve (D) was compressed. The slider valve was then opened and closed. Volumes should be chosen which require at least 100 sec to time, so that errors in time measurements will be negligible. The accuracy of this method is dependent on constant flow of the mobile phase during the course of the run.

A second variation of the volumetric method is to count a preset number of drops of eluent with an automated device such as is found in most fraction collectors. The device sends an electrical pulse to the event marker of the recorder, after a fixed number of drops pass through an orifice. The drops are counted by interrupting a light beam which impinges on a photoelectric cell. The accuracy of the method depends on producing drops with uniform volume. At constant flow rate and eluent composition, volumes can be measured with a standard error of ± 1.5% or better. The advantage of drop counting over the air bubble method is that flow rate can be measured periodically during the run if the time interval between drops is measured with a data logger containing a digital clock.

It is also possible to measure volume directly by a vessel with a syphon tube attached to it. When liquid in the vessel reaches a set volume, it syphons over and interrupts a light beam or breaks an electric circuit maintained by an electrode, thereby signaling that a fixed volume of eluent has been pumped through the chromatograph. Poor drainage of aqueous solutions from the glass syphoning vessel causes flow rates measured by syphon systems to be less reproducible than those measured by the bubble or drop counting method. Drainage is poor because the walls of the glass vessel become contaminated by adsorption of dissolved solute molecules, particularly proteins. Adsorption of solute molecules causes varying numbers of water droplets to adhere to the wall of the vessel each time it is drained. In the case of the drop counting method, it is possible to use an orifice made of a plastic such as Teflon which exhibits little or no adsorption of protein.

Measurement of Pressure

Measurement of the pressure at the head of the column, while not an absolute necessity, is extremely useful as an analytical troubleshooting device in the operation of a chromatograph. The pressure gauge (h) should be inserted between the pump (b) and the injector valve (i) (see Fig. 7.1). Increases in pressure indicate an increased resistance to flow usually caused by plugging of the column, particularly at the column inlet. Often, changing a bed support after a number of runs will decrease the pressure at the head of the column as it is the bed support which has become clogged by precipitated solute. A sudden decrease in pressure often indicates a leak in the system. The most inexpensive method of measuring pressure is to use a Bourdon gauge. A pressure transducer will measure pressure with higher sensitivity than the Bourdon type gauge, but it is more expensive.

Packing of Columns

Before packing the column, it should be positioned vertically with a level or plumb line. The length of outlet tubing should approximate 1½ column lengths. Eluents should be degassed. A simple degassing method is to aspirate magnetically stirred eluent in a stoppered vacuum filtration flask. About 5% of the empty column should be filled with degassed eluent and the outlet closed. A long tube (stiff polyethylene tubing is suitable) should be used to tamp down the filters on the bottom of the bed support. In this way bubbles trapped under the bed support will be forced out. The abscence of bubbles and clogged filters can be tested by observing a rapid flow of eluent from the open outlet which is lowered below the liquid level in the chromatography tube. The crosslinked polyacrylamide and dextran gels are supplied in dehydrated powder form and should be rehydrated according to the manufacturers' instruction prior to packing.

Manufacturers of soft gels recommend a slurry gravity sedimentation (SGS) method of packing columns (i.e., sedimentation is under the force of gravity). The SGS method applied to soft gels has been described in great detail in literature obtainable from the manufacturer (Anon. 1971, 1973). The SGS method produces a soft gel packing in which the pressure drop across the column is $\leq$3.5 kPa ($\leq$½ psi). Therefore the flow of the mobile phase can be driven by gravity or by peristaltic pump. Unfortunately, the SGS method applied to soft gels also produces metastable packings. If an event occurs which increases the resistance of the packing material, the flow rate will decrease inversely with the increase in resistance, if flow is gravity driven. If flow is driven by pump, an increase in gel resistance to flow will result in a proportionate increase in pressure, whereas flow will remain relatively constant. Eventually the gel will compress, causing a change in the column calibration. If the gel were allowed to compress far enough, the pressure at the column inlet would rise until the system developed a leak. Sudden compression of the gel in agarose columns after the application of several LPC samples has been observed in our laboratory. A possible explanation of such compressions is adsorption to the packing by LPC or gradual clogging of the filters at column ends by fine gel particles.

To minimize the number of such compressions and subsequent repackings and or recalibrations, we have adopted a slurry-pressure sedimentation (SPS) method of packing gel columns similar to the methodology used to pack ion exchange columns. Catsimpoolas (1972) by a similar method showed that rapid analytical gel chromatography could be performed with

G-25 and G-50 Sephadex by packing these gels into a 3 mm glass micropore column. Partial separations were obtained in 40 min. Experiments with G-100 Sephadex had to be terminated because the pressures which developed caused the system to leak. Moreover, resolution was rather poor because of tailing. Nevertheless, Catsimpoolas (1974) reported that pressure-packed G-50 Sephadex could be used to obtain the molecular weight distribution of polypeptides resulting from the enzymatic hydrolysis of glycinin, the major storage protein of soybeans.

Fishman and Burdick (1977) using the SPS method packed four gel columns in series to obtain the molecular weight distribution of the extractable proteins in Coastal Bermuda grass. The gels and packing parameters are in Table 7.1. This series of columns was found to separate proteins in the molecular weight range of 1 million to 426. Tailing of standard proteins was not found to be a problem. A column 6 mm in diameter was used, possibly eliminating the "wall effects" which Catsimpoolas (1972) speculated caused the tailing in his experiments with G-50 Sephadex in 3 mm columns.

TABLE 7.1. PACKING PARAMETERS OF FOUR COLUMN CHROMATOGRAPH

Column	Packing	Height (cm)	Vol (ml)
1	Sephadex G-10, 25[1]	13.1	3.70
2	Sephadex G-50, 75[1]	12.6	3.56
3	Bio-Gel A-0.5 m	11.7	3.31
4	Bio-Gel A-5 m	11.5	3.24
Total		58.9	13.82

Source: Fishman and Burdick (1977).
[1]Mixed to give equal bed volumes.

In the SPS packing method used by Fishman and Burdick (1977), the concentrated slurry was spooned into the column prepared as outlined at the beginning of this section. The gel was washed down the column with as little degassed solvent as possible, taking care that no bubbles were trapped in the gel. The pump was connected to the top of the column, the outlet opened, and the pump started. The concentrated slurry of gel and degassed solvent was pumped under a flow of 0.12 ml/min until all but the fine particles had settled and only a light blue or white haze (color depended on gel porosity) remained above the gel bed. Then, the outlet was closed and excess fluid was withdrawn until about 1 cm of liquid remained above the gel bed. The procedure was repeated until the desired length of the column was obtained.

We believe the SPS method of packing columns produces more stable columns than the SGS method because gels are densely packed at or near maximum deformation. The procedure detailed here minimizes particle size gradients from forming in the column by removing fines during the packing procedure and also prevents the formation of interfaces which increase resistance to flow. Moreover, gels packed to compression exhibit higher resolution than those packed under no compression (Edwards and Helft 1970; Fishman and Barford 1970). Hence, separations are more easily automated and more rapid. Fishman and Burdick (1977) analyzed five LPC samples with one loading of the chromatograph in less than 16 hr. They found that the major disadvantage of the SPS method over the SGS method is enhanced retardation, probably by adsorption, particularly of high molecular weight proteins such as apoferritin. Retardation of apoferritin was virtually eliminated by increasing NaCl content of the mobile phase to 0.8 *N*.

If initial pressures are significantly higher than 276–345 kPa (40–50 psi) by the SGS method, then decrease the flow rate during packing. Further, reuse the same gel when required to repack a column. Gels which are reused appear to have more stability and pack with smaller pressure drops than new ones. Just add new gel to replace that which is lost from the old.

Calibration of Columns

In gel chromatography, the elution volume is proportional to the product of a shape factor (i.e., the intrinsic viscosity) and the molecular weight (Coll and Gilding 1970). Hence, gel chromatography is a relative rather than an absolute technique for measuring molecular weight. Consequently, the elution volumes must be measured for a series of standards whose molecular weights are known. Moreover, sample and standards must have the same shape (i.e., rod, spherical, or random coil) and density. Furthermore, neither sample nor standard should undergo dissociation or aggregation during elution, or elute by a mechanism other than a separation based on molecular size.

The shape of a calibration curve relating elution volume or partition coefficient to molecular size or weight of the solute molecule is dependent upon the pore size distribution within the gel matrix. Soft gels will give an S-shaped curve for a plot of K_{AV} against the log of the molecular weight (log M) for a series of calibration standards of similar shape density (Determann and Brewer 1975). The central portion of such a plot is approximated by the linear relationship, (7.8).

$$K_{AV} = A + B \log M \tag{7.8}$$

Unfortunately, linearity does not extend much over one logarithmic cycle of molecular weight for any particular gel. Moreover, the selectivity of a gel (i.e., the slope K_{AV} plotted against log M) rapidly approaches zero at the upper and lower nonlinear portions of the curve. For a broad distribution of molecular weights such as found in LPC, it was necessary to use several gels in series to cover the entire molecular weight range. Fishman and Burdick (1977) found that the entire range of molecular weights in Coastal Bermuda grass LPC could be covered by using four columns in series (see Table 7.1). Figure 7.4 is the calibration curve for this series of columns. The useful

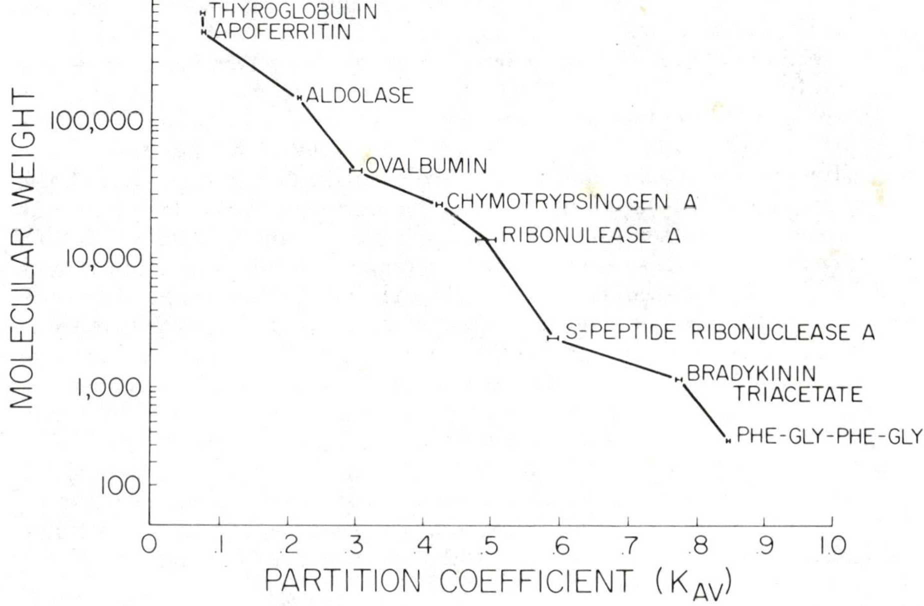

Fig. 7.4. Calibration curve for four column gel chromatograph.
From Fishman and Burdick (1977).

operating range has been extended to somewhat over three logarithmic cycles of molecular weight. The curve is the sum result of four S-shaped curves with overlapping ends and therefore nonlinear. For the case where the K_{AV} and molecular weight of the unknown are different from the standards, the molecular weight is obtained by assuming that segments between calibration standards are linear and interpolating the value of the unknown.

APPLICATIONS OF ANALYTICAL GEL CHROMATOGRAPHY TO LPC

Molecular Weight Determination

The most obvious use of analytical gel chromatography is to determine the molecular weight of an unknown sample. If the sample contains a pure macromolecule (e.g., a protein), molecular weight determination by gel chromatography is rather straightforward. A gel is chosen such that the K_{AV} of the unknown falls within the linear range of the gel (i.e., $0.1 \leq K_{AV} \leq 0.7$). A calibration curve is constructed according to equation (7.8). Once the constants of equation (7.6) have been determined, from a series of standards, a measurement of K_{AV} for the unknown would permit a calculation of its molecular weight from equation (7.8). Such a procedure could be used to characterize a major protein component from leaves such as 1,5-ribulose diphosphate carboxylase (RUDP-case), as found in plants which fix CO_2 via the phosphoglyceric acid pathway (i.e., C_3 plants), or phosphoenolpyruvate carboxylase (PEP-case), such as found in plants which fix CO_2 via the dicarboxylic acid pathway (i.e., C_4 plants).

Often, in food studies one is not interested in just one protein, but all the proteins found in the plant. Such is the case with LPC. Therefore one approach to characterizing LPC is by molecular weight distribution (MWD) analysis. In this case, the unknown sample is treated as a continuous distribution of molecular weights over the fractionation range of the column. The distribution often is characterized by as many as the first three normal moments of the distribution curve. If at each data point taken from the gel chromatogram, the abscissa value is transformed to its molecular weight equivalent, M_i, through a calibration procedure, and the corresponding ordinate value is transformed to C_i, the concentration of molecules with the molecular weight M_i, through an equation relating detector response to solute concentration, then the first three moments calculated according to equations (7.9), (7.10), and (7.11) will be the number average, $\overline{M}_n$, the weight average, $\overline{M}_w$, and the Z average molecular weight, $\overline{M}_z$.

$$\overline{M}_n \sum_{i=1}^{\alpha} C_i / \sum_{i=1}^{\alpha} (C_i/M_i) \tag{7.9}$$

$$\overline{M}_w = \sum_{i=1}^{\alpha} C_i M_i / \sum_{i=1}^{\alpha} C_i \tag{7.10}$$

$$\overline{M}_z = \sum_{i=1}^{\alpha} C_i M_i^2 / \sum_{i=1}^{\alpha} C_i M_i \tag{7.11}$$

Generally, these average weights are important because they can be determined by absolute techniques independent of gel chromatography. $\overline{M}_n$ can be obtained from osmometry, $\overline{M}_w$ from light scattering, and $\overline{M}_z$ from ultracentrifugation. In the specific case of LPC, Fishman (1976) noted that the values of $\overline{M}_n$, $\overline{M}_w$, and $\overline{M}_z$ obtained from gel chromatography for LPC would be apparent values, not true ones, because many of the conditions necessary to obtain the true values, as outlined by Catsimpoolas (1974), are not satisfied. Moreover, the finite resolution of gel columns will tend to give higher values for $\overline{M}_n$ obtained from gel chromatography than are obtained by osmometry (Ouano and Kaye 1974). The problem of limited resolution is particularly severe in the case of MWD analysis of LPC because of the broadness of the MWD. At constant column length, the resolution of a gel decreases as the molecular weight operating range increases.

The foregoing considerations have prompted us to abandon the procedure of calculating $\bar{M}_n$, $\bar{M}_w$, and $\bar{M}_z$ average molecular weight from gel chromatography and to adopt an MWD analysis more suited to the broadness of the MWD and the chemical heterogeneity of proteins found in LPC. In our procedure, the first and second moments in terms of retention volume, $\bar{V}_i$ and $\bar{V}_2$, are calculated according to equations (7.12) and (7.13) from the directly measured parameters: ΔR_i, the differential response (e.g., ultraviolet absorption or refractive index) of the i'th solute molecule and the solvent; and V_i, the retention volume of the i'th solute molecule.

$$\bar{V}_i = \sum_{i=1}^{j} \Delta R_i V_i / \sum_{i=1}^{j} \Delta R_i \tag{7.12}$$

$$\bar{V}_2 = \sum_{i=1}^{j} \Delta R_i V_i^2 / \sum_{i=1}^{j} \Delta R_i V_i \tag{7.13}$$

The first and second moment partition coefficients $\bar{K}_{AV_1}$ and $\bar{K}_{AV_2}$ are then obtained by substituting $\bar{V}_i$ or $\bar{V}_2$, respectively, for V_e in equation (7.5). The first and second moment apparent molecular weights M_{A_1} and M_{A_2} of the gel curve are then obtained from K_{AV_1} and K_{AV_2}, respectively, by interpolating from a calibration curve such as Fig. 7.4. There are several advantages to this method of MWD analysis compared to the conventional method of calculating $\bar{M}_n$, $\bar{M}_w$, and $\bar{M}_z$. Averages can be obtained prior to introduction of calibration molecular weights into the calculations. Therefore, calibrations need not be made prior to running samples, and calibration standards are easily changed. The effect of limited resolution on polydispersity is more clearly recognized by calculating it from the ratio of $\bar{K}_{AV_1}/\bar{K}_{AV_2}$ rather than $\bar{M}_w/\bar{M}_n$ because the ratio is not amplified by the molecular weight. Meaningful molecular weight averages are readily calculated even if the operating range of the gel is more narrow than the size distribution of sample, provided the molecular weight average falls within the operating range of the gel (Barford *et al.* 1977).

Fishman and Burdick (1977) applied MWD analysis to LPC obtained by extracting Coastal Bermuda grass with 0.1 *M* boric acid sodium borate buffer, mM sodium metabisulfite, and 0, 0.2, 0.5, or 1% sodium dodecylsulfate (SDS), a detergent. The flow diagram for the isolation of LPC (cut-1) from ground Coastal is shown in Fig. 7.5. The representative gel chromatograms which were obtained at 206 and 254 nm are shown in Fig. 7.6 and 7.7. These chromatograms exhibit a broad MWD which ranges from 1 million to 453 Daltons. First moment apparent molecular weights, M_{A_1}, and the ratio of $\bar{K}_{AV_1}/\bar{K}_{AV_2}$ are in Table 7.2. At 206 nm, the M_{A_1}-SDS relation passes through a minimum, whereas at 254 nm the M_{A_1}-SDS relationship is constant over the SDS concentration range 0–0.5%, but more than doubles at 1.0% SDS. Moreover, at 0 and 0.2% SDS, M_{A_1} is larger at 206 nm than at 254, whereas the reverse is true at 1% SDS. These trends in M_{A_1} occur because of changes in the amount of protein which eluted in the molecular weight range of 186,000 to 2400. At 0% SDS, the chromatogram taken at 206 nm (see Fig. 7.6) shows a peak at 50,000 which becomes less prominent with increasing SDS, whereas at 1% SDS, the chromatogram taken at 254 nm (see Fig. 7.7) exhibits a peak at 28,700 which is not apparent at 0%. The trends in molecular weight with change in SDS concentration can be explained by postulating that SDS breaks up chloroplasts and dissolves chloroplastic proteins by dissociating them and by providing an environment in the aqueous media which solubilizes the relatively nonpolar, hydrophobic membrane proteins found in chloroplasts.

Vander Zanden (1974) chromatographed LPC from alfalfa on a 2.5 × 31.5 cm column containing Bio-Gel P-100. The material chromatographed over the entire operating range of the column with six partially resolved peaks, including one at the void volume. Although no molecular weight calibration data for the columns were provided, several facts about the molecular weight distribution can be inferred from the gel pattern. According to the manufacturer's specifications (Anon. 1973), Bio-Gel P-100 fractionates globular proteins linearly over the molecular weight range of 5000 to 100,000 and nonlinearly over the range of 5000 to 0. Therefore, just as in the case of Coastal Bermuda grass LPC, alfalfa LPC is a broad distribution of molecular weights. The peak at the void volume indicates that the upper limit of the molecular weight range is in excess of 100,000.

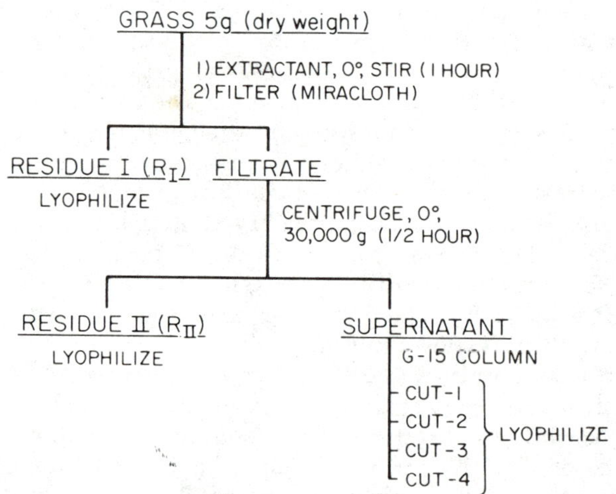

Fig. 7.5. Flow diagram for the preparation of fractions from Coastal Bermuda grass. LPC is equivalent to cut-1. *From Fishman and Burdick (1977).*

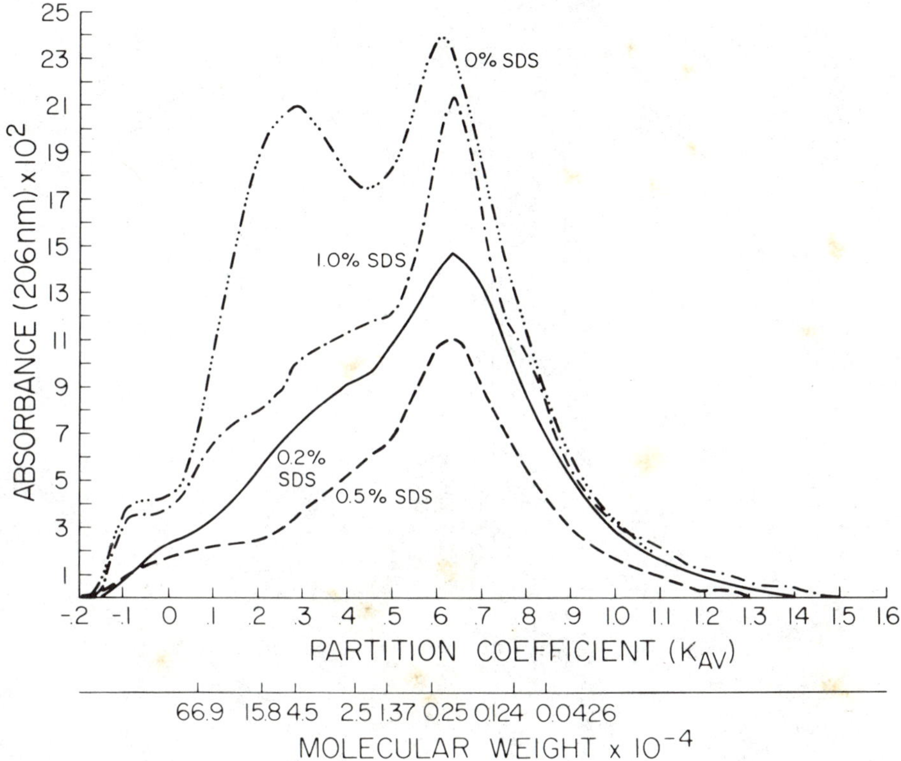

Fig. 7.6. Gel chromatograms of LPC extracted with various concentrations of SDS. Wavelength of detection 206 nm. Chromatograms have not been normalized for concentration (3–6 mg/ml).
From Fishman and Burdick (1977).

Sarkar *et al.* (1975), by a combination of ammonium sulfate precipitation and preparative gel filtration, separated the alfalfa LPC into Fraction I (F I) soluble protein, RUDPcase, and Fraction II (F II), proteins. The Fraction II proteins were chromatographed on a G-150 Sephadex column (5 × 90 cm), but no data were presented on molecular weight calibration of the column. According to the manufacturer's specification (Anon. 1973), G-150 Sephadex has a fractionating range of 400,000 to 5000 for globular proteins. Fraction II proteins eluted along the entire operating range of the G-150 Sephadex column, indicating that the protein had a broad molecular range weight. Gel electrophoresis gave a minimum of 15 bands for Fraction II of alfalfa LPC. Therefore, it appears that alfalfa LPC could be treated as a continuum of molecules in gel filtration characterization by MWD analysis.

TABLE 7.2. MOMENTS AND MOLECULAR WEIGHTS FROM GEL CHROMATOGRAPHY

% SDS	206 nm			254 nm		
(W/V)	$\bar{K}_{AV_1}$	$\bar{K}_{AV_1}/\bar{K}_{AV_2}$	$M_{A_1} \times 10^{-3}$	$\bar{K}_{AV_1}$	$\bar{K}_{AV_1}/\bar{K}_{AV_2}$	$M_{A_1} \times 10^{-3}$
0	0.446 ± 0.041	0.880 ± 0.021	21.2 ± 1.2	0.566 ± 0.059	0.907 ± 0.027	5.2 ± 6.7
0.2	0.520 ± 0.021	0.900 ± 0.020	10.5 ± 2.4	0.572 ± 0.024	0.883 ± 0.018	4.6 ± 2.7
0.5	0.565 ± 0.009	0.915 ± 0.003	5.4 ± 1.0	0.557 ± 0.015	0.870 ± 0.014	6.3 ± 1.7
1.0	0.525 ± 0.030	0.896 ± 0.009	9.9 ± 3.4	0.492 ± 0.037	0.870 ± 0.013	13.7 ± 5.0

Source: Fishman and Burdick (1977).

Knuckles *et al.* (1975) used a 2.4 × 46.5 cm column containing Bio-Gel P-60 to evaluate the efficiency of diafiltration in removing nonprotein and pigmented components from alfalfa juice which had insolubles removed by prior centrifugation. Gel chromatographic data in conjunction with UV absorption measurements, trichloracetic acid precipitation, and Kjeldahl nitrogen determination indicated that after 10 sample volumes had passed through the membrane, the dried material which was retained by the membrane contained 93% protein and only 5% of the original pigmented components present. Although no relative areas under the curve or molecular weight calibrations were given, it appears from the chromatogram taken at 280 nm that a majority of the area under the curve elutes as one peak at the column void volume, indicating one or more proteins were present with an apparent molecular weight in excess of 60,000.

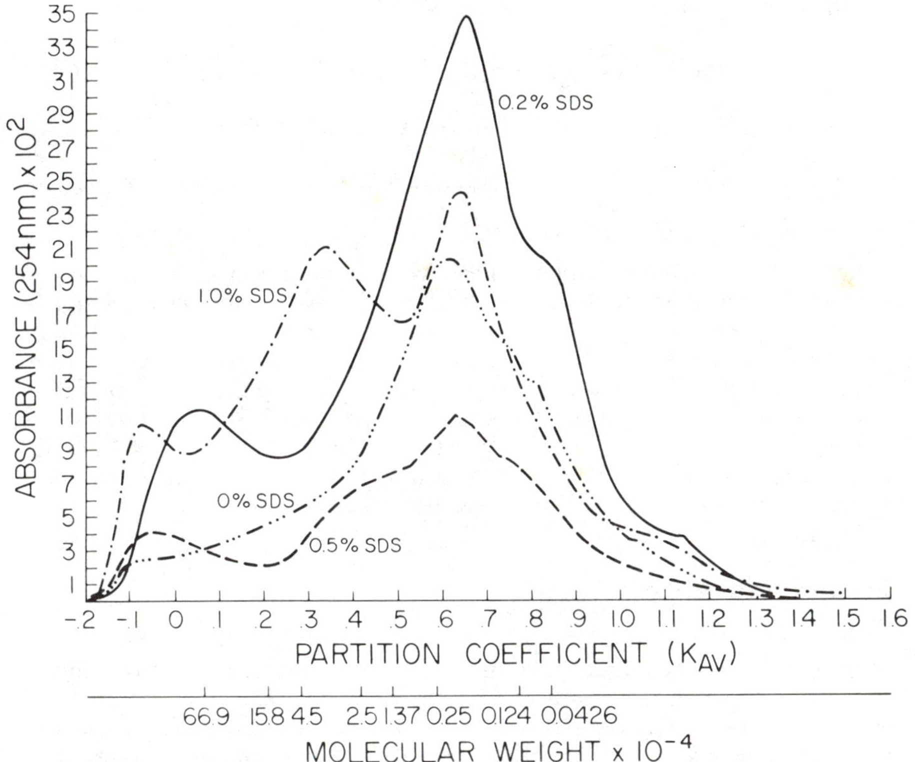

Fig. 7.7. Gel chromatograms of cut-1 extracted with various concentrations of SDS. Wavelength of detection 254 nm. Chromatograms have not been normalized for concentration (3–6 mg/ml).

From Fishman and Burdick (1977).

Protein Purity

Fishman (1976) extracted Coastal Bermuda grass with water in the presence of crosslinked polyvinylpyrrolidone and found that the molecular weight distribution and the area under the gel curve for LPC depended on the method or mode of detection. Thus, the apparent first moment molecular weights of water-soluble LPC were 5180, 10,800, and 32,000, as determined by refractive index measurements and by absorbance readings at 254 and 206 nm. These observations prompted Fishman and Burdick (1977), in subsequent studies on LPC produced by buffer and buffer-SDS extraction of Coastal Bermuda grass, to suggest that the parameter F_A could be used to measure changes in protein purity of LPC by extracting with different levels of detergent. The parameter, F_A, is the fractional change in absorbing functional groups by increasing the level of SDS in the extractant from 0 to finite SDS concentrations. Experimentally, F_A is obtained by equation (7.14).

$$F_A = (A_{206} / A_{254})_{SDS\,=\,0} \Big/ (A_{206} / A_{254})_{SDS\,=\,x} \qquad (7.14)$$

where $(A_{206}/A_{254})_{SDS\,=\,0}$ is the ratio of areas at 0% SDS

and $(A_{206}/A_{254})_{SDS\,=\,x}$ is the ratio of areas at finite SDS concentration

For proteins, the amide bond is the major contributor to A_{206}, whereas aromatic amino acids such as phenylalanine, tyrosine, and tryptophan are the major contributors to A_{254} (Scopes 1974). Therefore, when Fishman and Burdick (1977) found that F_A was 2.3 at 1% SDS in the extractant, they suggested that the increase in aromatic absorbance by the addition of SDS to the extractant was caused by the contamination of LPC with endogenous phenolics arising from the chloroplasts. Amino acid analysis of LPC obtained with and without SDS in the extractant strengthened the hypothesis as no change was found in the composition of aromatic amino acids (Fishman and Evans 1978).

Protein Solubility

Gel chromatography also can be used to determine changes in protein solubility from areas under the curve. Fishman and Burdick (1977) found that the cytoplasmic protein of Coastal Bermuda grass was completely soluble in 0.8 *N* NaCl after lyophilization, whereas the chloroplastic protein was not. The cytoplasmic protein was obtained by buffer extraction of Coastal Bermuda grass without SDS, whereas chloroplastic in addition to cytoplasmic protein was obtained by extracting Coastal with 1% SDS in buffer. The fractional change in the solubility, F_S, was obtained from A_{206} values at each level of SDS in the extractant by equation (7.15).

$$F_s = (A_{206})_{SDS\,=\,x} \Big/ (A_{206})_{SDS\,=\,0} \tag{7.15}$$

where $(A_{206})_{SDS\,=\,x}$ is the area at finite detergent (SDS) concentration

and $(A_{206})_{SDS\,=\,0}$ is the area at 0 detergent (SDS) concentration

The value of 0.28 for F_s which was found at 1% SDS in the extractant multiplied by the total LPC nitrogen extracted at 1% SDS gave the same value for LPC nitrogen as extracted at 0% SDS in the extractant, indicating that all the chloroplastic protein was insoluble.

Preparative Gel Chromatography

One of the primary goals of preparative gel chromatography is to obtain sample, whereas the main purpose of analytical gel chromatography is analysis. While resolution and speed are important in the analytical gel chromatography of LPC, capacity and speed are of utmost importance in its preparative gel chromatography. Hence, column capacity is increased at the expense of resolution. This is done by increasing the sample load. Therefore, the sample size is increased from about 0.2 to 2 mg/run in analytical gel chromatography up to about 3 g in preparative gel chromatography. A sample size in the range of 1.5–3 g enables further analysis of LPC by analytical gel chromatography, micro-Kjeldahl determination, and amino acid analysis.

Techniques and Equipment. The techniques and equipment of analytical gel chromatography must be modified to obtain the increased column capacity required in preparative chromatography. Generally, the degree of modification is proportional to the increase in sample size. Modification of preparative over analytical gel chromatography includes higher flow rates (3ml/min), larger injection volumes (50–100 ml), larger column volumes (500 ml, e.g., 2.5 × 100 cm columns), and less sensitive detection (e.g., 0–100% T, full scale for UV absorbance).

In addition to collecting sample, other major goals for the preparative gel chromatography of LPC are to separate proteins from lower molecular weight endogenous species of leaves and to concentrate protein. These goals are obtainable by using tightly cross-linked rigid gels such as G-15 and G-25 Sephadex. Columns packed with G-15 and G-25 Sephadex can be operated at higher flow rates and lower pressures than comparable columns packed with Sephadex of higher G values and with agarose gels such as those used in analytical gel chromatography of LPC.

Whereas the gels employed in preparative gel chromatography are easier to use than those in analytical gel chromatography of LPC, injecting 50–100 ml of sample rather than 0.2 ml onto the column is more difficult. A convenient method of injecting a large volume of sample onto the column is to pump it on with a peristaltic pump. The sample can be pumped onto the column without interrupting flow by changing the flow pattern of the six port rotary loop valve shown in Fig. 7.2A. The sample loop is disconnected, the 9 o'clock port is connected to drain and the 3 o'clock port is connected to a sample pump (peristaltic). If the valve is in the configuration shown in Fig. 7.2C, eluent from the reservoir passes through the column and the peristaltic pump is turned off. When the peristaltic pump is turned on, simultaneously the rotor of the valve is rotated manually through 60° (see Fig. 7.2D). The sample is sucked from its container past the rollers of the peristaltic pump and pumped onto the column. Simultaneously, eluent from the reservoir is directed to drain. When the desired volume of sample is pumped onto the column, the rotor of the sample valve is returned to the configuration of Fig. 7.2C. Once again, eluent from the reservoir is pumped through the column and liquid which passes through the peristaltic pump is directed to the drain. At this point, the sample delivery tubing can be washed with water. At no time is flow through the column interrupted.

Peristaltic pumps are well suited to sample introduction in that the sample never comes into direct contact with pump parts. Further, since wider columns with more rigid gels can be operated at head pressures of less than 345 kPa (50 psi), the relatively low upper pressure limit of peristaltic pumps is not a problem.

Applications of Preparative Gel Chromatography to LPC

Coastal Bermuda Grass. Fishman and Burdick (1977) used a 2.5 × 85 cm column packed with G-15 Sephadex to separate the extractable proteins, polypeptides, and amino acids from Coastal Bermuda grass into three major fractions and a minor one. The elution pattern from the column is shown in Fig. 7.8. The analytical gel chromatography of cut-1, which is equivalent to LPC, has already been discussed in the previous section. Amino acid analysis and Kjeldahl determination of these cuts (Fishman and Evans 1978; Fishman *et al.* 1978) indicate that protein quality based on the amino acid pattern is better for LPC (cut-1) than it is for the whole grass, the insoluble residue, the soluble polypeptide, or amino acids. Further isolation of the proteins from polypeptides and amino acids more than tripled the concentration of proteins in LPC compared to their initial concentration in grass (i.e., 13.5 to about 45% for crude protein).

Alfalfa. Free and Satterlee (1975) used a 2 × 90 cm column containing G-50 Sephadex to separate into four fractions alfalfa juice which was untreated, treated with 2% sodium sulfite, dialyzed against water, heat precipitated, and heat-acid precipitated. In each fraction, protein was determined by the Folin-Ciocalteu reagent and UV absorbance spectra were measured. Protein fractions were subjected to isoelectric focusing and SDS electrophoresis. It was found that sodium sulfite gave the highest yield of protein, followed by untreated, heat precipitated, heat-acid precipitated,

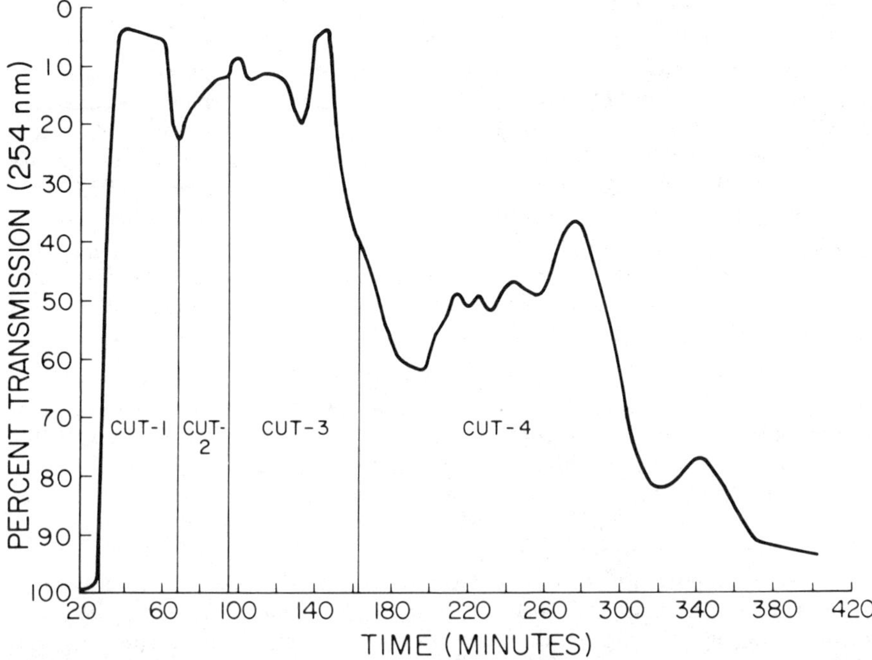

Fig. 7.8. Preparative gel chromatogram of soluble fractions of Coastal Bermuda grass. Column 2.4 × 85 cm, G-15 Sephadex. Sample size, 80 ml.
From Fishman and Burdick (1977).

and dialyzed juice, in that order. SDS electrophoresis indicated that 6.3% of the protein from alfalfa juice had a molecular weight of 600,000 with the remaining protein having a molecular weight in the range of 25,000–60,000. The gel chromatogram of the heat-acid precipitated juice contained none of the 600,000 molecular weight protein.

By combination of buffer extraction (pH 7.85), filtration through dacron cloth, centrifugation, precipitation with sodium sulfate, and gel chromatography on a 5 × 90 cm Sepharose 5B column, Sarkar *et al.* (1975) obtained nearly homogeneous Fraction I (F I) protein from ground alfalfa.

Sarkar *et al.* (1975) were able to obtain Fraction II (F II) proteins from ground alfalfa extracts by a combination of ammonium sulfate precipitation and gel chromatography on a 5 × 50 cm G-25 Sephadex column.

Jones and Mangan (1976) developed a method for large-scale production of Fraction I (up to 100 g/run) from alfalfa. Fraction I protein was separated from low molecular weight phenolics and salts by gel filtration on a 15 × 60 cm column containing G-75 Sephadex.

Maize, Cotton, Spinach, and Tobacco Leaves. Bahr *et al.* (1977) isolated Fraction I protein from maize, cotton, spinach, and tobacco leaves. The Fraction I was obtained from crude extracts by a combination of ammonium sulfate precipitation, gel chromatography on a 4 × 55 cm column of Bio-Gel A-5 m and DEAE-cellulose column chromatography. Purified Fraction I protein from tobacco, cotton, and spinach did not denature until it reached a temperature of 60°C, whereas maize Fraction I started precipitating at 43°C. It was concluded from activity and SDS-electrophoretic measurements that Fraction I from tobacco, cotton, and spinach, all C_3 plants, was 1,5-ribulose diphosphate carboxylase (RUDP-case) whereas Fraction I protein from maize, a C_4 plant, also contained about 25% phosphoenolpyruvate carboxylase (PEP-case). It was suggested that it was the PEP-case which precipitated from maize extracts at 43°C. Furthermore, they were unable to crystallize Fraction I protein from maize, cotton, and spinach, unlike that from tobacco.

Broad Bean Leaves and Stems. Clarke *et al.* (1968) extracted broad bean forage with ethanol and phenol-acetic acid-water (PAW) (2:1:1, w/v/v). The extracts were fractionated further on a G-75 Sephadex column with PAW as the eluent. Such a fractionation enabled them to separate pigmented from nonpigmented material. The PAW extract was subjected to prior fractionation by free-flow electrophoresis to eliminate matter with a net charge. In both cases, the nonpigmented material eluted first from the G-75 column followed by the pigmented matter. Amino acid analysis in all fractions indicated that the nonpigmented fraction from the ethanol fraction contained most of the protein material. They believed the pigmented fractions contained pheophytin, carotenoid, and lipids in addition to lower molecular weight polypeptides and amino acids.

REFERENCES

ANON. 1971. A Laboratory Manual on Gel Chromatography. Bio-Rad Laboratories, Richmond, CA.

ANON. 1973. Gel Filtration in Theory and Practice. Pharmacia Fine Chemicals, Piscataway, NJ.

ANON. 1978. TSK-Gel, SW Type, Technical Data. Toyo Sodo Manufacturing Co., Tokyo.

BAHR, J.T., BOURQUE, D.P. and SMITH, H.J. 1977. Solubility properties of Fraction I proteins of maize, cotton, spinach and tobacco. J. Agric. Food Chem. *25*, 783–789.

BARFORD, R., KUPEC, J. and FISHMAN, M.L. 1977. Monitoring Keratin Degradation in Activated Sludge by Rapid Gel Permeation Chromatography. J. Water Pollut. Control Fed. *49* (May) 764–767.

BELEW, M., PORATH, J. and FOHLMAN, J. 1978. Adsorption phenomena on Sephacryl S-200 Superfine. J. Chromatogr. *147*, 205–212.

CASSASSA, E.F. 1971. Gel permeation chromatography and thermodynamic equilibrium. Sep. Sci. *6*, 305–319.

CATSIMPOOLAS, N. 1972. Rapid analytical gel chromatography of proteins and peptides on Sephadex micropore columns. J. Chromatogr. *64*, 77–83.

CATSIMPOOLAS, N. 1974. Rapid analytical gel filtration chromatography. III. Apparent molecular weight distribution of peptides produced by proteolysis. Anal. Biochem. *61*, 101–111.

CHANG, S.H., GOODING, K.M. and REGNIER, F.E. 1976. High performance liquid chromatography of proteins. J. Chromatogr. *125*, 103–114.

CLARKE, E.M.W., ELLINGER, G.M. and SYNGE, R.L.M. 1968. Fractionation of plant material. IV. Distribution of amino acid residues in fractions obtained from leaves of broad bean (*Vicia faba* L.). J. Sci. Food Agric. *19*, 214–218.

COLL, H. and GILDING, D.K. 1970. Universal calibration in GPC: A study of polystyrene, poly-α-methylstyrene and polypropylene. J. Polym. Sci. Part A2: *8*, 89–103.

DE STEFANO, J.J. 1974. Large-scale separations. *In* Introduction to Modern Liquid Chromatography. L.R. Snyder and J.J. Kirkland (Editors). John Wiley & Sons, New York.

DETERMANN, H. 1968. Gel Chromatography, Gel Filtration, Gel Permeation, Molecular Sieves. Springer-Verlag, New York.

DETERMANN, H. and BREWER, J.E. 1975. Gel chromatography. *In* A Laboratory Handbook of Chromatographic and Electrophoretic Methods. E. Heftmann (Editor). Van Nostrand, New York.

EDWARDS, V.H. and HELFT, J.M. 1970. Gel chromatography: Improved resolution through compressed beds. J. Chromatogr. *47*, 493–498.

ENGELHARDT, J. and MATHES, D. 1977. Chemically bonded stationary phases for aqueous high performance exclusion chromatography. J. Chromatogr. *142*, 311–320.

FISHMAN, M.L. 1976. Semiautomated gel chromatography to characterize broad molecular weight distributions of cytoplasmic extracts from Coastal Bermudagrass. Anal. Biochem. *74*, 41–51.

FISHMAN, M.L. and BARFORD, R.A. 1970. Increased resolution of polymers through longitudinal compression of agarose gel columns. J. Chromatogr. *52*, 494–496.

FISHMAN, M.L. and BURDICK, D. 1977. Extractability, solubility, and molecular size distribution of nitrogenous constituents in coastal Bermudagrass. J. Agric. Food Chem. *25*, 1122–1127.

FISHMAN, M.L. and EVANS, J.J. 1978. Amino acid composition of Coastal Bermudagrass fractions. J. Agric. Chem. *26*, 1447–1451.

FISHMAN, M.L., EVANS, J.J. and BURDICK, D. 1978. The extraction of protein from Coastal Bermudagrass with detergent. *In* Proc. 8th Res. Ind. Conf., Coastal Bermudagrass Processors' Assoc. D. Burdick (Editor). R.B. Russell Agricultural Research Center, Athens, GA.

FREE, B.L. and SATTERLEE, L.D. 1975. Biochemical properties of alfalfa protein concentrate. J. Food Sci. *40*, 85–89.

GIDDINGS, J.C., BOWMAN, L.M. JR. and MYERS, M.N. 1977. Exclusion chromatography in dense gases: An approach to viscosity optimization. Anal. Chem. *49*, 243–249.

HALLER, W. 1965. Chromatography on glass of controlled pore size. Nature *206*, 693–696.

JONES, W.T. and MANGAN, J.L. 1976. Large-scale isolation of Fraction I leaf protein (18S) from Lucerne (Medicago sativa L.). J. Agric. Sci. (Cambridge) *86*, 495–501.

KNUCKLES, B.E., DE FREMERY, D., BICKOFF, E.M. and KOHLER, G.O. 1975. Soluble protein from alfalfa juice by membrane filtration. J. Agric. Food Chem. *23*, 209–212.

LAURENT, T.C. and KILLANDER, J. 1964. A theory of gel filtration and its experimental verification. J. Chromatogr. *14*, 317–330.

MOORE, J.C. 1964. Gel Permeation Chromatography. I. A new method for molecular weight determination of high polymers. J. Polym. Sci. Part A: *2*, 833–844.

OUANO, A.C. and KAYE, W. 1974. Gel permeation chromatography. X. Molecular weight detection by low-angle laser light scattering. J. Polym. Sci. Polym. Chem. Ed. *12*, 1151–1162.

PERONE, J.P. and JONES, D.O. 1973. Digital Computers in Scientific Instrumentation. McGraw Hill Book Co., New York.

PIRIE, N.W. 1971. Leaf Protein: Its Agronomy, Preparation, Quality, and Use. Blackwell Scientific Publication, Oxford.

PORATH, J. and FLODIN, P. 1959. Gel filtration—A method of desalting and group separation. Nature *183*, 1657–1659.

ROKUSHIKA, S., OHKAWA, T. and HATANO, H. 1978. Gel permeation chromatography of proteins on the TSK–Gel column. U.S.-Jpn. Semin. Adv. Techniques of Liq. Chromatogr. Univ. of Colorado, Boulder.

SARKAR, S.K., HOWARTH, R.E., HIKICHI, M. and McARTHUR, J.M. 1975. Soluble proteins of alfalfa (Medicago sativa) herbage. Fractionation by ammonium sulfate and gel chromatography. J. Agric. Food Chem. *23*, 626–630.

SCOPES, R.K. 1974. Measurement of Protein by Spectrophotometry at 205nm. Anal. Biochem. *59*, 277–282.

SNYDER, L.R. and KIRKLAND, J.J. 1974. Introduction to Modern Liquid Chromatography. John Wiley & Sons, New York.

VANDER ZANDEN, R. 1974. The partial characterization of an alfalfa leaf protein concentrate. Ph.D. Thesis. Kansas State University, Manhattan, KA.

WHEATON, R.M. and BAUMAN, W.C. 1953. Non-ionic separations with ion exchange resins. Ann. N.Y. Acad. Sci. *57*, 159–176.

8

Carbohydrates in LPC and Fractionated Leaf Extracts

Gerald N. Festenstein

Carbohydrates in large-scale extracts of leaves have been studied in two main fractions, the water-soluble carbohydrate in the uncoagulable component or liquor remaining after heat precipitation of the protein (Festenstein 1972) and the carbohydrate associated with the protein coagulum itself (Festenstein 1976).

CARBOHYDRATES IN LIQUOR

Some 62 liquors from a variety of crops, including alfalfa or lucerne *(Medicago sativa)*, barley *(Hordeum vulgare)*, cocksfoot *(Dactylis glomerata)*, fat hen *(Chenopodium album)*, field beans *(Vicia faba)*, fodder radish *(Raphanus sativus)*, maize *(Zea mays)*, mustard *(Sinapis alba)*, red clover *(Trifolium pratense)*, rye *(Secale cereale)*, ryegrass *(Lolium perenne)*, sugar beet *(Beta vulgaris)*, sweet clover *(Melilotus alba)*, wheat *(Triticum aestivum)* and mixed wheat and vetch *(Vicia sativa)*, were studied.

The soluble carbohydrate was about half of the 2% dry matter of the liquor; the fraction soluble in 80% ethanol contained on average three-quarters of the total carbohydrate, the sugars being fructose, glucose, and sucrose, with traces of xylose.

The polysaccharide fraction of the liquor, that insoluble in 80% ethanol, was more variable in composition than the ethanol-soluble fraction, depending on the presence of fructosan in the crop studied. Fructosan is the principal reserve carbohydrate of cereals and grasses, and there is less in legumes such as alfalfa and the clovers (McIlroy 1967). The composition of the liquors reflected this trend. Nonfructosan polysaccharide in 31 liquors on hydrolysis with 2 N H_2SO_4 released arabinose, glucose, galactose, and xylose, in order of abundance. The amount found in red clover and wheat liquors was 1 mg/ml, corresponding to about 1% of the dry matter of the leaf.

ANALYSIS OF CARBOHYDRATES IN LPC

Hydrolysis of LPC with 2 *N* H_2SO_4

Table 8.1 shows the total carbohydrate and reducing sugar content of extracts made by heating leaf protein with 2 *N* H_2SO_4, conditions which hydrolyze starch to glucose. The table shows that the sugars detected were mainly galactose, arabinose, and xylose, with smaller amounts of glucose.

TABLE 8.1. CARBOHYDRATE RELEASED FROM LEAF PROTEIN BY HEATING WITH 2 *N* H_2SO_4

	Total Carbohydrate	Reducing Sugar	Sugars Detected by TLC[1]			
Crop	% Dry Wt		Arabinose	Xylose	Galactose	Glucose
Barley	6.5	2.6	+++	+++	+++	tr
Rye	5.5	1.7	++	+	+++	—
Wheat	5.0	2.3	++	++	+++	—
Cocksfoot	5.0	1.5	+++	++	+++	—
Ryegrass	7.7	2.8	+++	++	+	—
Lucerne	6.0	2.5	++	++	+++	—
Maize	9.5	5.0	+++	+++	+++	+
Mustard	4.9	2.1	+++	+++	+++	—
Red clover	7.5	3.5	++	+	+++	+
Fat hen	6.0	2.3	++	tr	+++	tr
Fodder radish	5.2	1.5	++	+	++	—

Source: Festenstein (1976).
Leaf protein (0.5 g) was heated with 5 ml 2 *N* H_2SO_4 in stoppered tubes at 102°–103°C for 1.5 hr.
[1]TLC—Thin layer chromatography.
tr—Trace.

The only other report of analysis of LPC for carbohydrate content is that of Hove *et al.* (1974), who extracted alfalfa LPC with *N*-H_2SO_4 and then 72% H_2SO_4, according to the procedure of Bailey (1967) for "hemicellulose" and "cellulose," and found 2.4 and 1.6% carbohydrate as reducing sugar, respectively. The figure of 2.4% for *N*-H_2SO_4 extraction is within the range for reducing sugars of the 2 *N* H_2SO_4 hydrolysates shown in Table 8.1. Hove *et al.* (1974) did not study the sugars released.

The complete absence of fructose in the 2 *N* H_2SO_4 hydrolysates of LPC indicates that none of the liquor components, fructose, sucrose, or fructosan, were associated with the protein coagulum because sucrose and fructosan would both have given fructose on acid hydrolysis.

Appreciable amounts of fructose and glucose were found only in acid hydrolysates of some inadequately washed protein preparations, in crude laboratory preparations made by coagulating concentrated rather than diluted juice, and in preparations from juice coagulated an hour or more after expression (Arkcoll *et al.* 1972).

Starch Content. The sugars identified by thin layer chromatography (Table 8.1) showed that glucose was a minor component of only a few samples, indicating that the amount of starch present was small. Red clover protein contained the highest amount of glucose, 0.5%, but specific determination of starch by incubation of this red clover protein with the enzyme glucoamylase (Macrae and Armstrong 1968) gave a value of only 0.2%, suggesting that some other glucose-containing compound besides starch was present in the leaf protein sample. The LPC preparations studied here were made by the method of Morrison and Pirie (1961), where the juice was centrifuged to remove starch and leaf fragments before steam was passed in to coagulate the protein; if the centrifuging had been omitted, the starch content of the final products might have been higher.

Incubation of LPC with Enzymes

Pectinase and Snail Digestive Juice. Pectic enzymes have been used in structural studies of alfalfa pectin (Aspinall and Fanshawe 1961; Aspinall *et al.* 1968), releasing the neutral sugars arabinose, galactose, and rhamnose as well as galacturonic acid. A pectic enzyme preparation from *Aspergillus niger* has also recently been used by Nordin *et al.* (1975) in studies of soluble polysaccharides from wheat seedlings, which released mainly arabinose and galactose. Table 8.2 shows results for incubation of red clover and wheat LPC with pectinase and with snail digestive juice for 5 days. The proportion of reducing sugar increased during incubation to a large fraction of the total. The sugars detected were the same for both enzymes, mainly arabinose and galactose, with some xylose and including also glucose for red clover.

TABLE 8.2. CARBOHYDRATE AND NITROGEN RELEASED FROM RED CLOVER AND WHEAT LPC BY DIFFERENT ENZYMES AND BUFFERS
0.1 g LPC/2 ml volume was incubated at 37°C along with 0.1 ml toluene. The enzymes, supplied by L. Light and Co., Ltd., Colnbrook, England, were: Pectinase from *Aspergillus niger* (1 g/25 ml dialyzed, 0.2 ml used); Pronase 0.001 g; snail juice 0.025 ml.

	Red Clover		Wheat	
	CHO[1]	N	CHO	N
Enzymes and Buffers	% Dry Wt Protein			
0.075 *M* Na phosphate buffer, pH 4.5	0.8	0.5	0.4	0.4
Pectinase in buffer, pH 2.4 (5 days)	2.4	0.5	1.9	0.5
Snail juice in buffer, pH 4.5 (5 days)	2.0	0.6	2.1	0.6
0.075 *M* Na phosphate buffer, pH 7.3	1.2	0.7	0.8	0.5
Pronase digest in buffer, pH 7.3 (3 days)	3.1	6.7	1.6	5.9
5% TCA-soluble fraction	2.0	6.5	1.3	5.8
Dialyzed digest	2.9	3.2	1.3	1.9
Dialyzed TCA-soluble fraction	1.1	0.4	0.6	0.2

[1]CHO = Carbohydrate.

Proteolytic Enzymes. Pronase, a commercial preparation from *Streptomyces griseus*, solubilized 60–75% of the total nitrogen of LPC preparations from alfalfa, mustard, red clover, wheat, and white clover *(Trifolium* *repens)* and released carbohydrate from 1.5 to 3.5% of the dry weight of the protein. Buffer alone extracted about 1% carbohydrate in some cases; Table 8.2 shows that 0.075 *M* sodium phosphate buffer at pH 7.3 extracted more carbohydrate than at pH 4.5.

The carbohydrate digested by Pronase was not released as small fragments, as no soluble sugars or oligosaccharides were detected by thin layer chromatography. Graded acid hydrolysis of the digests showed that 0.2 N-H_2SO_4 released arabinose and xylose and that 2 N-H_2SO_4 yielded glucose and galactose as well. The amounts of xylose released by acid hydrolysis decreased considerably if the Pronase digests were dialyzed prior to hydrolysis, indicating preferential removal of xylose-containing components. These xylose-containing components would therefore seem to be different from those associated with arabinose and galactose.

The fraction from red clover extracted with buffer only (Table 8.2) is also different, as it yielded mainly glucose, with some arabinose and galactose, on hydrolysis with 2 N-H_2SO_4. There is evidently a spectrum of different carbohydrate molecules associated with the leaf proteins. Waite and Gorrod (1959) found a galacto-gluco-araban in aqueous extracts of cocksfoot leaves, but there is no evidence of its being linked to nitrogen.

The amounts of total carbohydrate released by pectinase or snail digestive juice from red clover and from wheat LPC were not affected by prior incubation of the LPC with Pronase. Residues, after successive incubations with buffer, Pronase, and pectinase, contained mainly galactose. Some carbohydrate released by Pronase is evidently bound initially in a protein-carbohydrate complex inaccessible to pectinase, as incubation of the Pronase digests with pectinase released arabinose, galactose, xylose, and glucose.

Fractionation of Red Clover Extracts on Sephadex.—*Sephadex G-25.* Figure 8.1 shows the separation of a Pronase digest and of a pH 7.3 buffer extract of red clover protein, analyses of which are given in Table 8.2. The carbohydrate from both eluted in two peaks with about 70% being excluded from the column for the Pronase digest and about half for the buffer extract.

The peaks for nitrogen in the Pronase digest coincided with those for carbohydrate, most of the nitrogen eluting with the second (smaller) carbohydrate fraction.

Sephadex G-75. Figure 8.2 shows the separation of a dialyzed TCA-soluble Pronase digest along with a dialyzed liquor.

The dialyzed TCA-soluble Pronase digest eluted as two fractions: the first, which was excluded from the column, contained one-third of the total carbohydrate. The second, with two-thirds of the carbohydrate, was associated with a brown color similar to that seen in the excluded fraction from G-25, which in this case contained 83% of the total carbohydrate.

The liquor gave three fractions besides fructosan: one-third of the total nonfructosan carbohydrate was excluded from the column and a second peak eluted in the same region as the second peak of the dialyzed TCA-soluble Pronase digest.

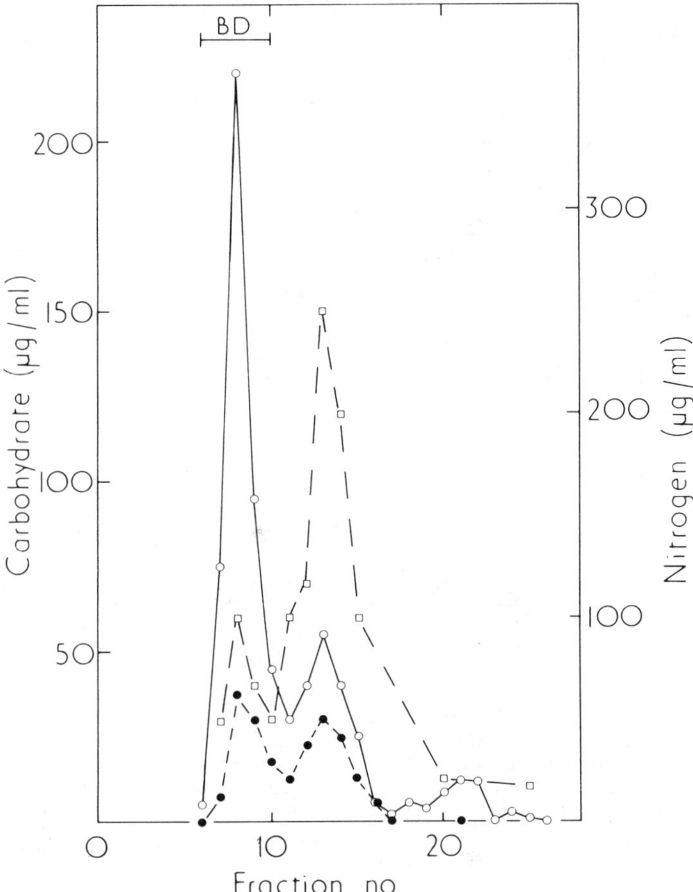

Fig. 8.1. Gel filtration of a buffer extract and a Pronase digest of red clover protein on Sephadex G-25. The buffer extract contained 0.8 mg carbohydrate and 0.2 mg N and the Pronase digest 1.8 mg carbohydrate and 3.3 mg N. Fraction volumes were 3.3 ml. BD shows the fractions in which Blue Dextran was eluted. ● Buffer extract carbohydrate. ○ Pronase digest carbohydrate. □ Pronase digest N.

The Pronase digest and liquor fractions excluded from G-75 both preferentially released pentose on hydrolysis with 0.2 N-H_2SO_4.

Sephadex G-100. The dialyzed TCA-soluble Pronase digest fraction excluded from G-75 was also excluded from G-100, indicating a molecular weight of at least 3×10^5; it contained one-third of the total carbohydrate and less than 10% of the nitrogen.

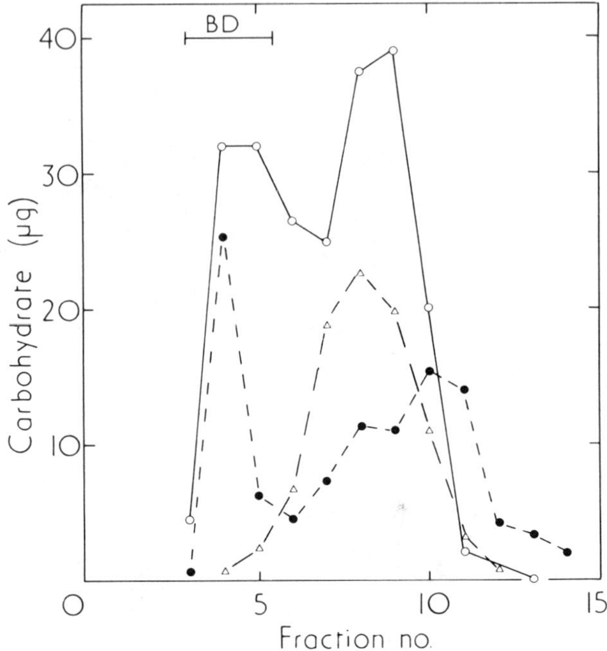

Fig. 8.2. Gel filtration of dialyzed red clover liquor and of a dialyzed TCA-soluble Pronase digest of red clover protein on Sephadex G-75. Both samples were concentrated and contained 10 mg carbohydrate and 3.3 mg carbohydrate, respectively. Fraction volumes were 17 ml. BD shows the fractions in which Blue Dextran was eluted. ○ Carbohydrate per ml of Pronase digest fraction. △ Total fructose per 0.25 ml liquor fraction. ● Nonfructose carbohydrate per 0.25 ml liquor fraction.

CARBOHYDRATE IN FRACTIONATED LEAF PROTEIN EXTRACTS

Fraction I Protein

There have been extensive studies of Fraction I (F I) protein, the major soluble protein in the chloroplasts of higher plants, which has a molecular weight of 500,000–600,000 (Bahr *et al.* 1977). In tobacco leaves, up to 50% of the soluble protein is Fraction I protein (Kawashima and Wildman 1970), but Sakano *et al.* (1973) found no carbohydrate present.[1] Fraction I protein of rice leaves has been shown Akazawa *et al.* (1965) to contain 5% carbohy-

[1]A more detailed discussion of Fraction I protein of tobacco is to be found in Chapter 4.

drate, consisting mainly of arabinose and galactose, and Ridley *et al.* (1967) found glucose and xylose, with traces of arabinose and galactose, in Fraction I protein of spinach beet leaves. Howarth *et al.* (1977) showed that Fraction I protein of alfalfa leaves stained with periodic-Schiff reagent, indicating the presence of carbohydrate; Fraction II (F II) stained only faintly.

"Cytoplasmic" Fractions of Barley and Lupine Leaves

Studies of "cytoplasmic" fractions from extracts of barley and lupine leaves were made in collaboration with Byers (1971); TCA-precipitated fractions of soluble protein obtained after centrifuging at 50,000 *g* gave carbohydrate contents between 1.8 and 3.2% for barley leaves and 1.7 to 2.1% for lupine leaves, expressed as % leaf dry matter. On acid hydrolysis, the preparations from the youngest barley leaves gave mainly xylose, with some galactose and arabinose; the oldest lupine leaves also yielded mainly xylose, with galactose, arabinose, and some glucose. Analysis of soluble lupine leaf cytoplasmic extracts after heat precipitation of crude extracts at 43°C was also made: TCA precipitates of the soluble fractions gave carbohydrate contents corresponding to 1.3–2.0% of the leaf dry matter; on acid hydrolysis the preparation from the oldest leaves gave mainly arabinose and galactose, with traces of glucose and xylose, the same sugars as before, but with xylose as a minor rather than a major component.

Oat and Wheat Seedling Extracts

Extracts of oat coleoptiles similar in composition to LPC and liquor have been described: Bishop *et al.* (1958) found that an aqueous extract of oat coleoptiles gave a nondialyzable fraction containing 10% nitrogen, corresponding to 60% protein, and also containing polysaccharide, which gave arabinose, xylose, galactose, and glucose on acid hydrolysis, the same sugars as found in LPC Morré and Olson (1965) extracted oat coleoptiles at pH 4.4 and, after heat coagulation of the protein, obtained a polysaccharide fraction which gave fructose, glucose, galactose, arabinose, and xylose on acid hydrolysis, as found in the liquors from leaf fractionation.

Nordin *et al.* (1975) separated wheat seedling extracts on Sepharose 6B to give two main fractions with molecular weights of 2×10^7 and 2×10^5, respectively, and containing mainly arabinose and galactose, with lesser amounts of glucose, xylose, mannose, and rhamnose.

CARBOHYDRATE IN LPC AS A PECTIN COMPONENT LINKED TO PROTEIN

The sugars detected in both the acid hydrolysates and also in the pectinase and snail juice digests of red clover and wheat LPC—galactose, arabinose, and xylose, with smaller amounts of glucose—are the neutral components of pectin. There is evidence from studies on cultured sycamore cells (Northcote 1969; Rubery and Northcote 1970; Stoddart and Northcote 1967) that the neutral arabinogalactan found is a precursor of arabinogalactan linked to uronic acid, the more complex acidic arabinogalactan, or pectin.

Acidic arabinogalactans attached to nitrogen have been isolated from 5% TCA extracts of broad bean leaves (Pusztai and Watt 1969; Pusztai *et al.* 1971). These TCA extracts are different from ordinary aqueous or water soluble extracts as they also contain hydroxyproline (Clarke and Ellinger 1967; Jennings and Watt 1967) and include carbohydrate not extracted by phenol-acetic acid-water (Jennings *et al.* 1968), a solvent which extracts protein of amino acid composition comparable with LPC (Gerloff *et al.* 1965; Byers 1971); hydroxyproline has not been reported in LPC.

Recent models of the cell wall by Talmadge *et al.* (1973) based on studies of extracellular polysaccharide in cultured sycamore cells, have postulated that neutral arabinogalactan is linked to the cell wall protein extensin (Lamport 1970) as well as being attached to acidic polyuronide. Aspinall and Molloy (1968) found that aqueous extracts of alfalfa leaves when chromatographed on DEAE-cellulose gave a neutral arabinogalactan containing 1% protein and acidic arabinogalactan fractions with up to15% protein, even after prior partitioning of the original extracts between phenol and water to remove protein; the residual nitrogen may have been linked to the carbohydrate.

Hillestad and Wold (1977) and Hillestad *et al.* (1977) found 1% water-soluble glycoproteins in *Cannabis* leaves. They extracted the leaves with water at 50–60°C and, by chromatography on DEAE-cellulose, separated fractions corresponding to neutral and acidic arabinogalactans and which were associated with 17–25% protein. There was no preliminary removal of protein by partitioning between phenol and water as done by Aspinall and Molloy (1968) for alfalfa leaf extracts, so the protein present may not all have been linked to the carbohydrate.

Arabinogalactans have been isolated from a variety of plant sources, cited by Fincher *et al.* (1974), who purified an arabinogalactan-peptide from aqueous extracts of wheat endosperm. As stated by Fincher *et al.* (1974), studies of the arabinogalactans were concerned mainly with the isolation and structure of the polysaccharide, and any associated protein was only of passing interest. Recently, two groups of workers have isolated different arabinogalactans from the same source, suspension-cultured tobacco cells: Hori and Sato (1977) isolated a hydroxyproline-rich glycoprotein with 21% uronic acid and 6% protein and Katō *et al.* (1977) isolated an arabinogalactan with 3% uronic acid and 1% protein. Both groups of workers fractionated extracellular extracts of the tobacco cells on DEAE-cellulose, but Katō *et al.* (1977) removed a "pectinic acid" fraction with cupric acetate beforehand, which may explain the different end products. Ford (1972) isolated an arabinogalactan from *Phaseolus atropurpureus* leaves (a Siratro cultivar) containing 14% uronic acid but little nitrogen; fractions from a

DEAE-cellulose column showing absorption at 280 nm, indicative of protein, were deliberately discarded.

The linkages between carbohydrate and protein have been studied for extensin, the hydroxyproline-rich glycoprotein of the primary cell wall of most green plants, and shown to be arabinosyl hydroxyproline (Lamport 1967) and galactosylserine (Lamport *et al.* 1973). Hydroxyproline was found in the water-soluble glycoprotein of South African *Cannabis sativa* leaves, but was absent from the corresponding Thailand leaves (Hillestad *et al.* 1977). However, serine-O-galactoside linkages were established in both kinds of leaves (Hillestad and Wold 1977; Hillestad *et al.* 1977) and it is possible that linkages of this type are present in the LPC preparations which do not contain hydroxyproline.

There are only two other reports of water-soluble hydroxyproline-containing glycoproteins from leaves: Wright *et al.* (1962) found an acidic arabinogalactan with 8% protein in aged tobacco leaves and Mani and Radhakrishnan (1974) purified a hydroxyproline-containing glycoprotein from the soluble fraction of sandal (*Santalum album* L.) leaves containing 16% carbohydrate, mainly arabinose, with a little galactose. Besides containing hydroxyproline, the sandal protein contained more aspartic and glutamic acids and glycine, but less leucine and valine, than is usual in LPC.

CARBOHYDRATE IN SEED GLYCOPROTEINS COMPARED WITH THAT IN LPC

Arabinogalactans in Lectins and β-Lectins

Glycoproteins from seeds which have been widely studied are the lectins or phytohemagglutinins which interact with cell surfaces and cause cells to agglutinate. The carbohydrates account for up to 20% of the glycoprotein and include mannose, glucosamine, and galactose, typical constituents of animal glycoproteins. Some lectins such as jack bean concanavalin-A and wheat germ agglutinin bind carbohydrate but do not contain carbohydrate themselves. Arabinose and xylose are only minor components of this class of compound (Sharon and Lis 1972). An exception is the lectin of potato tubers, isolated by Allen and Neuberger (1973), containing hydroxyproline and 50% carbohydrate, which was mainly arabinose, with small amounts of galactose, glucose, and glucosamine.

Jermyn and Yeow (1975) designated a new lectin type, "all-β" lectin, first isolated by Yariv *et al.* (1967) from soybean, jack bean, and maize seeds and shown to form precipitates with β-glycosides covalently attached to phloroglucinol. Jermyn and Yeow (1975) found this lectin type in 91 of 104 angiosperm and gymnosperm seeds studied; it contained mainly carbohydrate (arabinose and galactose with small amounts of xylose, rhamnose, and mannose) and up to 7% protein, rich in hydroxyproline, alanine, and serine.

The liquid suspension cultures of endosperm from *Lolium multiflorum* studied by Anderson *et al.* (1977) contained a similar carbohydrate-binding arabinogalactan-protein with molecular weight $2-3 \times 10^5$. The amount of carbohydrate in the all-β lectins, over 90%, is much higher than that in the ordinary lectins. The arabinogalactans resemble those of coniferous woods, with 1,3 and 1,6 branched linkages (Anderson *et al.* 1977).

Arabinoxylan and Galactoarabinoxylan Linked to Protein

The polysaccharides released by *Lolium multiflorum* endosperm cells in tissue culture include, besides the arabinogalactan-protein, a complex of arabinose and xylose and also galactose; these may represent arabinoxylans and possibly also galactoarabinoxylans (Anderson *et al.* 1977). Arabinoxylans are a major fraction of hemicellulose of cell walls of cereal endosperm (Mares and Stone 1973).

McNeil *et al.* (1975) found barley aleurone cell walls to consist mainly of arabinoxylan (85%) with 8% cellulose and 6% protein, but no hydroxyproline. Arabinoxylan was also found to be the major component of the cell wall suspension cultures of the monocotyledons bromegrass, oats, rice, ryegrass, sugarcane, and wheat (Burke *et al.* 1974). These cultures contained much less hydroxyproline (0.05–0.16%) in the cell wall than the 2% of bean and sycamore cell wall suspension cultures (Talmadge *et al.* 1973). The protein content of the monocotyledon cultures was in the range of 7–17% of the cell wall, somewhat higher than the 10% of sycamore. Serine and threonine may be more important than hydroxyproline in the linkage between carbohydrate and protein for monocotyledons; this may also be the case with LPC.

REFERENCES

AKAZAWA, T., SAIO, K. and SUGIYAMA, N. 1965. On the structural nature of fraction-1 protein of rice leaves. Biochem. Biophys. Res. Commun. *20*, 114–119.

ALLEN, A.K. and NEUBERGER, A. 1973. The purification and properties of a lectin from potato tubers, a hydroxyproline-containing glycoprotein. Biochem. J. *135*, 307–314.

ANDERSON, R.L., CLARKE, A.E., JERMYN, M.A., KNOX, R.B. and STONE, B.A. 1977. A carbohydrate-binding arabinogalactan-protein from liquid suspension cultures of endosperm from *Lolium multiflorum*. Aust. J. Plant Physiol. *4*, 143–158.

ARKCOLL, D.B., DAVYS, M.N.G., FESTENSTEIN, G.N. and PIRIE, N.W. 1972. Quality of the extracted protein. Rep. Rothamsted Exp. Stn. *1971*, 126.

ASPINALL, G.O. and FANSHAWE, R.S. 1961. Pectic substances from lucerne *(Medicago sativa)*. Part I. Pectic acid. J. Chem. Soc., 4215–4225.

ASPINALL, G.O., GESTETNER, B., MOLLOY, J.A. and UDDIN, M. 1968. Pectic substances from lucerne *(Medicago sativa)*. Part II. Acidic oligosaccharides from partial hydrolysis of leaf and stem pectic acids. J. Chem. Soc. C:, 2554–2559.

ASPINALL, G.O. and MOLLOY, J.A. 1968. Pectic substances from lucerne *(Medicago sativa)*. Part III. Fractionation of polysaccharides extracted with water. J. Chem. Soc. C:, 2994–2999.

BAHR, J.T., BOURQUE, D.P. and SMITH, H.J. 1977. Solubility properties of fraction 1 proteins of maize, spinach, and tobacco. J. Agric. Food Chem. *25*, 783–789.

BAILEY, R.W. 1967. Quantitative studies of ruminant digestion. II. Loss of ingested carbohydrates from the reticulo-rumen. N.Z. J. Agric. Res. *10*, 15–32.

BISHOP, C.T., BAYLEY, S.T. and SETTERFIELD, G. 1958. Chemical constitution of the primary cell walls of *Avena* coleoptiles. Plant Physiol. *33*, 283–289.

BURKE, D., KAUFMAN, P., McNEIL, M. and ALBERSHEIM, P. 1974. The structure of plant cell walls. VI. A survey of the walls of suspension-cultured monocots. Plant Physiol. *54*, 109–115.

BYERS, M. 1971. Amino acid composition and *in vitro* digestibility of some protein fractions from three species of leaves of various ages. J. Sci. Food Agric. *22*, 242–251.

CLARKE, E.M.W. and ELLINGER, G.M. 1967. Fractionation of plant material. II. Amino acid composition of some fractions obtained from the broad bean plant (*Vicia faba* L.) and chromatographic differentiation of hydroxyproline isomers. J. Sci. Food Agric. *18*, 536–540.

FESTENSTEIN, G.N. 1972. Water-soluble carbohydrates in extracts from large-scale preparation of leaf protein. J. Sci. Food Agric. *23*, 1409–1415.

FESTENSTEIN, G.N. 1976. Carbohydrates associated with leaf protein. J. Sci. Food Agric. *27*, 849–854.

FINCHER, G.B., SAWYER, W.H. and STONE, B.A. 1974. Chemical and physical properties of an arabinogalactan-peptide from wheat endosperm. Biochem. J. *139*, 535–545.

FORD, C.W. 1972. Arabinogalactan from Phaseolus Atropurpureus leaves. Phytochemistry *11*, 2559–2562.

GERLOFF, E.D., LIMA, I.H. and STAHMANN, M.A. 1965. Leaf proteins as foodstuffs. Amino acid composition of leaf protein concentrates. J. Agric. Food Chem. *13*, 139–143.

HILLESTAD, A. and WOLD, J.K. 1977. Water-soluble glycoproteins from *Cannabis sativa* (South Africa). Phytochemistry *16*, 1947–1951.

HILLESTAD, A., WOLD, J.K. and ENGEN, T. 1977. Water-soluble glycoproteins from *Cannabis sativa* (Thailand). Phytochemistry *16*, 1953–1956.

HORI, H. and SATO, S. 1977. Extracellular hydroxyproline-rich glycoprotein of suspension-cultured tobacco cells. Phytochemistry *16*, 1485–1487.

HOVE, E.L., LOHREY, E., URS, M.K. and ALLISON, R.M. 1974. Effect of lucerne-protein concentrate in the diet on growth, reproduction, and body composition of rats. Br. J. Nutr. *31*, 147–157.

HOWARTH, R.E., SARKAR, S.K., FESSER, A.C. and SCHNARR, G.W. 1977. Some properties of soluble proteins from alfalfa *(Medicago sativa)* herbage and their possible relationship to ruminant bloat. J. Agric. Food Chem. *25*, 175–179.

JENNINGS, A.C., PUSZTAI, A., SYNGE, R.L.M. and WATT, W.B. 1968. Fractionation of plant meterial. III. Two schemes for chemical fractionation of fresh leaves, having special applicability for isolation of the bulk protein. J. Sci. Food Agric. *19*, 203–213.

JENNINGS, A.C. and WATT, W.B. 1967. Fractionation of plant material. I. Extraction of proteins and nucleic acids from plant tissues and isolation of protein fractions containing hydroxyproline from broad bean (*Vicia faba* L.) leaves. J. Sci. Food Agric. *18*, 527–535.

JERMYN, M.A. and YEOW, Y.M. 1975. A class of lectins present in the tissues of seed plants. Aust. J. Plant Physiol. *2*, 501–531.

KATŌ, K., WATANABE, F. and EDA, S. 1977. An arabinogalactan from extracellular polysaccharides of suspension-cultured tobacco cells. Agric. Biol. Chem. *41*, 533–538.

KAWASHIMA, N. and WILDMAN, S.G. 1970. Fraction I protein. Annu. Rev. Plant Physiol. *21*, 325–358.

LAMPORT, D.T.A. 1967. Hydroxyproline-O-glycosidic linkage of the plant cell wall glycoprotein extensin. Nature *216*, 1322–1324.

LAMPORT, D.T.A. 1970. Cell wall metabolism. Annu. Rev. Plant Physiol. *21*, 235–270.

LAMPORT, D.T.A., KATONA, L. and ROERIG, S. 1973. Galactosylserine in extensin. Biochem. J. *133*, 125–131.

MACRAE, J.C. and ARMSTRONG, D.G. 1968. Enzyme method for determination of α-linked glucose polymers in biological materials. J. Sci. Food Agric. *19*, 578–581.

MANI, U.V. and RADHAKRISHNAN, A.N. 1974. Isolation and characterization of a hydroxyproline-containing protein from soluble extracts of the leaves of Sandal (*Santalum album* L.) Biochem. J. *141*, 147–153.

MARES, D.J. and STONE, B.A. 1973. Studies on wheat endosperm. I. Chemical composition and ultrastructure of the cell walls. Aust. J. Biol. Sci. *26*, 793–812.

McILROY, R.J. 1967. Carbohydrates of grassland herbage. Herb. Abstr. *37*, 79–87.

McNEIL, M., ALBERSHEIM, P., TAIZ, L. and JONES, R.L. 1975. The structure of plant cell walls. VII. Barley aleurone cells. Plant Physiol. *55*, 64–68.

MORRÉ, D.J. and OLSON, A.C. 1965. An analysis of *Avena* coleoptile pectin fractions. Can. J. Bot. *43*, 1083–1095.

MORRISON, J.E. and PIRIE, N.W. 1961. The large-scale production of protein from leaf extracts. J. Sci. Food Agric. *12*, 1–5.

NORDIN, P., JILKA, R., CHASE, P. and WHITLOCK, L. 1975. Extraction of polysaccharides from wheat seedlings with sodium dodecylsulfate. Phytochemistry *14*, 1355–1358.

NORTHCOTE, D.H. 1969. Growth and differentiation of plant cells in culture. Symp. Soc. Gen. Microbiol. *19*, 333–349.

PUSZTAI, A., BEGBIE, R. and DUNCAN, I. 1971. Fractionation and characterization of water-soluble polysaccharide-protein complexes containing hydroxyproline from the leaves of *Vicia faba*. J. Sci. Food Agric. *22*, 513–519.

PUSZTAI, A. and WATT, W.B. 1969. Fractionation and characterization of glycoproteins containing hydroxyproline from the leaves of *Vicia faba*. Eur. J. Biochem. *10*, 523–532.

RIDLEY, S.M., THORNBER, J.P. and BAILEY, J.L. 1967. A study of the water-soluble proteins of spinach beet chloroplasts with particular reference to fraction 1 protein. Biochim. Biophys. Acta *140*, 62–79.

RUBERY, P.H. and NORTHCOTE, D.H. 1970. Effect of auxin (2,4-dichlorophenoxyacetic acid) on the synthesis of cell wall polysaccharides in cultured sycamore cells. Biochim. Biophys. Acta *222*, 95–108.

SAKANO, K., PARTRIDGE, J.E. and SHANNON, L.M. 1973. Absence of carbohydrate in crystalline fraction I protein isolated from tobacco leaves. Biochim. Biophys. Acta *329*, 339–341.

SHARON, N. and LIS, H. 1972. Lectins: Cell-agglutinating and sugar-specific proteins. Science *177*, 949–959.

STODDART, R.W. and NORTHCOTE, D.H. 1967. Metabolic relationships of the isolated fractions of the pectic substances of actively growing sycamore cells. Biochem. J. *105*, 45–59.

TALMADGE, K.W., KEEGSTRA, K., BAUER, W.D. and ALBERSHEIM, P. 1973. The structure of plant cell walls. I. The macromolecular components of the walls of suspension-cultured sycamore cells with a detailed analysis of the pectic polysaccharides. Plant Physiol. *51*, 158–173.

WAITE, R. and GORROD, A.R.N. 1959. The comprehensive analysis of grasses. J. Sci. Food Agric. *10*, 317–326.

WRIGHT, H.E., BURTON, W.W. and BERRY, R.C. 1962. Isolation and characterization of a complex polysaccharide from aged Burley tobacco. Phytochemistry *1*, 125–129.

YARIV, J., LIS, H. and KATCHALSKI, E. 1967. Precipitation of arabic acid and some seed polysaccharides by glycosylphenylazo dyes. Biochem. J. *105*, 1C–2C.

9

Pigments in Leaf Protein Concentrates

Margaret Holden

The most obvious feature of unfractionated leaf protein concentrate (LPC) is its unattractive color. The appearance is unimportant for animal feeding, but it does cause problems for its acceptance as human food, although this aspect has often been exaggerated. LPC consists largely of chloroplasts and it is the chloroplast pigments (chlorophylls and carotenoids) and their degradation products that are mostly responsible for the color. The fresh green of undegraded chlorophylls is almost wholly acceptable as a food color, but the greenish-brown color of pheophytins and pheophorbides, which are formed from chlorophylls during processing, is much less attractive.

Problems that have arisen in animal feeding experiments due to the presence of chlorophyll-type pigments in LPC are photosensitization of albino rats and white pigs, which is discussed in the later section on chlorophyllase action, and green pigmentation in the yolks of eggs (Hughes and Eyles 1953). Morris (1977) has suggested that greenish yolks may only occur when hens are fed LPC in which lipid oxidation has taken place between harvesting and drying.

In contrast to the chlorophylls, the carotenoids (carotene and xanthophylls) seem to cause no problems. The presence of a vitamin A precursor, β-carotene, provides a useful bonus when LPC is used for feeding malnourished children (Pirie 1971). Some of the xanthophylls have commercial value as pigmenters for poultry skin and egg yolks, and the large amount present in LPC has helped create a market for it in the United States.

Chlorophyll-type Pigments

The amounts of undegraded chlorophylls and various degradation products differ according to variations in the way LPC is prepared and, also, from which species it is made. The following scheme illustrates the main changes in the chlorophylls that can occur during the preparation of LPC.

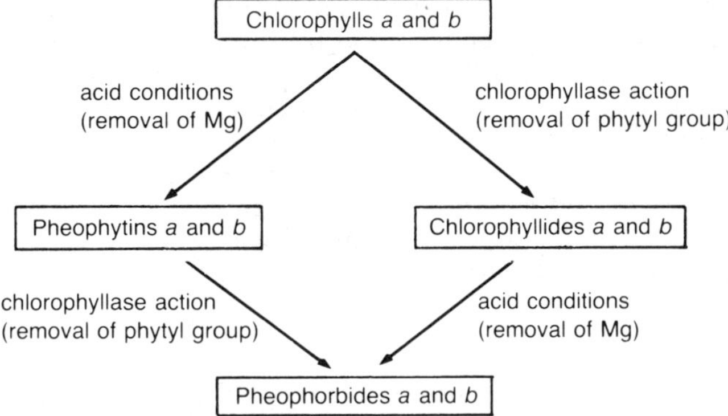

Up to eight pigments which are easily separable and recognizable by thin layer chromatography (TLC) (Bacon 1965) are thus formed. In addition, small amounts of the chlorophyll isomers *a′* and *b′* may be formed on heating and these too can be detected on TLC plates.

Chlorophyllase Action

Arkcoll and Holden (1973) found that with extracts from leaves rich in the enzyme chlorophyllase coagulation of protein at 80°C led to the formation of chlorophyllides. These are green like the chlorophylls so no color change results. The enzyme is inactive in the pigment-protein complex in leaf juice at 20°–30°C, but as the temperature is raised and the complex is denatured, chlorophyllase becomes active. The enzyme catalyzes the removal of the phytyl group from chlorophylls (and pheophytins) before it, too, is denatured. When protein was rapidly coagulated at a temperature near 100°C, chlorophyllide formation was almost completely prevented. However, Holden (1974), who investigated the conversion to chlorophyllide in more detail using a range of species, found that with sugar beet leaves, which have exceptionally high chlorophyllase activity, chlorophyllide formation was not entirely eliminated even at 100°C.

The formation of chlorophyllides was at first regarded as of only academic interest, but it soon assumed some importance. Workers in New Zealand found that LPC from lucerne (alfalfa) caused photosensitization in albino rats (Hove *et al.* 1974) and white cross bred pigs (Carr and Pearson 1976) which were exposed to daylight during feeding trials. LPC from ryegrass did not have this effect in rats.

Lohrey *et al.* (1974) obtained evidence that pigments derived from chlorophyll, especially the chlorophyllides and pheophorbides, were the photosensitizing agents in leaf protein. In these experiments the protein was coagulated slowly and the conditions were such that chlorophyllase action could have been expected if the extracts had had high enzyme activity. The difference between the LPCs from lucerne and ryegrass was due to the high chlorophyllase activity in the former species and the low activity in the latter. Tapper *et al.* (1975) confirmed that more rapid coagulation of protein in lucerne juice at a higher temperature than they had previously used diminished the content of phytyl-free pigments and found that the LPC did not cause photosensitization. Pheophorbide *a* was a strongly photosensitizing agent whereas pheophytin *a* was not, and it was suggested that the difference must be attributed to the phytyl-free pigment, pheophorbide, being more readily absorbed from the gut than the phytylated pigment, pheophytin. This is also a possible explanation for the occurrence of green egg yolks mentioned earlier.

Removal of Magnesium

Fresh leaf juice usually contains a trace of pheophytin *a*; the amount is increased and some pheophytin *b* appears during heat coagulation of protein in juices with low chlorophyllase activity. When the activity is high there may be no pheophytin at all because it is converted to pheophorbide.

When LPC is given an acid wash, as it often is, to allow preservation of moist cake, chlorophyllides formed by enzyme action are converted to pheophorbides and most of the remaining chlorophyll is converted to pheophytin. It is at this stage that the color of the LPC is changed from dark green to greenish-brown.

Other Changes in Chlorophyll-type Pigments

There is little or no change in the nature of the chlorophyll-type pigments when LPC is freeze-dried, but the pigments are less easily extracted by organic solvents from dry preparations than from moist cake. Some changes do occur, however, when LPC is stored. Arkcoll and Holden (1973) found little change with storage at −20°C or at room temperature in metal foil packs, but when polythene packs were used, there was both a decrease in the total amount of chlorophyll-type pigment extractable and an increase in the number of pigments present. The decrease in extractable pigment was thought to be due partly to bleaching by light and partly to pigments becoming more tightly bound to the protein.

Some of the extra pigments seemed to be identical with the "changed" chlorophylls described by Bacon and Holden (1967). These are oxidation products of chlorophylls and pheophytins and probably also of the pheophorbides; their presence is an indication of unsatisfactory storage conditions.

Carotenoids

At about the same time in the early 1970s interest in the carotenoids of LPC began to be shown in three different places. Pirie and colleagues at Rothamsted (England), Kohler's group at Albany (California), and Ramana and Singh in India all published papers on the carotenoids and their changes at various stages during the preparation of LPC from a number of species.

The carotenoids likely to be found in LPC are β-carotene and the xanthophylls lutein, violaxanthin, and neoxanthin. They are, however, all liable to breakdown during the processing, both enzymically and nonenzymically, leading to the formation of degradation products, some of which are colored and some not. Knuckles *et al.* (1971) and Arkcoll and Holden (1973) have described methods for determining carotenoids in LPCs.

Carotenoids are lost during pulping of the leaves and before the protein in the juice has been coagulated because enzymes are active at this stage. Several enzyme systems have been linked with carotenoid degradation, some of these being connected with the oxidation of unsaturated fats; different systems are probably operative in different plant species. After enzymes have been inactivated by heating, carotenoid losses during the later stages will be nonenzymic. However, if peroxides have already been formed enzymically, these may affect the subsequent stability of the carotenoids. In addition, the removal in the separated juice of any natural antioxidants that may be present will make the carotenoids more liable to breakdown.

Effect of pH During Pulping of the Leaves

In the Pro-Xan process which was developed as a commercial method for production of alfalfa LPC for animal feeds (Spencer *et al.* 1971), ammonia was added to keep the pH near 8 while the leaves were being pulped. One reason for adjusting the pH was because this was found to decrease xanthophyll losses (Kohler and Bickoff 1971). Preparations made by Arkcoll and Holden (1973) with NaOH added during grinding so as to produce a juice with pH 8.5–9 had higher carotenoid contents than those made without pH adjustment.

Effect of Heat Coagulation

Ramana and Singh (1971A) reported little loss of carotene during protein coagulation in juices from lucerne and *Dolichos* leaves. Using juices from a range of cereals, legumes, and wild plants, Arkcoll and Holden (1973) confirmed that coagulation of protein at 80°C caused little loss of carotene.

Although the carotene is remarkably stable during heat coagulation, the xanthophylls are much less so. Arkcoll and Holden (1973) found losses of up to 25% in the total xanthophyll in a wide range of plants; Ramana and Singh's losses (1971A) were even higher. Lutein, which accounts for nearly half the total xanthophyll, and neoxanthin were stable, but violaxanthin was considerably altered. Due mainly to the slight acidity of the juice, it was partly converted into luteoxanthin (with one furanoid and one epoxy group) and partly into auroxanthin (with two furanoid groups).

Effect of Acid Washing

Acid washing further diminished the violaxanthin content, most having been converted to auroxanthin. Neoxanthin too decreased in amount with neochrome (a 5,8-epoxide) being formed (Arkcoll and Holden 1973). The amount of lutein present was little altered and there was no eidence of its having been isomerized. If an acid wash is omitted, as in the Pro-Xan process, there will be a smaller loss of xanthophyll up to this stage. However, the loss of violaxanthin and neoxanthin is comparatively unimportant because lutein is much more effective as a pigmenter of poultry products than the other two xanthophylls (Kuzmicky *et al.* 1969).

Carotene was unaffected by acid washing; an apparent small increase in the carotene content was due to the removal of water-soluble consitituents. Ramana and Singh (1971B) gave values for the β-carotene content of freshly-made LPCs from five species, ranging from 0.37 mg/g dry weight for *Manihot utilissima* to 0.96 mg/g for *Dolichos lablab*. In small-scale preparations of lucerne LPC, Arkcoll and Holden (1973) found the carotene content ranged from 0.93 to 1.4 mg/g dry weight and total xanthophyll from 1.78 to 2.91 mg/g. Miller *et al.* (1972) reported lower values than these for "dejuiced coagulum" in a large-scale preparation.

Effect of Drying

On a small scale, LPC is dried satisfactorily by freeze-drying and there is little change in the nature or content of carotenoids in freeze-dried materials. With air drying at 40°C, losses amounted to only a few percent. Several different methods for drying alfalfa LPC on a large scale were compared by Miller *et al.* (1972). With all of them the carotenoid losses were fairly small, up to 15% for xanthophyll and 10% for carotene. Pirie (1971) suggested that 2 g of a fresh freeze-dried preparation of LPC per day should be enough to provide the 1.8 mg of β-carotene needed by a young child.

Effect of Storage

Conditions of storage are important for the retention of carotenoids. Witt *et al.* (1971) gave details of their stability in Pro-Xan after drum drying. Both xanthophyll and carotene were more stable in freeze-dried than in drum-dried LPCs stored at 38°C in open containers. The addition of the antioxidant ethoxyquin (0.125%) considerably diminished carotenoid breakdown; Wesson oil likewise had a protective effect. Carotenoids were more stable in unwashed than in water-washed Pro-Xan, presumably because natural antioxidants were removed in the washing. Adding back water-soluble material increased the stability of the carotenoids.

Arkcoll and Holden (1973) found that carotene was less stable than xanthophyll in stored LPCs when air was present. Both pigments were less stable in acid-washed than in unwashed preparations. Earlier, Arkcoll (1973) had found good retention of carotene when LPCs were stored in metal-foil bags that were impermeable to light and oxygen; xanthophyll too was satisfactorily retained under the same conditions. Morris (1977) suggested that LPC will probably be stored under inert gas if preservation of pigments is important.

REFERENCES

ARKCOLL, D.B. 1973. The preservation and storage of leaf protein preparations. J. Sci. Food Agric. *24*, 437–445.

ARKCOLL, D.B. and HOLDEN, M. 1973. Changes in chloroplast pigments during the preparation of leaf protein. J. Sci. Food Agric. *24*, 1217–1227.

BACON, M.F. 1965. Separation of chlorophylls *a* and *b* and related compounds by thin-layer chromatography. J. Chromatogr. *17*, 322–326.

BACON, M.F. and HOLDEN, M. 1967. Changes in chlorophylls resulting from various chemical and physical treatments of leaves and leaf extracts. Phytochemistry *6*, 193–210.

CARR, J.R. and PEARSON, G. 1976. Photosensitization, growth performance and carcass measurement of pigs fed diets containing commercially prepared leaf-protein concentrate. N.Z. J. Exp. Agric. *4*, 45–50.

HOLDEN, M. 1974. Chlorophyll degradation products in leaf protein preparations. J. Sci. Food Agric. *25*, 1427–1432.

HOVE, E.L., LOHREY, E., URS, K. and ALLISON, R.M. 1974. The effect of lucerne-protein concentrate in the diet on growth, reproduction and body composition of rats. Br. J. Nutr. *31*, 147–158.

HUGHES, G.P. and EYLES, D.E. 1953. Extracted herbage leaf protein for poultry feeding. I. Introduction and feeding trials with laying hens. J. Agric. Sci. (Cambridge) *43*, 136–143.

KNUCKLES, B.E., WITT, S.C., MILLER, R.E. and BICKOFF, E.M. 1971. Determination of carotene and xanthophyll in alfalfa protein concentrates. J. Assoc. Off. Anal. Chem. *54*, 769–772.

KOHLER, G.O. and BICKOFF, E.M. 1971. Commercial production from alfalfa in USA. *In* Leaf Protein: Its Agronomy, Preparation, Quality and Use. IBP Handb. *20*. N.W. Pirie (Editor). Blackwell Scientific Publications, Oxford.

KUZMICKY, D.D., KOHLER, G.O., LIVINGSTON, A.L., KNOWLES, R.E., and NELSON, J.W. 1969. Broiler pigmentation potency of neoxanthin and violaxanthin relative to lutein. Poult. Sci. *48*, 326–330.

LOHREY, E., TAPPER, B. and HOVE, E.L. 1974. Photosensitization of albino rats fed on lucerne-protein concentrate. Br. J. Nutr. *31*, 159–166.

MILLER, R.E., EDWARDS, R.H., LAZAR, M.E., BICKOFF, E.M., and KOHLER, G.O. 1972. PRO—XAN process: Air drying of alfalfa leaf protein concentrate. J. Agric. Food Chem. *20*, 1151–1154.

MORRIS, T.R. 1977. Leaf-protein concentrate for non-ruminant farm animals. *In* Green Crop Fractionation. R.J. Wilkins (Editor). Br. Grassl. Soc. Occas. Symp. *9*.

PIRIE, A. 1971. Carotene content of leaf protein preparations and their use as source of vitamin A. *In* Leaf Protein: Its Agronomy, Preparation, Quality and Use. N.W. Pirie (Editor). IBP Handb. *20*. Blackwell Scientific Publications, Oxford.

RAMANA, K.V.R. and SINGH, N. 1971A. Studies on carotene and xanthophyll pigments in leaf protein and their stability during storage. Indian J. Exp. Biol. *9*, 478–480.

RAMANA, K.V.R. and SINGH, N. 1971B. β-Carotene in leaf proteins. Curr. Sci. *40*, 293–294.

SPENCER, R.R., MOTTOLA, A.C., BICKOFF, E.M., CLARK, J.P. and KOHLER, G.O. 1971. The PRO-XAN process: The design and evaluation of a pilot plant system for the coagulation and separation of leaf protein from alfalfa juice. J. Agric. Food Chem. *19*, 504–507.

TAPPER, B.A., LOHREY, E., HOVE, E.L., and ALLISON, R.M. 1975. Photosensitivity from chlorophyll-derived pigments. J. Sci. Food Agric. *26*, 277–284.

WITT, S.C., SPENCER, R.R., BICKOFF, E.M., and KOHLER, G.O. 1971. Carotenoid storage stability in drum-dried PRO-XAN. J. Agric. Food Chem. *19*, 162–165.

10

Reactions of Phenolic Compounds with Proteins, and Their Relevance to the Production of Leaf Protein

W.S. Pierpoint

Plants produce an amazing array of phenolic compounds, many of which have the potential to react with proteins and other cytoplasmic components. Reaction is restricted during the life of a particular tissue and only becomes important as the tissue dies or is harvested and processed. In some cases, the subsequent reaction between phenols and proteins are highly appreciated since they will add significantly to the flavor, taste, and appearance of products such as tea, coffee, beer, and tobacco. It is conceivable that in the future the phenolic content of some preparations of edible leaf protein (LP) will be similarly appreciated for its contribution to their taste. However, in the present state of the art, the main concern with phenols in LP is the way in which they hinder its extraction and decrease its digestibility and nutritive value.

It is convenient to consider three types of reaction between proteins and plant phenols: first, the formation of adducts with tannins *(sensu stricto)* which are stabilized by H-bonds; second, absorptions which depend on other secondary valence forces such as hydrophobic attractions; and third, reactions forming covalent bonds, especially with quinones and other quinonoids generated from more innocuous phenols. These distinctions may prove somewhat arbitrary, and the complex reactions between proteins and tannins, for instance, may involve all three types of reaction to different degrees. However, in general, the products of the reactions are, initially at least, sufficiently different to justify the division. Phenols also form metabolic complexes with proteins such as the N-ferulyl-esters of barley and lucerne (van Sumere *et al.* 1975, 1980), and these may survive cell disruption. The frequency of their occurrence, like their disgestibility and metabolic significance is, however, unclear, and they will not be considered.

TANNINS *(SENSU STRICTO)* AND THEIR REACTION WITH PROTEINS

Although some authorities (Haslam 1977, 1978) disapprove of the chemical imprecision of the term tannin, with its overtones of the leather trade, it is very useful in the context of LP technology. Swain (1965) describes a tannin as any "naturally occurring compound with a high enough molecular weight (500–3000) containing a sufficiently large number of phenolic-OH or other suitable groups (1–2 per 100 MW) to enable it to form effective crosslinks between proteins and other macromolecules"; the formation of effective cross-links may be judged by the leathering of hides, the precipitation of soluble proteins, or the inhibition of enzymes.

For our purpose the molecular weight values may be unnecessarily restrictive. Smaller molecules may well form fewer bonds and not cross-link proteins, but larger and less soluble molecules, although unable to penetrate collagen fibrils and so tan hides, are likely to bind and retain soluble proteins. Their effect on extracting soluble proteins from leaves will be much the same as that of defined tannins, although, as Swain points out, these substances are difficult to characterize and estimate.

Structure and Distribution of Hydrolyzable Tannins

Two main classes of preformed tannins were distinguished by Freudenberg. The hydrolyzable tannins are based on a core of polyhydric alcohol, usually glucose, whose –OH groups are esterified either partly or wholly with gallic acid and/or a congenor. A general structure can be written

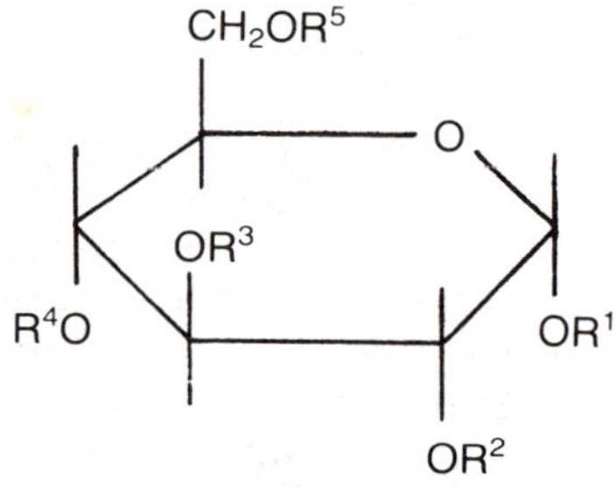

CH_2OR^5

O

OR^3

R^4O OR^1

OR^2

R may be a galloyl (2) or a number of galloyl residues linked as depsides (3) as in the gallotannins

(1) R = H—

(3) R = HO, HO—, —CO—[O—]n, HO, HO—, —CO—O—, HO, HO—, —C(=O)—, HO

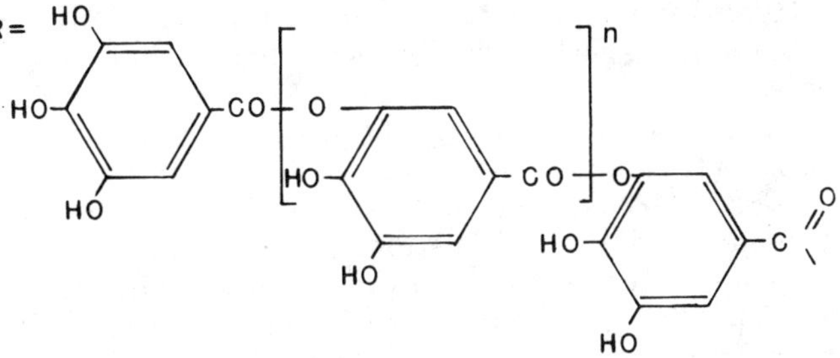

(2) HO, HO—, —CO—, HO

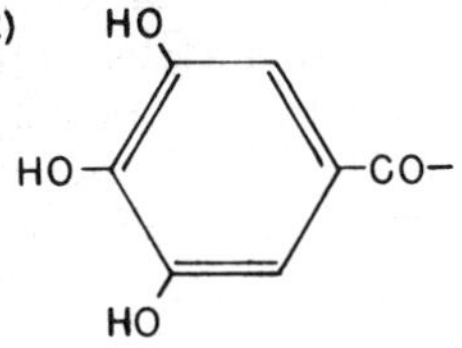

or, as in the ellagitannins, galloyl residues which have been oxidatively linked (4, 5), and which are often liberated as ellagic acid on hydrolysis

(4) HO, HO—, —CO—, HO, HO, HO—, —CO—, HO

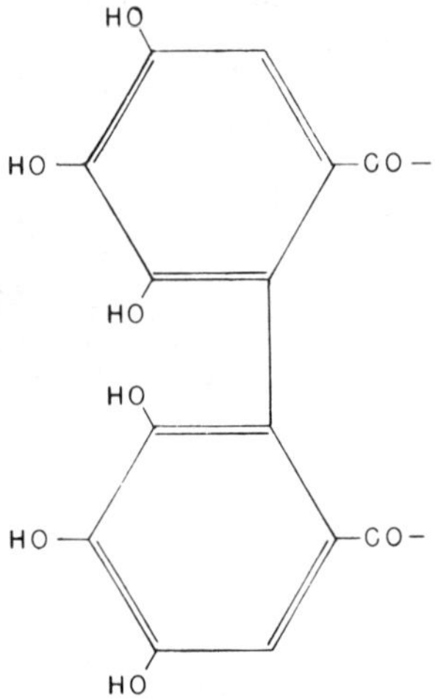

Hexahydroxydiphenyl Residue

(5) HO, HO—, —CO—, HO, HOOC, O, —CO—, O

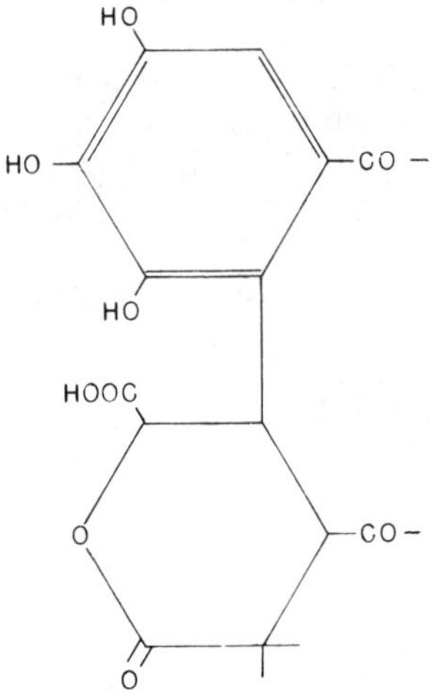

Chebulic Residue

In the commercial Chinese gallotannin obtained from insect galls on the leaves of *Rhus semialata*, $R^1 = R^3 = R^4 = R^5$ = gallic acid, and R^2 = polygallic acid (n = 0 , 1, or 2). The crystalline samples of "tannic acid" used in some studies (e.g., Goldstein and Swain 1965) are octa- or nona-galloyl derivatives of glucose, but likely to contain some gallic acid polymers (King and Pruden 1970). Gallotannins often have flat or disk-shaped molecules with –OH groups disposed toward the periphery of the disk. Ellagitannins are thought to be more spherical, but once again the –OH groups are arranged on the surface (Haslam 1978).

Hydrolyzable tannins are confined to a few "advanced" orders of cotyledonous plants such as the Rosales, which includes Leguminosae, the Sapindales, Geraniales, Parietales, and Myrtiflorae (or Myrtales). The have not been detected in monocotyledons, gymnosperms, ferns, or nonvascular species. As their name indicates, they are hydrolyzed by acids, alkalies, and tannases derived from fungi such as *Aspergillus* and *Penicillium* species. They are hydrolyzed intestinally in nonruminants, even though tannases have not been detected in animal tissues or intestinal bacteria (Glick and Joslyn 1970A). The products are absorbed and the sugar moiety metabolized, presumably usefully, whereas the phenols are hydroxylated, methylated, or conjugated before being excreted (Milic and Stojanovic 1972; McLeod 1974). This detoxication, of course, imposes a metabolic requirement for energy and a supply of methyl groups.

Structure and Distribution of Condensed Tannins

The other main group of tannins is the condensed tannins, and the most common members of this group are better described as procyanidins because of the red anthocyanidins that they give on heating in acid (Haslam 1977, 1978). These are oligomers of flavan-3-ols and flavan-3,4-diols with no carbohydrate core. The particular flavonoids involved depend on the species, and their hydroxylation pattern reflects that of the free flavonoids present in the species. Dimers and trimers based on stereoisomers of (+) catechin have been extracted from the fruits and vegetative parts of a number of species and well characterized. The dimers of (−)-epicatechin (A) have been extracted from apples, cherries, and horsechestnuts, while those of the trans isomer, (+)-catechin (B), are present in willow catkins, strawberries, rosehips, and hops.

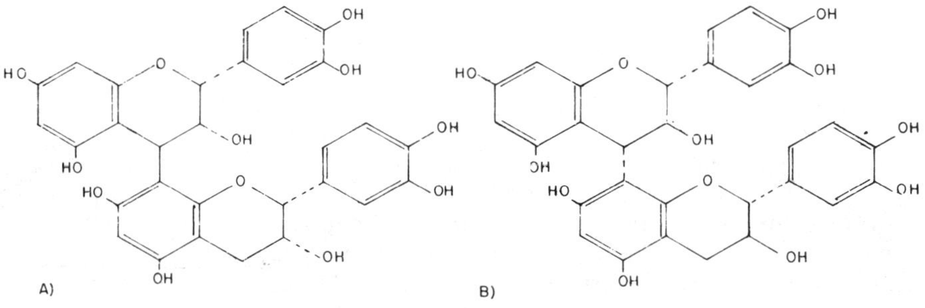

Mixed polymers based on both isomers are also known. Restriction of intramolecular rotation about the interflavan bond imparts a right- or left-handed helical configuration on higher polymers made wholly with one isomer or the other; once again, −OH groups are fully exposed on the periphery of the helix and this may be relevant to the close interaction of these tannins with proteins.

The condensed tannins of commerce may well be composed along different lines from the procyanidins, and their structure modified by post-mortem changes occurring either in dead tissue in the plant or during extraction. Oligomeric flavonoids in which the components are linked from A to B rings

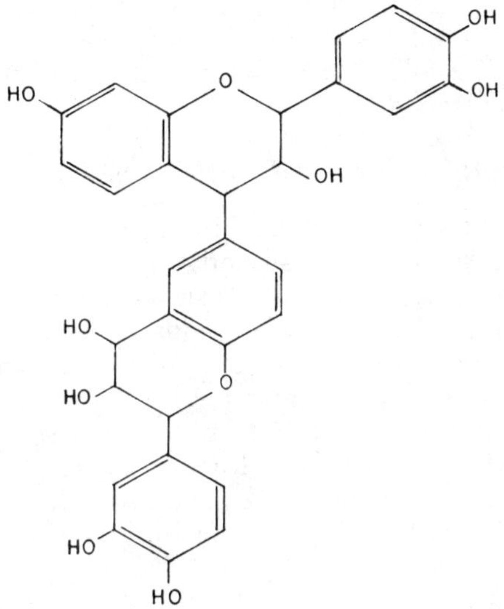

have been extracted from the wood of the leguminous tree *(Acacia mearnsii)* which is the source of commercial wattle (see Haslam 1978).

Condensed tannins are often considered to be less effective protein precipitants than hydrolyzable tannins. The ability of some purified procyanidins to precipitate hemolyzed blood is between 10 and 50% of that of an equal weight of tannic acid (Bate-Smith 1973). However, it is not always easy to measure this "relative astringency," especially for tannins of limited solubility; and some condensed tannins, the prodelphinidins of sainfoin *(Onobrychis viciifolia)* and red currant leaves (*Ribes* sp.), appear to be as astringent as tannic acid (Bate-Smith 1975).

Condensed tannins are more widely distributed than hydrolyzable ones. In surveys conducted by Bate-Smith and his colleagues (Bate-Smith 1962; Swain 1965), they were qualitatively detected by the anthocyanidin color produced by hydrolysis in 2 *N* HCl, and found in ferns, gymnosperms, and angiosperms, but not in nonvascular plants. In the angiosperms, they were present in 45% of dicotyledons tested and 30% of monocotyledons; about 15% of the same sample of dicotyledons gave ellagic acid after hydrolysis, indicating the probable presence of ellagitannins. Condensed tannins tend to characterize plants with a woody growth habit, and the tissues which contain enough tannin to be exploited commercially (10–40%) are usually barks and hardwoods. However, they occur in some cereals such as barley and sorghum (Ramachandra *et al.* 1977) and, along with hydrolyzable tannins, in forage crops such as lucerne, sainfoin (McLeod 1974), and the flowerheads of white clover (Bate-Smith 1975).

Condensed tannins are not readily broken down by enzymes either *in vivo* or *in vitro* and are unlikely to be digested or, under normal conditions, absorbed from the gut (Milic and Stojanovic 1972). Large amounts may, however, like large amounts of hydrolyzable tannins, produce intestinal damage (Texl and Konecny 1968), leading to their absorption and some toxic consequences (McLeod 1974).

Formation of Protein-Tannin Complexes

The forces responsible for the initial binding of tannins and other phenols to proteins are relatively weak secondary-valence forces. They can be broken by treatment with aqueous organic solvents, urea, detergents, and nonanionic polymers (Gustavson 1956; Goldstein and Swain 1965). Gustavson (1956) and Gustavson and Holm (1952) suggested that they are hydrogen bonds, and, because tannins also bind to polymers of urea-formaldehyde (Grassmann *et al.* 1937) and to nylons whose only reactive functions are peptide-like bonds, it was further suggested that the H-bonds linked unionized phenol groups to the peptide bonds of proteins. This idea has been widely accepted and can be formulated as follows (e.g., Haslam 1978).

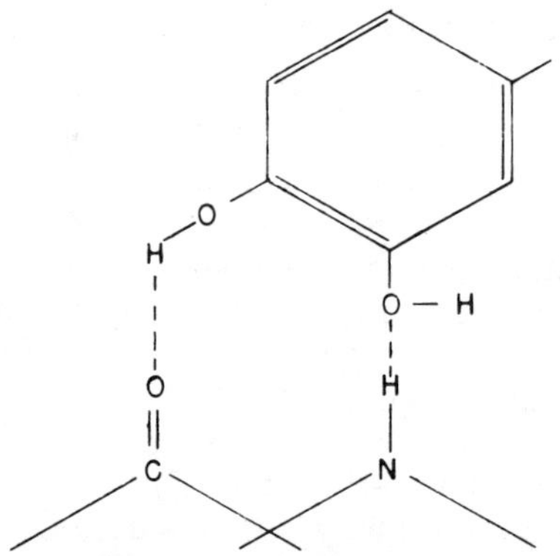

It is assumed that large numbers of such bonds are formed between the OH-groups suitably disposed on the surface of tannin molecules and the peptide groups of proteins. Since the size and shape of the tannin molecule allows it to bind to two or even more protein molecules, large molecular aggregates with a tendency to precipitate are formed. The H-bonds may be continuously broken and reformed in a random manner (Russell *et al.* 1968A). As the complex can only dissociate when all the bonds are broken simultaneously, tannins of large size, with many points of attachment, will form complexes of the greatest stability.

It is likely that the carboxyl groups of hydrolyzable tannins contribute to the binding of proteins by forming either ionic or nonionic links. This would help explain the way in which the binding of these tannins is affected by pH. The amount of either type of tannin that is bound by crude preparations of collagen (hide powder) is very low at pH's above which OH-groups would be expected to ionize (Fig. 10.1). The binding of condensed tannin does not change much at low pH's. The binding of hydrolyzable tannins increases as the pH is lowered, and is maximal when ionization of the carboxyl groups is suppressed. This suggests that the ionized carboxyl groups decrease the binding by electrostatic repulsion and solvation effects (Russell *et al.* 1968A, B), whereas in the unionized state they increase binding, possibly by forming H-bonds (Loomis and Battaille 1966). It is unlikely that the carboxyl groups become linked to side-chain residues of proteins, because synthetic polyamides bind tannic acid in the same pH-dependent way (Fig. 10.1).

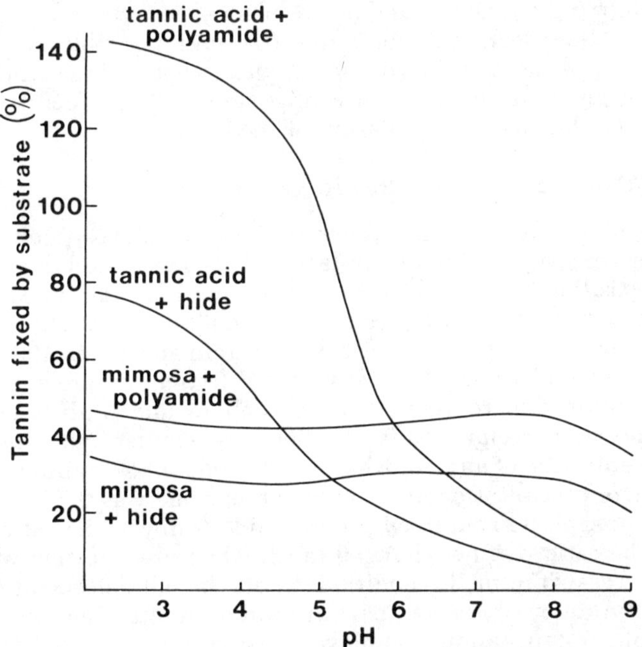

Fig. 10.1. Fixation of tannins by a crude collagen preparation (hide powder) and hydrated polyamide at different pH's. Tannic acid is the hydrolyzable tannin and mimosa extract the condensed one. Reaction with hide powder was done in 0.5 *M* NaCl to prevent effects due to swelling.
Redrawn from Gustavson (1956).

There is, however, some evidence that protein amino groups contribute to tannin binding at pH's below 3; thus crude collagen binds twice as much tannic acid at pH 2 as does deaminated collagen (Bowes and Kenten 1949).

Bonds other than H-bonds may also be involved in the binding of condensed tannins to proteins. Gustavson (1956) interpreted kinetic studies involving collagen with modified amino groups to indicate the rapid formation of ionic bonds between unmodified collagen and mimosa tannin. Some workers (Goldstein and Swain 1965), but not others (Russell *et al.* 1968A, B), have invoked forces other than H-bonds to explain the difficulty with which complexes between these tannins and proteins can be dispersed by detergents, tannin-adsorbents, and alkali.

Most of these general ideas on the initial interactions of protcins and tannins are based on older work which dealt with complex commercial tannins and crude protein preparations. It is likely that with newer techniques and more defined preparations they will receive even more chemical precision in the next decade. Haslam (1974) has identified the structures which, in a series of galloyl-glucose esters, lead to optimal reaction with the plant protein β-glucosidase, and he has shown that the resulting complex contains, on the average, 20 molecules of tannin per molecule of protein. Structural analysis of this type of product made between tannins and proteins of known structure and configuration should identify both the points of attachment and the nature of the bonds.

Precipitation of Protein-Tannin Complexes

Whatever the nature of the bonds in these complexes, their formation does not necessarily lead to precipitation. This depends on the pH and the ionic composition and concentration of protein and tannin. The effect of most of these factors is illustrated by the precipitation of β-glucosidase by a crystalline preparation of tannic acid (Goldstein and Swain 1965). Precipitation was virtually complete between pH 2 and 7.5, provided that the solution contained more than 10 m*M* phosphate; and at pH 8 some 25% of the complex was precipitated from a phosphate buffer, but none from the same concentration of an amine buffer. The amount of tannin required for the complete precipitation of 1 mg of the enzyme was 0.75 mg, and the resulting precipitate contained protein and tannin in the ratio of 2:1 by weight. The ratio was not changed much when precipitation was from a five-fold excess of tannin. In conditions where the salt concentration was too low to facilitate precipitation, partial inhibition of the enzyme indicated that soluble protein-tannin complexes existed.

Larger changes in the nature of the tannin-protein complexes were evident from the weight of precipitate formed when a preparation of crude nettle-leaf protein was mixed with the tannins extracted from oak leaves (Fig. 10.2; Feeney 1969). Precipitates were not formed, or formed only slowly, when the protein was in excess, and, although protein was almost completely precipitated by slightly less than its own weight of tannin, more

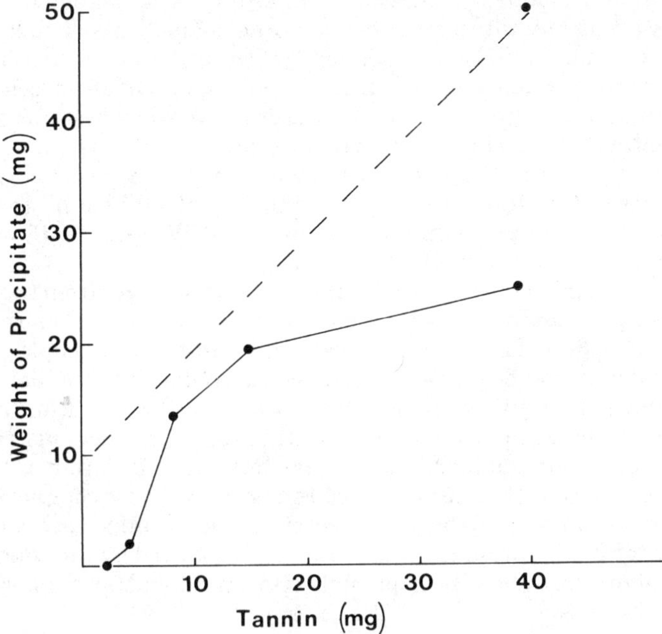

Fig. 10.2. Precipitation of nettle-leaf protein (9.6 mg) by increasing amounts of oak-leaf tannins. Solutions (approximately 12 ml) contained NaCl (approx. 0.05%) and citrate buffer (pH 5, 0.025 *M*) and were incubated at 20°C for 10 min before centrifugation.
Redrawn from Feeny (1969).

precipitate, containing almost 1½ times as much tannin as protein, was formed from a four-fold excess of tannin (Fig. 10.2). It is unlikely that precipitate formation was complete in the short incubation time used in this experiment: the precipitation of casein by oak-leaf tannins was complete after 15 hr at 25°C, but only 85% complete after 2 hr. Fraction I (F I) protein from lucerne complexes with almost its own weight of the condensed tannins of sainfoin, corresponding to 23 molecules of tannin per molecule of protein (Jones and Mangan 1977). However, it is completely precipitated by less than one-tenth of this amount. The complexes are stable in the pH range of 3.5–7, but are dispersed, especially in the presence of polyethylene glycol, both above and below this range. At an ionic strengh of 0.1, dispersal occurs more completely below pH 3 than above pH 7.5. This acid-lability, which also occurs with complexes of potato enzymes and tannins (Mejbaum-Katzenellenbogen and Morawiecka 1959), contrasts with the stability to acid of tanned collagen.

The reaction of tannins with a complex mixture of proteins will have aspects not readily appreciated from studies using individual proteins. The overall reaction will depend on the different affinities of the components for tannin, as well as any interaction between the components. The different affinities, which may well be a consequence of the different electrochemical properties of the proteins (Gustavson 1956), will be important in conditions where the amount of tannin is limited. Thus, the two whey proteins of milk, β-lactoglobulin and α-lactalbumin, when isolated, react with and are precipitated by tea tannins; however, when whole milk is infused with "normal" amounts of tea, the tea tannins are preferentially bound to α- and β-casein, forming soluble complexes (Brown and Wright 1963), and the whey proteins remain unmodified.

A dynamic picture of tannin-protein interactions emerges from the experimental manipulation of beers that form a haze or "trouble" as they age (Chapon *et al.* 1961). These hazes, mostly protein-tannin complexes containing metal ions, can be prevented and redissolved to different degrees by adding soluble polyvinylpyrrolidone (PVP) with a high affinity for tannins. Changes in the ease and completeness of this resolution demonstrate the existence of different complexes which are formed at different rates and whose interconversions are summarized in Fig. 10.3. These complexes may differ in conformation, in the presence of covalent links between their components, or by the presence of new tannins produced by the continuing oxidative polymerization of beer phenols (Harris 1965; Van Sumere *et al.*

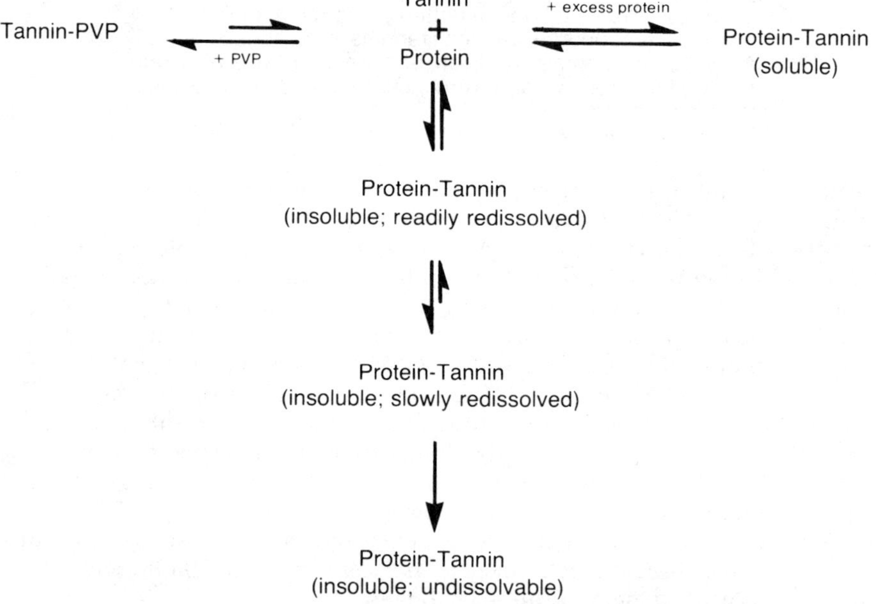

Fig. 10.3. Equilibria among proteins, tannins, and a tannin-absorbent, PVP, in beer.
Summarized from Chapon et al. (1961).

1975). The precipitates, unlike those between tannic acid and β-glucosidase, are formed quicker at lower ionic strengths ($\mu < 0.08$) than at higher ones.

ADSORPTION OF PHENOLS ONTO PROTEINS

The –OH groups of some phenols, especially when they are vicinal or otherwise suitably disposed, appear to form intramolecular H-bonds. These phenols, chlorogenic acid, for example, form intermolecular H-bonds less readily with polyamides or PVP and are therefore poorly absorbed by these polymers (Loomis and Battaille 1966). They are, however, strongly absorbed by uncharged polystyrene such as Amberlite XAD which has little or no affinity for condensed tannins (Gray 1978; Loomis *et al.* 1979). This absorption may involve a hydrophobic interaction between the aromatic rings of the phenols and those of the polymer. Such bonds, which would be expected to be formed independently of pH and to be stabilized by high salt concentrations, may contribute to the bonding of some phenols to the hydrophobic regions of proteins (e.g., Henneke and Wedding 1975); van Sumere *et al.* (1975) describe many situations in which they may be involved and Mohammadzadah *et al.* (1969) discuss structural aspects of the interactions.

REACTION OF PROTEINS WITH QUINONOIDS

Common features of protein-tannin complexes are that they contain a proportion of irreversibly bound tannin which increases with time (e.g., Chapon *et al.* 1961; Jones and Mangan 1977). This is sometimes attributed to conformation changes in the complex (Jones and Mangan 1977) but more often (Loomis and Battaille 1966; van Sumere *et al.* 1975) to a slow formation of covalent bonds linking tannins to proteins. The bonds most likely to form are those between *o*-quinones or other quinonoids slowly generated by the oxidation of phenolic residues, and suitable groups, especially $-NH_2$ groups, of proteins. Such bonds would be similar to those formed when *p*-benzoquinone chemically tans gelatin and hides, and which, since the 1920s have been attributed to protein-NH_2 substituted into the nuclei of polymerized quinone (see Gustavson 1956). Covalent links formed between proteins and phenols form in many diverse biological situations (Mason 1955; Pierpoint 1971; Synge 1975; van Sumere *et al.* 1975) and have been interpreted in a similar manner, although analytical difficulties have prevented their satisfactory characterization. Whatever their precise structure, their importance for LP technology is that, not only may they form between tannins and proteins, but they also occur between proteins and quinonoids generated from phenols which by themselves would have little affinity for the proteins.

Generation of Quinonoids

Quinones and other quinonoids can be produced from phenols in plant extracts by nonenzymic reactions such as the metal-catalyzed oxidations that occur in alkali (Pollard and Timberlake 1971). However, the major route by which they are formed is enzymic oxidation catalyzed either by *o*-diphenol oxidases (polyphenoloxidases, tyrosinases), monophenol or *p*-phenol oxidases (laccases), or by peroxidases in the presence of hydrogen peroxide. The *o*-diphenol oxidases are thought to oxidize dihydroxyphenols by the removal of two electrons, so that, initially, *o*-quinones are formed (Mason *et al.* 1961), whereas the other enzymes catalyze single electron transfers, producing initially semi-quinones (Young and Steelink 1973). Dismutation reactions of the type

$$Q + QH_2 \rightleftharpoons 2QH^{\cdot}$$

can bring quinones and semi-quinones into equilibrium. Because quinones can also oxidize phenols that are not oxidized enzymically, and because plants may contain a variety of phenols and oxidizing enzymes, it is clear that plant extracts have the potential for producing a complex series of quinonoids, many of which are highly reactive and of only transient occurrence in the extract.

Not all these quinonoids react with proteins. Some may react with low molecular weight components of plant extracts such as amino acids, indoles, or reducing agents, and some react with other polymers such as nucleic acids or carbohydrates. Some polymerize to stable compounds like the lignins produced from semi-quinones of ferulic acid derivatives. Some of these polymers may themselves have properties of tannins and combine with proteins much as do the preformed tannins already described. The best example of this is probably the tannins of tea *(Camellia sinensis)*. They are formed by phenolase-catalyzed oxidation of the flavonoids which may comprise as much as 40% of the dry weight of the leaf (see Berkowitz *et al.* 1971; Pierpoint 1971). The formation of such polymers is, of course, encouraged during the commercial production of tea, but they render the protein precipitated in the leaf of little food value. They are also formed in extracts of fresh leaves and make it difficult to extract enzymes, including the polyphenoloxidase responsible for their formation, without the addition of tannin-absorbents (Coggon *et al.* 1973).

Reaction of Quinonoids with Amino Acids

Amino acids and other compounds containing such nucleophilic groups as NH_2- and $SH-$ substitute into *p*-quinones; and products such as that formed between *p*-benzoquinone and the ethyl ester of glycine:

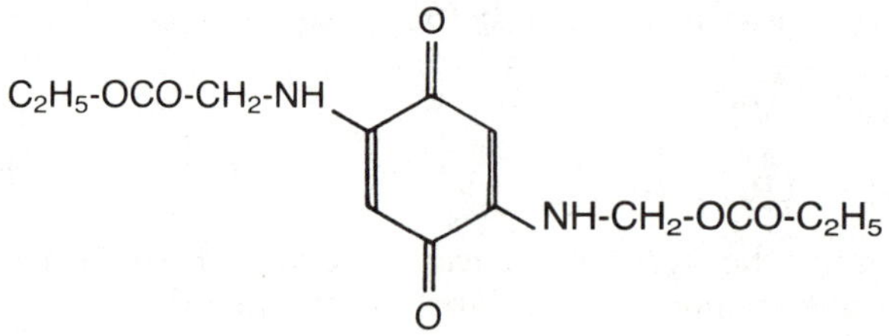

O

C_2H_5-OCO-CH_2-NH

NH-CH_2-OCO-C_2H_5

O

have been known since the time of Fischer and Schrader and well characterized by others (Horspool 1969; Finley 1974; Cranwell and Haworth 1971). Reactions with *o*-quinones are more complex and often produce many compounds of which only a few have been identified (Cranwell and Haworth 1971; Davies and Frahn 1977). It has, however, been shown (Davies and Pierpoint 1975) that chlorogenoquinone and caffeoquinone, the *o*-quinones produced enzymically from chlorogenic acid and caffeic acid (Pierpoint 1966), react differently with trapping reagents than do the synthetic compounds, suggesting possibly that the enzyme directs the course of the reaction.

We can, therefore, restrict discussion to those model systems in which only enzymically-generated quinonoids have been allowed to react with amino acids or proteins. Such studies are not numerous, and they have usually been concerned with systems which initially generate *o*-quinones. This restriction is unfortunate, but the results may be the most relevant to LP technology in view of the widespread occurrence of *o*-dihydroxyphenols and *o*-dihydroxyphenol oxidases and the great reactivity of *o*-quinones in leaf extracts.

Experiments using enzymically-generated *o*-benzoquinone and 4-methyl-*o*-benzoquinone (Mason and Peterson 1965) and chlorogenoquinone (Pierpoint 1966, 1969A), produced spectroscopic evidence for their reaction with the α-NH_2 groups of amino acids and the ϵ-NH_2 of lysine. However, not all *o*-quinones react with free amino acids, and dopa-quinone, derived from dihydroxyphenylalanine, preferentially cyclizes, being "internally" substituted by the $-NH_2$ in its side chain. Where reaction occurs, it can be a comparatively simple substitution, as with proline, followed by oxidation of the product to a quinone state.

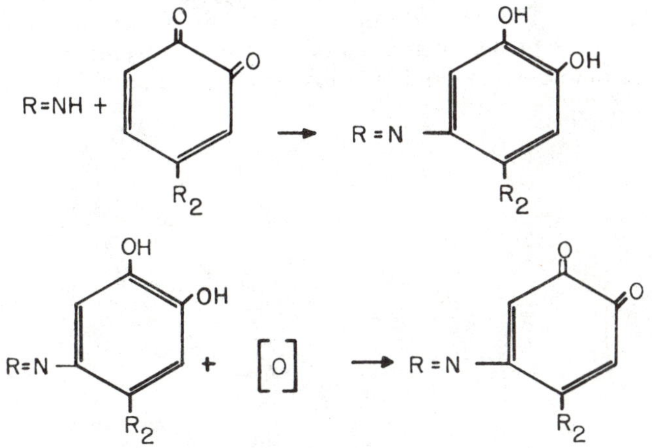

Usually, it is more complex because the newly produced quinone may be further substituted and reoxidized, and the $-NH_2$ of the amino acid can react with the quinone C=O to give an imine compound. Moreover, secondary reactions involving these compounds lead to the deamination of free amino acids (Trautner and Roberts 1950; Haider *et al.* 1965; Pierpoint 1971).

The experiments with enzymically-generated *o*-quinones also demonstrate that the –SH of cysteine substitutes into the quinone nucleus, giving colorless products presumably of the following nature.

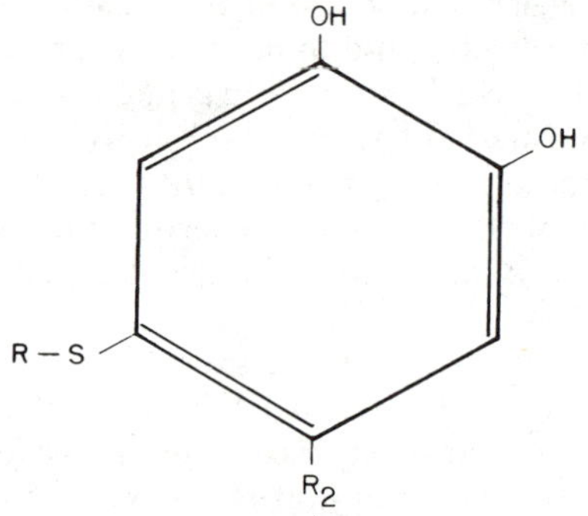

OH
OH
R – S
R_2

Such products that as depicted can also be oxidized by an excess of quinone to a quinone state. Substitution of a quinone nucleus by –SH seems to go more readily than substitution by $-NH_2$. S-substituted derivatives of dopaquinone such as S-(2,3-dihydroxyphenyl) cysteine could be produced, in spite of the tendency of this compound to cyclize (Mason and Peterson 1965; Sanada *et al.* 1972). Cysteine was also the only amino acid which could unequivocally be demonstrated to react with enzymically-generated quinones of flavonoids (Roberts 1959), giving compounds of presumed structure, as follows:

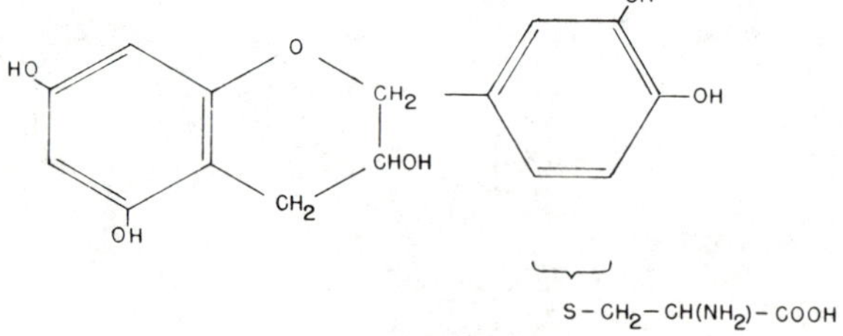

HO
O
CH_2
CHOH
CH_2
OH
OH
OH
$S-CH_2-CH(NH_2)-COOH$

Such substitution reactions occur in competition with the direct oxidation of amino acid thiol groups to disulfides by *o*-quinones.

o-Quinones can, potentially, react with other structures present in the side chains of amino acids. These could include the indole part of tryptophan, the imidazole of histidine, –OH groups, amide groups including those in peptide bonds, and the S-atom of methionine (Pierpoint 1966, 1969A; Synge 1978). However, experiments with amino acids and their N-acetyl derivatives in the aqueous, nearly neutral solutions in which the quinones were generated have, so far, given no unequivocal evidence for such reactions. Moreover, the reaction of chlorogenoquinone with small peptides (Pierpoint 1969A) could be explained by its reaction with their free $-NH_2$ or SH groups, even though the reaction of these groups was often quantitatively or qualitatively different from those observed with the corresponding free amino acids.

Reaction of Quinonoids with Proteins

The SH– and NH_2–groups of proteins are also, apparently, the primary targets of reaction with the enzymically-generated quinones. Serum albumin reacts with small amounts of chlorogenoquinone through its SH–group (Mason 1955; Pierpoint 1969B) to give colorless products.

$$\text{Protein}-\text{SH} + \text{Q} \rightarrow \text{Protein}-\text{S}-\text{QH}_2$$

The reaction is prevented by treating the protein with reagents which alkylate SH–. With excess of quinone, protein NH_2-groups also react

$$\text{Protein}-\text{NH}_2 + \text{Q} \rightarrow \text{Protein}-\text{N}-\text{QH}_2$$

and then both derivatives may be oxidized to quinones.

$$\text{Protein}-\text{S}-\text{QH}_2 + \text{Q} \rightarrow \text{Proteins}-\text{S}-\text{Q} + \text{QH}_2$$

$$\text{Protein}-\text{N}-\text{QH}_2 + \text{Q} \rightarrow \text{Protein}-\text{N}-\text{Q} + \text{QH}_2$$

These last two reactions appear not to go to completion, and it is possible that the oxidation of protein–S–QH_2 does not go to an appreciable extent. Both the α-NH_2 of the terminal aspartate and the ϵ-NH_2 of lysine are modified (Pierpoint 1969B; Haider *et al.* 1965). Reaction did not lead to any cross-linking of protein molecules.

Other studies emphasize the susceptibility of protein SH–groups to enzymically-generated quinones. Thus, a protein from the lens of bovine eyes loses –SH groups as it is exposed to tyrosine being oxidized by tyrosinase, and the modified protein contains a substance which resembles the product derived from cysteine after its exposure to quinones (A. Pirie 1968); a mutant of a plant virus (cowpea chlorotic mottle) which differs from the wild type only in possessing a cysteine group on its surface, is inactivated in leaf extracts as they brown (Bancroft *et al.* 1971). It is also germane that a protein isolated from the antennae of cockroaches *(Periplaneta americana)* and which is thought to be a sensory receptor of volatile naphthoquinones, is inactivated by −SH blocking reagents (Singer *et al.* 1975).

However, many proteins in their undenatured state have most of their SH−groups and some of the NH_2−groups "buried" in hydrophobic regions or otherwise rendered unreactive. This is illustrated in the reaction of chlorogenoquinone with the plant virus, potato virus X (PVX). The virus consists of approximately 1400 subunits arranged in a long thread-like helix. Each subunit has a molecular weight of about 27,000, and contains 12–14 lysine groups and 3 thiol groups. Reaction with an excess of chlorogenoquinone (Pierpoint 1973; Pierpoint *et al.* 1977) modifies only one site on each subunit and, judging from the way that the virus reacts with other protein-modifying reagents (Pierpoint 1974), this is a lysine residue. When the virus is disaggregated, the separated subunits expose more reactive $-NH_2$ and −SH residues (Pierpoint and Carpenter 1978) and in this condition would presumably react more extensively with chlorogenoquinone.

The formation of quinoned-PVX reveals two more features of the reaction of quinones with proteins. The reaction goes more readily at pH 7 than it does at pH 6 (Pierpoint *et al.* 1977). As it seems that free amino acids do not react with *o*-quinones below pH 6.5 (Haider *et al.* 1965), this may indicate the greater reactivity of protein-bound $-NH_2$. However, at pH's near 8, the reaction takes a different course and produces a different type of modified virus ($PVX-Q_2$); it is blue and contains two molecules of chlorogenoquinone bound per protein subunit. Similar blue products can be prepared from other proteins and macromolecules with free $-NH_2$ groups after exposure to chlorogenoquinone in alkaline solution. The blue chromophore is probably a quinone, as it is bleached by reducing agents; its structure is being investigated.

As expected, quinoned forms of PVX are less readily digested by trypsin than is unmodified PVX, and $PVX-Q_2$ contains a large undigestible portion. This may partly be because the peptide bond adjacent to modified lysine groups can no longer be split by the enzyme. However, it may be due partly to the cross-links that chlorogenoquinone introduces between adjacent subunits and which may hinder the approach of trypsin. Such cross-links affect 18% of the subunits of PVX−Q and 40% of those of $PVX-Q_2$; in $PVX-Q_2$, polymers containing eight or nine linked subunits could be detected. Such cross-linked polymers may contain groups such as protein−N−Q−N−protein or protein−N−Q−−Q−N−protein. Because such intermolecular links could not be detected in serum albumin after treatment with chlorogenoquinone, it is possible that they may be formed only between proteins which have a close and organized proximity in solution.

Some Natural Quinonoid-modified Proteins

Proteins modified by quinonoids have been extracted from silks and tissues of insects (Brunet and Coles 1974; Hackman and Goldberg 1977), rabbit eyes (van Heyningen and Pirie 1967), skin pigments, anise fruits (Brienskorn and Mosandl 1970), oak leaves (Alibert *et al.* 1968), and brown necrotic areas of leaves infected with viruses (Hampton 1970) and fungi (Spurr and Main 1974). The "brown pigments" from aging tobacco leaves and from cured tobacco have received much attention and been shown to contain protein, iron, and bound derivatives of the phenols chlorogenic acid and rutin (Wright *et al.* 1960, 1964; Weybrew and Long 1970; Chortyk 1972; Tso 1972; Sheen and Burton 1978), although the linkage between phenol and protein was not identified.

More recently, Synge and his colleagues have followed the binding of oxidizing chlorogenic acid to protein in autolyzing extracts of tobacco leaves by measuring the quinic acid fragment of bound chlorogenic acid that can be released by alkali (Davies *et al.* 1978; Synge 1978). Concomitant with the binding, there is a decrease in the amount of unmodified $-NH_2$ in the protein, suggesting that protein lysine is one of the main groups to react with the quinonoids. The modified lysine is, however, unstable during hydrolysis of the protein and cannot be isolated and identified (see also Pierpoint 1969B). Methods of reducing quinone-amino acid compounds and making them stable to hydrolysis have been devised (Davies *et al.* 1975; Eagles *et al.* 1980), and their application to quinone-modified proteins may well produce the long-awaited identification of the cross-links.

Experience with the quinone-modified forms of potato virus X made *in vitro* has prompted a search for them in senescent leaves of PVX-infected tobacco (Ireland and Pierpoint, unpublished). Although a modified form of virus can be extracted from these leaves, in amounts corresponding to about a fifth of the virus originally present, its properties are not identical to those of PVX−Q. It is brown and recognizable in the electron microscope, but it is uninfective. A moiety can be separated from it by alkali which resembles but is not quinic acid. Until more is known about this moiety, it is not clear how far PVX−Q can be regarded as a model for the virus, and other proteins, modified in tobacco leaves.

COVALENT REACTION BETWEEN PROTEINS AND PHENOLS NOT INVOLVING QUINONOID FUNCTIONS

Plant phenols may contain reactive groups, other than those derived from −OH groups, which react with proteins. The best known example is gossypol, the toxic phenolic di-aldehyde of cottonseeds *(Gossypium hirsutum)*. Although it is poorly soluble in aqueous media, it reacts with one or more of the $-NH_2$ groups of proteins, forming Schiff bases according to the equation:

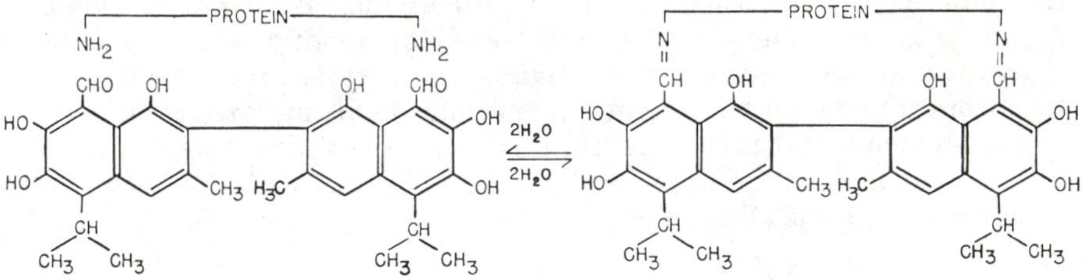

The resulting adducts are unexpectedly stable, suggesting that there is either a further rearrangement of the Schiff base, or, more likely, that there is a hydrophobic component to the binding (Finlay *et al.* 1973).

Gossypol, like many other phenols, is not randomly distributed through the cell of the cottonseed, but is confined to glandular hairs. These can be removed by controlled comminution followed by "liquid cyclone" centrifugation, leaving a relatively unmodified protein (Gardner *et al.* 1976).

FACTORS AFFECTING THE REACTION OF PHENOLS AND PROTEINS DURING THE FRACTIONATION OF GREEN CROPS

During their extraction, leaf proteins can combine with tannins, react with quinonoids, and absorb phenols. Covalent reaction with groups other than −OH on the phenols, although important for *Gossypium* and related species, is likely to be of less general occurrence. Since the proteins of most leaves are similar, modification will depend upon the phenols present, the oxidative systems functioning, and the conditions of the extraction. Modification will be less when only small amounts of phenols are present, and the phenolic content will depend upon the plant material and the conditions under which it was grown. High intensities of far-red light and such "stress" conditions as infection or N-deficiency increase the phenol content of tobacco leaves. Some cultivars of commercial crops, for example lucerne, contain much less phenol than do others and, consequently, are more suitable for extraction (Monties and Rambourg 1978A,B). New varieties containing little phenolic material can be developed and selected, but sometimes these, as with sorghum (see Griffiths and Jones 1977) and barley (von Wettstein *et al.* 1977), probably because of their low phenol content, are susceptible to predation or infection.

The conditions in the extract which control the extent to which these reactions occur are the temperature, the pH, the aeration, and the time during which the reactants are in contact. Low temperatures, fast extraction, and minimal aeration will restrict protein modification by these as well as other reactions. Moderate alkalinity will decrease precipitation with tannins but may increase the rate at which quinonoids are produced enzymically as well as the ease with which they react with proteins; it may also, as with PVX and chlorogenoquinone, affect the mechanism of the reaction. There are two further disadvantages of alkali: different types of phenols are known to be extracted from the fiber of apple pulp at different rates (van Burren *et al.* 1976), and alkali will almost certainly accelerate the solution of phenolic acids; secondly, it may increase the rate at which glycoside esters of phenols are hydrolyzed to more readily oxidized phenols. Alkalinity greater than pH 9 inactivates the enzymes that produce quinoids, but it increases the rate of non enzymic metal-catalyzed oxidation of phenols and probably encourages the products to react with proteins. Strong alkali, of course, in the absence of phenols, destroys both the lysine and cysteine of proteins (Nashef *et al.* 1977).

The net effect of the pH at which extraction takes place on the reaction of phenols with proteins will depend, therefore, on the predominant phenols present and on the type of reaction they undergo. LP extracted from *Lablab atropurpureus* at pH 11 has better digestibility, biological value, and protein efficiency ratio for rats than protein extracted at pH's 8, 9, or 10 (Nanda *et al.* 1977); this may be a consequence of a more complete dissolution of protein-tannin complexes at the higher pH. On the other hand, protein extracted from lucerne at pH 8.5 contains much more absorbed coumestrol than that extracted at lower pH's (Knuckles *et al.* 1976), probably because more of the isoflavonoid is extracted from the fibrous residue in alkali; LP preparations, satisfactorily free from the compound, could only be obtained by extracting at a lower pH and washing in alkali. Moderate amounts of alkali (1/10 weight of 0.5 *M* NaOH) did not significantly affect the solubility, amino acid composition, or *in vitro* digestibility of LP from grass or lucerne, but again increased (40–90%) its content of phenolic material that could be extracted with hot ethyl acetate (Fafunso and Byers 1977). The extracted phenols were tentatively identified as coumaric, caffeic, and chlorogenic acids, and also tannic acid. The first three compounds may well have been more completely solubilized at the higher pH, and, unlike the tannic acid, only weakly absorbed to the protein.

OTHER ATTEMPTS TO MINIMIZE REACTION DURING FRACTIONATION

Apart from adjusting the pH at which extraction takes place, there are other ways in which the reaction between phenols and proteins can, in principle, be minimized. Thus protein-tannin complexes can be prevented or, once formed, dispersed with reagents which break H-bonds, enzymes that hydrolyze tannins, or polymers that absorb tannins (van Sumere *et al.* 1975). Means of preventing quinonoids' reacting with proteins have been discussed previously (Pierpoint 1971; Loomis and Battaille 1966; Loomis, 1974; Anderson 1968). Some of these, such as excluding air or adding expensive adsorbents, are clearly inappropriate. Polyvinylpyrrolidone has, nevertheless, been tested in the laboratory preparation of LP from lucerne and grass (Fafunso and Byers 1977) and it decreased the amount of phenol that could be extracted with ethyl acetate by over 50%. As expected (Loomis and Battaille 1966), it was less effective at a higher (but unstated) pH. However, a more practical approach to preventing the quinonoid modification of proteins is the addition of substances, such as sulfite, which prevent the oxidation of phenols.

Sulfite is widely used in the food industry to prevent oxidation of phenols and may act by inhibiting oxidases, by reducing quinonoids, or by forming sulfite addition compounds with quinones. It is reported to be less effective at pH's above 7.5 (Anderson 1968). Sulfite is also likely to prevent any "nonenzymic" browning of amino acids and sugars that may occur as LP is processed. There are disadvantages to using it routinely (Pirie 1978), such as its destruction of S-containing amino acids and vitamins, and, moreover, some sulfited-diets develop toxicity as they age (see McWeeney *et al.* 1974). However, when added during the preparation of LP from lucerne, the product was both cleaner and of better nutritional quality (Edwards *et al.* 1975; Arkcoll 1973) and contained a smaller proportion of modified lysine (Allison 1971). Its addition also appears to improve the nutritive value of LP from clover and grasses in a way which suggests that it prevents destruction of cysteine and some methionine (Donnelly and McDonald, personal communication).

Diluting lucerne extracts two- or three-fold with water before protein is coagulated improves the product (Arkcoll 1973). Although there is no evidence, it is possible that some of the improvement is due to a diminished interaction between protein and phenols.

EFFECTS OF THE REACTION OF PROTEINS AND PHENOLS ON CROP FRACTIONATION AND ON THE PRODUCTS

(1) Effects of Tannins

Reaction of leaf proteins with the insoluble tannins of the leaves will lead to their precipitation and retention in fiber. Reaction with soluble tannins will have the same effect. A high tannin content will therefore be expected to decrease the yield of LP, and this probably accounts for part of the very poor extraction from tree leaves and, for example, from water hyacinth (Pirie 1978). If pulping is quick and conditions in the pulp retard precipitation, a proportion of the complexes may escape retention and pass into the extracted juice and so to the LP. This proportion may increase with tannins of low "astringency"; it may be large for leaves having a tannin content of less than 1/30 their protein content because complexes with a small content of bound tannin and hence a greater solubility will be formed. Heating to coagulate LP may well strip some tannin off the complexes and into the "whey," although there is little evidence to indicate to what extent this will occur. Judging from the stability of complexes between sainfoin tannins and lucerne protein (Jones and Mangan 1977), acid added to facilitate the filtration of LP, or used instead of heat to precipitate it, is unlikely to redissolve more than a fraction of bound tannin.

The nutritional consequences of tannins either in fiber or LP will presumably be the same as those observed for tannins in other foodstuffs (McLeod 1974). If there is enough to impart an astringent taste, the material will have a decreased acceptability. Complexed protein will be less readily hydrolyzed by digestive proteases, an effect which has been demonstrated *in vivo* as well as *in vitro*, and which is responsible for the negative correlation between the digestibility of many foodstuffs and their tannin content (e.g., Lindgren 1975; Ramachandra *et al.* 1977; Moseley and Griffiths 1979). A net loss of dietary protein is a common consequence of tannin in a diet (McLeod 1974). This occurs, for instance, with rats fed a diet containing tannic acid, and the resulting loss in weight can be prevented by supplementary casein. The effect may not be explained simply as the unaltered passage of complexed protein through the animals; although there is an increase in the protein N of the feces of tannin-fed rats, it appears to have an endogenous origin (Glick and Joslyn 1970B). Tannin-protein complexes may be dissociated in parts of the gut having a high enough (Feeney 1969) or low enough (Jones and Mangan 1977) pH; the tannin is then available to inhibit other digestive enzymes, including bacterial cellulases (Griffiths and Jones 1977), or to combine with other intestinal proteins. If the tannins are hydrolyzed and absorbed, they may impose an extra demand for methyl groups used to detoxify their components (Pirie 1978), and if, like condensed tannins they remain unmetabolized and unabsorbed, they may cause intestinal irritation. Toxic effects, especially on the liver, may result from the intake of large amounts of tannins or some of their components (McLeod 1974; Glick and Joslyn 1970A). The geographic distribution of esophageal cancer suggests that it is related to a high intake of food or drinks which are rich in condensed tannins (Morton 1978).

Ruminants are less sensitive to dietary tannins than are monogastric animals and may even benefit from their presence (McLeod 1974; Jones and Mangan 1977). This may be because complexed proteins are protected from deamination in the rumen, and are then released for less destructive digestion in the acid conditions of the intestine. Dietary tannins may also protect ruminants from "bloat" by complexing the surface-active proteins that are partly responsible.

(2) Effects of Quinonoids

Quinones and other quinonoids will discolor proteins with which they combine, making them brown under neutral conditions and, if the extracts contain chlorogenic acid, making them bluish in alkali. They may also, by making proteins less soluble, increase the proportion that is retained by the fibrous residue during extraction. This is a consequence of the formation of interprotein cross-links and of altered surface charge, and it will depend not only on the extent of reaction with quinonoid but also on the quinonoid involved: PVX is made much less soluble by *o*-quinone derived from caffeic acid than by chlorogenoquinone (Pierpoint, unpublished). Whichever fraction the affected protein is contained in, it will have a greater proportion of its lysine modified to a "chemically unavailable" form and, as a consequence, will be less readily digested by proteolytic enzymes and so have a lower nutritive value. The proportion of lysine which is chemically unavailable in a series of LP preparations is correlated with a low *in vivo* digestibility and low biological value (Allison 1971; Allison *et al.* 1973).

Many of these expectations have been confirmed with proteins that have been exposed, deliberately or adventitiously, to phenols undergoing oxidation. Casein, after deliberate exposure, has less lysine than can be recovered after hydrolysis, is less readily digested *in vitro* and *in vivo*, and has a lower biological value (Horigome and Kandatsu 1968A, 1971); protein from red clover is less readily digested by pepsin after a similar treatment (Horigome and Kandatsu 1966A), and adding chlorogenic acid to lucerne extracts increases the proportion of chemically unavailable lysine in the LP produced (Allison 1971). Unavailable lysine also increases in autolyzing extracts of leaves or seeds that are rich in chlorogenic acid, and is associated with an increase in the amount of protein-bound quinonoid (Davies *et al.* 1978). Such protein modification may, of course, occur in unfractionated tissue. It probably occurs in clover (Horigome and Kandatsu 1968B) and other forages (Horigome and Kandatsu 1966B) as they are dried, and its effect will depend on the concentration of phenols and oxidases. The reactions occur in stored samples of the African oilseed *Pentaclethra macrophylla*, in which the phenol involved is N-caffeoyl-putrescine and whose reaction with protein lowers its protein efficiency ratio (Mbadiwe 1975; Synge 1978). Thus the protein of vegetable material destined for fractionation may be modified during any long delay between harvesting and processing.

Although the biological value of some preparations of LP seems to be limited by availability of lysine (Allison *et al.* 1973), this is not true of all of them, and methionine is often the limiting amino acid (e.g., Donnelly and McDonald 1978). It is not clear if this is because of its comparatively low concentration or its biological unavailability (Pirie 1978; Byers 1971). The methionine of LP from clover and grasses is apparently protected by sulfite present during extraction (Donnelly and McDonald, personal communication) suggesting that it may be destroyed by the products of an oxidizing system, possibly quinonoids. Quinones are unlikely to form adducts with methionine in the nonacid conditions of leaf fractionation, although they may oxidize methionine to a sulfoxide or sulfone state of doubtful nutritional value (Pirie 1978). Quinones will almost certainly react with cysteine and so remove its methionine-sparing ability. Because of the affinity of quinones for SH-groups, this will occur with quinones that react poorly with lysine; it occurs in autolyzing extracts of potatoes where the quinones involved are derived mainly from the oxidation of tyrosine (Davies and Laird 1976). There is no reason to believe that the enzymic generation of *o*-quinones and consequent reaction with proteins will occur more readily in the debris of chloroplasts, although chloroplasts do contain some isozymes of phenoloxidases, and, therefore, no reason to believe that this type of reaction is responsible for the much discussed nutritional difference between "chloroplastic" and "cytoplasmic" proteins (Pirie 1978; Byers 1971; Horigome 1977).

The expectation that the principal effects of enzymically-generated quinonoids will be upon the lysine, cysteine, and probably methionine of proteins is based upon studies using a limited number of phenols and oxidizing systems. Synge (1975, 1978) has emphasized the potential reactivity of other amino acids, including that of the peptide bond itself (Horigome 1973; but compare Davies and Frahn 1977). The available information clearly needs augmenting, and augmentation may well revise this expectation.

(3) Effects of Loosely-attached, Unpolymerized Phenols

Leaf protein prepared from a number of sources, as well as protein extracted from sunflower seeds, contains appreciable quantities of unpolymerized phenols which can be extracted by methods unlikely to break covalent bonds. The amounts present and the strength of the attachment make it clear that their presence is not always the result of inadequate washing of the protein. The forces responsible may be H-bonds or hydrophobic attractions, depending on the phenol involved and the site to which it is attached; thus the forces may be different for different phenols and different for a single phenol attached to different sites.

LP from lucerne has been most closely examined in this respect. Some preparations (Lahiry *et al.* 1977) contain chlorogenic acid, only about half of which can be extracted with boiling alcohol; it is completely released only after digestion of the protein with pepsin and pancreatin. It is, judged by the methods used to separate and estimate it (Pomenta and Burns 1971), chemically unmodified. Much of the chlorogenic acid can be dissolved in a solution of buffered salt containing 2-mercaptoethanol, where it is apparently associated with a group of small proteins and peptides which make up only a tenth of the protein N of the preparation. In this respect it resembles the chlorogenic acid of flour from sunflower seeds which is also associated, partly by H-bonds, with peptides of molecular weight less than 5000 (Sabir *et al.* 1974). Other preparations of LP from lucerne contain flavones and coumestanes, but only traces of chlorogenic acid and dihydroxyphenols (Monties and Rambourg 1978A,B; Knuckles *et al.* 1976; Newby *et al.* 1979). Limited amounts of these compounds can be successively extracted with a series of solvents of increasing polarity, and the rest can be extracted only after the protein has been solubilized with acetyl bromide in acetic acid (Monties and Rambourg 1978A,B). These results clearly demonstrate the existence in the protein mixture of a range of absorption sites of different specificities and affinities. A chloroplast protein which is involved in energy transduction is known to have two different sites which specifically absorb the flavonoid quercetin (Cantly and Hammes 1976).

Small amounts of absorbed flavonoids may contribute to the keeping qualities of LP and other protein preparations by acting as antifungal agents (Naim *et al.* 1974) or as antioxidants (Naim *et al.* 1976). The objection to the large amount of chlorogenic acid absorbed to sunflower-seed preparations is the dark greenish colors that it produces on processing (Sabir *et al.*

1974). It may also decrease the *in vitro* digestibility of the protein (Free and Satterlee 1975). *p*-Coumaric acid attached loosely to casein does not affect the *in vivo* digestibility of the protein but it does decrease its biological value (Horigome and Kandatsu 1968A). However, in general, absorbed phenols would be expected to be released during *in vivo* digestion and be free to exert any pharmacological activities that they possess. These may be undesirable and necessitate attention. Thus, the isoflavones of washed LP made from red clover, principally formononetin and biochanin A, are estrogenic in ruminants, and they may constitute up to 1% of the dry material of the preparation (Glencross *et al.* 1972). The coumestrol of lucerne LP may have a similar activity, and extraction procedures have been adjusted to decrease its concentration in the product (Knuckles *et al.* 1976). On the other hand, the phenols may be beneficial for animals (see Lookhart *et al.* 1978) and, as has often been claimed for the phenols of tea, be useful human medicines; cynarin, the dicaffeyl ester of quinic acid, may well alleviate arteriosclerotic diseases (Mancini *et al.* 1960), but skepticism will greet any new claims for alleged "vitamin P" activity (Stagg and Millin 1975).

FINAL COMMENTS

A complete appreciation of how phenols have affected the fractionation of a particular crop and specifically affected the quality of the LP fraction would require information on

(1) The tannin (*sensu stricto*) content of the LP and fibrous residue, and the amount of protein bound to it
(2) The extent to which the protein has been covalently modified by quinonoids reacting with susceptible groups
(3) The amount, nature, and biological effects of absorbed unpolymerized phenols.

Some effort would be required to get this complete information. It should be possible to estimate bound tannins semiquantitatively either from a color reaction or from the gallic and ellagic acids released after hydrolysis (Bate-Smith 1977; McLeod 1974). Moreover, tannin-bound protein could be estimated after its semiquantitative recovery. Absorbed phenols may also be extracted, identified, and measured when attention is paid to the multiplicity of binding sites and the tenacity of absorption (Monties and Rambourg 1978A,B).

Perhaps the most difficult value to estimate is the extent to which quinonoids have modified proteins. At the present time, the amount of protein-bound quinonoid can only be determined for derivatives of chlorogenic acid or N-caffeoylputrescine which after hydrolysis liberate a moiety which can be estimated (Davies *et al.* 1978; Pierpoint *et al.* 1977). Estimates of the quinonoid-modified lysine can be made from the difference between lysine which is available to react with HNO_2 and the total lysine recovered after protein hydrolysis (Allison *et al.* 1973). These estimates depend upon the assumptions that reaction with quinonoids is the major way in which lysine has been modified, and that the modified lysine is completely regenerated during hydrolysis (but compare Cranwell and Haworth 1971). Perhaps the simplest way of evaluating the extent of modification by quinonoids is by preparing LP from a sample of leaves in the absence and in the presence of oxidase inhibitors, and comparing the apparent amino acid composition and nutritional properties of the two preparations.

Studies on the phenolic components of LP preparations that have been reported so far have, of necessity, restricted their attention to one class of phenols, or to the "total" phenol content that can be readily extracted and measured by unspecific methods. Nevertheless, the results are suggestive. Thus, the amount of protein that can be extracted from tree leaves of different ages changes as the phenol content of the leaves changes (Butler and Pirie 1978). Although there is, apparently, no direct relationship between the nutritional quality of a range of LPs and their content of extractable phenols there is an inverse relationship between nutritional quality and the ratio of extractable phenols to protein N (Subba Rau *et al.* 1972). It may well be that, in these preparations, nutritional quality is determined by tightly bound phenols and less so by less tightly bound ones. Such a direct relationship would be well worth searching for, but would require analytical methods that discriminate between the different types of phenols present.

There are two further points worth mentioning: When leaves from mixed pastures are fractionated, the effect of their mixed phenolic constituents may be more pronounced than the effects of the phenols in each species separately. Thus, a species rich in phenoloxidases may complicate extraction from a species rich in phenols but with little oxidase. Such an effect could well explain why LP extracted from a mixture of ryegrass and clover sometimes had a larger proportion of unavailable lysine and a lower cysteine- or methionine-limited, nutritive value than LP extracted from either crop separately (Donnelly and McDonald 1978).

The second point is more cautionary. Methods used to estimate "total" phenols are often based on a relatively nonspecific reduction of complex phosphomolybdic or phosphotungstic acids. Interference by reducing agents and by the tyrosine of proteins is well-appreciated. Methods of estimating protein based on the well-used procedure of Lowry use essentially the same reaction to estimate, among other things, protein-bound tyrosine, and their use in phenol-rich plant tissue has led to very large errors. There are other methods of estimating proteins both approximately and quickly which are less affected by phenols and other constituents of plant extracts (Loomis 1974; Esen 1978; Robinson 1979).

ENVOI

Impeccable authorities (Milton 1667) describe the results of eating of the Fruit of the Tree of Knowledge

"... whose mortal taste
Brought death into the World, and all our woe"

Surely part of this woe is that many people have too little to eat and that even it is of too poor quality. The question now is whether this woe can be alleviated in part, at least, by eating of the Leaves rather than of the Fruit of the Tree of Knowledge. The moral of these pages is that these leaves, like those of more readily available crops, may contain phenolic compounds and may, in consequence, be poorly fractionated. A study of these phenols and of the way in which they interact with proteins may give us a better appreciation of how to process and utilize these leaves. At the least, it will prevent us from approaching the Tree with quite the same naïveté as Eve.

ACKNOWLEDGMENTS

I am indebted to Drs. Haslam, Donnelly, Monties, Synge, and Pirie for access to unpublished manuscripts, and to the latter two for help and advice on many occasions.

REFERENCES

ALIBERT, G., MARIGO, G. and BOUDET, A. 1968. Presence of phenolic acids in a protein fraction isolated from leaves of *Quercus pedunculata*. C.R. Acad. Sci. Paris *267*, 2144–2146.

ALLISON, R.M. 1971. Factors influencing the availability of lysine in leaf protein. *In* Leaf Protein: Its Agronomy, Preparation, Quality and Use. N.W. Pirie (Editor). IBP Handb. *20*. Blackwell Scientific Publications, Oxford.

ALLISON, R.M., LAIRD, W.M. and SYNGE, R.L.M. 1973. Notes on a deamination method proposed for determining 'chemically-available lysine' of proteins. Br. J. Nutr. *29*, 51–55.

ANDERSON, J.W. 1968. Extraction of enzymes and subcellular organelles from plant tissue. Phytochemistry 7, 1973–1988.

ARCKOLL, D.B. 1973. Studies connected with the bulk production of leaf protein. Rothamsted Exp. Stn. Rep. *1972*, 117.

BANCROFT, J.B., McLEAN, G.D., REES, M.W. and SHORT, M.N. 1971. The effect of an arginyl to a cysteinyl replacement on the uncoating behaviour of a spherical plant virus. Virology *45*, 707–715.

BATE-SMITH, E.C. 1962. The phenolic constituents of plants and their taxonomic significance. I. Dicotyledons. J. Linn. Soc. London Bot. *58*, 95–173.

BATE-SMITH, E.C. 1973. Haemanalysis of tannins: The concept of relative astringency. Phytochemistry *12*, 907–912.

BATE-SMITH, E.C. 1975. Phytochemistry of proanthocyanidins. Phytochemistry *14*, 1107–1113.

BATE-SMITH, E.C. 1977. Astringent tannins of *Acer* species. Phytochemistry *16*, 1421–1426.

BERKOWITZ, J.E., COGGAN, P. and SANDERSON, G.W. 1971. Formation of epitheaflavic acid and its transformation of thearubigins during tea fermentation. Phytochemistry *10*, 2271–2278.

BOWES, J.H., and KENTEN, R.H. 1949. The effect of modification of the reactive groups of collagen on the fixation of tanning agents. J. Soc. Leather Trades Chem. *33*, 368–386.

BRIESKORN, C.H. and MOSANDL, A. 1970. A caffeic acid-containing protein from umbellifer fruits. Tetrahedron Lett. *1*, 109–111. (German)

BROWN, P.J. and WRIGHT, W.B. 1963. An investigation of the interactions between milk proteins and tea polyphenols. J. Chromatogr. *11*, 504–511.

BRUNET, P.C.J. and COLES, B.C. 1974. Tanned silks. Proc. R. Soc. London Ser. B: *187*, 133–170.

BUTLER, J.B. and PIRIE, N.W. 1978. Leaf protein extraction. Rothamsted Exp. Stn. Rep. *1977*, 291.

BYERS, M. 1971. The amino acid composition of some leaf protein preparations. *In* Leaf Protein: Its Agronomy, Preparation, Quality and Use. N.W. Pirie (Editor). IBP Handb. *20*. Blackwell Scientific Publications, Oxford.

CANTLY, L.C. and HAMMES, G.G. 1976. Investigations of quercetin binding sites on chloroplast coupling Factor 1. Biochemistry *15*, 1–7.

CHAPON, L. CHOLLOT, B. and URION, E. 1961. Physiochemical study on associations between vegetable proteins and polyphenolic substances. Bull. Soc. Chim. Biol. *43*, 429–441. (French)

CHORTYK, D.T. 1972. High molecular weight materials of tobacco. *In* Chemistry of Tobacco and Tobacco Smoke. I. Schmeltz (Editor). Plenum Press, New York, London.

COGGON, P., MOSS, G.A. and SANDERSON, G.W. 1973. Tea catechol oxidase: Isolation, purification and kinetic characterisation. Phytochemistry *12*, 1947–1955.

CRANWELL, P.A. and HAWORTH, R.D. 1971. Humic acid. IV. The reaction of α-amino acid esters with quinones. Tetrahedron *27*, 1831–1837.

DAVIES, A.M.C. and LAIRD, W.M. 1976. Changes in some nitrogenous constituents of potato tubers during aerobic autolysis. J. Sci. Food Agric. *27*, 377–382.

DAVIES, A.M.C., NEWBY, V.K. and SYNGE, R.L.M. 1978. Bound quinic acid as a measure of coupling of leaf and sunflower-seed proteins with chlorogenic acid congeners: Loss of availability of lysine. J. Sci. Food Agric. *29*, 33–41.

DAVIES, R. and FRAHN, J.L. 1977. Addition of primary aliphatic amines to 1, 2-benzoquinone: The absence of reaction between a secondary amide and 1, 2-benzoquinone. J. Chem. Soc., Perkin Trans. *1*: 2295–2297.

DAVIES, R., LAIRD, W.M. and SYNGE, R.L.M. 1975. Hydrogenation as an approach to study of reactions of oxidizing polyphenols with plant proteins. Phytochemistry *14*, 1591–1596.

DAVIES, R. and PIERPOINT, W.S. 1975. Problem of the reactive species from enzymic and chemical oxidations of *o*-diphenols: Anomalies in the trapping of *o*-quinonoids with benzene sulphinic acid. Biochem. Soc. Trans. *3*, 671–674.

DONNELLY, P.E. and McDONALD, R.M. 1978. The quality of leaf protein concentrates. Proc. N.Z. Nutr. Soc. *3*, 84–95.

EAGLES, J., MARCH, J.F. and SYNGE, R.L.M. 1980. Mass-spectrometric evidence for quinoid-lysine coupling products in cigar protein. Phytochemistry *19*, 1171–1175.

EDWARDS, R.H., MILLER, R.E., DE FREMERY, D., KNUCKLES, B.E., BICKOFF, E.M. and KOHLER, G.O. 1975. Pilot plant production of an edible white fraction leaf protein concentrate from alfalfa. J. Agric. Food Chem. *23*, 620–626.

ESEN, A. 1978. A simple method of quantitative, semi-quantitative, and qualitative assay of protein. Anal. Biochem. *89*, 264–273.

FAFUNSO, M. and BYERS, M. 1977. Effect of pre-press treatments of vegetation on the quality of extracted leaf protein. J. Sci. Food Agric. *28*, 375–380.

FEENY, P.P. 1969. Inhibitory effect of oak leaf tannins on the hydrolysis of proteins by trypsin. Phytochemistry *8*, 2119–2126.

FINLAY, T.H., DHARMGROMGARTAMA, E.D. and PERLMANN, G.E. 1973. Mechanism of the gossypol inactivation of pepsinogen. J. Biol. Chem. *248*, 4827–4833.

FINLEY, K.T. 1974. The addition and substitution chemistry of quinones. *In* The Chemistry of Quinonoid Compounds, Part 2. S. Patai (Editor). John Wiley & Sons, London, New York, Sydney, Toronto.

FREE, B.L. and SATTERLEE, L.D. 1975. Biochemical properties of alfalfa protein concentrate. J. Food Sci. *40*, 85–89.

GARDNER, H.K., HRON, R.J. and VIX, H.L.E. 1976. Removal of pigment glands (gossypol) from cottonseed. Cereal Chem. *53*, 549–560.

GLENCROSS, R.G., FESTENSTEIN, G.N. and KING, H.G.C. 1972. Separation and determination of isoflavones in the protein concentrate from red clover leaves. J. Sci. Food Agric. *23*, 371–376.

GLICK, Z. and JOSLYN, M.A. 1970A. Food intake depression and other metabolic effects of tannic acid in rats. J. Nutr. *100*, 509–515.

GLICK, Z. and JOSLYN, M.A. 1970B. Effect of tannic acid and related compounds on the absorption and utilisation of proteins in the rat. J. Nutr. *100*, 516–520.

GOLDSTEIN, J. and SWAIN, T. 1965. The inhibition of enzymes by tannins. Phytochemistry *4*, 185–192.

GRASSMANN, W., CHAUN-CHU, P. and SCHELZ, H. 1937. A nephelometric micromethod for determination and identification of vegetable tannins. Collegium (Darmstadt), 530–541.

GRAY, J.C. 1978. Absorption of polyphenols by polyvinyl-pyrrolidone and polystyrene resins. Phytochemistry *17*, 495–497.

GRIFFITHS, D.W. and JONES, D.I.H. 1977. Cellulose inhibition by tannins in the testa of field beans *(Vicia faba)*. J. Sci. Food Agric. *28*, 983–989.

GUSTAVSON, K.H. 1956. The Chemistry of Tanning Processes. Academic Press, New York.

GUSTAVSON, K.H. and HOLM, B. 1952. Reactions of polyamides with tanning agents. J. Am. Leather Chem. Assoc. *47*, 700–711.

HACKMANN, R.H. and GOLDBERG, M. 1977. Molecular crosslinks in cuticles. Insect Biochem. *7*, 175–184.

HAIDER, K., FREDERICK, L.R. and FLAIG, W. 1965. Reactions between amino acid compounds and phenols during oxidation. Plant Soil *22*, 49–64.

HAMPTON, R.E. 1970. An oxidation product of chlorogenic acid in tobacco leaves infected with tobacco streak virus. Phytopathology *60*, 1677–1681.

HARRIS, G. 1965. The polyphenol composition of non-biological hazes of beers. J. Inst. Brew. London *71*, 292–298.

HASLAM, E. 1974. Polyphenol-protein interactions. Biochem. J. *139*, 285–288.

HASLAM, E. 1977. Symmetry and promiscuity in procyanidin biochemistry. Phytochemistry *16*, 1625–1640.

HASLAM, E. 1978. Vegetable tannins. *In* Biochemistry of Plant Phenolics: Recent Advances in Phytochemistry, Vol. 12. T. Swain, J.B. Harborne and C.F. van Sumere (Editors). Plenum Press, New York.

HENNEKE, C.M. and WEDDING, R.T. 1975. NAD-phenol complex formation, the inhibition of malate dehydrogenase by phenols and the influence of phenol substituents on inhibitory effectiveness. Arch. Biochem. Biophys. *168*, 436–442.

HORIGOME, T. 1973. Nutritive value of N-acetylcasein and brown-coloured N-acetylcasein. Eiyo To Shokuryo *26*, 257–262. (Chem. Abstr., 1974, *80*, 35952).

HORIGOME, T. 1977. Nutritional studies on fractionated cytoplasmic and chloroplastic proteins from leaves of oats and ladino clover. Jpn. J. Zootech. Sci. *48*, 267–272.

HORIGOME, T. and KANDATSU, M. 1966A. Studies on the nutritive value of grass proteins. Part 13. Phenolic substances of red clover leaves and effects of *p*-coumaric, caffeic and chlorogenic acids on the digestibility of the leaf protein. J. Agric. Chem. Soc. Jpn. *40*, 246–251.

HORIGOME, T. and KANDATSU, M. 1966B. Studies on the nutritive value of grass proteins. Part 14. Lowering effect of phenolic compounds and *o*-diphenoloxidase on the digestibility of protein in pasture plants. J. Agric. Chem. Soc. Jpn. *40*, 449–455.

HORIGOME, T. and KANDATSU, M. 1968A. Biological value of proteins allowed to react with phenolic compounds in presence of *o*-diphenol oxidase. Agric. Biol. Chem. *32*, 1093–1102.

HORIGOME, T. and KANDATSU, M. 1968B. Studies on the nutritive value of grass proteins. Part 17. Biological value and digestibility of the leaf proteins of ladino clover and red clover. J. Agric Chem. Soc. Jpn. *42*, 471–478.

HORIGOME, T. and KANDATSU, M. 1971. Biological value of proteins allowed to react with phenolic compounds in presence of *o*-diphenol oxidase; effects of *o*-diphenol concentration on the biological value of protein-diphenol mixtures. J. Jpn. Soc. Food Nutr. *24*, 253–258.

HORSPOOL, W.M. 1969. Synthetic 1:2-quinones: Synthesis and thermal reactions. Q. Rev. Chem. Soc. *23*, 204–236.

JONES, W.T. and MANGAN, J.L. 1977. Complexes of condensed tannins of sainfoin (*Onobrychis viciifolia* scop) with fraction 1 leaf protein and with submaxilliary mucoprotein, and their reversal by polyethylene glycol and pH. J. Sci. Food Agric. *28*, 126–136.

KING, H.G.C. and PRUDEN, G. 1970. Lower limits of molecular weights of compounds excluded from Sephadex G-25 eluted with aqueous acetone mixtures. J. Chromatogr. *52*, 285–290.

KNUCKLES, B.E., DE FREMERY, D. and KOHLER, G.O. 1976. Coumestrol content of fractions obtained during wet processing of alfalfa. J. Agric. Food Chem. *24*, 1177–1180.

LAHIRY, N.L., SATTERLEE, L.D., HSU, H.W. and WALLACE, G.W. 1977. Characterisation of the chlorogenic acid binding fraction in leaf protein concentration. J. Food. Sci. *42*, 83–85.

LINDGREN, E. 1975. The nutritive value of peas and field beans for hens. Swed. J. Agric. Res. *5*, 159–161.

LOOKHART, G.L., JONES, B.L. and FINNEY, K.F. 1978. Determination of the coumestrol in soybeans by high-performance liquid and thin-layer chromatography. Cereal Chem. *55*, 967–972.

LOOMIS, W.D. 1974. Overcoming problems of phenolics and quinones in the isolation of plant enzymes and organelles. *In* Methods in Enzymology, Vol. 31. S.P. Colowick and M.D. Kaplan (Editors). Academic Press, New York, San Francisco, London.

LOOMIS, W.D. and BATTAILLE, J. 1966. Plant phenolic compounds and the isolation of plant enzymes. Phytochemistry *5*, 423–438.

LOOMIS, D.W., LILE, J.D., SANDSTROM, R.P. and BURBOTT, A.J. 1979. Absorbent polystyrene as an aid in plant enzyme isolation. Phytochemistry *18*, 1049–1054.

MANCINI, M., ORIENTE, P. and ANDREA, L.D. 1960. Therapeutic effect of 1,4-dicaffeyl quinic acid, the active principle of artichoke. Minerva Med. *51*, 2460–2463. Chem. Abstr. (1961) *55*, 12632.

MASON, H.S. 1955. Comparative biochemistry of the phenolase complex. Adv. Enzymol. *16*, 105–184.

MASON, H.S. and PETERSON, E.W. 1965. Melanoproteins: Reactions between enzyme-generated quinones and amino acids. Biochim. Biophys. Acta *111*, 134–146.

MASON, H.S., SPENCER, E. and YAMAZAKI, I. 1961. Identification by electron spin resonance spectroscopy of the primary product of tyrosinase-catalysed catechol oxidation. Biochem. Biophys. Res. Commun. *4*, 236–238.

MBADIWE, E. 1975. Biochemical and nutritional aspects of nitrogenous constituents of seeds of *Pentaclethra macrophylla*. Ph.D. Thesis. University of East Anglia, Norwich, England.

McLEOD, M.N. 1974. Plant tannins, their role in forage quality. Nutr. Abstr. Rev. *44*, 803–815.

McWEENY, D.J., KNOWLES, M.E. and HEARNE, J.F. 1974. The chemistry of non-enzymic browning in foods and its control by sulphites. J. Sci. Food Agric. *25*, 735–746.

MEJBAUM-KATZENELLENBOGEN, W. and MORAWIECKA, B. 1959. Studies on regeneration of protein from insoluble protein-tannin compounds. Acta Biochim. Pol. *6*, 453–465. (Polish)

MILIC, B.L. and STOJANOVIC, S. 1972. Lucerne tannins: Metabolic fate of lucerne tannins in mice. J. Sci. Food Agric. *23*, 1163–1167.

MILTON, J. 1667. Paradise Lost. Book 1, lines 2–3.

MOHAMMADZADAH, A., FEENEY, R.E. and SMITH, L.M. 1969. Hydrophobic binding of hydrocarbons by proteins; Parts I and II. Biochim. Biophys. Acta *194*, 246–264.

MONTIES, B. and RAMBOURG, J.C. 1978A. Presence and separation of flavonoids in protein preparations isolated from lucerne leaves. Bull. Liaison Groupe Polyphenols *8*, 25–30. (French)

MONTIES, B. and RAMBOURG, J.C. 1978B. Presence of flavonoids (flavones and coumestanes) in preparations of proteins extracted from lucerne (Medicago sativa var. Europe). Ann. Technol. Agric. *27*, 629–654. (French)

MORTON, J.F. 1978. Economic botany in epidemilogy. Econ. Bot. *32*, 111–117.

MOSELEY, G. and GRIFFITHS, D.W. 1979. Varietal variation in the antinutritive effects of field-beans *(Vicia faba)* when fed to rats. J. Sci. Food Agric. *30*, 772–778.

NAIM, M., GESTETNER, B., BONDI, A. and BIRK, Y. 1976. Antioxidative and antihemolytic activities of soybean isoflavones. J. Agric. Food Chem. *24*, 1174–1177.

NAIM, M. GESTETNER, B. ZILKAH, S., BIRK, Y. and BONDI, A. 1974. Soybean isoflavones, characterisation, determination and antifungal activity. J. Agric. Food Chem. *22*, 806–810.

NANDA, C.L., TERNOUTH, J.H. and KONDOS, A.C. 1977. Evaluation of the nutritive value of plant protein concentrates. J. Sci. Food Agric. *28*, 1075–1079.

NASHEF, A.S., OSUGA, D.T., LEE, H.S., AHMED, A.I., WHITAKER, J.R. and FEENEY, R.E. 1977. The effect of alkali on protein di-sulfides and their products. J. Agric. Food Chem. *25*, 245–251.

NEWBY, V.K., SABLON, R.M., SYNGE, R.L.M., CASTEELE, K.V. and VAN SUMERE, C.F. 1980. Free and bound phenolic acids of lucerne (Medicago sativa, cv. Europe). Phytochemistry *19*, 651–657.

PIERPOINT, W.S. 1966. The enzymic oxidation of chlorogenic acid and some reactions of the quinone produced. Biochem. J. *98*, 567–580.

PIERPOINT, W.S. 1969A. *o*-Quinones formed in plant extracts: Their reactions with amino acids and peptides. Biochem. J. *112*, 609–617.

PIERPOINT, W.S. 1969B. *o*-Quinones formed in plant extracts: Their reaction with bovine serum albumin. Biochem. J. *112*, 619–629.

PIERPOINT, W.S. 1971. Formation and behaviour of *o*-quinones in some processes of agricultural importance. Rothamsted Exp. Stn. Rep. *1970* (Part 2) 199–218.

PIERPOINT, W.S. 1973. PVX-Q: An infective product of potato virus X and a leaf *o*-quinone. J. Gen. Virol. *19*, 189–199.

PIERPOINT, W.S. 1974. Chemical modification of the lysine-amino groups of potato virus X. J. Gen. Virol. *25*, 303–312.

PIERPOINT, W.S. and CARPENTER, J.M. 1978. An infective pyridoxyl-derivative of potato virus X: PVX-PLP. J. Gen. Virol. *38*, 505–518.

PIERPOINT, W.S., IRELAND, R.J. and CARPENTER, J.M. 1977. Modification of proteins during the oxidation of leaf phenols: Reactions of potato virus X with chlorogenoquinone. Phytochemistry *16*, 29–34.

PIRIE, A. 1968. Reaction of tyrosine oxidation products with proteins of the lens. Biochem. J. *109*, 301–305.

PIRIE, N.W. 1978. Leaf Protein and Other Aspects of Fodder Fractionation. Cambridge University Press, London.

POLLARD, A. and TIMBERLAKE, C.F. 1971. Fruit juices. *In* Biochemistry of Fruits and Their Products, Vol. 2. F.C. Hulme, (Editor). Academic Press, London, New York.

POMENTA, J.V. and BURNS, E.E. 1971. Factors affecting chlorogenic, quinic and caffeic levels in sunflower kernels. J. Food Sci. *36*, 490–492.

RAMACHANDRA, G., VIRUPAKSHA, T.K. and SHADAKSHARASWAMY, M. 1977. Relationship between tannin levels and in vitro protein digestibility in finger millet. J. Agric. Food Chem. *25*, 1101–1104.

ROBERTS, E.A.H. 1959. The interaction of flavanol orthoquinones with cysteine and glutathione. Chem. Ind. (London), 995.

ROBINSON, T. 1979. The determination of proteins in plant extracts that contain polyphenols. Plant Sci. Lett. *15*, 211–216.

RUSSELL, A.E., SHUTTLEWORTH, S.G. and WILLIAMS-WYNN, D.A. 1968A. Further studies on the mechanism of vegetable tannage, Part IV. J. Soc. Leather Trades Chem. *52*, 220–238.

RUSSELL, A.E., SHUTTLEWORTH, S.G. and WILLIAMS-WYNN, D.A. 1968B. Further studies on the mechanism of vegetable tannage, Part V. J. Soc. Leather Trades Chem. *52*, 459–486.

SABIR, M.A., SOSULSKI, F.W. and FINLAYSON, A.J. 1974. Chlorogenic acid-protein interactions in sunflowers. J. Agric. Food Chem. *22*, 575–578.

SANADA, H., SUZUE, R., NAKASHIMA, Y. and KAWADA, S. 1972. Effect of thiol compounds on melanin formation by tyrosinase. Biochim. Biophys. Acta *261*, 258–266.

SHEEN, S.J. and BURTON, H.R. 1978. Amino acid composition in soluble tobacco fractions containing brown pigments. J. Agric. Food Chem. *26*, 380–385.

SINGER, G., ROZENTAL, J.M. and NORRIS, D.M. 1975. –SH groups and quinone-receptors in insect olfaction and gustation. Nature (London) *256*, 222–223.

SPURR, H.W. and MAIN, C.E. 1974. Brown-pigment formation in tobacco leaves infected with alternaria. Phytopathology *64*, 738–745.

STAGG, G.V. and MILLIN, D.J. 1975. The nutritional and therapeutic value of tea—A review. J. Sci. Food Agric. *26*, 1439–1459.

SUBBA RAU, B.H., RAMANA, K.V.R. and SINGH, N. 1972. Studies on nutritive value of leaf proteins and some factors affecting their quality. J. Sci. Food Agric. *23*, 233–245.

SWAIN, T. 1965. The tannins. *In* Plant Biochemistry. J. Bonner and J.E. Varner (Editors). Academic Press, London, New York.

SYNGE, R.L.M. 1975. Interaction of polyphenols with proteins and plant products. Qual. Plant. *24*, 337–350.

SYNGE, R.L.M. 1978. Polyphenol-protein reaction and their significance for agricultural practive. C.R. Assem. Gen. Groupe Polyphenols, May 1978, Nancy *8*, 13–24.

TEXL, A. and KONECNY, M. 1968. Hepatotoxic effect of tannic acid and rectobaryum in rats. Scr. Med. *41*, 301–312.

TRAUTNER, E.M. and ROBERTS, E.A.H. 1950. Chemical mechanism of the oxidative deamination of amino acids by catechol and by polyphenolase. Aust. J. Sci. Res. Ser. B: *3*, 356–380.

TSO, T.C. 1972. Physiology and Biochemistry of Tobacco Plants. Dowden, Hutchinson & Ross, Stroudsburg, PA.

VAN BURREN, J., DE VOS, L. and PILNIK, W. 1976. Polyphenols in Golden Delicious apple juice in relation to methods of preparation. J. Agric. Food Chem. *24*, 448–451.

VAN HEYNINGEN, R. and PIRIE, A. 1967. The metabolism of naphthalene and its toxic effect on the eye. Biochem. J. *102*, 842–852.

VAN SUMERE, C.F., ALBRECHT, J., DEDONDER, A., DE POOTER, H. and Pe, I. 1975. Plant proteins and phenolics. *In* The Chemistry and Biochemistry of Plant Proteins. J.B. Harborne and C.F. VAN Sumere (Editors). Academic Press, London, New York, San Francisco.

VAN SUMERE, C.F., HOUPELINE-DE COCK, H.L., VINDEVAGHEL-DE BACQUER, Y.C. and FOCKENIER, G. 1980. N-Feruloylglycine-L-phenylalanine isolated by partial hydrolysis of bulk leaf protein of lucerne, *Medicago sativa* cv. Europe. Phytochemistry *19*, 704–705.

VON WETTSTEIN, D., JENDE-STRID, B., AHRENST-LARSEN, B. and SORENSEN, J.A. 1977. Biochemical mutant in barley renders chemical stabilization of beer superfluous. Carlsberg Res. Commun. *42*, 341–351.

WEYBREW, J.A. and LONG, R.C. 1970. More on tobacco browning: The first pigment. Tob. Sci. *14*, 167–169.

WRIGHT, H.E., BURTON, W.W. and BERRY, R.C. 1960. Soluble browning reaction pigments of aged burley tobacco. I. The non-dialysable fraction. Arch. Biochem. Biophys. *86*, 94–101.

WRIGHT, H.E., BURTON, W.W. and BERRY, R.C. 1954. Soluble browning reaction of aged burley tobacco. II. The dialysable fraction. Phytochemistry *3*, 525–533.

YOUNG, M. and STEELINK, C. 1973. Peroxide catalysed oxidation of naturally-occurring phenols and hardwood lignins. Phytochemistry *12*, 2851–2861.

11

Lipids in Leaf Protein Concentrates

Steven Nagy and Harold E. Nordby

The term "lipid" is applied to a heterogeneous class of cellular compounds whose solubility in organic solvents and insolubility in water distinguishes them from other cellular components, such as carbohydrates, proteins, and nucleic acids. Chemically, the vast majority of leaf lipids are acyl lipids, that is, derivatives of long-chain fatty acids (Hawke 1973). Acyl lipids would include simple wax esters (esters of fatty acids and long-chain monohydroxy alcohols), simple fats (triacyl glycerols), sterol esters, triterpene alcohol esters, sphingosine-containing ester derivatives, glycolipids, phospholipids, and other complex lipids (e.g., phytoglycolipid; Carter and Koob 1969). Leaf polar acyl lipids contain active functional groups such as amino, amido, phosphate, and sulfate moieties. The nonacyl leaf lipids include free sterols and long-chain aliphatic compounds such as alcohols, aldehydes, ketones, and hydrocarbons. Other leaf compounds which may be included under the term "lipid" are fat-soluble pigments (discussed in a separate chapter of this book, Chapter 9) and fat-soluble vitamins.

Lipids of leaves and leaf protein concentrates (LPCs) may be separated into three principal classes. Class distinction is based both on chemical structure and on chromatographic resolution by silica gel columns (Rouser *et al.* 1967). Leaf lipids may be classified chemically as nonpolar, nonionic polar, and ionic polar. Nonpolar lipids (commonly referred to as neutral or simple) are extracted from leaf tissues and LPCs with organic solvents of low dielectric constants (<5), e.g., hexane, benzene, diethyl ether, and chloroform. Nonionic polar lipids refer to a group of sugar-containing lipids, and they are eluted from silica gel columns with acetone or 5% methanol in chloroform (Nordby *et al.* 1976). The ionic polar lipids generally contain phospho, sulfo, amino, or carboxyl reactive groups which cause these molecules to be strongly retained on silica gel columns. These lipids can be eluted from silica gel columns only by solvents of high dielectric constants (>20), e.g., methanol.

Comprehensive texts exist (Hitchcock and Nichols 1971; Galliard and Mercer 1975; Kolattukudy 1976) on the chemistry and biochemistry of plant lipids. It is the purpose of this chapter to critically evaluate the contribution of lipids to the quality of LPC preparations. Information for this review was gathered from research published between 1950 and mid-1978.

LIPIDS OF LEAVES

Leaves of higher plants contain up to 7% of their dry weight as acyl lipids, nonacyl long-chain lipids, chlorophyll, and other fat-soluble pigments (Hitchcock and Nichols 1971). Leaf lipids are components of two major morphological structures: (1) cuticular and epicuticular layers of tissue surfaces and (2) cellular and organelle membranes. The composition and distribution of leaf lipids are related to many factors, such as botanical leaf type, stage of maturity, and growing conditions (fertilization, soil type, climate, temperature, and rainfall).

Cuticular Lipids

All aerial parts of plants are bounded by protective outer skins or cuticles. The insoluble lipid polyester, called cutin, is the structural component of the outer skin of the plant's fleshy tissues (e.g., petals, leaves, and stems). On leaves, cuticles, which are noncellular, nonliving, and heterogeneous in chemical composition, are generally multilayered and lie over and merge into the outer wall of the epidermal cell layer (Martin and Juniper 1970).

Embedded within the cutin matrix and sometimes exuded over the surface of the cutin layer are numerous lipid compounds; collectively, these are called wax. The term "wax" has two meanings, one broad and one narrow: (1) it is used to denote a wide variety of nonpolar and weakly polar lipids which qualitatively have certain physical properties in common; and (2) by strict chemical definition, it is an ester of a monohydric long-chain alcohol with a long-chain acid. In this chapter, "wax" will be used according to its broadest meaning while "wax ester" will refer strictly to compounds with the ester structure.

Waxes embedded within the cuticle (cuticular) and layered above the cuticle (epicuticular) are complex lipid mixtures. Lipid components reported to be present in leaf waxes by Martin and Juniper (1970) and by Kolattukudy (1976) include: long-chain hydrocarbons (saturated and unsaturated, linear, iso-, anteiso-, and dimethyl-branched), alcohols (primary, secondary, α, ω-diols), ketones (monoketones, β-diketones, hydroxy-β-diketones), fatty acids (saturated and unsaturated linear, iso-, and anteiso-branched monocarboxylic; as well as hydroxy and dicarboxylic), esters (hydroxy, mono-, and di-esters), aldehydes, sterols, glycerides, and fat-soluble terpenoid compounds. While leaf waxes are complex, it should not be inferred that the lipid components enumerated are all found together. In fact, many leaf waxes are differentiated by the presence or absence of certain lipid components.

Cellular (Internal) Lipids

Internal lipids serve primarily a structural role in plant cells. As major membrane constituents of cell organelles, i.e., nucleus, mitochondria, microsomes, Golgi apparatus, chloroplast, peroxisomes, plasmalemma, and others, lipids interact with proteins by way of nonionic, hydrophobic bonding (Hitchcock and Nichols 1971) to impart structural integrity to the membrane. Due to the diverse function of each organelle, the lipid composition of each organelle's membrane will differ (Mazliak *et al.* 1975). Leaves contain comparatively small amounts of neutral lipids but large amounts of ionic and nonionic polar lipids.

Wintermans (1960) showed that the major classes of lipids in leaves are galactosyl diglycerides, sulfolipid, phosphatidyl choline, phosphatidyl glycerol, phosphatidyl ethanolamine, phosphatidyl inositol, and diphosphatidyl glycerol. Compositions of major glycerolipids in several plant leaves are shown in Table 11.1. As evident, the relative concentrations of the different lipids vary considerably among plants. Glycolipids (mono-, digalactosyl diglycerides, and sulfolipid) are the major acyl lipids in leaf tissue, and account for about 65 to 85% of the total, while phospholipids account for about 15 to 35%.

The distribution of polar lipids within the different membranes of the cell is quite striking. While the phospholipids are the major lipids in nonphotosynthetic membranes, e.g., mitochondria, nucleus, and endoplasmic reticulum, the glycolipids predominate in the limiting double membrane (envelope membrane) and the inner chlorophyll-containing lamellar membrane of the chloroplast (Table 11.2). Chloroplasts, by virtue of their size, number, and high membrane content, contain the bulk of the lipid of the plant cell (Thompson 1965). The numerous repeating unit membranes (lamellae) of the chloroplast account for the finding that over 50% of their dry mass is lipid. Poincelot (1973) reported that the envelope membranes of chloroplasts contain more galactosyl diglycerides and phosphatidyl choline, and less sulfolipid and phosphatidyl glycerol, than the lamellae, and that small amounts of cerebroside, sterol glucoside, acylated sterol glucoside, phosphatidyl ethanolamine, free sterol, and sterol esters are exclusive to the envelopes.

Lipids found in trace quantities in leaf tissues include phosphatidyl serine, phosphatidic acid, phytoglycolipids, mono-, di-, triglycerides, glucocerebrosides, sterol esters, carotenoid esters, and esterified sterol glucosides (Stumpf 1975; Galliard and Mercer 1975; Nagy *et al.* 1978A).

Fatty Acids. For the most part, the relative proportions of fatty acids isolated from leaves depend on the maturity and physiological state of the plant. The comparable function of plant leaves is often reflected in similar

TABLE 11.1. GLYCEROLIPID COMPOSITION OF SEVERAL PLANT LEAVES

	Galactosyl Diglycerides		Moles Lipid per g Fresh Tissue					
Plant	Mono-	Di-	Sulfolipid	Phosphatidyl Choline	Phosphatidyl Glycerol	Phosphatidyl Ethanolamine	Phosphatidyl Inositol	Diphosphatidyl Glycerol
White clover *(Trifolium repens)*	8.60	5.20	0.76	1.41	1.13	0.87	0.25	0.28
Lucerne *(Medicago sativa)*	8.60	5.20	1.72	0.75	0.67	0.50	0.28	0.58
Tomato *(Solanum esculentum)*	5.08	2.46	0.31	1.10	0.43	0.45	0.10	0.10
Squash *(Cucurbita pepo)*	4.10	2.70	0.30	1.60	0.91	1.00	0.14	0.09
Lettuce *(Lactuca sativa)*	0.68	0.68	0.03	0.31	0.10	0.21	0.06	0.13
Perennial ryegrass *(Lolium perenne)*	5.10	3.95	0.45	1.35	0.75	0.55	0.20	0.20
Maize *(Zea mays)*	3.10	2.30	0.35	0.45	0.48	0.24	0.12	0.24
Cocksfoot *(Dactylis glomerata)*	8.00	5.10	0.62	1.10	1.10	0.80	0.10	0.28

Source: Roughan and Batt (1969).

TABLE 11.2. LIPID, PIGMENT, AND QUINONE COMPOSITION OF CHLOROPLAST LAMELLAR MEMBRANES

Zea mays[1]		Spinach[2]	
Components	g per 100 g Lipid Materials	Components	g per 100 g Lipid Materials
Monogalactosyl diglyceride	26.9	Monogalactosyl diglyceride	22.0
Digalactosyl diglyceride	20.5	Digalactosyl diglyceride	15.0
Sulfolipid	4.5	Sulfolipid	7.0
Phosphatidyl glycerol	4.2	Phosphatidyl glycerol	7.8
Phosphatidyl choline	—	Phosphatidyl choline	2.9
Phosphatidyl inositol	0.7	Phosphatidyl inositol	1.3
Phosphatidyl ethanolamine	0.6	Phosphatidyl ethanolamine	—
Chlorophyll *a*	19.8	Chlorophyll	21.0
Chlorophyll *b*	3.8	Carotenoid	3.0
β-Carotene	1.2	Quinone	3.0
Lutein	1.4		
Violaxanthin	0.7		
Neoxanthin	0.4		
Plastoquinone 45	0.6		
Tocopherol quinone	0.1		
Tocopherol	0.2		
Naphthoquinone	0.2		

[1]Koenig (1971).
[2]Poincelot (1973).

fatty acid contents, i.e., the major acids of all leaves are linolenic (18:3), linoleic (18:2), and palmitic (16:0).[1] The preponderance of 18:3 in photosynthetic tissues and in chloroplastic glycolipids is apparently related to its role in chlorophyll synthesis (Rosenberg and Gouaux 1967; Nichols *et al.* 1967; Stumpf 1975). Minor, bound fatty acids found in leaves at levels below 5% are lauric (12:0), myristic (14:0), palmitoleic (16:1), *trans*-3-hexadecenoic (3t 16:1), hexadeca-7,10,13-trienoic (16:3), stearic (18:0), oleic (18:1), arachidic (20:0), and behenic (22:0).

LIPIDS OF LEAF PROTEIN CONCENTRATES

Laboratory and commercial methods for the expression of protein from leaves and the preparation of LPC have been extensively reviewed (Pirie 1971; Bickoff *et al.* 1975; Kohler *et al.* 1976; Nagy *et al.* 1978B). As outlined in Fig. 11.1, LPC is prepared by the following sequence: (1) rupture of leaf cells by grinding or mincing, (2) separation of the protein-laden juice from the insoluble fiber by pressing, filtration, and centrifugation, (3) coagulation of the soluble protein in the juice by heat or chemical means to form a protein curd, (4) separation of the protein curd from the supernatant fluid, and (5) washing, pressing, and drying the LPC. Figure 11.1 also shows the preparation of "crude lipids" from either the protein coagulum or the LPC fraction. The methodology used in the analyses of crude lipids will be presented later in this chapter.

[1] No. of carbons:No. of double bonds.

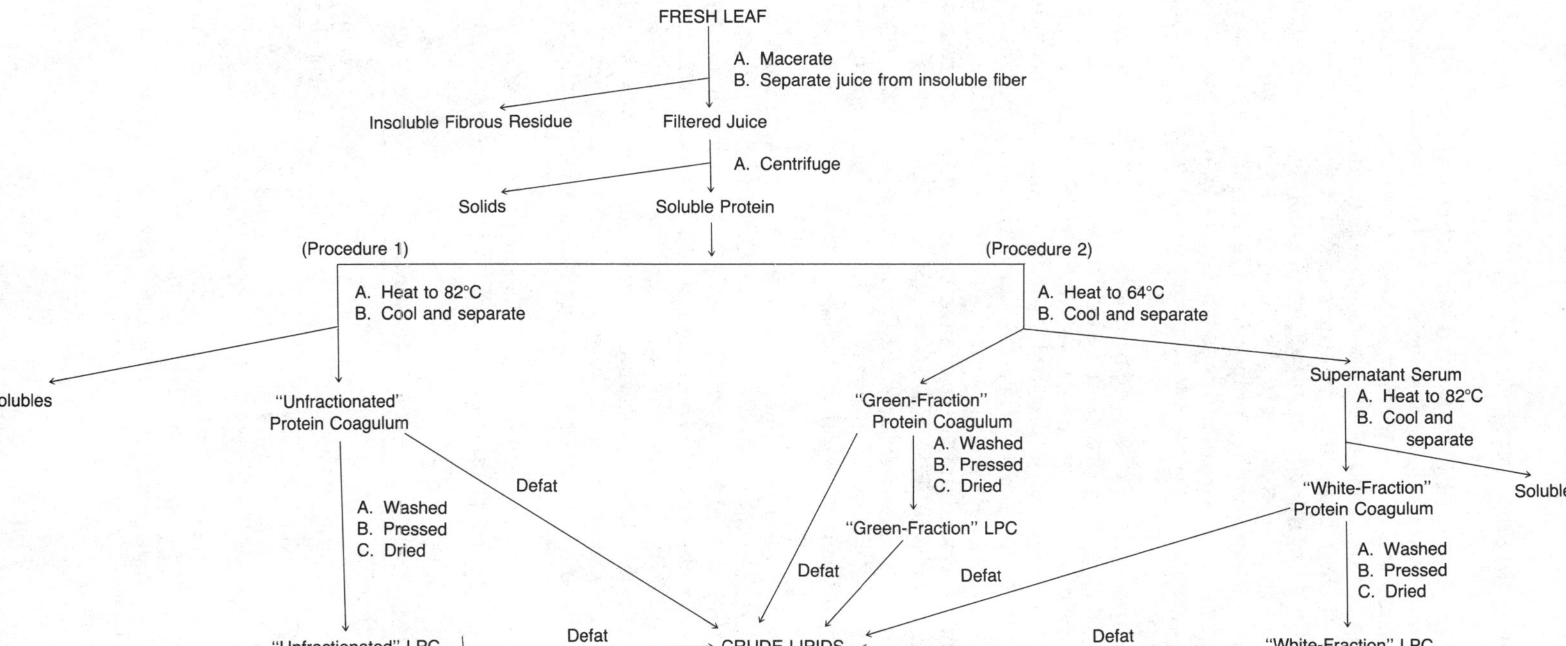

Fig. 11.1. Basic schematic for preparation of LPCs and crude lipids.
From Nagy et al. (1978B).

Lipids that are not tightly bound and those that are somewhat water-soluble (sugar-containing lipids, alcohols, free fatty acids) would be expected to predominate in the proteolipid fraction of the expressed juice. Most LPC preparations should contain relatively large amounts of glycolipids because of their high concentrations in leaf tissues and their high water solubility. Also, internal neutral lipids, chlorophyll, pigments, and some epicuticular wax constituents should appear in the expressed juice because of their weak bonding properties. Conversely, high contents of phospholipids and other complex lipids would not be expected in the expressed juice because of strong attachments to the membrane and poor water solubility.

The lipid compositions of LPC preparations will depend on leaf source, on stage of maturity, and on processing and fractionation procedures. The expressed green juice of leaves contains soluble proteins that are coaguable into different fractions by differential heat treatment. Juice heated between 50° and 64°C yields a green protein curd known as "green-fraction" LPC (Bickoff *et al.* 1975). Practically all chlorophylls, fat-soluble pigments, and most of the expressed lipids are co-precipitated with this protein coagulum (Hudson and Karis 1973). The co-precipitated lipids account for 10 to 30% by weight of the green-fraction LPC (Lea and Parr 1961; Buchanan 1969; Byers 1971A,B; Betschart and Kinsella 1974; Edwards *et al.* 1975) and contain high levels of palmitic, linoleic, and linolenic acids (Lima *et al.* 1965).

Comparatively few material balance studies have been conducted on the quantitative distribution of lipids during LPC production. In one study (Table 11.3), Hudson and Karis (1973) showed that polar lipids (aqueous butanol extracts) were present in greater amounts in all fractions than were nonpolar lipids (petroleum ether extracts) and that the LPC fractions had the highest contents of lipids. Material balance indicated that about half of the total leaf lipids remained in the insoluble fiber fraction, less than half were found in the LPC, and the remaining lipids were distributed in the LPC filtrate (whey).

In a study of LPC lipid distributions (Table 11.4; Nagy *et al.* 1978A), moist, freshly prepared, green-fraction LPCs were successively extracted

TABLE 11.3. LIPID CONTENTS OF LPC FRACTIONS[1]

	Turnip Tops % of Dry Matter			Kale % of Dry Matter		
LPC Fraction	Nonpolar	Polar	Total	Nonpolar	Polar	Total
Pulp	1.0	3.7	4.7	1.3	3.1	4.4
fiber	0.9	2.8	3.7	1.1	2.7	3.8
expressed juice	0.9	4.1	5.0	1.6	3.5	5.1
LPC	2.2	7.4	9.6	3.4	6.5	9.9
whey	0.4	1.9	2.3	0.2	1.1	1.3

Source: Hudson and Karis (1973).
[1]Nonpolar lipids extracted with petroleum ether; polar lipids extracted with water-saturated n-butanol.

TABLE 11.4. LIPID DISTRIBUTIONS OF FOUR GREEN PROTEIN FRACTIONS[1]

		Total Lipid Distribution (%)			Lipid Class Distribution (%)		
Tropical Leaves	Lipid/Crude Protein	Fatty Acids	Nonsaponifiables	Residuals[2]	Neutral[3]	Glycolipid	Phospholipid
Chaya	0.19	33.8	27.6	38.6	75.1	23.8	1.1
Sorghum × Sudan	0.23	35.3	28.5	36.2	67.3	30.7	2.1
Cassava	0.12	32.0	25.2	42.8	74.8	22.3	2.9
Sauropus	0.22	34.1	30.4	35.5	83.5	16.1	0.5

Source: Nagy *et al.* (1978A).
[1] LPCs extracted with 10% water in acetone.
[2] Includes lipid moieties not extracted by hexane and heptane after saponification and acidification (e.g., glycerol, galactosyl glycerol).
[3] Includes chlorophyll and other fat-soluble pigments.

with 10% water in acetone and 95% ethanol. Although $CHCl_3$-MeOH is the most widely used mixture for extraction of lipids, Nagy *et al.* (1978A) used an aqueous acetone mixture on their LPC preparations because: (1) it is recommended for chlorophyll extraction (Willstatter and Stoll 1913; AOAC 1965) and (2) it is one of the least toxic of industrial solvents, being comparable to ethanol in toxicity (Weissberger *et al.* 1955).

Lipids accounted for about 10 to 20% of the weight of the four tropical LPCs shown in Table 11.4. When the lipids that had been extracted with the green protein coagulum were saponified, about ⅓ of the reaction mixture was composed of fatty acids, less than ⅓ was due to nonsaponifiables, and the remainder or "residual" fraction consisted of compounds that could not be extracted with hexane. Lipid class separation by silica gel column chromatography showed that about ¾ of the total lipids were neutral lipids (includes chlorophyll and other fat-soluble pigments), about ⅕ to ¼ were glycolipids, and less than 1/20 were phospholipids. The low percentages of phospholipids might be explained by the fact that phospholipids are primarily structural components and are not readily freed from plant tissue by grinding or mincing, and by the poor extraction of phospholipids from LPCs by acetone (Shah 1971B). Low contents of phospholipids have also been reported of wheat (Hudson and Karis 1973) and ryegrass (Hudson and Warwick 1977) LPC preparations.

The most extensive distribution lists of lipid components in LPC preparations have been reported by Hudson and Warwick (1977) and by Nagy *et al.* (1978A). Lipid components of ryegrass LPC (Table 11.5) were reported to consist of simple lipids and pigments (60.0%), glycolipids (30.8%), and phospholipids (9.2%). Nagy and coworkers (1978A) reported not only the presence of those classes of lipids, but also long-chain ketones, aldehydes, triglycerides, primary alcohols, and triterpene alcohols in four tropical LPCs. Since many of these additional components originate in cuticle waxes, they would be expected to occur in LPCs prepared from waxy tropical leaves. The glycolipid fractions of LPCs account for about 15 to 30% of the total lipid (Tables 11.4 and 11.5) and contain five major glycolipids (Table 11.5). Two major acyl monogalactosyl diglycerides (AMGDG-1, -2) and two sphingolipids (Fig. 11.2) were also observed in tropical LPCs (Nagy *et al.*

TABLE 11.5. COMPOSITION OF TOTAL LIPID OF RYEGRASS LPC[1]

Simple Lipids (%)		Pigments and Others (%)		Glycolipids[2] (%)		Phospholipids[3] (%)	
Diglycerides	8.8	Chlorophylls	14.1	SQDG	4.4	PI	1.3
Fatty Acids	8.4	Carotenes	3.4	DGDG	10.5	PC	3.5
Sterols	3.2	Tocopherols	0.03	SG	1.6	PE	4.4
Sterol esters, waxes	3.0	Others	19.3	MGDG	10.5		
				ESG	3.8		

Source: Hudson and Warwick (1977).
[1]LPCs extracted with water-saturated n-butanol.
[2]SQDG—Sulfoquinovosyl diglycerides. DGDG—Digalactosyl diglycerides. SG—Sterol glucosides. MGDG—Monogalactosyl diglycerides. ESG—Esterified sterol glucosides.
[3]PI—Phosphatidyl inositol. PC—Phosphatidyl choline. PE—Phosphatidyl ethanolamine.

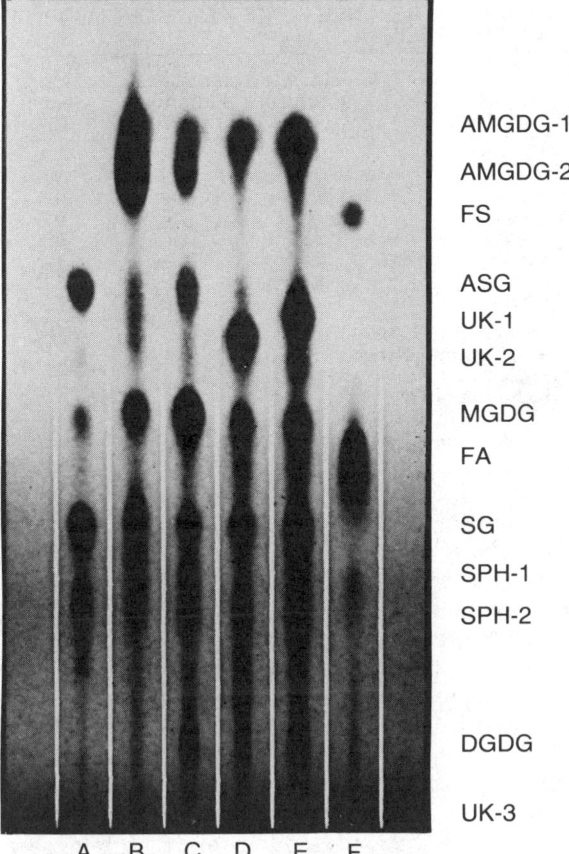

Fig. 11.2. LPC glycolipids from tropical plants. TLC separation of glycolipids on 250 μ silica gel G with $CHCl_3$-MeOH (85:15). Column identification: A—Reference glycolipid mixture from citrus vesicular lipids (Nordby *et al.* 1976). Glycolipids from green protein fractions of B—Chaya, C—*Sorghum* × Sudan, D—Cassava, and E—Sauropus. F—Standard free fatty acids and cholesterol. Lipid identifications: AMGDG-1, -2—Acylated monogalactosyl diglycerides. FS—Free sterols. ASG—Acylated sterol glucosides. UK-1, -2, -3—Unknowns. MGDG—Monogalactosyl diglyceride. FA—Free fatty acids. SG—Sterol glucosides. SPH-1, -2—Sphingolipids. And DGDG—Digalactosyl diglycerides.
From Nagy et al. (1978A).

1978A). AMGDG-1 and -2 are not naturally occurring glycolipids but are formed by the transfer of acyl from digalactosyl diglycerides to monogalactosyl diglycerides during tissue homogenization (Heinz 1967; Critchley and Heinz 1973; Heinz *et al.* 1974). It is important to recognize that during tissue maceration many hydrolases and transferases are released. These enzymes rapidly degrade and transform many principal lipid constituents.

Fatty acids comprise about 3 to 10% of the total weight of the LPC and about 30 to 40% of the LPC lipid (Lima *et al.* 1965; Hudson and Warwick 1977; Nagy *et al.* 1978A). The fatty acids of LPCs prepared from various leaves are predominantly unsaturated (Table 11.6). Linolenic acid (18:3), the predominant unsaturated acid, ranges from about 35 to 64%, while

TABLE 11.6. RELATIVE PERCENTAGE OF MAJOR FATTY ACIDS IN LPCs FROM VARIOUS SPECIES

Plant	Fatty Acid[6]					
	Palmitic 16:0	Palmitoleic 16:1	Stearic 18:0	Oleic 18:1	Linoleic 18:2	Linolenic 18:3
Chenopodium[1]	22.8	5.2	1.2	10.6	18.4	35.5
Soybean[2]	21.9	4.7	8.6	2.7	14.1	48.2
Lucerne[3]	13.8	—	0.9	0.7	10.7	64.0
Wheat[4]	15.5	—	0.8	2.5	10.4	52.5
Chaya[5]	25.1	Trace	2.5	2.9	7.3	62.2
Sorghum × Sudan[5]	31.5	Trace	1.7	3.7	13.0	50.1
Cassava[5]	33.7	Trace	3.3	4.9	8.7	49.4
Sauropus[5]	30.0	Trace	1.3	5.1	13.0	50.6

[1]Lima *et al.* (1965).
[2]Betschart and Kinsella (1975).
[3]Hudson and Karis (1976).
[4]Buchanan (1969).
[5]Nagy *et al.* (1978A).
[6]No. of carbons:No. of double bonds.

linoleic acid (18:2), the second most abundant unsaturated acid, ranges from about 7 to 18%. Palmitic acid (16:0), with a range from about 13 to 33%, is the most abundantly distributed saturated acid. The relative concentration and percentage distribution of LPC fatty acids are strongly influenced by the stage of plant maturity (Hudson and Karis 1973, 1974). Hawke (1973) reported higher proportions of 18:3 (74 to 79% of the total recovered fatty acids) and lower proportions of 16:0 (10 to 12%) in new growth of ryegrass than in grass that had aged (58 to 68% for 18:3; 14 to 22% for 16:0). Hawke also showed that the lipid content and yield of fatty acids of new grass were greater than in mature grass. Since fresh, succulent leaves are preferred for the preparation of LPC (Pirie 1971; Nagy *et al.* 1978B), LPC lipids would be expected to contain high levels of unsaturated fatty acids.

EFFECTS OF DRYING AND STORING LPC

Microbial spoilage and development of rancidity are the two major problems encountered during the storage of LPC (Lea and Parr 1961; Kinsella 1970; Arkcoll 1973). LPCs may be preserved by such conventional methods as pickling, salting, canning, freezing, and drying. Drying (freeze, roller, hot oven, air) is generally the preferred method because: (1) the dried LPC can be handled and transported more conveniently and cheaply and (2) drying the LPC to a water activity of 0.65 or less suppresses the growth of xerophilic fungi (Arkcoll 1973). For the purpose of this chapter, we will concentrate our discussion on subjects related to rancidity, i.e., on the relationships of LPC drying and storing to lipid extractability, lipid oxidation, protein-lipid reactions, and nutritive loss caused by lipid oxidative products.

Lipid Extractability

Removal of water from LPCs by air drying results in a decrease in the extractability of lipids (Buchanan 1969; Shah 1971A). As a typical example (Table 11.7), air drying of barley LPC at 100°C decreased total extractable lipid, lipid nitrogen, and lipid phosphorus. Chlorophyll showed the most dramatic reduction over the 24 hr drying period (12.8 to 1.2 mg/g of protein); about 34% of the chlorophyll could not be extracted from the sample heated for 2 hr, and about 86% from a 12 hr sample. Iodine value, a measure of fatty acid unsaturation, decreased about 50% in 24 hr.

TABLE 11.7. EFFECT OF DRYING AT 100°C ON THE EXTRACTABILITY AND COMPOSITION OF THE LIPIDS PRESENT IN BARLEY PROTEIN[1]

	mg/g of Protein				
Time of Drying in Air (hr)	Extractable Lipid	Lipid Nitrogen	Lipid Phosphorus	Chlorophyll	Iodine Value
Fresh cake	190	2.6	0.7	12.8	104
1	191	2.6	0.6	9.7	113
2	188	2.2	0.6	9.6	111
3	190	2.2	0.6	8.5	108
12	174	1.9	0.4	1.8	85
24	172	1.9	0.4	1.2	53

Source: Shah (1971A).
[1]Extracted with $CHCl_3$-MeOH (2:1).

As measured by oxygen absorption (Lea and Parr 1961), the loss in lipid extractability of LPC samples is apparently due to lipid oxidation caused by slow, high-temperature drying (Shah 1971A) and/or by high-temperature storage in air (Fig. 11.3; Buchanan 1969). The formation of insoluble complexes between autoxidized lipids and proteins (Pirie 1971) or the formation of lipid degradation products which are soluble in water (Buchanan 1969) has been postulated as the cause of the decreased levels of extractable lipids in stored LPC samples.

High-temperature drying and high-temperature storage in air appear critical to the formation of nonextractable lipid reaction products. Betschart and Kinsella (1974) showed that when soybean LPC was carefully prepared by freeze-drying and subjected to storage at 27°C, no change occurred in the extractability of LPC lipids. Betschart and Kinsella suggested that the natural antioxidants in soybean LPC might have inhibited oxidation of lipids under ambient storage conditions, and, if oxidation did occur, it was not sufficient to impair lipid extractability. While total lipid extractability was not affected, Betschart and Kinsella (1975) showed that the fatty acid composition was considerably altered. Marked decreases in the relative quantity of linolenic acid and relative increases in palmitic acid were observed after 12 weeks of storage.

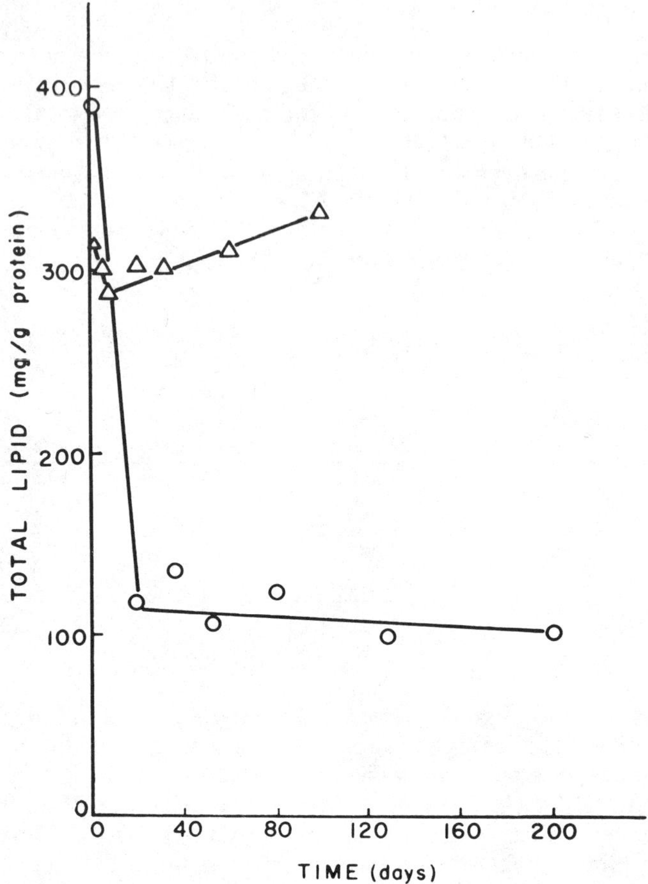

Fig. 11.3. Total lipid extracted from leaf protein stored at 100°C in air (○) and in nitrogen (△). The stored protein (2.5% moisture) was soaked overnight in 0.2 *N* HCl and then extracted with hot chloroform-methanol (2:1 v/v).
From Buchanan (1969).

Lipid Oxidation

Hudson and Karis (1976) utilized the linolenic-palmitic acid ratio (18:3/16:0) to monitor the effects of storage times, temperatures, and moisture levels on the destruction of LPC 18:3. Their studies showed that high storage temperatures and high moisture levels accelerated the rate of destruction of 18:3 (Table 11.8). Although well-defined trends in the effects of time and temperature were evident, no distinct first or second order reaction kinetics were observed. In contrast to the destructive effects

TABLE 11.8. EFFECT OF TEMPERATURE ON THE TRANSFORMATION OF LINOLENIC ACID OF LOW- AND HIGH-MOISTURE LPC SAMPLES

Temp (°C)	Time (hr)	Whole LPC[1]	
		6% Moisture	12% Moisture
50	0	3.76	3.76
	4	3.55	3.55
	6	3.54	3.35
	8	3.51	3.33
	10	3.48	3.29
	12	3.47	3.27
100	4	3.04	3.26
	6	2.88	3.03
	8	2.70	2.81
	10	2.62	2.69
	12	2.56	2.40
150	4	2.20	1.97
	6	1.98	1.82
	8	1.75	1.65
	10	1.70	1.44
	12	1.63	1.24
200	4	0.07	0.13
	6	0.04	0.06
	8	0.03	0.03
	10	0.02	0.02
	12	0.01	0.01

Source: Hudson and Karis (1976).
[1]Values expressed as 18:3/16:0 ratio.

of high-temperature storage, Hudson and Karis also reported that, if the LPC preparation was stored at room temperature, 18:3 was stable. Those workers suggested that 18:3 stability might have been the result of many causes, namely: (1) the presence of phospholipids which deactivate pro-oxidant trace metals, (2) the existence of a mesomorphic phase for glycolipids and phospholipids, and (3) the presence of natural antioxidants (carotenes, tocopherols, polyhydroxy flavones and their glycosides).

In a study of the autoxidation process of LPC 18:3, Hudson and Warwick (1977) showed that the induction period of oxygen absorption was out of phase with the fall of 18:3. Those workers suggested that 18:3 was not the lipid component most sensitive to oxidation. Apparently, the LPC preparation contained powerful antioxidants (not identified) which exerted a sparing action on 18:3. When the lipids were isolated from the LPC and vigorously purged of antioxidant activity, a classical autoxidation process was evident, with oxygen absorption in phase with 18:3 breakdown.

Oxidative rancidity in LPC preparations is related to the high content of unsaturated fatty acids within the various lipid fractions (Table 11.9). Fatty acid oxidation during juice extraction (lipoxidative enzymes) and during drying and storage of the LPCs (autoxidation and catalytic effects of pro-oxidants; Arkcoll 1973) results in the formation of numerous compounds. It is now widely accepted that hydroperoxides are the primary products of the reaction between oxygen and unsaturated fatty acids,

TABLE 11.9. RELATIVE PERCENTAGES OF FATTY ACIDS IN LIPID CLASSES FROM GREEN PROTEIN FRACTIONS OF FOUR TROPICAL LEAVES

	Fatty Acid				
Lipid Fraction	Palmitic 16:0	Stearic 18:0	Oleic 18:1	Linoleic 18:2	Linolenic 18:3
Neutral lipids					
chaya	37.8	4.2	5.2	13.5	39.3
Sorghum × Sudan	42.2	2.1	5.3	16.0	34.4
cassava	42.7	4.1	6.1	10.7	36.4
sauropus	30.8	1.6	5.1	12.3	50.1
Glycolipids					
chaya	12.1	1.7	1.1	3.2	81.9
Sorghum × Sudan	13.4	1.3	1.8	8.3	75.2
cassava	16.2	1.8	2.4	4.2	75.4
sauropus	14.5	0.8	7.2	20.6	56.9
Phospholipids					
chaya	34.1	5.6	6.0	4.7	49.6
Sorghum × Sudan	31.5	2.8	4.2	12.9	48.6
cassava	26.3	4.2	6.3	8.2	55.0
sauropus	31.0	3.7	9.1	10.1	46.1

Source: Nagy *et al.* (1978A).

whereas the secondary degradation products are formed largely by hydroperoxide dismutation and decomposition. An assessment of the number of different hydroperoxides that could be formed and the multiple mechanisms for their decay would show an enormous array of degradative compounds.

The alcohols, aldehydes, and unsaturated compounds which result from the degradation of hydroperoxides are susceptible to even further oxidation, for example, to acids. Aldehydes are the most troublesome of these degradation products because they are unstable, highly susceptible to polymerization and condensation reactions, and responsible for most of the off-flavors in rancid foods (Keeney 1962). Although no data are available on the quantity of carbonyls in a rancid LPC preparation, such data might be obtained if LPCs were tested for both off-flavor development and formation of volatile carbonyls. These could be measured either by the "carbonyl index" method of Chang and Kummerow (1955) or by the volatile carbonyl method of Dinsmore and Nagy (1971). Some oxidatively produced aldehydes found to contribute to the malodor of rancid foods are *n*-hexanal (fatty-green, grassy odor), 3-*cis*-hexenal (deep-green, leafy odor), 2-*trans*-hexenal (powerful green-fruity, grassy odor), 2-*trans*-octenal (rancid odor), 2-*trans*-nonenal (rancid odor), 2-*trans*-6-*cis*-nonadienal (cucumber odor), and alk-2,4-dienals (rotten, rancid, sweet aldehydic odors) (Hoffman 1962). *n*-Hexanal, which easily oxidizes in air, yields caproic acid (pervasive, rancid odor).

Protein-lipid Reactions

Lipids undergoing peroxidation (peroxidizing lipids) in other food and model systems have been associated with: (1) polypeptide chain scission

(Zirlin and Karel 1969), (2) decreased solubility of proteins because of cross-linking and formation of noncovalent, bound lipoprotein complexes (Schultz *et al.* 1962; Roubal and Tappel 1966; Jarenback and Liljemark 1975), and (3) the destruction of labile amino acid residues, namely, methionine, lysine, cysteine, and histidine (Roubal and Tappel 1966; Braddock and Dugan 1973; Karel *et al.* 1975; Yong and Karel 1978). These reactions might be expected to occur in LPC as a result of processing, drying, and storing.

Oxidation of methionine to methionine sulfoxide takes place during the processing and storage of LPCs, and is apparently due to the presence of peroxidizing lipids (which may be catalyzed by chlorophyll in the presence of light) or to the presence of quinones and/or H_2O_2 generated during the extraction and processing of LPC (Woldegiorgis 1976). The methionine sulfoxide content of unfractionated alfalfa LPCs prepared by heat coagulation, acid precipitation, or anaerobic fermentation (Stahmann 1976) was found to be about 10% of the total methionine content by Woldegiorgis (1976). Because methionine is the first limiting amino acid in all LPC preparations, the oxidation of peptide-bound methionine to methionine sulfoxide during storage may be one of the most important factors governing the nutritional quality of LPC. Cuq and coworkers (1973) reported that peptide-bound methionine sulfoxide was not readily liberated from proteins by *in vitro* enzymic digestion, whereas others (Slump and Schreuder 1973) reported that peptide-bound methionine sulfoxide was as available as peptide-bound methionine. Free methionine sulfoxide, on the other hand, has been reported to be less efficiently utilized by the animal than free methionine (Kuzmicky *et al.* 1972).

Transformation of lysine would also be expected to reduce the protein efficiency ratio (PER) (FAO 1970) of an LPC preparation (Allison 1971). Peroxidizing lipids react with the ε-amino groups of lysine to form polymers and Schiff's base condensation products (Butkus 1967; Tannenbaum *et al.* 1969). Limited studies, however, have been conducted on the relationship of oxidizing lipids to the destruction of lysine and, hence, to the reduction in PER values. In a dye-binding experiment which measured lysine availability, Hudson and Karis (1976) showed that defatted LPCs stored at 150° and 200°C for up to 12 hr had higher available lysine than the fat-containing preparations. Those authors concluded that highly reactive intermediates were formed during lipid oxidation and reacted with free amino groups to produce changes in protein quality.

Peroxidizing lipids also react with cysteinyl sulfhydryl groups to form aldehyde condensation products and products resulting from the addition to the double bonds of the hydroperoxide (Arya *et al.* 1972; Gardner *et al.* 1976), and with histidine to form imidazole acetic acid and imidazole lactic acid (Yong and Karel 1978). Apparently, no studies have been conducted on the reactivites and nutritional effects of peroxidizing lipids on cysteine and histidine in LPC preparations.

Nutritive Loss

Factors that affect the nutritive value of an LPC include (Woldegiorgis 1976): (1) amino acid composition, (2) the effect of processing conditions, (3) interaction of polyphenols with proteins, (4) lipid-protein interactions during processing and storage, and (5) other miscellaneous factors, e.g., toxic leaf components. Because of these factors, the nutritive value of a LPC preparation is usually lower than that expected on the basis of the essential amino acid pattern. In terms of nutritive value, it is usually the availability of the essential amino acids, rather than their absolute amounts, which determines a protein's effectiveness (Byers 1971A). *In vitro* enzymatic digestion (Akeson and Stahmann 1965; Saunders *et al.* 1973; Fafunso *et al.* 1976) and microbiological assay (Henry and Ford 1965; Smith and Pena 1977) have been used indirectly to assess the biological value (BV) of LPCs. Studies on wheat LPC by Oke and Umoh (1974) showed that the *in vitro* pepsin/trypsin and pepsin/pancreatin enzymic methods of Saunders *et al.* (1973) agreed closely with true digestibility as determined by the rat assay technique. The BV of wheat LPC was calculated by dividing net protein utilization (determined by rat assay) by true digestibility. Oke and Umoh (1974) concluded, however, that the *in vitro* enzymic methods were less sensitive in detecting the unavailability of some of the essential amino acids, like lysine, than the rat assay procedure.

The *in vitro* enzymatic method was used by Shah *et al.* (1967) to test the digestibility of LPC preparations that had been defatted (Table 11.10). With two exceptions, enzyme digestibilities were greater on the defatted LPCs. The decrease in trypsin digestibility of the 80°C defatted sample and decrease in pepsin digestibility of the 100°C defatted sample were attributed to the removal by chloroform-methanol of simple peptides that had formed during the drying process. In general, loss in protein digestibility was associated with both high-temperature drying and fat content. Shah and

TABLE 11.10. DIGESTIBILITY OF WHOLE AND DEFATTED LPC

		Percentage Digestibility of LPC					
	Enzyme Reaction	Dried at 60°C		Dried at 80°C		Dried at 100°C	
Enzyme	Time (hr)	Whole	Defatted	Whole	Defatted	Whole	Defatted
Trypsin	6	7.3	8.5	6.3	5.3	5.1	4.8
	9	8.6	9.8	7.4	8.2	5.9	6.7
	24	5.1	10.9	9.9	7.2	3.5	8.3
Pancreatic extract	6	8.1	12.1	8.4	10.6	4.2	4.8
	9	10.8	16.2	7.0	13.2	7.4	10.2
	24	26.9	28.7	21.7	24.0	15.6	20.3
Pepsin	6	11.8	16.0	10.4	13.1	14.7	9.3
	9	16.1	22.0	12.6	16.3	16.3	14.9
	24	25.6	41.8	18.0	26.3	25.8	20.6

Source: Shah *et al.* (1967).

co-workers (1967) concluded that lipid oxidative products formed during drying were toxic to trypsin, pepsin, and the pancreatic enzymes; and the loss in digestibility of the heated LPC samples was due mainly to these oxidative products. Since lipids do not react readily with protein in the absence of water, conditions which remove water from LPC preparations at low temperatures improve the nutritive value of the leaf protein.

Buchanan (1969) showed that the digestibility of LPC preparations could be improved by both low-temperature drying and by solvent extraction of lipids. He suggested that the loss in LPC digestibility caused by heating at 100°C was due to: (1) lipid-protein interactions which depend on the moisture content and (2) modification of the protein which depends on the moisture content and the duration of heating. Protein modification (as measured by digestibility with papain) was also apparent when the LPC was dried at a low temperature (60°C); however, the decrease in LPC digestibility caused by protein modification was lower than that of the sample dried at 100°C.

The lipids which co-precipitate with leaf proteins impart both positive and negative attributes to LPC. On the positive side, these lipids enhance the nutritional quality of the LPC by contributing important fatty acids, namely, linoleic and linolenic acids. Negatively, because more than half the fatty acids contain two or three double bonds (see Table 11.6), they are apt to oxidize during LPC preparation and storage. When lipid oxidation occurs, off-flavors and off-odors are produced which reduce the palatability of the LPC. In addition, and probably the most detrimental, oxidizing lipids react with the leaf protein and cause a decrease in nutritive value (Duckworth and Woodham 1961; Shah *et al.* 1967; Hudson and Karis 1976). Shah (1971A) also reported that oxidizing lipids caused a loss in protein solubility; however, Betschart and Kinsella (1974) concluded that lipids had no effect on the solubility profile of soybean LPC stored for up to six months. Delipidation would reduce the number of adverse nutritional effects and improve the shelf-life of the LPC, but the extra solvent extraction step would substantially increase the cost of the process. Removal of lipids can be feasible only if the fat-free LPC is cost justified and/or a market is available for the lipid by-products.

To obtain a palatable and nutritious lipid-containing LPC preparation, careful attention to processing and storage parameters must be taken into consideration. Processing should be rapid so that lipoxidative and proteolytic enzyme activities, and chemical reactions of lipid compounds with proteins, would be minimized. The protein cake obtained after coagulating, washing, and pressing should be stored at low temperatures. The addition of antioxidants to the fresh press cake might also be warranted (Shah 1969). If water is to be removed, desiccation should be conducted at low to moderate temperatures. Storage of the LPC product should always be at low temperatures (about 0°C) and preferably in the absence of air and light (Lea and Parr 1961).

EXTRACTION AND ANALYSIS OF LPC LIPIDS

The analysis of any lipid or lipid class is dependent upon the researcher's ability to isolate it from nonlipid materials. The four basic steps in lipid isolation involve (Burton 1974): (1) rapid and complete tissue maceration, (2) rapid and effective solvent penetration of the disrupted tissue, (3) removal of nonlipid materials, and (4) separation of lipids by classes and, subsequently, as specific molecular species. The schematic (see Fig. 11.1) for the preparation of LPC shows the different leaf protein fractions (either the protein coagulum or LPC but not both) which may undergo a defatting process. For the extraction of lipids, the solvent must penetrate the lipid-containing protein preparation and come in contact with the lipid. Therefore, the solvent should not only dissolve lipids effectively but also should be water miscible. Solvents commonly used for LPC lipid extractions include: acetone (Morrison and Pirie 1961), 10% water in acetone (Shah 1971A; Nagy *et al.* 1978A), water-saturated *n*-butanol (Hudson and Warwick 1977), and $CHCl_3$-MeOH, 2:1 (Lea and Parr 1961; Shah 1971A,B; Betschart and Kinsella 1974). In a comparative study on extraction of lipids from wheat LPC, Shah (1971B) showed that extraction with $CHCl_3$-MeOH (2:1) yielded more lipid nitrogen, lipid phosphorus, and total lipid per gram of protein than any other solvent (Table 11.11). Although Nagy *et al.* (1978A) recognized the superiority of $CHCl_3$-MeOH for lipid extraction, they selected 10% water in acetone as the solvent because, if delipidation of commercial LPCs becomes necessary, a solvent, such as acetone, with properties of low toxicity, easy recoverability, and low cost will be required.

A brief description of three methods used in extraction of lipids from LPC preparations is presented.

TABLE 11.11. COMPARATIVE STUDY OF LIPID EXTRACTION FROM WHEAT LPC[1]

Solvent	Extractable Lipid (mg)	mg/g Protein		
		Lipid N	Lipid P	Lipid Chl[2]
$CHCl_3$-MeOH (2:1)	252	3.2	2.2	12.2
$CHCl_3$-MeOH-H_2O (2:2:1)	243	2.6	1.8	12.0
Acetone (hot)	229	2.0	0.8	11.3
C_2H_5OH-$(C_2H_5)_2O$ (3:1)	207	2.1	1.2	8.2
Acetone (room temp.)	183	1.6	0.3	11.4

Source: Shah (1971B).
[1]Five grams of wheat LPC used in each extraction test.
[2]Lipid Chl = Lipid chlorophyll.

$CHCl_3$-MeOH, 2:1, Method (Shah 1971A)

The protein coagulum of LPC powder (Fig. 11.1) is adjusted to a moisture content of about 80%. The moist material is extracted three times at room temperature with a five-fold volume of $CHCl_3$-MeOH (2:1, v/v). The extracts are combined and washed with water (⅕ the volume of the $CHCl_3$-MeOH). The lower ($CHCl_3$) layer, which contains the lipid, is removed, dried over Na_2SO_4, and concentrated *in vacuo.*

Water-saturated *n*-Butanol Method (Hudson and Karis 1973)

Nonpolar lipids are extracted from 10 g LPC samples with four successive 30 ml aliquots of petroleum (pet.) ether. The samples, after solvent removal, are used for extraction of polar lipids with water-saturated *n*-butanol (30 ml per 10 g LPC). The solvents are removed *in vacuo* and the polar and nonpolar residues are dissolved in $CHCl_3$-MeOH (2:1). Nonlipid contaminants are removed by an aqueous wash of the $CHCl_3$-MeOH-lipid mixture by the method of Folch-Pi *et al.* (1957). Hudson and Warwick (1977) reported that this extraction method removes 98% of all lipids present in LPCs.

10% Water in Acetone Method (Nagy *et al.* 1978A)

The moist protein coagulum is vigorously stirred for 5 min with a solution of 10% water in acetone (1 ml/10 g protein coagulum) and centrifuged. The supernatant is decanted and the procedure repeated five or more times until the extract is devoid of the green chlorophyll color. A final extraction is made with 95% ethanol to remove residual acetone. The acetone and ethanol extracts are combined, the mixture is concentrated *in vacuo* to an aqueous slurry and the slurry is partitioned between equal volumes of $CHCl_3$ and water. The $CHCl_3$ layer is removed, and the aqueous layer is extracted three times with $CHCl_3$. The four $CHCl_3$ extracts are combined, dried over Na_2SO_4, and concentrated *in vacuo*. If the crude lipid is not immediately processed, it is stored in benzene-absolute ethanol (4:1) at about 0°C.

Figure 11.4 is a general scheme for analysis of the lipids extracted from leaf protein preparations. The lipid extract (200–300 mg) in 50 ml of benzene-absolute ethanol is divided and 20% is used for the preparation of fatty acid methyl esters (FAMEs). The FAMEs are prepared by the NaOH-BF_3-MeOH procedure of Nordby and Nagy (1971), and are purified by thin layer chromatography (TLC) on silica gel with hexane-ethyl ether (90:10). The purified FAMEs are separated by gas-liquid chromatography (GLC) on a glass column (1.52 m × 4 mm id) packed with 3% SP 1000 (manufactured by Supelco Co., Bellefonte, PA.), and are quantitated with an electronic integrator (Nagy *et al.* 1978A). Of the remaining crude lipids, 40% is purified by the method of Wuthier (1966), and 40% is used for chlorophyll, carotenoid, and other pigment analyses (AOAC 1965).

The purified lipid is divided as follows: 4% for dry weight determination, 2% for organic phosphate determination (Bartlett 1959), 80% for lipid class fractionation, and 14% for saponification. The lipid fraction for saponification is dissolved in 5 ml of 6% KOH in 95% ethanol, and the mixture is

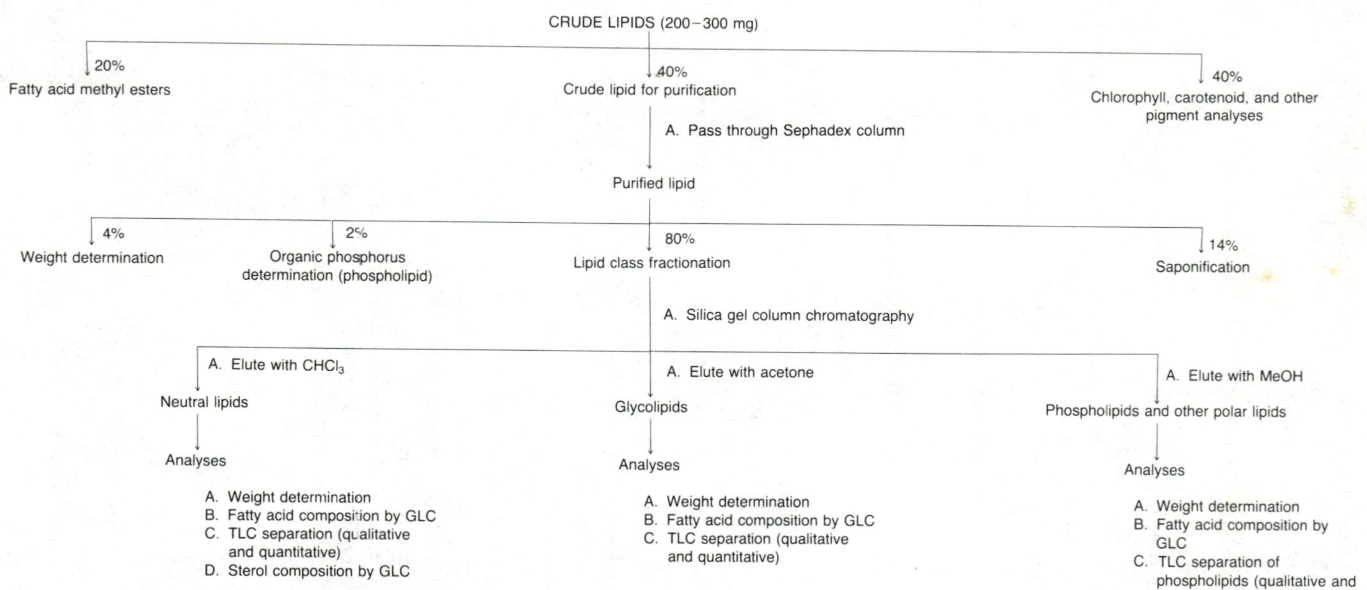

Fig. 11.4. Schematic for analysis of LPC lipids.

heated in a sealed acylation tube at 105°C for 1 hr. The mixture is then divided into saponifiable, nonsaponifiable, and residual fractions by a series of extraction and acidification steps, and a weight is obtained for each fraction (Nagy *et al.* 1978A). Further analyses of the saponifiable and nonsaponifiable fractions by TLC and GLC might be warranted if information were desired on the fatty acid, sterol, and hydrocarbon compositions.

Eighty percent of the purified lipid is fractionated into three principal classes—neutral lipids, glycolipids, and phospholipids and other polar lipids—by silica gel column chromatography (Rouser *et al.* 1967; Nagy *et al.* 1975). Weight determination, fatty acid analysis, and TLC separation are conducted on each of the three lipid classes. For TLC the individual lipid class is spotted, along with appropriate standards, onto a 250 μ silica gel G plate and developed in the following solvent systems: neutral lipids (hexane-diethyl ether-acetic acid, 88:10:2), glycolipids (chloroform-methanol, 17:3), and phospholipids and other polar lipids (chloroform-methanol-acetic acid-water, 170:30:20:7). After development, the plates are sprayed with nonspecific or specific reagents. Nonspecific reagents may be Rhodamine 6G, 2′, 7′-dichlorofluorescein, and iodine. Specific reagents may be Bail's orcinol reagent for sugars, Dittmer and Lester's reagent for phospholipids, ninhydrin reagent for primary amines, and 50% sulfuric acid with heating at 140°C for 10 min to produce specific colors for sugars and sterols. Quantitative TLC methods of analyzing the individual lipids that comprise a specific class are found in extensive detail elsewhere: neutral lipids (Blank *et al.* 1964; Mahadevan 1967; Nagy and Nordby 1970), glycolipids (Roughan and Batt 1968, 1969), and phospholipids (Blank *et al.* 1964; Rouser *et al.* 1970).

REFERENCES

AKESON, W.R. and STAHMANN, M.A. 1965. Nutritive value of leaf protein concentrate, an *in vitro* digestion study. J. Agric. Food Chem. *13*, 145–148.

ALLISON, R.M. 1971. Factors influencing the availability of lysine in leaf protein. *In* Leaf Protein: Its Agronomy, Preparation, Quality and Use. N.W. Pirie (Editor). Blackwell Scientific Publications, Oxford.

AOAC. 1965. Pigments. *In* Official Methods of Analysis of the Association of Official Agricultural Chemists, 10th Edition. Assoc. Off. Agric. Chem., Washington, DC.

ARKCOLL, D.B. 1973. The preservation and storage of leaf protein preparations. J. Sci. Food Agric. *24*, 437–445.

ARYA, S.S., PARIHAR, D.B. and NATH, H. 1972. Interaction of malonaldehyde in foods. I. Reaction with sulfur amino acids. J. Food Sci. Technol. *9* (4) 185–190.

BARTLETT, G.R. 1959. Phosphorus assay in column chromatography. J. Biol. Chem. *234*, 466–468.

BETSCHART, A.A. and KINSELLA, J.E. 1974. Influence of storage on composition, amino acid content and solubility of soybean leaf protein concentrate. J. Agric. Food Chem. *22*, 116–123.

BETSCHART, A.A. and KINSELLA, J.E. 1975. Changes in the relative concentration of fatty acids in stored soybean leaf protein concentrate. J. Food Sci. *40*, 271–273.

BICKOFF, E.M., BOOTH, A.N., DE FREMERY, D., EDWARDS, R.H., KNUCKLES, B.E., MILLER, R.E., SAUNDERS, R.M. and KOHLER, G.O. 1975. Nutritional evaluation of alfalfa leaf protein concentrate. *In* Protein Nutritional Quality of Foods and Feeds. M. Friedman (Editor). Marcel Dekker, New York.

BLANK, M.L., SCHMIT, J.A. and PRIVETT, O.S. 1964. Quantitative analysis of lipids by thin-layer chromatography. J. Am. Oil Chem. Soc. *41*, 371–376.

BRADDOCK, R.J. and DUGAN, L.R. 1973. Reaction of autoxidizing linoleate with Coho salmon myosin. J. Am. Oil. Chem. Soc. *50*, 343–347.

BUCHANAN, R.A. 1969. Effect of storage and lipid extraction on the properties of leaf protein. J. Sci. Food Agric. *20*, 359–364.

BURTON, R.M. 1974. Lipid extraction and separation procedures. *In* Fundamentals of Lipid Chemistry. R.M. Burton and F.C. Guerra (Editors). BI-Science Publications Division, Webster Groves, MO.

BUTKUS, H. 1967. The reaction of myosin with malonaldehyde. J. Food Sci. *32*, 432–434.

BYERS, M. 1971A. The amino acid composition of some leaf protein preparations. *In* Leaf Protein: Its Agronomy, Preparation, Quality, and Use. N.W. Pirie (Editor). Blackwell Scientific Publications, Oxford.

BYERS, M. 1971B. Amino acid composition and *in vitro* digestibility of some protein fractions from three species of leaves of various ages. J. Sci. Food Agric. *22*, 242–251.

CARTER. H.E. and KOOB, J.L. 1969. Sphingolipids in bean leaves *(Phaseolus vulgaris)*. J. Lipid Res. *10*, 363–369.

CHANG, S.S. and KUMMEROW, F.A. 1955. An instrumental method for measuring the degree of reversion and rancidity of edible oils. J. Am. Oil Chem. Soc. *32*, 341–344.

CRITCHLEY, C. and HEINZ, E. 1973. Characterization and enzymatic synthesis of acyl galactosyl monoglyceride. Biochim. Biophys. Acta *326*, 184–193.

CUQ, J.L., PROVANSAL, M., GUILLEUX, F. and CHEFTEL, C. 1973. Oxidation of methionine residues of casein by hydrogen peroxide. Effects of *in vitro* digestibility. J. Food Sci. *38*, 11–13.

DINSMORE, H.L. and NAGY, S. 1971. A rapid gas chromatographic method for studying volatile carbonyl compounds from orange juice and their changes during storage. J. Agric. Food Chem. *19*, 517–519.

DUCKWORTH, J. and WOODHAM, A.A. 1961. Leaf Protein concentrates. I. Effect of source of raw material and method of drying on protein value for chicks and rats. J. Sci. Food Agric. *12*, 5–12.

EDWARDS, R.H., MILLER, R.E., DE FREMERY, D., KNUCKLES, B.E., BICKOFF, E.M. and KOHLER, G.O. 1975. Pilot plant production of an edible white fraction leaf protein concentrate from alfalfa. J. Agric. Food Chem. *23*, 620–626.

FAFUNSO, M.A., BASSIR, O. and OKE, O.L. 1976. *In vitro* digestibility of some leaf protein preparations using papain. Nutr. Rep. Int. (Nuribl.) *14*, 353–358.

FAO. 1970. Amino Acid Content of Foods and Biological Data on Proteins. Food and Agriculture Organization of the United Nations, Rome.

FOLCH-PI, J., LEES, M. and SLOANE STANLEY, G.H. 1957. A simple method for the isolation and purification of total lipids from animal tissues. J Biol. Chem. *226*, 497–509.

GALLIARD, T. and MERCER, E.I. 1975. Recent Advances in the Chemistry and Biochemistry of Plant Lipids. Academic Press, New York.

GARDNER, H.W., WEISLEDER, D. and KLEIMAN, R. 1976. Addition of N-acetylcysteine to linoleic acid hydroperoxide. Lipids *11*, 127–134.

GODNEV, T.N. and EFREMOVA, R.V. 1958. The absorption spectra of chlorophyll in the living leaf tissue. Inzh. Fiz. Zh. Akad. Nauk Beloruss. SSR *1*, 91–95 (Chem. Abstr. *52*, 13015a).

HAWKE, J.C. 1973. Lipids. *In* Chemistry and Biochemistry of Herbage. G.W. Butler and R.W. Bailey (Editors). Academic Press, New York.

HEINZ, E. 1967. Acylgalactosyl diglyceride from leaf homogenates. Biochim. Biophys. Acta *144*, 321–332. (German)

HEINZ, E., RULLKOTTER, J. and BUDZIKIEWICZ, H. 1974. Acyl digalactosyl diglyceride from leaf homogenates. Hoppe-Seyler's Z. Physiol. Chem. *355*, 612–616.

HENRY, K.M. and FORD, J.E. 1965. The nutritive value of leaf protein concentrates determined in biological tests with rats and by microbiological methods. J. Sci. Food Agric. *16*, 425–432.

HITCHCOCK, C. and NICHOLS, B.W. 1971. Plant Lipid Biochemistry. Academic Press, New York.

HOFFMAN, G. 1962. Vegetable oils. *In* Lipids and Their Oxidation. H.W. Schultz, E.A. Day and R.O. Sinnhuber (Editors). AVI Publishing Co., Westport, CT.

HUDSON, B.J.F. and KARIS, I.G. 1973. Aspects of vegetable structural lipids. I. The lipids of leaf protein concentrate. J. Sci. Food Agric. *24*, 1541–1550.

HUDSON, B.J.F. and KARIS, I.G. 1974. Effect of crop maturity on leaf lipids. J. Sci. Food Agric. *25*, 1491–1502.

HUDSON, B.J.F. and KARIS, I.G. 1976. Stability of lipids and proteins in leaf protein concentrates. J. Sci. Food Agric. *27*, 443–448.

HUDSON, B.J.F. and WARWICK, M.J. 1977. Lipid stabilization in leaf protein concentrates from ryegrass. J. Sci. Food Agric. *28*, 259–264.

JARENBACK, J. and LILJEMARK, A. 1975. Ultrastructural changes during frozen storage of cod. III. Effects of linoleic acid and linoleic acid hydroperoxides on myofibrillar proteins. J. Food Technol. *10*, 437–452.

KAREL, M., SCHAICH, K. and ROY, R.B. 1975. Interaction of peroxidizing methyl linoleate with some proteins and amino acids. J. Agric. Food Chem. *23*, 159–163.

KEENEY, M. 1962. Secondary degradation products. *In* Lipids and Their Oxidation. H.W. Schultz, E.A. Day and R.O. Sinnhuber (Editors). AVI Publishing Co., Westport, CT.

KINSELLA, J.E. 1970. Evaluation of plant leaf protein as a source of food protein. Chem. Ind. *17*, 550–554.

KOENIG, F. 1971. Concentration of some lipids in the chloroplast of *Zea mays* and *Antirrhinum majus* (snapdragon). Z. Naturforsch. *26*, 1180–1187. (German)

KOHLER, G.O., BICKOFF, E.M. and DE FREMERY, D. 1976. Green leaves—A potential new source of protein for human nutrition. Univ. Calif. Spec. Publ. *3058*, 116–125.

KOLATTUKUDY, P.E. 1976. Chemistry and Biochemistry of Natural Waxes. Elsevier. New York.

KUZMICKY, D.D., KOHLER, G.O. and BICKOFF, E.M. 1972. Utilization of Pro-Xan as a protein source for broilers. 11th Tech. Alfalfa Conf. Proc., 1972, Berkeley, CA, U.S. Dep. Agric. *ARS-74-60*.

LEA, C.H. and PARR, L.J. 1961. Some observations on the oxidative deterioration of the lipids of crude leaf protein. J. Sci. Food Agric. *12*, 785–790.

LIMA, I.H., RICHARDSON, T. and STAHMANN, M.A. 1965. Fatty acids in some leaf protein concentrates. J. Agric. Food Chem. *13*, 143–145.

MAHADEVAN, V. 1967. TLC of neutral glycerides. *In* Lipid Chromatographic Analysis, Vol. 1. G.V. Marinetti (Editor). Marcel Dekker, New York.

MARTIN, J.T. and JUNIPER, B.E. 1970. The Cuticles of Plants. St. Martin's Press, New York.

MAZLIAK, P., DOUADY, D., DEMANDRE, C. and KADER, J.C. 1975. Exchange processes between organelles involved in membrane lipid biosynthesis. *In* Recent Advances in the Chemistry and Biochemistry of Plant Lipids. T. Galliard and E.I. Mercer (Editors). Academic Press, New York.

MORRISON, J.E. and PIRIE, N.W. 1961. The large-scale production of protein from leaf extracts. J. Sci. Food Agric. *12*, 1–5.

NAGY, S. and NORDBY, H.E. 1970. The effects of storage conditions on the lipid composition of commercially prepared orange juice. J. Agric. Food Chem. *18*, 593–597.

NAGY, S., NORDBY, H.E. and SMOOT, J.M. 1975. The lipid composition of commercially canned single-strength orange juice. J. Am. Oil Chem. Soc. *52*, 121–123.

NAGY, S., NORDBY, H.E. and TELEK, L. 1978A. Lipid distributions in green leaf protein concentrates from four tropical leaves. J. Agric. Food Chem. *26*, 701–706.

NAGY, S., TELEK, L., HALL, N.T. and BERRY, R.E. 1978B. Potential food uses for protein from tropical and subtropical plant leaves. J. Agric. Food Chem. *26*, 1016–1028.

NICHOLS, B.W., STUBBS, J.M. and JAMES, A.T. 1967. *In* Biochemistry of Chloroplasts, Vol. 2. T.W. Goodwin (Editor). Academic Press, New York.

NJAA, L.R., UTNE, F. and BRAEKKAN, O.R. 1968. Anti-oxidant properties of methionine esters. Nature *218*, 571–572.

NORDBY, H.E. and NAGY, S. 1971. Comparative citrus fatty acid profiles of triglycerides, monogalactosyl diglycerides, steryl esters and esterified steryl glucosides. Lipids *6*, 554–561.

NORDBY, H.E., NAGY, S. and HALL, N. 1976. Fatty acids of monogalactosyl diglycerides of *Citrus*. Phytochemistry *15*, 957–960.

OKE, O.L. and UMOH, I.B. 1974. Nutritive value of leaf protein: A note on the comparison of *in vitro* and *in vivo* methods. Nutr. Rep. Int. (Nuribl.) *10*, 397–403.

OSIPOVA, O.P. 1957. State of chlorophyll in chloroplasts. Fiziol. Rast. *4*, 28–32 (Chem. Abstr. *52*, 11188e).

PIRIE, N.W. 1971. Leaf Protein: Its Agronomy, Preparation, Quality and Use. Blackwell Scientific Publications, Oxford.

POINCELOT, R.P. 1973. Isolation and lipid composition of spinach chloroplast envelope membranes. Arch. Biochem. Biophys. *159*, 134–142.

ROSENBERG, A. and GOUAUX, J. 1967. Quantitive and compositional changes in monogalactosyl and digalactosyl diglycerides during light-induced formation of chloroplasts in *Euglena gracilis*. J. Lipid Res. *8*, 80–83.

ROUBAL, W.T. and TAPPFIL, A.L. 1966. Damage to proteins, enzymes and amino acids by peroxidizing lipids. Arch. Biochem. Biophys. *113*, 5–8.

ROUGHAN, P.G. and BATT, R.D. 1968. Quantitative analysis of sulfolipid (Sulfoquinovosyl diglyceride) and galactolipids (monogalactosyl and digalactosyl diglycerides) in plant tissues. Anal. Biochem. *22*, 74–88.

ROUGHAN, P.G. and BATT, R.D. 1969. The glycerolipid composition of leaves. Phytochemistry *8*, 363–369.

ROUSER, G., FLEISCHER, S. and YAMAMOTO, A. 1970. Two-dimensional thin-layer chromatographic separation of polar lipids and determination of phospholipids by phosphorus analysis of spots. Lipids *5*, 494–496.

ROUSER, G., KRITCHEVSKY, G. and YAMAMOTO, A. 1967. Column chromatographic and associated procedures for separation and determination of phosphatides and glycolipids. *In* Lipid Chromatographic Analysis, Vol. 1. G.V. Marinetti (Editor). Marcel Dekker, New York.

SAUNDERS, R.M., CONNOR, M.A., BOOTH, A.N., BICKOFF, E.M. and KOHLER, G.O. 1973. Measurement of digestibility of alfalfa protein concentrates by *in vivo* and *in vitro* methods. J. Nutr. *130*, 530–535.

SCHULTZ, H.W., DAY, E.A. and SINNHUBER, R.O. 1962. Lipids and Their Oxidation. AVI Publishing Co., Westport, CT.

SHAH, F.H. 1969. *Cited by* R.A. BUCHANAN. 1969. Effect of storage and lipid extraction on the properties of leaf protein. J. Sci. Food Agric. *20*, 359–364.

SHAH, F.H. 1971A. Effect of heat on the extractability of lipid from leaf protein meal. Pak. J. Sci. Ind. Res. *14*, 492–496.

SHAH, F.H. 1971B. Effect of solvents on the extractability of lipids from leaf proteins. Pak. J. Sci. Ind. Res. *14*, 207–210.

SHAH, F.H. UD-DIN, R. and SALAM, A. 1967. Effect of heat on the digestibility of leaf proteins. Part I. Toxicity of the lipids and their oxidation products. Pak. J. Sci. Ind. Res. *10*, 39–41.

SLUMP, P. and SCHREUDER, H.A.W. 1973. Oxidation of methionine and cystine in foods treated with hydrogen peroxide. J. Sci. Food Agric. *24*, 657–661.

SMITH, E.B. and PENA, P.M. 1977. Use of *Tetrahymena pyriformis* W to evaluate protein quality of leaf protein concentrates. J. Food Sci. *42*, 674–676.

STAHMANN, M.A. 1976. Coagulation of protein from the juices of green plants by fermentation and the preservation thereof. U.S. Pat. 3,975,546. Aug. 17.

STUMPF, P.K. 1975. Biosynthesis of fatty acids in chloroplasts. *In* Recent Advances in the Chemistry and Biochemistry of Plant Lipids. T. Galliard and E.I. Mercer (Editors). Academic Press, New York.

TANNENBAUM, S.R., BARTH, H. and LE ROUX, J.P. 1969. Loss of methionine in casein during storage with autooxidizing methyl linoleate. J. Agric. Food Chem. *17*, 1353–1354.

THOMPSON, G.A. 1965. Cellular membranes. *In* Plant Biochemistry. J. Bonner and J.E. Varner (Editors). Academic Press, New York.

WEISSBERGER, A., PROSKAUER, E.S., RIDDICK, J.A. and TOOPS, E.E. 1955. Technique of Organic Chemistry, Vol. 7. Interscience Publishers, New York.

WILLSTATTER, R. and STOLL, A. 1913. Investigations on Chlorophyll: Methods and Results. Springer Verlag, Berlin.

WINTERMANS, J.F. 1960. Concentration of phosphatides and glycolipides in leaves and chloroplasts. Biochim. Biophys. Acta *44*, 49–54.

WOLDEGIORGIS, G. 1976. Protein nutritional quality studies of leaf protein concentrates from alfalfa (*Medicago sativa* L.) and processed foods. Ph.D. Thesis. University of Wisconsin, Madison.

WUTHIER, R.E. 1966. Purification of lipids from nonlipid contaminants on Sephadex bead columns. J. Lipid Res. *7*, 558–561.

YONG, S.H. and KAREL, M. 1978. Reaction of histidine with methyl linoleate: Characterization of the histidine degradation products. J. Am. Oil Chem. Soc. *55*, 352–357.

ZIRLIN, A. and KAREL, M. 1969. Oxidation effects in a freeze-dried gelatin-methyl linoleate system. J. Food Sci. *34*, 160–164.

12

Toxic Substances in Potential Plant Sources for Leaf Protein Preparation

Lehel Telek

Extraction and heat fractionation of leaf proteins could offer a white protein concentrate for human nutrition as well as a green protein concentrate associated with lipids, carotenoids, and chlorophyll for nonruminant animal feed. In addition, the pressed fibrous residue could still be a good feed for ruminants in the form of pellets, silage, or direct consumption. With this new technology, one single plant species could serve man, ruminant, and nonruminant animals simultaneously.

However, the search for suitable plant sources for LPC extraction and fractionation must give special attention to the presence of potentially harmful toxic ingredients occurring naturally in many plants. This precaution is especially warranted when species of plants are selected which are not commonly cultivated. Thus, their chemical constitution usually has been studied only superficially or not at all.

The toxicity of plants has been of interest since prehistoric times. Some plants were extracted for direct use in killing fish and animals. They were used as weapons in the form of arrow poison or in the hands of the law; for example, the lethal extract of deadly hemlock (*Conium maculatum* L.) offered to Socrates. Plants were the sources of ancient medicine and even with the rapid advance in the use of synthetic chemotherapeutic agents, new types of medicines of plant origin are being found, such as reserpine, vinblastine, and vincristine, and plant sources of steroid hormones: diosgenine, hecogenine, and solasodine. The cardiac glycosides of digitalis, the antimalarial substances such as quinine, amebicides like emetine, and pain killers like the opiates and cocaine have been important natural medicaments since ancient times. Interest in the chemistry and toxicology of natural compounds predates the birth of systematic organic chemistry. The steady advance of analytical methodology spread to food analysis and later to animal feed toxicology. New, precise analytical procedures shed light on toxic, teratogenic, and antinutrient factors in plants used as human food or animal feed, and hundreds of injurious compounds have been recognized, isolated, and characterized.

It is interesting to note that some plants are shunned by animals. It was observed by the author that in the dry season in the arid pastures of southwestern Puerto Rico, the lush, thick leaves of *Calotropis procera* are the only green material left. It appeared that the emaciated cattle grazed more soil than grass, and completely ignored the luring toxic plants. Similarly, the author observed that grazing goats in the dry season avoided the lush leaves of *Crotalaria* and choose the brown, lifeless grasses instead.

Linnaeus remarked that all animals refused to eat the toxic water pepper, *Polyonum hydropiper*. However, this instinct of avoiding toxic plants is not always present. Poisonous plants endanger the health of man and animal. The yearly economic loss in livestock in the United States has been estimated to be over $50 million (Schmitz *et al.* 1968). There is a definite danger if animals cannot make their own selection, as is the case in feeding leaf protein concentrates. Toxic or antinutrient factors could be concealed when mixed with good-tasting feed ingredients; thus, the feed mixes could be toxic baits for animals. It is dangerous to assume that the presence of alkaloids in a leaf species is unlikely to be an obstacle to its use as a source of LPC. All the alkaloids are soluble in an acid medium since, through their phenolic hydroxy group, they can be attached by strong hydrogen bonds to proteins. They can be occluded by coagulated proteins and can be disguised by the flavor of other substances. Consequently, animals can accept a protein concentrate in spite of the presence of highly toxic ingredients.

The level of toxic ingredients cannot be predicted. It is influenced by many factors in diverse magnitudes. Seasonal variations in the concentration of toxicants are well known. Climatic conditions such as drought increase cyanogenesis in sorghum or cassava leaves, or the level of estrogens in trifoliums. The age of the plant part and the environment where it is growing may also affect concentration of toxins. The young leaves of sorghum are higher in cyanogen glycoside content than the old. Cassava leaves which are low in cyanogens in Colombia could have higher toxic contents in Puerto Rico. In leaf protein extraction, the toxic ingredient can be widely distributed in the products. Mimosine, a toxic amino acid, was found in every leaf protein fraction prepared from *Leucaena leucocephala* (Telek and Evans 1978).

Some toxic ingredients can be concentrated in the green protein fraction; others will remain, at least partially, in the fibrous residue. Some water-soluble toxic ingredients are concentrated in the deproteinized juice and can be washed out from the protein concentrates. In some processes this fraction is evaporated to a syrup and recycled with the fibrous residue. Care must be taken that toxic ingredients which affect ruminants are not present in this fraction.

The purpose of this presentation is to review those toxic plant ingredients which could have a role in leaf protein extraction and fractionation. In the following pages only the naturally potential toxic ingredients will be considered. Since the role of saponins is exceptionally important in alfalfa leaf proteins, it has been treated in a separate chapter by Cheeke, (Chapter 13). The well-known antinutrient effect of polyphenols and tannins is also discussed by Pierpoint in a separate chapter (Chapter 10). Pesticide residues will not be discussed in this study nor will mycotoxins. However, due to the widespread effect of the excessive use of nitrogen fertilizer, the dangerously high nitrate accumulation in plants will be discussed. Sudan grass was suggested as an important plant material for LPC production for the tropics because of its high protein content and impressive yields under good management and high-level nitrogen fertilization. However, nitrate accumulation in the leaves persists in the leaf protein extract.

The extraction of cassava leaves for LPC preparation is a logical attempt to utilize the by-product of the starchy, practically protein-free cassava root crop to prepare protein for food. The investigation of the fate of cyanogenic glycosides in the leaf protein process using cassava leaves is therefore important.

Chibnall (1939) extracted proteins from *Brassica oleracea* in the early 1920s. Potentials of leaf protein production from various leafy wastes in West Pakistan were studied by Hussain *et al.* (1968), who estimated that 30,000 metric tons (MT) of LPC could be produced from radish leaves in their country. Young leaves of *Brassica nigra* give good protein yields (Telek 1979). *Brassica carinata*, usually an oilseed crop, showed good potential in Texas (Brown *et al.* 1975) as a leaf protein source. Because of the early spring or late fall harvesting time of rape and mustard, the leaves are used in protein preparation in Hungary in order to prolong the manufacturing season. All *Brassica* species contain mild or potential goitrogenic glucosinolates which could even be transmitted to the milk of animals after ingestion. It is an important safeguard to follow the pathway and chemical changes during the process of leaf protein fractionation from brassicas.

Goodall in 1950 suggested that a high protein feed could be produced from sugar beet tops, and Pirie mentioned the possible use of wastes of sugar beet tops as an LPC source. In this species, the oxalic acid content is high. *Amaranthus* and *Chenopodium*, suggested as best LPC sources in Sweden (Carlsson 1975), are also very high in insoluble oxalates.

Protein of the leaves of potato was studied by Pirie at Rothamsted Experiment Station in Great Britain. The steroid glycoalkaloids solanine and chaconine could be present in LPC from the potato leaf. If the success of Fraction I (F I) protein prepared from tobacco expands the research to other *Solanum* species, the products will have to be checked for the presence of solasodine and tomatidine and, in the case of tobacco, nicotine.

Toxic amino acids are ingredients of some legume leaves. Mimosine is present in the leaves of the pantropical plant *Leucaena leucocephala*. *Indigo* species are high protein forage plants, but some species contain the hepatotoxic indospicine.

Toxins are often concentrated in seeds. During the harvesting of legumes, young seed pods could be processed, and the toxic ingredients could then enter the protein concentrate. Since temperatures are low (55° to 64°C) during protein coagulation, antinutrient factors could be coextracted and precipitated with the products.

The use of mixed sward or roadside grass cuttings as a source of LPC results in a double hazard: toxic plants and seed in which the toxic ingredients are highly concentrated could both be harvested. Thus, this source for protein concentrate should be rejected.

The presence of toxic ingredients should be noted and measured and analytical controls established; only with these safeguards should plants containing toxic substances be utilized as sources for protein concentrate for humans and animals.

In the following pages, specific toxic ingredients of potential plants for leaf protein concentrate production will be discussed. Their chemistry and toxicology and analytical methods for their detection and quantitative determination will be reviewed.

CYANOGENIC GLYCOSIDES

More than 1000 species of higher plants contain cyanogenic glycosides as secondary compounds. These are built according to a uniform structure from cyanhydrins or hydroxynitriles as aglycons to which a sugar component is attached by a glycosidic bond.

The first cyanogenic glycoside, amygdalin, was isolated in 1830 by Robiquet and Boultron-Charlard. Next, described was linamarin in 1891. Since then, not more than 20 other compounds have been characterized. Five amino acids, valine, leucine, isoleucine, phenylalanine, and tyrosine, are the primary precursors of the aglycons. The C-C=N moiety of these amino acids is incorporated intact into the cyanogenetic glycosides (Conn and Butler 1969) (Fig. 12.1).

Detailed studies of cyanogenic glycosides can be found in numerous reviews: Conn (1969, 1978, 1979A,B, Eyjolfsson (1970), Nahrstedt (1973), Miller (1973), Tapper and Reay (1973), and Seigler (1975, 1976).

This section will focus on those cyanogenic compounds which could be of importance in the preparation of LPC concentrates: namely, dhurrin of the grasses, and linamarin and lotaustralin of white clover and cassava leaves.

Dhurrin, (s)-*p*-hydroxymandelonitrile-β-D-glycopyranoside (Fig. 12.2), was first isolated by Dunstan and Henry (1902). It is found in *Sorghum vulgare*, *Panicum maximum* Jacq., and *Panicum muticans* Forsk. The first isolates were rather crude preparations and its chemical properties could not be defined. Mao *et al.* (1965) reported an improved preparation of this

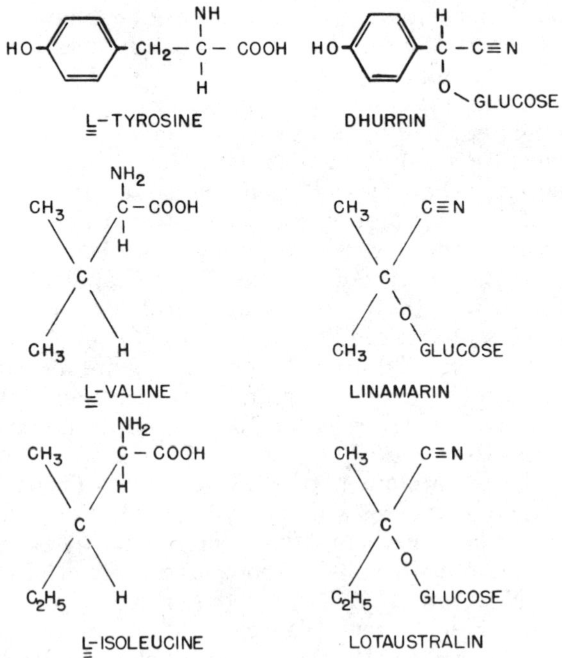

L-TYROSINE DHURRIN

L-VALINE LINAMARIN

L-ISOLEUCINE LOTAUSTRALIN

Fig. 12.1. Cyanogenic glycosides and their amino acid precursors.

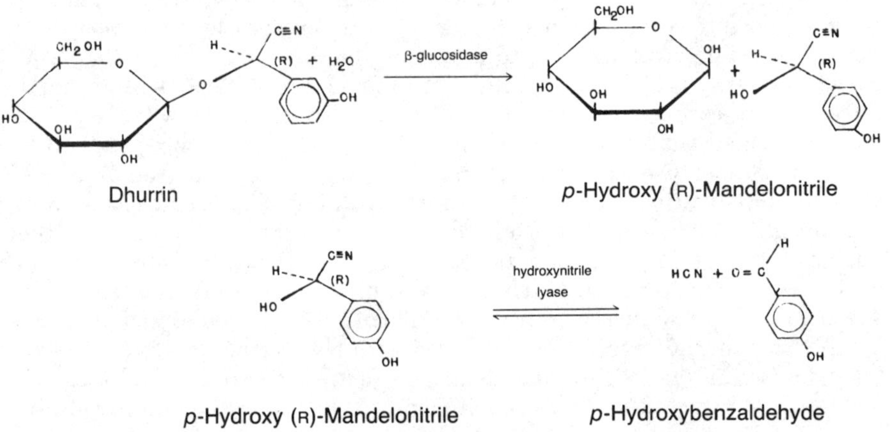

β-glucosidase

Dhurrin p-Hydroxy (R)-Mandelonitrile

hydroxynitrile lyase

p-Hydroxy (R)-Mandelonitrile p-Hydroxybenzaldehyde

Fig. 12.2. Enzymatic decomposition of dhurrin to p-hydroxybenzaldehyde.

cyanogen glycoside. In their method, the sugar impurities were removed by yeast fermentation, and other impurities by ion exchange resins or cellulose column chromatography. The prepared compound was crystalline and had a well-defined melting point of 163°–165°C. The purity was demonstrated by paper chromatography. UV absorption maxima in neutral and acidic solution is at 230 nm, E = 1.07×10^4. In alkaline solution there is a bathochromic shift to max = 255 nm, E = 1.5×10^4.

Another improved preparation for the isolation of dhurrin extracted from etiolated seedlings of *Sorghum vulgare* with MeOH:$CHCl_3$:H_2O (12:5:3) has been reported by Reay (1969). The extracts were treated with basic lead acetate, the excess Pb ions being removed by sparging with hydrogen sulfide. The solution was concentrated and mixed with isopropanol. The isopropanol extract was chromatographed on a polyvinyl-pyrrolidone column and eluted with methanol-isopropanol (30:70) + 1 drop acetic acid, and finally with the same mixture in a 40:60 ratio. The eluted dhurrin separated in crystalline form.

The level of dhurrin in sorghum is influenced by many factors. Genetic variation was found by Collison (1919) and later this was confirmed by many others (Harrington 1966; Alvarado and Sylva 1967; Lloyd and Gray 1970; Gorz *et al.* 1977; and McBee and Miller 1980).

Sorghum plant parts differ in dhurrin concentration, and the cyanide content decreases with age of the plant. Wolf and Washko (1967) found that leaf blades without midrib were high in cyanide in all growth stages; midrib, sheath, and stem portions contained less with maturity. Decrease in HCN potential (HCN-p) of the entire plant was due to the proportional increase in weight of low cyanide-containing parts.

Benson *et al.* (1969) studied the relation of HCN-p of leaf samples to that of whole plants of sorghum and found that small portions of various leaves could be used to compare varieties for HCN-p, but that leaf samples were not suitable for estimating the total amount of dhurrin in the whole plant. Lloyd and Gray (1970) studied the dhurrin content of various plant parts during the life cycle of three cultivars of high, medium, and low HCN-p, and also confirmed that cyanide content of tillers, leaves, stems, heads, and roots had generally decreased with maturity. It has been reported that high nitrogen fertilization increases the dhurrin content (Boyd *et al.* 1938; Patel and Wright 1958; Jung *et al.* 1964). Harms and Tucker (1973) reported the effects of nitrogen fertilization, phosphate application, light intensity, and curing conditions on total N, HCN-p, and nitrate concentration of Sudan grass forages. Yield increases from N applications were found insignificant for the first cut; however, they increased with N increments through 88 kg N/ha for second and third cuts. Nitrogen fertilization increased total N, HCN-p, and nitrate concentration at each cut. In a growth chamber study, increased light intensity had little effect on HCN-p, but decreased the concentration of nitrates. High levels of soil P decreased both the HCN-p and nitrate concentration. However, the effect of N levels was found to be insignificant in growth chamber and field experiments (Gorashi *et al.* 1980).

Linamarin and Lotaustralin

The tropical root crop cassava or manioc (*Manihot esculenta* Crantz) is a staple for more than 400 million people in the lowland humid tropics. The roots of cassava are practically devoid of proteins; the leaves in contrast are very rich in protein. Therefore, it seemed logical to consider the leaves as a source of leaf concentrate, which could be used to enrich the starchy foods prepared from the tubers.

Cassava roots and leaves contain the cyanogenic glycosides linamarin (2-hydroxyisobutyronitrile-β-D-glucopyranoside) and (R)-lotaustralin or methyl-linamarin, (R)-(2-hydroxy-2-methylbutyronitrile-β-D-glucopyranoside) (Fig. 12.3), which are hydrolyzed on injury of tissues by the endogenous enzyme, linamarase (EC 3.2.1.21, linamarin β-D-glycoside glycohydrolase). Dunstan *et al.* (1906) reported that the main cyanogenic glycoside of the cassava is linamarin, which was isolated by Clapp *et al.* (1966) 60 years later. Butler and Conn (1964) demonstrated the presence of small quantities of lotaustralin, methyllinamarin, in the alcoholic extracts of cassava tubers by paper chromatography. The extracts were chromatographed in a Me-Et ketone-acetone-water (30:10:4) system. A weak spot (Rf 0.66) corresponding to methyllinamarin and a strong spot (Rf 0.52) corresponding to linamarin were found. The separation of methyllinamarin (lotaustralin) by column chromatography on silica gel with 5:1 chloroform-methanol as eluting solvent remained unsuccessful (Clapp *et al.* 1966).

Bissett *et al.* (1969) described the isolation and synthesis of lotaustralin. The separation of the glycoside was achieved by column chromatography and gas chromatography. The β-D-glycopyranosides of the enantiomeric hydroxynitriles were synthesized from acetobromoglucose and methylethylcyanohydrine. The formed epimer tetraacetates were separated by chromatography on a silica gel column with a benzene-ether solvent system. The less levorotatory of the synthetic glycosides have the R configuration at the asymmetric center of the aglycon. The compound was shown to be

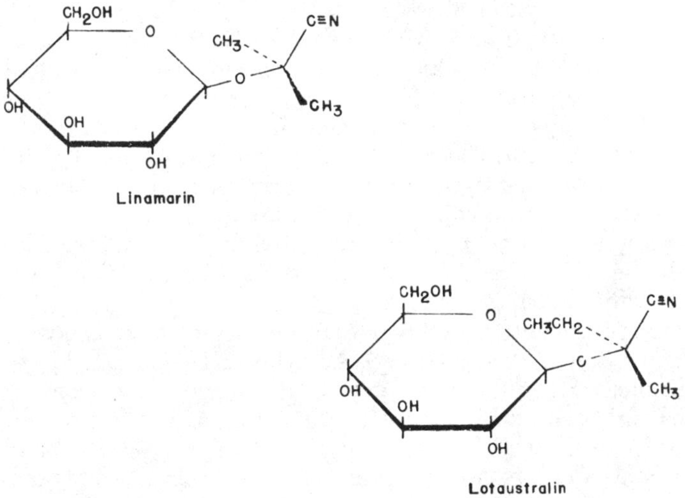

Fig. 12.3. Cyanogenic glycosides of cassava: Linamarin and lotaustralin.

identical with lotaustralin. Attempts to separate the small quantity of lotaustralin from the large main component, linamarin, remained unsuccessful. However, the presence of both was shown by gas-liquid chromatography (GLC). Trimethylsilyl (TMS) derivatives of known samples of linamarin and lotaustralin were separated efficiently on 6-, 10-, and 12-m SE30 columns. Samples of alcoholic extracts of cassava were prepurified on a silica gel column, trimethylsilylated, and chromatographed on an SE30 column. A weak peak with retention time equal to lotaustralin was obtained. After collecting the fractions in capillary tubes and mixing them in a 1:1 ratio, well-separated peaks appeared. Final positive identification of the lotaustralin was demonstrated with a mass spectrum of TMS derivative of authentic lotaustralin similarly collected from an SE30 column. The gas chromatograph method was found to be suitable for quantitative determination of linamarin and lotaustralin in cassava tubers.

Linamarin and lotaustralin have been reported to occur together in *Trifolium repens* in approximately equivalent amounts (Melville and Doak 1940). The total cyanogenetic glycoside content of 20 tested cultivars varied 100-fold: between 3.2 and 352 ng HCN released/g fresh weight (Butler 1965). The first preparative scale isolation of linamarin and lotaustralin from leaves of *Trifolium repens* involved continuous extraction of an aqueous syrup with ethyl acetate (Melville and Doak 1940). The method failed to give a crystalline product. Modified methods were reported in which the aqueous syrup was extracted with boiling ethyl acetate (Melville and Fraser 1951).

Detection of Cyanide in Plants

Guignard (1916) developed a simple method for determination of cyanide in beans based on reaction of cyanide with picric acid-saturated filter paper. Based on this procedure, Steyn (1977) described a test suitable for field testing cyanide (CN) content of plants. Filter paper was soaked in a solution of 5% sodium carbonate and 0.5% picric acid solution, dried, and cut to narrow strips. A few grams of shredded plants were placed in a small vial and 3 drops of chloroform were added. A strip of the test paper was inserted and the vial was closed tightly. If the CN content was relatively high, the paper turned red in few minutes. A similar qualitative test using paper strips impregnated with 1% picric acid and 10% sodium carbonate is included in the official methods of analysis AOAC (1975) for detection of cyanogenic glycosides in feeds.

A specific fluorometric method for the detection of cyanide was reported by Guilbault and Kramer (1965A). Addition of 0.5 ng cyanide to quinone monoxime benzene sulfonate ester yielded a highly fluorescent product. Of 30 anions, only cyanide reacted with fluorescence. In further development of fluorescence methods, Guilbault and Kramer (1965B) found that *p*-benzoquinone N-chloro-*p*-benzoquinonime and O-(*p*-nitrobenzene sulfonyl) quinone monoxime are powerful reagents for a simple, direct method for specific detection and determination of small quantities of cyanide by fluorescence. The fluorescence produced by *p*-benzoquinone with cyanide is proportional to the cyanide concentration over the range 0.2 to 50 ng. With calibration of fluorescence vs. cyanide concentration, the amount of cyanide present may be determined with a deviation of 5%.

In other experiments where high sensitivity and development of aqueous system were attempted, Guilbault and Kramer (1966) found an ultrasensitive colorimetric method for cyanide determination using *p*-nitrobenzaldehyde and *o*-dinitrobenzene. *p*-Nitrobenzaldehyde reacts with cyanide specifically to give an active reductant which can reduce various compounds, such as *o*-dinitrobenzene, to form a highly-colored blue compound with a wavelength of maximum absorbance of 560 nm. Cyanide is regenerated and catalytic reaction occurs. Only *p*-nitro- and *p*-cyanobenzaldehyde of over 30 aldehydes tested reacted to form the reductive cyanohydrine, and only cyanide anion is detectable by this method.

Bennet and Tapper (1968) reported a sensitive method for detecting cyanogenic glycosides on paper or cellulose thin layer, where as little as 0.005 micromole was detected. The cellulose layer or paper was spotted, then sprayed with the corresponding enzyme solution, and covered with a polyethylene film and rigid glass plate. It was incubated, then sprayed with 10% sodium carbonate, and with 0.05% *p*-nitrobenzene and *p*-nitrobenzaldehyde in 2-methoxyethanol. Isonitrosobenzoyl lactone spray of 0.02 *M* intensified the mauve-colored spots. Dhurrin gave a purple spot.

Zitnak *et al.* (1977) described a simple quantitative procedure for the direct detection of the intact glycoside. In a new paper chromatography method, the separated linamarin was reacted with *p*-anisaldehyde 2% in ethyl alcohol containing 6 ml 85% phosphoric and 2 ml sulfuric acid. At 88°C, the reaction produced a pink to cherry red visible color, coupled with a brilliant pink fluorescence when viewed in longwave (366 nm) UV light. The ascending paper chromatography was developed with a solvent mixture of 1-butanol:ethanol:water (8:1:2) (Rf: 0.52–0.54 for linamarin and 0.58–0.61 for lotaustralin). Another, faster moving solvent system is very useful: ethyl acetate:acetone:water (Rf: 0.71–0.73 for linamarin, 0.82–0.84 for lotaustralin). Linamarin concentration was estimated visually by comparison of fluorescence in the unknowns with a set of calibration standards.

Enzymatic Hydrolysis of Cyanogen Glycosides

Analytical methods are based on enzymatic hydrolysis of cyanogen glycosides. The plants containing cyanogenic glycosides also have the necessary enzymes for release of the HCN, converting the glycoside to the sugar moiety and acetone or an aldehyde. The reaction proceeds in two steps. First, the enzymatic hydrolysis by β-glucosidase produces cyanohydrine and sugar. The cyanohydrine is subsequently dissociated by the catalytic action of oxynitrilase to yield the corresponding aldehyde or ketone and

HCN (Mao and Anderson 1967; Bove and Conn 1961) (Fig. 12.2). The enzymes are specific; emulsin (β-glucosidase of amygdalin type) hydrolyzes only the glycosides with cyclic aglyca, with different rates of hydrolysis. Other types of glycosides will be hydrolyzed very slowly or not at all. Linamarase, the enzyme which hydrolyzes linamarin swiftly, hydrolyzes dhurrin very slowly. Mao and Anderson (1965) found that glucosidase I isolated from vegetative tissues of sorghum, even after 10-fold purification, had little activity against dhurrin. Glucosidase II was extracted from vegetative tissues with 50% ammonium sulfate solution and purified 85-fold. When extracted from seeds in which it occurs in higher concentrations, the purification was 4-fold. It was found that the rate of hydrolysis of dhurrin with glycosidase II was 5.8 times more active than with glycosidase I.

Butler *et al.* (1965) studied linamarase prepared from linseed flax, *Linum usitatissimum* L., and, using a DEAE-cellulose column, separated the disaccharase activity from glucosidase activity and purified it by a factor of 500 over the activity in the initial crude extract. This separation was further improved by purification on Sephadex columns. The most successful method for linamarase purification was column electrophoresis on Sephadex G-25. It was found that linamarase migrated with higher speed to the anode than the main protein band. Purification of 105-fold was achieved in one step alone and no advantage was found by prepurification by DEAE-cellulose column chromatography and Sephadex gel filtration.

Wood (1966) reported a procedure for preparing and assaying crude linamarase. Fresh cassava peel (100 g) was homogenized with 100 ml of ice-cold 0.1 *M* acetate buffer, pH 5.5. The homogenate was filtered and the filtrate was used to extract two more 100 g batches of peel. The enzyme was precipitated by cold acetone at 2°C, and the crude enzyme was then dialyzed to remove HCN.

Wood (1966) reported a new method for the isolation of linamarin from cassava. Fresh cassava peel (100 g) was homogenized in 130 ml of ice-cold *n*-perchloric acid in a blender. The homogenate was filtered through celite into a receptacle cooled in ice. The process was repeated two times, using the previous filtrate to homogenize two additional batches of 100 g of peel. The final filtrate was neutralized to pH 7 with 10 *N* KOH and maintained at 0°C to precipitate potassium perchlorate. After treatment with basic lead acetate, and removal of excess lead by H_2S, the clear solution was deionized through Zeokarb 225 H^+ column and De Acidite FF (OH-resin). The solution was vacuum concentrated and kept over H_2SO_4. The syrup was dissolved in a butane:acetic acid:water mixture and was column chromatographed on cellulose powder and eluted with the same solvent. Five ml fractions were collected. Fraction I and Fraction II (F II) contained the pure glycoside. After vacuum concentration, addition of absolute alcohol, and vacuum evaporation, a white crystalline compound was formed.

Linamarase was prepared from white clover (*Trifolium repens* L.) by stepwise DEAE-cellulose chromatography (Hughes 1968). Maher and

Hughes (1971) extracted frozen minced clover with a Waring Blendor with 5 vol. of 80% ethanol. The combined filtrates were reduced *in vacuo* at 40°C and clarified with 40% lead acetate. After centrifuging, the precipitate was washed. The liquid phase and washings were treated with hydrogen sulfide. The lead sulfide was filtered and the solution deionized on Zeokarb 225 (H^+) and De Acidite E (OH^-). The solution was concentrated in vacuum and chromatographed on a Whatman cellulose column. The glycosides were crystallized from *n*-butanol.

Cooke *et al.* (1978) purified linamarase from cassava parenchymal tissue by extraction with acetate buffer, fractional precipitation with ammonium sulfate, followed by column chromatograpy on DEAE-cellulose, and by gel filtration with Sepharose 6B. The specific activity by this method was increased 350-fold.

Quantitative Determination of Cyanide Content of Plants

Analytical Methods for the Determination of Dhurrin in Sorghum. With the early methods of colorimetric assays, the HCN content of *Sorghum bicolor* L. (Moench) and *S. sudanense* (Piper) Staph was based on reaction of NaCN and sodium picrate. The plant material was macerated and the indigenous glycoside hydrolyzed the cyanogen to HCN, which was distilled or aerated into sodium carbonate solution (Nowosad and MacVicar 1940; Hogg and Ahlgren 1942).

A simple and rapid procedure for the determination of cyanogenic glycosides of cassava was reported by Wood (1965). The HCN was liberated by autolysis, followed by treatment with acid, and distilled into sodium carbonate solution, then reacted with picric acid and heated for 12 min in boiling water. After cooling, the absorptivity was measured at 530 nm in a spectrophotometer.

Dhurrin is decomposed by two enzymes to *p*-hydroxybenzaldehyde (PHBA). First, the glucose is split off the molecule, then the aglycon, *p*-hydroxymandelonitrile, decomposes to PHBA and HCN (Fig. 12.2). Akazawa *et al.* (1960) found that HCN and PHBA in alkaline hydrolysates of dhurrin were equivalent; thus, the reaction is applicable for assaying HCN by the 2,4-dinitrophenylhydrazone method. PHBA can also be measured directly by UV spectrophotometry at 330 nm.

Gorz *et al.* (1977) applied this method for HCN determination in sorghums. The extraction and hydrolysis were performed by autoclaving samples of seedlings in water. However, it was found that in maturing plants other UV-absorbing compounds overshadow the spectrum of PHBA, making the measurement difficult (Telek, unpublished, 1982). It was recognized that a valid method for dhurrin determination should include chromatographic separation of PHBA. Recently, two new methods have been developed (Telek and Jones, unpublished, 1983). One, by HPLC on reversed phase column, shows the array of compounds absorbing in the 330 nm area, which makes the direct spectrophotometric method inaccurate and nonspecific. For practical analysis, a rapid, simple GLC method using capillary column was found. Methyl paraben was selected as the internal standard.

Determination of Cyanide in Cassava. The colorimetric determination of cyanide is based on oxidation of CN^- to a cyanogenehalide CN^+x-. The CN^+ reacts with pyridine to form glutatonin anhydride, which couples with primary amines or compounds having reactive methylene hydrogens (RH_2) to yield colored Schiff bases (Konigs salt).

Lambert *et al.* (1975), searching for stable reagents for the Konigs reaction, studies N-chlorosuccinimide as an oxidant, stabilized with excess succinimide as the oxidizing solution.

Aldridge (1944) reported a method based on conversion of cyanide by bromine water to cyanogen bromide: $HCN + Br_2 \rightarrow CNBr + HBr$. The excess bromine is removed by sodium arsenite, and the cyanogen bromide is reacted with benzidine in diluted pyridine hydrochloride to give an intense orange to red solution. Basically, the same principle is recommended for cyanide determination in feed by the German Agricultural Handbook (Handb. Exp. Res. Methods Agric. 1975) except that, for removal of excess bromine instead of toxic arsenite, 5% aqueous ascorbic acid is recommended. In the official method of the European Common Market, the free and bound cyanides in feeds and bean varieties (lima bean and especially cassava meal) are liberated by mixing with freshly milled sweet almond seed. The cyanide is distilled into a measured amount of 0.02 *N* silver nitrate solution. The silver cyanide formed is filtered, and the excess silver nitrate is back-titrated by 0.02 *N* ammonium thiocyanate solution. One ml 0.02 *N* $AgNO_3$ is equivalent ot 0.54 mg HCN (Off. Methods Eur. Common Market 1971).

Bark and Higson (1964A) tested 46 amines to replace the carcinogenic benzidine from the Aldridge method of cyanide determination, and selected *p*-phenylene diamine (1964B). The sensitivity was increased to 0.005 ng/ml. However, the phenylene diamines were found to be powerful allergens. Nahrstedt (1977) decided to replace the carcinogenic and allergenic amines of the Aldridge method by anthranilic acid (2-aminobenzoic acid). The resultant colored compound developed in 10 min and had a maximum at 520 nm.

Cooke (1978) described an enzymatic assay for cassava roots and leaves. The plant material was extracted with orthophosphoric acid and filtered. Neutralized aliquots were incubated with exogenous linamarase. The cyanide present was determined spectrophotometrically by a modified chloramine-pyridine-pyrolazone method.

Recently, ion-selective electrodes have been used to measure the cyanide content of NaCN which could be formed by volatilization of HCN after hydrolysis of the cyanogenic glycoside and trapped into NaOH or Na_2CO_3

solutions. Others used the electrode method for direct measurement (Blaedel *et al.* 1971; Eck 1976; Gorz *et al.* 1977). Analyzing low CN-containing samples by a direct potentiometric method was found to be difficult.

Toxicity of Cyanogenic Glycosides

Generally, plants with 2000 ppm of cyanogenic glycosides in fresh weight are considered lethally toxic. In sorghum-Sudan, the cyanide content of the whole leaf of different cultivars was found to be between 431 + 31 and 1398 + 68 ppm, measured by spectrophotometry as *p*-hydroxybenzaldehyde (Gorz *et al.* 1977).

The maximum level of cyanide on clover pastures can be as high as 1760 ppm (Butler 1965). Cyanide content of cassava leaves is in the region of 500 ppm. Wet leaf protein concentrate contains about 30 ppm (fresh weight basis). The average lethal single oral dose of hydrogen cyanide for humans, sheep, and cattle is about the same: 2 mg/kg body weight. Acute hydrocyanic acid poisoning has killed many thousands of sheep, goats, and cattle in the South African Union. The species responsible are principally grasses, of which *Cynodon* species are the most dangerous (Steyn 1977). In chronic poisoning, when small quantities of hydrogen cyanide are ingested for a prolonged time, the central nervous system is attacked. Tropical ataxic neuropathy occurs widely in the cassava belt (Osuntokun 1981). As antidote, sodium thiosulfate is used for cattle, and hydroxocobalamin for humans.

Four factors which are of importance in cyanide poisoning are: the concentration of cyanide content in the plant, amount of plant intake, speed of release of HCN from plant material, and the rate of detoxification by the animal. The cyanide content of plant material is not a stable characteristic. Due consideration should be given to the wide limits between which the HCN content of species varies under different soil, fertilizer, and climatic conditions, and even at different periods of the day. A very complicated phenomenon is that the HCN contents of plants may change from hour to hour. Drought conditions, heat, frost, and direct sunlight increase the HCN content of plants.

The amount of intake of HCN-containing plants is regulated by need; hungry animals are more susceptible to poisoning because they ingest large quantities of toxic material at a very rapid rate.

The speed of release of HCN depends on many factors. It is proportional to the quantity of enzymes in the plant. Not only can the endogenous enzymes split the hydrogen cyanide, but active enzymes in other plants that are consumed may do so as well. Higher acidity of the digestive tract will also increase the rate of hydrolysis. The presence of nitrate may act synergistically with HCN in reducing the oxygen-carrying capacity of red blood cells (Steyn 1977).

Animals differ in the rate of detoxification. Ruminants are more susceptible since the rate of hydrolysis is high in the rumen.

Toxicity Symptoms

Hydrocyanic acid forms cyanmethemoglobin in the red blood cells and also inactivates the cytochrome enzyme system essential for tissue respiration. When oxygen is not transferred from the hemoglobin to the tissue cells, acute anoxia develops, and death is caused by asphyxia.

GLUCOSINOLATES

The Cruciferae are a family of more than 3000 species widely distributed around the world. They are the source of many foods: cabbage, chard, Brussels sprouts, mustard greens, cauliflower, turnip, broccoli, radish, Chinese cabbage, and the condiment, prepared mustard. Some of the Cruciferae are important fodders for early spring and late fall. The leaves of all species of the Cruciferae family and their seeds contain glucosinolates, a class of sulfur compounds which can adversely affect growth and reproduction when fed to nonruminant animals (Ettlinger and Kjaer 1968). According to Wills (1966), goitrogens in cruciferous plants are transferred to the milk of cows consuming kale or turnip; humans who drink the milk produced by such cows sometimes develop goiter.

Chemical studies began in the last century; however, the systematic classification of these compounds started only in 1956 when Ettlinger and Lundeen proposed a new general structure of glucosinolates (Fig. 12.4). Kjaer (1960) reviewed the isolation and characterization of these compounds. Fifty different glucosinolates were described by Ettlinger and Kjaer (1968). Subsequently, several reviews have concerned the subject of glucosinolates (Eyjolfsson 1970; Walker and Gray 1970; Miller 1973; Tapper and Reay 1973; Van Etten and Wolff 1973; Van Etten and Tookey 1978, 1979; Tookey *et al.* 1978). The sugar moiety of all glucosinolates is D-glucose found in β-pyranoside form. The side chain R can be aliphatic with or without aromatic substitution. Based on these variations, about 70 glucosinolates were identified in nature, and in one plant species usually several compounds of this group are found.

In their idioblast cells, the plants also contain a hydrolyzing enzyme myrosinase (thioglucosidase, EC 3.2.3.1) which is released by cell injury during cutting, peeling, or maceration. Myrosinase activity increases with

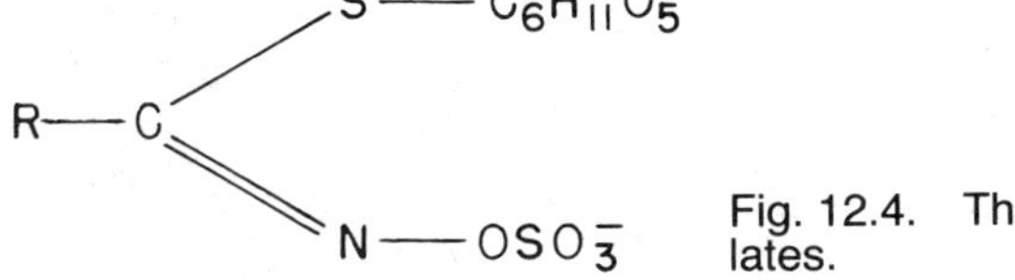

Fig. 12.4. The general formula of glucosinolates.

moderate heating up to 60°C and the enzyme is inactivated at 100°C (Björkman and Lonnerdale 1973). Glucosinolates and some of their hydrolysis products are water-soluble, and these compounds contribute to the flavor and pleasant characteristic aroma of the raw or cooked vegetables of the *Brassica* species (MacLeod and MacLeod 1970).

Figure 12.5 shows the scheme for enzymatic hydrolysis of glucosinolates, which leads to a number of products: β-D-glucose, acid sulfate ion, and a transitional organic aglycon form. The aglycon will hydrolyze to yield organic isothiocyanates, nitriles, elementary sulfur, and thiocyanates. However, if the glucosinolate is progoitrin, the aglycon R will be 2-hydroxy-3-butenyl, and the hydrolysis will take a different course, as illustrated in Fig. 12.6. Two nitriles and sulfur may form and, through a theoretical intermediate, a ring compound, 5-vinyl OZT (5-vinyl oxazolidine-2-thione, goitrin), forms, which is the most potent goitrogen known to occur in plants (Daxenbichler *et al.* 1968). It stimulates the secretion of thyrotropin by the pituitary (Wills 1966). This is why administration of iodine as potassium iodide will not prevent the process of goiter formation.

On the other hand, inorganic thiocyanates and organic isothiocyanates act by inhibiting the accumulation of iodine in the thyroid glands. Raising the iodine concentration of the blood by iodine supplementation of the diet has significant preventive and curative action of goiter formation by thiocyanates.

Some brassicas are important early or late fodder plants and also plant sources for leaf protein fractionation, especially in the Northern Hemi-

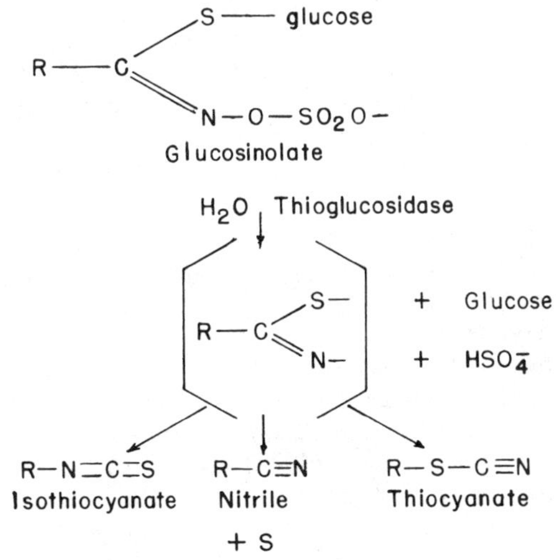

R—C(—S—glucose)=N—O—SO$_2$O$^-$
Glucosinolate

H_2O ↓ Thioglucosidase

R—C(—S$^-$)=N$^-$ + Glucose + HSO_4^-

R—N=C=S
Isothiocyanate

R—C≡N
Nitrile
+ S

R—S—C≡N
Thiocyanate

Fig. 12.5. Enzymatic decomposition of glucosinolates.

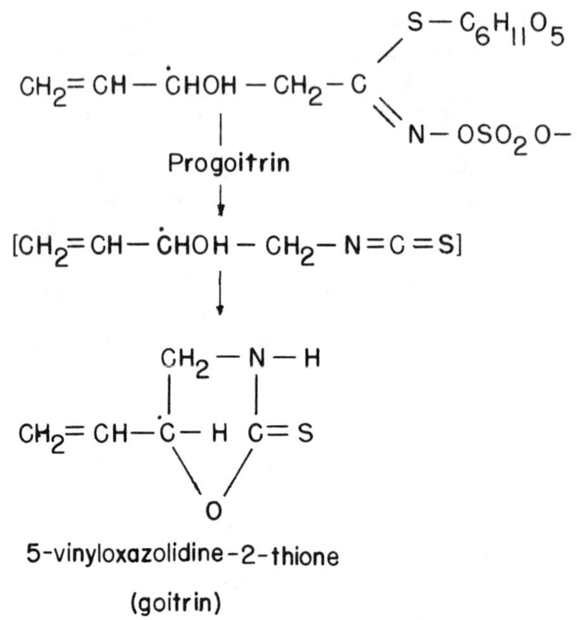

$$CH_2{=}CH{-}\dot{C}HOH{-}CH_2{-}C\begin{matrix}\diagup S{-}C_6H_{11}O_5\\ \diagdown\!\!\diagdown N{-}OSO_2O^-\end{matrix}$$

Progoitrin

↓

$$[CH_2{=}CH{-}\dot{C}HOH{-}CH_2{-}N{=}C{=}S]$$

↓

$$\begin{matrix} & & CH_2 & - & N-H \\ & & | & & | \\ CH_2{=}CH- & & \dot{C}-H & & C{=}S \\ & & \diagdown & O & \diagup \end{matrix}$$

5-vinyloxazolidine-2-thione

(goitrin)

Fig. 12.6. Enzymatic decomposition of progoitrin to goitrin.

sphere, where they help prolong the production time of the Vepex process when alfalfa is not available (Holló and Koch 1970). Rape or white mustard has been suggested as the best source. Brassicas were investigated in the humid hot tropics with high yield of proteins of good quality (Telek 1979).

During the cutting and disintegration of plants, the enzyme myrosinase is liberated from the cells. Since the glucosinolates and the enzyme are water-soluble, they are extracted with the leaf proteins. The activity of the enzyme will increase with increasing temperature of the extracts. The bulk of the protein precipitates at 55°C, the smaller white fraction at 64°C, and a third at 82°C, at which temperature the enzyme reaches its height of activity. Thus, enzymatic hydrolysis is at its optimum at 80°C, close to the highest temperature of protein precipitation. It will be inactivated only at 100°C. The hydrolysis products of the glucosinolates are water-soluble; however, they are adsorbed on the surface of the protein. It was noted that, even after prolonged drying, the proteins prepared from *Brassica alba* or kale had a pronounced "cabbage" smell. The influence of cooking of glucosinolates in cruciferous vegetables was reported by Mullin and Sahasrabudhe in 1978. In Brussels sprouts after cooking, OZT and *n*-butylisothiocyanate content increased approximately 100 to 200%, respectively, and in this study it was shown that boiling was not very effective in removing glucosinolates from the cooked solids. Only 10–30% of residual glucosinolates were leached out into the cooking water.

Determination of Glucosinolates

A GLC method for qualitative detection of glucosinolates has been reported by Underhill and Kirkland (1971). Silylation of 11 glucosinolates formed derivatives of corresponding desulfoglucosinolates and were well separated using two silicone columns (1.5% SE-52 on 80–100 mesh acid-washed DMGS-treated Chromosorb G, the other with 1.5% OV-225 on the same solid support). In the preliminary studies, it was observed that the retention times of TMS derivatives by glucosinolates were the same as the retention times of the TMS derivatives of the corresponding desulfoglucosinolates. Thus, desulfation occurred during derivation. The derivatives could be separated by treatment of myrosinase. Disappearance of the peak indicates that the compound is a glucosinolate; if the peak remains, the compound is a desulfoglucosinolate, since these compounds are not hydrolyzed by the enzyme.

The glucosinolate content can be determined by two methods. Either trimethylsilyl derivatives of the individual glucosinolates are measured directly by GLC (Persson 1974; Thies 1976), or they are hyrolyzed and their isothiocyanates are measured indirectly as oxazolidinethione or thiourea derivatives (Appelqvist and Josefsson 1967; Wetter and Youngs 1976). However, neither method measures the presence of sinalbin, or indolylglucosinolates, which are present in the vegetative part of rape. They are not recorded in gas chromatograms and also their isocyanates do not form thiourease with ammonium hydroxide. McGregor (1978) suggested that the present GLC methods of obtaining TMS derivatives of the glucosinolates should be complemented by thiocyanate analysis.

Thies (1976) removed the bulk of interfering cations on neutral substances from crude extracts of rapeseeds by ion exchange before gas chromatography. However, the method had a disadvantage: the relatively large solvent volume (10 ml), the concentration of which was a time-consuming operation. An improvement on this procedure was reported (Thies 1977), the concentration being facilitated on ion exchange resin and 89% of the undesired substances removed. This step is especially useful if a large number of samples with low level glucosinolates have to be analyzed. Olsson *et al.* (1976) reported a method for total glucosinolate determination of seed meal. The meal was extracted in an ultrasonic bath with 80% ethanol and hydrolyzed with myrosinase for 18 hr at 50°C. The released glucose was determined by GLC. The individual glucosinolates present in the 80% alcohol were converted to TMS derivatives and were identified from retention time of GLC and MS.

Van Etten *et al.* (1976) detected 12 different glucosinolates in each of 22 varieties of cabbage. The glucosinolates in an aliquot of the cabbage extract were adsorbed onto an anion exchange resin (Dowex 1-X2). The resin/glucosinolate complex was hydrolyzed with aqueous myrosinase at pH 7 and extracted with methylene chloride. The total glucosinolates were estimated from the quantity of released glucose. Individual glucosinolates were estimated by GLC. The stationary phases were 1% EGSS-X and 3% Apieson L on Gas-Chrom Q. Twelve glucosinolate aglycons were identified by Josefsson (1970). Bailey *et al.* (1961) had previously identified most of them. A newly identified compound, 4-methylsulfonyl glucosinate, had not been reported previously.

Van Etten and Daxenbichler (1977) described a GLC procedure for separation of total glucosinolates by ion exchange and enzymatic hydrolysis to measure the released glucose. The intact glucosinolates were extracted, and an aliquot was adsorbed onto an anion exchange resin, AG 1 × 2, 50–100 mesh. Then, the ion exchange resin was transferred quantitatively into a culture tube and hydrolyzed with thioglucosidase enzyme EC 3.2.3.1. The preparation of the crude enzyme was described in the procedures. Glucose was determined by Glostat X4 reagent (Worthington Biochemical Corp., Freehold, NJ) by the method of Van Etten *et al.* (1974).

The aglycons formed by the hydrolysis were extracted and determined by GLC. Using the previous enzymatic hydrolysis procedure, Daxenbichler and Van Etten (1977) determined the aglycon derivatives from cabbage. The resulting isothiocyanates and oxazolidinethiones were separated by GLC, and individual aglycons were identified and determined quantitatively with methyl palmitate as an internal standard and a flame ionization detector. The stationary phase was 3% Apiezon L on 8–100 mesh Gas-Chrom Q and 1% EGSS-X on 100–120 mesh Gas-Chrom Q. Ten isothiocyanates were identified and goitrin VOT (vinyl oxazolidinethione) was determined.

This procedure was extended to the analysis of nitriles (Daxenbichler *et al.* 1977). Autolysis of fresh cabbage at its natural pH (5.6–6.3) produced mostly nitriles instead of related isothiocyanates and goitrin. The sample was pulped and, after 30 min standing, was boiled, cooled, and filtered with celite filter. The filtrates were concentrated at reduced pressure and extracted with methylene chloride. The Na_2SO_4 dried extract was evaporated and weighed. This was redissolved in small amounts of methylene chloride, and the total nonvolatile nitriles were determined by IR spectrophotometry (Daxenbichler *et al.* 1966). The specific nitriles and goitrin from progoitrin were determined by GLC procedure, as reported previously. Goitrin was also measured by UV absorption at its maximum of 244 nm in ethanol. During the autolysis of cabbage, 10 different nitriles were formed from glucosinolates.

The separation of a series of glucosinolates by a reversed-phase, ion-pair, liquid chromatographic method was reported by Helboe *et al.* (1980) which, in combination with the ion exchange isolation method for the total glucosinolates of Olsen and Sorensen (1980), allows fast and reliable determination of individual glucosinolates. A rapid and effective separation was achieved on a Nucleosil 5 C18 column with a 0.01 *M* phosphate buffer at pH 7—methanol (3:7) containing 0.005 *M* tetraheptylammonium bromide as the mobile phase. Pyridinium salts of glucosinolates were analyzed. The modifier concentration, the nature of the counterion, and the pH greatly influenced the separation of the individual glucosinolates from each other and from nonionic impurities. The method permitted the rapid separation and quantitative determination of intact individual glucosinolates under gentle conditions; acidic and basic conditions which would lead to decomposition of glucosinolates were avoided.

Some authors have used the breakdown product, potassium hydrogen sulfate, for determination of total glucosinolate (Van Etten *et al.* 1965; Tookey 1973). Croft (1979) suggested that the titration of potassium hydrogen sulfate with 0.025 *N* NaOH and TLC would be a valuable and simple procedure for determination of the toxic glucosinolate constituents. TLC of glucosinolates has been described by Matsuo (1970).

Croft (1979) developed a method to identify glucosinolates in aqueous extracts. The solutions were spotted on EDTA-treated silica gel plates, which were heated on a hot plate and developed in an ethyl acetate-methanol-water-acetic acid 35:30:10:2 solvent system. The spray reagent consisted of 0.5 g diphenylamine and 0.5 ml aniline dissolved in 50 ml acetone and 8 ml orthophosphoric acid.

Determination of Goitrin

Goitrin, 5-vinyloxazolidine-2-thione (OZT) is a hydrolysis product of the glucosinolate progoitrin, found in rape, turnip, and cabbage (Astwood *et al.* 1949; Altamura *et al.* 1959; Austin and Wolff 1968; Lo and Hill 1972). Its antithyroid activity is similar to thiouracil (Astwood *et al.* 1949). The presence of this powerful goitrogen in food and feed is of critical importance since residues were reported and may occur in milk and other products from animals fed leafy vegetables of rape or protein supplement of oil cakes extracted from seeds of *Brassica* species.

Seeds and leaves of *Brassica* varieties contain two toxic components—OZT and isothiocyanate. A method for estimation of OZT has been reported by Astwood *et al.* (1949). The antithyroid compound was isolated from root and seed of turnip and from seed of cabbage and rape by steeping them in cold water from which the substance was extracted with ether. The colorless, biologically active crystals had an mp of 50°C. The compound proved to be 5-vinyl-2-thiooxazolidone. Using a quantitative UV spectrophotometric method, a strong UV absorption maximum at 240 nm, parallel with antithyroid activity, was observed.

Wetter (1955) described the determination of isothiocyanate of rapeseed meal by argentometric titration. The isothiocyanate was isolated by steam distillation from rapeseed meal. The distillate was reacted with ammonia and silver nitrate, forming substituted thiourea. On refluxing, the latter decomposed in ammoniacal silver nitrate, forming insoluble silver sulfide. The unreacted silver was backtitrated with 0.01 *N* potassium isothiocyanate by the Volhard method.

Wetter (1957) modified the method for estimation of thiooxazolidones described by Astwood (1949), and the reported method can be used in conjunction with the determination of isothiocyanates in a single sample of rapeseed. The procedure involves first the estimation of the isothiocyanate which was removed from the milled rapeseed by steam distillation. Then the filtered residue is shaken with diethyl ether, and the thiooxazolidone content is measured by UV spectrophotometry at 248 nm. The isothiocyanate/thiooxazolidone ratio varies considerably from sample to sample.

The total quantity of epithionitriles has been estimated by IR (Daxenbichler *et al.* 1966) based on nitrile absorption. A rapid quantitative GLC method was developed by Daxenbichler *et al.* (1970) for determination of the progoitrin degradation products in crambe and rapeseed meals. The samples were dissolved in methylene chloride and chromatographed on dual columns: column one was packed with 1% EGSS-X on 100–120 mesh Gas-Chrom, and column two with 3% Apiezon L on 80–100 mesh. Methyl palmitate was selected as the internal standard. Progoitrins in seed meals of *Brassica napus* and seven crambes were analyzed.

Appelqvist and Josefsson (1967) critically evaluated the UV determination of isothiocyanates on 5-vinyl oxazolidine-2-thiones (OZT's) in defatted seed cakes of rape and turnip rape. They determined the optimal temperature for the enzymatic formation of isothiocyanates and OZT. Using Wetter's UV spectrophotometric procedure, the results obtained by this improved method demonstrated that the OZT in rapeseed is considerably higher (4.6%) than that obtained by the earlier method, 3.1%.

The detection of low levels of antithyroid substances, especially OZT, in milk is extremely important because it is consumed in large quantities by infants and children. In the previous methods, 300 ml of milk had to be extracted to achieve detection of 5–10 μg of OZT by two-dimensional paper chromatography and consequent quantitization with spectrophotometry (Kreula and Kiesvaara 1959). McLeod *et al.* (1978) investigated the separation of a heptafluoroanhydride derivative of goitrin by two GLC columns. The nonpolar 3% OV-1 and the intermediate 4% SE 30/6% SP 2401 on 80–100 mesh Chromosorb W HP gave similar separations and were found to be interchangeable. The response of special detectors such as ^{63}Ni electron capture (ECD), Coulson electrolytic conductivity (CECO, nitrogen and halogen modes), and Melpar flame photometric emission (MFPD, sulfur 394 nm) were investigated and found to be inadequate for goitrin, itself; however, the technique was improved when HFBA derivatives were analyzed. Application of the method to determine 2 ppm goitrin and HFB derivative in milk was found satisfactory. A high performance liquid chromatography (HPLC) method for determination of OZT in milk was reported by Benns *et al.* (1979). The pH of the milk was adjusted to 8.5 with 2 *N* NaOH. It was treated with H_2S gas and extracted with diethylether. The residue of the ether extract was transferred with 1% ammonium hydroxide, neutralized to pH 6.7–7.5, and extracted with hexane. The pH of the aqueous phase was adjusted to 8.5 and the solution was extracted with diethylether. The ether phase residue was dissolved in isooctane containing 10% isopropropanol and applied to an LC column of Lichrosorb SiGO and eluted with the same solvent containing 0.1% ammonium hydroxide. The recovery of added OZT at a low level (5.6 ng) was found to be 62 and 81%. With this method, 1–2 ng/liter OZT can be detected in 50 ml of milk sample.

NITRATES, NITRITES, NITROSAMINES

Among the potential toxicants present naturally in herbage, nitrates and nitrites are the most widely distributed threats to animals and humans. Their concentrations in plants are increased by careless application of inorganic nitrogenous fertilizers. The increasing cost of natural gas, the initial ingredient of ammonium nitrate synthesis, will minimize this danger since the yield of managed grass production cannot support the expensive input. Grass as a source of LPC was considered in Britain (Pirie 1971). Fishman and Burdick (1977) studied the LPCs of Coastal Bermuda grass. Stahmann (1965) suggested pangola and Nagy *et al.* (1978) sorghum-Sudan as plant sources in the tropics.

The nitrate content of crops such as turnip can change considerably within weeks. The nitrate content can also vary within the same plot or field which will introduce heterogeneity into loose or baled hay.

Excessive fertilization can stimulate dangerous nitrate accumulation in brassicas such as kale (Wojtych *et al.* 1973), which is a recommended plant source for the Vepex system in early spring and late fall (Holló and Koch 1970). Ostgard (1973) studied the sowing, nitrogen fertilization, and yield of fodder rape, *Brassica napus* var. oleifera, and found that nitrate levels are very high in young plants. Harvesting should be 60–70 days after nitrate fertilization. Turnip leaves also accumulated high nitrate levels (Yoshida *et al.* 1969). Amaranth leaves were suggested as potential plant sources by Carlsson (1975). Their nitrate content can reach up to 3.25% on a dry weight basis, causing fatal methemoglobinemia in cattle (Steyn 1960). Extreme weather conditions such as prolonged cloudiness or drought can influence the nitrate level of many plants. Sorghum and other grasses can accumulate dangerous levels of nitrate under certain soil and climatic conditions.

The Analysis of Nitrates

The analysis of nitrates and nitrites at low levels has become more important in the last 15 years with the growing interest in the formation of N-nitrosamines. Classical methods for determination of nitrate and nitrite have been reviewed by Taras (1958). The progress in analytical methods was discussed by Boltz (1973). Usher and Telling (1975) published a critical review of the analysis of nitrates.

Existing assay methods can be grouped according to analytical techniques: spectrophotometry, fluorophotometry, GLC, TLC, and potentiometry by ion selective electrodes.

Spectrophotometric methods are based on nitration of phenolic compounds. The method for the determination of nitrate based on the nitration of 2,4-xylenol in the presence of sulfuric acid was devised by Blom and Treschow (1929). Balks and Reekers (1954) reported a method for nitrate determination, which they improved in 1960. The interference of water-soluble carbohydrates in plant extracts was eliminated by filtration through a column of alumina. Extraction with 1% copper sulfate in a shaking machine for 30 min was found to be as efficient as boiling with 2% copper sulfate solution. The filtered plant extract reacted for only a few seconds with the 1,2.4-xylenol-sulfuric acid mixture. The reaction mixture was extracted with ether. From the separated ether phase, the nitroxylenol was transferred to 5% aqueous sodium hydroxide, and the absorption of the yellow solution was determined spectrophotometrically at 430 nm.

Wiseman and Jacobson (1965) reported a method for the determination of nitrate in plant material whereby plant extracts were clarified by use of charcoal-Celite columns in which nitrate is retained, while the monosaccharides, chlorides, sulfates, and ammonium salts are eluted by water. Nitrate can be eluted by sodium bicarbonate solution. Dried aliquots of nitrate were treated with salicylic acid in concentrated sulfuric acid. After the nitrated salicylic acid was made alkaline, a yellow color formed which could be measured at 414 nm. Interfering nitrite could be removed by sulfanilic acid treatment before chromatography. Hatscher and Schall (1965) found that, in the analysis of samples that contain water-soluble organic compounds, the colorimetric nitrate determinations based on nitration and oxidation result in erratic results. They found high organic anion content in extracts of corn, soybean, and feeds which could not be separated by ion exchange purification as was previously recommended by Jones and Underdown (1953). TLC on Alumina-G was recommended as a cleanup procedure in the quantitization method by 3,4-xylenol nitration using colorimetry. Acetone 0.05 *N* NaOH 170:30 was the developing solvent and diphenylamine-sulfuric acid was the detecting agent.

Baker (1967) suggested the use of brucine to determine nitrates colorimetrically in plant extracts. To prevent the interference of sucrose and fructose present in plant extracts, a simple ion exchange procedure was suggested. The purified plant extract was reacted with 2% brucine in 0.05 *N* HCl in 50% sulfuric acid mixture. Absorptivity was determined at 410 nm. The procedure is fairly complicated, and the use of highly toxic brucine makes the assay inconvenient in routine determinations.

Other spectrophotometric methods are based on nitrite determinations after reduction of nitrates. Reduction of nitrate to nitrite can be achieved by various reagents: copper, zinc, cadmium (powder or sponge), hydrazine sulfate, or copper-coated cadmium wire in teflon tubing. Nitrite in aqueous solution can be determined by diazotization with a primary amine in acid solution. The resulting diazonium salt is coupled with aromatic compounds with active amino and hydroxyl substituents to form an azo dye, which can be measured spectrophotometrically. Follett and Ratcliff (1963) described a nitrate determination method by reduction to nitrite with cadmium, followed by production of the dye Orange I from nitrite with β-naphthol and sulfanilic acid reagent. The intensity of the color developed under the assay condition was measured spectrophotometrically at a wavelength of 474 nm. Adrianse and Robbers (1969) reported a quantitative procedure for determination of nitrite and nitrate content in plant material, meat products, and soil samples. The nitrate was reduced with a Cd column to nitrite. The spectrophotometric assay is based on red color formation, which is formed when sulfanilamide is diazotized by the nitrite, and then coupled to 1-naphthylamine-7-sulfonic acid. The color intensity was measured at 530 nm. The plant extracts were clarified with potassium ferrocyanide and zinc sulfate.

Stainton (1974) described a simple reduction column for autoanalyzers of nitrate, which has less dead volume, needs less wash time, and thus increases the rate of analysis considerably. The column was constructed from 1 m 1/32 in. teflon tubing with a 1 m long 1 nm diameter cadmium wire and fitted to a 4-way liquid chromatography valve and built into an autoanalyzer. The nitrite was determined colorimetrically by a diazotization reaction. The usual reducing agents are not sufficiently specific, and it is difficult to obtain quantitative reduction of nitrate to nitrite. Lowe and Hamilton (1967) suggested the use of soybean nodule bacteroids for reduction of nitrate to nitrite. The bacteroids possess an extremely active nitrate reductase which is highly specific and the reduction is quantitative. No sterile techniques or aseptic culturing procedures are necessary. The nodules were produced in 25 cm (10 in.) pots, which yielded sufficient bacteroids for 300–500 nitrate analyses. The analysis was performed with a Technicon Autoanalyzer. The nitrite was reacted with 1% sulfanilamide in 3 *N* HCl and coupled with 0.01% N-(1-naphthyl) ethylenediamine hydrochloride; the absorbance was determined at a wavelength of 540 nm. The method is sensitive to as little as 0.01 ng of nitrate nitrogen/ml and is adaptable to extensively wide ranges of nitrate concentrations. In the method of Lowe and Hamilton (1967), the preparation of reductase requires 6–8 weeks to produce suitable soybean nodules. McNamara *et al.* (1971) suggested the use of nitrate reductase from *Escherichia coli* in reduction for nitrate assay. *E. coli* strain B was readily available and was found to reduce nitrate to nitrite quantitatively. Procedures for culture of *E. coli*, extraction of enzyme, and assay of the enzyme activity were reported.

Axelrod *et al.* (1970) suggested a fluorometric determination of trace nitrates. Fluorescein was reacted with nitrate to produce a dinitro derivative of the dye. The reaction product does not fluoresce. Nitrate contents in concentrations as small as 0.01 mg/ml in the final assay solution were determined by measurement of the fluorescence suppression at 485 nm. The gas chromatographic methods of Glover and Hoffsommer (1974) and Ross *et al.* (1975) are based on nitration of benzene to nitrobenzene. *NOTE*: The use of the carcinogenic benzene in routine analysis is *not* recommended. Bhatty and Townshend (1971) recommended the use of the less toxic toluene in nitrate determinations. Müller and Siepe (1979) critically evaluated this method in analysis of nitrate content of food and determined nitrotoluene by GLC, using trichlorobenzene as an internal standard. For a routine laboratory control, GLC offers a fast and easy procedure. The same authors reported a thin layer chromatography method in which nitrate reacts with 3,4-dimethylphenol to 6-nitro-3,4-dimethylphenol in silver sulfate containing sulfuric acid. The nitrocompound can be extracted with toluene and chromatographed on silica gel plates with a 1:1 mixture of toluene and petroleum benzene. In analysis of milk products, the GLC method in general showed as much as 40 times greater sensitivity as was obtained by the xylenol method. The TLC method confirmed the low results obtained by the GLC determinations. The recovery assays of 100 ppm nitrates showed only 1 ppm difference. The method was tested in many baby food products, especially spinach and carrot purees. TLC is not disturbed by interferences, but it is more time consuming and requires a photodensitometer for quantitative measurements. These products were also analyzed by nitrate specific electrodes, which gave sufficient accuracy. This method is fast and specific. However, for the calculation a linear regression correlation had to be calculated by statistical analysis.

Paul and Carlson (1968) compared the nitrate-specific ion electrode to the phenoldisulfonic acid method of Johnson and Ulrich (1950) and found that the agreement was sufficiently close for practical purposes, and that the simple electrode method could be substituted for the colorimetric procedure. From the plant extracts, organic acid anions and HCO_3^- were eliminated by addition of Al-resin. Since the nitrate electrode responds to chloride, it increases the nitrate value. Cl^- should be eliminated when tissues contain 500 ppm of NO_3-N or less and 2% or more Cl^-. Chloride can be removed by addition of silver resin. The relative standard deviation for 16 plant materials for the electrode method was 3.1%. Baker and Smith (1969) studied extensively the use of nitrate ion-selective electrodes in analyses of a large number of grass, field corn, and corn silage samples, and compared the results with those obtained by the reduction procedure (Paul and Carlson 1968) and the colorimetric brucine method (Baker 1967). The simplicity, rapidity, precision, and apparent accuracy of the potentiometric method warrants the use of this procedure for routine analyses.

A solution of 0.025 *M* $Al_2(SO_4)_3$ containing 10 ng/ml of NO_3-N as preservative is used for extraction. The $Al_2(SO_4)_3$ acts as a buffer to pH 3.0, which depresses ionization of weak acids and thus interference from their anions. Maintenance of a minimum of 10 ng/ml of NO_3-N in extracts and standards resulted in more stable and rapid meter readings, linearity of the calibration curve, and a minimizing of interference of other ions. Aluminum ions strongly complex the organic acids, and nitrite is reacted with sulfanilic acid. At pH 3 the concentrations of HCO_3^- and organic acid anions are very low. In comparison with the Dewarda method in plant samples, the potentiometric determination shows lower nitrate levels, since the Dewarda method hydrolyzes some organonitrogene compounds. The rapidity and accuracy of the method have proved adequate for most useful applications in plant analysis.

The nitrate electrode is not specific. Chloride, nitrite, and organic anions interfere in the determination of nitrate concentration. Milham *et al.* (1970) proposed a procedure whereby the buffer used in extraction eliminates the disturbing ions and gives better recovery and reproductibility than the Dewarda method. The buffer solution concentration was 0.010 *M* with respect to aluminum sulfate, 0.010 *M* to silver nitrate, 0.020 *M* to boric acid, and 0.020 *M* to sulfamic acid. The final pH 3.0 was adjusted with 0.1 *M* sulfuric acid. The relationship between nitrate concentration and cell potential was plotted on a linear log chart and it was found to be linear from 5 to 1000 ppm of nitrate nitrogen. Chloride quantitatively precipitated with silver nitrate, which also removed other anions, cyanides, sulfide, and phosphate ions.

Ruminal microorganisms reduce nitrate to nitrite and, at a lower rate, nitrite to ammonia. However, when excess nitrate is ingested, toxic nitrite will accumulate, will be partially absorbed from the rumen, and will convert hemoglobin in the blood into methemoglobin, thus reducing oxygen transport from the lungs to the tissues (Ashbury and Rhode 1964). Although nitrite is the direct causative factor, the generally accepted terminology is nitrate poisoning. In forage and feed, nitrates are toxic only insofar as they may be reduced to nitrite; otherwise, nitrate ions are excreted in the urine.

Walker (1975) reviewed the occurrence of nitrate in unprocessed food and found high concentrations in leafy vegetables. Spinach and lettuce commonly contain 1000 ppm or more. Cabbage, cauliflower, celery, kale, and leeks usually contain nitrate at concentrations ranging from several hundred to over 1000 ppm (Achtzehn and Hawat 1969). Nitrite concentration was usually found to be very low in fresh, undamaged vegetables, even under adverse storage conditions. Vegetables rich in nitrate can accumulate nitrite up to toxic levels. Nitrate is nontoxic to mammals, but it can be reduced *in vivo* to nitrite in the rumen of cattle, in the gastrointestinal tract of infants, and by the microflora of the human mouth. Saliva contributes 6–12 mg nitrite/day. The nitrite, itself, is toxic, and can cause toxicity indirectly through formation of carcinogenic N-nitrosamines by reaction with amino compounds.

Nitrites

Recently, nitrites have been shown to accumulate in plant tissues as a result of herbicidal action (Klepper 1979). Nitrite has also been reported to accumulate in processed and raw food when nitrate content was associated with improper storage (Bassir and Maduagwu 1978).

The colorimetric determination of nitrite is based on reaction of nitrite with an aromatic amine in acid solution; the formed diazonium salt is reacted with a coupling reagent to form an azodye which can be measured spectrophotometrically. The methods were described in the previous section on nitrate determinations.

Nitrosamines

In humans and animals, the potential formation of nitrosamines is a dangerous threat to health. The prime source of nitrates is dietary, resulting from overfertilized vegetables. The nitrite can come from the saliva, produced by enzymes of the oral microflora from ingested nitrates. In lesser amount, nitrite can be formed by microbiological reduction during storage. Nitrite toxicity may act in two directions: by reaction with hemoglobin to form methemoglobin and with amines to form nitrosamines (Fig. 12.7). The nitrosamines are extremely carcinogenic compounds. They may be formed in food or feed from available precursors: nitriles, nitrates, amines, and amino acids.

The N-nitroso compound may be formed during digestion in the stomach or by bacteria during transit through the intestines. The dietary amines can form during heating of proteins since some free amino acids are always present. Nitrites can also be formed by bacterial reduction of nitrate.

The carcinogenic activity of dimethylnitrosamine was reported by Magee and Barnes (1956), who found that feeding a small quantity of this compound to test animals over prolonged periods resulted in the development of cancer of the liver, while a single high dose produced kidney tumors. Hepatotoxic disorders in farm animals in Norway were shown to be due to the presence of dimethyl-N-nitrosamine (DMN) in the fish meal.

Sen *et al.* (1972) found trace amounts of DMN in fish meal which was implicated in the liver disease of mink in Canada. The identity of the isolated compound was confirmed by both TLC and GLC. No nitrite could be detected in the samples.

DMN is extremely toxic to pigs, cattle, and sheep (Koppang 1974A,B,C). The analytical method for the determination of nitrosamines in food or feed must be very sensitive. Because of the high carcinogenic potential of many N-nitrosamines, their presence at even very low levels in food or feed could be physiologically detrimental. In preparation of suitable extracts for anal-

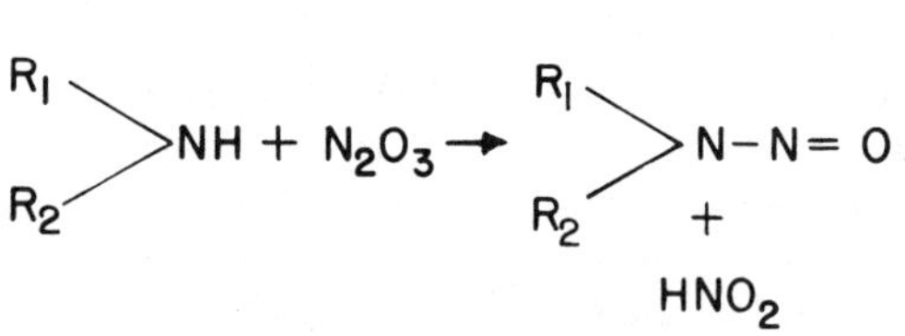

$$2HNO_2 \rightleftharpoons N_2O_3 + H_2O$$

$$R_1R_2{>}NH + N_2O_3 \rightarrow R_1R_2{>}N{-}N{=}O + HNO_2$$

Fig. 12.7. Formation of nitrosamines.

ysis, large samples must be processed in which an array of disturbing compounds could be present in the assay solutions. Therefore, a prepurification before instrumentation is suggested. The low molecular weight nitrosamines are volatile and can be isolated from the analytical sample by vacuum or steam distillation from alkali solution. Solvent extraction was studied by Neurath *et al.* (1964), and it was found that dichloromethane extracts the nitrosamines quantitatively. Eisenbrand *et al.* (1970A) and Neurath and Doerk (1964) suggested the use of UV for detection of nitrosamines. Later, Neurath *et al.* (1964) reported a method in which the nitrosamine was reduced to hydrazine. The hydrazine derivatives were separated by TLC, CCl_4-EtOH, or $CHCl_3$-MeOH solvent systems. Potassium ferricyanide was the detecting spray reagent.

Preussman *et al.* (1964) developed a simple, sensitive color reaction for detection of N-nitroso compounds separated by TLC. The spray reagent consists of 5 parts of a solution of 1.5% diphenylamine in EtOH and 1 part of a solution of 0.01% palladium chloride in 0.2% saline. The nitroso compounds viewed under short UV light are seen as violet spots. Separation of alkyl- and aryl-nitrosamines can be effected with hexane-ether-dichloromethane 4:3:2 using a silica gel layer. Using this procedure, 0.5 ng of nitrosamine was detected. Two-dimensional TLC was suggested by Serfontein and Hurter (1966).

Eisenbrand *et al.* (1970B) investigated the quantitative TLC of typical nitrosamines. They found that, to obtain reproducible results and good recoveries, the following conditions must be maintained. The solvent, dichloromethane, must be dry. A special evaporator (Kuderma-Danish) should be used in extract concentrations. The TLC chromatography should be performed in the dark and at 40°C. Layer thickness should be at least 0.6 mm. The volatile nitrosamines can be separated quantitatively from the spots by steam distillation. Only under these conditions can TLC be used as a partial cleanup procedure in the trace analysis of volatile nitrosamines. Silica gel with fluorescence ($\lambda = 254$ nm) was used for the chromatography; *n*-pentane-diethylether-dichloromethane 5:2:2 was used as a solvent mixture. During the chromatography, the tank was kept in a refrigerator at 4°C. The spots were revealed with a UV lamp.

An attempt to increase the sensitivity of the method by reducing nitrosamines to hydrazines prior to GLC analysis proved unsuccessful (Serfontein and Hurter 1966): the detection limit of hydrazines was not better than that of nitrosamines.

Foreman *et al.* (1970) reported a gas chromatographic method. Column packing was of microporous polymer beds (Chromosorb 101). With a prepurification with suitable concentration procedure. 0.01 ppm nitrosamine should be detectable. The nonvolatile nitrosamines should be separated from a complex mixture of nitrosamines by a solvent extraction procedure. Sen (1970) observed that the oxidation product of dimethyl-N-nitrosamine (DMN)—dimethylnitramine (DMNA)—is extremely sensitive to electron capture detection. The extracted sample was chromatographed on TLC, and the DMNA spot was extracted by methylene chloride and oxidized to DMNA in trifluoroacetic acid with 50% H_2O_2. The mixture was poured on ice, made alkaline with 30–40 ml K_2SO_4, and extracted with methylene chloride, passed through an alumina basic column, washed with pentane, and eluted with ethyl ether. The concentrated eluate was chromatographed on 100% Carbowax on 60–80 mesh Chromosorb W and measured with an electron capture detector. The sensitivity of the electron capture detector is about 1000 times greater than that of the hydrogen flame detector.

Telling *et al.* (1971) described a procedure for volatile nitrosamines based on vacuum distillation linked with gas chromatography and mass spectrometry. The GLC column was packed with 10% Carbowax 20 M on acid-washed, silanized Celite (100–200 mesh); the temperature was programmed from 100° to 200°C to shorten the time of analysis for separating the constituents of widely differing retention time. The limits of detection were 25 ppb for N-nitrosodimethylamine to 65 ppb for N-nitrosodipentylamine. This technique was found to be suitable only as a screening test, and it could not be used as a quantitative method for the determination of carcinogenic, volatile nitrosamines.

Bryce and Telling (1972) improved the previous method by selecting an ion characteristic of each nitrosamine for monitoring the effluents of GC, which enabled them to identify nitrosamines at 1 ppb level. The increased sensitivity has been achieved by changing the grid resistor of the electrometer and by monitoring for a characterisitic ion by peak matching, using perfluorotri-*n*-butylamine as the mass calibrant. A compound eluted from GC is identified as a nitrosamine if it has the correct retention time and possesses the characteristic ion in its mass spectrum.

Newell and Sisken (1972) presented an analytical method for determination of nitrosodimethylamine (NDMA) sensitive to 3 ppb in milk and apple. The method should be applicable to food or feed. The volatile components are separated by vacuum distillation, and the NDMA is removed from the water by percolation through a column of polymer beads (Porapak). NDMA is purged from the column by heat and carried into the gas chromatography, where a 100/120 mesh Porapak Q column with programmed temperature separates NDMA from other components. After catalytical reduction to ammonia, it is quantitized by microcoulometric titration and recorded.

Cox (1973) suggested high performance liquid chromatography (HPLC) for replacing two established gas chromatographic procedures for the determination of nitrosamines in foods. He was able to reduce the time of chromatographic analyses by a factor of approximately five. However, a rather complicated 2,4-dinitrophenyl derivatization and new, more costly equipment make this assay procedure less attractive. The authors, themselves, pointed out that the reported methods cannot give completely unequivocal results for identification of nitrosamines. Confirmation by high resolution mass spectrometry is required.

A membrane separator has been constructed by Gough and Webb (1972) and its use for transferring nanogram quantities eluted from a GC column to a mass spectrometer has been evaluated. The details of the construction of the membrane separator are given. By peak matching against reference standards, the detection limit was 2 mg/liter. By incorporating a peak-cutting system into the gas chromatograph, the detection limit is lowered to 0.2 mg/liter, which represents a limit of 0.2 ng/kg of sampled material. Gough and Webb (1973) reported a method for detection of traces of volatile nitrosamines using combined gas chromatography and mass spectrometry with carrier gas pressure programming and a peak-cutting method. The gas chromatograph and high-resolution mass spectrometer were coupled with a membrane separator, and the nitrosamines were detected by parent-ion monitoring with a detection limit of 1 mg/liter of injected sample. The pressure programming abbreviates the overall analysis time substantially compared with the temperature-programmed method. It was shown that the silicone membrane separator was suited to pressure programming than to temperature programming. The pressure-programming and peak-cutting system are described in detail. Gough and Webb (1974) improved the previously reported membrane separator and described a GLC-MS procedure based on characteristic ion monitoring. A silver frit interface and a modified mass spectrometer (MS)-inlet system were used to transfer the separated material from the GLC to the mass spectrometer. The nitrosamines were partitioned by 5% SE-52 on 80–100 mesh Chromosorb W. The detection limit for nonvolatile nitrosamines was found to be 10 ng/ml.

A simplified method for the screening of nitrosamine content in food and feed was reported by Riedmann (1974). Samples for GLC and high resolution MS must be processed with time-consuming, effective cleanup procedures. For routine screening, GLC with an N-flame-ionization detector (N-FID) or electrocapture detector is sufficiently sensitive; however, the N-flame ionization is superior in many aspects. The baseline is linear, an internal standard technique can be used, no derivatization is needed, and it is suitable for analysis of every nitrosamine. The selectivity of N-FID can be regulated so that the nonnitrogenous components appear as negative peaks, and the nitrosamines appear only as positive peaks. The following stationary phases gave good separations: 1% SE-30 or 5% Carbowax 20 M on Chromosorb G AW-DMCS, and 2% Carbowax 20 M on Haloport F. The limit of detection was found to be 0.20–0.005 ppb.

Fine *et al.* (1975) described the use of the thermal energy analyzer (TEA) for trace determination of volatile and nonvolatile N-nitroso compounds. The detector described is capable of selectively detecting sub-ng/kg amounts of N-nitroso compounds in complex biological materials. The dilute solution containing the N-nitroso compounds is injected into a catalytic pyrolyzer at 275°C. The N-nitroso compound is pyrolyzed into a nitrosyl and an organic radical, and swept into an evacuated chamber where the nitrosyl radical is reacted with ozone, yielding electronically excited NO_2^*, which falls back rapidly to the ground stage with the emission of light near the infrared region. The emission is recorded passing through a red optical filter by means of a photomultiplier tube, the response is amplified, and it is recorded on a chart.

Gough *et al.* (1977) compared various mass spectrometric and chemiluminescent methods for the estimation of volatile nitrosamines. Extracts of meat and vegetation have been analyzed for the presence of nitrosamines and analyzed by high and low resolution mass spectrometry and chemiluminescence. The data of the latter two methods are in good agreement; however, inconsistencies were observed using low-resolution mass spectrometric procedures.

Cross *et al.* (1978) described a method for the identification and determination of volatile N-nitrosamines. The technique is based on separation by double distillation, cleanup on a silica gel column, determination by cleavage by HBr in glacial acetic acid, and subsequent colorimetric determination of nitrite released or TLC of the 4-chloro-7-nitrobenzo-2-oxa-1,3-diazole derivatives of the corresponding amines. The limit of detection is in the order of ppb. The technique gave results comparable to the high-resolution GLC-MS method.

A simple screening method for determination of volatile nitrosamines was described by Cross and Bharucha (1979). The analysis is based on fluorescence densitometry of the nitrobenzo-oxadiazole amines produced by reaction of amines, liberated from nitrosamines by hydrogen bromide in glacial acetic acid or by hydrogen bromide in dichloromethane, with 4-chloro-7-nitrobenzo-2-oxa-1,3-diazole (NBD-Cl). The NBD amines are separated by TLC on silica gel.

OXALATES

Oxalates occur in plants at relatively high levels, mainly as the soluble sodium and potassium salt or as the insoluble calcium oxalate. Higher levels are in Chenopodiaceae, spinach, *Atriplex*, and portulacae. The highest is in *Halogeton*, which constitutes up to 34% of the dried plant (Clarke and Clarke 1967). Oxalates are widely distributed in plants suggested as sources for LPC preparation: *Chenopodium album*, *Amaranthus* varieties, sunflower leaves, sugar beet tops, and forage grasses such as the setarias, brachiarias, and digitarias. Oxalate-containing plants may also have high nitrates or cyanogenic glycosides, which can increase the severity of the toxic effect of methemoglobinemia, inducing degenerative changes in the kidney, which can lead to minimal excretion of the oxalates. Ingestion of large quantities of a high oxalate-containing plant may cause alkalosis, hypocalcemia, and acute uremia due to blockage of kidney tubuli by calcium oxalate crystals. Oxalic acid of 5 g or more can be fatal in man, causing corrosive gastroenteritis, shock, convulsions, and renal damage.

Oxalate poisoning in man has often been caused by eating rhubarb leaves. The poisoning is complex, and the sign of toxicity varies with the animal species. Oxalate poisoning can be aggravated when the calcium intake is low. Boyce *et al.* (1956) have shown that experimental animals died after eating spinach leaves when their diet was low in calcium. Ruminants, especially sheep, are less sensitive to oxalate poisoning than non-ruminants. It was suggested by Watts (1957) that enzymes in the rumen contents or a bacterium plays an important part in the breakdown of the oxalate. O'Halloran (1962) studied the effects of oxalates on 26 strains of bacteria isolated from the rumen and found only one of them that could effectively decompose oxalates. James *et al.* (1967) studied *in vitro* degradation of oxalate and cellulose fermentation by rumen liquor obtained from a sheep before and after feeding of *Halogeton glomeratus*, a high oxalate-producing plant. It was found that cellulose fermentation was inhibited when 240, 180, or 120 mg of oxalate were added to 100 ml of fermentation medium containing rumen liquor inoculum from a sheep that had not been fed *Halogeton*. When the fermentation media contained rumen liquor inoculum of *Halogeton*-fed sheep, cellulose fermentation took place at a slow rate; however, oxalate was degraded after 4 hr of fermentation when the rumen liquor inoculum was from the *Halogeton*-fed sheep, but there was a delay of 8 hr using rumen liquor inoculum from the sheep not fed *Halogeton*. Thus, the *in vitro* experiment suggests that oxalate poisoning may involve unpaired cellulose fermentation and rumen dysfunction. In ruminant digestion, the oxalates are converted to carbonate and bicarbonate, which, if produced in high concentration, may produce severe alkalosis. However, a certain amount of the ingested oxalate will be absorbed, causing calcium deficiency, kidney damage, and uremia. Seawright *et al.* (1970) reported the death of nine cows within 24 hr after grazing on a pasture of *Setaria sphacelata*.

James and Butcher (1972) studied the effect of high level oxalate intake in sheep, and concluded that up to 6% soluble oxalate had no effect on calcium, phosphorus, and magnesium balance.

Schneider *et al.* (1970) studied the milkfat depression in dairy cows fed Sudan grass and pearl millet grown with two levels of fertilization and found that only pearl millet caused milkfat depression. It contained higher percentages of nitrate N and high concentrations of oxalate and succinate, which increased with higher K and Ca fertilization. Oxalic acid was very high early in the season, then steadily decreased and varied directly with the K levels of the forage. Milkfat rose when soil moisture increased, whereas oxalate decreased during the same period.

Analytical Methods

The classical determination of oxalates in biological material has been the precipitation with calcium ions followed by gravimetry or titration. Later methods have utilized cerimetric and iodimetric titrations. Myers (1947) modified the permanganate titration method. Mitchell (1933) suggested a colorimetric method in which red color was produced by sodium vanadate reagent in the presence of water-soluble oxalate. Calkins (1943) reported a method by which oxalic acid was reduced to glycolic acid, then treated with 2,7-dihydroxynaphthalene in sulfuric acid to produce a violet color.

Burrows (1950) reported a colorimetric method for determination of oxalate in mushroom compost. The method is based on the fading effect of oxalates on various organic complexes of ferric 7-iodo-8-hydroxyquinoline-5-sulfonic acid. Removing the coloring matter with citric acid extraction and close control of acidity below pH 5 resulted in a reproducibility of ± 4%; however, the recovery of added oxalate only amounted to 90%.

GLC has been used for organic acid analyses in the form of volatile derivatives (De Sylva 1971). Roughan and Slack (1973) reported two simple methods for the extraction and determination of oxalate in plant material. From 0.2 g dry powdered plant material, the oxalic acid was extracted and converted to dimethyl oxalate simultaneously with a 5 ml solution of 5% sulfuric acid in a 2 + 1 (v/v) mixture of anhydrous chloroform and absolute methanol. For semiquantitative analyses, aliquots of 5 nl of the chloroform phase were spotted on thin layers of silica gel impregnated with hydroxylamine hydrochloride and ferric chloride and the chromatograms developed with benzene. The methyl oxalate appeared as a brown spot (Rf = 0.4) after exposing the thin layers to ammonia vapor in a closed developing tank for 5 min. The size and intensity of assay sample spots were compared visually with a series of standard spots equivalent to 1 to 10% oxalic acid on a dry weight basis for 0.2 g plant sample. Using this method, oxalic acid content could be estimated within 1 to 5% dry weight by visual observation. Samples containing concentrations higher than 5% were diluted and rechromatographed. The same sample solutions were analyzed by GLC at 200°C with a flame ionization detector on a 2 m stainless steel column containing 17% ethylene glycol succinate on Chromosorb W. The retention time was 4.5–5 min. The sample was injected without prior cleanup, and column life in continuous use lasted for several months.

PLANT ESTROGENS IN FORAGE LEGUMES

The choice plant material for large-scale industrial production of leaf protein concentrates by the Pro-Xan and Vepex processes is alfalfa. Clover varieties also offer a rich protein source. However, natural estrogens present in forages are found to be the cause of serious reproduction disturbances in ruminant animals. In the 1940s, a sudden decrease in fertility of ewes grazing for longer periods on subterranean clover, *Trifolium subterraneum*, was observed in Australia and New Zealand (Bennetts 1944). The compound partially responsible for the serious losses in lambing was characterized as an isoflavone: genistein (Curnow *et al.* 1948). Genistin, the glycoside of this compound, had earlier been isolated from defatted soybean meal (Walter 1941). The discovery of estrogenic isoflavonoids led to the isolation of genistein and formononetin from 9000 lb (4082 kg) subterranean clover (Bradbury and White 1951). Pope and Wright (1954) found that formononetin, genistein, and biochanin A are also present together in red clover, *Trifolium pratense*. Later, Guggolz *et al.* (1961) found daidzen in subterranean and red clovers, alfalfa, and ladino clover (Fig. 12.8).

The estrogenic activity of subterranean clover has been attributed to genistein; however, the presence of another, more powerful, estrogen was noted by Curnow (1954) on alkali treatment of the chloroplast of the clover. Bickoff *et al.* (1957) isolated this estrogen from ladino clover by solvent extraction, countercurrent distribution, and crystallization from methanol. Because of the coumarin structure of the molecule, the name coumestrol has been proposed for the new compound (Fig. 12.9). Lyman *et al.* (1951) found coumestrol in alfalfa, red clover, and subterranean clover (Table 12.1).

Isolation

Bickoff *et al.* (1957) isolated coumestrol by solvent extraction of dried alfalfa meal, followed by several countercurrent distributions, with final recrystallization from methanol. Coumestrol has a bright blue fluorescence in neutral and acid solution, turning to a greenish-yellow in strong alkali. Its UV spectrum in methanol shows maxima at 208, 243, and 343 nm. The

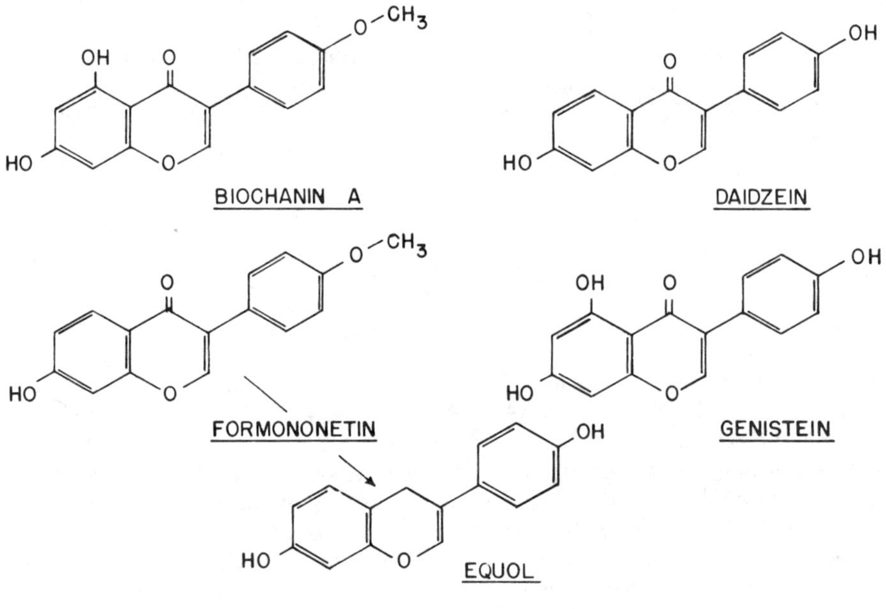

Fig. 12.8. Estrogenic isoflavonoids and equol, the rumen metabolite of formononetin.

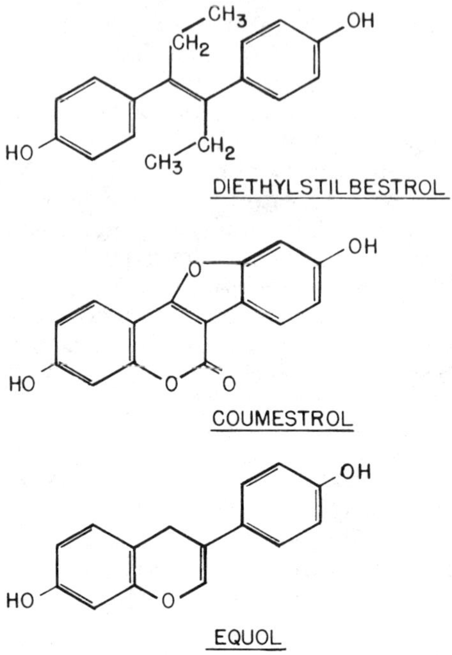

Fig. 12.9. The structural similarity of diethylstilbestrol and coumestrol.

TABLE 12.1. THE PRESENCE OF PLANT ESTROGENS IN FORAGE LEGUMES

Legume	Genistein	Biochanin A	Formononetin	Daidzen	Coumestrol
Subterranean clover	+[1]	+[2]	+[2]	+[3]	+[4]
Red clover	+[2]	+[2]	+[2]	+[3]	+[4]
Ladino clover	+[3]	–	+[3]	+[3]	+[5]
Alfalfa	+[3]	+[3]	+[3]	+[3]	+[4]

[1] Curnow *et al.* (1948)
[2] Pope and Wright (1954).
[3] Guggolz *et al.* (1961).
[4] Lyman *et al.* (1959).
[5] Bickoff *et al.* (1957, 1958A,B).

detailed, large-scale isolation of coumestrol from ladino clover has been reported by Bickoff *et al.* (1958A). Two hundred kg of reground meal were extracted first with hot water and skellysolve to remove impurities without estrogenic activity. Consequently, the residue was extracted with 1000 gal. of ether for 30 days. Even after this time, some estrogenicity still remained in the meal. The ether extract was concentrated to a solid residue weighing 5 kg. The residue was extracted with chloroform, of which the active principle was extracted with 5% sodium carbonate (pH 10–11). The aqueous alkaline extract was quickly acidified and extracted five times with a 1 liter portion of ether. After distilling off the ether, the residue was extracted with six different solvent mixtures by countercurrent distribution. The final pure isolate crystallized from chloroform and methanol as clumps of small needles. The empirical formula was found to be $C_{15}H_8O_5$. Formation of diacetate and dimethylation established the presence of two OH-groups. By mouse uterine weight assay, the crystalline compound was at least 30 times more estrogenic than genistein.

Estrogenic Activity of Phytoestrogens in Animals

The relative estrogenic activity of isoflavone derivatives was determined by Cheng *et al.* (1954).

In a later study, Cheng and Burroughs (1959) reported the estrogenic activity of isoflavones by the average uterine weight test, expressed as micrograms of diethylstilbestrol activity. The potency of genistein was found to be 0.019. Biochanin A was found to be very similar, 0.020. Daidzen was the most active with a potency of 0.042. Formononetin had the lowest activity. The potency by this test was very low, 0.009.

Genistein, biochanin A, and formononetin have been reported as causative factors for depressed fertility of ewes grazing subterranean clover pastures (Moule *et al.* 1963; Morley *et al.* 1968). Wong and Flux (1962) reported that genistein and biochanin A are estrogenic in mice. However, Millington *et al.* (1964) could not find support for estrogenic activity of hydroxyisoflavones of subterranean clover in sheep, but they found, surprisingly, a positive relationship with the formononetin content. A preliminary report on metabolism of isoflavones in sheep was published. Batterham *et al.* (1965) found that biochanin A was demethylated to genistein and further to *p*-ethylphenol. By contrast, Batterham *et al.* (1965) and Nilsson *et al.* (1967) have suggested that formononetin *in vivo* and *in vitro* incubated in sheep rumen fluid is first demethylated to daidzen and then reduced to equol. Biochanin A and genistein when administered parenterally to sheep showed much higher estrogenic potency than formononetin. Braden *et al.* (1967) studied the estrogenic activity and metabolism of certain isoflavones in sheep and found that pure genistein, biochanin A, and formononetin, when administered to ovariectomized ewes by intraruminal infusion (I.M.), appeared to have estrogenic activities of the same order. The activity of coumestrol was about 15 times greater than that of the isoflavones. Formononetin was the only one which was more active in I.M. than when injected intramuscularly.

Examining the urinary phenols before and after treatment showed that the administered isoflavones underwent metabolic degradation. Genistein and biochanin A were excreted as *p*-ethylphenol; only 5% of the formononetrin was accounted for as detectable metabolites, of which a major one was equol (Fig. 12.8). The negligible activity of formononetin administered orally in mice or intramuscularly to ewes was considered possible due to its low solubility. Nilsson *et al.* (1967) have shown that formononetin was metabolized *in vitro* to equol in urine ruminant fluid. Shutt *et al.* (1967) found equol in relatively high concentration in plasma of sheep after the ingestion of red and subterranean clover. Shutt and Braden (1968) reported that equol was estrogenic in mice. By subcutaneous administration, it had about one-fourth of the activity of genistein. In ewes grazing red clover, equol was found in the plasma and in the uterine tissue and represented in both instances more than 70% of the extracted phytoestrogens. It was concluded that equol is responsible for most of the estrogenic activity found in sheep after ingesting clover with high formononetin content. It was found that, in subcutaneous administration, at least 50% of the formononetin dose and 30% of the daidzen dose were precipitated near the injection site, making the assay of these two compounds unreliable. The solubility of genistein is much higher. Only 5% of the initial dose was recovered from the injection site. In another experiment, red clover pellets containing 0.4% formononetin and 0.2% biochanin A on a dry matter basis were fed to ovariectomized ewes and also to guinea pigs. Blood samples were analyzed for equol content. The results showed that, after ingestion of red clover pellets, equol was found in the blood of sheep and guinea pigs in relatively high concentration. It was established that conversion of daidzen to equol does not proceed in the tissues of sheep (Batterham *et al.* 1965; Braden *et al.* 1967); thus it appeared that the formation of equol in the digestive tract is the causative factor for the estrogenic activity of clovers containing formononetin.

Shutt *et al.* (1970) studied the quantitative aspects of phytoestrogen metabolism in Merino wethers fed on a subterranean clover *(Trifolium subterraneum)* cultivar or red clover *(Trifolium pratense)*. The dietary intake of isoflavones with both clovers was about 9 g/day. In subterranean clover, biochanin A and genistein indicated a low level of estrogenicity causing a slight teat length increase. With red clover, formononetin represented 60% of the isoflavone present and the wethers exhibited maximal teat length increases, indicating a high level of estrogenicity. Less than 1% of the daily intake of the isoflavones was excreted in urine. The isoflavones were metabolized or retained in the sheep. The isoflavones were found to disappear rapidly from the rumen, and isotope markers indicated that the removal of these compounds from the stomach was complete. Equol, the metabolite of formononetin, was the predominant compound excreted in the urine. It was 70% of the intake of formononetin. A large portion of equol produced in the rumen was absorbed from there in about 2 hr. The isoflavones were present in blood plasma in conjugated forms; only 1–2% was present in free form. The data support the conclusion that equol accounts for most of the estrogenic activity in sheep fed on clovers with a high level of formononetin. The free and conjugated isoflavones were determined by the method of Lindner (1967). Equol was also determined by UV spectrophotometry absorption at 280 nm, or by GLC using 3% OV-17 on Gas-Chrom Q. These experiments indicate that the estrogenicity of the two clovers was affected in opposite ways by digestion in the rumen. In the subterranean clover, biochanin A and genistein, which were found active when administered parenterally, were degraded to inactive simple phenols in the rumen. By contrast, on the red clover diet, formononetin was metabolized in the rumen to equol, which is estrogenic. Little is known about the factors determining the ability of the rumen microorganisms to cause these reactions to occur.

Estrogenic Activity of Plants

The estrogenic potency in forages varies according to cultivars, age of the plant, season of the year, number of cuttings, and climatic conditions (Pieterse and Andrews 1956A, B). Stob *et al.* (1957) analyzed 56 different cultivars of alfalfa and found wide differences in the level of estrogenic activity of various cultivars. Manda *et al.* (1971A, B) found that the estrogenic potency of alfalfa was low in the bud stage and increased markedly during growth. Estrogen level in ladino clover remained constant throughout growth, and it was always lower than that of alfalfa. According to Jorgensen and Fregmiller (1972), the estrogenic activity of alfalfa was significantly higher in first than second cuttings and the estrogenic level of sun-cured hay from second growth alfalfa was significantly lower than in fresh herbage and was not affected by rumen fermentation.

A similar study gave surprising results when Kitts *et al.* (1959) analyzed the estrogenic activity of first, second, third, and fourth cuttings of alfalfa. The estrogenic content was high in the first cutting, decreased in the successive cutting, but built up in the fall, before the fourth harvest.

Todd (1970) reported that estrogenic compounds are relatively stable, and their activity is not destroyed by drying in a current of hot air, although sometimes loss of activity does occur during haymaking.

Genistein and biochanin A are estrogenic, but their metabolite in the rumen, *p*-ethylphenol, is an inactive compound (Shutt and Braden 1968). Formononetin, itself, is a low estrogenic compound. However, its metabolite, formed in the rumen, 7,4′-dihydroxyisoflavan (equol), is a very active estrogen (Shutt 1976). According to Biggers (1958), Whalley has suggested that the estrogenic activity of coumestrol could be attributed to its stilbene-like structure (Fig. 12.9).

Because of the relatively higher potency of coumestrol compared with the other flavonoid estrogens, the relationship of its structure to its biological activity has been investigated by Bickoff *et al.* (1960). Twenty-nine closely related compounds were prepared and evaluated by the uterine weight response test. None of the compounds evaluated were more active than coumestrol. The most important groups for high activity are the two hydroxy groups at 4′ and 7 positions. The opening of the lactone ring and formation of an *o*-methoxycinnamic acid derivative only slightly decreased the activity.

The relative potencies of the five estrogenic compounds found in forages have been compared with diethylstilbestrol and estrone and reinvestigated by mouse uterine weight bioassay (Bickoff *et al.* 1962). Coumestrol was found to be 35 times more potent than genistein. Daidzen was 0.75%, biochanin A 0.46%, and formononetin 0.26% as potent as genistein. The relative potency of diethylstilbestrol and estrone was 10^5 times and 6.9×10^3 times higher, respectively, than the activity of genistein.

However, forage with even low-activity estrogens can cause serious physiological changes in animals if consumed in large quantity.

Analytical Methods

In the initial studies of estrogenic activity in fresh and dried forages, bioassays were used (Cheng and Burroughs 1953; Biggers and Curnow 1954). The first estrogenic reactions were measured by the biological assay of Doisy, as described in detail by Emmens (1950). Bickoff *et al.* (1959) reported an improved procedure for bioassay of estrogenic activity in plant extracts using uterine-weight response of immature mice. In their assay procedure, 400 g of freshly harvested frozen forage were extracted in 1400 ml acetone by disintegration in a commercial 4 liter (1 gal.) blender. The extract was filtered and concentrated under vacuum to 30 ml volume. The aqueous concentrate was extracted four times with ethyl ether. The ether extract was evaporated to dryness under vacuum. The solid residue was dissolved in a small volume of acetone and ethanol and added to the mouse ration. The solvent was removed with continuous stirring to assure uniform distribution of estrogens in the feed. The estrogenic activity was evaluated by feeding the best diets to immature female mice and determining the increase in weight of the freshly excised uteri. The animal assays are costly and complicated; thus, chemical assays have been developed for the phytoestrogenic compounds.

Analysis of Isoflavonoids

Curnow (1954) developed a method for estimation of genistein in plant material and a micromethod for its detection. In a one-leaf assay, the plant material was extracted with ethanol and, after addition of water to the extract, the chlorophyll was removed with benzene. The water phase was evaporated and reextracted in *n*-butanol containing 1% concentrated HCl. The extract was spotted on a Whatman No. 4 filter paper alongside 2.5 ng and 5 ng of genistein standard. The paper was developed by ascending method in *n*-butanol-acetic acid-water, 40:10:50. $FeCl_3$ was used as the spray reagent. The genistein formed pink spots.

Guggolz *et al.* (1961) reported a study of detection of daidzen, formononetin, genistein, and biochanin A in alfalfa, ladino clover, red clover, and subterranean clover. Dried forage samples (300 g) were defatted in a Soxhlet apparatus with skellysolve B for 24 hr. A subsequent extraction with acetone for 24 hr removed the estrogens. The acetone extract was concentrated in reduced pressure. An aliquot was chromatographed on paper with authentic daidzen and formononetin and developed by the ascending method in the upper phase of a benzene-acetic acid-water (2:2:1) solvent system. Daidzen and formononetin were detected with a UV lamp. Ammonia vapor greatly increased the intensity of fluorescence. After two subsequent re-chromatographies of the eluted fluorescing zones on silica gel thin layers, ultraviolet spectra were determined on a recording spectrophotometer. Formononetin, biochanin A, and genistein were separated on silica gel thin layers, using the ethyl acetate-skellysolve B (1:1) solvent system, and visualized with diazotized sulfanilic acid-sodium carbonate spray reagent. Semiquantitative estimation of each of the estrogenic compounds was made on two-dimensional paper chromatography. The paper was developed first in acetic acid-water (60:40), followed by formic acid-water (40:60) systems. Daidzen and formononetin were observed as blue-violet fluorescent spots under 360 nm UV light. Genistein and biochanin A were visualized by spraying with bis-diazotized benzidine. Coumestrol was measured by fluorescence.

Tablc 12.2 summarizes the approximate amounts of estrogenic substances found in the samples in each forage plant, showing the extremely high level of isoflavones in red and subterranean clovers, and the highest level of coumestrol in alfalfa.

TABLE 12.2. PLANT ESTROGENS IN DRY FORAGES (PPM)

Plant Estrogen	Alfalfa	Ladino Clover	Red Clover	Subterranean Clover
Daidzen	1	3	29	18
Formononetin	14	38	1700	900
Genistein	1	1	40	850
Biochanin A	1–5	0	1000	500
Coumestrol	57	49	18	26

Source: Guggolz *et al.* (1961).

A two-dimensional paper chromatographic separation and detection of isoflavones and coumestrol was reported by Wong and Flux (1962). The concentration of individual estrogenic constituents was determined by spectrophotometric measurements after elution from the paper chromatograms. The plant material was disintegrated in 95% ethyl alcohol in a Waring Blendor and refluxed for 15 min. The filtrates were concentrated, extracted with petroleum benzin, then with ether. The combined ether extracts were evaporated to dryness and taken up in ethanol, then spotted on Whatman No. 3MM paper and developed by descending method in benzene-acetic acid-water (125:72:3) in the first direction. Aqueous 2 *N* ammonia was used for the second direction. With a combination of fluorescence in UV (for formononetin, daidzen, and coumestrol) and color formation with diazotized sulfanilic acid (for biochanin A and genistein), less than 10 ng of each of the estrogenic constituents could be detected. The authors recognized that the method was poor for analysis of the most important estrogenic constituents: formononetin and coumestrol. The concentration of estrogens as mg % of red clover leaves was found to be 110 for formononetin, 140–150 for biochanin A, 2–3 for genistein, 0.6–1.8 for daidzen, 0–0.1 for coumestrol.

Bech (1964) found that isoflavones were in bound form as glycosides in the intact subterranean clover leaves and that crushing prior to ethanol extraction greatly enhanced the isoflavone results. The sample, about 3 g of green leaf, was crushed with sand in water. The resulting sludge was allowed to stand 30 min at 37°C and extracted twice with boiling ethanol. The alcohol was evaporated under vacuum and the residue extracted with ether. Sodium chloride was added to the aqueous phase. The extraction of formononetin was a long procedure (2 hr). The united ether extracts were evaporated to dryness, redissolved in benzene-ethanol for chromatography by TLC on silica gel plates, and developed in 11% v/v methanol in chloroform. Formononetin spots were compared with spotted standards under UV (257 nm). Genistein and biochanin A were made visible by spraying with diazotized sulfanilic acid and exposure to ammonia fumes. The Rf values for biochanin A_1, formononetin, and genistein were approximately 0.85, 0.75, and 0.55, respectively, when developed in an incompletely saturated tank.

Francis and Millington (1965) developed a microtechnique for determination of varietal variations in the isoflavone content of subterranean clover. The combination of the chromatographic method of Beck (1964) with the extraction method of Curnow (1954) was utilized in this study.

Francis *et al.* (1967) studied the distribution of estrogenic isoflavones in 100 *Trifolium* species and found that 14 had isoflavone content comparable to that of subterranean clover. In all species, genistein, biochanin A, and formononetin were in glycosidic form. TLC was used to detect isoflavone glycosides in ethanolic extracts from entire leaves of *Trifolium subterraneum* L. separated on silica gel G with the developing solvent ethyl acetate-methyl ethyl ketone-formic acid-water, 50:30:5:10. Formononetin was detected after exposure to ammonia gas under ultraviolet light (235.7 nm). Genistein and biochanin A were determined after spraying with a 2% solution of ferric chloride. The aglycons were liberated by hydrolysis with 4 *N* hydrochloric acid and extracted with amyl alcohol; the isoflavones were identified by the chromatographic methods of Beck (1964).

A method was developed by Dedio and Clark (1968) for quantitative estimation of the isoflavones—biochanin A and formononetin—in red clover. The isoflavones were separated by paper chromatography and evaluated by scanning with a densitometer for biochanin A and with a fluorimeter for formononetin. For biochanin A, 2–6 nl of extracts were spotted with reference standards of 1, 2, 3, 4, 5, and 6 ng in duplicate. The chromatograms were developed in formic acid-water (40:60) and, after drying, were sprayed with a solution of diazotized sulfanilic acid in 0.1% NaOH. After final drying, the chromatograms were scanned in a photodensitometer. Two to 6 μl of extract were chromatographed on Whatman No.1 paper for formononetin assay and developed by ascending method in 2 *N* NH_4OH. The formononetin reference standard was also spotted in 1–6 ng quantities. The chromatograms were scanned on a suitable fluorimeter. Studying the isoflavone content in red clover varieties at several maturity stages, the authors found that the highest isoflavone content (1% dry weight of each isoflavone) occurred in the leaves before flowering and then fell rapidly.

Lindner (1967) presented a comprehensive method for the specific determination of genistein, biochanin A, formononetin, daidzen, pratensein, and coumestrol in plasma or adipose tissue of sheep. The concentration of isoflavones in the plasma of sheep grazing estrogenic pastures is about 104–105 times lower than that in the plants. Therefore, new methods had to be developed for this analysis. The report presents detailed flow sheets for selective extractions and isolation of phytoestrogenic components in plasma, adipose tissue, and plant material.

The separation of isoflavones and coumestrol was performed by paper chromatography. Two solvent systems were selected for optimal separation. In toluene-petroleum benzin-methanol-water (5:5:7:3), the genistein was only slightly separated from the starting line, whereas in the system benzene-methanol-water (10:5:5), biochanin A moved close to the solvent front. The biochanin A and genistein spots were cut and eluted by methanol, and UV absorption spectra were determined over the range of 240–284 nm against paper blank eluates. For semiquantitative estimation of genistein, biochanin A, and pratensein, the paper chromatograms were stained with bis-diazotized benzidine, Folin-Ciocalteu reagent, and ferric-chloride-ferricyanide reagent. Formononetin, daidzen, and coumestrol were determined on paper by direct fluorophotometry at peak emission 254 nm, or after eluting the bands with 90% ethanol, evaporated to dryness, and redissolved in 1 *M* ammonium hydroxide in 4 ml methanol. Fluorescence was determined against a suitable paper blank in a fluorospectrophotometer.

Isoflavones and coumestrol were assayed by GLC. The sensitivity of the method was enhanced substantially by the assay for genistein, biochanin, and pratensein. Plant extracts can be applied directly to the gas chromatography column (0.75% SE-30) after derivatization to the trimethyl silyl ethers in pyridine. This method was applied to analyses of the plasma of sheep grazing subterranean clover and detected the presence of 2.6 genistein, 0.4 biochanin A, 2.3 formononetin, and 1.7 daidzen in ng units/100 ml. Coumestrol was found in traces only.

Batterham *et al.* (1971) studied the metabolism of intraruminally administered (4-^{14}C) formononetin and (4-^{14}C) biochanin A in sheep. A single intraruminal dose of labeled isoflavone was administered by stomach tube to two ovariectomized ewes, which were slaughtered 6 hr later. In the ewe given labelled biochanin A, labelled genistein was detected in addition to the labelled biochanin A in the blood plasma, urine, and in all parts of the body. *p*-Ethyl phenol, which is a metabolite of biochanin A, was present in the urine but not labelled, indicating that it originated from ring B of the isoflavone molecule. In the ewe given C^{14}-labelled formononetin, a similar distribution of the isoflavone and demethylation product, daidzen, was found. In addition, labelled equol was found in the blood plasma and urine. Another labelled metabolite, identified as O-desmethyl angolensin (4-dihydroxyphenyl-*p*-hydroxy-α-methylbenzyl ketone), was also found in the urine from both ewes. The isoflavones and their metabolites were separated by TLC on silica gel G with methanol-chloroform (1:9) (Beck 1964). Using Whatman No. 1 paper, the paper chromatograms were developed in hexane-butanol-methanol-water (10:5:5:4) and benzene-methanol-water (2:1:1) on both papers, and on TLC chromatograms, formononetin and daidzen were located by their fluorescence under UV light (257 nm). Other phenolic compounds were visualized by spraying first with diazotized sulfanilic acid and then with benzyltrimethylammonium methoxide (40% in methanol, diluted 1:1 with ethanol). TLC plates were sprayed with diazotized sulfanilic acid and exposed to ammonia fumes.

Glencross *et al.* (1972) used Sephadex G-25 column chromatography to remove the interfering chlorophyll and its breakdown products from the isoflavone-containing extracts of leaf protein concentrates. The protein concentrate was dispersed in water and extracted twice with boiling ethanol. The suspension was filtered in vacuum. As the ethanol content was lowered to about 30%, most of the chlorophyll precipitated. The filtrate was evaporated to dryness and then redissolved in 70% ethanol, while the lipids were extracted with petroleum benzin. The alcohol layer was filtered and concentrated in vacuum, and the isoflavones extracted with ether. After evaporating, the ether residue was dissolved in 0.1 *N* NaOH and reprecipitated as a fine suspension by adding 0.1 *N* HCl. The suspension was finally dissolved in 0.1 *N* NH_4OH. The ammoniacal solution was chromatographed on a Sephadex G-25 column and eluted with 0.1 *N* ammonium hydroxide. The eluates were collected in fractions of 4.5 ml. The isoflavones were well separated and determined by spectrophotometry in ethanol, ethanolic 0.1 *N* sodium hydroxide, and 0.1 *N* aqueous ammonia solvents. In the last solvent, the max of biochanin, daidzen, formononetin, and genistein was found to be 268, 258, 255, and 269.5 nm, respectively. The total isoflavone content of LPC was found to be 1% of its dry weight.

Sachse (1974) examined 32 varieties of white clover and red clover for isoflavones and coumestrol. Ten grams of plant material were extracted after hydrolysis with 1 *N* HCl in a boiling water bath, then extracted with acetone. The extracts were concentrated in vacuum and extracted with petroleum benzin. The aqueous phase was mixed with 0.5 g polyamide and transferred to a polyamide column. In another prepurification method, TLC was performed on polyamide layers using several partition solvent mixtures. Coumestrol was purified by TLC on silica gel G. The quantitative analysis was carried out spectrophotometrically. The low levels of formononetin and coumestrol in white clover were determined semiquantitatively on polyamide layers. For formononetin, the plates were developed in petroleum benzin-benzene-methyl ethyl ketone-methanol-acetic acid (30:30:20:20:2), and, for coumestrol, benzene-ethyl acetate-petroleum benzin-methanol (6:4:3:1). The plates were sprayed with 20% sodium carbonate and observed under UV light.

Gosden and Jones (1978) described a simplified method for determination of formononetin in red clover, using fluorophotometry as a routine method for a crude plant extract, without chromatographic purification. The direct fluorometric method gives reproducible results. The freeze-dried plant material (50 mg) was extracted in 3 ml water for 30 min, 7 ml ethanol was added, and the mixture was left for 1 hr with occasional shaking, then centrifuged. Fifty ml of the supernatant was mixed in 5 ml of a 2% ammonia in ethanol solution, and the fluorescence was compared with a standard solution. The direct method was compared to a chromatographic procedure in which the plant extract was prepurified by petroleum benzin extraction of lipids, chromatographed on a glass fiber plate, developed in chloroform, and exposed to ammonia vapor. A spot of formononetin was located under UV light as a pale blue fluorescence. This was cut out of the sheet and placed in a 5 ml ammonia-ethanol solution, and the fluorescence was compared with the co-chromatographed standard. High correlation was found between the direct and chromatographed method.

Determination of Coumestrol

A chromatographic and spectrophotometric method for detection of coumestrol in leguminous plants has been reported (Lyman *et al.* 1959). The method consisted of chromatographing the acetone extract of the dried, milled, plant material in two solvent systems sequentially on paper, followed by using rechromatography four times on silica gel thin layers in four different solvent systems. The identity and purity of coumestrol were established by its characteristic fluorescence, Rf value, and spectrophotometry. By this procedure, the coumestrol was measured in seven forage legumes and the results compared with the values obtained by mean uterine weight assays (Bickoff *et al.* 1959).

Livingston *et al.* (1960) developed a method for analyzing the pure compound by the quantitative measurement of coumestrol on paper chromatograms. The best solvent mixture for the paper chromatography was the water-acetic acid (1:1) mixture, and Whatman No. 1 was the final choice for paper from 17 analyzed samples. It was concluded that coumestrol can be determined in the applied range of 0.2 to 1.0 mg with a standard deviation of about 7%. The method was found to be reproducible from one operator to another.

A rapid, quantitative, paper chromatographic procedure has been developed by Livingston *et al.* (1961) for the determination of coumestrol in fresh and dried alfalfa. Dry or fresh samples were extracted by disintegrating the plant material in 95% ethanol. The alcohol extracts were purified by solvent extraction with petroleum benzin to remove chlorophyll, and the aqueous alcohol phase was extracted successively with ethyl ether. The dried and concentrated ether extracts were then applied to the paper in five different quantities by repeated spottings. The chromatograms were developed in acetic acid-water-hydrochloric acid mixture (50:35:15). By alternate procedures, the extract was chromatographed on silica gel thin layer. The coumestrol spot was detected by UV lamp, removed, and extracted with methanol. Absorbance was determined at 352 mμ.

Similarly, spots from previously described paper chromatograms could be eluted and their absorbances measured with a UV spectrophotometer. The coefficient of variation was 3.4% when analyzing dried alfalfa and 2.3% for the fresh alfalfa.

Knuckles *et al.* (1975) reported a quantitative method for determination of coumestrol in plant material. Freeze-dried samples were extracted with alcohol. Chlorophyll was removed by phase-distribution between chloroform and borate buffer at pH 10. The extracts and coumestrol standards were chromatographed on paper with acetic acid:water (1:1 v/v), and the concentration of coumestrol in spots was directly measured fluorimetrically without elution from the paper. The limit of lowest level that could be measured reliably was 0.1 μg/g. Knuckles *et al.* (1976) determined the coumestrol content of alfalfa leaf protein concentrates. It was reported that more than 80% of initial coumestrol of the alfalfa remained in the pressed residue in the Pro-Xan I process and 95% in the Pro-Xan II process. Coumestrol content of the alfalfa ranged from 11 to 18 μg/g: in the pressed alfalfa, 12 to 142 μg/g; in the green LPC, 18 to 121 μg/g; and in the solubles, 4 to 13 μg/g.

The coumestrol content of white LPC prepared by heat precipitation was found to be 1.1 ng/g, while LPC prepared by ultrafiltration contained 0.4 ng/g.

Lookhart *et al.* (1978) presented a rapid quantitative method for coumestrol determination by high performance liquid chromatography. The plant material was extracted in water for 3 min, allowed to hydrate for 1 hr, blended with methanol, solvated for ½ hr, and centrifuged for 20 min at 1000 *g*. The methanol-water fraction was extracted with *n*-pentane to remove lipids and concentrated on a rotary evaporator. The aqueous concentrate, after extraction with ethyl ether, was transferred quantitatively to a volumetric flask where it was diluted 1:1 with a 65:35 v/v mixture of methanol and water. The HPLC analyses were performed with a DuPont 5 mm particle Zorbax-ODS column, used in the reverse phase mode at room temperature. The solvent system was methanol and water (65:35 v/v). With a flow rate of 1.0 ml/min (13.11 kPa or 1.900 psi), the retention time of coumestrol was about 9 min. A dual pen recorder registered the UV and fluorescence traces. The UV absorption was recorded at 343 nm.

The same author reported a more simple method. TLC was performed on silica gel-G precoated plastic sheets cut to 5 × 5 cm. The developing solvent was chloroform and acetone (88:12 v/v). One ml aliquots of the extracts were concentrated 20-fold by drying under nitrogen. The residue was dissolved in 50 μl methanol, and 1 μl aliquots were spotted. Detection was by viewing under long wavelength UV. The fluorescence of standard and sample spot at Rf 0.50 was visually compared. Quick estimation of coumestrol could be quantitated in the 50–100 ppm range.

Lookhart (1979) reported an improved method of extracting and quantitating coumestrol from soybean which considered the effect of the lipid fraction and type of solvent on the recovery of added standards. About 3 g milled samples were defatted by petroleum benzin with Ultra-Turrax Model SDT and centrifuged. The petroleum benzin extract was back-extracted with 75:25 methanol-water. The defatted plant material was also extracted twice, subsequently with the same solvent mixture. The combined aqueous-methanol extract was concentrated on a rotary evaporator and extracted 3 times with small portions of ethyl ether. The ether fractions were dried under vacuum. The residue was redissolved in 65:35 methanol:water and stored for HPLC analysis.

Lookhart (1980) described a method for determination of coumestrol in animal feeds by HPLC. The air-dried feed samples were extracted by the method previously reported for soybeans (Lookhart 1979), and the separation performed on a 10 nm particle u Bondapak C_{18} column detection system, which included a variable wavelength detector, set at 343 nm, a filter fluorometer with an excitation filter peaking at 360 nm, and an emission filter passing wavelengths above 415 nm. At a flow rate of 1.0 ml, the solvent system, methanol:water (65:35 v/v), gave a retention time for coumestrol of about 9 min.

TOXIC AMINO ACIDS

At the present time, about 320 amino acids are found in plants, and only 20 of these are built into proteins. Some of the nonprotein amino acids are toxic. Because of their close similarity to the protein amino acids, they are able to antagonize basic functions by competing with normal amino acids at specific synthesis sites. In this review, only toxic amino acids which could be present in potential plants for leaf protein extractions (canavanine, mimosine, the lathyrogens, S-methylcysteine sulfoxide, and indospicine) will be discussed. The occurrence and chemical characteristics of these nonprotein amino acids have been reviewed by Murti and Seshadri (1967), Hegarty and Peterson (1973), and Hegarty (1978).

CANAVANINE

Leaves of *Canavalia ensiformis* (L.) DC. (jack bean) were found to be rich in protein (Telek 1979), and the yield of DM was impressive. However, the leaves can contain L-canavanine, 2-amino-4(guanidinoxy)butyric acid, a naturally occurring toxic structural analogue of L-arginine (Fig. 12.10). Kitagawa and Tomiyama (1929) discovered it in *C. ensiformis* and *C. lineata*. It is now known to be present in the seeds and leaves of a large number of species of the subfamily Lotoideae (Rosenthal 1977).

Analysis

Early development of a reliable analytical procedure helped the broad investigation of this toxic amino acid.

Pentacyanoammonioferrate (PCAF) derivatives react with guanidinoxy compounds only within the pH range of 5–7.5, whereas alkyl-substituted guanidines such as arginine react only in solutions more alkaline than pH 8 (Fearon 1946). The reaction in activated by exposure to daylight. Fearon and Bell (1955) reported the test procedure in detail and applied it to a wide variety of seeds, leaves, and fruits. It was only found positive with Leguminosae *Colutea arborescens*, *Medicago arborea*, *M. echinus*, and *Ornithopus perpusillus*. Canavanine has been isolated from *Colutea arborescens*. The Fearon-Bell procedure was slightly modified by Rosenthal (1977). The treatment of the plant extracts by cationic exchange chromatography resulted in a high level of specificity, and the use of persulfate as an oxidizing agent greatly improved the sensitivity of the PCAF canavanine colorimetric assay. The formed magenta color was measured at 530 nm in a spectrophotometer. The inhibition of the PCAF color reaction by ascorbic acid and creatinine makes its direct application to biological plant extracts

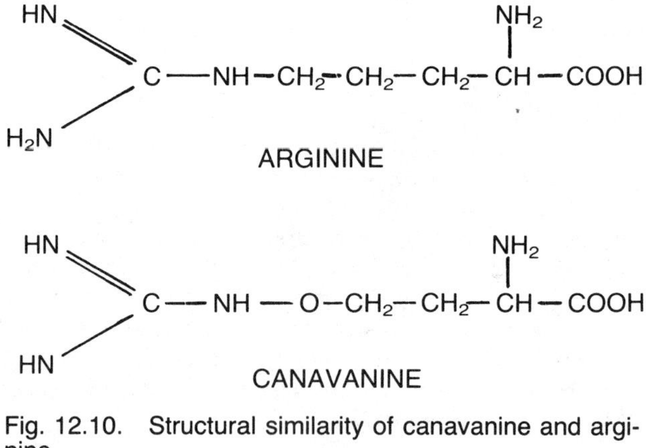

$$(HN{=})(H_2N)C{-}NH{-}CH_2{-}CH_2{-}CH_2{-}CH(NH_2){-}COOH$$

ARGININE

$$(HN{=})(HN)C{-}NH{-}O{-}CH_2{-}CH_2{-}CH(NH_2){-}COOH$$

CANAVANINE

Fig. 12.10. Structural similarity of canavanine and arginine.

of limited value. This difficulty was eliminated by using paper chromatographic determinations or paper electrophoresis to separate the PCAF reactive compounds from others which would inhibit or mask color production (Bell 1958).

The seeds were extracted with 0.1 *N* HCl at room temperature. The acid extract was applied to Whatman No. 1 paper and chromatographed in phenol-water 4:1 (w/w) and butanol-pyridine-acetic acid-water (4:1:1:2). The papers were sprayed with phosphate buffer pH 7 to eliminate pyridine and with PCAF reagent. The positive magenta color was found with extracts prepared from seeds of *Anthyllis vulneraria*, *Caragana arborescens*, *Coronilla emerus*, *C. valentia*, *Desmodium gyrans*, *Hedysarum coronarium*, *Indigofera gerardiana*, *Medicago echinus*, *M. lupulina*, *M. sativa*, *Ononis fructicosa*, *Trifolium dubium*, *T. hybridum*, *T. pratense*, *T. repens*, and *Vicia sativa*.

Miller and Smith (1973) used an amino acid analyzer for the determination of canavanine in indigo species and found 10–564 mg of canavanine/g of nitrogen in whole meal of the nonprotein nitrogen extracts of all the 17 species examined. The only negative reaction was found in the extract of *I. pilosa*.

Preparation

Rosenthal (1977) described a relatively simple method for preparation of L-canavanine from the jack bean. The defatted jack bean meal (350 g) was extracted with a 3 liter 1:1 mixture of ethanol and 0.4 *N* H_2SO_4 and filtered. Proteins were precipitated by adjustment to pH 7.3 with NH_4OH and removed by centrifugation. The pH of the liquid phase was adjusted with H_2SO_4 to 6.2 and stirred with Dowex 50–X8 (NH_4^+). L-Canavanine was eluted with ammonia and crystallized from 95% ethanol. The yield from jack bean was 3.2%.

Biosynthesis and Biochemistry

It was shown that the canavanine content of the leaves increased markedly in the first 13 days of growth (Rosenthal 1970). The biosynthesis of canavanine in developing jack bean leaves was studied by Rosenthal (1972). It was established that the leaf possesses the enzymes required for synthesizing canavanine by a cyclic series of reactions where canaline, O-ureidohomoserine, and canvanine succinate intermediates are involved. Canavanine was hydrolyzed by arginase to canaline, and urea was formed as a by-product (Rosenthal 1973). The arginase enzyme was isolated from the leaves of an 11 day jack bean plant. L-Canaline was isolated as dipicrate salt, which was converted to canaline sulfate by sulfuric acid. Its free base was liberated by the addition of barium hydroxide and precipitated with ice cold absolute ethanol. A new method for colorimetric determination of L-canaline was also presented by Rosenthal.

The biological effects and mode of L-canavanine were extensively reviewed by Rosenthal (1977). Production of canavanine-containing proteins can disrupt the important reaction of RNA and DNA metabolism. It also affects arginine metabolism. Thus canavanine changes essential biochemical reactions, and it becomes a potent antimetabolite of L-arginine. It was found that L-canavanine is a highly toxic secondary plant ingredient, functioning as an allelochemic agent which acts as a deterrent against feeding activity of insects and other herbivores.

LATHYROGENS

For a long time, the seeds and plants of some *Lathyrus* species have been known to cause severe toxic effects in man and animals. Selye (1957) recognized two pathological forms of lathyrism. One, neurolathyrism, refers to a nervous disorder in which the muscles of the legs are paralyzed. The other pathological form is osteolathyrism, in which permanent deformities take place in the bones. The toxic lathyrogen amino acids are shown in Fig. 12.11.

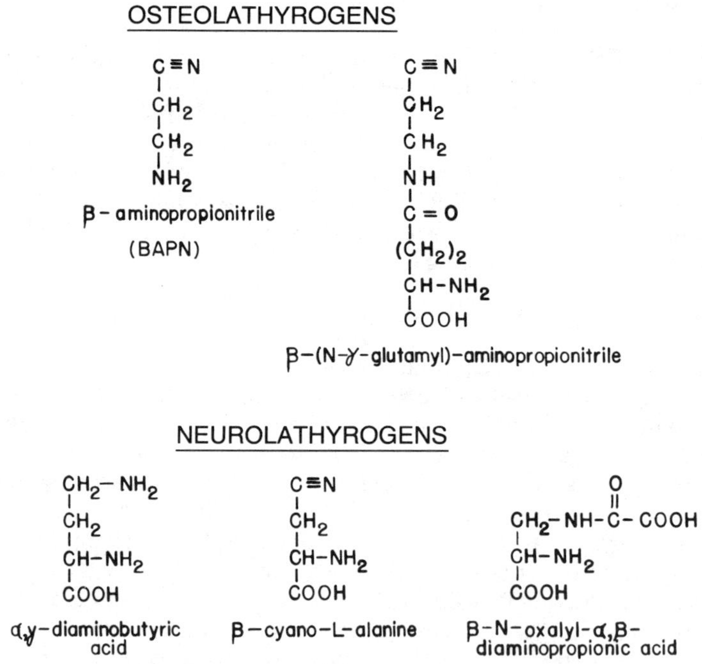

OSTEOLATHYROGENS

$C{\equiv}N$ | CH_2 | CH_2 | NH_2

β-aminopropionitrile (BAPN)

$C{\equiv}N$ | CH_2 | CH_2 | NH | $C=O$ | $(CH_2)_2$ | $CH{-}NH_2$ | $COOH$

β-(N-γ-glutamyl)-aminopropionitrile

NEUROLATHYROGENS

$CH_2{-}NH_2$ | CH_2 | $CH{-}NH_2$ | $COOH$

α,γ-diaminobutyric acid

$C{\equiv}N$ | CH_2 | $CH{-}NH_2$ | $COOH$

β-cyano-L-alanine

$CH_2{-}NH{-}C(=O){-}COOH$ | $CH{-}NH_2$ | $COOH$

β-N-oxalyl-α,β-diaminopropionic acid

Fig. 12.11. The osteo- and neurolathyrogens.

Neurolathyrogens

Lathyrus sativus seeds have long been suspected of causing the neurolathyrism prevalent in populations in some areas of India. The neurotoxic principle has been isolated in crystalline form and characterized as β-oxaloamino-alanine (Adiga *et al.* 1963). Bell (1964) reported that this compound occurs in 20 other *Lathyrus* species, and its higher homologue, β-amino-L-oxaloaminobutyric acid, occurs in 10 species. It was found by Ressler *et al.* (1961) that β-cyano-L-alanine at a 1% level in a standard rat diet produced severe nervous symptoms, hyperirritability, and convulsions, followed by death. Lewis and coworkers described the same symptoms in rats after feeding them with *Lathyrus latifolius* (perennial sweet pea) and *L. sylvestris* (flat pea). In their attempt to detect and isolate β-cyano-L-alanine from these plants, Ressler *et al.* (1961) suggested that the chief neurotoxic principle was its reduction product, L-diaminobutyric acid. Bioassay by administration of its aqueous extract by stomach tube into male rats showed that within 48 hr, after tremors and convulsions, the experimental animals died. The ground seed was extracted by hexane and 3 times with 30% ethanol. After charcoal purification, it was crystallized and was subjected in 2.7 g aliquots to preparative electrophoresis in pyridine acetate.

The activity was concentrated in the basic region. After several purifications by electrophoresis, the active principle was crystallized and identified as diaminobutyric acid. Quantitative determination of this toxic amino acid in *Lathyrus latifolius* seed indicated concentrations of 0.51–0.67% and, in *L. sylvestris*, 1.4%. This finding explains the high toxicity of immature flat pea plants consumed as forage by livestock.

Ressler (1962) reported the isolation and identification of crystalline β-cyano-L-alanine from *Vicia sativa* and *V. angustifolia* seeds as a factor of neurolathyrism. It was found to be neurotoxic to rats at the 1% level; the D-isomer was toxic also at about ⅓ of potency.

Osteolathyrogens

Schilling (1954) reported the isolation of a crystalline toxic compound from the sweet pea *(Lathyrus odoratus)* that was found to be active in the production of skeletal changes in rats. The same compound was prepared at higher purity by Dasler (1954), who described two procedures for isolation of toxic crystals from sweet peas. In the first method, the residue from alcoholic sweet pea extract was partitioned between ether and water. The aqueous phase was purified with basic lead acetate followed by passage of a strongly basic ion exchange resin [Amberlite IRA-400 (OH^-)]. The toxic factor was then adsorbed onto a strongly acidic cation exchange resin [Amberlite IR-105 H^+)], from which it was eluted with 5% H_2SO_4. Excess $SO_4^=$ was removed with barium hydroxide. After concentration of the solution, ethanol precipitated the alkali sulfates, which were filtered out of the warm solution. During cooling time, white needles separated.

In his second method, the coarsely ground sweet peas were extracted thoroughly with *n*-hexane to remove lipids. The dried peas were subsequently extracted with 95% ethanol for 7 hr. On standing in a refrigerator, dense rosettes of yellowish crystals formed. The crystals were washed with ethyl ether, dissolved in water, and treated with basic lead acetate. Following filtration, the excess lead was removed by sparging with H_2S gas, and the filtrate of the formed lead sulfide was evaporated to dryness in a vacuum. The white solid was dissolved in boiling ethanol and water added to cloud point. On cooling, crystals formed. Recrystallization from alcohol-water gave long, fine colorless needles melting at 209°C.

Schilling and Strong (1954) reported that the toxic compound isolated from the sweet pea and reported previously was β-(N-1-L-glutamyl) aminopropionitrile. The analysis gave the formula $C_8H_{13}O_3N_3$. It showed one ninhydrin positive spot on paper chromatography. After hydrolysis in HCl, this spot disappeared and was replaced by two others. On cooling of the hydrolysis mixture, L-glutamic acid precipitated and β-alanine formed in the remaining hydrolysis product. β-(N-1-L-glutamyl) aminopropionitrile was synthesized and found to be identical with the fine needles isolated from *Lathyrus odoratus*.

Wawzonek *et al.* (1955) determined that β-aminopropionitrile (BAPN) fed to weanling rats at concentrations of 0.1, 0.4, and 1% in their diet produced extensive degenerative damage in bones and connective tissues. Blood vessel lesions were observed in rats fed on diets containing 50%. *Lathyrus odoratus*. α-Aminopropionitrile did not produce lesions at 1.0 and 0.2% levels. With BAPN at the 0.2% level, no degenerative activity could be observed in rats. The experimental animals developed normally during the 34 days of the experiment. Dupuy and Lee (1954) demonstrated the presence of bound BAPN in *L. odoratus* and *L. pusillus*. The legumes were extracted for 12 hr in a Soxhlet extractor with absolute methanol. The concentrated extracts were chromatographed on paper by the butanol-acetic acid-water system. Ninhydrin spray (0.15% in acetone) formed a blue color with BAPN.

Garbutt and Strong (1957) developed a rapid method for the determination of BAPN in legume seed with ninhydrin, which produces a green color. As low as 50 ppm BAPN can be detected by this method. The ground sample was extracted with water and refluxed for 40 hr to hydrolyze the naturally occurring β-(N-1-L-glutamyl) aminopropionitrile. An aliquot was saturated with sodium chloride, and its pH adjusted to 9 with Na_2CO_3. It was extracted with ether and taken up in 1-butanol. Ninhydrin reagent was added (20 mg/ml acetone) to an aliquot. The absorption was measured at 620 nm. A calibration curve was prepared with BAPN standard (100 mg/ml butanol).

THE *BRASSICA* ANEMIA FACTOR

Brassicas are valuable cattle feed in winter. The crop may be cut periodically and transported to the stable or consumed in the field. With increasing feed prices, there is new interest in growing this low price crop again. However, ruminants fed mainly on *Brassica* crops may develop severe hemolytic anemia. Clegg (1966) reviewed the kale poisoning of cattle and discussed the first reports of this disease. Reports of later studies on kale anemia are thoroughly discussed in reviews by Greenhalgh (1969) and Greenhalgh *et al.* (1969, 1970, 1972). The first clinical signs of the disease appear after a few weeks of kale feeding. Granules develop in the red cells, the so-called Heinz-Ehrlich bodies. Severe anemia and hemoglobinuria develop. Jaundice appears, due to accumulation of heme products, and milk production decreases. Similar symptoms can be observed when rape, cabbage, and Brussels sprouts are fed to cattle.

Isolation of the toxic principle is described in detail by Smith (1974). The systematic investigation of kale to isolate and identify the toxic principle was started by N.A. Matheson. He isolated the compound by ion exchange column chromatography. However, the characterization of the compound was accomplished by Smith *et al.* (1974). They found in the isolates high contents of S-methylcysteine sulfoxide (SMCO), the hemolytic fraction (Fig. 12.12).

This compound had previously been isolated on a relatively large scale from cabbage by Synge and Wood (1956), who characterized the compound chemically in detail. Thus, the experiments could be continued with a pure compound. Smith *et al.* (1974) observed that volatile sulfur compounds were formed in high concentrations in the rumen of a kale-poisoned goat (Fig. 12.12). They identified the presence of dimethyl disulfide and methanethiol

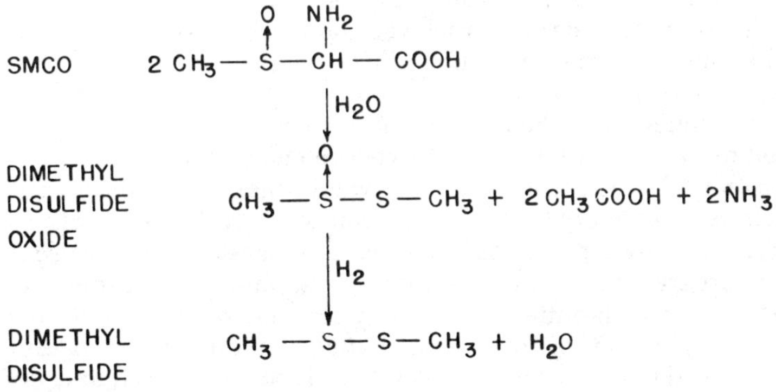

Fig. 12.12. The metabolism of S-methylcysteine sulfoxide to dimethyl disulfide in rumen.

by GLC and mass spectroscopy. Forty years ago, Gruhzit (1931) found hemolytic compounds in onion juice, of D-*n*-propyldisulfide which produced severe anemia in experimental animals. Using his dosage form, Smith *et al.* (1974) administered 1.4 g pure dimethyl disulfide to a 14 kg goat for 6 days. The response was characteristic of kale poisoning.

Analytical Methods

Morris and Thompson (1956) determined the SMCO content of turnip, cabbage, Chinese cabbage, cauliflower, kohlrabi, radish, and broccoli by two-dimensional paper chromatography. Whittle *et al.* (1976) presented a reliable method suitable for rapid screening of a large number of *Brassica* samples by electrophoretic separation of SMCO on a silica gel-impregnated glass-fiber sheet, visualized with ninhydrin/cadmium acetate reagent and measured quantitatively by photodensitometry. The results agreed well with those obtained by using the amino acid analyzer. The SMCO content of farm-grown kales varied by cultivar between 4.13 and 12.7 g/kg dry wt. The SMCO content of swedes varied from 5.0 to 18.7 g/kg dry matter.

Matheson and Moir (1976) reported a simple, semiquantitative TLC method for determination of SMCO. This method is suitable for fast preliminary screening of a large quantity of plant material. Ten grams of fresh weight sample were extracted by maceration with aqueous ethanol, evaporated to dryness, and redissolved in water. The extracts were chromatographed on a microcrystalline cellulose layer (MN-300) and developed by the solvent system isopropanol:20% formic acid (80:20). Visualization occurred with 0.2% ninhydrin in methanol. Standards were applied simultaneously in concentrations of 0.05, 0.1, 0.3, and 0.5 monograms on the TLC plates.

Matheson (1980) suggested some improvements in sample preparation over their previous method. Kale samples were extracted by single maceration with ethanol, and the extract was applied directly to thin layer plates. The ethanolic extraction simplified the procedure, and more samples could be processed at the same time.

A semiautomated method for the estimation of SMCO in forage kale was reported by Gosden (1979). This procedure enabled 36 samples to be analyzed in an 8 hr period. The apparatus was a simplified amino acid analyzer lab-built from commercially available components. The apparatus is fairly expensive to construct, and this method is suggested only for use in plant breeding programs with a large number of samples. The freeze-dried sample was treated with buffered hydrogen peroxide solution, and the extract chromatographed on a short ion exchange column containing Amberlite CG-120, type II resin. The method was found specific and reliable. Although the separation between SMCO and the neighboring amino acids was poor, the maximum of the SMCO peak was not affected. The accuracy of determinations was found to be about 5%.

The influence of SMCO on nonruminant animals was reviewed by Smith (1974). Itokawa *et al.* (1973) found that, in cholesterol-fed rats, SMCO was involved in lowering the cholesterol level of the plasma and liver. Smith (1978) reported that a daily intake of 5–10 g/100 kg generally led to a mild blood disturbance only, and the productivity of the animal was not affected. SMCO content is a heritable characteristic of the brassicas; breeding to lower the content of its active form would improve the value of this forage. As yet, no antidote has been found to counteract the physiological action of SMCO in ruminants; therefore, the limiting of intake is the only preventive measure that can be taken. The possible anticoronary action of SMCO in man was discussed by Smith (1978).

MIMOSINE

The toxic nonprotein amino acid, mimosine, β-[N-(3-hydroxy-4-pyridone)] -α-aminopropionic acid, is present in every variety of *Leucaena leucocephala*, a legume tree found throughout the tropics and in some subtropical areas. Mimosine is also present in the leaves of other trees of the Mimosa family. Haberland (1890) investigated the exudates of mimosas and their reaction with $FeCl_3$. Molisch (1915) recognized the phenolic nature of the compound. Renz (1936) reported that the crystalline material was formed from the exudate of young leaf stems of *Mimosa pudica*. After cutting the stems with sharp, nickel-plated scissors, he smeared the exudate on a watch glass. A short time later, the green-yellow slimy mass crystallized in different forms. The crude crystalline compound was washed with absolute alcohol, and the insoluble material was recrystallized in water to a white crystalline product with a constant melting point of 228°C. The empirical formula was found to be $C_4H_5O_2N$. It was noted that the isolated compound was insoluble in absolute alcohol, methanol, chloroform, ether, and xylene, but soluble in warm 50% ethanol and weak aqueous or methanolic alkali, and could be recrystallized in water. It was also established that it could be detected in 0.008% solution with 1% ninhydrin in ethanol and in 0.007% solution with 5% aqueous ferric chloride reagent. It gave a red color with diazotized benzene sulfonic acid. The compound was named mimosine.

Nienburg and Tauböck (1937) reported their independent results of isolation of mimosine from exudates of *Mimosa pudica*. They determined that the molecular formula should be $C_8H_{10}O_4N_2$ (molecular weight 198.09), since only half of the total nitrogen could be titrated according to the method of Van Slyke. They prepared several derivatives; however, their suggestion as to the molecular configuration of mimosine was not entirely faultless. Mascre (1937) isolated a crystalline solid, mp 287°C, by aqueous extraction of ground *Leucaena leucocephala* seed and named this compound leucenol. Its empirical formula was found to be ($C_4H_5O_2N$); it was shown experimentally to be an L-amino acid, and it contained a phenolic hydroxyl.

Adams *et al.* (1945) investigated the chemical structure of leucenol, extracting it from *Leucaena leucocephala* seed with 90% ethanol. The presence of a phenolic group was confirmed by ferric chloride and folin reagent tests. Its entity as an amino acid was confirmed by the ninhydrin test, half of the N content being found as an amino group by Van Slyke analysis. Absorption spectra in aqueous and diluted solutions resembled the spectra of the hydroxypyridines. Through degradation studies (Adams and Johnson 1949), the structural formula of leucenol was reported (Fig. 12.13). Leucenol has been synthesized by condensation of 3-methyl-4-pyridone with acetamidoacrylic acid and hydrolysis of the primary condensation product, which is the same as the mimosine isolated by Renz procedures (1936). The identity of mimosine and leucenol was also reported by Kleipool and Wibaut (1950) and Wibaut and Schumacher (1952).

Bickel and Wibaut (1946) isolated mimosine from seeds of *Leucaena leucocephala* (at that time *Leucaena glauca*) by hot water extraction. The vacuum-concentrated syrupy extract was poured into stirred 95% ethanol. With charcoal treatment, purified mimosine crystallized. One kg of seed yielded 16 g of pure mimosine.

Hegarty and Court (1964) reported an improved method for the isolation of mimosine from the seed of *Leucaena*. Seeds were milled and seed coat particles removed. A 100 g portion of milled material was mixed with 1250 ml of water. To this mixture was added a cellophane bag containing a slurry of Zeokarb 225 (110 ml of wet ion exchange resin) in 0.5% gum arabicum. The mixture and bag were shaken for 24 hr. The cellophane bag was

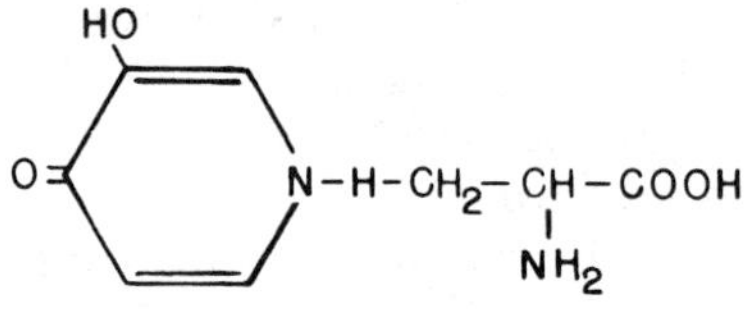

HO
O= N-H-CH_2-CH-COOH
NH_2

L-Mimosine

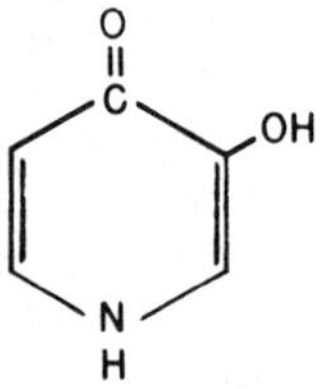

O
C
OH
N
H

3-hydroxy-4(IH)-pyridone

Fig. 12.13. Mimosine and its metabolite 3-hydroxy-4-pyridone.

exchanged for a new bag and shaking continued for another 12 hr. The resin from both bags was transferred to a glass column and washed with 1 liter water and 200 ml ethanol. Ethanol was removed with distilled water wash, and the organic cations were displaced by 2 *N* NH_4OH. The eluate was concentrated to a thick syrup, dissolved in 20–30 ml of water, and pH was adjusted to 4.5–5 with 6 *N* HCl. The suspension was stored overnight at 4.5°–5°C. The resulting crystalline mimosine was filtered, washed with cold water, and dried in vacuum. The third extract contained only 0.04 g mimosine.

The amino acid mimosine is not built into the proteins of Mimosaceae. Leaf protein concentrate prepared from *Leucaena leucocephala* contains up to 7% mimosine, which can be extracted by aqueous hydrochloric acid of low concentration. The distribution of mimosine during leaf protein fractionation can be monitored by an amino acid analyzer (Telek and Evans 1978).

Analysis

Quantitative determination based on the color reaction of mimosine with ferric chloride has been developed by Yoshida (1944). Matshumoto and Sherman (1951) modified this method by using activated carbon to remove interfering colored substances. Carangal and Catiding (1955) and Hegarty (1957) examined the free amino acids of *Leucaena leucocephala* by use of two-dimensional paper chromatography. A quantitative GLC analysis of mimosine was reported by Mee and Brooks (1971). Mimosine was extracted from *L. glauca* (now *L. leucocephala*) with cold 0.1 *N* HCl and derivatized by esterification and acylation according to Roach and Gehrke (1969). The glass column was packed with 0.325% EGA on 80–100 mesh HT Chromosorb G.

Mzik (1977) described two procedures for measuring the concentration of mimosine in sheep plasma by ion exchange chromatography, using a Technicon TSM amino acid analyzer. One of the methods, using a four-buffer system, analyzed all the acidic and neutral amino acids, including mimosine. The second, faster procedure resolved only isoleucine, leucine, mimosine, and thyrozine in plasma.

Hegarty *et al.* (1976) described a chromatographic method for quantitative determination of mimosine and its metabolite in leaves and seeds of *Leucaena leucocephala* and animal urine specimens. The plant material was extracted with 0.1 *N* HCl, the extracts were purified by ion exchange chromatography on Dowex 50-X4 cation exchange resin (H^+ form) and eluted with 2 *N* ammonium hydroxide. Aliquots of the prepared samples were spotted on Whatman No. 1 paper and chromatographed by descending chromatography with the solvent mixture mesityloxide:formic acid:water (41:7:6). The paper was lightly sprayed with ferric chloride, and the mimosine and 3-hydroxy-4-pyridone (DHP) appeared as orange-red spots. The spots were cut out and extracted with 5 ml $FeCl_3$ reagent in the dark for 15 min with several gentle agitations. Absorptivity was measured at 535 nm.

A colorimetric method for mimosine determination in *Leucaena* leaves developed by Megarrity (1978) is an automated version of the Matshumoto-Sherman procedure. Fresh leaf material was extracted with diluted HCl containing activated carbon, and the concentration of mimosine in the clarified solution was determined by colorimetry with ferric chloride reagent using an autoanalyzer. The recovery of mimosine was satisfactory, and the results were in agreement with the paper electrophoretic method of Reis *et al.* (1975B).

Biological Activity

The visible symptoms of mimosine toxicity are hair loss in horses, loss of part or all of their wool in sheep, loss of feathers and decreased growth in poultry, and reduced fertility and low growth rates in swine. Some toxicity is also reported in ruminants, but it is transitory and less severe in these animals. It has been reported by Hegarty *et al.* (1976) that the metabolite of mimosine, 3-hydroxy-4(1H)-pyridone (DHP), is a potent goitrogen (Fig. 12.13). Offspring with goiters have been born to sheep (Bindon and Lamond 1966) and cattle (Hamilton *et al.* 1971) fed during pregnancy on rations containing high percentage of *Leucaena*. Holmes (1976) found that goiters in cattle grazing *Leucaena* could not be reversed by a high iodine diet. Isomimosine prepared by Ward and Harris (1976) had a potency similar to mimosine for actively defleecing sheep. DHP given as an intravenous infusion was ineffective.

Hegarty *et al.* (1978) investigated the comparative toxicities of mimosine and chemically related compounds using mouse bone marrow cells in liquid culture. Thirteen compounds related to mimosine were studied. The preparation of these compounds was summarized and documented. Mimosine was shown to be a potent inhibitor of incorporation of (^{3}H)-thymidine into mouse bone marrow cells in liquid culture. For the inhibitory activity, the presence of the 3-hydroxyl-4-oxo function of the pyridone ring and an alanine or 2-aminoethyl side chain was necessary. The metabolite of mimosine, 3-hydroxy-4(1H)-pyridone (DHP), a potent goitrogen, was only slightly inhibitory. The inhibition could be used as a cytotoxicity index; it is a sensitive and reproducible method. Hegarty *et al.* (1979) studied the effect of DHP on mice and rats. Mice fed a diet containing 1% (w/w) DHP developed goiters even on a diet high in iodine; mimosine of 0.5% did not produce goiters even on a low-iodine diet. A single intragastric dose of DHP inhibited the absorption of ^{125}I by the thyroid of the rat. An equivalent dose of mimosine did not. The inhibition occurs at the iodine-binding step, similar to methylthiouracil. The metabolic form of DHP in animals (DHP-3-O-glucuronide) was almost as potent a goitrogen as the free compound when given orally; however, it was found to be considerably less active in the bloodstream than the free form.

Defleecing of Sheep

Consumption of seeds or leaves of *Leucaena leucocephala* causes loss of hair in various animals. Crounse *et al.* (1962) investigated the inhibition of growth of hair in mice by purified mimosine and by mimosine extracted from *L. leucocephala* and found that no hair regrowth could be observed in animals receiving 10% ground seed or 1% mimosine in their diet. They demonstrated that only the growing hair was affected. Hegarty *et al.* (1964B) showed that mimosine caused alopecia. The depilatory effect of *L. glauca* (now *Leucaena leucocephala*) was influenced by level and method of feeding. During the intravenous administration of 4.0 g of mimosine/day to a sheep weighing 32 kg, it was found that shedding was positive after 92 hr and stopped soon after 36 hr administration. The animal stopped eating at 36 hr and by 120 hr was lying down continuously. The dewclaws on the hind legs were shed at 144 hr, and the hooves were shed from the left foreleg and right hind leg on the eighth day. The sheep died after 190 hr. Abomasal infusion of about 35 g mimosine into two sheep over a period of 4–5 days resulted in shedding of the fleece and in the death of the experimental animals.

Reis (1975) measured the defleecing potential and wool regrowth after a continuous intravenous infusion of L-mimosine into Merino sheep for periods of 1½, 2, and 21 days. Infusions for 1½ and 2 days at a daily rate of 80–120 mg/kg caused a cessation of wool growth by 1½–2 days after the start of infusion, and all sheep were subsequently defleeced. Wool growth stopped for 10½–13 days in four sheep and 5½–9½ days in two sheep after infusion for 1½ days. The growth rate of wool fibers was greater post-treatment than it was pretreatment. Simultaneous infusions of tyrosine, phenylalanine, and cysteine with mimosine failed to prevent any of the effects.

Additional testing of the effects of mimosine on wool growth and the skin of sheep was reported by Reis *et al.* (1975A). Merino sheep were dosed with various amounts of L-mimosine by intravenous or intraperitoneal injections, or as a continuous intravenous infusion for periods of 1–4 days. Only injections of larger amounts (8–16 g) changed slightly the strength of the wool. Infusions of a total of 8 g either at a daily rate of 2 g/day or 8 g/day weakened the wool but not sufficiently for successful defleecing. Infusion at the higher rate for one day had a greater effect. Defleecing was effective with mimosine infusions at the daily rate of 77 mg/kg or higher. The skin was not affected by the dosing.

Reis *et al.* (1975B) investigated the fate of mimosine administered orally to sheep and its effectiveness as a defleecing agent. Isolated mimosine and foliage of *Leucaena leucocephala* were given orally to Merino sheep in single daily doses for periods of 1–3 days. A single dose of 450–600 mg/kg body weight was effective for defleecing sheep. A daily dose rate of 300 mg/kg was effective for defleecing sheep if given on two successive days. The effectiveness of an oral treatment depended on the concentration of mimosine in plasma, a concentration which should be maintained above 0.1 mmol/liter for at least 30 hr. Some of the mimosine was excreted in the urine; some was metabolized to 3-hydroxy-4(1H)pyridone (DHP) and began to be excreted 3 days after mimosine dosing. Small amounts of mimosine amine were also excreted. Following an intravenous infusion of mimosine, no DHP was detected in the urine. Most of the mimosine was excreted without any change; only 9% was transformed into mimosine amine.

Ward and Harris (1976) studied the inhibition of DNA synthesis in wool follicles by mimosine and related DHP. The *in vitro* incorporation of (^{3}H)-thymidine was examined in thin slices of sheep skin. Mimosine was shown to inhibit the incorporation at a concentration of 0.2 nm. The inhibition of (^{3}H)-thymidine incorporation is time dependent and completely reversible. Two hr of incubation are required for maximal inhibition of DNA synthesis. The 3-hydroxyl-4-oxo function of the pyridone ring appears to be the active center of the inhibition.

Reis *et al.* (1978) studied the defleecing effectiveness of oral doses of mimosine using two successive daily applications or a single dose. Two successive daily doses of 300 mg/kg allowed all sheep to be defleeced. For sheep consuming a daily intake of 600 g feed, a single oral dose of 400 mg/kg was sufficient for defleecing. When the daily feed intake was increased to 1200 g, a dose of 600 mg/kg was required to allow defleecing of most sheep. Fasting prior to dosing appeared to obviate the effects of previous feedings; however, it increased the risk of toxic effects and doubled or tripled the concentration of mimosine in plasma.

Effectiveness of intravenous and abomasal doses of mimosine for defleecing sheep and effects on subsequent wool growth have been studied by Reis (1978). Four Merino sheep were given intravenous infusions of mimosine for two days at a rate of 110–120 mg/kg/day. Wool growth stopped about 1 day after the start of the infusions, and the sheep could be manually defleeced. The wool growth ceased for about 12 days. Wool growth rates were above the pre-infusion rates in early regrowth (3–5 weeks after dosing), and fiber diameter was 2 nm above the pre-infusion values. In further experiments, it was found that the minimal rate of infusion to produce consistent defleecing was 80 mg/kg/day. The dosage of 160 mg/kg/day was found to be lethal to one sheep, and higher doses of 240–320 mg/kg were lethal to all animals. The concentration of mimosine in plasma was proportional to the rate of its infusion.

The influence of nutrition on the effectiveness of mimosine for defleecing sheep has been studied by Reis and Tunks (1978). It was reported that sheep receiving 600 g of roughage-based diet, followed by an 80 mg/kg/day infusion of mimosine, consistently were defleeced. With a 4-day fasting prior to the start of mimosine infusions, approximately half the amount was required to defleece sheep. Fasting enhances the concentration of mimosine in plasma. Nutritional status, especially amino acid supply, may influence the action of mimosine. High energy intake, together with large amounts of amino acids (such as casein) available for absorption from the small intestine, for at least 1 week prior to mimosine infusion, completely prevented defleecing with the standard amount of infusion of mimosine. It is interesting to note that a relatively larger amount of mimosine was required to defleece young lambs than adult sheep. Infusion of mimosine at a standard rate resulted in a concentration of 100 μ-moles/liter of plasma; however, this concentration did not ensure that defleecing would be successful.

INDOSPICINE

Warmke *et al.* (1952) studied the palatability of some tropical legumes and found that *Indigofera endecaphylla* was second best in acceptance (59% consumption) and showed good recovery after grazing. The yield was calculated as 5173 kg/ha DM from January 16 until September 30. However, after its introduction in Hawaii, it was observed that the plant was toxic to herds of dairy cattle (Nordfeldt *et al.* 1952). Feeding tests with guinea pigs in Puerto Rico indicated no toxicity, but pregnant females invariably aborted during early or middle pregnancy. Feeding tests with 1-week-old chicks showed that the lethal dose for them is 5 g of dry plant material. Rosenberg and Zoebisch (1952) suggested a chick test for toxicity in forage legumes, especially for routine checks of new, exotic forage plants. Only about 500 g of dry meal were needed to perform this test with *Indigo* species. The chicks responded by slow growth, paralysis, and eventually death. Morris *et al.* (1954) found that the toxic plant material is soluble in hot water. From water it could be extracted with ether. From melting points and UV absorption maxima, they concluded that the compound was hyptagenic acid, which was found to be β-nitropropionic acid (BNPA) by Carter and McChesney (1949).

Britten *et al.* (1959) studied the toxic effects of BNPA and sodium nitrite of *I. endecaphylla* on chicks. They stated that the characteristic symptoms of plant toxicity were caused by BNPA. Nothing could be observed with treatment with sodium nitrite. The authors wrongly concluded that BNPA was the sole toxic ingredient of creeping indigo. Coleman *et al.* (1960) studied the toxicity of *I. endecaphylla* and concluded that the liver damage observed in test animals was not caused by BNPA. They described the toxic ingredient as water-soluble and capable of being isolated on ion exchange resins. Hutton *et al.* (1958A) investigated the toxicity of *I. endecaphylla* and decided that the toxin was not BNPA. They found that rabbits fed green leaf or seed of creeping indigo developed severe liver damage. β-Nitropropionic acid could not be detected in the seed, although it was present in the leaf in a range of 6.5–13.2 mg/g of fresh plant weight. The feeding of plants with higher levels of BNPA had no visible effect on the liver damage induced by plants of low or high activity. Synthetic BNPA was found to be hepatotoxic to rabbits when force-fed in amounts comparable to that in the green leaf. The same workers (Hutton 1958B) evaluated mice as test animals for biological analysis of various fractions of *I. endecaphylla*. It was reported that severe liver damage could be produced in mice by feeding them the seeds of *I. endecaphylla*. Similar liver damage could be produced by feeding the chloroform-extracted residue of the leaf which is free from BNPA. The degree and type of histological liver damage produced are reliable indexes of the toxicity of the material fed.

Hegarty and Pound described the isolation, structure, and biological behavior of indospicine (1970) (Fig. 12.14). The isolation from seeds and leaves is presented in detail. The fresh leaves of *Indigofera specata* were extracted with 75% ethanol and concentrated in a rotary evaporator at 40°C. The extract was chromatographed on Zeokarb 225 in ammonia form equilibrated with ammonium acetate-acetic acid buffer at pH 5.9. The same buffer was used as eluent, and 25 ml fractions were collected. The presence of indospicine in the fractions was tested with TLC. The indospicine-rich fractions were united and crude indospicine isolated and purified through its flavionate salt, then crystallized from boiling water. The monohydrochloride monohydrate salt was crystallized from aqueous ethanol. Various plant parts were extracted with 75% ethanol, concentrated, and analyzed for indospicine content. The concentration was found highest in seeds (0.5–2%), slightly lower in tips, and lower in leaves (0.04–0.5%). Miller and Smith (1973) examined 17 different species of *Indigofera*. The occurrence of indospicine was determined by TLC. The seed meal was extracted with 0.1 *N* HCl in 70% ethanol. TLC was performed on silica gel G plates with a developing solvent mixture of chloroform-methanol-conc. NH_4OH-water (40:40:15:5). Spots were visualized with a solution of 500 mg of ninhydrin in 15–20 ml of acetone and 3 ml of acetic acid and then diluted to 100 ml with 1-butanol. Ion exchange chromatographic separation was achieved with 50–100 mesh Dowex 50-X2 cation exchange resin in H^+ form. Basic amino acids were eluted from the column with 250 ml of 2 *N* NH_4OH as one fraction and separated on Whatman 3 mm paper using 1-propanol-conc. ammonium hydroxide (70:30) as the partition solvent. The separation of the

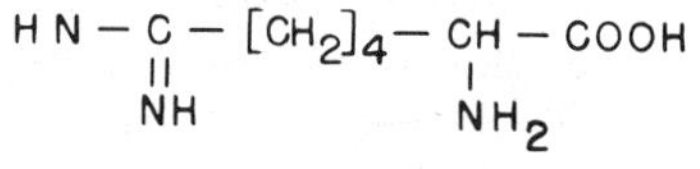

$$HN{-}\underset{\underset{NH}{\|}}{C}{-}[CH_2]_4{-}\underset{\underset{NH_2}{|}}{CH}{-}COOH$$

Indospicine

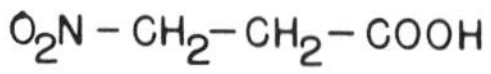

$$O_2N-CH_2-CH_2-COOH$$

β-nitropropionic acid (BNPA)

Fig. 12.14. Indospicine and β-nitropropionic acid (BNPA).

basic amino acids with pH 5.28 (0.35 *N* sodium citrate) buffer was performed by an amino acid analyzer using a 50 cm long column filled with Beckman UR 30 resin. Indospicine was eluted about 50 min after canavanine.

Charlwood and Bell (1977) described a qualitative and quantitative method for determination of free amino acids present in plant extracts by use of the amino acid analyzer. The analyzer was modified to allow the absorption of ninhydrin colors to be measured at various wavelengths, permitting the identification of amino acids by the formed ninhydrin colors and by the elution times. The method was used for analyzing free amino acids of extracts of 32 species of *Indigofera*. Christie *et al.* (1969) reported that a single dose (2 g/kg body weight) of indospicine HCl administered through a stomach tube caused an increase in liver triglycerides and nearly doubled the weight of the liver. It was found that the increase was caused by a sudden water uptake by the liver. Pearn and Hegarty (1970) found that indospicine caused infertility and teratogenic reactions in rats and mice. In rats, a 2 g/kg dose given on day 13 of gestation produced cleft palates in 80% of the test animals. Indospicine is an arginine analogue and antagonist; it inhibits the incorporation of arginine into liver protein, resulting in a secondary inhibition of other amino acid depositions (Madsen *et al.* 1970).

SOLANUM ALKALOIDS

Potato haulms were studied by Pirie (1978) as a source of leaf protein concentrate. The yield of extracted protein depends on the variety and the age of the haulm. It was estimated that, in Britain alone, 50,000MT LPC could be extracted from this unutilized by-product of potato harvest. Similarly, a large percentage of tomato leaves is removed and discarded during the growing season which could be a potential source for LPC extraction. The author himself has experimented with simultaneous utilization of leaves of *Solanum laciniatum* for solasodine and LPC production (Telek, unpublished).

The protein content of the *Solanum* leaves is sufficiently high for extraction; however, the leaves contain various levels of toxic and teratogenic steroid glycoalkaloids. The *Solanum* glycoalkaloids tomatine, solanine, and solasonine are water-soluble. It was anticipated that they may remain in solution in the deproteinized juice. However, when the author studied the leaf proteins of *Solanum laciniatum* containing solasonine, a preferred plant source for industrial synthesis of a wide range of steroidal hormones, it was noted that the compound was partially adsorbed on the leaf protein concentrates, which were heat-precipitated from the green juice of this plant.

Solanine was isolated about 160 years ago (Desfosses 1820), and it was known to be the causative factor of potato poisoning (Willimot 1933). The observation that some *Solanum* species were resistant to the attack of the potato beetle and that the sap of tomato stems was fungistatic to *Fusarium bulbigenum* stimulated a renewed effort in the research of *Solanum* steroid alkaloids. During the progress of this research, by application of new chromatographic methods, it was demonstrated that numerous *Solanum* glycoalkaloids could be found in nature because of the extensive variation in the carbohydrate side chain.

The second impetus in this research came after the report of Sato *et al.* (1951) that the side chain of solasodine and tomatidine could be eliminated by the Marker degradation (Marker and Rohrmann 1939) to form 3-β-acetoxypregnan-5,16-diene-20-one and its 5,6-dihydro derivative, which are starting intermediates for manufacturing a wide variety of steroidal drugs.

The chemistry of the *Solanum* alkaloids has been thoroughly reviewed by Prelog and Jeger (1953 and 1960) and Schreiber (1968). The biochemistry of glycoalkaloids has been discussed by Heftmann (1967) and Singh *et al.* (1969). The biosynthesis of steroids has been reviewed by Willuhn (1965) and Heftmann (1968).

SOLANINE

Solanine has been known since 1820, when Desfosses found it in *Solanum nigrum*. In 1826 Baup reported its isolation from potatoes. Potato sprouts are very rich in solanine, and they are a good source of this glycoalkaloid. Kuhn and Löw (1947) reported the isolation of solanine from potato sprouts. Freshly cut sprouts were soaked for 48 hr with 2% acetic acid and disintegrated in a blender. The slurry was centrifuged and filtered with celite. Concentrated ammonia was added, and the ammoniated slurry was placed in a refrigerator. The amorphous precipitate was separated in centrifuge bottles and extracted with ethyl ether (which removes the co-precipitated solanidine). The ether insolubles were extracted with 80% ethanol, after concentration in a rotary vacuum evaporator. On cooling, crude solanine separated. It was recrystallized from 80% ethanol or dioxane. Solanine was hydrolyzed in aqueous or alcoholic solution with HCl and yielded solanidine as aglycon and the sugars L-rhamnose, D-galactose, and D-glucose. During the hydrolysis, the dehydrated solanidine, 3,5-solanidine, may form in different quantities, which are always lower if the hydrolysis is performed in an alcoholic medium. Solanidine yields a sparingly soluble digitonid.

Demissine was found by Kuhn and Löw (1947) in the leaves of the wild potato species *Solanum demissium* Lind, which are resistant to the larvae of the potato beetle (*Leptinotarsa decemlineata* Say). The glycoalkaloid content of the fresh leaves was found to be 4.7 g/kg. The alkaloid could be extracted with diluted acetic acid and precipitated from the concentrated extract with ammonia. Demissine can be hydrolyzed to demissidine (solanidan-3-β-ol) and the sugar moiety: one mole each of D-xylose and D-galactose and two of D-glucose (Fig. 12.15). Kuhn and Löw (1954) found

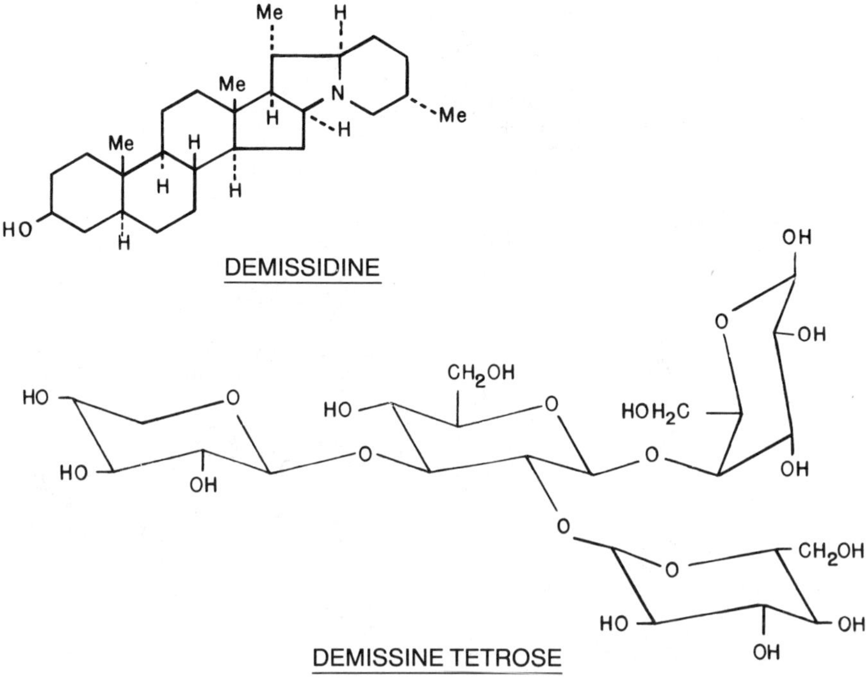

DEMISSIDINE

DEMISSINE TETROSE

Fig. 12.15. Demissine.

several glycosides in potato: α-solanine and α-chaconine were the major components (95% of the total glycoalkaloids present). These glycoalkaloids have the same aglycon but differ as to composition and structure of the trisaccharide chain attached to the C_3 of the solanidine molecule. The common aglycon solanidine (solanid-5-on-3-β-ol, ($C_{27}H_{43}NO$) can be obtained by hydrolysis of solanine (Fig. 12.16). They determined the sugar moiety of α-solanine to be β-solatriose, a branched-chain trisaccharide consisting of galactose, glucose, and rhamnose (Fig. 12.16). That of α-chaconine was found to contain one molecule of glucose and two molecules of rhamnose (Fig. 12.17). In addition, two disaccharides and two monosaccharides (all β-compounds) of solanine and chaconine were found as minor components. The formulas and composition of potato and tomato glycoalkaloids are summarized in Table 12.3. A high alkaloid content was found in the short tips of the leaves, and the flowers were rich in solanine (Bushway *et al.* 1980B).

It was observed by Street *et al.* (1946) that the total glycoalkaloid content in leaves of *Solanum tuberosum* increased during the growing season, but

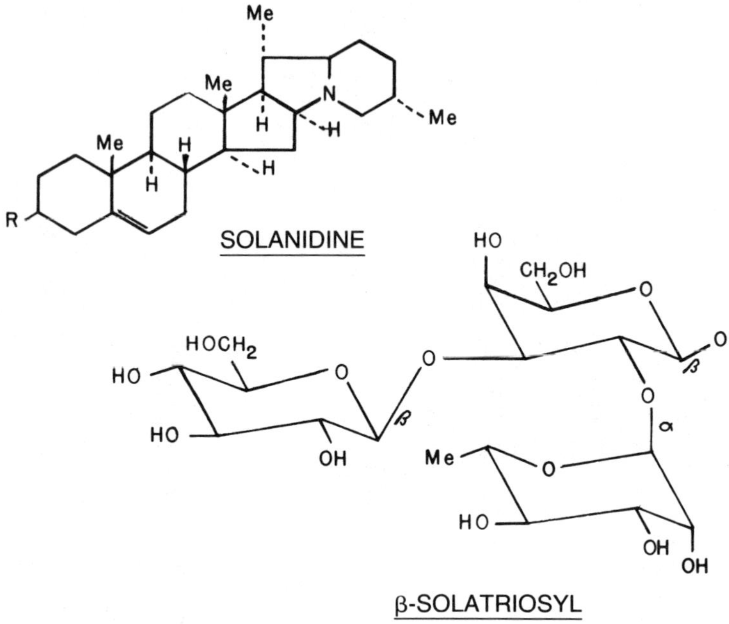

Fig. 12.16. Solanine: β-Solatriosyl solanidine.

in the tubers it declined steadily. Schreiber (1957) reported another glycoalkaloid, tomatidenol, in hydrolysates of extracts of potato sprouts. Two new major components were detected in leaves of Kennebec potato varieties (Shih and Kuč 1974). They were glycosides of tomatidenol and have been identified as α- and β-solamarine (Fig. 12.18). These were detected by TLC on silica gel plates, developed in 95% ethanol, sprayed with Carr-Price reagent ($SbCl_3$ in chloroform), and heated at 120°C for 5 min. The sugar component of β-solamarine is the same as that of α-chaconine, and that of α-solamarine is the same as that of α-solanine (Fig. 12.18). Salunkhe and Wu (1977) have reviewed intensively the studies of solanine contents of potato cultivars and the factors contributing to the biogenesis of glycoalkaloids.

Analytical Methods

Baker *et al.* (1955) described an improved method for extraction and determination of solanine in potato tubers. The potato tubers were disintegrated in a Waring Blendor and extracted in a Soxhlet apparatus. The color development of solanine with concentrated sulfuric acid and 1% formaldehyde was measured spectrophotometrically. However, it was found that solanine could not be determined exactly with sulfuric acid and formalde-

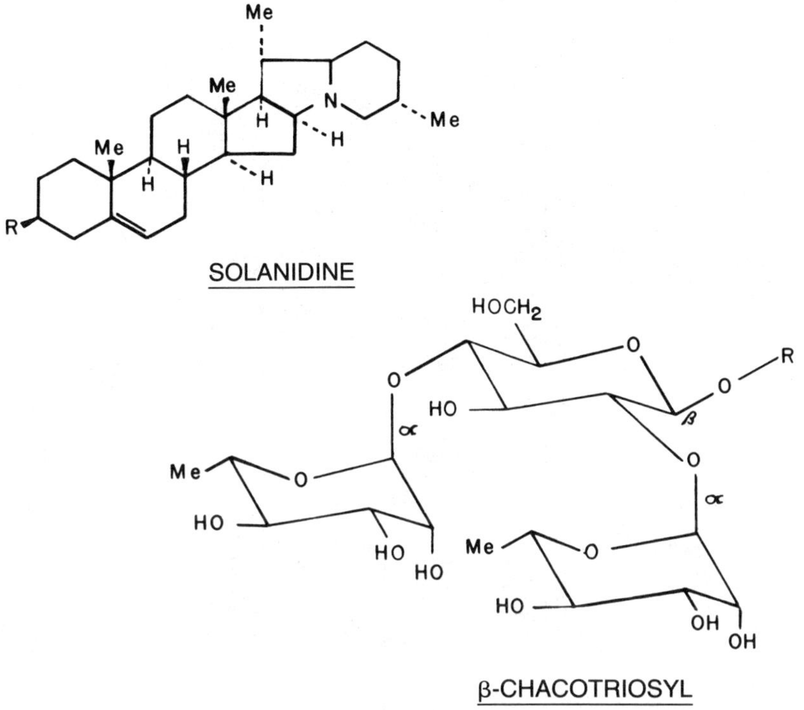

SOLANIDINE

β-CHACOTRIOSYL

Fig. 12.17. Chaconine: β-Chacotriosyl solanidine.

hyde because the crude components of the extract disturbed the color formation. Clarke (1958) modified the procedure, replacing the sulfuric acid with phosphoric acid, in which solanine produces a steel blue color with paraformaldehyde. The Clarke reaction was found to be specific to solanine. Patt and Winkler (1960) reported the preparation and determination of solanine using Duolite C-10 ion exchange resin. The purified alkaloid extracts were separated using horizontal circular paper chromatography after being sprayed with Dragendorf reagent. Seven alkaloid bands were shown. The eluted solanine zone was reacted with phosphoric acid and 0.2% paraformaldehyde at 50°C and determined spectrophotometrically at 670 nm.

Fitzpatrick and Osman (1974) developed a method for determination of glycoalkaloids in potato tubers. The tubers were extracted twice in a Waring Blendor with 2:1 methanol-chloroform mixed solvent and filtered. An aliquot of methanol layer was hydrolyzed with 2 N H_2SO_4. The aglycons were extracted into benzene, dried in vacuum, redissolved in methanol, and titrated with methanolic bromophenol blue solution.

Herb *et al.* (1975) developed a gas liquid chromatographic method for qualitative and quantitative analyses of potato glycoalkaloids. Permethyl-

TABLE 12.3. STEROID GLYCOALKALOIDS IN *SOLANUM TUBEROSUM* L. AND *LYCOPERSICON ESCULENTUM* MILL.

	Steroid Glycoalkaloid	Aglycon	Polysaccharides	Sugar Components of Polysaccharides
Solanum tuberosum	α-Solanine β-Solanine	Solanidine	β-Solabiose β-Solabiose	L-Rhamnose, D-glucose, D-galactose D-Glucose, D-galactose D-Galactose
	α-Chaconine β-Chaconine	Solanidine	β-Chacobiose β-Chacobiose	2 L-Rhamnose, D-glucose L-Rhamnose, D-glucose D-Glucose
	Demissine		Lycotetrose	D-Xylose, 2 D-glucose, D-galactose
Lycopersicon esculentum	Tomatine	Tomatidine	Lycotetrose	D-Xylose, 2 D-glucose, D-galactose
	α-Solamarine β-Solamarine	Tomatidenol	β-Chacobiose β-Solabiose β-Chacobiose β-Solabiose	L-Rhamnose, D-glucose, D-galactose 2 L-Rhamnose, D-glucose L-Rhamnose, D-glucose D-Glucose, D-galactose

β-SOLAMARINE (β-CHACOTRIOSYL TOMATIDENOL)

TOMATIDENOL = R

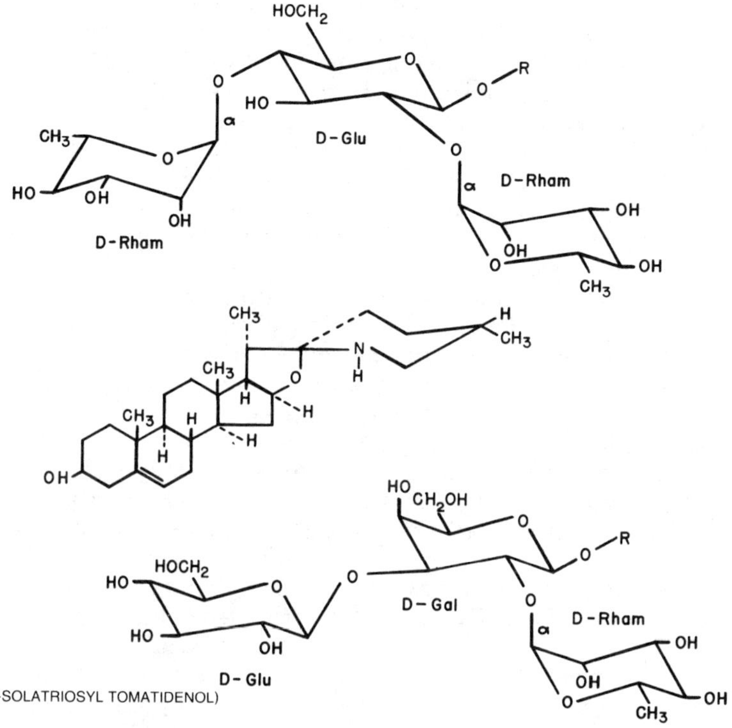

α-SOLAMARINE (β-SOLATRIOSYL TOMATIDENOL)

Fig. 12.18. α- and β-solamarine.

ated derivatives were prepared in dimethylsulfoxide in the presence of sodium hydride with methyliodide. The derivatives were chromatographed on OV-1 and Dexsil 300. Several cultivars of potatoes have been known for their high solanine content.

A rapid method for identification of steroidal alkaloids was reported by Hunter *et al.* (1976). On silica gel G thin layer, 26 alkaloids were spotted and sprayed with 50% aqueous sulfuric acid. The spots were observed with longwave (366 nm) UV light, while the plate was kept at 80°C on a hot plate. The color response and Rf values in 8 solvent systems are listed in the paper. Bushway *et al.* (1979) separated the three glycoalkaloids of the potato, α-chaconine, α-solanine, and solamarines by high-performance liquid chromatography (HPLC). The separation was achieved by using three different columns: u Bondapak C_{18}, u Bondapak NH_2, and a column for carbohydrate analysis. All samples and standards were dissolved in a tetrahydrofuran (THF)-water-acetonitrile mixture (50:30:20), and a 50 g sample was extracted. The extract was concentrated to dryness and redissolved in methanol.

The glycoalkaloids were precipitated at pH 0.5 with ammonium hydroxide. The precipitate was collected and redissolved in the tetrahydrofuran-water-acetonitrile solvent mixture and injected into the liquid chromatograph.

The u Bondapak C_{18} column is useful in separating glycoalkaloids according to the number of carbohydrate residues. α-Chaconine and α-solanine, the main glycoalkaloids of the potato, both contain three carbohydrate moieties which appear as a single peak, and β-chaconine, which is separated by this column, contains only two carbohydrates in its molecule. It was possible to separate β- and α-chaconine and α-solanine on a u Bondapak NH_2 column in the reversed-phase mode. The complex analysis was performed in 7 min.

The carbohydrate analysis column with THF-H_2O-CH_3CN (56:14:30) was found to be the best for analyzing glycoalkaloids. The chromatograph spread out for 17 min, and the components were separated with distinct baselines. α-Chaconine was separated from β-solanine in a 6 min interval. Bushway *et al.* (1980A), using the same method, determined the glycoalkaloid content of dried potato by-product meal and found 0.11–0.16% α-chaconine and 0.07–0.09% α-solanine. Bushway *et al.* (1980B) reported a procedure for the preparation of glycoalkaloids from potato blossoms. A mixture of tetrahydrofuran-water-acetonitrile (50:30:20) was used as the extractant for freeze-dried flowers, and a crude mixture of glycoalkaloids was isolated, of which the α-chaconine conent was 53% and the α-solanine content 47%. From HPLC analysis, the percentage recovery of chaconine was found to be 58% and of solanine 76%. Cadle *et al.* (1978) reported a TLC method for detection and determination of potato glycoalkaloids. The extracted alkaloids were separated on silica gel plates; the partition liquid was the organic phase of an HCl-95% EtOH-1% NH_4OH (2:2:1) mixture. The developed and air-dried plates were dipped in a saturated solution of $SbCl_3$ in chloroform and heated to 150°C for 4 min. The colored spots were quantitized with a densitometer. Sixteen to 22 mg of α-solanine and 25–43 mg of α-chaconine were found in 1 kg of fresh weight potato samples. The glycoalkaloids of potato foliage were more difficult to separate.

Clement and Verbist (1980) evaluated the colorimetric methods for determination of solanine in *Solanum tuberosum* L. tubers. A considerable variation in the results was found among the methods. These differences were attributed to the nonquantitative extraction of the glycoalkaloids or the unspecificity of the color formation of the reaction. The method proposed by Wang appears to be the most satisfactory.

Speroni and Pell (1980) modified the bisolvent extraction procedure from leaves using acetic acid and increased the percentage recovery from 27 to 97%. The new procedure was easily adapted to tuber total glycoalkaloid determination and demonstrated improved recovery of α-solanine from tuber tissue when compared with the bisolvent extraction.

Toxicity

Potato glycoalkaloids have caused poisonings and death. Renwick (1972) announced a hypothesis concerning a possible relationship between human anencephaly-spina bifida and teratogens from *Alternaria solani-* or *Phytophthora infestans*-blighted Russet Burbank potatoes. This proposal initiated new interest and increased research activities in toxicity and teratogenic potential of the *Solanum* alkaloids. The majority of the contributing scientists believe that the bulk of the epidemiologic evidence presented to date fails to support the Renwick hypothesis. Keeler *et al.* (1975) reported that, in feeding trials with *Phytophthora infestans-* or *Alternaria solani*-infected Russet Burbank potato, the preparation did not produce spina bifida or anencephaly in rats, mice, hamsters, or rabbits.

Keeler *et al.* (1976B) studied the teratogenicity of solanine and air-dried potato sprouts of Kennebec potato. A dose of 180 mg solasodine in 3 ml water administered to hamsters of 120 g average weight on the seventh or eighth day of gestation produced 48 deformed offspring in 23 of 89 (25.8%) of the litters from surviving pregnant dams. The potato sprout preparation, when fed at a 500 mg dose to pregnant hamsters on the seventh or eighth gestation day, produced 64 abnormal offspring in 26 of 113 (23%) litters. Control hamsters (183) produced only 3 litters with abnormalities. The tuber was found to be nonteratogenic at doses four times as high as the sprout preparation.

McMillan and Thompson (1979) reported an outbreak of suspected solanine poisoning in 78 London schoolboys. Seventeen of the boys required hospitalization with gastrointestinal, circulatory, and neurological complaints. The amount of α-solanine and α-chaconine in the flesh and peel of the potatoes, known to have been left in storage from the previous term, was high. The authors suggested that the low margin between the solanidine alkaloid content reported for acceptable and toxic potatoes might perhaps result from an excessive synthesis in the toxic varieties of additional compounds, such as saponins and sapogenins, which, by promoting gastrointestinal absorption, might enhance the toxicity of the solanidine alkaloid.

TOMATINE

The glycoalkaloid tomatine ($C_{50}H_{83}NO_{21}$) and its aglycon, tomatidine ($C_{27}H_{45}NO_2$) (Fontaine *et al.* 1951), are C_{27} steroids and have a heterocyclic secondary amine ring system, characteristic of the spirosolanes. The structural formula is defined by Schreiber (1968) as [25S]-5α,22β-N-spirosolan-3-β-ol. Tomatidine is present in the plant as a tetrasaccharide glycoside forming a branched structure (Kuhn and Löw 1953), which is attached at the C-3 position of the tomatine (Fig. 12.19).

Gottlieb (1943) observed that sap expressed from stems of three varieties of tomato retarded the growth of *Fusarium bulbigenum* var. lycopersici in proportion to the wilt resistance of the variety. The active principle in the sap was found to be stable at 100°C for 2 hr and was adsorbed by activated charcoal. This steroid alkaloid occurs in tomato species and was noticed first because of its fungistatic properties (Fisher 1935). Irving *et al.* (1945) notes its insect repellent action. Fontaine *et al.* (1948) isolated tomatine from the leaves of *Lycopersicon pimpinellifolium* by ethanol extraction. After distillation of the solvent, the aqueous residue was treated with ammonia. Af-

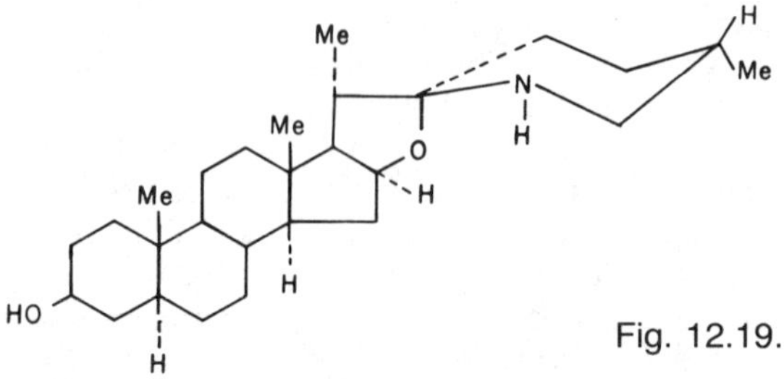

Fig. 12.19. Tomatidine.

ter centrifugation, the crude alkaloid was precipitated from acid solution and tomatine was crystallized from 80% dioxane or 70% ethanol. Acid hydrolysis yielded the tomatidine aglycon, one molecule each of D-xylose and D-galactose, and two of D-glucose (Ma 1950).

Camerino (1961) reported the preparation of tomatidine from four cultivars grown in experimental plantings in Italy. In the first experiments, it was established that the tomatine content remained stable during short storage and that drying in shade or sun did not cause any change. The tomatine content was lower in flowering and fruit-bearing plants than that in the corresponding vegetative plants, from which the flowers had been removed. The maximum tomatine level was reached in this group of plants in 3 weeks, compared with 5 weeks in the fruiting plants. The DM of cultivar San Marzano contained 0.79% tomatidine. In a cross of *Lycopersicon pimpinellifolium* × *L. esculentum* var. Pearsen, 1.8–2% tomatine was found.

Tomatine was extracted with diluted sulfuric acid introducing considerable savings to the process. The synthesis of prednisolone from solasodine using previously reported procedures was performed smoothly; however, some steps should be improved for developing an economical process. The experimental tomatoes were from commercial lines, and the process sought to utilize the large bulk of the by-product in Italy.

Bognár and Makleit (1956) described the preparation of tomatine and tomatidine from dry leaves of *Lycopersicon humboldtii* Dun. The milled leaf meal was extracted by shaking with 10-fold weight of 0.5% nitric acid. A second extraction used 5-fold weight of 0.5% nitric acid. The unified extracts were alkalized with concentrated ammonium hydroxide. After 24 hr the separated precipitate was filtered and dried at 70°C. From 1200 g air-dried plant material, 82 g tomatine could be isolated. Tomatidine was isolated after hydrolysis by refluxing with 1.5 *N* hydrochloric acid in 50% ethanol. The yield was 2.1 g tomatidine prepared from 1500 g dry plant material.

Crude tomatine can be purified by cholesterol precipitation according to Sander and Grisebach (1958). The crude tomatine was extracted under reflux in 95% ethanol, filtered, and precipitated with 45 ml of 1% cholesterol in 95% ethanol. The mixture was kept in a refrigerator to precipitate the cholesterol-tomatine complex. The precipitate was dissolved in 0.5 ml glacial acetic acid, then mixed with 0.5 ml of distilled water. The free tomatine was precipitated with 1.5 ml of 25% ammonium hydroxide.

Analysis

Tomatine can be determined by nonaqueous titration according to Gyenes (1953). The methanolic extract is dried in a water bath, extracted with 0.1 *N* HCl, and filtered. The filtrate is then made alkaline with 10% ammonium hydroxide. On cooling, the tomatidine separates. The filtered and dried glycoalkaloid is dissolved in a phenol-carbon tetrachloride mixture and, in the presence of dimethyl yellow indicator, is titrated with 0.005 *N p*-toluenesulfonic acid in chloroform to a permanent red color. One ml of 0.005 *N p*-toluenesulfonic acid is equivalent to 5.17/mg of tomatine.

Schreiber *et al.* (1963) developed a TLC method for separation of *Solanum* steroid alkaloids and steroid sapogenins. In a complicated system, a synthetic mixture of 7 *Solanum* steroid alkaloids, 4 of their derivatives, 10 steroid sapogenins, and 2 other steroid alkaloids (jervine and conessine) were subject to chromatographic separation. Four adsorbents, 5 developing solvent mixtures, and 4 spray reagents were listed. The preceding steroids can be resolved into groups on silica gel layer and further differentiations are possible by other adsorbents and solvent systems. Rönsch and Schreiber (1967) reported the analytical and preparative thin layer chromatographic separation of 5 α-saturated and Δ^5-unsaturated steroid alkaloids and steroid sapogenins on silver nitrate-impregnated silica gel G or alumina G layers. The silver nitrate-impregnated layers of silica gel G separated tomatidine from Δ^5-tomatidenol, and demissidine from solanidine. The developing solvent was chloroform-methanol (95:5). Ceric sulfate in 70% sulfuric acid spray reagent was found to be a sensitive spray reagent.

Heftmann *et al.* (1966) summarized the color formation reactions with 141 representatives of various classes of steroids.The steroids were dissolved in dichloromethane, and 4 ng of each compound were spotted on a silica gel G layer and sprayed with 50% sulfuric acid, then heated on a hot plate to a surface temperature of 78°C. Tomatidine in half a minute formed a pink color; after heating, the color changed to green; and, under longwave light (366 nm), the color was bright blue. Δ^5-Tomatidenol was found to be pink, purple, and blue, respectively. In all cases, the lower limit of detection was 0.01–0.05 ng.

Biological Activity

Irving *et al.* (1945) recognized the fungistatic potential of crude plant extract of tomato against *Fusarium oxysporum* var. lycopersici and developed a rapid bioassay to measure the fungistatic activity, using the cylinder-plate method. The inhibition zones surrounding the cylinders were sharply defined and could be measured accurately. McKee (1961) reviewed the toxicity of solanine and tomatine to fungi. Irving *et al.* (1946) showed that crude tomatine inhibited the growth of a number of bacteria and plant- and animal-pathogenic fungi.

Arneson and Durbin (1968) tested the α-tomatine sensitivities of 30 fungal species. Tomatine appears to be toxic to domestic animals. Forsyth (1968) observed that pigs died after they had eaten green tomato plants. The mechanism of toxicity is not fully understood.

Schreiber *et al.* (1961) reviewed the alkaloids of more than 200 experimentally produced mutants of *Lycopersicon esculentum* Mill (L) and *Lycopersicon pimpinellifolium* Mill. Some mutants showed a particularly high alkaloid content (4%).

Roddick (1974) has tabulated the occurrence of tomatine in solanaceous plants and reviewed extensively the chemistry and biological acitivity of tomatine.

TOXIC ALKALOIDS IN WEEDS OF PASTURES

Suggestions have been made for better utilization of grasslands by harvesting the material for leaf protein fractionation and utilizing the products on the farm, then reverting the harvested land back to pasture (Ostrowski-Meissner 1980). Mixed swards should be used with care; vegetation should be examined for toxic weeds such as crotalarias, veratrums, and lupines. If these toxic weeds are included in the plants used for LPC fractionation, their powerful poisons can cause malformations and death in animals consuming the products.

Crotalaria Alkaloids

Numerous crotalaria species have been held responsible for the poisoning of livestock, poultry, and swine. More than 40 pyrrolizidine alkaloids causing severe liver damage have been isolated from diverse crotalaria species. The pyrrolizidine alkaloids of crotalaria have been reviewed by Culvenor (1973) and lately by Jadhav *et al.* (1982). Mattocks (1978) reviewed the cytotoxic action of pyrrolizidine alkaloids. Chalmers *et al.* (1965) characterized the pyrrolizidine alkaloids by gas, thin layer, and paper chromatography.

Veratrum Alkaloids

Congenital malformations in lambs, with monstrous deformations in the head region, have been described by Binns *et al.* (1959). The deformation can distort the head of lambs so the cyclopian eye is located in the center of the head, or lambs can be born like monsters with enlarged legs, big bumps on the head, and hydrocephalic brains. It was noticed that the cyclopian type of malformation occurred in lambs from ewes that were bred in August or early September while on certain alpine meadow range areas in south central and southeastern Idaho. Binns *et al.* (1963) reported that the cyclopian malformation in lambs was induced by maternal ingestion of *Veratrum californicum*. The malformations were reproduced in controlled experimental conditions by feeding fresh and dried plants of *V. californicum*. Feeding experiments with *V. californicum* and grazing experiments on infested pastures demonstrated that, when ewes ingested the plants from the first to the tenth day of their gestation period, the fetus was not affected. Ingestion from the first to the fifteenth day caused cyclopian deformities to occur in lambs. If ingestion was continued after the fifteenth day, fetal death occurred with severe malformations.

Keeler and Binns (1966A,B) reported the preparation and characterization of fractions and alkaloids for biological testing and production of fetal cyclopia by fractions and isolated alkaloids. The data suggested that three alkaloids, veratrosine, alkaloid X, and alkaloid V (now cyclopamine), induced cyclopia, and that alkaloid V and jervine could induce fetal death.

The teratogenic effects of veratramine were reported by Keeler and Binns (1966C). The alkaloid veratramine produced congenital abnormalities in lambs; however, it did not produce the expected cyclopian and cephalic malformations but caused a typical deformation in the front legs and loss of skeletal muscular control in the hind legs. Surviving abnormal animals showed improvement within three weeks, with the exception of bowing legs. Similar malformations were reported by Keeler and Binns (1967) in ewes that ingested *V. californicum* plants and roots. TLC of benzene extracts showed the presence of veratramine. Keeler (1968) isolated veratrine, alkaloid Q, and cyclopamine from *V. californicum* (Durand). From the crude benzene extract, a colored product crystallized which showed 8–10 components on TLC. After recrystallization from acetone water and methanol water, the product contained three alkaloids: cyclopamine, veratramine, and an unknown designated as alkaloid Q. By column chromatography on silica gel, nearly pure cyclopamine was isolated. Pure veratramine and Q were prepared by rechromatography and recrystallization.

Keeler and Binns (1968) tested a wide variety of steroids for their ability to form cyclopia in sheep. Only cyclopamine, alkaloid X, jervine, and veratrosine were active. The structure of cyclopamine was established by Keeler (1969). Data by infrared (IR), NMR, and mass spectrometer (MS) confirmed that cyclopamine is 11-deoxyjervine, and that treatment of 11-deoxyjervine with acid yields veratramine. Deoxyjervine was synthesized by Wolf-Kishner reduction from jervine. Acetylation of isolated cyclopamine and 11-deoxyjervine produced identical compounds.

In further experiments, Keeler (1970) found that cyclopamine produced cyclopia and related malformations in rabbits when orally administered with $CaCO_3$, which prevents *in vivo* acid-induced conversion to veratramine, which does not cause cyclopia.

After structural investigations by IR, NMR, and spectrophotometry Keeler (1971) found that nonteratogenic alkaloid Q (one of the three benzene-extractable alkaloids of *V. californicum*) is 5-veratrine-3β,11-diol-11-acetate. The compound was named muldamine.

Keeler and Binns (1971) reported that the cyclopamine content of *V. californicum* varied among plants and various collection sites. A marked correlation was found in total alkaloid content and percentage of cyclopamine as a function of age of the plant. Both levels were highest in the early growing season in the leaves, in midgrowing season in the stem, and in aging plants in the root system.

Keeler (1971) defined the precise gestational insult period and the natural alkaloid specificity in rabbits. Fetal rabbits became malformed similarly to lambs upon maternal ingestion of cyclopamine and jervine; other veratrum alkaloids tested were inactive. The cyclopia and related malformations occurred when ingestion took place on the seventh day of gestation.

Binns *et al.* (1972) summarized, in an illustrated review, the severe congenital deformities in lambs, calves, and goats resulting from maternal ingestion of *V. californicum* roots and leaves at specific periods of embryogenesis. Keeler (1973C) described the limb deformities produced by cyclopamine after feeding pregnant ewes with veratramine, veratrosine, cyclopamine, and muldamine after the fifth week of gestation (Fig. 12.20). Only cyclopamine produced the same deformities of limbs previously produced by ingestion of the whole plant.

Keeler (1975) found that the golden hamsters were extremely sensitive to a laboratory animal assay of steroidal alkaloid teratogens. They required only a single small dose of the test material to respond to the action of cyclopamine and jervine. Rats were susceptible to cyclopamine but not to jervine. Mice were resistant to the teratogens.

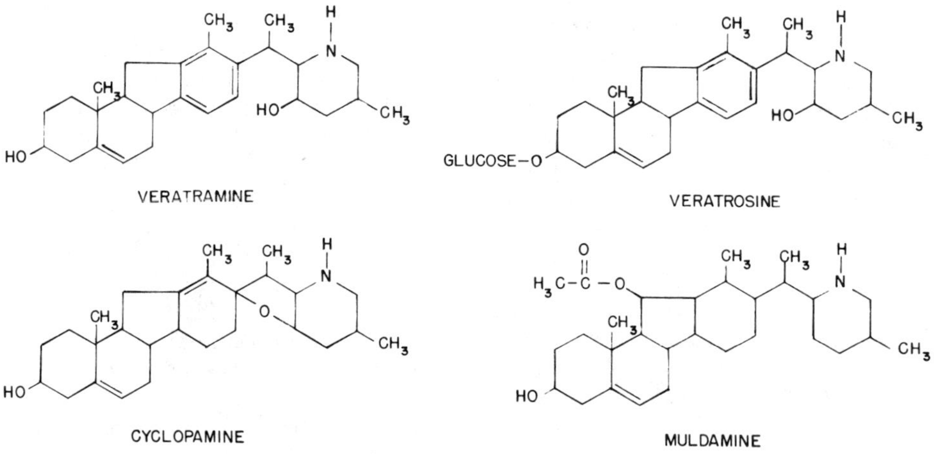

VERATRAMINE

VERATROSINE

CYCLOPAMINE

MULDAMINE

Fig. 12.20. Veratrine alkaloids.

Brown and Keeler (1978) have presented the relationship between structure and activity of steroidal amine teratogens in depth.

Lupine Alkaloids

Plants of the genus *Lupinus* in the tropical and subtropical areas of America are rich sources of seed oil and protein. Generally, they are grown as ornamentals and are represented by hundreds of species. Some species have been developed for use as high-yielding forages and cover crops. Lupines are adapted to low-nitrogen soils. Bitter lupines *(Lupinus cosenthini)* are self-regenerating over many thousands of hectares of the Western Australian sandplain, growing on an almost nitrogen-free deep sand. *Lupinus albus*, originating in the Mediterranean, shows promise in Southern Australia on soils generally too heavy for other lupine species (Gladstones 1975). The bitter lupines are toxic plants with up to 2% alkaloid content. The genetic structure for alkaloid synthesis is relatively simple. Brücher (1977) demonstrated that *Lupinus tauris*, introduced from the Andes to the Caracas area, produced high yields of biomass. If the alkaloid content in leafy lupines could be genetically lowered, similar to the level in European sweet varieties, the lupines could be potential leaf protein sources in the high altitude tropics. The European seed lupines *Lupinus albus* L. and *L. luteus* L. contain 34–38% crude protein, and 561–968 kg/ha protein yields have been reported in Hungary (Kiss 1978).

In an experiment in the Soviet Union, the plant produced 50 MT/ha of green vegetation containing 1.75 MT of protein/ha (Brücher 1968).

Wagnon (1960) observed congenital disorders caused by lupines in pregnant cows grazing on them during early fall, when seed pods were well developed. The disease in their offspring is characterized by bowed and deformed forelimbs, curved spine, and twisted neck. Shupe *et al.* (1967A,B,C) reported that the lupine plant is the cause of this dreadful disease. The critical period of teratogenic action was found to be between the fortieth and seventieth days of gestation. Two cows fed sparteine sulfate gave birth to a normal calf and one with questionable deformity.

Keeler (1973A) compared the distribution of alkaloid patterns of extracts of lupines that produced crooked calf disease experimentally with those which were not teratogens.

A similarity in the GLC pattern could be noticed in extracts of all active plants. Four major alkaloids were present in active form. A single peak designated the major teratogenic alkaloid responsible for the disease. The compound was identified as anagyrine. The other three alkaloids were identified by GLC and MS as teratogenic alkaloids of lupines (Keeler 1973B). The alkaloids were separated on 7.5% SE-30 on Chromosorb G, using a flame-ionization detector. The GC was attached to the mass spectrometer. It was found that anagyrine is sometimes contaminated by isolupanine. Other alkaloids present but not active in causing crooked calf disease were lupanine, epimethoxylupanine, and 5,6-dehydrolupanine (Fig. 12.21). Later, Keeler (1976), by feeding alkaloidal extracts to pregnant cows, proved that anagyrine is the active teratogen in lupines. Severity of the malformation of the offspring was directly proportional to the level of anagyrine administered to the experimental cow.

In general, the structures of the six lupine alkaloids are similar; however, sparteine is free of carbonyl function at carbon atom 2 in ring a, and anagyrine has double bonds in ring a and is different in the conformation of ring c at position 6.

Alkaloids of 21 *Lupinus* species indigenous to North and South America have been determined by Kinghorn *et al.* (1980). Nineteen quinolizidine alkaloids were identified, including some which had not previously been found in the genus. GC-MS was performed on a 2 m glass column with 3% OV-210 on Chromosorb W(HP), 80–100 mesh; temperature was programmed for 150 to 250°C. TLC on silica gel was separated with systems S_1, MeOH-28% NH_4OH (131:2), S_2, $CHCl_3$-MeOH-28% NH_4OH (85:15:1); and S_3, C_6H_{12}-diethylamine (7:3).

The concentrations of total alkaloids and major individual alkaloids were determined in various plant parts of teratogenic lupines of different maturity by Keeler *et al.* (1976A). The concentration of alkaloids was high in the early growth, decreasing as the plant aged and the alkaloids became concentrated in the seeds. It was lowest in the roots and mature leaves, and stems showed only a slightly higher concentration. Pregnant cows run the greatest risk of giving birth to deformed offspring when the concentration of anagyrine is highest and they are susceptible to the teratogen between the fortieth and seventy-fifth days of their gestation period.

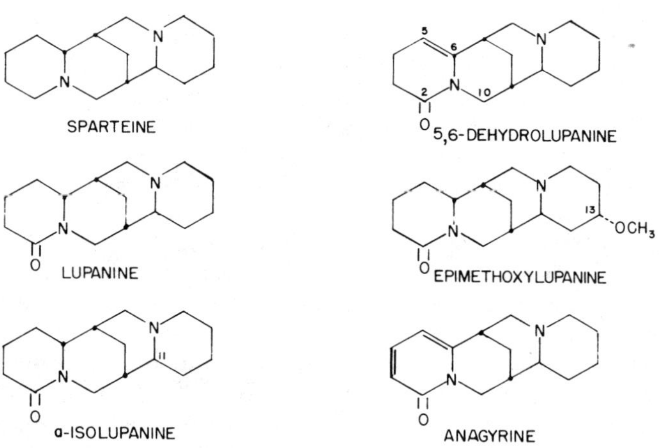

Fig. 12.21. Lupine alkaloids.

Burkett (1959) claimed that mineral supplements could reduce or even eliminate this disease. Keeler *et al.* (1977) followed the results of these treatments in six ranches and concluded that the mineral mixtures used were not responsible for variation in incidents from year to year. The valid explanation is that variation of incidence was related to the susceptible gestation period and relative level of teratogen in the lupine plants ingested. To avert toxic reactions, the best suggestion is that the range be foraged by nonpregnant cattle only.

REFERENCES

ACHTZEHN, M.K. and HAWAT, H. 1969. Nitrate content of vegetables. Nahrung *13*, 667.

ADAMS, R., CRISTOL, S.J., ANDERSON, A.A. and ALBERT, A.A. 1945. The structure of leucenol. J. Am. Chem. Soc. *67*, 89–92.

ADAMS, R. and JOHNSON, J.L. 1949. Leucenol: A total synthesis. J. Am Chem. Soc. *71*, 705–708.

ADIGA, P.R., RAO, S.L.N. and SARMA, P.S. 1963. Some structural features and neurotoxic action of a compound from *Lathyrus sativus* seeds. Curr. Sci. *32*, 153.

ADRIANSE, A. and ROBBERS, J.E. 1969. Determination of nitrite and nitrate in some horticultural and meat products and in samples of soil. J. Sci. Food Agric. *20*, 321.

AKAZAWA, T., MILJANICH, P. and CONN, E.E. 1960. Studies on cyanogenic glycoside of *Sorghum vulgare*. Plant Physiol. *35*, 535–538.

ALDRIDGE, W.N. 1944. A new method for the estimation of micro quantities of cyanide and thiocyanate. Analyst *69*, 262–265.

ALTAMURA, M.R., LONG, L., JR. and HASSELSTROM, T. 1959. Goitrin from fresh cabbage. J. Biol. Chem. *234*, 1847.

ALVARADO, D.G. and SILVA, P. 1967. Effect of fertilizers on the hydrocyanic content of 2 sorghum species. Agric. Trop. *23*, 469–476.

AOAC. 1975. Official Methods of Analysis of the Association of Official Analytical Chemists. W. Horwitz (Editor). Am. Assoc. of Analytical Chemists, Washington, DC.

APPELQVIST, L.A. and JOSEFSSON, E. 1967. Method for quantitative determination of isothiocyanates and oxazolidinethiones in digests of seed meals of rape and turnip rape. J. Sci. Food Agric. *18*, 510–519.

ARNESON, P.R. and DURBIN, R.D. 1968. The sensitivity of fungi to tomatine. Phytopathology *58*, 536–537.

ASHBURY, A.C. and RHODE, E.A. 1964. Nitrite intoxication in cattle. The effect of lethal doses of nitrite on blood pressure. Am. J. Vet. Res. *25*, 1010.

ASTWOOD, E.B., GEER, M.A. and ETTLINGER, N.G. 1949. 2,5-Vinyl-2-thiooxazolidone, an anti-thyroid compound from yellow turnip and *Brassica* seeds. J. Biol. Chem. *181*, 121–130.

AUSTIN, F.L. and WOLFF, I.A. 1968. Sinapin and related esters in seed meal of *Crambe abyssinica*. J. Agric. Food Chem. *16*, 132–135.

AXELROD, H.D., BONELLI, J.E. and LODGE, J.P. 1970. Fluorometric determination of trace nitrates. Anal. Chim. Acta *51*, 21.

BAILEY, S.D., BAZINET, M.L., DRISCOLL, J.L. and McCARTHY, A.I. 1961. The volatile sulfur components of cabbage. J. Food Sci. *26*, 163.

BAKER, A.S. 1967. Colorimetric determination of nitrate in soil and plant extracts with brucine. J. Agric. Food Chem. *15*, 802–806.

BAKER, A.S. and SMITH, R. 1969. Extracting solution for potentiometric determination of nitrate in plant tissue. J. Agric. Food Chem. *17*, 1284–1287.

BAKER, L.C., LAMPITT, L.H. and HEREDITH, O.B. 1955. Solanine, glycoside of the Potato. III. An improved method of extraction and determination. J. Sci. Food Agric. *6*, 197.

BALKS, R. and REEKERS, I. 1954. Nitrate determination in plant materials. Landwirtsch. Forsch. *6*, 121–126.

BALKS, R. and REEKERS, I. 1960. Nitrate determination in plant material with 1,2,4 xylenol. Landwirtsch. Forsch. *13*, 134–136.

BARK, L.S. and HIGSON, H.G. 1964A,B. Investigations of reagents for the colorimetric determination of small amount of cyanide. Talanta *11*, 471–479 and 621–636.

BASSIR, O. and MADUAGWU, E.N. 1978. Occurrence of nitrate, nitrite, dimethylamine and dimethylnitrosamine in some fermented Nigerian beverages. J. Agric. Food Chem. *26*, 200–203.

BATTERHAM, T.J., HART, N.K. and LAMBBERTON, J.A. 1965. Metabolism of oestrogenic isoflavones in sheep. Nature *206*, 509.

BATTERHAM, T.J., SHUTT, D.A., BRADEN, A.W. and TWEEDALE, H.J. 1971. Metabolism of intraruminally administered ($4^{14}C$) formononetin and ($4^{14}C$) biochanine A in sheep. Aust. J. Agric. Res. *22*, 131.

BAUP, M. 1826. Isolation of solanine from potato. Ann. Chim. Paris *31*, 108.

BECK, A.B. 1964. The oestrogenic isoflavones of subterranean clover. Aust. J. Agric. Res. *15*, 223.

BELL, E.A. 1958. Canavanine and related compounds in *Leguminosae*. Biochem. J. *70*, 617–619.

BELL, E.A. 1964. Relevance of biochemical taxonomy to the problem of lathyrism. Nature *203*, 378.

BENNET, W.D. and TAPPER, B.A. 1968. A sensitive method for detecting cyanoglycosides on paper and allulox thin layers. J. Chromatogr. *34*, 428.

BENNETTS, H.W. 1944. Two sheep problems on subterranean clover dominant pastures. 1. Lambing trouble (Dystokia) in Merinos. 2. Prolapse of the womb (inversion of the uterus). West. Aust. Dep. Agric. J. *21*, 104–109.

BENNS, G., L'ABBE, M.R. and LAWRENCE, J.F. 1979. High pressure liquid chromatography detection of the antihydroid compound 5-vinyloxazolidine-2-thione in milk. J. Agric. Food Chem. *27*, 426–428.

BENSON, J.A., GRAY, E. and FRIBOURG, H.A. 1969. Relation of hydrocyanic acid potential of leaf samples to that of whole plants of sorghum. Agron. J. *61*, 223–224.

BHATTY, M.K. and TOWNSHEND, A. 1971. Spectrophotometric determination of small amounts of nitrates and nitrite by conversion to nitrotoluene and extraction into toluene. Anal. Chim. Acta *56*, 55–60.

BICKEL, A.F. and WIBAUT, J.P. 1946. On the structure of leucaenine (Leucaenol) from *Leucaena glauca* Benthan. Rec. Trav. Chim. *65*, 65–68.

BICKOFF, E.M., BOOTH, A.N., LIVINGSTON, A.L., HENDRICKSON, A.P. and LYMAN, R.L. 1959. Determination of estrogenic activity in fresh and dried forage. J. Anim. Sci. *18*, 1000.

BICKOFF, E.M., BOOTH, A.N., LYMAN, R.L., LIVINGSTON, A.L., THOMPSON, C.R. and DE EDS, F. 1957. Coumestrol, a new estrogen isolated from forage crops. Science *126*, 969.

BICKOFF, E.M., BOOTH, A.N., LYMAN, R.L., LIVINGSTON, A.L., THOMPSON, C.R. and KOHLER, G.O. 1958A. Isolation of a new estrogen from Ladino clover. J. Agric. Food Chem. *6*, 536.

BICKOFF, E.M., LIVINGSTON, A.L. and BOOTH, A.N. 1960. Estrogenic activity of coumestrol and related compounds. Arch. Biochem. Biophys. *88*, 262.

BICKOFF, E.M., LIVINGSTON, A.L., HENDRICKSON, A.P. and BOOTH, A.N. 1962. Relative potencies of several estrogen-like compounds found in forages. J. Agric. Food Chem. *10*, 410.

BICKOFF, E.M., LYMAN, R.L., LIVINGSTON, C.R. and BOOTH, A.N. 1958B. Characterization of coumestrol, a naturally occurring plant estrogen. J. Am. Chem. Soc. *80*, 3969.

BIGGERS, J.D. 1958. Plant phenols possessing oestrogenic activity. *In* The Pharmacology of Plant Phenolics. J.W. Fairbairn (Editor). Academic Press, London.

BIGGERS, J.D. and CURNOW, D.H. 1954. The oestrogenic activity of subterranean clover. I. The oestrogenic activity of genistein. Biochem. J. *58*, 278–282.

BINDON, B.M. and LAMOND, D.R. 1966. Examination of tropical legumes for deleterious effects on animal reproduction. Proc. Aust. Soc. Anim. Prod. *6*, 109–116.

BINNS, W., JAMES, L.F., SHUPE, J.L. and EVERETT, G. 1963. A congenital cyclopian-type malformation in lambs induced by material ingestion of a range plant, *Veratrum californicum*. Am. J. Vet. Res. *24*, 1164–1175.

BINNS, W., KEELER, R.F. and BALLS, L.D. 1972. Congenital deformities in lambs, calves, and goats resulting from maternal ingestion of *Veratrum californicum*: Hare Lip, Cleft Palate, Ataxia, and Hypoplasia of metacarpal and metatarsal bones. Clin. Toxicol. *5* (2) 245–261.

BINNS, W., THACKER, E.J., JAMES, L.F. and HUFFMANN, W.T. 1959. Head deformities of ewes, fed *Veratrum californicum* on the 14th day of gestation. J. Am. Vet. Med. Assoc. *134*, 180–183.

BISSETT, F.H., CLAPP, R.C., COBURN, R.A., ETTLINGER, M.G. and LONG, L., JR. 1969. Cyanogenesis in manioc concerning lotaustralin. Phytochemistry *8*, 2235–2247.

BJORKMAN, R. and LONNERDALE, B. 1973. Studies on myrosinases. III. Enzymatic properties of myrosinases from *Sinapis alba* and *Brassica napus* seeds. Biochim. Biophys. Acta *327*,121.

BLAEDEL, W.J., EASTY, D.B., ANDERSON, L. and FARRELL, T.R. 1971. Potentiometric determination of cyanide with an ion-selective electrode. Application to cyanogenic glycosides in sudangrasses. Anal. Chem. *43*, 890–894.

BLOM, J. and TRESCHOW, C. 1929. Determination of nitrate using 2-4 xylenol. Z. Pflanzenernaehr. Dueng. Bodenkd. *13A*, 159.

BOGNÁR, R. and MAKLEIT, S. 1956. The alkaloid glycosides of *Lycopersicon humboldtii* Dun. Preparation and identification of tomatine. Pharmazie *11*, 376–378. (German)

BOLTZ, D.F. 1973. Nitrate determinations. Crit. Rev. Anal. Chem. *3*, 166.

BOVE, C. and CONN, E.E. 1961. Metabolism of aromatic compounds in higher plants. II. Purification and properties of the oxynitrilase in *Sorghum vulgare*. J. Biol. Chem. *236*, 207–210.

BOYCE, W.H., GARVEY, F.K. and STRAWCUTTER, H.E. 1956. Incidence of urinary calculi among patients in general hospitals 1948–1952. J. Am. Med. Assoc. *161*, 1437–1442.

BOYD, F.T,. AAMODT, O.S., BOHSTEDT, G. and TRUOG, E. 1938. Sudangrass management for control of cyanide poisoning. J. Am. Soc. Agron. *30*, 569–582.

BRADBURY, R.B. and WHITE, D.E. 1951. The chemistry of subterranean clover. Part I. Isolation of formononetin and genistein. J. Chem. Soc. 3447–3449.

BRADEN, A.W.H., HART, N.K. and LAMBERTON, J.A. 1967. The oestrogenic activity and metabolism of certain isoflavones in sheep. Aust. J. Agric. Res. *18*, 335.

BRITTEN, E.J., MATSUMOTO, H. and PALAFOX, A.L. 1959. Comparative toxic effects of 3 nitropropionic acid, sodium nitrite, and *Indigofera endecaphylla* on chicks. Agron. J. *51*, 462–464.

BROWN, H.E., STEIN, E.R. and SALDANA, G. 1975. Evaluation of *Brassica carinata* as a source of plant protein. J. Agric. Food Chem. *3*, 545.

BROWN, D. and KEELER, R.F. 1978. Structure-activity relation of steroidal teratogens. III. Solanidan epimers. J. Agric. Food. Chem. *26*, 566–569.

BRÜCHER, H. 1968. Protein rich, wild or semidomesticated leguminosae from Latin America and their future importance in nutrition. Qual. Plant. *26*, 71–106.

BRÜCHER, H. 1977. Tropical Crops. Origin, Evolution and Adaptation. Springer Verlag, Berlin, Heidelberg, New York. (German)

BRYCE, T.A. and TELLING, G.M. 1972. Semiquantitative analysis of low levels of volatile nitrosamines by GC-MS. J. Agric. Food Chem. *20*, 910–911.

BURKETT, W.H. 1959. Improve Your Roughage with Phosphorous Nutrition. Northwest Livestock Directory, Western Livestock Reporter, Billings, MT.

BURROWS, S. 1950. A colorimetric method for the determination of oxalate. Analyst *75*, 80–84.

BUSHWAY, A.A., BUSHWAY, A.V., BELYEA, P.R. and BUSHWAY, R.J. 1980A. The proximate composition and glycoalkaloid content of three potato meals. Am. Potato J. *57*, 167–169.

BUSHWAY, R.J., BARDEN, E.S., BUSHWAY, A.V. and BUSHWAY, A.A. 1979. High performance liquid chromatographic separation of potato glycoalkaloids. J. Chromatogr. *178*, 533–541.

BUSHWAY, R.J., BARDEN, E.S., BUSHWAY, A.V. and BUSHWAY, A.A. 1980B. The mass extraction of potato glycoalkaloids from blossoms. Am. Potato J. *57*, 175–180.

BUTLER, G.W. 1965. The distribution of the cyanglycosides linamarin and lotaustralin in higher plants. Phytochemistry *4*, 127–131.

BUTLER, G.W., BAILEY, R.W. and KENNEDY, L.D. 1965. Studies on the glucosidase "Linamarase." Phytochemistry *4*, 369–381.

BUTLER, G.W. and CONN, E.E. 1964. Biosynthesis of the cyanogenic glycosides: linamarin and isolinamarin. J. Biol. Chem. *239*, 1674–1679.

CADLE, L.S, STELZIG, D.A., HARPER, K.L. and YOUNG, R.J. 1978. Thin layer chromatographic system for identification and quantitation of potato tuber glycoalkaloids. J. Agric. Food Chem. *26*, 1453–1454.

CALKINS, V.P. 1943. Microdetermination of glycolic and oxalic acid. Ind. Eng. Chem. Anal. Ed. *15*, 762–763.

CAMERINO, B. 1961. Investigations of tomatine content, its extraction and degradation to pregnane derivatives. Tagungsber. Dtsch. Akad. Landwirtschaftswiss. Berlin *27*, 183–192.

CARANGAL, A.R. and CATIDING, A.D. 1955. The mimosine content of locally grown ipil ipil *(Leucaena glauca)*. Philipp. Agric. *39*, 249–254.

CARLSSON, R. 1975. Selection of centrospermae and other species for production of leaf protein concentrates. Ph.D. Thesis. University of Lund, Lund, Sweden.

CARTER, L. and McCHESNEY, W.J. 1949. Hyptagenic acid identified as β-nitropropionic acid. Nature *164*, 575–576.

CHALMERS, A.H., CULVENOR, C.C.J. and SMITH, L.W. 1965. Characterization of pyrrolizidine alkaloids by gas, thin-layer, and paper chromatography. J. Chromatogr. *20*, 270.

CHARLWOOD, B.V. and BELL, E.A. 1977. Qualitative and quantitative analysis of common and uncommon amino acids in plant extracts. J. Chromatogr. *135*, 377–384.

CHENG, E. and BURROUGHS, W. 1959. Estrogenic substances in forages. *In* Grasslands. H.B. Sprague (Editor). Am. Assoc. Adv. Sci. *53*, 195–202.

CHENG, E., STORY, C.D., PAYNE, L.C., YODER, L. and BURROUGHS, W. 1953. Detection of estrogenic substances in alfalfa and clover hays fed to fattening lambs. J. Anim. Sci. *12*, 507.

CHENG, E., YODER, L., STORY, C.D. and BURROUGHS, W. 1954. Estrogenic activity of some isoflavone derivatives. Science *120*, 575–576.

CHIBNALL, A.C. 1939. Protein Metabolism in the Plants. Yale Univ. Press, New Haven, CT.

CHRISTIE, G.S., MADSEN, N.P. and HEGARTY, M.P. 1969. Acute biochemical changes in rat liver induced by the naturally occurring amino acid indospicine. Biochem. Pharmacol. *18*, 693–700.

CLAPP, R.C., BISSET, F.H., COBURN, R.A. and LONG, L. 1966. Cyanogenesis in manioc: Linamarin and isolinamarin. Phytochemistry *5*, 1323–1326.

CLARKE, E.A.C. and CLARKE, M.L. 1967. Garners Veterinarian Toxicology, 3rd Edition. Bailliere, Tindall and Cassell, London.

CLARKE, E.G.C. 1958. Identification of Solanine. Nature *181*, 1152–1153.

CLEGG, F.G. 1966. Kale poisoning of cattle. Ber. Tag. Weltgesellschaft für Buiatrik Zurich *4*, 11.

CLEMENT, E. and VERBIST, J.F. 1980. The quantitation of solanine. A comparative study. Lebensm. Wiss. Technol. *13*, 202–206.

COLEMAN, R.G., WINDRUM, G.M. and HUTTON, F.M. 1960. Studies of the toxicity of *Indigofera endecaphylla.* III. Separation of toxic fractions from seeds and herbage. J. Nutr. *70*, 267.

COLLISON, S.E. 1919. Prussic acid in sorghum. Fla. Agric. Exp. Stn. Bull. *155*, 51–56.

CONN, E.E. 1969. Cyanogenic glycosides. J. Agric. Food Chem. *17*, 519–529.

CONN, E.E. 1978. Cyanogenesis, the production of hydrogen cyanide by plants. *In* Effect of Poisonous Plants on Livestock. R.F. Keeler, K.R. van Kampen and L.F. James (Editors). Academic Press, New York.

CONN, E.E. 1979A. Cyanide and cyanogenic glycosides. *In* Herbivores, Their Interactions with Secondary Plant Metabolites. G.A. Rosenthal (Editor). Academic Press, New York.

CONN, E.E. 1979B. Biosynthesis of cyanogenic glycosides. Naturwissenschaften *66*, 28–34.

CONN, E.E. and BUTLER, G.W. 1969. Cyanogen glycosides. *In* Perspectives in Phytochemistry. J.B. Harborne and T. Swain (Editors). Academic Press, London.

COOKE, A.R. 1955. The toxic effect of *Indigofera endecaphylla.* Arch. Biochem. Biophys. *55*, 114–120.

COOKE, R.D. 1978. An enzymatic assay for the total cyanide content of cassava (*Manihot esculenta* Crantz). J. Sci. Food Agric. *29*, 345–352.

COOKE, R.D., BLAKE, G.G. and BATTERSHILL, J.M. 1978. Purification of cassava linamarase. Phytochemistry *17*, 381.

COX, G.B. 1973. Estimation of volatile n-nitrosamines by high-performance liquid chromatography. J. Chromatogr. *83*, 471–481.

CROFT, A.G. 1979. The determination of total glucosinolates in rapeseed meal by titration of enzyme liberated acid and identification of individual glucosinolates. J. Sci. Food Agric. *30*, 417–423.

CROSBY, N.T. 1976. Nitrosamines in foodstuffs. Residue Rev. *64*, 77–135.

CROSS, C.K. and BHARUCHA, K.R. 1979. A simple screening method for determination of volatile nitrosamines in fried bacon rasher and cook out fat. J. Agric. Food Chem. *27*, 1358–1360.

CROSS, C.K., BHARUCHA, K.R. and TELLING, G.M. 1978. Determination of volatile n-nitrosamines in bacon cook out fat by nitrate release and T.L.C. of fluorescent amine derivatives. J. Agric. Food Chem. *26*, 657–660.

CROUNSE, R.G., MAXWELL, J.D. and BLANK, H. 1962. Inhibition of growth of hair by mimosine. Nature *194*, 694–695.

CULVENOR, C.C. 1973. Alkaloids. *In* Chemistry and Biochemistry of Herbage. C.W. Butler and R.W. Bailey (Editors). Academic Press, London, New York.

CURNOW, D.H. 1954. Oestrogenic activity of subterranean clover. The isolation of genistein from subterranean clover and methods of quantitative estimation. Biochem. J. *58*, 283–287.

CURNOW, D.H., ROBINSON, T.J. and UNDERWOOD, E.J. 1948. Oestrogenic action of extracts of subterranean clover (*T. subterraneum* L. var. *dwalganup*). Aust. J. Exp. Biol. Med. Sci. *26*, 171–180.

DASLER, W. 1954. Isolation of toxic crystals from sweet peas *(Lathyrus odoratus)*. Science *120*, 307.

DAXENBICHLER, M.E. and VAN ETTEN, C.H. 1977. Glucosinolates and derived products in cruciferous vegetables: gas-liquid chromatographic determination of the aglucon derivatives from cabbage. J. Assoc. Off. Anal. Chem. *60*, 950–953.

DAXENBICHLER, M.E., SPENCER, G.F., KLEIMAN, R., VAN ETTEN, C.H. and WOLFF, I.A. 1970. Gas-liquid chromatographic determination of products from the progoitrins in crambe and rapeseed meals. Anal. Biochem. *38*, 374.

DAXENBICHLER, M.E., VAN ETTEN, C.H. and SPENCER, G.F. 1977. Glucosinolates and derived products in cruciferous vegetables. J. Agric. Food Chem. *25*, 121–124.

DAXENBICHLER, M.E, VAN ETTEN, C.H. and WOLFF, I.A. 1966. (S)- and (R)-cyanohydroxy-3-butene from myrosinase hydrolysis of epi-progoitrin and progoitrin. Biochemistry *5*, 692.

DAXENBICHLER, M.E., VAN ETTEN, C.H. and WOLFF, I.A. 1968. Diastereomeric episulfides from epigoitrin upon autolysis of crambe seed meal. Phytochemistry *7*, 989–996.

DE SYLVA, E.M. 1971. Analysis of Krebs-cycle and related acids in guinea pigs tissues by G.L.C. Anal. Chem. *43*, 1031.

DEDIO, W. and CLARK, K.W. 1968. Biochanin and formononetin content in red clover varieties at several maturity stages. Can. J. Plant Sci. *48*, 175.

DESFOSSES, M. 1820. Abstract from a letter to Mr. Robiquet. J. Pharm. 6 (2) 374–376.

DUNSTAN, W.R. and HENRY, T.A. 1902. Cyanogenesis in plants. Part II. The great millet, *Sorghum vulgare*. Philos. Trans. R. Soc. London Ser. A: *199*, 399–410.

DUNSTAN, W.R., HENRY, T.A. and AULD, S.J.M. 1906. Cyanogenesis in plants. V. The occurrence of phaseolunatin in cassava, *Manihot aipi* and *M. utilissima*. Proc. R. Soc. London Ser. B: *78*, 152–158.

DUPUY, H.P. and LEE, J.G. 1954. The isolation of a material capable of producing experimental lathyrism. J. Am. Pharm. Assoc. Sci. Ed. *43*, 61–62.

ECK, H.V. 1976. Hydrocyanic acid potentials in leaf blade tissue of eleven grain sorghum hybrids. Agron. J. *68*, 349.

EISENBRAND, G., SPACZYNKI, K. and PREUSSMANN, R. 1970A. Separation of carcinogenic nitrosamines on Sephadex LH-20. J. Chromatogr. *51*, 304–306.

EISENBRAND, G., SPACZYNSKI, K. and PREUSSMANN, R. 1970B. Quantitative thin-layer chromatography of nitrosamines. J. Chromatogr. *51*, 503–509.

EMMENS, C.W. 1950. Hormone Assay. Academic Press, New York.

ETTLINGER, M.G. and KJAER, A. 1968. Sulfur compounds in plants. *In* Recent Advances in Phytochemistry, Vol. 1 T.J. Mabry, R.E. Alston and V.C. Runeckles (Editors). Appleton-Century-Crofts, New York.

ETTLINGER, M.G. and LUNDEEN, A.J. 1956. The structures of sinigrin and sinalbin; and enzymatic rearrangement. J. Am. Chem. Soc. *78*, 4172–4173.

EYJOLFSSON, R. 1970. Recent advances in the chemistry of cyanogenic glycosides. *In* Advances in the Chemistry of Organic Nature Products, Vol. 28. L. Zechmeister (Editor). Springer-Verlag, Vienna, New York. (German)

FEARON, W.R. 1946. Preparation of trisodium pentacyano amino ferrate. Analyst *71*, 562.

FEARON, W.R. and BELL, E.A. 1955. Canavanine: Detection and occurrence in *Colutea arborescens*. Biochem. J. *59*, 221–224.

FINE, D.H., RUFEH, F., LIEB, D. and ROUNBEHLER, D.P. 1975. Description of the thermal energy analyzer (TEA) for trace determination of volatile and nonvolatile N-nitroso compounds. Anal. Chem. *47*, 1188–1191.

FISHER, P.L. 1935. Fungistatic properties of expressed juice of tomato plant. Agric. Exp. Stn. Bull. *374*.

FISHMAN, M.L. and BURDICK, D. 1977. Extractability, solubility, and molecular size distribution of nitrogenous constituents in coastal Bermuda grass. J. Agric. Food Chem. *25*, 1122.

FITZPATRICK, T.J. and OSMAN, S.F. 1974. A comprehensive method for the determination of total potato glycoalkaloids. Am. Potato J. *51*, 318–323.

FOLLET, M.J. and RATCLIFF, P.W. 1963. Determination of nitrite and nitrate in meat products. J. Sci. Food Agric. *14*, 138–144.

FONTAINE, T.D., ARD, S.J. and MA, R.M. 1951. Tomatidine, a steroid secondary amine. J. Am. Chem. Soc. *73*, 878–879.

FONTAINE, T.D., IRWING, G.W., MA, R.M., POOLE, J.B. and DOOLITTLE, S.P. 1948. Isolation and partial characterization of crystalline tomatine, an antibiotic agent from the tomato plant. Arch. Biochem. *18*, 467.

FOREMAN, J.K., PALFRAMAN, J.F. and WALKER, E.A. 1970. Gaschromatographic determination of N-alkyl nitrosamine. Nature *225*, 554.

FORSYTH, A.A. 1968. British Poisonous Plants. HMSO, London.

FRANCIS, C.M. and MILLINGTON, A.J. 1965. Varietal variation in the isoflavone content of subterranean clover. Its estimation by a microtechnique. Aust. J. Agric. Res. *16*, 557–564.

FRANCIS, C.M., MILLINGTON, A.J. and BAILEY, E.T. 1967. The distribution of oestrogenic isoflavones in the genus Trifolium. Aust. J. Agric. Res. *18*, 47–54.

GARBUTT, J.T. and STRONG, G.M. 1957. Colorimetric determination of β-aminopropionitrile in mature legume seeds. J. Agric. Food Chem. *5*, 367.

GLADSTONES, J.S. 1975. Legumes and Australian agriculture. J. Aust. Inst. Agric. Sci. *41*, 227–240.

GLENCROSS, R.G., FESTENSTEIN, G.N. and KING, H.G.C. 1972. Separation and determination of isoflavones in protein concentrates from red clover leaves. J. Sci. Food Agric. *23*, 371.

GLOVER, D.J. and HOFFSOMMER, J.C. 1974. Gas chromatographic analysis of nitrate and nitrite ions in microgram quantities by conversion to nitrobenzene. J. Chromatogr. *94*, 334–337.

GOODALL, M. 1950. New high protein feed produced from sugar beet tops. Br. Sugar Beet Rev. *19*, 54.

GORASHI, A.M., DROLSOM, P.N. and SCHOLL, J.M. 1980. Effect of stage of growth, temperature, and N and P levels on hydrocyanic acid potential of sorghums in the field and growth room. Crop Sci. *20*, 45–46.

GORZ, H.J., HAAG, W.I., SPECHT, J.E. and HASKINS, F.A. 1977. Assay of p-hydroxybenzaldehyde as a measure of hydrocyanic acid potential in sorghums. Crop Sci. *17*, 578–582.

GOSDEN, A.F. 1979. An automated procedure for the estimation of S-methyl cysteine sulfoxide in kale, J. Sci. Food Agric. *30*, 892–898.

GOSDEN, A.F. and JONES, R. 1978. A routine method for predicting the formononetin content of red clover. J. Sci. Food Agric. *29*, 925–929.

GOTTLIEB, D. 1943. Expressed sap of tomato plants in relation to wilt resistance. Phytopathology *33*, 1111.

GOUGH, T.A. and SUGEN, K. 1975. Dual column gas chromatographic system for use in mass spectral determination of nitrosamines. J. Chromatogr. *109*, 265.

GOUGH, T.A. and WEBB, K.S. 1972. The use of a molecular separator in the determination of trace constituents by combined gas chromatography and mass spectrometry. J. Chromatogr. *64*, 201–210.

GOUGH, T.A. and WEBB, K.S. 1973. A method for the detection of traces of nitrosamines using combined GLC and MS. J. Chromatogr. *79*, 57–63.

GOUGH, T.A. and WEBB, K.S. 1974. Trace detection of some nonvolatile nitrosamines by combined gas chromatography and mass spectrometry. J. Chromatogr. *95*, 59–63.

GOUGH, T.A., WEBB, K.S., PRINGUER, M.A. and WOOD, B.J. 1977. Comparison of various mass spectrometric and chemiluminescent method for estimation of volatile nitrosamines. J. Agric. Food Chem. *25*, 663–667.

GREENHALGH, J.F.D. 1969. Kale anaemia. Proc. Nutr. Soc. *28*, 178–183.

GREENHALGH, J.F.D., AITKEN, J.N. and GUNN, J.B. 1972. Kale anaemia. III. A survey of kale feeding practices and anaemia in cattle on dairy farms in England and Scotland. Res. Vet. Sci. *13*, 15–21.

GREENHALGH, J.F.D., SHARMAN, G.A.M. and AITKEN, J.N. 1969. Kale anaemia. I. The toxicity to various species of animal of three types of kale. Res. Vet. Sci. *10*, 64–72.

GREENHALGH, J.F.D., SHARMAN, G.A.M. and AITKEN, J.N. 1970. Kale anaemia. II. Further factors concerned in the occurrence of the disease under experimental conditions. Res. Vet. Sci. *11*, 232–238.

GRUHZIT, O.M. 1931. The haemolytic principles of onion juice. Am. J. Med. Res. *181*, 815.

GUGGOLZ, J., LIVINGSTON, A.L. and BICKOFF, E.M. 1961. Detection of daidzein, formononetin, genistein, and biochanin A in forages. J. Agric. Food Chem. *9*, 330.

GUIGNARD, L. 1916. The detection and estimation of hydrocyanic acid in beans. Ann. Falsif. *9*, 301–305. (Chem. Abstr. *11*, 671. 1927.)

GUILBAULT, G.G. and KRAMER, D.N. 1965A. A specific fluorometric method for the detection of cyanide. Anal. Chem. *37*, 918.

GUILBAULT, G.G. and KRAMER, D.N. 1965B. Specific detection and determination of cyanide using various quinone derivatives. Anal. Chem. *37*, 1395–1399.

GUILBAULT, G.G. and KRAMER, D.N. 1966. Ultra-sensitive, specific method for cyanide using p-nitrobenzaldehyde and o-dinitrobenzene. Anal. Chem. *38*, 834–836.

GYENES, I. 1953. Volumetric determination of tomatin and tomatidine by means of 0.005 N p-toluene sulfonic acid. Magy. Kem. Foly. *59*, 159.

HABERLAND, H. 1890. The irritant tissues of mimosine. Leipzig.

HAMILTON, R.I., DONALDSON, L.E. and LAMBOURNE, L.J. 1971. *Leucaena leucocephala* as a feed for dairy cows: Direct effect on reproduction and residual effect on the calf and lactation. Aust. J. Agric. Res. *22*, 681–692.

HANDB. EXP. RES. METHODS AGRIC. 1975. Method Book. III. Feed research. Cyanides. Method *16.3.3*. Ludwig Schmitt (Editor). J. Neumann-Neudamm, Lesungen, Berlin. [Handbuch d. Landw. Versuchs. und Untersuchungs Methodik. Methoden Buch. III. Futtermittel Untersuchung. Cyanide.] (German)

HARMS, C.L. and TUCKER, B.B. 1973. Influence of nitrogen fertilization and other factors on yield, prussic acid, nitrate, and total nitrogen concentration of sudangrass cultivars. Agron. J. *65*, 21–26.

HARRINGTON, J.D. 1966. Hydrocyanic acid content of Piper, Trudan I, and six sorghum sudangrass hybrids. Pa. Agric. Exp. Stn. Bull. *735*.

HATCHER, D.W. and SCHALL, E.D. 1965. Nitrates in feeds. J. Assoc. Off. Anal. Chem. 648–653.

HEFTMANN, E. 1967. Biochemistry of steroidal saponins and glycoalkaloids. Lloydia *30*, 209–230.

HEFTMANN, E. 1968. The biosynthesis of plant steroids. Lloydia *31*, 293–312.

HEFTMANN, E., SKO, S.T. and BENNETT, R.D. 1966. Response of steroids to sulfuric acid in thin-layer chromatography. J. Chromatogr. *21*, 490–494.

HEGARTY, M.P. 1957. The isolation and identification of 5-hydroxy piperidine-2 carboxylic acid from *Leucaena glauca* Benth. Aust. Chem. J. *10*, 484–488.

HEGARTY, M.P. 1978. Toxic amino acids of plant origin. *In* Effects of Poisonous Plants on Livestock. R.F. Keeler, K.R. van Kampen and L.F. Jones (Editors). Academic Press, New York.

HEGARTY, M.P., CHEW, P.L., CHRISTIE, G.S., COURT, R.D. and HAYDOCK, K.P. 1979. The goitrogen 3-hydroxy-4 (1H)-pyridone, a ruminal metabolite from *Leucaena leucocephala*: Effects in mice and rats. Aust. J. Biol. Sci. *32*, 27–40.

HEGARTY, M.P. and COURT, R.D. 1964. A simple method for the isolation of mimosine from the seed of *Leucaena glauca* Benth. Aust. J. Agric. Res. *15*, 165–166.

HEGARTY, M.P., COURT, R.D., CHRISTIE, G.S. and LEE, C.P. 1976. Mimosine in *Leucaena leucocephala* is metabolized to a goitrogen in ruminants. Aust. Vet. J. *52*, 490.

HEGARTY, M.P., COURT, R.D. and THORNE, P.M. 1964A. The determination of mimosine and 2,4-dihydroxypyridine in biological material. Aust. J. Agric. Res. *15*, 168–179.

HEGARTY, M.P., LEE, C.P., CHRISTIE, G.S., DE MUK, F.G. and COURT, R.D. 1978. Comparative toxicities of mimosine and some chemically related compounds to mouse bone marrow cells in liquid culture. Aust. J. Biol. Sci. *31*, 115–121.

HEGARTY, M.P. and PETERSON, P.J. 1973. Free amino acids, bound amino acids, amines and ureides. *In* Chemistry and Biochemistry of Herbage, Vol. 1. C.W. Butler and R.W. Bailey (Editors). Academic Press, London.

HEGARTY, M.P. and POUND, A.W. 1970. Indospicine, a hepatotoxic amino acid from Indigofera spicata: Isolation, structure and biological studies. Aust. J. Biol. Sci. *23*, 831.

HEGARTY, M.P., SCHINCKEL, P.G., and COURT, R.D. 1964B. Reaction of sheep to the consumption of *Leucaena glauca* Benth. and to its toxic principle mimosine. Aust. J. Agric. Res. *15*, 153–167.

HELBOE, P., OLSEN, O. and SORENSON, H. 1980. Separation of glucosinolates by HPLC. J. Chromatogr. *197*, 199–205.

HERB, S.F., FITZPATRICK, T.J. and OSMAN, S.F. 1975. Separation of potato glycoalkaloids by gas chromatography. J. Agric. Food Chem. *23*, 520.

HOGG, P.G. and AHLGREN, H.L. 1942. A rapid method for determining hydrocyanic acid content of single plants of sudangrass. J. Am. Soc. Agron. *34*, 199–200.

HOGG, P.G. and AHLGREN, H.L. 1943. Environmental breeding, and inheritance studies of hydrocyanic acid in *Sorghum vulgare* var. *sudanense*. J. Agric. Res. *67*, 195–210.

HOLLÓ, J. and KOCH, L. 1970. Protein from green matter. Process Biochem. 5 (10) 37–39.

HOLLÓ, J., ZAGYVAI, I. and KOCH, L. 1971. Process for the production of fiberless green plant concentrate of full biological value. U.S. Pat. 3,637,396. Jan 25. (Vepex process).

HOLMES, J.H.G. 1976. Growth of Brahman cross heifers grazing *Leucaena*. Proc. Aust. Soc. Anim. Prod. *11*, 453–456.

HUGHES, M.A. 1968. Studies on the β-glucosidase system of *Trifolium repens* L. J. Exp. Bot. *19*, 427–434.

HUNTER, I.R., WALDEN, M.K., WAGNER, J.R. and HEFTMANN, E. 1976. TLC of steroidal alkaloids, J. Chromatogr. *118*, 259–262.

HUSSAIN, A., ULLAH, M. and AHMAD, B. 1968. Studies on the potentials of leaf proteins for the preparation of concentrates from various leaf wastes in West Pakistan. Pak. J. Agric. Res. *6*, 110.

HUTTON, E.M., WINDRUM, G.M. and KRATZING, C.C. 1958A. Studies on the toxicity of *Indigofera endecaphylla*. I. Toxicity for rabbit. J. Nutr. *64*, 321–328.

HUTTON, E.M., WINDRUM, G.M. and KRATZING, C.C. 1958B. Studies on the toxicity of *Indigofera endecaphylla*. II. Toxicity for mice. J. Nutr. *65*, 429–440.

IRVING, G.W., FONTAINE, T.D., JR. and DOOLITTLE, S.P. 1945. Lycopersicin, a fungistatic agent from the tomato plant. Science *102*, 9–11.

IRVING, G.W., FONTAINE, T.D., JR. and DOOLITTLE, S.P. 1946. Partial antibiotic spectrum of tomatine, an antibiotic agent from the tomato plant. J. Bacteriol. *52*, 601–667.

ITOKAWA, Y., INOUE, K., SASAGAVA, S. and FUJIWARA, M. 1973. Effect of SMCO, S-allylcysteine sulphoxide and related S-containing amino acids on lipid metabolism of experimental hypercholesterolemic rats. J. Nutr. *103*, 88–92.

JADHAV, S.J., SALUNKHE, D.K., KADAM, S.S., CHAVAN, J.K. and INGLE, U.M. 1982. Pyrrolizidine alkaloids: A review. J. Food Sci. Technol. *19*, 87–93.

JAMES, L.F. and BUTCHER, J.E. 1972. *Halogeton* poisoning of sheep: Effect of high oxalate intake. J. Anim. Sci. *35*, 1233–1237.

JAMES, L.F., STREET, J.C. and BUTCHER, J.E. 1967. *In vitro* degradation of oxalate and of cellulose by rumen ingesta from sheep fed *Halogeton glomeratus*. J. Anim. Sci. *26*, 1438.

JOHNSON, C.M. and ULRICH, A. 1950. Determination of nitrate in plant material. Anal. Chem. *22*, 1526.

JONES, G.B. and UNDERDOWN, R.E. 1953. Determination of nitrate in plant material. Anal. Chem. *25*, 806.

JORGENSEN, N.A. and FREGMILLER, D.D. 1972. Oestrogenic activity of fermented alfalfa. J. Dairy Sci. *55* (1) 80-82.

JOSEFSSON, E. 1970. Content of p-hydroxybenzylglucosinolate in seed meals of *Sinapis alba* as affected by heredity, environment and seed part. J. Sci. Food Agric. *21*, 94–97.

JUNG, G.A., LILLY, G., SHIH, S.C. and REID, R.L. 1964. Studies with sudangrass. I. Effect of growth stage and level of nitrogen fertilizer upon yield of dry matter; estimated digestibility of energy, dry matter and protein; amino acid composition; and prussic acid potential. Agron. J. *56*, 533–537.

KEELER, R.F. 1968. Teratogenic compounds of *Veratrum californicum* (Durand). IV. First isolation of veratramine and alkaloid Q and a reliable method for isolation of cyclopamine. Phytochemistry *7*, 303–306.

KEELER, R.F. 1969. Teratogenic compounds of *Veratrum californicum* (Durand). VI. The structure of cyclopamine. Phytochemistry *8*, 223–225.

KEELER, R.F. 1970. Teratogenic compounds of *Veratrum californicum* (Durand). X. Cyclopia in rabbits produced by cyclopamine. Teratology *3*, 175–180.

KEELER, R.F. 1971. Teratogenic compounds of *Veratrum californicum* (Durand). XIII. Structure of muldamine. Steroids *18*, 741–752.

KEELER, R.F. 1973A. Lupin alkaloids from teratogenic and nonteratogenic lupins. I. Correlation of crooked calf disease incidence with alkaloid distribution determined by gas chromatography. Teratology *7*, 23–30.

KEELER, R.F. 1973B. Lupin alkaloids from teratogenic and nonteratogenic lupins. II. Identification of the major alkaloids by tandem gas chromatography-mass spectrometry in plants producing crooked calf disease. Teratology, *7*, 31–36.

KEELER, R.F. 1973C. Teratogenic compound of *Veratrum californicum* (Durand). XIV. Limb deformities produced by cyclopamine. Proc. Soc. Exp. Biol. Med. *142*, 1287–1291.

KEELER, R.F. 1975. Teratogenic effect of cyclopamine and jervine in rats, mice and hamsters. Proc. Soc. Exp. Biol. Med. *149*, 302–306.

KEELER, R.F. 1976. Lupine alkaloids from teratogenic and nonteratogenic lupins. III. Identification of anagyrine as the probable teratogen by feeding trials. J. Toxicol. Environ. Health *1*, 887–898.

KEELER, R.F. and BINNS, W. 1966A. Teratogenic compounds of *Veratrum californicum* (Durand). I. Preparation and characterization of fractions and alkaloids for biologic testing. Can. J. Biochem. *44*, 819–828.

KEELER, R.F. and BINNS, W. 1966B. Teratogenic compounds of *Veratrum californicum* (Durand). II. Production of fetal cyclopia by fractions and alkaloid preparations. Can. J. Biochem. *44*, 829–838.

KEELER, R.F. and BINNS, W. 1966C. Possible teratogenic effects of veratramine. Proc. Soc. Exp. Biol. Med. *123*, 921–923.

KEELER, R.F. and BINNS, W. 1967. Teratogenic compounds of *Veratrum californicum* (Durand). III. Malformations of the veratramine induced type from ingestion of plant or roots. Proc. Soc. Exp. Biol. Med. *126*, 452–454.

KEELER, R.F. and BINNS, W. 1968. Teratogenic compounds of *Veratrum californicum* (Durand). V. Comparison of cyclopian effects of steroidal alkaloids from the plant and structurally related compounds from other sources. Teratology *1*, 5–10.

KEELER, R.F. and BINNS, W. 1971. Teratogenic compounds of *Veratrum californicum* as a function of plant part, stage, and site of growth. Phytochemistry *10*, 1765–1769.

KEELER, R.F., CRONIN, L.H. and SHUPE, I.L. 1976A. Lupine alkaloids from teratogenic and nonteratogenic lupins. IV. Concentration of total alkaloids, individual major alkaloids, and the teratogen anagyrine as a function of plant part and stage of growth and their relationship to crooked calf disease. J. Toxicol. Environ. Health *1*, 899–908.

KEELER, R.F., DOUGLAS, D.R. and STALLKNECHT, G.F. 1975. The testing of blighted, aged, and control Russet Burbank Potato tuber. Preparations for ability to produce spina bifida and anencephaly in rats, rabbits, hamsters, and mice. Am. Potato J. *52*, 125–132.

KEELER, R.F., JAMES, L.F., SHUPE, J.L. and VAN KAMPEN, K.R. 1977. Lupine induced calf disease and a management method to reduce incidence. J. Range Manage. *30*, 97–102.

KEELER, R.F., YOUNG, S. and BROWN, D. 1976B. Spina bifida, exencephaly, and cranial bleb produced in hamsters by the solanum alkaloid solasodine. Res. Commun. Chem. Pathol. Pharmacol. *13*, 724–730.

KINGHORN, D.A., SELIM, M.A. and SMOLENSKI, S.J. 1980. Alkaloid distribution in some new world *Lupinus* species. Phytochemistry *19*, 1705–1710.

KISS, T. 1978. Investigations of white sweet lupine varieties in species and variety trials (1974–1976). Novenytermeles *27*, 57–64. (Hungarian)

KITAGAWA, M. and TOMIYAMA, T. 1929. A new amino compound in the jack bean and a corresponding new ferment. J. Biochem. *11*, 265–271.

KITTS, W.D., SWIERSTRA, E., BRINK, V.C. and WOOD, A.J. 1959. The estrogenic substances in certain legumes and grasses. II. The effect of stage of maturity and frequency of cutting on the estrogenic activity of some forages. Can. J. Anim. Sci. *39*, 158–163.

KJAER, A. 1960. Naturally derived isothiocyanates (mustard oils) and their parent glucosides. Progr. Chem. Org. Nat. Prod. *18*, 122.

KLEIPOOL, R.J.C. and WIBAUT, J.P. 1950. Mimosine (leucaenine). Rec. Trav. Chim. Pays-Bas *69*, 37–44.

KLEPPER, L.A. 1979. An improved method for nitrite extraction from plants, J. Agric. Food Chem. *27*, 438–441.

KNUCKLES, B.E., DE FREMERY, D. and KOHLER, G.O. 1976. Coumestrol content of fractions obtained during wet processing of alfalfa. J. Agric. Food Chem. *24*, 1177.

KNUCKLES, B.E., MILLER, R.E. and BICKOFF, E.M. 1975. Quantitative determination of coumestrol in dried alfalfa and alfalfa leaf protein concentrates containing chlorophyll. J. Assoc. Off. Anal. Chem. *58*, 983.

KOPPANG, N. 1974A. Dimethylnitrosamine. Formation in fish meal and toxic effects in pigs. Am. J. Pathol. *74*, 95–106.

KOPPANG, N. 1974B. Toxic effect of dimethylnitrosamines in cows. J. Natl. Cancer Inst. *52*, 523–531.

KOPPANG, N. 1974C. Toxic effect of dimethylnitrosamines in sheep. Acta Vet. Scand. *15*, 533–543.

KREULA, M. and KIESVAARA, M. 1959. Determination of 1-5-vinyl-2-thioxazolidone from plant material in milk. Acta Chem. Scand. *13*, 1375.

KUHN, R. and LÖW, I. 1947. Demissin: A glycoalkaloid from the leaves of *Solanum demissium*. Chem. Ber. *80*, 406–410.

KUHN, R. and LÖW, I. 1953. Lycobiose and lycotriose: A disaccharide and a trisaccharide of tomatine. Chem. Ber. *86*, 1027–1034.

KUHN, R. and LÖW, I. 1954. The constitution of solanine. Angew. Chem. *66*, 639.

LAMBERT, J.L., RAMASAMY, J. and PAUKSTELIS, J.V. 1975. Stable reagents for the colorimetric determination of cyanide by modified König reactions. Anal. Chem. *47*, 916–918.

LINDNER, H.R. 1967. Study on the fate of phyto oestrogens in the sheep by determination of isoflavones and coumestrol in the plasma and adipose tissue. Aust. J. Agric. Res. *18*, 305–333.

LIVINGSTON, A.L., BICKOFF, E.M., GUGGOLZ, J. and THOMPSON, C.R. 1960. Fluorometric estimate of coumestrol on paper chromatograms. Anal. Chem. *32*, 1620–1622.

LIVINGSTON, A.L., BICKOFF, E.M., GUGGOLZ, J. and THOMPSON, C.R. 1961. Quantitative determination of coumestrol in fresh and dried alfalfa. J. Agric. Food Chem. *9*, 135.

LLOYD, R.C. and GRAY, E. 1970. Amount and distribution of hydrocyanic acid potential during the life cycle of plants of three sorghum cultivars. Agron. J. *62*, 394–397.

LO, M.T. and HILL, D.C. 1972. Glucosinolates and their hydrolytic products in intestinal contents, feces, blood and urine of rats dosed with rapeseed meals. Can. J. Physiol. Pharmacol. *50*, 962–966.

LOOKHART, G.L. 1979. Note on an improved method of extracting and quantitating coumestrol from soybeans. Cereal Chem. *56*, 386–388.

LOOKHART. G.L. 1980. Analysis of coumestrol, a plant estrogen, in animal feeds by high performance liquid chromatography. J. Agric. Food Chem. *28*, 667.

LOOKHART, G.L., JONES, B.L. and FINNEY, K.F. 1978. Determination of coumestrol in soybeans in high performance liquid and thin-layer chromatography. Cereal Chem. *55*, 967.

LOWE, R.H. and HAMILTON, J.L. 1967. Rapid method for determination of nitrate in plant and soil extracts. J. Agric. Food Chem. *15*, 359.

LYMAN, R.L., BICKOFF, E.M., BOOTH, A.N. and LIVINGSTON, A.L. 1959. Detection of coumestrol in leguminous plants. Arch. Biochem. Biophys. *80*, 61–67.

MA, M.R. 1950. Identification of the sugars in crystalline tomatine. Arch. Biochem. *27*, 461–462.

MacLEOD, A.J. and MacLEOD, G. 1970. Flavour volatiles of some cooked vegetables. J. Food Sci. *35*, 374.

MADSEN, N.P., CHRISTIE, G.S. and HEGARTY, M.P. 1970. Effect of indospicine on incorporation of L-arginine ^{14}C into protein and transfer ribonucleic acid by cell-free systems from rat liver. Biochem. Pharmacol. *19*, 853–857.

MAGEE, P.N. and BARNES, J.M. 1956. The production of malignant primary hepatic tumors in the rat by feeding dimethylnitrosamines. Br. J. Cancer *10*, 114–122.

MAGEE, P.N., MONTESANO, R. and PREUSSMANN, R. 1976. N-Nitroso compounds and related carcinogens. *In* Chemical Carcinogens. C.E. Searle (Editor). American Chemical Society, Washington, DC.

MAHER, E.P. and HUGHES, M.A. 1971. Isolation of linamarin-lotaustralin from *Trifolium repens*. Phytochemistry *10*, 3005–3007.

MANDA, T., MATSUMOTO, T. and SATO, K. 1971B. Studies on oestrogenic substances in herbage. 3. Seasonal and yearly variations in the oestrogenic activity of legumes. J. Jpn. Soc. Grassl. Sci. *17*, 205–211.

MANDA, T., SATO, K. and MATSUMOTO, T. 1971A. Studies on oestrogenic substances in herbage. 2. Oestrogenic activity of Ladino clover and alfalfa at various stages of development. J. Jpn. Soc. Grassl. Sci. *17*, 1-6.

MAO, C.H. and ANDERSON, L. 1965. Cyanogenesis in *Sorghum vulgare*. II. Mechanism of the alkaline hydrolysis of dhurrin (p-hydroxymandelonitrile glucoside). J. Org. Chem. *30*, 603–607.

MAO, C.H. and ANDERSON, L. 1967. Cyanogenesis in *Sorghum vulgare*. III. Partial purification and characterization of two β-glucosidases from Sorghum tissues. Phytochemistry *6*, 473–483.

MAO, C.H., BLOCHER, J.P., ANDERSON, L. and SMITH, D.C. 1965. Cyanogenesis in *Sorghum-vulgare*. I. An improved method for the isolation of dhurrin; physical properties of dhurrin. Phytochemistry *4*, 297–303.

MARKER, R.E. and ROHRMANN, E. 1939. Sterols. LXXXI. Conversion of sarsapogenin to pregnanediol-3 (α) 20 (α). J. Am. Chem. Soc. *61*, 3592.

MASCRE, M.M. 1937. Leucaenol: The active principle of seeds of *Leucaena glauca* Benth. Legumes, papilionaceae. R. Acad. Sci. Paris *204*, 890–891.

MATHESON, N.A. 1980. Improvements in the approximate determination of S-methylcysteine sulphoxide (kale anaemia factor). J. Sci. Food Agric. *31*, 260–261.

MATHESON, N.A. and MOIR, A.W. 1976. A simple method for the approximate determination of S-methylcysteine sulphoxide (kale anaemia factor). J. Sci. Food Agric. *27*, 959–961.

MATSHUMOTO, H. and SHERMAN, G.D. 1951. A rapid colorimetric method for the determination of mimosine. Arch. Biochem. *33*, 195–200.

MATSUO, M. 1970. New TLC solvent systems for glucosinolates (mustard oil glucosides.) J. Chromatogr. *49*, 323–324.

MATTOCKS, A.R. 1978. Recent studies on mechanism of cytotoxic action of pyrrolizidine alkaloids. *In* Effects of Poisonous Plants on Livestock. R.F. Keeler *et al.* (Editors). Academic Press, New York.

McBEE, G.G. and MILLER, F.R. 1980. Hydrocyanic acid potential in several sorghum breeding lines as affected by nitrogen fertilization and variable harvests. Crop Sci. *20*, 232–234.

McGREGOR, D.I. 1978. Thiocyanate ion, a hydrolysis product of glucosinolates from rape and mustard seed. Can. J. Plant Sci. *58*, 795–800.

McKEE, R.K. 1961. Observations on the toxicity of solanine and related alkaloids to fungi. Tagungsber. Dtsch. Akad. Landwirtschaftswiss. Berlin *27*, 277–289.

McLEOD, H.A., BENNS, G., LEWIS, D. and LAWRENCE, J.F. 1978. Detection of goitren and its heptafluorobutyril derivative by GLC with electron capture, electrolytic conductivity and sulfur detectors. J. Chromatogr. *157*, 255.

McMILLAN, M. and THOMPSON, J.C. 1979. An outbreak of suspected solanine poisoning in schoolboys. Examination of criteria of solanine poisoning. Q. J. Med. *48*, 227–244.

McNAMARA, A.L., MEEKER, G.B., SHAW, P.D. and HAGEMAN, R.H. 1971. Use of a dissimilatory nitrate reductase for *Escherichia coli* and formate as a reductive system for nitrate assays. J. Agric. Food Chem. *19*, 229–231.

MEE, J.M.L. and BROOKS, C.C. 1971. Gas-liquid chromatography of mimosine. J. Chromatogr. *62*, 141–143.

MEGARRITY, R.G. 1978. An automated colorimetric for mimosine in Leucaena leaves. J. Sci. Food Agric. *29*, 182–186.

MELVILLE, J. and DOAK, B.W. 1940. Cyanogenesis of white clover. II. Isolation of the glucosidase constituent. N.Z. J. Sci. Technol. Sect. B: *22*, 367–371.

MELVILLE, J. and FRASER, J.G. 1951. Preparation of the cyanogenetic glucoside of white clover. N.Z. J. Sci. Technol. Sect. A: *33*, 56.

MILHAM, P.J., AWAD, A.S., PAULL, R.E. and BULL, J.H. 1970. Analysis of plants, soils and waters for nitrate by using an ion-selective electrode. Analyst *95*, 751–758.

MILLER, L.P. 1973. Glycosides. *In* Phytochemistry, Vol. 1. L.P. Miller (Editor). Van Nostrand Reinhold Co., New York.

MILLER, R.W. and SMITH, C.R. 1973. Seeds of *Indigofera* species: Their content of amino acids that may be deleterious. J. Agric. Food Chem. *21*, 909–912.

MILLINGTON, A.J., FRANCIS, C.M. and McKEOWN, N.R. 1964. Wether biassay of annual pasture legumes. II. The oestrogenic activity of nine strains of *Trifolium subterraneum* L. Aust. J. Agric. Res. *15*, 527–536.

MITCHELL, G.A. 1933. Colorimetric determination of water soluble oxalates. Analyst *58*, 279.

MOLISCH, H. 1915. *Mimosa pudica*. Sitzungsber. Akad. Wiss. Wien Math. Naturwiss. Kl. Abt. 1: *124*, 507.

MORLEY, F.H.W., BENNETT, D., BRADEN, A.W.H., TURNBULL, K.E. and AXELSEN, A. 1968. Comparison of mice, guinea-pigs, and sheep as test animals for bioassay of oestrogenic pasture legumes. Proc. N.Z. Soc. Anim. Prod. *28*, 11.

MORRIS, C.F. and THOMPSON, J.F. 1956. The identification of (+) S-methyl-L-cysteine sulfoxide in plants. J. Am. Chem. Soc. *78*, 1605–1608.

MORRIS, M.P., PAGAN, C. and WARMKE, H.E. 1954. Heptagenic acid, a toxic component of *Indigofera endecaphylla*. Science *119*, 322–323.

MOULE, G.R., BRADEN, A.W.H. and LAMOND, D.R. 1963. The significance of oestrogens in pasture plants in relation to animal production. Anim. Breed. Abstr. *31*, 139.

MÜLLER, H. and SIEPE, V. 1979. Comparison of different methods for nitrate determinations in food. Colorimetry, GLC, TLC and potentiometry. Dtsch. Lebensm. Rundsch. *75*, 175–183.

MULLIN, W.F. and SAHASRABUDHE, M.R. 1978. Effect of cooking on the glucosinolates in cruciferous vegetables. J. Inst. Can. Sci. Technol. Aliment. *11* (1) 50–52.

MURTI, V.V.S. and SESHADRI, F.R.S. 1967. Naturally occurring less common amino acids of possible nutritional interest and their simple derivatives. Nutr. Abstr. Rev. *37*, 677–693.

MYERS, A.T. 1947. Seasonal changes in total and soluble oxalates in leaf blades and petioles of rhubarb. J. Agric. Res. *74*, 33.

MZIK, J. 1977. Estimation of mimosine in ovine plasma. J. Chromatogr. *144*, 146–148.

NAGY, S., TELEK, L., HALL, N.T. and BERRY, R.E. 1978. Potential food uses for protein from tropical and subtropical plant leaves. J. Agric. Food Chem. *26*, 1016–1028.

NAHRSTEDT, A. 1973. Cyanogenic glycosides in higher plants. Pharm. Unserer Zeit *2*, 147–155. (German)

NAHRSTEDT, A. 1977. Replacement of carcigenic and allergenic amines in the cyanid determination method of Aldridge. Dtsch. Apoth. Ztg. *117*, 1357–1360. (German)

NATL. ACAD. SCI. 1977. *Leucaena*: Promising Forage and Tree Crop for the Tropics. National Academy of Sciences, Washington, DC.

NEURATH, G. and DOERK, E. 1964. Identification and quantitative determination of some primary and secondary amines from mixtures as 4 L-nitroazobenzoic (4) amide. Chem. Ber. *97*, 172. (German)

NEURATH, G., PIRMAN, G. and DUNGER, M. 1964. Identification of N-nitroso compounds and asymmetric hydrazine as 5-nitro-2-hydroxy-benzol derivatives and utilization as micromethod. Chem. Ber. *97*, 1630–1631.

NEWELL, J.E. and SISKEN, H.R. 1972. Determination of nitrosodimethylamine in the low parts per billion. J. Agric. Food Chem. *20*, 711.

NIENBURG, H. and TAUBÖCK, K. 1937. The constitution of mimosine and some substituted phenylaminoacetic acids. Hoppe Seylers Z. Physiol. Chem. *245*, 80–86. (German)

NILSSON, A., HILL, J.L. and DAVIES, H.L. 1967. An *in vitro* study of formononetin and biochanin A metabolism in rumen fluid from sheep. Biochim. Biophys. Acta *148*, 92.

NORDFELDT, S.L., HENKE, L.A., MORITA, K., MATSUMOTO, H., TAKAHASH, M., YOUNGE, O.R., WILLERS, E.H. and CROSS, R.F. 1952. Feeding tests with *Indigofera endecaphylla* (Creeping Indigo) and some observations on its poisonous effect on domestic animals. Hawaii Agric. Exp. Stn. Tech. Bull. *15*.

NOWOSAD, F.S. and MACVICAR, R.M. 1940. Adaptation of the "picric-acid test" method for selecting HCN-free lines in sudangrass. Sci. Agric. *20*, 566–569.

OFF. METHODS EUR. COMMON MARKET. 1971. Cyanide determination. Amtsblatt der Europäischen Gemeinschaft *L 155/15*. European Communities, Brussels. (German)

O'HALLORAN, M.W. 1962. The effect of oxalate on bacteria isolated from the rumen. Aust. Soc. Anim. Prod. Proc. *4*, 18–20.

OLSEN, O. and SORENSEN, H. 1980. Sinalbin and other glucosinolates in seeds of double low rape species and *Brassica napus* var. Bronovski. J. Agric. Food Chem. *28*, 43–48.

OLSSON, K., THEANDER, D. and AMAN, P. 1976. Determination of total glucosinolate content in rapeseed and turnipseed meals by gas liquid chromatography. Swed. J. Agric. Res. *6*, 225–229.

OSTGARD, O. 1973. Fodder rape. The effect of sowing methods and nitrogen fertilization on yield and chemical composition at different times of harvesting. Forsk. Fors. Landbruket *24*, 577–599.

OSTROWSKI-MEISSNER, H.T. 1980. Protein extraction from pasture: A new concept in efficiency dairy farming in temperate and sub-tropical regions. 4th World Conf. Anim. Prod., Buenos Aires, Aug. 1978. L.S. Verde and A. Fernandez (Editors).

OSUNTOKUN, B.O. 1981. Chronic cyanide intoxication and neuropathy in the Nigerian Africans. *In* Human Nutrition and Diet. G.H. Bourne (Editor). S. Karger A.G., Basel. World Review of Nutrition and Dietetics *36*, 141–174.

PATEL, C.J. and WRIGHT, M.J. 1958. The effect of certain nutrients upon the hydrocyanic acid content of sudangrass grown in nutrient solution. Agron. J. *50*, 645–647.

PATT, P. and WINKLER, W. 1960. Preparation and determination of solanine using ion exchange. Arch,. Pharm. Paris, *293*, 846–853.

PAUL, J.L. and CARLSON, R.M. 1968. Nitrate determination in plant extracts by the nitrate electrode. J. Agric. Food Chem. *16*, 766.

PEARN, J.H. and HEGARTY, M.P. 1970. Indospicine: The teratogenic factor from *Indigofera spicata* extract causing cleft palate. Br. J. Exp. Pathol. *51*, 34–36.

PERSSON, S. 1974. A method for determination of glucosinolates in rapeseed as TMS derivatives. Proc. 4th Int. Rapeseed Congr., Giessen, West Germany, 1974.

PIETERSE, P.L. and ANDREWS, F.N. 1956A. The oestrogenic activity of alfalfa and other feedstuffs. J. Anim. Sci. *15*, 25–36.

PIETERSE, P.L. and ANDREWS, F.N. 1956B. The oestrogenic activity of legume grass and corn silage. J. Dairy Sci. *39*, 81–89.

PIRIE, N.W. 1971. Leaf Protein: Its Agronomy, Preparation, Quality, and Use. Blackwell Scientific Publications, Oxford.

PIRIE, N.W. 1978. By-product leaves. *In* Leaf Protein and Other Aspects of Fodder Fractionation. Cambridge University Press, Cambridge.

POPE, G.S. and WRIGHT, H.G. 1954. Oestrogenic isoflavones in red clover and subterranean clover. Chem. Ind. *33*, 1019–1020.

PRELOG, V. and JEGER, O. 1953. The chemistry of *Solanum* and *Veratrum* alkaloids. *In* The Alkaloids, Chemistry and Physiology, Vol. 3. R.H.F. Manske and H.L. Holmes (Editors). Academic Press, New York.

PRELOG, V. and JEGER, O. 1960. Steroid alkaloids. The *Solanum* group. *In* Alkaloids—Chemistry and Physiology, Vol. 7. R.H.F. Manske (Editor). Academic Press, New York.

PREUSSMAN, R., DAIBER, D. and HENGY, H. 1964. A sensitive color reaction for nitrosamines on thin-layer chromatograms. Nature *201*, 502–503.

REAY, P.R. 1969. An improved procedure for isolation of dhurrin. Phytochemistry *8*, 2259–2260.

REIS, P.J. 1975. Effects of intravenous infusion of mimosine on wool growth of Merino sheep. Aust. J. Biol. Sci. *28*, 483–493.

REIS, P.J. 1978. Effectiveness of intravenous and abomasal doses of mimosine for defleecing sheep and effects on subsequent wool growth. Aust. J. Agric. Res. *29*, 1043–1055.

REIS, P.J. and TUNKS, D.A. 1978. The influence of nutrition on the effectiveness of mimosine for defleecing sheep. Aust. J. Agric. Res. *29*, 1057–1064.

REIS, P.J., TUNKS, D.A. and CHAPMAN, R.E. 1975A. Effects of mimosine, a potential chemical defleecing agent, on wool growth and the skin of sheep. Aust. J. Biol. Sci. *28*, 69–84.

REIS, P.J., TUNKS, D.A. and DOWES, A.M. 1978. Mimosine, administered orally and two related compounds as chemical defleecing agents for sheep. Aust. J. Agric. Res. *29*, 1065–1075.

REIS, P.J., TUNKS, D.A. and HEGARTY, M.P. 1975B. Fate of mimosine administered orally to sheep and its effectiveness as a defleecing agent. Aust. J. Biol. Sci. *28*, 495–501.

RENWICK, J.H. 1972. Hypothesis: Anencephaly and Spina Bifida are usually preventable by avoidance of a specific but unidentified substance present in certain potato tubers. Br. J. Prev. Soc. Med. *26*, 67–68.

RENZ, J. 1936. Mimosin. Hoppe Seylers Z. Physiol. Chem. *244*, 153–158.

RESSLER, C. 1962. Isolation and identification from common vetch of the neurotoxin β-cyano-L-alanine, a possible factor in neurolathyrism. J. Biol. Chem. *237*, 733.

RESSLER, C., REDSTORE, P.A. and ERENBERG, R.H. 1961. Isolation and identification of a neuroactive factor from *Lathyrus latifolius*. Science *134*, 188.

RIEDMANN, M. 1974. Screening of nitrosamines in food, using nitrogen flame ionization detector. J. Chromatogr. *88*, 376–380.

ROACH, D. and GEHRKE, C.W. 1969. Direct esterification of the protein amino acids. GLC on N-TFA n butyl esters. J. Chromatogr. *44*, 269–278.

ROBIQUET, H.E. and BOULTRON-CHARLARD, A.F. 1830. Amygdalin in bitter almonds. Ann. Chem. Phys. *44*, 352. (French)

RODDICK, J.G. 1974. The steroidal glycoalkaloid α-tomatine. Phytochemistry *13*, 9–25.

RÖNSCH, H. and SCHREIBER, K. 1967. Analytical and preparative TLC separation of 5α saturated and D^5 unsaturated steroid alkaloids and sapogenins on silver nitrate containing layers. J. Chromatogr. *30*, 149.

ROSENBERG, M.M. and ZOEBISCH, O.C. 1952. A chick test for toxicity in forage legumes. Agron. J. *44*, 314–315.

ROSENTHAL, G.A. 1970. Investigation of canavanine. Biochemistry in the jack bean plant, *Canavalia ensiformis* (L.) DC. I. Canavanine utilization in the developing plant. Plant Physiol. *46*, 273–276.

ROSENTHAL, G.A. 1972. Investigations of canavanine. Biochemistry in jack bean plant, *Canavalia ensiformis* (L.) DC. II. Canavanine biosynthesis in the developing plant. Plant Physiol. *50*, 328–331.

ROSENTHAL, G.A. 1973. Preparation and colorimetric analysis of L-canaline. Anal. Biochem. *51*, 354.

ROSENTHAL, G.A. 1977. The biological effects and mode of action of L-canavanine, a structural analogue of L-arginine. Q. Rev. Biol. *52*, 155–179.

ROSS, W.D., BUTLER, G.W., DUFFY, T.G., REHG, W.R., WININGER, M.T. and SIEVERS, R.E. 1975. Analysis for aqueous nitrates and nitrites and gaseous oxides of nitrogen by electron capture gas chromatography. J. Chromatogr. *112*, 719–727.

ROUGHAN, P.G. and SLACK, C.R. 1973. Simple methods for routine screening and quantitative estimation of oxalate content of tropical grasses. J. Sci. Food Agric. *24*, 803–811.

SACHSE, J. 1974. Determination of estrogenic isoflavones and coumestrol in clovers (*Trifolium pratense* L. and *T. repens* L.). J. Chromatogr. *96*, 123.

SALUNKHE, D.K. and WU, M.T. 1977. Toxicants in plants and plant products. CRC Crit. Rev. Food Sci. Nutr. *8*, 265–324.

SANDER, H. and GRISEBACH, H. 1958. Preparation of ^{14}C labeled tomatine. Z. Naturforsch. *13b*, 755–756.

SATO, Y., KATZ, A. and MOSETTIG, E. 1951. Degradation of tomatidine. J. Am. Chem. Soc. *73*, 880.

SCHILLING, E.D. 1954. Crystalline substance from *Lathyrus odoratus* producing skeletal changes of lathyrism. Fed. Proc. Fed. Am. Soc. Exp. Biol. *13*, 290.

SCHILLING, E.D. and STRONG, F.M. 1954. Isolation structure and synthesis of a lathyrus factor from *L. odoratus* J. Am. Chem. Soc. *76*, 2848.

SCHMITZ, E.M., FREEMAN, B.N. and REED, R.E. 1968. Livestock Poisoning Plants of Arizona. Univ. of Arizona Press, Phoenix.

SCHNEIDER, B.A., CLARK, N.A., HEMKEN, R.W. and VANDERSALL, J.H. 1970. Relationship of pearl millet to milk fat depression in dairy cows. II. Forage organic acids as influenced by soil nutrients. J. Dairy Sci. *53*, 305–310.

SCHREIBER, K. 1957. *Solanum* alkaloids. V. Isolation of Δ^5 tomatidin-3 β-ol and yamogenin from potatoes. Angew. Chem. *69*, 483. (German)

SCHREIBER, K. 1968. Steroidal alkaloids: The *Solanum* group. *In* The Alkaloids, Vol. 10. R.H.F. Manske (Editor). Academic Press, New York.

SCHREIBER, K., AURICH, O. and OSSKE, G. 1963. Thin-layer chromatography of *Solanum* steroid alkaloids and steroidal sapogenins. J. Chromatogr. *12*, 63–69.

SCHREIBER, K., HAMMER, U., ITHAL, E. and RUDOLPH, W. 1961. Tomatin content of mutants of *Lycopersicon* varieties. Tagungsber. Dtsch. Akad. Landwirtschaftswiss. Berlin *27*, 75. (German)

SEAWRIGHT, A.A., GROENENDYK, S. and SILVA, K.I.N.G. 1970. Outbreak of oxalate poisoning in cattle grazing *Setaria sphacelata*. Aust. Vet. J. *46*, 293–296.

SEIGLER, D.S. 1975. Isolation and characterization of naturally occurring cyanogenic compounds. Phytochemistry *14*, 9–29.

SEIGLER, D.S. 1976. Plants of the northeastern United Stated that produce cyanogenic compounds. Econ. Bot. *30*, 395–407.

SELYE, H. 1957. Lathyrism. Rev. Can. Biol. *16*, 1.

SEN, N.P. 1970. GLC determination of dimethylnitrosamine as dimethylnitramine at picogram levels. J. Chromatogr. *51*, 301–304.

SEN, N.P. 1980. Nitrosamines. *In* The Safety of Foods, 2nd Edition. H.D. Graham (Editor). AVI Publishing Co., Westport, CT.

SEN, N.P. and DALPEC, C. 1972. A simple TLC technique for the semiquantitative determination of volatile nitrosamines in alcoholic beverages. Analyst *97*, 216.

SEN, N.P., SCHWINGHAMER, L.A., DONALDSON, B.A. and MILES, W.F. 1972. N-Nitrosodimethylamine in fish meal. J. Agric. Food Chem. *20*, 1281.

SEN, N.P., SMITH, D.C. and SCHWINGHAMER, L. 1969. Formation of N-nitrosamines from secondary amines and nitrite in human and animal gastric juice. Food Cosmet. Toxicol. *7*, 301–307.

SERFONTEIN, W.J. and HURTER, P. 1966. Method for identifying small amounts of nitrosamines in biological material. Nature *209*, 1238–1239.

SHIH, M. and KUČ, J. 1974. α and β solamarin in Kennebec *Solanum tuberosum* leaves and aged tuber slices. Phytochemistry *13*, 997–1000.

SHUPE, J.L., BINNS, W., JAMES, L.F. and KEELER, R.F. 1967A. Crooked calf syndrome, a plant-induced congenital deformity. Zuchthygiene *2*, 145–152.

SHUPE, J.L., BINNS, W., JAMES. L.F. and KEELER, R.F. 1967B. Lupine, a cause of crooked calf disease. J. Am. Vet. Med. Assoc. *151*, 198–203.

SHUPE, J.L., JAMES, L.F. and BINNS, W. 1967C. Observations on crooked calf disease. J. Am. Vet. Med. Assoc. *151*, 191–197.

SHUTT, D.A. 1976. Estrogenic substances in plants. Endeavour *35*, 110-113.

SHUTT, D.A., AXELSEN, A. and LINDNER, H.R. 1967. Free and conjugated isoflavones in the plasma of sheep following ingestion of oestrogenic clover. Aust. J. Agric. Res. *18*, 647.

SHUTT, D.A. and BRADEN, A.W.H. 1968. The significance of equol in relation to the oestrogenic responses in sheep ingesting clover with a high formononetin content. Aust. J. Agric. Res. *19*, 545.

SHUTT, D.A., WESTON, R.H. and HOGAN, J.P. 1970. Quantitative aspects of phyto-oestrogen metabolism in sheep fed on subterranean clover (*Trifolium subterraneum* cultivar Clare) or red clover *(Trifolium pratense)*. Aust. J. Agric. Res. *21*, 713.

SINGH, H., KAPOOR, V.K. and CHAWLA, S.A. 1969. Some aspects of the recent advances in plant steroid. J. Sci. Ind. Res. *28*, 339–354.

SMITH, R.H. 1974. Kale poisoning. Rep. Rowett Inst. *30*, 112–131.

SMITH, R.H. 1978. S-Methylcysteine sulphoxide, the *Brassica* anaemia factor (a valuable dietary factor for man?). Vet. Sci. Commun. *2*, 47–61.

SMITH, R.H., EARL, G.R. and MATHESON, N.A. 1974. S-Methylcysteine sulphoxide, the haemolitic toxin in kale. Biochem. Soc. Trans. *2*, 101.

SPERONI, J.J. and PELL, E.J. 1980. Modified method for tuber glycoalkaloid and leaf glycoalkaloid analysis. Am. Potato J. *57*, 537–542.

STAHMANN, M.A. 1965. The potential for protein production from green plants. Econ. Bot. *22*, 73.

STAINTON, M.P. 1974. Simple, efficient reduction column for use in the automated determination of nitrate in water. Anal. Chem. *46*, 1616.

STEYN, D.G. 1960. The problem of methaemoglobinaemia in man with special reference to poisoning with nitrates and nitrites in infants and children. Univ. Pretoria Publ. New Ser, Pretoria, S. Afr. Union Bull. *11*, 13.

STEYN, D.G. 1977. Modern trends in methods of food production, food processing and food preparation which constitute a potential hazard to human and animal health. Repub. S. Afr. Dep. Agric. (Pretoria) Tech. Serv. Tech. Commun. *136*, 13.

STOB, M., DAVIS, R.L. and ANDREWS, F.N. 1957. Strain differences in the estrogenicity of alfalfa. J. Anim. Sci. *16*, 850.

STREET, H.E., KENYON, A.E. and WATSO, G.M. 1946. The nature and distribution of various forms of nitrogen in the tomato. Ann. Appl. Biol. *33*, 1–12.

SYNGE, R.L.M. and WOOD, J.C. 1956. (+)-(S-Methyl-L-cysteine S-oxide) in cabbage. Biochem. J. *64*, 252.

TAPPER, S.A. and REAY, P.F. 1973. Cyanogenic glycosides and glucosinolates. *In* Chemistry and Biochemistry of Herbage, Vol. 1. G.W. Butler and R.W. Baily (Editors). Academic Press, London and New York.

TARAS, M.J. 1958. Colorimetric Determination of Nonmetals. Interscience, New York.

TELEK, L. 1979. Preparation of leaf protein concentrates in lowland humid tropics. *In* Tropical Foods: Chemistry and Nutrition, Vol. 2. G.E. Inglett and G. Charalambous (Editors). Academic Press, New York.

TELEK, L. and EVANS, J. 1978. Preparation of mimosine free leaf protein fractions. Presented in Annu. Meet. Am. Chem. Soc., Miami, Sept. 10–15, 1978.

TELLING, G.M, BRYCE, T.A. and ALTHORPE, J. 1971. Use of vacuum distillation and gas chromatography-mass spectrometry for determination of low levels of volatile nitrosamines in meat products. J. Agric. Food Chem. *19*, 937.

THIES, W. 1976. Quantitative gas liquid chromatography of glucosinolates on a microliter scale. Fette Seifen Anstrichm. *78*, 231–234. (German)

THIES, W. 1977. Analysis of glucosinolates in seeds of rapeseed (*Brassica napus* L.): Concentration of glucosinolates by ion exchange. Pflanzenzuechtung *79*, 331–335. (German)

TODD, J.R. 1970. Factors in white clover which affect animal health. Agric. Dig. *20*, 25–34.

TOOKEY, H.L. 1973. Solubilization and selected properties of crambe seed thioglucosidase (thioglucoside glucohydrolase EC 3.2.3.1). Can. J. Biochem. *51*, 1305.

TOOKEY, H.L., VAN ETTEN, C.H. and DAXENBICHLER, M.E. 1978. Goitrogens. *In* Toxic Constituents of Plant Foodstuffs, 2nd Edition. I.E. Liener, (Editor). Academic Press, New York.

UNDERHILL, E.W. and KIRKLAND, D.F. 1971. Gas chromatography of trimethylsilyl derivatives of glucosinolates. J. Chromatogr. *57*, 47–54.

USHER, C.D. and TELLING, G.M. 1975. Analysis of nitrate and nitrite in foodstuffs: A critical review. J. Sci. Food Agric. *26*, 1793–1805.

VAN ETTEN, C.H. and DAXENBICHLER, M.E. 1977. Glucosinolates and derived products in cruciferous vegetables: Total glucosinolates by retention on anion exchange resin and enzymatic hydrolysis to measure released glucose. J. Assoc. Off. Anal. Chem. *60* (4) 946–949.

VAN ETTEN, C.H., DAXENBICHLER, M.E., PETERS, J.E., WOLFF, I.A. and BOOTH, A.N. 1965. Seed meal from *Crambe abyssinica*. J. Agric. Food Chem. *13*, 24.

VAN ETTEN, C.H., DAXENBICHLER, M.E., WILLIAMS, P.H. and KWOLEK, W.E. 1976. Glucosinolates and derived products in cruciferous vegetables. Analysis of the edible part from twenty-two varieties of cabbage. J. Agric. Food Chem. *24*, 452.

VAN ETTEN, C.H., McGREW, C.E. and DAXENBICHLER, M.E. 1974. Glucosinolate determination in cruciferous seeds and meals by measure of enzymatically released glucose. J. Agric. Food Chem. *22*, 483–487.

VAN ETTEN, C.H. and TOOKEY, H.L. 1978. Glucosinolates in cruciferous plants. *In* Effects of Poisonous Plants on Livestock. R.F. Keeler, K. van Kampen and L.F. James (Editors). Academic Press, New York.

VAN ETTEN, C.H. and TOOKEY, H.L. 1979. Chemistry and biological effects of glucosinolates. *In* Herbivores, Their Interactions With Secondary Plant Metabolites. G.A. Rosenthal and D.H. Janzen (Editors). Academic Press, New York.

VAN ETTEN, C.H. and WOLFF, I.A. 1973. *In* Toxicants Occurring Naturally in Foods, 2nd Edition. National Academy of Sciences, Washington, DC.

WAGNON, K.A. 1960. Lupine poisoning as a possible factor in congenital deformities in cattle. J. Range Manage. *13*, 89–91.

WALKER, N.J. and GRAY, I.K. 1970. The glucosinolate of Land Crees *(Coronopus didymus)* and its enzymatic degradation products as precursors of off-flavor of milk: A review. J. Agric. Food Chem. *18*, 346–352.

WALKER, R. 1975. Naturally occurring nitrate/nitrite in foods. Review. J. Sci. Food Agric. *26*, 1735–1742.

WALTER, E.D. 1941. Genistin, an isoflavone glucoside and its aglucone, genistein, from soybeans. J. Am. Chem. Soc. *63*, 3273.

WARD, K.A. and HARRIS, R.L.N. 1976. Inhibition of wool follicle DNA synthesis by mimosine and related 4 (1H) pyridones. Aust. J. Biol. Sci. *29*, 189–196.

WARMKE, H.E., FREYRE, R.H. and MORRIS, M.P. 1952. Studies on palatability of some tropical legumes. Agron. J. *44*, 517–520.

WATTS, P.S. 1957. Decomposition of oxalic acid. *In vitro* by rumen content. Aust. J. Agric. Res. *8*, 266.

WAWZONEK, S., PONSETI, I.V., SHEPARD, R.S. and WIEDEMANN, L.G. 1955. Epiphyseal plate lesions, degenerative arthritis and dissecting aneurism of the aorta produced by amino nitriles. Science *121*, 63–65.

WETTER, L.R. 1955. The determination of mustard oils in rapeseed meals. Can. J. Biochem. Physiol. *33*, 980–984.

WETTER, L.R. 1957. The estimation of substituted thiooxazolidone in rapeseed meals. Can. J. Biochem. Physiol. *35*, 293–297.

WETTER. L.R. and YOUNGS, C.G. 1976. A thiourea U.V. assay for total glucosinolate content in rapeseed meals. J. Am. Oil Chem. Soc. *53*, 162–164.

WHITTLE, P.J., SMITH, R.H. and McINTOSH, A. 1976. Estimation of S-methylcysteine sulphoxide (kale anaemic factor and its distribution among *Brassica* and root crops. J. Sci. Food Agric. *27*, 633–642.

WIBAUT, J.P. and SCHUHMACHER, J.P. 1952. The optical activity of mimosine. Rec. Trav. Chim. 71, 1017–1020.

WILLIMOT, G.G. 1933. An investigation of solanine poisoning. Analyst *58*, 431–439.

WILLS, J.H., JR. 1966. Goitrogens in foods. Toxicants occurring naturally in foods. Natl. Acad. Sci. Nat. Res. Counc., Washington, D.C., Publ. *1354*.

WILLUHN, G. 1965. The biogenesis of important pharmaceutical plant steroids. Pharm. Ztg. *110*, 96–106.

WISEMAN, H.G. and JACOBSON, W.C. 1965. Determination of nitrate in silages and forages. J. Agric. Food Chem. *13*, 26–39.

WOJTYCH, B., PODUSOWSKA, I. and STRAWINSKA, Z. 1973. Effect of rate of nitrogen on the contents of nitrates and goitrogens (vinyl) thiooxazolidone and isothiocyanates) in kale (*Brassica oleracea* var. *acephala*) and winter rape *(Brassica napus)*. Acta Agrar. Silvestria Ser. Agrar. *13*, 87–93.

WOLF, D.D. and WASHKO, W.W. 1967. Distribution and concentration of HCN in a sorghum-sudan grass hybrid. Agron. J. *59*, 381–382.

WONG, E. and FLUX, D.S. 1962. The oestrogenic activity of red clover isoflavones and some of their degradation products. J. Endocrinol. *24*, 341.

WOOD, T. 1965. The cyanogenic glycoside content of cassava and cassava products. J. Sci. Food Agric. *16*, 300–305.

WOOD, T. 1966. The isolation, properties, and enzymatic breakdown of linamarin from cassava. J. Sci. Food Agric. *17*, 85–90.

YOSHIDA, R.K. 1944. A chemical and physiological study of the nature and properties of the toxic principle in Leucaena glauca (Koa haole). Ph.D. Thesis. Univ. of Minnesota, Minneapolis.

YOSHIDA, J., NAKAMURA, Y., HORI, S. and NAKAMURA, R. 1969. Feeding of high nitrate turnip leaves to the sheep. Sci. Rep. Fac. Agric. Ibaraki Univ. *17*, 31–36. Herb. Abstr. (1971) *41*, 55.

ZITNAK, A., HILL, D.C. and ALEXANDER, J.C. 1977. Determination of linamarin in biological tissues. Anal. Biochem. *77*, 310–314.

13

Biological Properties and Nutritional Significance of Legume Saponins

P.R. Cheeke

Saponins are glycosides widely distributed among plants of economic importance. Most forage legumes grown in temperate areas contain saponins; little is known of their distribution among the many tropical legumes being increasingly evaluated as human and animal foods. Saponins have a wide variety of biological effects, with both positive and negative implications. Of the former, their potential role in lowering serum cholesterol levels in humans, as a means of reducing the risk of atherosclerosis, is an area of much current investigation. Of the negative effects, reduction of growth rate of nonruminant animals fed alfalfa-containing diets is probably the major concern. Saponins are characterized by a bitter taste and foaming properties (honeycomb foam in water). They are well known for their hemolytic action, a property which has been exploited in analytical procedures for saponin content of plant material.

This chapter will deal primarily with recent studies on alfalfa saponins and their significance in alfalfa meal, alfalfa protein concentrate (APC), and other alfalfa fractions. Alfalfa saponins have previously been reviewed by several authors (Birk 1969; Cheeke 1971; Bondi *et al.* 1973; Cheeke 1976). These references should be consulted for further information on the early work with saponins.

ISOLATION, CHEMICAL STRUCTURE, AND MEASUREMENT OF ALFALFA SAPONINS

Alfalfa saponins are readily extracted from plant material with aqueous ethanol. Saponins may complex with leaf proteins, rendering them insoluble in water. The water-insoluble saponins may be precipitated by concentration of the alcohol extract; water-soluble saponins may be precipitated by complexing with cholesterol or other sterols. Following precipitation, the sterols can be removed with benzene. Purification of individual compounds has been achieved with thin layer and column chromatography (Bondi *et al.* 1973). Application of the high pressure liquid chromatography (HPLC) technique to saponin analysis should permit further elucidation of the saponins in alfalfa and be useful in preparation of pure compounds for further study.

Alfalfa saponins are glycosides, containing an aglycone (sapogenin) with a side chain of monosaccharides linked by an ether bond to the aglycone at carbon 3 (Fig. 13.1A). The principal saponins identified in common alfalfa cultivars are medicagenic acid, soyasapogenol A, soyasapogenol B, and lucernic acid (Fig. 13.1B, C, D). These differ in the hydroxyl and carboxyl groups attached to the sapogenin. Mediacagenic acid appears to be the major alfalfa saponin responsible for antinutritional effects (Hanson *et al.* 1973). While these are the major ones, at least 10 individual sapogenins may be found in common alfalfa cultivars (Horber *et al.* 1974).

With various combinations of sapogenin and side chains, a large number of individual saponins exist in alfalfa. Berrang *et al.* (1974) detected 33 saponins in DuPuits and 27 in Lahontan cultivars. Monosaccharides in the side chain include glucose, galactose, xylose, arabinose, and rhamnose (Horber *et al.* 1974). A detailed discussion of the relationships between the aglycone and side chain groups is provided by Berrang *et al.* (1974).

Quantitative estimates of saponin content of alfalfa may be made by chemical or biological analyses. Chemical methods have been reviewed by Bondi *et al.* (1973). Brawn *et al.* (1981) have reported on a rapid gas chromatographic method for the determination of medicagenic acid in alfalfa protein concentrate. Numerous bioassays are available; these are of particular application in plant breeding work. These methods include the well-known *in vitro* erythrocyte hemolysis bioassay, in which an alfalfa extract is serially diluted and a red blood cell suspension added. The concentration causing complete hemolysis is determined and compared with standard values obtained with isolated alfalfa saponin. Horber *et al.* (1974) describe the technique in detail. These workers also developed a bioassay based on the survival of larval potato leaf hoppers and pea aphids. These organisms are sensitive to alfalfa saponins. While the test gave satisfactory results, it does not appear to have been employed by other workers.

The most widely used bioassay at present is the *Trichoderma* assay developed by Pedersen at Utah State, and first reported by Zimmer *et al.* (1967). *Trichoderma viride* is an alfalfa pathogenic fungus which is sensitive to alfalfa saponins. The bioassay compares rates of growth of the fungus on potato dextrose agar with various levels of saponin or alfalfa extract, as compared to growth rate with no saponin present. Pedersen employed an ED_{50} to express saponin content, which is the effective dose of saponin or alfalfa extract that reduces growth rate of the fungus by 50%

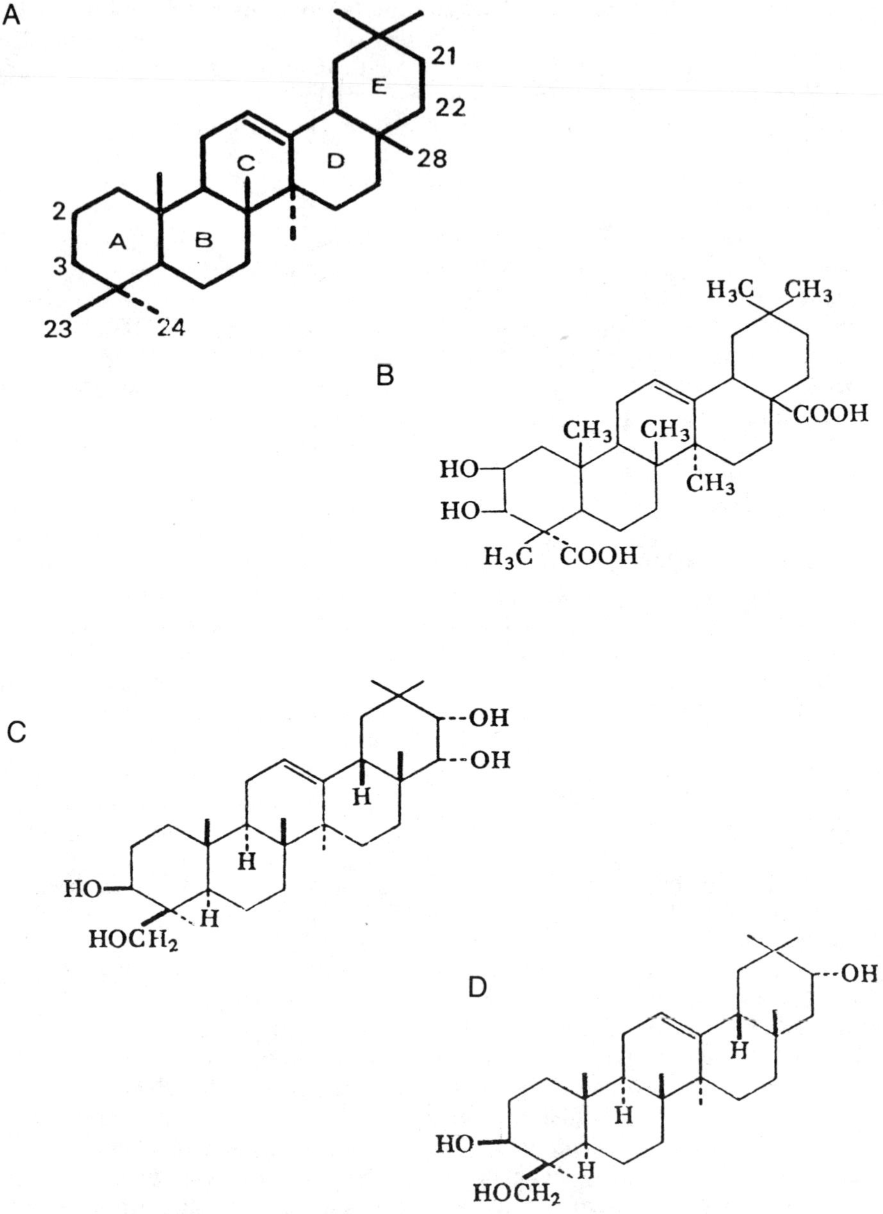

Fig. 13.1. Structures of some alfalfa saponin aglycons. A—General structure. B—Medicagenic acid. C—Soyasapogenol A. D—Soyasapogenol B.

(Pedersen and Wang 1971). This assay has been refined by Livingston *et al.* (1977B); saponin is extracted from alfalfa with aqueous ethanol and added to the agar. A standard curve is prepared with a saponin standard, and the saponin level of the plant extract is calculated by a slope ratio analysis.

Distribution of Saponins in Alfalfa

Cultivar differences in saponin content have been demonstrated. For example, DuPuits alfalfa is high in medicagenic acid, while the principal saponin in the Lahontan cultivar is soyasapogenol A (Hanson *et al.* 1973). Saponins are distributed in all parts of the plant. Pedersen (1975) reported that the foliage saponin of DuPuits alfalfa was more toxic to *Trichoderma* than that obtained from Lahontan foliage, but the root saponins of the two cultivars were of similar toxicity and much more toxic than the foliage saponin. Saponin in the root is concentrated in the outermost layer of the cortex, where it appears to have a role in resistance to root diseases (Pedersen 1975). Quazi (1976) has also demonstrated the concentration of saponin in the outer root, and suggested that this may be important in deterring the feeding of the grass grub.

Medicagenic acid and soyasapogenol A are not stored in seeds (Pedersen 1975), but other saponins (soyasapogenins B, C, and E) are found in alfalfa seeds. The toxicity of sprouted alfalfa seeds to *Trichoderma* increased rapidly in the first 48 hr of germination, and at a slower rate up to 192 hr (Pedersen 1975). Livingston *et al.* (1977B) also reported a very high saponin content of alfalfa sprouts. This may be of significance in human nutrition (to be discussed later) in terms of the hypocholesterolemic effects of alfalfa saponins.

The saponin content of alfalfa foliage is influenced by environmental factors. The saponin concentration follows a seasonal cycle, being high in midsummer and low in spring and fall (Pedersen 1979). As a consequence, the saponin content of second cutting alfalfa tends to be higher than for first or third cuttings (Pedersen 1979). Saponin in the roots is translocated to the tops in response to flowering and unidentified environmental factors (Pedersen 1979). The saponin content of the foliage is controlled by that in the roots, since grafting a top from a low saponin alfalfa plant onto a root from a high saponin plant produces foliage with a high saponin content, while grafting a high saponin top onto a low saponin root gives foliage with a low saponin content (Pedersen 1978).

Plant breeders have successfully modified the saponin content of several alfalfa cultivars by selection. Pedersen (1979) summarized an extensive breeding program, in which six cultivars were selected for seven generations for both low and high saponin content. The principal change in the low saponin selections is a decrease in medicagenic acid, the most toxic alfalfa saponin. Elliott at Michigan State (Scardavi and Elliott 1967) has developed a low saponin line of Vernal alfalfa, using erythrocyte hemolysis as the primary bioassay for saponin. Pedersen used the *Trichoderma* assay. The low saponin selections of both Pedersen and Elliott show potential as improved types of alfalfa for animal feeding.

Biological Effects of Saponins

The effects of saponins on animals may include:

(1) Effects on growth
(2) Effects on palatability and feed intake
(3) Effects on tissue cholesterol levels and cholesterol excretion
(4) Effects on cholesterol content of eggs
(5) Erythrocyte hemolysis
(6) Bloat in ruminants
(7) Inhibition of smooth muscle activity
(8) Effects on enzymes
(9) Effects on digestion and absorption
(10) Effects on fertility
(11) Other effects of saponins

Most of these have been reviewed by Cheeke (1971). This discussion will be concerned mainly with new information since that time.

(1) Effects on Growth. The growth-inhibiting effects of alfalfa saponins are important because of the contribution that alfalfa can make to world food supplies. Alfalfa produces more protein per hectare than any other temperate zone crop (Stahmann 1968). Efficient utilization of this protein source requires overcoming a number of problems, including those posed by saponins. Cheeke and Myer (1975) summarized the factors limiting the value of alfalfa for nonruminants such as swine and poultry as:

(1) Growth inhibitors such as saponins
(2) Fiber content
(3) Low digestible energy
(4) Low palatability
(5) Low digestibility of alfalfa protein

Knowledge that alfalfa saponins depress growth stems from the work of Peterson (1950A, B) and Kodras *et al.* (1951) who noted that the growth inhibition caused by alfalfa meal in chick diets was largely overcome by supplementation with 1% cholesterol. Since saponins bind cholesterol, this observation suggested an involvement of the saponin fraction. Heywang and Bird (1954), Heywang *et al.* (1959), Anderson (1957), and Coulson (1957) also reported growth depression due to alfalfa saponins. The development of alfalfa cultivars varying in saponin content (Pedersen and Wang 1971) allowed further evaluation of the effects of saponin on growth. Growth rate of chicks fed low saponin alfalfa exceeded that of chicks fed the unmodified alfalfa, while high saponin alfalfa meal markedly reduced growth (Pedersen *et al.* 1972).

The magnitude of the saponin effect varied with the alfalfa cultivar. Selection for low saponin content in DuPuits alfalfa gave more substantial improvement than was the case with the Lahontan cultivar. The major saponin in DuPuits alfalfa is medicagenic acid, while soyasapogenol A is the major one in Lahontan (Hanson *et al.* 1973). Medicagenic acid appears to be the principal saponin responsible for the detrimental effects of alfalfa saponins (Horber *et al.*1974) as assessed by several bioassays, and as suggested by the chick growth responses. Gestetner *et al.* (1972) also noted that biological activity reflected mainly the medicagenic acid content. The addition of 1% dietary cholesterol had a greater effect on improving chick growth when added to a diet with DuPuits alfalfa meal than when added to a diet containing Lahontan meal (Pedersen *et al.* 1967). This can be attributed to the fact that medicagenic acid forms an insoluble complex with cholesterol, whereas soyasapogenol A does not (Gestetner *et al.* 1972).

Superior growth performance of swine fed low saponin alfalfa has also been reported. Young pigs had similar gains on an alfalfa-free diet and a 15% low saponin alfalfa diet, while gain was depressed with 15% high saponin alfalfa (Cheeke *et al.* 1977). In further work (Cheeke *et al.* 1978), when young pigs were fed diets with 20 and 40% of low saponin, unselected, and high saponin alfalfa meal (saponin contents of 1.01, 1.91, and 2.80%, respectively), rate of gain and feed efficiency were correlated with saponin content (Fig. 13.2). When fed at the 40% level, the low saponin alfalfa gave results equivalent to 20% unselected alfalfa.

Recent studies with laboratory animals have also shown unfavorable effects of saponins on growth. Reshef *et al.* (1976) noted growth inhibition in mice and quail fed isolated alfalfa saponins. The growth inhibition was directly related to medicagenic acid content. Cheeke *et al.* (1977) noted a substantial difference in growth of rats fed low and high saponin alfalfa meals. Method of drying (air drying vs. freeze drying) did not influence the response to either type of alfalfa.

The growth-depressing properties of saponins are of interest with respect to leaf protein concentrates (LPC). Livingston *et al.* (1977A) studied the distribution of saponins in fractionation products of alfalfa. They observed that in some cases a substantial part of the plant saponin may be concentrated in the LPC fraction. This may be due to hydrogen bonding of alfalfa saponin to leaf proteins. The pH at coagulation and washing of the LPC affect its saponin content. The most biologically active alfalfa saponins contain carboxyl groups and therefore tend to be more soluble under alkaline conditions. As a consequence, coagulation at pH 8.5 results in much lower saponin contents of the LPC than precipitation at lower pH's. Thus biologically active saponins may be concentrated in LPC unless the processing conditions are controlled. Livingston *et al.* (1977A) recommend the use of alkaline coagulation and washing, as well as using low saponin alfalfa, as a means of producing food-grade LPC with a saponin content similar to that in many common vegetables. Saponin contents of LPC and several common vegetables are shown in Table 13.1.

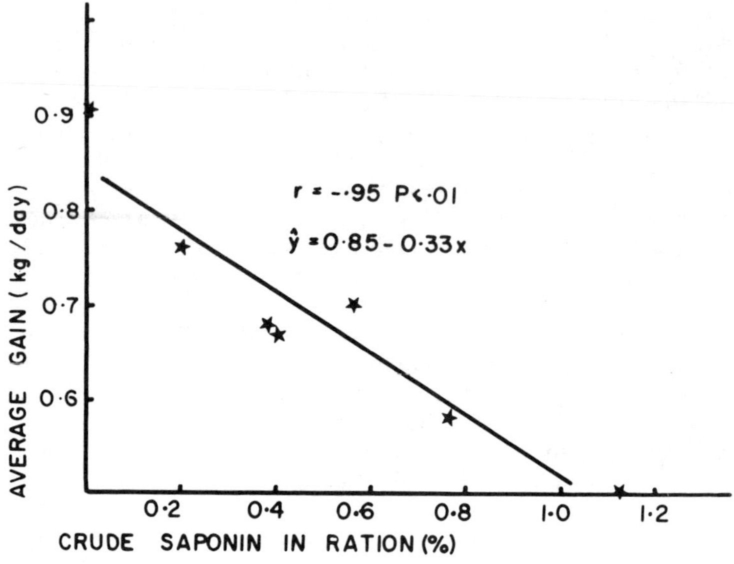

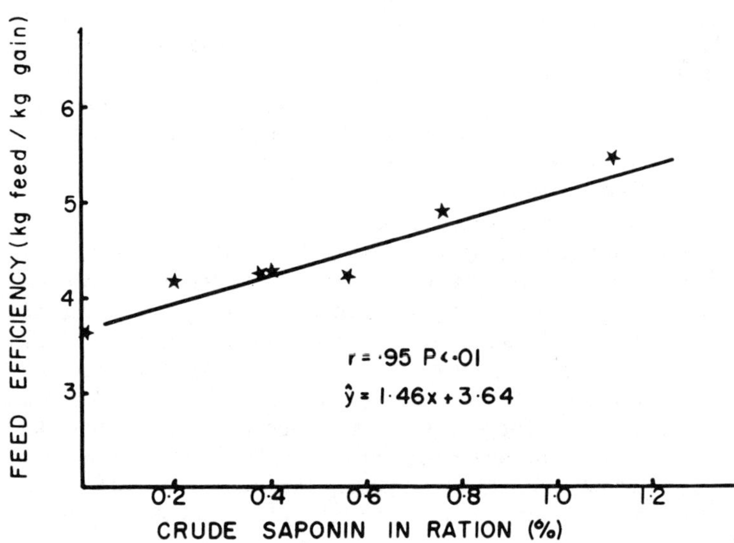

Fig. 13.2. Effect of dietary saponin level on growth rate (top) and feed efficiency (bottom) of pigs fed various dietary alfalfa levels. *From Cheeke et al. (1978).*

The high saponin content of alfalfa sprouts is noteworthy, and may have relevance in control of hypercholesterolemia (to be discussed later).

Tung *et al.* (1977) also studied the saponin content of alfalfa fractions. They prepared alfalfa protein concentrate (APC) from the high and low saponin lines of alfalfa developed in Utah (Pedersen and Wang 1971). The saponin content of the APC was higher in that prepared from high saponin alfalfa. Performance of chicks fed diets with 40% APC is shown in Table 13.2. The regular APC is from alfalfa unselected for saponin content. The results show very favorable performance with low saponin APC, while extremely poor growth and feed intake were obtained with the APC from high saponin alfalfa.

A recent trial with turkey poults fed APC from low and high saponin alfalfa showed similar results (Harper *et al.* 1980). Turkey poults were fed diets in which APC replaced all the soybean meal. The dietary APC level was 37%; saponin content was 0.11 and 1.12% for low and high saponin APC, respectively. Results are shown in Table 13.3. Representative poults of each group are shown in Fig. 13.3.

These studies have shown that saponins in alfalfa can adversely affect the quality of the LPC produced. Methods of preventing these effects would be to use low saponin alfalfa as the raw material and to coagulate at alkaline pH. Stahmann (1979) has suggested that using fermentation to coagulate the protein would result in microbial degradation of saponin, thus offering another approach.

TABLE 13.1. SAPONIN CONTENT OF ALFALFA PRODUCTS AND COMMON VEGETABLES

Product	% Saponin (Dry Wt Basis)
White alfalfa LPC	0.07
Alfalfa sprouts	7.93
LPC from low saponin alfalfa	0.10
LPC from high saponin alfalfa	1.90
Spinach leaves	0.07
Green beans	0.05
Brussels sprouts	0.03
Peas	0.03
Bean sprouts	0.01

Source: Livingston *et al.* (1977B).

TABLE 13.2. PERFORMANCE OF CHICKS FED ALFALFA PROTEIN CONCENTRATE (APC) VARYING IN SAPONIN CONTENT

Treatment	Average Daily Gain (g)	Average Daily Feed Intake (g)
Control (chick starter)	5.6	12.3
Low saponin APC	4.4	11.2
High saponin APC	0.3	4.6
Regular APC	0.9	7.4

Source: Tung *et al.* (1977).

TABLE 13.3. GROWTH AND FEED INTAKE OF TURKEY POULTS FED ALFALFA PROTEIN CONCENTRATE (APC) FROM HIGH AND LOW SAPONIN ALFALFA

Treatment	Avg 5 Week Body Weight (g)	Avg Daily Feed Intake (g)
Control	995	38.4
High Saponin APC	427	15.3
Low Saponin APC	735	24.3

Source: Harper *et al.* (1980).

There are a number of mechanisms which might account for the growth-depressing effects of saponins. These include:

(1) Depression of feed intake because of unpalatability (bitterness of saponin)
(2) Depression of feed intake because of effects of saponin on rate of passage of ingesta
(3) Irritation of membranes of mouth and digestive tract
(4) Effects on digestibility
(5) Impaired nutrient absorption
(6) Inhibition of cellular metabolism

Cheeke (1976) suggested that effects on feed intake may be the major mechanism by which saponins depress growth. A pair feeding trial (Cheeke *et al.* 1977) showed that rats that were pair-fed the same level of low saponin

Fig. 13.3. Turkey poults fed diets containing soybean meal (left), high saponin APC (middle), and low saponin APC (right) as the protein supplement.

alfalfa diet as that voluntarily consumed by rats fed a high saponin alfalfa diet had the same growth rate, suggesting that saponin affects growth mainly by limiting feed intake. In two choice feed preference tests, low saponin alfalfa is preferred over high saponin alfalfa in nonruminant species. Cheeke *et al.* (1977) found that rats preferred diets with low saponin alfalfa at all levels of alfalfa tested (10, 15, 20, 25, and 30%). Rabbits showed no discrimination between the two types at alfalfa levels of 30% or less; at higher levels they preferred the low saponin alfalfa. In similar studies with swine (LeaMaster and Cheeke 1979), diets with low saponin levels were preferred at all levels tested (1, 5, and 15%). Rats rejected diets containing alfalfa root saponin at dietary saponin levels of 0.8% and above (Cheeke *et al.* 1978). Kendall and Leath (1976) reported reduction in feed intake when alfalfa saponin was added to meadow vole diets. Quinine sulfate, a bitter compound, was considerably more unpalatable than alfalfa saponin on an equal diet concentration basis both to meadow voles (Kendall and Leath 1976) and to rats (Cheeke *et al.* 1978). When offered a choice of either low saponin or high saponin alfalfa pellets, Shetland ponies consumed only the low saponin alfalfa (Cheeke, unpublished observations). Marten (1978) conducted grazing trials with sheep to study effects of saponins on palatability of alfalfa. With the low and high saponin strains of Pedersen (Utah) and the low saponin alfalfa of Elliott (Michigan State), no palatability differences were noted. Marten concluded that since sheep are more discriminating than cattle in their selection of pasture plants, the observation that saponin content had no effect on palatability may apply to ruminants in general. In recent studies (Cheeke *et al.* 1981), geese, turkeys, quail, and chickens (Leghorn roosters) were fed diets with high or low saponin alfalfa meal, at levels from 1 to 20% of the diet. The only discrimination between the two alfalfa types was with geese fed 20% alfalfa; at this level they preferred the low saponin type.

These studies have indicated that in some nonruminant species, saponins are unpalatable and may adversely affect feed intake. Effects on feed intake are one of the major, if not the major, mechanisms by which legume saponins exert their growth-depressing effects.

(2) Effects on Palatability and Feed Intake. Recent studies on the effects of alfalfa saponins on palatability were discussed in the preceeding section. While taste sensations of animals are no doubt not the same as for humans, it is of interest that the high saponin alfalfa developed by Pedersen and Wang (1971) is bitter and astringent when chewed by humans. It has a pronounced irritating effect on the membranes of the mouth and throat. The low saponin alfalfa, by contrast, is bland with no discernible bitterness. While difficult to prove, common sense suggests that many animals are likely to experience similar sensations, and therefore find high saponin alfalfa unpalatable. The irritant effect of saponin has also been observed in laboratory personnel employed in grinding the alfalfa samples. Dust from the high saponin alfalfa irritates the mouths, throats, and eyes of these people.

If saponins reduce growth rate by causing reduced feed intake, and if cholesterol overcomes the growth depression (as discussed earlier), then it follows that the effect of cholesterol may be exerted via improvements in palatability. If the saponin mainly depresses feed intake, it is difficult to rationalize any other way that cholesterol could overcome the saponin effects. However, in the limited studies in this area, Cheeke (unpublished observations) found no difference in palatability, as assessed in two choice tests of high saponin alfalfa with or without added cholesterol. Thus at present the favorable effects of dietary cholesterol on reducing saponin-induced growth depression suggest that saponins act in other ways besides reducing feed intake.

(3) Effects on Tissue Cholesterol Levels and Cholesterol Excretion. Cheeke (1971, 1976) reviewed work on effects of dietary saponins on serum and tissue cholesterol levels. He suggested that further studies would be useful to determine the possible use of dietary saponin to lower serum cholesterol levels in humans, and to reduce cholesterol levels in animal products such as eggs. Significant recent advances in these areas have been made.

Cookson and Federoff (1968) reported that hypercholesterolemia in rabbits induced by cholesterol feeding could be prevented by inclusion of alfalfa meal in the diet. Other work also suggests a cholesterol-lowering effect of alfalfa in a variety of species, including humans. Kritchevsky *et al.* (1974) reported that feeding alfalfa meal to rats caused a reduction in serum and liver cholesterol levels, and reduced cholesterol absorption. Malinow *et al.* (1978) found that feeding 50% alfalfa diets to cynomolgus monkeys following a period of cholesterol loading caused a decrease in cholesterolemia and plasma phospholipid levels, normalization in the distribution of plasma lipoproteins, and reduction of aortic and coronary atherosclerosis. The alfalfa diet contained a cholesterol level similar to that of the "typical" American diet. This work provides strong evidence that alfalfa counteracts the atherogenic effect of dietary cholesterol in primates.

It is unlikely that humans would accept high dietary alfalfa levels for control of serum cholesterol. Therefore, Malinow's group has evaluated the use of alfalfa seeds. In a rat study, Malinow *et al.* (1980C) fed a diet with 15% alfalfa seeds. Plasma cholesterol levels and absorption of labeled cholesterol were reduced. Fecal excretion of neutral steroids and bile acids was increased. In a related study, alfalfa seeds were administered to human volunteers (Malinow *et al.* 1980B). The seeds were consumed in a fruit juice suspension at meal time, at dosage levels of 80 or 160 g of seed per day. Normal meal intake patterns were maintained. Serum parameters before, during, and after the period of alfalfa seed consumption were monitored. Both dosage levels of alfalfa seeds, for three weeks, caused a significant reduction in serum cholesterol levels (from about 250 mg/dl to 195 mg/dl).

There is strong evidence that the hypocholesterolemic effect of alfalfa is due to its saponin content. Malinow *et al.* (1977A) fed monkeys an atherogenic diet containing cholesterol and butter. The group receiving 1% alfalfa root saponins did not experience elevated serum cholesterol levels, while the control group did. In a rat study, radioactive cholesterol was administered with and without alfalfa root saponin. Cholesterol absorption was 70% in the controls and 32% in the group receiving saponin. In another rat experiment (Malinow *et al.* 1977B), the effect of alfalfa tip and alfalfa root saponins on cholesterol absorption and plasma cholesterol was studied. Saponins reduced cholesterol absorption from about 50 to about 22%. Root and top saponins had similar activity. Mild acid hydrolysis, which split off part of the side chain of monosaccharides, increased the activity. Conclusive evidence that the cholesterol-modifying effects of alfalfa are due to its saponin content was reported by Malinow *et al.* (1979). Rats received four dietary treatments: a control diet, control + 15% alfalfa meal, control + 15% extracted alfalfa meal (saponins removed), and control + 15% extracted alfalfa meal with saponin extract added back. Two replicates were conducted. Results are shown in Table 13.4. The results clearly show that alfalfa saponins reduce cholesterol absorption, and that the residue left after saponin extraction (alfalfa fiber) has no effect.

TABLE 13.4. EFFECT OF ALFALFA MEAL AND ALFALFA SAPONINS ON CHOLESTEROL ABSORPTION IN RATS

Treatment	% Absorption of Oral Dose of Cholesterol[1]	
	Trial 1	Trial 2
Control	77	76
Control + alfalfa meal	48	46
Control + alfalfa meal (saponins extracted)	81	80
Control + extracted alfalfa meal + saponin extract	55	48

[1] Malinow *et al.* (1979).

The mechanism(s) by which saponins modify cholesterol metabolism have been studied. Cholesterol is excreted in the bile, and then is largely reabsorbed from the intestine. Kritchevsky *et al.* (1974) suggested that alfalfa may bind cholesterol directly in the intestine, and prevent its reabsorption, or bind bile salts which are necessary for cholesterol absorption. In a comparison of several fiber sources, Kritchevsky and Story (1974) found that alfalfa meal bound more bile salts than any other fiber source tested. Oakenfull and Fenwick (1978) studied the ability of fiber sources to bind bile acids. Only those preparations containing saponins bound bile acids. When saponins were removed by extraction, the ability to bind bile acids was abolished. They suggested that the strong surface active properties of saponins may induce binding of bile salts to polysaccharides in fiber. In related studies (Topping *et al.* 1978), saponin feeding increased bile acid production and the excretion of neutral sterols and bile acids, supporting the hypothesis that saponins act by adsorption of bile acids in the intestines. In further studies (Hood *et al.* 1979), these workers showed that in both rats and pigs, dietary saponins increased fecal excretion of bile acids and neutral sterols, and partially reversed the hypercholesterolemia caused by feeding cholesterol. In both rats and pigs, saponin feeding increased the excretion of primary bile acids (particularly chenodeoxycholic).

Oakenfull *et al.* (1979) found that in rats given both saponins and cholesterol, chenodeoxycholic acid and its metabolites were major contributors to fecal bile acid excretion but were only a minor component of the bile. Saponins may inhibit the metabolism of bile acids by gut microflora since they increase primary and decrease secondary bile acids. Malinow *et al.* (1980A) administered alfalfa saponins to monkeys. Serum cholesterol and cholesterol absorption were reduced, while fecal excretion of neutral steroids and bile acids was increased. Sterol synthesis was increased from 0.3 mg/day in controls to 42.8 mg/day in the animals receiving saponin.

Saponins appear to have considerable potential as hypocholesterolemic agents. They are present in many natural foods, and at low levels do not have pronounced toxic properties, although their safety for this application needs thorough examination. In the recent work of Malinow *et al.* (1980B) with human volunteers given alfalfa seeds, several problems were noted. Some of the individuals found the preparations unpalatable. Moderate discomfort from intestinal gas and abdominal distention was noted. One volunteer experienced transitory hemolytic anemia. Therefore, full evaluation of possible toxic side effects is needed. Of particular interest is the very high saponin content of alfalfa sprouts (Livingston *et al.* 1977B). Sprouts are a widely accepted part of the diet of many Americans. Use of alfalfa sprouts may well be the most feasible way of utilizing the favorable effects of alfalfa saponins on serum cholesterol.

(4) Effects on Cholesterol Content of Eggs. The ability of saponins to lower serum cholesterol levels might have application in producing animal products, such as eggs, with a reduced cholesterol content. Turk and Barnett (1972) found that alfalfa was the most effective of several fiber sources tested in decreasing egg cholesterol levels when added to a corn-soy layer diet. McNaughton (1978) compared alfalfa meal to several fiber sources in their effects on egg yolk, liver, and plasma cholesterol levels. Alfalfa meal in the diet resulted in a significant decrease in plasma cholesterol, an increase in liver cholesterol, and a significant reduction in egg yolk cholesterol, from 13.8 mg cholesterol per g egg to 13.38 mg. Weiss and Scott (1979) in a similar study found that a high dietary alfalfa level significantly reduced plasma cholesterol in hens, but did not have a significant effect on egg cholesterol. However the value in the basal group was 16.7 mg/g egg, and 15.4 mg/g in the alfalfa-fed group. They suggested that ovarian synthesis, rather than transfer from plasma, was the principal determining factor in regulating egg cholesterol level. Nakaue *et al.* (1980) evaluated the effect on the egg cholesterol levels of feeding low and high saponin alfalfa meal to layers. Values were 15.5, 15.9, and 15.9 mg cholesterol per g egg for control, low, and high saponin alfalfa meal, respectively.

Considering these studies in total, it appears that any effect of alfalfa or alfalfa saponins on egg cholesterol levels is slight, indicating that use of alfalfa or saponin to attempt to produce eggs with a substantially lower cholesterol content is not a promising procedure.

(5) Erythrocyte Hemolysis. The hemolytic properties of saponins are well known. They have been reviewed by Birk (1969) and Cheeke (1971). The hemolytic effects occur primarily *in vitro*, as saponins are not absorbed to an appreciable extent. The primary practical implication of hemolysis is in the *in vitro* tests for saponins in plant tissue, in which the minimum concentration of plant extract which causes hemolysis is measured. The technique is described by Horber *et al.* (1974).

(6) Bloat in Ruminants. Saponins are one group of foaming agents that have been implicated in causing ruminant bloat. Cheeke (1971) reviewed a number of properties of saponins and experimental findings which suggested that saponins could contribute substantially to the complex of factors involved in bloat. Some of the factors implicated are saponins, tannins, pectins, cytoplasmic proteins, chloroplast membrane fragments, and rate of leaf digestion in the rumen. While some of the evidence linking saponins to bloat is attractive, it appears that saponins do not play a critical role in causing this condition. Canadian investigators have evaluated bloat incidence with the low and high saponin alfalfas developed by Pedersen. There was no difference in bloat incidence; the number of bloat cases was 86 with high saponin and 103 with low saponin alfalfa (Majak *et al.* 1980). Since low saponin did not reduce bloat, and high saponin did not intensify bloating, it must be concluded that saponins are not significantly involved in the bloat syndrome.

(7) Inhibition of Smooth Muscle Activity. Alfalfa saponins can inhibit smooth muscle activity (Cheeke 1971). The physiological significance is uncertain, but probably slight. Conceivably, saponins could reduce peristalsis, and, by reducing rate of passage, contribute to the reduced feed intake observed in nonruminants fed alfalfa or saponins.

(8) Effects on Enzymes. A number of cellular enzymes may be inhibited by saponins (Cheeke 1971). Injected alfalfa saponin alters activity of certain liver enzymes, such as aminopyrine demethylase (Cheeke 1976). Rats fed a 30% alfalfa diet had significantly elevated hepatic aminopyrine demethylase activity (Garrett *et al.* 1982). These findings suggest that saponins could, by modification of liver enzyme activity, alter the metabolism of other dietary toxins.

Because saponins are not appreciably absorbed, their effects on enzymes would most likely be in the digestive tract. Saponins form bonds with protein (Livingston *et al.* 1977A) so could conceivably "tie up" digestive enzymes. Ishaaya and Birk (1965) found that soybean saponins inhibit chymotrypsin and trypsin activity. Alfalfa saponins have been implicated as trypsin inhibitors (Mooijman 1965). However, recent work suggests that the trypsin inhibitor(s) in alfalfa is protein (Chang *et al.* 1978) rather than saponins.

There is at present little evidence to suggest that enzyme inhibition is a major toxic mode of action of saponins.

(9) Effects on Digestion and Absorption. Effects of saponins on digestive enzymes such as trypsin would imply the possibility of reduced digestive efficiency. Cheeke *et al.* (1978) found no difference in digestibility of crude protein or ether extract of low saponin or unselected alfalfa meal in rats. Addition of 1 and 2% alfalfa root saponin to a purified diet had no effect on protein or fat digestibility in rats (Cheeke *et al.* 1978). West *et al.* (1978) tested the ability of alfalfa saponins to complex with minerals and vitamins. Alfalfa leaf and root saponin extracts did not complex with fat-soluble vitamins. Alfalfa root saponins formed insoluble complexes with zinc and iron. Feeding 2% root saponin increased fecal losses of iron and magnesium.

(10) Effects on Fertility. Several reports, summarized by Cheeke (1976), indicate that various saponins may have infertility effects, such as abortion and fetal resorption, in rats and cattle. There is no evidence that alfalfa saponins have antifertility effects.

(11) Other Effects of Saponins. Saponins from various plants have a wide variety of industrial uses. As foaming agents, they have been used in beverages, fire extinguishers, shampoo, and in the manufacture of pharmaceuticals. These uses, which are beyond the scope of this review, have been summarized by George (1965). They may also have medical value as anti-inflammatory, antiexudative, and antiviral agents, and possibly as tumor inhibitors (Segal *et al.* 1977). Saponins have been used as adjuvants for foot and mouth vaccines (Egerton *et al.* 1978). Finally, a commercial saponin derived from yucca is being used as a feed additive in poultry rations to control ammonia, odors, and flies (Anon. 1979).

SUMMARY AND CONCLUSIONS

Present knowledge on biological properties and nutritional significance of alfalfa saponins has been reviewed. Saponins appear to be a major factor limiting the use of alfalfa meal by nonruminant animals, with their effects mediated primarily by reduced palatability and feed intake. The development of cultivars of alfalfa low in saponin content should be beneficial. The recent work on the favorable effects of alfalfa saponins on reducing serum cholesterol in humans is especially exciting.

REFERENCES

ANDERSON, J.O. 1957. Effect of alfalfa saponin on the performance of chicks and laying hens. Poult. Sci. *36*, 873–876.

ANON. 1979. Feed additive reduces ammonia, odors and flies. Poult. Dig. *38*, 612.

BERRANG, B., DAVIS, K.H., WALL, M.E., HANSON, C.H. and PEDERSON, M.D. 1974. Saponins of two alfalfa cultivars. Phytochemistry *13*, 2253–2260.

BIRK, Y. 1969. Saponins. *In* Toxic Constituents of Plant Foodstuffs. I.E. Liener (Editor). Academic Press, New York.

BONDI, A., BIRK, Y. and GESTETNER, B. 1973. Forage saponins. *In* Chemistry and Biochemistry of Herbage. G.W. Butler and R.W. Bailey (Editors). Academic Press, New York.

BRAWN, P.R., LINDER, N.M., MILLER, J.M. and TELLING, G.M. 1981. A gas chromatographic method for the determination of medicagenic acid in lucerne (alfalfa) leaf protein concentrate. J. Sci. Food Agric. *32*, 1157–1162.

CHANG, H-Y., REECK, G.R. and MITCHELL, H.L. 1978. Alfalfa trypsin inhibitor. Agric. Food Chem. *26*, 1463–1464.

CHEEKE, P.R. 1979. Unpublished observations. Oregon State University, Corvallis.

CHEEKE, P.R. 1971. Nutritional and physiological implications of saponins: A review. Can. J. Anim. Sci. *51*, 621–632.

CHEEKE, P.R. 1976. Nutritional and physiological properties of saponins. Nutr. Rep. Int. *13*, 315–324.

CHEEKE, P.R., KINZELL, J.H. and PEDERSEN, M.W. 1977. Influence of saponins on alfalfa utilization by rats, rabbits and swine. J. Anim. Sci. *45*, 476–481.

CHEEKE, P.R. and MYER, R.O. 1975. Protein digestibility and lysine availability in alfalfa meal and alfalfa protein concentrate. Nutr. Rep. Int. *12*, 337–344.

CHEEKE, P.R., PEDERSEN, M.W. and ENGLAND, D.C. 1978. Responses of rats and swine to alfalfa saponins. Can. J. Anim. Sci. *58*, 783–789.

CHEEKE, P.R., POWLEY, J.S., NAKAUE, H.S. and ARSCOTT, G.H. 1981. Feed preferences of poultry fed alfalfa meal, high and low saponin alfalfa, and quinine sulfate. Proc. West. Sect. Am. Soc. Anim. Sci. *32*, 426–427.

COOKSON, F.B. and FEDEROFF, S. 1968. Quantitative relationships between administered cholesterol and alfalfa required to prevent hypercholesterolemia in rabbits. Br. J. Exp. Pathol. *49*, 348–355.

COULSON, C.B. 1957. Properties of lucerne and other saponins. Biochem. J. *67*, 10 p.

EGERTON, J.R., LAING, E.A. and THORLEY, C.M. 1978. Effect of Quil A, a saponin derivative, on the response of sheep to alum precipitated *Bacteroides nodosus* vaccines. Vet. Sci. Commun. *2*, 247–252.

GARRETT, B.J., CHEEKE, P.R., MIRANDA, C.L., GOEGER, D.E. and BUHLER, D.R. 1982. Consumption of poisonous plants (*Senecio jacobaea, Symphy-*

tum officinale, Pteridium aquilinum, Hypericum perforatum) by rats: Chronic toxicity, mineral metabolism, and hepatic drug-metabolizing enzymes. Toxicol. Lett. *10*, 183–188.

GEORGE, A.J. 1965. Legal status and toxicity of saponins. Food Cosmet. Toxicol. *3*, 85–91.

GESTETNER, B., HENIS, Y., TENCER, Y., ROTMAN, M., BIRK, Y. and BONDI, A. 1972. Interaction of lucerne saponins with sterols. Biochim. Biophys. Acta *270*, 181–187.

HANSON, C.H., PEDERSON, M.W., BERRANG, B., WALL, M.E. and DAVIS, K.H. 1973. The saponins in alfalfa cultivars. *In* Antiquality Components of Forages. Crop Science Society of America, Madison, WI.

HARPER, J.A., CHEEKE, P.R. and KOHLER, G.O. 1980. Unpublished data. Oregon State University, Corvallis.

HEYWANG, B.W. and BIRD, H.R. 1954. The effects of alfalfa saponin on the growth, diet consumption and efficiency of diet utilization of chicks. Poult. Sci. *33*, 239–241.

HEYWANG, B.W., THOMPSON, C.R. and KEMMERER, A.R. 1959. Effect of alfalfa saponin on laying hens. Poult. Sci. *38*, 968–971.

HOOD, R.L., OAKENFULL, D.G. and TOPPING, D.L. 1979. Dietary saponins and plasma cholesterol. Proc. Nutr. Soc. *38*, 78A.

HORBER, E., LEATH, K.T., BERRANG, B., MARCARIAN, V. and HANSON, C.H. 1974. Biological activities of saponin components from DuPuits and Lahontan alfalfa. Entomol. Exp. Appl. *17*, 410–424.

ISHAAYA, I. and BIRK, Y. 1965. Soybean saponins. IV. The effect of proteins on the inhibitory activity of soybean saponins on certain enzymes. J. Food Sci. *30*, 118–120.

KENDALL, W.A. and LEATH, K.T. 1976. Effect of saponins on palatability of alfalfa to meadow voles. Agron. J. *68*, 473–476.

KODRAS, R., COONEY, W.T. and BUTTS, J.S. 1951. Chick growth depressing factor in sun-cured and dehydrated alfalfa meals. Poult. Sci. *30*, 280–292.

KRITCHEVSKY, D. and STORY, J.A. 1974. Binding of bile salts in vitro by nonnutritive fiber. J. Nutr. *104*, 458–462.

KRITCHEVSKY, D., TEPPER, S.A. and STORY, J.A. 1974. Isocaloric, isogravic diets in rats. III. Effects of nonnutritive fiber (alfalfa or cellulose) on cholesterol metabolism. Nutr. Rep. Int. *9*, 301–308.

LeaMASTER, B.R. and CHEEKE, P.R. 1979. Feed preferences of swine: Alfalfa meal, high and low saponin alfalfa, and quinine sulfate. Can. J. Anim. Sci. *59*, 467–469.

LIVINGSTON, A.L., KNUCKLES, B.E., EDWARDS, R.H., MILLER, R.E., de FREMERY, D. and KOHLER, G.O. 1977A. Distribution of saponins in alfalfa protein recovery systems. Proc. Annu. Meet. Am. Soc. Agric. Eng., 1977, Chicago, Pap. *77–6502*.

LIVINGSTON, A.L., WHITEHAND, L.C. and KOHLER, G.O. 1977B. Microbiological assay for saponin in alfalfa products. J. Assoc. Off. Anal. Chem. *60*, 957–960.

MAJAK, W., HOWARTH, R.E., FESSER, A.C., GOPLEN, B.P. and PEDERSEN, M.W. 1980. Relationships between ruminant bloat and the composition of alfalfa herbage. II. Saponins. Can. J. Anim. Sci. *60*, 699–708.

MALINOW, M.R., CONNER, W.E., McLAUGHLIN, P., STAFFORD, C., LIN, D.S., LIVINGSTON, A.L. and KOHLER, G.O. 1980A. Effects of alfalfa saponins on sterol balance in cynomolgus monkeys. Fed. Proc. Fed. Am. Soc. Exp. Biol. *39*, 1039.

MALINOW, M.R., McLAUGHLIN, P., KOHLER, G.O. and LIVINGSTON, L. 1977A. Prevention of elevated cholesterolemia in monkeys by alfalfa saponins. Steroids *29*, 105–110.

MALINOW, M.R., McLAUGHLIN, P., NAITS, H.K., LEWIS, L.A. and McNULTY, W.P. 1978. Effect of alfalfa meal on shrinkage (regression) of atherosclerotic plaques during cholesterol feeding in monkeys. Atherosclerosis *30*, 27–43.

MALINOW, M.R., McLAUGHLIN, P., PAPWORTH, L., STAFFORD, C., KOHLER, G.O., LIVINGSTON, A.L. and CHEEKE, P.R. 1977B. Effect of alfalfa saponins on intestinal cholesterol absorption in rats. Am. J. Clin. Nutr. *30*, 2061–2067.

MALINOW, M.R., McLAUGHLIN, P. and STAFFORD, C. 1980B. Personal communication. Oregon Regional Primate Center, Beaverton.

MALINOW, M.R., McLAUGHLIN, P. and STAFFORD, C. 1980C. Alfalfa seeds: Effects on cholesterol metabolism. Experimentia *36*, 562–564.

MALINOW, M.R., McLAUGHLIN, P., STAFFORD, C., LIVINGSTON, A.L., KOHLER, G.O. and CHEEKE, P.R. 1979. Comparative effects of alfalfa saponins and alfalfa fiber on cholesterol absorption in rats. Am. J. Clin. Nutr. *32*, 1810–1812.

MARTEN, G.C. 1978. Personal communication. University of Minnesota, St. Paul.

McNAUGHTON, J.L. 1978. Effect of dietary fiber on egg yolk, liver and plasma cholesterol concentrations of the laying hen. J. Nutr. *108*, 1842–1848.

MOOIJMAN, J.G. 1965. Purification and characterization of the trypsin inhibitor in alfalfa. Diss. Abstr. *25*, 4390.

NAKAUE, H.S., LOWRY, R.R., CHEEKE, P.R. and ARSCOTT, G.H. 1980. The effect of dietary alfalfa of varying saponin content on egg cholesterol level and layer performance. Poult. Sci. *59*, 2744–2748.

OAKENFULL, D.G. and FENWICK, D.E. 1978. Absorption of bile salts from aqueous solution by plant fibre and cholestyramine. Br. J. Nutr. *40*, 299–309.

OAKENFULL, D.G., FENWICK, D.E. and HOOD, R.L. 1979. Effects of saponins on bile acids amd plasma lipids in the rat. Br. J. Nutr. *42*, 209–216.

PEDERSEN, M.W. 1978. Personal communication. U.S. Dep. Agric., Logan, Utah.

PEDERSEN, M.W. 1975. Relative quantity and biological activity of saponins in germinated seeds, roots, and foliage of alfalfa. Crop Sci. *15*, 541–543.

PEDERSEN, M.W. 1979. Low saponin alfalfa for nonruminants. Proc. 2nd Int. Green Crop Drying Congr., Univ. Saskatchewan, Saskatoon, Canada, 1978.

PEDERSEN, M.W. and WANG, L.C. 1971. Modification of saponin content of alfalfa through selection. Crop Sci. *11*, 833–835.

PEDERSEN, M.W., ZIMMER, D.E., McALLISTER, D.R., ANDERSON, J.O., WILDING, M.D., TAYLOR, G.A. and McGUIRE, C.F. 1967. Comparative study of saponin of several alfalfa varieties using chemical and biochemical assays. Crop Sci. *7*, 349–352.

PEDERSEN, M.W., ANDERSON, J.O., STREET, J.C., WANG, L.C. and BAKER, R. 1972. Growth response of chicks and rats fed alfalfa with saponin content modified by selection. Poult. Sci. *51*, 458–463.

PETERSON, D.W. 1950A. Effect of sterols on the growth on chicks fed high alfalfa diets or a diet containing Quillaja saponin. J. Nutr. *42*, 597–607.

PETERSON, D.W. 1950B. Some properties of a factor in alfalfa meal causing depression of growth in chicks. J. Biol. Chem. *183*, 647–653.

QUAZI, H.M. 1976. Distribution of saponins in roots of lucerne. N.Z. J. Agric. Res. *19*, 347–348.

RESHEF, G., GESTETNER, B., BIRK, Y. and BONDI, A. 1976. Effect of alfalfa saponins on the growth and some aspects of lipid metabolism of mice and quails. J. Sci. Food Agric. *27*, 63–72.

SCARDAVI, A. and ELLIOTT, F.C. 1967. A review of saponins in alfalfa and their bioassay using *Trichoderma* sp. Q. Bull. Mich. Agric. Exp. Stn. *50*, 163–177.

SEGAL, R., MILO-GOLDZWEIG, I. and KAPLAN, G. 1977. The protective action of glycyrrhizin against saponin toxicity. Biochem. Pharmacol. *26*, 643–645.

STAHMANN, M.A. 1968. The potential for protein production from green plants. Econ. Bot. *22*, 73-79.

STAHMANN, M.A. 1979. Anaerobic fermentation for coagulation of plant juice protein and preservation of the protein and fiber residues. Proc. 2nd Int. Green Crop Drying Congr., Univ. Saskatchewan, Saskatoon, Canada, 1978.

TOPPING, D.L., HOOD, R.L., ILLMAN, R.J., STORER, G.B. and OAKENFULL, D.G. 1978. Effects of dietary saponins on bile acid secretion and plasma cholesterol in the rat. Proc. Nutr. Soc. Aust. *3*, 68.

TUNG, J.Y., STRAUB, R.J., SCHOLL, J.M. and SUNDE, M.L. 1977. Methods used to evaluate biological protein quality and saponin concentration of various alfalfa juice proteins. Proc. Annu. Meet. Am. Soc. Agric. Eng., 1977, Chicago, Pap. *77–1010*.

TURK, D.E. and BARNETT, B.D. 1972. Diet and egg cholesterol content. Poult. Sci. *51*, 1881.

WEISS, F.G. and SCOTT, M.L. 1979. Effects of dietary fiber, fat and total energy upon plasma cholesterol and other parameters in chickens. J. Nutr. *109*, 693–701.

WEST, L.G., GREGER, J.L. and NONNAMAKER, B.J. 1978. Saponin-mineral interactions. Fed. Proc. Fed. Am. Soc. Exp. Biol. *37*, 667.

ZIMMER, D.E., PEDERSEN, M.W. and McGUIRE, C.F. 1967. A bioassay for alfalfa saponins using the fungus Trichoderma viride. Crop Sci. *7*, 223–224.

14

The Nutritional Evaluation of Leaf Protein Concentrates

Anthony A. Woodham

It is probable that green leaves were consumed directly by man from the time of his emergence some millions of years ago, and they continue to form part of the diet of all of those races which have access to them. For many animals they constitute the major portion of the diet and for the herbivores, of course, they are the only source of nutrients. The protein in leaves is nutritious, and though the levels in individual leaves may not be high, when complemented by the products of microbial action in the case of herbivores or by other protein-containing foods, in the case of nonruminants and man, leaf protein can make a useful contribution to the diet. The value of this contribution would clearly be enhanced if the protein could be concentrated. Leaves may contain around 4 to 5% of so-called "crude protein" (N × 6.25). A product containing 50–60% crude protein in the dried material can be obtained by a process involving maceration of the leaves, followed by heating the separated juice to around 80°C. The product thus obtained is comparable in quantity of protein to conventional protein concentrates such as fish and meat meals and to oilseed residues after removal of the oil.

FACTORS AFFECTING NUTRITIVE VALUE

First, we are concerned with ascertaining whether procedures applied to the leaves have any effect upon the quality of the protein in the product. In the case of oilseed processing, it is known that the application of heat may affect the quality of the product adversely, and since heat is applied in leaf protein extraction processes during protein precipitation and again during dying of the product, tests are necessary to find the minimum heating needed to produce a good yield of a concentrate having satisfactory nutritional qualities.

Secondly, we wish to know if particular species of plants yield products of better nutritional value than others. Some species may contain undesirable substances and, if these are not excluded from the product by the procedure employed, then steps must be taken to either exclude or inactivate them, if these species are to be used as practical sources of protein supplements.

Thirdly, we must discover whether it is possible to enhance the quality of the product, particularly if we are dealing with a plant species which is known to yield poor concentrates.

Finally, it is important to know if leaf protein concentrates are more suitable for inclusion in diets containing certain ingredients than others. This requires a study of the composition of the products in order to see which particular amino acids are present in abundance, for example, thereby allowing LPC to make up for deficiencies in those amino acids in particular staple foods.

METHODS USED FOR EVALUATION OF PROTEIN QUALITY OF LEAF PROTEIN CONCENTRATES (LPC)

All of the "standard" protein quality tests have been used. These include procedures which assess the test material alone, such as the Protein Efficiency Ratio (PER) test (Derse 1960) and the estimation of net protein utilization (NPU) (Miller 1963). In their original form, both of these are rat tests and both suffer from the drawback that the protein levels employed are unrealistically low. Furthermore, because the protein concentrates are tested alone, the effects of other constituents which could be present under practical feeding conditions are not taken into consideration. In spite of these shortcomings, these tests are popular and have been much used. The reason is, essentially, their suitability for routine use and the existence of well-established, published procedure. Furthermore, both tests can discriminate well among protein test materials, and reproducibility is generally good, providing the tests are carried out under carefully controlled conditions.

Because of its sensitivity to shortfalls in sulfur-containing amino acids, the net protein utilization procedure is particularly suitable for comparing leaf protein concentrates, whose main disadvantage, nutritionally, is the under provision of methionine and cystine. The widespread use of the PER test led to its adoption as a biological criterion for assessing leaf protein concentrates (Pirie 1971A). It is especially useful when samples are required to be compared on the basis of their lysine availability and, consequently, the PER test can distinguish well those samples which have been subjected to harsh processing treatment.

Distinct from the type of test described above are those in which the test protein does not provide all of the nitrogen in the diet. As in normal feeding practice, the high protein material to be tested is mixed with another protein source or sources, usually cereals. In these circumstances, the test protein is evaluated as a supplementary protein source, and, providing that the experimental conditions are controlled so that the overall protein level, the ratio of supplementary protein to cereal protein, the provision of vitamins, and the ratio of dietary energy to protein are maintained constant, useful comparisons can be made. One such test which was used in much of the earlier work with leaf proteins was the gross protein value (GPV) test using chickens. Devised by Carver and his co-workers in the 1930s (Heiman *et al.* 1939), this test suffered from the disadvantages that the overall protein level and the ratio of supplementary to cereal protein were unrealistic. The overall protein level of 11% is close to that normally used in the PER and NPU tests—usually 10%—and is far below the optimum level for a growing chick. It is also based upon an assumption, the validity of which is doubtful, that the value of the high protein test component can be assessed by subtracting the weight gains of chickens fed only the cereal portion of the diet. Variability was found to be often unacceptably high and, though capable of distinguishing between "good" and "poor" specimens of the same type of concentrate, discrimination between samples which were rather similar was often doubtful. This was true in spite of the fact that the impractically low overall level of protein in the diet tended to exaggerate differences.

These criticisms led to the development of an alternative test of supplementary protein value which was called the total protein efficiency (TPE) test (Woodham 1968). In this test the overall protein level of the diets was either 18 or 18.5% and the ratio of supplementary, i.e., test, protein to basal cereal protein was 2 to 1. Employing chickens 2–4 weeks old, the test measures weight gain over the 14 day test period in relation to the amount of protein consumed. Broiler chickens of this age would normally receive diets providing around 21% protein, and the lower protein level chosen was designed to avoid feeding an excess while still allowing a very good rate of growth. In fact, birds fed a good GPV diet in which the supplementary protein source was good quality fish meal grew as well as on a similar 21% protein diet. However, the protein source was of poorer quality—an overheated fish meal or a groundnut meal, for example—then the additional 3% of crude protein in the 21% protein diet caused a considerable improvement in chick growth compared to that with the 18% protein diet. Thus, the choice of an 18% protein level for the diets permitted discrimination among a range of fish meals as well as among proteins of generally poor quality. The 2:1 ratio of test protein to cereal protein is in line with many commercial broiler diets. Good discrimination at the high protein level was achieved by careful management of the experiments, including the avoidance of any unnecessary disturbance of the birds during the course of the test, the use of bright red lighting which permitted good visibility of food while discouraging undue wastage of effort, and careful control of the *ad libitum* feeding arrangements to minimize spillage.

The TPE test is not dependent solely on either lysine or sulfur amino acid provision. In fact, it has been shown that TPE correlates with either, depending upon which is in shorter supply (Carpenter and Woodham 1974).

Thus, the test will rank a series of leaf protein concentrates on the basis of overall nutritive value, regardless of whether the defects are inherent and resulting from differences in the plant species concerned, or whether they have been introduced as a result of unsatisfactory processing treatments. A modification of the TPE procedure in which rats are given 16% crude protein diets for three weeks, half of the protein being provided by the test protein and half by cereals, has also proved useful for evaluating protein sources both conventional and novel, and has the advantage of requiring more modest amounts of test materials than does the chick test. This is important in cases where difficulties of processing large quantities of leaves limits the scale of the extraction and the resulting yield of concentrate. In general, growth of chicks and rats in the early weeks of life runs parallel for a particular protein source so that either may be used satisfactorily for predicting overall nutritive value.

Emphasis has been placed upon biological methods for estimating protein quality in leaf protein concentrates. Simple laboratory procedures such as *in vitro* nitrogen solubility, dyestuff absorption, and the estimation of total amino acid composition have not proved to be especially useful. Measurable differences in the amino acid composition of leaf protein fractions have been found, but they are so small that they are unlikely to be responsible for the observed differences in animal growth (Byers 1971). It has been suggested that the latter might be attributable to differences in the availability of lysine and of the sulfur-containing amino acids, or alternatively, that the relative proportions of individual amino acids might have a significant effect. The biological techniques described have been used to study the quality of leaf protein concentrates prepared from different plant species and by various processing methods.

EVALUATION OF LPC PREPARED FROM DIFFERENT PLANT SPECIES

Before the mid-1950s, variable results for the quality of LPC produced from different plant species suggested that there were marked differences among species. In particular, grasses and lucerne yielded poorer products than cereal leaves. More recent work has tended to show that much of the variability found was due to processing factors, and the need for rigorous control of the conditions used only then became apparent. While lucerne is now known to be capable of yielding a product of high quality, clover and some grasses, notably cocksfoot, undoubtedly do not yield a product comparable to that which can be extracted from cereal leaves. Information is still lacking on the extent to which protein quality, as distinct from digestibility, is influenced by the stage of maturity of the leaf, and Singh has suggested that differences among the concentrates produced from different plant species may be attributable to variations in feed intake and digestibility rather than to protein quality. He confirmed our observations and those of others that the nutritional variations were not explicable on the basis of minor differences in amino acid pattern which were observed. Horse gram, French bean, and groundnut leaves all yielded products inferior to lucerne while material prepared from carrot and from *Dolichos lablab* failed entirely to support growth in rats (Singh 1969). A great amount of work on different tropical species from India appears to leave little doubt that different plant species do yield products of quite different protein quality (Woodham 1971). An interesting aspect of the Indian work is the apparently conflicting results of growth and nitrogen balance studies. Some samples of LPC which supported little or no growth in rats (PER = 0 to 0.91) showed biological values ranging from 70 to 77.

EFFECT OF HEAT DURING PREPARATION OF LPC

Although the protein dissolved in the juice pressed from the leaves may be precipitated and fine particles flocculated without the use of heat, in practice it is usual to apply heat. Mere aging of the juice for 1–2 days will bring about coagulation, and adjustment of the pH of the juice by acidification to near the isoelectric point can also be used (Pirie 1971B). It has been claimed that flocculation using polyelectrolytes assists separation of the precipitate (Annelli *et al.* 1977). Heating, however, diminishes the risk of microbial contamination and inactivates some undesirable enzymes. Subba Rau and Singh (1970) have reported that rats fed acid-coagulated LPC grow more slowly than those fed material coagulated by heat. Maximum precipitation is achieved by heating to 80°C, and this is most readily done by passing live steam into the juice. The precipitated protein should by separated from the liquors with the least possible delay. Oxidative processes leading to production of *o*-quinones which could affect lysine availability and the polymerization of polyphenols into tannin-protein complexes could render a number of essential amino acids unavailable to nonruminant animals (Horigome and Kandatsu 1968). Lysine is, of course, the most important amino acid provided by leaf protein concentrates, and the amount contributed is comparable with that in good quality animal protein concentrates such as fish meal.

While 80°C is an adequate temperature for precipitating all of the useful protein in the juice, a nutritionally superior fraction can be obtained by raising the temperature first to 60°C. The protein precipitated at this temperature consists largely of the somewhat inferior chloroplastic protein. Subsequently raising the temperature of the juice to 80°C precipitates the superior cytoplasmic protein (Kohler and Bickoff 1971). This double precipitation procedure has the additional advantage that the green color which is associated with the chloroplasts is removed in the first fraction and the product obtained on raising the temperature to 80°C is off-white in color. It is not necessary to restrict the temperature of precipitation to 80°C. Recent experiments have shown that precipitation at 100°C does not cause any deterioration in the quality of the ultimate product (Table 14.1).

The wet product obtained by draining or centrifuging the precipitated protein contains 60–70% water and, unless it is dried quickly, a rich growth of mold soon develops. Sun drying is feasible in the tropics. Elsewhere, artificial means must be adopted. Various procedures were tried experimentally on samples of leaf protein concentrate prepared from either barley or rye leaves, and treating the concentrate alone or mixed with an equal weight of ground barley. These included freeze-drying the washed protein slurry, either by a laboratory procedure or by a commercial "accelerated" freeze-drying process; acetone drying, followed by removal of the residual at 30°C *in vacuo*; absorption of the moisture of the wet LPC by mixing with barley meal previously dried so as to contain less than 4% of moisture; and air drying LPC both alone and mixed with the same weight of barley meal at various oven temperatures ranging from 44° to 100°C (Table 14.2). The products were evaluated using a modification (Duckworth *et al.* 1961) of the chick growth procedure for the determination of the gross value of proteins (GPV) originated by Heiman *et al.* (1939). This procedure is designed to evaluate protein concentrates as supplements to cereals in diets for growing chicks.

Nearly all of the drying procedures yielded products of roughly the same quality and equivalent to that of well processed soybean meals which exhibit gross protein values of 80–90. The single exception was that of the rye LPC-barley meal sample heated at 100°C where the temperature of the sample itself reached a maximum of 94°C. The rye LPC heated alone at 100°C reached a maximum of only 78°C because drying was stopped when the residual moisture content reached 12.9%. The residual moisture of the corresponding LPC-barley meal sample was as low as 6.7%. From these results it would seem that damage occurs to the leaf protein concentrate when its temperature reaches a point between 82° (when no harm is apparent) and 94°C. From other work with cereals (Woodham and Bailey 1977), there is a suggestion that the critical temperature would lie between 90° and 94°C.

TABLE 14.1. NET PROTEIN UTILIZATION (NPU) OF LEAF PROTEIN CONCENTRATE SAMPLES PRECIPITATED AT 80° AND 100°C

Sample	Temperature of Precipitation (°C)	NPU
1	80	56
2	80	52
3	80	58
4	100	57
5	100	57
6	100	59
7	100	58
8	100	54

Source: Woodham *et al.* (1974).

TABLE 14.2. GROSS PROTEIN VALUE (GPV) OF LEAF PROTEIN CONCENTRATE (LPC) DRIED IN VARIOUS WAYS

LPC	Drying Procedure	GPV
Barley	Freeze-dried (laboratory)	87
Rye	Freeze-dried (commercial, "accelerated" freeze-drying)	86
Barley	Moisture absorbed by dried diet	83
Barley	Acetone dried; final heating *in vacuo* at 30°C	80
Barley/barley meal (1:1)	Air dried; oven temp 40°C	80
Rye	Air dried; oven temp 44°C; max LPC temp 42°C	81
Rye	Air dried; oven temp 66°C; max LPC temp 66°C	83
Rye	Air dried; oven temp 83°C; max LPC temp 82°C	83
Rye	Air dried; oven temp 100°C; max LPC temp 78°C	86
Rye/barley meal (1:1)	Air dried; oven temp 44°C; max LPC temp 42°C	88
Rye	Air dried; oven temp 66°C; max LPC temp 66°C	83
Rye	Air dried; oven temp 83°C; max LPC temp 82°C	85
Rye	Air dried; oven temp 100°C; max LPC temp 94°C	65

EFFECT OF OTHER PROCESSING VARIABLES ON NUTRITIVE VALUE OF LPC

For most leaves, pressing alone or with added water yields a juice with a pH of 5–6. Some leaves, notably the Cucurbitaceae, yield alkaline extracts. In all cases, it is desirable to acidify somewhat before precipitating and coagulating the protein, and a pH of 4–5 has been found satisfactory from the point of view of giving good yields of a readily filterable and good quality product upon subsequent steaming. Extraction of the leaves at an alkaline pH gives somewhat better yields and, in the case of lucerne, a better product. With cocksfoot grass, however, the quality of the product as measured by NPU was unchanged. An early cut of Italian ryegrass yielded a superior quality product on alkaline extraction, but a later cut gave a poorer product than the control sample extracted at pH 5 (Table 14.3). Although more evidence relating age of leaf to extraction pH is desirable, it seems reasonable to infer that the more thorough extraction consequent upon the use of alkali is desirable for young leaves but less so in the case of the aging leaf. The relative insolubility of the good quality cytoplasmic protein present in spinach and tobacco leaves below pH 6 renders the use of alkali essential in the case of these plants, failure to do so resulting in the loss of between 25 and 50% (Singer *et al.* 1952). The Chayen procedure for protein extraction involved hammer milling in an alkaline aqueous phase and formed the basis of a process which was operated commercially (Chayen *et al.* 1961). Some of these commercial products were evaluated by the pepsin-pancreatin digestion method and found to be potentially of high quality. Values obtained were higher than those given by soybean, beef, or casein (Akeson and Stahmann 1965).

TABLE 14.3. EFFECT OF pH OF EXTRACTION UPON THE QUALITY OF LPC PREPARED FROM LUCERNE, COCKSFOOT, AND ITALIAN RYEGRASS

Sample	Leaf Species	Extraction pH	NPU
1[1]	Lucerne	6	38
2[1]	Lucerne	8.5	49
3[1]	Cocksfoot	6	31
4[1]	Cocksfoot	7.5	31
5[1]	Cocksfoot	6	30
6[1]	Cocksfoot	8.5	32
7	Italian ryegrass (early cut)	4.5	30
8	Italian ryegrass (early cut)	5	29
9	Italian ryegrass (early cut)	9	38
10	Italian ryegrass (late cut)	5	34
11	Italian ryegrass (late cut)	8	29

[1] Woodham *et al.* (1974).

The addition of detergent during the pulping of lucerne leaves had no beneficial effect upon the quality of the product. The product from untreated leaves had an NPU value of 38, and that from the treated leaves a value of 37.

The quantity of water added, either during or prior to pulping, had no measurable effect upon the quality of the product from lucerne leaves as judged by NPU. The addition of water at the rate of 1 liter/kg of lucerne leaves yielded a product with NPU of 45, while tripling the quantity of water resulted in a product with NPU of 43.

The avoidance of delays during the extraction procedure is undoubtedly desirable. Only in one case involving cocksfoot leaves was no difference in quality noted between slowly and rapidly processed leaves (Table 14.4).

TABLE 14.4. THE EFFECT OF SPEED OF PROCESSING UPON THE QUALITY OF LPC PREPARED FROM LUCERNE, COCKSFOOT, AND WHEAT LEAVES

Sample	Leaf Species	Speed of Processing	NPU
1	Lucerne	Slow[1]	44
	Lucerne	Fast[2]	48
2	Lucerne	Slow	32
	Lucerne	Fast	40
3	Cocksfoot	Slow	41
	Cocksfoot	Fast	40
4	Cocksfoot	Slow	33
	Cocksfoot	Fast	44
5	Wheat	Slow	37
	Wheat	Fast	42
6	Wheat	Fast	55
	Wheat	Fast	57
7	Wheat	Slow	46
	Wheat	Fast	58

Source: Woodham *et al.* (1974).
[1] Slow—Total time for precipitation and filtration is 6 hr or longer.
[2] Fast—Total time for precipitation and filtration is less than 2¼ hr.

EFFECT OF SULFITE ADDITION DURING PROCESSING UPON QUALITY OF ISOLATED LPC

The most consistent and significant changes in nutritional value effected by processing technique were those caused by the use of sulfite. This was introduced with a view to inhibiting the oxidation of phenolic compounds (Anon. 1972).

Improvements in quality were noted on sulfite treatment of lucerne and cocksfoot grass and these were marked when the treatment was carried out under alkaline conditions (Table 14.5). That these were the most important changes found on attempting various modifications to the standard extraction procedure was emphasized by Woodham *et al.* (1974). Similar improvements were found in the growth performance of rats given the "white" LPC fraction prepared with the use of bisulfite when compared with the growth of rats given ordinary "white" LPC (Bickoff *et al.* 1975).

The reasons for the improvement are not rigidly established as yet. It has not been possible to link the beneficial effect of sulfite specifically to its bacteriostatic action. An alternative reducing agent, ascorbate, did not produce the same effect. However, both in our work and in that carried out

TABLE 14.5. EFFECT OF SULFITE AND ALKALI ADDITION ON THE QUALITY OF LPC PREPARED FROM LUCERNE AND COCKSFOOT

Sample	Leaf Species	Additions	NPU
1	Lucerne	None	38
2	Lucerne	Sulfite	53
3	Lucerne	None	51
4	Lucerne	Sulfite; NH_3	59
5	Lucerne	None	36
6	Lucerne	Sulfite	49
7	Lucerne	Sulfite (leaves soaked overnight)	57
8	Lucerne	Sulfite; NaOH	54
9	Lucerne	Sulfite; NaOH	57
10	Lucerne	Sulfite; NaOH	49
11	Lucerne	Sulfite; NaOH	50
12	Cocksfoot	None	31
13	Cocksfoot	Sulfite	45
14	Cocksfoot	None	30
15	Cocksfoot	Sulfite	50

at the Western Regional Research Laboratory of the U.S. Dept. of Agriculture, higher amounts of methionine and cystine were found in samples of LPC produced by the sulfite or bisulfite methods (Karmali 1973; Bickoff *et al.* 1975). These results are summarized in Table 14.6.

One sample of lucerne did not show a change on sulfite treatment and the reason for this is not understood.

Sulfite addition increases the nutritive value and also lowers the extra gain in weight of experimental animals when methionine is also given (Bickoff *et al.* 1975). These authors have suggested that the higher analytical values for methionine and cystine in the concentrates from sulfite-processed leaves may be related to an instability of some compounds partially oxidized to acid during the performic acid oxidation. Certainly, the results suggest that methionine or cystine—perhaps both—are lost to some extent during normal processing.

It seems clear that, while considerable progress has been made in our understanding of the optimum conditions for processing green leaves to get

TABLE 14.6. METHIONINE AND CYSTINE CONTENTS (G/16 G N) FOR LEAF PROTEIN CONCENTRATES PRODUCED WITH AND WITHOUT THE USE OF SULFITE (2000 PPM) OR BISULFITE (1000 PPM)

Reference	LPC and Treatment	Methionine	Cystine
Bickoff *et al.* (1975)	White lucerne LPC (control)	2.27	1.44
	White lucerne LPC (bisulfite-treated)	2.65	1.68
Karmali (1973)	Whole lucerne LPC (control)	1.62	1.01
	Whole lucerne LPC (sulfite-treated)	2.03	1.06
Karmali (1973)	Whole lucerne LPC (control)	1.87	1.04
	Whole lucerne LPC (sulfite-treated)	1.84	1.10
	Whole lucerne LPC (sulfite-treated)	1.67	1.04
Karmali (1973)	Whole cocksfoot LPC (control)	1.76	0.85
	Whole cocksfoot LPC (sulfite-treated)	2.02	1.16
	Whole cocksfoot LPC (sulfite-treated)	2.02	1.19

a product with good yield and of superior nutritional quality, some questions still remain to be answered before the full potential of the raw material can be realized. It is perhaps unnecessary to reiterate the importance of increasing world protein supplies. Nevertheless, leaves represent the most abundant primary protein source the world possesses, and it seems inevitable that as increasing populations exert heavier demands upon the products of the earth, constantly improved technology will be demanded to keep pace. In this scheme, there is little doubt that further developments in the production methods for leaf protein concentrates will take a prominent place.

PROTEIN EVALUATION PROCEDURES FOR LEAF PROTEIN CONCENTRATES (LPC)

(1) Protein Efficiency Ratio (PER)

Weanling male rats (19–21 days of age) of the same strain and within a maximum weight range of 10 g are divided into groups of 10 animals each on the basis of weight. The rats are housed in individual screen-bottomed cages and supplied with test diets and water *ad libitum*. Body weights and food consumption data are collected at weekly intervals over a 4-week test period and PER, the ratio of total weight gain to total protein consumption, is calculated for each group.

Test Diets.
Test sample to contribute 10% of protein (N × 6.25) to diet

Maize oil	10% of diet
Cellulose	2% of diet
Salt mixture (follows)	4% of diet
Vitamin mixture (follows)	1% of diet
Maize starch	to 100% of diet

Salt Mixture.

NaCl	1393.5 g
KI	7.9 g
KH_2PO_4	3891 g
$MgSo_4 \cdot 7H_2O$	573 g
$CaCO_3$	3814 g
$FeSO_4 \cdot 7H_2O$	270 g
$MnSO_4 \cdot 4H_2O$	40.1 g
$ZnSO_4 \cdot 7H_2O$	5.5 g
$CuSO_4 \cdot 5H_2O$	4.8 g
$CoCl_2 \cdot 6H_2O$	0.23 g
Total	10,000 g

Incorporate the salt mixture in the diet at the rate of 4 g to 100 g total diet.

Formulation is based on AOAC (1965), p. 779.

Vitamin Mixture.

Vitamin A (stabilized)	2,000,000	IU
Vitamin D (stabilized)	200,000	IU
Vitamin E (stabilized)	10,000	IU
Choline	200	g
Menadione	0.5	g
p-Aminobenzoic acid	10	g
Inositol	25	g
Niacin	4	g
Ca-D-pantothenate	4	g
Riboflavin	1	g
Thiamin HCl	0.5	g
Pyridoxine HCl	0.5	g
Folic acid	0.2	g
Biotin	0.04	g
Vitamin B_{12}	0.003	g
Dextrose	to 1000	g

Incorporate in the diet at the rate of 1 g to 100 g total diet.

Formulation is based on AOAC (1965), p. 785. Inositol and riboflavin have been increased to levels recommended in *Evaluation of Protein Quality*, p. 31 (Miller 1963).

(2) Net Protein Utilization (NPU)

Rats of the Hooded Lister strain are weaned at 19–20 days of age and given a stock diet until they are 28–30 days old and weigh 50–60 g. Four litters of 8 rats each are divided into 8 groups of 4 so that each group contains one rat from each litter and totals the same weight within 1–2 g. If unusually large or small rats are present in the litters, they are discarded and the number of experimental groups is reduced accordingly.

One group is given a nonprotein diet and each of the others receives test protein diets for 10 days, after which the animals are killed with carbon dioxide or coal gas. The carcasses, dried to constant weight, are minced and ground to provide a uniform powder, and 350 mg samples are analyzed for nitrogen content by the Kjeldahl method. The nitrogen content of the feces collected during the latter 5 days of the experimental period are similarly analyzed for nitrogen in order to provide a digestibility value for the test proteins. Food uneaten during the experiment is dried at 105°C and weighed, and the nitrogen intake of the animals is calculated.

Nonprotein Diet.

Margarine	15%
Potato starch	10%
Glucose	15%

Vitamin mixture	5%
Salt mixture	5%
Rice starch	50%

Test Diets.
Test sample to contribute 10% of protein (N × 6.25) to diet

Margarine	15%
Potato starch	10%
Glucose	15%
Salt mixture	5%
Vitamin mixture	5%
Rice starch	to 100% of diet

Salt Mixture.

Calcium citrate	616.7	g
$Ca_4(PO_4)_2 \cdot H_2O$	225.5	g
K_2HPO_4	437.5	g
NaCl	154.1	g
KCl	249.5	g
$CaCO_3$	137.2	g
$MgCO_3$	71.4	g
$MgSO_4$(anhydrous)	76.7	g
Ferric citrate	19.0	g
$MnCl_2 \cdot 4H_2O$	10.0	g
Copper carbonate (basic)	2.3	g
Zinc carbonate	1.0	g
NaF	1.0	g
KI	0.08	g
Total	2000	g

Incorporate in the diet at the 5% level.

Vitamin Mixture.

Vitamin B_{12}	0.002	g
Folic acid	0.080	g
Biotin	0.080	g
Pyridoxine HCl	0.080	g
Thiamin HCl	0.120	g
Riboflavin	0.400	g
Ca-D-pantothenate	2.40	g
Nicotinic acid	8.0	g
Inositol	8.0	g
p-Aminobenzoic acid	24.0	g
Chlorine chloride (50%)	48.0	g
Maize starch	1909	g
Total	2000	g

Incorporate in the diet at the 5% level.

Calculation of NPU:

$$NPU = \frac{B - (B_K - I_K)}{I}$$

where: B and B_K are the total body nitrogen values for the test and non-protein diets, respectively
and I and I_K are the intakes of nitrogen for the same groups

(3) Gross Protein Value (GPV)

Four hundred 1-day-old cockerels are housed in wire-floor hovers and given cracked wheat and maize for 3 days followed by an 8% crude protein (N × 6.25) depletion diet, 6.5% of which is provided by cereals and the remainder by yeast and whey. All birds are weighed at 2 weeks of age and the heaviest and lightest discarded to leave 192 birds as even in weight as possible. The selected birds are divided randomly into 32 groups of 6 and allocated to single tier cages and to one of 8 experimental diets. These include six 11% protein diets containing proteins under test, one 11% protein diet in which casein replaces the test proteins, and one 8% protein diet which contains cereal protein only. The diets are given for a further 14 days and weight gain and food consumption for each group are measured.

Basal Diet.

Wheat offals	40.0 kg
Maize meal	28.0 kg
Barley meal	40.0 kg
Sussex-ground oats	26.6 kg
Whey	13.4 kg
Yeast	8.0 kg
Salt	1.2 kg
Vitamin supplement[1]	2.8 kg
Total	160 kg

Depletion and Control Diets (8% Crude Protein).

Basal mix, Oat feed	to provide 8% crude protein and 7% crude fiber in the diet
$Ca_3(PO_4)_2$	to raise the dietary phosphorus level to 0.72%
$CaCO_3$	to raise the dietary calcium level to 1.10%
Vitamin E	360 mg
Maize starch	to 140 kg of total diet

[1]Provides 1000 IU of Vitamin A and 200 IU of Vitamin D_3 per g.

Test Diets (11% Crude Protein).
Test protein or casein to contribute 3% of crude protein to final diet

Basal diet } Oat feed }	quantities calculated to contribute 8% of crude protein and 7% of fiber to the final diet
$Ca_3(PO_4)_2$	to raise the phosphorus level of the diet to 0.72%
$CaCO_3$	to raise the calcium level of the diet to 1.10%
Vitamin E	60 mg
Maize starch	to give 20 kg of total diet

Calculation of GPV:

$$\text{GPV} = \frac{\text{Wt gain/g of supplementary protein in test diet (g)}}{\text{Wt gain/g of supplementary protein in casein diet (g)}} \times 100$$

where Wt gain/g of supplementary protein =

$$\frac{\text{Extra wt gain (g)}}{\text{Food eaten/head (g)}} \times \frac{100}{\text{\% Supplementary protein}}$$

Extra wt gain = Wt gain/head for test group − Wt gain/head for control group

% Supplementary protein = Crude protein (N × 6.25) content of test diet (by analysis) − Crude protein content of control diet

(4) Total Protein Efficiency (TPE)—Chick

Four hundred 1-day-old broiler chickens in tier brooders are given a diet consisting of equal parts of cracked wheat and maize for 3 days followed by a normal 21% protein chick starter for 10 days. The birds are weighed individually at 14 days of age and 192 selected of similar weight and as near to the heavier end of the available weight range as possible. Usually the selected birds cover a range of about 20 g. The birds are then distributed evenly over 16 or 32 single-tier wire-floored cages and the total weight of each group of 6 or 12 birds is recorded.

Experimental diets are given to duplicate groups of 12 birds or quadruplicate groups of 6 birds for 14 days, at which time groups are weighed and food consumption is recorded. Lighting for 13 hr daily is by 150 watt red bulbs hung 25 cm above each feeding compartment. Spillage is minimized by the provision of 2.5 cm grids laid on the surface of the powdered food in the troughs, and spilled food amounting to 20–30 g over the entire 14-day test period is collected in trays 5 cm wide placed beneath the feeders. Cage temperatures are lowered gradually from 32° to 27°C during the experimental period and the house temperature from 24° to 21°C. Deaths are rare and weights of dead birds are added to the final group live-weight before calculating TPE. TPE is the weight gain of the group divided by the weight of protein eaten by the group. A standard fish meal is usually included in each experiment as a check on between-experiment variability, and is desirable because of differences between successive lots of chickens.

Test Diets (18% Crude Protein).

Barley or barley + wheat offals	to provide 6.0% crude protein in diet
Test sample	to provide 12.0% crude protein in diet
Steamed bone flour	3.0% of total diet
Vitamin supplement	0.31% of total diet
NaCl	0.19% of total diet
Lard Maize starch	appropriate combinations used to achieve equivalence of energy provision in all diets

Vitamin-Mineral-Antibiotic Supplement.

NaCl	2260 g
$MnSO_4 \cdot H_2O$	148 g
Riboflavin (94%)	8 g
Vitamin A (500,000 IU/g) + Vitamin D_3 (100,000 IU/g)	52 g
Vitamin D_3 (200,000 IU/g)	6.5 g
Pyridoxine HCl	8.8 g
Vitamin B_{12} (1000 mg/kg)	213 g
Vitamin E (50%)	52 g
Menadione	2.6 g
Ca D-pantothenate (45%)	22.4 g
Nicotinamide	63 g
Biotin (1%)	8.8 g
Aurofac 100	282 g

Diet Balancing Procedure. The combination of barley and wheat offals used is dependent upon the crude protein content of the test protein. If high, then barley alone can be used as the cereal source, but, if below about 40%, then the replacement of some barley by high protein wheat offals will be necessary to allow inclusion of the necessary amount of test protein concentrate. Leaf protein samples are normally above 50% crude protein so that the inclusion of wheat offals is optional.

The procedure for achieving isocaloric diets is as follows:

(1) Sum all ingredients except lard and starch and subtract from 100 to give figure A.

(2) Calculate the total energy content of the diet from tables or from analytical values, assuming that A comprises only starch.

(3860 × A) + metabolizable energy (ME) (Kcal/kg) of cereals and additives gives figure B.
(3) Subtract B from the desired total ME of the diet to give figure C.
(4) % of lard required in the diet (D) is 2.025 × C.
(5) % of starch required in the diet is A − D.
(6) Check that ME values for all dietary ingredients add up to the chosen figure for the diet.

(5) Total Protein Efficiency (TPE)—Rat

Sixty weanling Hooded Lister rats are selected for evenness of weight from approximately 80 animals and distributed evenly to 6 groups of 10 so that each group totals approximately the same weight. Six experimental diets, each providing 8% of crude protein (N × 6.25) from wheat offals and 8% from the protein under test are given to the individually caged rats *ad libitum* for 21 days. Weight gain and food consumption are measured weekly for each animal and the TPE is calculated from the means for each group after 1, 2, and 3 weeks.

Test Diets (16% Crude Protein).
Wheat offals to contribute 8% of protein (N × 6.25) to the diet
Test protein sample to contribute 8% of protein (N × 6.25) to the diet

Mineral mix	4% of diet
Vitamin supplement	1% of diet
Lard } Maize starch }	appropriate combinations to achieve equivalence of energy provision in all diets

Vitamin and mineral supplements are as described for the rat Protein Efficiency Ratio (PER) test (#1). Balancing of lard and maize starch additions are carried out in the same manner as described for the chick TPE test (#4).

REFERENCES

AKESON, W.R. and STAHMAN, M.A. 1965. Nutritive value of leaf protein concentrate, an *in vitro* digestion study. J. Agric. Food Chem. *13*, 145–148.

ANELLI, G., FIORENTINI, R., MASSIGNAN, L. and GALOPPINI, C. 1977. The poly-protein process: A new method for obtaining leaf protein concentrates. J. Food Sci. *42*, 1401–1403.

ANON. 1972. Annu. Rep. Rothamsted Exp. Stn. *1972* (Part 1) 117. Harpenden, Herts., U.K.

AOAC. 1965. Official Methods of Analysis, 10th Edition. Association of Official Agricultural Chemists, Washington, DC.

BICKOFF, E.M., BOOTH, A.N., DE FREMERY, D., EDWARDS, R.H., KNUCKLES, B.E., MILLER, R.E., SAUNDERS, R.M. and KÖHLER, G.O.

1975. Nutritional evaluation of alfalfa leaf protein concentrate. *In* Protein Nutritional Quality of Foods and Feeds, Vol. 2, Part 2. M. Friedman (Editor). Marcel Dekker, New York.

BYERS, M. 1971. The amino acid composition of some leaf protein preparations. *In* Leaf Protein: Its Agronomy, Preparation, Quality and Use. IBP Handb. *20*. N.W. Pirie (Editor). Blackwell Scientific Publications, Oxford and Edinburgh.

CARPENTER, K.J. and WOODHAM, A.A. 1974. Protein quality of feedingstuffs. 6. Comparisons of the results of collaborative biological assays for amino acids with those of other methods. Br. J. Nutr. *32*, 647–660.

CHAYEN, I.H., SMITH, R.H., TRISTRAM, G.R., THIRKELL, D. and WEBB, T. 1961. The isolation of leaf components. 1. J. Sci. Food Agric. *12*, 502–512.

DERSE, P.H. 1960. Evaluation of protein quality (biological method). J. Assoc. Off. Agric. Chem. *43*, 38–41.

DUCKWORTH, J., WOODHAM, A.A. and McDONALD, I. 1961. The assessment of nutritive value in protein concentrates by the Gross Protein Value method. J. Sci. Food Agric. *12*, 407–417.

HEIMAN, V., CARVER, J.S. and COOK, J.W. 1939. A method for determining the gross value of protein concentrates. Poult. Sci. *18*, 464–474.

HORIGOME, T. and KANDATSU, M. 1968. Biological value of proteins allowed to react with phenolic compounds in presence of *o*-diphenol oxidase. Agric. Biol. Chem. *32*, 1093–1102.

KARMALI, R.A. 1973. Effect of some aspects of processing on the composition and nutritive value of some leaf protein concentrates. M.Sc. Thesis. Univ. of Aberdeen, Aberdeen, Scotland.

KOHLER, G.O. and BICKOFF, E.M. 1971. Commercial production from alfalfa in U.S.A. *In* Leaf Protein: Its Agronomy, Preparation, Quality and Use. IBP Handb. *20*. N.W. Pirie (Editor). Blackwell Scientific Publications, Oxford and Edinburgh.

MILLER, D.S. 1963. A procedure for the determination of NPU using rats: Body N technique. *In* Evaluation of Protein Quality. Natl. Acad. Sci.-Natl. Res. Counc., Washington, DC. NAS-NRC Publ. *1100*.

PIRIE, N.W. 1971A. Conclusions. *In* Leaf Protein: Its Agronomy, Preparation, Quality and Use. IBP Handb. *20*. N.W. Pirie (Editor). Blackwell Scientific Publications, Oxford and Edinburgh.

PIRIE, N.W. 1971B. Equipment and methods for extracting and separating protein. *In* Leaf Protein: Its Agronomy, Preparation, Quality and Use. IBP Handb. *20*. N.W. Pirie (Editor). Blackwell Scientific Publications, Oxford and Edinburgh.

SINGER, S.J., EGGMAN, L., CAMPBELL, J.M. and WILDMAN, S.G. 1952. The proteins of green leaves. IV. A high molecular weight protein comprising a large part of the cytoplasmic proteins. J. Biol. Chem. *197*, 233–239.

SINGH, N. 1969. Leaf proteins in nutrition: Studies on production, nutritive value and utilisation. Voeding *30*, 710–713.

SUBBA RAU, B.H. and SINGH, N. 1970. Studies on nutritive value of leaf proteins from lucerne *(Medicago Sativa)*. Part II. Effect of processing conditions. Indian J. Exp. Biol. *8*, 34–36.

WOODHAM, A.A. 1968. A chick growth test for the evaluation of protein quality in cereal-based diets. 1. Development of the method. Br. Poult. Sci. *9*, 53–63.

WOODHAM, A.A. 1971. The use of animal tests for the evaluation of leaf protein concentrates. *In* Leaf Protein: Its Agronomy, Preparation, Quality and Use. IBP Handb. *20*. N.W. Pirie (Editor). Blackwell Scientific Publications, Oxford and Edinburgh.

WOODHAM, A.A. and BAILEY, P.H. 1977. The effect of drying temperatures upon the nutritive value of barley for growing chickens. Proc. Nutr. Soc. *36*, 50A.

WOODHAM, A.A., KARMALI, R.A., CLARKE, E.M.W. and ARKCOLL, D.B. 1976. The effect of processing conditions on the nutritive value of protein concentrates prepared from green leaves. Proc 4th Int. Congr. Food Sci. Technol., Vol. 1, Madrid 1974.

Part III

Preparation of LPC

15

Protein Concentrates from Pasture Herbage and Their Fractionation into Feed- and Food-grade Products

Henry T. Ostrowski-Meissner[1]

FRACTIONATION OF PROTEINS EXTRACTED FROM PASTURE HERBAGE

Although green vegetation represents an ample source of good quality protein, only a few species, notably leafy vegetables, are at present utilized by man. The main reason for the limited direct consumption of plant material by monogastric organisms is the low protein/fiber ratio and indigestibility of the cellulosic cell walls in green plant leaves. However, since green vegetation is the primary replenishable source of food in the world, numerous technologies have been developed over the last 50 years which have made it possible to separate the protein from the accompanying fibrous plant material, making the extracted plant proteins available and more usable for direct consumption by man and monogastric animals (Pirie 1971).

Grasslands, of all crops, have been found to be most outstanding, being high-yielding performers in terms of dry matter and protein production, particularly in temperate and subtropical agricultural ecosystems (Ostrowski-Meissner 1976A,B, 1978A). Therefore, grasslands have been involved in the protein extraction process in order to recover highly concentrated protein fractions for use in monogastric farm animals' nutrition and to utilize the partially deproteinized herbage as fodder for ruminants (Ostrowski-Meissner 1978A,C, 1979C).

The processing of pasture is accomplished when the pasture herbage, after harvesting, is mechanically disintegrated in the macerator and the

[1] Balai Penelitian Ternak, Project for Animal Research and Development, Bogor, Indonesia (Commonwealth Scientific and Industrial Research Organization—Australia).

pulp is fractionated in the press (belt or screw-type) into green liquor (herbage juice) and fiber residues. The partially deproteinized herbage is then used for feeding cows, and the herbage juice is processed in order to recover proteins in a concentrated form which is chemically and biologically equivalent to soybean protein and can be used in monogastric farm animal nutrition. The typical protein extraction process from pasture herbage and distribution of dry matter, protein, minerals, and soluble carbohydrates is shown in Fig. 15.1.

Applying protein extraction to irrigated pasture already involved in dairy farming in Australia, the conversion of pasture protein into meat, milk, and LPC protein increases from some 13% in conventional farming operations, based on pasture grazing, to more than 75% in the alternative operation with the protein extraction system (Ostrowski-Meissner 1978C). Depending on the stocking rates (cows per hectare of grassland), annual yields of recoverable protein (N $\times$ 6.25) amounted to 1.7 kg $\times$ 10^3 ha^{-1}. It has been estimated that the involvement of subtropical topdressed grasslands in the protein extraction system may result in yields of up to 4.5 $\times$ 10^3 kg protein per ha. This amount is recoverable in leaf protein concentrate (LPC) form.

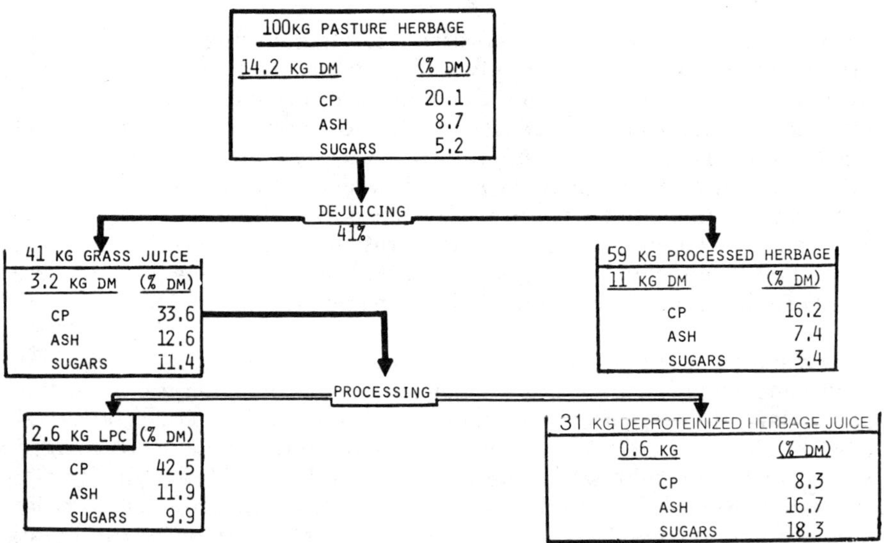

Fig. 15.1. Efficiency of pasture herbage processing as achieved in typical protein extraction operation with heat coagulation at 85°C, and the distribution of dry matter (DM), crude proteins (CP), ash, and soluble carbohydrates among the fractions of the original herbage subject to mechanical and chemical processing.

In general practice, acid and/or heat coagulation is used for the recovery of protein from herbage extract (juice) mainly for use as a feed for poultry. However, such a product, due to its dark green color, bitter taste, and strong grassy smell, is not acceptable for direct human consumption (Ostrowski-Meissner 1978B). Therefore, in order to prepare protein concentrates from herbage which would be more acceptable as a potential novel high protein food supplement, a system of protein extraction from pasture herbage has been developed with alternative separation of a protein fraction suitable for direct human consumption (Fig. 15.2). Within such a system, the chloroplastic material responsible for the green color and much of the grassy flavor is separated by differential heating at 55°C followed by sedimentation, centrifugation, or filtration. The remaining soluble proteins—cytoplasmic protein fraction—can be precipitated by heat at 85°C or concentrated without heat precipitation by the use of membrane filtration (Ostrowski-Meissner 1975). As a result of the protein extraction and fractionation operation, two distinctive protein fractions are separable: the dark green chloroplastic "animal fraction" and the cream-white cytoplasmic "human fraction."

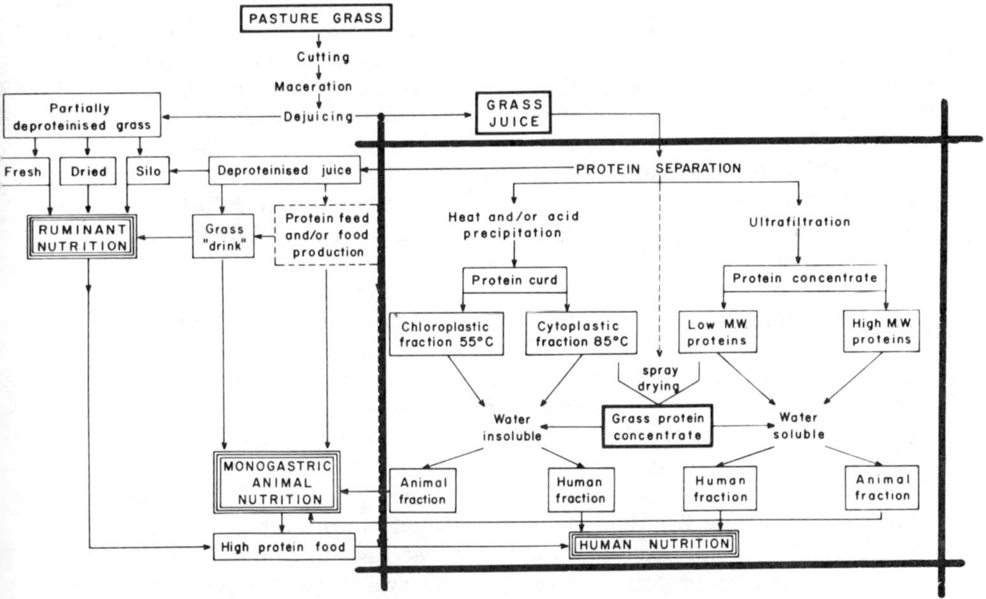

Fig. 15.2. Diagram of protein extraction system from pasture herbage with ultrafiltration being alternative to heat coagulation used for isolation of proteins from herbage and protein fractionation into "human" and "animal" fractions (framed part of the process).

TECHNIQUES FOR FRACTIONATION OF HERBAGE PROTEINS

In the whole system of protein extraction from pasture herbage, one of the factors restricting the efficiency of protein recovery during the extraction process is the method of protein separation from the juice (Ostrowski-Meissner 1976A, 1978C). Despite the fact that the most commonly used method to isolate protein from plant extracts is that based on heat and/or acid precipitation (Pirie 1971), such treatments cause the denaturation of proteins, which become water-insoluble. In such form they are not favored in modern food and feed technology and also may have a restricted application to farm practice (e.g., as milk replacer). Thus, looking at the different methods and techniques for protein recovery from herbage juice, a membrane filtration technique (ultrafiltration) has been chosen as a possible alternative to the precipitation procedure (Ostrowski-Meissner 1979A,B,C, 1980A,B,C; Ostrowski-Meissner *et al.* 1980).

In recent years, when suitable commercial ultrafiltration membranes appeared on the market (Abcor, Romicon, DDS, IOPOR-CIP, and others), ultrafiltration became one of the cheapest protein isolation and concentration methods (Payne *et al.* 1973). Thus, the ultrafiltration technique has been applied for protein isolation, fractionation, and concentration as an alternative method to heat (at 55°C and 85°C) and/or acid coagulation for separating proteins from herbage juices processed within the system of protein extraction from pasture (Ostrowski-Meissner 1975, 1976C).

Ultrafiltration has already been reported by Singh *et al.* (1974), Knuckles *et al.* (1975), and Ostrowski-Meissner (1975, 1978A,B, 1979C) as useful in concentrating proteins in herbage juices by removing 80 to 90% of the water and nonprotein components. The final product obtained after drying (protein concentrate) still remains water soluble.

There are several alternatives which can be applied to herbage juice concentration and fractionation. To concentrate juice proteins by membrane filtration without protein fractionation, one can apply membranes of 1 to 2×10^4 molecular weight (MW) cutoff. As a result, the protein concentrate of feed-grade which is obtained contains chloroplastic and cytoplasmic proteins and, except for the solubility, has similar chemical characteristics to acid/heat precipitated (pH 3.5/85°C) concentrates (Table 15.1). When the chloroplastic fraction is removed by heat precipitation at 55°C, then proteins (cytoplasmic fraction) not precipitated at this temperature can be recovered by precipitation at 85°C as a water-insoluble product or by ultrafiltration, without protein denaturation, as a water-soluble product. Different membranes used in the ultrafiltration process result in slightly different efficiency levels. Since ultrafiltration of the whole herbage juice is a long and high energy consuming process, the most advantageous method of protein separation appeared to be steam coagulation of the chloroplastic (feed-grade) fraction at 55°C followed by membrane filtration (ultrafiltration) for recovery of the cytoplasmic (food-grade) fraction (Ostrowski-Meissner 1976D; 1979C). Figure 15.3 presents a schematic diagram of the

TABLE 15.1. EFFICIENCY OF PROTEIN SEPARATION PROCEDURE AND CHEMICAL COMPOSITION OF THE LPCs OBTAINED BY DIFFERENT METHODS USED FOR PROTEIN SEPARATION FROM HERBAGE JUICE

Protein Separation Method[1]	Protein Fraction	Yield of LPC (kg DM) from 100 Liters of Juice	Total Nitrogen (% DM)	Total Ash (% DM)	Soluble Sugars (% DM)	Water Solubility (Dispersivity)
Acid (pH 3.5) and heat (85°C)	chloroplastic and cytoplasmic	9.72 (0.52)	7.41 (0.47)	12.2 (0.62)	7.3 (0.54)	−
ABCOR 2×10^4 MW (whole) juice ultrafiltration at 39°C)	chloroplastic and cytoplasmic	9.57 (0.64)	7.10 (0.68)	15.5 (0.56)	11.7 (0.66)	+
Heat (55°C)	chloroplastic	6.60 (0.38)	7.23 (0.36)	12.9 (0.46)	6.4 (0.43)	−
Heat (55°/ 85°C)	cytoplasmic	1.91 (0.12)	8.90 (0.51)	8.9 (0.41)	11.1 (0.58)	−
ABCOR 2×10^4 MW membrane (55°C filtrate processing at 39°C)	cytoplasmic	1.70 (0.21)	9.90 (0.72)	12.5 (0.63)	7.5 (0.39)	+
ROMICON 1×10^4 MW membrane (55°C filtrate processing at 39°C)	cytoplasmic	1.87 (0.14)	10.33 (0.55)	11.6 (0.44)	8.2 (0.35)	+

Source: Ostrowski-Meissner (1976D).
[1]Each value represents the mean of four recovery procedures (± standard deviation).

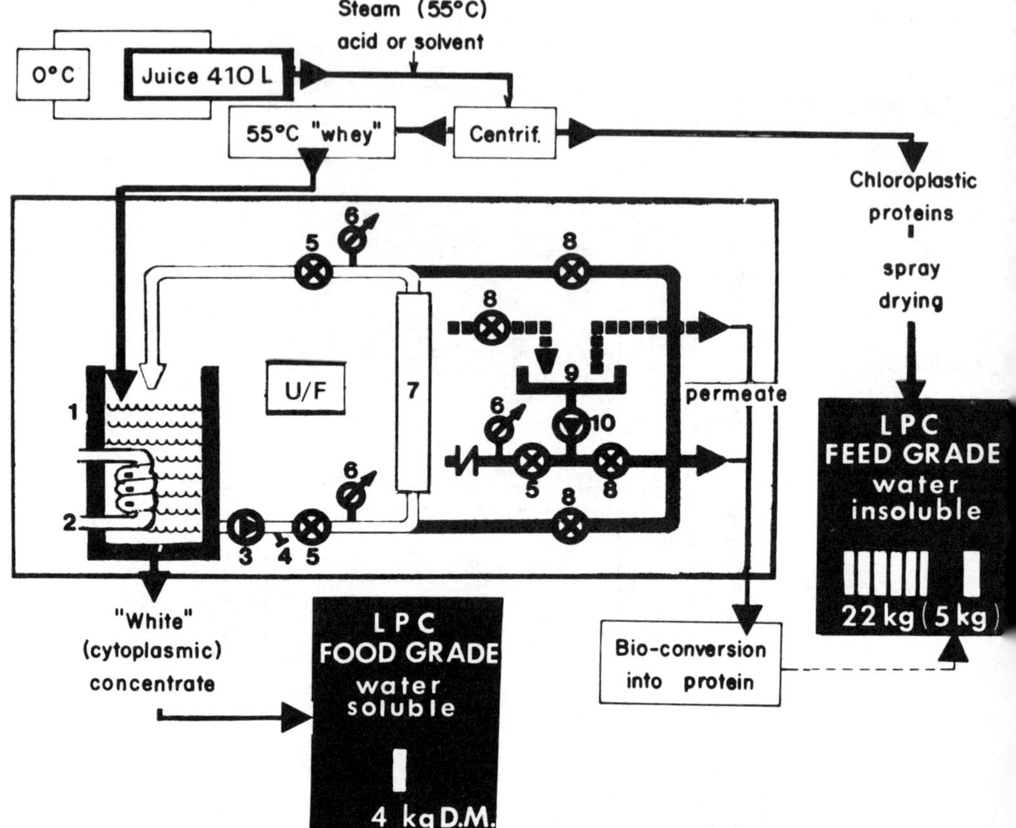

Fig. 15.3. Processing of juice extracted from pasture herbage and average yields of chloroplastic (feed-grade) and cytoplasmic (food-grade) protein fractions as achieved during fractionation using heat coagulation at 55°C for chloroplastic protein separation, followed by concentration and separation of the cytoplasmic proteins using ultrafiltration technique. Framed part of the process represents "batch-type" ultrafiltration system: 1—Process tank. 2—Heat exchanger. 3—Process pump. 4—Strainer. 5—Pressure control valve. 6—Pressure gauge. 7—Ultrafiltration module. 8—Ball valve. 9—Permeate tank. 10—Permeate pump. (Based on processing of juice extracted from 1 MT of fresh weight herbage as in Fig. 15.1).

separation of protein fractions from herbage juice extracted from 1 MT of fresh weight herbage showing approximate recoveries of feed- and food-grade protein fractions. The diagram also indicates one of the possible ways of utilizing the deproteinized liquor in farm animal nutrition through its use as a substrate for microbial growth, allowing for the production of approximately 14 to 20 g of microbial protein from 1 liter of deproteinized herbage juice. When not used, the liquor containing minerals and nitrogen compounds is returned to pasture as topdressing.

PROTEIN FRACTIONS AS RECOVERED FROM PASTURE HERBAGE

In practice, there are three major fractions which can easily be separated from herbage juice. This occurs when the permeate (filtrate) is removed from the whole juice filtration process using the membrane with a nominal 6.5×10^4 MW cutoff level. The largest fraction represents proteins of a molecular weight above 6.5×10^4 (approximately 75–80% of total recoverable proteins) and the smallest fraction, being approximately 5% of the total, represents proteins below 6×10^3 MW. In addition to precipitable proteins, the fraction below 6×10^3 MW contains nonprecipitable amino-nitrogen compounds in the form of free amino acids, peptides, and polypeptides as well as macromolecules formed through condensations of amino -nitrogen. The protein fraction of molecular weight below 6.5×10^4, being approximately 20–25% of the total recoverable protein, is, after concentration, cream-white in color and tasteless. It is comparable to the cytoplastic fraction which is separated from juice using fractionated steam coagulation. The distribution of the protein fractions in concentrates and permeates, separated in the two-stage ultrafiltration (UF) procedure, with the two membranes of 6.5×10^4 and 6×10^3 MW cutoff levels, in reference to the whole juice and supernatants obtained from fractionation by heat coagulation at 55°C and 85°C, is demonstrated on the polyacrylamide gel electrochromatograms shown in Fig. 15.4.

Five proteins were observed on the gel to which a sample of herbage juice was added. Proteins labelled as 4 and 5 and a small portion of the 3 were separated from the juice with the permeate using ultrafiltration membrane of molecular weight cutoff 6.5×10^4. Ultrafiltered juice concentrate contained proteins labelled as 1, 2, and 3 with traces of 4 and 5 which indicate that a majority of proteins present in the herbage juice are those of high molecular weight category. Similarly, in the electrochromatograms of the UF permeate and supernatant from 55°C precipitation (during which the chloroplastic protein fraction was separated), it was indicated that the chloroplastic fraction is not a homogeneous protein but a mixture of proteins representing high molecular weight proteins above 6.5×10^4 MW.

Further ultrafiltration of the permeate from the 6.5×10^4 MW process using a membrane with 6×10^3 MW cutoff level resulted in the separation of the concentrate composed of two proteins labelled as 4 and 5 representing MW in the range between 6×10^3 and 6.5×10^4. Comparing the permeate from the membrane filtration and supernatant from the heat precipitation (85°C), it may be concluded that the so-called cytoplasmic fraction commonly recoverable in several protein extraction procedures as human protein fraction represents the mixture of two proteins exhibiting a molecular weight below 6.5×10^4.

Free and Satterlee (1975), studying the biochemical properties of alfalfa protein concentrate using polyacrylamide gel electophoresis, indicated several proteins in chloroplast-free juice and six in the dialyzed one. This difference may be due to different plant material (pasture herbage mixture

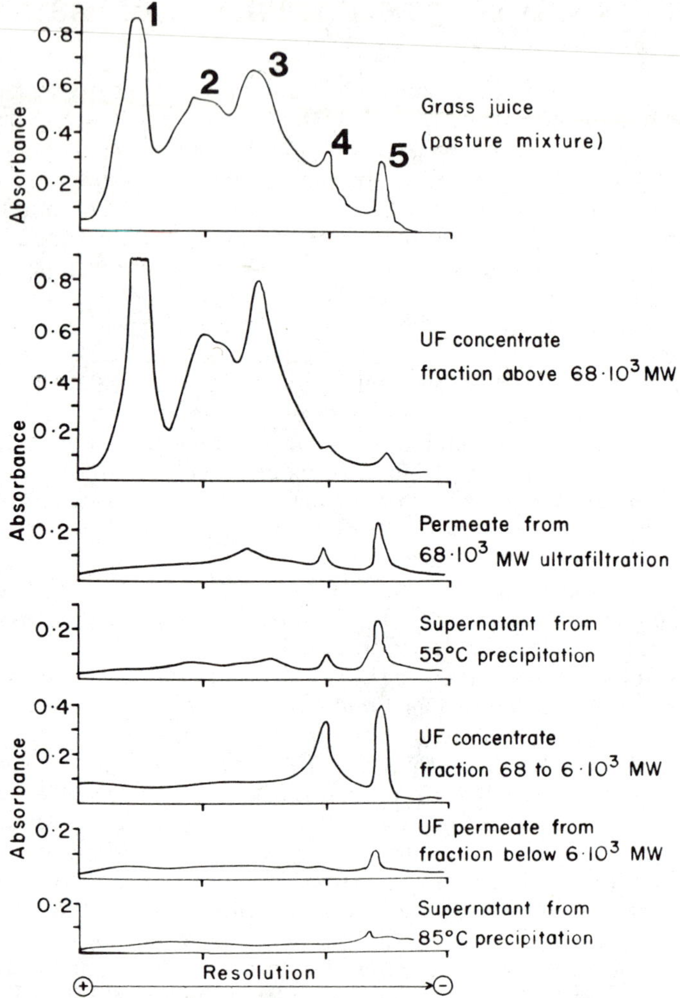

Fig. 15.4. Protein fractions as determined by polyacrylamide gel electrophoresis in concentrates and permeates from two ultrafiltration procedures and comparison with fractions determined in supernatants obtained by protein fractionation using heat precipitation (55° and 85°C).

instead of alfalfa monoculture) since protein fraction distribution has been found to be different in the juices extracted from the various pasture herbage species (Ostrowski-Meissner *et al.* 1980). There were substantial differences in protein fractions among the perennial grasses, clover, and alfalfa.

In the supernatant obtained from heat precipitation at 85°C, there are much smaller quantities of free amino acids such as lysine, glycine, and methionine as compared to premeate obtained from the ultrafiltration procedure of the same herbage juice (Fig. 15.5). This may be due to the endogenous proteolytic and oxidative enzymes which may, to some extent, impair the recovery of protein during the 2 to 3 hr ultrafiltration process at higher temperatures (39°C). Knuckles *et al.* (1975) reported a decrease in the protein content during the ultrafiltration process due to proteolytic activity. This may explain the slightly lower yields of LPCs obtained from ultrafiltration at 39°C as compared with the heat precipitation procedure (see Table 15.1). However, when ultrafiltration was done at lower temperatures (22°C), yields of recoverable protein fractions were higher than those achieved by heat precipitation (Table 15.2).

CHEMICAL AND BIOLOGICAL CHARACTERISTICS OF PROTEIN FRACTIONS

As a result of different methods of protein separation and/or fractionation of proteins extracted from pasture herbage, ultrafiltration (UF) appeared to be a superior procedure to heat precipitation. Protein concentrates obtained by the latter procedure are also inferior to UF from the chemical composition point of view.

Both the chloroplastic fraction and unfractionated LPCs have similar biochemical characteristics as opposed to the cytoplasmic fraction's (food-grade) being superior to LPC feed-grade. It has been noted that the cytoplasmic protein fraction contained more lysine, histidine, and tryptophan

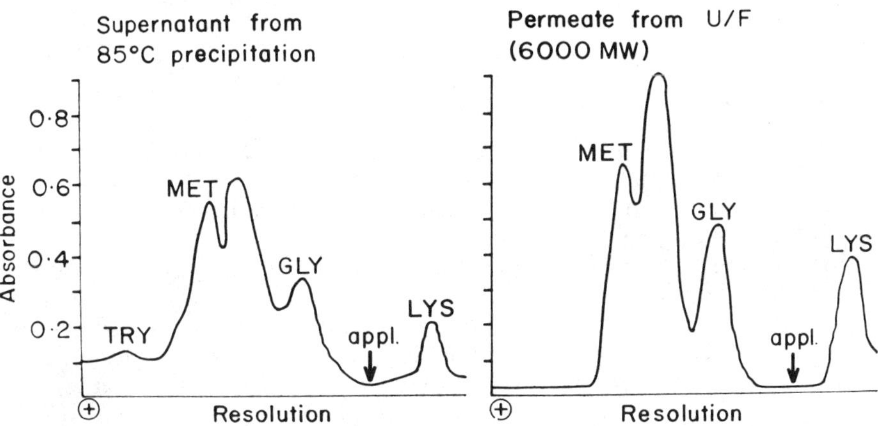

Fig. 15.5. Some of the essential amino acids in deproteinized herbage juice obtained as a result of heat coagulation (85°C) or ultrafiltration (6000 MW cutoff) procedures.

TABLE 15.2. PRODUCTION EFFICIENCY AND CHEMICAL CHARACTERISTICS OF LPC OBTAINED FROM PASTURE HERBAGE PROCESSED ALTERNATIVELY WITHOUT OR WITH FRACTIONATION INTO CONCENTRATES OF FEED- AND FOOD-GRADE PRODUCTS USING DIFFERENT PROCESSING AND FRACTIONATION TECHNIQUES

	Protein Concentrate from Pasture Herbage				
	Heat Precipitation			Membrane Filtration	
		Fraction			
Measurement[1]	Without Fraction-ation (85°C)	Chloro-plastic (55°C)	Cyto-plasmic (55°/ 85°C)	Without Fraction-ation	Cytoplasmic Fraction
Protein Concentrate (Grade)	Feed	Feed	Food	Feed	Food
LPCs production efficiency					
Yield of LPC (kg DM from 100 kg of fresh herbage)	2.6	2.2	0.4	3.3	0.4
Protein nitrogen recovery (recovered protein as % of the total N × 6.25 in herbage)	38.7	32.1	6.2	44.1	6.6
Protein yield (g per kg herbage DM)	77.8	64.6	12.5	89.7	13.2
Chemical characteristic of LPC (% DM)					
Crude protein (N × 6.25)	42.5	41.2	57.4	46.8	52.0
Ash	11.9	13.1	5.5	9.6	3.6
Soluble carbohydrates	9.9	11.7	9.1	6.7	6.4
Total essential amino acids (EAA)[2] (g per 100 g recovered)	44.8	44.3	47.4	48.7	49.0

Source: Ostrowski-Meissner *et al.* (1980).
[1]Each value represents the mean from eight processed herbages.
[2]Cystine excluded.

and less leucine as compared with chloroplastic protein fractions (Table 15.3). Methionine and other amino acids were in both fractions at similar levels. In general, ultrafiltered protein concentrates contained more amino acids than heat-precipitated ones.

The biological value of the chloroplastic protein fraction, as measured by the Protein Efficiency Ratio (PER), was substantially lower than that recorded with the cytoplasmic fraction. Supplementation of the diets for chickens with lysine, methionine, and tryptophan indicated methionine as the first limiting amino acid in the cytoplasmic fraction, but lysine and tryptophan were limiting, too, in the chloroplastic fraction (Table 15.4).

Despite the total lysine "sufficiency" in both LPCs (feed-grade), the response of chickens to lysine added may be an indication of loss in lysine availability during processing which was greater in the fractionated chloroplastic LPC as opposed to the unfractionated LPC. This can be explained by heat processing (Lund 1973) since in the presence of reducing sugars, proteins are degraded via the Maillard reaction, basic amino acids being

TABLE 15.3. THE AMINO ACID COMPOSITION OF LPCs RECOVERED FROM PASTURE HERBAGE BY: EITHER UNFRACTIONATED HEAT COAGULATION (85°C) AND MEMBRANE FILTRATION; OR BY FRACTIONATING WITH THE USE OF HEAT (55°C) FOLLOWED BY MEMBRANE FILTRATION; AND COMPARISON WITH THE RANGE OF AMINO ACID CONCENTRATIONS IN SEVERAL LEAF PROTEINS (BYERS 1971B) AND WITH FAO (FAO/ WHO 1965) PROVISIONAL RECOMMENDATIONS (G AMINO ACID PER 100 G RECOVERED AMINO ACIDS)

	Protein Concentrate from Pasture Herbage[1]					References		
	Heat Precipitation			Membrane Filtration				
	Without Fractionation (85°C)	Fraction						
Amino Acid		Chloroplastic (55°C)	Cytoplasmic (55°/85°C)	Without Fractionation	Cytoplasmic Fraction	Byers (1971B) (Range)		FAO (FAO/WHO 1965)
Histidine	2.2	2.0	2.6	2.0	2.9	1.8	2.8	—
Isoleucine	4.6	4.5	4.7	4.6	4.6	4.5	5.5	4.2
Leucine	9.5	9.9	9.3	9.9	8.7	8.8	10.2	4.8
Lysine	4.8	4.6	5.7	6.2	6.6	5.6	7.3	4.2
Methionine	1.9	1.8	2.0	2.0	1.9	1.6	2.6	2.2
Phenylalanine	6.1	6.2	6.0	5.9	5.9	5.5	6.8	2.8
Threonine	4.3	4.0	4.8	5.0	6.3	4.7	5.8	2.8
Tryptophan	1.3	1.3	1.8	2.0	2.1	1.2	2.3	1.4
Tyrosine	3.9	3.8	4.0	4.3	4.1	3.7	4.9	2.8
Valine	6.2	6.2	6.5	6.7	6.3	5.9	6.9	4.2

Source: Ostrowski-Meissner *et al.* (1980).
[1]Each value represents the mean of four determinations.

especially reactive. Even though the heat-coagulated LPCs were supplemented with methionine and lysine, they had a lower PER value than that observed with casein (2.8). An increase in PER due to tryptophan supplementation may indicate that, due to processing, tryptophan became limiting, too, in feed-grade LPCs. This may be due to the lowering in tryptophan availability. From all the essential amino acids, lysine and threonine were pointed out by Lund (1973) as the most heat labile, but it was shown by Meredith *et al.* (1974) that during processing, histidine, threonine, and valine also are subject to an even higher degree of degradation than are methionine and lysine. Wallace (1973), however, indicated that processed protein products tend to be limiting by the sulfur amino acids rather than by lysine and so damage to the sulfur amino acids and supplementation with these is generally more significant than damage to lysine and supplementation with lysine. The results presented in Table 15.4 would indicate that

TABLE 15.4. NUTRITIONAL CHARACTERISTICS OF LPC OBTAINED FROM PASTURE HERBAGE PROCESSED ALTERNATIVELY WITHOUT OR WITH FRACTIONATION INTO CONCENTRATES OF FEED- AND FOOD-GRADE PRODUCTS USING DIFFERENT PROCESSING AND FRACTIONATION TECHNIQUES

	Protein Concentrate from Pasture Herbage[1]				
	Heat Precipitation			Membrane Filtration	
		Fraction			
Measurement[1]	Without Fractionation (85°C)	Chloroplastic (55°C)	Cytoplasmic (55°/85°C)	Without Fractionation	Cytoplasmic Fraction
Protein Concentrate (Grade)	Feed	Feed	Food	Feed	Food
Protein digestibility (%)					
in vivo	73	71	80	78	82
in vitro	85	78	84	80	93
Availability (%)					
lysine	77	73	82	81	86
methionine	82	80	81	85	91
tryptophan	78	75	80	72	94
Protein Efficiency Ratio (PER)[2]					
LPC supplemented with DL-methionine (0.2%)	1.4	1.1	2.0	2.2	2.6
LPC supplemented with DL-methionine (0.2%) and L-lysine (0.5%)	2.2	1.9	2.4	2.7	2.6
LPC supplemented with DL-methionine (0.2%), L-lysine (0.5%), and L-tryptophan (0.3%)	2.7	2.6	2.8	2.6	2.8

Source: Ostrowski-Meissner *et al.* (1980).
[1]Each value represents the mean from five processed herbages.
[2]Casein control group PER: 2.8; all groups of rats fed LPC without amino acid supplementation gave negative weight gains.

this is so. Fetuga *et al.* (1973), on the other hand, showed that apart from methionine, both lysine and tryptophan are the amino acids in shortest supply in most proteins of plant origin. However, both these amino acids in the analyzed LPCs were above the FAO (FAO/WHO 1965) amino acid standard.

In general, concentrations, of the essential amino acids, detected in LPCs—despite the technique used for their production—were in the range of concentrations as reported by Byers (1971B). Byers (1971A) reported, however, that the method of protein separation from juice may influence the amount of lysine in the final product. This influence was also distinctive in LPCs recovered by different methods in reference to lysine.

The total essential amino acids and microbiologically determined availability correspond with the nutritional value of LPCs measured in biological tests. A similar relationship between PER values and amino acid composition of LPCs was shown by Hansen and Eggum (1973) and Sikka *et al.* (1975), and between PER and lysine availability by Ostrowski-Meissner *et al.* (1972). However, chemically determined lysine availability showed large variation due to the method being used for availability determination (Table 15.5). Variation in availability was greater due to the method of determination within the analyzed protein concentrate rather than due to the technique used for protein recovery.

Both *in vivo* and *in vitro* digestibilities of both LPCs feed-grade obtained by different production procedures are in the range of values reported by

TABLE 15.5. AVAILABILITY OF LYSINE IN VARIOUS PROTEIN CONCENTRATES RECOVERED FROM PASTURE HERBAGE AS DETERMINED BY DIFFERENT CHEMICAL PROCEDURES

	Protein Concentrates (Grade)					
		Extracted from Herbage				
	Soybean Meal	Heat Precipitation			U/F[1]	
		85°C	55°C	55°/85°C	(A)	(B)
Measurement	Feed	Feed	Food	Food	Feed	Food
N × 6.25 (% DM)	44.6	42.5	41.2	57.4	46.8	52.0
Total lysine (mg/g)[2]	19.8	20.4	18.9	32.7	29.0	34.3
Lysine availability (%) as measured by method[3]						
FDNB-reactive lysine (direct method)	92	83	78	82	75	88
FDNB-reactive lysine (different method)	93	72	72	77	74	80
TNBS-reactive lysine (direct method)	94	79	75	81	79	86
Dye-binding method (Acid Orange 12)	105	117	122	110	108	103

Source: Ostrowski-Meissner *et al.* (1980).
[1]Ultrafiltration procedure using DIAFLO membrane: (A)—Without fractionation. (B)—Cytoplasmic fraction from juice after 55°C precipitation.
[2]As determined by short column chromatography.
[3]FDNB—Fluorodinitrobenzene. TNBS—Trinitrobenzene sulfonic acid.

Byers (1971B), Subba Rau *et al.* (1969, 1972), and Hartmann *et al.* (1967) to be satisfactory for such a type of product, but lower than those reported by Akeson and Stahmann (1965) and Saunders *et al.*(1973). Digestibilities *in vitro*, however, when determined in various experimental conditions, were substantially higher with longer duration of the digestion and/or with higher enzyme concentrations (Table 15.6).

Irrespective of the type of enzyme and its concentration, one- or two-step digestion procedure, and the duration of the digestion, the protein digestibilities in ultrafiltered LPC—food-grades were similar to those recorded with LPC precipitated at 85°C. Protein digestibilities in ultrafiltered concentrate determined at both lower enzyme concentrations and shorter digestion durations were slightly higher than in heat-coagulated LPC.

ULTRAFILTRATION SYSTEMS FOR CONCENTRATION OF PROTEINS FROM PASTURE HERBAGE WITHOUT FRACTIONATION

The efficiency of the three commercial ultrafiltration modules (Table 15.7) measured by the ultrafiltrate flux (permeation rate) as a result of the increase in juice DM content, showed the Romicon PM-50 hollow fiber system as the most effective at the range of low juice DM concentrations (Fig. 15.6) with notably lower ultrafiltrate fluxes at DDS-500 UF module (Fig. 15.7) and the lowest fluxes recorded with Abcor HFA-180 module (Fig. 15.8). With an increase in juice DM to approximately 5% with the DDS module and to approximately 8% with Romicon hollow fiber cartridge, a rapid decrease in the permeation rate occurs which is followed by unrecoverable blockage (clogging) of both of the modules at ranges of 9.7 and 12%, respectively. The Abcor tubular membrane is not subject to the blockage and the gradual decrease in permeate fluxes is recorded up to the level of approximately 25% DM, i.e., until ultrafiltrated concentrate is stopped in its recirculation in the system due to excessive juice thickening.

The degree of both total (TN) and protein nitrogen (PN) concentrations which was related both to DM content in the concentrated herbage juice and to the ultrafiltrate flux indicates that, despite the UF system, a gradual and steady increase in gradient of protein concentration accrues until approximately 6% TN in concentrated DM. In using the Abcor system within the range of approximately 17 to 24% DM during the ultrafiltration process, a rapid increase in both TN and PN concentration is observed while the other two systems cannot operate due to membrane blockage. The concentration of the TN beyond the limit of 6% DM was below the permeation rate acceptable as satisfactory in plant-scale operation. With the progress in herbage juice concentration, notable changes occurred in the ratio of TN to PN. More protein nitrogen remained in the ultrafiltrated concentrate, with the nonprotein nitrogen being removed with the permeate from the concentrate during the UF procedure. The chemical composition and yields of the protein concentrates obtained as a result of juice concentration to the extent when permeate fluxed decreased below 10 liters m^{-2} hr^{-1} are given in Table 15.8.

TABLE 15.6. THE EFFECT OF THE TYPE AND QUANTITY OF ENZYME USED IN THE *IN VITRO* DIGESTION PROCEDURES USING TWO DIGESTION LENGTH INTERVALS ON PROTEIN DIGESTIBILITY OF HEAT-COAGULATED AND ULTRAFILTERED LPCs—FOOD-GRADE

	One-step Digestion						Two-step Digestion					
	Papain			Pepsin			Pepsin/Trypsin			Pepsin/Pancreatin		
		% Digestibility			% Digestibility			% Digestibility			% Digestibility	
Duration of Digestion	mg	55°/85°C	UF	mg	55°/85°C	UF	mg	55°/85°C	UF	mg	55°/85°C	UF
12 hr	1	77	80	1	94	95	5/5	95	96	1/4	96	96
	10	93	93	10	95	95	10/5	96	96	2.5/4	97	97
24 hr	1	80	85	1	95	95	5/5	96	96	1/4	97	97
	10	97	97	10	95	96	10/5	96	97	2.5/4	97	99

Source: Ostrowski-Meissner *et al.* (1980).
UF—Ultrafiltration.

TABLE 15.7. CHARACTERISTICS OF ULTRAFILTRATION MEMBRANES USED IN THE PLANT-SCALE PROTEIN CONCENTRATION AND PROTEIN FRACTIONATION FROM PASTURE HERBAGE

Membrane	Type	Nominal MW Cutoff	Characteristics
Abcor	HFA-180 (polyethylene)	20,000	tubular membrane
DDS-500	DDS-500 plate membrane (cellulose acetate)	65,000	plate membrane
Romicon	HF 30-20-XM-50 (polysulfonate)	50,000	hollow fiber cartridge
Romicon	HF 30-20-XM-10 (polysulfonate)	10,000	hollow fiber cartridge

Source: Ostrowski-Meissner (1976D).

Knuckles *et al.* (1975) and Singh *et al.* (1974) showed the levels of 5.5% protein in alfalfa juice and 7 to 8%, respectively, as critical for the ultrafiltration efficiency. Exceeding these levels caused a rapid decrease in the permeation rate with a simultaneous decrease in the rate of protein concentration. The decrease in permeate fluxes as observed with the three different systems as shown in Fig. 15.6, 15.7, and 15.8 may be ascribed to a

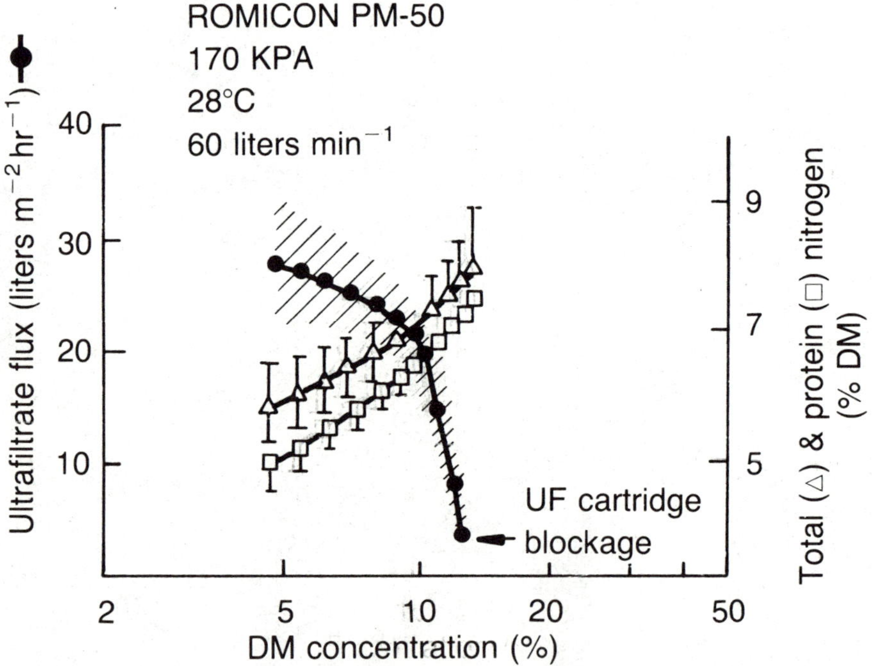

Fig. 15.6. Variation in ultrafiltrate fluxes with concentration of herbage juice using Romicon PM-50 (5×10^4 MW nominal cutoff) hollow fiber cartridge (mean ± S.E.), and gradient of total and protein concentration.

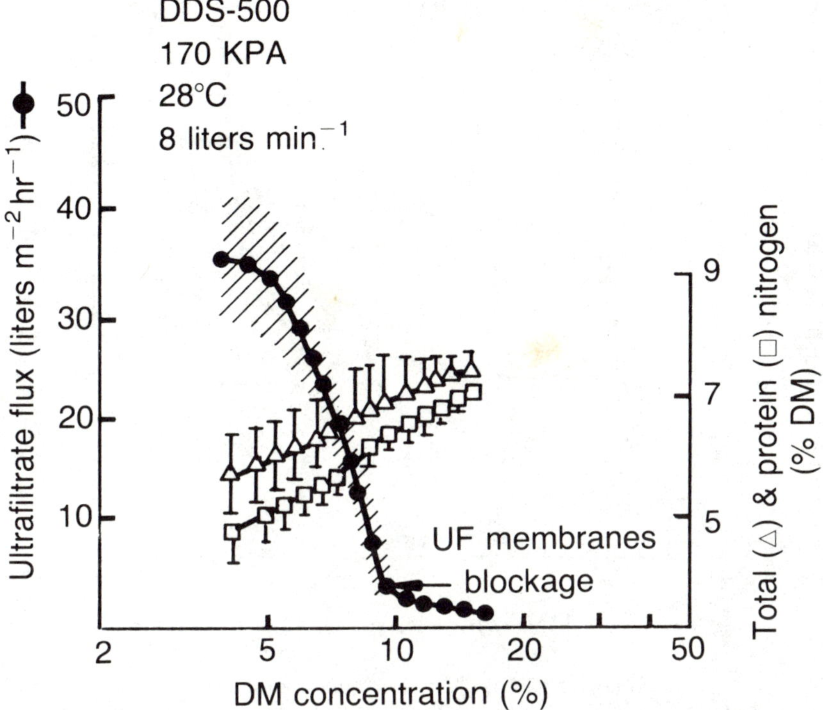

Fig. 15.7. Variation in ultrafiltrate fluxes with concentration of herbage juice using DDS-500 (5.8×10^4 MW nominal cutoff) membrane (mean ± S.E.), and gradient of total and protein nitrogen concentration.

number of factors reported in the literature (Horton 1973; Payne *et al.* 1973; Singh *et al.* 1974). The most obvious factors reported by Porter and Michaelis (1971) are the increase in viscosity of the concentrated proteinaceous material and protein-gel formation on the membrane's surface.

It appears from the results presented so far that the most efficient ultrafiltration procedure takes place with juices of low DM content. Thus, to obtain a high degree of protein nitrogen concentration and the high protein concentration rate, the "Hold-Up-Volume" UF system is recommended. In such a system a constant volume of processed herbage juice is maintained by water addition during the UF processed resulting in a constant volume of low DM juice recirculating through the UF plant from which sugars and ash are gradually rejected, causing gradual concentration and purification of herbage proteins. Horton (1973) reported that, using this system, the crude protein concentration achieved with ultrafiltration of proteins was as high as 80–82% in concentrate of 30% DM. With the addition of water to equate the volume of permeate being passed through the UF membrane, the Romicon hollow fiber cartridge could be used for efficient protein concentra-

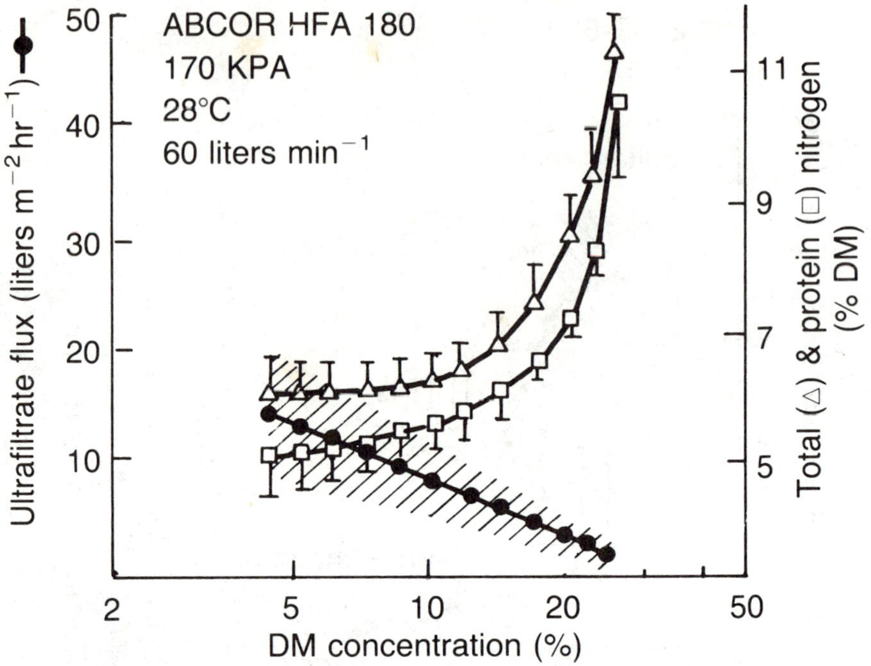

Fig. 15.8. Variation in ultrafiltrate fluxes with concentration of herbage juice Abcor HFA-180 (2×10^4 MW nominal cutoff) membrane (mean ± S.E.), and gradient of total and protein nitrogen concentration.

TABLE 15.8. CHEMICAL COMPOSITION OF THE HERBAGE PROTEIN CONCENTRATES OBTAINED BY ULTRAFILTRATION PROCEDURE WITH THE USE OF THE THREE ULTRAFILTRATION SYSTEMS

Ultrafiltration System (Membrane Type)	Yield of LPC from 100 Liters of Juice[1] (kg DM)	Composition (% DM)[2]			
		Total Nitrogen (TN)	Protein Nitrogen (PN)	Total Ash	Soluble Sugars
Abcor (2×10^4 MW)	7.72a[3]	6.16b	5.49bB	24.1aA	19.3aA
Romicon (5×10^4 MW)	7.24a	6.57ab	6.08abAB	18.5bAB	12.8bB
DDS (6.5×10^4 MW)	7.01a	7.53a	7.06aA	12.3aA	11.4bB
S.E.(d)[4]	0.21	0.38	0.31	1.74	1.33
(N = 7) Significance	*	*	**	**	**

Source: Ostrowski-Meissner (1976D).

[1]Juice of the average composition (%): DM = 7.02, TN = 0.384, and PN = 0.344.

[2]The composition of the concentrate as recovered after juice concentration to the degree in which permeate fluxes decreased below 10 liters $m^{-2}hr^{-1}$.

[3]Values with unlike letters following differ statistically (P = 0.05 = small letters and P = 0.01 = capital letters) according to multiple Duncan's test.

[4]S.E.(d)—Standard error of the mean difference. *—Significance at P = 0.05 level. **—Significance at P = 0.01 level.

tion and purification from sugars and ash followed by secondary concentration (dewatering) in the Abcor UF tubular system, up to approximately 20% DM content, before the final spray- or freeze-drying. In such a system, the DDS membrane module and the Romicon hollow fiber system would be prevented from clogging (blockage) occurring with these two systems during batch-type herbage juice concentration.

FRACTIONATION OF HERBAGE PROTEINS BY ACID/STEAM COAGULATION AND ULTRAFILTRATION

Of the total recoverable proteins, approximately one-third to one-quarter was represented by cytoplasmic protein fraction (white cream one) which has been shown by Pirie (1971), Oke (1973), and Parrish *et al.* (1974) to be suitable for human nutrition. While there are no consistent differences in yield and chemical composition of LPCs due to the system used for protein separation, i.e., Romicon UF or acid/heat coagulation (see Table 15.1) there is a notable difference in yields of the UF cytoplastic fraction as obtained by the use of Abcor or Romicon PM-10 system. The latter gives a bigger yield of LPC of higher nitrogen concentration than the Abcor system.

As opposed to Abcor, the Romicon PM-10 hollow fiber system appeared to be much more efficient for cytoplasmic protein fraction concentration and separation from the chloroplastic-free supernatant from which chloroplastic proteins were removed by centrifugation of the raw herbage juice previously heated up to 55°C (Fig. 15.9). Also, nitrogen concentration in the cytoplasmic fraction is much faster with the Romicon PM-10 cartridge than with the Abcor unit (Fig. 15.10). These two UF units have different physical characteristics which can explain the differences in the UF efficiency. While the Romicon cartridge has a nominal 1×10^4 MW cutoff membrane, the Abcor membranes represent 2×10^4 MW nominal cutoff level. Singh *et al.* (1974) and Knuckles *et al.* (1975), who used membrancs with different molecular weight cutoff values for cytoplastic protein isolation from alfalfa, also showed higher retention values for membranes with the lower MW cutoff characteristics.

The reason for high performance with chloroplastic-free juice of the Romicon PM-10 hollow fiber system as compared with Romicon PM-50 used for protein recovery from juice without fractionation is the low DM content in the chloroplast-free juice (2.6 to 3.5%) which does not cause a membrane clogging problem (even by 19% DM), as opposed to the whole juice, generally of a much higher initial DM content (4–11%).

No attempt has been made to determine the economics of the ultrafiltration procedure, in its application either to whole grass processing or to the cytoplastic protein fraction concentration. At this stage, it is extremely difficult to conclude whether the UF procedure would be a viable means of concentrating and purifying herbage proteins in large-scale operations for protein concentrate production. Much research has yet to be done on a

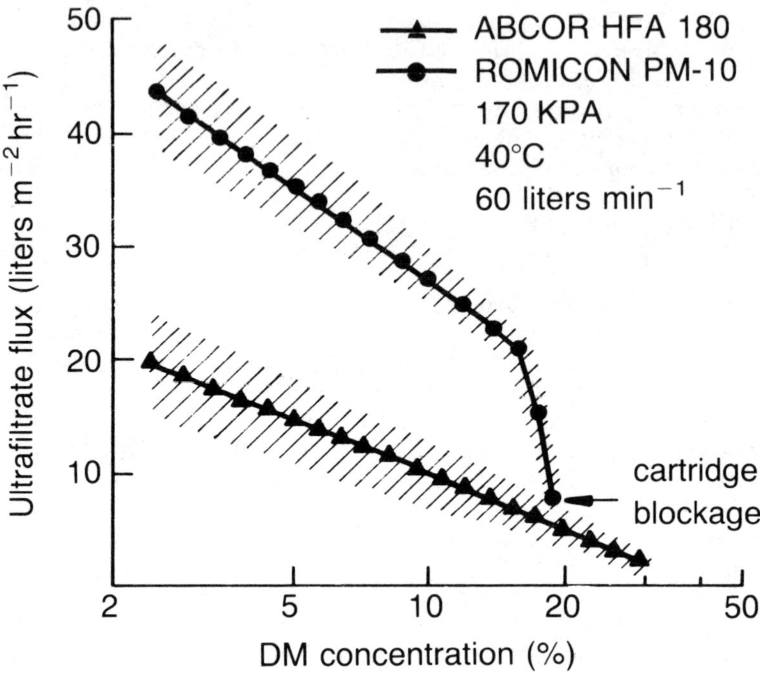

Fig. 15.9. Variation in flux rates with dry matter concentration in chloroplast-free herbage juice (centrate from heat precipitation at 55°C) using either Abcor HFA-180 membrane or Romicon PM-10 hollow fiber cartridge.

variety of herbage juices obtained from different pastures of various botanical compositions and grown during different seasons of the year. It has been observed, for example, that juice extracted from Tama ryegrass grown during the winter season is of very high DM content (13 to 14%) and of high viscosity, and that ultrafiltration of such juice results in extremely low permeate flux rates (2 to 5 liters m^{-2} h^{-1}). However, after juice pretreatment (freezing and thawing; mixing with water; pH changes, etc.), the ultrafiltration rate was similar to that observed with low DM (5–6%) juices.

Ultrafiltration of the chloroplast-free protein fraction appeared to be a very efficient process, despite the UF system used, with Romicon PM-10 hollow fiber system being superior to the Abcor HFA-180 one. The spray-dried product obtained from the UF procedure was water-soluble (dispersible) and reconstituted easily and readily. Knuckles *et al.* (1975), Singh *et al.* (1974), and Tragardh (1974) also found the UF technique to be the most interesting with regard to cytoplastic protein separation and concentration as an unconventional protein source for human consumption.

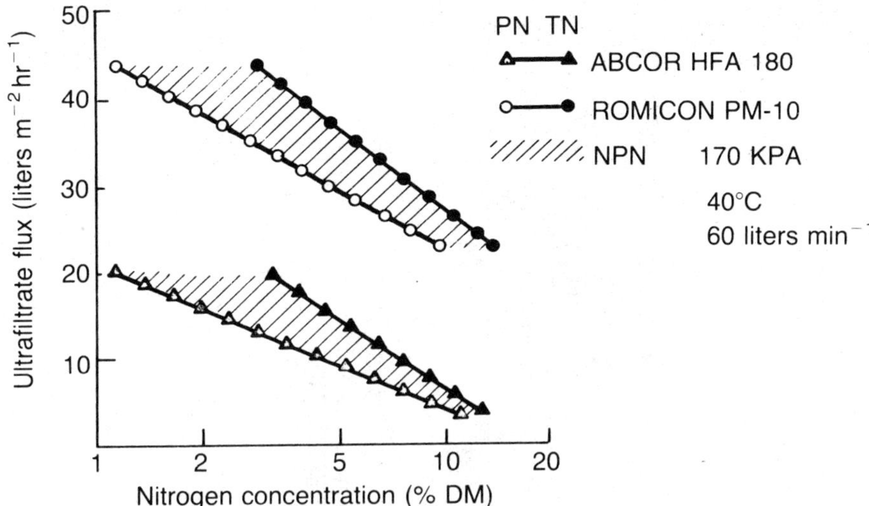

Fig. 15.10. Relationship between ultrafiltrate fluxes and the degree of total and protein nitrogen concentration in chloroplast-free herbage juice using either Abcor HFA-180 membrane or Romicon PM-10 hollow fiber cartridge.

However, there are a number of factors affecting the ultrafiltration process (Horton 1973; Payne *et al.* 1973; Singh *et al.* 1974) which may alter efficiency of the commercial ultrafiltration procedure with the herbage juice.

SOME FACTORS AFFECTING HERBAGE JUICE ULTRAFILTRATION EFFICIENCY

The effect of some factors which alter the efficiency of protein extraction was investigated in batch concentration procedures in relation to average permeate flow rate, volume, DM, and total nitrogen concentration factors, as well as efficiency of protein (protein N × 6.25) recovery.

Temperature

There is a highly significant increase in the speed of ultrafiltration as measured by the permeate flow rate with the rise in average temperature of the UF grass juice from 20°C to 38°C (Table 15.9). The increase in the temperature of the UF is generally known as a factor improving the rate of the UF procedure (Horton 1973; Payne *et al.* 1973). By ultrafiltration of the juice at 38°C, just below the protein precipitation range, nearly twice as much juice could be concentrated as compared with the procedure running at 20°C.

TABLE 15.9. CONCENTRATION OF HERBAGE PROTEINS USING FOUR HFA-180 ABCOR UF MEMBRANES AS AN EFFECT OF UF TEMPERATURE
Feed flow rate—60 liters/min. Pressure—170 kPa.

Measurement Temperature	Average Permeate Flow Rate (Liters $m^{-2}hr^{-1}$)	Volume Concentration Factor	Dry Matter (%)		DM Concentration Ratio	Total Nitrogen (% DM)		Protein Recovery Efficiency[1] (%)
			Feed (Juice)	Concentrate		Feed (Juice)	Concentrate	
20°C	12	4.3	6.1	20.4	3.3	5.76	6.07	24.8
40°C	21	4.3		21.3	3.5		6.62	24.4
S.E.(d)[2]	0.11	—		0.97	0.24		0.44	0.3
(N = 6) Significance	***			NS	NS		**	NS

Source: Ostrowski-Meissner (1976D).

[1]In this and subsequent tables: Protein Recovery Efficiency (%) = $\frac{\text{(protein nitrogen in juice} \times 100)}{\text{(protein nitrogen in final concentrate)}}$

[2]S.E.(d)—Standard error of the mean difference. **—Significance at P = 0.01 level. ***—Significance at P = 0.001 level. NS—Not significant.

Recirculation Rate

An increase in the recirculation rate from 30 to 60 liters min^{-1} (without increasing the pressure) resulted in a significant rise in the average permeate rate and efficiency of protein recovery (Table 15.10) without affecting either the DM and/or the TN concentration in the final product. An increase in the permeate flux rate with the recirculation rate has a well-established relationship in the UF procedure and is related to the influence of concentration polarization and the problem of the gel layer formation on the UF membrane surface (Payne *et al.* 1973). An increase in the recirculation rate results in a substantial increase of UF efficiency, a factor which was also shown by Knuckles *et al.* (1975) in reference to alfalfa juice.

Pressure

An increase in pressure during the UF procedure resulted in an increased permeation flow rate with a simultaneous increase in both DM concentration and protein recovery, with the TN concentration not being affected by the pressure (Table 15.11). The increase in UF efficiency due to higher pressure during the UF procedure was also reported by Horton (1973), Payne *et al.* (1973), and Singh *et al.* (1974). This is also connected with the problem of the protein gel layer or "cake" on the membrane surface thickening with the increase in pressure. Thus, it is important to adjust the recirculation rate in parallel with the pressure applied on the UF membrane. According to Horton (1973), it is necessary to optimize simultaneously the recirculation rate and pressure, which are both functions of the changeable viscosity of the gradually concentrated material and thus variable in every stage of the UF procedure.

Degree of Volume Concentration

The higher the volume concentration, then the more the permeate flow rate is significantly reduced (Table 15.12), together with simultaneous significant increases in DM, TN, concentration, and efficiency of protein recovery. Singh *et al.* (1974) reported a similar tendency in reference to alfalfa juice.

pH

A slight decrease in the grass juice pH—from original 6.2 to 5.5—meant a significant increase in the rate of UF process. This was accompanied by a lowering in the degree of DM concentration with a simultaneous significant increase in both the degree of TN concentration and the efficiency of protein recovery (Table 15.13). Horton (1973) reported that change in the pH of the UF material (whey) increases flux without any other real benefits experienced elsewhere. He emphasized, however, that the one most variable and peculiar factor within the UF is pH, and that its effect on the UF procedure can be quite dramatic (Horton 1973).

TABLE 15.10. CONCENTRATION OF HERBAGE PROTEINS USING FOUR HFA-180 ABCOR UF MEMBRANES AS AN EFFECT OF RECIRCULATION RATE
Temperature—28°C. Pressure—170 kPa.

Measurement Recirculation Rate (Liters/min)	Average Permeate Flow Rate (Liters $m^{-2}hr^{-1}$)	Volume Concentration Factor	Dry Matter (%)		DM Concentration Ratio	Total Nitrogen (% DM)		Protein Recovery Efficiency[1]
			Feed (Juice)	Concentrate		Feed (Juice)	Concentrate	
30	27	2.7	5.8	13.0	2	5.44	5.95	11.6
60	48.3	2.7		12.8	2		5.97	14.8
S.E.(d)	4.1	—		0.1			0.02	0.9
(N = 6) Significance	**			NS			NS	*

[1]See Table 15.9.

TABLE 15.11. CONCENTRATION OF HERBAGE PROTEINS USING FOUR HFA-180 ABCOR UF MEMBRANES AS AN EFFECT OF AVERAGE PRESSURE IN THE UF TUBES
Temperature—28°C. Flow rate—60 liters/min.

Measurement Pressure (kPa)	Average Permeate Flow Rate (Liters $m^{-2}hr^{-1}$)	Volume Concentration Factor	Dry Matter (%)		DM Concentration Ratio	Total Nitrogen (% DM)		Protein Recovery Efficiency[1]
			Feed (Juice)	Concentrate		Feed (Juice)	Concentration	
85	23	1.9	8.3	13.4	1	5.28	5.77	12.7
170	31	1.9		14.2	1		5.81	15.3
S.E.(d)	1.8	—		0.08	0		0.02	0.77
(N = 5) Significance	**			**			NS	*

[1]See Table 15.9.

TABLE 15.12. CONCENTRATION OF HERBAGE PROTEINS USING FOUR HFA-180 ABCOR UF MEMBRANES AS AN EFFECT OF DEGREE OF CONCENTRATION

Temperature—28°C. Flow rate—60 liters/min. Pressure—170 kPa.

Measurement Volume Concentration	Average Permeate Flow Rate (Liters $m^{-2}hr^{-1}$)	Volume Concentration Factor	Dry Matter (%)		DM Concentration Ratio	Total Nitrogen (% DM)		Protein Recovery Efficiency[1]
			Feed (Juice)	Concentrate		Feed (Juice)	Concentration	
4-fold	21	4.3	6.1	21.3	3.5	5.76	6.62	24.4
6-fold	14	5.8		24.6	4.3		7.40	33.1
S.E.(d)								
(N = 6) Significance	**	—		*	**		**	**

[1]See Table 15.9.

TABLE 15.13. CONCENTRATION OF HERBAGE PROTEINS USING FOUR HFA-180 ABCOR UF MEMBRANES AS AN EFFECT OF JUICE pH

Temperature—28°C. Flow rate—60 liters/min. Pressure—170 kPa.

pH	Average Permeate Flow Rate (Liters $m^{-2}hr^{-1}$)	Volume Concentration Factor	Dry Matter (%)		DM Concentration Ratio	Total Nitrogen (% DM)		Protein Recovery Efficiency[1]
			Feed (Juice)	Concentrate		Feed (Juice)	Concentrate	
6.2	31	1.9	8.3	14.2	1	5.28	5.81	15.3
5.5	45	1.9		13.4	1		6.12	19.6
S.E.(d)	2.2			0.17			0.07	0.9
(N = 5) Significance	**	—		*			*	**

[1]See Table 15.9.

TABLE 15.14. CONCENTRATION OF MEMBRANE PROTEIN USING FOUR HFA-180 ABCOR UF MEMBRANES AS AN EFFECT OF THE SIZE OF THE UF PLANT

Temperature—28°C. Recirculation rate—60 liters/min. Pressure—170 kPa.

Size of the UF Plant (No. of Tubes)	Average Permeate Flow Rate (Liters $m^{-2}hr^{-1}$)	Volume Concentration Factor	Dry Matter (%)		DM Concentration Ratio	Total Nitrogen (%) DM		Protein Recovery Efficiency[1]
			Feed (Juice)	Concentrate		Feed (Juice)	Concentrate	
4	48.3	2.7	5.8	12.8	2	5.44	5.97	14.8
10	46.1	2.7		13.2	2		5.93	14.4
S.E.(d)	1.6			0.2			0.02	0.4
(N = 6) Significance	NS	—		NS			NS	NS

[1]See Table 15.9.

Size of the UF Plant

An increase in the number of UF tubes connected in line from 4 to 10 does not result in any significant change in the efficiency of the UF process (Table 15.14) as calculated on the standard UF section size basis. Thus the size of the plant is linearly related to the volume of the juice in the batch being processed within the standard time unit.

Further experiments are in progress to determine the differences in the efficiency of protein extraction and fractionation as a result of different herbage species growing in mixed pasture sward and/or pure legumes and other crops growing as monocultures.

ACKNOWLEDGMENTS

The author acknowledges the receipt of a Research Fellowship from the New Zealand National Research Advisory Council, which enabled him to undertake this research in the Ruakura Research Centre in New Zealand, and also a Research Grant from the Bendigo College of Advanced Education, Victoria, Australia, where research was completed.

Appreciation is also expressed to Dr. Sanderson and Dr. Marshall, both from DRI, Palmerston North (N.Z.), for giving the opportunity to use their equipment for ultrafiltration and spray-drying at the initial stage of the project, and also Mr. M. Parkin of the same institute for his help and cooperation during practical operations of the UF plant. The author is grateful also to Mr. R. Dive of Chemac Laboratories, Auckland, N.Z., for his assistance and generous help when dealing with electrophoretic separations of proteins and amino acids.

REFERENCES

AKESON, W.R. and STAHMANN, M.A. 1965. Nutritive value of leaf protein concentrate, an *in vitro* digestion study. Agric. Food Chem. *13*, 145–148.

BYERS, M. 1971A. The amino acid composition and *in vitro* digestibility of some protein fractions from three species of leaves of various ages. J. Sci. Food Agric. *22*, 242–247.

BYERS, M. 1971B. The amino acid composition of some leaf protein preparations. *In* Leaf Protein: Its Agronomy, Preparation, Quality and Use. IBP Handb. 20. N.W. Pirie (Editor). Blackwell's Scientific Publication, Oxford.

FAO-WHO. 1965. Joint Expert Group on Protein Requirements. FAO Nutr. Meet. Rep. Ser. *37*. Food Agric. Organ. U.N., Rome.

FETUGA, B.L., BABATUNDE, G.M. and OYENUGA, V.A. 1973. Protein quality of some Nigerian feedstuffs. II. Biological evaluation or protein quality. J. Sci. Food Agric. *24*, 1505–1514.

FREE, B.L. and SATTERLEE, L.D. 1975. Biochemical properties of alfalfa protein concentrate. J. Food Sci. *40*, 85–89.

HANSEN, N.G. and EGGUM, B.O. 1973. The biological value of proteins estimated from amino acid analysis. Acta Agric. Scand. *23*, 247–251.

HARTMANN, G.H., JR., AKESON, W.R. and STAHMANN, M.A. 1967. Leaf protein concentrate prepared by spray drying. J. Agric. Food Chem. *15*, 74–79.

HORTON, B.S. 1973. Experiences with ultrafiltration in the Dairy Industry. Pap. presented Scientific Int. Dairy Fed. (IDF) Symp. Dairy Effluent Treatment, Kollekolle, Denmark, May 1973.

KNUCKLES, B.E., DE FREMERY, D., BICKOFF, E.M. and KOHLER, G.O. 1975. Soluble protein from alfalfa juice by membrane filtrations. J. Agric. Food Chem. *23*, 209–212.

LUND, D.B. 1973. Effects of food processing. Food Technol. *27*. (Jan.) 16–18.

MEREDITH, F.I., GASKINS, M.H. and DULL, G.G. 1974. Amino acid losses in turnip greens during handling and processing. J. Food Sci. *39*, 689–691.

OKE, O.L. 1973. Leaf protein research in Nigeria: A review. Trop. Sci. *15*, 139–155.

OSTROWSKI-MEISSNER, H.T. 1975. Concentration of grass proteins by ultrafiltration and reverse osmosis. *In* Leaf Protein Concentrate (New Zealand Scene). G.M. Wallace (Editor). Ruakura Agric. Res. Centre Publication, Palmerston North, Hamilton, New Zealand.

OSTROWSKI-MEISSNER, H.T. 1976A. Pasture production in protein extraction system. Proc. N.Z. Soc. Anim. Prod. *36*, 31–41.

OSTROWSKI-MEISSNER, H.T. 1976B. Protein extraction from pastures in temperate regions—Present and potential capabilities. Proc. 1st Int. Congr. Eng. Food, Boston, Aug. 1976.

OSTROWSKI-MEISSNER, H.T. 1976C. Ultrafiltration as a method for recovery of proteins from grass—Their fractionation and purification. Proc. 1st Int. Congr. Eng. Food, Boston, Aug. 1976.

OSTROWSKI-MEISSNER, H.T. 1976D. Final Report on the Research on Protein Extraction from Pastures, 1973 to 1976. (Relevant papers.) Final Rep. N.Z. Res. Advisory Counc. Res. Fellowship. Ruakura Research Centre, Hamilton, New Zealand.

OSTROWSKI-MEISSNER, H.T. 1978A. Protein extraction from herbage: New development and its potential. Proc. 3rd Conf. Sci. Technol., Aust. N.Z. Assoc. Adv. Sci. (ANZAAS), Canberra, May 1978.

OSTROWSKI-MEISSNER, H.T. 1978B. Fractionation of chloroplast-free proteins from herbage for human consumption. Proc. 3rd Conf. Sci. Technol., Aust. N.Z. Assoc. Adv. Sci. (ANZAAS), Canberra, May 1978.

OSTROWSKI-MEISSNER, H.T. 1978C. Protein extraction from pasture: A new concept in efficient dairy farming in temperature and sub-tropical regions. Proc. 4th World Conf. Anim. Prod., Buenos Aires, Augs. 1978.

OSTROWSKI-MEISSNER, H.T. 1979A. Membrane filtration for isolation, fractionation and purification of food- and feed-grade proteins from pasture herbage. J. Food Processing Preserv. *3*, 59–84.

OSTROWSKI-MEISSNER, H.T. 1979C. Protein extraction from grasslands. Sci. Technol. *16*, 4–11.

OSTROWSKI-MEISSNER, H.T., MORSTIN, E. and KOSCINSKA, A. 1972. A comparison of nutritional value of feed mixtures for pigs in experiments on rats and pigs. Zesz. Probl. Postepow Nauk Roln. *126*, 143–149. (Polish)

OSTROWSKI-MEISSNER, H.T. 1980A. Quantities and qualities of protein extracted from pasture herbage using heat precipitation or ultrafiltration procedures. J. Sci. Food Agric. *31*, 177–187.

OSTROWSKI-MEISSNER, H.T. 1980B. Protein degradation in herbage extract during membrane filtration process: The effect of reducing agents addition. Food Processing Preser. *4*, 261–279.

OSTROWSKI-MEISSNER, H.T. 1980C. Quantities and quality of protein extracted from pasture herbage using heat precipitation or ultrafiltration procedures. J. Sci. Food Agric. *31*, 177–187.

OSTROWSKI-MEISSNER, H.T., CARLSON, R. and TRAGARDH, C. 1980. Isolation and purification of proteins from green vegetation for direct human consumption. *In* Food Process Engineering. P. Linko, Y Maiki, and J. Olkku (Editors). Applied Science Publisher, London.

PARRISH, G.K., KROGER, M. and WEAVER, J.C. 1974. The prospects of leaf protein as a human food and a close look at alfalfa. Crit. Rev. Food Technol. *5*, 1–13.

PAYNE, R.E., HILL, C.G. and AMUNDSEN, C.H. 1973. Concentrations of egg white by ultrafiltration. J. Milk Food Technol. *36*: (7) 359–363.

PIRIE, N.W. 1971. Leaf Protein: Its Agronomy, Preparation, Quality and Use. IBP Handb. *20*. Blackwell's Scientific Publishers, Oxford.

PORTER, M.C. and MICHAELS, A.S. 1971. Membrane ultrafiltration. Chem. Technol. *1*, 56–63.

SAUNDERS, R.M., CONNOR, M.A., BOOTH, A.N., BICKOFF, E.M. and KOHLER, G.O. 1973. Measurement of digestibility of alfalfa protein concentrates by in vivo and in vitro methods. J. Nutr. *103*, 530–535.

SIKKA, K.A., JOHARI, R.P., DUGGAL, S.K., AHUJA, V.P. and AUSTIN, A. 1975. Comparative nutritive value and amino acid content of different extractions of wheat. J. Agric. Food Chem. *23*, 24–26.

SINGH, R., WHITNEY, L.F. and CHEN, C.S. 1974. Recovery of alfalfa protein by membrane ultrafiltration. Proc. Annu. Meet. Am. Soc. Agric. Eng., Oklahoma City, June 1974, Pap. *74-6003*.

SUBBA RAU, B.H., MAHADEVIAH, S. and SINGH, N. 1969. Nutritional studies on whole-extract coagulated leaf protein and fractionated chloroplastic and cytoplasmic proteins from lucerne. J. Sci. Food Agric. *20*, 355–358.

SUBBA RAU, B.H., RAMANA, V.R. and SINGH, N. 1972. Studies on nutritive value of leaf proteins and some factors affecting their quality. J. Sci. Food Agric. *23*, 233–245.

TRAGARDH, C.H. 1974. Productions of leaf protein concentrate for human consumption by isopropanol treatment. A comparison between untreated raw juice and raw juice concentrated by evaporation and ultrafiltration. Lebensm. Wiss. Technol. 7, (4) 199–201.

WALLACE, G.M. 1973. Nutrient loss during food processing. Food Technol. N.Z. *8* (Mar.) 11–12.

16

On-farm Forage Harvesting: Plant Juice Protein Production System in a Humid Temperate Climate[1]

H.W. Ream, N.A. Jorgensen, R.G. Koegel, and H.D. Bruhn

Forage harvesting in the humid areas of the world is a risky operation and often results in very high losses of forage dry matter and feed nutrients. Rain and poor drying weather, as well as a lack of satisfactory harvesting methods, have been the chief causes of poor preservation of forages in these areas where rainfall occurs frequently during harvest. Sometimes this results in complete loss of the harvest. It is estimated that field dry matter losses under present alfalfa harvesting methods in the humid midwestern United States amount to an average of 17% of the first crop (Hundtoft and Winkelblech 1966). In Wisconsin alone with alfalfa at $55.56 per metric ton (MT) [$50 per short ton (ST)] this represents an average annual loss of $37 million.

Direct harvesting and dehydration of forage by heat reduce these harvesting losses to 3% or less. However, research and experience in many countries have shown this method to be uneconomic. The present outlook on fuel cost and availability is particularly depressing in terms of further development. After many investigations of other methods, such as barn-drying forages with forced air, or pelleting, or wafering them, these countries have adopted silage making as the most practical method of minimizing losses in harvesting and preserving legume and grass forages; but even here losses are often substantial since the forage must be left in the field for at least

[1] A contribution from the Plant Juice Protein Team, Wisconsin Agricultural Experiment Station, Madison. Research supported by the College of Agricultural and Life Sciences, University of Wisconsin-Madison, by Hatch Proj. *7026* and the Research Committee of the Graduate School Proj. *140640* with funds supplied by the Wisconsin Alumni Research Foundation and by National Science Foundation Grants No. *AEN75-13078* and *AER-76-12339*.

one good drying day between cutting and storage to reduce moisture to a proper level for ensiling. Recent research at the University of Wisconsin has concentrated on development of a weather independent, on-farm forage harvesting system employing a fractionation process, involving maceration, juice expression, protein separation, and protein concentrate preservation, with the main product a pressed forage that can be directly ensiled, Fig. 16.1.

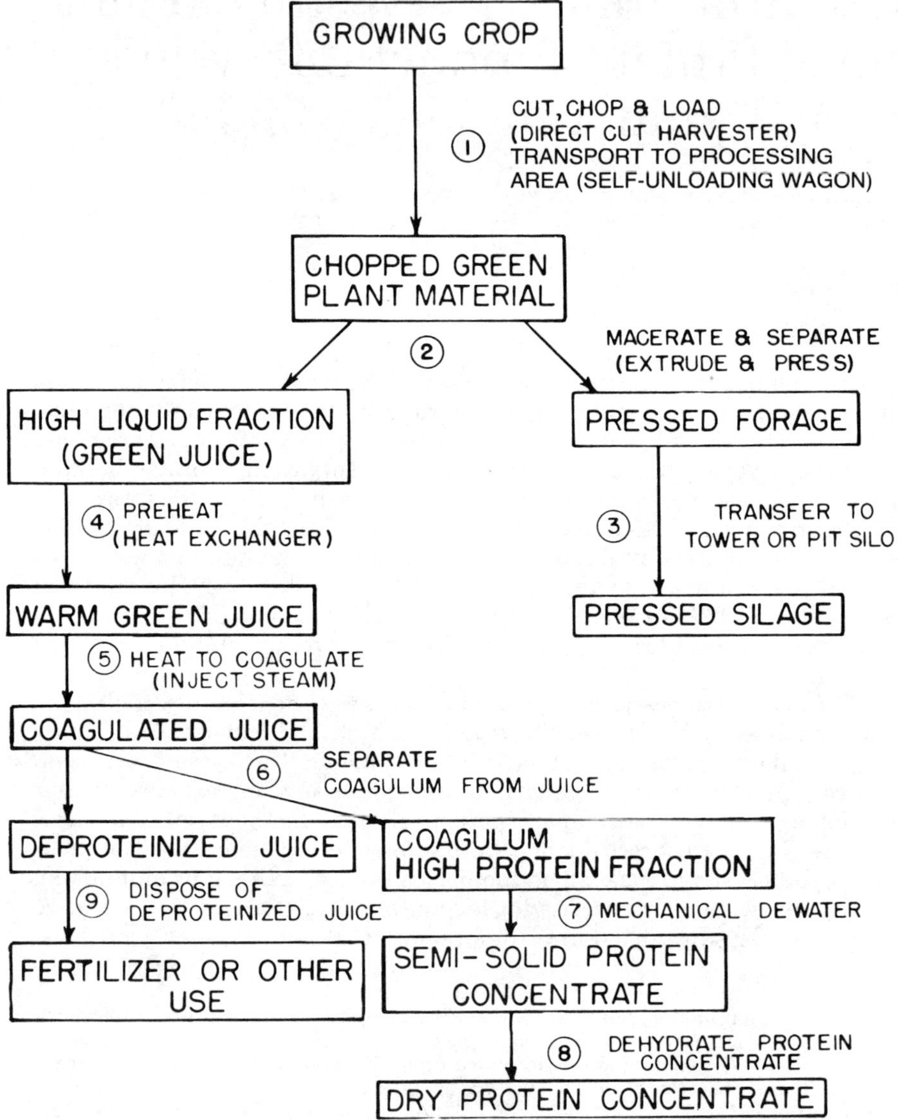

Fig. 16.1. On-farm forage harvesting—Plant juice protein production system.

The prime objective is a quick reduction in moisture content of the fresh green forage from the initial 80% range to approximately 65% moisture, wet basis (W.B.), which is a desirable moisture for proper fermentation in the silo (Hibbs *et al.* 1968).

By this direct harvesting system, field losses can be reduced to about 2% compared with losses of up to 35% or more when the crop is handled as baled hay. In addition, the process provides a weather independent harvesting system which will allow harvesting to be conducted at the proper times to ensure maximum nutrient yields, especially energy and protein. The pressed forage remains the major product and contains 70 to 75% of the original plant protein (15 to 17%, dry basis). This is generally higher than the protein content of stored forages because of overmaturity due to delays caused by bad weather conditions or actual weather damage. The maceration step (rupture of cells) may partially delignify the fiber and/or open the fibers to greater attack by the rumen bacteria which makes it more digestible by ruminants; thus, the nutrients extracted in the whole juice may serve as a bonus over and above the quantity of nutrients normally available in conventionally prepared forages. Research conducted on the various phases of this sytem and the results to date are presented in the following sections.

FIELD HARVESTING

Conventional field harvesters equipped with a cutter bar and either cylinder or flywheel chopping mechanisms are most satisfactory. The selection of this type of machine is based on low harvest field loss, minimum trash pickup, more uniform and controlled length of cut, and less severe bruising of the material than that resulting from flail cutter mechanisms. Crop bruising should be minimized to prevent excessive enzymatic action after chopping and prior to processing. Bruising and delay between chopping and processing reduce the protein quality and also make the separation of coagulated protein from brown juice more difficult. Well developed reliable commercial field forage harvesters meeting these established requirements are readily available.

Conventional self-unloading "chopper wagons" are satisfactory for transporting forage. The size selection may be based to some extent on the anticipated harvest rate. Wagons with a hauling capacity of 4.5–5.5 MT (5 or 6 ST) can be filled rapidly enough to prevent excessive enzymatic action while loading is in progress. A wide selection of good commercial self-unloading wagons with more than adequate unloading rates is available. The pertinent dimensions of these wagons are covered in ASAE Standards S328.1, ASAE Yearbook, page 355 (Am. Soc. Agric. Eng. 1977).

MACERATION

Feeding the forage into the macerator from the forage wagon is a first step in processing. The feeder mechanism should have a minimum capacity of 18 MT (20 ST) per hr with a possibility of future increases to 32 or 36

MT (35 or 40 ST) per hr. It should have a receiving hopper sufficiently low to accommodate the self-unloading wagons. These dimensions are provided in ASAE Standards S328.1 section on blower hopper dimensions, ASAE Yearbook, page 356 (Am. Soc. Agric. Eng. 1977).

To readily remove appreciable quantities of juice from plant material requires the rupturing of a large number of plant cells and can require the use of considerable energy (Koegel 1971; Koegel *et al.* 1973A,B; Pirie 1971). There are numerous means of rupturing plant cells, such as passing material between rolls, random chopping, chopping combined with random impact such as hammer mill action, abrasion combined with a pressure gradient applied by single or multiple screw presses, and pressure gradient applied by extrusion through a perforated plate.

Each of these mentioned devices is currently in use in some process either as a method of particle size reduction or moisture extraction (Koegel *et al.* 1973A,B). Many of the early investigators have provided excellent reports on power requirements in using various types of equipment in their experimental juice extraction activity. For background purposes, a few excerpts from these reports are quoted. In each case, for the convenience of the reader, the quoted energy requirement is also listed in both SI and English units.

(1) *Pirie's Pulper:* "One ton of crop per hour with the expenditure of 10–40 kWhr of energy" (40–160 kJ/kg or 14–54 hp hr/ton) (Pirie 1971).

(2) *Hungarian Process:* "A considerable amount of electrical energy is required in the disintegration procedure and in the separation of the raw material, in order to obtain two phases. The pilot plant production figures show that 45–55 kWhr of electricity are required to process one ton of green matter" (180–220 kJ/kg or 60–74 hp hr/ton) (Pirie 1971).

(3) *Screw Press or Hammermill-Roller Press Combination:* "McDonald found that the power consumption depended to some extent on the nature of the crop, but in general about 20 kWhr per ton of fresh crop were expended" (80 kJ/kg or 27 hp hr/ton) (Tilley and Raymond 1957).

(4) *Hammermill-Screw Press Combination:* "Tilley and Raymond (1957) reported less than 30 kW hr/ton for most crops using a hammermill followed by a screw expeller" (120 kJ/kg or 40 hp hr/ton).

The high energy requirement and wide discrepancy in the various reports indicated the need for basic study not only to discover the reason for the discrepancy but also to reduce the energy requirement to a level acceptable in an operation of commercial size.

Analysis of the fundamental process of cell rupture on an individual cell basis led to the theory that pressure gradient over the length of a cell resulted in rupture (Koegel *et al.* 1973B). This led to the theory of cell rupture or maceration by extrusion.

While the energy required in roller maceration of lucerne in research at the University of Wisconsin-Madison is comparable to that of some of the early investigators, 72 kJ per kg (24.6 hp hr/ST (Koegel *et al.* 1973B), the energy range for extrusion through perforated plates in laboratory apparatus varied from 16 kJ per kg (5.3 hp hr/ST) for a 6.4 mm (¼ in.) orifice to 7.7 kJ per kg (2.6 hp hr/ST) for a 12.7 mm (½ in.) orifice (Schirer 1973). A small rotary extruder equipped with a cylindrical die with a 12.7 mm (½ in.) orifice required 7.2 kJ per kg (2.4 hp hr/ST) at a rate of 2350 kg/hr (2.6 ST/hr) (Basken *et al.* 1975).

The energy input to a recently constructed experimental high capacity rotary macerator, at normal working capacity, 22,000 kg (24 ST) per hr, averaged well under 6 kJ per kg (2 hp hr/ST). Energy consumption for maceration probably cannot be reduced much below these values unless a lower degree of maceration is acceptable. With no throughput there is an energy requirement of about 7.0 kW (9.5 hp). As throughput is increased, energy required increases essentially as a linear function. In the working range the total energy requirement averages slightly under 6 kJ per kg (2 hp hr/ST). A larger orifice in the die ring would reduce both the energy requirements and the degree of maceration. Tests on juice and fiber separation equipment (presses) as well as dairy cattle feeding trials will indicate the advisability of more or less intensive maceration (Nelson 1977).

In view of what is known now, the high power requirements reported by early investigators appear to have resulted from using very inefficient equipment not suitable for the process, and this suggests the potential for progress in other phases.

JUICE EXTRACTION

Fundamental data on press design criteria for green plant fractionation are rapidly being made available. Early laboratory research indicated the energy of separation is minor compared to maceration (Koegel *et al.* 1973A).

The rate of juice expression from the macerated material has been shown to be dependent on the combination of pressing variables chosen. Time, pressure, and material thickness can be varied in numerous combinations to achieve the desired end result. Material thickness was shown to be the least important variable of these three. Laboratory studies indicate that the energy required for juice expression is less than 0.75 kJ/kg (0.25 hp hr/ST) if the expression is accomplished by pure compression (Koegel and Bruhn 1972). However, it has also been shown that reorientation of the plant material during the dewatering process can result in greater press throughput, but only at the expense of greater energy input. This increased energy appears prohibitive, except for very low rates of reorientation (Floyd *et al.* 1975).

Research using various press configurations has shown that the conventional roller press has low throughput relative to its size, high power consumption, and presents problems in separating the expressed liquid and incoming macerated forage. The screw press has better separation characteristics, but only at a very high expenditure of energy. Rotary presses with drainage through the pressing surfaces, such as the double cone or "vee" press, appear promising.

In the double cone press, material is compressed between the faces of perforated cones whose central axes are at an angle. This angle determines the degree of compression the material undergoes. Reorientation of the material being pressed is possible by driving the two cones at slightly different angular velocities. Preliminary data indicate power requirements of only 3.0 to 4.5 kJ/kg (1.0–1.5 hp hr/ST). A prototype press is being designed to press approximately 20 MT per hr. The press will be designed to allow changing the compression ratio, as well as the relative cone velocities so that their effects on juice expression rate may be evaluated and optimal operating conditions determined (Pitt *et al.* 1977).

PROTEIN SEPARATION

Protein separation has been accomplished primarily by heat coagulation at 80°C and flotation of the coagulum. Heating is accomplished by automatically metered steam injection into the whole juice (Straub and Bruhn 1975). The high energy cost associated with this has been reduced by approximately 50% by installation of a shell and tube heat exchanger for regenerative heating from the soluble fraction. Use of the heat exchanger requires extra precautions during operation and cleanup to prevent fouling problems. In order to prevent coagulation in the heat exchanger the temperature is monitored, and if it approaches 60°C, regenerative heating is automatically shut down. Following operation, an alkali wash is followed by an acid rinse to remove any fouling.

The heated juice is then run into a flotation trough where the protein floats to the surface and is skimmed off by a chain-driven paddle mechanism. Flotation has been successful in varying degrees for the crops processed, except for aquatic vegetation, which formed a very fine grained curd and did not all float. It has been found that injection of finely divided air into the juice as it is heated and into the flotation tank helps to alleviate separation problems when they occur, for example, when the alfalfa has had to stand for a long period of time between harvesting and processing.

After the coagulated protein has been skimmed from the flotation trough, it is drained on a vibratory screen to remove excess moisture. Laboratory studies have indicated that this coagulum probably can be mechanically dewatered from the 80% moisture level, as it leaves the vibratory screen, to less than 65% moisture. This would reduce to less than half the amount of moisture which needs to be dehydrated for preservation. Research has shown that very low pressure is required to dewater the protein curd, but material thickness must be kept low. A pressure of 34.5 kPa (5 psi) is sufficient if the material thickness is less than 1 kg dry matter/m^2 of screen area (Straub and Bruhn 1975). At present, the possibility of large-scale dewatering by direct pressure or vacuum dewatering is being explored.

Precipitation of plant juice protein by anaerobic fermentation of the whole juice is being studied as an alternative to heat coagulation. The bacteria normally resident on leaves and stems provide the inoculum for the fermentation. Experiments utilizing this method were carried on by Stahmann in the mid-1960s (Stahmann 1977). He was able to maintain fermented juice samples from many different plants in small sealed containers at room temperature for up to three or four years without appreciable spoilage. Recent experiments have been conducted utilizing large airtight tanks of from 303 to 3785 liters (80 to 1000 gal.) capacity.

Juice samples expressed from alfalfa, corn, oats, lawn clippings, pea vines, and pangola, elephant, brome, and Sudan grasses all had initial pH between 5.5 and 6.0. After anaeorbic fermentation for from 24 to 48 hr, the pH dropped from 5.5 to 4.5 and the protein in the juice separated as a precipitate. Amino acid analysis of spray-dried alfalfa protein concentrate precipitated by anaerobic fermentation was found to contain 40% more cystine (as cysteic acid) and 12% more methionine (as methionine sulfone) than similar material produced by heat coagulation. Thus, there appears to be some destruction of the sulfur amino acids during the heat coagulation process, or synthesis of these amino acids by the microorganisms during the fermentation process.

Ajibola (1981) investigated the dynamics of the anaerobic fermentation of alfalfa juice. He concluded that the variable length lag phase at the beginning of the fermentation process could be eliminated if the population of lactic acid bacteria was at least 10^7 cells per ml. On a practical basis, this could be accomplished by adding an inoculant to the fresh juice consisting of 5% by volume of supernatant from the previous day's fermentation. If allowed to stand for longer periods, however, this inoculum lost its effectiveness.

The time rate of change of pH increased as temperature was increased. However, for all temperatures above 24°C (75°F), it was possible to reach the pH of 4.5, at which the protein precipitates in less than 24 hr.

The minimum pH attained during the fermentation depended on the concentration of nonstructural carbohydrates in the fresh juice. If the minimum pH attained in a given fermentation was not as low as desired, it could be reduced to the desired level by adding a readily fermentable carbohydrate and allowing the fermentation to restart and continue.

Anaerobic fermentation of alfalfa juice yielded only 67 to 88% as much protein concentrate compared with heat coagulation. However, with many of the grasses the fermentation process produced more. Alfalfa juice is high in proteolytic enzymes which convert some insoluble protein into soluble peptides or amino acids during fermentation, particularly if the fermentation continues for more than several days. This decreases protein yield. On the other hand, most grass juices contain carbohydrates and nonprotein nitrogen; and, in the fermentation process, these are converted to single cell protein, thereby increasing the yield of protein.

Precipitation of plant juice protein by anaerobic fermentation can result in significant energy savings when compared with heat coagulation (Koegel and Bruhn 1978). It is estimated that less than 0.5 Kcal of energy are required to coagulate alfalfa juice by fermentation as compared with heat coagulation. However, the fermented protein concentrate from alfalfa is very difficult to separate from the deproteinized juice, whereas alfalfa protein coagulum from the heat process floats and is easily skimmed off. Separation of the fermented protein concentrate can be accomplished with a centrifuge, but the latter equipment is presently too expensive for farm-scale operations. Research is continuing on economical methods of separating the fermented protein.

PRESERVATION OF PROTEIN CONCENTRATE

An economic analysis of the plant juice protein process has shown one of the major costs to be that of drying the wet protein concentrate, the common method of preserving it (Koegel *et al.* 1974).

Dehydration has normally been accomplished by using a spray dryer or a double drum dryer. Both pieces of equipment require the material to be at relatively high moisture, which increases drying costs. Both types of dryers are relatively expensive, especially the spray dryer. While the drum dryer is less costly, it can reduce the quality of the protein unless drum temperatures are carefully controlled. Throughput of the drum dryer is also low, being about 3.7 kg/m^2-hr (0.75 lb/ft^2-hr) of drum area.

A study has shown that plant juice protein concentrates can be successfully dried using a drum or roller drier. Selection of roll temperature, roll speed, and nip clearance can drastically affect performance. Drum temperature of 110°C to 130°C proved most practical in this experiment, with the final moisture content dependent on the drum speed at any given temperature. Efficiency of the drum dryer proved to be very acceptable. Protein quality can be maintained when drying on a drum dryer as indicated by enzyme digest results and by chick growth studies (Straub *et al.* 1977).

Alternatives to drying include reducing the pH of the wet protein to pH 3.5 and storing for further use, and the mixing of the protein with dry grain for pelleting or ensiling. The latter alternative seems the most feasible since drying costs are reduced. This technique would only be practical for the production of animal feeds. Such use could, however, be realized in the immediate future if costs are competitive.

PRODUCTION OF ALFALFA FRACTIONS AND ENERGY REQUIREMENTS OF ON-FARM SYSTEM

Normal alfalfa forage harvesting and ensiling operations for making low moisture silage (LMS) on midwestern United States farms, at present, involves handling about 18,144 kg (20 ST) per hr of green crop equivalent. Machinery for macerating, pressing, and coagulating the juice in the proposed on-farm forage dewatering system has been designed for this capacity. Quantities of products formed at various steps in the processing of 18,144 kg of alfalfa to produce pressed alfalfa silage or dehydrated alfalfa and dried alfalfa protein concentrate by heat coagulation are shown in Fig. 16.2. The

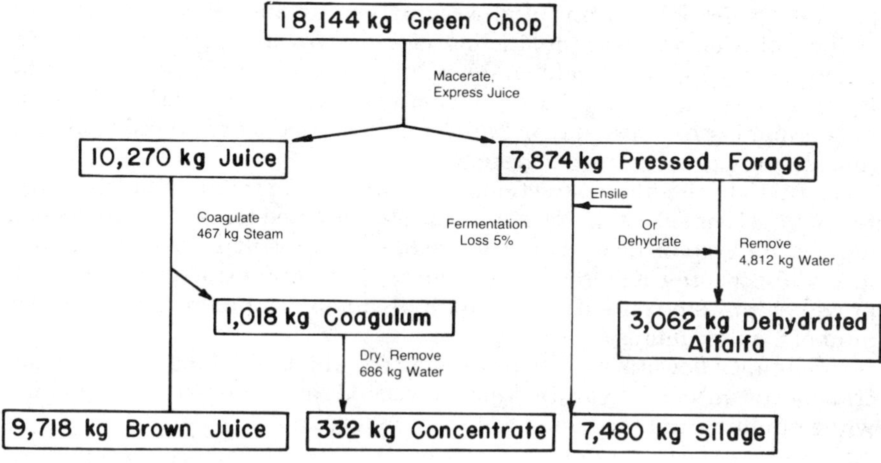

Fig. 16.2. Quantities of products formed at various steps in the processing of 18,144 kg of alfalfa.

18,144 kg green weight is about the average per ha yield of first harvest alfalfa in the midwestern United States. Energy requirements, based on research results to date, for these various steps are shown in Fig. 16.3. Total energy requirements for production of dried protein concentrate and pressed alfalfa silage amount to 123.2 to 127.7 kw and 110 liters/hr of fuel oil and for production of dehydrated pressed alfalfa 112.2 to 116.7 kw and 526 liters/hr of fuel oil, with 1977 corrections on macerating power requirement. Direct

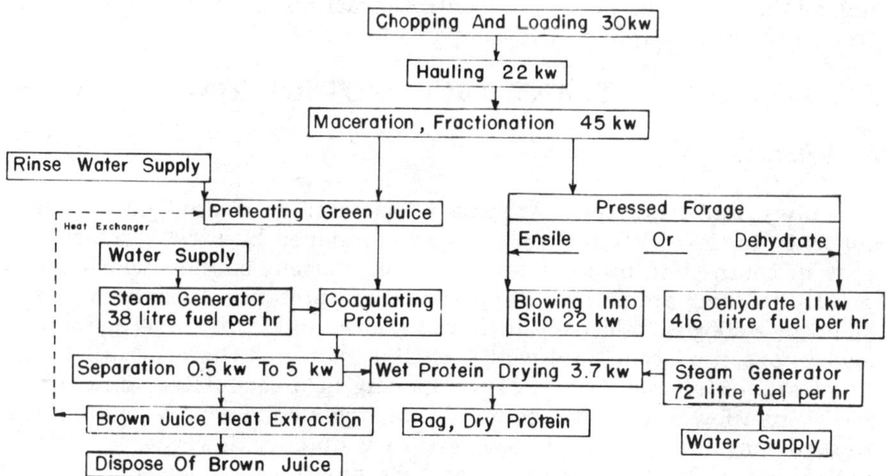

Fig. 16.3. Energy requirements for processing 18,144 kg (20 MT) fresh alfalfa per hour.

harvesting and dehydrating alfalfa requires about 56 kw and 1287 liters/hr of fuel oil. Conventional production of LMS, involving cutting, wilting, chopping, drying in the field, and ensiling requires only 82 kw. While the latter is less demanding in total energy, the risk of weather damage, harvesting losses, and delay in harvest with subsequent reduced quality is considerably greater in this system.

Adoption of the alfalfa fractionation-plant juice protein production system will: (1) ensure a uniform, high quality pressed forage as a result of a harvesting system independent of weather, (2) result in reducing forage losses and saving a higher proportion of the protein produced, and (3) provide a protein concentrate for high-producing ruminants, monogastric animals, and humans.

Mechanical dewatering and processing the plant juice for protein concentrate in the alfalfa dehydration industry could save as much as 50% in fuel, while doubling the throughput of the dehydrators.

CHEMICAL ANALYSES OF ALFALFA FRACTIONATION PRODUCTS

Concentration of chemical constituents, including total nonstructural carbohydrates (TNC), in alfalfa herbage, protein concentrate, and deproteinized juice is shown in Table 16.1. Alfalfa herbage is shown as: (1) green chopped alfalfa fresh from the field just before pressing, (2) alfalfa pressed forage just before ensiling, (3) alfalfa after drying in the field for making low moisture silage (LMS), (4) LMS after fermentation in the silo, and (5) pressed alfalfa after fermentation in the silo.

Percentages of N and K are high, Ca moderately high, with P and Mg somewhat lower in the alfalfa herbage components. Nitrogen is much higher than K in the protein concentrate fraction, whereas the reverse is true in the deproteinized juice component.

EVALUATION OF PLANT JUICE PROTEIN CONCENTRATES

In Vitro

Amino Acid Analyses. Analysis of 30 samples of plant juice protein concentrate (PJPC) from English plants provided by Pirie revealed: (1) that in contrast to proteins of seeds from various species, which differ greatly in their amino acid composition, the proteins of leaves from the 10 species showed relatively little difference, and (2) the average amino acid composition compared well with that of meat (Gerloff *et al.* 1965). Later studies (Tung *et al.* 1977) comparing heat-coagulated, spray-dried PJPC from low and high saponin alfalfa strains and from Vernal alfalfa showed that amino acid profiles were very similar. However, the sulfur-containing amino acids, cystine, and methionine were low in all three alfalfas. Methionine contents varied from 1.4 to 1.8%, while cystine was present in negligible quantity in the hydrolysates. Wang and Kinsella

TABLE 16.1. CONCENTRATIONS OF CHEMICAL CONSTITUENTS IN ALFALFA HERBAGE, PROTEIN CONCENTRATE, AND DEPROTEINIZED JUICE. AVERAGE OF FIRST HARVEST, FIRST FLOWER ALFALFA FOR 3 YEARS (1972–1974)

	Concentrations (Dry Wt at 70°C)													
	TNC[1]	N	P	K	Ca	Mg	S[2]	Na	Al	Fe	B	Cu	Zn	Mn
	(%)								(ppm)					
Green chopped alfalfa before pressing	6.04	2.95	0.31	3.22	0.90	0.25	0.25	0.029	108	138	18	14	33	45
Pressed alfalfa before ensiling	4.63	2.51	0.26	2.17	0.70	0.16	0.20	0.030	88	131	15	13	23	34
Alfalfa after field drying for LMS[3]	5.95	2.95	0.30	3.37	0.88	0.25	0.27	0.021	101	126	18	15	29	42
LMS-silage	2.17	2.99	0.30	3.47	0.99	0.28	0.27	0.034	86	104	18	6	21	40
Pressed alfalfa silage	1.22	2.39	0.25	2.61	0.90	0.21	0.20	0.030	95	182	17	7	23	36
Protein concentrate	4.88	7.30	0.51	3.56	1.24	0.32	0.56	0.044	611	900	23	107	113	103
Deproteinized juice	17.97	2.74	0.40	9.33	1.39	0.61	0.18	0.048	38	53	27	8	55	60

Source: Unpublished data by Dale Smith and N.A. Jorgensen, University of Wisconsin-Madison.
[1] TNC—Total nonstructural carbohydrates.
[2] S—Average of 2 years.
[3] LMS—Low moisture silage.

(1975) reported that precipitation of the alfalfa juice protein by acid at pH 3.7 in lieu of heat coagulation resulted in higher recovery of methionine. These studies suggest the PJPC would have high nutritive value for monogastric animals including man, if supplemented with methionine. Temperatures at which heat-coagulated AJPC is dried, particularly when drum dried, affect methionine and lysine contents. Studies of drum drying with subsequent air drying at different temperatures showed that drum drying temperatures of 100° to 140°C had little effect on amino acid content resulted in a reduced methionine content; methionine content was 1.2, 1.1, and 0.8%, respectively, at temperatures of 105°, 120°, and 140°C. Subsequent air drying temperatures had a significant effect on lysine content. There was a drastic decrease in lysine content from an average of 6.5% to 4.7% when air drying temperatures were increased from 50° to 150°C, regardless of whether the material was previously drum dried at 105°, 120°, or 140°C (Tung *et al.* 1977).

Anaerobic fermentation of alfalfa juice resulted in more methionine in the AJPC than when heat was used to coagulate the protein (Stahmann 1977). Enzymatic hydrolyses with pepsin and pancreatin released twice as much methionine from the fermented coagulum as from that coagulated by heat. No cystine was released from the heat-coagulated AJPC, but there was good release from the fermented product. Since sulfur amino acids limit growth, these data suggest that anaerobic fermentation should give AJPC of better nutritive value than that coagulated by heat. This was confirmed by protein efficiency ratio assays (PER) with rats.

Digestibility and Biological Value. To estimate the digestibility and biological value for animals, the amino acids released by hydrolyzing samples of PJPC from nine species of green plants with the digestive enzymes pepsin and pancreatin were measured. The data from Akeson and Stahmann (1964, 1965) showed that: (1) the biological value from enzyme hydrolysis correlated well with that from rat growth, and (2) that the PJPC should have a high nutritive value when fed to monogastric animals.

Saponin Content. Alfalfa selections and cultivars vary in their saponin content. Pedersen and Wang (1971) were successful in selecting alfalfa cultivars with low and high saponin content. Low and high saponin strains from these selections were grown at Madison, Wisconsin. AJPC was extracted from them and compared with AJPC from Vernal, the variety commonly grown in Wisconsin. These were assayed by the hemolysis test (Jones and Elliot 1969) with the end point set at 30% hemolysis of chicken blood cells. The high saponin strain and Vernal were found to contain 3 to 3½ times as much saponin as the low saponin selection (Tung *et al* 1977). Hemolysis tests with red clover and oat coagulated juice protein concentrate showed low saponin content, but that from *Cicer* milk vetch had a rather high level.

Vitamin and Xanthophyll Content. Because green plants in our foods are an important source of vitamins, alfalfa juice protein concentrate (AJPC) was analyzed for its vitamin content. The results showed a high content of thiamin, riboflavin, and especially carotene. Xanthophyll, which is used to pigment poultry products, was also very high. These data indicated that AJPC would be of value as a supplement in foods and feeds to increase both protein and vitamin intake.

In Vivo

Chicken Feeding Trials. Initial chick feeding trials resulted in 100% mortality at 11 days of age when a ration containing 40% dried AJPC was fed to day-old chicks; cause of death was believed to be due to saponin content of the AJPC. Subsequent trials were conducted in which AJPC from low and high saponin selections and from Vernal alfalfa fed as 40% of the diet were compared. Chicks gained an average of 82, 5, and 21 g in 14 days when fed APJC from low, high, and Vernal alfalfa, respectively. The average daily grams of feed consumed were 11.2, 4.6, and 7.4, respectively, for the low, high, and Vernal AJPC. The weight gains of the chicks fed low saponin AJPC were somewhat less than weight gains of those fed practical chick starter, but the difference was not significant. Saponins materially depressed the growth of day-old chicks to 14 days of age, and the primary effect is found in the palatability of the feed, thus reducing the voluntary intake of the animals.

Supplementation of low saponin AJPC with 0.3% methionine improved chick growth significantly; similar AJPC not supplemented produced only 18% of the weight gains compared with those of chicks fed a standard chick starter, whereas the supplemented material produced at a 95% level (Tung *et al.* 1977).

When AJPC from Vernal alfalfa made up 5% of the ration fed to laying hens, yolk color development in eggs was excellent; as a source of xanthophyll for this purpose, AJPC was three times as active as alfalfa meal. Protein extracted from alfalfa is currently being used commercially in rations for laying hens to supply the required xanthophyll.

Swine Feeding Trials. Utilization of whole alfalfa juice in wet-feeding systems for pigs has been practiced with some success in England (Foot 1974). Wet-feeding systems of growing pigs were studied at Wisconsin with both fresh alfalfa juice and with fermented alfalfa juice. Pigs, having access to a conventional dry ration, were given fresh raw juice free choice in troughs. Water was withheld from 8:00 A.M. to 5:00 P.M. each day. The juice was found to be unpalatable as the pigs would become thirsty each day, yet fail to consume over 0.9 kg (2 lb) of juice, including evaporation and spillage. It was necessary to discontinue the experiment after one week. Anaerobically fermented alfalfa juice was mixed in various ratios with corn or with corn and soybean meal and fed to 27 kg (60 lb) pigs. After an initial setback the first week, gains improved the second week, only to drop off again by the third week. Performance declined with increasing amounts of the fermented juice in the diet. Acceptance was never good, especially at the higher juice levels. After the third week, the amount of dry feed to juice was increased, but after three weeks, performance was still poor and the experiment was discontinued. Apparently, the introduction of air into the storage tanks allowed the growth of detrimental organisms, thereby altering the quality of the juice and affecting pig performance.

Mixed results were obtained when 22.5–27 kg (50–60 lb) pigs were fed dried, heat-coagulated Vernal AJPC in trials conducted in three different years. In the first year, performance was adversely affected by the inclusion of 10% AJPC in the diet. Feed intake, growth rate, and feed conversion were significantly poorer than for pigs on a control diet of corn and soybean meal. Pig performance in a second year trial, with either 5 or 10% of the ration made up of AJPC, was equally as good as the control diet. Again in a third year, experiment total and average daily gains and feed consumption were less where either 5 or 10% of the ration was made up of AJPC as compared to the control ration. Why performance was affected unfavorably by the addition of AJPC in the first and third year trials and not in the second is not known, but heat damage when drying the coagulum may be the cause. Other studies have shown that when wet AJP coagulum is dried at different temperatures and the dried AJPC is fed to young pigs, growth rate declines as drying temperatures increase (Cheeke *et al.* 1977).

In another experiment, pigs were fed fresh alfalfa juice, anaerobically fermented alfalfa juice, and wet heat-processed coagulum which were extruded with corn, along with a protein supplement free choice. All pigs performed well during the trial. The extruded corn-alfalfa products appeared to be palatable as was indicated by the level of protein the pigs selected under free-choice feeding.

It appears that with proper processing a juice protein concentrate can be prepared from green alfalfa that can be incorporated into swine rations.

Ruminant Feeding Trials. In a feeding trial beginning with three-day-old calves, when APJC replaced none, half, or all of the casein in a 24% milk replacer (of which ¾ of the protein was normally from casein), during the first 35 days, average daily weight gains were 0.39, 0.38, and 0.28 kg/day, respectively. Initial gains were lower for the AJPC, but where half of the protein in the ration was from this source, the calf weight gains were nearly equal to the normal 18% casein ration at the end of 35 days. Milk proteins are the best source of proteins in calf rations during the first 14 days, after which other protein sources may be substituted in milk replacers. Indications from this study are that AJPC could be gradually introduced into the milk replacer after about 14 days and that all of the casein could be replaced after 21 days.

Digestibility studies were conducted with goats to determine protein digestibility of alfalfa juice proteins. Wet alfalfa juice protein coagulum was blended with dry shelled corn (1:2 ratio) and ensiled. When fed with corn silage to supply 20, 35, and 50% of the dietary protein, digestibility of the alfalfa protein was found to be 73, 76, and 78%, respectively. Digestibility of the protein in drum dried AJPC was 77%. Since intake was not reduced in these studies and since digestibility of the protein averaged over 75%, substitution for other protein supplements for ruminants appears feasible.

Functional Properties

Major damage to the functional properties of AJPC was found to occur during the heat coagulation process. Additional heat damage was minimized if spray drying was used for final water removal. Acid precipitation of alfalfa juice gave yields of AJPC comparable to those with heat coagulation and also maintained the solubility characteristics of fresh juice protein. Polyphosphate precipitation held no advantage over either acid precipitation or heat coagulation with respect to AJPC yield. Gravity sedimentation was not acceptable because of extensive proteolysis. Filtration experiments indicated that fiber removal and curd separation require different filter media for adequate removal or recovery.

Treatment of the heat-coagulated AJPC with alkali for resolubilization or solvent extraction for pigment removal was less beneficial than acid precipitation and filtration. Filtration followed by acid precipitation yielded a less colored, more functional protein product than heat coagulation.

PRESSED FORAGE UTILIZATION

The major product, and one of utmost importance, in the proposed on-farm forage harvesting-plant juice production system, is the pressed forage. Since ensiling alfalfa, particularly the first cutting, is a commonly practiced method of forage preservation and one which provides maximum conservation of nutrients at the lowest energy cost; it is the method used in preserving the pressed forage. Determination of the feeding value of pressed forage silage as compared with field wilted alfalfa silage (the conventional method) in the production of milk from dairy cows is a necessary step in evaluating the feasibility of this proposed new system. Research, involving lactation and digestion trials comparing these two silage-making methods, was conducted in each of four years, 1973–1976, with cows from the University of Wisconsin dairy herd (Jorgensen 1978). First growth alfalfa (*Medicago sativa* L.) was harvested at late bud to first flower stage of growth by either the conventional field-wilting process (experimental control) for making silage or by direct harvesting followed by maceration and pressing according to the method of Bruhn and Koegel (1978) in each of four successive years; year 1-Trial 1; year 2-Trial 2; year 3-Trial 3; Year 4-Trial 4. In years 1, 2, 3, and 4 dry matter percentage of the wilted silage (control) was 46.1, 41.1, 39.1, and 47.3%, respectively. The resulting forages were stored in 3.0 × 7.6 m conventional concrete stave silos, the top covered with a 6 mil polyethylene sheet, and stored 90 days before initiation of the feeding trials.

Lactation Trials

Pressed Alfalfa Silage vs. Field Wilted Silage. Three trials (1, 2, and 3) compared these two types of alfalfa silage. The average composition of the two types as initially stored and when fed as silage together with that of freshly harvested alfalfa for the three trials is presented in Table 16.2.

TABLE 16.2. MEAN COMPOSITION OF FRESH, PRESSED, AND WILTED ALFALFA FORAGES AND RESULTING SILAGES[1]

Composition	Forage as Harvested or Stored			Silages		SE of Mean
	Fresh	Control	Pressed	Control	Pressed	
Component						
dry matter, %	20.0[2]	43.5[3]	32.0[4]	42.1[3]	30.5[4]	0.80
% of Dry Matter						
crude protein	18.7[2]	18.3[2]	15.0[3]	18.5[2]	15.9[3]	0.16
cell wall constituents (CWC)	48.1[2]	45.5[2]	58.6[3]	47.2[2]	57.8[3]	0.75
acid-detergent fiber (ADF)	35.1[2,3]	33.9[2]	42.2[4]	37.6[3]	47.4[4]	0.50
estimated hemicellulose (CWC-ADF)	13.0[2]	11.6[2,3]	16.4[4]	9.6[3]	10.4[3]	0.31
acid-detergent lignin	6.2[2]	6.3[2]	7.2[3]	6.6[2,3]	8.2[4]	0.12
ash	9.6[3]	9.5[3]	7.0[3]	9.7[2]	7.9[3]	0.19
calcium	1.02	0.92	0.84	1.09	0.91	—
phosphorus	0.26	0.21	0.22	0.27	0.21	—
magnesium	0.28	0.25	0.20	0.30	0.22	—
potassium	3.05	2.43	2.30	3.36	2.50	—

[1] All values are the means of three years with the exception of wilted alfalfa (control), the values of which are the mean of the first two years.
[2,3,4] Means, in the same row, with different footnote numbers were significantly ($P < 0.05$) different.

When compared with the fresh material, the pressed forage contained a significantly ($P < 0.05$) greater concentration of dry matter, cell wall constituents, acid-detergent fiber, estimated hemicellulose, and acid-detergent lignin at the expense of crude protein and ash. The pressing operation removed 58, 22, and 37%, respectively, of the moisture, dry matter, and protein present in the fresh plant material. As indicated by a rapid fall in pH and a marked increase in organic acid content of the ensiled pressed silages, an extensive fermentation will take place in macerated and pressed materials even though much of the soluble carbohydrate has been removed. The pressed silage contained significantly ($P < 0.05$) greater concentrations of each individual volatile fatty acid, total volatile fatty acids, total organic acids, and nonprotein nitrogen.

The feeding of pressed silage in these first three lactation trials was associated, to varying degrees, with a reduced silage intake; resulting in a depressed total dry matter intake. The mean consumption of the pressed silage was 91.1% of that for the control over the three trials. As a result of the depressed intake of the pressed silage, production of milk and 4% fat correct milk (FMC) were an average of 6.3 and 7.5% lower in animals fed pressed silage. However, these differences were not significant in any of the trials. Addition of dry hay to the ration in Trial 3 improved the milk fat test, which was depressed when pressed forage alone was fed.

Formic Acid Treatment of Pressed Silage. Since high levels of butyric acid and ammonia are undesirable end products of fermentation, control of fermentation is important. Addition of 0.5% formic acid to the pressed ensiled forage improved the quality of the forage. In pilot silo studies, it was observed that 0.3 to 0.4% formic acid was adequate to control butyric acid and ammonia production. Addition of 20 to 40% dry grain also controlled fermentation and resulted in a high quality semicomplete feed for ruminants. Addition of enzymes which act on carbohydrates to increase the yield of glucose was not beneficial. Formic acid treatment of the pressed forage before ensiling improved intake when fed to dairy cows and resulted in a slightly higher output of 4% FCM when compared with conventional wilted silage. This suggests that the pressed forage resulting from this system can be of equal value to the original material if properly preserved.

Digestion Trials

Digestibility of the alfalfa silages from years 1, 3, and 4 (Lactation Trials 1, 3, and 4) was determined in 15 day single reversal trials with four male castrated goats or sheep in which silages were the only feed. With the year 1 silages, an increased protein and decreased acid-detergent fiber digestibility in the pressed silage were the only significant ($P < 0.05$) differences observed. Digestibility of the protein was greater for the pressed silage than predicted by the equation of Holter and Reid (1959). With year 3 silages the digestibilities of these components tended to be reversed. Digestibility of the crude protein was lower, 64.3 vs. 69.6%, for the pressed silage (with 15.2% CP) that for the control (with 18.5% CP). The coefficient of 64.3 for the pressed forage was lower than the 69.7 predicted by the Holter and Reid (1959) equation.

The disagreement may be due to the effect of processing, which increased structural carbohydrates while reducing the protein component. Although total dry matter digestibility tended to be reduced in the pressed silage, a nonsignificant ($P < 0.05$) trend for increased digestibility of estimated hemicellulose in both trials and of cell wall constituents, acid-detergent fiber, and cellulose in Digestion Trial 2 indicated a possible greater availability of these constituents due to fractionation. The digestibility of the dry matter (DDM) in the formic acid-treated silage, (year 4 silages) was about equal to that for the control silage (66.3 vs. 67.1% DDM). Digestibility of the protein was lower (71.9 vs. 76.5%), while that for hemicellulose was higher (69.4 vs. 57.4%) in the formic acid-pressed silage. The increased digestibility of the crude protein, cell solubles, and estimated hemicellulose in year 1 pressed silage and of the cell wall constituents, acid-detergent fiber, estimated hemicellulose, and cellulose in the pressed silages of years 3 and 4 may indicate greater availability of the components of the plant materials to microbial attack following pressing. The differences between the trials could be due to differences in the degree of maceration of the plant material in the different trials, allowing a more complete extraction of the plant's more soluble components and breakdown of the structural components.

Potential for Pressed Alfalfa Silage

These studies have shown that production per unit of feed consumed by dairy cows was not significantly different between alfalfa silage made after field wilting and pressed alfalfa silage. Intake of the pressed alfalfa silage appears to be a limiting factor in its productive value. Intake is highly related to the moisture content of a forage. Using presently available pressing equipment, it has not been possible to reduce the moisture percentage of the pressed alfalfa below the 68–70% range. Pilot studies with small experimental silos have shown that if the moisture content can be reduced to 65%, satisfactory silage can be made from pressed alfalfa. This moisture content is in the very upper limit of that recommended for ensiling field wilted alfalfa (50–65% moisture content). However, in the maceration and pressing process, the cell walls of the alfalfa plant are broken and enzymes released, which cause a rapid fermentation and quick drop in pH, resulting in a good preservation of the pressed alfalfa, even though the moisture level is high. Treatment of the pressed forage at ensiling with 0.3 to 0.5% formic acid will alter the fermentation pattern and ensure the making of a satisfactory silage when moisture levels are questionable.

It should also be noted that in all four years of these studies the field-wilted control alfalfa silage was ensiled without weather damage and at an ideal growth stage. Normally, silages made in this way may be rain damaged or their harvest delayed, resulting in much reduced quality. When such silage is fed to lactating dairy cows, poorer performance can be expected when compared with that made from alfalfa harvested at the proper stage of maturity and without field losses. The real advantage of dewatering alfalfa is that farmers can be ensured of ensiling a forage of the highest quality with virtually no losses.

Pressed Forages from Other Crops

Small experimental silos were used to study preservation of residues from other crops. Good silages have been made in these silos from legumes such as alfalfa, red clover, and pea vines, from bromegrass and oats, and from vegetable crop wastes—carrot tops and potato vines. Preservation of the latter affords an opportunity to utilize large quantities of otherwise wasted materials as shown by a study in which potato vines were macerated, pressed, and ensiled. Preservation quality was excellent as based on smell, freedom from mold, pH, and organic acid levels. The pressed potato vine silage was compared with pressed and with field-wilted alfalfa silages. The dry matter in the potato silage was lower in crude protein and hemicellulose and was higher in cellulose. When fed to goats, average dry matter intake was lower than the field-wilted, but higher than the pressed alfalfa silage. Apparent dry matter and crude protein digestibility were much lower than that of the alfalfa silages. While the acceptability of pressed potato vine silage was good, the low digestibility of the components limits its use as a satisfactory forage for high-producing ruminants; however, it could serve as a good source of nutrients for ruminant animals on maintenance types of rations. No toxicity problem was noted with goats fed potato vine silage.

DEPROTEINIZED JUICE UTILIZATION

The system of plant juice protein-forage production has as an end product a large volume of residual juice, which must be disposed of in some manner, to avoid serious environmental pollution. This product has been termed deproteinized plant juice (DPJ). It constitutes about 50% of the weight of the harvested green plant before pressing, with most crops. DPJ generally contains from 4 to 5% solids and generally is very high in concentration of potassium (0.45%) and nitrogen (0.12%). Several methods of disposing of DPJ have been under investigation. These include use as a fertilizer and production of protein by using single cell organisms.

Use as a Fertilizer

Field Studies. Field experiments were conducted to determine the effects of utilizing DPJ as a fertilizer on alfalfa, *Medicago sativa* L.; bromegrass, *Bromus inermus* Leyss.; and corn, *Zea mays* L. Deproteinized alfalfa juice (DAJ) was applied to: (1) an alfalfa-bromegrass mixture, (2) to bromegrass, and (3) to corn at depths of 0, 0.625, 1.25, and 2.50 cm. Increased yields of all three crops were obtained with the annual application of 1.25 cm of DAJ. However, plant damage and yield reductions occurred to alfalfa and corn when DAJ was applied at rates of 2.5 cm, with only minor damage to bromegrass. Per hectare yields of crude protein were increased and concentration of K in the herbage of alfalfa, bromegrass, and corn was higher where DAJ was applied. Available P and exchangeable K in the soil generally increased with each increment of DAJ applied, and soil pH was maintained at satisfactory levels as a result of Ca and Mg additions from DAJ.

When oats followed corn in the rotation, with no further fertilization with DAJ, the residual yields of grain were higher wherever DAJ previously had been applied (Ream *et al.* 1977).

Greenhouse Studies. Studies with alfalfa were conducted to observe more closely the possible causes of plant damage when DAJ is applied as a fertilizer. In one series of experiments, DAJ was applied to alfalfa at depths of from 0.16 to 10.0 cm. Plants fertilized with DAJ at depths of 1.25 cm or more showed chlorotic symptoms and growth retardation. Only a few plants survived at the 5.0, 7.5, and 10.0 cm rates. When DAJ was applied to timothy plants, results were similar to those when alfalfa was fertilized with DAJ, but timothy plants appeared to survive better than alfalfa under the higher rates of DAJ. Yields of the test plants decreased when more than 1.25 cm of DAJ was applied (Walgenbach *et al.* 1977).

There was some speculation that saponin, a glycoside that occurs in alfalfa and other plants, caused the damage when DAJ was applied to alfalfa, bromegrass, timothy, or corn. In another series of greenhouse experiments, DAJ extracted from low and high saponin alfalfa strains was applied back to alfalfa growing in pots of soil. Yields were not significantly different whether DAJ from low or from high saponin alfalfa was applied. It was concluded that saponin was not the causal agent in the injury or death of alfalfa or other plants when fertilized with DAJ.

In another greenhouse experiment, results were similar where deproteinized juice extracted from oats (DOJ) was compared with DAJ when applied to alfalfa. Yields declined and damage occurred when either DOJ or DAJ was applied to alfalfa at depths greater than 1.25 cm. Yield decline and injury to alfalfa was not as great when DOJ was applied at 2.5 cm as with DAJ, but practically all plants were killed with either DOJ or DAJ at 3.75 cm.

It is hypothesized from these experiments that a possible cause of injury and/or death to plants from applications at high rates of DPJ could be a lack of oxygen supply to the roots. Saturation of the soil by the large amounts of liquid applied, together with excessive growth of fungi, which use up the oxygen and further exhaust the oxygen supply, may result in no oxygen available for normal functioning of the roots. Another possible cause of the damage could be phytotoxic compounds in the DPJ, or soluble and/or volatile microfloral breakdown products of the DPJ.

USE AS A MEDIUM FOR SINGLE CELL ORGANISMS

Deproteinized alfalfa juice was aerobically fermented with various organisms using a variety of batch and continuous procedures. Yeast or single bacterial species were much less efficient in reducing the biological oxygen demand (BOD) than a mixed culture of bacteria. Dilution of the DAJ was necessary to reduce foaming and ensure adequate oxygen transfer. Results from a series of 2 kl (500 gal.) batch fermentations of DAJ resulted in 41% more microbial protein/acre-year from low saponin DAJ than from the DAJ of Vernal alfalfa. The development of lower-saponin alfalfa strains will be advantageous for production of single cell protein from DAJ in a fermentation process.

Preliminary chick feeding trials with cells produced from the 2 kl (500 gal.) batch fermentations of either the low saponin or Vernal DAJ showed no toxic effects at the 40% level of incorporation in the diet.

Fermentations of deproteinized juice from pea vines, sorghum-Sudan grass hybrid, and bromegrass were superior to either Vernal or low saponin alfalfa with respect to yield and BOD removal.

ECONOMIC EVALUATION

Preliminary economic research has concentrated on modeling the alfalfa harvesting-protein extraction technology (AJP) in comparison with the conventional production of low moisture silage (LMS) on a typical Wisconsin dairy farm (McGuckin and Hughes 1978). Linear programming and modeling of the two harvesting systems were used to determine the increase, if any, in net annual revenues attributable to the AJP system and then, discounting these revenues over an expected investment period, to estimate the amount a farmer could invest in the system.

The typical dairy farm had 80 ha (200 acres) of cropland with 100 cows each producing 6800 kg (15,000 lb) of milk valued at $0.198 per kg ($9 per cwt). One-half of the cropland was in alfalfa, one-third in corn, and one-sixth in oats.

In order to focus on the differences between the two systems, the following components of dairy operations were extensively modeled:

(1) The impact of weather delays and damages on the two systems.
(2) The types and quality of feeds produced with the two systems.

It was assumed that with the AJP system the alfalfa crop was harvested at mid-bud, whereas the LMS was harvested at varying maturity stages with 8 of the 40 alfalfa ha (20 of the 100 acres) rain-damaged during two five-day harvesting periods with a weather sequence based on probabilities in Wisconsin. In the AJP system it was assumed that the coagulum was separated from the DAJ by fermentation, ensiled with grain, and fed as a high protein concentrate to the dairy subsector, the deproteinized juice being valued at its fertilizer replacement value of $26.20 per ha ($10.48 per acre). Storage in both systems was assumed to have a 10% dry matter loss.

Since dairy farm machinery, equipment, and storage facilities used for current wilted silage technology can be simply converted to an AJP system with the addition of the macerator, press, and fermentation tanks for the coagulum separation, the increases in net revenue of this system over LMS can be attributed to the capitial investments required. To estimate the investment value, or what a farmer can afford to spend on the system, requires that the increase in annual cash flow between the two systems be discounted over the expected investment period. It was assumed that useful life of the investment is 10 years and that the appropriate interest rate is 10%. On this basis, with corn at $94.50 per MT ($2.40 per bu) and soybean oil meal at $244 per MT ($220 per ST), a farmer could afford to invest $40,271 in an AJP system. While machinery and equipment for this system are not fully developed, current estimates are that the cost will be below this amount. As further research is completed, a more precise economic evaluation will be possible.

REFERENCES

AJIBOLA, O.O. 1981. Separation of protein concentrate from plant juice by means of pH adjustment. Ph.D. Thesis. Univ. of Wisconsin-Madison.

AKESON, W.R. and STAHMANN, M.A. 1964. A pepsin pancreatin digest index of protein quality evaluation. J. Nutr. *83*, 257–261.

AKESON, W.R. and STAHMANN, M.A. 1965. Nutritive value of leaf protein concentrate, an in vitro digestion study. J. Agric. Food Chem. *13* (2) 145–148.

AM. SOC. AGRIC. ENG. 1977. ASAE Yearbook. American Society of Agricultural Engineers, St. Joseph, MI.

BASKEN, K.E., SCHIRER, D.K., KOEGEL, R.G. and BRUHN, H.D. 1975. Reducing the energy requirements of plant juice protein production. Am. Soc. Agric. Eng. Pap. *75–1056*.

BRUHN, H.D. and KOEGEL, R.G. 1978. More usable protein per acre by a modified forage program. Annu. Meet. North Atlantic Region, Cornell Univ., Ithaca, NY. Am. Soc. Agric. Eng. Pap. *NA 75–004*.

BRUHN, H.D., STRAUB, R.J. and KOEGEL, R.G. 1977. A systems approach to the production of plant juice protein concentrate. Proc. Int. Grain and Forage Harvesting Conf., Ames, IA, Sept. 25–29, 1977.

CHEEKE, P.R., KINSELLA, J.H., DE FREMERY, D. and KOHLER, G.O. 1977. Freeze dried and commercially prepared alfalfa protein concentrate evaluation with rats and swine. J. Anim. Sci. *44*, 772.

FLOYD, S.L., KOEGEL, R.G. and BRUHN, H.D. 1975. Press throughput and energy as affected by pulp reorientation. Am. Soc. Agric. Eng. Pap. *75–1058*.

FOOT, A.S. 1974. Lucerne juice for pigs. Pig Farm. *22* (9) 71.

GERLOFF, E.D., LIMA, I.G. and STAHMANN, M.A. 1965. Amino acid composition of leaf protein concentrates. J. Agric. Food Chem. *13*, 139–143.

HIBBS, J.W., CONRAD, H.R. and JOHNSON, W.H. 1968. Macerated, dewatered vs. wilted alfalfa grass silage for dairy cows. Ohio Res. Dev. Cent. Res. Bull. *1013*.

HOLTER, J.A. and REID, J.T. 1959. Relationship between the concentration of crude protein and apparent digestible protein in forages. J. Anim. Sci. *18*, 1339.

HUNDTOFT, E.B. and WINKELBLECH, C.S. 1966. Hay harvesting losses. Am. Soc. Agric. Eng. Pap. *66:502*.

JONES, M. and ELLIOT, F.C. 1969. Two rapid assays for saponin in individual alfalfa plants. Crop Sci. *9*, 688–691.

JORGENSEN, N.A. 1978. Preservation and utilization of products resulting from green plant fractionation. Proc. Conf. Non-Conventional Pro. and Foods. Natl. Sci. Found. and Univ. Wisconsin-Madison, Oct. 1977.

KOEGEL, R.G. 1971. Pressure fractionation of alfalfa. Unpublished Ph.D. Dissertation. Univ. of Wisconsin-Madison.

KOEGEL, R.G., BARRINGTON, G.P. and BRUHN, H.D. 1974. Harvesting and processing equipment for alfalfa juice protein concentrate. Proc. 4th Alfalfa Symp., Madison, WI, Apr. 9, 1974.

KOEGEL, R.G. and BRUHN, H.D. 1972. Pressure fractionation characteristics of alfalfa. Trans. ASAE *15* (5) 856–860.

KOEGEL, R.G. and BRUHN, H.D. 1978. Energy economics of alfalfa juice protein. Trans. ASAE *21* (4) 605–609.

KOEGEL, R.G., FOMIN, V.I. and BRUHN, H.D. 1973A. Roller maceration and fractionation of forages. Trans. ASAE *16* (2) 236–240.

KOEGEL, R.G., FOMIN, V.I. and BRUHN, H.D. 1973B. Cell rupture properties of alfalfa. Trans. ASAE *16* (4) 712–716.

McGUCKIN, T. and HUGHES, H.G. 1978. The economics of the alfalfa dewatering and protein extraction technology. Proc. Conf. Non-conventional Prot. and Foods. Natl. Sci. Found. and Univ. Wisconsin-Madison, Oct. 1977.

NELSON, F.W. 1977. A functional investigation of forage maceration mechanism. M.Sc. Thesis. Univ. of Wisconsin-Madison.

PEDERSEN, M.W. and WANG, L.C. 1971. Modification of saponin content of alfalfa through selection. Crop Sci. *11*, 833–835.

PIRIE, N.W. 1971. Equipment and methods for extracting and separating protein. *In* Leaf Protein: Its Agronomy, Preparation, Quality and Use. IBP Handb. *20*. Blackwell's Scientific Publishers, Oxford.

PITT, R.E., STRAUB, R.J., KOEGEL, R.G. and BRUHN, H.D. 1977. Plant fractionation press design criteria. Am. Soc. Agric. Eng. Pap. *77-6503*.

REAM, H.W., SMITH, D. and WALGENBACH, R.P. 1977. Effects of deproteinized juice applied to alfalfa-bromegrass, bromegrass and corn. Agron. J. *69*, 685–689.

SCHIRER, D.K. 1973. Extrusion as a forage maceration technique. Unpublished M.S. Thesis. Univ. of Wisconsin-Madison.

STAHMANN, M.A. 1977. Anaerobic fermentation for coagulation of plant juice protein and preservation of both the protein and fibrous residues. Pap. presented at Int. Workshop on Utilization of Agric. Wastes for Feed and Food. Belo Horizonte, Brazil, Dec. 1977.

STRAUB, R.J., BASKEN, K.E., KOEGEL, R.G. and BRUHN, H.D. 1977. Instrumentation and controls for automated plant juice protein concentration production. Trans. ASAE *20* (4) 649–652.

STRAUB, R.J. and BRUHN, H.D. 1975. Mechanical dewatering of alfalfa protein concentrate. Am. Soc. Agric. Eng. Pap. *75-6519*.

STRAUB, R.J., TUNG, J.Y., KOEGEL, R.G. and BRUHN, H.D. 1977. Drum drying of plant juice protein concentrates. Am. Soc. Agric. Eng. Pap. *77–1061*.

TILLEY, H.M.A. and RAYMOND, W.F. 1957. The extraction and utilization of leaf protein. Herb. Abstr. *27* (4) Dec. 235–245.

TUNG, J.Y., STRAUB, R.J., SCHOLL, J.M. and SUNDE, M.L. 1977. Methods used to evaluate biological protein quality and saponin concentration of various alfalfa juice proteins. Am. Soc. Agric. Eng. Pap. *77-1010*.

WALGENBACH, R.P., SMITH, D. and REAM, H.W. 1977. Growth and chemical composition of alfalfa fertilized in greenhouse trials with deproteinized alfalfa juice. Agron. J. *69*, 690–694.

WANG, J. and KINSELLA, J.E. 1975. Composition of alfalfa leaf protein isolates. J. Food Sci. *40*, 1156–1161.

17

Mechanical Parameters in Leaf Cell Rupture for Protein Production

T.O. Addy, L.F. Whitney, and C.S. Chen

Some of the limitations in the commercial production of leaf protein can be related to fundamental factors in the rupture of cells to obtain their protein content. This chapter considers the significance of some of these factors, related to both raw materials and process methods. Experiments are also described which evaluate the effectiveness of dynamic forces of shear and compression in cell rupture, on the basis of the energy required.

The benefits of production of edible protein from inedible plant sources, without the rather inefficient ruminant intermediaries, have been well demonstrated. With direct conversion, the usual 10–18% animal conversion efficiency could potentially be considerably improved. Commercial production of leaf protein, however, has been hampered by low production efficiencies, with yields too low to render leaf protein competitive with present available sources of edible protein. Commercial production has therefore been limited in the main to the use of leaf proteins as animal feed supplements. The current concern over world hunger underscores the need for methods to improve process efficiency and thus introduce a potentially abundant novel source of food.

To extract leaf protein, the protein-containing intracellular contents of the leaves have to be ultimately separated from the fibrous cellulosic material of the leaf cell skeleton. Although this task could be accomplished by biochemical methods, as, for instance, the disintegration of the cells with enzymes, the most economical and feasible methods are considered to be those involving mechanical maceration of the leaf to rupture the cells, followed by, or simultaneously with, mechanical separation of the protein-rich juice from the fibrous material.

The most significant factors limiting protein yields can be classified into three basic groups of parameters, described by Kohler and Bickoff (1971) as follows:

(1) Only 70–75% of the nitrogen in the leaf is in the form of true protein, and although 60% of the nonprotein nitrogen is in the form of free amino acids, these are not recoverable in the usual coagulation step to obtain protein.
(2) The ultimate yield depends on the number of cells broken in the maceration process, and hence on the amount of nitrogen made available from the plant material.
(3) During mechanical separation of the nitrogen-rich juice from the fiber, a filtration system (internal binding) develops as a result of the fibrous mat which is formed on pressing the pulped mat. Protein, especially that protein held in the chloroplasts, may then be held back, and thus limit production yields.

The first group of parameters, controlling the ratio of protein to nonprotein nitrogen, is an agronomic factor and is not discussed here. From a mechanical standpoint, the second and the third parameters are of particular interest.

A considerable amount of energy is required in the disintegration process and the separation of raw materials to obtain two phases. Holló and Koch (1971) reported that in order to process 1 MT of forage material, 45 to 55 kwh and 40 kg of fuel were required. Pirie (1970) determined that in processing similar amounts of leaves, only 0.75 kwh or less was required in mechanical separation ("expression") of the juice from the fiber, while Koegel (1971), investigating power requirements for the separation of juice from macerated alfalfa, found that only about 1% of the total power required for both maceration and "expression" by present methods is consumed in the "expression" operation. These observations underscore the significance of the maceration process, and indicate that in efficiency considerations, the cell rupturing step may be the most critical unit operation in the process. This chapter considers some of the fundamental factors which would potentially influence the effectiveness of maceration for protein production.

It is clear that the nature and physical characteristics of the raw material would be a factor in maceration. For instance, it has been shown that protein yields are dependent on the conditions of growth and time of harvest (Byers and Sturrock 1965). It has also been generally observed that an increase in leaf age causes a decline in extracted protein. Furthermore, different species of forage material respond differently to the same mechanical treatment. Since the cell is the basic unit of leaf structure, these differences could be correlated with the physical and mechanical properties of the cells, as well as the general microstructure of the leaf. The raw material parameters evaluated herein include changes in leaf weight and thickness, number of cells per unit weight of leaf, and intercellular space.

From the standpoint of machine and process design, the task of improving the competitive position of leaf protein should include the evaluation of the specific causes of the present limitations, as well as the effects of various factors, such as machine geometry, types of force applied, and rates of loading, which have been generally considered as important in leaf protein production.

If the critical process design criterion is to minimize the input of energy per unit of protein produced, the need for quantification of the factors cited in the preceding paragraphs becomes obvious. Since alfalfa is one of the most abundant potential sources of leaf protein production, it becomes a natural choice for the study of processing problems. The discussion, however, could easily be extended to other forage materials.

Specifically, this chapter considers the implications of the microstructural characteristics of alfalfa leaves in the mechanics of rupture and protein production, and evaluates the effectiveness of dynamic shear and compressive impact in maceration by estimating the energy requirements for cell rupture. The leaf cell characterization was accomplished by a microscopic sectioning technique for the study of the microstructure of "representative" leaves from a test plot as a function of time (stage of growth). Energy requirements were determined by imparting energy to a sample of leaves by a pendulum and determining the effectiveness of rupture at various loading speeds. The implications of the results in leaf protein production are then discussed.

STRUCTURAL CHARACTERISTICS

The experimental method for structural analysis is similar to that used by Turrell (1942) in his study of the "internal surface of alfalfa leaves," by which sections from leaf samples were mounted on microscopic slides for a permanent recording of cellular characteristics. However, rather than following the development of a particular group of leaves, here "representative" leaves are studied with the developmental stage of a group of plants as reference.

Each whole plant from the sample was divided into three parts along the stem, and representative leaf triads were selected from the upper two-thirds. These are defined as "upper" and "lower" leaves, respectively. No samples were taken from the bottom third of the plant, thus ensuring that only the larger primary leaves were used for analysis.

The leaves were found to be generally composed of seven layers of cells, consisting of a layer of epidermal cells on either side, constituting about 20% of the total thickness, two layers of cylindrical palisade cells, and usually about three layers of spongy cells. The spongy cells are quite irregular in shape and arrangement, and the lines of distinction between the cell layers are not as clearly defined as those in the epidermis and palisade.

Details of the experimental procedures and methods of computations are presented elsewhere (Addy 1974). The description of specific results obtained from the evaluation of physical characteristics follows.

LEAF WEIGHT

Changes in leaf weight constitute one of the obvious characteristics of growth. The average weights of both upper and lower leaves on each sample plant were determined over the experimental period, and the results showed that for both upper and lower leaves, it is clear that the average leaf weight increased till about the sixteenth or seventeenth day, after which there occurred a gradual decline in the weight of upper leaves. The decline was most probably attributable to the progressively smaller sizes of leaves that were formed after the period of maximum leaf weight. The lower leaves, however, continued to increase in size and weight. However, at the latter stages of growth, some of the lower leaves deteriorated and fell off, leaving them in smaller numbers compared with the upper leaves. The net effect of these factors was a gradual decline in the weight of an "average" leaf on the plant.

The period of maximum leaf weight coincided with the period when, from qualitative observation, plant growth was fastest and the foliage most abundant. For this, and for other reasons which will become apparent after discussion of other morphological characteristics, this period is defined as the "peak period."

CELL NUMBERS

Cell multiplication is generally presumed to be an important factor in protein yields, having possible mechanical as well as biochemical implications. As Arkcoll (1971) stated, rapid cell division and extension usually imply a high protein content. In mechanical and structural terms, fast growth would tend to assure succulent leaves, the cell walls of which would be relatively free from secondary thickening and lignification, thus making cell rupture and protein release easier. Analysis of the experimental data suggests, however, that although the number of cells generally increased with time, the major period of extensive cell division had occurred before the test period. Dramatic effects of cell division were therefore not observed. Nevertheless, changes in a related parameter with regard to mechanical behavior were observed. This parameter is characterized by the number of cells per unit weight of leaf, and it is evaluated as a function of time. As with other factors, data were obtained for both upper and lower leaves, and "plant average" values were computed from these. Figures 17.1 and 17.2 are representative plots of these results.

It is clear from Fig. 17.1 that upper leaves have a higher cell density than lower leaves on the same plant. This suggests that, during the growth stages covered by the experimental period, as a particular leaf matures, the increase in its weight is greater than the corresponding increase in the number of cells, demonstrating that cell expansion is more important during this period than cell division. It is of particular interest to note that

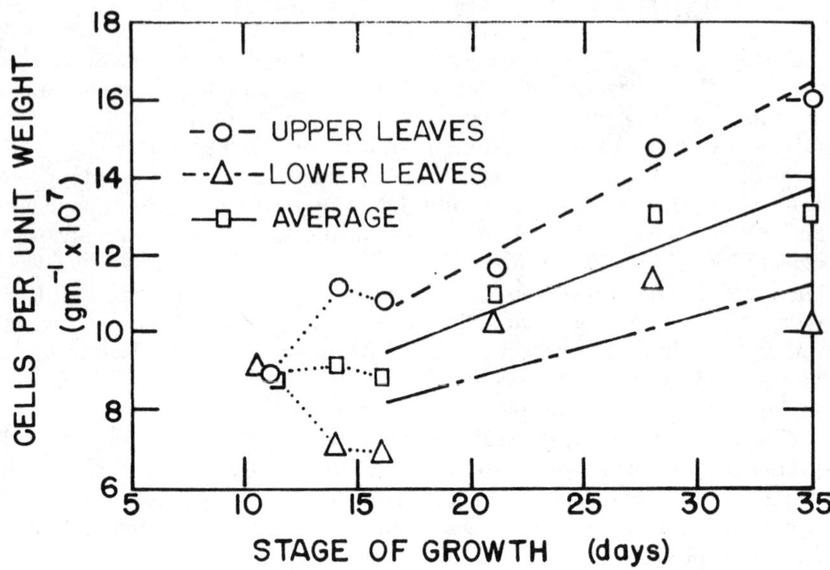

Fig. 17.1. Total number of cells per unit weight vs. time.

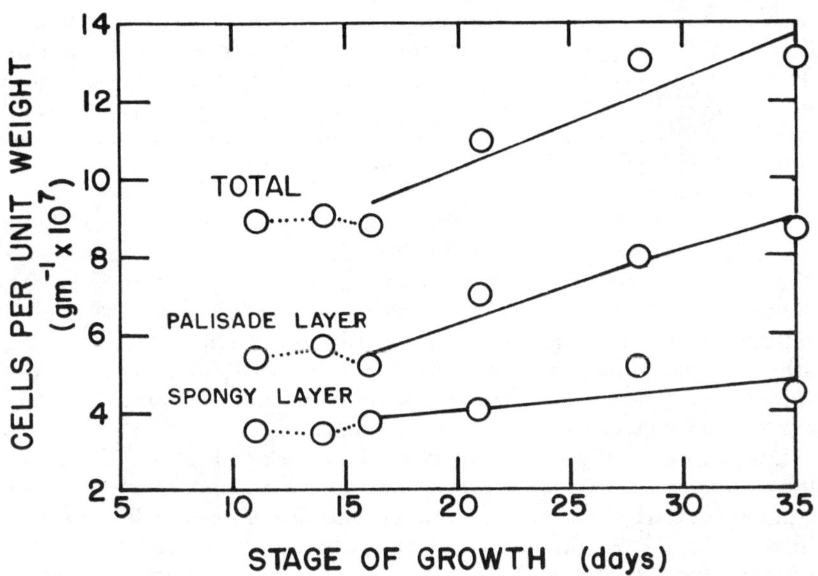

Fig. 17.2. Comparison of average numbers of cells per unit weight.

before the peak period the curves show a different trend than shown during the period after. It is clear, however, that the peak period displays the minimum cell density. The curves also show that although the spongy tissue displays the same trends as the palisade, the changes, especially prior to the peak period, are not as distinctive as shown by the latter.

LEAF THICKNESS

Leaf thickness is of fundamental importance in the design and analysis of leaf maceration processes. Not only does leaf thickness indicate the sizes of cell layers, but in forage maceration equipment such as hammer mills, the design of the shearing gap between the hammers and housing involves some consideration of leaf thickness. Leaf thickness is computed here simply by the summation of the thicknesses of all cell layers. Figure 17.3 shows the plot of leaf thickness as a function of time. It is again noted that the curves show maxima during the peak period. After this period, the average thickness of leaves begins to decline, with upper and lower leaves showing similar behavior. As expected, the older leaves are thicker than younger ones, implying the expected phenomenon of cell expansion as well as cell wall growth as a particular leaf matures. Possible explanation for these trends are discussed by Addy (1974).

INTERCELLULAR SPACE

The amount of intercellular space should be of considerable significance in the evaluation of the structural characteristics of the leaf. Comparison

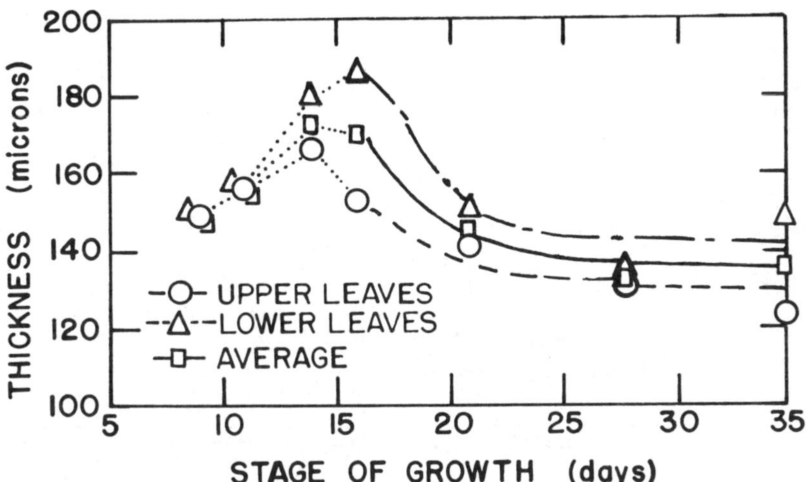

Fig. 17.3. Leaf thickness as a function of time.

with most engineering materials, one should expect a higher air-space fraction to indicate a less rigid structure, while a tightly cell-packed leaf would exhibit greater strength characteristics.

The extent of intercellular space was estimated by the computation of cell "packing density." Packing density is defined as the ratio of the total actual volume of cells to the volume of the particular tissue layer. Cell volumes were computed from their diameter measurements. Figure 17.4 shows the variations of packing density with plant age. It is clear that the palisade tissue is much more closely packed than the spongy tissue. The plots also indicate the general increase of packing density with time, with the minimum occurring around the peak period. Again, it should be noted that although the spongy tissue shows similar trends, these changes are more detectable in the palisade tissue.

PROTEIN CONTENT

In addition to its significance with regard to leaf physical characteristics, the peak period is again found to be important in terms of the available protein in the leaves. The leaf protein content, determined by micro-Kjeldahl analysis, is plotted as a function of time and shown in Fig. 17.5. Percentage protein was obtained by multiplying the percentage nitrogen by 6.25. The results demonstrate that the upper, newer leaves are generally richer in protein than the lower leaves, implying that as a particular leaf matures its potential protein content eventually decreases. It is also

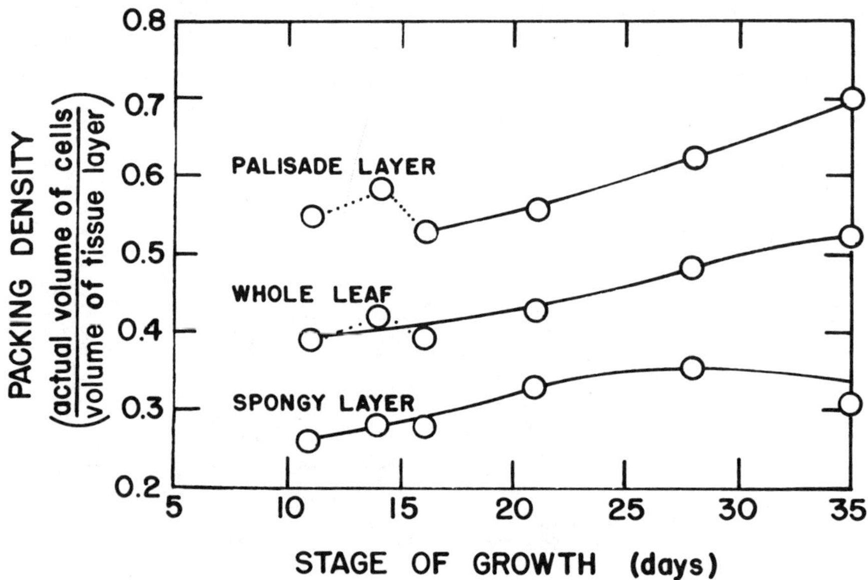

Fig. 17.4. Comparison of average packing densities.

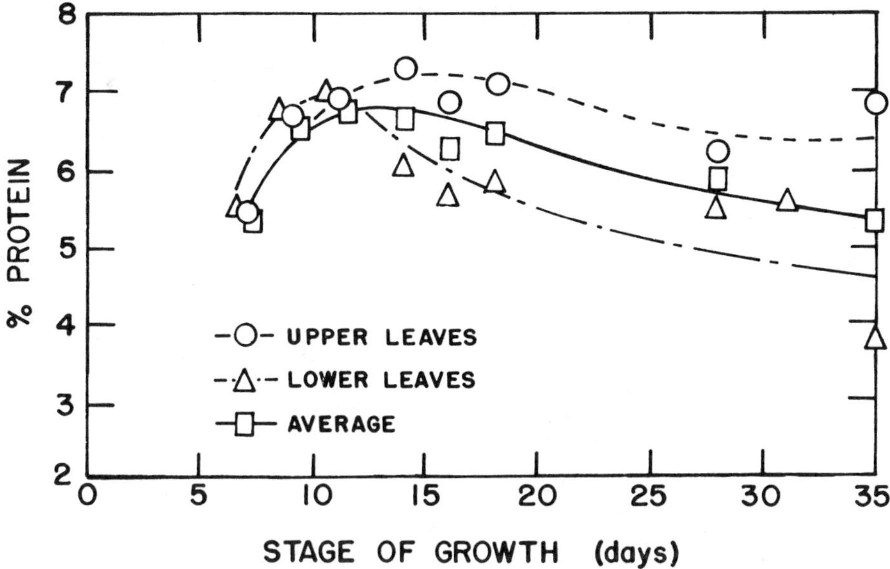

Fig. 17.5. Protein content of leaves as a function of time.

clear that as the whole plant ages, the average protein content rises to a maximum during the peak period and then declines thereafter, with the lower leaves declining in nitrogen content much faster than upper leaves. Reasons for the decline in protein content have been discussed by Addy (1974). The maximum available protein measured is consistent with values generally cited in the literature, (e.g., Akeson and Stahmann 1966).

The implications of the preceding morphological characteristics in leaf protein process design will be discussed shortly in a later section.

ENERGY REQUIREMENTS

Experimental Methods and Procedures

The test leaf samples for the determination of energy characteristics were obtained from a test crop of 1-year-old alfalfa plants, at a stage of growth corresponding to the peak period.

The basic requirement for the evaluation of energy characteristics is the transfer of a determinable amount of energy to the leaves under relatively standardized conditions, and the determination of the effectiveness of the transferred energy with regard to cell rupture. The two types of forces considered, dynamic shear and compression, are those most likely to be encountered in mechanical processing. The energy transfer technique employed was similar to that used by Prince and Wheeler (1960) in studies on shear cutting of alfalfa stalks. The apparatus, a diagram of which is shown in Fig. 17.6, basically consisted of a 1.3 cm (½ in.) diameter aluminum

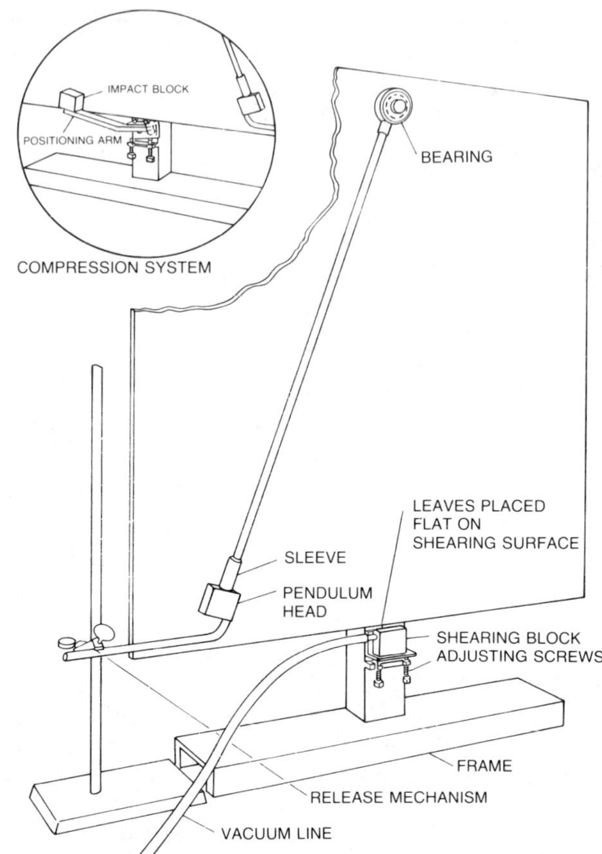

Fig. 17.6. Perspective diagrams of shear and compressive systems.

tubing arm, on which was mounted a fixed "head" and a precision ball bearing on the opposite end to form a 91.4 cm (36 in.) long pendulum. For the shearing system, a stainless steel shearing block was designed to provide a shearing surface and hold leaves in place. The block was mounted in such a manner that the gap between the pendulum head and the shearing surface (shear gap) could be adjusted.

The transferred energy was obtained by determination of the change in potential energy after contact with the leaf sample. (Bearing losses were considered.)

For the determination of potential energy changes, the travel of the pendulum was photographically recorded, and the height differentials were determined from the photographs.

The dynamic compression system was a slightly modified version of the shearing system. In place of the shearing block was bolted an inclined steel plate on which was mounted a stainless steel anvil, which was positioned such that on impact, the pendulum was at an angle of 10° beyond the vertical as shown in Fig. 17.6.

Measurement of the extent of rupture was performed by an indirect method. It is generally known that the protein in a leaf is almost completely contained in its individual cells. The amount of protein (or total nitrogen) released from a leaf sample could thus be related to the percentage of cells ruptured, if the available nitrogen in the sample were known. If the number of cells in a given weight of sample can be estimated, then the number of cells ruptured would be readily obtained. In order to estimate the effectiveness of the forces, the protein-rich juice from ruptured leaves was obtained by mechanical pressing of the leaf sample by an "Instron" in an "expression," or liquid separation device, the details of which are shown in the diagram of Fig. 17.7.

Shearing

Separate tests were performed for upper and lower leaves, and for each group of samples, the available nitrogen was also estimated. For each test

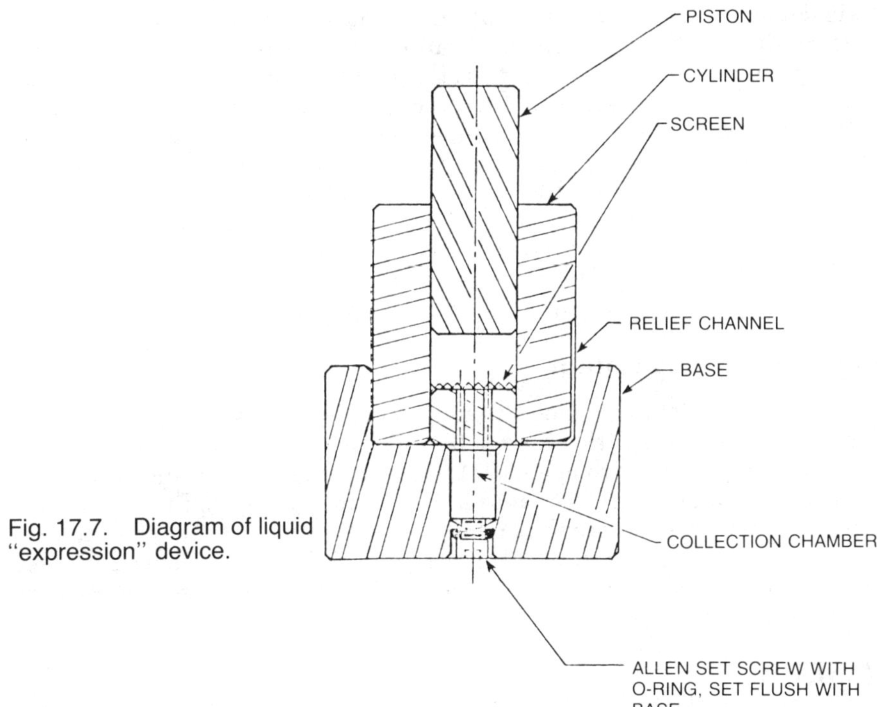

Fig. 17.7. Diagram of liquid "expression" device.

the shearing surface was covered with the leaf sample and a small vacuum was activated to hold the leaves in place. The pendulum was then released from a prescribed position, and the camera triggered simultaneously to record its peak-to-peak travel. The ruptured leaves were placed in breakers with some water for subsequent fiber juice separation.

It has been reported that in forage maceration hammer mills, for instance, the tips of the hammers travel at speeds of the order of 2 m per sec (Pirie 1963). The experimental loading speeds were therefore designed to be in this range, and the shearing energy characteristics were determined at four loading speeds, from 0.5 to 2.4 m/sec (21 to 94 in./sec). Preliminary tests indicated that higher loading rates than those employed caused unacceptable instability in the system (vibrations, etc.). It should be noted, however, that the loading speed in this discussion refers to the maximum attainable linear speed of the tips of the pendulum when released from a prescribed angle (or height) rather than the actual speed of shearing, which would involve deceleration processes, and therefore vary across the leaf.

Compression

The procedure for the evaluation of energy characteristics in dynamic compression was quite similar to that described for shearing. Preliminary tests demonstrated that at pendulum speeds greater than 1.52 m/sec (60 in./sec), the leaf sample "exploded" on impact, spattering pieces of leaves and ruptured cells. Furthermore, at these higher speeds, vibration effects became severe. Tests were therefore not performed beyond that speed.

Prior to each series of tests, the impact system was calibrated by measuring the restitution of the pendulum after impact on the uncovered surface of the block. With leaves on the surface, the difference in absorbed energy could then be considered as the energy transferred to the leaves. The loading speeds ranged from 0.06 to 1.52 m/sec. At the highest loading speed, additional tests were performed to evaluate the extent of rupture when a double layer of leaves was placed on the impact surface.

Liquid/Fiber Separation

Preliminary tests confirmed that quasi-static loads, as applied by an Instron, caused very little damage by themselves, consistent with the observations reported by Koegel (1971). The mechanical pressing of the ruptured leaves would therefore cause insignificant damage to the intact cells. For separation, the system shown in Fig. 17.7 was loaded at a constant rate of 0.5 cm/min to a maximum load of 113.4 kg (250 lb), then relaxed for 90 sec before raising the load cell. The separated juice was then analyzed for nitrogen content.

RESULTS

Three series of experiments were conducted with three groups of samples which were obtained from the test plot over a period corresponding to the peak period, as related to growing season and environmental conditions.

Shearing

Preliminary test demonstrated the interdependency of leaf thickness, shear gap, and loading speed on the effectiveness of shearing. With an average thickness of leaves between 150 and 170 μ, and for the range of speeds employed, the most effective shear gaps were found to be between 90 and 100 μ, and for the tests described here the gap was nominally set at 95 μ.

For all three groups the results generally showed an increase of transferred energy with loading speed. The trend shown by the percentage released nitrogen, however, was not as direct, the results strongly suggesting that nitrogen yields may peak at some loading speed, and then actually decline thereafter. Figure 17.8 shows the plots of the average transferred energy and percentage released nitrogen as a function of loading speed for an average leaf. Although some of the data suggested that for comparable amounts of energy the upper leaves might yield higher amounts of nitrogen, one sample group showed an opposite trend, and the confidence level of the data does not permit conclusive inferences about the differences. Figure 17.8 illustrates the apparent extremum behavior of released nitrogen.

Compression

The initial series of compression tests was performed with loading speeds ranging from 0.06 to 1.5 m/sec (16.5 to 60 in./sec). Due to the unavoidably large energy losses upon impact, it was determined that at speeds below 0.75 m/sec, the transferred energies were so small that the potential error of measurement was relatively large. Generally, both released nitrogen and

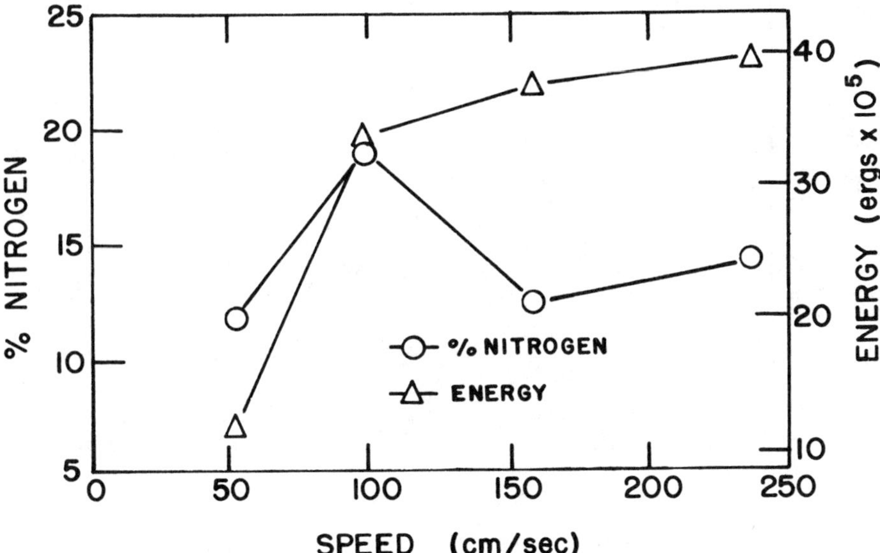

Fig. 17.8. Shearing energy and released nitrogen for an "average" leaf.

transferred energy showed increases with loading speed. At the highest loading speed, there seemed to be a rather consistent drop in absorbed energy for both upper and lower leaves. Possible explanations for this phenomenon will be presented shortly. The average results for the three sample groups are plotted in Fig. 17.9.

Effectiveness of Rupture

In order to reduce the preceding results to a common base for comparison, the actual effectiveness of the transferred energy in cell rupture has to be evaluated. This parameter is determined by dividing the energy input by the estimated number of cells ruptured, and it constitutes the estimated energy required to rupture a single cell, defined here as "energy per cell." For each sample of leaves, the estimated number of cells can be determined from Fig. 17.1 and, recalling the assumption that all the nitrogen is contained within the cells, the number of cells ruptured can be directly ob-

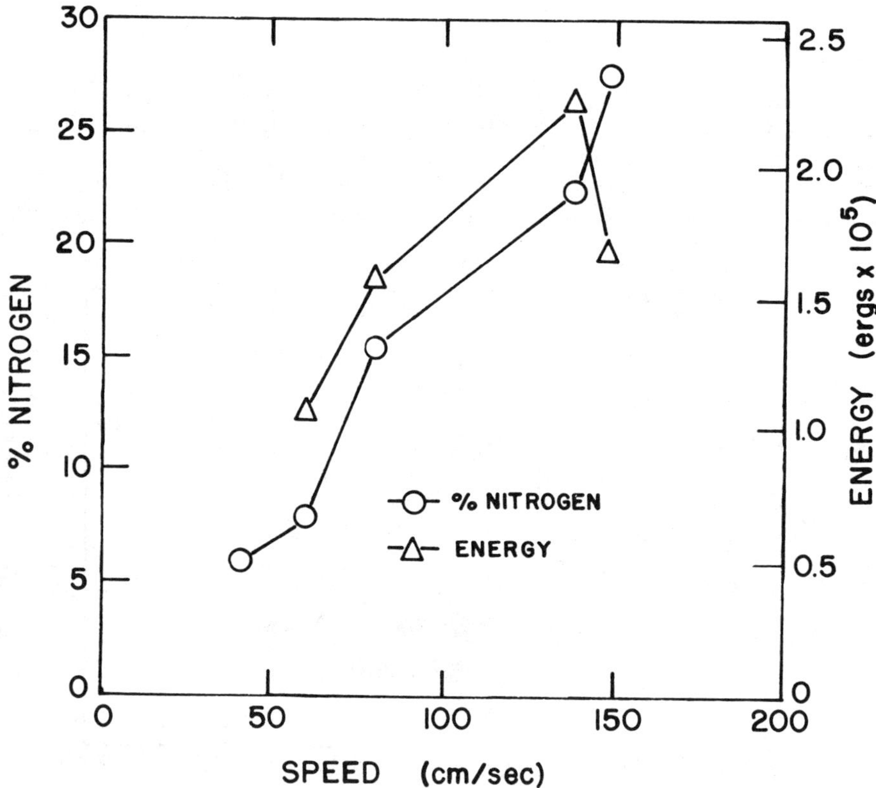

Fig. 17.9. Impact energy and released nitrogen for an "average" leaf.

tained. From Fig. 17.1, the number of cells per gram during the peak period is estimated to be 11.7×10^7 and $8.7 \times 10^7\ g^{-1}$ for upper and lower leaves, respectively. The number of cells per sample was thus determined and the energy per cell evaluated. The average results for the experimental period are shown in Fig. 17.10 and 17.11. For shearing, the average energy per cell is shown to generally increase with loading speed, consistent with the trends shown by the individual test groups. As previously noted, the apparent difference between upper and lower leaves cannot be regarded as conclusive.

The individual compression tests showed energy requirements that are quite consistent with those illustrated in Fig. 17.11. Although the differences are not large, the upper leaves consistently showed lower energy requirements, as would be intuitively expected. Figure 17.11 also indicates that for compression, the energy requirements apparently decrease with loading speed. Tests with a double layer of leaves on the impact block showed results similar to those with a single layer.

Comparison of Fig. 17.10 and 17.11 vividly demonstrates the differences

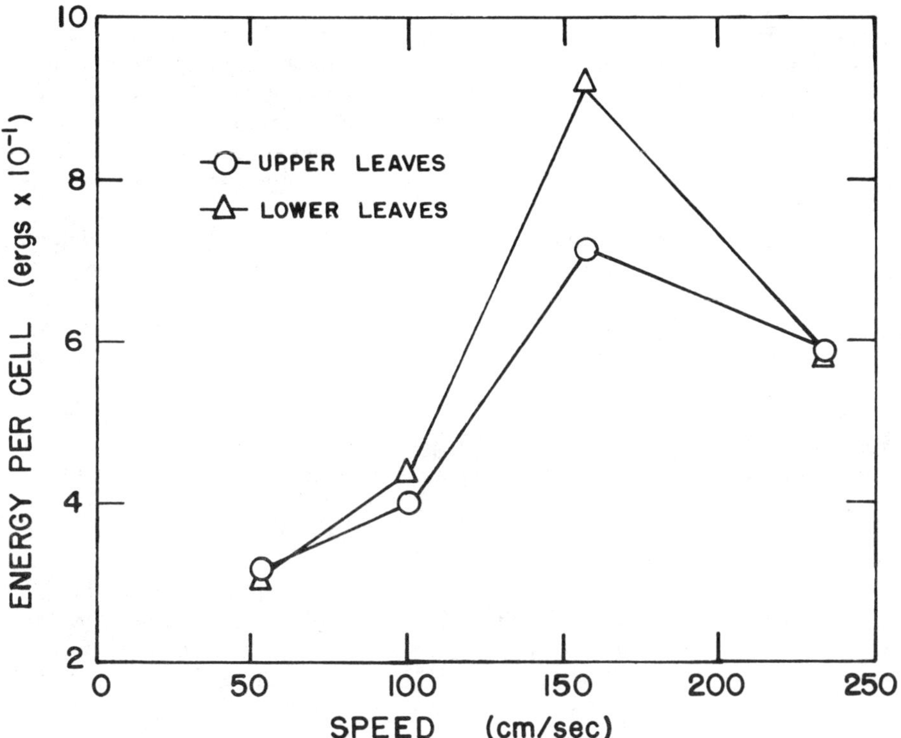

Fig. 17.10. Average shearing energy per cell vs. speed.

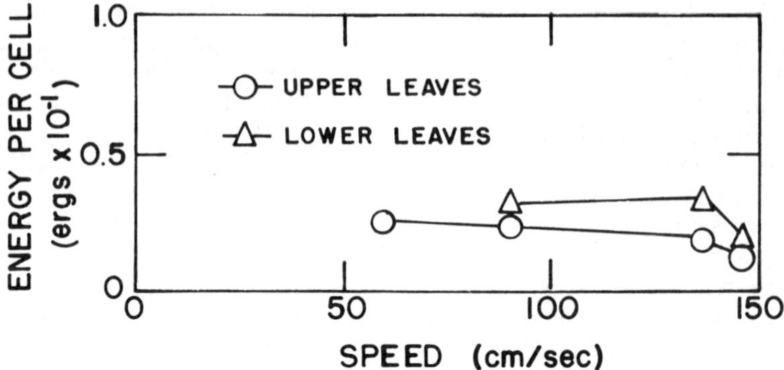

Fig. 17.11. Average impact energy per cell vs. speed.

in energy requirements for shear and compression, with the latter being approximately an order of magnitude more effective than shear.

IMPLICATIONS IN LEAF PROTEIN PRODUCTION

A significant observation from the study of morphological characteristics was the identification of the "peak period," during which foliar growth and average nitrogen content were apparently at a maximum. Leaf deterioration was noticed soon after this period, and the average nitrogen content declined. On the basis of quantity and quality of leaves, and the availability of protein alone, forage material processed during this period would maximize protein yields.

The incidence and duration of the peak period are apparently dependent on the total age of the crop, as well as on the environmental conditions. A comparison of the samples used in the present study, obtained from the beginning and end of the growing season (May and October, respectively), shows that for the early-season samples, the peak period occurred during the twelfth and seventeenth days, while the late-season group showed a peak period after 28 days, and a duration longer than 10 days. It is quite reasonable to suggest that these differences can be related to the growth rate of plants, with slower growing plants having delayed-peak periods of longer duration. It is obvious that these factors will also vary from species to species, and the need for their consideration in protein production is quite evident.

The period of abundant foliage and maximum protein availability is also accompanied by several physical and structural factors pertinent to the rupture of leaf cells, and/or to protein production. It was shown, for instance, that maximum leaf weights were obtained during the peak period. Crops harvested during this period would, therefore, have higher total weights and the largest quantities of available protein.

Analysis of the number of cells per unit weight of leaf revealed an apparent decline of values during the peak period, followed by a gradual increase till flowering. This trend is consistent with the observation that the average leaf thickness was at a maximum during the peak period, and examination of the plotted data for packing density indicates that the fraction of air space was also highest during this period. The implication of these observations is that during the peak period, the leaf cells are relatively loosely packed, making deformation and rupture easier. It was also shown that during the peak period the palisade cells are much more elongated and slender than during the periods before and after. Slender configurations are more unstable in buckling under compressive-type loads than are shorter, wider columns. Consequently, the configuration of the palisade cells renders them more amenable to rupture during the peak period.

The results of several tests indicate that there is a rather rapid loss of moisture from leaves (especially younger leaves) once they are harvested. This phenomenon could have adverse effects in rupture considerations. The loss of moisture would cause protoplasm to withdraw from the cell walls, leaving them unsupported. The walls would lose their rigidity, and the cells could then withstand considerably larger deformation without rupturing. This factor, among others involving enzymatic changes in the leaves with subsequent low protein yields (Arkcoll 1971), imposes limitations on the elapsed time between harvest and the extraction of protein from the raw material.

From the standpoint of force application, the limited rupture caused by quasi-static loading, as effected by the "Instron," is consistent with earlier suggestions of the ineffectiveness of quasi-static loads. Some probable reasons for limited rupture follow.

Most biological cells are viscoelastic in nature, with the ability to sustain relatively large plastic deformation under static loads. A quasi-static load may thus cause large deformations without rupturing the cell. A second factor is that in quasi-static loading the possibility of liquid transfer through the semipermeable membrane of the cell wall is increased. When the rate of load application is very small, this factor may become quite significant. Liquid will be expelled from the cell on loading, thus continuously decreasing the cells' resistance to the applied load. Large deformation could then occur without rupture. The "expressed" juice would contain little protein, since the cellular particles' chloroplasts in which most of the protein is contained would not pass through the cell wall.

Since dynamic loads are known to be more effective in causing failure (rupture) than corresponding static loads, the increased level of nitrogen yields obtained with the dynamic shear and compression are completely to be expected. In shearing, the optimum loading rate was found to be dependent on the shear gap. It is clear that for each shear gap to leaf thickness ratio, the speed characteristics for minimum energy expenditure would change. It was observed, for instance, that for each shear gap setting, there was a threshold loading speed below which shearing could not be completed over the whole surface. In Figure 17.10, it is shown that the energy requirements increase with loading speed. In design for the optimum speed it is not feasible to just select the lowest speed, which showed the lowest energy requirement, since at that speed the amount of nitrogen actually released is relatively small. By comparison with the characteristics at the loading speed of approximately 102 cm/sec ((40 in./sec), it is observed that the percentage of released nitrogen is much higher. This implies that although it would require somewhat larger energy expenditures, the latter speed would minimize the number of times a group of leaves is subjected to rupturing forces from input to output of a machine. This consideration could have impact on both the size of machinery and energy losses in the process. Proper design would therefore require the optimization between "energy per cell" and percentage released nitrogen.

For the impact tests, it is shown that the percentage released nitrogen increases with loading speed, while the energy requirements for rupture decrease. As previously noted, at the highest speed of loading (approximately 147 cm/sec or 58 in./sec), there was a consistent drop in transferred energy, while nitrogen yields continued to rise. This loading speed seems to be greater than a threshold value beyond which the energy absorbed by the leaves in deformation alone is at a minimum, thus making the transferred energy more efficient in rupture. These observations suggest that for impact systems, processes would potentially be most effective at the highest feasible speeds.

In order to compare the estimated process energy expenditure from the present study with values cited in the literature, it is recalled that, as an average, a modern hammer mill would macerate 0.9 MT (1 ST) of material with an energy input of 30 to 40 kwh, while liberating between 55 and 75% protein (Pirie 1970). Here, 35 kwh and 75% protein are assumed for the purposes of comparison. Using the average of the highest values of energy requirements as shown in Fig. 17.10, the estimated energy expenditure, based on the results of this study, would be less than 5% of the previously reported pilot scale values. The difference provides an indication of the fraction of input energy apparently expended due to process and machine limitations.

CONCLUSION

The discussion presented in this chapter has demonstrated the significance of various structural and mechanical factors in process design for leaf protein production. From a materials standpoint, the existence of a identifiable peak period would have considerable impact in production. From a mechanical perspective, the types of force, as well as loading rates and shear gaps, have been shown to influence rupture characteristics. For the purposes of rupture, dynamic compression has been shown to be more effective than shearing, and if its main drawbacks such as vibrations, heat, and noise can be minimized, it would be potentially superior in commercial processes. The discussion also illustrates that, in spite of the simplicity of the test methods, the evaluation of fundamental factors could be quite valuable in ultimate wide-scale commercialization of leaf protein.

REFERENCES

ADDY, T.O. 1974. Mechanical parameters in leaf cell membrane rupture for protein extraction. Unpublished Ph.D. Thesis. Food Engineering Dep., University of Massachusetts, Amherst.

AKESON, W.R. and STAHMANN, M.A. 1966. Leaf protein concentrates: A comparison of protein production per acre of forage with that from seed and animal crops. Econ. Bot. *20*, 3.

ARKCOLL, D.B. 1971. Agronomic aspects of leaf protein production in Great Britain. *In* Leaf Protein. IBP Handb. *20*. Blackwell Scientific Publications, Oxford.

BYERS, M. and STURROCK, T.W. 1965. The yields of leaf protein extracted by large-scale processing of various crops. J. Sci. Food Agric. *12*, 1.

HOLLÓ, J. and KOCH, L. 1971. Commercial production (of leaf protein) in Hungary. *In* Leaf Protein. Blackwell Scientific Publications, Oxford and Edinburgh.

KOEGEL, R.G. 1971. Pressure fractionation of alfalfa. Unpublished Ph.D. Thesis. Agricultural Engineering Dep., University of Wisconsin.

KOHLER, G.O. and BICKOFF, E.M. 1971. Commercial production (of leaf protein) from alfalfa in the U.S.A. *In* Leaf Protein. Blackwell Scientific Publications, Oxford and Edinburgh.

PIRIE, N.W. 1963. Non-conventional protein sources. *In* Advances in Food Science, Vol. 3. J.M. Leitch and D.M. Rhodes (Editors). Academic Press, New York.

PIRIE, N.W. 1970. Thirty years of progress with leaf protein. Unpublished Bulletin from the Rothampsted Exp. Stn., Harpenden, Herts., England.

PRINCE, R.P. and WHEELER, W.C. 1960. Factors affecting the cutting of forage crops. Am. Soc. Agric. Eng. Pap. *60–611*.

TURRELL, F.M. 1942. A quantitative morphological analysis of large and small leaves of alfalfa with special reference to internal surface. Am. J. Bot. *29*, 400.

18

LPC for Feeds and Foods: The Pro-Xan Process

George O. Kohler, Richard H. Edwards, and Donald de Fremery

Of the leafy plants grown as forages in the United States, alfalfa is dominant because of its high productivity, high nutritive value, and low production costs (Kohler *et al.* 1978). In this chapter, we shall be speaking largely of alfalfa, realizing that the technologies discussed have broad application to a wide variety of leafy crops.

The earliest reference to alfalfa as a feed dates back to about 1300 B.C., although it has been speculated that it was used in Eastern Mediterranean countries as early as 4000–7000 B.C. (Bolton *et al.* 1972).

During the millenia which have passed, the primary usage of forages has been as feed for cattle, sheep, and horses, since these animals have the ability to digest most of the fibrous components of forages. Poultry and swine do not have comparable digestible capabilities. With the advent of heat dehydration, the higher quality products resulting have found some usage in poultry and swine rations, but as special purpose supplements to grain-based rations rather than as a primary ration component. One of the important components of alfalfa leading to usage in poultry rations has been its content of xanthophyll, the yellow pigment responsible for coloration of egg yolks and the skin of broiler and fryer chickens. However, even with dehydrated alfalfa, the high fiber and low energy content have limited its usage in nonruminant animals. In ruminants, alfalfa when fed as the primary feed contains more protein than necessary to meet the animal requirements. Furthermore, xanthophyll has no value in cattle rations and may even lead to downgrading of carcasses due to castiness (yellow fat). Thus, removal of the surplus protein and xanthophyll by juicing and recovery in a separate product would lead to greatly improved utilization of this basic crop, providing products specifically designed for different types of livestock.

The earliest reference we have found on the use of alfalfa in the human diet is an 1882 article which reported that "the Chinese eat it (alfalfa) as a vegetable" (Bretschneider 1882). During World Wars I and II, some work was done in Germany to use alfalfa as a food by washing out the bitter principle(s) with hot water (Haberlandt 1916; Henpke and Scholler 1942). However, there seems to have been little general usage of products prepared in this manner. In Germany and in the United States, dried alfalfa grasses have been incorporated into bread and other foods, but acceptability has been poor largely because of the green color (i.e., "green bread" appears moldy) (Lommel 1939; Kohler 1947). Dried alfalfa has been sold in health food stores for many years, generally in the form of tablets or tea.

In recent years, fresh alfalfa sprouts have become quite popular with consumers. In spite of the interest and enthusiasm of some scientists and "health food" enthusiasts, whole green alfalfa and other forages, fresh or dried, do not constitute a significant part of the human diet anywhere in the world. We see no evidence which indicates that this situation will change in the future. Here, of course, we are speaking specifically of whole plant material, not of isolates derived from leafy crops.

From the early 1930s through the 1960s, research was carried out in several countries, including Great Britain, the United States, and Hungary, to prepare low-fiber protein concentrates or isolates for food or feed from a wide variety of leaves (Pirie 1971B; Kohler *et al.* 1978). During this time, suitable equipment for some of the unit operations was not available, yields were low, and knowledge regarding the nature and utility of the products was inadequate. Also, at the yields then achievable, whole green leaf protein concentrates (LPC) could not compete as a feed ingredient during those years of agricultural surpluses. For these reasons, no lasting commercial or other large-scale production of LPC was realized.

If leaf protein is to play a substantial role in the protein economy of the United States and other countries, it will have to compete on an economic basis with corn gluten meal, soybean meal, and other protein sources presently used for both animals and man.

PRESSING AND PRESS CAKE UTILIZATION

When alfalfa is ground and pressed (Fig. 18.1), the juice contains 35–60% of the crude protein and 20–40% of the dry matter of the original alfalfa, depending on the quality of the alfalfa and the effectiveness of the process and equipment used. The press cake, which is quantitatively the major product of the process, must be used effectively as a feed if protein recovery from the juice is to be economically feasible. The press cake, with or without added urea, can be utilized in the same way as whole alfalfa. Due to its relatively low moisture content, several advantages are apparent for the press cake utilization systems shown in Fig. 18.2. (1) In direct feeding (treatment a), the higher nutrient density permits greater nutrient intake by cattle and reduces hauling costs; (2) in ensiling (treatment b), the low-moisture press cake produces equivalent or superior silage compared with whole alfalfa (Hibbs *et al.* 1968; Stahmann 1975; Russell *et al.* 1978) and

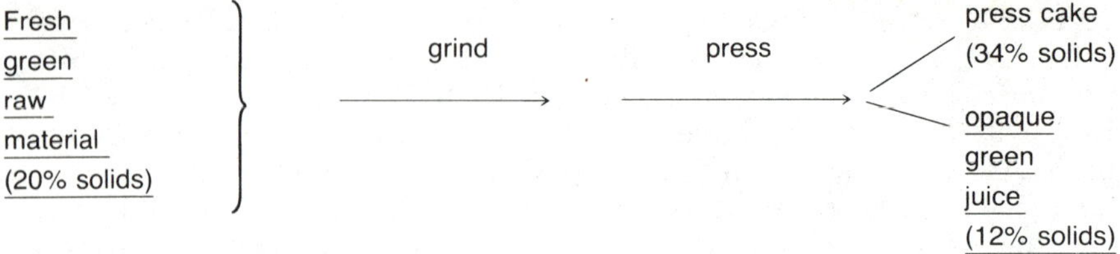

Fig. 18.1. Basic wet process steps.
From Kohler (1975).

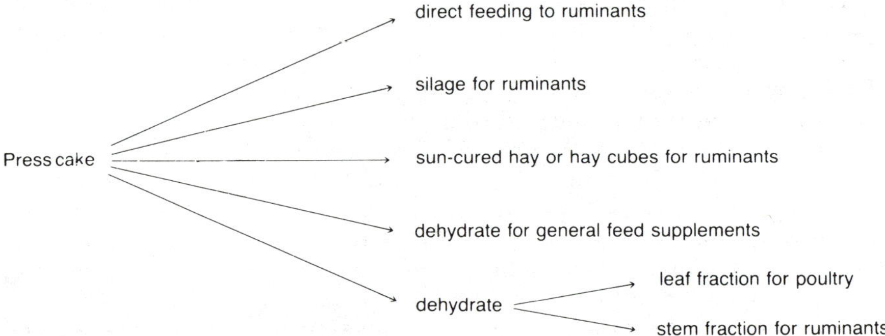

Fig. 18.2. Alternative treatments and uses for the press cake.
From Kohler (1975).

eliminates the field wilting step conventionally used to reduce moisture content of ensiled alfalfa; (3) in haying (treatment c), the lower moisture and crushed stems of the pressed alfalfa lead to much more rapid sun curing and, therefore, reduced exposure to possible rain damage; and (4) in dehydration (treatments d and e), the lower moisture content requires less fuel energy for drying (Casselman *et al.* 1965; Kohler *et al.* 1973).

While the composition of the protein fractions and the solubles does not vary greatly with high or low extraction levels, the protein content of the press cake is affected. When the yield of LPC is 18%, the press cake contains about 10.3% protein as compared with 20% for the raw material (dry basis). This level of protein may be raised to 11.6% by adding back the solubles, preferably after concentration in a multiple-effect evaporator. The press cake has a much higher digestibility than would be expected from a forage with this protein content. This results because the lignin-cellulose ratio is the same as that of the original 20% protein raw material and also because the cells have been opened up by grinding (Connell and Houseman 1977; Kohler *et al.* 1973; Kohler *et al.* 1979B). The dehydrated press cake may be marketed, as is, in competition with sun-cured alfalfa hay pellets or cubes, or by blending with higher protein material to give products equivalent to standard grades of dehydrated alfalfa (e.g., 15 or 17% protein).

Having obtained a juice which contains from 30 to 60% of the protein of the original alfalfa, let us consider recovery of this protein in a form suitable for feed or food.

PHASE I—LPC FOR FEED

Several approaches to press juice utilization are shown in Fig. 18.3. In treatment (a), the whole juice is fed to pigs. Research has been carried out along this line in Ireland (Maguire and Brookes 1973) and England (Braude 1973). The product distribution is limited in this case by the excessive weight per unit of nutrient and by susceptibility to spoilage. A second treatment (b) is to dry the whole juice for use as a poultry or swine supplement (Hartman *et al.* 1967). The advantage of (b) over (a) is that the dried product is microbiologically stable and can be shipped at low cost. However, since the whole protein-rich juice cannot be processed effectively in multistage evaporators, drying costs are even greater than those for drying whole alfalfa. Further, dried whole juice is high in ash and not high enough in protein (about 33%) to compete readily with soybean meal as a source of protein. Therefore, alternative (c) of Fig. 18.3 has been our preferred method for juice treatment (Kohler *et al.* 1968; Kohler and Bickoff 1971).

The system which we use and describe as the Pro-Xan process (named for the LPC product, Pro-Xan, which has a high content of both protein and xanthophyll) is designed to give large-scale, low-cost leaf protein production while complementing current forage utilization systems (Kohler *et al.* 1979A; Knuckles *et al.* 1972; Edwards *et al.* 1975A). The Pro-Xan (feed-grade) system is evolving as continuing research is done. The current system is shown in Fig. 18.4. Fresh field-chopped alfalfa is treated with

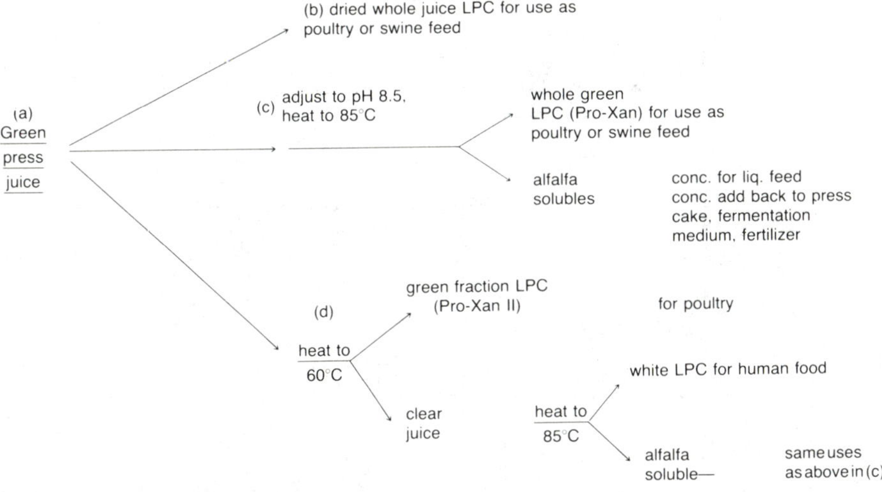

Fig. 18.3. Alternative treatments and uses for the press juice.
From Kohler (1975).

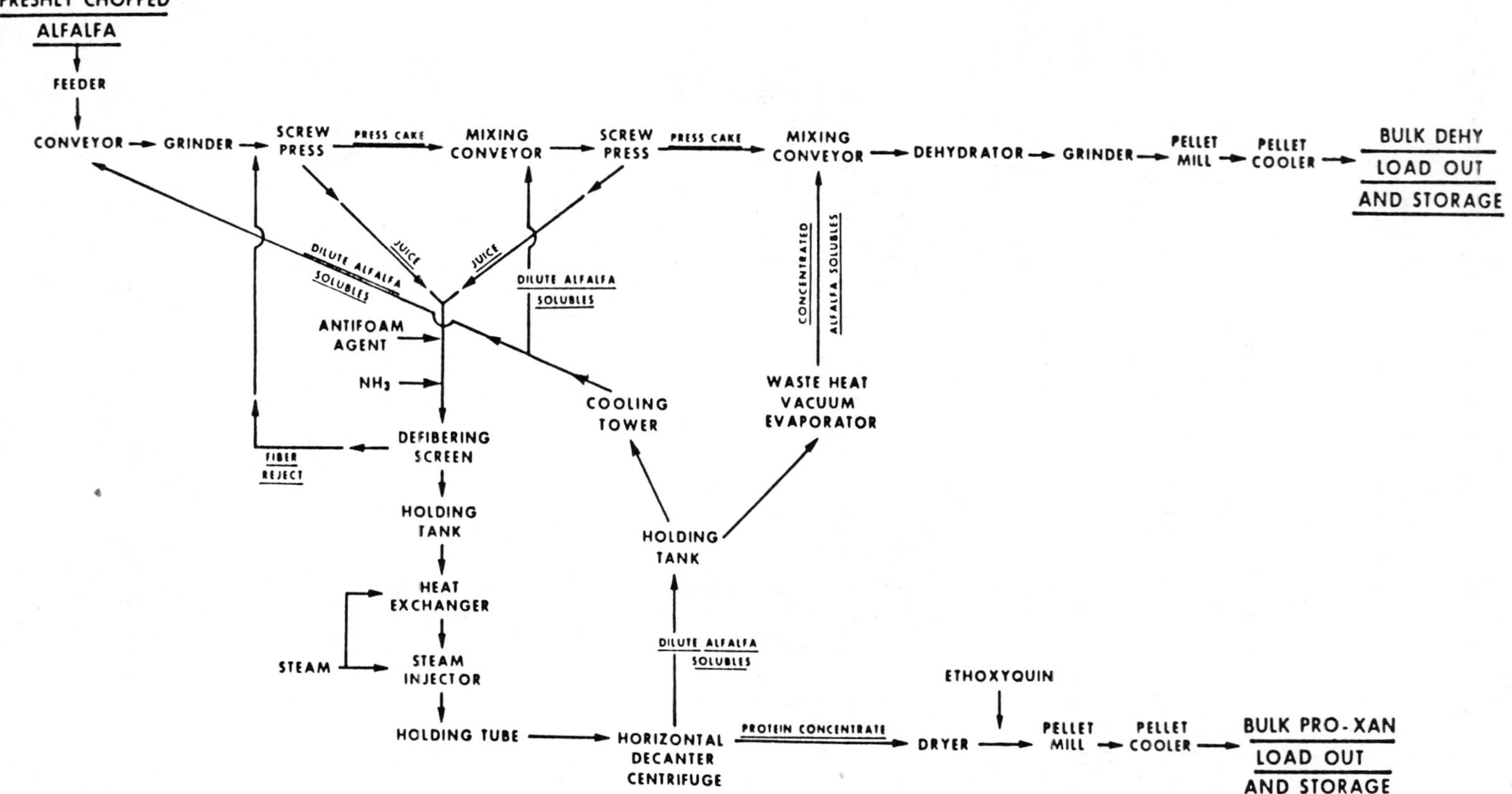

Fig. 18.4. Flow diagram for production of Pro-Xan from alfalfa.

gaseous ammonia to raise the pH of the press juice to 8.5. This treatment markedly inhibits the proteolytic enzymes of the plant which would otherwise hydrolyze the leaf proteins at a rapid rate (de Fremery *et al.* 1972). (If time between harvesting and pressing is short, the ammonia may be applied to the press juice rather than to the chopped alfalfa.)

The alfalfa is then ground in a screenless hammer mill to rupture the leaf cells (Edwards *et al.* 1976, 1978B). The ground alfalfa is pressed and then repressed in tandem screw presses to extract protein and water from the raw material (Kohler *et al.* 1979A). A part of the alfalfa solubles from a later step is cooled and added to the raw material before grinding and also between pressings to increase protein extraction (Edwards *et al.* 1978A). The protein in the juice is coagulated by heating to 80°–90°C for 10–20 sec using direct steam injection. The bright green curd is separated from the brown whey-like juice (alfalfa solubles fraction) by means of a scroll-type centrifuge (Smith 1966; Edwards *et al.* 1976). The centrifuged curd contains 40–50% dry matter. It is then granulated or extruded prior to drying in a rotary drier, tunnel drier, or fluidized bed drier, maintaining product temperature below 60°–80°C (Smith 1966; Miller *et al.* 1972). The press cake is dehydrated and pelleted by conventional means. Normally the brown juice is vacuum concentrated and added to the wet press cake prior to dehydration. Use of the waste heat evaporator is desirable to conserve energy (Giroud and Vinconneau 1979).

The protein concentrate (whole LPC, Pro-Xan) is a dark green granular product which is very low in fiber and high in protein and xanthophyll. Xanthophyll gives the product special value as a chicken feed ingredient, especially in the United States, since it is this pigment which gives egg yolks and broiler skins their desirable golden yellow color (Kuzmicky and Kohler 1977; Kuzmicky *et al.* 1977).

PHASE II—LPC FOR FOOD

Whole green LPC has been unacceptable to most people as a food because of its color and flavor characteristics. Such a product might be acceptable (a) in times of famine (war or crop failure), (b) where the material is incorporated into foods which mask its flavor and color, and (c) in protein-deficient areas where it might be used for infants and young children whose food acceptance patterns have not been established. In the last category, projects on feeding acid-washed whole green LPC (prepared according to Pirie 1971A) to children have been undertaken. The work in Nigeria has shown that feeding 10 g/day cures kwashiorkor (protein deficiency disease) in children consuming diets high in cassava (Olatunbosun *et al.* 1972). Results of the Coimbatore (India) project (Devadas *et al.* 1978) showed good acceptance by 3–4 year old children when LPC was incorporated into a candy-like product. Children receiving the LPC showed superior growth in both height and weight as compared with controls.

When Phase I of the program was well along, we initiated Phase II research with the objective of producing a white, bland leaf protein (white

LPC) for human consumption. Exploratory experiments on solvent extraction to remove the green color of whole LPC were discouraging. Nonpolar solvents are ineffective. Polar solvents such as aqueous acetone, alcohols, etc., could be used to extract chlorophyll from the green heat coagulate or to precipitate the protein from the green juice and extract the chlorophyll from the precipitate. However, very large amounts of solvents were needed to remove enough chlorophyll so that no green color remained (Miller *et al.* 1977). Even when such exhaustive extraction was carried out, the protein tended to be gray in color rather than white.

Another approach to white LPC production is separation of the green juice protein into two parts, a green fraction (green LPC) and a white fraction (white LPC) (Kohler and Bickoff 1971; Subba Rau *et al.* 1969; de Fremery *et al.* 1973; Edwards *et al.* 1975B; Bickoff and Kohler 1974). This separation may be accomplished without solvents by fractional heat precipitation. The juice from the press contains protein in two forms. About half of the true protein consists of insoluble, colloidally dispersed lipoproteins associated with the chloroplasts, the subcellular particles which contain all of the chlorophyll in the leaves. The other half of the juice protein is in true solution and is not associated with chlorophyll. This soluble protein is a mixture of cytoplasmic protein and a chlorophyll-free protein (Fraction I protein) derived from the breakdown of chloroplasts during juicing (Kohler *et al.* 1978). By adjusting the conditions of temperature, time, and pH, the colloidal green particles can be agglomerated sufficiently to permit their centrifugal separation using commercially available equipment. In the pilot plant, we heat the fresh juice by direct steam injection for 10–20 sec at 60°–65°C as in Fig. 18.3, treatment (d) (de Fremery *et al.* 1973; Bickoff and Kohler 1974). The solids, containing the insoluble proteins, are centrifuged out in a two-stage system as a pasty green sludge. The centrate, or liquid phase from the centrifuge, contains the soluble proteins as well as sugars, salts, water-soluble vitamins, etc. After removing final traces of green particles by filtration, the white protein is recovered from the clarified juice by heat, acid precipitation, ultrafiltration, or gel filtration. After washing to remove the residual non-protein solubles, the white protein is dried.

Ultrafiltration of the green press juice has been studied as an alternative procedure to separate the green protein from the press juice, but it appears that further work will be necessary to obtain practical results (Singh *et al.* 1974; Eakin *et al.* 1978).

The green protein by-product of the preceding separations is brought to pH 8.5 with ammonia and heated to 95°C. This treatment further denatures the protein to form a harder curd which can be dewatered in a centrifuge prior to drying. This green fraction LPC, which we call Pro-Xan II, is very rich in carotene and xanthophyll and is valuable as a poultry supplement.

Let us next consider the several procedures for white protein recovery from the clarified juice and their effects on product quality. Important white LPC quality factors which are controlled by process steps are: (1) the nutritional value of the product (including digestibility, amino acid composition, and the presence of undesirable impurities), and (2) the functional properties of the protein (including solubility, fat binding capacity, gelling, foaming, etc.). The nutritional quality of the protein has been discussed by Bickoff *et al.* (1975). Briefly, the white protein fraction is comparable to casein in chemical score and Protein Efficiency Ratio (PER) measured with weanling rats. Addition of sodium metabisulfite at the chopping or grinding step not only increases the PER value to values greater than those of casein, but also improves the color of the dried product, presumably by preventing oxidation of some polyphenols present in the juice.

Turning to the matter of functional properties, Fig. 18.5 shows the pH solubility profiles of several white LPC products (Betschart and Kohler 1975). The heat-coagulated product, in either freeze-dried or spray-dried form, showed practically no solubility from pH 2 to 10. The acid-precipitated product showed acid and alkali solubility but with a broad range of low solubility between pH 3 and pH 8.

A further study of acid precipitation (Miller *et al.* 1975; Bickoff *et al* 1976) showed that much of the solubility at pH 7 could be retained in the acid-precipitated white LPC if the temperature was reduced to close to 0° C prior to the addition of the acid (Fig. 18.6). A pH solubility profile (Fig. 18.7) showed that even the cold acid-precipitated white LPC was fairly insoluble at pH 6. This suggests that the protein was altered (or denatured) by even the cold acid treatment, since undenatured white protein is soluble at pH 6

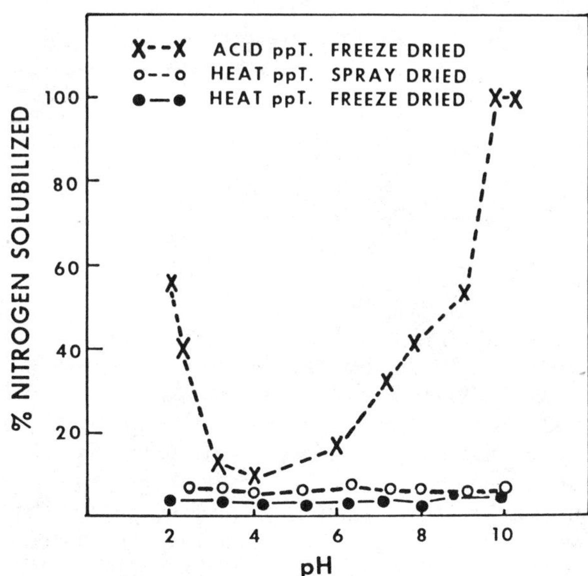

Fig. 18.5. Nitrogen solubility of heat- and acid-precipitated alfalfa protein isolates as a function of pH.

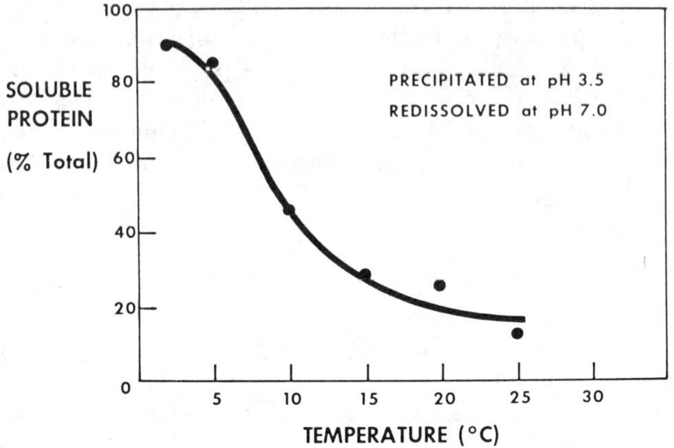

Fig. 18.6. Solubility of alfalfa protein precipitated at pH 3.5 and redissolved at pH 7.0. Temperature was maintained at indicated level during precipitation, washing, and redissolving.

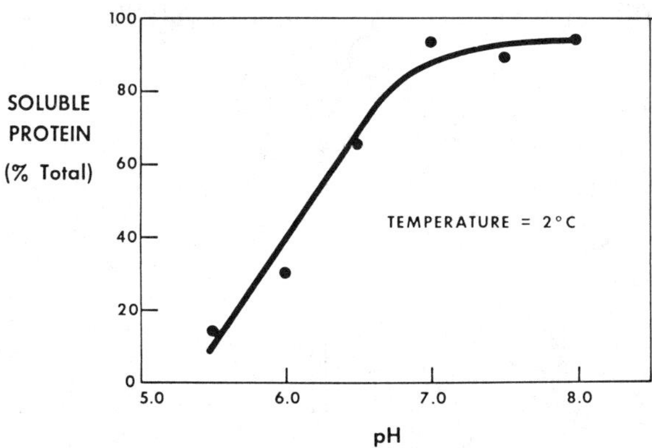

Fig. 18.7. Solubility of alfalfa protein precipitated at pH 3.5 and redissolved at various pH levels. Temperature was maintained at 2°C during precipitation, washing, and redissolving.

and at pH 3.5 and below (Fig. 18.8) (Knuckles *et al.* 1975). Diafiltration (washing in the ultrafiltration unit) yielded products soluble at pH 3.5. Gel filtration using Sephadex G-50 yields comparable or superior products. The properties of the ultrafiltered and gel-filtered products appear to be the most desirable yet obtained. Hence, these processes are currently being expanded to pilot plant scale.

The alfalfa solubles from the Pro-Xan (whole LPC) process and the Pro-Xan II (fractionation) process are identical. The thin solubles may be concentrated in a waste heat evaporator to produce a stable molasses-like

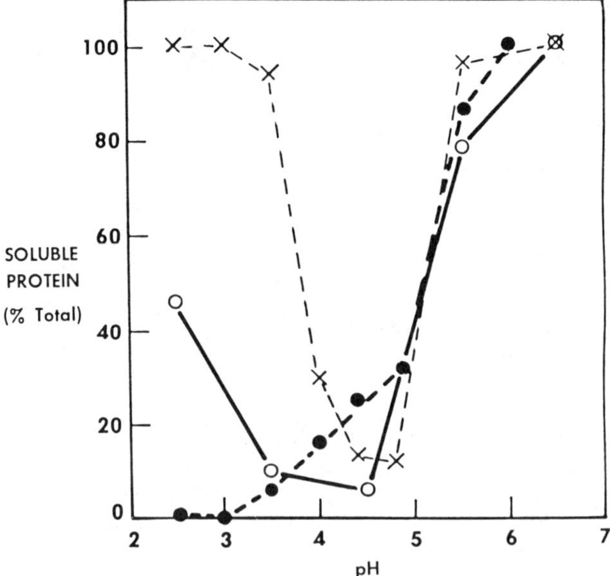

Fig. 18.8. Effect of ultrafiltration and diafiltration on acid solubility of protein. ●——● Centrate. o——o Retentate (ultrafiltration). x——x Retentate (diafiltration).

product. It is suitable for use in liquid feed supplements (Perry *et al.* 1974); it may be added back to the press cake or to the protein coagulate prior to drying; it has potential use as a fermentation medium (Paredes-Lopez and Camargo 1973); or, where economics dictate, it may be pumped back on the fields for its fertilizer and irrigation value (Ream *et al.* 1975).

Typical product yields from the two processes (Pro-Xan and Pro-Xan II) are shown in Table 18.1. The data are based on recycling of brown juice to the grinder so that yields of fractionated LPC are higher than reported earlier (Kohler and Knuckles 1977). If we look at the recovery of the process products, we see that 65% of the dry weight of the alfalfa was recovered in the press cake. Of the 35% removed in the juice, 17% was recovered in the solubles fraction. In the Pro-Xan process, the remaining 18% was recovered as whole LPC (Pro-Xan). In the Pro-Xan II process, 14% was recovered as green LPC (Pro-Xan II) and 4.2% as white LPC. A look at the crude protein distribution column shows that pressing removed 67% of the crude protein in the juice. Of this, 52% was recovered in the Pro-Xan, the remaining 15% in the brown juice. When the split was made in the Pro-Xan II process, about two-thirds of the recoverable protein was in the green fraction, and one-third in the white. The latter represents about 58% of the soluble protein present in the original alfalfa. These figures represent substantial in-

TABLE 18.1. DISTRIBUTION OF SOLIDS IN THE PRO-XAN SYSTEM[1]

Solids	Dry Weight %	Crude Protein (% of Original)	Soluble Protein (% of Original)
Raw material			
solids	100	—	—
crude protein	20	100	—
soluble protein	7	—	100
Recovery of Pro-Xan process products[2]			
whole LPC	18	52	—
press cake	65	33	—
brown juice	17	15	—
Recovery in Pro-Xan II products[3]			
white LPC	4.2	20	58
green LPC	14	33	—

[1] 18% yield basis with 50% brown juice recycle.
[2] Based on pilot plant runs.
[3] Calculated.

creases in yield over our previously published results. The improvement is due largely to improved cell disruption in the grinder, double pressing, and recycling of solubles during grinding and pressing. The degree of cell disruption achieved in the grinder and press is estimated to be about 75% (Anaya-Serrano 1978).

All of our yield data are calculated on a dry basis and corrected to a standard soluble solids basis. This "standard" product contains about 8% soluble solids and 62% protein (Table 18.2). If the product contains more brown juice solids so as to lower the product protein content to 44% (either by leaving more brown juice in the curd going to the drier, or by adding back concentrated brown juice), the yield of the product is increased by about 33%. Thus, the achievable yield of a 44% protein, whole, green, feed-grade LPC is about 24% of the dry weight of the starting material. The yields, of course, would be lower if poorer quality raw material were used. Higher quality raw materials can be obtained at specific times of the growing season, by harvesting the plants at an earlier stage of growth or by harvesting the leaves or the tops of the plants separately from the bottom

TABLE 18.2. PROXIMATE COMPOSITION OF ALFALFA LPC PRODUCTS[1]

Product	Crude Protein[2] %	Fat[3] %	Crude Fiber %	Ash %	Nitrogen-free Extract %	Soluble Solids %
Whole LPC (Pro-Xan)	61.9	8.9	1.7	11.1	16.5	8.1
Green fraction LPC (Pro-Xan II)	45.3	13.3	4.4	15.6	21.5	7.9
White LPC (heat coagulate)	88.7	0.6	1.0	0.4	9.3	0.3

[1] Dry basis.
[2] %N × 6.25.
[3] Ether extract.

stem portions. Proportionately higher yields of Pro-Xan have been obtained from such raw materials (Edwards *et al.* 1979).

Since soybean meal currently dominates the market as a source of protein for feeds and for plant-derived food protein additives, it seems appropriate to compare the yields of alfalfa protein products with soybean products recoverable on a per hectare or per acre basis. The data in Table 18.3 show that the crude protein yields from alfalfa ranged from 2 to 4 times that obtained from soy seeds or meal. The Pro-Xan recovered from 1 acre (0.4 ha) of alfalfa was 1620 to 3600 lb/acre (1822 to 4050 kg/ha) as compared with 1496 lb of soybean meal from 1 acre (1683 kg/ha) of soybeans in Illinois. Comparable or greater yields of white protein isolate are recoverable from alfalfa as compared with protein isolate from soy. However, the alfalfa simultaneously yields 486 to 1080 lb of protein per acre (547 to 1215 kg/ha) in the form of Pro-Xan II, feed-grade green LPC. Thus, we see that alfalfa has substantial product yield advantages over soybeans in addition to its superior ability as a crop to prevent soil erosion and to fix nitrogen.

Ecomomic analyses of the Pro-Xan process (whole green LPC) have been made at several stages of its development and are presented in Chapter 20 of this book.

TABLE 18.3. RELATIVE YIELD/ACRE OF SOY AND ALFALFA PROTEIN PRODUCTS

Protein Product	Relative Yield/Acre[1]	
Soy	United States Avg (1975) lb (Soybeans)/Acre	Illinois (1975)[2] lb/Acre
seed	1728	2160
crude protein (38.4%)	663	829
50% protein meal	1247	1496
concentrate (70% protein)	748	935
concentrate protein	524	655
isolate (33% of protein meal, 96% protein)	412	515
isolate protein	395	493
Alfalfa	Nebraska[3] lb/Acre	Southwest[4] lb/Acre
harvested crop (db)[5]	9000	20000
crude protein (20%)	1800	4000
true protein (80% of crude protein)	1440	3200
Pro-Xan (18% of crop)	1620	3600
Pro-Xan protein (57%)	923	2052
white protein in crop (55% of true protein)	792	1760
recoverable "white protein" (5% of crop)[6]	450	1000
"white protein" protein (90%)	405	900
by-product Pro-Xan II (12% of crop)	1080	2400
Pro-Xan II protein (45%)	486	1080

Sources: Soybean yields: U.S. Dep. Agric. (1977); soybean protein yields: Cater *et al.* (1978); alfalfa yields: American Dehydrators Assoc., Mission, KS.

[1] 1 lb/acre = 1.125 kg/ha.

[2] Illinois had the highest average yield in the United States.

[3] Based on 1 ST per acre (2.25 MT/ha) per cutting = 4½ cuttings/season.

[4] Based on 1 ST per acre (2.25 MT/ha) per cutting (irrigated) = 10 cuttings/season.

[5] Based on yields of alfalfa grown for dehydration on bottomlands comparable to that used for soybean production.

[6] Based on present state of technology.

The Pro-Xan process is presently in commercial operation in France where a 44 MT per hr (40 ST per hr) plant has been operating since June 1976. A 33–44 MT per hr (30–40 ST per hr) plant has been constructed and is operating in the United States (Valley Dehydrating Company, Sterling, Colorado). The operation of the latter plant will be studied over a three-year period by researchers from the U.S. Department of Agriculture with partial funding from the U.S. Department of Energy.

The Pro-Xan II process (fractionated green and white LPC) is not ready for detailed economic analysis. The increase in yields from 2% two years ago to over 4% of the dry weight of the alfalfa is encouraging, and further improvements in yield are expected.

SUMMARY

The Pro-Xan process for feed-grade green leaf protein concentrate has been greatly improved by grinding and pressing of the raw material in the presence of recycled deproteinized brown juice from a later step in the process. Average yields of 18% of the raw material (dry basis) are attainable using large pilot scale equipment [i.e., 11–13 MT (10–12 ST) fresh alfalfa per hr].

Food-grade protein can be prepared by fractionating the protein contained in the press juice by differential heat coagulation. This removes the green pigment (with some of the protein) from a brown solution containing the soluble protein. The latter is recovered by heat coagulation or, in soluble form, by ultrafiltration or gel filtration.

Economic studies show rapid capital payback for the feed-grade product (Pro-Xan). The research on the white food-grade protein has not progressed far enough for economic evaluation. Further research is needed on increasing yield, application of the protein product in various food systems, and obtaining data necessary for clearance by the U.S. Food and Drug Administration (FDA).

REFERENCES

ANAYA-SERRANO, H. 1978. Measurements of the degree of cell rupture in alfalfa and its relationship with energy consumption. M.S. Thesis, Univ. of California, Davis.

BETSCHART, A.A. and KOHLER, G.O. 1975. Certain functional properties of alfalfa protein isolates prepared and dried by various methods. 12th Tech. Alfalfa Conf. Proc. 1974, Overland Park, KS, U.S. Dep. Agric/Agric. Res. Serv., Berkeley, CA.

BICKOFF, E.M., BOOTH, A.N., DE FREMERY, D., EDWARDS, R.H., KNUCKLES, B.E., MILLER, R.E., SAUNDERS, R.M. and KOHLER, G.O. 1975. Nutritional evaluation of alfalfa leaf protein concentrate. *In* Protein Nutritional Quality of Foods and Feeds, Part 2. M. Friedman (Editor). Marcel Dekker, New York.

BICKOFF, E.M., DE FREMERY, D., EDWARDS, R.H., KNUCKLES, B.E., KOHLER, G.O. and MILLER, R.E. 1976. Preparation of soluble edible protein from leafy green crops. U.S. Pat. 3,959,246. May 25.

BICKOFF, E.M. and KOHLER, G.O. 1974. Preparation of edible protein from leafy green crops such as alfalfa. U.S. Pat. 3,823,128. July 9.

BOLTON, J.L., GOPLEN, B.P. and BAENZIGER, H. 1972. World distribution and historical developments. *In* Alfalfa Science and Technology. American Society of Agronomy, Madison, WI.

BRAUDE, R. 1973. Feeding grass juice to pigs. Presentation at Natl. Inst. for Dairying, Sinfield, England, Apr. 12, 1973.

BETSCHNEIDER, E. 1882. Quoted in HEDRICK, U.P. 1919. Sturtevant's Notes on Edible Plants. N.Y. State Dept. Agric. 27th Annu. Rep. *2*. (Pt. II) 358.

CASSELMAN, T.W., GREEN, V.E., JR., ALLEN, R.J., JR. and THOMAS, F.H. 1965. Mechanical dewatering of forage crops. Fla. Agric. Exp. Stn. Univ. Fla., Gainesville, Tech. Bull. *694*.

CATER, C.M., CRAVENS, W.W., HORAN, F.E., LEWIS, C.J., MATTIL, K.F. and WILLIAMS, L.D. 1978. Oilseed proteins. *In* Protein Resources and Technology. M. Milner, N.S. Scrimshaw and D.I.C. Wang (Editors). AVI Publishing Co., Westport, CT.

CONNELL, J. and HOUSEMAN, R.A. 1977. The utilisation by ruminants of the pressed green crops from fractionated machinery. *In* Green Crop Fractionation. Br. Grassl. Soc., Grassland Research Inst., Hurley, England.

DE FREMERY, D., BICKOFF, E.M. and KOHLER, G.O. 1972. Pro-Xan process: Stability of proteins and carotenoid pigments in freshly expressed alfalfa juice. J. Agric. Food Chem. *20*, 1155–1158.

DE FREMERY, D., MILLER, R.E., EDWARDS, R.H., KNUCKLES, B.E., BICKOFF, E.M. and KOHLER, G.O. 1973. Centrifugal separation of white and green protein fractions from alfalfa juice following controlled heating. J. Agric. Food Chem. *21*. (5) 886–889.

DEVADAS, R.P., KAMALANATHAN, G. and VIJAYALAKSHMI, P. 1978. Report on leaf protein feeding trial conducted at Coimbatore, South India, 1975–1977. Find Your Feed, London.

EAKIN, D.E., SINGH, R.P., KOHLER, G.O. and KNUCKLES, B.E. 1978. Alfalfa protein fractionation by ultrafiltration. J. Food Sci. *43*, 544–547, 552.

EDWARDS, R.H., DE FREMERY, D. and KOHLER, G.O. 1975A. The Pro-Xan process: Production of leaf protein from alfalfa. 12th Tech. Alfalfa Conf. Proc., 1974 Overland Parks, KS, U.S. Dep. Agric. Agric. Res. Serv., Berkeley, CA.

EDWARDS, R.H., DE FREMERY, D. and KOHLER, G.O. 1978A. Use of recycled dilute alfalfa solubles to increase the yield of leaf protein concentrate from alfalfa. J. Agric. Food Chem. *26*, 738–741.

EDWARDS, R.H., DE FREMERY, D., MACKEY, B.E. and KOHLER, G.O. 1978B. Factors affecting juice extraction and yield of leaf protein concentrate from ground alfalfa. Trans. ASAE *21*, 55–59, 62.

EDWARDS, R.H., DE FREMERY, D., MILLER, R.E. and KOHLER, G.O. 1978C. Pilot plant production of alfalfa leaf protein concentrate (Pro-Xan). *In* Food, Pharmaceutical and Bioengineering—1976/77. Inst. Chem. Eng. Symp. Ser. *74*. (172) 158–165. American Institute of Chemical Engineering, New York.

EDWARDS, R.H., KNUCKLES, B.E., MILLER, R.E., CURRENCE, D.H., DE FREMERY, D. and KOHLER, G.O. 1979. Use of leaf enriching harvesting methods to increase the yield of leaf protein concentrate from Lucerne. J. Sci. Food Agric. *30* (6) 558–565.

EDWARDS, R.H., MILLER, R.E., DE FREMERY, D., KNUCKLES, B.E., BICKOFF, E.M. and KOHLER, G.O. 1975B. Pilot plant production of an edible white fraction leaf protein concentrate from alfalfa. J. Agric. Food Chem. *23*, 620–626.

GIROUD, P. and VINCONNEAU, M.F. 1979. Industrial production of alfalfa protein and energy economy. Proc. 2nd Int. Green Crop Drying Congr., Saskatoon, Sask., Aug. 20–25, 1978. Ext. Div., Univ. of Saskatchewan, Saskatoon, Canada.

HERBERLANDT, G. 1916. Legume leaves as a food component. Naturwissenschaften *4*, 361–363. (German)

HARTMAN, G.H., JR., AKESON, W.R. and STAHMANN, M.A. 1967. Leaf protein concentrate prepared by spray-drying. J. Agric. Food Chem. *15*, 74–79.

HENPKE, W. and SCHOLLER, R. 1942. About the utilization of alfalfa as a human food component. Ernaehrung *7* (A6) 162–166. (German)

HIBBS, J.W., CONRAD, H.R. and JOHNSON, W.H. 1968. Macerated, dewatered vs. wilted alfalfa-grass silage for dairy cows. Ohio Agric. Res. Dev. Cent., Wooster, Res. Bull. *1013*.

KNUCKLES, B.E., BICKOFF, E.M. and KOHLER, G.O. 1972. Pro-Xan process: Methods for increasing protein recovery from alfalfa. J. Agric. Food Chem. *20*, 1055–1057.

KNUCKLES, B.E., DE FREMERY, D., BICKOFF, E.M. and KOHLER, G.O. 1975. Soluble protein from alfalfa juice by membrane filtration. J. Agric. Food Chem. *23*, 209–212.

KOHLER, G.O. 1947. Personal communication. Berkeley, CA.

KOHLER, G.O. 1975. Wet processing of alfalfa. 12th Tech. Alfalfa Conf. Proc., 1974, Overland Parks, KS, U.S. Dep. Agric./Agric. Res. Serv., Berkeley, CA.

KOHLER, G.O. and BICKOFF, E.M. 1971. Leaf protein. 3rd Int. Congr. Food Sci. Technol. 1970, Washington, DC. Inst. of Food Technology, Chicago.

KOHLER, G.O., BICKOFF, E.M. and DE FREMERY, D. 1973. Mechanical dewatering of forage and protein byproduct recovery. 1st Int. Green Crop Drying Congr. Proc., 1973, Oxford. E. & E. Plumridge, Linton, Cambridge.

KOHLER, G.O., BICKOFF, E.M., SPENCER, R.R., WITT, S.C. and KNUCKLES, B.E. 1968. Wet processing of alfalfa for animal feed products. 10th Tech. Alfalfa Conf. Proc., 1968, U.S. Dep. Agric./Agric. Res. Serv. *ARS-74-46*, Berkeley, CA.

KOHLER, G.O., EDWARDS, R.H. and DE FREMERY, D. 1979A. Increasing yields of feed grade LPC (Pro-Xan). Proc. 2nd Int. Green Crop Drying Cong. Saskatoon, Sask., Aug. 20–25, 1978. Ext. Div., Univ. of Saskatoon, Sask., Canada.

KOHLER, G.O. and KNUCKLES, B.E. 1977. Edible protein from leaves. Food Technol. *31* (5) 191–195.

KOHLER, G.O., WALKER, H.G. and KUZMICKY, D.D. 1979B. Processing and use of crop residue including alfalfa press cake. Fed. Proc. Fed. Am. Soc. Exp. Biol. *38*, 1934–1938.

KOHLER, G.O., WILDMAN, S.G., JORGENSEN, N.A., ENOCHIAN, R.V. and BRAY, W.J. 1978A. Leaf protein in relation to forage crop production and utilization. *In* Protein Resources and Technology. M. Milner, N.S. Scrimshaw and D.I.C. Wang (Editors). AVI Publishing Co., Westport, CT.

KUZMICKY, D.D. and KOHLER, G.O. 1977. Nutritional value of alfalfa leaf protein concentrate (Pro-Xan) for broilers. Poult. Sci. *56*, 1510–1516.

KUZMICKY, D.D., LIVINGSTON, A.L., KNOWLES, R.E., KOHLER, G.O., GUENTHER, E., OLSON, O.E. and CARLSON, C.W. 1977. Xanthophyll availability of alfalfa leaf protein concentrate (Pro-Xan) for broilers and laying hens. Poult. Sci. *56*, 1504–1509.

LOMMELL, F. 1939. Enrichment of food with plant protein. Klin. Wochenschr. *18* (51) 1596–1598. (German)

MAGUIRE, M.F. and BROOKES, I.M. 1973. The effects of juice extraction on the composition and yield of grass crops for dehydration. 1st Int. Green Crop Drying Cong. Proc., 1973, Oxford. E. & E. Plumridge, Linton, Cambridge.

MILLER, R.E., DE FREMERY, D., BICKOFF, E.M. and KOHLER, G.O. 1975. Soluble protein concentrate from alfalfa by low-temperature acid precipitation. J. Agric. Food Chem. *23*, 1177–1179.

MILLER, R.E., DE FREMERY, D. and KOHLER, G.O. 1977. Unpublished data. Western Regional Research Center, Berkeley, CA 94710.

MILLER, R.E., EDWARDS, R.H., LAZAR, M.E., BICKOFF, E.M. and KOHLER, G.O. 1972. Pro-Xan process: Air drying of alfalfa leaf protein concentrate. J. Agric. Food Chem. *20*, 1151–1154.

OLATUNBOSUN, D.A., ADADEVOH, B.K. and OKE, O.L. 1972. Leaf protein: A new protein source for the management of protein calorie malnutrition in Nigeria. Niger. Med. J. *2*, 195–199.

PAREDES-LOPEZ, O. and CAMARGO, E. 1973. The use of alfalfa residual juice for production of single-cell protein. Experientia *29* (10) 1233–1234.

PERRY, T.W., BEESON, W.M., DABELL, W.R., KOHLER, G.O. and GOUGH, F.A. 1974. Effect of alfalfa solubles on urea utilization by beef cattle. J. Anim. Sci. *39*, 1158–1164.

PIRIE, N.W. 1971A. Equipment and methods for extracting and separating protein. *In* Leaf Protein: Its Agronomy, Preparation, Quality and Use. N.W. Pirie (Editor). IBP Handb. *20*. Blackwell Scientific Publications, Oxford and Edinburgh.

PIRIE, N.W. 1971B. Leaf Protein: Its Agronomy, Preparation, Quality and Use. IBP Handb. *20*. Blackwell Scientific Publications, Oxford and Edinburgh.

REAM, H.W., KOEGEL, R.G., JORGENSEN, N.A. and ROHWEDER, D.A. 1975. Progress report-Harvesting, processing, and feeding alfalfa juice protein concentrate and pressed alfalfa silage and utilizing deproteinized plant juice. 5th Annu. Alfalfa Symp. Proc., 1975, Hershey, PA. Pennsylvania State Univ., University Park.

RUSSELL, J.R., HURST, J.P., JORGENSEN, N.A. and BARRINGTON, G.P. 1978. Wet plant fractionation: Utilization of pressed alfalfa silage. J. Anim. Sci. *46* (1) 278–287.

SINGH, R., WHITNEY, L.F. and CHEN, C.S. 1974. Recovery of alfalfa protein by membrane ultrafiltration. Presented at 1974 Am. Soc. Agric. Eng. Meet., Stillwater, OK.

SMITH, R.H. 1966. Lipid-protein isolates. *In* World Protein Resources. American Chemical Society, Washington, DC.

STAHMANN, M.A. 1975. The Wisconsin work. 12th Tech. Alfalfa Conf. Proc., 1974, Overland Park, KS, U.S. Dep. Agric./Agric. Res. Serv., Berkeley, CA.

SUBBA RAU, B.H., MADADEVIAH, S. and SINGH, N. 1969. Nutritional studies on whole-extract coagulated leaf protein and fractionated chloroplastic and cytoplasmic proteins from lucerne *(Medicago sativa)*. J. Sci. Food Agric. *20*, 355–358.

U.S. DEP. AGRIC. 1977. Agricultural Statistics 1977. U.S. Dep. of Agric., Washington, DC.

VOSLOH, C.J., JR., EDWARDS, R.H., ENOCHIAN, R.V., KUZMICKY, D.D. and KOHLER, G.O. 1976. Leaf protein concentrate (Pro-Xan) from alfalfa: An economic evaluation. U.S. Dep. Agric., Econ. Res. Serv. Berkeley, CA, Agric. Econ. Rep. *346*.

19

Economics of Producing LPC for Feed with the Pro-Xan Process

Robert V. Enochian, George O. Kohler, Richard H. Edwards, Donald D. Kuzmicky, and Carl J. Vosloh, Jr.

For many years, researchers have attempted to develop products from alfalfa and other forage crops which would improve the utilization and increase the value of these crops. Initial work in this field was reported over 25 years ago and numerous approaches and techniques for obtaining high protein fractions (which also contain xanthophyll[1]) from green leaves have been thoroughly reviewed (Pirie 1971; Kohler *et al.* 1978B). The Western Regional Research Center (WRRC), U.S. Dept. of Agriculture (USDA), Albany, California, has been active in this research and has made considerable progress. Initially, a process for air separation of dehydrated alfalfa into high and low protein fractions was developed and an economic evaluation of this process showed commercial possibilities (Chrisman *et al.* 1971; Vosloh *et al.* 1974). Systems for producing and utilizing leaf protein on the farm have been developed by the University of Wisconsin and by the National Institute of Agricultural Engineering, Silsoe, England. The economics of these systems have been analyzed by Bruhn and Koegel (1977), Dumont and Boyce (1976), and McGuckin and Hughes (1977). The economics of green crop fractionation and leaf protein production under different situations has also been analyzed by Bray (1977).

In recent years, industrial processes for wet extraction of leaf protein concentrate from alfalfa have been receiving considerable attention, and five or six plants both in the United States and abroad are now producing leaf protein concentrates from alfalfa. A process developed at WRRC has been named the Pro-Xan process. A complete description of this process, including a flow diagram, is contained in Chapter 18 of this book and in the

[1] Xanthophyll is a naturally occurring pigment present in several feed ingredients which, when ingested by chickens, results in yellow skins and egg yolks.

papers cited in its reference list. The Pro-Xan process results in a better separation of the fiber from the high protein-high xanthophyll fraction than does air separation of dehydrated alfalfa. In 1975, pilot plant data on material balances and processing variables were used as a basis for an economic evaluation of the Pro-Xan process. That evaluation showed potentially favorable returns on capital investment (Vosloh *et al.* 1976).

Several developments have occurred since 1975 which could affect returns on investment in the Pro-Xan process. These developments include the following: (1) there have been modifications in the process which make possible the extraction of up to 18% of the total solids in alfalfa, in the form of Pro-Xan, instead of only 12% as in the 1975 study[2]; (2) process modifications also have resulted in a xanthophyll content of 450 mg per lb (1 g per kg) of Pro-Xan rather than 350 mg (0.778 g per kg) as was used in the 1975 study; (3) a waste-heat evaporator has been introduced into the process which saves on natural gas usage[3]; (4) broiler and layer feeding trials have shown that the xanthophyll in Pro-Xan is utilized 1.7 times more efficiently than the xanthophyll in dehydrated alfalfa[4] (Kuzmicky *et al.* 1977); and (5) there have been changes in the prices of feed ingredients that would compete with Pro-Xan as well as increases in the prices of equipment, utilities, and other inputs.

The effects of these developments on return on investment have been discussed in a paper presented at the 1977 annual meeting of the American Society of Agricultural Engineers (Enochian *et al.* 1977) and in a report published by the U.S. Department of Agriculture (Enochian *et al.* 1980). The material presented in this chapter is based largely on these sources.

PROCEDURES USED IN ECONOMIC ANALYSES OF THE PRO-XAN PROCESS

The potential costs and earnings of four systems of producing Pro-Xan were analyzed by Vosloh *et al.* (1976). The basic differences among these four systems were the way in which the juice was expressed from the alfalfa and the yield of Pro-Xan, which ranged from 8.5 to 12% of the total dry weight of the starting alfalfa. In addition to the four systems, the effect of four important processing variables on costs and earnings also was evaluated. These variables were the method of disposition of the alfalfa solubles; the method of handling the press cake; the length of operating season; and the size or capacity of the processing plant. Four different lengths of

[2] Pro-Xan yields of over 20% have been obtained in pilot plant operations, but for purposes of this report, 18% Pro-Xan yield is the maximum considered.

[3] Waste heat evaporators have been used for a number of years for the concentration of liquids, especially orange juice (Rebeck and Cook 1977). Recently a patent was issued to a French firm for concentration of alfalfa solubles by waste heat evaporation (de Mathan 1978).

[4] These feeding trials were made with rations containing from 9 to 10 mg of xanthophyll.

season—130, 180, 230, and 280 days—and three plant capacities in metric tons of green chop input per hour—18, 36, and 72 MT (20, 40, and 80 ST)—were analyzed. On the basis of the findings of this analysis, subsequent analyses of the modified Pro-Xan process (Enochian *et al.* 1977, 1980) evaluated only one basic system. Table 19.1 shows the principal differences in the four systems analyzed in the 1975 study compared with the system analyzed in 1977.

As might be expected, the system with the greatest yield of Pro-Xan, operating for the longest season and with the largest capacity, had the highest return on investment. With regard to the method of disposition of the solubles and the method of handling the press cake, the highest return accrued to those plants in which it was assumed that the dilute solubles were added to the press cake and the press cake dehydrated in a dehydration drum. This was the case even though the quantity of gas used for this

TABLE 19.1. PRINCIPAL DIFFERENCES IN PRO-XAN SYSTEMS ANALYZED, 1975 AND 1977

System and Year	Method of Extracting Juice from Green Chop	Recycling of Dilute Solubles	Pro-Xan Yield (%)	Final Treatment of Solubles and Press Cake (p.c.)
				A, B, C, Below Used with Systems I–IV
I (1975)	No grinder Twin screw press	Not recycled	8.5	(A) Dilute solubles added to p.c. and p.c. dehydrated
II (1975)	No grinder Twin screw press	Recycled to green-chop prior to pressing	9.0	(B) Dilute solubles pumped to field (1) p.c. fed wet (2) p.c. dehydrated
III (1975)	No grinder Double twin screw press	Recycled to green-chop between presses	12.0	(C) Solubles concentrated with triple effect evaporator
IV (1975)	Grinder plus twin screw press	Not recycled	12.0	(1) Added to p.c. (a) p.c. fed wet (b) p.c. dehydrated (2) Used as a liquid feed supplement
V (1977)	Grinder plus 4 single screw presses	Recycled to green-chop prior to grinding and between presses	12–18[1]	Solubles concentrated with waste heat evaporator, added to p.c.; p.c. dehydrated

[1]Pro-Xan yields of over 20% have been obtained in pilot plant operations, but for purposes of this report, 18% Pro-Xan yield is the maximum considered.

method of water removal was nearly double that required when it was assumed the dilute solubles were concentrated in a triple effect vacuum evaporator before being added to the press cake for final drying. As the price of gas increases, however, the relative costs of these two approaches to water removal would eventually result in the concentration approach's becoming the most profitable. This effect was illustrated in Vosloh *et al.* (1976).

Since the price of natural gas has increased rapidly since 1975, and is expected to continue to increase, the concentration approach to water removal from the dilute solubles, which is then added to the press cake prior to final dehydration, was the only approach considered in subsequent economic evaluations of the process.

The effect of several variables, including length of season, on annual return on investment is evaluated in this chapter. Length of season has a significant effect on costs per unit of output in a given size plant. The reason is that annual fixed costs remain the same but are spread over a greater output the longer the plant operates. Alfalfa is grown in many areas of the United States and the production season varies widely, ranging from about 130 to 280 days. Emphasis in this chapter is given to plants operating for 130 days per season, which is typical in the Kansas-Nebraska area where the alfalfa dehydration industry is concentrated.[5]

The analysis consists of computing rates of return on investment for a "synthesized" or "model" plant when producing Pro-Xan yields of 12, 15 or 18%. To compute these rates of return, estimates were made of requirements and costs for equipment, buildings, and land; annual fixed and operating costs; and sales values for Pro-Xan and dehydrated press cake.

EQUIPMENT AND LAND REQUIREMENTS

In the most recent economic analysis of the Pro-Xan process (Enochian *et al.* 1980), harvesting, hauling, and processing equipment requirements were determined for the model Pro-Xan plant with a green-crop input of 36 MT (40 ST) per hr.[6] This model plant was based on manufacturers' equipment specifications and material balance determinations. The same plant is used for recovering all levels of Pro-Xan. Material balances were based on pilot scale experimental work done at the Western Regional Research Center and are given in Table 19.2 for 12, 15, and 18% Pro-Xan recovery.

Green chop input rates were determined by a least cost matching of the capacities of the screw presses and the press cake dehydration drum. At different Pro-Xan yields, all equipment may not be fully utilized but the best balance of available equipment capacity was designed into the model plant.

[5]The actual harvest season lasts for about 150 days but 20 days are allowed for nonproductive time.

[6]Tons in this report refer to U.S. short tons (2000 lb).

TABLE 19.2. MATERIAL BALANCE DESCRIPTION OF MODEL PRO-XAN PLANT WITH GREEN-CHOP INPUT OF 40 ST (36 MT) PER HR[1]

	Pro-Xan Yield[3]		
	12%	15%	18%
Item[2]		lb per hr	
Green-chop input	80,000	80,000	80,000
Green juice[4]	120,047	121,600	123,153
Wet press cake	36,753	35,200	33,647
Heating steam used	8,334	8,433	8,522
Wet Pro-Xan cake	5,280	6,600	7,920
Dilute alfalfa solubles to evaporator	46,301	46,633	46,955
Concentrated alfalfa solubles	5,089	5,812	6,543
Alfalfa solubles (dry basis)	2,992	2,992	2,992
Water evaporated from dilute solubles	41,212	40,821	40,423
Press cake drier input	41,842	41,012	40,179
Water evaporated from press cake in drier	24,242	24,012	23,779
Water evaporated from press cake in grinder	765	739	713
Water evaporated from Pro-Xan	2,933	3,667	4,400
Pro-Xan (10% water)	2,347	2,933	3,520
Dehydrated press cake (8% water)	16,835	16,261	15,687

[1]Green-chop contains 22% dry matter, which is 20% protein.
[2]Does not include 80 lb of anhydrous ammonia per hr which is added to enhance processing behavior.
[3]Pro-Xan yield is the percentage (34,836 kg) of dry matter recovered as Pro-Xan; 1 lb per hr = 0.45 kg per hr.
[4]Includes 76,800 lb of recycled dilute alfalfa solubles.

All driers in the model plant were assumed to be equipped with exhaust gas recycling systems. Recent experience suggests that EPA (Environmental Protection Administration) standards for the drying operation can be met by use of recycling systems and by careful control of the drying cycle.

The model plant contains equipment, not shown in Fig. 18.4, Chapter 18, to permit conversion of the Pro-Xan operation to a straight dehydration operation in case of mechanical failure or other emergency. In this event, the green-crop input per hour would have to be reduced from 36 to 18 MT (40 to 20 ST).

Estimates of equipment requirements for harvesting and hauling green-chop were based on an earlier study of alfalfa harvesting costs (Vosloh 1971) and confirmed by alfalfa dehydration industry experience. A list of all harvesting and processing equipment, with specifications, is given in Table 19.3.

Building space requirements for the model plant were based on estimates of the space required for the equipment layout. Construction was assumed to be a combination of masonry and steel sheeting having reinforced concrete roofs with beam supports and concrete floors and foundations. There were variations in construction within the building depending upon whether space was to be used for the processing operation, office space, maintenance shop, or boiler room. Total space required for the model plant was estimated at 747 m^2 (8300 ft^2).

TABLE 19.3. HARVESTING AND PROCESSING EQUIPMENT REQUIREMENTS FOR A PRO-XAN PROCESSING SYSTEM WITH A CAPACITY OF 40 ST (36 MT) GREEN-CHOP INPUT PER HR

Item	Number Required	Specifications	Connected Horsepower (Electric Motors)[1]
Harvester	4	Self-propelled, 14 ft (4.3 m) header	—
Truck	5	15 ST (13.5 MT) tandem axle 24 ft (7.3 m) bed, diesel powered	—
Truck	2	¾ ST (0.675 MT) pickup	—
Truck scale	1	60 ST (54 MT)	—
Hydraulic truck lift	1	35 ft (10.7 m) long	10
Feeder	1	40 ST (36 MT)/hr	20
Grinders (green-chop)	4	10 ST (9 MT)/hr	400
Single screw press	4	20 ST (18 MT)/hr	400
Hydrasieve	1	72 in. (183 cm) wide	—
Steam injector	2	3 in. (7.6 cm) diameter	—
Centrifuge	2	130 gal. (492 liters) feed/min	330
Heat exchanger, plate type	1	147 ft^2 (13.2 m^2) plate surface	—
Extruder (Pro-Xan)	1	8000 lb (3629 kg) wet curd/hr	20
Drier (Pro-Xan) with recycle system	1	9000 lb (4082 kg) H_2O evap./hr	60
Waste heat evaporator with cooling tower (4 stage, 3 effect)	1	51,000 lb (23,134 kg)/hr	352
Pneumatic conveyor (Pro-Xan)	1	5 ST (4.5 MT)/hr	25
Drier (press cake) with recycle system; 185°F (85°C) wet bulb	1	30,000 lb (13,608 kg) H_2O evap./hr	164
Pneumatic conveyor (press cake)	1	12 ST (10.8 MT)/hr	50
Grinder (press cake)	2	6 ST (5.4 MT)/hr	400
Pellet mill	2	6 ST (5.4 MT)/hr	420
Transfer system (hot press cake pellets)	2	6 ST (5.4 MT)/hr	10
Pellet cooler	2	6 ST (5.4 MT)/hr	80
Transfer system (cold pellets)	2	6 ST (5.4 MT)/hr	100
Automatic weigh scale (100 lb or 45.4 kg bags)	1	5 bags/min	1
Boiler	1	400 boiler hp (3923.8 kW)	55
Air compressors	1	36 SCFM (standard ft^3/min)	10
Pumps	6	1 to 275 gal. (3.8 to 1041 liters)/min	48.25
Conveyors	14	4 to 45 ST (3.6 to 40.5 MT)/hr	50.5
Tanks (with agitators)	4	1000 to 10,000 gal. (3785 to 37,854 liters)	2
Well	1	250 gal. (946 liters)/min	20
Total horsepower			3027.75

[1] 1 horsepower (electric) = 746.0 W.

Land requirements for the model plant were based on the space required for the building and on the area required for truck movement. This was estimated to be 1.6 ha (4 acres).

INVESTMENT COSTS

Costs of the model plant were based on prevailing costs in Kansas and Nebraska. Harvesting and hauling equipment and processing plant equipment costs represent delivered costs to the Kansas-Nebraska area and, in the 1975 study (Vosloh *et al.* 1976), were based on manufacturers' estimates. These costs were updated to 1977 by using the net increases in the wholesale price index for equipment, reported by the Bureau of Labor Statistics (U.S. Dep. Labor 1975 and 1977). The increases were 17, 15, and 14% for harvesters, trucks, and plant equipment, respectively.

Installation of processing plant equipment and plant engineering costs were estimated by firms involved in this type of construction to be 40% of the total delivered costs of equipment. These estimates include all electrical wiring, piping, valves, and controls.

Estimated building costs in 1975 ranged from \$1.52 to \$2.31 per m^2 (\$16.68 to \$25.70 per ft^2), depending on intended use. In 1977, these costs had increased 20% (American Appraisal Associates 1972, 1975 and 1977).

Land costs were assumed to be \$1600 per ha (\$4000 per acre) in 1975, with an estimated increase of 30% in 1977 (U.S. Dep. Agric. 1977).

The total 1977 investment costs for a Pro-Xan operation with a capacity of 36 MT (40 ST) of green-chop input per hr is given in Table 19.4. Total investment is over \$3.3 million, with over 80% being the cost of plant equipment.

OPERATIONAL SPECIFICATIONS AND ANNUAL COSTS FOR THE MODEL PLANT

The model plant was assumed to operate at capacity rates for 130 days per season and 22 hr per day. The remaining 2 hr in each day were allowed for slack or down-time due to breakdown, poor coordination of raw product delivery, and cleanup time.

Annual operating costs are based on operational specifications and the rates or costs of raw material, labor, depreciation, interest, taxes, insurance, fuel, utilities, chemicals, maintenance, repairs, administration, supervision, storage, marketing, transportation, and working capital. The rates or costs of these inputs have been discussed in Enochian *et al.* (1980), and are summarized in Table 19.5 for both 1977 and 1975.

The annual cost for harvesting and hauling green-chop is the same for all levels of Pro-Xan recovery. In 1977, this annual cost amounted to \$401,796, with the major portion being the variable costs of labor, fuel, and maintenance and repairs. A breakdown of these costs can be found in Enochian *et al.* (1980).

Annual plant operating costs, with 12, 15 and 18% Pro-Xan yields, ranged from \$995,377 to \$1,001,543, respectively. Since the same plant is used to achieve all levels of Pro-Xan recovery, the only cost items that are affected

TABLE 19.4. INVESTMENT COSTS FOR PRO-XAN SYSTEM WITH CAPACITY OF 40 ST (36 MT) GREEN-CHOP INPUT PER HR, 1977

Item	Investment Cost (Dollars)
Harvesting and hauling equipment	395,790
Processing plant equipment	1,941,405
installation[1]	776,562
Subtotal	2,717,967
Buildings[2]	
dehydraton and pelleting	44,400
Pro-Xan processing	70,800
office	43,200
maintenance shop	26,040
boiler room	15,480
Subtotal	199,920
Land[3]	20,800
Total	3,334,477

[1] Based on 40% of equipment cost and includes plant design and engineering.
[2] Buildings include space for all operations except for product storage, which is treated as a separate cost item.
[3] Land area is 4 acres (1.6 ha).

by the higher Pro-Xan yields are those for natural gas and chemicals, with differences being relatively minor. The major cost items are the variable costs of utilities and maintenance and the fixed costs of depreciation and repairs. See Enochian *et al.* (1980) for a breakdown of these cost factors.

PRO-XAN PRODUCTS AND THEIR SALES VALUES

As indicated before, the current Pro-Xan process results in the recovery of Pro-Xan and dehydrated press cake, the latter of which contains the alfalfa solubles. The nutrient composition of Pro-Xan is independent of Pro-Xan yield and is shown in Table 19.6.

The amount and composition of press cake recovered from the Pro-Xan process depend upon the Pro-Xan yield. As the yield of Pro-Xan increases, protein and dry matter are essentially transferred from the press cake fraction to the Pro-Xan fraction. The protein content of dehydrated press cake (8% moisture) ranges from 14.4%, when the yield of Pro-Xan is 12%, to 11.6%, when the Pro-Xan yield is 18%.

Pro-Xan and dehydrated press cake are not currently being marketed in the United States; therefore, their sales values had to be estimated so that potential earnings and returns on investment from the Pro-Xan model plant could be computed. These values were based on market prices of

TABLE 19.5. FACTOR INPUTS AND THEIR RATES OR COSTS PER UNIT, 1975 AND 1977

Item	Rate or Cost[1]	
	1975	1977
Green-chop (standing in field)	\$5.15/ST (\$5.72/MT)	\$6.70/ST (\$7.44/MT)
Labor (includes fringe benefits and overtime for two 12-hr shifts)		
harvest and haul (8 workers/shift)	\$3.30/hr	\$4.30/hr
processing plant (5 workers/shift)	\$3.75–\$4.00/hr	\$4.75/hr
Fuel and oil (for harvesters and trucks)	\$0.75/ST (\$0.83/MT) of green-chop	Same
Maintenance and repairs		
harvesters and trucks	\$1/ST (\$1.11/MT) of green-chop	Same
processing equipment and buildings	7.0% of investment cost/year	Same
Administrative costs (management, office expenses, etc.)	\$23,000/year allocated 33.3% for field operations, 40% for plant operations, and 26.7% for storage operations	\$26,680/year; same allocation
Supervisor's salary	\$20,000/year allocated 45% for field operations and 55% for plant operations	\$23,200/year; same allocation
Depreciation		
harvesters	10% of cost/year	Same
trucks	16.67% of cost/year	Same
plant equipment	6.67% of cost/year	Same
buildings	4.0% of cost/year	Same

(continued)

TABLE 19.5. *(Continued)*

Item	Rate or Cost[1]	
	1975	1977
Insurance		
all equipment	1.0% of cost/year	Same
buildings	0.5% of cost/year	Same
Property		
Taxes	1.0% of assessed value which is assumed to be 35% of cost	Same
Working capital	Annual interest on 25% of all annual costs	Same
Interest on investment	9.0%/year (4.5% of cost for depreciable property)	Same
Natural gas	\$0.66/1000 ft^3 (\$0.022 per m^3)	\$0.97/1000 ft^3 (\$0.032 per m^3)
Electricity	\$0.021/kwh (75.6 kJ)	\$0.027/kwh (75.6 kJ)
Anhydrous ammonia (2 lb/ST or 1 kg/MT of green chop)	\$150/ST (\$166/MT)	Same
Silicone, antifoam agent (2 lb/40 ST or 0.025 kg/MT of green-chop)	Not considered	\$0.85/lb (\$1.88/kg)
Ethoxyquin, antioxidant (added to Pro-Xan at rate of 0.015%)	Not considered	\$12.95/gal. (\$3.42/liter) (6 lb/gal. or 0.719 kg/liter)
Inert gas storage (½ annual production stored for 6 months)	\$1.50/ST/month (\$1.66/MT/month)	\$1.75/ST/month (\$1.94/MT/month)
Marketing costs	\$1.50/ST (\$1.66/MT)	\$1.75/ST (\$1.94/MT)
Transport to market (Alfalfa Center, NE to Kansas City, MO)	\$10/ST (\$11.11/MT)	\$11.30/ST (\$12.56/MT)

[1] 1 ST = 0.9 MT

TABLE 19.6. NUTRIENT COMPOSITION OF PRO-XAN

Nutrient	Unit	Content in Pro-Xan
Dry matter	%	90.0
Metabolizable energy	Kcal/lb	1175.0
Protein	%	51.7
Arginine	%	3.34
Glycine	%	2.86
Isoleucine	%	2.90
Lysine	%	3.06
Methionine	%	1.19
Methionine and cystine	%	1.80
Threonine	%	2.64
Tryptophan	%	0.77
Phosphorus	%	0.54
Calcium	%	1.39
Fiber	%	1.83
Fat	%	8.47
Xanthophyll	mg/lb	450.0

commercially available feed ingredients that would provide comparable nutrients and were calculated separately for press cake and for Pro-Xan as described in the following sections.

Press Cake Value

Discussions with alfalfa dehydration industry representatives have led to the conclusion that dehydrated press cake from a Pro-Xan operation would be comparable to sun-cured alfalfa pellets at protein contents of either 13 or 15%. The price difference between 13 and 15% protein sun-cured alfalfa pellets is very small but the price level of both is generally lower than for dehydrated alfalfa of 17% protein content.

Using reported prices in Kansas City for the third week of each month, an average annual value was computed for sun-cured alfalfa pellets of 13 and 15% protein content for 1974 through 1977. These prices are given in Table 19.7 which, for comparison purposes, also gives the average prices for

TABLE 19.7. AVERAGE ANNUAL PRICES FOR DEHYDRATED SUN-CURED ALFALFA PELLETS, AND ALFALFA HAY, KANSAS CITY, 1974 THROUGH 1977

Item	Average Annual Prices			
	1974	1975	1976	1977
	Dollars per ST			
Dehy pellets, 17%[1]	86.80	80.87	106.19	91.74[2]
Sun-cured pellets, 15%[1]	77.92	74.15	92.67	82.38[2]
Sun-cured pellets, 17%[1]	77.83	74.07	92.42	82.25[2]
Alfalfa hay[3]	47.50	49.50	54.00	51.50

[1] Based on prices reported by Feedstuffs.
[2] Based on the first 8 months of 1977.
[3] Based on average prices received by Kansas farmers for baled alfalfa hay as reported in Agricultural Prices, U.S. Dept. of Agriculture, ESCS. Does not include costs for pelleting and transportation to Kansas City, both of which are included in the prices for the other ingredients.
1 ST = 0.9 MT.

dehydrated alfalfa pellets of 17% protein content, and for alfalfa hay.

The prices of sun-cured pellets of 15 and 13% content were interpolated and extrapolated to obtain estimated prices for press cake when Pro-Xan yields were 12, 15, and 18%. These prices are given in Table 19.8 and are believed to be conservative because research studies have shown that the digestibility of the fiber in dehydrated press cake from the Pro-Xan process is significantly better than that in the unprocessed alfalfa from which it was made (Kohler *et al.* 1978A). Chapter 18 of this book and its references contain information on the composition and nutritional value of press cake.

Pro-Xan Value

The estimated sales value of Pro-Xan was determined by computer, using parametric linear programming (PLP). A complete description of the use of parametric linear programming for estimating sales values of new feed ingredients can be found in other sources (Enochian *et al.* 1971; Halloran 1959; Taylor *et al.* 1968).

Requirements for broiler finisher rations were considered to be the most appropriate for valuing a high energy, high protein, high xanthophyll ingredient such as Pro-Xan. The nutritional requirements for a broiler finisher ration and the nutritional values of the ingredients used in poultry rations are given in Vosloh *et al.* (1976).

Using Kansas City feed ingredient prices for the third week of each month, two different PLP sales values, based on different assumptions, were calculated for each month of 1974, 1975, 1976, and the first eight months of 1977.[7] These monthly values were then averaged to arrive at annual sales values for Pro-Xan. The two different sales values were based on the following assumptions: (1) no xanthophyll was specified in the ration, thus the value of Pro-Xan would be based on the value of its protein, energy, and other nutrients, excluding xanthophyll; and (2) the ration specification for xanthophyll was 29 mg per kg (13 mg per lb) of ration and the xanthophyll content of the Pro-Xan was 1 g per kg (450 mg per lb). The average annual PLP prices for Pro-Xan, based on these assumptions, are given in Table 19.9. See Enochian *et al.* (1980), for computations of the PLP value of Pro-Xan when the ration specification for xanthophyll is 29 mg per kg (13 mg per lb) of ration and the xanthophyll in Pro-Xan is 1.7 g per kg (765 mg per lb) (1.7 times the analytical content) based on pigmentation results when Pro-Xan was used in broiler and hen feeding trials (Kuzmicky *et al.* 1977).

---

[7] All ingredients which could be used in broiler finisher rations for which prices were reported were used in the PLP analysis. The major sources of xanthophyll for satisfying the requirement in broiler finisher rations are corn, corn gluten meal, dehydrated alfalfa, and marigold meal. Marigold meal prices were not reported, therefore it was not included in the analysis. However, the prices of marigold meal are generally too high for it to be competitive in rations having the specifications of those used in this study.

TABLE 19.8. PROTEIN CONTENT AND ESTIMATED VALUE OF DEHYDRATED PRESS CAKE FROM A MODEL PLANT WITH 3 DIFFERENT YIELDS OF PRO-XAN, 1974 THROUGH 1977

Pro-Xan Yield (%)	Protein Content of Press Cake[1] (%)	Estimated Annual Values of Press Cake[2]			
		1974	1975	1976	1977[3]
		Dollars/ST[4]			
12	14.4	77.91	74.13	92.60	82.34
15	13.0	77.83	74.07	92.42	82.25
18	11.6	77.77	74.01	92.24	82.16

[1] Assumes green-chop contains 18.4% protein on an 8% moisture basis and that dehydrated press cake contains 8% moisture.
[2] Based on Kansas City prices.
[3] Based on the first 8 months of 1977.
[4] 1 ST = 0.9 MT.

ANNUAL RETURNS ON INVESTMENT

Prices determined by PLP cannot substitute for prices determined in the market where the forces of supply and demand are operating. PLP prices computed for Pro-Xan, when used in rations specifying 29 mg of xanthophyll per kg (13 mg per lb), are what might be received by initial processors whose production would be too small to have a significant effect on the demand for competing feed ingredients. Thus, this was the value selected to estimate total annual earnings and returns on investment for the model plant.

Table 19.10 summarizes total annual sales values, costs, earnings, and returns on investment for the model Pro-Xan plant. The estimated annual returns on investment, before income taxes, using 1976 product sales values and 1977 costs, are 28.7, 37.0, and 45.4% for 12, 15, and 18% Pro-Xan recovery, respectively. These returns on investment are not only illustrative of what initial processors might have received in that year, but also illustrate the sensitivity of returns on investment to different yields of Pro-Xan.

TABLE 19.9. AVERAGE ANNUAL PLP VALUES FOR PRO-XAN, WHEN USED IN BROILER FINISHER RATIONS WITH DIFFERENT SPECIFICATIONS FOR XANTHOPHYLL, KANSAS CITY, 1974 THROUGH 1977

Year	No Xanthophyll Specified in Ration	13 mg Xanthophyll Specifed per lb (29 mg per kg) of Ration
	Dollars per ST[1]	
1974	184.02	344.74
1975	163.06	349.97
1976	211.15	432.65
1977[2]	277.99	524.25

[1] 1 ST = 0.9 MT.
[2] Based on the first 8 months of 1977.

TABLE 19.10. ANNUAL RETURNS ON INVESTMENT FOR A PRO-XAN PLANT PROCESSING 40 ST (36 MT) GREEN-CHOP PER HR, AND OPERATING FOR 130 DAYS PER SEASON, 1977[1]

Item	Unit	Pro-Xan Yield		
		12%	15%	18%
Dehydrated press cake				
production per hour	lb	16,835	16,261	15,687
annual production	ST[2]	24,074	23,253	22,452
price per ST[2]	Dollars	92.60	92.42	92.24
annual sales value	Dollars	2,229,252	2,149,042	2,069,128
Pro-Xan				
production per hour	lb	2,347	2,933	3,520
annual production	ST[2]	3,356	4,194	5,034
price per ST[2]	Dollars	432.65	432.65	432.65
annual sales value	Dollars	1,451,973	1,814,534	2,177,960
Annual sales value of all products	Dollars	3,681,225	3,963,756	4,247,088
Annual costs (fixed and variable)				
green-chop	Dollars	766,480	766,480	766,480
harvesting and hauling	Dollars	401,796	401,796	401,796
processing	Dollars	995,377	998,809	1,001,543
storage	Dollars	143,992	144,098	144,197
marketing	Dollars	47,997	48,033	48,066
transport to market	Dollars	309,927	310,155	310,367
interest for working capital	Dollars	59,975	60,061	60,130
Total costs	Dollars	2,725,544	2,629,432	2,732,579
Annual earnings	Dollars	955,681	1,234,324	1,514,509
Total investment	Dollars	3,334,477	3,334,447	3,334,477
Annual return on investment	%	28.7	37.0	45.4

[1] All product sales values based on 1976 estimates. All costs based on 1977 estimates.
[2] 1 ST = 0.9 MT.

It may be difficult to regularly achieve an 18% yield of Pro-Xan in a commercial operation. Furthermore, since the protein content of the press cake from this high a Pro-Xan yield is lower than any pelleted alfalfa products now on the market—either dehydrated or sun-cured—it is uncertain how the market would value such a product. On the other hand, it is believed that 15% Pro-Xan yield could readily be achieved under most commercial conditions; therefore, the return on this yield of Pro-Xan is considered to be the most realistic for most situations, at least for initial investors.

The wide variation in the estimated annual prices for press cake pellets (Table 19.8) as well as for Pro-Xan (Table 19.9) means that the annual return on investment would fluctuate, being higher in some years and lower in others. The sensitivity of returns on investment to these price variations is illustrated in Table 19.11. These data show the annual returns on investment for 1974 through 1977 when the prices computed for Pro-Xan and press cake pellets for those years are used in conjunction with 1977 cost estimates. These estimated returns of investment can be assumed to be representative of the range of returns on investment in a Pro-Xan process

TABLE 19.11. ESTIMATED ANNUAL RETURNS ON INVESTMENT FOR A PRO-XAN PLANT PROCESSING 40 ST (36 MT) OF GREEN-CHOP PER HR, OPERATING FOR 130 DAYS PER SEASON, AND RECOVERING 15% PRO-XAN, 1974–1977[1]

Year	Return on Investment (%)
1974	16.1
1975	14.0
1976	37.0
1977[2]	41.4

[1] See Tables 20.8 and 20.9 for press cake and Pro-Xan prices. See Table 20.10 for press cake and Pro-Xan yields and for processing costs for plants yielding 15% Pro-Xan.
[2] Based on the first 8 months of 1977.

that might be expected in future years. The sensitivity of returns on investment to other variables is discussed in the next section.

Effect of Processing Variables on Returns on Investment

The return on investment from a Pro-Xan operation would be dependent not only on variations in prices of Pro-Xan and press cake but also on the size or capacity of the plant, the length of operating season, the yield of Pro-Xan and its xanthophyll content, and the prices of processing inputs, especially natural gas.

The effects of plant capacity and length of operating season on return on investment were computed for plants yielding 15% Pro-Xan, with a xanthophyll content of 1 g per kg (450 mg per lb) using constant prices for all ingredients and production inputs. The results are shown in Fig. 19.1. The annual return on investment ranges from about 30% for a plant processing 18 MT (20 ST) green-chop per hr and operating for 130 days a year, to about 110% for a plant processing 72 MT (80 ST) of green-chop per hr and operating for 230 days. The different lengths of season are representative of what would be experienced in different geographic regions. The short season (130 days) is representative of the midwest, the medium season (180 days), the Texas high plains, and the long season (230 days), the southwest. All returns are before income taxes.

The effects of Pro-Xan yield and xanthophyll content of Pro-Xan on return on investment using constant prices are shown in Fig. 19.2 for plants processing 36 MT (40 ST) of green-chop per hr and operating 130 days per year. The annual return on investment ranges from about 6% for a plant yielding 12% Pro-Xan, with zero xanthophyll content, to about 70% for a plant yielding 18% Pro-Xan and containing 1.7 g of xanthophyll per kg (765 mg per lb).

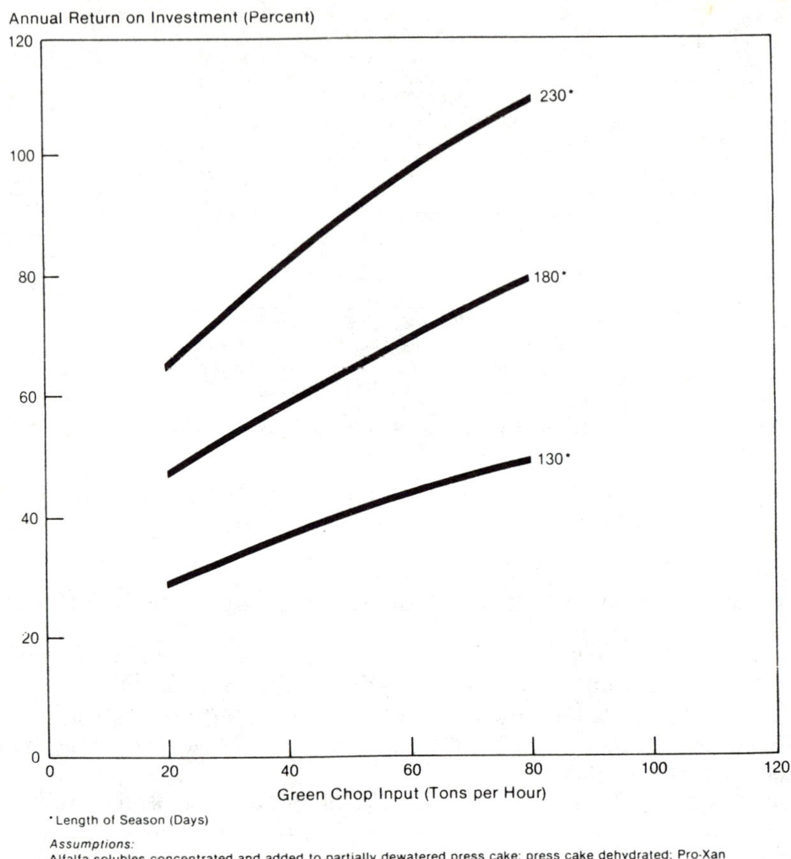

Fig. 19.1. Effect of Pro-Xan plant capacity and length of operating season on return on investment, 1977.

With different prices for ingredients and production inputs, the rates of return on investment would be different.

Natural gas is a major cost factor in a Pro-Xan operation. Thus, changes in the price of natural gas would have a significant effect on return on investment. For plants processing 36 MT (40 ST) of green-chop per hr, operating for 130 days per year, and yielding 15% Pro-Xan, with a xanthophyll content of 1 g per kg (450 mg per lb) of Pro-Xan, when natural gas is \$0.032 per m^3 (\$0.97 per 1000 ft^3)—as it was in the Kansas-Nebraska area in 1977—the annual return on investment was 37% (Table 19.10). If the price of natural gas had been \$0.017 per m^3 (\$0.50 per 1000 ft^3), the annual return on investment would have been about 40%. As the price of natural gas increases, the annual return on investment would decrease, until at

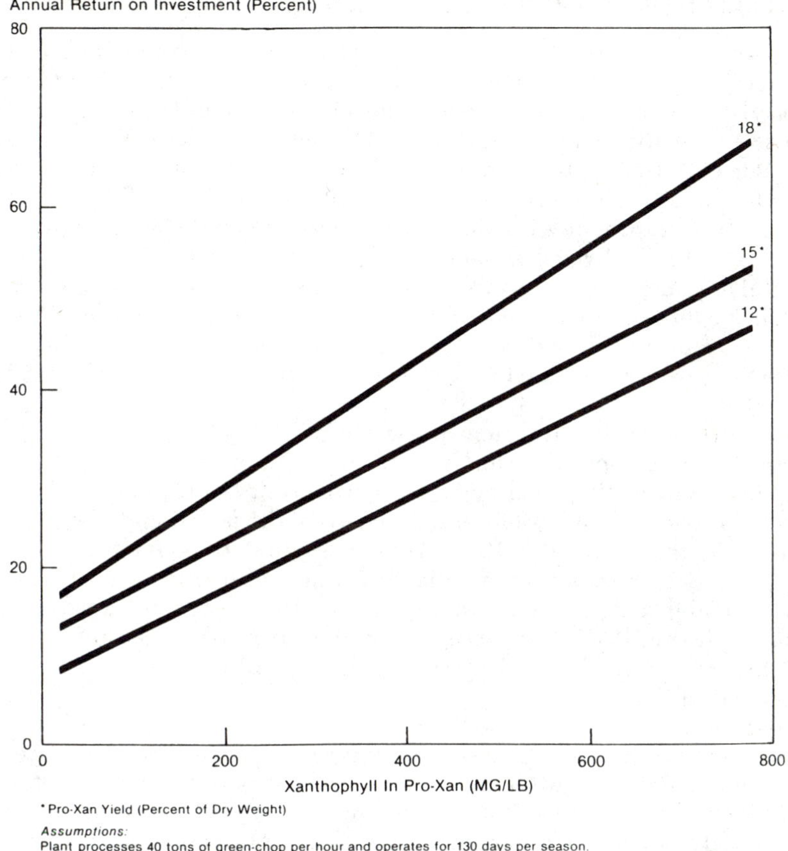

Fig. 19.2. Effect of Pro-Xan yield and its xanthophyll content on return on investment, 1977.

\$0.067 per m^3 (\$2 per 1000 ft^3), the annual return would be about 30%. Thus, because of rapidly escalating prices for natural gas, methods to reduce gas usage for Pro-Xan processing are of great importance.

Because of the variations in prices of feed ingredients and production inputs, each potential investor in a Pro-Xan system would have to evaluate the projected profitability based on his own particular situation. This can be done using the engineering data and physical relationships used in this study.

In addition, dehydrators of alfalfa who are potential investors in a Pro-Xan system will want to compare the relative profitability of dehydrated alfalfa and Pro-Xan operations. Such a comparison has been made by Enochian *et al.* (1980).

UNITED STATES MARKET POTENTIAL FOR PRO-XAN

In a recent study of the economics of green crop fractionation in the United Kingdom, the authors concluded that with the exception of certain special circumstances, the fractionation of alfalfa would be no more attractive economically than dehydration (Wilkins *et al.* 1977). This conclusion was based on the assumption that leaf protein concentrate would be valued only for its crude protein and energy content, with no value given to its pigmenting (xanthophyll) value. The authors' rationale for giving no value to the xanthophyll was based on the apparently small demand for supplemental pigmenting materials in poultry feeds in the United Kingdom. When the authors included a value for the xanthophyll, their estimates of the return on investment were considerably higher and, according to the authors, were comparable to the returns which were computed by Vosloh *et al.* (1976).

In contrast to the situation in the United Kingdom, there is a sizable market for xanthophyll in the United States. The apparent reason for this is that U.S. consumers prefer yellow-skinned broilers and yellow-colored egg yolks. The cost for this preference in terms of the additional cost per ton of feed is illustrated in Table 19.12. This table shows the comparative costs of computer-determined broiler finisher rations with xanthophyll specifications of 0 and 29 mg per kg (0 and 13 mg per lb) of ration in Kansas City, by months, during 1976. The average annual cost was $5.91 per MT ($5.32 per ST) higher for the ration with 29 mg per kg (13 mg per lb) xanthophyll specification.

Assuming that about half of all broiler rations contain a specification for xanthophyll that averages 29 mg per kg (13 mg per lb), the estimated total costs for including xanthophyll in broiler rations in the United States in 1976 were $48.5 million.[8] Although this is a significant cost factor, the estimated cost per kg (lb) of ready-to-cook broilers amounted to only slightly more than $0.011 per kg ($0.005 per lb). Therefore, it is assumed that the use of xanthophyll for pigmenting broiler skins and egg yolks in the United States will continue to be the accepted practice for the foreseeable future. Pro-Xan should be able to share in this demand for xanthophyll.

Broiler and laying hen rations are the only rations formulated in the United States which have a xanthophyll specification. The specification varies widely depending on the specific ration, the use of the end product, and the market demand. In some broiler and laying hen rations, corn provides all of the specification for xanthophyll. In others, the specification for xanthophyll can be satisfied only by use of another (supplemental) source.[9] It has been estimated that the combined annual requirement for all

[8] 18.24 million ST of broiler feed used in the United States ÷ 2 × $5.32; (16.42 million MT ÷ 2 × $5.91).

[9] These sources are corn gluten meal, dehydrated alfalfa, marigold meal, and Pro-Xan.

TABLE 19.12. COMPARATIVE COSTS OF COMPUTER-DETERMINED BROILER FINISHER RATIONS WITH AND WITHOUT XANTHOPHYLL, KANSAS CITY, 1976

	Cost of Least-cost Ration with 0 and 13 mg Xanthophyll per lb (0.45 kg) of Ration		
	0 mg	13 mg	Cost Difference
Month	Dollars per ST[1]		
January	123.01	127.87	4.96
February	122.29	128.37	6.08
March	123.71	129.28	5.57
April	126.00	132.23	6.23
May	133.82	136.49	2.67
June	148.57	150.91	2.34
July	154.95	160.30	5.35
August	140.65	146.23	5.58
September	140.55	147.88	7.33
October	134.10	141.27	7.17
November	130.17	135.52	5.35
December	139.67	145.01	5.34
Average	134.79	140.11	5.32

[1] 1 ST = 0.9 MT.

of the supplemental xanthophyll in United States broiler and laying hen rations could be satisfied by about 270,000 MT (300,000 ST) of Pro-Xan (Enochian *et al.* 1980) if all supplemental xanthophyll were supplied by Pro-Xan.

As production of Pro-Xan increases to satisfy the potential demand, the return on investment in a Pro-Xan plant may not be as high as that realized by initial investors because of possible competition from other ingredients that supply xanthophyll. Therefore, firms considering entry into production of Pro-Xan should monitor the growth in production of Pro-Xan and its market prices to assist them in deciding if this would be a profitable decision.

REFERENCES

AM. APPRAISAL ASSOC. 1972. Boeckh Building Valuation Manuals, Vol. 1, Agricultural; Vol. 2, Commercial; Vol. 3, Industrial. American Appraisal Associates, Milwaukee.

AM. APPRAISAL ASSOC. 1975 and 1977. Boeckh Building Cost Index Numbers. American Appraisal Associates, Milwaukee.

BRAY, W.J. 1977. A consideration of the economics of green crop fractionation and leaf protein production. Int. Workshop on the Utilization of Agric. Waste for Feed and Food, Belo Horizonte, Brazil, Dec. 12–16, 1977.

BRUHN, H.D. and KOEGEL, R.G. 1977. More usable protein per acre by a modified forage program. Trans. ASAE *20* (4) 653–656.

CHRISMAN, J., KOHLER, G.O., MOTTOLA, A.C. and NELSON, J.W. 1971. High and low protein fractions by separation milling of alfalfa. U.S. Dep. Agric., Agric. Res. Serv., Rep *74–57*.

DE MATHAN, O. 1978. Process for the treatment of vegetable matter with recovery of calories from the dehydration stack gases and applications thereof. U.S. Pat. 4,070,351. Jan. 24.

DUMONT, A.G. and BOYCE, D.S. 1976. Leaf protein production and use on the farm: An economic study. J. Br. Grassl. Soc. *31*, 153–163.

ENOCHIAN, R.V., EDWARDS, R.H., KUZMICKY, D.D. and KOHLER, G.O. 1977. Leaf protein concentrate (Pro-Xan) from alfalfa: An updated economic evaluation.Winter Meet. Am. Soc. Agric. Eng., 1977, St. Joseph, MI. Dec. Mimeo. Pap. *77-6538*.

ENOCHIAN, R.V., KOHLER, G.O., EDWARDS, R.H., KUZMICKY, D.D. and VOSLOH, C.J., JR. 1980. Producing Pro-Xan (leaf protein concentrate) from alfalfa: Economics of an emerging technology. U.S. Dep. Agric., Econ. Stat. Coop. Serv., Agric. Econ. Rep. *445*.

ENOCHIAN, R.V., KOHLER, G.O. and KUZMICKY, D.D. 1971. Evaluating research improvements on livestock feeds through parametric linear programming. Cereal Sci. Today *16* (6) 181–184, 189.

HALLORAN, H.R. 1959. Determination of least-cost formulas with electronics. Feedstuffs *31* (18) 39–40.

KOHLER, G.O., WALKER, H.G., JR. and KUZMICKY, D.D. 1978A. Potential use and processing of crop residues. Proc. Fed. Am. Soc. Exp. Biol., 19th Annu. Ruminant Nutr. Conf., Atlantic City, NJ, Apr. 9, 1978.

KOHLER, G.O., WILDMAN, S.G., JORGENSEN, N.A., ENOCHIAN, R.V. and BRAY, W.J. 1978B. Leaf protein in relation to forage crop production and utilization. *In* Protein Resources and Technology. M. Milner, N.S. Scrimshaw, and D.I.C. Wang (Editors). AVI Publishing Co., Westport, CT.

KUZMICKY, D.D., LIVINGSTON, A.L., KNOWLES, R.E., KOHLER, G.O., GUENTHER, E., OLSON, O.E. and CARLSON, C.W. 1977. Xanthophyll availability of alfalfa leaf protein concentrate (Pro-Xan) for broilers and laying hens. Poult. Sci. *56*, 1504–1509.

McGUCKIN, T. and HUGHES, H. 1977. The economics of the alfalfa dewatering and protein extraction technology: A comparative study. Proc. Nonconventional Prot. and Foods Conf., Natl. Sci. Found., Univ. Wisconsin, Madison, Oct. 18, 1977.

PIRIE, N.W. 1971. Leaf Protein: Its Agronomy, Preparation, Quality, and Use. IBP Handb. *20*. Blackwell Scientific Publications, Oxford.

REBECK, H.M. and COOK, R.W. 1977. Manufacture of citrus pulp and molasses. *In* Citrus Science and Technology, Vol. 2. S. Nagy, P.E. Shaw and M.K. Veldhuis (Editors). AVI Publishing Co., Westport, CT.

TAYLOR, R.D., KOHLER, G.O., MADDY, K.H. and ENOCHIAN, R.V. 1968. Alfalfa meal in Poultry Feeds—An economic evaluation using parametric linear programming. U.S. Dep. Agric., Econ. Res. Serv., Agric. Econ. Rep. *130*.

U.S. DEP. AGRIC. 1977. Farm real estate market developments. U.S. Dep. Agric. Econ. Res. Serv. *CD-82*.

U.S. DEP. LABOR. 1975 and 1977. Bureau of Labor Statistics, Wholesale Price Index. Annual Reports. U.S. Dep. Labor, Washington, DC.

VOSLOH, C.J., JR. 1971. An alfalfa dehydrating plant on the Colorado River Indian Reservation—A feasibility study. U.S. Dep. Agric., Econ. Res. Serv., Unnumbered Rep., June.

VOSLOH, C.J., JR., EDWARDS, R.H., ENOCHIAN, R.V., KUZMICKY, D.D. and KOHLER, G.O. 1976. Leaf protein concentrate (Pro-Xan) from alfalfa: An economic evaluation. U.S. Dep. Agric., Econ. Res. Serv., Agric. Econ. Rep. *346*.

VOSLOH, C.J., JR., KUZMICKY, D.D., KOHLER, G.O. and ENOCHIAN, R.V. 1974. Air separation of alfalfa into high and low protein fractions—An economic evaluation. U.S. Dep. Agric., Econ. Res. Serv., Agric. Econ. Rep. *259*.

WILKINS, R.J., HEATH, S.B., ROBERTS, W.P., FOXELL, P.R. and WINDRAM, A. 1977. Green crop fractionation: An economic analysis. Br. Grassl. Res. Inst., Hurley, U.K., Tech. Rep. *19*.

20

Utilization of Press Cake from LPC Operations

H.G. Walker, Jr. and George O. Kohler

Research workers have envisioned production of leaf protein concentrate (LPC) in a variety of systems with primary objectives, or, in some cases, multiple objectives (Kohler *et al.* 1978B). Thus LPC might be the by-product of an on-the-farm forage dewatering system with the main product, pressed forage, being fed directly to ruminants or ensiled for later feeding (System A). It might be produced as the main product in village-scale operations in developing countries for use as a human food supplement (System B). Or it might be produced as a co-product along with pressed alfalfa and concentrated deproteinized juice to provide a high value feed product for nonruminants in a system designed to reduce the energy required to produce dehydrated alfalfa for ruminants (System C). Only System C has been shown to be economically sound and is currently being applied commercially (in the United States, France, Denmark, and Hungary).

The different system approaches and constraints necessarily lead to different equipment and operating conditions with a resultant difference in LPC yields. Consequently, the composition and nutrient values of the press cakes vary widely. For example, in considering the establishment of a green crop fractionation plant in England, it was necessary to insist that the crude protein of dried press cake be at least 14% in order to receive the European Economic Community subsidy (Thring 1976). Similarly, work in the United States at the University of Wisconsin has been aimed at removing only as much protein in the pressing operation as will leave a press cake with a crude protein content suitable for the preparation of high quality silage for dairy use (e.g., 15% protein, dry basis) (Stahmann 1974). On the other hand, economics of LPC production in commercial multiple product forage dehydration plants (Pro-Xan process) indicate that protein removal from the green crop should be as complete as possible for maximal return on investment (Vosloh *et al.* 1976; Enochian *et al.* 1980). No matter how press cake is generated, it is generally agreed that it must be utilized effectively in order that the overall economics of an LPC process be favorable (Kohler *et al.* 1978B). The only use developed thus far has been as an alternative forage for ruminants. In 1957, Raymond and Harris noted that pressed residue might also be used as an industrial raw material for the production of paper, fiberboard, or even methane. At that time, however, several factors weighed against the likelihood that this could become an economic reality, and the picture seems little changed since then.

As a feedstuff, the composition of press cake from LPC operations is influenced by four factors: (1) composition of starting material; (2) and (3) the amount of leaf solids removed by pressing as determined by the nitrogen extraction ratio:

$$(\text{NER}) = 100 \times \frac{\text{N in press juice}}{\text{N in raw material}}$$

and the dry matter extraction ratio:

$$(\text{DMER}) = 100 \times \frac{\text{dry matter in press juice}}{\text{dry matter in raw material}}$$

and (4) whether residual liquor after deproteinization is added back to the cake. Table 20.1 shows analyses of two low DMER press cakes (20% range for alfalfa) and the raw materials from which they were made (Connell and

TABLE 20.1. COMPOSITION (%) OF FORAGE AND LOW DMER[1] PRESS CAKE[2,3]

Composition	Alfalfa		Ryegrass	
	Crop	Press Cake	Crop	Press Cake
Dry matter	20.5	23.9	30.9	28.1
Total nitrogen	3.3	2.7	3.5	3.2
Crude protein	20.6	16.9	21.9	20.0
Nonprotein N	0.8	0.8	1.0	1.3
True protein	15.6	11.9	15.6	11.9
NH_4-N (× 100)	1.3	1.1	16.2	16.4
Ash	8.9	7.7	8.2	8.6
Fat (ether extract)	2.6	2.0	2.1	2.4
Neutral detergent fiber	39.6	46.7	59.7	59.8
NFE (nitrogen-free extract)	28.5	26.5	8.5	9.2
Cellulose	27.0	31.9	26.2	26.6
Water-soluble carbohydrate	9.7	9.0	20.7	19.0
Hexosans	23.1	24.3	26.8	25.0
Pentosans	8.6	10.3	15.9	16.0
Galacturonic acid	0.8	0.8	0.9	0.7
Pectin	0.6	0.7	0.4	0.2
Protopectin	2.4	2.6	0.7	0.6
Total uronides	3.9	4.0	2.0	1.5
Total carbohydrates	41.3	46.1	60.8	59.9
Nitrogen-free lignin	8.7	10.0	9.8	11.1

[1] ca 20%.
[2] Dry matter basis.
[3] Connell and Foxell (1976).

Foxell 1976). The data show a decrease in protein and an increase in cell wall constituents in the alfalfa press cake. The smaller differences between ryegrass and ryegrass press cake would seem to indicate a lesser degree of pressing although DMER data are not presented in the paper. Compositional differences between pressed and unpressed material are rather small. In the same study, the only significant compositional changes detected after 48 hr of storage of the press cakes were a large increase in ammonia nitrogen and a large decrease in water-soluble carbohydrate, both presumably caused by enzymatic and/or microbial action. No amino acid compositional data for press cake were reported in this study.

After deproteinization, most of the ash and carbohydrate of the juice remain in the residual liquor (brown juice, BJ), so that the deficit of these components in the press cake can be restored by adding the BJ back to it. An example of this is given in Table 20.2 which shows the analysis of press cakes made from alfalfa using a high DMER (ca 30%) (Kohler *et al.* 1978A). Brown juice was added back to a portion of the press cake prior to dehydration. The higher protein, nitrogen-free extract (NFE), and ash values of the press cake with added BJ compared with untreated press cake reflect the nutrient enhancement obtained with the add-back process. Factors which affect the NER and DMER and thus press cake composition were studied by Edwards *et al.* (1977). Using a twin screw press operated under standard conditions on ground alfalfa, they established that DMER's were controlled by the raw material dry matter and fiber contents. LPC yields (a function of NER) were influenced by raw material protein, fiber, and dry matter content and alfalfa temperature.

Since the goal in the United States has been to maximize yield of LPC (Enochian *et al.* 1980), several strategies have been developed to increase the amount of juice and protein extracted from the raw forage (Edwards *et al.* 1978A). The data in Fig. 20.1 were obtained from experimental lots of alfalfa with about 20% protein that were pressed after recycle of part of the

TABLE 20.2. ANALYSIS OF ALFALFA AND HIGH DMER[1] PRESS CAKES[2,3]

Variables	Control	Press Cake	Press Cake with Brown Juice
Proximate analysis (%)			
crude protein	19.6	13.1	14.9
crude fiber	25.7	36.0	29.9
nitrogen-free extract	42.3	42.2	44.3
ether extract	3.0	2.3	1.5
ash	9.4	6.3	9.4
Van Soest analysis (%)			
acid detergent fiber	30.4	46.4	37.0
neutral detergent fiber	41.8	57.7	49.9
lignin	6.7	10.0	7.4
cellulose	28.2	36.8	31.2

[1] ca. 30%.
[2] Dry matter basis.
[3] Kohler *et al.* (1978A).

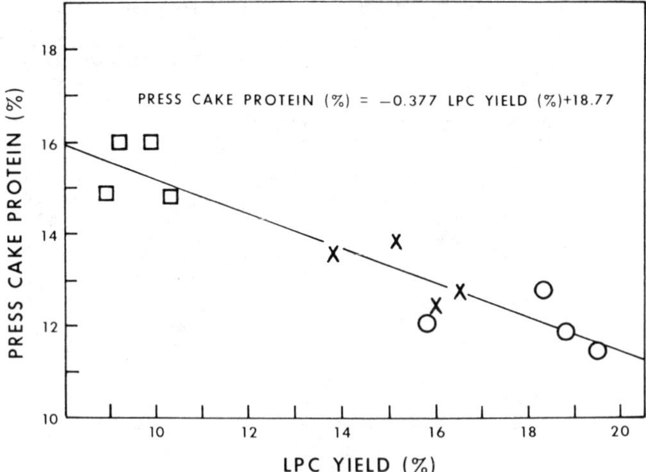

Fig. 20.1. Alfalfa press cake protein content as a function of pressing (LPC yield). Protein content of fresh chops = 20%.
From Edwards et al. (1978B).

BJ to the grinder to increase the extent of extraction (Edwards *et al.* 1978A). They show that, as expected, there is an inverse correlation between yield of LPC and residual pulp protein content. Other yield-increasing improvements include further grinding of chopped forage (Edwards *et al.* 1978B) and tandem dual pressing with juice add-back after the first pressing (Edwards and Kohler 1978C). A process combining all of these improvements gives a press cake containing 10–13% residual protein.

How to evaluate the forage quality of these low protein press cakes presents a problem. Table 20.3 shows the chemical composition of each of the hay grades proposed for legume hay (Rohweder *et al.* 1978) and the forage analytical values determined on two press cakes made from high quality alfalfa (Kohler *et al.* 1978A). Press cake with solubles added back apparently falls within the grade #3 definition and press cake alone would have to be rated in grade #4. However, there are good reasons to believe that the values of both of these legume press cakes as forages are better than indicated by the analytical data. Various researchers (Phillips and Loughlin 1949; Meyer and Lofgreen 1959; Oh *et al.* 1966; Lema 1972; Rohweder *et al.* 1978) have shown that total dry matter digestibility of legume type roughages is positively correlated with total N content, so that the digestibility of the energy components (cellulose and hemicellulose) of the press cakes should be that of the high grade starting material, and not that of more highly lignified, aged material of grade 3 and 4 quality (Kohler *et al.* 1973). It should be noted that the foregoing reasoning does not necessarily apply to the case of press cakes made from grasses since the

TABLE 20.3. COMPOSITION OF PROPOSED MARKET HAY GRADES FOR LEGUMES[1] AND WRRC SAMPLES[2]

Grade Forage Product	Stage of Maturity International Term	Typical Chemical Composition-%[3]		
		CP[4]	ADF	NDF
1 Legume hay	Prebloom	>19	<31	<40
2 Legume hay	Early bloom	17–19	31–35	40–46
3 Legume hay	Midbloom	13–16	36–41	47–51
4 Legume hay	Full	<13	>41	>51
5 WRRC alfalfa samples				
control		19.6	30.4	41.8
press cake[5]		13.1	46.4	57.7
press cake with solubles added back[5]		14.9	37.0	47.9

[1] Rohweder *et al.* (1978).
[2] Kohler *et al.* (1978A).
[3] Dry matter basis.
[4] CP—Crude protein. ADF—Acid detergent fiber. NDF—Neutral detergent fiber.
[5] DMER = 30%.

correlation between dry matter digestibility and total nitrogen is not nearly as good with grasses as it is with legumes (Rohweder *et al.* 1978). In addition, the comminution involved in the processing operation should increase the digestibility of the fibrous constituents of the press cake to that of unpressed material (Greenhalgh and Reid 1975). The problem of the relative value of press cake can only be clarified by further animal research studies.

FEED USE OF PRESSED FORAGE

As it leaves the press, the moisture content of press cake may range from 60 to 75%, so that it must be consumed immediately or preserved for subsequent use. On the farm, operations favor feeding fresh or ensiled material; large-scale factory operations have so far favored dehydration in conventional forage dehydrators (Kohler *et al.* 1978B), but future needs for energy savings may make it necessary to forego dehydration of press cake with fossil fuels. In a dehydration operation with press cake, there is a considerable reduction in energy required compared with fresh material. This was pointed out (Raymond and Harris 1957; Kohler *et al.* 1973) as being due to lower moisture content and easier diffusion of water through the crushed material. Figure 20.2 shows that, depending on the extent of juice removal, gas savings for water evaporation of 45% or more over conventional dehydration of fresh crop can be achieved with a well run pressing operation (Kohler *et al.* 1973). At present, all commercial operations take advantage of these fuel economies to produce a dehydrated pelleted press cake which is easy to handle and store. Obviously, if dilute brown juice is added back to the press cake before dehydration, the fuel savings are essentially eliminated. In commercial practice, the BJ is evapo-

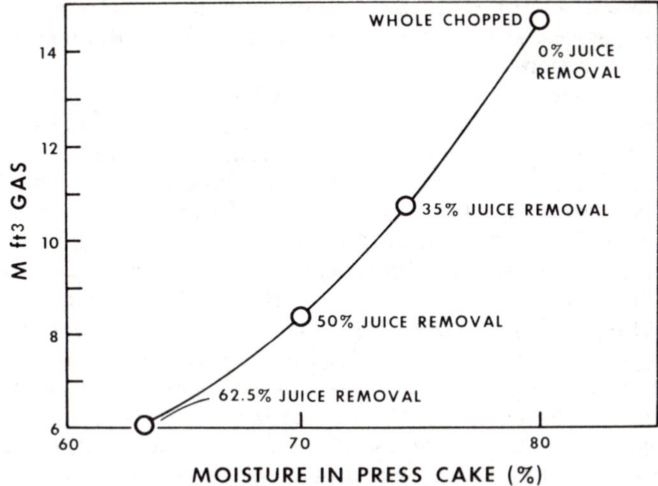

Fig. 20.2. Fuel required to produce 0.9 MT (1 ST) of dehydrated product (93% dry matter) from alfalfa press cakes of different moisture contents. Assumed fuel requirement—0.133 m^3 gas per kg (2 ft^3 per lb) of water evaporated.
From Kohler et al. (1973).

rated to about 50% solids by use of a waste heat evaporator using stack gases from the dehydrator. The molasses-like concentrate is then added back to press cake prior to dehydration and adds only slightly to the dehydrator load.

Many animal experiments have been carried out to determine the nutritive value of the press cakes made in different LPC operations, and results of some will be reviewed here. No claim of completeness can be made for this section, however, since some of the research reports are in periodicals or other experiment station or other institutional reports not readily available in most library collections.

DRIED PRESS CAKE EXPERIMENTS

Early lamb feeding work by Raymond and Harris (1957) showed that dry matter digestibility of dried residue from a lightly pressed grass mixture (DMER not given) was about 9 percentage points lower than that of unprocessed material (55.6 vs. 64.3%). Dry matter intake was the same for both feeds. Using a very high extraction dried press cake from mixed pasture (judged to be a high extraction ratio but DMER not given), Ulyatt (1970) showed that adequate nitrogen was present to maintain sheep in balance at normal feed intakes, but that calcium, phosphate, and soluble carbohydrate were deficient. He suggested that adding back the liquor left after protein separation could help alleviate the observed nutrient deficiencies. Vartha *et al.* (1973) indicated that dried press cakes from high quality alfalfa and ryegrass are satisfactory substitutes for alfalfa hay for feeding dry (pregnant) sheep.

In a series of dairy trials carried out at the National Institute for Research in Dairying (U.K.) over a period of three years, Connell and Foxell (1976) compared the performance of dried wafered alfalfa press cake (DMER estimated to have been about 20%) with whole crop material. Results indicated no significant difference in feeding value of the two materials. Dry matter intakes were similar, but milk yields tended to be lower with press cake even though the differences were not significantly so. It was assumed that the trend to lower production with the press cake was a reflection of its slightly lower overall digestibility. It is interesting to note that in one of their trials where pulped pressed Italian ryegrass was compared with whole crop, the grass press cake out-performed the whole crop material in regard to milk yield, fat, and lactose production.

Jones *et al.* (1977) studied the use of dried press cake (DMER estimated to have been about 20%) from chopped perennial ryegrass in a steer feeding trial. Some of the press cake was ground further in a hammer mill. The two press cake materials were compared with high quality, long-dried grass. Even though the digestibility of the whole crop was significantly better than that of either of the press cakes (established in a digestibility trial with lambs), the steer feeding trial showed no statistical differences in feed intake or live weight gains among the three feedstuffs.

Garrett *et al.* (1977) (cited by Kohler *et al.* 1979) investigated the composition and digestibility of press cakes made from alfalfa at two different juice solids removal levels (DMER = ca 22% and 30%, respectively), with BJ added back on one case. Digestibility data are tabulated in Table 20.4. At the low level of juice solids removal, the digestibilities of organic matter, protein, acid detergent fiber, and cellulose, and the digestible energy of press cake were similar to those of the dehydrated whole alfalfa. At the higher level of juice solids removal, with no add-back of juice solubles, the

TABLE 20.4. DIGESTIBILITY[1] OF DEHYDRATED ALFALFA PRESS CAKES

Component	Dehydrated Control	Low Extraction Press Cake[2]	High Extraction Press Cake[3]	High Extraction Press Cake with Solubles Added Back[3]
	Digestibility Coefficient (%)			
Organic matter	60.6	61.5	57.7	59.2
Crude protein	70.9	69.3	62.2	61.1
Acid detergent fiber	36.7	41.7	44.9	42.1
Cellulose	52.2	55.4	57.0	55.7
Digestible energy (Kcal/g)	2.7	2.6	2.4	2.4

Source: Garrett *et al.* (1977).
[1]Determined with lambs.
[2]DMER = ca 22%.
[3]DMER = ca 30%.

digestibility of organic matter and protein decreased, but the digestibility of acid detergent fiber and cellulose increased materially. Even though about 30% of the solids of the original alfalfa were removed in the high extraction pressing operation, the digestible energy of the dried residual press cake was only 9% lower than that of the dehydrated unfractionated alfalfa. Add-back of juice solubles to high extraction press cake gave a material whose digestibility characteristics were closer to those of regular press cake than those of the untreated control.

FRESH PRESS CAKE EXPERIMENTS

A number of trials have shown that wet fresh or frozen press cake is a satisfactory forage replacement. Vartha *et al.* (1973) determined that the organic matter digestibility of wet fresh alfalfa press cake (72.8%) was about 9 percentage points higher than that of dried press cake (63.6%). They found that the wet material was eaten readily, but spoiled so rapidly that, unless the press cake was prepared daily, it was preferable to convert it to silage.

Work at the Rowett Institute (Houseman *et al.* 1977) showed that the dry matter and organic matter digestibility of fresh ryegrass press cake (71–73%) were less than that of unpressed grass (78–80%). Results of a beef cattle performance trial at the same institute are given in Table 20.5 in which paddock grazing, fresh cut grass, and fresh pressed grass cake were compared (Jones and Houseman 1975). Paddock grazing resulted in an average weight gain of 0.72 kg/day. Fresh cut grass was about the same. Feeding fresh press cake resulted in an increase in daily gain to about 0.83 kg/day from a significantly lower dry matter intake. The press cake was from a low extraction rate pressing; even so, the excellent performance of the press cake was surprising considering that about 20% of the nonfiber solids were removed in the single-screw pressing operation. Digestibilities of fresh grass and press cake were essentially the same and showed no indication of change due to a seasonal effect.

In a later beef trial at the same institute comparing fresh press cake from red clover with fresh whole clover, Houseman *et al.* (1978A) found that

TABLE 20.5. BEEF CATTLE[1]—FRESH PRESS CAKE[2] GRASS VERSUS PADDOCK FEEDING

Type of Feed	Live Wt Gain (kg/Day)	Dry Matter Intake (kg/Day)	Fresh Matter Intake (kg/Day)
Paddock grazing	0.72	—	—
Fresh cut grass	0.73	6.78	40.9
Fresh press cake	0.83	6.26	23.8
Standard error	±0.05	±0.20	±0.97

Source: Jones and Houseman (1975).
[1] 12 cattle per treatment—about 4½ months.
[2] DMER = ca 20%.

animal performance was similar with both materials. Daily dry matter intake, weight gain, feed conversion, and digestibility were only slightly better with whole clover than with press cake.

Russian workers (Eidrigevich *et al.* 1978) reported that they fed bulls for 116 days on diets consisting mainly of fresh alfalfa or wet fresh alfalfa press cake at two different levels. Results listed in Table 20.6 show that press cake at either feeding level gave higher daily gain and overall feed efficiency than fresh material. Carcass yields were the same for all diets.

Trigg and Bryant (1978) fed pressed pasture (DMER = 20%) to dairy cows to evaluate the nutritive potential of press cake. In general, the pressing operation caused apparent reduction in all chemical constituents except fiber; this was especially important in the case of magnesium and sodium since their levels were already considered marginal in the unpressed forage. Dry matter intake and overall milk production were significantly less with press cake diets than with unpressed forages. Milk fat or lactose production was not different, but milk protein was significantly reduced on the press cake diets. Magnesium supplementation did not improve performance of animals on press cake diets. The authors suggest that the observed differences probably result from the lowered intake and digestibility of press cake components compared with unpressed pasture.

Greenhalgh and Reid (1975) showed that comminution of fresh roughage had a beneficial effect on overall feed intake and on press cake digestibility. Ryegrass was chopped (Treatment C) and pressed twice in a screw press to give a press cake (Treatment P) and juice. When whole green juice and press cake were recombined, a new feed was obtained (Treatment R). Intake of the Treatment R diet was about 25–50% greater than that of either Treatment C or Treatment P. Since dry matter digestibility of all treatments was essentially the same, comminution must have increased the digestibility of the press cake portion.

Yu *et al.* (1975) at Michigan State University subjected thawed alfalfa press cake to a number of chemical and physical treatments (i.e., chlorine compounds, alkalis, enzymes, electron irradiations, and several combinations of these) in efforts to increase its digestibility. None of the treatments gave outstanding results, but in many cases, *in vitro* neutral detergent fiber (i.e. cell wall) digestibility of the press cake was raised from 40 to 50–55%.

TABLE 20.6. RUSSIAN BULL FEEDING TRIAL—FRESH ALFALFA VS. FRESH ALFALFA PRESS CAKE

Material	Daily Gain (g)	FU/kg Gain
Alfalfa		
fresh (33 kg/day)	618–632	10.24–10.47
Press cake (6 kg/day)	689	9.36
Press cake (11 kg/day)	744	8.83

Source: Eidrigevich *et al.* (1978).
FU—Feed units.

SILAGE PRESS CAKE EXPERIMENTS

Many whole crop forages have such high moisture levels (80% and over) that they frequently incur seepage losses and unfavorable clostridial fermentations due to high water activity when ensiled (McDonald 1973). Indeed, in past years, several groups investigated use of machines to field press alfalfa and other forages to reduce moisture to levels more favorable for silage production (Derbyshire *et al.* 1969; Casselman *et al.* 1965; Hibbs *et al.* 1968). The magnitude of the nutrient losses in such schemes made them economically inferior to wilting procedures, but did demonstrate that good silages could be made from pressed high moisture leafy crops. LPC pressing operations give a press cake moisture content comparable to that of wilted roughages, and hence a level which favors rapid lactic acid fermentation.

Raymond and Harris (1957) were unable to ensile press cake made from an alfalfa LPC operation without the addition of molasses or sulfuric acid, presumably because of the low level of soluble carbohydrate. Even with these additions, the products they obtained were unpalatable so that they could not be used for animal trials. On the other hand, Oelshlegel *et al.* (1969) were able to make a satisfactory silage with very small seepage losses from alfalfa press cake, using a vacuum packing technique in plastic bags. Analysis of the organic acids in the silage indicated that no detrimental clostridial growth took place. They postulated that pulping and pressing may have had a beneficial effect on the silage fermentation by distributing the plant enzymes more widely through the material mass, aiding the degradation of hexoses to lactic acid. Using the vacuum pack process, Vartha *et al.* (1973) reported that it was necessary to add sulfuric acid and molasses to produce a satisfactory silage from alfalfa press cake. The silage had about the same organic matter digestibility as dried press cake but voluntary intake of dry matter was 20% greater for the ensiled product.

A sheep digestibility trial by Buchanan-Smith (1977) compared silage from alfalfa press cake with silage from field-wilted alfalfa. Apparent organic matter and nitrogen digestibilities were appreciably lower for the press cake than for the wilted silage, but too few animals were used to quantitate the results in a substantial manner. Houseman *et al.* (1978B) compared the performance of steers fed ensiled whole ryegrass with that of animals fed ensiled ryegrass press cake. Dry matter and organic matter digestibility (sheep) were higher for ensiled whole grass, but daily dry matter intake and gain were slightly higher for ensiled press cake. Feed conversion was essentially the same for both materials, as was overall animal performance.

Extensive studies of the ensiling of alfalfa press cake residue have been carried out by the LPC task force at the University of Wisconsin. In all cases, press cake from relatively low LPC extractive pressing was used (DMER = ca 24%). Results of dairy trials running for three successive years using alfalfa press cake silage have been reported (Russell *et al.* 1978).

Control silage was made from field-wilted alfalfa. Composition of the two silage types averaged over three years is shown in Table 20.7. Compared with the wilted forage silage, the press cake silage had significantly less ($P < 0.05$) dry matter, crude protein, and ash, and more fiber components. The silage from press cake had significantly greater concentrations of all the individual and total volatile fatty acids. Lactic acid contents were not significantly different but that of press cake material was numerically lower. Results of digestion trials run in years 1 and 3 are shown in Table 20.8. Significantly higher crude protein and lower ADF digestibilities were obtained for press cake silage in year 1, but no significant differences in digestibility of any component were found in year 3. The improved

TABLE 20.7. MEAN COMPOSITION OF ALFALFA SILAGE

Component	Control[1]	Pressed[2]
Dry matter, %	42.1	30.5
% of dry matter		
crude protein	18.5	15.9
cell wall constituents (CWC)	47.2	57.8
acid detergent fiber (ADF)	37.6	47.4
estimated hemicellulose (CWC−ADF)	9.6	10.4
acid detergent lignin	6.6	8.2
ash	9.7	7.9
Organic acids, % of DDM		
acetic	2.1	3.8
propionic	0.2	0.5
butyric	0.1	1.2
total volatile acids	2.4	5.5
lactic	3.8	2.7
total organic	6.2	8.2
% of total N		
nonprotein N	20.4	27.2
ammonia N[3]	8.6	3.2

Source: Russell *et al.* (1978).
[1]Means of years 1 and 2.
[2]Mean of 3 years.
[3]Year 3.
DDM—Digestible dry matter.

TABLE 20.8. APPARENT DIGESTIBILITY[1] OF CONTROL AND PRESSED SILAGE DRY MATTER AND ITS COMPONENTS FROM YEARS 1 AND 3

	Silages, Year 1, Trial 1		Silages, Year 3, Trial 2	
	Control	Pressed	Control	Pressed
Component	Digestibility, %			
Dry matter	64.6	63.3	60.9	60.4
Crude protein	72.6	78.0	69.6	64.3
Cell wall constituents (CWC)	59.5	57.1	56.8	61.6
Acid detergent fiber (ADF)	55.6	52.5	57.1	58.2
Cell solubles (100 − CWC)	68.9	69.0	65.5	58.3
Estimated hemicellulose (CWC − ADF)	79.4	80.2	64.8	71.1
Cellulose (ADF − lignin)	56.5	55.4	64.9	69.1

Source: Russell *et al.* (1978).
[1]Determined with 3 animals.

digestibility of fiber constituents in year 3 suggests improved maceration techniques were aiding fiber digestion.

Results of the lactation tests showed slightly poorer performance on press cake silage but the differences were not statistically significant in most cases. This trend to lowered performance seemed to be linked with decreased intake of press cake silage. In one trial (results shown in Table 20.9), both silage diets were supplemented with 2 kg of hay. This increased

TABLE 20.9. MEAN[1] DAILY DRY MATTER INTAKE AND PRODUCTION OF COWS FED CONTROL AND PRESSED SILAGES WITH AND WITHOUT HAY

	Period 1			Period 2		
	Silages			Silages Plus Hay		
Parameter	Control	Pressed	S.E.of Mean	Control	Pressed	S.E.of Mean
Dry matter intake						
silage (kg)	12.2	11.6	—	11.0	10.1	0.22
hay (kg)	—	—	—	2.0	2.0	—
total forage (kg)	12.2	11.6	0.37	13.0[2]	12.1	0.22
grain (kg)	7.8	7.8	—	7.8	7.8	—
total dry matter (kg)	20.1	19.4	0.44	20.9	19.9	0.23
% of body weight	3.2	3.0	0.08	3.3	3.1	0.04
Production						
milk (kg)	24.0	23.6	0.55	23.9	22.9	0.30
fat (%)	3.8[2]	3.4	0.08	3.6	3.9	0.15
4% FCM (kg)	23.3[2]	21.3	0.54	22.6	22.6	0.06
protein (%)	3.3	3.1	0.08	3.5	3.5	0.06
Weight change (kg/day)	0.1	0	—	0	0	4.48

Source: Russell *et al.* (1978).
[1]All values adjusted by covariance.
[2]Means in same row and period are significantly different ($P < 0.05$).
FCM—Fat corrected milk.

TABLE 20.10. DRY MATTER INTAKE AND PRODUCTION OF COWS FED LOW MOISTURE SILAGE (LMS) OR PRESS CAKE SILAGE TREATED WITH FORMIC ACID (FPS)

	LMS		FPS		
Parameter	Mean	S.E.	Mean	S.E.	Significance
n	5		5		
Dry matter intake					
silage (kg/day)	10.5	0.7	13.3	0.9	NS
grain (kg/day)	7.1	0.8	7.1	0.7	NS
total (kg/day)	17.6	1.3	20.4	1.4	NS
% of body weight	2.8	0.2	3.2	0.1	NS
Production					
milk (kg/day)	21.9	1.9	22.8	3.5	NS
fat (kg/day)	0.9	0.1	0.9	0.1	NS
fat (%)	4.1	0.1	4.0	0.1	NS
4% FCM (fat corrected milk)(kg/day)	22.7	2.3	22.7	3.5	NS
protein (kg/day)	0.8	0.1	0.8	0.1	NS
protein (%)	3.4	0.1	3.5	0.1	NS
kg feed/kg 4% FCM	0.8	0.1	1.0	0.2	NS
weight change (kg/day)	0.1	0.04	0.3	0.10	[1]

Source: Lu *et al.* (1979).
[1]$P < 0.05$.
NS—Not significant.

total dry matter intake for both groups and alleviated the depressed production of milk fat and protein by the press cake silage-fed animals. Another report from this research group indicates that addition of 0.2–0.65% formic acid to press cake during the ensiling step improves the silage quality materially (Lu *et al.* 1979). The lactation trial data in Table 20.10 show silage made from press cake with 0.5% added formic acid was indistinguishable in performance from high quality, low moisture silage.

SUMMARY

The roughage obtained by mechanical pressing of alfalfa or other leafy materials may be considered to be a dewatered forage, or a by-product or a co-product of leaf protein concentrate (LPC) production, depending on the primary objectve of the operation. The nutritive value of press cakes depends upon the dry matter extraction ration (DMER) (% of the raw material dry matter which is removed in the press juice) and the quality of the raw material (e.g., protein and fiber content). The DMER, which is a function of raw material quality and of equipment and process design, may range from 7 to 40%. In operations where the press cake is dehydrated, the residual deproteinized brown juice may be concentrated using a waste heat evaporator and added back to the press cake prior to dehydration to increase its feed value. When the press cake is to be used as silage, this is of course not possible without an expensive evaporation step.

The several variables mentioned make it possible to have press cakes of widely varying compositions and nutritive value. Nonetheless, an important generalization can be drawn from the literature on ruminant digestibility and feeding trials: namely, that the press cakes are only slightly lower in feed value than the forages from which they were produced. This is somewhat surprising since 20 to 30% of the most digestible nutrients are removed in the juicing operation. The explanation for the high nutritive value of the press cake is that the grinding and/or pressing operation tears open most of the forage cells, making the cell wall components more accessible to the cellulolytic organisms in the rumen. This is reflected in higher fiber digestion coefficients in press cake as compared with unpressed raw material.

While present commercial LPC operations are converting the press cake to dehydrated pellets, the ever-increasing fuel costs can be expected to result in greater press cake use as a fresh feed or a silage in the near future.

REFERENCES

BUCHANAN-SMITH, J.G. 1977. Dewatering alfalfa. Technical problems in preparing, preserving, and feeding liquid protein concentrate. Dairy Ind. Res. Rep, 3–6.

CASSELMAN, T.W., GREEN, V.E., JR., ALLEN, R.J., JR. and THOMAS, F.H. 1965. Mechanical dewatering of forage crops. Agric. Exp. Stn. Univ. Fla., Gainesville, Tech. Bull. *694*.

CONNELL, J. and FOXELL, P.R. 1976. Green crop fractionation, the products and their utilization by cattle, pigs and poultry. Bienn. Rev. Natl. Inst. Res. Dairy, 21–41.

DERBYSHIRE, J.C., GORDON, C.H., HALDREN, R.D. and MENEAR, J.R. 1969. Evaluation of dewatering and wilting as moisture reduction methods for hay crop silage. Agron. J. *61*, 928–931.

EDWARDS, R.H., DE FREMERY, D. and KOHLER, G.O. 1978A. Use of recycled dilute alfalfa solubles to increase the yield of leaf protein concentrate from alfalfa. J. Agric. Food Chem. *26*, 738–741.

EDWARDS, R.H., DE FREMERY, D., MACKEY, B.E. and KOHLER, G.O. 1977. Factors affecting juice extraction and yield of leaf protein concentrate from chopped alfalfa. Trans. ASAE *20*,423–428.

EDWARDS, R.H., DE FREMERY, D., MACKEY, B.E. and KOHLER, G.O. 1978B. Factors affecting juice extraction and yield of leaf protein concentrate from ground alfalfa. Trans. ASAE *21*, 55–59., 62

EDWARDS, R.H. and KOHLER, G.O. 1978C. Personal communication. Western Regional Research Center, Berkeley, CA 94710.

EIDRIGEVICH, E.V., KINZBURGSKII, Z.S., PIDORENKO, L.D., NAUMENKO, V.I. and PASECHNIK, G.I. 1978. Nutritive value of the fractionation products of lucerne. Vestn. Skh. Nauki Moscow *6*, 95–102; Nutr. Abstr. Rev. Ser. B: *48*, 5102.

ENOCHIAN, R.V., KOHLER, G.O., EDWARDS, R.H., KUZMICKY, D.D., and VOSLOH, C.J., JR. 1983. Economics of producing LPC for feed with the Pro-Xan process. *In* Leaf Protein Concentrates. L. Telek and H.D. Graham (Editors). AVI Publishing Co., Westport, CT.

GARRETT, W.N., KOHLER, G.O. and WALKER, H.G., JR. 1977. Unpublished results. Univ. of California, Davis, CA 95616 and Western Regional Research Center, Berkeley, CA 94710.

GREENHALGH, J.F.D. and REID, G.W. 1975. Mechanical processing of wet roughage. Proc. Nutr. Soc. *34*, 74A.

HIBBS, J.W., CONRAD, H.R. and JOHNSON, N.H. 1968. Macerated, dewatered vs. wilted alfalfa grass silage for dairy cows. Ohio Agric. Res. Dev. Cent., Wooster, Res. Bull. *1013*.

HOUSEMAN, R.A., BAIRD, B.A., TRUSCOTT, S.A. and JONES, A.S. 1977. The fractionation of winter rye and the nutritional evaluation of rye juice and pulp. Anim. Prod. *24*, 141 (Abstr. *38*).

HOUSEMAN, R.A., PIRIE, R. and TRUSCOTT, S.A. 1978A. The performance of beef animals given pressed clover and pigs given fresh clover juice. Anim. Prod. *26*, 393, Abstr. (Nutr. Abstr. Rev. Ser. B: *49*, 892, 1979.)

HOUSEMAN, R.H., TRUSCOTT, S.A. and JONES, A.S. 1978B. The performance of beef animals given ensiled pressed grass and of pigs given fresh grass juice. Anim. Prod. *26*. 378. Abstr. (Nutr. Abstr. Rev. Ser. B: *49*, 908, 1979).

JONES, A.S. and HOUSEMAN, R.A. 1975. Annual Report of Studies in Animal Nutrition and Allied Sciences, Vol. 31. The Rowett Research Institute, Bucksburn, Aberdeen, Scotland.

JONES, A.S., HOUSEMAN, R.A., MACDEARMID, A. and TRUSCOTT, S.A. 1977. The nutritive value of dried grass for ruminants. Anim. Prod. *24*, 140.

KOHLER, G.O., BICKOFF, E.M. and DE FREMERY, D. 1973. Mechanical dewatering of forage and protein byproduct recovery. Proc. 1st Int. Green Crop Drying Congr., Oxford, England, Apr. 9–13, 1973. Br. Assoc. Green Crop Driers, 16 Lansdale Gardens, Tunbridge Wells, Kent, England.

KOHLER, G.O., DE FREMERY, D. and EDWARDS, R.H. 1983. LPC for feeds and foods—The Pro-Xan process. *In* Leaf Protein Concentrates. L. Telek and H.D. Graham (Editors). AVI Publishing Co., Westport, CT.

KOHLER, G.O., WALKER, H.G., JR. and GARRETT, W.N. 1978A. Unpublished results. Western Regional Research Center, Berkeley, CA 94710.

KOHLER, G.O., WALKER, H.G., JR. and KUZMICKY., D.D. 1979. Processing and use of crop residues including alfalfa press cake. Fed. Proc. Fed Am. Soc. Exp. Biol. *38*, 1934–1938.

KOHLER, G.O., WILDMAN, S.G., JORGENSEN, N.A., ENOCHIAN, R.V. and BRAY, W.J. 1978B. Leaf protein in relation to forage crop production and utilization. *In* Leaf Protein Resources and Technology. M. Milner, N.S. Scrimshaw and D.I.C. Wang (Editors). AVI Publishing Co., Westport, CT.

LEMA, M.F. 1972. *In vivo* and *in vitro* measures as predictors of the nutritive value of alfalfa and bromegrass hays. Ph.D. Thesis. Univ. of Wisconsin, Madison.

LU, C.D., JORGENSON, N.A. and BARRINGTON, G.P. 1979. Wet fractionation process: Preservation and utilization of pressed alfalfa forage. J. Dairy Sci. *62*, 1399–1407.

McDONALD, P. 1973. The ensilage process. *In* Chemistry and Biochemistry of Herbage, Vol. 3. G.W. Butler and R.W. Bailey (Editors). Academic Press, New York.

MEYER, J.H. and LOFGREEN, G.P. 1959. Evaluation of alfalfa hay by chemical analysis. J. Anim. Sci. *18*, 1233–1242.

OELSHLEGEL, F.G., SCHROEDER, J.R. and STAHMANN, M.A. 1969. Protein concentrates. Use of residues as silage. J. Agric. Food Chem. *17*, 796–798.

OH, H.K., BAUMGARDT, B.R. and SCHOLL, J.M. 1966. Evaluation of forages in the laboratory. V. Comparison of chemical analyses, solubility tests, and *in vitro* fermentation. J. Dairy Sci. *49*, 850–855.

PHILLIPS, T.G. and LOUGHLIN, M.E. 1949. Composition and digestible energy of hays fed to cattle. J. Agric. Res. *78*, 389–395.

RAYMOND, W.F. and HARRIS, C.E. 1957. The value of fibrous residue from leaf protein extraction as a feeding-stuff for ruminants. Br. Grassl. Soc. J. *12*, 166–170.

ROHWEDER, D.A., BARNES, R.F. and JORGENSEN, N. 1978. Proposed hay grading standards based on laboratory analyses for evaluating quality. J. Anim. Sci. *47*, 747–759.

RUSSELL, J.R., HURST, J.P., JORGENSEN, N.A. and BARRINGTON, G.P. 1978. Wet plant fractionation: Utilization of pressed alfalfa silage. J. Anim. Sci. *46*, 278–287.

STAHMANN, M.A. 1974. The Wisconsin work. 12th Tech. Alfalfa Conf. Proc., 1974, Overland Park, KS. West. Reg. Res. Cent., Berkeley, CA.

THRING, J.M. 1976. The BOCM-Silcock green crop fractionation process. Br. Grassl. Soc. Occas. Symp. *9*, 171–174.

TRIGG, T.E. and BRYANT, A.M. 1978. The nutritive value of protein extracted pasture for lactating dairy cows. Proc. Nutr. Soc. N.Z. *3*, 97–106.

ULYATT, M.J. 1970. The nutritive value of the residue from protein-extracted herbage. Proc. N.Z. Soc. Anim. Prod. *30*, 92–93.

VARTHA, E.W., FLETCHER, L.R. and ALLISON, R.M. 1973. Protein extracted herbage for sheep feeding. N.Z. J. Exp. Agric. *1*, 171–174.

VOSLOH, C.J., JR., EDWARDS, R.H., ENOCHIAN, R.V., KUZMICKY, D.D. and KOHLER, G.O. 1976. Leaf protein concentrate (Pro-Xan) from alfalfa. An economic evaluation. U.S. Dep. Agric., Econ. Res. Serv., Agric. Econ. Rep. *346*.

YU, Y., THOMAS, J.W. and EMERY, R.S. 1975. Estimated nutritive value of treated forages for ruminants. J. Anim. Sci. *41*, 1742–1750.

21

Optimization of the Protein Extraction Process from Grasslands in Temperate and Subtropical Regions

Henry T. Ostrowski-Meissner[1]

FACTORS LIMITING PROTEIN RECOVERY FROM HERBAGE

Several new technologies have already been developed and applied to both feed and food manufacturing operations, on an experimental basis, in order to increase yields of protein recoverable from agricultural ecosystems (Pirie 1971; Jones 1977; Ostrowski-Meissner 1976A, 1978A,B). Of these, protein extraction from green vegetation, particularly from grasslands grown in temperate and subtropical climates, has come to be considered the most attractive and promising alternative to conventional farming operations (Ostrowski-Meissner 1978A,B, 1979, 1980).

However, the quantities of protein which can be extracted from grasslands and various green crops depend on a number of factors which limit protein recovery from green vegetation (Arkcoll 1971; McKenzie 1977; Oke 1973; Ostrowski-Meissner 1975; Ostrowski-Meissner *et al.* 1975; Pirie 1971). Also, the protein fractions (feed- and food-grade) recoverable from the herbage grown and/or processed in various conditions vary in both quantities and proportions (Ostrowski-Meissner 1976A).

The limitations have been conveniently grouped into four categories:

(1) Factors related to the ecology and the agronomy of grasslands
(2) Factors limiting protein recovery at the herbage harvesting stage
(3) Factors limiting protein recovery at the herbage processing stage
(4) Factors restricting protein recovery depending on the system of juice processing

[1]Balai Penelitian Ternak, Project for Animal Research and Development, Bogor, Indonesia (Commonwealth Scientific and Industrial Research Organization—Australia).

Due to these factors, the yields and subsequent protein recoveries vary considerably—the extent of variation (Fig. 21.1) not being acceptable in agricultural practice (Ostrowski-Meissner 1976A,B). In addition to the variation in protein recovery from herbage, the final product—leaf protein concentrates (LPC)—is marked by differences in both chemical composition and biological value (Table 21.1).

In order to optimize the protein extraction process and make it a feasible and reliable proposition for wide and practical applicability, the effects of various factors which can limit the entire extraction operation have been studied in climatic conditions characteristic of temperate and subtropical areas (Ostrowski-Meissner 1975, 1976B) in order to establish relationships

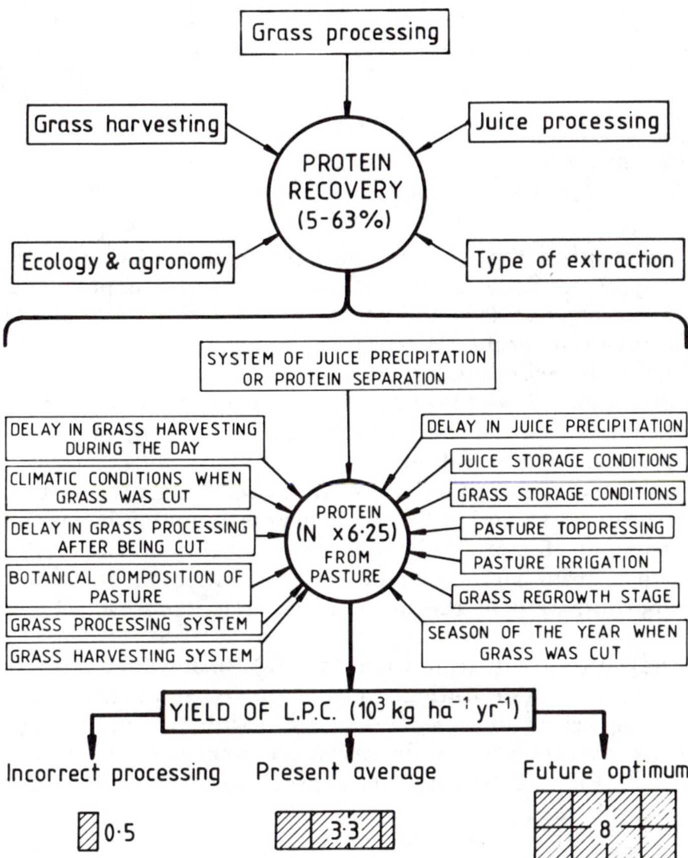

Fig. 21.1. Factors limiting protein recovery from pasture herbage and their overall effect on protein recovery and annual production of protein concentrates (LPC), as achieved during incorrect extraction procedure, average as observed at present, and future "optimum" yields possible to be recovered from grasslands.

TABLE 21.1. BIOCHEMICAL AND BIOLOGICAL CHARACTERISTICS OF SPRAY-DRIED PROTEIN CONCENTRATES PRODUCED BY THE USE OF DIFFERENT EXTRACTION METHODS

Characteristics	Formic Acid (pH 3.5)	Heat (85°C)	Ultrafiltration
Crude protein (N × 6.25)	40.5	33.2	43.2
Ash	9.6	20.9	11.5
Crude fiber	14.5	22.2	17.3
Soluble sugars	10.4	9.7	6.6
Amino acids content (g/16 g N)			
lysine and its availability (%)	3.0 (72)	4.4 (66)	2.8 (79)
methionine	1.6	1.3	1.9
sum of the essential amino acids	52	49	51
Protein digestibility (%)			
in vivo	61	62	67
in vitro	66	58	71
PER			
(a)0.2% DL-methionine suppl.	2.41	1.31	2.01
(b)0.2% DL-methionine and 0.5% L-lysine suppl.	2.33	1.70	2.33

Source: Ostrowski-Meissner (1976A).

among the single factors which can possibly limit the efficiency of the extraction process. Recognizing such relationships, the protein extraction operation can be optimized and programmed, with prediction being made as to the yields of protein possible to recover from the plant material grown and/or processed under certain conditions. By the use of a simple mathematical model, yields of protein recoverable from grassland can be made optimal in terms of the maximal efficiency of the protein extraction operation under field conditions.

The research carried out in New Zealand and Australia on the optimization of the protein extraction process from grasslands has been concentrated within two areas: factors limiting protein recovery of both feed- and food-grade proteins from herbage, and the mathematical model which could be used for optimization of the protein extraction process in agricultural practice.

Characteristic climatic conditions (Fig. 21.2), on which a series of trials on protein extraction limitations were conducted, indicate climate which is typical of temperate/subtropical areas. As a result, production of dry matter (DM) on pasture involved in dairy operation reached the level of 17 MT DM ha^{-1} $year^{-1}$ (Fig. 21.3), which is characteristic of high DM-producing grasslands.

LIMITATIONS IN PROTEIN EXTRACTION FROM HERBAGE

Aspects Related to Ecology and Agronomy of Grasslands

Pasture Regrowth Stage. As pastureland matures, regardless of its botanical composition, topdressing, and/or irrigation, herbage cut for protein

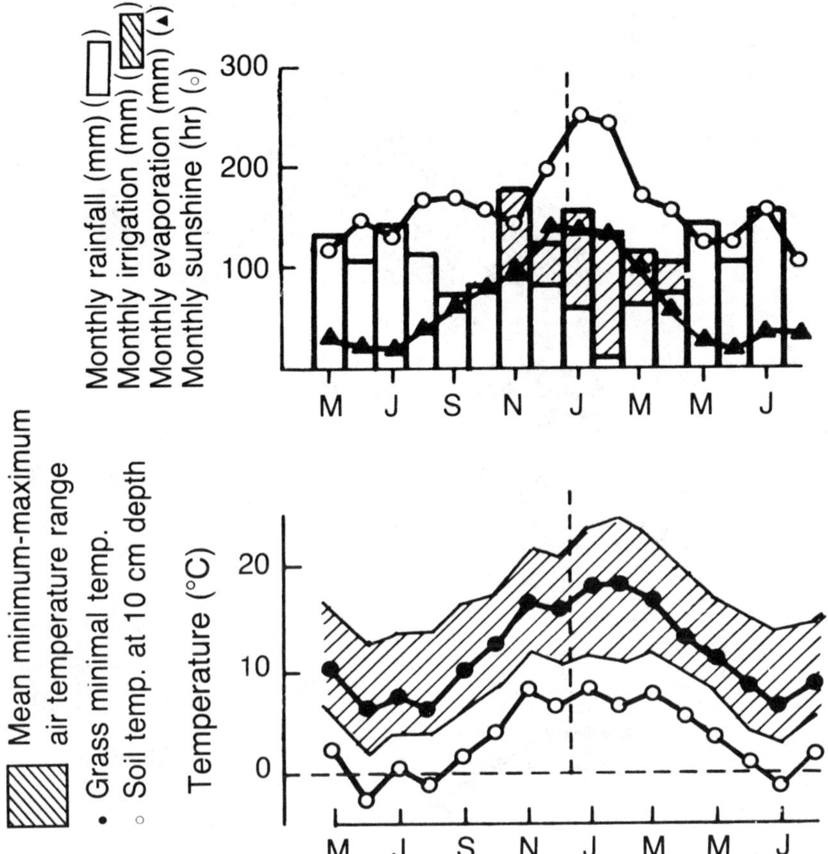

Fig. 21.2. Climatic conditions in which factors limiting protein recovery from pasture herbage have been investigated. Shadowed area enclosed within two solid lines indicates difference between mean monthly highest and lowest recorded air temperature. Black columns built on rainfall figures indicate irrigation (mm).

extraction increases in DM content. As a result of this increase, crude protein (N × 6.25) concentration, on a dry matter basis, increases at the initial herbage regrowth stage, followed by a notable decrease in more mature plants (Fig. 21.4).

The decrease in concentration of protein in more mature herbage is associated with a significant reduction in protein recovery during the protein extraction procedure (Table 21.2). However, with herbage maturity the ratio of the chloroplastic protein fraction to cytoplasmic proteins decreased notably.

With herbage processing, after washing in water in order to restore plant moisture saturation, the yields and protein recoveries were much higher

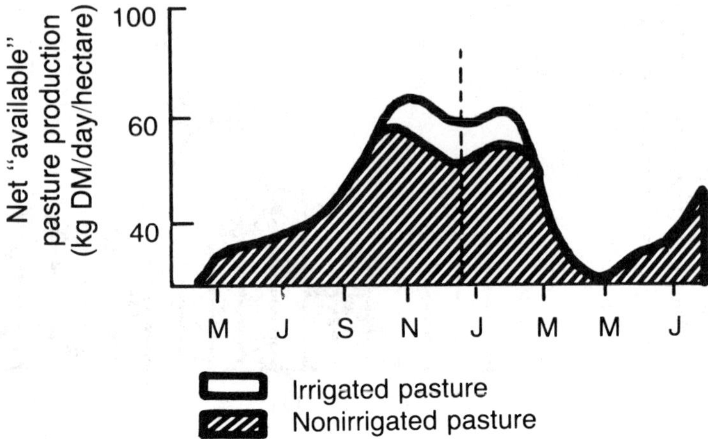

Fig. 21.3. Productive characteristic of irrigated and topdressed pasture composed of white clover and perennial grasses (approximate average ratio 1:1) which has been involved in the study of the limitations restricting the efficiency of protein extraction from grasslands.

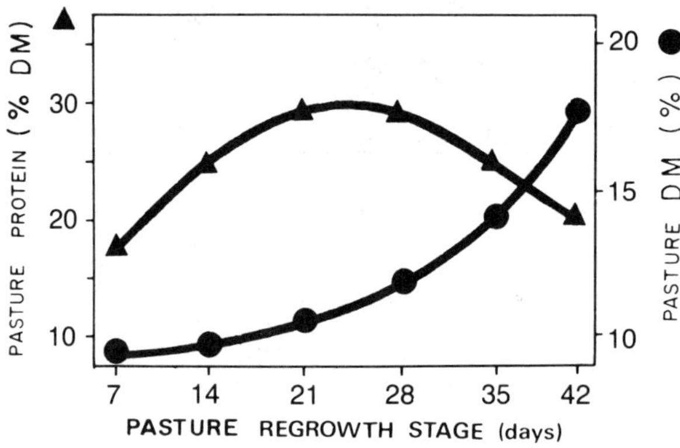

Fig. 21.4. Changes in crude protein (N × 6.25) and dry matter content of herbage cut from pasture at different regrowth stages.

and less variable as compared with herbage processed "as cut"—without any water treatment. Also, the amounts of the cytoplasmic protein fraction recovered from water-treated herbage were much higher than in herbage without water treatment in terms of both yields and proportions to the chloroplastic protein fraction.

The reduction in extractability of protein from herbage of increasing maturity, as presented in Table 21.2, is consistent with observations made under different agricultural conditions by Allison and Vartha (1973), Ark-

TABLE 21.2. THE EFFECT OF HERBAGE REGROWTH STAGE AND HERBAGE TREATMENT WITH WATER PRIOR TO PROCESSING ON PROTEIN EXTRACTION EFFICIENCY AND RECOVERY OF CYTOPLASMIC (FOOD-GRADE) PROTEIN FRACTION

		Yield of Protein (g/kg Herbage DM)		Recovery of Cytoplasmic (Food-grade) Protein Fraction (% of the Total Recoverable Protein)	
Treatment*		Processing Without Water Treatment	Processing After Treatment with Water	Processing Without Water Treatment	Processing After Treatment with Water
Herbage regrowth stage (weeks)					
3		77	123	22	29
4		46	127	25	31
5		32	111	26	31
6		24	72	27	33
(N = 4)[1]	S.E.[2]	4.7 **	5.3 **	1.0 **	1.4 NS

Source: Ostrowski-Meissner (1976D).
* In this and subsequent tables:
[1] N—Number of observations (separate extractions) within the treatment.
[2] S.E.—Standard error of mean differences between the treatments:
*—Significance at the level P = 0.05.
**—Significance at the level P = 0.01.
NS—Not significant.

coll (1971), Arkcoll and Festenstein (1971), Pirie (1971), Oke (1973), and Vartha and Allison (1973), in reference to different pure crops of herbages. Higher fiber content with increasing maturity reduces the efficiency of cell rupture in the macerator and protein may also be trapped by fibrous material during dejuicing in the press (Arkcoll and Festenstein 1971; Vartha and Allison 1973; Lexander *et al.* 1970). However, a longer period of pasture regrowth produced higher herbage dry matter yield. Thus, the decision on the optimum stage of herbage at which it should be used for the purpose of protein extraction has to be a compromise between the yield of dry matter and the diminishing protein rate (as measured by both protein recovery and yield of protein per unit of processed herbage dry matter). In this presentation, those optima were established as the fifth week of pasture regrowth. One week's delay in pasture cutting beyond the established "optimum" regrowth stage resulted in approximately a 15 to 25% decrease (depending on season) in quantities of protein recovered from the unit of pasture area—even though the herbage dry matter yield increased progressively. At the same time, yield expressed per unit of processed herbage dry weight decreased as much as approximately 25 to 42%. This indicates that the maturity of herbage used for the protein extraction study is one of the more important factors from the extraction-efficiency point of view. This is also emphasized by Allison and Vartha (1973), Arkcoll and Festenstein (1971), McKenzie (1977), Oke (1973), and Pirie (1971), who studied several pure stands of herbages, both perennial and legumes, in different agronomic conditions.

Significant interactions between the pasture regrowth stage and the DM and nitrogen content in herbage, as well as protein recovery from pasture during its regrowth, indicate that protein extraction efficiency is dependent on the season of the year when extraction takes place.

Season of the Year. Winter- and spring-grown pasture herbage showed a higher degree of protein recovery as compared with the other seasons (Table 21.3). An earlier survey of pasture species in Victoria conducted by McKenzie (1977) showed that, despite the topdressing, recovery of protein from mixed pasture in Victoria decreased substantially as the season progressed toward the summer. Extractability of protein from spring-grown pasture obtained in its fifth week of regrowth (59 g/kg herbage dry matter, respectively) was consistent with corresponding figures recorded earlier by McKenzie (1977) (61 g dry weight) for roughly similar season and both cutting time and percentage white clover in the sward. However, it has been reported by Maguire and Brookes (1973) that, in Irish climatic conditions, a variation in both the total and protein nitrogen concentration, in herbage cannot be ascribed exclusively to seasonal variations but rather to single cuts within the spring, summer, and autumn seasons. This is similar to results obtained in Australia indicating a variation in the protein extraction pattern in quite different climatic conditions.

Herbage treatment with water (soaking) before processing resulted in no difference in efficiency of protein extraction between the seasons, but had notably higher proportions and yields of cytoplasmic protein fraction in autumn-grown herbage as compared with other seasons.

TABLE 21.3. THE EFFECT OF THE SEASON OF THE YEAR AND HERBAGE TREATMENT WITH WATER PRIOR TO PROCESSING ON PROTEIN EXTRACTION EFFICIENCY AND RECOVERY OF CYTOPLASMIC (FOOD-GRADE) PROTEIN FRACTION

Treatment[1]	Yield of Protein (g/kg Herbage DM)		Recovery of Cytoplasmic (Food-grade) Protein Fraction (% of the Total Recoverable Protein)	
	Processing Without Water Treatment	Processing After Treatment with Water	Processing Without Water Treatment	Processing After Treatment with Water
Season				
Spring	70	118	20	29
Summer	45	110	23	28
Autumn	59	126	21	30
Winter	81	121	25	32
(N = 4) S.E.	3.6 **	3.9 NS	1.1 *	1.4 NS

[1] See Table 21.2.

Irrigation. Precipitable protein recovery from a nonirrigated pasture is significantly lower as compared with an irrigated one (Table 21.4) and, due to significantly higher dry matter and protein production from an area of irrigated herbage, yields of protein recovered from the unit of pasture area are even more favorable.

Pirie (1971) reported that only in the summer season is there a substantial improvement in herbage yield with an irrigation which is parallel to the yield of extracted protein, while, in general, yields of protein, as a percentages of herbage yields, are similar under irrigation and dry land conditions. The results presented in Table 21.4 show irrigation to be an important factor in grass protein concentrate production from the area of pasture. To keep the optimal water status in plants exposed to the time-varying soil-water potential and atmospheric transpiration demands, particularly in temperate and warm climates (subtropical conditions), and to equate plant transpiration demands as well as soil water depletion, irrigation is one of the most important factors optimizing plant productivity in the dry season of the year.

Herbage treatment with water before or during the extraction process reduces the differences in efficiency of protein extraction due to irrigation.

Nitrogen Topdressing. Topdressing had no significant effect on protein extraction results as measured by yields of precipitable DM and precipitable nitrogen recovery (Table 21.5). Most of the results obtained with various herbage species in different climatic conditions indicate topdressing as being without significant effect on protein extractability based on a unit of either fresh or dry weight herbage (Arkcoll and Festenstein 1971; Vartha and Allison 1973). On the other hand, MacLeod and MacLeod (1974) reported that N and K fertilization increased both the organic matter and protein yields in herbage. However, this protein represented mainly a

TABLE 21.4. THE EFFECT OF IRRIGATION AND HERBAGE TREATMENT WITH WATER PRIOR TO PROCESSING ON PROTEIN EXTRACTION EFFICIENCY AND RECOVERY OF CYTOPLASMIC (FOOD-GRADE) PROTEIN FRACTION

		Yield of Protein (g/kg Herbage DM)		Recovery of Cytoplasmic (Food-grade) Protein Fraction (% of the Total Recoverable Protein)	
Treatment[1]		Processing Without Water Treatment	Processing After Treatment with Water	Processing Without Water Treatment	Processing After Treatment with Water
Nonirrigated		56	112	23	28
Irrigated		80	126	20	27
(N = 4)	S.E.	5.6	5.9	1.2	0.8
		*	NS	NS	NS

[1]See Table 21.2.

TABLE 21.5. THE EFFECT OF NITROGEN TOPDRESSING AND HERBAGE TREATMENT WITH WATER PRIOR TO PROCESSING ON PROTEIN EXTRACTION EFFICIENCY AND RECOVERY OF CYTOPLASMIC (FOOD-GRADE) PROTEIN FRACTION

	Yield of Protein (g/kg Herbage DM)		Recovery of Cytoplasmic (Food-grade) Protein Fraction (% of the Total Recoverable Protein)	
Treatment[1]	Processing Without Water Treatment	Processing After Treatment with Water	Processing Without Water Treatment	Processing After Treatment with Water
Without topdressing	45	93	26	30
Topdressed	80	126	20	27
(N = 4) S.E.	8.6 *	5.9 *	1.1 *	1.1 NS

[1]See Table 21.2.

soluble nitrogen fraction which cannot be recovered during the heat precipitation process. This may account for the reduced protein recovery. observed with topdressed herbage. It was also observed that the response of pasture to N topdressing is much better with irrigation and/or during the rainy season. This would suggest that an increase in the water absorption capacity of the plant during the active growing season ensures a way of equilibrating the osmotic pressure of the N and other mineral-enriched cells.

Therefore, such factors as irrigation during intensive water evaporation from the soil, regrowth stage of grass treated as a mixture or as pure grass species crops, and pasture botanical composition factors which, due to their multiple interaction, can introduce several alterations to the original simple relationship between NPK topdressing and protein extraction efficiency, should be taken into consideration when topdressing is investigated as a factor limiting protein extraction efficiency. Pasture botanical composition in particular has been shown to be a factor altering the recovery of protein from topdressed pastures. McKenzie (1977) demonstrated that reduced protein yields from topdressed spring-grown pastures could be ascribed to the reduction in clover participation with a simultaneous increase in perennial grass proportions in the mixed pasture sward, all being a result of nitrogen topdressing.

Herbage treatment with water before the extraction procedure notably increased recoveries and yields of protein as opposed to herbage processed without water treatment. Simultaneously, there were more distinctive differences in efficiency of the process between topdressed and pasture without topdressing.

Pasture Botanical Composition. White clover appears to be the most suitable species in terms of protein yield. *Paspalum* shows lowest, and mixed pasture and perennial ryegrass show intermediate extraction efficiency figures (Table 21.6). The most notable increase in the efficiency of protein extraction due to water treatment before herbage processing was observed with *Paspalum*, perennial ryegrass, and mixed pasture, while clover was a much less responding species.

TABLE 21.6. THE EFFECT OF HERBAGE SPECIES GROWING IN COMPETITION IN MIXED PASTURE SWARD AND HERBAGE TREATMENT WITH WATER PRIOR TO PROCESSING ON PROTEIN EXTRACTION EFFICIENCY AND RECOVERY OF CYTOPLASMIC (FOOD-GRADE) PROTEIN FRACTION

	Yield of Protein (g/kg Herbage DM)		Recovery of Cytoplasmic (Food-grade) Protein Fraction (% of the Total Recoverable Protein)	
Treatment[1]	Processing Without Water Treatment	Processing After Treatment with Water	Processing Without Water Treatment	Processing After Treatment with Water
Herbage species				
Mixed pasture herbage	73	122	29	33
Perennial ryegrass	31	58	35	32
Paspalum	12	36	40	34
White clover	158	189	31	37
(N = 4) S.E.	7.1 **	6.5 **	2.4 *	2.2 *

[1]See Table 21.2.

With an increase in white clover participation in a mixed pasture sward with a simultaneous decrease in the percentage of perennial grasses, the yields of protein increased notably despite the water treatment (Table 21.7). Proportions of cytoplasmic (food-grade) protein fraction were relatively stable as a result of both clover participation in pasture sward and herbage water treatment.

Since the "monoculture" plant species growing within a mixed sward have their own optimum regrowth periods in terms of protein extractability which differ from that of the mixed sward (Arkcoll 1971; Pirie 1971; Oke 1973) and which again are related to the prevailing environmental conditions (Oke 1973; Pirie 1971), it is more correct to treat pasture species as a mixture of pasture species rather than as individual herbage species. Therefore, optimization of protein extraction efficiency from grasslands should be related to the pasture sward of a known botanical composition.

Herbage Species Grown as a Crop. *Atriplex hortensis* and *Chenopodium quinoa* were superior to lucerne and mixed pasture herbage (Table 21.8); the latter two did not differ in protein yields, while lucerne, in each case, showed substantially higher proportions of cytoplasmic proteins as compared with mixed pasture herbage. *Atriplex hortensis* was the most favorable crop in terms of protein yields and recovery of food-grade protein fraction.

TABLE 21.7. THE EFFECT OF WHITE CLOVER PERCENTAGE IN THE PASTURE SWARD AND HERBAGE TREATMENT WITH WATER PRIOR TO PROCESSING ON PROTEIN EXTRACTION EFFICIENCY AND RECOVERY OF CYTOPLASMIC (FOOD-GRADE) PROTEIN FRACTION

		Yield of Protein (g/kg Herbage DM)		Recovery of Cytoplasmic (Food-grade) Protein Fraction (% of the Total Recoverable Protein)	
Treatment[1]		Processing Without Water Treatment	Processing After Treatment with Water	Processing Without Water Treatment	Processing After Treatment with Water
White clover in the pasture sward (%)					
0		23	41	31	30
30		72	102	29	31
50		108	149	30	34
80		124	161	31	36
100		158	189	31	37
(N = 4)	S.E.	18.7 **	13.2 **	1.8 NS	2.0 NS

[1]See Table 21.2.

TABLE 21.8. THE EFFECT OF HERBAGE SPECIES GROWN AS A CROP AND HERBAGE TREATMENT WITH WATER PRIOR TO PROCESSING ON PROTEIN EXTRACTION EFFICIENCY AND RECOVERY OF CYTOPLASMIC (FOOD-GRADE) PROTEIN FRACTION

		Yield of Protein (g/kg Herbage DM)		Recovery of Cytoplasmic (Food-grade) Protein Fraction (% of the Total Recoverable Protein)	
Treatment[1]		Processing Without Water Treatment	Processing After Treatment with Water	Processing Without Water Treatment	Processing After Treatment with Water
Mixed pasture herbage		73	122	29	33
Lucerne		89	134	44	46
Atriplex hortensis		131	183	47	56
Chenopodium quinoa		114	166	40	45
(N = 4)	S.E.	6.3 **	7.5 **	2.3 **	2.5 **

[1]See Table 21.2.

Despite small differences in precipitable protein recovery from pasture and from lucerne, the absolute amounts of extractable protein, as measured by yield of protein from a kg of herbage dry weight, are much higher from lucerne than from pasture grasses. Allison (1973), Arkcoll (1971), Byers (1971), Joshi (1971), Pirie (1971), Ostrowski-Meissner (1975), and McKenzie (1977) reported legumes (clover and/or lucerne) as being superior to perennial grasses from the protein extraction efficiency point of view. This is so despite the prevailing agricultural conditions at the place of the extraction operations.

Other Agronomical Factors. Neither the pasture management system (Table 21.9) nor the long-term effect of protein extraction from pasture (Table 21.10) appeared to be critical for final efficiency of protein extraction from herbage as measured by yields of protein. This indicates the possibility of standardization of the extraction system in farm practice, based on those factors which significantly altered the efficiency of protein extraction, i.e., the stage of herbage maturity, which can be more precisely characterized by a certain DM to TN (total nitrogen) ratio.

Herbage Harvesting Stage

Harvesting Machine. Protein yields were notably lower when the flail harvester was used, as opposed to a hatchet-type harvester (Table 21.11). This can be ascribed to differences in ash content in the herbage harvested by the flail-type harvester (23.5%) and the hatchet-type harvester (8.3%). Cutting herbage with the flail harvester to 1.5 cm stubble height results in large amounts of soil being collected as well as herbage usually being partially macerated and leaf blades bruised. Herbage cut with the blade-type (hatchet) harvester is more efficiently dejuiced (40 to 50%) than when cut with the flail harvester (20 to 32%).

Herbage cut with the flail harvester, without or after treatment with water, shows much lower yields of protein with smaller proportions of the

TABLE 21.9. THE EFFECT OF THE SYSTEM OF PASTURE MANAGEMENT AND HERBAGE TREATMENT WITH WATER PRIOR TO PROCESSING ON PROTEIN EXTRACTION EFFICIENCY AND RECOVERY OF CYTOPLASMIC (FOOD-GRADE) PROTEIN FRACTION

		Yield of Protein (g/kg Herbage DM)		Recovery of Cytoplasmic (Food-grade) Protein Fraction (% of the Total Recoverable Protein)	
Treatment[1]		Processing Without Water Treatment	Processing After Treatment with Water	Processing Without Water Treatment	Processing After Treatment with Water
"0 grazed" pasture (2 years involvement in protein extraction without grazing cows)		33	97	24	23
Conventionally grazed pasture involved in occasional extractions		29	101	25	25
(N = 4)	S.E.	1.6 NS	1.5 NS	0.8 NS	0.8 NS

[1]See Table 21.2.

TABLE 21.10. THE EFFECT OF LONG-TERM PASTURE INVOLVEMENT IN THE PROTEIN EXTRACTION PROCESS AND HERBAGE TREATMENT WITH WATER PRIOR TO PROCESSING ON PROTEIN EXTRACTION EFFICIENCY AND RECOVERY OF CYTOPLASMIC (FOOD-GRADE) PROTEIN FRACTION

	Yield of Protein (g/kg Herbage DM)		Recovery of Cytoplasmic (Food-grade) Protein Fraction (% of the Total Recoverable Protein)	
Treatment[1]	Processing Without Water Treatment	Processing After Treatment with Water	Processing Without Water Treatment	Processing After Treatment with Water
Long term effect of protein extraction from pasture ("0 grazing")				
After 1 year	31	104	25	25
After 2 years	33	97	24	23
(N = 4) S.E.	2.1 NS	2.6 NS	0.9 NS	1.3 NS

See Table 21.2.

TABLE 21.11. THE EFFECT OF THE HARVESTING MACHINE AND HERBAGE TREATMENT WITH WATER PRIOR TO PROCESSING ON PROTEIN EXTRACTION EFFICIENCY AND RECOVERY OF CYTOPLASMIC (FOOD-GRADE) PROTEIN FRACTION

	Yield of Protein (g/kg Herbage DM)		Recovery of Cytoplasmic (Food-grade) Protein Fraction (% of the Total Recoverable Protein)	
Treatment[1]	Processing Without Water Treatment	Processing After Treatment with Water	Processing Without Water Treatment	Processing After Treatment with Water
Flail harvester	46	83	21	20
Hatchet-type (blade) harvester	77	122	26	29
(N = 4) S.E.	7.4 *	6.8 **	1.0 *	1.2 **

[1]See Table 21.2.

cytoplasmic protein fraction being recovered as opposed to herbage cut with the hatchet-type harvester. With the hatchet-type harvester, herbage had been cut with minimal bruising as opposed to the marked bruising found in herbage cut with the flail harvester. In bruised grass, protein has a tendency to coagulate on the fiber and to autolyze in the extract (Pirie 1971). This may explain differences observed with protein extraction efficiency as a result of different harvesters' being used for herbage cutting in the field.

Weather Conditions During Herbage Harvest. The reduction in yields and the recovery of the cytoplasmic protein fraction observed with herbage cut during sunny days (Table 21.12) may be ascribed to poorer dejuicing of the drier plant material harvested under these conditions. Herbage, after treatment with water, shows an increase in yields of protein and recovery of the food-grade protein fraction. This increase is always higher with herbage harvested during hot, dry and sunny days with extraction efficiency figures being equal to those achieved with herbage cut during cloudy weather and similarly treated with water. Also, Chayen *et al.* (1961) and Pirie (1971) have noticed beneficial effects of the additional moisture on leaf surfaces on the efficiency of protein extraction from plant material.

TABLE 21.12. THE EFFECT OF WEATHER CONDITIONS DURING HERBAGE HARVEST AND HERBAGE TREATMENT WITH WATER PRIOR TO PROCESSING ON PROTEIN EXTRACTION EFFICIENCY AND RECOVERY OF CYTOPLASMIC (FOOD-GRADE) PROTEIN FRACTION

	Yield of Protein (g/kg Herbage DM)		Recovery of Cytoplasmic (Food-grade) Protein Fraction (% of the Total Recoverable Protein)	
Treatment[1]	Processing Without Water Treatment	Processing After Treatment with Water	Processing Without Water Treatment	Processing After Treatment with Water
Weather conditions during herbage harvest				
Sunny day	48	117	19	30
Cloudy day	72	120	23	31
(N = 4) S.E.	4.7	5.9	0.8	0.9
	*	NS	*	NS

[1] See Table 21.2.

Time of Day of Herbage Harvest. Herbage cut at 9:00 A.M. was, despite the treatment with water, characterized by both lower protein yields and protein recoveries as compared with grass cut at 6:00 A.M. (Table 21.13). As a result, herbage cut from pastures 3 hr after sunrise during a bright, sunny summer day resulted in the processing of approximately two times more herbage to obtain similar protein extraction efficiency as compared with herbage cut at sunrise.

Lower efficiency of protein extraction from pasture, as a consequence of delay in its cutting from the paddock during the day, may be ascribed to the increase in both herbage and juice moisture content during the day (Fig. 21.5) and the lowering in degree of herbage dejuicing (Pirie 1971; Ostrowski-Meissner 1975). Herbage which was processed early in the morning was wet due to dew, which improved dejuicing, and, in consequence, the degree of protein recovery was significantly higher as compared with herbage cut 3 hr later. Herbage harvesting time from pasture during the day can be

TABLE 21.13. THE EFFECT OF TIME DURING THE DAY WHEN HERBAGE GRASS IS CUT FOR PROCESSING (HOT, DRY SUMMER DAY) AND HERBAGE TREATMENT WITH WATER PRIOR TO PROCESSING ON PROTEIN EXTRACTION EFFICIENCY AND RECOVERY OF CYTOPLASMIC (FOOD-GRADE) PROTEIN FRACTION

Treatment[1]		Yield of Protein (g/kg Herbage DM)		Recovery of Cytoplasmic (Food-grade) Protein Fraction (% of the Total Recoverable Protein)	
		Processing Without Water Treatment	Processing After Treatment with Water	Processing Without Water Treatment	Processing After Treatment with Water
Time during the day when herbage is cut for processing (hot, dry summer day)					
6 A.M.		79	128	26	29
9 A.M.		48	109	22	27
(N = 4)	S.E.	5.1 **	4.3 *	0.8 **	0.9 NS

[1]See Table 21.2.

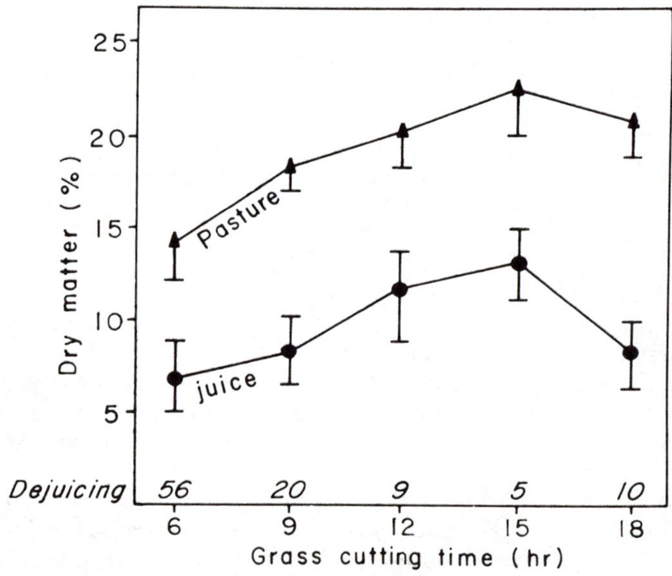

Fig. 21.5. The effect of the time of day when herbage is cut from pasture on dry matter content in the herbage and the juice expressed from pasture processed without treatment with water. Dejuicing figures indicate volume of juice expressed from 100 kg of fresh weight herbage processed "as cut" from pasture at different times during the day.

eliminated as a variable in the protein extraction process by treatment of the herbage with water prior to processing (Fig. 21.6).

Herbage Processing Stage

Herbage Dejuicing Method. A single pair of rubber rolls is much more effective, in terms of extractability of protein from herbage, as compared with the cylindrical wine press or belt press (Table 21.14). Single rubber rolls and the belt press were the most efficient means by which highest yields of protein were obtained from water-treated herbage. These two methods of herbage dejuicing also maintained a high recovery of the food-grade protein fraction.

The lower dejuicing, DM and PN (protein nitrogen) recovery figures obtained with the cylindrical wine press and hand squeezing are explicable since the grass fiber were tightly packed on the boundary of the portion of pulp in contact with the perforated stainless steel screen or with the muslin, while the inner portion of grass was still not dejuiced. According to Chayen *et al.* (1961), this fiber layer with further pressing begins to act as a semipermeable membrane, causing a decrease in the degree of dejuicing followed by a lowering in the protein recoveries from herbage.

Dejuicing Conditions Using Belt Press. With a faster belt speed, wet herbage throughput substantially increases with a simultaneous decrease

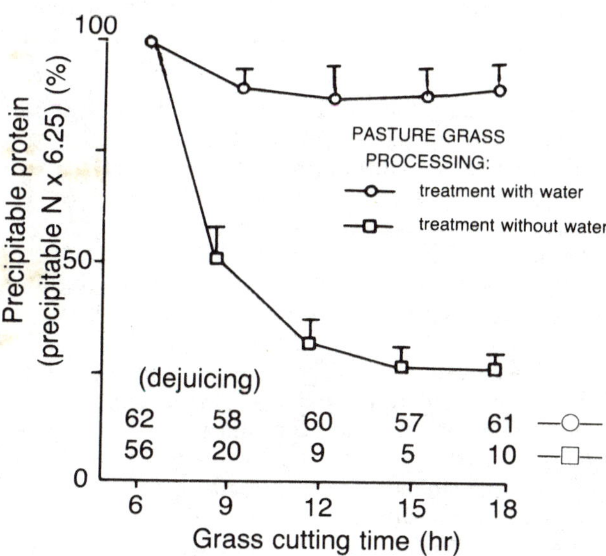

Fig. 21.6. Herbage harvested from the pasture at different times during the day and percentage changes in yields of precipitable protein (ppt N × 6.25) as an effect of herbage processing either after treatment with water (30 min soakage in a tank with cold water) or without water treatment. Dejuicing figures indicate volume of juice expressed from 100 kg fresh weight herbage "as cut" from pasture.

TABLE 21.14. THE EFFECT OF METHOD OF HERBAGE DEJUICING AND HERBAGE TREATMENT WITH WATER PRIOR TO PROCESSING ON PROTEIN EXTRACTION EFFICIENCY AND RECOVERY OF CYTOPLASMIC (FOOD-GRADE) PROTEIN FRACTION

	Yield of Protein (g/kg Herbage DM)		Recovery of Cytoplasmic (Food-grade) Protein Fraction (% of the Total Recoverable Protein)	
Treatment[1]	Processing Without Water Treatment	Processing After Treatment with Water	Processing Without Water Treatment	Processing After Treatment with Water
Method of herbage dejuicing				
Wine press	21	29	26	24
Rubber rolls	44	133	29	32
Belt press	41	121	28	32
Hand squeeze	28	37	22	23
(N = 4) S.E.	2.6 **	7.8 **	1.2 *	1.3 *

[1] See Table 21.2.

in the degree of herbage dejuicing (Fig. 21.7) and reduction in both protein yields and protein recovery values (Fig. 21.8). This occurs despite the water treatment before herbage processing (maceration and dejuicing) (Table 21.15). The choice of the optimal speed of the belt press is always a compromise between the throughput of herbage through the processing unit and the yield and recovery of protein during the extraction operation.

With an increase in pressure applied on the macerated herbage layer during its dejuicing, yields of protein extracted from herbage increase notably with a simultaneous enhancement of the cytoplasmic protein fraction recovery.

Herbage Processing with Reducing Agents. The addition of water alone or together with one of two reducing agents to the herbage during its processing improved the yields and recovery of protein (Table 21.16). Protein recoveries, as achieved with the addition of reducing agents, were, however, much lower than could be expected from juice protein nitrogen analysis. According to Free and Satterlee (1975), this can be explained by the high proportion of soluble protein which are not precipitated during the extraction procedure and, therefore, cannot be recovered in a protein concentrate (LPC) form.

Of the two reducing agents tested, sodium sulfite appeared to be superior to ascorbic acid. Both of them, however, improved the precipitable protein recoveries as compared with herbage without the addition of reducing agents. The LPCs obtained from herbage to which ascorbic acid or sodium sulfite was added were lighter in color, which, according to Free and Satterlee (1975), may be due to the prevention of the oxidation of chlorogenic acid (responsible for a color problem in LPC) to its quinone form in

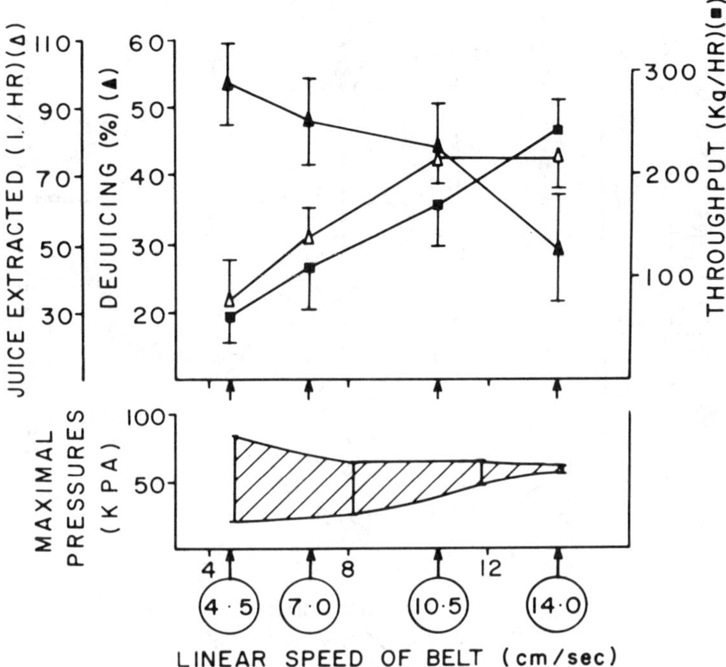

Fig. 21.7. Efficiency of herbage processing at different linear speeds of the belt press as expressed by percentage of herbage dejuicing and grass throughput (kg/hr) in relation to maximal pressures applied during dejuicing.

which it covalently binds to protein-forming chromophores in the juice expressed from the macerated herbage pulp.

pH of the Macerated Herbage. Addition of ammonia solution to the herbage in order to change the pH of the macerated pulp from its usual range of approximately 6.3 to pH 8.0 resulted in improvement in yield and cytoplasmic protein fraction recovery (Table 21.17).

Herbage Processing in the Frozen State. Herbage processed in the frozen state causes a substantial reduction in protein yield (Table 21.18). A higher degree of dejuicing from herbage cut during a frosty morning in the winter season was associated with more "aqueous" juice as compared with juice from nonfrozen herbage cut from an area sheltered with shrubs and trees. This can be explained by water crystallization in the frozen plant material. Due to the increase in volume by the formation of the ice crystals, plant cells rupture. According to Rolfe (1970), the ice crystals can modify or even damage the structure of the protein due to ice formation in cell

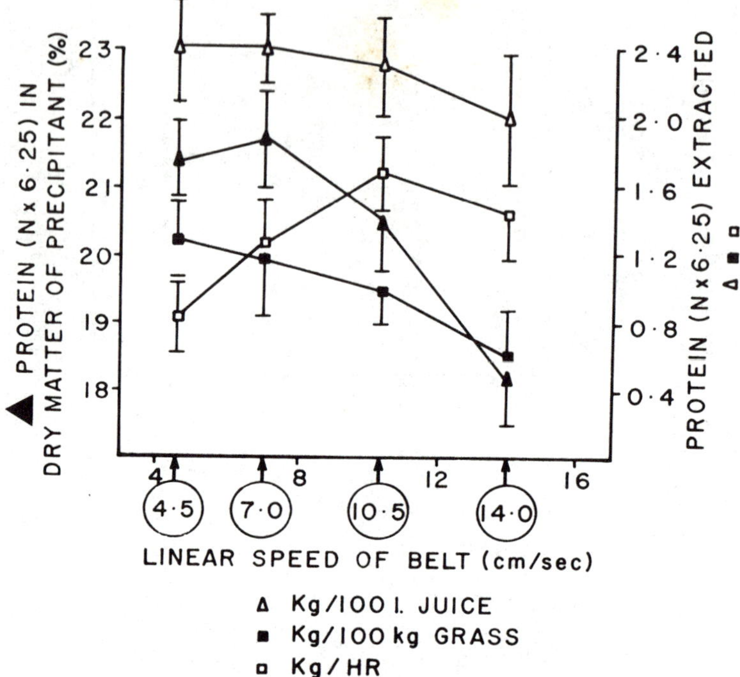

Fig. 21.8. Efficiency of protein extraction from pasture herbage processed at different speeds of the belt press as expressed by concentration of protein in dry matter of precipitated protein curd and by amount of protein extracted from the area of grassland and/or within time limits.

protoplasm. The decrease in protein yields and an increase in cytoplasmic protein fraction recovery can be ascribed to the physiochemical changes such as aggregation or cross-linking of undenatured protein, denaturation of proteins followed by aggregation, or interaction of the native or denaturated proteins with lipids or carbohydrates, all of which occur in cells of herbage during freezing and following thawing. In addition the frozen state facilitates energy transfer, which causes polymer breaks and free radical formation during freezing stress (Patat and Hoegner 1964). This may initiate herbage protein change to such an extent that it becomes extensive and irreversible during herbage thawing.

Also, slow freezing causes a high salt concentration by a simultaneous protein dislocation and aggregation, with water being able to act as a solvent reactant (in hydrolysis), a product (in condensations), or a modifier of catalytic or inhibitory activity of other substances. The proteolytic enzymes may be active even in the frozen state, catalyzing protein breakdown in both frozen and thawed plant material.

TABLE 21.15. THE EFFECT OF LINEAR SPEED OF BELT AND AN EXTRA PRESSURE APPLIED DURING HERBAGE DEJUICING AND HERBAGE TREATMENT WITH WATER PRIOR TO PROCESSING ON PROTEIN EXTRACTION EFFICIENCY AND RECOVERY OF CYTOPLASMIC (FOOD-GRADE) PROTEIN FRACTION

	Yield of Protein (g/kg Herbage DM)		Recovery of Cytoplasmic (Food-grade) Protein Fraction (% of the Total Recoverable Protein)	
Treatment[1]	Processing Without Water Treatment	Processing After Treatment with Water	Processing Without Water Treatment	Processing After Treatment with Water
Linear speed of belt (cm/sec)				
5.0	71	104	30	28
10.5	59	101	27	28
10.5 (with an extra pressure applied—15 kPa	83	130	32	31
(N = 4) S.E.	2.2 *	2.8 **	0.9 *	0.7 *

[1] See Table 21.2.

TABLE 21.16. THE EFFECT OF REDUCING AGENT ADDITION DURING HERBAGE MACERATION AND HERBAGE TREATMENT WITH WATER PRIOR TO PROCESSING ON PROTEIN EXTRACTION EFFICIENCY AND RECOVERY OF CYTOPLASMIC (FOOD-GRADE) PROTEIN FRACTION

	Yield of Protein (g/kg Herbage DM)		Recovery of Cytoplasmic (Food-grade) Protein Fraction (% of the Total Recoverable Protein)	
Treatment[1]	Processing Without Water Treatment	Processing After Treatment with Water	Processing Without Water Treatment	Processing After Treatment with Water
Herbage macerated with an addition[2]				
Ascorbic acid (1%)	50	127	24	28
Sodium sulfite (2%)	47	135	28	29
No reducing agent	49	112	25	27
(N = 4) S.E.	1.9 NS	2.8 *	1.2 NS	1.3 NS

[1] See Table 21.2.
[2] Reducing agents were dissolved in the water used during herbage treatment with water at the maceration stage.

Bryant and Newth (1975), who analyzed herbage fresh or after being frozen and thawed, showed that less soluble protein nitrogen is present in frozen herbage, which may indicate that, in frozen leaves, more protein was in precipitable form and, as such, could not be recovered in the herbage dejuicing process.

TABLE 21.17. THE EFFECT OF pH OF THE MACERATED HERBAGE AND HERBAGE TREATMENT WITH WATER PRIOR TO PROCESSING ON PROTEIN EXTRACTION EFFICIENCY AND RECOVERY OF CYTOPLASMIC (FOOD-GRADE) PROTEIN FRACTION

		Yield of Protein (g/kg Herbage DM)		Recovery of Cytoplasmic (Food-grade) Protein Fraction (% of the Total Recoverable Protein)	
Treatment[1]		Processing Without Water Treatment	Processing After Treatment with Water	Processing Without Water Treatment	Processing After Treatment with Water
pH 6.3		52	108	24	27
pH 8.5		75	131	29	33
(N – 4)	S.E.	6.8 *	7.3 *	1.4 *	1.5 *

[1]See Table 21.2.

TABLE 21.18. HERBAGE PROCESSING IN THE FROZEN STATE AND HERBAGE TREATMENT WITH WATER PRIOR TO PROCESSING ON PROTEIN EXTRACTION EFFICIENCY AND RECOVERY OF CYTOPLASMIC (FOOD-GRADE) PROTEIN FRACTION

		Yield of Protein (g/kg Herbage DM)		Recovery of Cytoplasmic (Food-grade) Protein Fraction (% of the Total Recoverable Protein)	
Treatment[1]		Processing Without Water Treatment	Processing After Treatment with Water	Processing Without Water Treatment	Processing After Treatment with Water
Fresh herbage		42	112	26	24
Frozen herbage		17	19	38	38
(N = 5)	S.E.	6.8 *	7.7 **	1.3 **	1.2 **

[1]See Table 21.2.

Delay in Herbage Processing After Harvest and Storage Conditions. A 3 hr delay in processing herbage stored at 22°C lowered the protein yields and protein recovery as compared with herbage processed immediately after harvest (Table 21.19). This was accompanied by an increase in soluble nitrogen concentration (Fig. 21.9).

Herbage stored for 3 hr at 0°C before being processed shows similar protein yields and protein cytoplasmic fraction recovery to that processed immediately after harvesting. This may be due to inhibition of polyphenoloxidases (Allison 1973) and proteolysis at the low temperature. Also, Pirie (1971) showed that there were no deleterious effects in terms of protein extractability when the herbage was stored for a few hours in a cool climate or for half an hour in a hot environment.

TABLE 21.19. THE EFFECT OF DELAY IN HERBAGE PROCESSING AND HERBAGE TREATMENT WITH WATER PRIOR TO PROCESSING ON PROTEIN EXTRACTION EFFICIENCY AND RECOVERY OF CYTOPLASMIC (FOOD-GRADE) PROTEIN FRACTION

	Yield of Protein (g/kg Herbage DM)		Recovery of Cytoplasmic (Food-grade) Protein Fraction (% of the Total Recoverable Protein)	
Treatment[1]	Processing Without Water Treatment	Processing After Treatment with Water	Processing Without Water Treatment	Processing After Treatment with Water
Processing				
No delay	51	125	26	29
3 hr delay (storage at 22°C)	27	74	22	21
3 hr delay (storage at 0°C)	50	126	25	28
(N = 4) S.E.	2.9 **	4.3 **	0.9 *	0.8 *

[1]See Table 21.2.

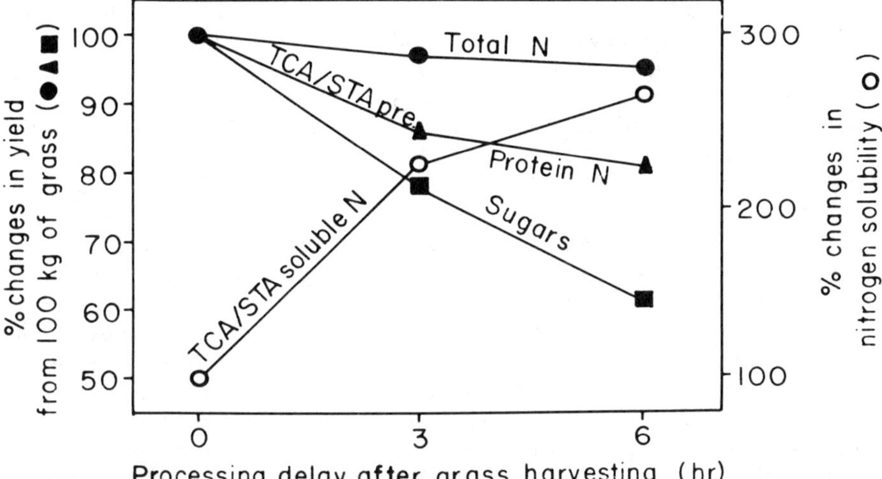

Fig. 21.9. Percentage changes in yields of total, soluble, and precipitable protein nitrogen and sugars extractable from 100 kg of herbage as an effect of delay in pasture processing.

Herbage Juice Processing

Juice Storage Conditions. Juice storage at room temperature (22°C) for over 24 hr resulted in up to a 20% decrease in recoverable protein content (Fig. 21.10). The degree of reduction of protein recovery is not greatly

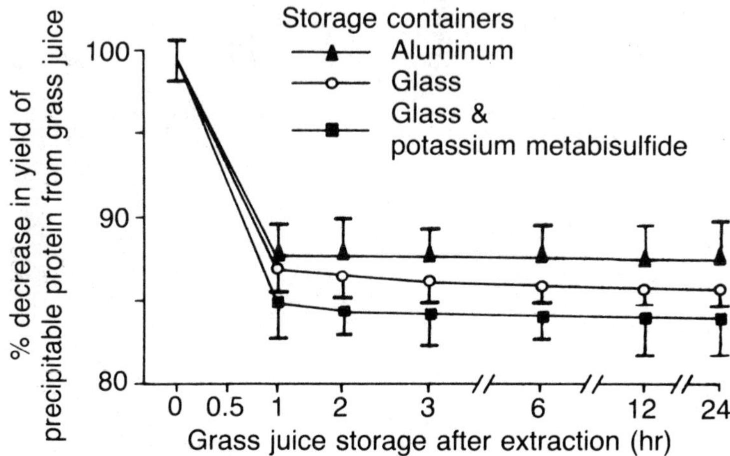

Fig. 21.10. The effect on the precipitable protein content of herbage juice storage during 24 hr at 22°C in aluminum and glass containers with potassium metabisulfide supplement.

affected by the presence of potassium metabisulfide (0.05% w/v), which is used as a preservative. There is some indication, however, that storage of the juice in aluminum and stainless steel containers, as opposed to glass and plastic ones, retarded protein degradation, resulting in slightly higher yields of LPC from the volume unit of juice (Fig. 21.11). Storing the juice at 0°C over a 24 hr period resulted in a much lower reduction of protein recovery. This was so irrespective of the material of which the storage containers was made, as compared with storage at room temperature.

The substantial decrease in protein recovery from the stored pasture herbage juice is similar to that observed by Singh (1962) with plant extracts in hot climates, where a decrease of up to 40% in the yield of precipitable protein was recorded. De Fremery *et al.* (1972) also reported a reduction of up to 50% in protein recovery from alfalfa juice stored at 50°C. The reduction in protein recoverable in precipitable form from stored juice was ascribed to the activity of proteolytic, endogenous enzymes which in juice cause degradation of precipitable protein particles into soluble peptides and amino acids, which in turn cannot be recovered in the precipitation procedure (Singh 1962; Ching Geh 1970; de Fremery *et al.* 1972). At lower temperatures these enzymes, according to Pirie (1971), are not so active as to cause a notable reduction in the final protein yield as recovered during the protein extraction procedure.

None of the aforementioned workers, dealing with enzymatic protein degradation in extracts from green plants indicated that protein degradation can be ascribed to any particular proteolytic enzyme. However, when overall enzymatic activity was measured by the bioluminescence tech-

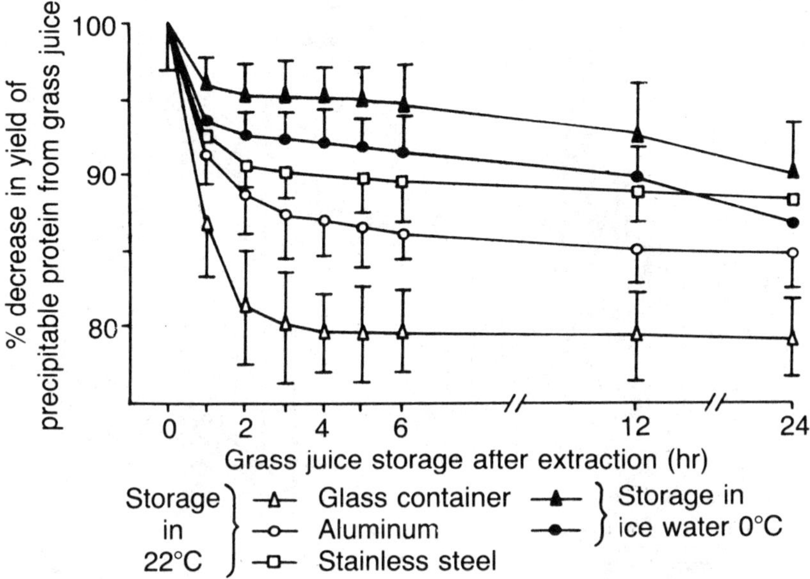

Fig. 21.11. The effect on the degree of decrease in precipitable protein content of herbage juice storage in glass, aluminum, and stainless steel containers at either 22° or 0°C.

nique, a reduction in protein concentration during juice storage at different conditions was accompanied by a similar decrease in the intensity of the photon emission in the model luminescence reaction (Fig. 21.12). Therefore, the problem of inhibition of the proteolytic activity of the endogenous herbage enzymes during storage becomes important in large-scale protein extraction processes as well as in juice processing when storage and/or processing of the juice at ambient temperature is envisaged (i.e., ultrafiltration procedure, which normally takes a few hours to complete when working in a large batch system). To prevent losses in recoverable proteins, it is necessary to refrigerate juice or to apply preservatives by adding them to freshly extracted herbage juice (Fig. 21.13). Reducing agents used as preservative to inhibit the activity of the proteolytic enzymes in the juice during its storage and/or its long processing prevent the loss in recovery of protein from the juice.

Protein Precipitation Method. The most effective procedures for protein nitrogen precipitation are those (1) with formic acid (pH 3.5), heating to 85°C, and ferric chloride supplement (1.37%); and (2) with trichloroacetic acid (10%), silicotungstic acid (1%) (TCA/STA), with or without ferric chloride supplement (Fig. 21.14). However, due to simultaneous high dry mat-

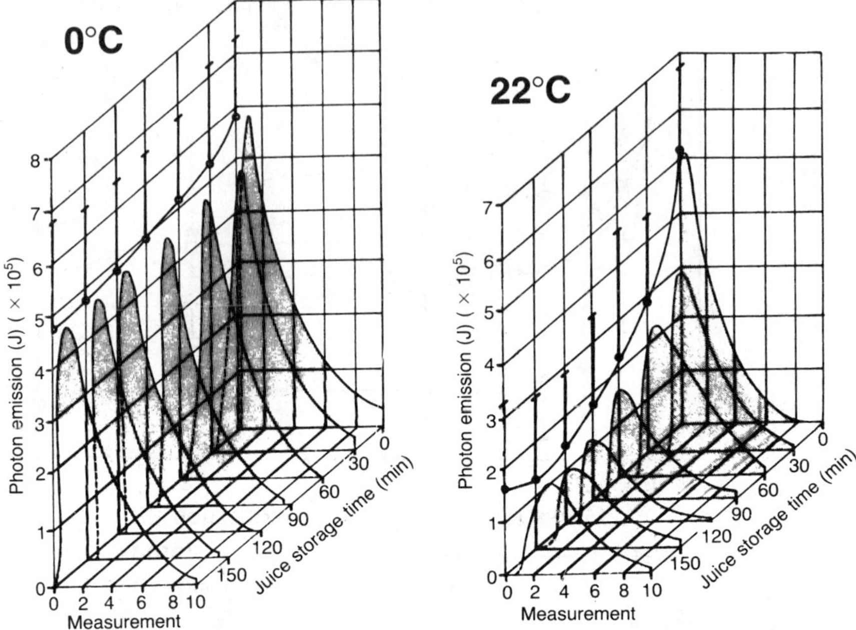

Fig. 21.12. The overall enzymatic activity of the grass juice stored during 3 hr either at 0° or at 22°C without reducing agents present, as measured by chemiluminescence technique.

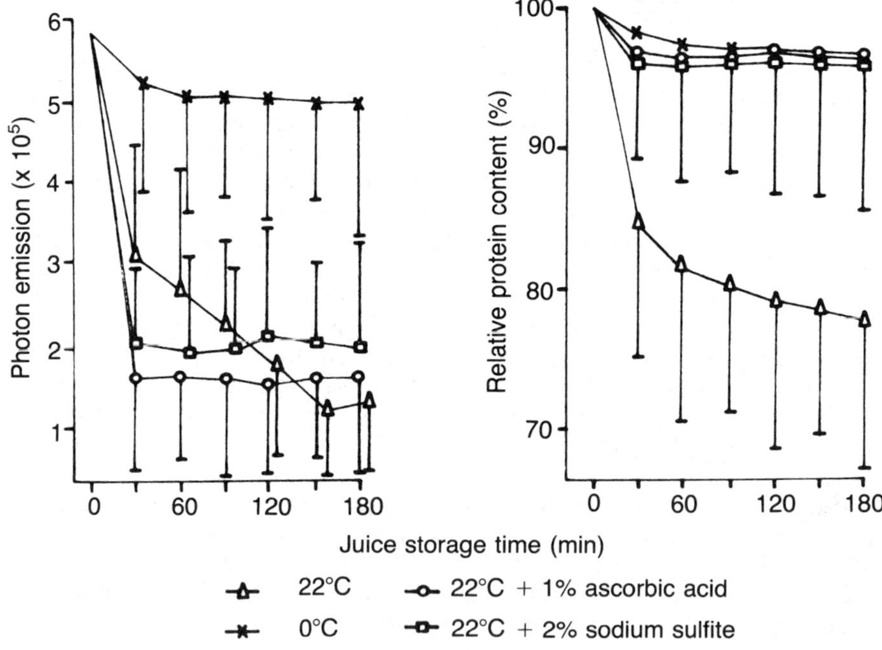

Fig. 21.13. The overall enzymatic activity and relative protein content in herbage juice stored during 3 hr either at 0° or at 22°C and without or with reducing agent supplements. Ascorbic acid (1%). Sodium sulfite (2%).

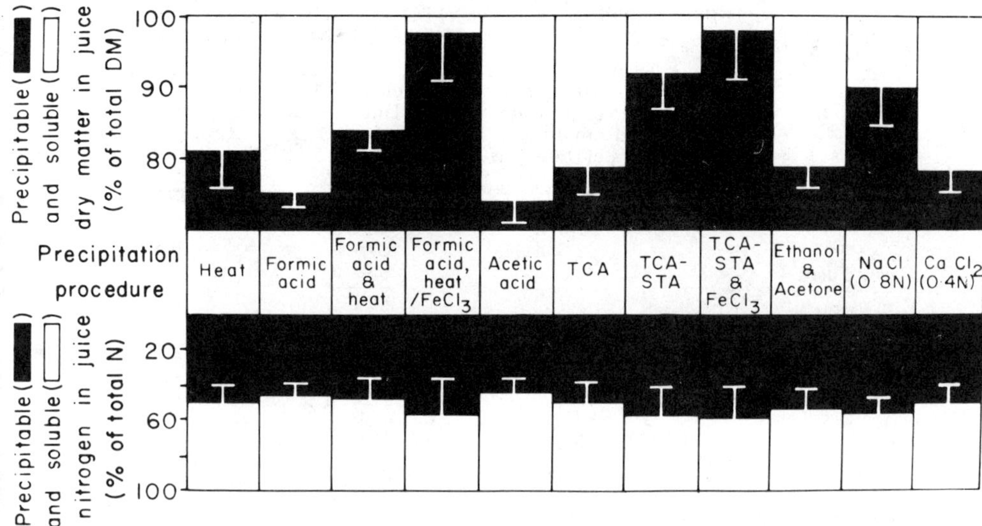

Fig. 21.14. Percentage distribution of both dry matter and nitrogen in precipitable and soluble fractions of the herbage juice using different precipitation procedures. Each value represents the mean of five determinations ± standard deviation.

ter yield obtained with these methods, protein concentration in the final product—leaf protein concentrate (LPC)—was much lower than in LPC produced by the use of heat and/or formic acid, acetic acid, ethanol, acetone, or $CaCl_2$.

The maximum degree of protein precipitation from pasture herbage juice by the use of the three different methods appeared to be at pH 3.0 (Table 21.20). However, individual acids give different maxima for protein precipitation (Fig. 21.15).

Heat (85°C) and TCA alone precipitated less nitrogen and lower quantities of LPC DM as compared with mixtures of TCA with STA or phosphotungstic acid (PTA) (Table 21.21). The high degree of protein N and DM precipitation, with TCA/STA or TCA/PTA, resulted, however, in the final LPC product of low protein concentration. STA added to TCA accelerates protein nitrogen and DM precipitation rates (Fig. 21.16).

Removal of the chemicals such as TCA, STA, and $FeCl_3$ from the precipitated coagulum—before its application in nutritional practice—might be a tedious and time- and energy-consuming process. Therefore, it appears that simultaneous juice acidification to pH 3.0–3.5 and heat coagulation at 85°C is the most reliable method for practical application for unfractionated LPC production (Table 21.21). Using juice expressed from more mature herbage, the degree of protein precipitation and yield of LPC, despite the precipita-

TABLE 21.20. THE EFFECT OF PRECIPITATION PROCEDURE AND DEGREE OF ACIDIFICATION OF THE HERBAGE JUICE ON THE EFFICIENCY OF PROTEIN EXTRACTION

	Nitrogen Precipitation from Juice[1] (% of the Juice TN)	Yield of LPC (g DM) from 100 ml of Juice (g DM)	Protein Nitrogen in LPC (% DM)
Precipitation method			
TCA	81.0 a[2]	4.58 a	7.00 a
TCA/STA	82.6 a	4.78 a	6.85 a
Formic acid	77.9 a	4.29 a	7.07 a
S.E. of mean differences	2.72	0.24	0.28
Precipitation at pH			
5.0	82.9	4.97	6.59
4.0	81.5	4.88	6.66
3.5	79.8	4.47	6.99
3.0	84.7	4.39	7.53
2.0	73.6	4.02	7.10
S.E. of mean differences	3.51	0.31	0.261

Source: Ostrowski-Meissner (1976D).
[1]Juice of average 8.32% DM (S.E. = 0.35) and 0.572% TN (S.E. = 0.078) was expressed from herbage of average 19.9% DM (S.E. = 0.29) and 0.684% TN (S.E. = 0.017) in a processing operation with 53% dejuicing (S.E. = 2.38).
[2]Values in the same column with unlike letters following them showed significant differences at P = 0.05 as determined by Duncan's multiple range test.

tion procedure, is much lower as compared with juice obtained from less mature herbage (Table 21.22). When fractionation of protein is envisaged, the most appropriate procedure is acidification to pH 5.5 with heating up to 55°C, followed by chloroplastic protein separation and further precipitation at 85°C, or ultrafiltration of cytoplasmic protein—human-grade fraction. Small quantities of acids added to juice during precipitation act as a preservative for deproteinized juice, which is expected to be used as a drink for farm animals or as a medium for microbial bioconversion. It was proven that, after acidification to pH 3.5, deproteinized juice was accepted as a drink by cattle and sheep. The LPCs obtained from this as a result of heat/acid coagulation after supplementation with synthetic lysine and methionine were of high nutritive value as measured by PER on rats and chickens (Ostrowski-Meissner 1976A, 1978A,B, 1979).

Results presented in this paper in reference to juice from pasture herbage are supported by the work of de Fremery *et al.* (1972). It was shown that the chemical (TCA) precipitation procedure does not correspond with heat coagulation used for protein nitrogen recovery from alfalfa juice. Differences in the degree of protein precipitation with the use of TCA alone or as a mixture with STA (TCA/STA mixture) were reported by McGrath (1972), who ascribed them to the difference in the degree of precipitation of basic proteins, which are soluble in TCA but are precipitated by 1% TCA solution. So, too, as is the case with LPC recovered from herbage, protein

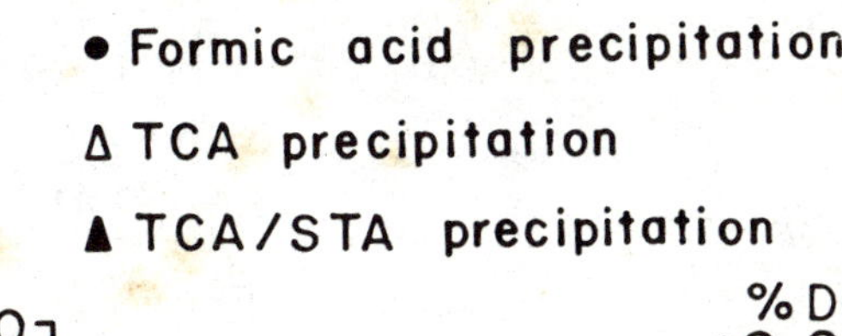

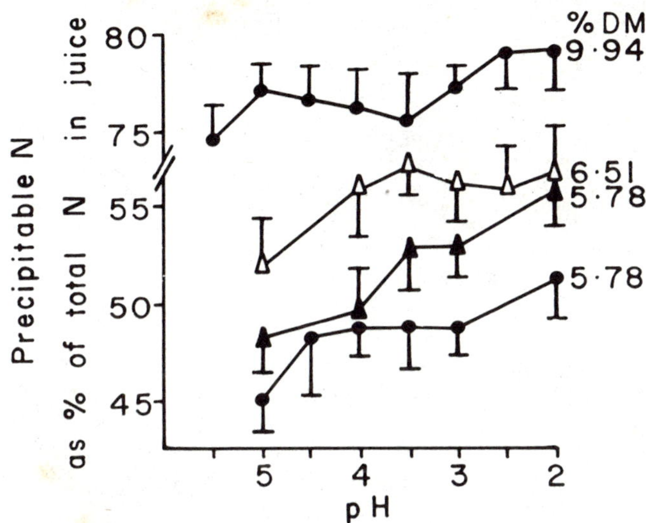

Fig. 21.15. Precipitation curves indicating degree of nitrogen (N) precipitation from herbage juices of different DM content as an effect of different acids used for juice coagulation at different pH's.

extracts from oilseed produced by either TCA or ethanol coagulation in addition to protein-containing peptides contain different quantities of basic amino acids (Bhatty and Finlayson 1973). On the other hand, the increase in LPC yields with TCA or PTA and ferric chloride additions to the herbage juice was due mainly to higher ash content found in coagula.

The highest degree of nitrogen precipitation in herbage juice at pH 3.0 is close to the range reported by Betschart and Kinsella (1973), who observed the lowest nitrogen solubility of the soybean leaf proteins (i.e., highest precipitation degree) at pH 3.2 and 3.7. In a number of studies on leaf protein precipitation (Chayen *et al.* 1961; Cowlishaw *et al.* 1956; Subba Rau and Singh 1970), values between 4.0 and 4.5 are quoted. The reason for the differences may be due to the origin of the plant material since they referred mainly to protein extracted from pure crops while juice from pasture herbage is a mixture obtained from various herbage species.

Protein Fractions in Herbage Juice. The difference in the degree of protein nitrogen precipitation due to different precipitation agents (method)

TABLE 21.21. THE EFFICIENCY OF PROTEIN EXTRACTION AS A RESULT OF THE NITROGEN PRECIPITATION METHOD FROM HERBAGE JUICE

Precipitation Method	Nitrogen Precipitation from Juice (% of the Juice TN)	Yield of LPC (kg DM) from 100 Liters of Juice	Protein Nitrogen in LPC (% DM)
Heat (85°C)	83.9 a[1]	4.3 cC	8.14 aA
Heat (85°C) and formic acid (pH 3.5)	85.2 a	5.6 bB	6.47 bB
TCA	84.5 a	4.5 cC	8.21 aA
TCA/STA	84.9 a	6.4 aA	5.67 cC
TCA/PTA	86.0 a	6.6 aA	5.61 cC
S.E. of mean differences	1.72	0.20	0.24

Source: Ostrowski-Meissner (1976D).
[1]See footnote [2] in Table 21.20.

may be ascribed to the protein fractions which can be precipitated to different degrees by the various precipitants applied (Girault 1973). Proteins which are present in the freshly extracted herbage juice are in solution in soluble form and are representative of two major protein groups—one composed of high molecular weight proteins, readily precipitated by most of the precipitation techniques, and the second group of basic, low molecular weight proteins precipitable only with great difficulty (Girault 1973). Ishino and Ortega (1975) also showed four major protein fractions in the "negro mecental" bean.

Five main protein fractions were observed in the herbage juices, as determined through a gel electrophoretic study (Fig. 21.17). However, with the use of different membrane sizes in the membrane filtration module, three major fractions (being mixtures of proteins) can be practically separable. The largest fraction is a mixture of three types of proteins with a molecular weight greater than 68,000 (approximately 75–80% of the total proteins) and the smallest fraction is below 6000 MW (approximately 5%). The fraction between 6000 and 68,000 MW is composed of two types of proteins recovered either by heat precipitation at 55°C or by ultrafiltration with the use of membranes of 5 to 10 $\times$ 10^3 MW cutoff. Protein fractions concentrated by ultrafiltration are still water-soluble (dispersible) after spray-drying. This is as opposed to an insoluble product obtained as a result of heat and/or acid precipitation.

OPTIMIZATION OF THE PROTEIN EXTRACTION PROCESS

The tremendous variation in protein extraction efficiency, due to limitations discussed earlier, cannot be accepted in agricultural practice where any new form of farming or industrial protein food and feed production has to be justified in both productive and economic terms. Therefore, an attempt has been made to optimize the protein extraction process from pasture herbage, taking into account various factors restricting the efficiency of protein recovery from grasslands.

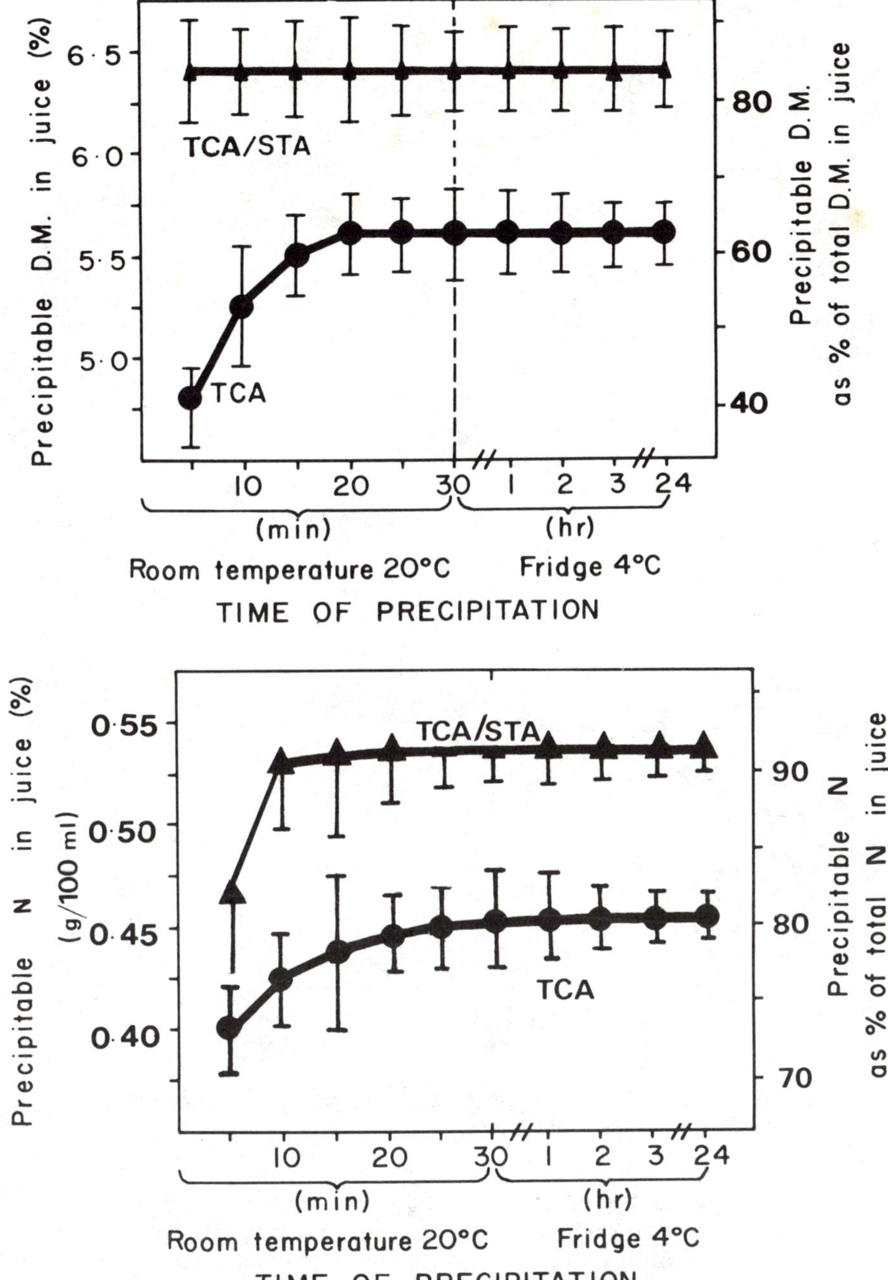

Fig. 21.16. Precipitation curves for dry matter and protein nitrogen extracted from herbage juice using either 10% trichloroacetic acid (TCA) or 10% TCA plus 1% silicotungstic acid (STA). Values represent means each of five determinations ± standard deviation.

TABLE 21.22. THE EFFICIENCY OF PROTEIN EXTRACTIONS AS A RESULT OF PROTEIN PRECIPITATION IN JUICE EXPRESSED FROM HERBAGE HARVESTED AT THREE DIFFERENT REGROWTH STAGES

	Nitrogen Precipitation from Juice (% of the Juice TN)	Yield of LPC (kg DM) from 100 Liters of Juice	Protein Nitrogen in LPC (% DM)
Precipitation method			
Heat (85°C) and acid (pH 3.5)	87.5 a[1]	5.0 bB	6.49 a
Ethanol (75%)	80.1 b	4.6 cB	6.42 a
TCA/STA (10%/1%)	88.8 a	6.3 aA	5.21 b
S.E. of mean differences	1.56	0.10	0.26
Herbage regrowth stage (week of regrowth)			
4	90.6 aA	7.36 aA	6.67 aA
7	80.4 bB	4.23 bB	5.43 bB
8	81.1 bB	4.22 bB	5.28 bB
S.E. of mean differences	2.1	0.11	0.29

Source: Ostrowski-Meissner (1976D).
[1]See footnote [2] in Table 21.20.

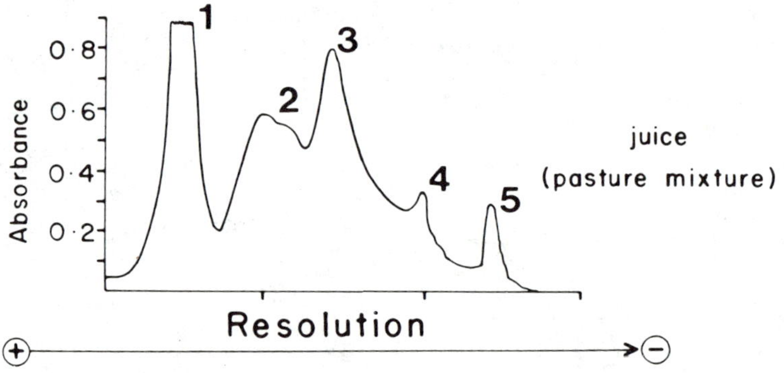

Fig. 21.17. Protein fractions in the whole herbage juice as determined by gradient gel electrophoresis.

Preliminary field and laboratory studies were conducted on mixtures of pasture herbage with the perennial grasses to clover ratio being approximately 1:1. The analysis of the results obtained in a series of trials on factors limiting the efficiency of protein extraction from pasture, as well as studying the kinetics of biological reactions in pasture herbage species during their regrowth, reveals that, due to complicated biological and physiological characteristics and the physiochemical structure of the pasture herbage mixture in the extraction process, the most distinctive factor restricting protein recovery from grasslands is the maturity of herbage used for processing.

Table 21.23 shows correlation coefficients among the characteristics of herbage and efficiency of the protein extraction process as expressed by various measurements. There is a very distinctive—statistically highly significant—relationship among pasture regrowth stage, its dry matter and protein content, and protein recovery during the extraction operation. However, these relationships are significant only in the case when herbage is processed after previous treatment with water.

The relationship between maturity of herbage, expressed as herbage regrowth stage in days (X), and protein recovery, expressed as g of protein extracted from 1 kg of herbage DM (Y), is characterized by the regression equation:

(1) $Y = 120.6 - 0.227X^2$ $(R^2 = 67)$

Despite a certain convenience in using formula (1) in agricultural practice, without the necessity of analyzing pasture herbage before processing it, it is, however, much more accurate and therefore more appropriate to conduct a simple analysis for dry matter content using an infrared moisture tester. This measure of herbage maturity done under field conditions could be completed within 15 to 20 min. Thus, in substituting an independent variable X—herbage regrowth stage (days)—with dry matter results (%), a yield of protein (g) from the unit of DM (1 kg) could be calculated (Y) from equation (2):

(2) $Y = -219 + 39.08 \times - 0.08X^3$ $(R^2 = 0.84)$

TABLE 21.23. CORRELATIONS AMONG RESULTS CHARACTERIZING EFFICIENCY OF PROTEIN EXTRACTION PROCESS AND REGROWTH STAGE, DRY MATTER, AND CRUDE PROTEIN CONTENT IN PASTURE HERBAGE (BASED ON THE RESULTS FROM 44 TRIALS)

	Pasture Herbage			
	Regrowth Stage	Dry Matter	Crude Protein (N × 6.25)	
Item	(Days)	(%)	(%)	(% DM)
Herbage dry matter (%)	0.880**			
Herbage crude protein				
%	0.600**	0.841**		
% DM	−0.003	−0.163	0.732**	
Protein recovery[1]				
g/kg herbage DM (−)	−0.122	−0.264	0.515**	0.841**
($+H_2O$)	−0.733**	−0.793**	0.693**	0.958**
kg/100 kg fresh herbage				
(−)	0.233	−0.256	0.490**	0.362
($+H_2O$)	0.179	0.236	0.246	0.081
% of the herbage TN				
(−)	−0.207	−0.263	0.114	0.384*
($+H_2O$)	0.512**	0.045	0.672**	0.831**
kg/ha (−)	0.954**	0.833**	0.599**	0.010
($+H_2O$)	0.973**	0.908**	0.611**	0.874**

[1](−) Herbage processed "as cut." ($+H_2O$) Herbage processed after being washed in water.

Predictions of the efficiency of protein extraction from fresh crop based on the crop DM have also been considered by Heath and King (1977) as a reliable proposition for the commercial extraction operation. Also, Jones and Houseman (1975) stressed dependence of both DM and protein extractability on the stage of maturity and the moisture content; the relationship is expressed by the following equation:

CP (crude protein) extraction (%) = 0.42 − 0.63 DM of grass [residual standard deviation (R.S.D.) = ±10.62%]

However, many factors may change the herbage DM within a similar maturity stage, and this includes the herbage juice to fiber ratio, as well as the protein nitrogen (PN) to nonprotein nitrogen (NPN) ratio at a given herbage dry matter (Arkcoll 1971).

Therefore, the relationship between Z—the herbage crude protein (TN × 6.25)—and the yield of recoverable protein from the unit of herbage DM, as expressed by equation (3), appears to be the more accurate measure indicating the efficiency of protein extraction as predicted from herbage chemical analysis as compared with the regrowth stage and/or dry matter content of the pasture herbage.

$$(3)\ Y = -25.38 + 5.6Z \qquad (R^2 = 0.92)$$

Using equations (1), (2), and (3), a prediction of protein yields possible to recover from pasture herbage in 35 protein extraction operations has been made. There was considerable error involved in the protein yield predictions in an "on the farm" extraction system, amounting to 37, 21, and 15%, respectively. This is the case especially when recoveries from calculations using appropriate regression equations are compared with practically achieved yields of protein in LPC form.

The least error in the predicted amount of protein (g) possible to recover from the unit of herbage dry matter has been achieved with the use of equation (3) when an independent variable protein content (Z) was used. The errors were much less when herbage was processed after previous washing with water (29, 14, and 9%, respectively). The additional operation of herbage treatment with water in extraction process, as was shown in Tables 21.2 to 21.22, enables the elimination of the deleterious effects of numerous factors limiting protein extraction from the herbage being processed "as cut."

Herbage washing and treatment with water for approximately 15 to 30 min before processing has been shown to be advantageous from the point of view of standardizing the extraction process. As a result, constantly high yields of protein from herbage are ensured despite various ecological and agronomical factors and different herbage harvesting and processing conditions.

To provide the field laboratory with the appropriate formula which would have wide application in general agricultural practice, irrespective of geographic location or climatic, ecological, and agronomic conditions, pasture maturity has been chosen as an independent variable in terms of regrowth stage (days) related to pasture herbage dry matter content and crude protein (N × 6.25) concentration.

Since: (i) Dry matter (DM) content of herbage shows a close relationship with crude protein (CP) concentration in herbage, the relationship being expressed as a correlation coefficient, and

(ii) Results of both crude protein and dry matter analysis in pasture herbage are closely related to protein yields (g/kg herbage DM) as recovered in LPC form [equations (2) and (3)]

Therefore, by knowing crude protein and dry matter concentration in pasture herbage which is going to be used for processing, a fair prediction of the protein extraction efficiency from pasture can be made before the start of a large-scale extraction operation in agricultural practice.

As a result, a simple mathematical model has been developed for predicting protein yields from pastures based on basic-routine analysis: dry matter and crude protein concentration in the herbage. This can be used in order to predict the "optimum" regrowth stage of the pasture herbage at which it should be used for the protein extraction purpose. A three-dimensional model of protein extraction from pasture has been built in which both dry matter and crude protein concentration in herbage were used as independent variables for projection of protein extraction efficiency as measured by g of protein recovered from 1 kg of dry weight of pasture herbage (Fig. 21.18). The three-dimensional model based on herbage CP and DM content may help to make a decision (within the limit of statistical confidence) as to the particular "productive position" of the pasture herbage in terms of the expected efficiency of protein extraction as obtained from the projection of DM and CP being determined—prior to the protein extraction operation.

From crude protein content (Z) and herbage dry matter concentration (X), a fair prediction of protein extraction efficiency can be made (1) by using the diagram (Fig. 21.18) or (2) from the regression equation characterizing the surface type response of protein yield (g/kg DM) as expected to be achieved (Y) in protein extraction operation from pasture.

$$(4)\ Y = -63.5 + 6.98X + 5.38Z + 0.08XZ - 0.02Z^2 - 0.35X^2 (R^2 = 0.96)$$

Since in well-defined local agricultural conditions, dry matter of pasture of certain botanical composition (Y) can be more or less accurately predicted from the herbage maturity stage expressed as days or regrowth (X), and the relationship between them being characterized by the regression equation (5):

$$(5)\ Y = 9.60 + 0.13X \qquad (R^2 = 0.89)$$

therefore, for convenient use in protein extraction operations in farm practice, the model presented in Fig. 21.18 refers to both herbage DM and/or regrowth stage; the former, of course, is more appropriate for use with latter, giving prediction of herbage DM in the case of lack of analytical facilities on farms where processing is carried out without outside analytical assistance.

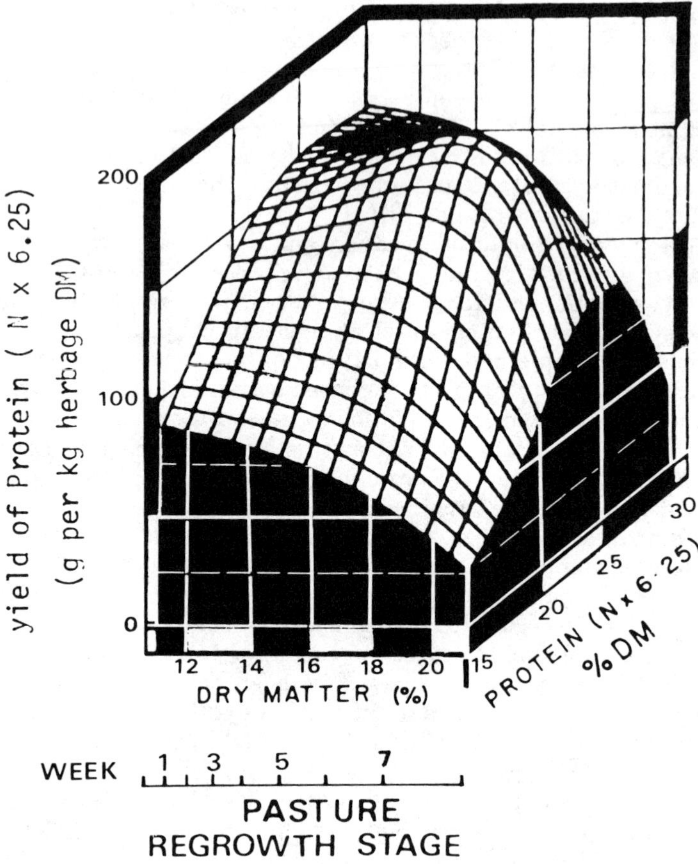

Fig. 21.18. Graphic representation of the relationships between dry matter and crude protein in pasture herbage in relation to herbage regrowth stage (days after last harvest and/or grazing). The graph allows projection of the yield of protein possible to be removed from pasture during its processing by using routine DM and nitrogen analysis of herbage.

Once the optimum point (maximum yield of extracted protein) on the "yield surface" (Fig. 21.18) has not been reached in relation to the pasture regrowth stage, then a decision can be made for how much longer herbage should be left on the pasture before it will produce the maximum yields of extracted protein in LPC form. This will ensure a most efficient protein extraction process in terms of yields of LPC being recovered from the unit of pasture dry weight and/or from the related pasture area.

The surface of the function characterized by equation (4) and depicted in Fig. 21.18 indicates that the dry matter concentration in processed herbage has a major influence on the preparation of herbage protein which can be extracted as LPC. Moisture in herbage provides the carrier for protein during the extraction process (Heath and King 1977); therefore, it explains why herbage washed in water before processing and absorbing as much water as possible, as determined by physiological plant moisture capacity, can yield much more protein as compared with herbage processed without any water treatment before or during the extraction process.

At present, research is being concentrated on the development of the computerized model of the protein extraction operation involving all factors, as described in the first part of this chapter (Tables 21.2 to 21.22), as well as the more detailed meteorological and agronomical data from the herbage regrowth stage so as to predict and control the protein extraction process from pasture involved in dairy farming operations.

The complicated model for the protein extraction efficiency evaluation based on the various factors having been assessed by multiple regression analysis does not increase the accuracy of predictions as compared with expectations based on CP content in herbage DM [equation (3)] when pasture herbage is subject to water treatment prior to the protein extraction process. However, mulitple regression analysis with the involvement of the various factors (as discussed earlier in this chapter) is necessary for the development of the general model in which both ecological and agronomical factors as well as processing conditions are extremely variable and herbage is processed without previous water treatment. Such a model, which is under construction, also takes into account the efficiency of dairying in certain systems of farming, giving as a result an estimation of the efficiency of the protein extraction process, carried out in connection with dairy farming operation—under conditions characteristic of temperate and subtropical regions.

REFERENCES

ALLISON, R.M. 1973. Leaf protein as an animal and human foodstuff. *In* Chemistry and Biochemistry of Herbage. G.W. Butler and R.W. Bailey (Editors). Academic Press, London and New York.

ALLISON, R.M. and VARTHA, E.W. 1973. Yields of protein extracted from irrigated lucerne. N.Z. J. Exp. Agric. *1* (1) 35–38.

ARKCOLL, D.B. 1971. Agronomic aspects of leaf protein production in Great Britain. *In* Leaf Protein: Its Agronomy, Preparation, Quality and Use. IBP Handb. *20*. N.W. Pirie (Editor). Blackwell's Scientific Publications, Oxford.

ARKCOLL, D.B. and FESTENSTEIN, G.N. 1971. A preliminary study of the agronomic factors affecting the yield of extractable leaf protein J. Sci. Food Agric. *22*, 49–56.

BETSCHART, A. and KINSELLA, J. 1973. Extractability and solubility of leaf protein. J. Agric. Food Chem. *21* (1) 60–65.

BHATTY, R.S. and FINLAYSON, A.J. 1973. Extraction of nonprotein nitrogen from oilseed meals with different solvents. Cereal Chem. *50*, 329–335.

BRYANT, A.M. and NEWTH, R.P. 1975. Evaluation of high-moisture forages with ruminants: II. Changes in the chemical composition of herbage after freezing and thawing. N.Z. J. Agric. Res. *18*, 375–378.

BYERS, M. 1971. The amino acid composition of some leaf protein preparations. *In* Leaf Protein: Its Agronomy, Preparation, Quality and Use. IBP Handb. *20*. N.W. Pirie (Editor). Blackwell's Scientific Publications, Oxford.

CHAYEN, T.H., SMITH, R.H., TRISTRAM, G.R., THIRKELL, D. and WEBB, T. 1961. The isolation of leaf components. J. Sci. Food Agric. *12*, 502–509.

CHING GEH, C.H. 1970. The degradation of lucerne proteins and their distribution in the plant. B.Sc. Thesis. University of Canterbury, New Zealand.

COWLISHAW, S.J., EYLES, D.E., RAYMOND, W.F. and TILLEY, J.M.A. 1956. Nutritive value of leaf protein concentrates. II. Effects of processing methods. J. Sci. Food Agric. *7*, 775–780.

DE FERMERY, D., BICKOFF, E.M. and KOHLER, G.O. 1972. PRO-XAN Process: Stability of proteins and carotenoid pigments in freshly expressed alfalfa juice. Agric. Food Chem. *20* (6) 1155–1158.

FREE, B.L. and SATTERLEE, L.D. 1975. Biochemical properties of alfalfa protein concentrate. J. Food. Sci. *40*, 85–89.

GIRAULT, A. 1973. The study of some properties of rapeseed protein with a view to protein concentrate production J. Sci. Food Agric. *24*, 509–513.

HEATH, S.B. and KING, M.W. 1977. The production of crops for green crop fractionation. *In* Green Crop Fractionation. R.J. Wilkins (Editor). Br. Grassl. Soc. Occas. Symp. *9*, 9–21.

ISHINO, K. and ORTEGA, D.M.L. 1975. Fractionation and characterization of major reserve proteins from seeds. J. Agric. Food Chem. *23* (3) 529–533.

JONES, A.S. 1977. The principles of green crop fractionation. *In* Green Crop Fractionation. R.J. Wilkins (Editor). Br. Grassl. Soc. Occas. Symp. *9*, 1–8.

JONES, A.S. and HOUSEMAN, R.A. 1975. Forage crop fractionation. Rep. Rowett Inst. *31*, 136–149.

JOSHI, R.N. 1971. The yield of leaf protein that can be extracted from crops of Aurangabad. *In* Leaf Protein: Its Agronomy, Preparation, Quality and Use. IBP Handb. *20* N.W. Pirie (Editor). Blackwell's Scientific Publications, Oxford.

LEXANDER, K., CARLSSON, R., SHALEN, V., SIMONSSON, A. and LUNDBERG, T. 1970. Quantities of leaf protein concentrates from wild species and crop species grown under controlled conditions. Ann. Appl. Biol. *66*, 193–216.

MACLEOD, L.B. and MACLEOD, J.A. 1974. Effects of N and K fertilization on the protein, nitrate and nonprotein reduced N fractions of timothy and bromegrass. Can. J. Plant Sci. *54*, 331–341.

MAGUIRE, M.F. and BROOKES, I.M. 1973. The effect of juice extraction on the composition and yield of grass crops for dehydration. Proc. 1st Int. Crop Drying Congr., Oxford, Apr. 1973. C.L. Skidmore (Editor). E. & E. Plumridge, Linton, Cambridge.

McGRATH, R. 1972. Protein measurement by ninhydrin determination of amino acids released by alkaline hydrolysis. Anal. Biochem. *49*, 95–102.

McKENZIE, D.R. 1977. Yields of protein extracted from a range of Northern Victorian herbage. Aust. J. Exp. Agric. Anim. Husb. *17*, 268–276.

OKE, O.L. 1973. Leaf protein research in Nigeria: A review. Trop. Sci. *15*(2) 139–155.

OSTROWSKI-MEISSNER, H.T. 1975. Factors limiting protein extraction from pasture—summary. *In* Leaf Protein Concentrate (New Zealand Scene). G.M. Wallace (Editor). Ruakura Agric. Res. Centre Publication, Palmerston North, Hamilton, New Zealand.

OSTROWSKI-MEISSNER, H.T. 1976A. Pasture production in protein extraction system. Proc. N.Z. Soc. Anim. Prod. *36*, 31–41.

OSTROWSKI-MEISSNER, H.T. 1976B. Protein extraction from pastures in temperate regions—Present and potential capabilities. Proc. 1st Int. Congr. Eng. Food, Boston, Aug. 1976.

OSTROWSKI-MEISSNER, H.T. 1976C. Limitations in protein extraction efficiency from grasses due to technology applied in processing. Proc. 1st Int. Congr. Eng. Food, Boston, Aug. 1976.

OSTROWSKI-MEISSNER, H.T. 1976D. Protein Extraction from Pastures,1973–1976. (Relevant papers.) Final Rep. N.Z. Res. Advisory Counc. Fellowship. Ruakura Agric. Res. Center, Hamilton, New Zealand.

OSTROWSKI-MEISSNER, H.T. 1978A. Protein extraction from herbage: New development and its potential. Proc. 3rd Conf. Sci. Technol. Aust. N.Z, Assoc. Adv. Sci. (ANZAAS), Canberra, May 1978.

OSTROWSKI-MEISSNER, H.T. 1978B. Protein extraction from pasture: A new concept in efficient dairy farming in temperate and subtropical regions. Proc. 4th World Conf. Anim. Prod., Buenos Aires, Aug. 1978.

OSTROWSKI-MEISSNER, H.T. 1979. Protein extraction from grasslands. Sci. Technol. *16*, 4–11.

OSTROWSKI-MEISSNER, H.T. 1980. Quantities and qualities of protein extracted from pasture herbage using heat precipitation or ultrafiltration procedures. J. Sci. Food Agric. *31*, 177–187.

OSTROWSKI-MEISSNER, H.T. 1981. Optimization of protein extraction from pasture herbage and qualitative considerations. J. Food Processing Preserv. *5*, 7–22.

OSTROWSKI-MEISSNER, H.T., HALL, R.I., HUGHES, J.W. and NEWTH, R.P. 1975. Field studies on protein recovery limitations during protein extraction from pasture grass. *In* Leaf Protein Concentrate (New Zealand Scene). G.M. Wallace (Editor). Ruakura Agric. Res. Centre Publication, Palmerston North, Hamilton, New Zealand.

PATAT, F. and HOEGNER, W. 1964. Degradation of linear macromolecules during freeze-drying. Macromol. Chem. *75*, 85–97.

PIRIE, N.W. 1971. Leaf Protein: Its Agronomy, Preparation, Quality and Use. IBP Handb. *20*. Blackwell's Scientific Publishers, Oxford.

ROLFE, E. 1970. Characteristics of preservation process as applied to proteinaceous foods. *In* Proteins as Human Food. R.A. Lawrie (Editor). Butterworths, London.

SINGH, N. 1962. Proteolytic activity of leaf extracts J. Sci. Food Agric. *13*, 325–329.

SUBBA RAU, B.H., and SINGH, N. 1970. Studies on nutritive value of leaf protein from lucerne (Medicago sativa): Part II. Effect of processing conditions. Ind. J. Exp. Biol. *8*, 34–41.

VARTHA, E.W. and ALLISON, R.M. 1973. Extractable protein from "Grasslands Tama" Westerworlds rye grass. N.Z. J. Exp. Agric. *1*, 239–244.

WILKINS, R.J., HEATH, S.B., ROBERTS, W.P. and FOXELL, P.R. 1977. A theoretical economic analysis of systems of green crop fractionation. *In* Green Crop Fractionation. R.J. Wilkins (Editor). Br. Grassl. Soc. Occas. Symp. *9*, 131-142.

22

The Vepex Process

Lehel Koch

The basic principles and goals for the procedures utilizing green plants were formulated in the early 1960s. Further research and development have taken place, within this framework, unchanged.

The Tamási (Hungary) production plant was established in 1972 with the concept of using the "total leaf protein" as a suitable basis for industry. It is evident from the general characteristics of our production plant that our basic principles of processing differ from those of Pirie (1966) and of Kohler *et al.* (1968). Piric's experiments were aimed at village-type units (Davys and Pirie 1963) in which the extracted leaf proteins could be used directly to enrich the diets of those living in developing areas, whereas U.S. Department of Agriculture researchers were interested primarily in the alfalfa-dehydration industry.

The basic aims of green plant processing for LPC fractionation can be briefly summarized as follows:

(1) To develop a process for the preparation of green protein which could be used as a partial substitute for conventional grain protein. This is based on the premise that, since green leaves can yield very high amounts of protein in a given area, protein shortage in critical areas could possibly be relieved.
(2) To prepare from the isolated protein a fraction with increased nutritional value and very high acceptance.
(3) To develop flexible processing methods which can be readily adapted to varying environmental conditions and nutritional requirements.

The system should be suitable for a variety of plant materials and the energy requirements should be low. One of the limiting goals of our green leaf processing is the fractionation of the raw material into various leaf protein concentrates with the expenditure of a minimum amount of energy.

Our research and development are progressing according to the previously set goals. Their state at present, and results, are reported in this chapter. Some of the work is in the pilot plant stage; other processes are ready for industrial development.

ISOLATION AND PURIFICATION OF LEAF PROTEIN CONCENTRATES

Yields of 1500–2000 kg of leaf proteins/ha from vegetative green plants even in temperate zones have been reported (Stahmann 1968; Arkcoll and Festenstein 1971). Similar results have been obtained in Hungary, using agricultural practices without irrigation. The Tamási leaf protein manufacturing plant produced 3.0–3.6% leaf protein concentrate on a wet basis from alfalfa as raw material. Based on a yield of 33–35 MT fresh green plant material, 1100–1200 kg leaf protein concentrate were produced per ha with 48–50% crude protein content.

The quantity of extractable leaf protein varies according to species and agricultural conditions (Lexander *et al.* 1970; Pirie 1970; Carlsson 1975). However, under different climatic conditions and growing practices, one can find numerous plants which are suitable for preparation of leaf protein concentrates (Byers 1961; Joshi 1971; Telek 1979).

The quality of the extractable protein is good, and, based on their amino acid pattern, is comparable to seed proteins, with the limiting amino acids being methionine and lysine (Akeson and Stahmann 1965; Byers 1971). In our experiments with 17 species of amaranths, performed during 1967 and 1968, we found significant variations in lysine concentrations. We consider this of secondary importance for the time being since, according to our experience thus far, the amino acid profile of leaf protein concentrates is comparable to seed proteins, but their real biological values can only be assessed by the combined effects of the content of secondary plant ingredients and by their methods of processing.

The nonfractionated leaf protein isolate naturally exhibits the characteristic properties of the system of photosynthesis. Its color is green because of its chlorophyll content, and, because of the plant metabolic materials, its color and flavor are typical. The lipid content of leaf protein and of fractions separated by heat treatment is high, generally 18–22%, which is due primarily to the high lipid content of the chloroplast. This high lipid content and the secondary plant ingredients, especially the phenolic compounds, can lower the biological value of the isolated proteins.

Some of the interesting components of this product are β-carotene and xanthophyll, which are important if the leaf protein concentrate is to be used to feed laying hens and broiler chickens. Unfractionated leaf protein concentrate is best utilized in chicken rations, and in this case its use is tailored to reach the necessary xanthophyll concentration of 4–5%. Thus, it is not utilized primarily as a protein supplement. In swine nutrition we were able to replace 50% of the needed soybean meal without any production loss. However, in this case the xanthophyll content was of less nutritional significance.

Direct utilization of the green protein concentrate for human consumption has several drawbacks, and experiments along these lines are in progress (Oke 1966). This is due partially to the by-products and to the organoleptic characteristics of the fraction produced by the simple extraction method.

In the past few years, research and development trends have been directed toward the distinct separation of chloroplastic and cytoplasmic proteins (Bickoff and Kohler 1974; Lexander *et al.* 1970; Telek 1979). This development is without a doubt of great importance. The composition of the white fraction, its secondary ingredients, and organoleptic characteristics are very favorable. Therefore, we can regard this fraction as being a more suitable protein source for human consumption.

The differential heat fractionation of the two protein fractions has been theoretically recognized in earliest research (Rouelle 1773).

The research and development goals were directed primarily toward the solution of the following problems:

The coagulation temperature of the two protein fractions overlaps to a certain extent and is a function of the time period of heat treatment. A part of the cytoplasmic fraction coagulates along with the chloroplastic fraction. It should also be noted that, among various plant types, the temperature of coagulation of the chloroplastic protein fraction shows slight variations.

The prerequisite for the preparation of a good quality cytoplasmic protein fraction is the quantitative separation of the chloroplastic fraction. Because of the intensive color of chlorophyll, even slight traces of chloroplastic residue could substantially decrease the value of the cytoplasmic fraction. The difficulty in this separation process is the low temperature of coagulation. Flocculation and agglomeration are somewhat hindered, so perfect separation is difficult to attain. For complete separation, separators alone or in combination with filters must be used.

The fractionation of green and white proteins fits logically into our green leaf utilization system, especially since one of our goals is to break up the initial material as far as possible in order to increase the values of the final product. Thus, the use of separators has been one of the basic unit processes in our upgraded manufacturing method since 1963, and they have been adapted in our manufacturing processing in the Tamási plant (Holló *et al.* 1969).

In order to fully utilize our successful separation techniques, we developed a fractionation method which can be adapted without major technical changes. The basic principles are the following:

(1) The green juice is heated to 53°–55°C to ensure optimum conditions for separation of the chloroplastic fraction. Separation is achieved after a 3–5 min waiting period. Separation of the cytoplasmic fraction is delayed by the addition of 300–800 ppm of surfactant before the

heat treatment. Under these circumstances there is no need to cool the green juice subsequently for the coagulation step. The flocculated chloroplastic protein is easily separable. In alfalfa extractions, the ratio of green protein fraction to the white is 3:1.

(2) The basic principle of our other separation method is the low temperature flocculation of the chloroplastic protein, which ensures the separation and also enhances slightly the yield of the white protein fraction. The chloroplastic protein fraction can be flocculated at 38°–42°C, which is the actual temperature of the green juice after a repeated double pressing. With the addition of polyvinylpyrrolidone at the level of 100 mg/liter, there is no need for additional heat treatment (Koch, unpublished data). Naturally, the perfect performance of separation with the differential heat fractionation or with the precipitation by additives of chloroplastic protein is a prerequisite.

Following the separation of the chloroplastic proteins, the cytoplasmic protein fraction can be coagulated by additional heating, by controlled pH adjustment, or by addition of polar solvents. The functional properties and composition of the wet or dried product are considerably influenced by the method of isolation.

Naturally, chloroplast is dominant among the leaf proteins. Among plants rich in cytoplasmic protein, the white protein represents 30–40% of total extractable protein; in the majority of plants, however, it is under 20%. Correspondingly, the utilization of a plant source and the value of the prepared product are defined mainly by its physical, chemical, and biological characteristics. Furthermore, it is defined by those potentials which can provide increased refinement in the process and thus can reach enhanced values.

Numerous data are available concerning the structure of the chloroplast organelles, their characteristics, and chemical composition. However, the area is not yet fully understood, especially the purification of the protein fractions. Those anomalies, which pertain to the extractability of chlorophyll from plant material, also indicate that we are confronted with a complex problem which cannot be generally characterized by the properties of any individual component of the system. Thus, for example, chlorophyll can be extracted from fresh or dry plant matter with alcohol or aqueous alcohol, and from the alcohol phase it can be transferred without any difficulty into a benzene phase; however, chlorophyll cannot be extracted directly even from dry plant material by benzene, despite its greater solubility in this solvent. Similarly, the extraction of chlorophyll by petroleum benzin remains unsuccessful, while concurrently the crude chlorophyll extracts are soluble in this solvent, as they can be separated from this solution only after purification. Acetone or aqueous acetone is a good solvent for chlorophyll.

Our experiences have shown that in practical application it is difficult to achieve good results with solvent extraction of the chloroplast fraction or of the complete protein fraction isolated at 82°C using acetone, isopropanol, or methanol. A grayish end product was obtained even with a solvent ratio of 1:30 or 1:50, based on dry matter content of the coagulum. When the product was mixed with water, it resulted in a brown or gray-brown suspension. Similar results were obtained by other researchers (Arkcoll 1973; Bray *et al.* 1978).

We suspect that the causes for the aforementioned anomalies and the slow and imperfect extractability can be found in the colloidal structures and composition of the lipid system of the chloroplast. The composition of the chloroplast is 50–60% protein and 20–30% lipid. The difficulties in the extraction can be caused by the colloidal aggregates of the fibrous molecules and by the individual lipid components' having entirely different characteristics toward each solvent. We conducted our experiments accordingly, and a brief summary follows:

Our experiments concentrated on two different areas:

(1) The structural modification of the colloid structure of the coagulum prepared by heat fractionation with humectant plasticizer additives, which could also be used as solvents in certain situations. Polyols and some of their derivatives such as Cellosolve (ethylene glycol monomethyl ether) were found to be useful.

(2) Alteration of the lipid ratios of the chloroplastic protein with fatty additives and fatty acid derivatives.

This process will modify the structure of the protein-lipid colloid system in such a manner that lipid extraction becomes a simple and complete operation. As one variation, the substitution of the lipids of the chloroplast fraction with edible fats was also investigated.

MICROSCOPIC EXAMINATIONS

The behavior of the green juice with heat treatment and different additives was investigated. The pressed green juice was made from spinach. The additives were: ethylene glycol monoethylether, tallow, stearic acid monoglyceride (SMG), or the 1:1 mixture with tallow, acetone, petroleum benzin, alcohol, and benzene.

Procedure. The green juice of spinach was coagulated under a cover glass. After the heat treatment, the extraction solvents were siphoned under the cover glass, and the material was examined at 60°–90°C and microscopic photographs were taken. When the action of tallow and stearic acid monoglyceride was studied, a smear was prepared on the slide onto which a drop of spinach green juice was added, and the photograph was taken after heating. A brief summary of the microscopic examination follows.

In the green juice, particle movement was seen at 45° and 50°C, and in the course of further warming, the formation of sharply contoured floccular structures and webs could be observed.

If Cellosolve is siphoned to the coagulated green protein even at room temperature, brownish-green diffuse areas are noticeable. The floccules are swollen and green drops are unwinding from them and, to a lesser degree, also from the web-like structures. The color of the floccules behind the solvent front is yellow and light brown.

If Cellosolve is siphoned to the coagulated protein and the system is warmed, results similar to the previous experiment are observed. The floccules swell greatly, and the green droplets are in motion and, in part, coalesce to form larger drops.

The floccules formed in the green juice which was added to the tallow smear and consequently heated also swell, and on the boundaries of the floccules and tallow, a diffuse brown phase is seen.

A comparable picture is obtained with the stearic acid monoglyceride smear.

Over a mixture of tallow and stearic acid monoglyceride, the coagulum of green juice filtrate forms a swollen, weblike structure, and a globular texture can be observed. In contrast, the heat-treated green juice without additives has a sharply contoured filamental structure.

If Cellosolve is siphoned to the protein coagulum found on a stearic acid monoglyceride (SMG) smear, large green- and brown-colored drops are formed adjacent to the light yellow-colored fibrous floccules.

The effect of Cellosolve on the coagulum formed on a tallow-SMG smear is comparable to the observation just described.

Alcohol or acetone is a good solvent for extraction of the green pigments from the protein coagulum. However, the floccules and web-like structures keep their formations, having sharp contours, and they are dark brown.

The microscopic picture obtained using benzene or petroleum benzin is similar to the preceding; the only difference noted is that the extraction of green pigments cannot be seen at all.

The conclusion of the microscopic investigation is that Cellosolve alters the solubility of the green protein coagulum lipids. This solvent makes radical changes in the associated polydispersed colloid system, so that at 60°–80°C its lipids separate from the proteins as a result of an increased pressure gradient.

Both the tallow and SMG show similar effects with one notable difference, namely, that Cellosolve could also be considered a solvent, and not simply have the property to change the structure of the colloid system. The tallow and SMG primarily have the effect of changing the associated colloid structure.

MODEL EXPERIMENTS IN THE LABORATORY

Based on the results of the microscopic examination, it was reasonable to do similar experiments on a laboratory scale. These are briefly summarized.

Experimental Materials

Spinach chloroplastic proteins coagulated at 50°–53°C, having 28.6% DM content

Alfalfa chloroplastic protein coagulated at 50°–55°C, having 33% DM

Vepex dried green protein concentrate (82°C) with added water to have 33% DM

Additives and extractions used: Cellosolve, tallow, tallow and SMG mixture in ratio of 3:1, and the combination of this with Cellosolve, isopropanol, and acetone

The amount of solvent and additives calculated on dry matter basis 50 or 100%

The temperatures of extractions were 20°, 60°, and 100°C; in the case of tallow and SMG, it was 60° and 100°C. Extraction with acetone and isopropanol was performed at reflux temperature. The homogenization and heat treatment were performed with an ultra-turrax apparatus which was equipped with a heated vessel. The treatment lasted for 15 min.

Experimental Data

The experimental data conform to the microscopic findings and are summarized as follows:

Although the extract can be separated only with some difficulty from the extracted material due to the plasticizer property of the Cellosolve, it still has a considerable effect on the lipid extraction.

The same extent of lipid extraction can be achieved with tallow and with tallow and SMG mixture. Lipid extraction is considerably enhanced if Cellosolve is used with tallow or tallow-SMG combination. It was found that, in the dry matter of the filtrate, the total lipid content and the crude fat content are practically equal. Thus, materials which are otherwise not extractable from the colloidal structure by petroleum benzin even in the dry stage, in the presence of fatty additives will be soluble in the same solvent. In these experimental-model tallow, Cellosolve-tallow, and SMG-Cellosolve systems, 90% of the lipids which were resistant to petroleum ether extraction can be separated from the protein-lipid complex.

The homogenized mixture was filtered through a G_2 glass filter. The filtrate and the residue were dried, both were analyzed for *lipid* content, extracted by a mixture of chloroform-methanol (2:1), and crude fat content was determined with normal extraction with petroleum benzin (bp = 70°C). The data of the experiments are summarized in Tables 22.1A, 22.1B, and 22.1C.

To summarize the experimental data:

(1) Although it is difficult to separate Cellosolve by filtration because of its plasticizing behavior, it still ensures a considerable amount of lipid extraction.
(2) The same amount of lipid extraction can be achieved with a tallow and SMG mixture.

(3) Further, the amount of lipid extraction is considerably enhanced if Cellosolve is used in combination with tallow or SMG.

Data conforming to the initially set conditions show that in the dry matter of the filtrate the total lipid and crude fat determination did not show any real difference. Thus, such materials, which are otherwise not

TABLE 22.1A. THE TREATMENT OF SPINACH GREEN PROTEIN CONCENTRATE

Treatment	Total Lipid-Crude Fat (%) Extract	Extracted Material	Extracted Material Total Lipid-Crude Fat (%) Control = 100
Cellosolve 100% t: 80°C	32.11	7.79	58.9
Cellosolve 100% t: 60°C	32.20	7.54	57.0
Cellosolve 100% t: 100°C	35.42	7.02	53.0
Tallow + Cellosolve 100%; t: 60°C	0.05	4.02	31.8
Tallow + Cellosolve 100%; t: 100°C	0.74	1.40	10.6
Acetone 100% t: 57°C	31.21	8.07	61.1
Isopropanol 100% t: 83°C	19.15	7.03	53.2
Starting Material (Control)	Total Lipid Content 24.27%	Added Crude Fat 11.06%	Difference 13.21%

t = Temperature.

TABLE 22.1B. THE TREATMENT OF ALFALFA GREEN PROTEIN CONCENTRATE

Treatment	Total Lipid-Crude Fat (%) Extract	Extracted Material	Extracted Material Total Lipid-Crude Fat (%) Control = 100
Cellosolve 100% t: 60°C	22.77	6.98	50.7
Cellosolve 100% t: 100°C	35.84	7.12	51.7
Tallow 100% t: 60°C	0.02	8.03	65.4
Tallow 100% t: 100°C	0.04	7.38	60.1
Tallow + Cellosolve 100%; t: 60°C	0.01	4.68	38.1
Tallow + Cellosolve 100%; t: 100°C	0.51	5.02	40.8
Acetone 100% t: 57°C	19.27	9.61	69.8
Isopropanol 100% t: 83°C	13.55	11.71	85.0
Starting Material (Control)	Total Lipid Content 22.25%	Added Crude Fat 9.97%	Difference 12.28%

t = Temperature.

TABLE 22.1C. THE TREATMENT OF VEPEX GREEN PROTEIN CONCENTRATE

Treatment	Total Lipid-Crude Fat (%) Extract	Total Lipid-Crude Fat (%) Extracted Material	Extracted Material Total Lipid-Crude Fat (%) Control = 100
Cellosolve 100% t: 20°C	12.15	7.11	57.8
Cellosolve 100% t: 60°C	11.43	8.68	70.6
Tallow 50% t: 60°C	0.05	7.64	62.2
Tallow 50% t: 100°C	0.01	8.43	68.6
Tallow + Cellosolve 100% t: 60°C	1.10	7.17	58.4
Tallow + Cellosolve 100% t: 100°C	0.11	7.71	62.8
Tallow + Cellosolve 100% t: 60°C	0.02	3.11	25.3
Tallow + SMG + Cellosolve 50%; t: 100°C	0.64	4.49	36.6
Acetone 100% t: 57°C	16.10	7.52	61.2
Isopropanol t: 83°C	11.73	9.35	76.1
Starting Material (Control)	Total Lipid Content 22.30%	Added Crude Fat 9.98%	Difference 12.32%

t = Temperature.

extractable from the colloid structure with petroleum benzin in the presence of added fat, will dissolve with the same solvent even in the anhydrous state.

In some instances, in the experimental model, the lipids which are insoluble in petroleum benzin alone could be extracted up to 90% from the protein-lipid complex using tallow and Cellosolve-tallow or SMG or Cellosolve mixtures. The tannin content determined by the Folin-Denis Method in the residue showed considerable decrease. The decrease of phenol content is substantially greater with the use of Cellosolve and fatty additives than with straightforward acetone and isopropanol extraction.

In subsequent experiments the conditions were modified. Less Cellosolve was used and its primary use was for the plasticization of the coagulum. The extraction and the modification of chloroplasts were achieved with the tallow and tallow and SMG mixtures.

The fatty additive was separated by centrifuging; the tallow-SMG-containing residue was processed in two ways:

(1) The purpose of the first variation was to determine to what degree the preliminary treatment with Cellosolve and fatty additives will change the organic solvent extractability of the original lipids from the protein coagulum. Acetone and isopropyl alcohol (isopropanol) were used in these experiments. Using these solvents slightly in excess, the extraction was easily achieved.

In the unsatisfactory solvent extractions using pure solvents, a 30- to 50-fold amount of solvent was used for extraction. By contrast, when using tallow additives with 6-fold extractions, the data in Table 22.2A were obtained.

The color of the product corresponds to the heat-fractionated white protein fraction; its aqueous suspension is not greenish, but brown and rather pale in color; and its protein total lipid content is satisfactory.

TABLE 22.2A. COMPOSITION OF TALLOW- AND SOLVENT-EXTRACTED LPC

	% (DM)			
Treatment	Crude Protein	Crude Fat	Total Lipid	Tannin
Tallow/ Cellosolve/ + acetone	68.4	1.33	5.36	0.54
Tallow/ Cellosolve/ + isopropanol	73.7	0.42	2.27	0.32

(2) The purpose of the second variation is the modification of the green protein fraction without use of solvents, and also by lipid exchange of the original lipids of the chloroplast. In our first experiment, the alfalfa green protein fraction was extracted with tallow or with tallow-SMG mixtures in two sequential steps. The melted fat was removed by centrifugation, and the residue was then suspended in warm water (80°C) and separated from the occluded tallow particles.

The same experiment was performed with the addition of a small amount of Cellosolve to the tallow for plasticization. The analytical data of the products are summarized in Table 22.2B.

Our work in the modification, extraction, and standardization of chloroplastic protein has advanced the development to such a degree that it can easily and rationally be adapted to very broad variations in technological and environmental factors.

By thc previously discussed developmental process, the major fraction of leaf protein concentrates, the chloroplastic protein, can be utilized on a wider scale, even replacing some other proteins of good quality. The limiting ingredients are extractable and the carotenoid pigments could also be utilized as another product of the process.

FRACTIONATION OF THE GREEN CROP

Utilization of the photosynthesis potential depends largely on the method of conversion as well as the characteristics of the applied agricultural practices. In the prevalent methods of food production, generally only cer-

TABLE 22.2B. COMPOSITION OF TALLOW-EXTRACTED LPC

Treatment	% (DM)			
	Crude Protein	Crude Fat	Total Lipid	Tannin
Tallow 100%/ + water wash 80°C	59.4	14.8	20.9	0.10
Tallow 100%/ + Cellosolve + water wash 80°C	62.1	12.6	18.9	0.07

tain parts of the plants are utilized, and the production methods are geared toward this end. According to investigations, the plant parts used (such as seeds or grains) comprise only 40% of the organic material formed during the growing season. It is a greater drawback that, under these circumstances, the agricultural productivity differs considerably from the maximum possible biological production (Table 22.3).

Consequently, the primary goal in present agricultural practice is plants for directly edible parts only. Thus, natural restrictions are placed on the total productivity of the growing area, as well as restricting the utilization of the radiant energy, which is the greatest factor in the difference between biological productivity and the practical crop yield under identical local conditions (Table 22.4). However, we must also take into consideration those secondary processes in which the primary metabolites formed during the photosynthesis are transported, polymerized, and deposited. This process naturally requires energy.

The accumulation of storage nutrients is also affected by the development of storage organs, whose formation is strongly influenced by environmental factors. Thus, it could be of great advantage if the plants were utilized during thc part of their growing stage corresponding as closely as possible to their maximum biological nutrient production.

It is evident from the given experimental and practical agricultural data that, under identical conditions, considerably more organic matter can be produced by these methods than with the traditional agricultural method of seed production. This fact can be used advantageously in production of feed

TABLE 22.3. THE BIOLOGICAL AND COMMERCIAL YIELD OF WHEAT AND CORN

Ripening Class	Wheat (Mexico)			Corn (Uganda)		
	Yr	Yc	Ic	Yr	Yc	Ic
Early	13.64	5.38	32.9	13.51	3.98	29.4
Medium	15.56	5.58	35.9	18.66	3.69	19.7
Late	17.09	5.80	33.9	21.44	3.50	16.7

Source: Holliday (1976).
Yr = The optimal biological yield in MT ha^{-1}.
Yc = Commercial yield in MT ha^{-1}.

$$Ic = \frac{Yc}{Yr} \times 100$$

TABLE 22.4. YIELD PER YEAR OF DIFFERENT AGRICULTURAL PLANTS

Species	Location	Yield MT/ha/Year	Notes
Corn			
(Zea mays)	Peru (12° N)	25.8	10.3 MT/ha seed (40%)
(Zea mays)	Egypt (30° N)	29.1	11.6 MT/ha seed (40%)
(Zea mays)	Italy (45° N)	34.0	140 days; 40 MT/ha (85% vegetative parts standing)
Sugarcane			
(Saccharum officinarum)	Swaziland (27° S)	63.0	365 days; 23.7 MT/ha (38%)
Sorghum-Sudan grass			
(*Sorghum* sp.)	United States (33° N)	46.6	210 days
Bermuda grass			
(*Cynodon* sp.)	Puerto Rico (18° N)	37.3	365 days
Coastal Bermuda grass			
(*Cynodon* sp.)	United States (34° N)	27.0	365 days
Napier grass			
(Pennisetum purpureum)	El Salvador (14° N)	85.3	365 days
Alfalfa			
(*Medicago* sp.)	Israel (31° N)	18.6	
(*Medicago* sp.)	United States (38° N)	27.6	6–8 cuttings
Soybean			
(Glycine max)	Japan (33° N)	6.3	
Wheat			
(Triticum vulgaris)	Mexico (27° N)	18.3	7.3 MT/ha seed (40%)
(Triticum vulgaris)	United States (46° N)	29.8	209 bu (7.357 kl) seed (40%)
Italian ryegrass			
(Lolium multiflorum)	Netherlands	22.0	

Source: Loomis and Gerakis (1975).

proteins. In this case, the plants are processed during their period of greatest photosynthetic activity. Using plants with good regrowth potential and our developed system, more organic matter and an increased amount of protein can be produced per unit area than with the utilization of storage nutrients.

However, the agricultural system which could be organized according to these new views allows the inclusion of a variety of factors which would benefit its use in other important areas:

(1) Utilization of land area for maximum biological productivity
(2) With further processing of the plant material, the difference between useful and waste products ceases
(3) The processing of plant material can be conducted in such a way that each fraction should be of increasing qualitative value and thus optimally utilized (Koch 1973). Under this kind of integrated agricultural system, the entire crop production is used for raw material. By-products obtained in the course of processing can be recycled or used as energy sources. Such a quasi-reversible system can also be

developed which functions very efficiently and can be kept practically in balance with the utilization of solar energy. In green matter, water is the major component of plant raw materials. Thus its elimination determines the energy requirements for the processing and yield of various fractions. One of the characteristics of our plant processing system is our endeavor to produce the largest amount of pressed juice. This is advantageous, even if the utilization of all possible fractionation is not contemplated.

The most important characteristics and techniques of our processing system are summarized in the following sections.

DISINTEGRATION

In order to assure maximum yield from the raw material, adequate maceration is necessary. This disintegration must be achieved under such conditions that protein coagulation should not occur due to heat produced during the grinding process. Maceration must be so effective that the pressing process can be carried out without difficulties. Fiber length of the disintegrated plant material decreases only slightly during the process. This is important for easy pressing as well as for an efficient classification process after drying of the pressed residue. Our disintegrator, designed and developed to satisfy these requirements, can process 50 liters of plant material per hr with a very favorable energy utilization of 2.0–2.5 kWh/MT green plant material.

PRESSING

The maximum juice production from the disintegrated material is accomplished with two presses. First—the low pressure preliminary press—for this a variety of equipment operating on different principles can be used (belt press, double screw press). The selection can be made according to the requirements and conditions of the individual establishments. The double screw presses, such as of Strid Stord Co., Norway, have advantages in their dependable performance, considerable expandability, and degree of control. Depending on plant material and the operating characteristics of the first press, the yield of liquid, based on the fresh weight, can be between 50 and 55%, yielding a pressed residue with a dry matter content of 28–32%.

The second press is a high pressure expeller, which increases the dry matter content of the sufficiently prepressed fibrous residue to 50–60%. With this double-press process, a juice yield of 70% was achieved. In this preparatory process of disintegration and pressing, 75% of the starting raw material will be transferred to the liquid phase, which is preferred over the solid state for fractionation and also for heat economy.

ISOLATION OF PROTEIN FRACTIONS

The temperature of the pooled green juices after the double pressing is 35°–40°C. Starting at this temperature, one can proceed with the separation of the proteins by several procedures. The simplest method is the combined separation of the chloroplastic and cytoplasmic proteins with direct steam injection at 82°C. The separation of the green and white proteins requires different equipment. However, the basic principle of the fractionation, as mentioned previously, is differential heat treatment. In our fractionation process, with an interest in obtaining the largest amount of white protein fraction possible, we carried out the quantitative separation of the chloroplast fraction at lower temperatures and delayed the separation of the white protein fractions by the use of suitable reagents. The following methods were employed in our process:

(1) For the coagulation of the chloroplastic protein of the press juice at process temperature, soluble polyvinylpyrrolidone was used.
(2) The filtrate was heated from the basic process temperature of 30°–40° to 48°–50°C with waste heat energy and using 50–100 ppm of two or three metal salts of 2 or 3 valence or hydroxides for the flocculation of the chloroplast fraction.
(3) Heat treatment at 55°C with the addition of surfactants as described previously.
(4) In case of flocculation, the juice was passed through a decanter centrifuge, removing the greater portion of the wet precipitate. The process juices of the decanter, which still contained 1.5% of protein precipitate, were then centrifuged with separators. The white protein fraction was separated from the chlorophyll-free process juice at 80°C by direct steam injection and separated by a decanter centrifuge from the mother liquid.

PROCESSING OF THE DEPROTEINIZED JUICE

After the separation of protein fractions, the deproteinized juice was transferred to a multistage vacuum evaporator and evaporated to a 40–45% DM content. If a larger capacity is required, the use of a four-stage condenser is suggested, in which the thin juice could be evaporated to a syrup with 50% dry matter.

In the case of green plant processing by disintegrator, effective pressing is the key factor to obtaining the maximum yield of juice production and effective evaporation in the vacuum evaporator, and is also the decisive factor for energy conservation in this process. The deproteinized juice still contains a significant quantity of dry matter, 2–2.5% of the dry matter weight of original plant material, and can be used advantageously as animal feed. The dilute liquid is very good substrate for yeast production. However, only enterprises with large capacity can afford to use this method successfully because of the considerable investment needed for aeration equipment and other expenses in the final processing. If the deproteinized juice is considered as a yeast fermentation medium according to our manufacturing experiences, a yield of 18–22 g/liter dry yeast can be expected from the alfalfa process. Thus, according to the present state of the art, evaporation of the deproteinized juice is the simplest method of utilization. In our current process, the concentrated deproteinized juice is mixed before drying to the fibrous press residue, and during the pelletizing.

At present, the decrease of heat energy requirement in water evaporation is one of the key factors in the processing of green plants. There are processes in which the hot humid vapor energy of the drum dryer is utilized in heating another vacuum evaporator or is used in another type of heat exchanger. These methods are quite useful on a lesser scope, but in reality this system cannot be integrated into the optimal processing of green plants.

PROCESSING OF THE PRESSED RESIDUE

According to the present industrial procedures, the pressed residue, having 30–35% dry matter, is dried in a drum dryer with the added deproteinized juice concentrate. Thus, 35–40% of the water content of the starting raw material is present in the drum dryer and about 40% of this water content will be evaporated in the vacuum dryer.

The double-pressing process will increase the juice yield to 75% and will yield a pressed residue with a temperature of 70°–80°C and containing only 40–50% water. Because of the modified ratio of pressed residue and quantity of juice, only 10–20% of the original water content will be present in the material to be dried. With the change of the material distribution, a potential is created for further improvement of heat energy conservation. The pressed residue at high fiber content is transferred directly to the dryer. This could be the commonly used drum dryer, where the product could be dried to 15–20% water content with flue gas. The dried fibers will be classified through one or two screening systems (5–9 mesh). Fifty to 60% will pass these screens. The rest (40–50%) will be used as fuel for the boilers. We must emphasize that a basic prerequisite for the classification is a satisfactory disintegration and the double-press procedure. The composition of the dried, pressed residue is in the two fractions resulting from classification as shown in Table 22.5.

The heat energy value of the classified pressed residue is 4000–4500 Cal/kg, depending on its water content, and for its utilization suitable heating equipment is available, even for smaller capacities. Depending on the exactness of the classification process, 30–40% dry matter of the pressed residue can be utilized for energy production.

The fiber content is greater than 70% and its heat energy value is 320–360 Mcal/MT of the material. This provides for a greater portion of the energy requirements in the course of processing.

The simplified flow sheets in the following figures illustrate the two characteristic variations of the technology of green plant processing. Figure 22.1A shows the setup of simplified unit processes and material bal-

TABLE 22.5. THE COMPOSITION OF THE DRIED PRESSED RESIDUE, AND THE TWO FRACTIONS RESULTING FROM CLASSIFICATION ON 5 MESH SCREEN

Component	% (DM)		
	Crude Protein	Crude Fiber	Ash
Dried pressed residue	11–12	50–55	6.5–7.5
Dried pressed residue sifted, residue on 5 mesh screen	3–4	75–80	4–5
Dried pressed residue sifted, passed 5 mesh screen	16–17	28–30	9–10

ances. Figure 22.1B shows the energy requirements by unit processes of the technology illustrated in Fig. 22.1A. Figure 22.2A illustrates the process of lipid extraction from the proteins. Figure 22.2B shows the step-by-step energy requirements of this process.

The flowsheets represent certain variations of the process. We consider as important the use of one part of the fibrous residue as an energy source, because we are convinced that the ever-increasing cost and diminishing availability of fossil fuel will make this process the only feasible one in the near future. Naturally, there are no obstacles to processing the whole, unclassified fibers by the traditional methods.

In the flowsheet in Fig. 22.2A, we illustrate more process variations. Among them, one is the chloroplast lipid exchange and the combination of the extractable fat into the green protein fraction. The second is the production of a pigment concentrate by the regeneration of the extracted fat, and the third variation is the solvent extraction of the green protein coagulate treated with fat addition. The energy requirement in Fig. 22.2B refers to the procedures for fat recovery. We must note that the simplified flowsheets show the major process steps. The specific use values were defined by data of industrial or semi-industrial measurements. The use times of the auxiliary equipment, such as pumps and transport systems, are appraised values which can show great variations depending on the capacity of the plant. In the simplified material balance, losses were not listed. Based on our experiences, the loss of the processed dry matter is only around 1%.

According to the data just presented, our fractionation procedure can meet very broad utilization demands. The number of products can be increased to six, if the deproteinized juice is used as a fermentation medium. Besides the possibilities of energy saving during the process, significant advantages are gained from the increased values of certain products, including the fact that the protein fraction or some protein fractions can be used for direct human nutrition. The spread and feasibility of fractionation of green plants are strongly influenced by the duration of processing, which depends on the availability of plant material, a function of climatic and environmental factors.

This is especially important under temperate zone conditions, where the protein extraction could be prolonged to six months by working up plant waste materials and cold-tolerant crops. The processing technology can,

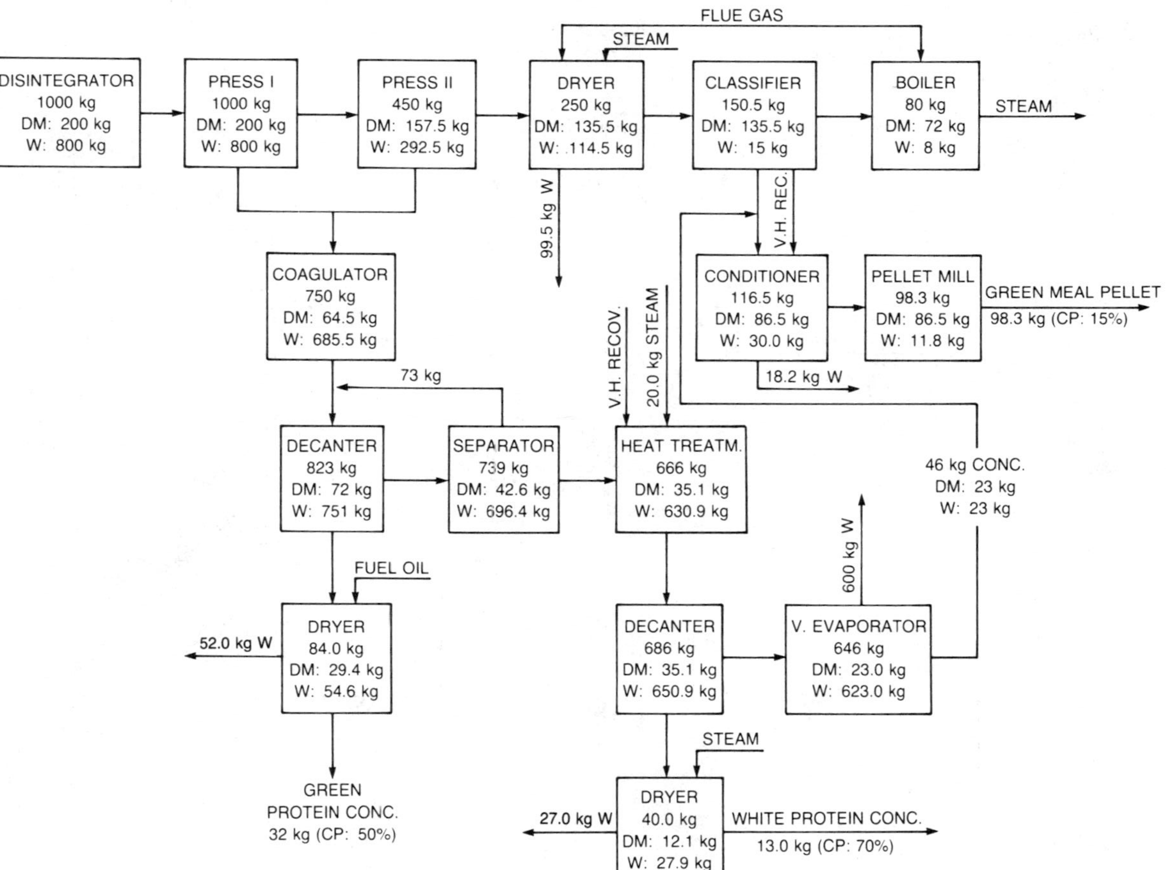

Fig. 22.1A. Simplified flow sheet of the Vepex process and material balance of the protein fractionation. Raw material—Alfalfa, DM: 20%, CP: 21%.

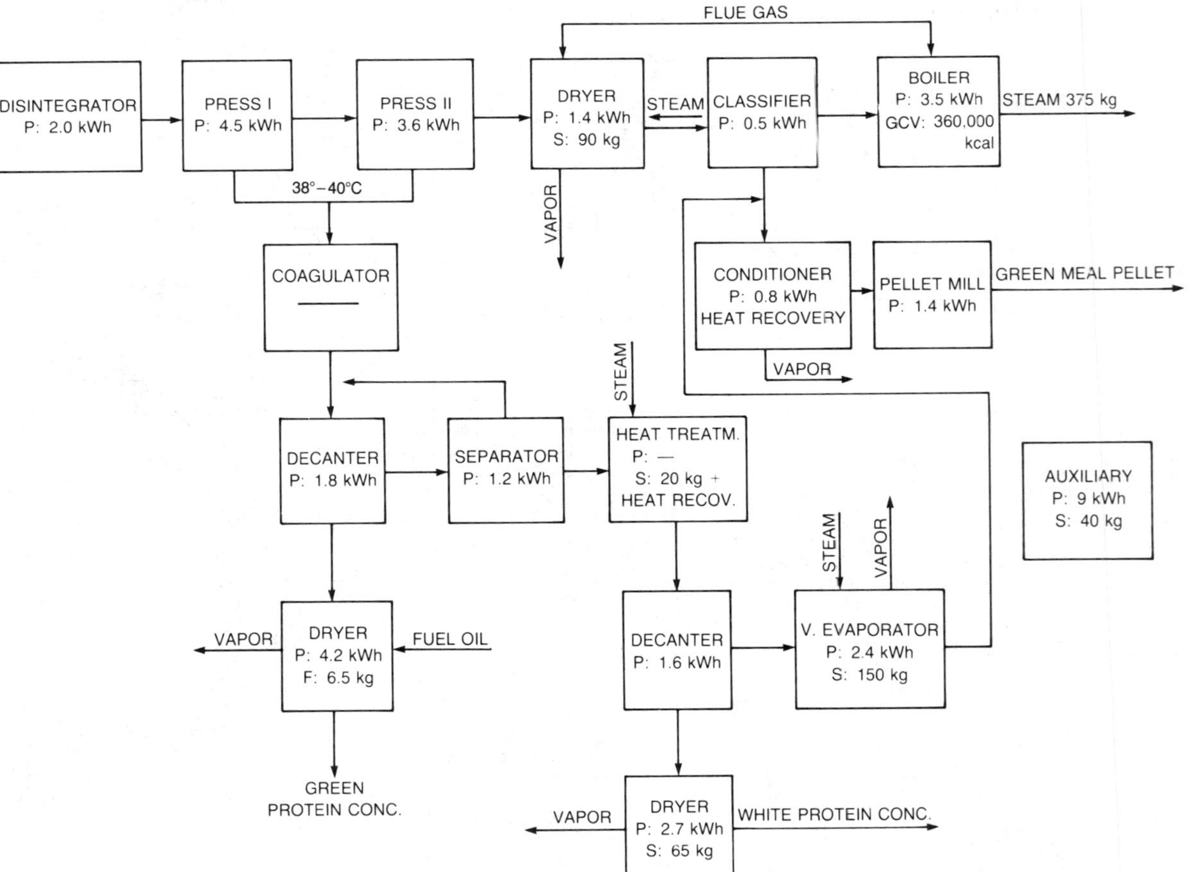

Fig. 22.1B. Energy requirements in unit processes in the protein fractionation. Energy requirement/MT raw material—Electric energy 40.6 kWh; heating oil 6.5 kg.

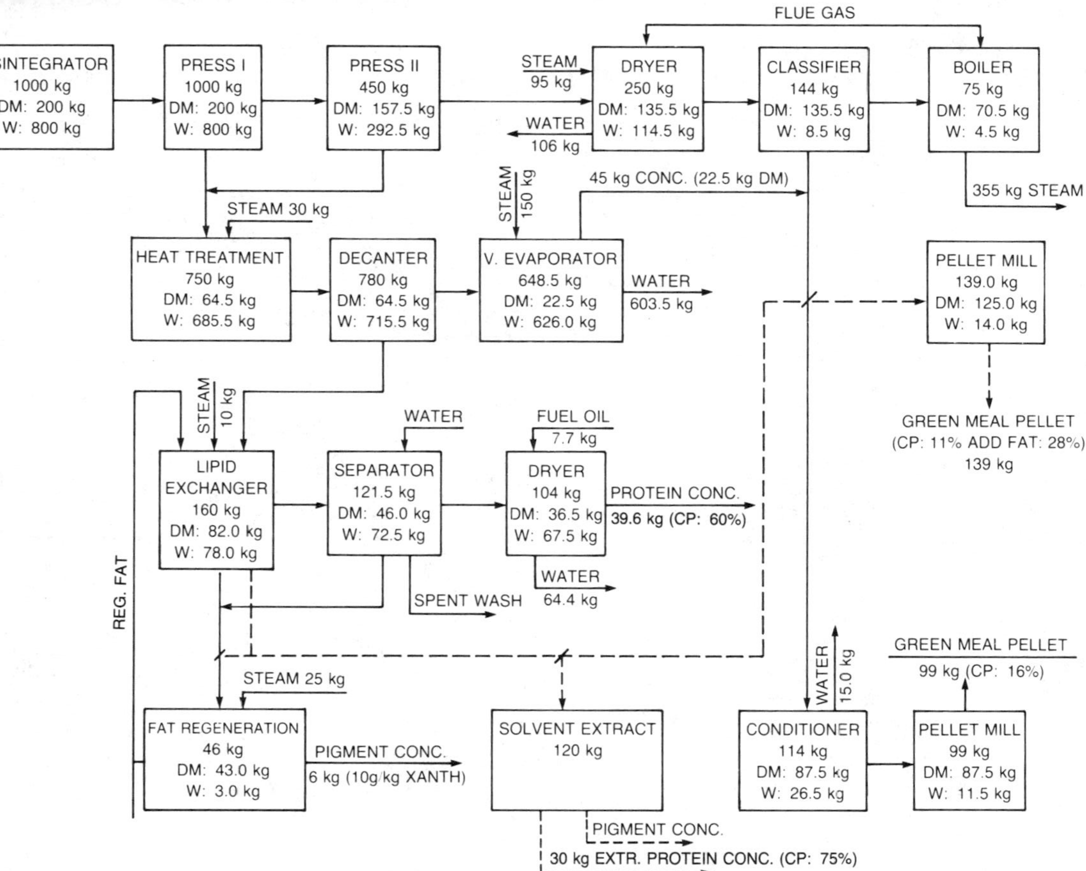

Fig. 22.2A. Simplified flow sheet of the Vepex process with lipid extraction of green proteins during the production. Raw material—Alfalfa, DM: 20%, CP: 21%.

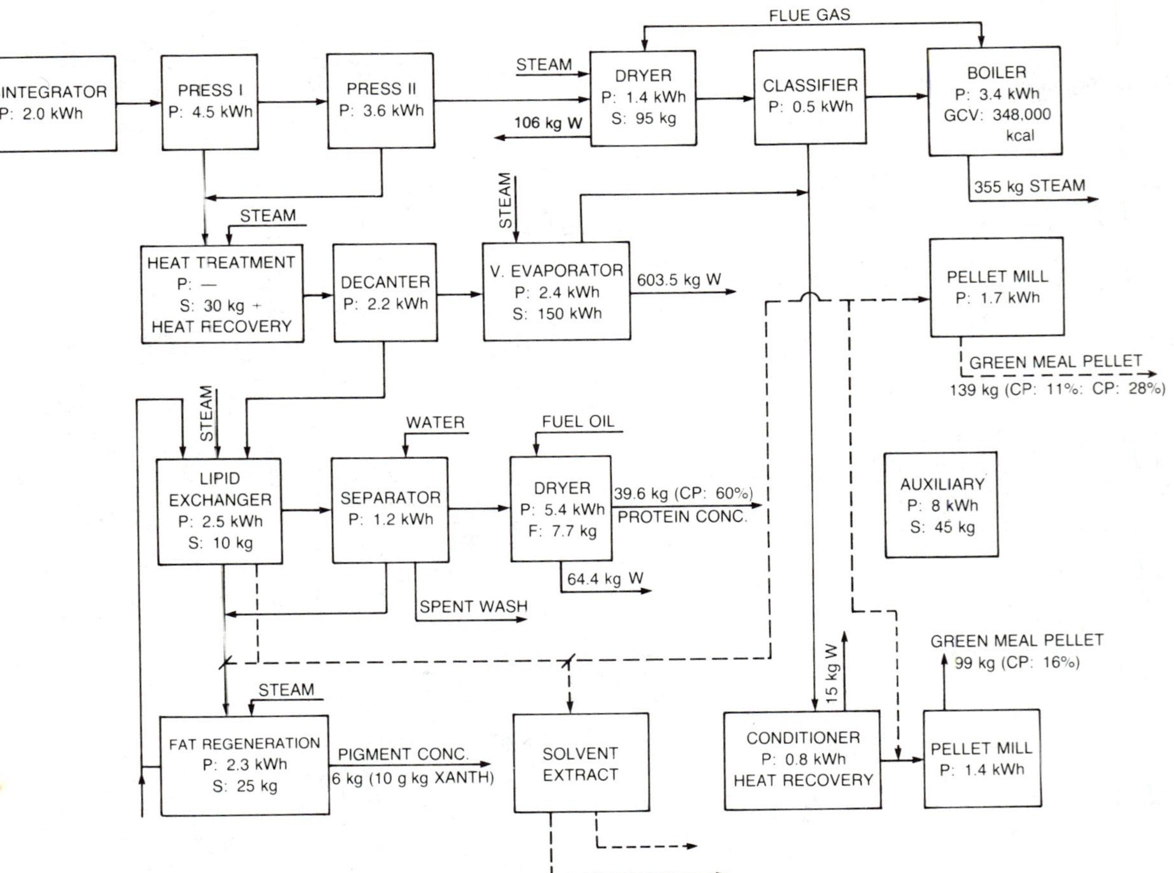

Fig. 22.2B. Energy requirements in unit processes in the simplified Vepex process with lipid extraction of green proteins during the production. Energy requirement/MT raw material—Electric energy 40.8 kWh; heating oil 7.7 kg.

however, be interrupted at some half-finished products and these products may be isolated without final processing. This means that protein coagulants with 30–35% dry matter content can be stored with preservatives and the final processing can be continued after the growing season. The same applies to the concentration of deproteinized juice. The leaf protein can be precipitated from the green juice and preserved by anaerobic fermentation (Stahmann 1974). The coagulum obtained by heat fractionation can be stored with additional preservatives (Pirie 1970; Arkcoll 1973).

We examined the shelf-life of the green precipitate having 33% dry matter prepared by decanter separation. Satisfactory results were obtained in six months storage at 25°C through the addition of 0.5–1% formic acid. The product remained suitable for further processing. It was interesting to find satisfactory levels of β-carotene (630 mg/kg) and xanthophyll (1170 mg/kg). This applies also to changes in the iodine, bromine, and Lea numbers. Similarly, perhaps even slightly less favorable values were obtained with 2% acetic acid preservation. For the workup of these preserved half-finished products, some departments of the factory could remain on steam even after the end of harvesting of the plant material. The unit processes can be separated into various phases. Freshly processed or preserved half-finished products can be finished in different refining process steps.

THE INTEGRATION OF LEAF PROTEIN PRODUCTION INTO THE AGRICULTURAL FEED PRODUCTION SYSTEM

It is predicted that at the turn of the next century the demand for animal feed will be considerably increased. According to some opinions, a 2-fold increase in grain and a 10-fold increase in the production of high quality protein feeds will be necessary. Considering the main elements of the chain of food production, this feed requirement will not be met by traditional sources. Under all circumstances this generalization is valid with respect to the future protein demand; this prediction is evident from two facts:

Population increase is exponential, while the traditional food production increase is linear. In the coming years the improvement of nutrition quality and increasing living standards will place a greater demand on food production and, primarily, a higher need for protein production. To satisfy the new protein requirements, new sources will have to be found. However, production by traditional agricultural methods occurs according to the law of diminishing returns, with a disproportional input of energy. For example, the average protein yield of soybeans in the United States, 400–571 kg/ha/year, is produced with an energy intensity of 1.03–1.21 kcal/ha/year. However, if the protein yield is increased to 2284 kg/ha/year, the energy intensity is 37 kcal/ha/year (Slesser 1973). These unrealistically high input values cannot be supported economically anymore because the traditional energy supplies will not be available in sufficient quantity at low price. For this reason, every developmental method which combines increased food or feed production with considerable energy savings has very significant importance. One of the important prerequisites in the development of our method of green plant processing is the considerable reduction of the energy used in protein production. With this aim we have presented one of the methods of fractionation in which we utilized the heat energy of one of the by-products derived from the raw material. These energy-saving potentials and present status of our process developments are summarized in the flowsheets (Fig. 22.1 and 22.2) and Table 22.7.

From the data of Table 22.6 it may be seen that not only is the protein production justified in terms of energy assessment but it presents considerable advantages over other agricultural food production systems. The total energy input for plant production is only 7.7 Mcal, and for leaf protein fraction is calculated to be 12.2 Mcal, which is considerably lower than, for example, the input in intensive corn production. The energy ratio is also advantageous because the process itself provided 10 Mcal energy. Taking this energy saving into account, E = 2.77 Mcal.

TABLE 22.6. ENERGY REQUIREMENT FOR PROCESSING OF GREEN PLANTS GROWN ON 1 HA OF LAND BY FIG. 22.1A PROCESS

Energy input for plant production			
(a) Fertilizer	Ammonium nitrate	1.380	Mcal
	Superphosphate	1.161	
	Potash	0.128	
(b) Pesticide		0.124	
(c) Machinery	Tractor (60.000 kcal/ha)	0.480	
	Harvester (190.00 kcal/ha)	0.380	
	Others	0.120	
(d) Transportation		0.378	
Total		4.15	Gcal/ha
Workup energy input			
Electrical energy (3100 kcal/kWh)		4.405	Mcal
Heating oil (9600 kcal/kg)		2.184	
Total		6.59	Gcal/ha
Total energy input for plant production and workup		10.75	Gcal
Energy output from plant material			
35 MT green plant/20% DM, 21% CP/7 MT DM/4.25 Gcal/MT		29.75	Gcal/ha
Product output			
3440 kg green pellet (CP 15%)			
1120 kg green protein concentrate (CP 50%)			
455 kg white protein concentrate (CP 70%)			
Total energy input (Gcal ha^{-1} $year^{-1}$)		10.75	
Total energy output (Gcal ha^{-1} $year^{-1}$)		19.05	
Energy input/kg total protein (Mcal)		7.7	
Energy input/kg LPC (Mcal)		12.2	

$$\text{Energy}\,\frac{\text{output}}{\text{input}} = E$$

Source: Specific energy data according to Slesser (1973).
kcal = kilocalorie = calorie $\times 10^3$.
Mcal = Megacalorie = calorie $\times 10^6$.
Gcal = Gigacalorie = calorie $\times 10^9$.

TABLE 22.7. ENERGY REQUIREMENT FOR PROCESSING OF GREEN PLANTS ACCORDING TO FIG. 22.2A PROCESS

Energy input for plant production (according to Table 22.6)	4.16 Gcal/ha
Energy output from plant yields (according to Table 22.6)	29.75 Gcal/ha
Energy input during the process	
Electrical energy (3100 kcal/kWh)	4426 Mcal
Heating oil (9600 kcal/kg)	2587 Mcal
Total	7.01 Gcal/ha
Product output	
3465 kg of green flour pellet	CP = 15%
1386 kg of LPC	CP = 60%
210 kg pigment concentrate	10 g/kg xanthophyll
Total energy input (Gcal ha^{-1} $year^{-1}$)	11.2
Total energy output (Gcal ha^{-1} $year^{-1}$)	19.2
Protein yield (kg ha^{-1} $year^{-1}$)	1401
Energy input (kg total protein/Mcal)	7.99
Energy input (kg LPC/Mcal)	15.5
Energy $\frac{\text{output}}{\text{input}} = E$	1.71

Source: Specific energy data according to Slesser (1973).
kcal = kilocalorie = calorie $\times 10^3$.
Mcal = Megacalorie = calorie $\times 10^6$.
Gcal = Gigacalorie = calorie $\times 10^9$.

Leaf protein production is also advantageous in comparison with the data on soybeans, especially if one assesses the area requirements for the production of an identical quantity of protein. In the case of low per ha production of soybeans, the yield intensity is 2–3 Mcal/kg of protein. However, in the 1000–2000 kg/ha protein yield, this value rises to 16–19 Mcal. In the comparison of cultivation systems, we may consider the fact that the leaf protein fraction, or at least a considerable part of it, produced by the mentioned energy data is suitable for direct human nutrition, which emphasizes further the energy considerations. In the comparison of the leaf protein system with soybean production, data were computed based on the protein content of the yield of soybeans. If this protein is to be used as feed or isolate for human nutrition, the energy needs for further processing such as grinding, pressing, and extraction isolation unit processes should be added to the previously given data. The energy needs of different protein isolates prepared from various seed proteins are 10–15 Mcal/kg, if we take into account that the energy requirement of leaf protein processing is only one-third of the other sources.

If the energy required for processing LPC is compared with that needed for producing single cell protein, an even more favorable comparison is obtained.

In the energy requirement of this process the extraction of leaf protein is not included, only the regeneration cost of the added fat is accounted for. The 55 MT/ha fresh yield of alfalfa is the average harvest of farms supplying the plant at Tamási. With a yearly precipitation of 550–600 mm, this area cannot be considered an ideal location for alfalfa cultivation. With favorable climatic conditions and supplemental irrigation, protein yield/ha/year could improve considerably. The results of energy evaluation of this fractionation process, which is practically identical with the production method outlined in Fig. 22.1A, are favorable.

SUMMARY

In this chapter we have summarized our efforts in the process of leaf protein production, which is progressing in three major areas:

(1) Increase in utilization value of the leaf protein fraction, especially of the chloroplastic fraction, and broadening the range of its utilization.
(2) The development of unit processes of the technology of fractionation with the aim of increasing the value of products made from the green plant material.
(3) Overall energy requirements of the process are lowered because plant residues may be used as combustible material.

On the basis of available data and experience there can be no further dispute that considerably more organic matter (including protein) can be produced from green plants per unit area/year than with traditional agricultural systems. This higher yield is also the result of the fact that the growing area can be utilized to its maximum biological productivity with a better degree of photosynthetical effect.

However, the obtainable nutrient or increased protein yield can be adequately utilized only under certain conditions:

The utilization value of the protein quality obtainable from green plants should be at least equal to the traditional sources of protein. If we consider the composition and organoleptic properties of the chloroplast protein fraction and take into account that this fraction is ⅔–¾ of the total extractable protein, then, at present, this condition has not been met. Precisely for this reason, this product has been utilized in a more restricted field of poultry nutrition, where its superior carotenoid pigment concentration produces yellow chicken carcasses and egg yolks.

In the initial stages of the development of this new protein source, this aim was acceptable as progress in the course of least resistance. At present, however, this is no longer the situation. Namely, there is a method for the modification of the green protein fraction whereby an increase in biological and utilization values can be achieved.This can also be accomplished in areas with less technological advancement. By supplementing the original process with an additional extraction procedure, it is possible to improve proteins to a level comparable to traditional sources.

Actually this could indicate such generalization of the leaf protein production methods that the differences and some disadvantages of this new protein source compared with the traditional ones could be resolved. The potential gains, such as increasing of protein production by species of raw material and the decrease of energy requirement, could then become primary factors.

The other stipulation is that the technology of fractionation of the green plant sources should be developed for different plant sources and should be suitable for local cultivation patterns. To evaluate these factors, we have collected sufficient industrial and semi-industrial data, and, in the framework of our developmental programs, the technology of utilization of various plant species is ready for industrial exploitation. It is extremely important to clear up the energy problems as well as consumer and marketing requirements in any given interval when examining the long-range viability of a new production system. This would provide a basis of comparison with other nutrient or protein production systems and offer some indication as to how a specific production method will meet the decrease in availability of fossil fuels, especially oil, as well as how these production methods can be utilized in those countries where the direct or indirect use of energy is already at a low level. The previously mentioned data, although not exam-

Fig. 22.3. Variable speed conveyor belt for plant material.

Fig. 22.4. The disintegrator.

ined in detail, demonstrate that the production of leaf protein concentrates from extraction and fractionation of green plants is viable from this point of view also. This process not only requires considerably less energy input per unit production of protein than other intensive and high energy-requiring processes, but there is a possibility that the energy requirement of the process can be supplied from the process itself. With some further process development, the energy requirement can be decreased more.

In examining the long-range possibilities of the green plant processing systems and leaf protein concentrate production, they appear to be the most useful for approximating and maintaining the steady state in comparison with other agricultural methods. Naturally, this extends into the coming decade. In the interest of utilizing these potentials as soon as possible, of primary importance is the dissemination of our available results for practical application.

Since 1977, in a pilot plant at the Institute of Agricultural Chemical Technology of the University of Technical Sciences, Budapest, the preparation of leaf protein concentrates for animal and human nutrition has been studied.

The processing capacity of this modern pilot plant is 600 kg fresh leafy

Fig. 22.5. Single screw press and expeller press for double pressing of pulp. Both are variable speed.

Fig. 22.6. Flottweg decanter for separating coagula.

Fig. 22.7. Westfalia separator for separating coagula.

Fig. 22.8. Filter aid-coated drum filter for filtering mother liquor after separating green protein.

Fig. 22.9. Wiegand vacuum evaporator for concentrating brown juice to syrup after coagulation of white protein.

Fig. 22.10. Anhydro spray dryer for drying protein coagula.

Fig. 22.11. Central control unit for directing entire operation of the production line.

plant material per hour. All the production steps are analyzed on a semi-industrial scale.

The plant material is carried along a conveyor belt of variable speed (Fig. 22.3) into the production line. The first unit process is the disintegration (Fig. 22.4). The disintegrator was designed and built by the university. The pulp is then taken to a single screw press (Model P-Special, Hans Vetter Maschinenfabrik, D-3500 Kassel-Bettenhausen, West Germany) and to an expeller press (Model No. 6, Anderson IBEC, Strongsville, Ohio 44136, U.S.A.) (presses are shown in Fig. 22.5). The speed of both presses is variable. With this double pressing, the dry matter of the pressed residue is increased to 50%. This step is very important for increasing LPC yield and energy saving during the drying of the pressed residue. The green juice is heat fractionated, and green protein is separated at 40°C, white protein at 75°C. The coagula are separated by a Flottweg decanter (Type Z 23-3, Flottweg Werk GmbH, D-8313 Vilsbiburg, West Germany, Fig. 22.6) and by a Westfalia separator (Type NA-7, Westfalia Separator AG, D-4740 Oelde 1, West Germany, Fig. 22.7). The mother liquor, after separation of the green protein, is filtered through a filter aid-coated drum filter built by the university (Fig. 22.8). After coagulation of the white protein, the brown juice is concentrated to a syrup in a Wiegand vacuum evaporator with a 400 kg/hr water evaporation capacity (Wiegand one-step evaporator, Wiegand

Karlsruhe GmbH, D-7505 Ettlingen, West Germany, Fig. 22.9). The syrup is mixed with the pressed residue and pelleted using a Kahl press (Type G/Z 20-28 Amandus Kahl Nachf. Maschinenfabrik, Reinbek/Hamburg, West Germany). The protein coagula are dried with an anhydro spray dryer (compact model, Anhydro A/S, DK-2860 Søborg-Kopenhagen, Denmark, Fig. 22.10).

The entire operation is directed from a central control panel (Fig. 22.11).

REFERENCES

AKESON, W.R. and STAHMANN, M.A. 1965. Nutritive value of leaf protein concentrate, an in vitro digestion study. J. Agric. Food Chem. *13*, 145.

ARKCOLL, D.B. 1973. The preservation and storage of leaf protein preparations. J. Sci. Food Agric. *24*, 437.

ARKCOLL, D.B. and FESTENSTEIN, G.M. 1971. A preliminary study of the agronomic factors affecting the yields of extractable leaf protein. J. Sci. Food Agric. *22*, 49.

BICKOFF, E.M. and KOHLER, G.O. 1974. Preparation of edible protein of leafy green crops such as alfalfa. U.S. Pat. 3,823,128. July 9.

BRAY, W.J., HUMPHRIES, C. and INERITEI, M.S. 1978. The use of solvents to decolourise leaf protein concentrate. J. Sci. Food Agric. *29*, 165.

BYERS, M. 1961. The extraction of protein from leaves of some plants growing in Ghana. J. Sci. Food Agric. *12*, 20.

BYERS, M. 1971. The amino acid composition of some leaf protein preparations. *In* Leaf Protein: Its Agronomy, Preparation, Quality and Use. N.W. Pirie (Editor). Blackwell Scientific Publications, Oxford.

CARLSSON, R. 1975. Centrospermae species as raw material for production of leaf protein. Ph.D. Thesis. Dept. Plant Physiology, Univ. of Lund, Fack, S-220 07, Lund, Sweden.

DAVYS, M.N.G. and PIRIE, N.W. 1963. Batch production of protein from leaves. J. Agric. Eng. Res. *8*, 70.

HOLLIDAY, R.H. 1976. The efficiency of solar energy conversion by the whole crop. *In* Food Production and Consumption. A.N. Duckham, J.G.W. Jones and E.H. Roberts (Editors). North-Holland Publishing Co., Amsterdam, Oxford. American Elsevier Publishing Co., New York.

HOLLÓ, J., KOCH, L. and KOCH, B. 1969. Some aspects of using leaf proteins in increasing the production of nutritive substances. Voeding *9*, 489.

JOSHI, R.M. 1971. The yields of leaf protein that can be extracted from crops of Aurangabad. *In* Leaf Protein: Its Agronomy, Preparation, Quality and Use. N.W. Pirie (Editor). Blackwell Scientific Publications, Oxford.

KOCH, L. 1973. Producing protein concentrates from green plants. Vaxtodling *28*, 129.

KOHLER, G.O., BICKOFF, E.M., SPENCER, R.R., WITT, S.O. and KNUCKLES, B.E. 1968. Wet processing of alfalfa for animal feed products. 10th Tech. Alfalfa Conf., Reno, July 1968, U.S. Dep. Agric. Proc. *ARS-74-46*.

LEXANDER, K., CARLSSON, R., SCHALEN, V., SIMONSSON, A. and LUNDBORG, T. 1970. Quantities and qualities of leaf protein concentrates from wild species and crop species grown under controlled conditions. Ann. Appl. Biol. *66*, 193.

LOOMIS, R.S. and GERAKIS, P.A. 1975. Productivity of agricultural ecosystems. *In* Photosynthesis and Productivity in Different Environments. IBP Handb. *3*. J.P. Cooper (Editor). Cambridge Univ. Press, Cambridge.

OKE, O.L. 1966. The introduction of leaf protein into the Nigerian diet. Nutrition (Paris) *20*, 18.

PIRIE, N.W. 1966. Leaf protein as a human food. Science *152*, 1701–1705.

PIRIE, N.W. 1971. Leaf Protein: Its Agronomy, Preparation, Quality and Use. IBP Handb. *20*. Blackwell Scientific Publications, Oxford.

ROUELLE, N.M. 1773. Observations on starches or green fractions of plants, and on glutinous or vegetable-animal substances. J. Med. Chir. Pharm. *40*, 59. (French)

SLESSER, M. 1973. Energy subsidy as a criterion in food policy planning. J. Sci. Food Agric. *24*, 1193.

STAHMANN, M.A. 1968. The potential for protein production from green plants. Econ. Bot. *22*, 73.

STAHMANN, M.A. 1974. Coagulation of protein from the juices of green plants by fermentation and the preservation thereof. U.S. Pat. 3,975,546. Aug. 17.

TELEK, L. 1979. Preparation of leaf protein concentrates in lowland humid tropics. *In* Tropical Foods, Vol. 2. G.I. Inglett and G. Charalambous (Editors). Academic Press, New York.

23

The Economics of Green Crop Fractionation and Leaf Protein Production

Walter J. Bray

The direct fractionation of fresh green crops represents the means by which it is possible to obtain the maximum yield of usable protein per unit area of land cultivated (Akeson and Stahmann 1966). In addition, the resultant leaf protein product has a nutritional quality superior to that of other vegetable proteins (Akeson and Stahmann 1965). However, this product will only be used in foods and feeds if it offers the consumer cost benefits over other proteins. Thus, the desirability of fractionating green crops and producing leaf protein is, in the final analysis, simply a matter of economics.

(1) Operations must be profitable from both the agricultural and the processing standpoints.
(2) The overall process must make efficient use of resources such as raw materials, labor, and energy.
(3) There must be a market for all products.
(4) Their selling prices must be both realistic and competitive.

From a general standpoint, ventures directed toward the production and sale of forage fractionation products must be more profitable and give a higher return on investment than others in the agribusiness area, otherwise there is no incentive for anyone to undertake them.

It is intended herein to consider the overall economics of green crop fractionation, to establish a guide relating to product selling prices, and to investigate the major process variables as they affect economics. It is hoped, thereby, to show the need for improving the efficiency of certain operations and reducing certain costs in order to increase the profitability and competitiveness of fractionation products.

However, it is desirable to first review previous work on leaf protein economics.

PREVIOUS WORK

Until recently, the matter of economics was almost completely overlooked by workers interested in leaf protein. Occasionally a possible price for the product was mentioned but it was usually not substantiated with data. In two early papers that did investigate the subject (Raymond and Tilley 1956; Mendes 1965), leaf protein was assumed to be the only product of value. Since it represented only about 10% of the dry weight of the crop, the conclusion, as one would expect, was that leaf protein concentrate would be very expensive and therefore the process would not be viable.

In spite of this, by 1970 there was limited commercial production of leaf protein concentrate by Batley-Janss Enterprises of Brawley, California (Bray 1973A), with the product being sold profitably to poultry producers at a price about 25% above that of soybean meal (Batley 1978). Yet at the same time the Protein Advisory Group of the United Nations (1970) was issuing Statement No. *11* in which they quoted a very high price for LPC, implying it could not be made profitably. In retrospect, politics was a major factor in the issuance of this statement.

An annotated bibliography of the major papers on the subject of leaf protein production economics is presented in Appendix Table A.1. Fifteen papers are listed with the first two primarily of historical interest. Of the remaining papers, nine deal with fractionation in conjunction with commercial forage crop dehydration, while the others are concerned with economics in relation to large farming operations.

Of the papers concerned with the effect of fractionation on the economics of forage dehydration, the most significant are the study of Vosloh *et al.* (1976), updated by Enochian *et al.* (1977), and the work by Wilkins *et al.* (1977). The Vosloh *et al.* (1976) paper considers the U.S. Dept. of Agriculture's Pro-Xan fractionation process applied to a large alfalfa dehydration operation. The economic analysis showed a return on the multimillion dollar investment required. It also showed that the return was very little better than for a regular dehydration plant.

The Enochian *et al.* (1977) paper updates in great detail the work of Vosloh *et al.* (1976). It particularly points out the very favorable effects that increasing the yield of LPC has on economics. At a 12% yield, the ROI (return on investment) is 47.7%, about the same as was found by Vosloh, while with an 18% yield, the ROI is 71.0%. The conclusion of both studies was that the economics of leaf protein production are highly favorable.

The Wilkins *et al.* (1977) paper reports on the development of a computer model in which 1480 possible systems related to the fractionation of green crops were studies. They found that the best system gave a return on capital only equal to that obtained with conventional green crop dehydration. However, when a fractionation operation was added to an existing drying operation, high returns were obtained on the extra capital. In general, the authors did not present an optimistic view of the economic possibilities of green crop fractionation.

Of the papers dealing with the "on-farm" use of the forage fractionation process, the most detailed is the work by Dumont and Boyce (1976). Using a linear programming model the authors showed that forage fractionation has an economic advantage over present forage conservation methods if low cost, high throughput machinery is developed. The other papers related to "on-farm" fractionation operations also reach an optimistic conclusion as to the economics of the process.

At this point it is important to realize that while a great amount of work has been done on green crop fractionation, there is much more to be done, work that will increase the yield and quality of the products, and that will substantially reduce the cost of the equipment needed. All of this will improve the economics of the process.

Based on the analyses of green crop fractionation that have been published to date, one can conclude that the process has the potential to improve the economic viability of a crop drying operation, and to substantially boost income when applied "on-the-farm."

CONTEXT OF EVALUATION

It is important to recognize that green crop fractionation can be applied in three general situations: (1) an "on-farm" operation in which the farmer would utilize all the products himself or sell only the leaf protein concentrate; (2) a commerical crop drying operation in which all the products would be sold; and (3) a village industry in a developing country in which the products would be sold or used as best suited the local situation.

Although the application of fractionation in a village setting is of extreme interest in areas perennially short of nutritious foodstuffs, no basic data are currently available to evaluate economics in this context.

An evaluation of on-farm economics also presents problems, particularly as to the relative value of the various fractions when the farmer utilizes them himself. Barring a variety of specific experiences in this area, the only approach that can be taken seems to be the one used by Dumont and Boyce (1976) in which a relationship is developed between the size of the farm and the justifiable investment in fractionation equipment.

On the other hand, the crop drying industry is well established. A market exists for the dehydrated forage product and fairly detailed cost information is available from a number of operations. Since green crop fractionation can beneficially be applied as part of the overall dehydration process, this provides a convenient basis upon which to evaluate economics.

It may be assumed that a market also exists for leaf protein concentrate based on the earlier sale of the product to the poultry industry in the United States (Bray 1973A) and the current marketing of LPC in France (de Mathan 1977). It thus seems reasonable to calculate the expected selling prices for the various products of green crop fractionation, and to apply these prices to an economic evaluation of the effects of the major process variables.

PRODUCT VALUES

In the standard crop drying operation there is only one product, but when fractionation is applied as a first stage in the process there will be three: a protein-containing fibrous material, a leaf protein product, and a solubles fraction. Economics dictate that all must be utilized in some way and command a price based on competitive value.

The fiber fraction is generally equivalent to regular dehydrated forage, but since its protein content is below the standard 17% of Dehy, it is expected to find application only in cattle feeding, probably in direct competition with hay. The price obtainable will depend on both protein content and roughage value.

Over a prolonged period of time, the protein value is determined primarily by the price of 44% protein soybean meal. Roughage value is determined by the price of dry forage crops extrapolated to a zero protein level.

A comparative analysis of prices of 44% soybean meal, 17% protein dehydrated alfalfa, and 13% protein hay over the past several years reveals the relationship shown graphically in Fig. 23.1. From this, given the pro-

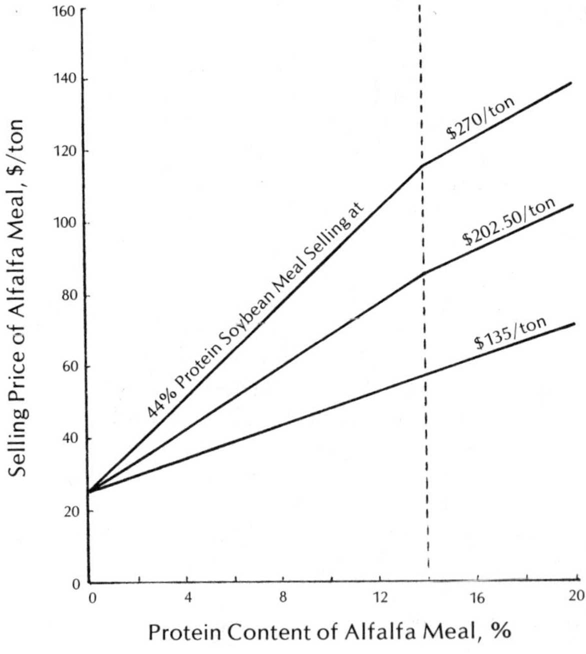

Fig. 23.1. Relationship between selling prices of various protein content alfalfa meals and 44% protein soybean meal.

tein content of the fresh crop, the degree of fractionation, and the current cost of soybean meal, it is possible to determine the expected selling price of the dried fiber fraction or of regular dehydrated forage if fractionation is not used.

The value of the leaf protein concentrate will depend on the end use. It can be used as food for humans or for feeding nonruminant animals and poultry. At this stage, however, consumption by man is not sufficiently advanced to be considered in an economic evaluation.

LPC has proven to be a good source of protein for pigs and other nonruminants (Cheeke 1974), but in such applications its value would be essentially the same as that of soybean meal. On the other hand, when used for poultry, the contained xanthophyll is also of value, and this the product would command a premium over other protein sources (Kuzmicky *et al.* 1977).

The relationship between xanthophyll content and protein content for a range of alfalfa products is shown in Fig. 23.2. Using these data and assuming that the price of contained xanthophyll ranges from $0.07 to

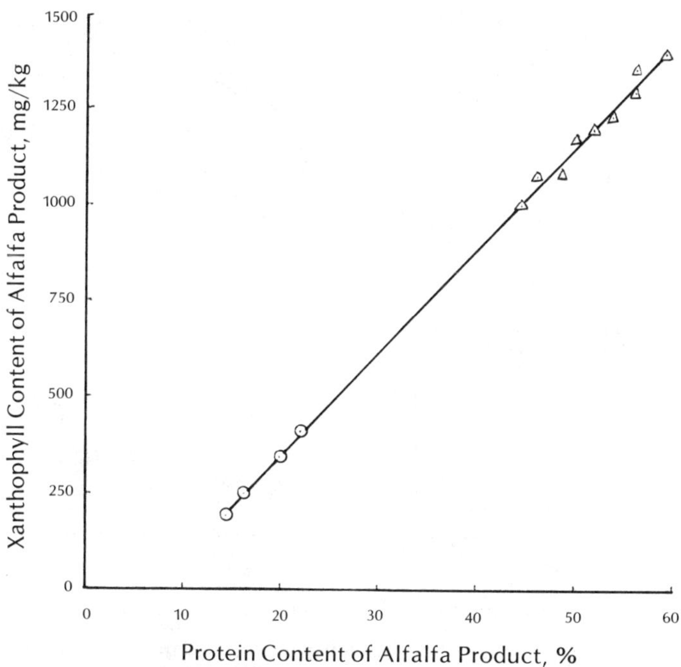

Fig. 23.2. Relationship between protein and xanthophyll contents of alfalfa products. ⊙ *Am. Dehydrators Assoc. (1965).* △ *Bray (1973B).* Note: Values are on a 7% moisture product.

$0.21 per g per MT of product, as the price of 44% soybean meal varies from $100 to $300 a MT, it is possible to calculate an expected selling price for leaf protein concentrate. This is presented graphically in Fig. 23.3.

The third product resulting from fractionation is the solubles: nonprotein nitrogen compounds, sugars, and soluble minerals such as potassium. This material can be used as a fertilizer, but in this case its value is comparatively low (Koegel *et al.* 1974). In all probability the cost of application would counterbalance the value of the contained minerals so that utilized in this manner the fraction would have an actual net worth of zero. In practice, this application would be of interest mainly with fractionation operations directly adjacent to farmland.

Alternatively, the solubles can be concentrated in a multiple effect evaporator to yield a molasses which could be sold as such for animal feeding. The utility of the concentrated alfalfa solubles in this application has been demonstrated by Perry *et al.* (1974).

An analysis of the prices of molasses and dehydrated alfalfa over the past several years reveals that alfalfa is usually worth somewhat more than

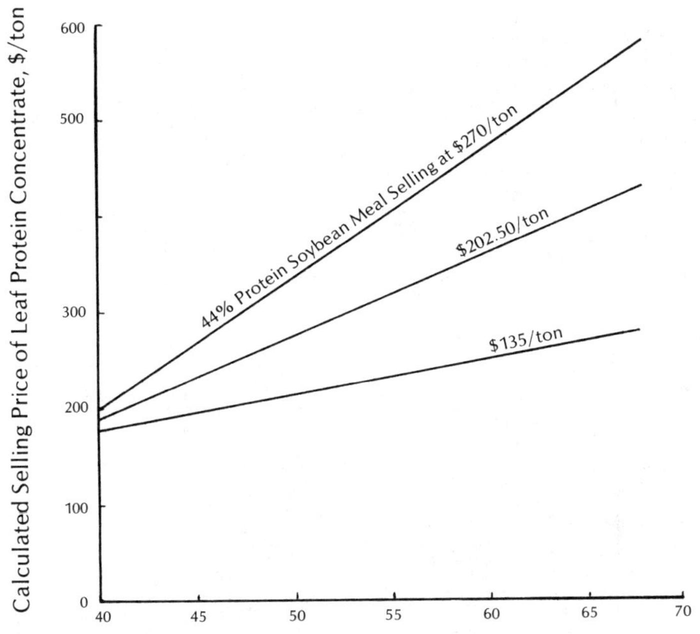

Fig. 23.3. Calculated relationship between selling prices of alfalfa leaf protein concentrate and 44% protein soybean meal.

molasses on a solids basis. Accordingly, the solubles, following concentration, should be applied back to the fiber and sold as part of this fraction rather than as a separate product.

In the evaluations that follow, the solubles have been assumed both at zero net value and at the value of the fiber in order to provide a means to compare the economics of concentrating the residual liquor.

ECONOMICS IN RELATION TO FORAGE DEHYDRATION

In order to determine the economic effect that green crop fractionation would have on a forage dehydration operation, it is necessary first to calculate or assume certain base conditions. This has been done, and the data are shown in Table 23.1.

TABLE 23.1. BASIC DATA FOR ECONOMIC ANALYSIS

Crop
Alfalfa with 80% moisture, 20% protein (DB, dry basis)
Cost: $25/ST (DB)
Dehydration operation
Production: 12,500 ST/year; 20 ST/hr green feed
Manufacturing cost: $85.70/ST
Selling price: $97/ST
Fractionation-dehydration operation
Fiber fraction manufacturing cost: $83.75/ST
Fiber fraction selling price: $86.50/ST
LPC yield: 13.5% of dry matter
LPC manufacturing cost: $122.50/ST
LPC selling price: $310/ST
Capital investment: $500,000 LPC; $250,000 solubles concentration
Other data
Price of 44% protein soybean meal: $202.50/ST
Price of fuel: $1/million BTU

1 ST (short ton) = 0.9 MT (metric ton).

When the solubles are used as fertilizer, i.e., no value, annual sales with a fixed amount of crop increase by about 8%, and because of the added value of the leaf protein, the profit increases by over 90%. The gross return on investment for the fractionation equipment of 25.9% makes the process of interest to a commercial operator.

On the other hand, if the solubles are concentrated with the dryer waste heat and returned to the fiber, sales increase by 20% and profitability by almost 150%. The gross return on the capital investment is 27.7%, only marginally higher than when the solubles are used for their fertilizer value.

Even more important than the case-specific comparison just given is the effect fractionation will have on the dehydration operation when there is a change in some of the uncontrollable variables such as the cost of fuel and the price paid for the crop.

In the case of increased crop cost, Fig. 23.4, the combination of frac-

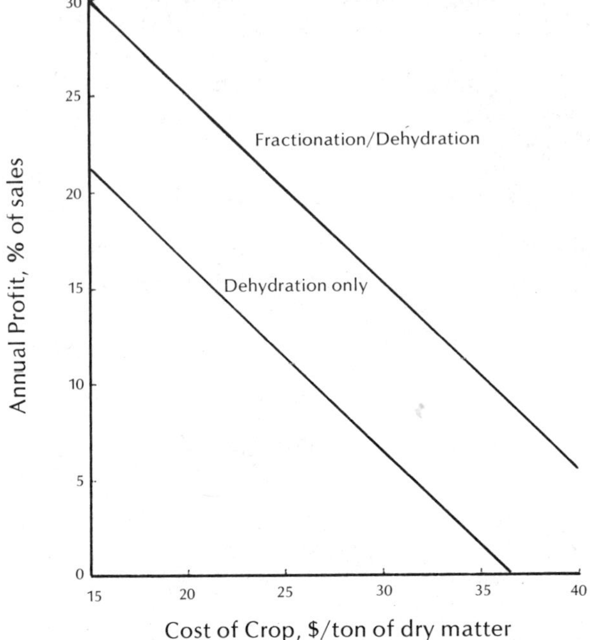

Fig. 23.4. Effect of crop cost on profitability of dehydration and fractionation/dehydration operations. No value assumed for residual liquor solids.

tionation and dehydration gives a larger profit than dehydration alone at all values of the crop. At the point at which there is no profit from a regular operation, there is still almost a 10% profit on sales with the combination. Fractionation thus protects the operator to some degree against a loss of profits when the increased cost of raw material cannot be compensated for by increasing the product price.

Fuel is another major cost item in the production of dehydrated forage. Since far less fuel is required to dry the fiber following dewatering, increased fuel costs have a much less disastrous effect of operational profitability, Fig. 23.5. When there is no profit from a plain dehydration plant, the combination of fractionation and dehydration will still return a 16% profit on sales. It is also to be noted that the higher the fuel cost, the greater return on the investment in fractionation equipment.

Owners of dehydration plants have, of course, recognized the problem of increasing fuel costs and turned to field wilting or partial field drying to overcome it. By this technique the moisture content of the crop is reduced before dehydration so that fuel consumption is lowered.

Reducing crop moisture also has the economically beneficial effect of permitting more material to be processed in a given time in a particular dryer since dryer capacity is primarily a function of evaporative loading. In

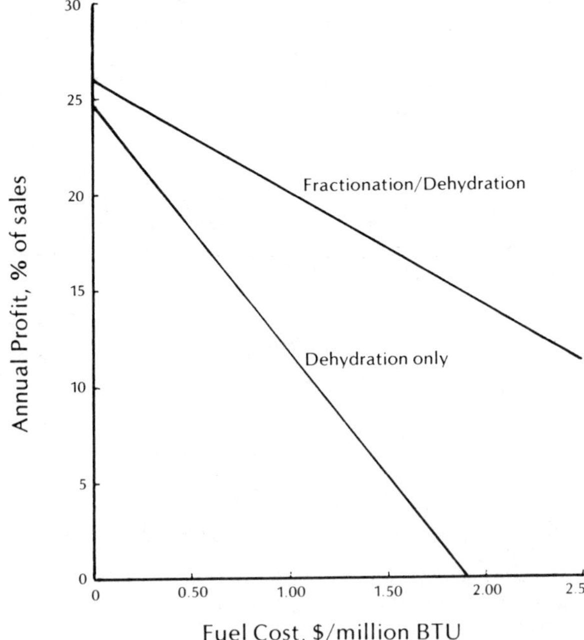

Fig. 23.5. Effect of fuel cost on profitability of dehydration and fractionation/dehydration operations. No value is assumed for residual liquor solids.

fact, if enough moisture is removed by pre-drying, the dryer throughput can be increased by about 50% (Bray 1977), provided, of course, the crop is available to the dryer operator. The result is more product resulting in more sales and increased annual profits.

Fractionation, in which the moisture content of the fiber is reduced by dewatering, accomplishes the same result. As shown in Fig. 23.6, the annual profit and the return on investment both increase dramatically as crop availability and hence annual production increase up to the capacity of the dryer to physically handle the dry matter.

FACTORS RELATED TO FRACTIONATION ECONOMICS

In order to fully understand fractionation economics and to consider the impact of the process on a dehydration operation, it is also necessary to evaluate the effect of fractionation variables. The more important of these are the percentage yield of the leaf protein concentrate product and the investment required for fractionation equipment.

As has already been seen, the leaf protein concentrate is a more valuable product than either the fiber or the solubles. Accordingly, the more LPC produced through fractionation, the more profitable the overall operation.

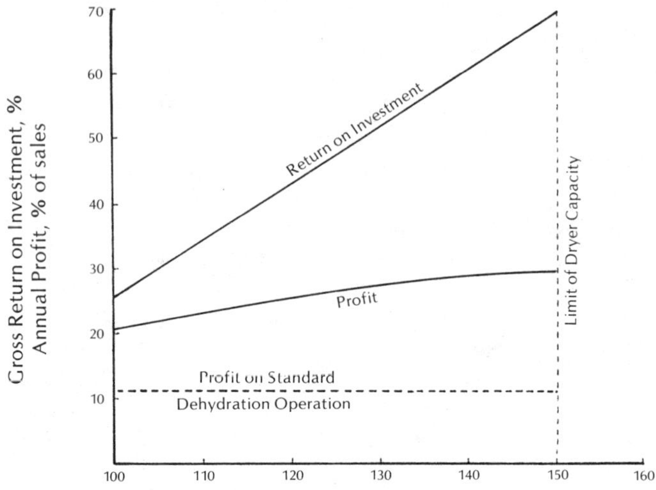

Fig. 23.6. Effect of increased crop availability on economics of fractionation/dehydration operation. No value assumed for residual liquor solids.

The effect of leaf protein yield on both profitability and return on investment is shown graphically in Fig. 23.7.

In regard to this, note that LPC yield is affected by three main factors: (1) the degree of cell rupture of the crop, (2) the percentage extraction of available proteins, and (3) the split between the solubles and the protein fraction in the juice. Improved equipment to give more cell rupture and techniques such as the application of liquor to the pulped crop prior to dewatering will have a very beneficial effect on process economics (Enochian *et al.* 1977). Likewise, minimizing proteolysis in the cut crop and in the juice will help to increase the amount of recoverable protein concentrate from the juice.

The other major factor affecting the economics is the cost of the equipment. Fig. 23.8 shows the relationship between the capital investment and both profitability and return on investment for a case in which the solubles are used for their fertilizer value and one in which they are concentrated and added back to the fiber. As would be expected, equipment cost has comparatively little effect on profitability but is by far the most significant factor in determining return on investment and, thus, the economic desirability of the process.

The desirability of concentrating the solubles fraction is determined by balancing the cost of the heat recovery equipment against the value of the

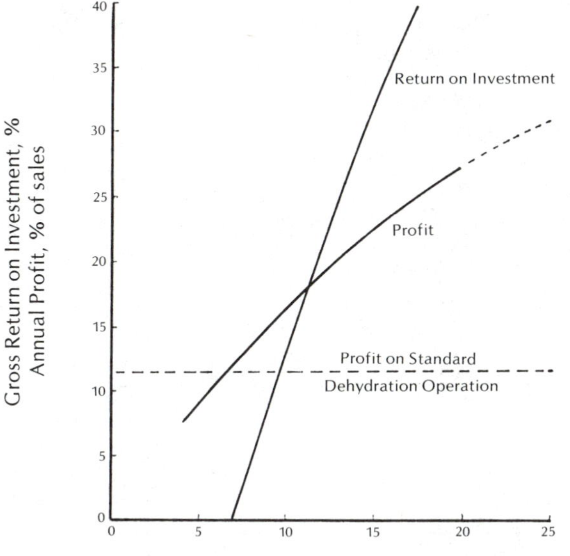

Fig. 23.7. Effect of leaf protein concentrate yield on economics of fractionation/dehydration operation. No value assumed for residual liquor solids.

extra product recovered by this procedure. For the standard case, there is only a marginal increase in the return on investment with the incorporation of a waste heat recovery unit resulting from the increased production of the fiber, Table 23.2.

OTHER APPLICATIONS OF FRACTIONATION

The economics of green crop fractionation have been examined specifically as they relate to the crop drying industry. However, the process can be applied in other ways to the processing of forages and leafy crops. In some cases, the fiber could be sold as such for cattle feeding, while the solubles could be applied back to the fiber following protein extraction, and the wet mixture used for ruminant animal feeding. In both cases the fiber would probably have to be consumed within one day. It may be assumed that the leaf protein would be processed in the normal manner and sold as a dry product with either variation.

The economic effects of these two alternatives are compared in Table 23.3 with that for "standard" fractionation-dehydration. Although total sales decrease slightly with the marketing of moist or wet, rather than dried, fiber, profit as a percentage of sales increased markedly. And although there is the same capital investment in all three cases, the return on this

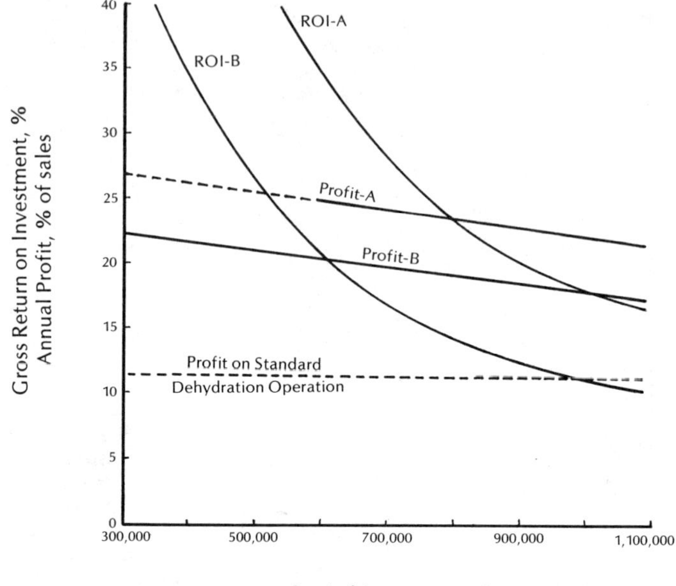

Fig. 23.8. Effect of total capital cost on economics of fractionation/dehydration operation. ROI-A—Return on investment with residual liquor concentrated to molasses, assumed at value of meal. ROI-B—Return on investment with residual liquor assumed at no value. Profit A—Profit with residual liquor concentrated to molasses, assumed at value of meal. Profit B—Profit with residual liquor assumed at no value.

TABLE 23.2. COMPARATIVE PROFITABILITIES

Forage dehydration		
Annual sales	$1,212,500	
Annual profit	$ 141,250	(11.6% of sales)
Fractionation and dehydration		
Solubles used for fertilizer		
Annual sales	$1,312,437	
Annual profit	$ 270,624	(20.6% of sales)
Return on investment	25.9%	
Solubles concentrated and added to fiber		
Annual sales	$1,458,406	
Annual profit	$ 349,342	(24.0% of sales)
Return on investment	27.7%	

investment is increased dramatically if the dehydration operation is eliminated.

When storage of the forage is required before feeding it to ruminants, fractionation can still be used with very beneficial results. The dewatered

TABLE 23.3. ECONOMIC COMPARISON[1] OF FRACTIONATION ALTERNATIVES

Sale of Dehydrated Fiber		
Fiber selling price	$ 86.50/ST	
Solubles selling price	zero—used as fertilizer	
Annual sales	$1,312,437	
Annual profit	$ 270,000	(20.6% of sales)
Capital investment	$ 500,000	
Return on investment	25.9%	
Sale of Moist Fiber		
Fiber selling price	$ 66.60/ST (dry basis)	
Solubles selling price	zero—used as fertilizer	
Annual sales	$1,130,850	
Annual profit	$ 289,787	(25.6% of sales)
Capital investment	$ 500,000	
Return on investment	58.0%	
Sale of Wet Fiber		
Fiber selling price	$ 49.50/ST (dry basis)	
Solubles selling price	same as fiber	
Annual sales	$1,058,344	
Annual profit	$ 316,406	(29.9% of sales)
Capital investment	$ 500,000	
Return on investment	63.3%	

[1]General data given in Table 23.1.

fiber can easily be ensiled with the advantage of reduced silo losses compared with fresh forage and increased field yields over partially sun-dried material (Koegel *et al.* 1974). Alternatively, the forage can be sun-dried after fractionation by spreading it on a prepared pad. It is anticipated that the usual respiratory losses associated with haymaking (Bray 1977) would be greatly reduced by such a procedure, and the profitability from fractionation would be high.

CONCLUSION

Green crop fractionation in conjunction with dehydration greatly increases the profitability of operations, as has been shown. In order to obtain the greatest economic benefit from fractionation, the leaf protein yield should be maximized, the throughput of the plant should be as high as possible, and the capital investment kept to a minimum.

However, commercial dehydration is only a minor part of the forage processing industry. Accordingly, for green crop fractionation to have a major impact, ways must be found to broaden its application. The "on-farm" use of the process in conjunction with either silage or haymaking represents ways to accomplish this. New ventures involving the direct feeding of the moist or wet fiber to cattle and the outside sale of leaf protein products are others. At this point, the economic potential of green crop fractionation and leaf protein production is excellent. But to realize this potential it remains for more innovative individuals to apply the process.

REFERENCES

AKESON, W.R. and STAHMANN, M.A. 1965. Nutritive value of leaf protein concentrate, an in vitro digestion study. Agric. Food Chem. *13*, 145–148.

AKESON, W.R. and STAHMANN, M.A. 1966. Leaf protein concentrate: A comparison of protein production per acre of forage with that from seed and animal crops. Econ. Bot. *20*, 244–250.

AM. DEHYDRATORS ASSOC. 1965. A Study of the Major Nutritional Constituents of Dehydrated Alfalfa. American Dehydrators Association, Kansas City, MO.

BATLEY, W.R. 1978. Personal communication. Brawley, CA.

BRAY, W.J. 1973A. Leaf protein recovery. Chem. Eng. *80*, (2) 76–77.

BRAY, W.J. 1973B. Unpublished data. El Centro, CA.

BRAY W.J. 1977. A consideration of wilting in the crop drying industry. Grass-J. Br. Assoc. Green Crop Driers *19*, 28–30.

CHEEKE, P.R. 1975. Nutritional evaluation of alfalfa protein concentrate with rats, swine, and rabbits. Proc. 12th Tech. Alfalfa Conf., Overland Park, Kansas, Nov. 1974. ARS-ADA-1.

DE MATHAN, O. 1977. Techno-economic comparison of alfalfa treatments. 7th Eur. Symp. Food Product and Process Selection in the Food Ind. Eindhoven, Netherlands, Sept. 1977.

DUMONT, A.G. and BOYCE, D.S. 1976. Leaf protein production and use on the farm: An economic study. J. Br. Grassl. Soc. *31*, 153–163.

ENOCHIAN, R.V., KOHLER, G.O., EDWARDS, R.H., KUXMICKY, D.D. and VOSLOH, C.J., JR. 1977. Leaf protein concentrate (Pro-Xan) from alfalfa: An updated economic evaluation. Am. Soc. Agric. Eng. Pap. *77-6538*.

KOEGEL, R.G., BARRINGTON, G.P. and BRUHN, H.D. 1974. Harvesting and processing equipment for alfalfa juice protein concentrate. 4th Annu. Alfalfa Symp. Univ. Wisconsin, Madison.

KUZMICKY, D.D., LIVINGSTON, A.L., KNOWLES, R.E., KOHLER, G.O., GUENTHNER, E., OLSON, O.E. and CARLSON, C.W. 1977. Xanthophyll availability of alfalfa leaf protein concentrate (Pro-Xan) for broilers and laying hens. Poult. Sci. *56*, 1504–1509.

MENDES, C.B. 1965. Investigation into the production of a high protein concentrate from leaves for inclusion into the diets of infants and children. Sci. Res. Counc. (Jamaica) Tech. Rep. *1/65*.

PERRY, T.W., BEESON, W.H., DABELL, W.R., KOHLER, G.O. and GOUGH, F.A. 1974. Effect of alfalfa solubles on urea utilization by beef cattle. J. Anim. Sci. *39*, 1158–1164.

PRO. ADVISORY GROUP U.N. 1970. PAG statement on leaf protein concentrate. Protein Advisory Group of the U.N., PAG Statement *11*.

RAYMOND, W.F. and TILLEY, J.M.A. 1956. The extraction of protein concentrates from leaves. Colon. Plant Anim. Prod. *6*, 3–19.

VOSLOH, C.J., JR., EDWARDS, R.H., ENOCHIAN, R.V., KUZMICKY, D.D.

and KOHLER, G.O. 1976. Leaf protein concentrate (Pro-Xan) from alfalfa: An economic evaluation. Econ. Res. Ser., U.S. Dep. Agric., Econ. Rep. *346*.

WILKINS, R.J., HEATH, S.B., ROBERTS, W.P., FOXELL, P.R. and WINDRAM, A. 1977. Green crop fractionation: An economic analysis. Br. Grassl. Res. Inst., Hurley, U.K., Tech. Rep. *19*.

Part IV

LPC Research Around the World

24

Introducing a Protein Extraction System to Agricultural Practice in Developing Countries

Henry T. Ostrowski-Meissner[1] *and Teresa M. Ostrowski-Meissner*

POTENTIAL AND SOME LIMITATIONS

In recent years, intensification of both food production and agricultural practices has become a complex, multidisciplinary, worldwide project, and various approaches to this internationally important problem—not only in developing countries—are demonstrated continuously in the literature. From studying reports from a number of conferences conducted under the auspices of various international bodies and recognized institutions in various parts of the world, it appears that the most sensible concept with the greatest potential for intensification of food production is that based on the integration of various types of animal husbandry within physically well-defined local ecosystems. Such animal production is referred to as complex integrated production across the woodland-nonwoodland and aquatic ecosystems, where various animal species, treated as variants of intensive (and extensive as well) cultures (polyculture), and growing together as compatible species, utilize to the utmost such a polyculture by using the variety of types and forms of feed available and the wastes produced within such ecosystems.

Since protein extraction from grasslands in subtropical regions was shown as a potentially promising operation leading to substantial improvement in protein recovery from the agricultural ecosystem (Ostrowski-Meissner 1979A,C), an attempt has been made to assess the potential of

[1]This work was done while the author was at Balai Penelitian Ternak, Project for Animal Research and Development, Bogor, Indonesia (Commonwealth Scientific and Industrial Research Organization—Australia).

protein extraction from grasslands under agricultural conditions characteristic of developing countries in the Southeast Asian region.

In the Southeast Asian region, agriculture plays a predominant role in the economy, providing not only the staple food for the population but also vital exports and animal production, although it still is primarily a subsistence enterprise (Robinson 1977). A major goal of livestock production is to increase meat, milk, and egg production in order to bridge the protein gap that exists in the diet of the majority of people living in the area.

Practical examples of intensification of animal production within the specific ecosystem reported by Ho (1961), Woynarovich (1976), and Bardoch and Santerre (1979) have shown integrated polyculture systems as being extremely attractive and efficient forms of intensification of animal production which may easily be introduced to the agriculture practice in Southeast Asia.

Looking at resources of green vegetation and herbage available in developing countries in the Southeast Asian region, one can find waste areas of rubber plantations in which mixed herbage is grown. Mixed herbage grown in temperate and subtropical regions has been shown to be a valuable product for protein extraction purposes (Ostrowski-Meissner 1976, 1979A), yielding substantial quantities of leaf protein concentrate (LPC) from a unit of fresh weight herbage (Ostrowski-Meissner 1979C). Approximately two-thirds of the total recoverable proteins represent feed-grade, with the remaining one-third a food-grade product. While LPC feed-grade may be used as a source of protein, in the main substituting for the soya in poultry rations, LPC food-grade may be used as a proteinaceous food for direct human consumption. LPC food-grade may be used in various forms, i.e., as a protein food for schoolchildren in the form of a soy cake, custard, pie, or milkshake, and/or the like. Several school feeding schemes have proved to be successful among schoolchildren in India (Bray 1977; Kamalanathan and Devadas 1975) and in Nigeria (Olatunbosun *et al.* 1972). Taking into account both the efficiency of protein extraction from green vegetation in subtropical conditions and the typical agricultural ecosystem as demonstrated by Ho (1961), a theoretical model has been prepared (Fig. 24.1) schematically showing how protein extraction may be incorporated into the integrated polyculture in developing countries in the Southeast Asian region.

By integrating protein extraction from herbage grown in rubber plantations, in the alternative presented in Fig. 24.1, individual farmers would cut and process herbage before taking it home for goat and sheep feeding (as is customary at present). By removing the juice from the herbage, a farmer, carrying the same weight as usual, would carry nearly twice as much herbage DM (dry matter) as with unprocessed herbage. Hence, there would be more roughage DM for the farmer's sheep in the private small-scale holding.

Partially deproteinized herbage which still remains a full productive roughage for ruminants may be used as fresh, dried, or ensilaged. With

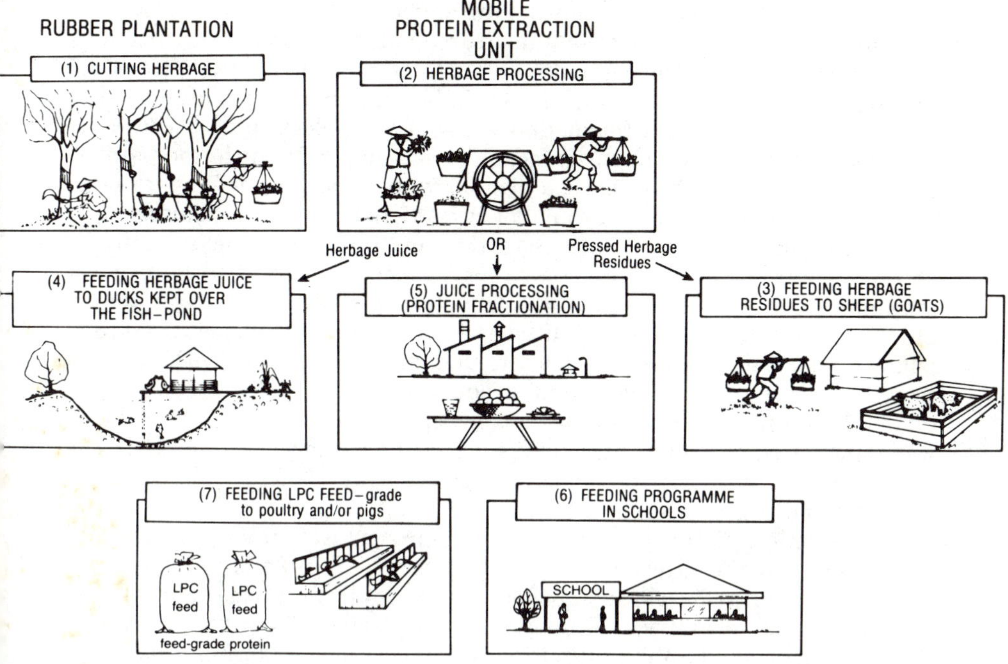

Fig. 24.1. Suggested integration of protein extraction into village-scale animal production (duck farming above the fishpond) with an alternative extension of the system into a village (school) feeding scheme and large-scale intensive poultry production.

more roughage DM available, as a result of protein extraction from herbage, for more sheep or goats in the private holding, an increase in productivity on the individual farm level may be expected with the possibility of the farmer's labor in herbage dejuicing bringing him an overall increase in income as well. This would be more likely when the herbage juice is used for protein recovery purposes, or, without processing, as a protein source, in duck farming. Duck farming may be combined with fish farming, as is the case on a number of farms in the Philippines, since duck droppings appear to be a suitable complementary feed for fish; hence, further intensification of animal production along the chain: agro-aquatic system (duck-fish).

Ho (1961) demonstrated an example of an integrated agro-aquatic system pioneered in Malaysia in which, instead of ducks, pigs were placed over the ponds. Water hyacinths grown on the part of the pond surface were incorporated into the pigfeed with water from the pond also being used to irrigate market garden crops. Such an integrated farming system, according to Ho (1961), can amortize itself and bear profit after three years—based on a year-round production basis.

It is reasonable to suggest that the introduction of the protein extraction system to the integrated agro-aquaculture should be connected with duck husbandry, using fast-growing ducks which reach their market size of 2.5 kg in 45 days, being convertors of protein of plant origin into high quality protein of animal origin (meat and eggs). The ducks could be grown or kept for egg production in sheds located over the ponds on slotted bamboo floors. Mutual benefits of such a system were reported by Woynarovich (1976), who showed the mutual benefits of fish and bird rearing, i.e., low capital investment—lower than that for intensive chicken culture, shortened growing time for ducks, better utilization of feed (ducks eat organisms not ordinarily eaten by fish such as aquatic weeds, frogs, snails, etc.), duck manure being distributed evenly throughout the pond and fish-pond, ducks being healthier, leaner, and having cleaner feathers than ducks raised in other conventional production systems. Bardoch and Santerre (1979) referred to the duck-*cum*-fish culture in Hungary where ducks were stocked in ponds after the fish reached fingerling size. As a result, the presence of ducks led to an increase of fish biomass of 0.3 to 0.4 MT/ha over conventional ponds without ducks.

Incorporation of the protein extraction procedure into the integrated polyculture, in the alternatives as presented in Fig. 25.1, indicates tremendous potential for further development, with the prospect of substantial increase in net primary protein production derived from the ecosystem for both human and animal nutrition. Using the model of integrated polyculture demonstrated by Ho (1961) in Malaysia, and including protein extraction from mixed herbage grown on rubber plantations, with ducks being used (instead of pigs as in the original Ho system), an agro-aquatic system has been suggested which is summarized schematically in the diagram in Fig. 24.2.

Despite the fact that sufficient information on the biological and engineering aspects of protein extraction from green vegetables is available to justify application of the system in agricultural practice in developed countries (Wilkins *et al.* 1977; Vosloh *et al.* 1976; Ostrowski-Meissner 1980), the prospects for the future adoption of the protein extraction system are inhibited by the relatively high costs of energy used for protein precipitation and optional drying of protein coagulum. There is still controversy as to the profitability of the protein extraction systems analyzed under the variety of economic circumstances. While Brown *et al.* (1975) concluded that for U.K. conditions the production of leaf protein concentrate was not economic, Wilkins *et al.* (1977) considered the protein extraction process a feasible alternative operation in a wide range of economic circumstances as examined in the U.K. in 1976.

According to Vosloh *et al.* (1976), who evaluated the economics of the large commercial-scale Pro-Xan process used for leaf protein concentrates production from alfalfa, the production of LPC in the United States was still economic under the price circumstances at that time.

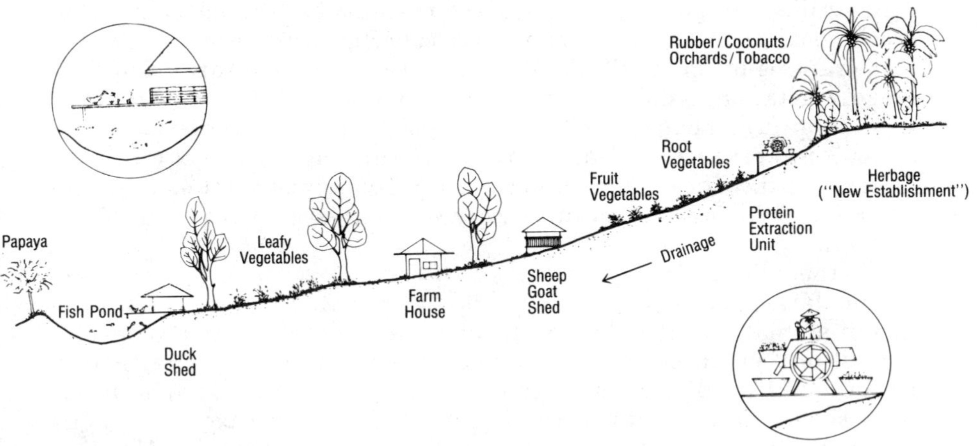

Fig. 24.2. A hypothetical integrated aqua-agricultural system (polyculture) in Southeast Asian productive circumstances, with the inclusion of the protein extraction operation on mixed herbage processing in the rubber plantation (with options for other leafy crops) and utilization of herbage juice in duck farming combined with fish farming.

The high price of fuel necessary for steam generation makes the protein extraction process strongly dependent upon fossil fuels, and because of this cannot be regarded as soundly based for the future (Spedding 1977). Taking into account that the supply of support energy required for the protein extraction purpose is limited in may countries, including developing ones, and that the cost of conventional energy sources is likely to increase rapidly, solar energy (and/or geothermal—if available) has been considered as a cheap alternative to fuel, which in subtropical and tropical regions would make the protein extraction process relatively independent of support energy input. At present, only 1.8% of the photosynthetically-active radiation (PAR) is recoverable from grasslands as a highly proteinaceous product. This is approximately only 1% of the total solar radiation available on the pasture surface. At the same time, approximately 60% of the total energy input in the protein extraction process has to be supplied in the form of fuel energy in order to recover protein from pasture herbage during the heat precipitation procedure. This part of the fuel energy can be easily replaced by the solar (and/or geothermal) energy obtained from the solar collectors of low grade (25° to 80°C) and/or medium grade heat (80° to 200°C). Several models of collectors have already been designed in Australia and have been proved to be an efficient means for supplying both low and high grade heat for use on small farms or in the large commercial units (Harding 1977).

Australian-designed flat plate collectors suited to the production of low grade heat and evacuated tubular glass collectors capable of operating at temperatures of up to 200°C, when involved in protein extraction from green vegetation, could make the process of protein recovery from green vegetation an economically attractive proposition for application in modern agricultural practice: at least, in terms of both the economy of the entire process and the efficient utilization of natural energy and protein resources available within any agricultural ecosystem—irrespective of geographical location.

Whether efficient protein extraction will be achieved in real practice—in routine farm operations—and can therefore contribute to the intensification of animal production in developing countries is a matter to involve agricultural engineering in the whole protein extraction process and in the optimization of the efficiency of the entire extraction system. It has been shown that the efficiency of protein extraction depends on many factors limiting the final protein recovery from pasture (Ostrowski-Meissner 1975) and other green herbage (Arkcoll and Festenstein 1971). Further research, however, is needed in order to develop a whole system of protein extraction feasible to be introduced to farming practice under various agriculture conditions specific to a particular country and/or climatic region.

SOCIOECONOMIC CONSIDERATIONS

There is always a danger in any developing country that any intensification of animal production and an introduction and incorporation of new farming forms into village communities will alter the well-established balance within the local agricultural ecosystem and within the well-established socioeconomic regional microcosm. However, it is reasonable to assume that there is a high possibility of social acceptance of the introduction of the protein extraction system into a well-integrated agricultural practice in the Southeast Asian region, where traditionally plant and animal husbandry have been complementary and interdependent. There is also a growing demand for an expanding animal industry (poultry, pigs) to cater to the simultaneous growth in the demand for protein concentrates. Hence, LPCs could well be the answer.

In Southeast Asia, tradition has secured the countryside's orientation toward the production of such food crops as rice, corn, and cassava, rather than intensive animal husbandry. The attitudes do not change easily and these limitations are very real, especially if the new concepts and innovations happen to conflict with traditional patterns in the village economy. Another area for experimental work which would benefit the animal husbandry industry in Southeast Asia is not only to introduce new grasses, better suited to the tropical conditions of constant high temperatures and heavy annual precipitation, but also to look into a more efficient use of the grasses in the fields, on the sides of the dykes, and at the roadsides, which at present tend no to be grazed by the animals but rather are cut by farmers and carried to the animals locked up in the village pen. This system of herbage harvest, transport, and subsequent use as a fodder by the vast majority of individual farmers in Southeast Asian countries forms the basis for the introduction of the protein extraction system into the village communities as a part of the already well-established and familiar routine. It goes without saying that to build onto the social concepts already understood is halfway to having an innovation communally accepted.

It is not difficult to theorize about the socioeconomic benefits which the introduction of the protein extraction system would bring to the countryside. In practice, however, the new development and modern technology would be limited by the very nature of the country itself in terms of regional differences and varying attitudes of indifference toward any new technological concepts, even though they are related to the efficient use of the available natural resources within the ecosystem in which the people live, for their self-benefit and material advantage.

The question arises how these attitudes would limit the effective introduction of an integrated protein extraction operation to the ecosystem and whether such a scheme has any chance to fit into the particular social milieu of the different regions of Southeast Asia. The declining capacity of the village unit to cope effectively with underemployment and the general subsistence level of its population does not necessarily provoke the inhabitants to question the validity of the prevailing social structure which for generations has dictated the use of available resources and manpower, thereby establishing the present balance between the community and ecosystem. One can assume that traditions remain strong in the interdependence between man and nature, especially in the countryside. The introduction of the protein extraction system into a village, after obtaining the necessary clearance from the local officials in the region and then the approval and consent of the village elders, would immediately affect that community.

To "softpeddle" the issue would perhaps pacify the former suspicions and be the first step to ensure the acceptance of the new system into the community. Hence, it appears that the most appropriate first step in introducing the new technology into an area would be the construction of a mobile protein extraction unit for demonstration purposes in villages. Initially an attraction, it would gradually become a daily or routine practice, with the involvement of the local administration to maintain its operation within the existing socioeconomic structure in the village, the mechanisms with which the inhabitants are familiar. It is also reasonable to suppose that the introduction of new machinery may effect a change in the manual labor ratio therein, perhaps causing some interpersonal frictions due to an increase in income which often accompanies technical work of sorts. The introduction and requirement of different skills could be re-allocate traditional village authority in terms of prestige and wealth in that the organization and related responsibilities for the operations of that machinery may be taken on by either appropriately trained or simply enthusiastic persons. Being aware of, and taking serious account of, the on-going village social system with its hierarchy of elders will ensure that the change in economic activity in the village will not necessitate administrative tension, thereby questioning the validity of the enterprise and its initial acceptance by the community as a whole.

ETHICAL AND HUMANITARIAN CONSIDERATIONS

In March of 1979, Pope John Paul II in his first Encyclical drew contrasting pictures between the consumer civilization of the rich, highly developed societies and the remaining societies, many of whose people are suffering and dying of starvation and malnutrition. So widespread is this phenomenon that it brings into question the financial, productive, monetary, and commercial mechanisms that, resting on various political pressures, support the world economy. These, however, are proving incapable either of remedying the unjust social situations inherited from the past or of dealing with the urgent challenges and ethical demands of the present.

The introduction of protein extraction from green vegetation into agricultural practice in developing countries may be a simple and acceptable system which can easily be integrated into a particular ecosystem, with the local people and communities being an integral part of it. Such a new technology offered to those who are in the process of development has a chance to be morally, politically, and socially acceptable. Once the new technology introduced to the developing country is accepted by the society and can resist socioeconomic rejection, then the new project may be an instrument of challenge—not for economically-advanced commonwealths—but for local communities which will assimilate modern technology into the ecosystem as part of an already well-established socioeconomic microcosm. Hence, naturally occurring intensification of production as an integral part of their daily routine in the supervised process of development—this according to Gurnett-Smith (1978)—appears to be the most effective form of help for the developing nations. Such assistance would thus become a positive vehicle for peaceful international relations based on ethical and humanitarian grounds.

REFERENCES

ARKCOLL, B.D. and FESTENSTEIN, G.N. 1971. A preliminary study of the agronomic factors affecting the yield of extractable leaf protein. J. Sci. Food Agric. *22*, 49.

BARDOCH, J.E. and SANTERRE, M.T. 1979. Use of organic residues in aquaculture. Food Nutr. Bull. *1*, 8.

BRAY, W. 1977. The processing of leaf-protein to obtain food-grade products. *In* Green Crop Fractionation. R.J. Wilkins (Editor). Br. Grassl. Soc. Occas. Symp. *9*, 107–116.

BROWN, G.D., THELWALL, A.D., MARLOW, G.B. and DEVINE, D.F. 1975. Leaf protein concentrate production. An economic assessment. Grass J. Br. Assoc. Green Crop Dryers *15*, 19–22.

BYERS, M. 1971. The amino acid composition and *in vitro* digestibility of some protein fractions from three species of leaves of various ages. J. Sci. Food Agric. *22*, 242–247.

FAO-WHO. 1965. Protein requirements. Report of a joint FAO/WHO Expert Group. FAO Nutr. Meet. Rep. Ser. *37*. Food Agric. Organ. U.N., Rome.

GARNETT-SMITH, A.F. 1978. Australia's contribution to overseas animal production in developing countries. Proc. Aust. Soc. Anim. Prod. *12*, 13–22.

HARDING, G.L. 1977. Solar energy as a low and medium grade heat source. Proc. 48th Aust. N.Z. Assoc. Adv. Sci. (ANZAAS) Congr. 1977, Melbourne, Vol. 1.

HARDJONO, J. 1971. Indonesia, Land and People. P.T. Gunung Agung, Jakarta.

HO, R. 1961. Mixed farming and multiple cropping in Malaya. Proc. Symp. on Land Use and Mineral Deposits in Hong Kong, Southern China and Southeast Asia, 1961, Singapore, Pap. *11*.

KAMALANATHAN, G. and DEVADAS, R.P. 1975. Leaf protein as a supplement in preschool feeding programs. Presented at 10th Int. Congr. Nutr. Kyoto, Aug. 1975, Int. Union Nutr. Sci.

MISSEN, G.H. 1972. Viewpoint on Indonesia: A Geographical Study. Thomas Nelson (Australia), Melbourne.

NAT. RES. COUNC. 1971. Nutrient Requirements of Dairy Cattle, 4th Revised Edition. National Research Council, National Academy of Science, Washington, DC.

OLATUNBOSUN, D.A., ADADEVOK, B.K. and OKE, O.L. 1972. Leaf Protein: A new protein source for the management of protein calorie malnutrition in Nigeria. Niger. Med. J. *2*, 195–199.

OSTROWSKI-MEISSNER, H.T. 1975. Factors limiting protein extraction from pasture—Summary. *In* Leaf Protein Concentrate (New Zealand Scene). G.M. Wallace (Editor). Ruakura Agric. Res. Center Publication, Palmerston North, Hamilton, New Zealand.

OSTROWSKI-MEISSNER, H.T. 1976. Pasture production in protein extraction system. Proc. N.Z. Soc. Anim. Prod. *36*, 30–41.

OSTROWSKI-MEISSNER, H.T. 1979A. Grasslands as a source of unconventional protein for direct animal and human consumption. Proc. 49th ANZAAS Congr., Auckland, Jan. 1979, Conf. Ser. *10*. W. Moran, P. Hosking and G. Aitken (Editors). N.Z. Geographical Soc., Auckland.

OSTROWSKI-MEISSNER, H.T. 1979B. The isolation of protein concentrates from pasture herbage and their fractionation into feed- and food-grade products. J. Food Sci. Preserv. *3*, 105–124.

OSTROWSKI-MEISSNER, H.T. 1979C. Protein extraction from grasslands. Sci. Technol. *16*, 4–11.

OSTROWSKI-MEISSNER, H.T. 1980. Protein extraction from pasture: A new concept in efficient dairy farming in temperate and sub-tropical regions. 4th World Conf. Anim. Prod., Buenos Aires, Aug. 1978. L.S. Verde and A. Fernandez (Editors). World Assoc. Animal Prod., Buenos Aires.

OSTROWSKI-MEISSNER, H.T., CARLSSON, R. and TRAGARDH, C. 1980. Isolation and purification of protein from green vegetation for direct human consumption. *In* Food Process Engineering. P. Linko, Y. Maiki and J. Olkku (Editors). Applied Science Publishers, London.

PIRIE, N.W. 1971. Leaf Protein: Its Agronomy, Preparation, Quality and Use. IBP Handb. *20*. Blackwell's Scientific Publishers, Oxford.

PIRIE, N.W. 1978. Leaf Protein: New Considerations. University Press, Oxford.

ROBINSON, D.W. 1977. Livestock in Indonesia. Cent. Anim. Res. Dev., Bogor, Indonesia, Res. Rep. *1*.

SPEDDING, C.R.W. 1977. An assessment of the future developments of the process of green crop fractionation in the U.K. *In* Green Crop Fractionation. R.J. Wilkins (Editor). Br. Grassl. Soc. Occas. Symp. *9*, 177–180.

VARTHA, E.W. and ALLISON, R.M. 1973. Protein extracted herbage for sheep feeding. N.Z. J. Exp. Agric. *1*, 171–177.

VINCENTE-CHANDLER, J. 1973. Fertiliser unlocks the potential of tropical grasslands. World Farming *15* (Jan.) 20–24.

VOSLOH, C.J., JR., EDWARDS, R.H., ENOCHIAN, R.V., KUZMICKY, D.D. and KOHLER, G.O. 1976. Leaf protein concentrate (Pro-Xan) from alfalfa: An economic evaluation. U.S. Dep. Agric. Econ. Res. Serv., Berkeley, Ca. Agric. Econ. Rep. *346*.

WILKINS, R.J., HEATH, S.B., ROBERTS, W.P. and FOXELL, P.R. 1977. A theoretical economic analysis of systems of green crop fractionation. *In* Green Crop Fractionation. R.J. Wilkins (Editor). Br. Grassl. Soc. Occas. Symp. *9*, 131–142.

WOYNAROVICH, E. 1976. The feasibility of combining animal husbandry with fish farming with special reference to duck and pig production. FAO Tech. Conf. Aquaculture, Kyoto, 1976, Pap. *R6*.

25

Leaf Protein Research in Brazil

Enio C. Vieira

Leaf protein research in Brazil is at an incipient stage. Some work has been done on analysis of leaves of many plants, especially those used as ruminant forage. Nevertheless, the country has a high potential in this field since it is located in the subtropical, tropical, and equatorial regions with sunshine during the entire year. The Amazon region with its native plants properly exploited may be a transformer of solar energy into good quality protein. In Brazil, leaf protein research has been carried out mainly in two plants: *Pereskia aculeata* and cassava. More recently, some work has been done on other plants.

PERESKIA ACULEATA

This plant is popularly known as *ora pro nobis* (from Latin: pray for us). It is a native bushlike perennial cactacea from tropical America that reaches 1 m high. The leaves are consumed largely as a vegetable. Its nutritive value is traditionally known by the people, who call it "meat of the poor." No agronomical data are available since there is no formal cultivation of the plant.

Almeida Filho and Cambraia (1974) first reported on analysis of *Pereskia* leaves showing their high protein content. Leaves were washed, dried at 60°C in a ventilated oven, ground, and finally dried at 105°C for 24 hr. Leaves collected in Viçosa, Minas Gerais (MG), and Guiricema, MG, contained 25.4 and 17.4%, respectively, of protein on a dry matter basis. These authors showed that 85% of the protein was digested by pepsin on incubation for 48 hr at 38°–40°C. The amino acid analysis reported by Almeida Filho and Cambraia was nearly the same for both samples. The results obtained for the Viçosa sample are shown in Table 25.1.

Dayrell and Vieira (1977A) reported on the extraction and composition of leaf protein concentrate (LPC) of *P. aculeata*, collected in Sete Lagoas, MG. The leaves were washed, and homogenized with three volumes of water at pH 7–8. The residue was removed through filtration in cheesecloth and

TABLE 25.1. AMINO ACID COMPOSITION OF *PERESKIA ACULEATA* LEAVES[1] OF *P. ACULEATA* LEAF PROTEIN CONCENTRATE (LPC)[2] AND OF FAO ESSENTIAL AMINO ACIDS REFERENCE PATTERN

Amino Acid (g/100 g of Protein)	*P. aculeata* Leaves	*P. aculeata* LPC	FAO Reference Protein
Lysine	5.32	5.44	4.2
Arginine	5.36	5.58	
Aspartic acid	7.28	9.46	
Threonine	3.60	4.34	2.8
Serine	2.41	4.30	
Glutamic acid	10.00	11.53	
Proline	6.69	4.20	
Glycine	4.81	8.89	
Alanine	4.58	5.94	
Cysteine	1.21	1.35	
Valine	5.52	5.83	4.2
Methionine	2.03	1.46	2.2
Isoleucine	4.23	4.45	4.2
Leucine	8.03	8.75	4.8
Tyrosine	4.37	4.83	
Phenylalanine	5.06	6.33	2.8
Histidine	2.54	1.53	
Tryptophan	—	2.2	1.4

[1]Source: Almeida Filho and Cambraia (1974).
[2]Source: Dayrell and Vieira (1977B).

re-extracted with two volumes of water. The filtrates were combined and passed through a 325-mesh sieve. Precipitation of proteins was done at pH 3. The precipitate was collected either by filtration under vacuum or by centrifugation at 3000 rpm for 10 min. The precipitate was washed and dried at 60°C in a ventilated oven.

Several parameters which would affect the efficiency of the extraction were studied. The optimum ratio water volume: leaf weight was 2:1 for both the first and the second extractions. Further increases in water volume did not affect the yield. No difference was found when either water or 1% NaCl was used as the extractant. The efficiency was significantly decreased when leaves were stored at −20°C for 8 days. However, storage at 4°C for the same period did not affect the yield. The best and the worst pH's of extraction were 8.0 and 4.0, respectively. The yield

$$\frac{\text{protein nitrogen in LPC}}{\text{protein nitrogen in leaves}} \times 100$$

obtained was above 50% in most experiments.

Table 25.1 shows the amino acid composition of *Pereskia* obtained by Dayrell and Vieira (1977B), the amino acid composition of one of the two lots of "*ora pro nobis*" reported by Almeida Filho and Cambraia (1974), and the essential amino acid composition of FAO reference protein. Except for methionine, *Pereskia* LPC has a higher proportion in all amino acids when compared with FAO reference protein. The values of the ratio leucine:isoleucine in LPC and in the reference protein are approximately 2 and 1, respectively.

The nutritive value of *Pereskia* LPC was also determined by Dayrell and Vieira (1977B) through the evaluation of protein efficiency ratio (PER), apparent digestibility (D_{app}), and apparent net protein utilization (NPU_{app}). The values of these parameters for diets whose protein sources were casein, LPC, and LPC fortified with DL-methionine are shown in Table 25.2. LPC had a low nutritive value. However, fortification with methionine raised the values to levels comparable with casein. The PER value of the diet containing LPC may be due to the deficiency of sulfur-containing amino acids, as evidenced by the PER value obtained when LPC was fortified with DL-methionine. Fortification of LPC with both methionine and lysine did not improve the nutritive value of methionine-fortified LPC.

Pereskia protein deserves further investigation. Its use by people and the results reported by Dayrell and Vieira (1977A,B) are good recommendations for future work.

CASSAVA

Cassava leaves are consumed in Brazil in several parts of the country. Preparation of the dishes requires heating and a certain period of aging to remove the hydrogen cyanide formed.

The first report in Brazil on determination of protein level of cassava leaves was published in 1962 by Pechnik *et al.* A meal prepared from cassava leaves contained 29% protein. A diet containing this meal as the sole source of protein was prepared and its efficiency in promoting growth in rats during 35 days was measured. The results obtained are shown in Table 25.3. The nutritive value of leaf meals is certainly lower than that of casein. However, the rats gained weight. When rats were fed on a diet made with cooked meal, there was weight loss. Fortification with both methionine and lysine did not improve the quality of the latter meal. The results shown in Table 25.3 indicate that cassava leaf may be a good source of protein if properly supplemented.

Many investigators outside Brazil became interested in the potentialities of cassava leaves as a protein source and many papers have been published on that subject (see Chapter 3).

In Brazil, Figueiredo and Maciel do Rego (1973) evaluated the protein and mineral content of seven varieties of cassava leaf. The values for protein content ranged from 15.9 to 21.88 g%.

Recently, the Brazilian government started a large program aimed at the utilization of cassava roots as a source of ethanol for fuel through hydrolysis with amylase and further fermentation with *Saccharomyces cerevisiae*. In 1976, Brazil had 2,082,000 ha of cassava under cultivation with a production of 25,812,000 MT of tuber (Mendes 1977). The yield of leaves is similar to that of roots (about 10 MT/ha). The utilization of cassava tops will be, therefore, of great potentiality if collection is proven to be feasible.

TABLE 25.2. WEIGHT GAIN, FOOD INTAKE, NITROGEN GAIN, PROTEIN EFFICIENCY RATIO (PER), APPARENT NET PROTEIN UTILIZATION (NPU_{app}), AND APPARENT DIGESTIBILITY (D_{app}) FOR DIETS WHOSE PROTEIN SOURCES WERE: Casein—Diet A. *Pereskia* leaf protein concentrate (LPC)—Diet B. LPC + 0.5% DL-methionine—Diet C. The figures represent the average ± S.D. of 5 female rats.

Diet	Food Intake (g)	Weight Gain (g)	Nitrogen Gain (g)	PER	NPU_{app}	D_{app}
A	314.76 ± 10.52	86.80 ± 6.97	2.47 ± 0.18	2.56 ± 0.27^{a}	46.51 ± 2.05^{a}	94.03 ± 0.44^{a}
B	105.52 ± 5.94	−3.44 ± 1.68	0.10 ± 0.03	-0.35 ± 0.32^{b}	5.82 ± 1.85^{b}	63.40 ± 2.42^{b}
C	287.88 ± 7.20	70.50 ± 3.85	2.04 ± 0.10	2.04 ± 0.21^{a}	$43.42 \pm 1.50^{a,c}$	63.72 ± 1.44^{b}

Source: Adapted from Dayrell and Vieira (1977B).
NOTE: Different superscript letters in the same column indicate significant difference at the level of 5%.

TABLE 25.3. WEIGHT GAIN, INGESTED PROTEIN, AND PROTEIN EFFICIENCY INDEX FOR DIETS WHOSE PROTEIN SOURCE WAS:
Casein—Diet A. Raw cassava leaf meal—Diet B. Experiments were carried out in 4 rats during 35 days.

Diet	Average Weight (g)			Ingested Protein per Rat (g)	Protein Efficiency Index
	Initial	Final	Gain		
A	41	124	83	41	2.0
B	53	78	25	35	0.7

In 1976, Kling *et al.* reported on the isolation of cassava leaf protein. Leaves reported to contain about 30% protein on a dry matter basis were ground and pressed. The juice was collected. The residue was extracted three times in succession with water. The extracts were combined. Heating at 80°C produced coagulation of the protein. The yield of the leaf protein recovered in the coagulum was 14.9%.

In 1974, a research program on the isolation of cassava leaf protein began at the Department of Biochemistry, Universidade Federal de Minas Gerais. A report on it has been published (Tupynambá and Vieira 1979). Extraction and precipitation of the proteins was done by the same procedure described before for *Pereskia*. The amino acid analysis of the cassava leaf protein concentrate (LPC) is shown in Table 25.4 and is compared with the amino acid analysis of the whole leaf as reported by Kling *et al.* (1976). The protein recovery in the coagulum varied from 20.2 to 61.5%, with most of the values over 50%. The protein content in the coagulum was above 40% in most runs.

TABLE 25.4. AMINO ACID COMPOSITION OF CASSAVA LEAF PROTEIN CONCENTRATE (LPC), OF CASSAVA LEAVES[1], AND FAO ESSENTIAL AMINO ACIDS REFERENCE PATTERN (G/100 G OF PROTEIN)

Amino Acid	Cassava LPC	Cassava Leaves	FAO Essential Amino Acid (EAA) Reference Pattern
Alanine	6.72	5.35	
Arginine	6.53	6.12	
Aspartic acid	10.8	8.04	
Cysteine	0.49	—	
Glutamic acid	13.1	15.45	
Glycine	5.96	6.93	
Histidine	2.26	3.00	
Isoleucine	3.93	4.75	4.2
Leucine	10.1	9.35	4.8
Lysine	5.31	7.08	4.2
Methionine	0.57	0.82	2.2
Phenylalanine	6.14	7.73	2.8
Proline	5.75	5.75	
Serine	6.43	4.81	
Threonine	5.41	4.62	2.8
Tryptophan	—	—	1.4
Tyrosine	4.63	4.84	
Valine	5.41	5.30	4.2

Source: Adapted from Tupynambá and Vieira (1979).
[1]Kling *et al.* (1976).

TABLE 25.5. WEIGHT GAIN, FOOD INTAKE, PROTEIN EFFICIENCY RATIO (PER), FOOD EFFICIENCY (FE), APPARENT NET PROTEIN UTILIZATION (NPU_{app}), AND APPARENT DIGESTIBILITY (D_{app}) FOR DIETS WHOSE PROTEIN SOURCES WERE:

Casein—Diet A. Cassava leaf protein concentrate (LPC)—Diet B. LPC + 0.6% DL-methionine—Diet C. The figures represent average ± S.D. for 5 male rats.

Diet	Weight Gain (g)	Food Intake (g)	PER	FE	NPU_{app}	D_{app}
A	103.86 ± 19.36	331.06 ± 31.06	2.97 ± 0.27	0.31 ± 0.03	62.69 ± 3.52	89.16 ± 4.33
B	−12.56 ± 2.30	122.28 ± 10.42	—	—	−6.90 ± 3.92	30.72 ± 5.09
C	4.92 ± 3.47	167.22 ± 27.98	0.28 ± 0.17	0.55 ± 0.23	19.12 ± 20.08	31.72 ± 6.98

Source: Tupynambá and Vieira (1979).

Analysis of the nutritive value of cassava LPC was performed. The results are shown in Table 25.5. The PER value for cassava LPC was negative. Fortification with methionine improved the nutritive value of the product, but still the values were low. Further research is being conducted on the utilization of whole cassava tops. The amino acid patterns of the extracted protein obtained either from the ramification zone (green stalks plus leaves) or from the whole aerial part of the plant were nearly the same, not very different from cassava LPC (Table 25.4). However, their methionine content was 2.06 compared with 0.57 g/100 g of protein for cassava LPC (Table 25.4). The biological assay, however, revealed that the isolated protein did not support the growth of rats. The low apparent digestibility (approximately 50%) and the possible presence of antinutritional factors may explain these results (C.R.L. Chaves and E.C. Vieira, in preparation) (see Chapter 3).

More recently, Fernandes and Nicoli (1981) reported on the production of single cell protein through fermentation of the brown juice, by-product of cassava LPC extraction. The biomass production after 48 hr of fermentation was the same with or without salt fortification of the medium. The salt fortification, however, increased the protein level from 19 to 26 g% and affected the amino acid pattern of the biomass.

OTHER PLANTS

Recently, Carlsson's group has worked on leaf protein fractionation in Brazil.

The legumes *Canavalia ensiformis*, *C. gladiata*, *Glycine wightii*, and *Stizolobium* sp. and the tree leaves of *Eucalyptus saligna* and *Lecytis pisonis* were processed. The protein content of the LPC varied from 6.9 to 52.4% (Carlsson *et al.* 1981B). The best results of protein efficiency ratio were obtained with *Canavalia* LPC, with values ranging from 1.42 to 1.81 (Jokl and Carlsson 1981).

The tropical C_4 grass *Pennisetum purpureum* cv Napier was used as a source of LPC. The crude protein content of the LPC varied from 25.8 to 49.0% (Carlsson *et al.* 1981A).

Future research on leaf protein in Brazil will most likely be centered on cassava. This crop is widely grown in the country, and now has the prospective production of ethanol from its roots.

REFERENCES

ALMEIDA FILHO, J. and CAMBRAIA, J. 1974. Studies of the nutritional value of leafy cactus, cv. *Ora pro nobis* (*Pereskia aculeata* Mill). Ceres *21*, 105–111.

CARLSSON, R., JOKL, L. and AMORIM, C. 1981A. Effects of processing conditions on the chemical composition of leaf protein concentrate from *Pennisetum purpureum* cv. Napier. 12th Int. Congr. Nutr., Aug. 16–21, 1981, San Diego, Abstr. *359*.

CARLSSON, R., JOKL, L. and SANTOS, R.C. 1981B. Effects of processing conditions on the chemical composition of leaf protein concentrates from tropical legumes and from leaves of forest trees. 12th Int. Congr. Nutr. Aug. 16–21, 1981, San Diego, Abstr. *358*.

DAYRELL, M.S. and VIEIRA, E.C. 1977A. Leaf protein concentrate of the cactacea *Pereskia aculeata* Mill. I. Extraction and composition. Nutr. Rep. Int. *15*, 529–537.

DAYRELL, M.S. and VIEIRA, E.C. 1977B. Leaf protein concentrate of the cactacea *Pereskia aculeata* Mill. II. Nutritive value. Nutr. Rep. Int. *15*, 539–545.

FERNANDES, V.M.V. and NICOLI, J. 1981. Production of protein from the thermotolerant fungus *Phanerochaete chrysosporium*, using the brown juice from a protein extract of cassava leaves as substrate. Rev. Bras. Microbiol. *12* (1981). *(In press)*.

FIGUEIREDO, A.A. and MACIEL DO REGO, M. 1973. Protein and mineral content of roots and leaves of cassava. Biol. Tec. Cent. Tecnol. Agric. Aliment. Rio de Janeiro *5*, 23–25. (Portuguese)

JOKL, L. and CARLSSON, R. 1981. Nutritive value of leaf protein concentrates from tropical legumes and from leaves of forest trees. 12th Int. Congr. Nutr. Aug. 16–21, 1981, San Diego, Abstr. *761*.

KLING, S.H., SOLEWCZ, E., DAUMAS, M.S.P., SILVA, G.H., MARTINS, M.R.J., MOURA, R.M.B. and PERRONE, J.C. 1976. Industrial evaluation of cassava leaves. Inf. Inst. Nac. Tecnol. Rio de Janeiro *9* (11) 13–18. (Portuguese)

MENDES, R.A. 1977. Cassava and its production in Brazil. Int. Workshop on the Utilization of Agric. Wastes for Feed and Food. Belo Horizonte, Brazil, Dec. 1977. (Proceedings to be published)

PECHNIK, E., GUIMARÃES, L.R. and PANEK, A. 1962. Evaluation of cassava leaves (*Manihot* sp.) for human nutrition. II. Arq. Bras. Nutr. *18*, 11–23. (Portuguese)

TUPYNAMBÁ, M.L.V.C. and VIEIRA, E.C. 1979. Isolation of cassava leaf protein and determination of its nutritive value. Nutr. Rep. Int. *15*, 529–537.

26

Experimental Studies on Leaf Proteins in Egypt

H.A. El-Alaily and H.S. Soliman

Like many, if not all developing countries, there is an ever increasing shortage of protein sources for human consumption in Egypt. The introduction of single cell proteins (SCP) and leaf protein concentrates (LPC) into animal feed and possibly human food appears to be one of the most promising attempts achieved by the scientific community to partially overcome the problem of world food supplies. However, in developing countries the production of protein from green plants appears to be more suitable than SCP because the former requires much less sophisticated technology. Furthermore, although the quality of LPC might differ among different species of plants, it appears to be comparable to that of protein sources known to be of high quality, such as casein or soybean (Duckworth and Woodham 1961; Henry and Ford 1965; Woodham and El-Alaily 1976).

IMPORTANCE OF LPC IN EGYPT

The area of irrigated land in Egypt is very limited and represents only about 4% of the whole area of the country. About one-third of this area (2.7 million feddan or 1.1 million ha) is cultivated with clover *(Trifolium alexandrinum)*. Production of clover amounts to about 40 million MT/year, all of which is produced during the winter season. It is a common practice in Egypt to maintain most, if not all, farm animals on clover as the main ration during the winter. Such practice usually results in an excess of protein intake of about one-third to one-half above the requirements of these animals (O. Shehata, personal communication). During the summer season, however, feedstuffs are scarce and inadequate for animal feeding. The production of LPC from a conventional plant such as clover would, therefore, offer an efficient and excellent approach to make the best use of such a crop. Firstly, it would eliminate losses of the excess protein and, secondly, the extracted protein could be recycled in animal feeds or could be used directly in human nutrition.

EXPERIMENTS ON LPC IN EGYPT

Although most of the work reported in the literature has been devoted to the production of LPC from nonconventional plants such as *Amaranthus, Atriplex*, and *Chenopodium* species (Carlsson 1977), little information is available on the production and quality of LPC extracted from local conventional plants such as clover. Satisfactory values for the extraction ratio of LPC from clover (34%) have been obtained by El-Bahnasy (1969). When the extracted LPC was included in Nicols chick diets to replace about 13% of dietary protein (23%), the chicks grew poorly up to 28 days of age, and the rate of mortality was high.

Much lower extraction rates from sweet potato leaves *(Ipomoea batatas)* (11%) and from turnip leaves *(Brassica rapa)* (18%), have been reported by Saad (1977). Apart from possible differences in the methods of extraction, the leaves were collected from mature plants (after being harvested) which would have a much lower rate of extraction than would younger plants (see Pirie 1969). Biological evaluation was carried out on LPC from turnip leaves only, because of the very low extraction ratio of sweet potato. Net protein utilization (NPU) of LPC from turnip leaves was 54, while that of casein was 55, using growing rats. Here again, it is difficult to interpret the results obtained with the turnip LPC because of the poor results obtained with casein, possibly due to its low quality.

Recently (1978), employing a liquidizer, we have extracted LPC from clover using fresh plants and tap water (1:2). The protein was coagulated from the extracts by steam injection at 80°C. The coagulated proteins were kept at 4°C overnight, separated by filtration, spread over plates, and dried in an oven at 60°C for 24 hr. The dried LPC was included in chick diets for biological evaluation tests of metabolizable energy (Hill and Renner 1960) and protein efficiency ratio (Buamah and Singsen 1975) using soybean meal (49% protein) as a reference protein.

Extraction ratio and chemical composition of LPC extracted from clover are presented in Table 26.1. Protein efficiency ratios (PER) and metabolizable energy (ME) values of clover LPC are presented in Table 26.2.

It should be appreciated that little attention has been paid to obtaining a high extraction ratio since it is desirable under our conditions to produce

TABLE 26.1. CHEMICAL COMPOSITION[1] OF CLOVER LEAVES AND LPC AND ITS EXTRACTION RATIO[2]

Composition	Leaves	LPC	Extraction Ratio (%)
Weight (g)	1000 (fresh)	30	40
Dry matter (%)	14.3	89.8	(oven dried)
Crude protein (%)	31.6	67.7	
Ether extract (%)	—	9.7	
Crude fiber (%)	—	2.3	
Ash (%)	—	9.9	

[1]On dry matter basis.
[2]Amount of extracted protein as % of protein of the sample (Carlsson 1978).

TABLE 26.2. PROTEIN EFFICIENCY RATIO (PER) AND METABOLIZABLE ENERGY VALUE (ME) OF CLOVER LPC

	PER (g Protein/g Gain)	ME (Kcal/g)
Control soybean meal + 0.2% DL-methionine	3.76	2.50
LPC	3.45	2.20
LPC + 0.2% DL-methionine	3.65	2.20

pulp containing about one-half of its original nitrogen to be used as a complete diet for ruminants.

Unlike the results obtained by El-Bahnasy (1969), all our chickens remained healthy during the experiment. Considering the level of substitution used in his experiment (13% of the dietary protein) and that used in our experiments (40%), it seems possible that factors other than LPC were responsible for the high rate of mortality recorded in his experiments.

However, our results showed that LPC extracted from clover had an ME value quite close to that of soybean protein. Also, the results obtained for the PER have demonstrated that LPC from clover can be successfully used to replace soyprotein in chicken diets at a level of up to 40% of dietary protein. The chicken breed used in our experiments (Dokki 4), however, was a slow-growing breed and it is possible that this may have masked differences in protein quality. Work is underway to examine the effect of including clover LPC in diets for fast-growing broiler chicks.

FUTURE STUDIES

Experiments on the possibility of using LPC from clover in milk replacers for newly born ruminants and in diets for laying hens are being conducted in our laboratories. It is hoped that an easily controlled machine can be developed for the cutting and pulping of clover on the field for large-scale production of LPC. Such a machine will certainly have a deep impact on the production of LPC in Egypt. This is supported by the fact that about 1.8 million MT of LPC/year (720 kg/feddan/year or 1735 kg/ha/year) can be produced if the entire area cultivated with clover is to be used for the production of LPC. With these figures in mind, with rising prices of clover making it unrealistic to afford losses of this crop in the winter season, and, furthermore, the acute shortage of animal feed in the summer season, we believe that there is a great scope for future production of LPC in Egypt.

REFERENCES

BUAMAH, T.F. and SINGSEN E.P. 1975. Studies on the protein efficiency ratio method for the evaluation of poultry feed supplements modifications associated with choice of dietary protein level for assay. J. Nutr. *105*, 688–700.

CARLSSON, R. 1978. Leaf protein from non-agricultural plants. Proc. Int. Workshop Utilization Agric. Waste for Feed and Food, CETEC, Belo Horizonte, Brazil, Dec. 1977.

DUCKWORTH, J. and WOODHAM, A.A. 1961. Leaf Protein concentrates. I. Effect of source of raw material and method of drying on protein value for chicks and rats. J. Sci. Food Agric. *12*, 5–15.

EL-BAHNASY, M.T. 1969. Leaf protein as a substitute for animal protein in poultry nutrition. M.Sc. Thesis. University of Alexandria, Egypt.

HENRY, K.M. and FORD, J.H. 1965. The nutritive value of leaf protein concentrates determined in biological tests with rats and microbiological methods. J. Sci. Food Agric. *16*, 417–422.

HILL, F.W. and RENNER, R. 1960. The metabolizable energy of soybean oil meal, soybean millfeeds and soybean hulls for the growing chicks. Poult. Sci. *39*, 579–583.

PIRIE, N.W. 1960. The production and use of leaf protein. Proc. Nutr. Soc. *28*, 85–91.

SAAD, S.A. 1977. Biochemical and biological studies on some leaf protein. M.Sc. Thesis. University of Ain-Shams, Shoubra El-Khaima, Cario.

WOODHAM, A.A. and EL-ALAILY, H. 1976. Unpublished data. Rowett Research Institute, Aberdeen, Scotland.

27

Leaf Protein Research in India

R.N. Joshi

As early as 1943, during the Bengal femine in India, Guha (1960) used leaf protein (LP) from water hyacinth (*Eichhornia crassipes* Solms.) and other species for human feeding. In the early 1950s, Subrahmanyan and his colleagues initiated some work at the Central Food Technological Research Institute (CFTRI), Mysore. Sur and Subrahmanyan (1955) and Sur (1961) reported the beneficial effects of lucerne (*Medicago sativa* L.) LP when used as a supplement to poor rice diets. The work was, however, discontinued as the product was considered unacceptable from various points of view (Singh 1975).

In 1959, the Indian Sarvodaya leader, Jayaprakash Narayan, had discussions in London with N.W. Pirie on LP research and development (R & D). On his return to India, Jayaprakash Narayan handed over some of Pirie's publications to the then Prime Minister, Jawaharlal Nehru. The Prime Minister directed the Council of Scientific and Industrial Research to look into the matter. Consequently, Pirie was invited to visit India at the beginning of 1961. He submitted a report on his five week study of the possibilities of making protein for human foods from lush vegetation to the Ministry of Food and Agriculture, Government of India. As a result of this study, research on LP was started at the National Botanic Gardens, Lucknow, in the Agricultural College (now University), Coimbatore, and was revived at the CFTRI, Mysore. In the late 1960s, leaf protein research began in the Punjab Agricultural University, Ludhiana, and some investigations were also conducted at the University Home Science College, Tirupathi, in Women's Christian College, Madras, and in Assam Agricultural College, Jorhat.

The LP work in Marathwada University, Aurangabad, and at the Indian Statistical Institute, Calcutta, formed a part of the Indian contribution to the International Biological Programme (IBP) and was undertaken in collaboration with the Rothamsted Group of the IBP in the United Kingdom. In 1966, R.P. Devadas, Director of the Sri Avinashilingam Home Science College for Women, Coimbatore, initiated studies on the presentation, nutritive value, and acceptability of LP in human diets. From November 25 to 27, 1970, Devadas organized in her college an IBP "Working Group" meeting. This meeting was sponsored and financed by the IBP and resulted in the IBP handbook on LP (Pirie 1971). This publication brought together the state of knowledge in 1970 on the agronomy, preparation, quality, and use of LP. The status of LP research in India has been summarized from time to time by Singh (1969A,B, 1974A,B, 1975) and Joshi (1978).

PRELIMINARY SCREENING WORK FOR THE CHOICE OF PLANTS

The local vegetation, cultivated and wild, available at Delhi (Kaur and Vijayaraghavan 1961), Lucknow (Singh 1964), Jammu (Singh, unpublished), Mysore (Valli Devi *et al.* 1965; Mahadeviah and Singh 1968), Jorhat (Majumdar, unpublished), Aurangabad (Dev and Joshi 1969A,B; Deshmukh and Joshi 1969), and Ludhiana (Garcha *et al.* 1970) was screened for LP extraction. The extractability of protein from leaves and protein content of the product prepared from the extracts by heat coagulation were taken as two criteria for recommending suitable plant species. A domestic meat mincer was used for making leaf pulp, and the juice was expressed by squeezing the pulp through a cotton cloth. A second extract was often made by adding water to the fibrous residue, remincing, and squeezing again. The procedure outlined by Byers (1961) was adopted for the analysis, calculation, and classification of results. Screening work in different regions indicated that lush legume fodder plants such as lucerne, berseem (*Trifolium alexandrinum* L.), and cowpea [*Vigna sinensis* (L.) Savi ex Hassk.] were the most suitable raw materials for bulk production of leaf protein. The tops of several green-manure legumes, the unused green foliage of the commercially cultivated vegetable and other crops, and a few wild plants were also suggested as supplementary raw materials. The following résumé includes the major contributions on various aspects of LP research from different centers in this country.

DEPARTMENT OF APPLIED CHEMISTRY, UNIVERSITY COLLEGE OF SCIENCE & TECHNOLOGY, CALCUTTA

In this department, special attention was paid to a detailed investigation of water hyacinth, said to cover 200,000 ha in India (cf. Pirie 1978), as a source of leaf protein. A blade-type hammer mill was used for pulping, and, of the several extractants tried, 2% sodium carbonate solution was found to extract over 60% of the total protein present in the leaves. Acetone was found to be the best solvent for removing the color and odor of the leaf protein concentrate (LPC). Experiments on rats showed that protein extracted without carbonate was more digestible and had a greater biological value (BV) than protein made by carbonate extraction (Datta *et al.* 1966A, B). The beneficial effect of adding methionine to LPC from water hyacinth was demonstrated (Ghosh 1967). In another experiment, Ghosh (cf. Pirie 1978) found that LP from this troublesome weed was a good supplement when added to rice at levels of 30, 40, and 50%, based on the protein content of the diet; its value diminished when more was used.

CENTRAL FOOD TECHNOLOGICAL RESEARCH INSTITUTE, MYSORE

The work undertaken by N. Singh and his colleagues falls into two periods. From 1965 to 1972, this group was mainly concerned with the use of green LP in human food and provided valuable information on nutritive value of leaf proteins from rat experiment feeding trials and with children. A batch extractor (Davys and Pirie 1963) was used for making leaf extracts and the process outlined by Morrison and Pirie (1961) was followed for obtaining the wet LP cakes.

In the reoriented program since 1975, emphasis is being given, on the one hand, to obtain a bland and depigmented LPC for versatile use, and, on the other, to develop an integrated technology for LP-*cum*-fodder fractionation suitable for small-scale production in Indian villages. Simple chemical methods are being standardized for screening leaf protein concentrates and quality norms. The work carried out at Mysore is summarized in three sections.

(1) Raw Material Choice

The batch extractability of N from 24 species was found to vary between 25 and 60% (Singh 1969B,C). The vegetation of eight species gave low yields of LPC, containing less than 5% N of dry matter (DM). The N content of leaf protein concentrates prepared from the following plants was over 5%; these plants were found suitable for batch production as they yielded over 1 kg of LPC DM per 100 kg fresh vegetation: lucerne, horse gram (*Dolichos uniflorus* Lam.), water hyacinth, French bean (*Phaseolus vulgaris* L.), amaranth (*Amaranthus* sp.), jowar (*Sorghum vulgare* Pers.); green-manure crops: pillipesara (*Phaseolus trilobus* Ait.), kolinji (*Tephrosia purpurea* Pers.), dhaincha [*Sesbania cannabina* (Retz.) Pers.], and *Sesbania speciosa* Taub. ex Engler; and by-product vegetation of green vegetable crops: turnip (*Brassica rapa* L.), knol khol (*Brassica caulorapa* Pasq.), cauliflower (*Brassica oleracea* L. var. botrytis L.), radish (*Raphanus sativus* L.), beetroot (*Beta vulgaris* L.), and cabbage (*Brassica oleracea* var. capitata L.).

(2) Process and Technology

Coagulation Studies. Subba Rau *et al.* (1969) standardized the fractional heat-coagulation process. The procedure included coagulation of the chloroplastic protein by bringing the temperature of the juice to 55°C and its subsequent separation in a high-speed Sharples centrifuge. The supernatant fluid was steam-injected for coagulation of the cytoplasmic material. The two fractions had 7 and 12% N (DM basis), respectively, when the whole unfractionated LPC had 9.6% N. A steam injection unit was designed by Ahmed and Singh (1969) for coagulating the LP from juice.

Preservation and Solvent Extraction of Leaf Protein. Subba Rao *et al.* (1967) observed that the wet LPC cake could be preserved by salting to a final salt concentration of 12%. The product could be preserved for years by pickling it with vinegar or dilute acetic acid to a final residual 2% acid concentration. Preliminary screening of solvents was done for obtaining a nongreen LPC (Singh, unpublished). Wet cake was found more suitable than the dried one, and a mixture of 90:10 acetone:hexane gave promising results.

Studies on Hot Water Pre-pulp Treatments of Lucerne Vegetation. On the processing side, post-1975 investigations have been concerned with the pre-pulp hot water treatments of the vegetation in relation to the residual nitrogen in the pressed residue (PR). Among the various temperature and time combinations studied, the following two were selected for batches up to 15 kg of vegetation: (1) holding for 1 min in 60°C hot water, and (2) an instantaneous dip in 80°C hot water. The two treatments improved the N-content of the PR: for example, vegetation DM-N 4.4–4. 6%, PR (control) 3.16%, PR (60°C) 3.74%, and PR (80°C) 4.29%. LPC yields decreased progressively with higher temperature treatments. The proximate composition did not show variations among the three leaf protein concentrates, suggesting no preferential coagulation of chloroplastic material in the tissue, as was assumed (Singh 1977).

Development of Machinery for Fodder Fractionation. In recent studies aimed at developing indigenous technology suitable for integrated small-scale farm-based operations in Indian villages, Singh (1977) has found a vertical cutter, formerly used for coconut, good for preparing pulps from leafy materials. This cutter is like a meat-mincing machine without its usual worm. Its energy consumption is less than the IBP pulper (Davys and Pirie 1969), and its efficiency of extraction is as good, while still keeping the fiber coarse, when a plate with about 15 mm diam. holes is used. The cutter could be made locally and is easy to clean.

For pressing the pulp, a commercially available table model oil expeller has been found satisfactory. Singh (1977) feels that these two machines, capable of processing from 60 to 100 kg vegetation per hr, would cost around Rs[1] 10,000 per 100 ha (≈$12.50 per 250 acres), therefore suitable for integrated small-scale farm-based operations.

(3) Quality Aspects

Protein Quality of Lucerne Leaf Protein—Rat Experiments. Lysine adequacy in lucerne LP was demonstrated, and methionine was found to be the most deficient amino acid. Supplementation of LP with methionine led

[1] Rs 8.00 = $1 (approximately).

to significant improvements in growth and protein-efficiency ratio (PER), and its best responses were in diets containing 10% protein levels; the diet intake also usually increased with methionine fortification (Shurpalekar *et al.* 1969).

Growth and PER studies with leaf protein dried under varying conditions showed no significant differences even when the material was dried at 100°C (Subba Rau and Singh 1970). However, some damage to quality in a baking oven indicated that drying in a fast current of hot air was preferable to preclude the possibility of rise in the material temperature, since at high material temperatures some deleterious lipoprotein interactions might occur (Buchanan 1969).

There was no improvement when diets were supplemented with cholesterol, indicating the absence of the growth-suppressing saponins in leaf protein preparations.

The quality of leaf protein coagulated with acid at pH 4–4.5 was found to be nutritionally inferior to that coagulated by steam injection. A hot water wash of the acid-precipitated LP caused some improvement in the quality, while heating the acidified extracts and then separating the LP led to deterioration (Subba Rau and Singh 1970).

Spray-dried leaf extract was found unsuitable as food, being toxic and failing to support good growth. The cytoplasmic material, separated from the cholorplastic one by fractional heat coagulation, was found to be nutritionally superior to the latter and to unfractionated LP (Subba Rau *et al.* 1969).

The results from low protein rice diet supplementation studies showed that even under a state of vitamin and mineral deprivation, leaf protein incorporation at 5% protein levels led to significant improvements. In diets adequate with respect to vitamins and minerals, the responses to LP were comparable to skim milk powder (SMP) at similar protein levels. In terms of protein metabolism, as reflected in liver fat levels, LP appeared to be a better supplement than SMP (Shurpalekar *et al.* 1969).

Growth and PER studies were also done on supplementation of wheat diets with leaf protein at different levels (Subba Rau and Singh 1971). The diets adequate in vitamins and minerals were used for both the 8-week growth studies on female rats and 4-week growth and PER studies on male rats. In the 8-week growth study, the four diets used had 12.5, 14.8, 16.2, and 18.0% protein, respectively, based on wheat and the three wheat + leaf protein mixtures containing 80:20, 70:30, and 60:40 protein ratios from the two sources. The data showed significant growth improvements due to supplementation, greater with higher protein up to 4 weeks, and later levelling off. However, the liver N indicated that the diet containing the highest proportion of LP, contributing 40% of the total protein in the mixtures, was the best of all. The 4-week growth and PER studies showed that a leaf protein + wheat mixture containing equal proportions of protein from both sources was nutritionally better in all respects than all other combinations. The most likely explanation for this seemed to be the improvements in the levels of essential amino acids in the mixture.

Protein Quality of Different Leaf Proteins—Rat Experiments. Subba Rau *et al.* (1972) conducted growth and PER experiments on leaf proteins prepared from 19 different kinds of vegetation. From an overall assessment of the results, leaf proteins were placed into four different categories: (1) five of no food value, causing loss or negligible gain in weight of rats, viz. *Tecoma stans* Juss., *Dolichos lablab*, *Sesbania speciosa*, carrot (*Daucus carota* L.), and horse gram; (2) six of poor quality, inducing a weight gain of less than 15 g in 4-week periods and showing a PER below 1.0, viz. groundnut (peanut) (*Arachis hypogaea* L.), French bean, kolinji, pillipesara, dhaincha, and beetroot; (3) three of medium quality, inducing a weight gain of 20–35 g with PER in the range of 1.3–1.75, viz. lucerne, *Amaranthus* sp., and potato (*Solanum tuberosum* L.); and (4) five of good quality, inducing a weight gain of more than 40 g with a PER greater than 1.75, viz. cauliflower, cabbage, knol khol, turnip, and radish (all brassicas). The last five, all of them cruciferous leaf proteins, were, with reference to growth response and PER, nutritionally 66% as efficient as SMP.

The apparent digestibility (D) and true digestibility (TD) values, from experiments with either young and growing or adult rats, were close to each other for the medium and good quality categories of leaf proteins. The values differed considerably for the poor quality leaf proteins and were lower than those for good quality leaf proteins. The TD values for carrot, beetroot, lucerne, and cauliflower leaf proteins in adult rats were around 40, 74, 87, and 89%, respectively, with that for SMP about 90%. The BVs were in a narrower range than the TDs, falling between 70 and 77 in growing rats and between 55 and 59 in adults (Subba Rau *et al.* 1972).

Some Factors Affecting the Protein Quality. When differences were apparent in the nutritive value among the proteins coagulated by different methods from similar leaf extracts, and also among leaf proteins prepared from different plant species by a common heat-coagulation technique, attempts were made to explain the differences in nutritive value of different leaf proteins with reference to the availability of the limiting amino acids. However, no consistent picture emerged. Subba Rau *et al.* (1972) also could not establish any consistent relationship between the trends in the metabolic values and the computed essential amino acid indices or the chemical scores calculated from the most limiting amino acid. Therefore, investigations into the factors which were probably responsible for the differences in the quality of different leaf proteins were undertaken. Leaf proteins were analyzed for total ash, hot water-soluble solids, total phenolics, and different sulfur fractions.

The analyses suggested that the likely factors, singly or in combination, affecting the quality of leaf proteins adversely were associated with the occurrence of low N, high ash, high soluble solids, high phenolic:N ratios, and/or low organic sulfur:N ratios. In carrot LP, the ash content was as high as 37.3%. A pre-extraction wash of carrot vegetation decreased the ash content in extracted LP and greatly enhanced its digestibility without changing its BV, while a hot acid wash of the heat-coagulated LP caused some improvement in BV, but none in digestibility. Among different leaf proteins, the nutritional inferiority was also associated with reduced diet intake.

Lucerne Leaf Protein—Metabolic Studies and Feeding Trials with Children. Metabolic studies with 10 to 12-year-old children showed that the quality of the low-protein diet improved remarkably on addition of LP, as reflected in the digestibility and N-retention. There were no differences between the cooked and uncooked LPC. Subsequently, a six-month long feeding trial with children on ragi (*Eleusine coracana* L.)-based diets was undertaken to compare the supplementary efficiency of synthetic lysine, LP, and sesame (*Sesamum indicum* L.) flour (Doraiswamy *et al.* 1969).

Four groups of 20 children, 6 to 12 years old, were given, per child, per day: (1) the basal diet containing ragi flour, beans, vegetables, SMP, oil, and sugar; it supplied 39 g of protein per day and 7 MJ; (2) the basal diet supplemented with 0.5 g of synthetic lysine (lysine deficiency is the principal shortcoming of ragi); (3) the basal diet supplemented with 15 g of LP; and (4) basal diet supplemented with 25 g sesame flour. The last two supplements contributed 10 g of protein to the daily diet, and sugar was withdrawn from all supplemented diets to compensate for the energy in the supplement. All three supplemented diets brought about improvements in height, weight, general nutritional status, apparent digestibility, and N-retention. The diet supplemented with LP led to the greatest growth response (Table 27.1). The apparent digestibility of the lysine-supplemented diet was less than that of the diets supplemented with LP and sesame flour, while the differences in N-retention in children among the three supplemented diets were not significant. However, the N-retentions, as % of ingested N with lysine and LP supplements, were similar and better than on sesame supplement.

TABLE 27.1. MEAN MEASUREMENTS ON FOUR GROUPS OF BOYS, 6 TO 12 YEARS OLD, GIVEN DIFFERENT DIETS FOR SIX MONTHS

Dietary Supplement	Height (cm)	Weight (kg)	Increase in Hemoglobin (g per 100 ml)	Red Cell Count (Millions per mm^3)
None (control)	2.2	0.47	0.29	0.06
0.5 g lysine (sugar withdrawn)	4.25	1.05	0.64	0.22
10 g protein in sesame flour (sugar withdrawn)	3.51	0.86	0.73	0.19
10 g protein in LP (sugar withdrawn)	4.84	1.28	0.87	0.23

Source: Doraiswamy *et al.* (1969).

Nutritionally Important Pigments in Leaf Proteins. The β-carotene in LP was found to be as effective as synthetic for replenishing retinol in the serum and liver of rats that had been on a retinol-deficient diet (Ramana and Singh 1971A,B). Storage studies on LP were also done to understand the problems of stability of carotenes and xanthophylls (Ramana and Singh 1971C).

PUNJAB AGRICULTURAL UNIVERSITY, LUDHIANA

Garcha *et al.* (1970) estimated crude protein, ether extract, ash, iron, phosphorus, and methionine contents of leaf proteins prepared from 20 plant species grown in Punjab. The quality of protein was assessed from the BV calculated by the "Chemical Score Method" of Block and Mitchell (1946). Leguminous plants gave highest yields of LP, and samples from only five species contained adequate amounts of methionine. The BV of LP was lowest (58.7) for senji (*Melilotus parviflora* Desf.) and highest (80.3) in berseem. In another communication, Garcha *et al.* (1970) reported the amounts of total and available lysine, histidine, arginine, and tryptophan in these samples. In general, the levels of amino acids compared favorably with those reported earlier by Gerloff *et al.* (1965) for LP samples.

Investigations were undertaken to evaluate the quality of the leaf protein concentrates prepared from cowpea, sarson (*Brassica campestris* L.), palak (*Beta vulgaris* L. syn. *Beta bengalensis* Roxb.) (Garcha *et al.* 1971), berseem (Kawatra *et al.* 1974), and cauliflower (Goel *et al.* 1977) and their effects when supplementing wheat flour diets on the growth rate of rats and the PER. Leaf protein from cauliflower replaced 10 or 20% of protein, whereas LP from the other plants provided 30% of a 10% protein diet. Casein was used as the reference diet. The growth rate of rats and PER values of leaf protein-supplemented diets were better than that of the wheat flour-fed group. The addition of DL-methionine along with palak, sarson, and cowpea leaf proteins brought about further improvements in these values (Garcha *et al.* 1971). It was concluded that LP could be used as a supplement to the nutritionally poor cereal diets with beneficial effects.

Studies were carried out on organoleptic evaluation of leaf protein as a component of biscuits. Two types of biscuits, viz. sweet and salted, were prepared containing sarson LP at a 5% level. The organoleptic score of a panel of 30 individuals showed that sweet biscuits were liked more than the salted ones (Garcha *et al.* 1971).

SRI AVINASHILINGAM HOME SCIENCE COLLEGE FOR WOMEN, COIMBATORE

Devadas *et al.* (1970) carried out a study on albino rats to evaluate the effects of LPC supplementation on the nutritive quality of the diets of a selected group of rural families. Kamalanathan and Devadas (1971) tried several methods of presentation of LPC using taste panels and observed that at 5–10 g levels, incorporation of LP in dhal balls, leaf chutney,

chutney powder, and ragi addai was acceptable. At the level of 15 g, all the samples were reported to have a leafy flavor, sawdust texture, and bitter taste. LPC was more acceptable when its strong flavors were masked by spices or fully ripe bananas.

In a six month feeding trial, both LP and groundnut (peanut) meal were found equally good as supplements for preschool children. Since the cost of LP was 1 rupee per kg, compared with 2 rupees per kg for the groundnut meal, Kamalanathan *et al.* (1975) felt that LP has very good scope for further testing and use.

The efficiency of absorption of β-carotene from amaranth, LPC, and standard β-carotene by preschool children was determined by Krishnamurthy *et al.* (1976). All three sources supplied 1200 μg of β-carotene per child per day for a period of three months. The percentage absorption of β-carotene from amaranth, LPC, and standard carotene was 61.4 ± 9.35, 76.7 ± 8.48, and 85.4 ± 6.14, respectively. There was a significant increase in serum vitamin A levels after feeding the different sources of β-carotene. The serum total proteins and albumin levels showed a positive correlation with serum vitamin A levels.

The leaf protein trial, sponsored by the charitable organization "Find Your Feet, Ltd.," U.K., and operated by Sri Avinashilingam College, from July 21, 1975, for a period of two years, is the most comprehensive LP feeding trial hitherto undertaken, involving 360 children of both sexes aged 2 to 5. The results of this trial are not yet published and this account is therefore based on personal communications and information from N.W. Pirie (1978). Six villages were chosen that are within 9 km of Coimbatore and as similar as possible in character, type of employment, and average income. A nursery school (balwadi) was set up in each village, and in this, on six days per week, about 60 children spent nine hours of the day. On the six school days, they got three meals containing 80 to 90% of their daily energy and protein supply. The children also received elementary training in hygiene and were taught to play and sing. The mothers were invited once a week to discuss their children's progress. Actual feeding thus took place as a part of an integrated nutrition and education program.

One of the balwadis was primarily educational and the food served in it was modelled, in quantity, character, and quality, on food usually eaten at home. In five of the balwadis, the food served contained 1.3 MJ more energy than the food served in the control balwadi. In one of these five, most of the energy came from tapioca, which supplies only 1 g of protein. The food given in the other four balwadis contained about 10 g of extra protein given in the form of horse gram, maize + Bengal gram, skim milk powder, or lucerne LP. The energy contents of the supplements were equalized by suitable adjustment of tapioca and sugar (jaggery). The mixture used for the daily helping contained 18 g of lucerne LPC, 40 g tapicoa, 10 g ragi, 2 g sesame, and 30 g jaggery. Enough moisture was added to shape it into a ball which resembled a sweetmeat called "laddu." The molasses flavor of the jaggery counteracts the taste of lucerne. In India, laddus are used for festivals and feasts and hence have "prestige" value. The children have, without exception, willingly accepted the LP supplement.

The children were checked periodically for height and weight gain, hemoglobin count, and serum retinol level. There were no medical problems. Clinical examinations of the children showed that there were considerable improvements in clinical status in all the balwadis; it was particularly striking in the one receiving LP. Symptoms of mild and moderate malnutrition disappeared, as did symptoms of vitamin A deficiency. A summary of the results after 18 months (Table 27.2) shows that milk is a better supplement than LP, which, in turn, is marginally better than the other two sources of protein. Devadas (1977) and Pirie (1978) feel that the trial has estabished that, contrary to the widely held belief, green LP does not present an acceptability problem with children.

The supplementary values of leaf protein, leaf protein + sesame meal, and coconut meal in the diets of preschoolers were compared by Devadas *et al.* (1978A). In each group there were 20 children. The supplements were planned to be isocaloric, each supplying 274 kcal, and isoproteinic, containing 7.1 g protein, and given in the form of laddus. The cost of each laddu was estimated at 15 or 16 paise[2]. The amino acid patterns of the leaf protein + sesame meal and the leaf protein supplements were better than that of the FAO (FAO/WHO 1965) reference protein. However, the amounts of lysine, tryptophan, and methionine were below the recommended level in the coconut meal supplement.

The effect of the supplements was evaluated by the assessment of the nutritional status of the preschoolers by anthropometry, clinical examination, and biochemical studies, which included the determination of blood hemoglobin level by the cyanmetheglobin method and urinary creatinine estimation. The study revealed that the children fed on all three supplements showed remarkable improvement in nutritional status over the control group. The combination of leaf protein and sesame meal gave the best results and LP was found to be a better supplement than the coconut meal.

In another experiment, Devadas *et al.* (1978B) evaluated the protein quality of leaf protein by a human nitrogen retention study. In this trial, five preschool children of five years of age, and of the same height, weight, blood hemoglobin level, and clinical status, were chosen from a balwadi. The children were from the same socioeconomic background, with a family income of Rs 100 to 200 ($12.50 to $25) per month. Their dietary and food consumption patterns were also similar. The experimental period was 14 days, in two phases. During the first phase, a basal diet which contributed 2008 kcal and 20.79 g of protein was fed, whereas during the second phase, a supplement prepared from leaf protein in the form of laddus contributing 280 kcal and 7.5 g of protein was provided. In each phase, the three-day collection period followed a four-day adjustment period.

---

[2]100 paise = 1 rupee.

TABLE 27.2. INTERIM RESULTS OF AN 18-MONTH COMPARISON OF DIFFERENT SUPPLEMENTS TO THE DIETS OF PRESCHOOL CHILDREN

			Diets Supplemented with 1.3 MJ				
				Diets Supplemented with 10 g Protein			
	Age (Months) at the Start	No Supplement	Tapioca	Horse Gram	Maize + Bengal Gram	Milk	Leaf Protein
Increased height (cm)	24–30	9.6	10.0	10.3	10.8	12.0	10.6
	36–42	9.3	9.4	9.8	10.3	11.8	10.3
	48–54	8.8	8.3	8.9	10.1	10.8	10.1
Increased weight (kg)	24–30	2.7	2.8	3.0	3.0	3.4	3.2
	36–42	3.0	3.1	2.9	3.3	3.6	3.2
	48–54	2.9	2.9	3.0	3.0	3.4	3.0
Increased hemoglobin (g per 100 ml)	24–30	2.3	2.1	2.3	1.6	2.2	2.5
	36–42	2.4	2.9	2.4	3.1	3.2	3.5
	48–54	2.4	2.5	3.0	3.7	4.3	4.2

The results of the study indicated that the nitrogen retention on the basal and supplemental diets was 425 mg and 1026 mg, respectively. The retention of nitrogen on the supplemental diet (38.5%) was statistically significant at the 1% level over the nitrogen retention (17.5%) observed on the basal diet. The mean apparent digestibility and apparent biological values of the basal diet were 80.0 ± 4.4 and 33 ± 19.0, respectively. The corresponding figures for digestibility and BV for supplemental diet were 86.6 ± 2.8 and 36 ± 4.6, respectively. The Creatinine/Height Index of both groups ranged from 1.66 to 1.78, indicating that the selected children were not victims of protein-calorie malnutrition.

DEPARTMENT OF BOTANY, MARATHWADA UNIVERSITY, AURANGABAD

(1) Agronomic Studies on Leaf Protein Production

Agronomic research has been undertaken over the past decade to work out a system of cropping that will yield the maximum amount of extracted protein per unit area per year. The technique and equipment devised for the IBP (Davys and Pirie 1969; Davys *et al.* 1969; Joshi 1971) were used for this study. The experimental farm is situated at an altitude of 650 m and lies 19° 52′ N latitude and 75°20′ E longitude. The climatic year is divided into three seasons: the monsoon from June to September, during which Aurangabad gets most of the total annual rainfall of 760 mm from the southwest monsoons, winter from October to February, and the hot dry summer from March to May. Soils of the experimental plots are black and clayey with alkaline pH. The farm is provided with adequate lift irrigation facilities.

Data obtained over a period of 12 years have shown that lucerne is a highly productive crop of consistent performance, capable of yielding over 150 MT of fresh vegetation, 25 MT dry matter (DM), 6 MT of crude protein (CP), and 3.2 MT of extracted protein per ha, when harvested 14 to 16 times a year (Mungikar *et al.* 1976A; Joshi 1978). In experiments conducted during 1969 to 1972 (Dev *et al.* 1974, 1975), lucerne responded with increased yields of dry matter and extracted protein to both NPK and farmyard manure + P_2O_5, simazine, and micronutrients + urea. The crop sown at the normal time, i.e., during October, produced more dry matter and protein than when sown in March, and six or eight harvests were found to give greater yields than five harvests in 180 days. The yield was increased by sowing in rows that were 30.5 rather than 46 cm apart.

The yields of extracted protein from lucerne were lower by 10 to 28% in the summer than in either the monsoon or winter. The early flowering of the plant with the rise in daily temperatures (Smith 1969) probably accounts for the decline in the extractability of protein N during the summer (Arkcoll and Festenstein 1971; Dev *et al.* 1974). Savangikar and Joshi (1976) observed that frequent irrigations increased the yields and also improved the protein N extractability of lucerne. Another finding, that the yields of extractable protein are highly correlated with the fresh vegetation yields, would be helpful in predicting the extractability of protein N from the harvested lucerne in the field itself by using a regression equation.

From 1969 to 1973, the effects of fertilizers, frequency of cutting (Gore *et al.* 1974), and simazine (Gore and Joshi 1976A) on the yields of dry matter and extractable protein were studied with hybrid Napier grass *(Pennisetum purpureum* × *Pennisetum typhoideum)*. The protein N extracted ranged from 21 to 38%. Extractability was not affected greatly by either the fertilizer or simazine treatment, but there were seasonal variations. With liberal dressings of fertilizers, the crop can be expected to yield from 200 to 250 MT fresh vegetation, 40 MT DM, 6 MT CP, and about 2 MT extractable protein from a hectare per year on irrigated lands. Large dressings of fertilizer N, however, increased the amounts of nonprotein N in the crop considerably, due to the shortage of water for irrigation during the summer. The process of extracting protein from Napier grass helps to remove considerable quantities of nitrates and oxalates in the soluble fraction (Mungikar, unpublished).

Cowpea is best adapted to the monsoon climate since it grows quickly, forming a thick surface cover, the dense foliage smothering weeds. The rate of 11.2 kg per ha per day extracted protein from cowpea during a monsoon of 1970 is the highest ever recorded for a season so far in this laboratory (Deshmukh *et al.* 1974). The crop is not suitable for cultivation during the winter, but, when irrigated, gives high yields during the hot, dry summer (March–May). It responded consistently to rhizobial inoculation (Deshmukh and Joshi 1973) and to micronutrient sprays (Dev *et al.* 1975), but not to simazine treatment (Deshmukh *et al.* 1974).

Although from 40 to 52% protein N was extractable from *Sesbania sesban* (Linn.) Merr. var. picta (Prain) Sant., the plant was not considered preferable to lucerne or cowpea (Gore and Joshi 1976B). With 110 kg N, the yields of dry matter and extracted protein were 8.8 and 0.89 MT per ha when the crop was cut five times in 221 days.

Berseem is one of the best winter fodder crops of North India and yields from 40 to 95 MT/ha green vegetation of green fodder in five or six cuttings. The yields of leaf protein from berseem, grown with three fertilizer treatments and harvested at three frequencies of cutting, were determined in this region by Mungikar *et al.* (1976B). The extractability of protein N declined very rapidly as the crop matured. The yields of extracted protein were maximum when the crop was harvested at intervals of 15 to 22 days, whereas dry matter yields were maximum with regrowth cutting frequency of 32 to 40 days. The yields of fresh vegetation and dry matter per ha reached 70 and 14.5 MT, respectively, in 190 days and those of extracted protein 700 kg in 140 days.

Mungikar *et al.* (1976A) studied the effects of fertilizer N on the yields of extracted protein from seven crops. Large dressings of N produced greater succulence, increased the amount of juice, and lowered the fiber content in most plants, increased the nitrogen content (as percentage of DM) in five species, improved the extractability of protein N in three, and gave significant increase in both dry matter and protein yields of nonlegumes. However, the yields were affected more by the climate than by N fertilizer; e.g., dry matter and protein yields from *Tithonia tagetiflora* Desf. showed significant increases with the application of 60 and 120 kg N/ha during the summer, but gave no response to even 180 kg N/ha during the monsoon. The maximum percentage of applied fertilizer N recovered as protein N was 60.0% from mustard, which received 120 kg N/ha. The maximum yields of dry matter (MT/ha) and extracted protein (kg/ha) from *Tithonia*, pearl millet (*Pennisetum typhoideum* Rich., cv Tift 23 A), mustard (*Brassica nigra* Koch.), wheat (*Triticum aestivum* L. cv Kalyan Sona), and maize (*Zea mays* L.) reached 6.4 and 689, 12.8 and 325, 3.7 and 609, 6.9 and 766, and 4.9 and 125 in 98, 93, 71, 70, and 71 days, respectively.

The yields of extractable protein from leaves taken at the time of harvest of the edible parts from brassicas, beetroot, turnip, and radish ranged from 76 to 170 kg/ha (Tekale and Joshi 1976). Defoliation at 80 or 90 days after sowing adversely affected the grain yields of groundnut; the extractability of protein N from these leaves was also very poor (Jadhav and Joshi 1977). Good yields of LP could be obtained from a number of weeds which grow exuberantly during the monsoon (Gore and Joshi 1972).

In all the agronomic trials reported so far, the plants have been grown very near the laboratory, harvested early in the morning, and processed soon afterward. These conditions would change if the crop or the expressed juice were to be transported over long distances. Hence, experiments have been conducted to study: (1) deterioration of protein and carotenoid pigments because of delay between harvesting the crop and processing it; (2) whether the extractability of protein and the amount of carotenoids vary at different times of the day; and (3) the stability of proteins, carotene, and xanthophyll in juices stored at different temperatures and pH.

Batra *et al.* (1976) measured the extractability of LP from seven crops kept at room temperature (28° to 38°C) for various times after harvesting. The yield from most of them was nearly halved after 9 hr. They attributed most of this diminution to the evaporation of water from the crop so that there was insufficient juice to extract the LP adequately. It was also observed that the condition of the crop early in the morning and late in the afternoon is not the same, especially during the summer; the protein N extractability was maximum early in the morning and declined as the day advanced. The carotene and xanthophyll contents of lucerne vegetation showed more or less the same trend (Tekale and Joshi 1977). When the juices were kept at room temperature, the loss of protein varied with the leaf species from 4 to 15% in 4 hr (Batra *et al.* 1976). The carotene and xanthophyll losses in juices of lucerne (Tekale and Joshi 1977) and the alien weed *Parthenium hysterophorus* L. (Joshi and Joshi 1979) were very high even at room temperature. Carotenoid stability increased markedly when the juice was stored at alkaline pH.

Experiments conducted (Jadhav *et al.* 1979) in 1974 and 1975 with sannhemp (*Crotalaria juncea* Linn.) and *Sesbania sesban* showed that these green-manure crops could be utilized more profitably for wheat production if part of the protein was extracted from them and the fiber remaining after protein extraction was buried in the soil, instead of the whole plant, as in conventional practice. The results showed that *per se* the ploughed-in vegetation led to greater wheat yields than the ploughed-in fibrous residue; however, on a relative nitrogen basis of the two treatments, the fibrous residue gave better responses than the whole vegetation. The underlying assumptions in undertaking these trials were that in the tropics and subtropics, the rapid decomposition of the softer vegetation probably does not lead to the expected benefits of organic matter enrichment of the soils. Pirie (1969) feels that under tropical conditions microbial denitrification is so rapid that protein from green-manure crops contributes little to the nitrogen content of the soil. There is, therefore, an obvious need for more detailed systematic investigations on green manuring in different regions.

(2) Silage from Lucerne and Napier Grass Fibers

The fibers left after LP extraction from various crops contained from 8 to 16% of CP (N × 6.0). These fibers should, therefore, provide an adequate maintenance diet for ruminants. Mungikar and Joshi (1976) observed that fibers from lucerne and Napier grass produced better silage than the fresh vegetation. Their findings confirmed those of Oelshlegel *et al.* (1969) that there is a definite relationship between pH and lactic acid concentration in the silage. The dry matter digestibility altered little with the age of silage samples and also was not affected by the pulping process.

(3) Leaf Protein from the Weed *Parthenium*

Parthenium hysterophorus L., an alien weed, is believed to have been introduced into this country with PL 480 foodgrains imported from the United States of America. The plant is now growing wild in many parts, creating agricultural and health hazards; it causes contact dermatitis in humans and livestock. Hand-weeding and hoeing are the simple, safe, and cheap methods for the control of *Parthenium.*

Studies have been undertaken to see whether *Parthenium* picked up from fields could be used as a protein-pigment source. The optimum age for getting the maximum extractability of protein from the plant was determined (Joshi and Savangikar 1977). Comparison with the FAO (FAO/WHO 1965) reference protein showed that sufficient quantities of essential amino acids are present in the product. The digestibility of protein *in vitro* (Buchanan and Byers 1969; Saunders *et al.* 1973) ranged from 62 to 78%. The true digestibility and BV from experiments with growing rats were above 80 and 86%, respectively. The product contained 0.4 to 0.6 mg of carotene per g and 0.7 to 0.9 mg of xanthophyll (Savangikar and Joshi 1978A).

(4) Modification of Leaf Protein Concentrate by the Use of the Plastein Reaction

A new approach was used (Savangikar 1977) to modify the unfavorable organoleptic properties of lucerne LPC prepared by the Morrison and Pirie (1961) method. This approach involved the initial peptic hydrolysis of the LPC and subsequent re-incubation of this hydrolysate with additional pepsin. A cream-colored, chocolate-flavored, protein-rich product produced by this plastein reaction was isolated from the incubated material. The various steps involved in this process were optimized with an emphasis on the simplest possible techniques. The products obtained and their possible uses are: (1) undigested pigment-rich LPC as a source of pigments for poultry; (2) leaf protein hydrolysate which may be useful in pharmacy; (3) a fraction insoluble in either water or 50% alcohol for incorporation into human diets or in medicines; and (4) a water- or alcohol-soluble product for which, at present, no specific use is envisaged. These preliminary studies have indicated that more flexibility is offered by plastein reactions for getting protein-rich products from leaves of desirable qualities than by other methods used hitherto.

However, the plastein reaction involves the use of proteolytic enzymes, which are expensive, and considerable quantity of enzyme is needed, particularly for hydrolyzing the protein concentrate. Hence, efforts were made to increase the efficiency of utilization of pepsin. One method would be to re-use the enzyme originally added. In the course of experimenting, a way was found (Savangikar 1977) in which the initial quantity of enzyme added to LPC along with 0.1 *N* HCl could be used repeatedly. After allowing the LPC to digest under predetermined optimum conditions, a further sample of LPC and HCl was added to the reaction mixture. After a further 24 hr incubation, more LPC and HCl were added and so on. It was possible to digest a minimum of six batches of LPC using the same quantity of enzyme added initially.

Another way of using the enzyme repeatedly would be in an immobilized state, i.e., after coupling it in active form to solid insoluble supports (carriers). A simple and inexpensive method was devised (Savangikar and Joshi 1978B) in which paraffin wax was used for the immobilization of pepsin. The enzyme was mixed with molten paraffin wax and the resultant mixture was solidified. The molten paraffin wax could be applied as a film on solid supports before solidifying. The excess pepsin on the surface, whenever present, was washed with an aqueous medium at or below pH 5.4 to leave, on the surface, immobilized pepsin in active and readily usable form. It was found that the immobilized pepsin could be used several times for the hydrolysis of LPC.

INDIAN STATISTICAL INSTITUTE, CALCUTTA

From among a number of plants processed with the IBP pulper and press, in addition to the commonly grown legume fodders, grasses, and vegetables, some water weeds [e.g., water hyacinth, *Pistia stratiotes* L., and *Ipomoea reptans* (L.) Poir.], wild plants (*Cestrum diurnum* L., *Amaranthus gangeticus* L., *Chrozophora plicata* Juss., *Croton sparsiflorus* Mor., and *Heliotropium indicum* L.), and two species occurring on marshy lands (*Polygonum hydropiper* L. and *Oldenlandia corymbosa* L.) have been suggested as suitable sources for LP extraction in West Bengal (Matai *et al.* 1971; Matai and Bagchi 1974).

In agronomic investigations, the effects of age of crop, seed rate, and fertilizer on the yields of extracted protein from tetrakalai, the tetraploid form of *Phaseolus aureus* Linn., local varieties of mustard, turnip, bajra, ragi, cowpea, and lucerne were studied. The land on which this agronomic work was carried out was of poor quality. The fields are reclaimed ground made by filling ponds with rubble over which there is a 30–40 cm layer of alluvial loam. The lower yields of LP at Calcutta, compared with those achieved at Aurangabad, in spite of the more humid climate, are attributed to the quality of the land (Matai *et al.* 1976; Pirie 1976).

The LP yield from mustard and turnip was studied in the winter season of 1970 (Matai *et al.* 1973). In mustard, the percentage extractability (49 to 62%) as well as the protein yield remained more or less constant even up to the late flowering stage. The rate of extracted protein of 8.8 kg/ha/day on mustard plots with 40 kg/ha seed rate and 180 kg fertilizer N/ha is the highest rate recorded for a season from this institute. The yield from turnip was 265 kg/ha in 52 days with 32 kg/ha seed rate and at the same fertilizer N level.

In experiments conducted during 1971–1972 with bajra, mustard, ragi, and turnip, generally 4–5 times the normal seed rates were tried to ensure quick ground cover (Matai *et al.* 1976). The maximum yields of extracted protein from these plants were (in kg/ha): 228, 319, 211, and 274 in 38, 42, 39, and 48 days, respectively. In mustard, ragi, and turnip, the extractability of protein N ranged from 40 to 60%. Harvesting just before the initiation of flowering produced the highest yields in the first two plants and bajra. The yield of extracted protein was not increased by giving mustard more than 60, ragi more than 160, and bajra more than 240 kg N/ha. Larger yields with higher seed rates, even at low N level, were observed with bajra and ragi. With turnip, the maximum yield of extracted protein was obtained 45–52 days after sowing and the conventional seed rate of 8 kg/ha was found to be optimum with 120 kg N/ha. Hybrid Napier grass gave 468 kg extracted protein/ha in 272 days. The N level for maximum response with turnip and Napier grass was not reached with 180 and 320 kg N/ha, respectively.

Tetrakalai grows well during the monsoon in West Bengal where it is used as fodder. It produces LP at rates that would correspond to an annual yield of 1760 kg/ha if growth had been maintained by irrigation during the dry season. Of the two seed rates tried, 100 kg/ha, i.e., four times the conventional rate, gave a greater yield of protein than 50 kg/ha. Bagchi and Matai (1976) concluded that tetrakalai is an admirable crop which on better soils would give large yields.

The normal seed rate of 30 kg/ha was found optimum for LP extraction from lucerne; the crop yielded 944 kg extracted protein/ha when cut six times in 151 days. The green-manure crop, dhaincha, deserves further trials as it gave 149 kg LP/ha in 23 days when grown in low-lying areas before the paddy transplantation in the rainy season. The yields of LP from the by-product leaves of three varieties of radish, Pusa Himani, Jap White, and Pusa Rashmi, were 223, 318, and 286 kg/ha, respectively, when root yields ranged from 140 to 150 kg/ha (Matai 1977). A fodder variety of cowpea, EC 4216, was found to be quite promising; it gave 313 kg extracted protein per ha in 65 days at the seed rate of 80 kg/ha and 180 kg P_2O_5/ha (Matai *et al.* 1978).

TAMIL NADU AGRICULTURAL UNIVERSITY, COIMBATORE

Equipment suitable for large-scale extraction of LP (Davys and Pirie 1960, 1965) was used for raw material choice and agronomic work. The plants reported suitable for LP extraction from Mysore and Aurangabad were also found useful at Coimbatore (Balasundaram *et al.* 1974A,B).

At Aurangabad, Deshmukh *et al.* (1974) found that sweet potato (*Ipomoea batatas* Lam.) is not an ideal crop for LP extraction because the presence of mucilage in the leaves complicates the processing. At Coimbatore, however, this plant yielded 700 kg extracted protein per ha. The green-manure crops, *Gliricidia maculata* H.B. & K., which was not found suitable at Aurangabad, and dhaincha yielded 600 and 500 kg LP per ha, respectively, (Samuel, unpublished).

Although the yields of DM and extractable protein from sannhemp increased by the treatment of different concentrations of benedyne to seeds and soil (Krishnamoorthy *et al.* 1975), these increases were statistically insignificant (Krishnamoorthy 1977).

The yields of extractable protein from all 15 varieties of fenugreek (*Trigonella foenumgraecum* L.) were maximum when the age cut was taken 40 days after sowing (Chandramani *et al.* 1975).

The results obtained on the extraction of LP from by-product leaves of cotton (*Gossypium hirsutum* L.) and cassava (*Manihot esculenta* Crantz) are very interesting. Leaves of cotton were removed when the crop was 45, 60, or 90 days old. These leaves are either used to make compost or go to waste. A study (Krishnamoorthy 1977) showed that cotton leaf tops removed on the forty-fifth day were suitable for LP extraction. In earlier trials (Samuel, unpublished), leaves gathered after the second picking of the bolls from the Russian varieties 84/4 and 72/2 yielded 510 kg of extracted protein per ha.

Leaves from cassava, picked at the time of the harvest of the tubers, contain appreciable amounts of protein. However, the main objection for the use of the leaves from cassava for LP production has been the presence of hydrocyanic acid (HCN) in them. A study undertaken by Balasundaram *et al.* (1976) revealed that from among the different fractions obtained in the LP production process, the maximum amount of HCN was contained in the juice. In dry LPC, the HCN content was well below the toxic levels.

Yields of DM extracted protein from three grasses, *Panicum maximum* Jacq., *Brachiaria mutica* (Forssk.) Stapf., and *Cenchrus glaucus* Mud. et Sund., depended on the frequency of cutting. *P. maximum* gave 1.3 MT of LP per ha when the first cut was taken 75 days after planting and 11 successive regrowths were cut at every 30 days. In one month, the daily yield was as high as 15.8 kg/ha. The yield was only 0.5 MT/ha when the interval between harvests extended to 45 days (Balasundaram *et al.* 1975; Chandramani *et al.* 1975).

Effect of manuring and frequency of cutting on the yields of LP from four grasses were measured by Balasundaram *et al.* (1977). The first cut was taken 60 days after planting. Six successive harvests were taken from *P. maximum* and *B. mutica* at intervals of 30 days and five successive harvests from *C. glaucus* and *Cenchrus ciliaris* L. at intervals of 45 days. *C. glaucus* was found superior to the other grasses tried and it gave the maximum yield of DM (16.9 MT/ha) and extractable protein (466 kg/ha). Farmyard manure at 10 MT/ha along with ammonium sulfate at 33 kg N/ha proved to be the best fertilizer and resulted in the highest yields. For all the grasses, the maximum yield was found to range within the first three cuttings.

THE BHARATIYA AGRO-INDUSTRIES FOUNDATION, URLI-KANCHAN

Most of the work at this foundation has focused on studying the efficacy of lucerne juice as calf feed. Fresh juice was obtained every day by crushing lucerne in a medium-sized sugar cane crusher fitted with two 17.5 × 22.5 cm rollers which yielded juice (10% DM) at the rate of 8 liters/hr with 35% efficiency (35 liters/100 kg of lucerne).

In one study (Prasad *et al.* 1977A), the calves were fed on a diet containing lucerne juice (40% DM basis) as a milk replacer. These calves grew at the rate of 420 g/day as against 484 g/day by those fed whole milk at 10% of their body weight. The cost of the milk replacer feeding was 55% lower than the whole milk feeding. In the second experiment (Prasad *et al.* 1977A), 24 newborn crossbred calves were divided into 3 groups of 8 each and given 3 different dietary treatments for 3 months: (1) milk replacer with lucerne juice (at 50% DM basis); (2) skim milk + limited whole milk; and (3) whole milk alone. The results indicated that calves tolerated the higher level of lucerne extract and grew at the rate of 410 g/day as compared with the 390 g/day of the skim milk group and 476 g/day in whole milk group. The cost of feeding (in rupees) per calf for the three groups was 434, 561, and 1050, respectively.

In another study (Prasad *et al.* 1977B), 20 crossbred (Holstein × Gir) male calves were weaned on the first day after birth, fed colostrum for 3 days, and whole milk during the subsequent 6 days (both at the rate of 10% of body weight). The calves were divided into 4 groups, and from the tenth day onward, they were given 4 different dietary treatments: (1) milk replacer with lucerne juice (40% DM); (2) milk replacer with skim milk powder; (3) skim milk; and (4) whole milk. Both the milk replacers were isoproteinous (23.5% DCP) and isocaloric (75% TDN). The calves in the first two groups received 1.15 liters of milk/head/day besides the required amount of milk replacer to meet the nutritional requirements. From three weeks of age onward, calves from all groups were given a calf starter containing 20% crude protein and a limited amount of fresh lucerne. In 3 months, the average weight gain per calf in the 4 groups was 41.5, 44.0, 37.3, and 46.0 kg, respectively. The treatment differences in the growth rate were significant at the 1% level. The cost of feeding in rupees per day per calf in the four groups was 4.90, 6.20, 6.13, and 10.20, respectively.

An experiment was conducted with two rumen-fistulated Jersey bulls to compare the digestibility coefficients of feeding fresh lucerne and fibrous residue. Joshi *et al.* (1979) suggested that: (1) the increase in digestibility of nondetergent fiber and acid-detergent fiber in residue (58.55 and 59.37%, respectively) relative to that in fresh crop (52.05 and 52.76%, respectively) could have been due to the physical effect *per se* of the crushing of the crop; (2) the removal of soluble nutrients during fractionation helped in increasing the residence time of all of the fractions in the residue; and (3) the higher levels of ammonia N and bacterial N in the animals fed fresh lucerne could have been due either to the differences in solubility of protein in both the feeds or simply to the higher CP in lucerne (20.26% DM basis) compared with residue (18.12% DM).

CURRENT THINKING

Fifteen Indian teams and institutions, already engaged in or planning LP research, participated in a meeting held at the CFTRI, Mysore, on July 4–5, 1977. In the stocktaking, it was noted that, despite over three decades of research, there is no regular production and use of LP in this country. So far, almost all work in India has been carried out using the equipment imported from Rothamsted with the sole objective of maximum possible extraction of green LPC for use as a cheap source of protein to overcome malnutrition among the poor. No attempt has been made to develop technology suitable for use in Indian villages. There was common agreement on the need for practical orientation in the field of LP to make the program more successful.

It was felt that efforts should now be made toward developing noncapital-intensive, simple, and nonlabor-saving technologies for an integrated approach for maximal utilization of LP and other products of processing. Further research must aim at evaluating, modifying, and simplifying the indigenous, commercially available, and easily serviceable machinery, such as the oil-expelling screw presses and sugarcane rollers. There are excellent prospects for the development of LP projects in India in conjunction with the dairy development programs undertaken for the benefit of small and marginal farmers. The farm-based small village units should produce fodder-grade fiber for the cattle and LPC for nonruminants. Production and utilization trials must be given top priority in future programming to assess the economics of this integrated approach.

REFERENCES

AHMED, S.Y. and SINGH, N. 1969. A heat coagulation unit for leaf protein. Indian J. Technol. *7*, 411–412.

ARKCOLL, D.B. and FESTENSTEIN, G.N. 1971. A preliminary study of the agronomic factors affecting the yield of extractable leaf protein. J. Sci. Food Agric. *22*, 49–56.

BAGCHI, D.K. and MATAI, S. 1976. Studies on the performance of tetrakalai (*Phaseolus aureus* Linn.) as a leaf protein crop in West Bengal. J. Sci. Food Agric. *27*, 1–6.

BALASUNDARAM, C.S., CHANDRAMANI, R., BALAKRISHNAN, T. and KRISHNAMOORTHY, K.K. 1977. Effect of manuring and frequency of cutting on the yield of leaf protein from some fodder grasses. J. Sci. Food Agric. *28*, 598–601.

BALASUNDARAM, C.S., CHANDRAMANI, R., KRISHNAMOORTHY, K.K. and BALAKRISHNAN, T. 1975. Optimum time of cutting for maximum yield of extractable protein from some fodder grasses. Madras Agric. J. *62*, 431–434.

BALASUNDARAM, C.S., CHANDRAMANI, R., MUTHUSWAMY, P. and KRISHNAMOORTHY, K.K. 1976. Distribution of hydrocyanic acid different fractions during the extraction of leaf protein from cassava leaves. Indian J. Nutr. Diet. *13*, 11–13.

BALASUNDARAM, C.S., KRISHNAMOORTHY, K.K., BALAKRISHNAN, T., RAMADOSS, C. and CHANDRAMANI, R. 1974A. Screening plant species for leaf protein extraction. Indian J. Home Sci. *8*, 1–3.

BALASUNDARAM, C.S., KRISHNAMOORTHY, K.K., CHANDRAMANI, R., BALAKRISHNAN, T. and RAMADOSS, C. 1974B. The yield of leaf protein extracted by large scale processing of various crops. Indian J. Home Sci. *8*, 6–8.

BATRA, U.R., DESHMUKH, M.G. and JOSHI, R.N. 1976. Factors affecting extractability of protein from green plants. Indian J. Plant Physiol. *19*, 211–216.

BLOCK, R.J. and MITCHELL, H.H. 1946. The correlation of the amino acid composition of proteins with their nutritive value. Nutr. Abstr. Rev. *16*, 249–278.

BUCHANAN, R.A. 1969. Effect of storage and lipid extraction on the properties of leaf protein. J. Sci. Food Agric. *20*, 359–364.

BUCHANAN, R.A. 1969. Interference by cyanide with measurements of papain hydrolysis. J. Sci. Food Agric. *20*, 364–367.

BYERS, M. 1961. Extraction of protein from the leaves of some plants growing in Ghana. J. Sci. Food Agric. *12*, 20–30.

CHANDRAMANI, R., BALASUNDARAM, C.S., KRISHNAMOORTHY, K.K. and BALAKRISHNAN, T. 1975. Effect of nitrogen and the frequency of cutting in guinea grass (*Panicum maximum* L.). Madras Agric. J. *62*, 155–157.

CHANDRAMANI, R., KRISHNAMOORTHY, K.K., BALASUNDARAM, C.S. and BALAKRISHNAN, T. 1975. Optimum time of cutting for obtaining maximum yield of extractable protein from fenugreek *(Trigonella foenum-graecum)* varieties. Madras Agric. J. *62*, 230–231.

DATTA, R.K., CHAKRABARTY, P.R. GUHA, B.C. and GHOSH, J.J. 1966A. Protein concentrates from leaves of water hyacinth. Indian J. Appl. Chem. *29*, 7–13.

DATTA, R.K., CHAKRABARTY, P.R., GUHA, B.C. and GHOSH, J.J. 1966B. Studies on leaf proteins—Preparation of protein concentrate from leaves of water hyacinth. Sci. Cult. *32*, 247–249.

DAVYS, M.N.G. and PIRIE, N.W. 1960. Protein from leaves by bulk extraction. Engineering (London) *190*, 274–275.

DAVYS, M.N.G. and PIRIE, N.W. 1963. Batch production of protein from leaves. J. Agric. Eng. Res. *8*, 70–73.

DAVYS, M.N.G. and PIRIE, N.W. 1965. A belt press for separating juices from fibrous pulps. J. Agric. Eng. Res. *10*, 142–145.

DAVYS, M.N.G. and PIRIE, N.W. 1969. A laboratory-scale pulper for leafy plant material. Biotechnol. Bioeng. *11*, 517–528.

DAVYS, M.N.G., PIRIE, N.W. and STREET, G. 1969. A laboratory-scale press for extracting juice from leaf pulp. Biotechnol. Bioeng. *11*, 529–538.

DESHMUKH, M.G., GORE, S.B., MUNGIKAR, A.M. and JOSHI, R.N. 1974. The yields of leaf protein from various short-duration crops. J. Sci. Food Agric. *25*, 717–724.

DESHMUKH, M.G. and JOSHI, R.N. 1969. Leaf protein from some leguminous plants. Sci. Cult. *35*, 629–631.

DESHMUKH, M.G. and JOSHI, R.N. 1973. Effect of rhizobial inoculation on the extraction of protein from the leaves of cowpea (*Vigna sinensis* (L.) Savi ex Hassk.). Indian J. Agric. Sci. *43*, 539–542.

DEV, D.V., BATRA, U.R. and JOSHI, R.N. 1974. The yields of extracted leaf protein from lucerne (*Medicago sativa* L.). J. Sci. Food Agric. *25*, 725–733.

DEV. D.V., DESHMUKH, M.G. and JOSHI, R.N. 1975. Effects of micronutrients and urea on the extraction of protein from lucerne (*Medicago sativa* L.) and cowpea (*Vigna sinensis* (L.) Savi ex Hassk.). J. Indian Biosci. Assoc. *1*, 75–76.

DEV. D.V., and JOSHI, R.N. 1969A. Extraction of protein from some plants of Aurangabad. J. Biol. Sci. *12*, 15–20.

DEV. D.V. and JOSHI, R.N. 1969B. Proteins from green plants. Maharashtra Med. J. *15*, 611–617.

DEVADAS, R.P. 1977. Leaf protein feeding research report. Presented at Indian Leaf Prot. Res. Get-together, Mysore, July 4–5, 1977.

DEVADAS, R.P., KAMALANATHAN, G., KUPPUTHAI, U. and RENUKAVATHY, V. 1978A. Supplementary value of leaf protein, leaf protein and sesame meal and coconut meal in the diets of preschoolers. Indian J. Nutr. Diet. *15*, 175–180.

DEVADAS, R.P. KUPPUTHAI, A. and SEBASTAIN, S. 1978B. Effect of leaf protein on nitrogen retention in pre school children. Indian J. Nutr. Diet. *15*, 107–111.

DEVADAS, R.P., LYZAMMA, M. and RADHA RUKMANI, A. 1970. Evaluation of the supplementary value of the leaf protein concentrates using albino rats. Indian. J. Nutr. Diet. 7, 234–239.

DORAISWAMY, T.R., SINGH, N. and DANIEL, V.A. 1969. Effects of supplementing ragi *(Eleusine coracana)* diets with lysine or leaf protein on the growth and nitrogen metabolism of children. Br. J. Nutr. *23*, 737–743.

FAO/WHO 1965. Protein requirements. FAO Nutr. Meet. Rep. Ser. *37*. Food Agric. Organ. U.N., Rome.

GARCHA, J.S., KAWATRA, B.L. and WAGLE, D.S. 1970. Evaluation of different leaf protein concentrates for some essential amino-acids. Curr. Sci. *39*, 269–270.

GARCHA, J.S., KAWATRA, B.L. and WAGLE, D.S. 1971. Nutritional evaluation of leaf proteins and the effect of their supplementation to wheat flour by rat feeding. J. Food Sci. Technol. *8*, 23–25.

GARCHA, J.S., KAWATRA, B.L., WAGLE, D.S. and BHATIA, I.S. 1970. Studies on extraction and isolation of leaf proteins of various crops grown in the Punjab. J. Res. Punjab Agric. Univ. *7*, 211–215.

GERLOFF, E.D., LIMA, I.H. and STAHMANN, M.A. 1965. Amino acid composition of leaf protein concentrates. J. Agric. Food Chem. *13*, 139–143.

GHOSH, J.J. 1967. Leaf protein concentrates: Problems and prospects in the control of protein malnutrition. Trans. Bose Res. Inst. Calcutta *30*, 215–223.

GOEL, U., KAWATRA, B.L. and BAJAJ, S. 1977. Nutritional evaluation of a cauliflower leaf protein concentrate by rat feeding. J. Sci. Food Agric. *28*, 786–790.

GORE, S.B. and JOSHI, R.N. 1972. The exploitation of weeds for leaf protein production. *In* Symposium on Tropical Ecology. P.M. Golley and P.B. Golley (Editors). University of Georgia, Athens.

GORE, S.B. and JOSHI, R.N. 1976A. Effect of simazine on the yield of dry matter and crude protein, and on the extractability of the protein from hybrid napier. Indian J. Agron. *21*, 491–492.

GORE, S.B. and JOSHI, R.N. 1976B. Effect of fertilizer and frequency of cutting on the extraction of protein from *Sesbania*. Indian J. Agron. *21*, 39–42.

GORE, S.B., MUNGIKAR, A.M. and JOSHI, R.N. 1974. The yields of extracted leaf protein from hybrid napier grass. J. Sci. Food Agric. *25*, 1149–1154.

GUHA, B.C. 1960. Leaf protein as a human food. Lancet (7126) (Mar. 26) 704–705.

JADHAV, B. and JOSHI, R.N. 1977. Extractability of leaf protein from the green tops of groundnut (*Arachis hypogaea* L.) J. Food Sci. Technol. *14*, 179–180.

JADHAV, B., TEKALE, N.S. and JOSHI, R.N. 1979. Green-manure crops as a source of leaf protein. Indian J. Agric. Sci. *49*, 371–373.

JOSHI, A.L., MUNGIKAR, A.M., SANE, M.S., BADAVE, V.C., PARSAD, V.L., KHARAT, S.T. and RANGNEKAR, D.V. 1979. Comparative evaluation of whole lucerne *(Medicago sativa)* and lucerne pulp for ruminants. Pap. submitted to 5th Int. Symp. Ruminant Physiol. Inst. Natl. Rech. Agron. (I.N.R.A.), Paris, 1979.

JOSHI, K.G. and JOSHI, R.N. 1979. A study on the stability of proteins and carotenoid pigments in the juice of *Parthenium hysterophorus* L. Indian J. Bot. *2*, 32–36.

JOSHI, R.N. 1971. The yields of leaf protein that can be extracted from crops of Aurangabad. *In* Leaf Protein: Its Agronomy, Preparation, Quality and Use. N.W. Pirie (Editor). Blackwell, Oxford.

JOSHI, R.N. 1978. Status of green crop fractionation in India. *In* Proc. 2nd Int. Green Crop Drying Congr., Univ. Saskatchewan, Saskatoon, Canada, Aug. 20–25, 1978.

JOSHI, R.N. and SAVANGIKAR, V.A. 1977. Preliminary studies on the extraction of protein from *Parthenium hysterophorus* L. Proc. Weed Sci. Conf. Indian Soc. Weed Sci., Hyderabad, 1977.

KAMALANATHAN, G. and DEVADAS, R.P. 1971. Acceptability of food preparations containing leaf protein concentrates. *In* Leaf Protein: Its Agronomy, Preparation, Quality, and Use. N.W. Pirie (Editor). Blackwell, Oxford.

KAMALANATHAN, G., KARUPPIAH, P. and DEVADAS, R.P. 1975. Supplementary value of leaf protein and groundnut meal in the diet of preschool children. Indian. J. Nutr. Diet. *12*, 203–205.

KAUR, S. and VIJAYARAGHAVAN, P.K. 1961. Leaf proteins in nutrition. Curr. Sci. *30*, 298–299.

KAWATRA, B.L., GARCHA, J.S. and WAGLE, D.S. 1974. Effect of supplementation of leaf protein extracted from berseem *(Trifolium alexandrinum)* to wheat flour diet. J. Food Sci. Technol. *11*, 241–242.

KRISHNAMOORTHY, K.K. 1977. Leaf protein project—Status Report, Tamil Nadu Agricultural University, Coimbatore. Presented at Indian Leaf Prot. Res. Get-together, Mysore, July 4–5, 1977.

KRISHNAMOORTHY, K.K., BALASUNDARAM, C.S., CHANDRAMANI, R. and BALAKRISHNAN, T. 1975. Effect of benedyne on the dry matter and extractable protein yields in sunnhemp (*Crotalaria juncea* L.). Madras Agric. J. *62*, 29.

KRISHNAMURTHY, N., GEETHA, S. and DEVADAS, R.P. 1976. Biological utilization of β-carotene from Amaranth and leaf protein in preschool children. Indian J. Nutr. Diet. *13*, 293–295.

MAHADEVIAH, S. and SINGH, N. 1968. Leaf protein from the green tops of *Cichorium intybus* L. (chicory). Indian J. Exp. Biol. *6*, 193–194.

MATAI, S. 1977. Status report on leaf protein research. Presented at Indian Leaf Prot. Res. Get-together, Mysore, July 4–5, 1977.

MATAI, S. and BAGCHI, D.K. 1974. Some promising legumes for leaf protein extraction. Sci. Cult. *40*, 34–37.

MATAI, S., BAGCHI, D.K. and CHANDA, S. 1973. Optimal seed rate and fertilizer dose for maximum yield of extracted protein from the leaves of mustard (*Brassica nigra* Koch) and turnip (*Brassica rapa* L.). Indian J. Agric. Sci. *43*, 165–169.

MATAI, S., BAGCHI, D.K. and CHANDA, S. 1976. Effects of seed rate, nitrogen level and leaf age on the yield of extracted protein from five different crops in West Bengal. J. Sci. Food Agric. *27*, 736–742.

MATAI, S., BAGCHI, D.K. and CHANDA, S. 1978. Yield of extracted leaf protein from EC 4216, a fodder variety of cowpea. Indian J. Agron. *23*, 163–166.

MATAI, S., BAGCHI, D.K. and RAYCHAUDHURI, S. 1971. Leaf protein from some plants in West Bengal. Sci. Eng. *24*, 102–105.

MORRISON, J.E. and PIRIE, N.W. 1961. The large scale production of protein from leaf extracts. J. Sci. Food Agric. *12*, 1–5.

MUNGIKAR, A.M., BATRA, U.R., TEKALE, N.S. and JOSHI, R.N. 1976A. Effects of nitrogen fertilisation on the yields of extracted protein from seven crops. Exp. Agric. *12*, 353–359.

MUNGIKAR, A.M. and JOSHI, R.N. 1976. Studies on the ensilage of the residues left after extraction of leaf protein from lucerne and hybrid napier grass. Indian J. Nutr. Diet. *13*, 39–43.

MUNGIKAR, A.M., TEKALE, N.S. and JOSHI, R.N. 1976B. The yields of leaf protein and fibre that can be obtained from fractionation of berseem (*Trifolium alexandrinum* L.). Indian J. Nutr. Diet. *13*, 114–118.

OELSHLEGEL, F.J., SCHROEDER, J.R. and STAHMANN, M.A. 1969. Protein concentrates: Use of residues as silage. J. Agric. Food Chem. *17*, 796–798.

PIRIE, N.W. 1969. The present position of research on the use of leaf protein as a human food. Plant Foods Hum. Nutr. *1*, 237–246.

PIRIE, N.W. 1971. Leaf Protein: Its Agronomy, Preparation, Quality and Use. N.W. Pirie (Editor). IBP Handb. *20*. Blackwell, Oxford.

PIRIE, N.W. 1976. Food protein sources. Philos. Trans. R. Soc. London Ser. B: *274*, 489–496.

PIRIE, N.W. 1978. Leaf Protein and Other Aspects of Fodder Fractionation. Cambridge University Press, London.

PRASAD, V.L., DEV, D.V., PATIL, R.E., JOSHI, A.L. and RANGNEKAR, D.V. 1977B. A note on feeding of lucerne extract to pre-ruminant calves as part of milk replacer. Indian J. Dairy Sci. *30*, 154–156.

PRASAD, V.L., PATIL, B.R., JOSHI, A.L. and RANGNEKAR, D.V. 1977A. Lucerne extract for calves. *Indian Dairyman 29*, 669–671.

RAMANA, K.V.R. and SINGH, N. 1971A. β-carotene in leaf proteins. Curr. Sci. *40*, 293–294.

RAMANA, K.V.R. and SINGH, N. 1971B. Nutritional efficiency of lucerne leaf protein as a source of β-carotene in rat diets. Indian J. Exp. Biol. *9*, 378–380.

RAMANA, K.V.R. and SINGH, N. 1971C. Studies on carotene and xanthophyll pigments in leaf protein and their stability during storage. Indian J. Exp. Biol. *9*, 478–480.

SAUNDERS, R.M., CONNOR, M.A., BOOTH, A.N., BICKOFF, E.M. and KOHLER, G.O. 1973. Measurement of digestibility of alfalfa protein concentrates by *in vivo* and *in vitro* methods. J. Nutr. *103*, 530–535.

SAVANGIKAR, V.A. 1977. Studies on leaf proteins—II. Ph.D. Thesis. Marathwada University, Aurangabad, India.

SAVANGIKAR, V.A. and JOSHI, R.N. 1976. Influence of irrigation and fertiliser on the yields of extracted protein from lucerne. Forage Res. *2*, 125–130.

SAVANGIKAR, V.A. and JOSHI, R.N. 1978A. Edible protein from *Parthenium hysterophorus* L. Exp. Agric. *14*, 93–94.

SAVANGIKAR, V.A. and JOSHI, R.N. 1978B. Immobilization of pepsin in active form in paraffin wax. J. Food Sci. *43*, 1616–1618.

SHURPALEKAR, K.S., SINGH, N. and SUNDARAVALLI, O.E. 1969. Nutritive value of leaf protein from lucerne *(Medicago sativa)*: Growth responses in rats at different protein levels and to supplementation with lysine and/or methionine. Indian J. Exp. Biol. 7, 279–280.

SHURPALEKAR, K.S., SUNDARAVALLI, O.E. and SINGH, N. 1969. Supplementary effects of lucerne leaf protein in rice diets fed to rats. Sci. Cult. *35*, 644–645.

SINGH, N. 1964. Leaf protein extraction from some plants of northern India. J. Food Sci. Technol. *1*, 37–39.

SINGH, N. 1969A. Leaf protein as food. Sci. Rep. *6*, 404–407.

SINGH, N. 1969B. Leaf protein research in India. J. Food Sci. Technol. *6*, 165–168.

SINGH, N. 1969C. Leaf proteins in nutrition—Studies on production, nutritive value and utilization. Overdruk uit Voeding *30*, 710–713.

SINGH, N. 1974A. Prospects for leaf protein research and development. J. Sci. Ind. Res. *33*, 51–54.

SINGH, N. 1974B. A bibliography of relevance to leaf protein research and development. J. Sci. Ind. Res. *33*, 55–59.

SINGH, N. 1975. Status of leaf protein in India. J. Sci. Ind. Res. *34*, 538–542.

SINGH, N. 1977. Leaf protein research at CFTRI, Mysore—Status report. Presented at Indian Leaf Prot. Res. Get-together, July, 4–5, 1977.

SMITH, D. 1969. Influence of temperature on the yield and chemical composition of Vernal alfalfa at first flower. Agron. J. *61*, 470–473.

SUBBA RAO, M.S., SINGH, N. and PRASANNAPPA, G. 1967. Preservation of wet leaf-protein concentrates. J. Sci. Food Agric. *18*, 295–298.

SUBBA RAU, B.H., MAHADEVIAH, S. and SINGH, N. 1969. Nutritional studies on whole-extract coagulated leaf protein and fractionated chloroplastic and cytoplasmic proteins from lucerne *(Medicago sativa)*. J. Sci. Food Agric. *20*, 355–358.

SUBBA RAU, B.H., RAMANA, K.V.R., and SINGH, N. 1972. Studies on nutritive value of leaf proteins and some factors affecting their quality. J. Sci. Food Agric. *23*, 233–245.

SUBBA RAU, B.H. and SINGH, N. 1970. Studies on nutritive value of leaf protein from lucerne *(Medicago sativa)*: II. Effect of processing conditions. Indian J. Exp. Biol. *8*, 34–36.

SUBBA RAU, B.H. and SINGH, N. 1971. Studies on nutritive value of leaf protein from lucerne *(Medicago sativa)*: III. Supplementation of rat diets based on wheat. J. Sci. Food Agric. *22*, 569–571.

SUR, B.K. 1961. Nutritive value of lucerne-leaf proteins. Biological value of lucerne proteins and their supplementary relations to rice proteins measured by balance and rat growth methods. Br. J. Nutr. *15*, 419–424.

SUR, B.K. and SUBRAHMANYAN, V. 1955. Utilization of calcium and phosphorus in the poor rice diet supplemented with lucerne or milk powder. Indian J. Med. Res. *43*, 231–235.

TEKALE, N.S. and JOSHI, R.N. 1976. Extractable protein from by-product vegetation of some cole and root crops. Ann. Appl. Biol. *82*, 155–157.
TEKALE, N.S. and JOSHI, R.N. 1977. Studies on stability of carotenoid pigments in lucerne vegetation and juice. Indian J. Nutr. Diet. *14*, 161–166.
VALLI DEVI, A., RAO, N.A.N. and VIJAYARAGHAVAN, P.K. 1965. Isolation and composition of leaf protein from certain species of Indian flora. J. Sci. Food Agric. *16*, 116–120.

28

Village Leaf Protein Production: A Cost Analysis[1]

Walter J. Bray

Recent large feeding programs in India (Martin 1977) and Pakistan (Shah 1978) have shown the benefits that accrue to children who regularly consume a nutrient concentrate made from plant leaves. These programs have also shown that this product can easily be presented so as to be wholly acceptable to the children. Nevertheless, questions remain concerning leaf nutrient. Paramount among them is the cost of production in developing countries, particularly in village operations.

A study was carried out in November 1979 by the Meals for Millions/Freedom from Hunger Foundation in three locations in India to establish the economics of fractionating green crops and the cost of various items related to the production of leaf protein concentrate. The findings are summarized here:

(1) Scale of Operation

Initially a very small operation was considered, one which would provide 15 g of LPC a day for each of 100 children. It was found, however, that such a unit would not be economic. An operation which would process about 1 MT of green crop a day was then selected as one that would be economically viable and yet still constitute a village unit, i.e., require less than 10 hp and allow most of the operations to be performed manually.

(2) Processes and Yield

Juice can be separated from the pulped crop by either pressing or extraction (Pirie 1978). Both processes were considered since they give significantly different yields (Bray 1977), do not use the same equipment

[1]Excerpted from Bray (1980).

Fig. 28.1. Indian children outside their home.

throughout, and have different energy requirements. Process 1, pressing, is detailed in Fig. 28.2; it produces an average of 25 kg of LPC from 1 MT of fresh crop. Process 2, in which aqueous extraction replaces the pressing step, could be expected to yield 40 kg of leaf nutrient.

(3) Equipment Costs

These were very similar for the two processes, totaling Rs 25,500 ($3185)[2] for Process 1 and Rs 25,000 ($3125) for Process 2. The most expensive single item in both cases was the pulper, at about Rs 5500 ($700). The addition of several other pieces of equipment to the processes, primarily a boiler and a dryer, would increase costs by Rs 11,500 ($1400), boosting the total to about Rs 37,000 ($4550). This unit would provide a nutrient supplement for 2000 children a day; the total capital investment would be only Rs 18.50 ($2.30) per recipient. It is noted that this investment is only one-tenth of that required for other food processing operations such as extrusion cooking plants and roasting/grinding facilities.

(4) Crop and Crop Costs

Alfalfa was the crop used to prepare the protein concentrate in the Mysore feeding trials (Doraiswamy *et al.* 1969) and more recently was the source material in the Coimbatore project (Martin 1977). Since alfalfa is also

[2] $1 (U.S.) equals Rs 8.00 (rupees).

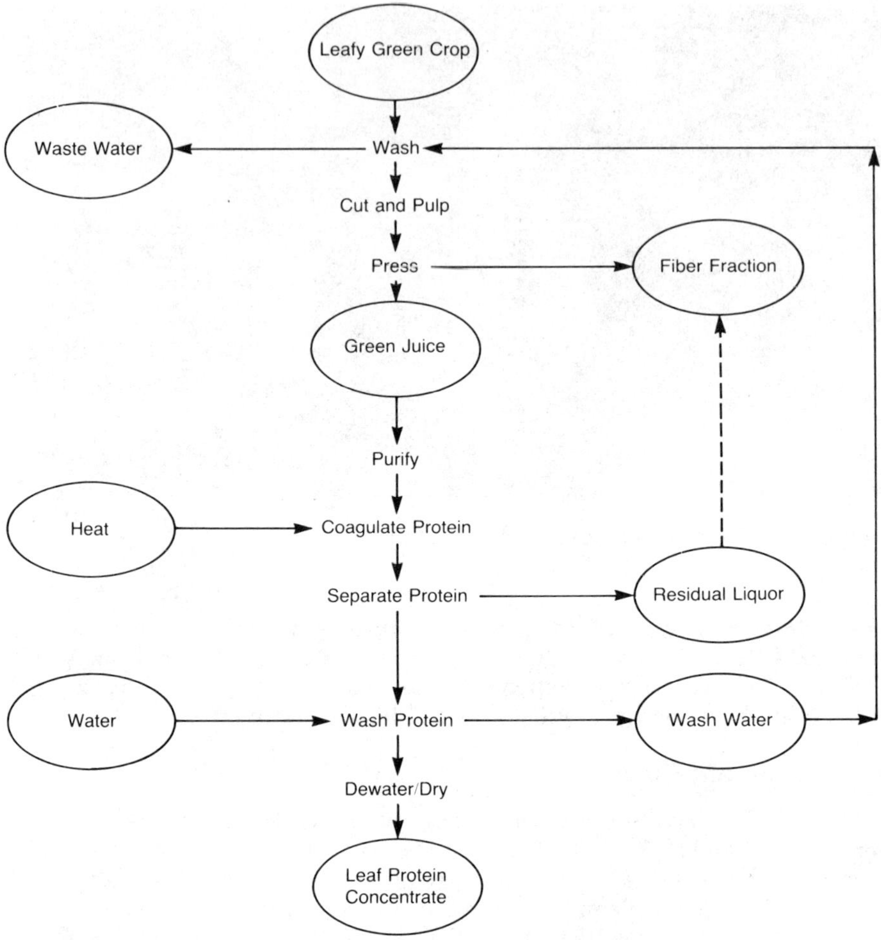

Fig. 28.2. Leaf protein/green crop fractionation process flow chart for Process 1—pressing.

widely grown in India, it is the crop considered in this study. Current prices for alfalfa vary widely in India and are not deemed meaningful in relation to a year-round operation with a guaranteed market as feed for the fractionation unit. The farmers should, of course, receive a good price for the crop, equivalent to that which they might receive raising sugarcane, rice, or other staples. Thus, with an expected annual yield of 100 MT of fresh alfalfa per ha (Joshi 1979), it was calculated that a farmer should be paid Rs 130 per MT for the alfalfa.

Fig. 28.3. A small-scale pulper/press.

(5) By-product Value

Both the fiber and solubles fractions can be used as feed for ruminant animals and as such have a real value. Processes 1 and 2 would remove 30 to 50% of the protein in the fresh crop, respectively; however, the value of the by-products as feed would only be reduced by 15 to 25% since straw, with essentially no protein, sells for half the price assigned to the fresh alfalfa.

It is noted that when using leaf nutrient in feeding programs, it is desirable to tie a small dairy into the nutrition activities (Devadas 1979). The fiber-solubles fractions from 1 MT of fresh green crop would provide the bulk of the daily forage for about 30 cows. These cows would be expected to produce 75 to 100 liters of milk each day.

(6) Labor Requirements and Wage Rate

Both Processes 1 and 2 were analyzed in detail to determine their labor requirements. Both would need a supervisor/lead operator. The extraction process would employ an additional three operators and two helpers. The use of a continuous press, in Process 1, simplifies operations so that only two operators and two helpers are required. Depending on the local supply of and demand for labor, a man now earns Rs 5–7 for a 10 hr day in India, with

Fig. 28.4. Pulper/press in operation.

women and boys paid less. On this basis, it was determined that the pay in the fractionation plant should be Rs 7.50 for an 8 hr day for the operators and Rs 6 for helpers. The supervisor should have an effective pay of Rs 300 a month or about Rs 12 a day.

(7) Power Requirements and Cost

For the fractionation of 1 MT of fresh crop a day, Process 1 would have a connected electrical load of 9 hp (6.75 kw per hr), while Process 2 would require 7.5 hp (5.6 kw per hr), i.e., extraction does not require the electrical power that pressing does. The cost of power varies considerably from one

Fig. 28.5. A field of alfalfa.

part of India to another as well as with the user category. A "light industry" rate of Rs 0.27 per kwh was assumed in the cost calculations.

(8) Fuel Requirements and Costs

Prices were obtained on the standard fuels in India (excepting cow dung). Low quality coal was found to be the least expensive based on the amount of heat recoverable from a controlled fire. Wood was the next least expensive fuel. In the fractionation process, the leaf protein concentrate is recovered from the juice after heating it to 85°C to coagulate the protein. To heat the juice from Process 1 would require the burning of approximately 11 kg of coal a day. On the other hand, Process 2, in which a considerable amount of residual liquor is recycled in order to extract the protein from the pulped crop, would require that 90 kg of coal be burned. A biogas plant connected with an associated dairy operation would eliminate the need to purchase fuel.

(9) Other Costs

Maintenance costs and the expense of supplies were calculated from the general experience of workers in the field (Devadas 1979; Joshi 1979). Depreciation was taken at 20% of the total equipment cost each year. While low cost interest loans might be available, a commercial rate of 12% was assumed in the calculations.

Fig. 28.6. Washing the alfalfa prior to processing.

(10) Production Cost Summary

A summary of the cost of production of leaf nutrient is presented in Table 28.1. For Process 2, the total is just over Rs 5 per kg, while for Process 1 it is about Rs 6.35 per kg.

(11) Possible Cost Variances

The manufacturing costs summarized in Table 28.1 were developed on a best judgment basis. It is recognized, however, that the individual cost items may vary for a number of reasons. Accordingly, the items were examined in detail and the possible variability determined. Yield is the most critical item in the cost calculation (see Fig. 28.9). Yields might be 10% lower than assumed previously, and this would increase the leaf protein cost by 10%. Some other costs such as raw materials, depreciation, and interest rates might actually be lower than has been assumed so far. Others such as labor, fuel, and maintenance costs possibly might be higher. The net result is that the calculated manufacturing costs for leaf nutrient shown in Table 28.1, could be underestimated by no more than 17.5%. For Process 1,

Fig. 28.7. Dewatering the protein curd.

TABLE 28.1. LEAF PROTEIN PRODUCTION COST SUMMARY

Costs	Process No. 1	Process No. 2
Raw material	Rs 5.20/kg	Rs 3.25/kg
less by product credit	4.18/kg	2.28/kg
Net raw material cost	1.02/kg	0.97/kg
Plant labor	1.14/kg	0.86/kg
Supervision	0.58/kg	0.36/kg
Water	—	—
Power	0.58/kg	0.30/kg
Fuel	0.13/kg	0.68/kg
Maintenance	0.66/kg	0.42/kg
Supplies, etc.	0.29/kg	0.26/kg
Total variable cost	Rs 4.58	Rs 3.85
Depreciation	Rs 0.91	Rs 0.56
Interest expense	0.60	0.38
Other fixed charges	0.25	0.25
Total fixed costs	1.76	1.19
Production cost	Rs 6.34/kg	Rs 5.04/kg

Rs = Rupees.

Fig. 28.8. Coagulating the protein in the leaf juice.

the production cost might rise to a maximum of Rs 7.45 per kg, while for Process 2, it might reach Rs 5.95 per kg.

(12) Leaf Nutrient Selling Price

The fractionation plant could operate to produce the nutritious food supplement for a group of schools or nutrition centers. Alternatively, the product could be made for sale in village shops. In the former case, the product price would be between Rs 5.50 and 6.75 per kg, depending on the production process used. When sold through a shop, the expected price to a customer would be Rs 6.50 per kg or higher, perhaps up to Rs 7.50 per kg. Based on the daily consumption of 15 g of leaf nutrient per child, i.e., the amount that would provide a three-year-old with 50% of his or her daily protein and iron requirements (Bray 1976A) and 100% of the Vitamin A (Bray 1976B), the cost to the nutrition center would be Rs 0.08 to Rs 0.10 per child per day ($0.010 to $0.0125). From this it can be seen that the product would be readily affordable by a center or nursery school. When purchased in a shop, the cost for a 15 g portion would only be about Rs 0.11. For a family with three small children and Rs 7 a day to spend on food, the purchase of leaf protein concentrate would represent less than 5% of the food budget.

(13) Relative Value of Leaf Nutrient

It is necessary to show not only that the price of leaf nutrient is low, as has been done, but also how it compares with other nutritious foods available in India. Taken on the basis of the cost per unit of protein, horse gram is the least expensive source, leaf nutrient is second, and cowpea third from a list of Indian legumes. As a source of protein, LPC is estimated to cost only about two-thirds as much as the average of the eight most commonly consumed Indian legumes. It should be noted that horse gram proved to be inferior to leaf protein in the Coimbatore feeding trials (Martin 1977). It is also to be noted that dried skimmed milk costs about five times as much as leaf protein concentrate and that whole milk is even more expensive.

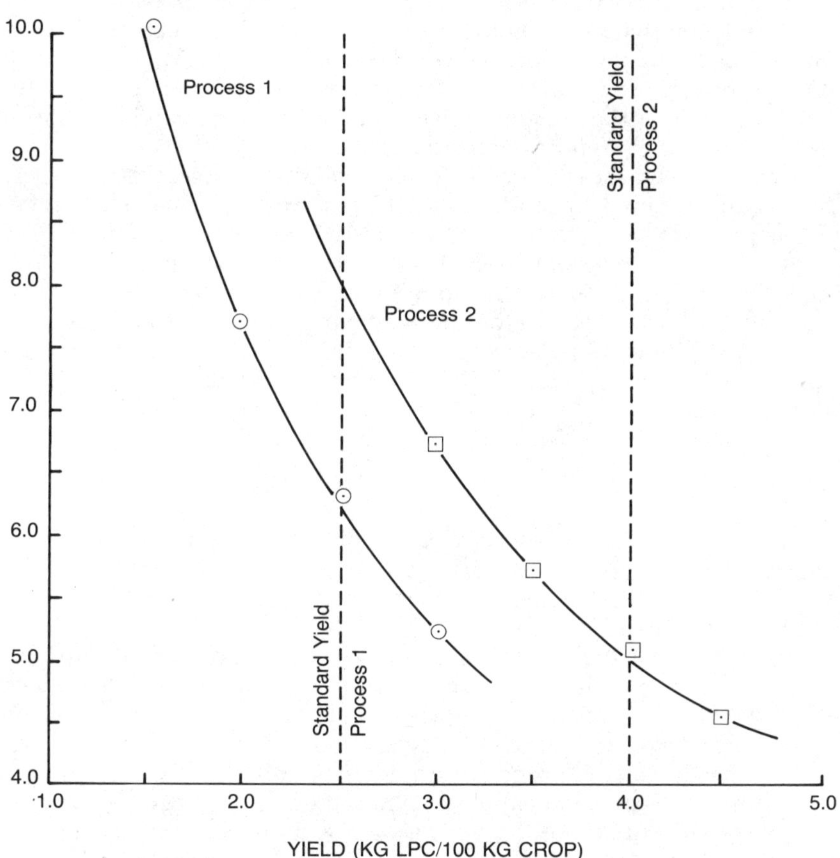

Fig. 28.9. Effect of yield on leaf protein production cost.

(14) Use of Leaf Nutrient Concentrate

The question remains as to how leaf protein concentrate could best be marketed. For balwadies (nursery schools) and nutrition centers, the product would probably be delivered to the site as produced, i.e., as a moist powder. The people in charge of food preparation would then mix it with other ingredients such as sugar, flour, and flavoring to make a product acceptable to children. This was done in Coimbatore (Martin 1977) where the LPC was mixed with jaggery (crude sugar) dissolved in hot water, with cassava flour, ragi flour (pearl millet, *Eleusine coracana*), and a little sesame added, then molded into soft balls, laddus, which were fed to the children as snacks. In local markets, leaf nutrient would almost certainly have to be presented in a form which would permit direct consumption, either as a snack food like the laddu, or as a formed product which could be added to traditional dishes such as curries. [The latter proved highly successful in Pakistan (Toosy and Shah 1974; Shah 1978).]

If the leaf nutrient concentrate were combined with sugar and flour and made into a laddu, this product would cost less than Rs 3 per kg to produce. It could be sold very profitably at Rs 4 to 4.50 per kg, or between Rs 0.20 and Rs 0.25 for 50 g, the amount which would contain enough LPC to provide 50% of the daily protein requirement of a child.

Alternatively, the concentrate could be formed and texturized to convert it into a chewy product similar to a dark green pea or a small chunk of meat. Such products would probably overcome the main problem in gaining acceptance for leaf nutrient concentrate in ordinary diets, namely the color of the powder. The texturized leaf protein concentrate, which could be mixed directly with steamed rice or added to curry sauces without coloring the entire dish green, would be expected to sell for about Rs 9 per kg. In this case the cost of 15 g would be Rs 0.135. For a family spending only Rs 7 a day on food, less than 2% of the total budget would feed a single child the amount needed to provide half of his daily nutrient requirements.

(15) Conclusions

The following general conclusions are drawn from this study of the cost of producing leaf nutrient concentrate in a village unit in India:

(1) A green crop fractionation/leaf protein production unit could easily be operated in a village.

(2) The equipment cost is low enough to be affordable by a group running a number of nutrition centers or by a village nutrition cooperative (possibly a women's cooperative which would be motivated by maternal as well as material considerations).

(3) The leaf nutrient concentrate would be only slightly more costly than many of the commonly consumed protein-rich legumes, and on an overall nutritional basis, it would be much less expensive.

(4) An LPC-containing product that would provide 50% of the daily protein requirements of a child would be affordable by most low income groups in India.

REFERENCES

BRAY, W.J. 1976A. Leaf protein concentrate as a source of minerals. Proc. Nutr. Soc. *35* (1) 35A.

BRAY, W.J. 1976B. Leaf protein concentrate as a source of vitamins. Proc. Nutr. Soc. *35* (1) 6A.

BRAY, W.J. 1977. The processing of leaf protein for human use. Ph.D. Thesis. University of Reading, Reading, England.

BRAY, W.J. 1980. A Study of the Cost of Producing Leaf Protein Concentrate in an Indian Village Operation. Meals for Millions/Freedom from Hunger Foundation, Davis, CA.

DEVADAS, R.P. 1979. Personal communication. Coimbatore, India.

DORAISWAMY, T.R., SINGH, N. and DANIEL, V.A. 1969. Effect of supplementing ragi diets with lysine or leaf protein on the growth and nitrogen metabolism of children. Br. J. Nutr. *23*, 737–743.

JOSHI, R.M. 1979. Personal communication. Aurangabad, India.

MARTIN, C. 1977. Report of Leaf Protein Feeding Trial Conducted at Coimbatore, South India, 1975–1977. Find Your Feet Ltd, London.

PIRIE, N.W. 1978. Leaf Protein and Other Aspects of Fodder Fractionation. Cambridge University Press, Cambridge.

SHAH, F.H. 1978. Fortification of the Human Diet with Leaf Protein Concentrate. PCSIR Laboratories, Lahore, Pakistan.

TOOSY, R.Z. and SHAH, F.H. 1974. Leaf protein concentrate in the human diet. Pak. J. Sci. Ind. Res. *17*, 40–42.

29

Leaf Protein Resource Development in New Zealand

R.W. Bailey and E.L. Hove

Physical Scene

Grassland farming is the base of New Zealand's economy. A temperate climate with mild winters, cool summers and good, well distributed rainfall permits year-round grazing of sheep and cattle. Of the country's 20 million ha of agricultural land, 41% (8.5 million ha) is improved pastureland of mixed perennial ryegrass-white clover swards. When topdressed with superphosphate and with irrigation, the annual yield of dry matter is 18,000 to 23,000 kg/ha. Depending on the frequency of cutting and grazing, the annual phytoproduction of protein can be as high as 4000 kg/ha. To illustrate the size of this production, the annual renewal of improved pasture growth in New Zealand contains protein in amounts equivalent to 50 g daily for 2×10^9 people, or half the present population of the world.

Another green leafy material, lucerne (*Medicago sativa* L. var. Wairau), is grown on 100,000 ha. Two major industrial organizations and some smaller ones are involved in drying and pelleting lucerne meal, mainly for export. In 1975 the export of lucerne pellets was 19,200 MT. The dry matter and protein renewal from lucerne over the six-month growing season are about the same as the annual pasture renewal.

Need for Leaf Protein Concentrate (LPC) in New Zealand

Over the past decade, serious attention has been directed in New Zealand to the possibility of converting a portion of the annual renewal of green leafy material to a protein concentrate for use in feeds of monogastric animals for the following two reasons. First, the efficiency in producing and exporting all of the fractions of pastoral protein-foods (dairy products, beef, and sheep meats) has been so great that the country is short of protein concentrates for pigs and poultry feeds. As a result, substantial amounts of fish meal and soybean meal have been imported to fill the gap. Second, as a converter of high protein leaf to usable animal products, the ruminant is not very efficient (10–30% of the protein consumed). Siphoning off some of the leaf protein and feeding the residue to ruminants should enable the production of the remaining LPC for pigs, poultry, or humans to be used at a much greater protein efficiency (50–60%).

An annual production of 30,000 MT of a 50% leaf protein concentrate would be needed for inclusion in the feed of the 5 million poultry and the 0.5 million swine which currently satisfy the internal demand for such foods. Possibly, a strong LPC industry would permit the development of export quantities of pig meat, poultry products, or LPC as a stock food. Sufficient LPC might be produced either from the pasture swards or from the lucerne production with little impact on the other uses of these green materials.

Approaches to LPC Production

The New Zealand Department of Scientific and Industrial Research (DSIR) undertook a research and development project in 1968 as a feasibility study aimed at establishing an LPC industry as an adjunct to the lucerne pelleting industry and tied to the current system of contracting lucerne production to fit the need and capacity of the industry. The residue after partial protein extraction from fresh lucerne was to be fed into the drying and pelleting stream or fed to ruminants. Although the initial concern was LPC for pigs and poultry, it was accepted that the ultimate aim would be a purified LPC suitable for human consumption.

The New Zealand Ministry of Agriculture and Fisheries (MAF) launched a program in 1972 to develop LPC production as an "on-farm" operation, integrated into normal farming operations to use surplus pasture growth. The residue after partial protein extraction of the green feed would be fed directly to ruminants or ensilaged.

Prior to these approaches, an exploratory trial had been carried out on a local farm by the Food Technology Department of Massey University in Palmerston North. The difficulties met in this early effort have been recorded by Latimer (1968A,B).

In the following account it is convenient to consider New Zealand's work in terms of LPC first from lucerne and other plants grown as crops, and second from pasture. This conveniently divides the work into the activities of the two major agricultural research organizations in New Zealand.

PROTEIN FROM LUCERNE

From Pressed Green Juice

The Procedure. A small pilot plant to prepare leaf protein concentrate from chopped lucerne and other forage crops was established at the DSIR research unit in Lincoln in Canterbury, the district that was at that time (1968) the center of lucerne growing in New Zealand. It was proposed to follow the procedures developed by N.W. Pirie at Rothamsted (see Pirie 1971), which are based on the green leaf juice. A Pirie pulper was obtained to macerate the fresh green plant cells, and a Pirie belt press to squeeze the green juice from the pulped material. The throughput of this operation was 70 kg of fresh lucerne per hr. The green juice was clarified with a desludging centrifuge and steam was injected through a nozzle into batches of 10 liters to raise the temperature to 80°C within 10 min. The coagulated protein was separated in a basket filter centrifuged and dried.

The head of the LPC pilot plant project was the late Dr. R.L. Allison, who had spent some time at Rothamsted to familiarize himself with the techniques. Later, he reviewed the current knowledge on LPC (Allison 1973). The development and use of Dr. Allison's pilot plant and modifications to the pulper and belt press were described by Hove and Bailey (1975). Allison's procedure for LPC has been published (Hove *et al.* 1974).

A typical flow chart and yield data are given in Fig. 29.1. The green juice pressed from the pulped lucerne has 10% solids (range 8.8 to 10.9%); and the range in pH was 6.1 to 6.3. Clover and ryegrass green juices had similar solids contents, but sainfoin *(Onobrychis viciifolia)* juice had less than 5% solids. Within 5 min of pressing at room temperature (18°C), the sainfoin juice separated into a green precipitate and a brown protein-free whey. Sainfoin has a particularly high tannin content. Undoubtedly, the tannins reacted rapidly with the protein, rendering much of it insoluble in the pulped material and rapidly precipitating the portion that did get into the juice. The experience with sainfoin emphasizes the importance of the tannin content of green crops in determining the yield of protein in fractionating fresh green forage crops.

The solids of the green lucerne juice were about equally partitioned between the coagulated protein curd and the whey. The representative data in Fig. 29.1 show that the whey plus the washings from the curd contained 18.8% of the solids of the original lucerne crop. Barnes (1976) looked at the possibility of growth of yeasts on this nutrient media.

The green juice contained 45% of the crude protein of the original lucerne. As Morrison and Pirie (1961) showed, higher protein yields can be obtained by repeated moistening and repressing of the residue cake, but this was not considered germaine to product development in New Zealand. The washed and dried LPC represented about 13.5% of the original solids and about 34% of the original crude protein. The press cake residue had 74.5% moisture; this was substantially less than the 83.0% moisture in the original crop. To dehydrate this press cake to a product with 10% moisture would require the removal of 259 kg water for every 100 kg of final product; this compares with the requirements to remove 429 kg water per 100 g of final product (with 10% moisture) when starting with the original lucerne. Thus, substantial savings in dehydration costs should be realized. Feeding trials showed that the residue was acceptable to ruminants (Vartha and Allison 1971).

Separation. The coagulated lucerne protein was easiest to separate when it had a strong curd and large particle size. Generally, the filter

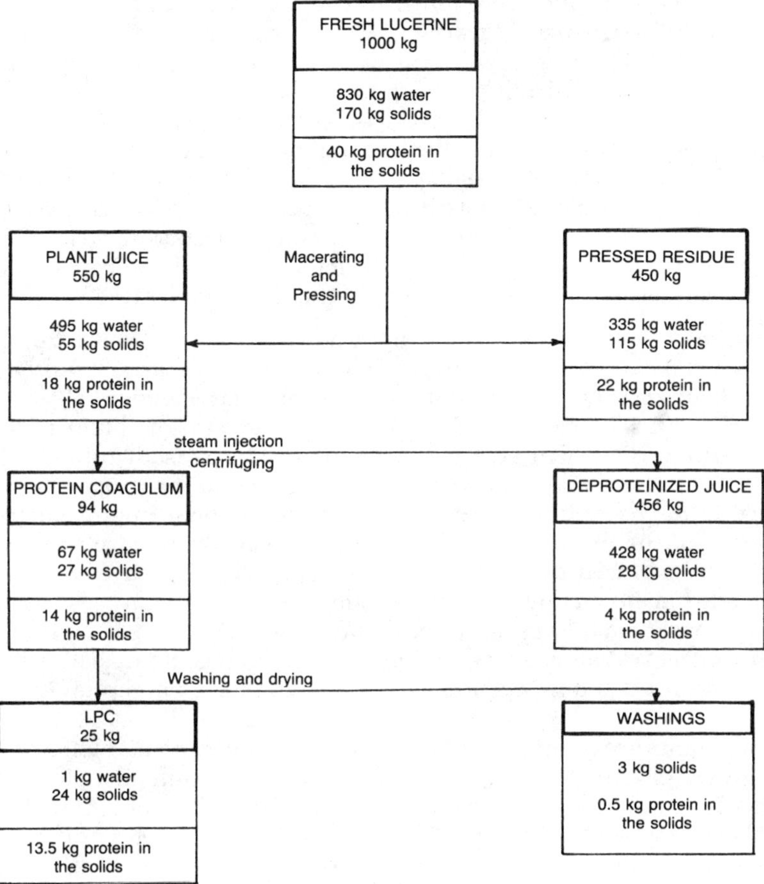

Fig. 29.1. Flow chart and yield data from a typical run of LPC preparation from lucerne at the Lincoln pilot plant.

(basket) centrifuge worked adequately with lucerne. However, the gelatinous fine precipitate obtained with Tama ryegrass clogged the filter, so a decanting centrifuge was used. A simple rotary press as used in producing casein was not very suitable for the weak LPC curds. Whatever way it was separated, the lucerne protein had to be washed with large volumes of warm (45°C) water to remove saponins known to be present in the variety of lucerne used.

Drying. The protein curd was freeze-dried. Obviously, this procedure is too costly (estimated at $1/kg of product) for commercial animal feed production. However, it was thought best to first establish the maximum nutritional potential of the product uncomplicated by possible secondary damage through drying procedures. In the period of 1971 through 1973, about 80 kg of freeze-dried lucerne LPC was prepared for nutritional testing. The possibility of spray-drying was examined; 15 kg sample of the washed protein curd with 28% dry matter was spray-dried by D.J. Woodhams of the Dairy Research Institute in Palmerston North. The material was first passed through a colloid mill to get proper particle size, diluted to 25% solids, and put through an experimental drier. The inlet air temperature was 189°C and the exhaust air temperature was 103°C. The maximum product temperature was 60°C. Dr. Woodham's evaluation was, "The lucerne product was comparatively easy to dry and we anticipate no problems on a commercial scale." Other drying methods were not tried.

Additives. It has been claimed by American workers that addition of alkali to pH 8–10 during pulping of the green leafy material resulted in a slight (about 5%) increase in protein yield that was commercially worthwhile. However, Morrison and Pirie (1961) had earlier found that the increased protein yield at pH 8 was accompanied by a disadvantage. At the Lincoln pilot plant, one trial with ammonia added to the chopped lucerne resulted in no discernible increase in yield and without improvements in separation of the protein curd. Extensive oxidation of plant phenolics occurred, as evidenced by a very dark product, residue and whey. It was concluded that no advantage, and possibly some disadvantages, resulted from the ammonia addition. Fafunso and Byers (1977) reported that leaf protein concentrates made by any process involving alkali had a larger phenolic content, and this depressed lysine availability and protein digestion.

Antioxidants are commonly added during pulping of the plant material or to the green juice immediately on pressing. At the Lincoln pilot plant, 0.5% of potassium metabisulfite was added routinely to the juice. One experimental run in which the metabisulfite was omitted produced a product with no detectable differences in nutritional protein quality.

The Product. ***Chemical Analyses.*** In common with many earlier reports on LPC, the lucerne LPC prepared at the Lincoln pilot plant had a well balanced amino acid profile rich in lysine and other essential amino acids except methionine and cystine (Hove *et al.* 1974). After thorough washing, the crude protein (N × 6.25) was 60% (56 to 66% in different batches). Without washing, the protein content was 52–54% on a dry matter basis. Some materials, possibly soluble carbohydrate and minerals, were removed by washing.

The ash, at 4.4%, was lower than frequently observed. Initial values of about 20% ash led to care in harvesting, with higher cuts to avoid soil and dust, and this was effective in lowering the crude ash value. A sample of commercial, imported lucerne LPC (X-Pro) had an ash of 23% (Hove *et al.* 1974).

Saponifiable lipid was 3.5% and nonsaponifiable lipid 11.8%. Much of the latter was chlorophylloid and carotenoid pigments. Of total fatty acids in the product, 51% was linolenic acid and 11% linoleic acid. In other words, over 2% of the LPC product was polyunsaturated fatty acids; this tends to create oxidative instability if anitoxidant levels are inadequate. Tocopherol levels in the product were not determined, but α-tocopherol was obviously low because fatal tocopherol deficiency occurred when the product was fed to rats in a diet without added vitamin E. In two experiments (Table 29.1), a total of 11 young rats fed the LPC product at 20% in a diet without added vitamin E or selenium died within 3 weeks, showing the syndrome of lung-hemorrhage/liver necrosis described by Hove *et al.* (1949). All 11 of the

TABLE 29.1. FATAL LIVER NECROSIS IN RATS FED PROTEIN CONCENTRATES FROM LUCERNE OR MILK, AND PROTECTION BY VITAMIN E OR SELENIUM SUPPLEMENTS

Diet Protein Source		Diet Supplements			Deaths	
Material	Level[1] (%)	Toco-pherol (mg/kg)	Se (mg/kg)	Liver Necrosis Incidence	No. Rats	Days
Lucerne LPC	15	0	0	11/11	11	14–29
Lucerne LPC	15	50	0	0/6	0	—
Lucerne LPC	15	0	0.1	0/5	0	—
Lactalbumin[2]	11	0	0	4/5	4	18–32
Lactalbumin[2]	11	50	0	0/5	0	—
Lactalbumin[2]	11	0	0.1	0/5	0	—
Casein[2]	9	0	0	3/5	1	16
Casein[2]	9	50	0	0/5	0	—

[1] Level to supply 9% protein in a diet without added vitamin E or selenium; but otherwise with complete vitamin and mineral mix; 5% olive oil and sucrose to 100%.
[2] Lactalbumin and casein were commercial products from Manawatu Co-op Dairy Co., Ltd.

control rats on the same diet, but with either DL-α-tocopherol or sodium selenite added, survived with no pathological lesions. The LPC product obviously was deficient in selenium as well as vitamin E. It has been known since 1957 that selenium can replace vitamin E in preventing the fatal syndrome. New Zealand is well known to suffer from selenium deficiency in soils, plants, and animals (Robinson 1975). This is demonstrated by the data in Table 29.1 which show fatal selenium deficiencies, not only in the lucerne grown in the Canterbury Plains of the South Island, but also in the milk protein products produced commercially in the Manawatu of the North Island. However, these deficiencies present no practical problems since pig and poultry feeds are routinely fortified with these two essential nutrients, as was done also for all subsequent rat feeding trials.

Carbohydrates in the lucerne LPC included about 3% of cellulose plus hemicelluloses and about 13% of undetermined material assumed to be insoluble carbohydrates, possibly existing as glycoproteins.

Rat Feeding Trials. Protein quality was determined by the widely accepted 4-week PER growth procedure. The sole dietary protein, at about

10% supplied by LPC products prepared from lucerne, white clover, or pasture swards, showed PER values of 1.5 to 1.9; supplements of DL-methionine or L-cystine increased these values to 2.6 to 3.1 (control casein at 2.50) as shown in Table 29.2. Hove *et al.* (1974) also showed that lucerne LPC was an excellent supplement to the protein of barley.

Long-term and high levels of LPC feeding to rats (Hove *et al.* 1974) revealed a few problems. At levels to supply 10% protein, LPC produced the same rate of weight gains as casein over six months (methionine added in all cases). However, at 20 to 30% dietary protein levels, the rats fed LPC grew slower than casein control rats, although they eventually reached nearly the same weight. The apparent protein digestibility was low at about 80% in all LPC-fed animals as compared with 93% in casein-fed rats. Body composition of LPC-fed rats differed from casein control rats in that body water was higher and body fat was lower. No pathological lesions (gross or histological) were observed in liver or kidneys, and all other organs were normal in weight. At all three levels of LPC (10, 20, and 30% protein), reproduction was normal; males were fertile and females bore and raised their young to weaning in a normal way.

A rat growth bioassay for available lysine showed that the lysine of lucerne LPC was 79% available in the freeze-dried product from the Lincoln pilot plant, but was only 54% available in "X-Pro," the commercial imported product. In line with these values, the PER of the "X-Pro" was significantly lower (Table 29.2).

TABLE 29.2. NUTRITIONAL QUALITY OF VARIOUS LEAF PROTEIN CONCENTRATES (LPC) AND THE EFFECT OF METHIONINE OR CYSTINE SUPPLEMENTS, AS DETERMINED BY THE STANDARD PER 4-WEEK RAT GROWTH METHOD

	Without Added Sulfur Amino Acids		With Added Methionine (M) or Cystine (C)	
Source of LPC (% Protein Content)	Gain (g)	PER ± sem	Gain (g)	PER ± sem
Lucerne—Lincoln LPC[1] (60% protein)	58	1.92 ± 0.08	(M) 106 (C) 101	3.02 ± 0.16 3.13 ± 0.21
Lucerne—"X-Pro" LPC[1] (38% protein)	53	1.60 ± 0.09	(M) 99	2.23 ± 0.06
Lucerne—white protein[2] (40% protein)	—	—	(M) 58	2.59 ± 0.11
White clover LPC (53% protein)	53	1.80 ± 0.07	(M) 148 (C) 136	310 ± 0.13 3.14 ± 0.11
Summer pasture LPC (54% protein)	51	1.52 ± 0.10	(M) 144	2.81 ± 0.12
Casein control	106	(2.50 ± 0.08)[3]	(M) 142	2.79 ± 0.07
Zero protein control	−19	—	(M) −17	—

[1]As previously reported by Hove *et al.* (1974).
[2]White protein fraction prepared by Allison's amyl alcohol procedure.
[3]Casein PER was 2.7–3.12 for different assays: all other PER values were adjusted to a common casein value of 2.50.
sem—Standard Error of the Mean.

Pig Feeding Trials. In a preliminary study, young pigs on a standard diet were offered coagulated green juice made from Tama ryegrass. Voluntary consumption replaced only 7% of the total diet dry matter. Weight gains of these animals were about 11% lower than controls to market weight (Allison, quoted by Hove and Bailey 1975).

At Massey University, Carr and Pearson (1976) found that pigs fed the commercial imported LPC, "X-Pro," instead of the usual fish meal with meat and bone meal, showed slower gains from weaning (25 kg) to 55 kg body weight, but showed normal gains thereafter to 80 kg market weight. It should be pointed out that "X-Pro" had lower protein quality and available lysine than locally produced (freeze-dried) lucerne LPC.

Chick Feeding. Allison reported (quoted by Hove and Bailey 1975) that lucerne LPC could replace up to 25% of the protein in a standard broiler diet with no adverse effect on growth or feed efficiency of the birds.

Photosensitivity. During initial rat-feeding trials, Hove *et al.* (1974) noted severe disfiguring photosensitivity in animals fed all three levels of lucerne LPC (10, 20, and 30% dietary protein). Casein-fed rats were not affected. The lesions included necrosis and sloughing of ears and tails, with extensive open sores on face, back, and paws. The severity of the lesions was correlated with the closeness of the rat to a fixed glass window admitting diffuse summer daylight, but no direct sunlight. Subsequently, it was established (Lohrey *et al.* 1974) that the active photosensitizing agent was pheophorbide formed from chlorophyll by enzymatic removal of the phytyl side chain during the preparation of the LPC. Pheophorbide was found in blood and liver of the rats; the amount of pheophorbide in various LPC preparations was correlated with their photosensitizing potential. Later, Tapper *et al.* (1975) prepared pure chlorophyll-derived pigments and established by feeding trials that pheophorbide *a* (but not pheophorbide *b*) was the photosensitizing agent.

The conversion of inert chlorophyll to the highly photosensitizing pheophorbide *a* was brought about by the enzyme chlorophyllase, present in lucerne leaves. The enzymatic conversion was very rapid at 70° to 80°C, the temperature used to coagulate protein, and increased with the time held at that temperature. The original Pirie process (Morrison and Pirie 1961) had emphasized rapidity in the heating to 80°C to coagulate protein, followed by rapid cooling. Their motivation was to prevent heat damage to the nutritional quality of the protein. An unexpected benefit of the rapid action was minimal formation of the dangerous pheophorbide *a*.

Formation of pheophorbide *a* could be minimized either by rapid heating of the green juice to about 90°C, which destroyed the chlorophyllase enzyme (Tapper *et al.* 1975) or by flash heating to 80°C and rapid cooling. Not realizing the danger, it had been the custom at the Lincoln plant to hold the juice at 70°–80°C for about 10 min to ensure complete coagulation; this permitted rapid buildup of pheophorbide *a*. Tapper *et al.* (1975) used high levels of dietary pheophorbide and more intense illumination which caused the death of rats after a few hours illumination. The animals showed severe facial edema and signs of physiological shock. Thus, the photosensitizing problem can be lethal for the animals and not merely a cosmetic effect.

Not all plants have chlorophyllase in their leaves. LPC prepared from ryegrass and pasture grass had little or no photosensitizing action at the levels fed. For safety, LPC preparations should be monitored for pheophorbide *a*. We have found that LPC preparations with less than 0.9 mg/g of pheophorbide *a* (as in ryegrass LPC) are safe. Products with over 6 mg/g were severely dangerous; less than 5% of such a product in the diet caused severe lesions or death in animals exposed to simulated daylight.

Only light-skinned animals were subject to the photosensitizing effects. White mice fed lucerne LPC died quickly under illumination, whereas black mice in the same cages showed no ill effect.

White crossbred pigs were fed "X-Pro," a lucerne LPC which contained 2 mg/g of pheophorbide. The photosensitized lesions that occurred in the pigs correlated with the level of LPC in the diet but were not permanent or disfiguring (Carr and Pearson 1976).

Saponins. We have assumed that saponins were responsible for the poor initial growth we always observed in animals fed unwashed lucerne LPC, and in mice fed freeze-dried "whey" (Hove *et al.* 1974). However, the actual nature of these growth suppressants was not established.

White Protein Products. Proteins in the green leaves occur in two major fractions: insoluble protein associated with the chloroplast fraction (green protein, which also contains all of the leaf pigments), and soluble protein associated with the cell sap fraction (white protein). The green juice produced by pulping and pressing the leafy material has at least half of the total protein of the original plant, the amount depending on the degree of cell rupture. Both protein fractions are present in in this juice. It is said (Pirie 1971) that the green and white proteins are present in ratios of from 2:1 to 1:1 when separated by differential heat (60° to 80°C). The two fractions can also be separated by differential pH, centrifugation, fractional ammonium sulfate precipitation, or combinations of these (Menke 1938). While pigs and poultry can consume the total LPC, for texturizing for direct human consumption, a white fraction is desirable.

Allison (1969, quoted in Hove and Bailey 1975) described a novel method of separating the green and white fractions of leaf juice. n-Butanol added (3% v/v) to the green juice resulted in an immediate precipitate of the chloroplastic green fraction. After this, the green fraction is separated by centrifugation, and the supernatant can be heated to 80°C or adjusted to a pH of between 4.3 and 4.6, to coagulate the white protein. Precipitation at the isoelectric point without heat has the advantage of producing a soluble protein which can be spray-dried or freeze-dried to retain valuable technological properties of use in food formulations. The nutritive value of this white protein fraction suffers for the great difficulty of removing all traces of solvent. The PER was less than it should have been because of this (Table 29.2).

The mechanism by which n-butanol flocculates the pigmented material is not understood. Possibly the small amount of lipid solvents acts on the membranes to eliminate the electrostatic charges, thus destroying their colloidal properties. Solvents other than n-butanol have been examined; iso-amyl alcohol, at 2% v/v, is more active than n-butanol. The flocculation effect of higher alcohols on pigmented material relates to the water solubility characteristics of such alcohols. Highly insoluble products (octanol) were inactive. Isobutanol is less soluble than n-butanol and was inactive. Chloroform was active but carbon tetrachloride was not. The range of solubility of effective compounds appears to be between 1 and 8 g/100 g water. Probably, the lipophilic portion of the molecule penetrates the chloroplast membrane, while the polar hydrophilic portion brings the material into solution to permit a phase separation.

Other procedures for separating white and green proteins have been tried. A promising one was described by Hove (1975). Total protein of the green juice was precipitated at pH 2.5 in the presence of polyphosphates (sodium hexaphosphate). The white protein was extracted from the precipitate by adjusting to pH 9, leaving the green protein behind. After separation, the white protein was then reprecipitated by adjusting the extract to pH 4.7. However, the yield of soluble white protein was only 12% of the protein of the juice (or 6% of the original lucerne protein), and this was thought to be too low to justify further study.

Summary and Evaluation. Although a protein concentrate can be produced from green juice pressed from pulped lucerne without obviously difficult engineering problems, no industrial organization in New Zealand has undertaken the commercial production of LPC as a factory operation. The balance sheet appears to show little or no financial advantage of this extra set of procedures, as compared with the straight production of lucerne pellets for export. The yield of the 50% protein LPC is about 15% of the original dry matter, and there is an unavoidable (at present) loss in dry matter of about 15% in the "whey." Thus, if the pellets sell for $100/MT, then the LPC would have to sell for $200/MT just to maintain the same inflow of cash. Some benefits in kiln drying costs of the pellets can be anticipated, but not as much as widely believed. If half of the weight of fresh lucerne (with 85% moisture) is pressed out as the green juice, the residue to be kiln dried would be 100 kg water (or 80% moisture content). A greater water loss than this 5% can be attained by field wilting. In addition, the new type of pellets after "dewatering" are lower in protein (17% as compared with 22%), higher in fiber, and lower in minerals and other nutrients.

From the viewpoint of the potential uses of LPC, there is no advantage in price or nutrition over common protein concentrates such as soybean meal or lupine meal, and there appear to be some distinct disadvantages in the form of heat damage to lysine during drying, photosensitivity dangers, and initial growth suppressants.

All-in-all, there ought to be a better way to bring the truly remarkable nutritional assets of leafy materials into use by monogastric animals.

Using the Whole Leaf

A new look at procedures to utilize the nutritional value of fresh leafy material was prompted by the difficulties with green juice, as described in the previous section. As Osborne *et al.* (1921) said more than 50 years ago, water and fiber prevent fresh leaves from being an excellent food for man. He should have added the occasional toxin to this short list.

It is well known that lucerne leaf as compared with stem has high protein, up to 34% dry basis, and low fiber (Bailey *et al.* 1970). Similarly, Hove (1977) reported lupine leaves to have 32% crude protein and 9% acid-detergent fiber, as compared with values for stem of 7 and 46%, respectively. Procedures to concentrate leaf *vis-à-vis* stem are evident in leaf-stripping harvesters, and in air classification and cyclone centrifuging of dried materials. Thus, if the stem can be avoided or eliminated from products, many of the difficulties in digestion caused by fiber (especially lignins) will be overcome.

Removal of water from fresh forage by heat is costly and damages the nutritional quality. Why not dehydrate with water-miscible organic solvents such as methanol or ethanol? Several benefits are immediately apparent. The full nutritional quality of the proteins would be retained; pigments (chlorophyll and carotenoids) would be removed; most of the lipid would be removed resulting in greater stability; and possibly saponins and other toxins would be removed. Since the alcohols penetrate the cells, the leafy material need not be minced or pulped to break cells; and the bulk of the protein and carbohydrates of the material would be retained for nutritional use.

The Procedure. A procedure for alcohol drying and mechanical removal of fiber was reported by Hove (1977). The laboratory procedure described was on a batch basis, but could no doubt be converted to a continuous countercurrent process.

The ratio of methanol (or ethanol) to fresh material was 8:1 (v/v). For the process to be economical, this large amount of alcohol would need to be recovered. Unfortunately, the heat of vaporization of ethanol is 204 Cal/g, which is high as compared with hexane used in oil seed defatting (80 Cal/g), but is lower than the figure for water of 540 Cal/g. The recovery would be expensive in terms of energy for distillation, but has the advantage that the alcohol-soluble fraction, a dark green sludge, has market value as a pigmenter in poultry diets.

Residual alcohol was removed from the dehydrated leafy material in a stream of warm air (50°C). The material was then fractionated according to fiber content by a system of screening and rolling. The object was to crumble the dry leaves while gathering the stemmy fibers into a wool ball. Two screen sizes were used (about 10 and 29 mesh) with the result that fine, medium, and coarse decolorized plant products were obtained, but, in practice, the medium fraction was reprocessed into fine and coarse.

The Products. The process worked well with young fresh lucerne, resulting in three products that would have commercial value, and that accounted for all the dry matter of the original plant. About half the dry matter is in the main product "leaf powder," a high protein food for monogastrics, including humans; about a quarter of the dry matter is in a fibrous product "leaf fiber" for ruminant feeds; the final quarter (approx.) of the dry matter was in the alcohol-extracted dark green sludge, which can supply carotenoids and xanthophylls to poultry rations.

The lucerne leaf powder was light tan in color, with 38% crude protein and 18% acid-detergent fiber. It represented 47% of the original dry matter and 72% of the original protein. The secondary "leaf fiber" (39% acid-detergent) accounted for 80% of the total fiber in the original plant; its protein level was 18%. The third product was the dark green sludge recovered from the ethanol. It had some protein, most of the lipid, and all of the pigments of the original plant. There was no waste fraction to be discarded.

For a variety of reasons the process did not work well for some other fresh materials such as white clover, lupine, rape, or lawn clippings (Hove 1977). However, with spinach the alcohol dehydration worked very well. Since spinach is all leaf as used, no fiber fractionation was necessary.

Nutritional Quality of the Leaf Powders. The leaf powders from various leafy materials were evaluated for growth (toxins) and protein quality by the usual rat-growth procedures. At amounts in the diet to supply 9% protein as the only source, and with added DL-methionine at 0.1%, all products except that from rape permitted four-week weight gains equal to casein control. Rats fed the rape leaf powder gained at only half the rate of casein. Obviously, the alcohol extraction had not removed all of the toxins (presumed to be glucosinolates).

The PER for the spinach and lupine leaf powders (with methionine) were not significantly different from the PER of casein, but all other products had PER values less than casein. The inefficient use of protein could be explained in part by the impaired digestion of protein at 80% or less.

However, as a supplement to the protein of white flour, the lucerne leaf powder was equal to food grade dry skim milk (Hove 1977).

Conclusion. Alcohol drying of fresh green leafy materials resulted in high quality products that still retained significant amounts of fiber. Selection of the starting material will affect the amount of fiber remaining, particularly the lignin fraction of the fiber. The use of leaf-enriched or leaf only (as spinach) produces the best products, with little or no fiber. A certain amount of fiber is now considered acceptable by nutritionists, for health reasons. An economic appraisal of the procedure may show costs are not too different from oil-fired kiln drying for pellet production, especially if alcohol recovery is efficient. The product has yet to be evaluated for its use in formulated foods and for its technological properties.

PROTEIN FROM PASTURE

New Zealand's high producing ryegrass-white clover pastures are devoted largely to dairying for export markets. The modern dairy cow is probably the most efficient ruminant converter of grass protein to usable animal products (25–30%), especially when operated in association with modern, multiproduct dairy factories recovering most of the milk solids. Up to the mid-1950s it would probably have been considered almost heretical for any New Zealand agricultural scientist to have suggested any means other than the grazing animal to convert this grass protein to edible products for man. However, in the late 1960s a growing awareness of the limits of the grazing process was leading some New Zealand scientists to look for ways of achieving a greater conversion of pasture protein to human food, preferably as an adjunct to the conventional grazing system. Thus, Hutton (1970), leader of the Ministry of Agriculture's major unit devoted to the nutrition of the dairy cow, advocated LPC production with feeding of the residue to livestock as the best way of increasing edible protein production from New Zealand pastures. Following this advocacy, a pilot scale development unit was set up in 1972 at the Nutrition Centre, Ruakura Agricultural Research Centre, Ministry of Agriculture, initially under Dr. Hutton's leadership. This unit now has a staff of 5 scientists and 12 support staff plus extensive land and animal feeding facilities under the leadership of Mr. P. Donnelly. The following account covers the basic philosophy and goals of the unit plus its achievements to date.

Aims, Philosophy, and Farming Implications

The main aims of the unit are to research the technical and economic viability of the extraction from pasture of protein which is surplus to livestock feed requirements and the preparation of this protein as a potentially exportable feed for poultry and pigs. The basic philosophy may be summed up as follows: First, to siphon off some of the pasture leaf protein with minimal or no effect on dairy production; second, to do this within the conventional high production dairy farm unit; i.e., 50–100 ha, milking 100–300 cows with daily tanker collection of whole milk; third, to recognize that production of LPC for pig and poultry feeding is a much more immediate prospect than production for direct human consumption. An important implication of the system is that, instead of moving harvested whole leaf to a central processing plant, leaf juice will be extracted in the field by a mobile processor with the residue immediately available to the grazing dairy herd or ensiled. In addition, unless residue is ensiled or dried, the area harvested each day will be determined by the feed needs of the dairy herd.

Each farmer would presumably have his own harvester. Whole juice or a coagulation produced on the farm would be transported by tanker to a central drying unit. The simplest and cheapest form of coagulation and drying is envisaged. While nutritional quality of the LPC is important, high pigmentation is not considered a problem as likely export markets are countries such as Japan where there is already a preference for very yellow-yolked or yellow-fatted eggs or meat.

Development of the LPC Harvesting Process

Initial assessments are largely concerned first with the measurement of LPC yields from the pastures and the effect of various factors on these yields and, secondly, with the nutritive value of both the LPC and the residue. During this stage, a standard stationary pulper and juice extractor are used to give a juice from which dried LPC is prepared by the usual methods. All yields are, therefore, based on pilot-scale operations rather than laboratory-scale tests. Developmental aspects are concerned with the production of a suitable mobile processor and with a harvester-juice extractor, for on-farm coagulation processes, and with nutritional problems associated with either the LPC or extracted residue. Although McDonald (1975) has calculated that the process on a suitable scale should be economically viable, full economic assessments can only be made once the complete pilot-scale process is operational.

It is convenient to consider results so far in terms of (1) the mechanical juicing and protein recovery system, (2) yields of LPC under various conditions, and (3) nutritive value of the products.

Juice Production and Protein Recovery

The stationary system in present use consists of an IBP pulper fed by a constant rate elevator system and an IBP type of belt press. Grass is wetted to 10% dry matter (DM). The compressed juice is filtered and protein coagulated by steam injection. The protein coagulate is harvested to 10–15% DM by conventional centrifuging or to 40–50% DM by means of a decanting centrifuge. Using a Westfalia CA220 decanter, McDonald (1978) obtained, at a flow rate of 31 liters/m, a solid of 57% DM with a loss of only 1.5% at an operating temperature of 98°C. He considers the high operating temperature to be essential. Coagulated concentrates are dried by either a spray drier (conventionally centrifuged coagulation) or a fluid bed drier (decanting centrifuge material). The product from the latter process is preferred for its handling properties in stock food formulations. The processes are shown schematically in Fig. 29.2. As operated, the process has a throughput of 800 kg fresh pasture per hr (Donnelly, personal communication). This throughput not only gives a yield assessment on a suitable scale of the process but also produces sufficient LPC and pasture residue for adequate feeding trials and permits direct comparisons of pasture residue with original grass in feeding trials with a small dairy herd.

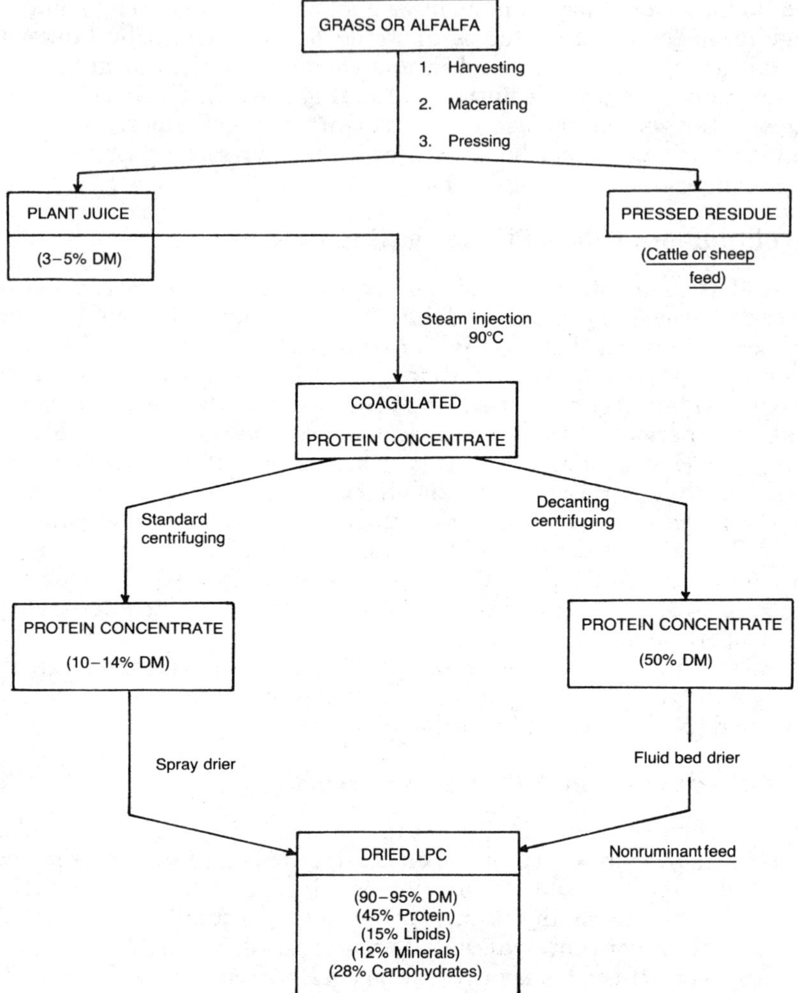

Fig. 29.2. System of protein extraction in use at Ruakura Research Station, New Zealand. Plant processing capacity—800 kg fresh grass per hr.

LPC Yields from Pasture

Initial results (Ostrowski 1976) showed ready extraction of protein from ryegrass and clover, with higher yields from irrigated compared with non-irrigated pasture, pasture harvested at 6 A.M. compared with 9 A.M., and after 4 weeks regrowth as opposed to 7 weeks regrowth. An extensive series of processings (Donnelly, personal communication) has examined the effect of pasture species and regrowth periods on LPC yields. They showed that, using the standardized process, 30% of the protein can be easily extracted and, of the extracted nitrogen, two-thirds can be recovered as dried LPC. Ryegrass gave lower extraction values than clover or lucerne. The effect of regrowth period was small, with nearly 30% extraction up to the seventh week of regrowth in spring and summer and up to the twelfth week in autumn and early winter. Observations of Ostrowski (1976) indicated that extraction was easier in the early morning compared with later in the day. This appears to be because of better turgor in the early morning and a higher moisture content, as Foster (1977) has shown that a moisture content of 90% facilitates extraction compared with lower moisture content. For these reasons harvesting between 6 A.M. and 9 P.M. is preferred for ease of extraction.

Nutritive Quality of Products

LPC. The nutritional quality of spray-dried LPC has been evaluated in rat feeding trials with lactalbumin as a standard protein. Results (Donnelly and McDonald 1978) given in Table 29.3 show relative nutritive values (RNV's) of LPC from lucerne, ryegrass, and pasture of 0.62, 0.53, 0.46, respectively, which on supplementation with methionine rise to 0.90, 0.85, and 0.84. Protein digestibility is 72–80% with a lysine availability of 85–90%. Preliminary trials with chickens have shown that the leaf protein was slightly inferior to soybean. More extensive trials with pigs and chickens are planned as well as trials using fluid bed dried material. Temperature conditions during protein processing are such as to eliminate chloropyllase activity and photosensitivity in the LPC.

A key part of the process as planned is the production of a residue of sufficient quality to maintain normal dairy production. While most workers recognize the need to use the ruminant's ability to digest the fiber in extracted plant residue, there appear to have been few trials involving a direct comparison of the nutritive value of the extracted residue with original herbage on a production as opposed to a maintenance basis. Two large-scale stall feeding trials comparing fresh, extracted pasture residue with the original pasture have been done at Ruakura using identical twin

TABLE 29.3. PROTEIN QUALITY, PROTEIN DIGESTIBILITY, AND LYSINE CONTENT OF LPC PRODUCED AT RUAKURA

	Pasture Types			
Parameter	Lucerne	White Clover	Ryegrass	Ryegrass White Clover[1]
Relative nutritive value (RNV)[2] (unsupplemented LPC)	0.62	0.50	0.53	0.46
RNV (LPC + methionine)	0.90	0.91	0.85	0.84
True protein digestibility (%)	78	80	72	71
Total lysine (g/16 g N)	6.07	6.00	5.73	5.40
Available lysine (g/16 g N)	5.55	5.42	5.13	4.62
Lysine availability (%)	91.5	90.2	89.3	85.5

Statistical analysis indicates: total lysine levels to be lower in mixed pasture than lucerne (0.67 ± 0.23*); available lysine to be lower in mixed pasture than lucerne (0.93 ± 0.29*) and a *calculated* ryegrass-white clover average (0.65 ± 0.25*). Lysine availabilities were lower in pasture than lucerne (6.0 ± 1.6*) and a *calculated* ryegrass-white clover average (4.25 ± 1.43*).

[1] Ryegrass/white clover was from typical dairying mixed pasture.

[2] RNV is the slope-ratio rat growth procedure.

*—Significance at the level P = 0.05.

lactating cows. The results (Trigg and Bryant 1978) show 12–14% less intake and 7–10% less milk production for the residue relative to the original pasture. Residue had a digestibility of 70–80%. Ca and Mg supplementation did not eliminate this difference. The cause of the milk production loss must be defined and eliminated. Future trials will include access to some whole pasture in an effort to overcome the problem.

Mobile Harvesting

Forage harvesters suitable for modification are available, while presses can be designed of a size and power need that can be accommodated on a mobile system. A prototype of such a machine was under design and testing at the unit (Mills, personal communication) and was to be ready for field trials during the 1978–1979 dairy season. A detailed account of this harvester and its evaluation is given by Mills (1980). Using a 67 kW tractor drive, the harvester-juice processor can handle 5 MT fresh crop per hr, producing a juice containing 30% of the crop protein. Further technical progress of the Ruakura concept centers around the successful development of this harvester. Other aspects which could well be important in the economic viability of the project include some form of initial on-farm protein coagulation and use of the whey as a by-product, a feedstuff molasses, or fermented to alcohol.

THE FUTURE OF LPC IN NEW ZEALAND

New Zealand's agricultural system is at present largely geared to pastures for production of ruminant products, with pig and poultry production only for the local market. While the feed requirements of this pig and poultry industry are quite sizeable, it seems that an LPC industry of viable size would inevitably be linked to an export market. Costs of transport to distant markets must, therefore, be added to the high costs of energy used to produce LPC. LPC production from lucerne crops could give a significant transport economy for the present lucerne meal export industry, provided energy costs were controlled. Likewise, LPC production as an adjunct to dairy production could produce a competitively priced product if energy costs were reasonable. The viability of either process in producing pig or poultry feed depends, therefore, on energy costs and transport costs to export markets, particularly in terms of competitiveness with feeds such as soybeans, other legume and cereal grains, or meat meal. In the final issue, these possibilities will be resolved only in the operation of either process on a large scale with a full marketing situation.

The production of LPC for direct human food in New Zealand is a different matter. This involves the production of white protein material of suitable flavor and free of the problems of acceptability of a new food. At present, the LPC from most processes seems to be uncompetitive compared with the use of soybean proteins for use in textured protein foods. New Zealand production is again faced with the problem of producing for distant export markets.

Research on possible better methods of producing purified LPC must be continued and is being continued in New Zealand. The one important factor in favor of LPC from legume-based forages is that it does represent a more efficient harvesting of plant proteins from the plant species which have the ability to fix nitrogen.

In the New Zealand pastoral system, there is growing evidence of pressure from cropping pushing the ruminant off the rolling, cultivable pasturelands and onto the less cultivable hill country. It may well be that LPC production could tip the scale either way by either contributing to this pressure or, as in the Ruakura model, helping to keep the ruminant on this land. From an energy point of view, the latter may be preferred. Continuing work at Ruakura 1978–1982 has led to a pilot scale plant for producing leaf protein for stock food which is now being commercially developed. Research is now concentrated on the fibrous residue from the crop. While this can be used to make good silage, the plans are to use it for producing higher value products.

REFERENCES

ALLISON, R.M. 1973. Leaf protein as an animal and human foodstuff. *In* Chemistry and Biochemistry of Herbage. R.W. Bailey and G.M. Butler (Editors). Academic Press, London.

ALLISON, R.M., LAIRD, W.M. and SYNGE, R.L.M. 1973. Notes on a deamination method proposed for determining "chemically available lysine" or proteins. Br. J. Nutr. *29*, 51–55.

BAILEY, R.W., ALLISON, R.M. and O'CONNOR, K.F. 1970. Protein and carbohydrate composition of lucerne grown in Canterbury. Proc. N.Z. Grassl. Assoc. *32*, 127–136.

BARNES, M.F. 1976. Growth of yeasts on spent lucerne whey and their effectiveness in scavenging residual protein. N.Z. J. Agric. Res. *19*, 537–541.

CARR, J.R. and PEARSON, G. 1974. Nutritive values of lucerne leaf-protein concentrate and lupin seed meal as protein supplements to barley diets for growing pigs. Proc. N.Z. Soc. Anim. Prod. *34*, 95.

CARR, J.R. and PEARSON, G. 1976. Photosensitisation, growth performance, and carcass measurements of pigs fed diets containing commercially prepared lucerne leaf-protein concentrates. N.Z. J. Exp. Agric. *4*, 45–50.

DONNELLY, P.R. and McDONALD, R. 1978. The quality of leaf protein concentrates. Proc. N.Z. Nutr. Soc. *3*, 84–95.

FAFUNSO, M. and BYERS, M. 1977. Effect of pre-press treatments of vegetation on the quality of the extracted leaf protein. J. Sci. Food Agric. *28*, 375–380.

FOSTER, R.P. 1975–1976. Stabilisation of protein yields from pasture herbage. Agricultural Research in New Zealand. Annu. Rep. Res. Div., N.Z. Minist. Agric. Fish., Wellington, N.Z.

HOVE, E.L. 1975. Green leaves as a source of food. N.Z. J. Dairy Sci. Technol. *10*, 138–141.

HOVE, E.L. 1977. High-protein food prepared from fresh leafy material by alcohol drying and mechanical defibring. N.Z. J. Agric. Res. *20*, 309–313.

HOVE, E.L. and BAILEY, R.W. 1975. Toward a leaf protein concentrate industry in New Zealand (A memorial to Dr. Russel M. Allison). N.Z. J. Exp. Agric. *3*, 193–198.

HOVE, E.L., COPELAND, D.H. and SALMON, W.D. 1949. A fatal vitamin E deficiency disease in rats characterised by massive lung haemmorrhage and liver necrosis. J. Nutr. *39*, 397–412.

HOVE, E.L., LOHREY, E., URS, M.K. and ALLISON, R.M. 1974. The effect of lucerne-protein concentrate in the diet on growth, reproduction and body composition of rats. Br. J. Nutr. *31*, 147–157.

HUTTON, J.B. 1970. Comparative efficiency of pastures and crops. Proc. 11th Int. Grassl. Assoc., 1970, Surfers Paradise, Queensland, Australia, A78–A87. M.J.T. Norman (Editor). Univ. of Queensland Press, St. Lucia, Queensland, Australia.

LATIMER, G.B. 1968A. Protein direct from grass may help solve world food shortage. N.Z. J. Agric. *116* (May) 78–83.

LATIMER, G.B. 1968B. Extraction from grass of protein for direct consumption. N.Z. J. Agric. *116*, (June) 73–75.

LOHREY, E., TAPPER, B. and HOVE, E.L. 1974. Photosensitisation of albino rats fed on lucerne-protein concentrate. Br. J. Nutr. *31*, 158–166.

McDONALD, R. 1975. Some aspects of leaf protein economics. *In* Leaf Protein Concentrates (Workshop Report). G.M. Wallace (Editor). Ruakura Agric. Research Centre, Hamilton, N.Z.

McDONALD, R. and DONELLY, P.E. 1978. Processing pasture juice to a protein concentrate. Proc. N.Z. Nutr. Soc. *3*, 70–83.

MENKE, W. 1938. Investigations of the particles in spinach leaves by chemical preparative methods. Z. Bot. *32*, 273–295. (German)

MILLS, R.A. 1980. A forage harvester/dejuicer for leaf protein extraction research. Proc. 5th Int. Conf. Mechanisation Field Exp. Neth. *5*, 246–255.

MORRISON, J.E. and PIRIE, N.W. 1961. The large scale production of protein from leaf extracts. J. Sci. Food Agric. *12*, 1–5.

OSBORNE, T.B. and WAKEMAN, L.I. 1920. Proteins of green leaves. I. spinach. J. Biol. Chem. *42*, 1–26.

OSBORNE, T.B., WAKEMAN, A.J. and LEAVENWORTH, C.S. 1921. Proteins of the alfalfa plant. J. Biol. Chem. *49*, 63–91.

OSTROWSKI, H.T. 1976. Pasture production in a protein extraction system. Proc. N.Z. Soc. Anim. Prod. *36*, 30–42.

PIRIE, N.W. 1971. Equipment and methods for extracting and separating proteins. *In* Leaf Protein: Its Agronomy, Preparation, Quality and Use. IBP Handb. *20*, N.W. Pirie (Editor). Blackwell Scientific Publications, Oxford.

ROBINSON, M.F. 1975. The Moonstone: More About Selenium. The Muriel Bell Memorial Lecture of the Nutrition Society of New Zealand. M.J. Ulyatt (Editor). D.S.I.R., Nutrition Society of New Zealand, Palmerston North, N.Z.

TAPPER, B., LOHREY, E., HOVE, E.L. and ALLISON, R.M. 1975. Photosensitivity from chlorophyll-derived pigments. J. Sci. Food Agric. *26*, 277–284.

TRIGG, T.E. and BRYANT, A.M. 1978. Nutritive value for dairy cows of extracted residues from pasture. Proc. N.Z. Nutr. Soc. *3*, 96–106.

VARTHA, E.W. and ALLISON, R.M. 1971. Digestibility of protein-extracted forages. Proc. N.Z. Soc. Anim. Prod. *31*, 64.

30

Leaf Protein Research and Development in Japan

T. Horigome

The annual importation of corn, milo, soybean oil meal, fish meal, and other feed ingredients to Japan from abroad in 1979 amounted to 16,297,000 MT. The annual total amount of formula feeds produced in Japan in this same year was about 22,438,000 MT. Therefore, about 73% of the total amount of feed ingredients was imported from abroad. This situation has encouraged us to study leaf protein production. In Japan, on-farm-scale experiments on green crop fractionation and leaf protein production have been conducted by the research teams of the National Grassland Research Institute at Nishi-Nasuno, Tochigi, and of Nagoya University at Nagoya since 1980. Now, the process of green crop fractionation has been put into production by several pilot plants in Japan. Studies on leaf protein in Japan have not been conducted so far from a nutritional point of view.

A similarity in amino acid composition between leaf proteins made from different crops has been confirmed by many researchers, but it has been noted that there were some marked differences between crops in the nutritional quality of the leaf protein. Henry and Ford (1965) suggested the method of drying leaf protein and the maturity of the leaf at harvesting affected the nutritional quality of leaf protein. However, the problem of the difference in leaf protein quality between crops has not yet been completely solved. The following factors possibly partially explain the problem, according to our studies: (1) occurrence of phenolic compounds and *o*-diphenoloxidase in plants; (2) ratio of lamellar and soluble proteins; (3) methionine content of leaf protein.

OCCURRENCE OF PHENOLIC COMPOUNDS AND *o*-DIPHENOLOXIDASE IN PLANTS

Eleven pasture plants were studied for the occurrence of *o*-diphenoloxidase and *o*-diphenol (Horigome and Kandatsu 1966). Arnow's method was used for the determination of *o*-diphenol and the results were expressed in terms of chlorogenic acid. The activity of *o*-diphenoloxidase in the acetone powder of fresh leaves was assayed by the Warburg technique at pH 6.3 with chlorogenic acid as substrate. From Table 30.1, it can be seen that the quantity of phenolic compounds and amount of *o*-diphenoloxidase activity varied with the plant species and that the occurrence of *o*-diphenoloxidase was accompanied by the occurrence of *o*-diphenolic compounds.

Leaf protein prepared from red clover or orchard grass was brown-colored after extraction with acetone followed by ethyl ether, while leaf protein from oats was white. Since red clover and orchard grass had large amounts of diphenolic compounds and a high activity of *o*-diphenoloxidase, this suggested that the brown-colored protein was produced by the interaction of protein with phenolic compounds undergoing enzymic oxidation. The phenomenon was demonstrated by the exposure of casein to phenolic compounds in the presence of *o*-diphenoloxidase, and it was shown that the resulting brown casein was nutritionally impoverished (Horigome and Kandatsu 1968, 1971). Further, it was shown that the browning of N-acetylcasein in which free amino groups were blocked by acetyl groups was caused by the caffeic acid-*o*-diphenoloxidase system, and the resulting brown acetylcasein had lower nutritional values than the original acetyl-

TABLE 30.1. *o*-DIPHENOLIC CONTENT AND *o*-DIPHENOLOXIDASE ACTIVITY IN FRESH LEAVES

Type of Leaf	Content of *o*-Diphenol[1] (% on Dry Basis)	Activity of *o*-Diphenoloxidase[2] (O_2 μl/hr)
Oats (*Avena sativa,* L.)	0.22	0
Italian ryegrass (*Lolium multiflorum,* Lam.)	1.71	112
Orchard grass (*Dactylis glomerata,* L.)	2.62	159
Genge (*Astragalus sinicus,* L.)	0.75	0
Common vetch (*Vicia sativa,* L.)	1.13	0
Hairy vetch (*Vicia villosa,* Roth.)	0	0
Red clover (*Trifolium pratense,* L.)	2.58	64
Ladino clover (*Trifolium repens,* L.)	0.76	5
Alfalfa (*Medicago sativa,* L.)	0	0
Mulberry (*Morus latifolia,* Pollet)	3.15	82
Sweet potato (*Ipomoea batatas,* (L) Lamk.)	7.79	118

[1] Expressed in terms of chlorogenic acid.
[2] Determined on 0.5 ml of the filtrate from the mixture of acetone powder (200 mg) and phosphate buffer of pH 8 (10 ml).

casein (Horigome 1973). Therefore, it was suggested that in addition to free amino groups, other groups such as –CO–NH– were involved in the reaction of protein with phenolic compounds undergoing enzymic oxidation. These are shown in Tables 30.2 and 30.3. The nutritional implication of phenolic compounds on protein quality is presumably relevant to brown-colored leaf protein.

Igarashi and Yasui (1978) reported the interaction of protein with biochanin A which was contained in leaves of red clover. Their results showed that the digestibility of casein with trypsin decreased in the presence of biochanin A.

RATIO OF LAMELLAR AND SOLUBLE PROTEINS

From the standpoint of nutritional study, it is generally accepted that most protein in the leaf is divided into two fractions, lamellar (chloroplastic) and soluble (cytoplasmic) proteins. Many investigators have demonstrated the superiority of soluble protein over lamellar protein from nutritional studies with rats (Davies *et al.* 1952; Henry and Ford 1965; Subba Rau *et al.* 1969; Bickoff *et al.* 1975; Horigome 1977; Clifford *et al.* 1977).

The ratio of lamellar and soluble proteins in leaf juice was measured with several crops (Horigome *et al.* 1978). Lamellar protein was separated from the leaf juice by using high-speed centrifugation, and the soluble protein by acidifying and heating the chloroplast-free juice. Since chloroplasts are mostly ruptured during the pulping of the leaf, it is presumed that the isolated soluble protein consists of cytoplasmic protein and stromal protein in chloroplasts, and that the isolated lamellar protein consists mainly of lamellar and grana proteins (Ellis 1978). Table 30.4 shows that there is more soluble protein than lamellar protein in the leaf juice from ladino clover, alfalfa, Italian ryegrass, and turnip, while the reverse is found for the leaf juice from Japanese radish, carrot, corn, and sorghum. Corn and sorghum belong to C_4-plants which have bundle sheath cells containing chloroplasts besides mesophyll cells lacking in Fraction I (F I) protein in their leaves (Hatch *et al.* 1967; Ellis 1978), and hence it is reasonable that the leaf juice from both crops contained more lamellar protein than soluble protein.

Next, unfractionated leaf proteins prepared from Italian ryegrass and from sorghum leaf were compared for nutritional quality in an experiment with rats (Horigome *et al.* 1981). Two percent ascorbic acid solution, which was adjusted to pH 7.8, was used during the pulping of leaves in order to prevent the browning of the proteins. As shown in Table 30.5, the leaf protein from Italian ryegrass had higher nutritional quality than from sorghum leaf. The high nutritional quality of the leaf protein from Italian ryegrass was assumed to be due to its having a higher soluble protein content than lamellar protein content.

TABLE 30.2. NUTRITIONAL VALUE OF CASEIN EXPOSED TO PHENOLIC COMPOUNDS UNDERGOING ENZYMIC OXIDATION[1]

Phenolic Compound					Relative Value[3]		
Designation	Amount g/100 g Casein	Enzyme Source	Drying[2] Method	Color	True Digestibility	Biological Value	Available Lysine
(Control)	0	—	B	White	100	100	100
Caffeic acid	3.60	—	B	White	99.6	97.2	99.7
Caffeic acid	3.60	Orchard grass	A	Brown	95.8	94.7	89.5
Caffeic acid	3.60	Orchard grass	B	Brown	96.2	89.4	87.4
iso-Chlorogenic acid	5.56	Orchard grass	A	Green-brown	96.7	91.5	90.8
Red clover	6.05	Red clover	A	Brown	95.1	90.9	86.3
Red clover	6.01	Red clover	B	Brown	95.8	85.8	81.7

[1] Casein was made to react with the phenolic compound at pH 6.5 and 25°–30°C for 4 hr, and then casein was precipitated by adjusting the pH of the reaction mixture to 4.3–4.5.
[2] A—Washed with acetone. B—Dried in a current of warm air without acetone washing.
[3] The values of control casein are taken as 100. Digestibility and biological value were measured with young male rats of the Wister strain at the level of 7–7.5% dietary protein.

TABLE 30.3. TRUE DIGESTIBILITY AND BIOLOGICAL VALUE OF N-ACETYLCASEIN AND BROWN-COLORED N-ACETYLCASEIN

Parameter	Starting Casein	N-Acetyl Casein	Brown-colored N-Acetylcasein
True digestibility (%)	98.1 ± 0.5	97.0 ± 0.5	93.9 ± 0.6
Biological value (%)	74.7 ± 1.3	65.2 ± 1.5[1]	60.8 ± 1.3[2]

Each value is the mean of 9 rats ± S.E.
[1] Significantly different from the starting casein group ($p < 0.01$).
[2] Significantly different from the N-acetyl casein group $p < 0.05$).

TABLE 30.4. RELATIVE AMOUNT OF LAMELLAR AND SOLUBLE PROTEINS IN GREEN JUICE PREPARED FROM LEAVES OF VARIOUS CROPS

Crop Leaf	Extractable Protein N% of Total Leaf N	Relative Amount in Green Juice: Lamellar Protein	Relative Amount in Green Juice: Soluble Protein
Ladino clover (*Trifolium repens,* L.)	61.4	61	100
Alfalfa (*Medicago sativa,* L.)	61.3	69	100
Italian ryegrass (*Lolium multiflorum,* Lam.)			
first cut: Leafy	68.7	64	100
Leafy	65.3	74	100
Early heading	56.6	81	100
second cut: Leafy	52.1	73	100
Turnip (*Brassica rapa rapifera,* Metzger)	65.6	86	100
Radish (*Raphanus sativus,* L.)	51.5	132	100
Carrot (*Daucus carota,* L. var. sativa DC.)	50.7	132	100
Corn (*Zea mays,* L.)	47.3	213	100
Sorghum (*Sorghum* spp.)			
height: 1.0 m	38.1	233	100
0.9	39.4	238	100
1.4	37.5	270	100
2.0	28.4	244	100

TABLE 30.5. WEIGHT GAIN, DIET INTAKE, AND PROTEIN EFFICIENCY RATIO OF RATS FED DIET CONTAINING ITALIAN RYEGRASS OR SORGHUM LEAF PROTEIN

	Weight Gain for 14 Days, (g)	Diet Intake for 14 Days, (g)	Protein Efficiency Ratio
Italian ryegrass leaf protein	36.9 ± 1.0	113.7 ± 0.2	3.85 ± 0.11
Sorghum leaf protein	32.4 ± 1.8[1]	113.3 ± 0.4	3.30 ± 0.17[1]

Each value is the mean with its standard deviation for 5 rats. Diets contained leaf protein at protein 9.3% and were fortified with methionine.
[1] Significantly different from the corresponding value of Italian ryegrass ($P < 0.01$).

METHIONINE CONTENT OF LEAF PROTEIN

It has been established that methionine is the first limiting amino acid in leaf protein. Ohshima and Oouchi (1976) also reported that the first limiting amino acid of the ladino clover leaf protein for growing rats was methionine. Therefore, it is obvious that the nutritional quality of leaf protein is influenced in part by its methionine content. Leaf protein from grasses seems to contain slightly more methionine than leaf protein from legumes (Byers 1971). Horigome (1977) found that fractionated leaf proteins from oats, which contained 2.16–2.49% of methionine (g amino acid per 100 g recovered amino acids), had significantly higher values in biological value than fractionated leaf proteins from ladino clover, which contained 1.65–1.66% of methionine. On the average for four rats, the biological value for oats was: soluble (cytoplasmic) protein 83.7 and lamellar (chloroplastic) protein 63.0, and for ladino clover 58.1 and 45.8, respectively.

The leaf proteins from ladino clover were prepared by using 2% ascorbic acid solution (pH 7.8) to prevent the interaction of protein with phenolic compounds. However, there was no difference in the protein efficiency ratio of unfractionated leaf protein between the two crops when the diets containing leaf protein were supplemented with methionine (Table 30.6). The result shows definitely that the low nutritional value of leaf protein from ladino clover was due to low methionine content, compared with leaf protein from oats. Furthermore, it may be concluded that a small difference in methionine content brings about a large difference in nutritional quality among leaf proteins since methionine is the first limiting amino acid in all leaf proteins. As can be seen from Table 30.7, this is also the case for a difference in the protein efficiency ratio between ladino clover and Italian ryegrass leaf proteins (Horigome and Uchida 1980). It also can be seen from Table 30.6 that leaf proteins supplemented with methionine were equal in protein efficiency ratio to soybean seed protein supplemented with methionine.

CONCLUSION

The interaction of protein with phenolic compounds undergoing oxidation may be inhibited to some extent by the addition of an appropriate

TABLE 30.6. WEIGHT GAIN, PROTEIN INTAKE, AND PROTEIN EFFICIENCY RATIO OF RATS FED UNFRACTIONATED LEAF PROTEIN FORTIFIED WITH METHIONINE

	Weight Gain for 20 Days, (g)	Total Protein Intake (g)	Protein Efficiency Ratio
Oats leaf protein	53.1 ± 1.4	15.9	3.34 ± 0.16
Ladino clover leaf protein	54.9 ± 1.6	15.8	3.47 ± 0.24
Soybean seed protein	53.4 ± 1.8	15.7	3.40 ± 0.15

Each value is the mean with its standard deviation for 5 rats.
Diets contained test protein at protein level 8.25–8.35%.

TABLE 30.7. BODY WEIGHT GAIN, DIET INTAKE, AND PROTEIN EFFICIENCY RATIO OF RATS FED UNFRACTIONATED LEAF PROTEIN WITHOUT OR WITH METHIONINE

	Weight Gain During 15 Days (g)	Diet Intake During 15 Days (g)	Protein Efficiency Ratio
Ladino clover: leaf protein	28.0 ± 4.1[1]	129.9 ± 6.7[1]	2.59 ± 0.27[1]
Italian ryegrass: leaf protein	41.0 ± 2.1[2]	138.5 ± 2.1[1,2]	3.50 ± 0.08[2]
Ladino clover: leaf protein + methionine	42.3 ± 1.3[2]	140.9 ± 0.2[2]	3.47 ± 0.10[2]
Italian ryegrass: leaf protein + methionine	43.0 ± 3.0[2]	141.0 ± 3.1[2]	3.58 ± 0.26[2]

Each value is the mean with its standard deviation for four rats.
[1,2] Values followed by a common superscript number did not differ significantly ($P < 0.05$).
Diets contained leaf protein at protein level 8.29–8.65%.

reducing reagent during extraction and by quick processing of the leaf juice. Since there was a difference in nutritional quality between unfractionated leaf proteins prepared from Italian ryegrass (C_3-plant) and sorghum (C_4-plant), it seems that the ratio of lamellar and soluble proteins is implicated to a certain degree in the nutritional quality of unfractionated leaf protein. The defect of low methionine content in leaf protein can be remedied by the addition of synthetic methionine. Of these three problems, however, the most difficult to prevent is the browning of leaf protein caused by the interaction with phenolic compounds during the processing of leaf juice.

REFERENCES

BICKOFF, E.M., BOOTH, A.N., DE FREMERY, D., EDWARDS R.H., KNUCKLES, B.E., MILLER, R.E., SAUNDERS, R.M. and KOHLER, G.O. 1975. Nutritional evaluation of alfalfa leaf protein concentrate. *In* Protein Nutritional Quality of Foods and Feeds, Part 2. M. Friedman (Editor). Marcel Dekker, New York.

BYERS, M. 1971. The amino acid composition of some leaf protein preparations. *In* Leaf Protein: Its Agronomy, Preparation, Quality and Use. IBP Handb. *20*. N.W. Pirie (Editor). Blackwell Scientific Publications, Oxford and Edinburgh.

CLIFFORD, A.J., VASCONCELLOS, J.A., FORMAN, L.P., LUMIJARVI, D. and WEIR, W.C. 1977. Nucleic acid content and nutritional value of green and white leaf proteins of alfalfa. Nutr. Rep. Int. *15*. 511–518.

DAVIES, M., EVANS, W.C. and PARR, W.H. 1952. Biological values and digestibilities of some grasses, and protein preparations from young and mature species, by the Thomas-Mitchell method, using rats. Biochem. J. *52*, xxiii.

ELLIS, R.J. 1978. Chloroplast proteins and their synthesis. *In* Plant Proteins. G. Norton (Editor). Butterworths, London.

HATCH, M.D., SLACK, C.R. and JOHNSON, H.S. 1967. Further studies on a new pathway of photosynthetic carbon dioxide fixation in sugarcane and its occurrence in other plant species. Biochem. J. *102*, 417–422.

HENRY, K.M. and FORD, J.E. 1965. The nutritive value of leaf protein concentrates determined in biological tests with rats and by microbiological methods. J. Sci. Food Agric. *16*, 425–432.

HORIGOME, T. 1973. Nutritive value of N-acetylcasein and brown-colored N-acetylcasein J. Jpn. Soc. Food Nutr. *26*, 257–262. (Japanese)

HORIGOME, T. 1977. Nutritional studies on fractionated cytoplasmic and chloroplastic proteins from leaves of oats and ladino clover. Jpn. J. Zootech. Sci. *48*, 267–272.

HORIGOME, T. and KANDATSU, M. 1966. Lowering effect of phenolic compounds and *o*-diphenoloxidase on the digestibility of protein in pasture plants. J. Agric. Chem. Soc. Jpn. *40*, 449–455. (Japanese)

HORIGOME, T. and KANDATSU, M. 1968. Biological value of proteins allowed to react with phenolic compounds in the presence of *o*-diphenoloxidase. Agric.

HORIGOME, T. and KANDATSU, M. 1971. Biological value of protein allowed to react with phenolic compounds in the presence of *o*-diphenoloxidase; effect of *o*-diphenol concentration on the biological value of protein-diphenol mixture. J. Jpn. Soc. Food Nutr. *24*, 253–258. (Japanese)

HORIGOME, T., MURAKAMI, A. and UCHIDA, S. 1981. Effect of ratio of lamellar and soluble proteins on the nutritional quality of unfractionated leaf protein. J. Jpn. Soc. Grassl. Sci. *27* (Suppl.) 201–202. (Japanese)
Biol. Chem. *32*, 1093–1102.

HORIGOME, T. and UCHIDA, S. 1980. An observation on the nutritional quality of leaf protein on connection with its methionine content. Jpn. J. Zootech. Sci. *51*, 429–435.

HORIGOME, T., UCHIDA, S., SUGAWARA, T. and HIRATA, M. 1978. Effect of ratio of chloroplastic and cytoplasmic proteins on the nutritional quality of unfractionated leaf protein. J. Jpn. Soc. Grassl. Sci. *24* (Suppl.) 195–196. (Japanese)

IGARASHI, K. and YASUI, T. 1978. Impurities of protein isolate from leaves of red clover and their effect on the protein digestibilties. J. Agric. Chem. Soc. Jpn. *52*, 241–246. (Japanese)

OHSHIMA, M. and OOUCHI, K. 1976. The order of limitation of amino acids in ladino clover leaf protein concentrate for growing rats. Nutr. Rep. Int. *14*, 611–620.

SUBBA RAU, B.H., MAHADEVIAH, S. and SINGH, N. 1969. Nutritional studies on whole-extract coagulated leaf protein and fractionated chloroplastic and cytoplasmic proteins from lucerne. J. Sci. Food Agric. *20*, 355–358.

31

Leaf Protein Research in Nigeria

Olusegun Ladimeji Oke

Nigeria is the largest country in West Africa, with an area of 928,200 km^2 (357,000 mi^2) and a population of about 80 million. It is divided into 19 states. The coastal area is swampy and at sea level. This is adjoined by a rain forest zone along the southern part, where it is evergreen. In the northern part is the open grassland or savannah, where the grass is lush; but this area becomes more narrow toward the extreme north, where there is scrub vegetation. It is drier in this area. There are two seasons, wet (rainy) and dry. During the rainy season, the heaviest downpour is along the coast and delta, where records show as much as 432 cm (170 in.) of precipitation a year, with most of it occurring between May and September.

The diet is largely vegetarian, roots and tubers being the staple in the south and cereals in the north. Both staples supply about 78% of the energy requirement. Animal sources supply only about 3% of the energy and 8% of the protein requirement, while pulses supply another 6% of the protein. In the northern part, where millet and sorghum are the staple foods, the mean protein intake was found in 1959 to be 85 g, with a protein score of 77, while in the south, where yam and cassava are the staples, the protein intake was 51 g, with a protein score of 50. It is noteworthy that in the north there was a deficiency of vitamin A and also of vitamin B_2. None of the children consumed enough food to meet their energy and protein requirements.

Proteins are of prime importance to health. However, they are often deficient in the diets of people in developing countries, particularly those in the vulnerable groups: nursing and expectant mothers, weanlings, and preschool children. Lack of protein may lead to high mortality and lowered resistance to disease, especially in childhood.

Deficiencies occur mainly in developing countries that are unable to produce enough inexpensive animal protein for their populations. This aspect of malnutrition is increasing due partly to the rapid growth of populations.

In Nigeria, the average yearly increase in population is about 3%. In the capital city, Lagos, the population has been estimated as increasing at about 8.2%/year (Okonjo 1962). Part of this is due to heavy migration from the rural areas to the city.

Since the Second World War, emphasis has been placed on the need for increasing dietary protein, particularly by the use of locally grown vegetable protein, as well as by the increased use of edible fish meals.

It is not sufficient to supply food without considering its nutritive value. The staple food in southern Nigeria is cassava, which contains very little protein, most of which is lost during processing. High-protein foods such as soybeans have limited distribution and are not eaten, whereas rice, maize, and Guinea corn are available, but their protein content is not sufficient to give a balanced diet. Animal proteins are very expensive and are not normally purchasable by lower-income groups.

In view of the economic situation in the rural areas and because kwashiorkor is rife in Nigeria, it is essential to look for inexpensive sources of good quality protein that can be used as alternatives to expensive animal protein. Since the high cost of animal protein is due mainly to the price of feeds, which are often imported into the country, it was felt that a local substitute such as leaf protein concentrate (LPC) might decrease the cost of animal protein.

In spite of the fact that green vegetables contain a high percentage of crude protein (15–30%), in Nigeria only about 100 g/person are consumed each day, supplying about 1–2 g/day of protein. The consumption of green vegetables would need to be increased to about 400 g/person/day to provide sufficient protein, but other factors, such as high-fiber content, are also responsible for keeping the consumption low. If, however, the fiber could be separated mechanically and the protein isolated, plants could supply as much as 10–20 g of protein per person per day. This can be achieved by the preparation of leaf protein concentrates (LPC) which, depending on the plant source, may be suitable for human consumption.

Leaf protein research in Nigeria is centered principally at the University of Ife with the primary objective being to produce an inexpensive and acceptable protein concentrate which can be used for food and/or animal feed.

The initial protein extraction work was done with a household meat mincer. Later on, the Village Unit (Davys and Pirie 1963) was bought and then the IBP pulper and press (Davys and Pirie 1969; Davys *et al.* 1969). Work is now in progress on the adaptation of the Posho mill for leaf protein extraction. Most of the results given in this review, however, were obtained with the use of the IBP pulper and press.

The Village Unit machine has a circular base, fabricated of angle-section steel, which stands on four legs. It can be driven by a motor or be belt-driven from an external source. The total weight of the running gear, with motor drive, which is borne by the leaves being processed, is 291 kg. This may be increased by 45 kg by filling the roller with water. A sheet metal tray is attached underneath the circular base to collect the juice, which is drained into a container through a spout. At the beginning of an extraction, 23–27 kg (fresh weight) of leaves are put quickly into the machine and, during the next 10–40 min, leaves are added as the machine will take them.

The IBP pulper and press has 58 beaters in 6 rows arranged as opposing pairs. The pulper can be fed uniformly at rates of up to 1.5 kg/min. It can be used with as little as 2 kg of fresh crop (or better still 3 kg) and is well adapted to agronomic work on plots that have been subjected to different types of husbandry.

The IBP press consists of two platens with square vertical grooves on their working faces. One is captive but hinged to the top edge of the back plate. During pressing, it hangs vertically. A funnel, fixed between the side plates, directs the juice into a collecting vessel.

The Posho mill is very similar in principle to the IBP pulper except that it has sharp blades which can be adjusted to carry out the pulping. The leaves are fed in from a tray above the pulper. The mill is available in every village in Nigeria and is used mainly for grinding corn and beans. Since there is no electricity in the villages, the mill is designed to run on a diesel engine.

Results similar to those from the IBP pulper have been obtained with the Posho mill. For example, in some trials with *Vernonia amygdalina*, the following results were obtained:

	% TN	% PN
Posho mill	40	35
IBP pulper	45	39

TN = Total nitrogen in the leaves.
PN = Protein nitrogen (total nitrogen precipitated when 10% trichloroacetic acid is added to the solution).

EXTRACTION OF PROTEIN FROM A VARIETY OF LEAVES

In the initial stages of the work, about 500 g of various leaves from Nigerian plants were extracted on a small scale in the laboratory with a household mincer, and the juice was squeezed out through a muslin cloth. Samples of the residue were dried in an oven overnight at 98°C. Nitrogen content was determined in the dry samples and in the juice by the Kjeldahl (digestion) method. The results are given in Table 31.1.

In 1975, a pilot plant based on the IBP pulper and press was purchased and housed in a building at the Institute of Church and Society through a grant obtained from the Christian Aid in London. By this time it had been decided to concentrate on three plants, *Amaranthus caudatus*, *Celosia argentea*, and *Vigna unguiculata*.

Extraction of the same leaves on a larger scale was carried out with the IBP pulper. The protein in the juice was precipitated by heating it to 80°C; it was then centrifuged and dried. Again, nitrogen was determined by the

TABLE 31.1. EXTRACTION OF PROTEIN FROM 500 G BATCHES OF SOME NIGERIAN LEAVES

Type of Leaf	Protein N Extracted (mg)	Protein N Extracted (%)	N in Coagulum After Heating to 80°C (%)
Cassava	1800	70.0	8.9
Cocoyam	1400	85.0	9.5
Maize	1632	74.0	11.0
Guinea corn	1580	79.5	10.1
Rice	1948	72.0	10.0
Fodder cane	1200	77.5	9.3
Pangola grass	1110	77.0	8.4
Elephant grass	704	56.0	9.2
Guatemala grass	980	71.5	8.3
Tamba grass	601	80.0	8.5
Papaya	1800	69.0	9.8
Banana	600	53.5	10.0

Kjeldahl procedure. Large-scale extractions were done with cereals, legumes, and green vegetables.

Maize was used as a typical cereal grown in Nigeria. The nitrogen in the dry matter increased from 3.0 to 3.5% in the first five weeks after planting, and then started to decrease gradually until the eleventh week, when the lowest figure of 2.5% was obtained. The true protein followed the same pattern. The dry matter increased progressively from 18.1 to 24.0% in 11 weeks. The amount of protein extracted was low, ranging from 35 to 50%.

The extractability of protein from maize leaves on a large scale was relatively low, and yet on a small scale these leaves gave the best results. Only the local white maize (Nigerian Synthetic Variety No.1) has been used so far, and no fertilizers have been applied. (There are several other types of maize which have not been tried, and the effect of fertilizer application has not been tested.) Cereals are known to give very poor yields when they are not fertilized, and this may have some effect on the extractability.

In legumes, unlike cereals, the percentage of nitrogen in the dry matter and the protein nitrogen increased up to 8 weeks after planting before they started to decline. In groundnut (peanut), the total nitrogen increased from about 120 to 648 kg/ha. Over 70% of this was extractable within the first 8 weeks after planting. Extractability then decreased to about 20% after 11 weeks (Fig. 31.1). About 80% of the total nitrogen extracted within the first 7 weeks was protein nitrogen, and this decreased to about 30% after 11 weeks.

Legumes gave high extractability values. They have the added advantage of being able to fix atmospheric nitrogen and so enrich the soil as well. As much protein as 500 kg/ha was obtained in 8 weeks, or about 3000 kg/ha/year. This is probably about three times the amount of protein that would be obtained if the plants were grown for seeds only. The decrease in extractability coincided with the period of seed development. For maximum leaf extraction, legumes should be planted close together (instead of at the

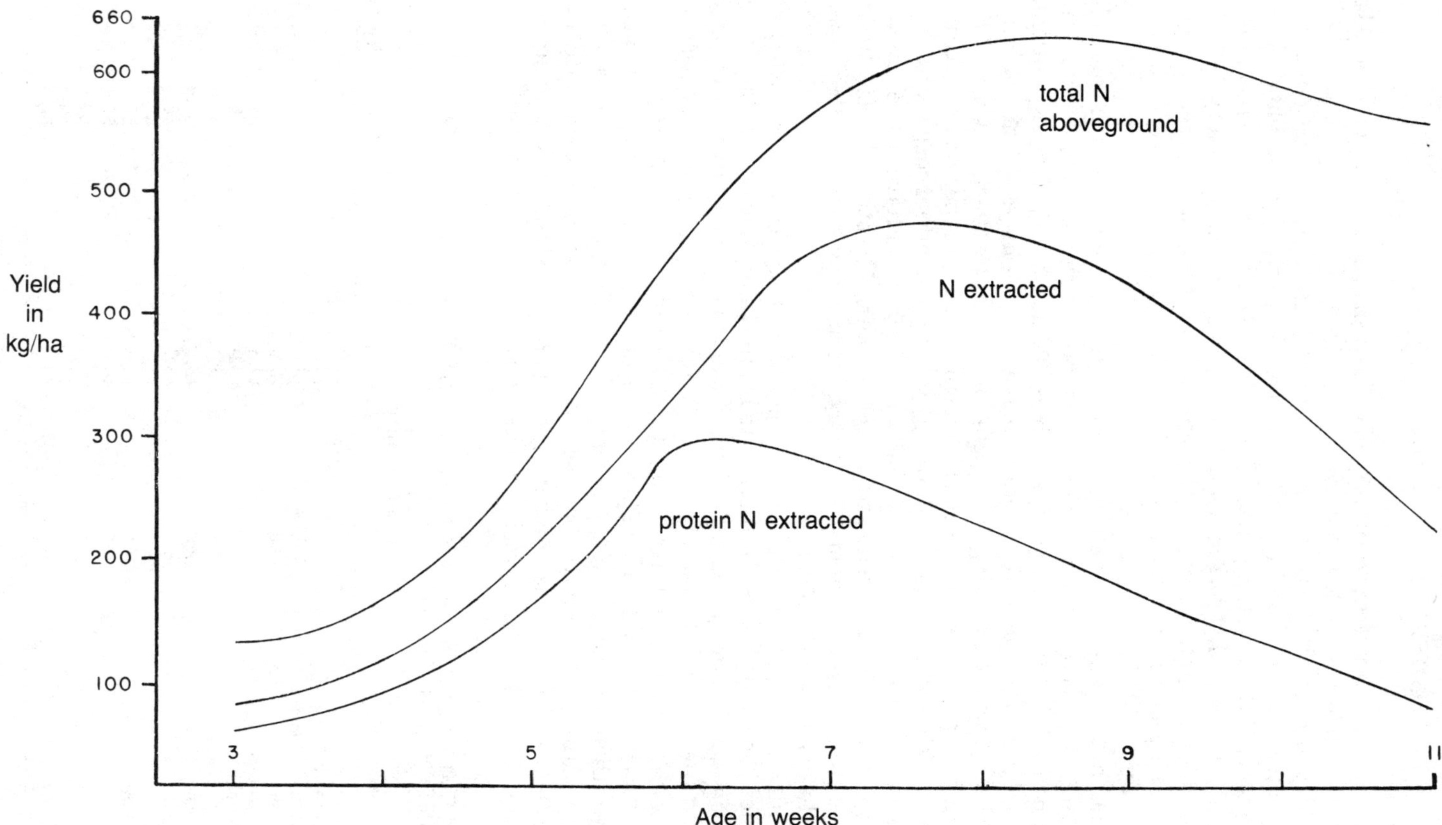

Fig. 31.1. Nitrogen content of aboveground dry matter of unfertilized groundnut (peanut), Nigeria.

usual spacing, which maximizes seed yields), and the harvesting should be done just before seed development.

In green vegetables, as with legumes, the percentage of nitrogen in the dry matter and the protein nitrogen increased for up to 7 weeks but dropped more steeply than with legumes. The total nitrogen started to decrease after about 9 weeks. The percentage of nitrogen extracted was very high in vegetables, as high as about 90% up to 8 weeks. Most of the total nitrogen extracted was true protein (about 80–90%) up to 6 weeks; this decreased to low values (40–50%) in 11 weeks.

The leaves of green vegetables offer a good source of easily extractable protein, as much as 90% being extracted in some cases. Protein yield from green vegetable leaves can be as high as 300 kg/ha in 5–6 weeks without the application of fertilizers, that is, about 3000 kg/ha/year. This quantity can be increased by using fertilizers and by closer spacing. Up to 2014 kg/ha/year of protein have been obtained in sequence experiments in Great Britain using winter wheat followed by two crops of either fodder radish or mustard (Arkcoll 1971), while in India 3000 kg/ha/year have been extracted from alfalfa, without special attention to manurial treatment (Joshi 1971). Generally, increased yields of extractable protein have resulted when fertilizer has been applied.

Fifteen varieties of cassava were planted at the University Research Farm. The young leaves were harvested at the same time from plants at the same stage of growth. About 1½ kg of the leaves of each were extracted using the IBP pulper and press. The protein was precipitated by passing steam into the juice to give a final temperature of 80°C. The supernatant juice was filtered and the leaf protein concentrate washed with dilute acid. It was then filtered through a muslin bag and allowed to drain dry at room temperature for two days. Samples were taken for the determination of nitrogen and for digestibility using the papain method of Buchanan and Byers (1969) with thioglycolic acid as activator (Table 31.2).

TABLE 31.2. EXTRACTABILITY AND DIGESTIBILITY OF PROTEIN FROM DIFFERENT VARIETIES OF CASSAVA

Cassava Variety	Extractability (%) Total N	Protein N	Papain Digestibility (%)
Afugba	59.7	44.0	52.8
Uboma II	60.3	45.3	60.9
Manihot palmata	56.8	43.6	58.3
Romba	60.9	45.9	57.7
Sweet cassava	57.7	44.3	54.9
Ugo-ocha	60.2	46.0	56.7
Ozu-nwagwe	59.1	44.9	58.8
Birakpo	59.9	46.1	58.9
Mikpa	58.7	45.0	58.6
Ife	55.8	44.5	53.1
Ogbomoso	57.3	44.8	56.8
53101	56.9	44.2	55.4
60447	59.4	45.4	54.3
Okobo	58.5	44.7	54.8
Imo	59.6	45.6	56.9

The Romba variety gave the highest value for total extractable nitrogen (60.9%), which is very similar to Uboma II (60.3%) and Ugo-ocha (60.2%), and the lowest was the Ife variety (55.8%). The difference in extractability was not significant, the average being 58.7%. Most of the nitrogen extracted was found to be protein nitrogen, with a range of 43.6 to 46.1% and an average of 44.9%. Uboma II, which had a high extractability, also had the highest digestibility (60.9%), with Afugba giving the lowest (52.8%). The average digestibility amounted to 56.6%.

COMPOSITION OF LEAF PROTEIN CONCENTRATE

Apart from protein, leaf protein concentrate contains 2.5–8.4% fatty acids, which play a very important role in its nutritive properties. The predominant unsaturated fatty acid is linolenic (21–54% of the total), while palmitic is the most abundant saturated fatty acid (15–40%). Large amounts of β-carotene, vitamin B_2, xanthophyll, and carbohydrate are also present.

Leaf protein concentrate can be separated, by fractional coagulation, into two fractions loosely termed chloroplastic and cytoplasmic protein. The chloroplastic protein precipitates when the leaf extract is heated to 55°–60°C. The precipitate is separated by centrifugation. If the supernatant is then heated to 80°C, the cytoplasmic protein precipitates. The chloroplastic fraction, with about 8% nitrogen, has more ash, fat, carbohydrate, and crude fiber than the cytoplasmic fraction, with 12–15% nitrogen.

The amino acid patterns in four Nigerian vegetables, *Amaranthus caudatus*, *Celosia argentea*, *Solanum nodiflorum*, and *Solanum incanum*, were studied. Two methods of hydrolysis were used for comparison, the sealed tube and the open flask methods (Oke 1971).

Details of the results are given in Table 31.3. The protein content of the leaves varied from 50.40 to 58.98%. The amino acid pattern was the same in the different leaves. This suggests that protein of a uniform composition can be extracted from a wide variety of green leaves. The proteins were high in such amino acids as aspartic acid, glutamic acid, leucine, and lysine.

The main difference in the overall result between hydrolysis in sealed tubes for 18 hr and ordinary refluxing for 22 hr was the amount of cystine destroyed: only some was destroyed in the first method but most was destroyed in the second. In order to obtain any values for cystine, a performic acid oxidation had to be carried out before hydrolysis. In the case of methionine, some was oxidized to the sulfoxide, and the result is expressed as the sum of both.

Apart from the amino acid pattern of a particular protein, which determines whether it is adequate for nutrition, the true nutritive value also needs to be determined by means of feeding trials with animals.

Since in Nigeria there is a variety of green leaves that could be used almost year-round for the extraction of protein, an attempt was made to

TABLE 31.3. AMINO ACID PATTERNS OF FOUR NIGERIAN VEGETABLES
Two methods of hydrolysis were used: open flask and sealed tubes.

	Amaranthus caudatus		*Celosia argentea*		*Solanum nodiflorum*		*Solanum incanum*	
Nitrogen (as % of dry matter)	9.83		8.65		8.40		9.16	
Protein (N × 6.0)	58.98		57.90		50.40		54.96	
Amino Acids (g/100 g)	Open	Sealed	Open	Sealed	Open	Sealed	Open	Sealed
Aspartic acid	10.12	9.91	10.23	9.79	9.53	9.76	10.43	10.61
Threonine	5.39	5.08	5.20	4.95	5.72	5.17	5.30	5.13
Serine	5.61	5.34	4.65	4.61	4.24	4.71	5.05	5.35
Glutamic acid	11.30	11.56	11.88	11.75	11.57	11.51	11.71	11.68
Proline	4.96	4.94	5.25	4.69	5.05	5.01	5.08	4.94
Glycine	5.57	5.13	4.73	5.43	5.83	5.65	5.61	5.24
Alanine	5.74	5.85	6.85	7.11	6.32	6.18	5.68	5.92
Valine	6.01	6.09	6.10	6.16	6.07	6.12	6.10	6.18
Cystine	1.95	2.03	1.33	1.35	1.55	1.55	1.98	1.96
Methionine	2.20	2.19	2.05	2.13	1.89	1.76	2.30	2.11
Isoleucine	5.38	5.37	5.09	4.98	4.77	5.07	5.02	5.13
Leucine	9.17	9.51	8.92	9.06	9.71	9.66	9.05	9.07
Tyrosine	4.43	4.64	5.00	4.91	4.66	4.83	4.78	4.80
Phenylalanine	6.01	6.06	6.08	6.12	6.42	6.42	6.09	6.04
Ammonia	0.98	0.95	1.22	1.29	1.08	1.06	1.00	1.03
Lysine	6.38	6.75	6.57	6.62	6.50	6.46	6.72	6.57
Histidine	2.61	2.37	2.60	2.73	2.73	2.66	2.17	2.26
Arginine	6.16	6.26	6.23	6.33	6.36	6.43	5.95	6.00
Totals	99.97	100.03	99.98	100.01	100.00	100.01	100.02	100.02

Source: Oke (1971).

extract protein from different leaves and determine digestibility by papain, using the method of Buchanan and Byers and a modification of it.

The leaves used in this experiment were obtained from the University Farm. They were harvested and the protein was extracted using Pirie's IBP pulper and press. The protein was precipitated by passing steam into the juice to give a final temperature of 80°C. The supernatant juice was filtered and the leaf protein concentrate (LPC) washed with dilute acid. It was then filtered through a muslin bag and allowed to drain dry at room temperature for two days. Samples were then taken for the determination of nitrogen by the Kjeldahl method and digestibility using the papain method of Buchanan and Byers with thioglycolic acid activator. In the modified method, nitrogen was determined directly in the residue after papain digestion.

Table 31.4 shows the extractability of protein from the different leaves. The highest values were given by edible leaves such as *Amaranthus* (73.5%), *Celosia* (72.9%), and *Solanum* (71.4%). The majority of the other leaves (most of which are not normally eaten) gave a range of 48–68%. Most of the nitrogen extracted was protein nitrogen, with a range of 73–90%.

The digestibility of the various kinds of LPC, using both the original and

TABLE 31.4. EXTRACTABILITY OF PROTEIN FROM VARIOUS LEAVES

Leaf Source	Common or Local Name	% Total N Extracted	% Protein N Extracted	Extractability % of Protein N
Musa spp.	Banana	68.4	61.6	90.06
Solanum africana	Igbagba	71.4	64.5	90.33
Anacardium occidentale L.	Cashew	59.8	50.8	84.95
Vernonia amygdalina	Bitter leaves, ewuro	48.8	42.1	86.27
Telfairia occidentalis	Fluted gourd, ugwu	70.1	63.1	90.01
Manihot esculenta	Cassava	59.7	44.0	73.70
Celosia argentea	Quail grass	72.9	66.2	90.80
Mangifera indica	Mango	60.6	52.8	87.13
Colocasia esculenta	Cocoyam	52.2	45.3	86.78
Amaranthus sp.	Tete	73.5	66.4	90.34
Abelmoschus esculentus L.	Okra	59.7	44.0	73.70

modified methods, was low. In the original method, casein gave 94.6% digestibility followed by *Amaranthus*, 72.7%, and *Celosia* and cashew, 71%. The lowest figure obtained was 50.9% for cocoyam. The range seems to be wide—50 to 73%. The figures are lower still in the modified method, with casein giving 82.4%, *Amaranthus*, *Celosia*, and cashew, 61%. Again, cocoyam gave the lowest value, 40%. However, when these figures are compared with casein as 100%, a more realistic result similar to the original method was obtained, and this is highly significant with $r = 0.977$.

One particular plant of interest is carrot *(Daucus carota)*, whose leaves Joshi (1971) reported failed to support growth. In a detailed report embodying rat growth tests and metabolic studies, Joshi found wide variations in the nutritive value of protein extracted from the leaves of different plants: lucerne, cabbage, knol, and radish all yielded PER's ranging from 1.5 to 1.9, while rats lost weight on *Dolichos lablab*, *Sesbania* species, carrot, and horse gram, with PER's ranging from 0 to 0.91.

Because the carrot is cultivated mainly for its roots while the leaves are wasted, and because it is now widely grown in the middle belt of Nigeria, preliminary work was carried out to ascertain whether the results obtained by Joshi for carrot leaves were due to toxic effects or to other causes. In a rabbit feeding experiment, carrot leaf was compared with the leaf of a *Stylosanthes* species *(Stylosanthes gracilis)*, a forage legume.

Seeds of carrot were grown on a plot in the University of Ife farm. Leaves were harvested at intervals of three weeks. *Stylosanthes* used in the experiment was obtained from the feed depot of the University of Ife farm.

Drying of *Stylosanthes* and carrot leaves was done at a temperature range of 50° to 60°C for three days. The dried materials were ground to pass through a 20 mm mesh. Weighing, mixing, and pelleting of ration were done at the feed depot of the University of Ife farm.

Forty-eight New Zealand white rabbits of 13 weeks average initial age, equalized as to sex and weight, were randomly allotted to two treatment groups of carrot and *Stylosanthes*. The resulting 24 rabbits per treatment were further subdivided into four Brewer's Dry Grains (BDG) replacement level groups. Experimental animals were housed individually and maintained in cages with wire screen floors raised to a height of 90 cm from the floor. Row cages of size 76 cm × 62 cm × 42 cm were used. The mesh wire screen floor had openings large enough to permit feces to fall out of reach of the rabbits, hence coprophagy was avoided. The animals were weighed at weekly intervals, while daily feed consumption was recorded by the weigh-back technique.

Feed and water were available *ad libitum* in all trials. Rabbits were slaughtered 8 weeks after the commencement of the experiment, and the carcass data obtained were the dressing value, skin weight, and weight of offal. The data were examined statistically by analysis of variance and Duncan's multiple range test as outlined by Steele and Torrie (1960).

In both carrot leaf- and *Stylosanthes*-supplemented diets, intake appeared to be influenced by the level of dietary BDG. Animals fed high levels (30 and 45%) of BDG significantly ($P < 0.05$) consumed more food than animals fed low levels (0%, 15%) of BDG (Table 31.5). However, at high levels of dietary BDG, intake was significantly ($P < 0.05$) higher by inclusion of carrot leaf in the diet than when *Stylosanthes* was fed. On the whole, animals fed carrot leaf ate 4.0 g more food per day than animals fed *Stylosanthes*; the carrot leaf-supplemented diets may have been more acceptable to the animals, and this could have influenced food intake.

In the overall experiment, animals fed supplemental carrot leaf gained 14.9 g of body weight per day as compared with 14.1 g body weight gained by animals on the *Stylosanthes* treatment. However, this difference was not statistically significant ($P < 0.05$). From the study, it appears that carrot leaves support better body weight gains than *Stylosanthes* in rabbits fed high levels of dietary BDG. This may be related to the low feed consumption by the animals on diets with supplemental stylo and the higher crude fiber content of *Stylosanthes* as compared with carrot leaves.

For both carrot leaf and *Stylosanthes* supplementation, efficiency of feed utilization was significantly depressed ($P < 0.05$) as the dietary BDG increased. Diets with carrot leaves were more efficiently utilized than those containing *Stylosanthes*, though the overall average values of 6.30 and 6.89 for carrot leaves and stylo, respectively, were not significantly different. The conversion efficiency may have been affected by the higher levels of minerals and lower level of crude fiber in carrot leaves as compared with stylo.

In general, feeding carrot leaves as supplement in diets of growing rabbits resulted in increased feed consumption, daily weight gain, and efficiency of feed utilization as compared with supplemental stylo.

Next, the nutritive value of the most commonly used staples in Nigeria, cassava, yam flour, ogi (ogi-starch) and rice powder, supplemented with leaf protein concentrate (LPC) was determined by feeding trials with rats. The formulations were highly digestible, with cassava showing the highest digestibility (94.77%). Ogi gave the highest PER of 2.01, followed by cas-

TABLE 31.5. EFFECT OF CARROT LEAVES OR *STYLOSANTHES GRACILIS* ON LIVE PERFORMANCE OF FRYER RABBITS

Animal Performance	Carrot Leaf Treatment[1]				*Stylosanthes* Treatment[1]				Average Values for Animal Performance	
	1	2	3	4	1	2	3	4	Carrot	Stylo
Number of rabbits	6	6	6	6	6	6	6	6	24	24
Average initial weight (g)	1447.2	1418.8	1447.2	1390.4	1362.0	1390.4	1390.4	1390.4	1425.9	1383.3
Average final weight (g)	2156.8	2270.0	2298.4	2270.0	2213.6	2355.2	2100.0	2014.8	2248.8	2170.9
Average daily feed consumption (g)	69.17d	82.61c	98.08a	102.24b	73.02c	87.58d	84.24a	91.08b	88.0	84.0
Average daily weight gain (g)	12.89	14.35	15.47	16.84	15.92	16.83	12.89	10.75	14.9	14.1
Mean efficiency of feed conversion	5.83	5.94	6.65	6.69	4.84	5.24	7.78	9.70	6.3	6.89

Values in Row 4 with a common letter are significantly different at $P < 0.05$.

[1]Treatment: 1 = 0% BDG (Brewer's Dry Grains)
2 = 15% BDG
3 = 30% BDG
4 = 45% BDG

sava (PER 1.66), then rice powder and yam flour with PER values of 1.21 and 1.12, respectively. These supplemented foods have enhanced NPU (net protein utilization) and BV (biological value) values. Supplemented ogi (wet milled fermented corn) appeared most nutritious and efficient. This was closely followed by the cassava diet. It is possible, therefore, to conclude that, despite the cyanide in cassava, this staple will still continue to play a significant role as a foodstuff for humans and farm livestock in many of tropical and subtropical countries.

The results of the trials showed that leaf protein could be used as an inexpensive source of protein to supplement a ration containing 20% of the common cereal and tuber staples (maize, rice, yam, and cassava). Among these staples, cassava is the most inexpensive and the least nutritious, yet it is the most important staple in Nigeria. It is the most inexpensive source of calories for man, the most widely grown crop (representing about 57% of the total tropical root and tuber production), and is the most productive farm crop, yielding an edible nutrient equivalent on average of over 136 kJ/ha (13 million kcal/acre) compared with 94 (9 million) for yam and 10.4 (1 million) each for Guinea corn and maize. Since cassava gave the highest digestibility (94.77%) and was next in PER to maize (1.66), it could be used mainly as an energy source in animal feed as a substitute for cereals. The more nutritious cereals could then be released for human nutrition.

THE CAROTENOID PIGMENTS IN NUTRITION

Unlike the water-soluble vitamins, the fat-soluble vitamins are usually from animal sources. Vitamin A, which is one of the most important, is found in milk, eggs, meat, liver, and butter. In Nigeria, these are all expensive sources of this vitamin. Fortunately, β-carotene, which can be converted in the body to vitamin A, occurs in palm oil, green leaves, and fruits, and so we have less expensive, indirect sources. If, as in some developing countries, children are not given animal sources of the vitamin and they have no access to green vegetables, they will develop a deficiency leading first to night blindness and then dryness of the corneas and conjunctivitis, i.e., xerophthalmia, and finally keratomalacia, or blindness (Oomen 1961). Xerophthalmia is endemic in countries where rice is the main staple such as South and East Asia. In some parts of the Middle East, Africa, and Latin America, where green leaves are not incorporated into the diet of children, it has assumed importance in the field of public health (Oomen 1961).

An attempt was made to find the distribution of carotenoids and their stability under tropical conditions during the processing of green leaves for LPC.

Leaves from different plants were collected from the University Farm, and their protein was extracted using the IBP pulper and press. The protein from the juice was precipitated by heating to 80°C and filtering through stockings. The LPC obtained was then freeze-dried. Samples were kept in polyethylene bags and stored on the shelves in the laboratory for various lengths of time. Carotenoids were determined from the samples using the modified method of Knowles *et al.* (1972). The distribution of β-carotenes of the process fraction is shown in Table 31.6. The highest value for β-carotene was obtained from *Gnetum buccholzianum* with 11.14 mg/100 g. On pulping, about 98% of it went into the juice while 10% remained in the fiber. The supernatant liquor, after precipitation of the leaf protein, contained only 6% of the β-carotene in the juice, while most of it (85%) was precipitated with the green proteins. This means that about 75% of the β-carotene in the fresh leaves was recovered in the LPC. The cassava leaves contained the least amount of β-carotene in the LPC. In general, about 86–97% of the β-carotene of the fresh leaves was extracted into the juice, 1–13% was left in the fiber, and 69–85% of the amount present in the fresh leaves was found in the green protein concentrate.

The stability data are compiled in Table 31.7. The freeze-dried samples were uniformly high in β-carotene, ranging from 744 to 1413 mg/kg initial weight, with that of *Solanum nodiflorum* having the highest amount and *Corchorus olitorius* the lowest. This did not follow the order in which β-carotene occurred in the leaves. The xanthophyll contents were even

TABLE 31.6. DISTRIBUTION OF β-CAROTENE OF LEAVES IN THE PREPARATION OF LEAF PROTEIN CONCENTRATE
Expressed as mg/100 g on a wet weight basis.

Leaves							
Common [Local] Name	Scientific Name	% Dry Matter	Pulped Leaves	Juice	Fiber	Super-natant	Wet LPC
Quail grass [soko]	*Celosia argentea* L.	19	8.54	7.66	0.77	0.38	6.89
Edible amaranthus [tete]	*Amaranthus hybridus*	16	7.62	7.39	0.08	0.59	6.50
Surinam spinach [gbure]	*Talinum triangulare* (Jacq.) Willd.	12	6.81	5.86	0.89	0.23	5.33
Jute mallow [ewedu]	*Corchorus olitorius* L.	19	5.93	5.57	0.24	0.56	4.79
Bitter leaf [ewuro]	*Vernonia amygdalina* Dal.	21	7.44	6.40	0.96	0.70	5.10
[Ogunmo]	*Solanum nodiflorum* Jacq.	22	9.26	8.56	0.56	0.60	6.93
[Igbo]	*Solanum africana*	20	8.84	7.77	0.97	0.78	6.22
Fluted gourd [ugwu]	*Telfairia occidentalis* Hook. f.	20	10.72	9.22	1.29	0.65	7.74
[Ukazi]	*Gnetum buccholzianum*	30	11.14	9.80	1.10	0.60	8.33
Cassava	*Manihot esculenta*	10	5.99	5.39	0.42	0.54	4.31

TABLE 31.7. STABILITY OF STORED β-CAROTENE (C) AND XANTHOPHYLL (X) OF LPC WITH TIME
mg/kg of freeze-dried sample.

Source of LPC	Initial Quantity		3 Months		6 Months		9 Months		12 Months		% Loss in 12 Months	
	C	X	C	X	C	X	C	X	C	X	β-Carotene	Xanthophyll
Celosia argentea [soko]	1016	2828	701	2715	528	2403	210	1309	164	1273	84	55
Amaranthus hybridus [tete]	984	2066	748	1963	432	1673	284	1171	208	1136	79	45
Talinum triangulare [gbure]	1205	3205	964	2917	566	2499	199	1392	172	1346	86	58
Corchorus olitorius [ewedu]	744	2306	528	2052	372	1914	250	1218	163	1153	78	50
Vernonia amygdalina [ewuro]	868	2083	729	1854	520	1666	173	1224	130	1167	85	44
Solanum nodiflorum [ogunmo]	1413	3532	1088	3226	749	2861	296	1780	228	1713	84	52
Solanum africana [igbo]	1087	2217	848	1995	533	1796	267	1301	175	1264	84	43
Telfairia occidentalis [ugwu]	1119	2526	929	2299	627	1996	285	1118	198	1065	82	58
Gnetum buccholzianum [ukazi]	948	2939	739	2645	513	2439	221	2086	177	2057	81	30
Manihot esculenta [cassava]	847	2004	660	1804	491	1703	219	1253	183	1202	78	40

higher, ranging initially from 2004 to 3532 mg/kg. Again, *Solanum nodiflorum* had the highest level, but cassava (which also had the lowest β-carotene) had the lowest. On exposure to light and air, the β-carotene content of *Solanum nodiflorum* decreased uniformly from 1413 to 228 mg/kg in 12 months, a loss of 84%. The corresponding figures for xanthophylls were 3532–1713 mg/kg, or 52% loss. On the whole, the loss of β-carotene ranged from 78 to 86%, while that of xanthophyll was much less, 30–58%.

One potential significant bonus of LPC in human nutrition is its high carotene content. Originally, kwashiorkor was regarded as a nutritional disease caused mainly by lack of protein. Often associated with this disease are eye lesions, especially in areas where sources of β-carotene are not accessible and where animal sources are not within the economic range of the common man. Thus, in Indonesia, where rice with no β-carotene is the main staple, about 75% of the kwashiorkor cases develop eye lesions (xerophenesia), whereas in Uganda, where yellow maize rich in carotene is available, such lesions occur in not more than 1% of the cases. Likewise, in West Africa, where red palm oil (which is high in β-carotene content) is used, the incidence of eye lesions associated with kwashiorkor is low.

In our experiments at Ibadan, 30 ml (2 tbsp) of LPC three times a day were recommended to mothers for their children, to be mixed with their food (Olatubosun *et al.* 1972), which amounts to about 20 g a day. This means an intake of β-carotene in excess of the requirement, which, in this case, is a very good practice. There will still be enough for the child, even if we assume a loss of 80% due to oxidation, which emphasizes the importance of LPC as a good source of β-carotene. Ramana and Singh (1971) have confirmed this in rats and found LPC to be better than the synthetic source in respect to growth (141 and 138 g, respectively) and serum content of vitamin A (68 and 59 mg/100 ml), as well as liver vitamin A content. It is possible to exhaust the liver stores of vitamin A long before clinical signs of deficiency appear. McLaren *et al.* (1965) found that children with severe protein-energy malnutrition (PEM) in Jordan showed no clinical sign of vitamin A deficiency, in spite of the fact that they had exhausted their liver stores and showed low serum levels. When eye lesions accompanied PEM, the mortality was usually about four times greater than with PEM alone (McLaren *et al.* 1965). High intake of LPC will help ensure a sufficiency of the vitamin in the liver.

Since β-carotene is so sensitive to destruction (up to 80% loss in 12 months), it is advisable to store LPC in a dark receptacle such as a plastic bag.

Our main interest in xanthophylls arose from the fact that we are considering replacing the nutritious maize in chick ration with cassava tubers as the source of energy. Cassava is mainly carbohydrate with very few or no nutrients, especially carotene and protein. This means that the ration has to be well-balanced with a rich source of protein and a source of carotene. When cassava replaced maize, the chicks became pale-colored and the egg yolk was dull. However, it was found that the color could be improved by adding synthetic carotenoids or cassava leaf meal to the diet. Hutagalung *et al.* (1973), Syed *et al.* (1975), and Agudu (1972) compared the efficiency of cassava and Madras thorn *(Pithecellobium dulce)* leaf meals, a synthetic xanthophyll material, and two sources of yellow corn as sources of egg yolk pigments in pullets. Cassava leaf meal had higher total and pigmenting xanthophyll content than Madras thorn leaf meal but could not be compared with the synthetic material used, which had an unusually low content of xanthophyll with no significant effect on egg yolk. If the LPC from cassava leaves had been used as the source of protein for the chicks [this has proven to be a more effective source than fishmeal (Adegbola and Oke 1973)], the amount in the ration would have been more than sufficient to satisfy their requirement for β-carotene. Arnold (1972) fed starter diets to birds from 0 to 5 weeks with different sources of xanthophylls and found no visual differences in those on diets of corn gluten meal, dehydrated alfalfa, or Pro-Xan, but those on marigold petals had poorer performance than the others.

CLINICAL TRIAL WITH CHILDREN

The results obtained from the preceding animal experiments were sufficiently encouraging to justify some clinical trials with leaf protein. Kwashiorkor, protein-calorie malnutrition, is prevalent in developing countries such as Nigeria. It can be controlled mainly by the addition of protein to the diet and the treatment of skin infections. Since not all affected children can be treated in the hospital, the vast majority are sent home with advice on nutrition and, in some cases, a diet sheet. The provision of animal protein is beyond the financial means of many parents, and there is a cultural reluctance to give meat and eggs to children. Furthermore, milk is believed to induce diarrhea in children who are deficient in lactase. There is, therefore, a need in Nigeria for an inexpensive, effective, and culturally acceptable form of protein supplement to overcome kwashiorkor.

An outpatient trial of feeding leaf protein supplements to 22 children with kwashiorkor was conducted, and the preliminary results are summarized here. Clinical diagnosis was established by the presence of peripheral edema, hair and skin changes, and mental apathy. The home diets to which the mothers were instructed to add the leaf protein powder consisted of maize gruel, yam flour pudding, cassava pudding, rice ewedu *(Corchorus olitorius)*, and okra soup. The total dose of leaf protein was approximately 10 g (7 g protein) per day. Chest infections when present were treated with tetracycline, but no other drugs were given. Diarrhea was not treated.

The results showed that, within 10 days, edema disappeared, appetite improved, and the children became more mentally alert. Diarrhea subsided spontaneously.

Results of changes in body weight, serum proteins, and serum albumin are given in Fig. 32.2. There was a good increase in body weight in view of the fact that the children had to shed a lot of excess water originally

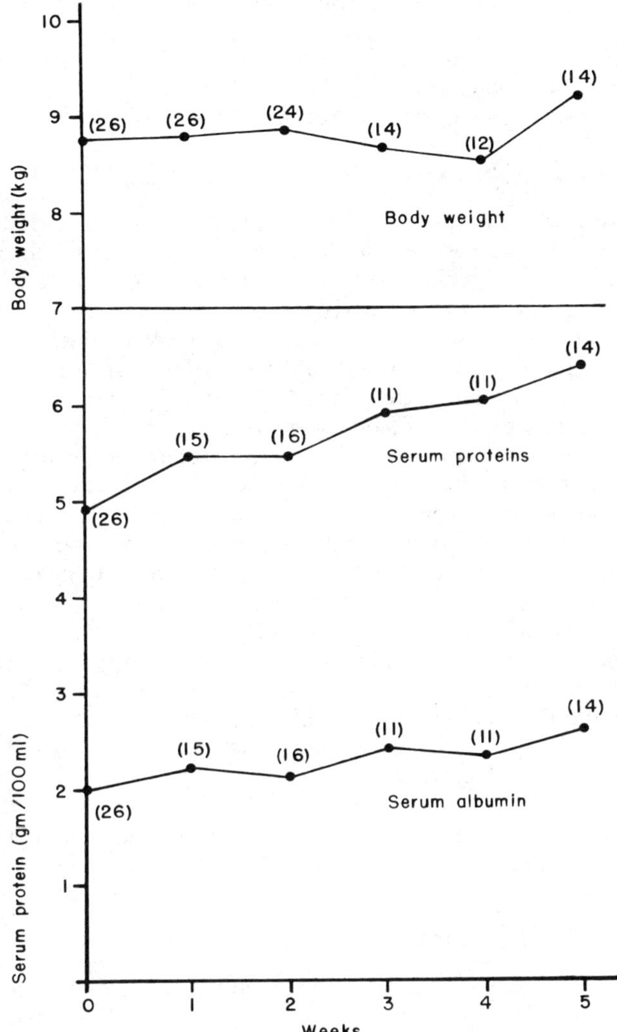

Fig. 31.2. Changes in body weight, serum proteins, and serum albumin in children fed leaf protein supplements. Number of children in brackets.

accumulated as edema. The serum proteins and albumin also increased markedly.

These results indicate that leaf protein supplements may prove to be inexpensive, effective, and culturally acceptable for the treatment and prevention of protein-calorie malnutrition.

INCORPORATION INTO TRADITIONAL FOODS

The most important aspect of the work being done with leaf protein concentrate is creating acceptance for it in various groups of the population. One advantage in Nigeria is that the villagers are used to taking maize gruel every morning with food mixtures ranging from black to dark green in color, and so the color of the leaf protein has not been a major problem. A high supplementation was acceptable with maize gruel, especially with farmers. It seem the older they are, the more supplementation they can tolerate. Virtually all the food prepared for lunch and supper is taken with green vegetable stew, which contains a bountiful amount of other food items such as crayfish, locust bean, pepper, tomatoes, etc. The product looks like a mass of green leaves. Sometimes, palm oil is used (this depends on the vegetable), but usually it is omitted. In some cases, the pepper soup is cooked separately, and a little bit of it is added to the vegetable soup. Vegetable soups afford a good medium for supplementation, and, as long as the supplementation does not exceed about 60%, there is no change in taste or color. With certain foodstuffs, however, especially those that are usually colored red by palm oil (e.g., jolloff rice), the green color and gritty feel may make the food less acceptable. Still, conservatism in food habits is not exclusively a Nigerian problem; with perseverance, the problem of acceptability may eventually be solved.

The quantity of leaf protein to be used in three Nigerian food mixtures—oyo soup (a kind of vegetable stew), yam flour (a popular lunch and supper dish), and maize gruel—has been determined. Recipes and nitrogen content of the dishes follow.

Oyo or Vegetable Stew

Cut and wash leaves. Add to boiling water and stir. Add cooked beans and crayfish and leaf protein concentrate. Stir. Leave to cool for a short time.

Contents	Weight Taken (g)	Dry Weight (g)	N Content (g)
Leaves of *Corchorus olitorius* or oyo	190.00	25.0	0.900
Locust bean	4.0	1.5	0.040
Crayfish	15.0	12.0	1.080
Leaf protein	24.0	23.6	2.400
	233.0	62.1	4.420

Nitrogen as % of dry matter:
Calculated = 7.20%
By analysis = 6.55%
% of nitrogen due to leaf protein = 54.30%

Yam Flour

Add the yam flour a little at a time to some boiling water and continue stirring until it forms a semisolid mass. Add the leaf protein and stir again until it is homogeneous.

(1) Contents	Weight Taken (g)	Dry Weight (g)	N Content (g)
Yam flour	60	48.0	0.72
Water	400	—	—
Leaf protein	10	10.0	1.00
	470	58.0	1.72

Nitrogen as % of dry matter:
Calculated = 2.97%
By analysis = 3.31%
% of nitrogen due to leaf protein = 58.1%

(2) Contents	Weight Taken (g)	Dry Weight (g)	N Content (g)
Yam flour	60	48.0	0.72
Water	400	—	—
Leaf protein	5	5.0	0.50
	465	53.0	1.22

Nitrogen as % of dry matter:
Calculated = 2.30%
By analysis = 1.98%
% of nitrogen due to leaf protein = 41.0%

Maize Gruel

Dissolve the maize flour in the minimum amount of cold water. Pour in boiling water, stirring until it forms a semisolid paste. Add the leaf protein and stir again.

(1) Contents	Weight Taken (g)	Dry Weight (g)	N Content (g)
Maize flour	132	7.92	0.088
Water	525	—	—
Leaf protein	5	5.00	0.500
	662	12.92	0.588

Nitrogen as % of dry matter:
Calculated = 4.60%
By analysis = 5.65%
% of nitrogen due to leaf protein = 85.0%

(2) Contents	Weight Taken (g)	Dry Weight (g)	N Content (g)
Maize flour	79	4.74	0.053
Water	300	—	—
Leaf protein	5	5.00	0.500
	384	9.74	0.553

Nitrogen as % of dry matter:
Calculated = 5.70%
By analysis = 5.97%
% of nitrogen due to leaf protein = 90.5%

COST

In India, alfalfa has been estimated to cost about 1 shilling per kg (1982) to process into leaf protein concentrate. This could provide 10–12 g of supplementary protein per day for an adult, which would cost about 4 new pence (British) a month. It is premature to give any costs for the inclusion of leaf protein in human diets in Nigeria since its use still has to be assessed under village conditions. However, leaf protein concentrate is almost certain to be a relatively inexpensive source of protein since machines such as the Posho mill can be used for LPC production and for other purposes. In addition, certain costs of production, such as labor, are relatively low, and some of the leaf material is obtained as a by-product of other operations.

REFERENCES

ADEGBOLA, A.A. and OKE, O.L. 1973. Preliminary observations on the value of leaf protein/fishmeal mixtures as protein supplement for white leghorn. Nutr. Rep. Int. *8*, 313–318.

AGUDU, E.W. 1972. Preliminary investigation on some unusual feedstuffs as yolk pigmenters in Ghana. Ghana J. Agric. Sci. *5*, 33–38.

ARKCOLL, D.B. 1971. Agronomic aspects of leaf protein production in Great Britain. *In* Leaf Protein: Its Agronomy, Preparation, Quality and Use. IBP Handb. *20*. N.W. Pirie (Editor). Blackwell Scientific Publications, Oxford.

ARNOLD, W.L. 1972. Comparison of xanthophyll sources. 11th Tech. Alfalfa Conf. Proc., U.S. Dep. Agric., July 29–30, 1971, Albany, CA. *ARS-74-60*.

BUCHANAN, A.R., and BYERS, M. 1969. Interference by cyanide with the measurement of papain hydrolysis. J. Sci. Food Agric. *20*, 364–369.

DAVYS, M.N.G. and PIRIE, N.W. 1963. Batch production of protein from leaves. J. Agric. Eng. Res. *8*, 70–74.

DAVYS, M.N.G. and PIRIE, N.W. 1969. A laboratory-scale pulper for leafy plant materials. Biotech. Bioeng. *11*, 517–528.

DAVYS, M.N.G., PIRIE, N.W. and STREET, G. 1969. A laboratory-scale press for extracting juice from leaf pulp. Biotech. Bioeng. *11*, 529–538.

HUTAGALUNG, R.I., HING, P.C. and FONG, H.V. 1973. The utilization of cassava (tapioca) in livestock feeding. Proc. 3rd Symp. Int. Soc. Trop. Root Crops, Ibadan, Nigeria.

JOSHI, R.N. 1971. The yields of leaf protein that can be extracted from crops of Aurangabad. *In* Leaf Protein: Its Agronomy, Preparation, Quality and Use. IBP Handb. *20*. N.W. Pirie (Editor). Blackwell Scientific Publications, Oxford.

KNOWLES, R.E., LIVINGSTON, A.L. and KOHLER, G.O. 1972. Methodology in the determination of xanthophyll. 11th Tech. Alfalfa Conf. Proc., U.S. Dep. Agric., July 29–30, 1971, Albany, CA. *ARS-74-60*.

McLAREN, D.S., SHIRAJIAN, E., TACHLAIN, M. and KHORNY, G. 1965. Xerophthalmia in Jordan. Am. J. Clin. Nutr. *17*, 117–121.

OKE, O.L. 1971. Some aspects of amino acid composition of leaf protein. Indian J. Nutr. Diet. *8*, 81–85.

OKONJO, C. 1962. Preliminary medium estimate of 1962 midyear population of Nigeria. Ph.D. Dissertation. University of Gottinger, Germany.

OLATUBOSUN, D.A., ADADEVOH, B.K. and OKE, O.L. 1972. Leaf protein: A new protein source for the management of protein-calorie malnutrition in Nigeria. Niger. Med. J. *2*, 195–199.

OOMEN, H.A.P.C. 1961. An outline of xerophthalmia. Int. Rev. Trop. Med. *1*, 131–150.

RAMANA, K.V.R. and SINGH, N. 1971. Nutritional efficiency of lucerne leaf protein as a source of β-carotene in rat diets. Indian J. Exp. Biol. *9*, 378.

STEELE, R.G. and TORRIE, J.H. 1960. Principles and Procedures of Statistics. McGraw-Hill Book Co., New York.

SYED, A.B., YEONG, S.W. and SEET, C.P. 1975. Performance of layers fed high level of broken rice and tapioca as a direct substitute for maize. MARDI Res. Bull. *3*, 63–70.

32

The Future of Leaf Protein Concentrate in Pakistan

F.H. Shah

Inadequacy of the available and potential food supplies and the anticipated increase in the world population have been the focus of attention of planners, nutritionists, and food technologists. Even though a controversy is raging over whether there is a shortage of calories or of protein in the human diet, there is no doubt that much larger supplies of protein will be needed to meet demands of the increasing population.

The population of Pakistan has risen from 42.88 million in 1961 to 72.45 million in 1977 and is expected to be 360 million by the turn of the century (Shah 1975). The production of cereals and pulses in the year 1974–1975 was 9.46 and 0.56 million metric tons (MT), respectively (Shah 1977B) (Table 32.1), and protein-rich food of animal origin in the year preceding was 550,000 MT (Kidwai 1978) (Table 32.2).

Production of pulses, the poor man's supplementary source of protein, decreased by 11% in 10 years (Table 32.1). This was mainly due to poor economic returns to the farmer. The economic returns to the farmer propagating proteinaceous foodstuffs range up to −284.69% in the rainfed areas which form 50% of the total area of the Punjab (Anon. 1976) (Table 32.3).

Percentage increase in the prices of protein-rich foodstuffs in the last 15 years (Khan 1978) (Table 32.4) is an indication that the supply and demand gap is widening and that the situation may be further aggravated with the population explosion.

Seventy-five percent of Pakistan's population is rural and poor. Fifty-five million of the country's 73 million inhabitants live in villages. A study conducted by the Institute of Development Economics in 1976 has revealed that 80% of the population lives below the annual expenditure level of U.S. \$31.50[1] per person per annum and that this income level does not provide

[1] \$1 U.S. = 11.1 Pakistani Rs (November 1982).

TABLE 32.1. PRODUCTION OF COMMON CROPS IN PAKISTAN
In 1000 MT.

Crop	Year		% Increase or Decrease	Year		% Increase or Decrease
	1964–1965	1974–1975		1974–1975	1980–1981	
Rice	1141	2272	+99	2272	3,080	+36
Wheat	4087	7184	+76	7184	11,340	+58
Pulses	629	559	−11	559	735	+32

TABLE 32.2. PRODUCTION OF ANIMAL PROTEINS 1973–1974

Animal Protein	1000 MT
Animal and poultry meat	84
Milk	389
Eggs	30
Fish	47
Total	550

TABLE 32.3. ECONOMIC RETURNS TO FARMERS

Crop	Irrigated (%)	Rainfed (%)
Gram *(Cajanus cajan)*	+56.98	+ 12.12
Black gram *(Phaseolus mungo)*	+82.32	−105.67
Green gram *(Phaseolus aureus)*	+52.77	−142.97
Lentil	+65.86	−212.37
Soybean		−284.59

TABLE 32.4. INCREASE IN THE PRICES OF ANIMAL PROTEINS

Commodities	Percentage Increase in Prices Since 1962
Beef	600
Mutton	528
Live poultry	361
Milk	324
Eggs	167

for even the minimum subsistence of a household (Mohammad 1977). Thus, the principal problem of the country is quantitatively insufficient food consumption by a vast majority of the population.

This problem is particularly pronounced in nutritionally vulnerable groups with high protein requirements, such as infants, children, and pregnant and lactating women. In Pakistan, 60% of the rural preschool children in the sample population were reported to be suffering from protein calorie malnutrition (PCM) on the basis of biochemical analysis, according to the 1965–1966 Nutrition Survey (Anon. 1970A). Anthropometric measurements also showed various degrees of PCM. About 20% of all the children examined had subnormal body weights (more than 40% below the international standards). The average body weight growth curve for Pakistani children between 5 and 15 years of age falls well below the third percentile of the international standards.

The situation in Pakistan has been clearly stated in the fourth Five Year Plan (Anon. 1970B). "The basic truth is that Pakistan is so poor that a large section of the population lives at sub-human standards. What they need is not marginal adjustment in nutrition, health and education, but a qualitative leap which will make them recognizable members of a dignified society. The average weight of an adult Pakistani is about 120 lb; this is about 30 lb less than an average European" (1 lb = 0.45 kg).

The average level hemoglobin is two-thirds lower than in Europe. In this anemic state, people are readily prone to infectious diseases. At any one time, about one-third of the population is infested with hookworms. The life expectancy is less than 50 years, which is 20 years less than in Europe. Fifteen percent of Pakistani children die at birth or in the first year of life.

The grave shortage of calories and protein and the rapid explosion of the population need immediate attention and call for firm steps. It is hoped that with an increase in the production of cereals, caloric needs of the population will be met. The approach for boosting protein production must be multipronged and should be based on indigenous resources. Recent experiences show that borrowed technologies with imported raw materials have little chance of success in the developing countries.

RESOURCES

Land

The land area of Pakistan is 80 million ha or 198 million acres. About 65 to 70% of this constitutes rangeland, 20.86% constitutes cultivated area, 1.54% forests, and 12.13% is reported as agricultural wasteland.

Climate

Pakistan is blessed with diverse climatic conditions and plenty of sunshine. Most of the countryside is far removed from the moderating influence of the sea. The northwestern part has high mountain ranges with alpine climate. The plains have low irregular rainfall and extremes of temperature. It is very hot during the summer and very cold during the winter over most of the country except the coastal belt. The country can be divided into the following major ecological zones: (1) alpine, (2) subalpine, (3) temperate moist, (4) temperate dry, (5) subtropical humid, (6) subtropical semi-arid, (7) tropical semidesert, (8) tropical desert and, (9) continental Mediterranean.

Irrigation

The irrigation resources of Pakistan have been developed recently and the country has the largest canal network. Of the total 30.4 million ha (76 million acres) of cultivable area [19 million ha (47.5 million acres) cultivated and 11.4 million (28.5 million) available for cultivation], about 13 million ha (32.5 million acres) are currently being irrigated from different sources. The irrigated area is expected to increase when the Tarbella Dam on the Indus River starts a full supply of water.

Availability of Machines for Protein Extraction

Traditional technology for extraction of juice from sugarcane and its concentration is widely employed in the rural areas of Pakistan. Almost 70% of the sugarcane is processed at the farm and village level. These sugarcane crushers are available in almost all the villages and can be used for extraction of juice from fodder crops, especially Persian or Egyptian clovers, which are grown over more than 80% of the irrigated area under fodder crops.

Large-scale extraction of protein-mineral-vitamin concentrate can be commenced once low energy-consuming machines are available.

EXTRACTABILITY OF PROTEINS FROM LEAVES

Extraction of protein concentrate from leaves was initiated in 1964 in Pakistan. Nazir and Shah (1966) determined the extractability of proteins from fresh leaves of 25 plants. Plants were pulped in a mincing machine and juice was extracted by pressing the pulp through double-fold muslin cloth. The residue left after the first extraction was mixed with distilled water equal to the volume of the juice, then minced and re-extracted. A third extraction was made in a similar fashion.

The results (Table 32.5) indicated that the extractability of protein varied from family to family and even from species to species. Relative extraction of nonprotein and protein nitrogen also varied in the different species. In addition, these observations indicated that extractability of protein varied with the age of the plant and was affected adversely when the pH was low. Thus, percentage of N extracted as protein nitrogen increased from 2.80 to 21.14% when the pH of *Embelica officinalis* was adjusted to 7.5.

Nazir (1975) determined the extractability of protein nitrogen (TCA-insoluble or heat-coagulated) as well as total nitrogen from 20, 30, 40, 60, 80, and 100-day-old cuts and regrowths of Persian clover *(Trifolium resupinatum)*. The pattern of extractable and protein nitrogen was irregular and varied with the age of the cut, the number of regrowths, and the climatic conditions. However, extractable as well as protein nitrogen decreased to a minimum in the last regrowth, i.e., when the temperature was high and the relative humidity was low (Table 32.6A,B). The percentage of nonprotein nitrogen (NPN) in the plant juice increased not only with age but also in the successive regrowths, thus indicating progressive autolytic breakdown of proteins of the leaf with increase in age (Table 32.7) and favorable climatic conditions.

TABLE 32.5. EXTRACTABILITY OF NITROGEN FROM FRESH LEAVES

Series No.	Latin Name	% of Nitrogen in Dry Matter	Mean pH	% N Extracted		
				Non-protein	Protein	Total
	(A) Family Leguminosae					
1	*Mimosa pudica*	3.66	6.5	4.87	9.72	14.59
2	*Bauhinia variegata*	3.44	6.6	14.70	17.62	32.32
3	*Sesbania aegyptica*	4.57	6.5	11.03	22.97	34.00
4	*Trifolium resupinatum*	5.48	6.3	8.95	45.84	54.79
5	*Medicago denticulata*	5.15	6.4	14.23	54.71	68.94
6	*Cassia fistula*	2.77	6.0	15.30	54.77	70.07
7	*Melilotus parviflora*	4.80	6.8	15.03	62.79	77.82
8	*Cassia absus*	3.63	6.4	16.13	66.38	82.51
9	*Trigonella foenum-graecum*	6.58	6.8	20.42	62.88	83.30
	(B) Family Cruciferae					
10	*Brassica oleracea*	6.24	6.3	13.75	35.50	49.25
11	*Raphanus sativus*	6.11	6.1	11.94	45.12	57.06
12	*Brassica campestris*	6.69	6.2	14.04	53.01	67.05
13	*Brassica napus*	4.05	6.0	12.22	60.56	72.78
	(C) Family Chenopodiaceae					
14	*Spinacea oleracea*	4.98	6.3	16.61	56.01	72.62
15	*Beta vulgaris*	4.68	6.5	15.83	63.12	78.95
	(D) Family Compositae					
16	*Lactuca sativa*	3.28	6.3	19.30	41.77	61.07
17	*Cinchorium intybus*	4.88	6.3	10.69	50.09	60.78
	(E) Family Gramineae					
18	*Cynodon dactylon*	3.06	6.2	17.28	44.91	62.19
19	*Avena sativa*	3.90	6.3	27.58	45.44	73.02
	(F) Family Umbelliferae					
20	*Daucus carota*	3.16	6.5	8.26	29.68	37.94
21	*Coriandrum sativum*	4.16	6.5	13.52	71.97	85.49
	(G) Families Rutaceae and Amarantaceae					
22	*Murraya exotica*	4.36	6.0	41.36	46.61	87.97
23	*Celosia cristata*	4.30	6.0	13.88	49.58	63.46
	(H) Families Rosaceae and Euphorbiaceae					
24	*Rosa indica*	2.57	5.9	16.71	21.02	37.73
25	(a) *Embelica officinalis*	1.90	3.7	11.89	2.80	14.69
	(b) Extraction with Na_2CO_3	1.80	7.5	18.18	21.14	39.32

EXTRACTABILITY FROM COMMON GRASSES OF PAKISTAN

Extractability of protein from 17 species of grasses was determined by Shah *et al.* (1976B,C). It was observed that 10 species gave maximum extractable proteins in the first regrowths. Extractable protein then decreased with an increase in the age of the crop. Maceration of these grasses with water, after pulping, increased the extractability of proteins up to

183%, which clearly indicated that presence of moisture was a critical factor in the extraction of protein from the grasses. The yield of the extractable proteins/ha/year was up to 502 (Shah *et al.* 1976B). The percentage of extractable protein in the other seven species was maximum first in the spring and then at the onset of winter, while it was minimum in the summer (Shah *et al.* 1976C).

EFFECT OF FERTILIZERS

The effect of nitrogen and phosphorus fertilizers on the extractability of protein from Egyptian clover *(Trifolium alexandrinum)* was studied by Shah *et al.* (1975). It was observed that nitrogen treatment resulted in higher extractability of juice and nitrogenous matter as compared with phosphorus treatment. This seemed to be due to the tender texture of the plants as a result of succulent and luxurious growth caused by the nitrogen supply (Arkcoll and Festenstein 1971).

Phosphorus alone or when applied with nitrogen resulted in an increase in the NPN and a decrease in PN contents of the juice. The decrease in PN of the juice seemed to be due to an increase in fibrous content of the plant, which retained the chloroplasts (Davys and Pirie 1965). The treatment of Egyptian clover with fertilizers containing nitrogen or a nitrogen-phosphorus mixture increased the yield of leaf protein concentrate (LPC) from 1977 to 2122 and 2269 kg/ha, respectively.

EFFECT OF EXTRACTION TECHNIQUES

The effect of different pulping and pressing techniques on the extractability of LPC was determined by Shah *et al.* (1976D). The IBP pulper with IBP press (International Biological Programme) was found to be the most efficient commercial technique (Table 32.8). The Crypto meat mincer and sugarcane crushers (hand- or power-operated) caused incomplete rupturing of the cell and disintegration of the plant tissue which resulted in retention of chloroplastic proteins. The IBP press was found to be slightly less efficient than hand pressing but far more efficient than belt pressing. However, the technique of hand pressing cannot be applied for bulk production of LPC.

Extractability of protein also varied considerably with changes in temperature. Maximum extractability, i.e., 60%, was observed during January, but extractability decreased to 35% during May. The decrease in the extraction rate of juice and protein appeared to be due to a decrease in moisture content of the plant which was due to a rise in the temperature.

Time used during the extraction process was also found to be an important factor. Total extractability of protein by hand and IBP pressing was higher than with belt pressing. However, the conversion of PN to NPN was also higher due to greater time consumed during hand or IBP pressing (Table 32.9).

TABLE 32.6A. CHANGES IN TOTAL NITROGEN (TN) IN THE DRY MATTER OF PULP, EXTRACTABLE NITROGEN (EN), AND PROTEIN NITROGEN (PN) IN THE JUICE OF THE CROP (PERSIAN CLOVER, *TRIFOLIUM RESUPINATUM*) HARVESTED AFTER AN INTERVAL OF 20 TO 40 DAYS

Type of Harvest	20 Days				30 Days				40 Days			
			PN %				PN %				PN %	
	TN %	EN %	TCA-insoluble	Heat-coagulable	TN %	EN %	TCA-insoluble	Heat-coagulable	TN %	EN %	TCA-insoluble	Heat-coagulable
1st cut	4.13	53.80	45.14	37.27	3.95	51.74	42.82	39.56	3.77	52.16	42.38	38.90
1st regrowth	4.51	52.95	44.59	37.83	3.40	51.36	44.18	42.66	4.00	49.04	38.35	34.35
2nd regrowth	4.90	46.51	40.03	36.54	4.20	49.14	40.06	36.44	3.65	51.97	40.18	36.14
3rd regrowth	4.66	47.32	39.86	34.55	4.00	50.69	40.06	34.78	3.40	50.71	32.81	29.88
4th regrowth	4.61	46.62	38.10	34.70	3.93	50.25	35.50	30.25	2.70[1]	36.79[1]	19.66[1]	18.84[1]
5th regrowth	4.24	53.13	42.24	39.61	2.50	41.38	17.88	17.00	—	—	—	—
6th regrowth	4.45	53.80	42.48	39.29	—	—	—	—	—	—	—	—
7th regrowth	3.80	46.55	33.82	29.51	—	—	—	—	—	—	—	—
8th regrowth	3.10	38.04	23.41	22.50	—	—	—	—	—	—	—	—

[1] Regrowth harvested after 20 days, as the season was over.

TABLE 32.6B. CHANGES IN TOTAL NITROGEN (TN) IN THE DRY MATTER OF PULP, EXTRACTABLE NITROGEN (EN), AND PROTEIN NITROGEN (PN) IN THE JUICE OF THE CROP (PERSIAN CLOVER, *TRIFOLIUM RESUPINATUM*) HARVESTED AFTER AN INTERVAL OF 60 TO 100 DAYS

Type of Harvest	60 Days				80 Days				100 Days			
			PN %				PN %				PN %	
	TN%	EN%	TCA-insoluble	Heat-coagulable	TN%	EN%	TCA-insoluble	Heat-coagulable	TN%	EN%	TCA-insoluble	Heat-coagulable
1st cut	3.55	51.63	41.31	38.35	3.52	49.09	32.30	30.81	3.25	42.67	25.67	24.01
1st regrowth	3.45	52.77	38.82	33.05	3.20	47.21	26.96	25.82	2.00	25.00	1.50	1.42
2nd regrowth	2.66	27.11	7.88	7.33	2.80[1]	41.38[1]	24.16[1]	23.74[1]	—	—	—	—

[1] Regrowth harvested after 20 days as the season was over.

TABLE 32.7. CHANGES IN PERCENTAGE OF NONPROTEIN NITROGEN (NPN) IN THE JUICE OF CROP HARVESTED AFTER DIFFERENT INTERVALS

Harvesting Intervals (Days)	1st Cut	Regrowths							
		1	2	3	4	5	6	7	8
20	16.3	15.5	14.2	15.4	18.3	20.5	20.7	22.6	40.7
30	17.0	14.1	18.4	21.0	29.7	60.7	—	—	—
40	18.8	21.9	22.7	35.4	46.4[1]	—	—	—	—
60	20.0	26.7	65.1	—	—	—	—	—	—
80	34.4	43.0	41.5[1]	—	—	—	—	—	—
100	37.8	94.0[2]	—	—	—	—	—	—	—

[1] Regrowths harvested after 20 days, as the season was over.
[2] Regrowth harvested after 80 days, as the season was over.

TABLE 32.8. EFFECT OF EXTRACTION TECHNIQUES ON THE EXTRACTION OF PROTEIN FROM *TRIFOLIUM ALEXANDRINUM*

Pulping Machines	Extractability of Protein (%)[1]					
	January			March		
	Belt Pressing	Hand Pressing	IBP Pressing	Belt Pressing	Hand Pressing	IBP Pressing
IBP pulper	51.7	60.2	57.8	44.7	50.5	50.0
Crypto meat mincer	43.6	50.0	50.0	34.0	44.1	40.0
Power-operated sugarcane crusher	—	—	—	20.0	24.0	21.0
Hand-operated sugarcane crusher	—	—	—	15.5	16.0	15.5

[1] Extracted protein N expressed as % of the total N of the leaf.

TABLE 32.9. EFFECT OF EXTRACTION TECHNIQUES ON PN AND NPN OF JUICE OF *TRIFOLIUM ALEXANDRINUM*

Pulping Machines	Percentage of Protein Nitrogen (PN) and Nonprotein Nitrogen (NPN)											
	January						March					
	Belt Pressing		Hand Pressing		IBP Pressing		Belt Pressing		Hand Pressing		IBP Pressing	
	PN	NPN	PN	NPN	PN	NPN	PN	NPN	PN	NPN	PN	NPN
IBP pulper	90.00	10.0	89.0	11.0	87.1	12.9	89.0	11.0	87.0	12.0	85.1	12.9
Crypto meat mincer	87.0	13.0	86.1	13.9	85.0	15.0	84.8	15.0	84.5	15.5	83.3	16.7
Power-operated sugarcane crusher	—	—	—	—	—	—	83.8	16.2	81.0	79.0	79.0	21.0
Hand-operated sugarcane crusher	—	—	—	—	—	—	80.7	19.3	71.6	28.4	70.0	30.0

Extractability thus depends on many factors, such as:

(1) Nature of species
(2) Moisture content of leaves
(3) Temperature
(4) Nature of fertilizers used
(5) Extraction techniques applied

LEAF PROTEIN CONCENTRATE

Yield

The yield of LPC from different species of grasses was determined by Shah and his associates (Shah 1977A). The yield varied with the species and the number of cuts. Maize varieties gave poor yield (42.70–46.80 kg/ha/year) because they gave only one cut (Table 32.10). Other grasses yielded more cuts/year and thus gave a high yield of extractable protein which varied from 141.0 kg/ha/year in the case of millet (Ex-Borneu) to 1451.09 kg/ha/year in the case of Napier millet hybrid. Low yield of LPC could be due to the fact that the grasses were grown without the application of fertilizer or manure. An increase in protein extraction after application of fertilizer has been reported by various workers (Byers 1961; Chayen *et al.* 1961; Filimonov *et al.* 1973). Gore *et al.* (1974), with liberal application of fertilizers, have reported 2000 kg/ha/year of LPC from hybrid Napier grass in India.

TABLE 32.10. LEAF PROTEIN CONCENTRATE YIELD FROM GRASSES

No.	Grass	Total Cuts/Year	Yield kg/ha/Year
1	*Cenchrus ciliaris*	7	682.50
2	*Chloris gayana*	9	1042.92
3	*Cymbopogon jwarancusa*	9	221.84
4	*Dicanthium annulatum*	7	243.95
5	(a) Maize (Neelum)	1	46.80
	(b) Maize (Syn. 200)	1	45.70
	(c) Maize (Syn. 545)	1	42.70
6	(a) Millet (B-18)	5	186.80
	(b) Millet (Ex-Borneu)	5	141.00
	(c) Millet (Giant)	5	502.90
7	Napier millet hybrid	8	1451.09
8	*Panicum antidotale*	7	991.91
9	*Sorghum almum*	7	644.11
10	Sudan grass	7	351.20

Nazir (1974) determined total yield (kg/ha/year) of LPC from 20, 30, 40, 60, 80, and 100-day-old cuts and regrowths of Persian clover *(Trifolium resupinatum)*. A progressive decrease from 1507.40 to 246.3 kg/ha/year was observed in LPC when the harvesting interval increased from 20 to 100 days. The amount of extractable protein also decreased from 901.2 to 135.2 kg/ha/year (Table 32.11).

TABLE 32.11. EFFECT OF DIFFERENT HARVESTING INTERVALS ON THE TOTAL YIELD OF LEAF PROTEIN CAKE (LPC) AND ITS PROTEIN CONTENT

No. of Harvests/Year	Harvesting Intervals (Days)	Yield of LPC kg/ha/Year	Protein Content (N × 6) kg
9	20	1507.40	901.2
6	30	1443.11	810.0
5	40	1319.50	715.2
3	60	761.50	436.0
3	80	769.90	431.2
2	100	246.30	135.2

Composition

Proximate analysis of LPC was carried out by Shah and his associates (Shah 1977A). The LPC samples were found to contain 37.26 to 50.22% protein, 8.02 to 17.69% ash, 5.39 to 10.35% lipids, and 0.49 to 7.23% fiber (Table 32.12).

Nazir (1975) showed that protein contents of LPC from Persian clover depended upon the age of cuts and number of regrowths and it varied between 51.0 and 63.0%. It was also found that lipid contents varied from 24.01 to 27.88% (on dry matter basis) when extracted with chloroform-methanol (Table 32.13).

Amino Acid Composition. Leaf protein concentrates prepared from various cuts of grasses were analyzed for their essential amino acid contents by the method of Ford (1962) using *Streptococcus zymogenes* as the test organism. The results indicated a similar pattern of amino acid makeup in 14 samples from different cuts of six grasses (Table 32.14).

Digestibility of LPC

The enzymic digestibility of LPC *in vitro* was determined after 3, 6, 9, and 24 hr with trypsin, pepsin, torula yeast, and the enzymes present in the aqueous extracts of the berries of *Withania coagulans*. The enzymes present in the berries showed weak proteolytic activity and converted only 10.36% protein nitrogen (PN) of the concentrate into nonprotein nitrogen. Enzymes in the pancreatic extract showed the maximum rate of digestion for the LPC and digested up to 50.7% of PN after 24 hr of incubation (Sheikh and Shah 1967). Shah *et al.* (1967) showed that heating at elevated temperatures adversely affected the enzymic digestibility of LPC. It was concluded that lipids and their oxidation products produced during heating were toxic to trypsin, pepsin, and the enzymes present in the pancreatic extract. Removal of the lipids enhanced the digestibility of all the samples.

Nazir (1975) determined the total and available amino acids of LPC as such and dried by different methods. It was observed that the amounts of total leucine, isoleucine, valine, methionine, arginine, histidine, tryptophan, phenylalanine, and threonine was almost the same in all the samples,

TABLE 32.12. PROXIMATE ANALYSIS OF LPC

Variety No.	Species	Age in Months	Ash %	Lipids %	Fiber %	Protein % (% N × 6.00)
I	*Digitaria eriantha*	3.6	10.62	10.35	4.98	39.90
II	*Eragrostis superba*	3.6	10.91	9.25	3.31	46.80
III	Napier millet hybrid	2.5	13.58	5.48	3.87	46.68
	Napier millet hybrid (acid wash)	2.5	11.74	5.39	2.68	47.70
	Napier millet hybrid	1.0 (month regrowth)	16.79	6.04	7.23	39.60
	Napier millet hybrid	1.5 (months regrowth)	17.69	9.83	2.22	37.26
IV	*Panicum vergatum*	1.6 (months regrowth)	9.21	6.25	0.81	48.54
	Panicum vergatum (acid wash)	1.0 (month regrowth)	8.02	6.07	0.49	50.22
	Panicum vergatum	1.0 (month regrowth)	16.20	7.35	1.49	39.84
V	Pearl millet	2.2	16.20	7.35	1.54	39.84

TABLE 32.13. COMPOSITION OF THE LEAF PROTEIN SAMPLES

Sample No.	Moisture, %	Nitrogen, % in Dry Matter	Protein, % in Dry Matter N × 6	Lipids, % in Dry Matter	
				Extraction with Chloroform:Methanol (2:1)	Extraction with Acetone
LPC	73.53	9.95	59.70	27.88	26.22
FD	6.51	10.00	60.00	27.19	26.36
OD_1	5.68	9.87	59.22	26.69	24.25
OD_2	5.85	9.84	59.04	26.50	24.22
OD_3	5.10	9.92	59.52	25.30	22.48
OD_4	5.09	9.91	59.45	24.20	21.70
RD	5.10	10.00	60.00	24.01	21.30

FD—Freeze-dried.
RD—Roller-dried.
OD_1—Oven-dried at 70°C.
OD_2—Oven-dried at 80°C.
OD_3—Oven-dried at 90°C.
OD_4—Oven-dried at 100°C.

TABLE 32.14. AMINO ACID CONTENT OF SIX GRASSES

Amino Acid	Range (g/16 g N)
Arginine	6.08–7.88
Histidine	1.35–3.18
Isoleucine	3.90–5.96
Leucine	4.89–9.84
Methionine	2.90–5.83
Valine	2.96–7.68

but that the total lysine content varied considerably. Freeze-dried samples of LPC contained the maximum amount of lysine, i.e., 7.55 g/16 g N, whereas samples dried in an oven at 70° and 100°C contained 7.22 and 6.89 g/16 N of lysine. Roller-dried sample was found to contain 6.80 g/16 g N of lysine. Heat-dried samples showed that decreases in the availability of different amino acids when papain was used for digestion varied from 4.4 to 28.7%. Extraction with chloroform-methanol increased the availability of most of the amino acids.

Storage Life of LPC

LPC has been found to contain a considerable amount of lipids, most of which have two or three double bonds (Buchanan 1969; Lima *et al.* 1965). These lipids provide the essential fatty acids for the body. However, at the same time, these lipids affect the shelf-life of LPC adversely (Lima *et al.* 1965; Shah 1968). Shah showed that the lipids present in different LPC samples oxidized rapidly at 37°C. Deterioration of LPC was attributed to the oxidative enzymes present in the freshly prepared samples which could not be checked by most of the synthetic antioxidants. Addition of synthetic antioxidants is restricted by law, so natural antioxidants were tried. "Amla" *(Embelica officinalis)* fruit powder was successfully used to retard the rate of oxygen uptake. The effectiveness of the "Amla" powder was attributed to the combined presence of gallic acid, its condensation products, and high vitamin C content, which among them possess antioxidant, antibacterial, and chelating properties.

Removal of lipids has been studied as a possible method to increase the shelf-life of LPC. Different solvents were used for the extraction of lipids, including acetone, acetone-water mixture, chloroform-methanol-water mixture, and chloroform-methanol (Shah 1971A). The best extraction was obtained with a 2:1 mixture of chloroform-methanol. It was also observed that drying of LPC at elevated temperatures resulted in a decrease in the extractability of lipids (Shah 1971B). This was attributed to oxidation of free lipids and formation of insoluble complexes by phospholipids and oxidation products of the lipids with proteins.

Degradation of chlorophyll during storage is another aspect which has recently been spotlighted (Holden 1974). Water-washed and acid (1.5 *N*, pH 4)-washed LPC samples were stored in amber-colored and colorless packages at 5°C and ambient temperatures. Loss of chlorophyll during drying as well as during storage was determined (Shah *et al.* 1976A) (Table 32.15). Loss of chlorophyll during drying was 47.0 and 48.1% in the water- and acid-washed samples, respectively. The rate of chlorophyll decomposition during storage appeared to be lower in the acid-washed sample, which may be due to the removal of hydrolyzable sugars and carbohydrates, which have been reported to catalyze the decomposition of chlorophyll (Khudairi 1970). The rate of decomposition of chlorophyll in LPC samples stored in amber-colored packages was always found to be lower than that in colorless packages. Shah and Afzal (1970) made extensive studies on the preservation of LPC and suggested that for checking microbial growth, the concentration of acetic acid in LPC cake should be 2% and it should not be pressed—as pressing would leach out certain antioxidants.

Animal Feeds

LPC when added to broiler feed, as a substitute for animal protein, showed an increase in dressing percentage from 68.03% in the control to 72.01% in case of poultry on feed containing 6% LPC supplemented with 0.2% lysine (Table 32.16).

Complementary value of LPC with wheat flour is depicted in Table 32.17). It is evident that at the 25% level, the PER, NPR (net protein retention), TD, and NPU were comparable and BV was better than casein.

Feeding Trials with LPC. Leaf protein concentrate from Egyptian clover *(Trifolium alexandrinum)* was found to have the following composition:

Ingredients	Quantity
Protein	48–62%
Fat	25–28%
Carbohydrates (by diff.)	10–24%
Fiber	0.5–5%
Carotene	1.01–1.41 mg/g

LPC has a fairly balanced amino acid profile which is comparable with the FAO reference protein (Shah 1975). The concentrate was incorporated into 22 acceptable Pakistani dishes. (Toosy and Shah 1974; Shah *et al.* 1979). The protein contents of these dishes were raised up to 96% (Table 32.18).

These dishes were subjected to organoleptic evaluation by a panel of judges and were graded for appearance, texture, taste, and flavor. All these dishes were found to be acceptable (Table 32.18). A feeding trial with 10–14-year-old subjects was successfully carried out at the All Pakistan Women Association colony and, as a continuation of the experiment, a feeding trial was conducted on 100 subjects in "Katchi Abadi," Garden Town, Lehore. LPC-fortified dishes were compared with isonitrogenous and isocaloric amounts of pure milk. The results of weight and height gain,

TABLE 32.15. CHLOROPHYLL CONTENTS OF FRESH AND STORED LEAF PROTEIN CONCENTRATE

		Fresh Cake			Stored											
					30 Days				60 Days				90 Days			
Storage Temperature	LPC Sample	Wet mg/g	Dry mg/g	Loss on Drying %	ACP[1] mg/g	Loss on Storage %	CLP[2] mg/g	Loss on Storage %	ACP[1] mg/g	Loss on Storage %	CLP[2] mg/g	Loss on Storage %	ACP[1] mg/g	Loss on Storage %	CLP[2] mg/g	Loss on Storage %
5°C	Water-washed	2.89	1.53	47.0	1.53	0.0	1.48	3.2	1.53	0.0	1.45	5.2	1.53	0.0	1.33	13.0
	Acid-washed	2.93	1.52	48.1	1.52	0.0	1.50	1.3	1.52	0.0	1.50	1.3	1.52	0.0	1.46	3.9
Ambient Temperature	Water-washed	2.89	1.53	47.0	1.07	30.0	0.98	36.0	0.78	49.0	0.75	50.9	0.71	53.6	0.65	57.5
	Acid-washed	2.93	1.52	48.1	1.37	9.9	1.12	26.0	1.22	19.7	0.89	41.4	1.11	27.0	0.85	44.0

[1] ACP—Amber-colored package.
[2] CLP—Colorless package.

TABLE 32.16. WEIGHT GAIN, FEED CONSUMPTION, FEED EFFICIENCY, AND DRESSING PERCENTAGE OF BROILER CHICKS

Parameter	Control	6% LPC	6% LPC + Lysine	8% LPC	8% LPC + Lysine
Avg initial wt/chick (g)	43.5	42.70	42.31	42.89	42.17
Avg final wt/chick (g)	932.1	734.63	1016.81	764.41	1003.60
Avg wt gain/chick (g)	888.6	691.93	974.50	721.52	961.43
Avg feed consumed/chick (g)	2232.6	1898.4	2173.70	1954.8	2212.0
Avg dressing percentage	68.03	66.08	72.01	66.24	69.18
Avg feed efficiency	2.51	2.71	2.23	2.70	2.30

TABLE 32.17. SUPPLEMENTATION OF WHEAT FLOUR WITH LPC

Description	Protein Source in Diets	
	Casein	25% Protein (LPC)
Gain in weight/group (g)	84.0	92.30
Protein efficiency ratio	2.53	2.65
NPR	3.59	3.69
TD%	93.00	84.6
BV%	77.00	86.0
NPU	72.00	72.5

TABLE 32.18. SUPPLEMENTATION OF PAKISTANI DISHES WITH LEAF PROTEIN CONCENTRATE

Series No.	Name of Product	Protein Percentage		
		Unfortified Product	Fortified Product	Increase in Protein %
1	"Aloo Paratha" (stuffed fried bread)	6.4	12.3	89.2
2	"Pappar" (unleavened saltish bread)	7.2	11.1	54.2
3	Cutlets	5.5	5.9	7.3
4	"Samosas" (stuffed snack)	3.7	5.6	51.4
5	"Sewian" (vermicelli dish)	7.8	15.3	96.2
6	Bread and potato sandwich	11.1	16.8	51.4
7	Vegetable sandwich	5.6	6.9	23.2
8	"Eahi Bhale" (gram flour balls in yogurt)	20.8	26.1	25.5
9	"Pakoras" (spiced gram flour balls)	8.1	8.3	2.5
10	"Chutney" (mint sauce)	11.4	19.4	70.2
11	Macaroni	9.4	12.9	37.2
12	Corn "Maroonda" (corn snack)	6.6	10.1	53.0
13	Wheat "Maroonda" (wheat snack)	7.7	9.9	28.6
14	"Murma" (puffed rice snack)	10.0	13.9	39.0
15	Rice "Maroonda" (rice snack)	4.4	6.3	43.2
16	Groundnuts "Maroonda" [groundnut (peanut) snack]	11.4	14.4	26.3
17	"Pat" (groundnut snack)	7.8	11.5	47.4
18	"Kachori" (stuffed dough)	10.0	13.4	34.0
19	Doughnuts	9.4	11.0	22.2
20	"Missi Roti" (spiced chapati)	16.2	19.3	19.1
21	Mungch Parat	14.0	16.0	14.3
22	Spinach curry	12.1	17.1	41.3

improvement in hemoglobin contents and blood film, and improvement in general alertness and tone of skin showed that LPC-fortified dishes are comparable to or even better than pure milk.

LARGE-SCALE HUMAN FEEDING TRIALS

Selection of the Subjects

Children from 46 families were screened by a preliminary medical survey. A total of 100 children from 7 to 14 years of age were selected. In terms of age, a more compact group was desired, but the ages quoted by the mothers, on a memory basis, were not reliable and it was difficult to obtain subjects of the same known age.

Socioeconomic Background of the Subjects

Socioeconomic backgrounds of the children were ascertained by door-to-door visits. The questionnaire was completed by using data obtained by direct interview and from discussions with the bread-earner and the welfare officer of the locality.

The average family size ranged from 7.3 to 7.7 (Table 32.19). The number of wage-earning members per family varied from 1.2 to 1.3 and the number of dependents ranged from 5.8 to 6.4. The average income share of a person per month was U.S. \$5.45, \$5.85, and \$5.50[2] in the case of control, milk, and LPC groups, respectively.

Deworming of the Infested Children

Children suffering from roundworms, hookworms, and threadworms were given 2–5 tablets (125 mg each) of Combantrin (pyrantel) according to their weight (10 ml/kg body weight) just before retiring to bed (Raz 1975). The procedure was repeated after one month. Children suffering from cysts were given Flagy1® (metronidazole) as prescribed by Todd (1967). Excreta were subjected to clinical examination and the medicine was administered in the case of a cyst's being detected.

Preparation of Dishes

Mixed grasses and "barseem" *(Trifolium alexandrinum)* were used for extraction of protein by using the IBP (International Biological Programme) pulper and press (Davys and Pirie 1969). LPC was air-dried at 50°C in an oven, a procedure which has little effect on nutritional value (Nazir 1975; Shah *et al.* 1967).

Dishes popular in the local diets were prepared with and without supplementation with LPC (Shah *et al.* 1979; Toosy and Shah 1974). Representative samples of these dishes were homogenized and subjected to chemical analysis. Dry matter, ash, fat, and fiber were determined by using AOAC methods (AOAC 1970). Protein was estimated by a micro-Kjeldahl method using a selenium mixture, i.e., K_2SO_4, $CuSO_4$, and SeO_2, 9:1:0.02 (Markham 1942). The crude protein contents were calculated as % N × 6 (Pirie 1966). Carbohydrates (other than fiber) were calculated by difference.

Organoleptic Evaluation

Standard dishes and dishes with LPC incorporated were evaluated organoleptically by a panel of five experienced judges. Samples were indepen-

[2]\$1 U.S. = 11.1 Pakistani Rs (November 1982).

TABLE 32.19. SOCIOECONOMIC BACKGROUND OF SUBJECTS

Groups	No. of Selected Subjects			No. of Families	No. of Family Members		No. of Earning Members		No. of Persons Supported by Each Earning Member	Average Monthly Income (U.S. $)[1]	Amount per Person per Month (U.S. $)[1]
	Male	Female	Total		Total	Average	Total	Average per Family			
Control	10	10	20	19	146	7.7	23	1.2	6.4	41.99	5.45
Milk	20	20	40	31	226	7.3	39	1.3	5.8	42.66	5.85
LPC	20	20	40	35	256	7.3	43	1.2	6.0	40.17	5.50
Total	50	50	100	46	326	7.1	55	1.2	5.9	42.31	5.96

[1]$1 U.S. = 11.1 Pakistani Rs (November 1982).

dently graded by scoring (0–10) for their color, taste, texture, and flavor (IFT Comm. Sensory Evaluation 1964).

Fortification of Dishes with Leaf Protein Concentrate

Fortification of the dishes with LPC increased their protein content from 8.8% in the "Halwa" to 45.0% in the case of "Kachori" (Table 32.20). The increase in protein content was generally more than 15%, except in the case of the halwa. Fortification with LPC caused a decrease in the relative amount of fat in most of these dishes. This resulted in the improvement of the texture of the product. A similar decrease in the amount of fat in textured protein beef patties, compared with all-meat patties, was observed by Anderson and Lind (1975).

For most of the dishes, there were small increases in their fiber contents after fortification with LPC. These minor increases in the fiber content were in no way found to be inconvenient. LPC was found to be rich in mineral

TABLE 32.20. CHEMICAL COMPOSITION[1] OF PREPARED[2] PRODUCTS

Ser. No.	Products		Protein (%)	Protein Increase (%)	Fat (%)	Fiber (%)	Ash (%)	NFE[3] (%)	Cal/100 g Prepared Products
1	Bread potato sandwich	A	11.1	—	10.0	4.8	0.9	73.1	427.2
		B	12.8	15.3	7.8	5.4	1.4	72.6	411.8
2	Dahi Bhalle (cultured milk cutlets)	A	9.8	—	8.5	5.7	1.1	74.9	415.3
		B	12.7	29.6	8.0	6.3	1.7	71.3	408.0
3	Halwa	A	14.7	—	18.7	0.2	0.6	65.8	490.3
		B	16.0	8.8	20.5	0.4	0.8	62.3	497.7
4	Kachori (stuffed dough)	A	10.0	—	18.3	4.4	1.8	65.5	466.7
		B	14.5	45.0	16.5	4.0	2.6	62.4	456.1
5	Laddu (solid sweet balls)	A	11.5	—	13.2	2.7	1.1	71.5	450.8
		B	14.4	25.2	14.1	3.1	1.5	66.9	452.1
6	Missi Roti (spiced chapati)	A	16.2	—	5.1	2.1	1.8	78.8	409.8
		B	19.2	18.5	5.2	2.2	2.2	71.2	408.4
7	Murmara (mixed snack)	A	10.0	—	9.9	7.3	1.1	71.7	415.9
		B	13.9	39.0	9.7	7.5	1.6	67.3	412.1
8	Pakoras (fried gram flour balls)	A	8.1	—	9.9	10.2	1.9	69.9	401.1
		B	11.5	43.0	9.2	11.0	2.4	65.9	392.4
9	Peanut Maroon-da (peanut snack)	A	11.4	—	26.6	7.7	1.8	52.5	495.0
		B	14.4	26.3	25.6	6.5	2.3	51.2	492.8
10	Wheat Maroonda (wheat snack)	A	7.7	—	3.0	7.5	2.3	79.5	375.8
		B	10.8	40.3	3.2	7.3	2.9	75.8	375.2

[1] On dry matter basis.
[2] Most of these dishes were prepared earlier by Toosy and Shah (1974) and Shah *et al.* (1979).
[3] Nitrogen-free extract.
A—Standard dishes.
B—LPC-supplemented dishes.

TABLE 32.21. CHEMICAL COMPOSITION OF THE DISHES PER SERVING
Containing 8.6 g protein.

Ser. No.	Name of the Product	Weight of the Sample (g)	Protein (g)	Fat (g)	Fiber (g)	Ash (g)	NFE (g)	Calories
1	Bread potato sandwich	67	8.6	5.2	3.6	0.9	48.7	276.0
2	Dahi Bhalle (cultured milk cutlets)	68	8.6	5.4	4.3	1.2	48.5	277.0
3	Halwa	54	8.6	11.1	0.2	0.4	33.7	269.1
4	Kachori (stuffed dough)	59	8.6	9.7	2.4	1.0	36.8	268.9
5	Laddu (solid sweet balls)	60	8.6	8.5	1.9	0.9	40.1	271.3
6	Missi Roti (spiced chapati)	45	8.6	2.4	1.0	1.0	32.0	184.0
7	Murmara (mixed snack)	62	8.6	6.0	4.7	1.0	41.7	225.2
8	Pakoras (fried gram flour balls)	75	8.6	6.9	8.3	1.8	49.4	294.1
9	Peanut Maroonda (peanut snack)	60	8.6	15.4	3.9	1.4	30.7	295.8
10	Wheat Maroonda (wheat snack)	80	8.6	2.6	5.8	2.3	60.7	300.6
	Milk	200	8.6	17.6	—	—	10.2	233.6 + 40.0[1] = 273.6

[1]Calories provided by 10 g sugar.

content (Shah 1977A). The fortification thus supplemented the mineral content of these dishes as well. Low nitrogen-free extract (NFE) content of LPC caused a slight decrease in the NFE content of the dishes upon fortification.

Calories provided by 100 g of the prepared dish decreased slightly in some cases, mainly due to variations in composition. The maximum decrease was only 3.6%. Per serving quantity (Table 32.21) of each dish varied between 45 g in the case of "Missi Roti" (spiced "chapati") and 80 g in the case of wheat "Maroonda" (wheat snack).

Individual servings of five of the dishes were within the range of ± 2.0% of 273.6 Cal (equivalent to the calories supplied by 200 g of milk). These dishes were supplied as such. Others were supplied in combination in such proportions that the calories supplied per day were within ± 2% of 273.6 Cal. All the dishes were considered acceptable in appearance, texture, taste, and flavor (Table 32.22).

Five dishes were highly acceptable (with a source of 8 or more) in appearance. LPC-fortified dishes also scored high in texture. Four dishes with an overall score of 32 or more were considered highly acceptable. All other dishes were acceptable with aggregate scores above 25. The children became fond of the LPC-fortified dishes and appeared to really relish them.

TABLE 32.22. ORGANOLEPTIC EVALUATION OF LPC-CONTAINING DISHES[1]

Ser. No.	Products	Appearance	Texture	Taste	Flavor	Total Score
1	Bread potato sandwich	9.0	9.0	6.0	6.8	30.8
2	Dahi Bhalle	10.0	9.0	9.8	9.0	37.8
3	Halwa	6.8	8.0	6.5	6.2	27.5
4	Kachori	9.0	8.5	7.3	7.3	32.1
5	Laddu	7.0	6.8	7.3	7.3	28.4
6	Missi Roti	6.5	6.5	7.8	6.5	27.3
7	Murmara	8.8	8.8	8.3	8.0	33.9
8	Pakoras	8.6	9.0	8.4	8.0	34.0
9	Peanut Maroonda	7.5	7.0	7.3	7.2	29.0
10	Wheat Maroonda	6.3	6.8	6.3	6.0	25.4

[1] These dishes were compared with the standard unsupplemented dishes (top grade = 10) for each evaluation.

Feeding Program

Where possible, two or three children from the same family were selected to be placed in different groups. The feeding program was continued for a period of 8 months without any break. Milk and LPC-fortified dishes were given as supplements to the normal diet, i.e., actually more food and calories were provided. The children were fed daily in the afternoon according to the following program:

Group I	(control)	Children (20) were allowed to continue their normal diet as usual.
Group II	(milk)	Children (40) were given 200 g of sweetened milk in addition to their regular diet.
Group III	(LPC)	Children (40) were given LPC-fortified dishes, isoproteinous and isocaloric with milk, in addition to their normal regular diet.

Attendance of the Subjects

Attendance of children fed on milk and LPC-fortified dishes was recorded daily. Children of group I (control) were not getting an additional diet, so their attendance was needed only during the anthropometric measurements and clinical tests.

The percentage attendance of children receiving LPC was lower than for those receiving milk during the first three months of the trial. Later, LPC-receiving children showed better attendance than the children receiving milk. The difference in attendance was slight during May 1978, but during the following months (i.e., June–July 1978), the popularity of the LPC-fortified dishes increased with the passage of time (Fig. 32.1).

Anthropometric Measurements

Weight and height measurements of the children were taken at regular intervals.

Initially, the average weight and height of the groups were almost the same (Table 32.23). The average increases in weight at the end of the 8-month period were 1.08 (5.01%), 2.45 (11.48%), and 2.62 kg (11.96%) for the control, milk, and LPC groups, respectively (Fig. 32.2). The average increases in height of the children in the control, milk, and LPC groups were 2.64 (2.15%), 4.87 (3.99%), and 5.33 cm (4.35%), respectively. Thus, children fed on milk and LPC showed similar weight and height gains, which were better than the control group.

It can be seen (Table 32.23) that the initial weights and heights of the children of all the groups were lower than the corresponding standard values for Pakistani children. The average increases in weight (1.08 kg) and height (2.64 cm) of the control group were less than the standard values for expected increases in weight (2.07 kg) and height (4.02 cm). Supplementation of the diet with milk or with LPC improved the rate of weight gain and height increase of the children. Thus, the average increases in weight and height were better than the standard values (calculated from the nutritional tables for the Pakistani children) for both the milk and the

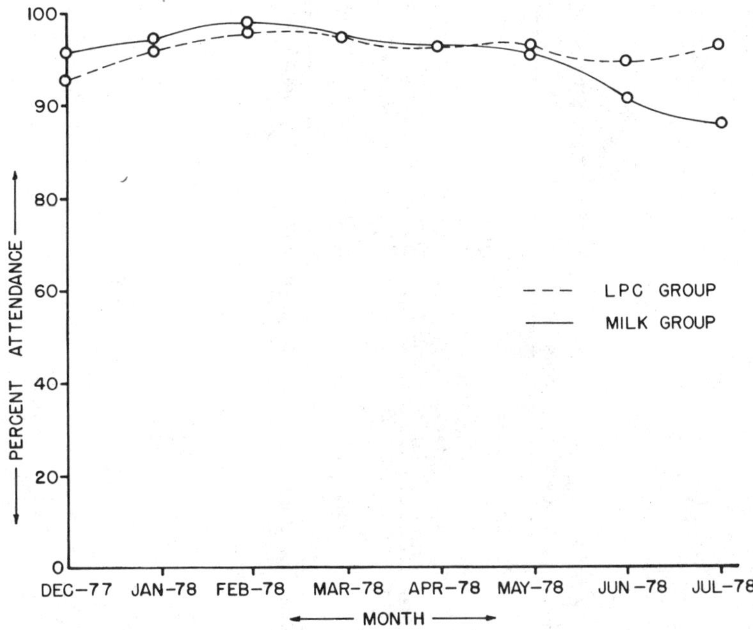

Fig. 32.1. Percentage attendance of children fed milk and LPC-fortified diets.

TABLE 32.23. AVERAGE WEIGHT AND HEIGHT GAINS BY DIFFERENT GROUPS
Compared with the standard data.

	Control				Milk				LPC			
	Initial	Initial Standard[1]	Increase (in 8 Months)	Standard Comparative Increase	Initial	Initial Standard[1]	Increase (in 8 Months)	Standard Comparative Increase	Initial	Initial Standard[1]	Increase (in 8 Months)	Standard Comparative Increase
Weight (kg)	21.34	24.95	1.08	2.07	21.34	24.17	2.45	2.30	21.90	25.55	2.62	1.98
Height (cm)	123.05	126.9	2.64	4.02	122.18	128.70	4.87	4.54	122.41	129.20	5.33	4.63

Source: Directorate of Nutrition Survey and Research, Islamabad (1970).
[1] Calculated for 8 months for a similar group from the data available for urban Pakistani children [Nutritional Survey of (West) Pakistan].

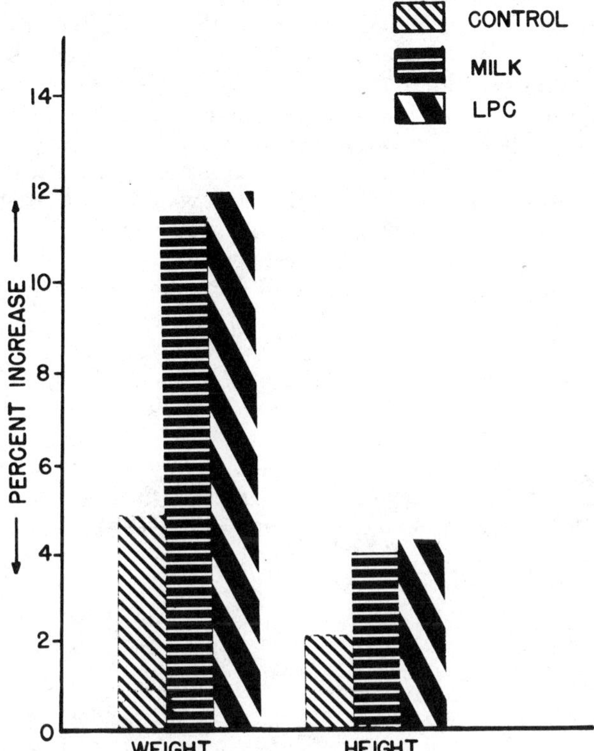

Fig. 32.2. Percentage increases in weight and height in 8 month period for groups of children given milk and LPC-fortified diets.

LPC groups (Table 32.23). These children were basically suffering from malnutrition, so the supply of good-quality protein, vitamins, and minerals triggered the key points of their metabolism, which was thus accelerated.

The weight- and height-increase data show that children on the control diet continued to suffer from malnutrition. Thus, it can be concluded that children of the lower middle class are suffering from acute malnutrition in regard to their body weight and height. However, this malnutrition is of a remedial nature and can be overcome with the supply of good-quality nutrients.

Growth Rates

Based on the weights taken at 40-day intervals, the control children had a slower rate of growth (Fig. 32.3). The growth rate curve of LPC and milk groups showed a slight decrease in the later months, being maximum during the first 80 days and then slowing down. The trial was started during the winter (December) and ended in midsummer (July). Excessive sweating and dehydration generally caused a relatively smaller increase in weight during the hot months. Furthermore, the children's original diet was deficient in high-quality protein, minerals, and vitamins. The inclusion of foodstuffs rich in these nutrients naturally accelerated the growth rate. With the passage of time, the malnutrition diminished and the assimilation of these nutrients was normalized, giving a slower growth rate in the later months. Comparison of growth rate curves of LPC and milk groups (Fig. 32.3) confirms that, throughout the trial period, the LPC groups showed a slightly better growth rate than the milk group.

Blood Examination

Blood examinations were carried out at the Research Cell, Ganga Ram Hospital, Lahore. Blood samples were taken at the start and at the termination of the feeding trial.

Hemoglobin (Hb) percentage was determined by the cyanomethemoglobin method (Damm 1965). Packed cell volume and mean corpuscular hemoglobin concentration were also determined (Long 1961).

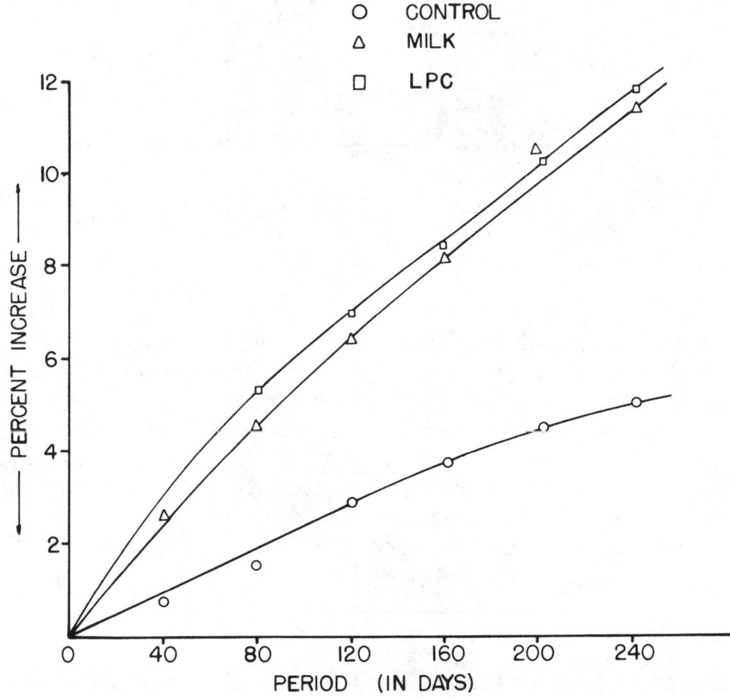

Fig. 32.3. Growth rates of children on milk and LPC-fortified diets.

Blood film, stained by Wright's stain, was microscopically examined to determine hypochromic cells, target cells, anisocytes, and poikilocytes in blood (Damm 1965).

Improvement in Hemoglobin and Red Blood Cell Status

Initial hemoglobin contents of control, milk, and LPC groups were 11.17, 11.12, and 10.93 g/100 ml, respectively (Table 32.24). The minimum acceptable hemoglobin content for children has been suggested to be 12.6 g/100 ml (Wintrobe 1961). By these standards, most of the children were anemic. After eight months, the corresponding values for the control, milk, and LPC groups were 11.67, 12.62, and 12.51 g/100 ml, respectively. Thus, all groups showed an increase in their hemoglobin content. The control group had an increase of 0.5 g/100 ml (i.e., 4.48% of the original hemoglobin content). This increase was expected because the hemoglobin content of the children increases with an increase in age. Moreover, deworming of the children could be a factor responsible for the increase in hemoglobin content. The milk and LPC groups showed an increase of 1.50 and 1.58 g/100 ml, respectively. These values correspond to an increase of 13.50% in the case of the milk group and 14.46% in the case of the LPC group. Again, hemoglobin results comparable to weight and height results were obtained for the milk and LPC groups (Fig. 32.4).

Packed cell volume (PCV) or hematocrit reading is a measure of the proportion of the whole blood which consists of red cells (Damm 1965). PCVs of the three groups in the beginning of the trial were 34.70, 34.82, and 34.42% for the control, milk, and LPC groups, respectively (Table 32.24). The corresponding values at the end of the trial were 36.15, 37.77, and 37.58%. These values represent percentage increases of 4.20, 8.47, and 9.18% in PCV content for the control, milk, and LPC groups, respectively. PCV was expected to increase with an increase in the hemoglobin content. Generally speaking, hemoglobin is one-third of PCV (Nutrition Cell 1977). This relation did not exist among the children of all groups at the beginning of the trial. It did, however, exist in all groups at the end of the trial. Differences in the ratio have been attributed to deficiency diseases (Nutrition Cell 1977). It can safely be concluded that the hemoglobin and red blood cell content of all groups improved during the trial period. As noted before, this was expected because all the children, including the control group, were dewormed before the trial. However, the improvement was maximum in the case of the LPC group (Fig. 32.4).

Mean corpuscular hemoglobin concentration (MCHC) is the percentage of hemoglobin per unit volume of packed cells. The normal range is 32–38% (Long 1961). Initially, MCHC values were 32.19, 31.94, and 31.75% for the control milk, and LPC groups, respectively. At the end of trial, the corresponding values were 32.28, 33.41, and 33.29% (Table 32.24). Although the initial MCHC value for the LPC group was slightly lower than that of the milk group, the increase in MCHC value of LPC group (1.54%)

TABLE 32.24. IMPROVEMENT IN BLOOD PICTURE OF THE CHILDREN UNDER TRIAL

Groups	Age (Years)	Hemoglobin, g/100 ml				PCV, %[1]				MCHC, %[2]			
		Initial	Final	Increase	% Increase	Initial	Final	Increase	% Increase	Initial	Final	Increase	% Increase
Control	9.4	11.17	11.67	0.50	4.48	34.70	36.15	1.45	4.20	32.19	32.28	0.09	0.28
Milk	9.7	11.12	12.62	1.50	13.50	34.82	37.77	2.95	8.47	31.94	33.41	1.47	4.60
LPC	9.7	10.93	12.51	1.58	14.46	32.42	37.58	3.16	9.18	31.75	33.29	1.54	4.85

[1] Packed cell volume.
[2] Mean corpuscular hemoglobin concentration.

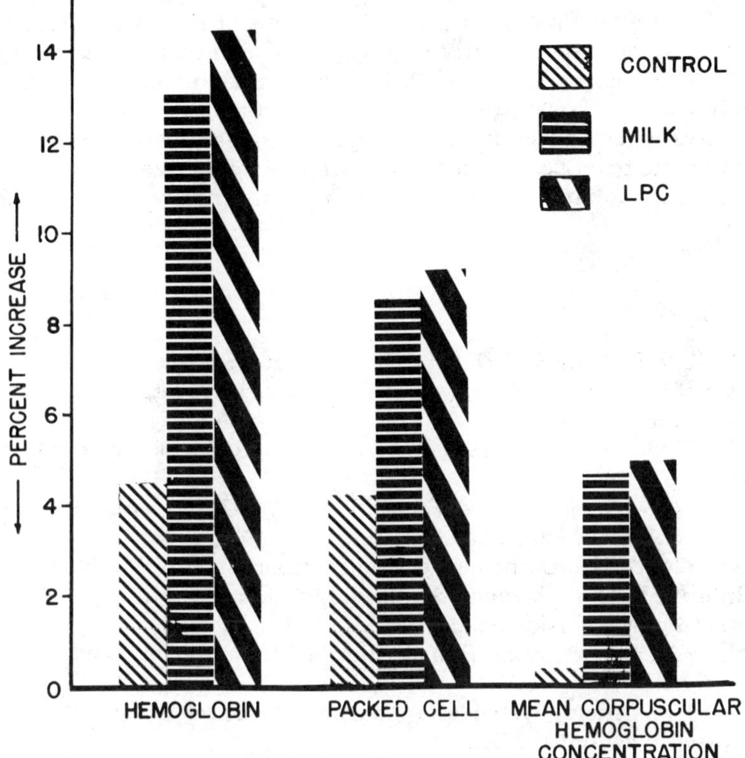

Fig. 32.4. Percentage increases in hemoglobin (Hb) content, packed cell volume (PCV or hematocrit), and mean corpuscular hemoglobin concentration (MCHC) in 8 month period for children on milk and LPC-fortified diets.

was slightly better than that of the milk group (1.47%). The LPC group thus showed the maximum improvement in the MCHC value (Fig. 32.4).

Pakistani children of the lowest social stratum seldom drink milk, so the production of lactase slows down with the passage of time (Fernandes *et al.* 1978; Johnson *et al.* 1978; Lacassie *et al.* 1978). This could be one of the reasons that children receiving milk did not show better results than those receiving LPC. However, for the children studied, on the basis of anthropometric measurements and hemoglobin-red blood cell status, it can be concluded that LPC-fortified dishes were comparable to milk as a food supplement.

ECONOMIC FEASIBILITY OF LPC PRODUCTION

Economic feasibility of the large-scale production of LPC in Pakistan was studied in 1974 by the Intermediate Technology Services (London) under assignment by the Ministry of Overseas Development. The report submitted to the Ministry of Finance of the Government of Pakistan stressed that the process should be urgently investigated for implementation as intermediate technology (Anon. 1974). It was estimated that the concentrate production costs of approximately U.S. \$0.40–\$0.60/kg were readily feasible. It was suggested that further investigation leading to correct choice of technique and good design should ensure more effective extraction rates, generate employment, and produce protein concentrate at more competitive prices.

REFERENCES

ANDERSON, R.H. and LIND, K.D. 1975. Retention of water and fat in cooked patties of beef and of beef extended with textured vegetable proteins. Food Technol. *29*, 44–45.

ANON. 1970A. Nutrition Survey of West Pakistan 1965–66. Govt. of Pakistan, Islamabad.

ANON. 1970B. The Fourth Five Year Plan (1970–75) Planning Commission. Govt. of Pakistan, Islamabad.

ANON. 1974. Techno-Economic Feasibility Report on Mini-Plants in Pakistan by Intermediate Technology Services, Ltd., London. Ministry of Finance, Govt. of Pakistan, Islamabad.

ANON. 1976. Report of the Punjab "Barani" Commission, Govt. of Punjab, Lahore.

AOAC. 1970. Official Methods of Analysis. Assoc. of Official Agricultural Chemists, Washington, DC.

ARKCOLL, D.B. and FESTENSTEIN, G.N. 1971. A preliminary study of the agronomic factors affecting the yield of extractable leaf protein. J. Sci. Food Agric. *22*, 49.

BUCHANAN, R.A. 1969. Effect of storage and lipid extraction on the properties of leaf protein. J. Sci. Food Agric. *20*, 359.

BYERS, M. 1961. Extraction of proteins from the leaves of some plants growing in Ghana. J. Sci. Food Agric. *12*, 20.

CHAYEN, I.H., SMITH, R.H., TRISTRAM, G.R., THIRKELL, D. and WEBB, T. 1961. The isolation of leaf components. I. J. Sci. Food Agric. *12*, 502.

DAMM, H.C. 1965. Practical Manual for Clinical Laboratory Procedure. Chemical Rubber Co., Cleveland.

DAVYS, M.N.G. and PIRIE, N.W. 1965. A belt press for separating juices from fibrous pulps. J. Agric. Eng. Res. *10*, 141.

DAVYS, M.N.G. and PIRIE, N.W. 1969. A laboratory scale pulper for leaf plant material. Biotechnol. Bioeng. *11*, 517–528.

FERNANDES, J., VOS, C.E., DOUWES, A.C., SLOTEMA, E. and DEGENHART, H.J. 1978. Respiratory hydrogen excretion as a parameter for lactose malabsorption in children. Am. J. Clin. Nutr. *31*, 597–601.

FILIMONOV, D.A., ZAKHAROV, V.N. and PAPILOVA, S.S. 1973. Effect of fertilizers on the extractability of proteins from leaves. Khim. Selsk. Khoz. *10* (5) 62.

FORD, J.E. 1962. A microbiological method for assessing the nutritional value of proteins. 2. The measurement of available methionine, leucine, isoleucine, arginine, histidine, tryptophan and valine. Br. J. Nutr. *16*, 409.

GORE, S.B., MUNGIKAR, A.M. and JOSHI, R.N. 1974. Yields of extracted leaf protein from Hybrid Napier Grass. J. Sci. Food Agric. *25*, 1149.

HOLDEN, M. 1974. Chlorophyll degradation products in leaf protein preparations. J. Sci. Food Agric. *25*, 1427.

IFT COMM. SENSORY EVALUATION. 1964. Guide for panel evaluation of foods and beverages. Food Technol. *18*, 1135–1138.

JOHNSON, J.D., SIMOONS, F.J., HURWITZ, R., GRANGE, A., SINATRA, F.R., SUNSHINE, P., ROBERTSON, W.V., BENNET, P.H. and KRETCHMER, N. 1978. Lactose malabsorption among adult Indians of the Great Basin and American South West. Am. J. Clin. Nutr. *31*, 381–387.

KHAN, M.A. 1978. Poultry industry of Pakistan. P.I.A. Shaver's Newslett. *8* (3) 8.

KHUDAIRI, A.K. 1970. Decomposition of chlorophyll. Physiol. Plant. *23*, 613.

KIDWAI, A. 1978. Proteins and human health. P.I.A. Shaver's Newslett. *8* (3) 9.

LACASSIE, Y., WEINBERG, R. and MONCKEBERG, F. 1978. Poor predictability of lactose malabsorption from clinical symptoms of Chilean populations. Am. J. Clin. Nutr. *31*, 799–804.

LEA, C.H. and PARR, L.J. 1961. Some observations on the oxidative deterioration of the lipids of crude leaf protein. J. Sci. Food Agric. *12*, 785.

LIMA, I.H., RICHARDSON, T. and STAHMANN, M.A. 1965. Fatty acids in some leaf protein concentrates. J. Agric. Food Chem. *13*, 143.

LONG, C. 1961. Biochemists Handbook. E. and F.N., London.

MARKHAM, R. 1942. A steam distillation apparatus suitable for micro-Kjeldahl analysis. Biochem. J. *36*, 790–791.

MOHAMMAD, A. 1977. Report on the Consultation on Improving Nutrition of the Rural Poor in Asia and the Far East. Food Agric. Organ. U.N., Rome.

NAZIR, M. 1975. Production of edible protein from Persian clover *(Trifolium resupinatum)*. Ph.D. Thesis. Punjab University, Lahore.

NAZIR, M. and SHAH, F.H. 1966. Extractability of proteins from various leaves. Pak. J. Sci. Ind. Res. *9*, 235.

NUTRITION CELL. 1977. Micro-nutrient survey of Pakistan 1976–1977. Planning and Development Div., Govt. of Pakistan, Islamabad.

PIRIE, N.W. 1966. Leaf protein as a human food. Science *152*, 1701–1705.

RAZ, A. 1975. Practical Medicine. Maktaba Tibbi Shahkar, Lahore. (Urdu)

SHAH, F.H. 1968. Changes in leaf protein lipids *in vitro*. J. Sci. Food Agric. *19*, 199.

SHAH, F.H. 1971A. Effect of solvents on the extractability of lipids from leaf proteins. Pak. J. Sci. Ind. Res. *14*, 207.

SHAH, F.H. 1971B. Effect of heat on the extractability of lipid from leaf protein meal. Pak. J. Sci. Ind. Res. *14*, 492.

SHAH, F.H. 1975. Proteins from leaves. Proc. Symp. Nutr. Deficiencies and Their Remedies. Pak. Acad. Sci., Islamabad, 1974.

SHAH, F.H. 1977A. Grasses as food and feed. Final Rep. on Investigation of the Preparation and Composition of Protein Concentrate from Grasses Common to Pakistan and the United States for Possible Food Use. Pak. Counc. Sci. Ind. Res. (PCSIR) Lab., Lahore. *PL-480* Proj. *UR-A 17-(10)-6*.

SHAH, F.H. 1977B. Country Report on Mycotoxins. Submitted to Food Agric. Organ. U.N., Rome. (In press)

SHAH, F.H. and AFZAL, M. 1970. Preservation of leaf protein concentrate. Proc. IBP Meet. 1970, Coimbatore, India.

SHAH, F.H., MAHMUD, B.A. and ZIA-UR-REHMAN. 1975. The effect of nitrogen and phosphorus on the yield and extractability of proteins from *Trifolium alexandrinum*. Pak. J. Sci. Ind. Res. *18*, 57.

SHAH, F.H., MALIK, S.K. and SHEIKH, A.S. 1976A. Degradation of chlorophyll during drying and storage of leaf protein concentrate. Pak. J. Sci. Ind. Res. *19*, 193.

SHAH, F.H., RIAZ-UD-DIN and SHEIKH, A.S. 1967. Effect of heat on the digestibility of leaf proteins. Part I: Toxicity of lipids and their oxidation products. Pak. J. Sci. Ind. Res. *10*, 39–41.

SHAH, F.H., SEDI, M.H. and NADIM, B.A. 1976B. Extraction of proteins from grasses. I. Effect of harvesting conditions on nutritive value of grasses. Pak. J. For. *26*, 1–6.

SHAH, F.H., SEDI, M.H. and NADIM, B.A. 1976C. Extraction of proteins from grasses. II. Pak. J. For. *26*, 147.

SHAH, F.H., TOOSY, R.Z. and SHEIKH, A.S. 1979. Leaf protein concentrate in human diet. II. Pak. J. Sci. Ind. Res. *23*, 76–78.

SHAH, F.H., ZIA-UR-REHMAN and MAHMUD, B.A. 1976D. Effect of extraction techniques on the extraction of proteins from *Trifolium alexandrinum*. Pak. J. Sci. Ind. Res. *19*, 39.

SHEIKH, A.S. and SHAH, F.H. 1967. Digestibility of leaf protein concentrates. Pak. J. Sci. Ind. Res. *10*, 181.

TODD, R.G. 1967. Metronidazole. *In* Matrindale's Extra Pharmacopoeia. London Pharmaceutical Press, London.

TOOSY, R.Z. and SHAH, F.H. 1974. Leaf protein concentrate in human diet. I. Pak. J. Sci. Ind. Res. *17*, 40–42.

WINTROBE, M.M. 1961. Clinical Haematology. Lea and Febiger, Philadelphia.

33

Leaf Protein Research in Poland

Piotr Hanczakowski

THE PROTEIN GAP

Unlike tropical countries, Poland does not have many plant materials abundant in protein. Neither soybean nor peanut is cultivated. *Brassica napus* (rape) plays an important part in animal feeding in Poland, but the presence of toxic substances, glucosinolates, limits its use. There are difficulties in obtaining feeds of animal origin, e.g., fish meal, and the results of the investigation on the production and use of single cell protein such as algae or yeasts are still not conclusive. Under these conditions the production of valuable protein concentrates from a cheap local raw material, such as green crops, becomes appropriate in bridging the protein gap.

SUITABLE RAW MATERIALS

Polish investigations along this line started in the 1970s and have continued in some research institutes. The focus was on the selection of plant species most suitable as raw material for the production of concentrates in Poland. Special attention was paid to grasses, considering the existence of great areas of meadows, and to the utilization of waste products, such as potato haulms or mangold (mangel-wurzel) leaves. Attempts were made to increase the amount of protein obtained per unit area by using agrotechnical procedures, and also, as far as possible, to increase the nutritive value.

Efforts were made to install factories in Poland for the needs of the food industry. The natural conclusion of these investigations is feeding experiments carried out on laboratory and farm animals with the aim of determining the nutritive value of the products obtained.

FEEDING EXPERIMENTS

The composition and feeding value of concentrates from various plant species cultivated in Poland were first reported by Hanczakowski (1975).

Using the Thomas-Mitchell method, the best results were obtained for cereals, with a biological value (BV) of 67 for wheat and 69 for rye. Also, the concentrate from potato haulms proved good with a BV of 60, much better than that of clover (BV 48) and grass (BV 44). The high protein value of the concentrate from potato haulms encouraged us to examine a number of varieties of this plant. It was found that significant differences occurred between them. The biological value of proteins of concentrates ranged from 40 to 60 according to the variety. Distinct differences were found in the content of another important component of the concentrates, i.e., the β-carotene. The lowest value found was 84.5 mg/kg, and the highest, 272 mg/kg.

We are paying much attention to the concentrate from potato haulms because the leaves of this plant, which are very popular in Middle and East Europe, are at present in general not utilized. Assuming the area of potato cultivation in Poland to be about 2.5 million ha, and the haulms about 1.5 MT from 1 ha, with a 2% protein content in the fresh matter of haulms, then annually about 75,000 MT of valuable protein are lost. There is no doubt that a considerable part of this protein could be regained in the form of a concentrate made from haulms collected simultaneously with the potato crop.

While looking for new plant varieties for Poland, which could be used as raw material for the production of leaf protein concentrates, attention was paid to the species of hogweed, *Heracleum sosnowskyi*, which was originally from Caucasus (Hanczakowski and Lutyńska 1976). This plant has large, sappy leaves and gives crops of about 200 MT/ha yearly. However, because of the characteristic sharp odor, the concentrate from the leaves of this plant was not readily eaten by rats and the biological value of protein was low (BV = 37), although as regards the amino acid composition, it was not inferior to the protein of the alfalfa concentrate. The low value was most likely caused by the presence of toxic substances in the concentrate, and this was confirmed by the fact that washing the concentrate before drying increased the biological value of 56.

INCREASING PROTEIN YIELD

Nitrogen Fertilizers

One of the methods employed for increasing the protein yield per unit area was the application of a high nitrogen fertilizer. We examined the effect of three kinds of nitrogen fertilizers, calcium nitrate, ammonium sulfate, and urea at levels of 60, 240, and 480 kg N/ha, on extractability, amino acid composition, and nutritive value of protein of LPC from grass, *Loliofestuca* (Hanczakowski *et al.* 1975). In spite of considerable increase of total nitrogen content in the green crop under the influence of fertilization, the amount of concentrate obtained from 100 kg of green crops did not increase. The extra nitrogen showed up in the nonprotein compounds in the green forage, which are not subject to heat coagulation. Also, the amino acid composition and biological value of protein concentrates were not affected by the kind of fertilizer applied or the level.

Similar results were obtained using a high nitrogen fertilization in the cultivation of various fodder cabbage varieties and hogweed (Hanczakowski 1977). With potatoes the application of 180 kg N/ha diminished the amount of concentrate and the β-carotene obtained from 100 kg of haulms, but the amino acid composition and the nutritive value of protein were not affected.

The results obtained showed that from the point of view of protein concentrate production, the use of an intensified nitrogen fertilization is advisable only when the green matter yield per unit area is increased.

INCREASING PROTEIN CONTENT

Herbicides

An increase of protein content in the plant may also be obtainedusing low herbicide doses, chiefly derivatives of S-triazine. We have examined the effect of two herbicides: gesatop (simazine, S-triazine derivative), and aphalon (linuron, urea derivative) on the composition and the nutritive value of leaf protein concentrate prepared from lupine. The results (shown in Table 33.1) raise the question of justifying the use of low doses of herbicides in the cultivation of plants designed for raw material in the production of LPC. Herbicides did indeed cause a distinct increase of protein content in the concentrates obtained, most likely as a result of an increase in easily soluble fractions (Elek *et al.* 1974), yet their biological value was decreased.

SUPPLEMENTATION OF LPC

Amino Acids. It is well known that methionine is an amino acid limiting the nutritive value of protein of LPC. In our investigation (Hanczakowski 1974), supplementation with this amino acid increased the biological value of protein concentrate from potato haulms from 60 to 69. A

TABLE 33.1. THE EFFECT OF HERBICIDES (GESATOP AND APHALON) ON PROTEIN CONTENT AND NUTRITIVE VALUE OF LEAF PROTEIN CONCENTRATES FROM LUPINE

	Experimental Groups		
Specification	Gesatop (0.2 kg/ha)	Aphalon (0.2 kg/ha)	Control (No Herbicide)
Protein content (%)	47.2	45.1	41.7
Biological value (BV)	57	62	69
True digestibility (TD)	87	79	80
Net protein utilization $\frac{BV \times TD}{100} = NPU$	50	49	55

lysine supplement caused a further increase of the BV to 78, i.e., to the level of the biological value of casein protein used as control. As the analyses showed a high lysine content in the protein of potatoes, most likely its availability decreased during the course of preparation.

Sulfur. Byers (1976) suggests that probably almost all the sulfur contained in the leaf protein concentrates is in the form of methionine and cystine. If the sulfur could be used for other purposes, then supplementation could be done using inorganic sulfur sources, which are cheaper than the synthetic methionine. We have examined the effect of a sulfur supplement in the form of methionine, methionine hydroxyanalog, and sodium sulfur on body weight gains and food conversion in broilers. The main source of protein in the feed was the commercially produced alfalfa protein concentrate "Vepex." Besides, the dose contained maize and beef tallow as well as vitamin and mineral supplements (only in the form of chlorides). The results of the experiment are shown in Table 33.2. A sulfur supplement slightly improved the weight gains of chickens. The best results were obtained with inorganic sulfur, but the differences were not statistically significant. The fattening figures were low in all groups, especially in the first period of the experiment, and the feed consumption relatively high.

ALFALFA LPC

Chicken Feed

The results of further experiments also showed that the use of alfalfa LPC as chicken feed should be carried out with great caution. In the second

TABLE 33.2. THE EFFECT OF VARIOUS SULFUR SUPPLEMENTS ON BODY WEIGHT GAIN AND FEED CONVERSION IN CHICKENS FED DIETS BASED ON LPC FROM LUCERNE

	Experimental Groups				
Effect on Chickens	Control (No Sulfur Added)	DL-Methionine (350 g/100 kg of Feed)	Methionine Hydroxyanalog (377 g/100 kg of Feed)	Sodium Sulfate (330 g/100 kg of Feed)	F
Body weight gain (g)					
1–3 weeks (starter)	187	196	204	200	—
4–8 weeks (finisher)	820	895	914	957	—
1–8 weeks	1005	1104	1121	1163	—
Feed conversion [kg/kg of body weight gain/ 1–8 weeks (whole fattening period)]	2.4	2.2	2.2	2.3	—

experiment (Hanczakowski *et al.* 1976) carried out on chickens, we replaced soybean meal at 25, 50 and 100% levels by an alfalfa protein concentrate in simplified doses, as in the previous experiment, but these feed mixtures contained all supplements, including methionine, according to the Polish norms. Simultaneously, soybean meal was replaced at 50 and 100% levels by the same concentrate in the Polish commercial seed mixture DKA, containing besides soybean meal powdered skim milk and fish meal. The results are shown in Table 33.3. The increase of LPC content in the simplified ration caused a significant decrease in weight gains. However, the replacement of a half of soybean meal in a richer commercial mixture by an alfalfa concentrate had no effect on fattening. The same feed consumption for 1 kg of body weight gain indicates that the poor results could be the result of low feed intake, probably due to poor palatability. Simultaneously, a considerable increase of vitamin A level in the livers of chickens receiving LPC was found, and, in the experiment carried out on laying hens, an increase of this vitamin in egg yolks was observed. Hens obtaining the concentrate laid slightly more eggs, but their average weight was smaller (Młodkowski *et al.* 1977).

Pig Rations

In 1975, a piece of equipment for the production of leaf protein concentrates, consisting of universal feed mill, screw press, coagulant, and a cylinder drier, was completed in the Experimental Station at Czechnica, Institute of Zootechnics (Glapś *et al.* 1975). In this way, it was possible to obtain a few tons of the concentrate yearly, making it possible to extend the investigations to pigs. It was found in an experiment carried out on porkers (Glapś and Korniewicz 1975) that soybean meal may be entirely replaced in a commercial feeding mixture by alfalfa protein concentrate without any deleterious effect on the weight gain, and, in addition to replacing 85% of the soybean, about half of the fish meal could also be replaced. However, the LPC supplement lowers the meatiness of the animals and increases the weight of their bones. In the second experiment (Ryś *et al.* 1977) in which "Vepex" was used, replacing the whole soybean meal in the feed mixture and partially replacing meals of animal origin, no negative changes in the carcass dressing were found. Maybe the better quality of "Vepex" was the result of its better production method, especially a more precise separation of coagulum from "brown juice" and the spray-drying.

LPC DRYING

Considering the possibility of LPC overheating, drying is the most critical stage of its production. The deleterious effect of heat may be eliminated by using the method proposed by Foot (1974), mixing of the wet protein coagulum with ground grain and drying in a moderate temperature. Such preparations give satisfactory products, except their humidity exceeds 16%.

TABLE 33.3. BODY WEIGHT GAIN AND FEED EFFICIENCY IN BROILERS AT DIFFERENT LEAF PROTEIN CONCENTRATE LEVELS IN DIETS

Specification	Experimental Diets (Protein Sources in Ration)						
	Simple Diets				Commercial Mixture (DKA)		
	100% Soybean	75% Soybean 25% LPC	50% Soybean 50% LPC	100% LPC	100% Soybean	50% Soybean 50% LPC	100% LPC
Mean body weight gain per 7 weeks of experiment (g)	1378	1336	1242	1030	1248	1264	1084
Feed efficiency (kg of feed for 1 kg of body weight gain)	1.9	2.0	1.9	2.0	2.2	2.0	2.2

We tried out this method using ground wheat, ground barley, and wheat bran as well as a protein coagulum from alfalfa juice. Grain was mixed with a wet coagulum in the ratio 1.5:1 and dried by air at a temperature lower than 40°C. A part of the coagulum was dried separately. The nutritive value of the products was determined in a balance experiment on rats. Grains were also mixed with a separately dried coagulum so that the individual components in the mixture gave the same amount of protein as in the previous preparations. The results are shown in Table 33.4. It indicates that a supplement of dried coagulum to the grain was more advantageous than to cover them with a wet coagulum, although in both cases the biological value of the protein of the mixtures was higher than that of each component separately. Most likely, including ground grain in a coagulum of comparatively low digestibility diminished the availability of its protein. The reduction of the protein digestibility of the mixture was particularly distinct in the case of wheat bran. It seems also that better results were obtained using an LPC supplement to barley than to wheat. This may partly account for the better results of LPC trials with pigs, for which the fodder was based on barley, than those with poultry, fed chiefly with wheat or maize.

EFFECT OF PRESERVATIVES ON LPC

The risks connected with concentrate drying may also be avoided by wet coagulum conservation. Comparing the protein nutritive value of alfalfa concentrate dried, frozen, and preserved by means of acetic acid and propionic acid as well as by sodium benzoate and sodium sorbate, we obtained the best results in the case of concentrate dried and preserved with propionic acid (Hanczakowski 1976). Sodium benzoate and sodium sorbate did not protect fresh coagulum from molding. It must be considered, however, that wet, preserved coagulum complicates the preparation of food rations for animals and if not used at the production site will result in transporting a considerable quantity of water.

TABLE 33.4. NUTRITIVE VALUE OF GROUND CEREALS COATED OR MIXED WITH LEAF PROTEIN COAGULUM (LPC)

Specification	Biological Value (BV)	True Digestibility (TD)	Net Protein Utilization $\frac{BV \times TD}{100}$
Ground wheat	57	89	51
Ground wheat coated with LPC	58	87	51
Ground wheat mixed with dried LPC	60	88	53
Wheat bran	61	92	56
Wheat bran coated with LPC	62	84	52
Wheat bran mixed with dried LPC	65	85	55
Ground barley	62	86	53
Ground barley coated with LPC	66	85	56
Ground barley mixed with dried LPC	68	85	58

FEEDING GREEN FORAGE JUICE

In order to avoid the expenses of drying and also of heat coagulation, the green forage juice could be fed directly to animals (Braude *et al.* 1977). Our preliminary investigations carried out on rats showed that under certain conditions alfalfa juice may be a valuable protein supplement to barley. We found an increased biological value from 63 to 71 of the protein of barley × alfalfa juice mixture using a juice stored during 48 hr at a temperature about 20°C without any preservatives (Hanczakowski 1979). This suggests that some delay may be advisable in giving alfalfa juice directly to animals. Such a delay is harmful in the production of a dried concentrate, causing a decrease in the true protein and an increase in the nonprotein nitrogen due to proteolysis (Antoniewicz and Hanczakowski 1978). An increased biological value of protein to 74 was also obtained by using the centrifugate from the brown juice and coagulum × barley mixture. A supplement of the condensed brown juice to the casein diet reduced the nutritive value of its protein. This supplement caused also such symptoms as diarrhea and caecum enlargement, characteristic of the presence of low-digestible substances in the ration (Leegwater *et al.* 1974). Also, feeding rats with fresh juice caused a diarrhea in the initial stage of the experiment. This confirms the presence in the alfalfa juice of substances decreasing the protein availability, which after its coagulation pass to the filtrate, and after a longer juice-keeping are subject to a decomposition or inactivation. Such substances, for example, may be low-available carbohydrates.

SUMMARY

The production and use of leaf protein concentrates in Poland are a part of the State Protein Problem and the experiments are carried out in several Agricultural and Technical Research Institutes. However, only a part of the results has so far been published in scientific journals and so a comprehensive report is not yet possible.

REFERENCES

ANTONIEWICZ, A. and HANCZAKOWSKI, P. 1978. The rate of proteolysis in juice extracted from alfalfa and grass. Rocz. Nauk Roln. Ser. B: Zootech. *5*, 155–163. (Polish)

BRAUDE, R., JONES, A.S. and HOUSEMAN, R.A. 1977. The utilization of the juice extracted from green crops. Proc. Br. Grassl. Soc. Occas. Symp. *9*, 47–55.

BYERS, M. 1976. Determination of S in extracted leaf protein. J. Sci. Food Agric. *27*, 131–134.

ELEK, E., BORBÉLY, I., BORBÉLY, F. and KECSKÉS, M. 1974. Herbicides increasing the protein content in lupin. Acta Agron. Acad. Sci. Hung. *23*, 456–459.

FOOT, A.S. 1974. Lucerne juice for pigs. Pig Farm. *22* (9) 71.

GLAPŚ, J. and KORNIEWICZ, A. 1975. Protein concentrates made from green plant juice as supplements for pig fattening. Rocz. Nauk Roln. Ser. B: Zootech. *2*, 221–239. (Polish)

GLAPŚ, J., KORNIEWICZ, A., PRZYSIECKA, M. and RYŚ, R. 1975. Production of protein concentrates from green plant juice. Rocz. Nauk Roln. Ser. B: Zootech. *2*, 201–220. (Polish)

HANCZAKOWSKI, P. 1974. The influence of the addition of synthetic methionine and lysine on the nutritive value of leaf protein concentrates. Rocz. Nauk Roln. B: Zootech. *1*, 139–145. (Polish)

HANCZAKOWSKI, P. 1975. The composition and nutritive value of leaf protein concentrates. Rocz. Nauk Roln. Ser. B: Zootech. *97*, 85–95. (Polish)

HANCZAKOWSKI, P. 1976. An attempt to preserve lucerne leaf protein concentrate. Rocz. Nauk Roln. Ser. B: Zootech. *3*, 107–113. (Polish)

HANCZAKOWSKI, P. 1977. Composition and nutritive value of leaf protein concentrates from four varieties of cabbage grown at various N-fertilizer levels. Rocz. Nauk Roln. Ser. B: Zootech. *4*, 227–235. (Polish)

HANCZAKOWSKI, P. 1979. The nitrogen retention from lucerne juice in rats. J. Sci. Food Agric. *30*, 27–30.

HANCZAKOWSKI, P. and LUTYŃSKA, R. 1976. Leaf protein extraction from hogweed (Heracleum Sosnowskyi) grown at various N-fertilizer levels. Rocz. Nauk Roln. Ser. B: Zootech. *3*, 143–150. (Polish)

HANCZAKOWSKI, P., RYŚ, R. and BARABASZ, J. 1976. Leaf protein concentrates from lucerne in poultry feeding. Acta Agrar. Silvestria Ser. Zootech. *16*, 21–32. (Polish)

HANCZAKOWSKI, P., RYŚ, R. and PIRÓG, H. 1975. The effect of nitrogen fertilizers on amino acid composition and nutritive value of leaf protein concentrates from Loliofestuca grass. Acta Agrar. Silvestria Ser. Zootech. *15*, 17–26. (Polish)

LEEGWATER, D.C., GROOT, A.P. and KOLMTHOUT-KUYPER, M. 1974. The aetiology of caecal enlargement in the rat. Food Cosmet. Toxicol. *12*, 687–697.

MŁODKOWSKI, M., HANCZAKOWSKI, P. and KUCHTA, M. 1977. The use of leaf protein concentrate from lucerne (Vepex) as protein and carotene source in poultry feeding. Zesz. Probl. Postepow Nauk Roln. *192*, 249–254. (Polish)

RYŚ, R., URBAŃCZYK, J., HANCZAKOWSKA, E. and SOCHA, A. 1977. Leaf protein concentrate from lucerne (Vepex) as protein supplement for swine. Zesz. Probl. Postepow Nauk Roln. *192*, 185–193. (Polish)

34

Production of Leaf Protein Concentrates from the Green Plant Biomass in the USSR

M. Bekeris, A. Upītis, I. Ievin, M. Daugavietis, O. Polis, and J. Keviņš

AGRICULTURAL GREEN CROPS

Climate and soil conditions in a number of regions in the Soviet Union, including the Baltic republics and Byelorussia, ensure high yields of perennial grasses for green forage. The nutritional value of hay prepared at the proper time from qualitatively fertilized perennial grasses is almost equal to that obtained from grain crops, but the contents of protein and carotene of green forage legumes are even higher than those in grain crops. Red clover *(Trifolium pratense)*, the most widely cultivated forage legume (and the most abundant crop) in the Baltic republics, is utilized as either hay or leaf meal (Lielmanis and Eidemanis 1960).

Red Clover

The composition of the green forage of red clover is given in Table 34.1 (Brencis and Ozols 1963).

Hay from red clover harvested during the blossoming period contains an average per kg of 0.52 kg of feed units, 32 g of available protein, and 25–35 mg of carotene. Red clover in the Latvian SSR yields up to 4000–5000 kg/ha of hay and is cultivated in the same fields for 2 consecutive years. Clover increases the nitrogen level in soil by 150–160 kg/ha, thus positively affecting the growth of subsequent crops.

Alfalfa

The area under alfalfa *(Medicago sativa)* is expanding each year in the Latvian SSR. This forage legume had begun to be cultivated in the territory

TABLE 34.1. COMPOSITION OF RED CLOVER GREEN FORAGE (PER KG)

Phase of Development	Nutritious Units (kg)	Available Protein (g)	Calcium (g)	Phosphorus (g)	Carotene (mg)
Stemming, at 82% moisture	0.22	46	3.2	0.7	104
Budding, at 81% moisture	0.21	36	3.8	0.9	66
Blossoming, at 78% moisture	0.23	25	2.7	0.4	56

of Latvia by the middle of the last century. According to the statistical data, in 1961 only 5000–6000 ha of land were planted with alfalfa, while in 1976 alfalfa was planted on 22,000 ha. Under the climatic conditions in the Baltic, the high level of precipitation during the blossoming phase makes it difficult to obtain alfalfa seeds, although in the western regions of the republic, it is possible to gather the seeds of this plant at that time.

Composition. The content of alfalfa green forage with 80% moisture is given in Table 34.2 (Brencis and Ozols 1963).

Yield. In the Latvian SSR, alfalfa is grown in the same fields for 4–10 years. It is harvested 3 or 4 times per year. The total yield of forage comprises 30–50 MT/ha (Gailums *et al.* 1959). Adding fertilizers, treating seeds with nitragin, and poldering lands are practices widely used to obtain good hay harvests.

The investigations carried out at the A. Kirchenstein Institute of Microbiology, Latvian SSR Academy of Sciences, show that a considerable influence upon alfalfa development can be exerted by inoculation of seeds with nitragin as well as by application of Mo, B, and lysine feed concentrate (Klincāre 1961). The production of nitragin from local active strains isolated from alfalfa nodules is, therefore, of considerable importance. Active cultures of nodule bacteria have been collected in the Latvian SSR, and

TABLE 34.2. COMPOSITION OF ALFALFA GREEN FORAGE PER KG, AT 80% MOISTURE

Phase of Development	Feed Units (kg)	Available Protein (g)	Calcium (g)	Phosphorus (g)	Carotene (mg)
Vegetative (stemming)	0.22	42	4.4	1.2	63
Budding	0.22	36	4.0	0.9	51
Flowering (blossoming), at 75% moisture	0.23	31	4.2	1.0	44

original technology of production either on agar media or as dry nitragin has been developed. Yearly observations on the farms of the LSSR demonstrate that nitragin treatment of alfalfa seeds increases hay yield by 20–60% during the first year and in subsequent years by 18–45%.

The application of nitrogen, phosphorus, and potassium fertilizers (30, 60, 60 kg/ha, respectively) under the conditions of the Byelorussian SSR increased the alfalfa hay yield from 8.5 to 11.6 MT/ha, an additional 3.1 MT/ha, equivalent to 36.7% increase in yield. Nitrogenous fertilizers, however, are less effective if nitragin is applied.

Alfalfa can be successfully grown with clover. The dry matter (DM) and crude protein (CP) yields of these legumes alone or in mixed swards under conditions of the Latvian SSR are summarized in Table 34.3 (Jansons and Jansons 1979).

TABLE 34.3. DRY WEIGHT AND CRUDE PROTEIN YIELD OF ALFALFA AND CLOVER IN THE LATVIAN SSR

Plant	Standard Quantity of Seed per ha (kg/ha)	Dry Weight (kg/ha)	Crude Protein Content (kg/ha)
Alfalfa	20	12,810	2360
Clover	20	9,430	1660
Alfalfa + clover	10 + 5	12,500	2330
Alfalfa + clover	10 + 10	12,450	2290
Alfalfa + clover	5 + 15	12,020	2200

The data show that half of the alfalfa can be replaced by clover without lowering the yield and the protein level of the forage. This condition is of great importance in the Baltic republics where the seeds of clover are easier to obtain than those of alfalfa.

Alfalfa may also be grown with timothy grass. However, in such a mixture, the grass will gradually overgrow the alfalfa and lower the protein yield of the harvested forage.

Soil Moisture and Composition. Soil moisture conditions have exerted a considerable influence upon alfalfa harvest in the northwestern zones of the USSR as well as in the Moldavian SSR, Bulgaria, Czechoslovakia, and other East European countries. By irrigating alfalfa lands, 60–100 MT/ha of green forage (12–25 MT/ha of hay) can be obtained annually. Good farm machinery and irrigation of alfalfa promote high forage production and protein yield. Climatic influences are also important. In the Baltic republics, the plant is mowed 3 times during the vegetative period, but in Bulgaria it may be cut 4–6 times.

Alfalfa affects the soil composition positively. After 3 years of alfalfa cultivation, 200 kg/ha of nitrogen and substantial amounts of organic substances accumulate in the soil.

Production of leaf meal and pellets from clover and alfalfa green forage is widespread in the USSR. The use of leaf meal ensures losses of only 5–8% of nutritious substances as compared with 35–50% in hay production (Ulanov and Fomin 1976). Equipment consisting of a mower, mill, means of transportation, and a dryer is used to obtain leaf meal. High-temperature dryers of ABM-04, ABM-1.5, and CB-1.5 types are used most.

Protein Concentrates Solve Cellulose Limitation. In 1975, over 4 million MT of leaf meal were produced in the USSR, including 20,000 MT in the Latvian SSR. One kg of good quality alfalfa leaf meal contains 150–220 g available protein, 150–300 mg carotene, 210–250 g cellulose, 13.1 g calcium, 1.7 g phosphorus, and various amounts of B group vitamins. The leaf meal is widely used as a source of protein and carotene to enrich diets of domestic animals and poultry (Janševskis 1974). Leaf meal prepared from alfalfa and grasses is a high-quality protein source for animal feed. However, its application in pig and poultry feeding is limited due to its high cellulose content (up to 25%). This is why various countries, including the USSR, have studied the preparation of protein concentrates from green forage. Leaf protein concentrates may be utilized for poultry and pig feeds and in human nutrition.

Protein Concentrate Production

In the USSR, the Fodder Institute began studies in 1942 on the protein-vitamin concentrates prepared from leaves (Zubrilin and Zafren 1942; Zubrilin *et al.* 1952).

At present, the fractionating process of leaves is being developed at the Rostov-on-Don Institute of Agricultural Machine Building, the Central Scientific Research and Planning Technological Institute of Mechanization and Electrification of Animal Breeding in the Southern Zone of the USSR, the USSR Scientific Research Institute of Complex Engineering Problems for Cattle Breeding and Fodder Production, the Don Zonal Scientific Research Institute of Agriculture, the Central Scientific Research Institute of Mechanization and Electrification of Agriculture (CSRIMEA), and elsewhere (Fomin *et al.* 1974; Ulanov and Fomin 1976).

At the Academy of Sciences of the Latvian SSR, in conjunction with the complex scientific-technical program, "Transformation of Photosynthesis Products," the problem of efficient production of forage has been studied by a number of research institutes, including the August Kirchenstein Institute of Microbiology, the main organization dealing with the program.

According to the data given by the Central Scientific Research and Planning Technological Institute of Mechanization and Electrification of Animal Breeding in the Southern Zone of the USSR at Zaporozhye, attention must be paid not only to the problem of protein concentrate production from green plant mass but also to its mechanical dehydration before drying, since energy consumption for mechanical dehydration is considerably lower than that for drying. In screw presses, the water content of the alfalfa mass before drying can be lowered from 75–78% to 57–60%. A partial mechanical dehydration of green forage by 10% increases the profitability of the drying equipment 1.7 times at the same energy expenditure.

Press cakes, high in cellulose and containing almost 12–15% protein, are fed to ruminants either fresh, conserved, or dried. The separated alfalfa juice can be fed to pigs and young cattle either fresh or concentrated.

Green Crop Fractionation and Juice Expression. Green crop fractionation is a means of increasing the resources of fodder protein for monogastric animals. Methods of leaf protein concentrate production have been studied in Great Britain since 1942 (Pirie 1942), in Hungary (Holló and Koch 1971), and the United States (Edwards *et al.* 1974; Bickoff *et al.* 1976). The 40 years of research in this field were recently reviewed by Pirie (1978).

Equipment. Extensive investigations of green crop fractionation and juice expression using the developed equipment have been carried out in the USSR. Thus, along the experimental lines for green crop fractionation at the Rostov-on-Don Institute of Agricultural Machine Building and Special Construction Bureau of Electrotechnology, the double-step fractionation machines "Volgarj-5" and KDU-2.0 were used. Later, an improved fractionation machine, the IZM-10, was built that ensures productivity of 6 MT/hr with energy consumption of about 6 kWh/MT. Single-screw horizontal presses PND-5 and VPND-10 were used for juice separation. The latter one separated 45–55% juice from a green crop of 75% moisture content. The holding time of the crop in the VPND-10 press was 7–10 minutes (Jatsko *et al.* 1975) (Table 34.4).

TABLE 34.4. CHARACTERISTICS OF THE VPND-10 PRESS IN ALFALFA FRACTIONATION

		Contents of Dry Matter			
Product	Amount of Dry Matter (%)	Protein (%)	Cellulose (%)	Fat and Non-N Substance (%)	Carotene (mg/kg)
Alfalfa green crop	24.5	19.5	28.6	39.5	137.0
Press cakes	45.0	16.0	34.5	39.0	75.0
Juice	9.0	35.5	2.2	47.3	116.0

A double-screw press has been constructed and tested at the Rostov Institute of Agricultural Engineering (Fomin *et al.* 1975A). The studies showed that single pressing of a fractionated alfalfa crop harvested in the budding stage having 75–79% moisture content and a mass of 450–550 kg/m^3 permits mechanical separation of up to 42% of the initial moisture. Multiple pressing of alfalfa is not profitable, since, in second pressing, the productivity of the equipment decreases and its energy requirement increases. Some characteristics of this double-screw press when fractionating alfalfa crop of the second and third cuts in the phases of blossoming and budding are given in Table 34.5.

The results show that the amount of juice from alfalfa depends upon crop moisture.

TABLE 34.5. EFFICIENCY OF THE DOUBLE-SCREW PRESS

Alfalfa Cuttings	Moisture (%)	Productivity (kg/hr) Green Crop	Productivity (kg/hr) Juice	Juice from Green Crop (%)	Dry Matter in Juice (%)
Second cut, during blossoming	69.0	2346	276	11.75	17.3
Third cut, during budding	78.6	2710	1125	41.60	10.3

Good results were also obtained when testing the 7-screw press B6-PTA. After disintegrating alfalfa in an aggregate of the "Volgarj-5" type, the productivity of the press was raised to 6 MT of green crop per hour (Fomin *et al.* 1975A).

The investigations carried out at the Institute of Microbiology of the Latvian SSR and collective farm "Uzvara" of the Bauska region in the LSSR showed that grape presses of mass production can be applied successfully in fractionating alfalfa leaves and sugar beet tops. Grape presses operate comparatively well when the green crop has been previously disintegrated by machine. Up to 50% of the juice containing 6–15% dry matter, including 4–6% reducing sugars, can be extracted from sugar beet tops (Upītis *et al.* 1978).

USSR scientists have numerous experimental data on isolating juice from up to 50% of the total green mass. Fomin *et al.* (1974) worked out technical principles for pressing green forage and presented mathematical equations for regulations and methods of calculation.

Fractionating Vegetable Juice

Alfalfa juice contains 6–17% dry matter. According to Novikov *et al.* (1977), this juice contains 0.4–0.7% nitrogen, 60–70% of which is protein nitrogen. Thus, proteins make up to 3–4% of alfalfa juice. It is well known that vegetable proteins are highly heterogeneous and differ considerably in their amino acid composition and chemical and physiological properties. The isoelectric point of most vegetable proteins is in a low acid zone. To obtain better results in precipitating proteins, it is of great importance that coagulation be done within the isoelectric zone.

Cytoplasmic (White) and Chloroplastic (Green) Proteins. To separate white and green proteins, a 2-step coagulation was used. At 53°C, green protein was coagulated and at 80°C, white protein. The pH was varied within the interval 4.2–6.0. The best fractionation occurred at pH 5.8–6.3, the white fraction dry matter making up 12.8–13.4% of the juice dry matter, with the yield of the green fraction being 50.8–52.0%. The maximum coagulation occurred at pH 4.0–4.2 and 53°C. The composition of fractions is summarized in Table 34.6.

Eighty-eight percent of juice proteins coagulated at pH 4.2 and 53°C, and the yield of the coagulated dry matter exceeded by 42.9% that of the analogue prepared at pH 5.4. The carotene contents at pH 4.2 were lower than in other pH variations.

Equipment. At the Rostov Institute of Agricultural Machine Building, the milk pasteurizer OPB-1 was used for protein coagulation. Productivity of 1900–2200 kg/hr was obtained, the juice temperature reaching 68°–70°C. However, the pasteurizer had to be washed with hot water for 10–15 min. after every 4–6 hr of operation.

The best results were obtained at the Institute when testing a steam jet coagulator with a fixed screw. The temperature of the juice and steam mixture was maintained within 65°–75°C. Kotovsky and Protsenko (1975) consider it sensible to use a conductive heat exchanger with a steam jet (contact-over) coagulator when green juice is first heated in a heat exchanger up to 50°–55°C and then brought to 75°C by pointed steam in a steam jet coagulator.

NOGSH-325, a new screw centrifuge for separating coagulated protein, was tested in the USSR and found to be less effective than previous separators. When testing a vacuum filter, a protein coagulum of 72% moisture was obtained. The productivity of the filter, which had a 1.6 m^2 surface area, reached 220 kg/hr. Flotation separation of green juice components after steam jet treatment using a specially designed flotator gave a protein concentrate of 82% moisture. The yield of the protein mass reached 30% of the green juice mass. Protein losses in the brown juice did not exceed 3–5% (Ulanov and Fomin 1976).

Further dehydration of the protein coagulum after flotation is possible by using vacuum filters, which results in a decrease of moisture of up to 72% (Isahanov and Titarenko 1975). Mathematical equations were formulated for the qualitative estimation of the coagulated juice fractional composition and its phases for any applied method of juice separation into protein concentrate and brown juice (Titarenko and Isahanov 1975).

Protein Storage. The protein separated from the brown juice can be used in the form of a paste for enriching feeds. For storage of the paste, adding 0.4% sodium pyrosulfite and maintaining a storage temperature of 8° to 10°C are recommended (Ulanov and Fomin 1976). However, the most suitable form of protein concentrate is the dry one, with a residual moisture of 8–10%.

TABLE 34.6. COMPOSITION OF ALFALFA GREEN CROP FRACTIONATION PRODUCTS

Product	Content of Dry Matter (%)	Composition of the Dry Matter (%)								
		Crude Protein (N × 6.25)	Protein	Fat	Cellulose	Ash	Ca	P	Nonnitrogenous Matter	Carotene (mg/kg)
Green crop	13.7	24.11	17.36	3.81	23.60	8.07	1.58	0.289	40.41	219.30
Press cakes	27.5	16.65	13.24	1.24	23.24	6.07	1.24	0.240	42.49	117.85
Juice	8.5	37.53	24.35	4.75	0.04	15.28	2.46	0.620	42.35	230.90
Coagulum at pH 4.2 and 53°C	20.1	48.45	38.24	11.0	0.05	8.05	1.66	0.450	32.45	307.72
Coagulum at pH 5.4 and 53°C	19.0	54.26	41.67	12.16	0.03	8.37	1.79	0.420	25.21	507.84
Coagulum at pH 6.0 and 53°C	20.0	51.55	38.13	10.75	0.03	7.85	1.79	0.360	29.75	526.20

Drying Equipment. When working out a method for drying the protein concentrate, the main difficulties were its peculiar consistency and the presence of fibers in the paste. The SDA-250 double-roller drier was found to be inefficient because it was difficult to lay the paste uniformly and keep it on the surface of the rollers.

In the case of spray-drying of green protein concentrate with a disk sprayer, the removal of fibrous admixtures is of great importance.

At the Rostov Institute of Agricultural Machine Building, the mechanics of spray drying were worked out. The spray dispersion and distribution of the protein paste were studied (Protsenko 1975).

Press Cake. The handling of the green crop press cake does not cause any considerable difficulty. One of the easiest ways is to ensile it. Leaf meal may also be produced from it. Both ways have been tested successfully in the USSR. In the case of ensiling press cakes, after separation of green juice with a moisture content of 55–60%, the press cakes should be dried to a moisture content of 45–55%. Drying of press cakes by active ventilation was worked out by Mironov (1974).

Brown Juice. Most technological schemes for fractionating green crop assume that the brown juice will be concentrated to a syrup-like consistency. The purpose of evaporation is to increase the shelf-life and decrease the product volume of the juice. The problems of utilizing brown juice in the process of microbiologal fermentation were studied at the August Kirchenstein Institute of Microbiology. Table 34.7 gives the contents of natural and 5-fold steam-concentrated brown juice.

TABLE 34.7. COMPOSITION OF ALFALFA BROWN JUICE

Component	Natural Brown Juice	Concentrated Brown Juice
Dry matter, %	7.1	33.8
Reducing matter, %	0.5	2.5
Nitrogen, %	0.5	2.6
Methionine, μ/ml	76	280
Threonine, μ/ml	900	3650
Biotin, μ/ml	1420	5270
Thiamin, μ/ml	2620	7110

Composition. It is well known that brown juice contains biologically active substances—amino acids and vitamins—that are essential components of nutritious media for microorganism cultivation. The presence of carbohydrates in the juice makes this substrate a promising source of raw material for microbiological biomass production for fodder use. Yet, the content of reducing matter in brown juice is subject to great change, depending upon the maturity of the plants used. It varies within the limits of 0.5–3.0% for alfalfa and 2–6% for the juice of sugar beet tops. The content of nitrogenous substances varies widely also.

Nutrient Medium for Yeast. Yeast from *Hansenula* species can be bred on nutrient substrates from brown juice under aerobic conditions (Marauska *et al.* 1978). It is possible to obtain 20 kg/m^3 dry biomass, containing up to 50% protein, by cultivating yeast in neutral or acidic alfalfa brown juice or in the juice of sugar beet tops in standard experimental equipment. In biological experimentation with animals, the biomass produced a growth effect similar to hydrolyzed yeast (Upītis *et al.* 1978). This result substantiates the reported data of Polish scientists Voitatovich and Sobeschansky (1978).

Industrial Methods of Green Forage Fractionation

Ulanov and Fomin (1976) reviewed the industrial methods of green forage fractionation in several research institutes of the USSR. A technological line was designed and tested at the Rostov Institute. Productivity and products of alfalfa fractionation were analyzed, and the following results were obtained for productivity (MT/hr):

green juice	6.0
protein concentrate of 80% moisture content	0.8
brown juice	2.0

The moist concentrate contained 7% protein and 9.8 mg% carotene.

The research institutes recommended a plan for large-scale production and utilization of leaf protein concentrates of green crops. On farms possessing machines for drying leaf meal, the installation of additional equipment is planned for working up 15–18 MT of green crop per hour. With the equipment, the farms can mow the green crop, press it to separate the juice, coagulate the protein, and obtain the protein concentrates in the form of a paste. Using this procedure, the productivity of the drying of green crop is increased 1.5 to 2 times. Press cakes can be used on the farms for silage or leaf meal. A part of the protein concentrate is utilized on the farm; the remainder of the concentrate and the brown juice are transported to the central mill for further work-up. Here the green protein concentrate is dried by spray drying, and the brown juice is concentrated in vacuum evaporators or used in yeast production.

The Central Scientific Research and Planning Technological Institute of Mechanization and Electrification of Animal Breeding in the Southern Zone of the USSR has planned to consolidate the fractionation of green forage and work-up of press cake and juice in one place. Equipment for these operations has been installed on the experimental farm of their institute, "Rassvet." The productivity (MT/hr) of the plant is as follows:

green mass	10
press cakes	5
green juice	5
protein paste	2–2.5

dry protein concentrate	0.4–0.5
electrical energy requirement, kWh	650
steam requirement, kg/hr	300
personnel	6 men
investment return:	2–3 years

The fodder of the experimental farm "Rassvet" is cut and collected with a self-propelled SKA-30 harvester and two or three trailer carts with tractors of the "Belorusj" type.

The green crop fractionation line is equipped with a KTU-10 accumulation-dosage machine, three Volgarj-5 disintegrators, VPO-20 and VPND-10 winemaking screw presses, and a number of conveyers and pumps. For protein paste drying, the SRC-6.5/165 NK spray-dryer is used.

Experimental Farm. Following the suggestions of the August Kirchenstein Institute of Microbiology, an experimental industrial complex for breeding 20,000 pigs per year is under construction on the collective farm "Uzvara," Bauska region, Latvian SSR. The complex includes a fodder mill, a plant for protein extraction and fractionation, and a fermentation unit for preparation of single cell protein. Nitragin production by bacterial fermentation is planned for this unit. A goal of 600 MT of protein concentrate has been set.

Economic Efficiency of Green Crop Fractionation

The experience of various organizations in the USSR shows that fractionation of green crop doubles protein content and more than doubles the carotene content in products made from the green crop. The fractionation of green crop compared with the production of leaf meal increases yield from the growing area unit by 7.5%; digestible protein, 5%; and carotene, 13% (Fomin *et al.* 1975B).

Protein concentrates from the green crop are effective substitutes for skim milk in pig raising. The data presented by the Don Zonal Scientific Research Institute of Agriculture show that a partial substitution of skim milk with green juice or protein paste from alfalfa in the ration of pigs during 140 days of fattening resulted in a mean daily weight gain 12% higher than that in the test group, which received an equivalent quantity of skim milk as a protein source. Thus, each MT of juice replacing an equal quantity of skim milk yields an additional 25 kg of meat. It has been calculated that one medium-size juice production line, the cost of which is 7000 rubles (approximately $5072 as of March 1, 1982), working in two shifts during the period of alfalfa harvest, can produce sufficient juice for a complete substitution of skim milk in the ration of 4000–5000 pigs, resulting in savings of more than 14,000 rubles ($10,145) a year. The protein paste production line, costing 25,000 rubles ($18,116), supplies protein the year round to the same number of pigs, juice during the growing period, and preserved protein paste afterwards (Fomin *et al.* 1975B).

The technology of milk substitute production on the basis of alfalfa green crop protein concentrate has been worked out by the Central Scientific Research and Planning Technological Institute of Mechanization and Electrification of Animal Breeding in the Southern Zone of the USSR. In these whole milk substitutes, up to 50% of the milk products can be replaced with leaf protein concentrates. Mills with a capacity of handling 45 MT/hr of green crop are projected. All the protein production (dry protein concentrate, containing 3096 MT of protein) will be used to prepare milk substitutes, which will replace 93,800 MT of whole milk. This will free 31,300 cows for milk production for human use. The tentative cost of a mill is 5.2 million rubles ($3.77 million), which will be repaid in 1.2 to 1.7 years (Novikov and Tkač 1975).

A number of organizations in the USSR are conducting scientific research and planning to elaborate efficient technology and equipment for obtaining protein concentrates from various sources of green crops and utilizing them in cattle feed.

TREE VERDURE

Tree needles, leaves, and nonlignified shoots have been considered as new sources for cattle feed. Many investigations of the chemical composition of tree verdure suggest potential application of this material for cattle feed and biologically active feed supplements.

Composition of Tree Verdure

According to the investigations made by the Byelorussian Research Institute, 1 kg of needle meal contains 0.64 feed units and 36 g of digestible protein (Gnoyanik 1972).

Amino acid composition in tree verdure (percentage of protein), as given by Volinova and Valdman (1975) and Kudashev and Shostak (1973), is listed in Table 34.8.

Protein content in needles is lower than in leaves; and, depending on the season, it lies within the range of 9.4 to 11.8% for pine and 5.6 to 8.3% for spruce by dry weight.

As a rule, 1-year-old needles are richer in amino acids than older ones. The composition and content of amino acids in needles varies by seasons, too (Ladinskaya and Hudasheva 1974).

Studies of LPC content in pine and spruce needles have been conducted in the Krasnoyarsk region by Repiah *et al.* (1976) and Repiah and Levin (1976). It was determined that crude protein content in 1-year-old pine needles was 8.81% on a dry weight basis. The pine needle crude protein consists of the following subunits (in %): albumins, 17.00; prolamines, 2.16; globulins, 4.99; glutelin, 35.53; and others, 40.30. The presence of 18 amino acids was determined.

TABLE 34.8. AMINO ACID PERCENTAGE IN TREE VERDURE AND ALFALFA
% of protein.

Species	Cysteine	Lysine	Methionine	Threonine	Arginine	Histidine	Tyrosine	Phenylalanine	Serine	Glycine	Protein (%)
Gray poplar	0.6	4.3	1.1	3.5	1.8	1.5	1.8	2.0	2.7	3.2	11.0
Lime	0.7	5.5	1.0	3.0	3.2	2.1	1.7	2.3	2.6	3.4	17.5
Ash	0.95	2.0	1.5	3.0	4.0	1.8	1.7	2.5	3.0	3.7	15.7
Maple	1.4	3.9	1.5	4.5	5.9	0.95	1.4	1.9	3.3	3.4	21.1
Acacia	0.5	4.5	0.5	3.7	3.7	1.0	0.6	1.6	3.0	3.2	24.9
Elm	1.4	4.8	2.2	4.5	5.2	2.6	1.9	0.98	2.9	3.3	21.4
Birch	0.8	3.6	1.8	3.6	2.7	1.4	2.0	1.5	2.7	3.0	13.3
Spruce needles	1.8	2.7	0.8	4.5	5.8	2.6	3.5	7.2	5.3	4.8	6.7
Alfalfa leaves	1.4	4.2	1.9	4.6	4.3	2.1	5.7	4.5	1.3	5.0	20.0

Content of Tree Verdure

Besides LPC, tree verdure is rich in vitamins, micro- and macro-elements, and nitrogen-free extractives which are biologically active and significantly increase the feed value of this raw plant material. For example, according to the data of Mateikiene (1971), the content of some group B vitamins in needles of different age is (mg/kg of dry weight): nicotinic acid, 16.9–38.3; thiamin, 0.3–3.5; pantothenic acid, 3.78–13.66; pyridoxine, 7.35–31.13; and biotin, 0.51–1.29.

The content of physiologically active substances in 1 kg dry weight of softwood and hardwood tree verdure in comparison with alfalfa is given in Table 34.9 (Terzič 1970). The content of different substances in tree verdure depends on many factors; hence, the data given in Table 34.9 should be regarded as rough estimates.

Limiting Substances

The comparatively high content of tannins, resinous substances, toxic glucosides, and lignins must be mentioned as substances limiting wide application of tree verdure for cattle feed.

Biologically Active Substances

There are biologically active substances of an unknown nature in tree verdures. Fresh needles and needle extractives enhance cattle sexual activity and eliminate infertility. Also, the intact verdure of many different species shows antimicrobial, cytotoxic, and antiblastic activity (Kalninš and Valdman 1978).

Industrial Production

According to Ievin and Dikelson (1963), harvesting 1 solid m^3 of stemwood in the Latvian SSR results in 36, 32, 74, and 60 kg of fresh tree verdure from aspen, birch, spruce, and pine trees, respectively. Large amounts of tree verdure can be produced in thinnings, too (Table 34.10). In early thinnings, Ievin and Dikelson (1963) found that tree verdure for birch resulted in 35% and for spruce and pine 39% of the total aboveground biomass harvested. Consequently, in final cuttings, 9 to 24 MT/ha of fresh tree verdure can be produced; in thinnings, 2 to 16 MT.

The chemical composition data show that tree verdure could compete with fodder plants for LPC production. The supplies are sufficient for industrial production, justifying research and development in the USSR of tree verdure for leaf protein concentrate.

Trends of Utilization. On an industrial scale, tree verdure is worked up by two processes:

(1) Conservation by drying and vitamin meal production for cattle feed.
(2) Processing by chemical methods: extraction of biologically active substances for cattle feed, medicine, and cosmetics.

TABLE 34.9. PHYSIOLOGICALLY ACTIVE SUBSTANCES IN 1 KG DRY WEIGHT OF TREE VERDURE AND ALFALFA

Substance	Spruce		Pine		Fir		Oak	Beech	Alfalfa
	Summer	Winter	Summer	Winter	Summer	Winter			
Carotenes, mg	35.5	53.7	56.7	64.7	42.08	69.82	67.5	58.26	160
Vitamin C, g	3.55	1.77	6.15	2.56	2.51	1.55	2.83	2.81	—
Riboflavin, mg	6.51	3.75	8.56	7.08	8.23	5.25	9.03	8.56	12.3
Vitamin K, mg	18.50	8.56	18.33	6.08	22.28	9.46	16.16	12.13	8.7
Vitamin E, mg	71.00	22.70	117.20	28.00	85.74	26.60	95.73	67.43	127.8
Chlorophyll, g	7.96	5.25	7.20	3.62	10.12	8.17	11.40	10.37	—
Iron, mg	427.20	108.40	385.40	47.00	229.10	181.90	624.20	664.50	454.0
Manganese, mg	429.90	329.10	41.20	40.10	227.60	204.10	773.30	1204.10	29.0
Zinc, mg	139.20	70.7	138.80	45.10	91.80	54.30	153.50	136.60	16.0
Cobalt, mg	9.41	14.27	8.67	14.76	7.53	8.88	31.91	30.84	0.36
Copper, mg	33.96	19.06	6.85	7.13	3.82	1.95	17.61	9.84	9.90
Molybdenum, mg	0.33	0.29	0.07	0.13	0.25	0.22	0.59	0.33	—
Lipids, %	31.31	31.44	49.02	47.28	33.07	28.39	4.17	3.23	—
Ash, %	5.01	3.60	2.70	2.90	7.17	3.78	4.50	3.33	9.0
Protein, g	9.30	5.20	11.70	6.90	10.80	5.20	14.90	10.40	17.0

TABLE 34.10. YIELD OF FRESH TREE VERDURE IN THINNINGS COMPARED WITH TOTAL BIOMASS OF BRANCHES (%)

Species	% Yield of Verdure					
Diameter, cm	2.1–4.0	4.1–6.0	6.1–8.0	8.1–10.0	10.1–12.0	12.1–14.0
Spruce	42.8	26.4	20.6	20.4	22.0	18.7
Pine	24.6	20.4	11.5	12.1	13.6	10.3
Birch	21.2	12.6	6.3	6.0	5.6	4.3
Aspen	16.8	8.4	5.2	4.6	5.5	5.3

Source: Ievin *et al.* (1971).

Vitamin Meal Production. Technology and equipment for the production of vitamin meal from tree verdure have been developed by the researchers of the Wood Chemistry Institute of the Academy of Sciences of the Latvian SSR, the Latvian Scientific Research Institute for Forestry Problems, and the Latvian Academy of Agriculture.

The first industrial mill for the production of needle vitamin meal was built in 1955 in Kuldiga forest district, Latvian SSR. The output of the mill was about 45 MT of meal per year (Āboliņš 1960). The simplicity of the technological process and the high market demand accelerated the development of this industry, which now exceeds 140,000 MT/year production. The production of vitamin meal from tree verdure in comparison with leaf meal has several advantages: production is not inhibited by seasonal impact—there is no necessity to store large inventories; also, because of lower moisture content, the fuel needed in production is decreased; and logging wastes can be used as an energy source. Compared with other methods of tree verdure processing, the production of vitamin meal has a number of advantages: simplicity of the technological process; utilization of the whole tree verdure biomass and the absence of industrial wastes; and availability of efficient manufacturing equipment. The quality of vitamin meal in the USSR is regulated by State Standards 13797-78 (Ievin *et al.* 1978). Vitamin meal is used as a 3–5% supplement to mixed feed. It is regarded as a substitute in crude feed or as a biologically active vitamin supplement (Kalniņš and Valdman 1978).

Limitations to Tree Verdure Utilization

The limiting factor for increased development of tree verdure utilization is the comparatively low level of mechanization and the high labor intensiveness of the collecting and separating process using branchwood and small size trees.

Mechanized Equipment. To overcome the difficulties, self-loading trucks are built with special equipment for loading and compressing branches. Separation of tree verdure from branches takes place in a mill using IPS-1.0 chipping and pneumosorting equipment. The basic operations of the IPS-1.0 involve chipping branches and small trees and "green chip" separation by airstream for merchantable tree verdure and fuel chips. Capacity of the equipment is 600 to 1000 kg of tree verdure per hour (Ievin *et al.* 1971).

For meal production from tree verdure, ABM-0.4 (ABM-0.65) equipment, initially designed for leaf meal production, is used. Meal pellets are also manufactured. The profit amounts to 30%. A standard mill for production of vitamin meal was developed at the Scientific and Industrial Research Association, "Silava," with a capacity of 800 to 1000 MT of meal per year.

Meal Composition

Composition of meal from tree verdure and alfalfa is given in Table 34.11 (Kalninš and Valdman 1978).

Industrial Extracts and Their Uses

The theoretical basis and technology for preparation of different substances have been developed at the Leningrad Academy of Forest Techniques. In 1949, the technology for obtaining chlorophyll-carotene paste was developed. Its production is now on an industrial scale. Chlorophyll-carotene paste is also used as a medicine in surgery, in gynecology, and other fields of medical and veterinary practice (Anderson and Fisher 1969).

Scientists of the Latvian Academy of Agriculture have proposed using volatile oils from coniferous species as growth stimulants for calves. In large-scale feeding trials, use of the oils resulted in weight gain (Anderson and Millers 1971; Kalninš and Valdman 1978).

Drawbacks. The main drawbacks of these processes are the low utilization of biomass and the great amount of industrial waste. Trials have been

TABLE 34.11. MEAL COMPONENTS FROM SPRUCE AND BIRCH VERDURE AND ALFALFA

Components	Spruce Needle Meal	Birch Leaf Meal	Alfalfa Meal
Protein, %	8.79	8.0	17.0
Lipids, %	6.54	8.2	3.2
Cellulose, %	35.6	18.0	26.2
Nitrogen-free substances, %	34.0	56.8	41.8
Ash, %	4.4	4.2	9.6
Carotenes, mg/kg	139	380	172
Riboflavin, mg/kg	6	4	13.2
Calcium, %	0.72	0.78	1.13
Phosphorus, %	0.17	0.26	0.31
Potassium, %	0.44	0.73	1.34
Magnesium, %	0.59	0.30	0.20
Iron, mg/kg	158.5	101.0	212.0
Manganese, mg/kg	292.0	30.0	29.0
Copper, mg/kg	5.6	8.0	9.9
Zinc, mg/kg	31.5	121.0	16.0
Cobalt, mg/kg	158.0	90.0	360.0

started in the utilization of the treated tree verdure for the production of single cell protein for cattle feed (Kostroma and Ladinskaya 1975). Results of the studies are given in Table 34.12.

Feed Products and LPC

Recently in the USSR, studies have been initiated for preparation of feed products of higher protein content from tree verdure, and different processes have been proposed.

In the Leningrad Academy of Forest Techniques, a laboratory method was developed in which the proteins of the pressed plant juice were coagulated by heat treatment. The LPC pastes obtained contained 5–6 times more protein than the untreated starting material, the needles (Hudasheva *et al.* 1973). Results of this study are summarized in Table 34.13.

TABLE 34.12. PROTEIN PRODUCTION FROM TREATED TREE VERDURE AFTER 20 DAYS FERMENTATION AT 26°C

Species	Tree Verdure Treatment Method	Type of Fungus	Output of Crude Protein (% of Dry Weight) When Raw Material Moisture Was		
			55%	65%	80%
Pine	Extraction with petrol and strong steam	*Panus tigrinus*	7.70	8.15	14.30
		Pleurotus ostreatus	6.48	7.30	11.25
Spruce	Treatment with petrol and strong steam	*Panus tigrinus*	7.89	10.35	18.25
		Pleurotus ostreatus	6.17	11.10	14.82
Maple	Treatment with ethyl ether	*Panus tigrinus*	6.57	7.78	17.45

TABLE 34.13. PROTEIN CONTENT OF THE PINE NEEDLE, ITS PRESSED JUICE, AND PROTEIN PASTE

Samples	% of Nitrogen on Dry Weight Basis	
	Nitrogen	Protein
Needle	0.8–1.2	5.0–7.5
Pressed needle juice	1.1–1.6	7.0–10.0
LPC paste		
from needle juice	3.2–4.8	20.0–30.0
from water extract	1.6–3.2	10.0–20.0

In the Scientific and Industrial Research Association, "Silava," birch, aspen, and gray alder leaves were studied as LPC sources under laboratory conditions. The disintegrated starting material was extracted with 0.2% NaOH, followed by heat coagulation in an acid medium (Bruvere *et al.* 1978). The LPC product was obtained in a 10% yield from the leaves on a dry basis.

Content and Composition. Chemical analysis indicates that, apart from crude protein, the product contains a number of substances which are useful in cattle feed (Table 34.14). Seventeen amino acids were measured in the protein concentrate, with highest levels of glutamic acid, leucine, aspartic acid, phenylalanine, and lysine (Table 34.15). Essential amino acids

TABLE 34.14. CHEMICAL COMPOSITION OF LPC PRODUCTS FROM TREE LEAVES
% of dry weight.

Components	Birch (*Betula pubescens*)	Aspen (*Populus tremula*)	Gray Alder (*Alnus incana*)
Crude protein	17.76	17.70	23.16
Lipids	15.35	12.91	10.38
Starch	2.10	1.10	2.70
Ash	12.74	6.53	3.31
Cellulose	10.70	16.30	7.85
Free sugar	1.74	4.87	0.47
Saccharose	1.68	0.57	trace
Tannin	0.58	1.13	0.22
Pectin	5.19	—	—

TABLE 34.15. AMOUNT OF AMINO ACIDS IN THE LPC PRODUCT FROM BIRCH AND ASPEN LEAVES

	Birch		Aspen	
Amino Acids	mg/g of Dry LPC Product	% of Crude Protein in LPC Product	mg/g of Dry LPC Product	% of Crude Protein in LPC Product
Lysine	16.6	6.3	17.5	4.4
Histidine	6.9	2.6	8.7	2.0
Arginine	11.5	4.4	20.0	5.1
Aspartic acid	20.5	7.8	31.9	8.1
Threonine	10.0	3.8	16.1	4.1
Serine	9.7	3.7	15.8	4.0
Glutamic acid	23.5	8.9	34.2	8.6
Proline	15.2	5.7	20.7	5.2
Glysine	13.1	4.9	20.3	5.1
Alanine	12.3	4.6	19.7	5.0
Valine	14.3	5.3	22.8	5.8
Methionine	3.6	1.1	5.0	1.3
Isoleucine	13.6	4.9	19.7	5.0
Leucine	22.5	8.5	33.4	8.5
Tyrosine	7.8	3.0	11.5	3.0
Phenylalanine	17.8	6.8	30.9	7.8
Tryptophan	2.0	0.8	2.1	0.5
Total	219.6	49.4	330.5	49.7

made up 60% of the total amount of amino acids, or 13.2% of the crude leaf protein. The antinutrient tannin was also present in various amounts. Material and energy balance of the process have yet to be determined.

Prospects for LPC from Tree Verdure

Nutritional quality of the protein concentrate in nonruminant feeding and the feeding value of pressed residue in ruminant feeds will have to be determined before tree verdure utilization can be considered alongside the protein concentrates prepared from agricultural plant sources.

REFERENCES

The reference section contains all information that was available at press time.

ĀBOLINŠ, JA.T. 1960. Needle and wood meal production plant. Trudi ILP i HD. AN. Latv. SSR *18*, 157–174.

ANDERSON, P.L. and MILLERS, A.JA. 1971. The chemical SM-k, a growth stimulator for calves. *In* Chemistry and Biology in Agriculture, Vol. 1. Zinatne, Riga, Latvian SSR, USSR.

ANDERSON, P.P. and FISHER, V.JA. 1969. Use of chlorophyll-carotene paste as a growth stimulator of cattle and poultry. *In* Stimulators of Organism Growth. Vilnius, USSR.

BICKOFF, E.M., DE FREMERY, D., EDWARDS, R.H., KNUCKLES, B.E., KOHLER, G.O. and MILLER, R.E. 1976. Preparation of soluble edible protein from leafy green crops. U.S. Pat. 3,959,246. May 25.

BRENCIS, K. and OZOLS, A. 1963. The Tables of Cattle Feed Content. Latvian State Publishing House, Riga, USSR.

BRŪVERE, V.A., ALKSNE, A.J., GALVANS, U.I. and POLIS, O.R. 1978. Studies on extraction of protein of tree leaves. Chimia Drevesini *4*, 106–108.

EDWARDS, R.H., DE FREMERY, D. and KOHLER, G.O. 1975A. The Pro-Xan process: Production of leaf protein from alfalfa. 12th Tech. Alfalfa Conf. Proc., Nov. 6–7, 1974, Overland Park, KS, U.S. Dep. Agric., Agric. Res. Serv., Berkeley, CA.

FOMIN, V.I. 1974. Calculation basis for the process of mechanical dehydration of green feeds. Trakt. Selkhozmashiny *3*, 8–12.

FOMIN, V.I., ISAHANOV, S.N. and MIRONOV, V.A. 1973. Studies of the mechanical dehydration process of alfalfa in double screw-press. Trakt. Selkhozmashiny *4*, 26–28.

FOMIN, V.I., VIACHESLAVOV, M.V. and GRIGORIAN, E.JU. 1975A. Studies of the semiworm press. *In* The Preparation of Green Feed Concentrates, Vol. 2, pp. 31–48. Rostov-on-Don Institute of Agricultural Machine Building, Ministry of Higher and Middle Special Education of the RSFSR [Russian Soviet Federal Socialist Republic], Rostov-on-Don, USSR.

FOMIN, V.I., ZAUHICIN, V.E., DANILOV, V.I., BLAGODATOV, O.A. and TUTAROV, G.A. 1975B. Practical introduction of the technology of preparation of green feed from fresh forage. *In* Works of Rostov-on-Don Institute of

Agricultural Machine Building, Vol. 2, pp. 5–12. Ministry of Higher and Middle Special Education of the RSFSR [Russian Soviet Federal Socialist Republic], Rostov-on-Don, USSR.

FOMIN, V.I., ZAUSHICIN, V.E., NOVIKOV, I.F. and DANILOV, V.I. 1974. The technology of green feed processing applying mechanical dehydration. *In* Industrial Methods of Feed Production, Vol. 1, pp. 5–40. Rostov-on-Don Institute of Agricultural Machine Building, Ministry of Higher and Middle Special Education of the RSFSR [Russian Soviet Federal Socialist Republic], Rostov-on-Don, USSR.

GAILUMS, F., LAURA, A. and STIKANS, J. 1959. Growing of Alfalfa Under the Conditions of the Latvian SSR. Latvian State Publishing House, Riga, USSR. 114 pp.

GNOYANIK, A. 1972. Wood vitamins. Zhivotnovodstvo *12*, 64–65.

HOLLÓ, J. and KOCH, L. 1971. Commercial production in Hungary. *In* Leaf Protein: Its Agronomy, Preparation, Quality and Use. IBP Handb. *20*, pp. 63–68. N.W. Pirie (Editor). Blackwell's Scientific Publishers, Oxford.

HUDASHEVA, G.S., GRACIANOVA, O.V., LADINSKAJA, S.I. and MEDNIKOV, F.A. 1973. Protein content in pine and spruce needles. Lesohimia Podsochka *9*, 13–14.

IEVIN, I., DAUGAVIETIS, M. and DERUMA, V. 1978. Vitamin Meal from Tree Verdure. GOST [State Standard] *13797-78*, Standartizdat, Moscow.

IEVIN, I., DAUGAVIETIS, M. and KEVINŠ, J. 1971. Mechanical Treatment of Tree Verdure in Latvian SSR. Latvian Institute of Scientific and Technical Information, Riga, USSR. 50 pp.

IEVIN, I. and DIKELSON, O. 1963. Estimation of the amount and composition of small-sized trees in forest enterprises of the Latvian SSR. Rep. Inst. For. Probl. Wood Chem., Riga *26*, 81–87.

ISAHANOV, S.I. and TITARENKO, V.M. 1975. Experimental equipment for coagulated alfalfa juice separation. *In* The Preparation of Green Feed Concentrates, Vol. 2, pp. 87–97. Rostov-on-Don Institute of Agricultural Machine Building, Ministry of Higher and Middle Special Education of the RSFSR [Russian Soviet Federal Socialist Republic], Rostov-on-Don, USSR.

JANŠEVSKIS, R. 1974. Studies of storage conditions and utilization efficiency of stabilized grass meal. Synopsis of Thesis degree. Candidate of Technical Sciences. Latvian Agricultural Academy, Jelgava, USSR.

JANSONS, F. and JANSONS, A. 1979. Let Us Increase Alfalfa Crops. Zinatne, Riga, USSR. 62 pp.

JATSKO, M., BALAN, G., NAGORNII, A. and KORINECHAIA, L. 1975. Juice pressing from the green feed biomass in worm grape press. *In* Preparation of Green Feed Concentrates, Vol. 2, pp. 54–60. Rostov-on-Don Institute of Agricultural Machine Building, Ministry of Higher and Middle Special Education of the RSFSR [Russian Soviet Federal Socialist Republic], Rostov-on-Don, USSR.

KALNINŠ, A.J.A. and VALDMAN, A.P. 1978. Forest for agriculture. Lesn. Promst. (Moscow), 192.

KLINCĀRE, A.J. 1961. Symbiosis of tuber bacteriums and papilionaceous plants. *In* Biological Collection Microorganisms in Agriculture. Publishing House of the Latvian SSR Academy of Sciences, Riga, USSR.

KOSTROMA, E.JU. and LADINSKAYA, S.I. 1975. Use of processed tree verdure for obtaining food protein concentrates. Lesohimia Podsochka *10*, 16.

KOTOVSKY, A.K. and PROTSENKO, G.I. 1975. Coagulation of green juice. *In* The Preparation of Green Feed Concentrates, Vol. 2, pp. 74–86. Rostov-on-Don Institute of Agricultural Machine Building, Ministry of Higher and Middle Special Education of the RSFSR [Russian Soviet Federal Socialist Republic], Rostov-on-Don, USSR.

KUDASHEV, A.V. and SHOSTAK, S.S. 1973. Amino acid composition of tree leaves feed [spring forage]. Zhivotnovodstvo *9*, 44–45. (Russian)

LADINSKAYA, S.I. and HUDASHEVA, G.S. 1974. Pine and spruce needle protein and possibilities of its extraction. Izv. Vyssh. Uchebn. Zaved. Lesn. Zh. [For. J.] *4*, 100–103. (Russian)

LIELMANIS, J. and EIDEMANIS, B. 1960. Red Clover. Latvian State Publishing House, Riga, USSR. 232 pp.

MARAUSKA, M.K., POPOVA, M.V. and UPITE, D.JA. 1978. Selection of yeast cultures for growing on substratom of plant origin. Proc. Symp. Biotechnol. Bioeng., Vol. 2. Zinatne, Riga, USSR, March 1978.

MATEIKIENE, I. 1971. Dynamics of bios-group vitamins in the aboveground parts of Scotch pine *(Pinus silvestris)* in the course of their development. Thesis degree. Candidate of Chemical Sciences. Vilnius State University, Vilnius, USSR.

MIRONOV, V.A. 1974. Drying of husk by active ventilation. *In* Collection: Individual Methods of Feed Industry, Vol. 1, pp. 121–138. Rostov-on-Don Institute of Agricultural Machine Building, Ministry of Higher and Middle Special Education of the RSFSR [Russian Soviet Federal Socialist Republic], Rostov-on-Don, USSR.

NOVIKOV, JU.F. 1977. Personal communication.

NOVIKOV, JU.F., KASIAN, S.S. and SUKHININ, V.N. *et al.* 1977. Determination of alfalfa green juice optimum acidity for a more complete coagulation and fractionation of proteins. Sci. Tech. Bull. on Mechanization and Electrification of Animal Breeding. Zaporozhye 7, 18–31.

NOVIKOV, JU.F. and TKAČ, G.F. 1975. Economic analysis of production and use of concentrates from green leaves. *In* The Preparation of Green Feed Concentrates, Vol. 2. Rostov-on-Don Institute of Agricultural Machine Building, Ministry of Higher and Middle Special Education of the RSFSR [Russian Soviet Federal Socialist Republic], Rostov-on-Don, USSR.

PIRIE, N.W. 1942. Direct use of leaf protein in human nutrition. Chem. J. Ind. *61*, 45.

PIRIE, N.W. 1978. Leaf Protein and Other Aspects of Fodder Fractionation. Cambridge University Press, Cambridge, England.

PROTSENKO, G.I. 1975. Sawing fineness of protein-vitamin feed paste by means of mechanical spurt sawing. *In* The Preparation of Green Feed Concentrates, Vol. 2, pp. 110–118. Rostov-on-Don Institute of Agricultural Machine Building, Ministry of Higher and Middle Special Education of the RSFSR [Russian Soviet Federal Socialist Republic], Rostov-on-Don, USSR.

REPIAH, S. and LEVIN, D. 1976. Protein content in spruce needles. Chimia Drevesini *4*, 114–116.

REPIAH, S.M., RAHMILEVICH, V.A. and LEVIN, E.D. 1976. Needle protein content of different-aged pine trees. Chimia Drevesini *4*, 111–113.

TERZIČ, D. 1970. A study of chemical composition of greens of forest trees as raw material for production of bovine feed concentrates. Sarajevo. 91 pp.

TITARENKO, V.M. and ISAHANOV, S.N. 1975. Quality evaluation of the effect of coagulated juice on protein-vitamin paste and the brown juice. *In* The Preparation of Green Feed Concentrates, Vol. 2, pp. 98–109. Rostov-on-Don Institute of Agricultural Machine Building, Ministry of Higher and Middle Special Education of the RSFSR [Russian Soviet Federal Socialist Republic], Rostov-on-Don, USSR.

ULANOV, B.P. and FOMIN, V.I. 1976. The Production of Protein Concentrate from the Juice of Green Plants. Ministry of Agriculture of the USSR, Moscow.

UPĪTIS, A., KRAUZE, I., BEKER, M. and PINTE, A. 1978. Processing products of green plants as a promising raw-material for obtaining of microbial protein. Proc. Symp. Biotechnol. Bioeng., Vol. 2. Zinatne, Riga, USSR, March 1978.

VOITATOVICH, M. and SOBESCHANSKY, E. 1978. Yeast cultivation on juice obtained after extracting protein from plants. Proc. Symp. Biotechnol. Bioeng., Vol. 2. Zinatne, Riga, USSR, March 1978.

VOLINOVA, P.M. and VALDMAN, A.R. 1975. Composition and Nutrition Value of Ingredients, Applicable in Development of Combined Foods in the Latvian SSR. Zinatne, Riga, USSR, p. 36.

ZUBRILIN, A. and ZAFREN, S. 1942. How to Prepare the Concentrate of Provitamin A Carotene from Green Plants. Selhozgiz [State Publishers on Agriculture], Moscow, p. 7.

ZUBRILIN, A.A., ZUBRILINA, Z.I. and GOLDBERG, G. 1952. Recent developments in the technology of production of protein-vitamin paste. Sov. Tehnika 7, 92–94.

Appendix

Walter J. Bray

AN ANNOTATED BIBLIOGRAPHY ON ECONOMICS OF GREEN CROP FRACTIONATION AND LEAF PROTEIN PRODUCTION

(1) RAYMOND, W.F. and TILLEY, J.M.A. 1956. The extraction of protein concentrates from leaves. Colon. Plant Anim. Prod. *6*, 3–19.

Discusses some early estimates of the cost of producing LPC and gives the author's estimate. Leaf protein is assumed to be the only product of value and, as a consequence, its cost is very high. Conclusion is that the process is not economically viable.

(2) MENDES, C.B. 1965. Investigations into the production of a high protein concentrate from leaves for inclusion into the diets of infants and children. Sci. Res. Counc., Jamaica, Tech. Rep. *1/65*.

This long presentation includes a section on economics. Calculations are based on a very low yield of leafy matter per acre (0.4 ha). No value is assumed for either the fiber or the solubles, and as a result, the cost of the LPC is very high.

(3) ARKCOLL, D.B. and DAVYS, M.N.G. 1973. Mechanical fractionation as an aid to crop drying. Proc. 1st Int. Green Crop Drying Congr., Oxford, April 1973.

This work shows that the drying load in a dehydration operation is greatly reduced when the crop is dewatered first as part of a fractionation procedure. Increasing the percentage extraction of juice from the crop also increases profits as a result of increased production of leaf protein.

(4) KOEGEL, R.G., BARRINGTON, G.P. and BRUHN, H.D. 1974. Harvesting and processing equipment for alfalfa juice protein concentrate. Proc 4th Annu. Alfalfa Symp., Apr. 9, 1974. Madison, WI.

Data presented on the investment and annual operating costs for an on-farm fractionation system. The production cost for the LPC is developed and the amount and value of the products including the solubles determined. A comparison is then made among haymaking, low moisture silage, and dewatered silage plus LPC in regards to yield and expected profit, showing the latter to be best.

(5) VOSLOH, C.J. *et al.* 1974. Economics of the Pro-Xan process. 12th Tech. Alfalfa Conf. Proc., U.S. Dep. Agric.-Agric. Res. Serv., Feb. 1, 1975.

This is a preliminary report on the more detailed evaluation given by Vosloh *et al.* (1976). Three different size dehydration plants and four different operating seasons are considered. Total capital investment with and without fractionation is reported and the production costs are developed for all systems.

(6) BRAY, W.J. 1975. The economics of leaf protein production. 169th Natl. Meet. Am. Chem. Soc., Philadelphia, April 1975.

Presented is a case-specific investigation of the economics of a crop drying plant with and without the application of fractionation. Fractionation more than doubles profitability and gives a gross return on investment of about 38% for the extra capital required.

(7) BROWN, G.O., THELWALL, A.D., MARLOW, G.B. and DEVINE, D.F. 1975. An economic assessment of leaf protein concentrate production. Grass J. Br. Assoc. Green Crop Driers *15*, 15–19.

Authors investigated the large-scale production of leaf protein with two different extraction levels. Acreage requirements, capital investments, and operating cost data are presented. It is concluded that the overall return on investment would be low.

(8) BRAY, W.J. 1976. Green crop fractionation. New Sci. *70* (995) (9 Apr.) 66–68.

This is an updating of the data of the Bray (1975) paper. It also investigates the effect of increased raw material cost and capital investment, as well as product price changes on the economics of fractionation.

(9) VOSLOH, C.J., JR., EDWARDS, R.H., ENOCHIAN, R.V., KUZMICKY, D.D. and KOHLER, G.O. 1976. Leaf protein concentrate (Pro-Xan) from alfalfa: An economic evaluation. U.S. Dep. Agric. Econ. Res. Serv., Econ. Rep. *346*.

The potential costs and earnings from four systems using the Pro-Xan process are analyzed and four processing variables are evaluated: method of handling the press cake, method of disposing of the solubles, length of operating season, and capacity of the plant. The unit operating with the highest yield for the longest season and having the highest capacity was the most profitable. The most economic means of handling solubles is to return them to the press cake prior to dehydration. Return on investment was found to be high, approaching 50%, but not significantly better than that for a standard dehydration plant.

(10) DUMONT, A.G. and BOYCE, D.S. 1976. Leaf protein production and use on the farm: An economic study. J. Br. Grassl. Soc. *31*, 153–163.

Reports on the use of a linear programming model which provided information on the economic feasibility of on-farm production and use of leaf protein. Results indicated that under a wide range of farm sizes and situations, forage fractionation shows an economic advantage over standard forage conservation methods if machinery of the required throughput and cost is available.

(11) McGUCKLIN, T. and HUGHES, H. 1977. The economics of the alfalfa dewatering and protein extraction technology: A comparative study. Non-Conventional Prot. and Foods Conf. Proc., Natl. Sci. Found., Oct. 18, 1977, Madison, WI.

A linear programming model is used to compare the economics of low moisture silage and dewatered silage plus LPC production for a dairy farm. The latter increases revenues and thus is a potentially profitable investment. It also reduces the risk from weather and soy price fluctuations.

(12) WILKINS, R.J., HEATH, S.B., ROBERTS, W.P., FOXELL, P.R. and WINDRAM, A. 1977. Green crop fractionation: An economic analysis. Grassl. Res. Inst., Hurley, U.K., Tech. Rep. *19*, Nov.

Reports on a computer analysis made on 1480 systems related to green crop fractionation. The work considers the scale of operation, type of crop, product form and output, length of season, price paid for the crop, capital cost, and depreciation period. The best systems only give a return on investment equivalent to that from standard green crop dehydration. When fractionation is added to an existing drying plant, the returns on the extra capital are high, however.

(13) BRAY, W.J. 1977. A consideration of the economics of green crop fractionation and leaf protein production. Workshop on the Utilization of Agricultural Waste, Natl. Sci. Found., Dec., Belo Horizonte, Brazil.

This paper develops the relationship between the price of soy and the expected price of leaf protein concentrate. The effects of fuel and crop costs on the economics of both dehydration and fractionation plus dehydration are investigated. The effects of capital investment cost and LPC yield on fractionation economics are also shown.

(14) ENOCHIAN, R.V., KOHLER, G.O., EDWARDS, R.H., KUZMICKY, D.D. and VOSLOH, C.J., JR. 1977. Leaf protein concentrate (Pro-Xan) from alfalfa: An updated economic evaluation. Am. Soc. Agric. Eng., Dec., Pap. *77–6538*.

A very detailed updating of the work of Vosloh *et al.* (1976). The capital investment required, the operating costs, and the product values are investigated for fractionation/dehydration systems giving yields of LPC of 12, 15, and 18%. The return on investment increased from 48% for the lowest yield to 71% for the highest.

(15) DUMONT, A.G. and BOYCE, D.S. 1977. Forage fractionation and leaf protein production on dairy farms in England and Wales; an economic study of the potential of a weather independent method of forage conservation. Natl. Inst. Agric. Eng., Silsoe, U.K., Dep. Note *DN/SY/646/1959*.

This paper expands on the work given in Dumont and Boyce (1976). It concludes that for fractionation to be widely applied on the farm, the equipment should be capable of throughputs of 2 metric tons of dry matter an hour and should cost less than $10,000. A market for undried leaf protein needs to be developed.

(16) EDWARDS, R.H., MILLER, R.E., KOHLER, G.O. and McDONALD, D.R. 1979. Commercial scale production of alfalfa leaf protein concentrate (Pro-Xan): A progress report. Am. Soc. Agric. Eng., Dec., Pap. *79–6533*.

This is a report on the work being done at the Valley Dehydrating Company, Sterling, Colorado, where a commercial Pro-Xan plant is being constructed. Some preliminary data on economics are included.

(17) ENOCHIAN, R.V., KOHLER, G.O., EDWARDS, R.H., KUZMICKY, D.D. and VOSLOH, C.J., JR. 1980. Producing Pro-Xan (leaf protein concentrate) from alfalfa: Economics of an emerging technology. U.S. Dep. Agric. Agric. Econ. Rep. *445*.

This paper supercedes the 1976 publication by Vosloh *et al.* (Ref. 9) and updates the economics presented in the earlier paper. The return on investment is calculated for three different yields of LPC and with three different xanthophyll contents in the product. With 450 mg of xanthophyll per pound and a 15% yield (dry matter basis), the return is calculated to be 37.0% before taxes. This paper gives a very favorable picture of LPC economics.

(18) EDWARDS, R.H., KOHLER, G.O., MILLER, R.E., LYON, C.K. and KUZMICKY, D.D. 1982. Wet fractionation of forage to reduce energy requirements of dehydration. Natl. Tech. Inf. Serv. Rep. *DOE/CS40090*.

This report provides updated information about the economics of Valley Dehydrating Co. after three years of operation. It points out that the VDC plant consumed 25% less energy than a conventional dehydration plant and projected that with future plants the energy saving would be 35%. The rate of return on a new plant is presented as a function of the number of operating days per year: 26.2% for 180 days per year, which is quite favorable.

Index